This Is Who We Were:
1880–1899

This Is Who We Were: 1880–1899

Based on material from Grey House Publishing's
Working Americans Series by Scott Derks

Grey House Publishing

PUBLISHER: Leslie Mackenzie
EDITORIAL DIRECTOR: Laura Mars
ASSOCIATE EDITORS: Diana Delgado; Sandy Towers
PRODUCTION MANAGER: Kristen Thatcher
MARKETING DIRECTOR: Jessica Moody
COMPOSITION: David Garoogian

Grey House Publishing, Inc.
4919 Route 22
Amenia, NY 12501
518.789.8700
FAX 845.373.6390
www.greyhouse.com
e-mail: books @greyhouse.com

While every effort has been made to ensure the reliability of the information presented in this publication, Grey House Publishing neither guarantees the accuracy of the data contained herein nor assumes any responsibility for errors, omissions or discrepancies. Grey House accepts no payment for listing; inclusion in the publication of any organization, agency, institution, publication, service or individual does not imply endorsement of the editors or publisher.

Errors brought to the attention of the publisher and verified to the satisfaction of the publisher will be corrected in future editions.

Publisher's Cataloging-In-Publication Data
(Prepared by The Donohue Group, Inc.)

This is who we were. 1880-1899 / [edited by] Grey House Publishing. — [First edition].

   pages : illustrations ; cm

Edition statement supplied by publisher.
"Based on material from Grey House Publishing's Working Americans Series by Scott Derks."
Includes bibliographical references and index.
ISBN: 978-1-61925-755-9

   1. United States—Economic conditions—1865-1918. 2. United States—Social conditions—1865-1918. 3. United States—Civilization—1865-1918. 4. United States—History—1865-1921. 5. Eighteen eighties. 6. Eighteen nineties. I. Based on (work) Derks, Scott. Working Americans. II. Grey House Publishing, Inc. III. Title: 1880-1899

HC105 .T45 2015
330.973

TABLE OF CONTENTS

Section One: Profiles

This section contains 29 profiles of individuals and families living and working in the 1880s and 1890s. It examines their lives at home, at work, and in their neighborhoods. Based upon historic materials, personal interviews, and diaries, the profiles give a sense of what it was like to live in the years 1880 to 1899.

Section Two: Historical Snapshots

This section includes lists of important "firsts" for America, from technical advances and political events to new products and top selling books. Combining serious American history with fun facts, these snapshots present an easy-to-read overview of America in the 1880s and 1890s.

Section Three: Economy of the Times

This section looks at a wide range of economic data, including food, clothing, transportation, housing and other selected prices, with reprints of actual advertisements for products and services of the time. It includes figures for the following categories, plus a valuable year-by-year listing of the value of a dollar.

Section Four: All Around Us—What We Saw, Wrote, Read & Listened To

This section includes reprints of newspaper and magazine articles, speeches, and other items designed to help readers focus on what was on the minds of Americans in the 1880s and 1890s. These original pieces show how popular opinion was formed, and how American life was affected.

Section Five: Census Data

This section includes state-by-state comparative tables and original reprints from the 1890 Census.

ESSAY: AMERICA, 1880-1899

The 20 years leading to the twentieth century were shaped by major change: the movement of people from farm to factory, the rapid expansion of wage labor, the explosive growth of cities and massive immigration. Nearly everywhere, the economic and social life of working people was changing. Beneath the glitter and exuberant wealth of the Gilded Age swirled an ocean of discontent yearning for the gold laden streets of America promised to millions of immigrants. Health for commoners was primitive and infectious disease was rampant in crowded cities. Children of the working class routinely left school in their teens to work beside their parents. The middle class was small, and college was largely an institution reserved for the elite and wealthy men of America. Farmers, merchants and small town artisans found themselves increasingly dependent on market forces. The new emerging capitalistic order was quickly producing a continent where only few were very rich and many were very poor. Child labor laws were largely non existent, and on-the-job injuries were common, even expected. It was an economy on a roll with few rudders or regulations—an economy ripe for unrest, reform and new ideas.

The rapid expansion of railroads, along with other technology, opened up the nation to new industries, new markets and the formation of monopolistic trusts that catapulted a handful of corporations into positions of unprecedented power and wealth. At the same time, professionally trained workers were reshaping American' economy alongside business managers or entrepreneurs eager to capture their piece of the American pie.

Across America, the economy—along with its work force—was running away from the land. Before the Civil War, the United States was overwhelmingly an agricultural nation. By the end of the century, nonagricultural occupations employed nearly two thirds of workers. As important, two of every three Americans came to rely on wages instead of self employment as farmers or artisans. At the same time, industrial growth began to center around cities, where wealth accumulated for a few who understood how to harness and use railroads, crate new consumer markets, and manage a ready supply of cheap, trainable labor. Jobs offering steady wages and the promise of a better life for workers' children drew people from the farms into the cities, which grew at twice the rate of the nation as a whole. A modern, industrially based work force emerged from the traditional farmlands, led by men skilled at managing others and the complicated flow of materials required to keep a factory operating. This led to an increasing demand for attorneys, bankers, and physicians to handle the complexity of the emerging urban economy. In 1890, newspaper editor Horace Greeley remarked, "We cannot all live in cities, yet nearly all seem determined to do so."

The new cities of America were home to great wealth and poverty, both produced by the massive migration and influx of immigrants willing to work at any price. It was a time symbolized by Andrew Carnegie's steel mills, John D. Rockefeller's organization of the Standard Oil monopoly, and the manufacture of Alexander Graham Bell's life-changing invention—the telephone. By 1894, the United States had become the world's leading industrial power, producing more than England, France and Germany—its three largest competitors—combined. For much of this period, the nation's industrial energy focused on providing railroads large quantities of labor, iron, steel, stone, and lumber. In 1883, nine tenths of the nations' entire production of steel went into rails. The most important invention of the period—in an age of tremendous change and innovation—may have been the Bessemer converter, which transformed pig iron into steel at a relatively low cost, increasing steel output 10 times from 1877 to 1892.

The greatest economic event during the last two decades of the nineteenth century was the tidal wave of immigration that swept America. It is believed to be the largest worldwide population movement in human history, bringing more than 10 million people to the United States, at a time when the need for workers was great and ever expanding. In the 1880s alone, 5.25 million immigrants arrived, more than in the first six decades of the nineteenth century. This number was dominated by Irish, German, and English immigrants, with those from Scandinavia, Italy, and China following close behind. To attract this much needed labor force, railroad and steamship companies advertised throughout Europe and China the glories or American life. To an economically depressed world, it was a welcomed call.

Despite the signs of economic growth and prosperity, America's late-nineteenth-century economy was profoundly unstable. Industrial expansion was undercut by a depression from 1882 to 1885, followed in 1893 by a five-year-long economic collapse that devastated rural and urban communities across the country. As a result, job security for workers just climbing onto the industrial stage was often fleeting. Few wage earners found full time work year round. The unevenness in the economy was caused specifically by the level of change underway and irresponsible speculation, but also, more generally, by the federal government's stubborn adherence to a highly inflexible gold standard as the basis of value for currency.

Between the very wealthy and the very poor emerged a new middle stratum, whose appearance was one of the distinctive features of late-nineteenth-century America. The new middle class fueled the economy—they purchased one million light bulbs a year by 1890, flocked to buy Royal Baking Powder instead of longer-acting yeast, and supported the emergence and spread of department stores. This new middle class was largely composed of old American stock, and immigrants from the British Isles who worked as either self-employed businessmen or at professional jobs. Merchant tailors, for example, who once labored alongside their employees, now dressed more elegantly, received their customers in well-appointed shops, and hid the actual manufacturing process in a back room.

In the midst of these changes, working men and women began to embrace the idea of collectivity and strength in numbers. Unions emerged, along with energetic reform movements designed to protest the abuse of workers. Between 1800 and 1900, unions organized 23,000 strikes, involving 6.5 million workers.

INTRODUCTION

This Is Who We Were: 1880-1899 is an offspring of our 13-volume *Working Americans* series, which was devoted, volume by volume, to Americans by class, occupation, or social cause. This new edition is devoted to the two final decades of the nineteenth century. It represents various economic classes, dozens of occupations, and all regions of the country. This comprehensive look at the turn of the century is through the eyes and ears of everyday Americans, not the words of historians or politicians.

This Is Who We Were: 1880-1899, presents 29 profiles of individuals and families—their life at home, on the job, and in their neighborhood—with lots of photos and historical images of the time. These stories portray both struggling, and successful Americans, and capture a wide range of thoughts and emotions. From the many government surveys, social worker histories, economic data, family diaries and letters, newspaper and magazine features, this unique reference assembles a remarkable personal and realistic look at the lives of a wide range of Americans between the years 1880 and 1899.

The profiles, together with additional sections outlined below, present a complete picture of what it was like to live in America from 1880 to 1899.

Section One: Profiles

Each of the 29 profiles in Section One begins with a brief introduction. Each profile is arranged in three categories: Life at Home; Life at Work; Life in the Community. Photographs, original advertisements, and contemporary articles round out each chapter.

Section Two: Historical Snapshots

Section Two is made up of three long, bulleted lists of significant events and milestones. In chronological order—Early 1880s, Late 1880s/Early 1890s and Late 1890s—these offer an amazing range of firsts and turning points in American history, including a few "can you believe it?" facts.

Section Three: Economy of the Times

One of the most interesting things about researching an earlier time is learning how much things cost and what people earned. This section offers this information in two categories—Annual Income of Standard Jobs, and Selected Prices—with actual figures from three specific years for easy comparison and study.

At the end of Section Three is a Value of a Dollar Index that compares the buying power of $1.00 in 2014 to the buying power of $1.00 in every year prior, back to 1860, helping to put the economic data in *This Is Who We Were: 1880-1899* into context.

Section Four: All Around Us

There is no better way to put your finger on the pulse of a country than to read its magazines and newspapers. This section offers 86 original articles, book excerpts, speeches, and advertising copy that influenced American thought from 1880 to 1899.

Section Five: Census Data

This section includes invaluable data to help define the last two decades of the nineteenth century—State-by-State comparative tables, and actual reprints from the Census of Population, including a Progress of the Nation report and detailed statistics on various topics, such as Color or Race, Conjugal Condition, School Attendance, Inability to Speak English, and Dwellings and Families.

This Is Who We Were: 1880-1899 ends with a comprehensive Bibliography, arranged by thoughtful topics, and a detailed Index.

The editors thank all those who agreed to be interviewed and share their personal photos for this book. We also gratefully acknowledge the Prints & Photographs Collections of the Library of Congress.

Farmer and Community Leader in 1880

Henrik Lunden and his family immigrated to Iowa from Norway to grow wheat and corn. First-generation immigrants, they lived in a close-knit community of fellow Norwegians who depended on one another for support, labor, and friendship. Henrik, the father in this family, helped his neighbors read letters from home and also preached in the community.

Life at Home

- The Lunden family left Norway in 1870 on a ship carrying 284 immigrants to North America. Their journey took 49 days, or seven weeks. One immigrant child died during the journey.
- On arrival in Quebec, Canada, the passengers were found to have a total of $6,300 among them with which to begin their new life.
- The Lunden family included 11 people: Eva, a 53-year-old grandmother; her son Henrik and his wife, Sigrid, both in their early thirties; Henrik's brothers Knut and Peter; two of his aunts; and Henrik and Sigrid's four children. None spoke English.
- The trip to northeastern Iowa, where the Lundens planned to settle, required a train ride to Detroit, Michigan, and a boat trip to Milwaukee, Wisconsin. Henrik's aunt Inga later wrote to a niece in Norway, "The speed of the train proved quite disturbing."
- The boat the family used to reach Milwaukee had arrived with a cargo of cattle shortly beforehand. No effort was made to clean the boat before loading the human passengers for the return trip. "For a boatload of immigrants, no one could be expected to provide first-class accommodations," Inga wrote. "At any rate none such were provided."
- In the late summer of 1870, the Lundens bought a farm near Forest City, Iowa, to the west of Decorah, where Norwegian settlement in Iowa was most concentrated.
- In 1880 the family moved into a new house, their third in Iowa. For the first time since they arrived in the United States, the family enjoyed a wood-frame, two-story house, not a log home. By this time Henrik and Sigrid had eight children.
- Farm work was clearly divided. The cows and the hens-the milk, butter, and eggs-were

Henrik Lunden immigrated with his family from Norway.

The Lunden family was large, and everyone worked on the farm.

Sigrid's province. The farming of wheat was Henrik's responsibility.

- Sigrid recognized Henrik as the head of the house, but "only in the rarest instances did he oppose her will," according to Inga.
- Because of the size of her family, Sigrid's labor was hard and her days long.
- The most important meal of the day was at noon. In the evening the women of the farm had so many duties that they were able to serve only a simple supper.
- Meals often included potato mash and "something resembling American hasty pudding."
- Sunday afternoons were reserved for social gatherings at which very strong, Norwegian-strength coffee was served.
- In the fall the family made trips into the surrounding countryside to pick grapes, plums, cherries, and walnuts.
- Dried fruits, including apples, peaches, currants, and raisins, could be purchased throughout the year. Currants occasionally were served as a dessert, but raisins were too expensive to be eaten often.
- Following Norwegian tradition, Christmas was celebrated from December 23 to January 6; gifts were never exchanged, although the food served was the best the family could afford.
- The father often assisted his neighbors in writing letters. "Most of our neighbors were industrious readers," Henrik later reported, "but they did not trust themselves to write letters."
- Henrik also served as the unofficial notary for the settlement, especially when letters came from Norway, where Latin and German both were still used. Henrik could read and write in both languages in addition to Norwegian.

- Many of the homes in the settlement had books; almost all of them were religious in nature. John Bunyan's *Pilgrim's Progress* was popular, along with works by the German Pietists Philipp Jakob Spener and August Hermann Francke.
- Almanacs-published free by patent medicine makers such as Ayer's, Green's, and Hostetter's-were popular reading material.
- Hostetter's contained amusing pictures; Hostetter's Stomach Bitters contained large amounts of alcohol and was widely sold, especially in areas where alcohol was prohibited.
- The family occasionally read a Chicago-based Norwegian newspaper or the *Decorah Posten*; the older children, who had learned to read English, occasionally got their news from the *Chicago Tribune*.
- Norwegian was spoken within the family and throughout the community, but English was taught at school.
- Schools emphasized the ability to read and write, but the mark of an educated person was quality penmanship. Some schools use the Lamson's New American System of Penmanship to teach penmanship.
- The family had become Lutheran after immigration, drawn by the faith's doctrine that the evidence of "conversion must and will appear in the daily conduct of a living Christian."
- Henrik was opposed to drinking, dancing, and card playing. Social relaxation was permitted on the Sabbath, but unnecessary labor and noisy activities such as baseball games were strongly discouraged. Sigrid was less strict.
- Henrik served as a lay preacher in the community; formal services conducted by ordained ministers were rare in rural communities.
- The Lundens avoided visits to the doctor's office because of the language barrier; they preferred to visit the druggist, who employed a Norwegian clerk to whom they could describe their symptoms.
- Recognizing the language problem, druggists in the community had begun stocking and prescribing products Norwegians were familiar with, such as oil of spike to help "morbid conditions" or Hoffman's Anodyne, a plaster designed to help rheumatism.
- Henrik voted Republican, as did most Scandinavians.

Life at Work

- In the area where the Lundens lived, the principal crops were corn and wheat, both of which were planted by hand using a mule and a steel plow. Small children often followed the plow, sowing the seed.
- The Lunden family also raised cows for milk and butter.
- Tough strains of wheat, resistant to cold and drought, were imported from Russia for the Western farmers.
- When the Norwegian newspaper out of Chicago advertised the Walter A. Wood self-binder machine for binding grain, it generated much excitement; binding with twine was an important agricultural advance.
- Newspaper reports indicated that haying went well in 1880, with a heavy crop and a lower-than-usual proportion of clover.
- Farmers still had to contend with the hazards of weather and climate. One newspaper warned, "The excessive rains of the past three or four weeks have overflowed some marshes and low meadows, which may prevent cutting upon them for some time yet."
- The speed of harvesting wheat was immensely increased in the 1880s by the combination reaper-thresher, known as a combine, which had to be drawn by 20 to 40 horses.
- Wild grass fires remained an ever-present danger to the farmers on the plains. Control of such fires usually meant building a counter fire to circumscribe the damage.
- Farmers were also plagued with locusts, which formed huge swarms. An observer wrote, "On clear days one could see them passing before the sun in darkening clouds. Where they alighted to feed, nothing was left to harvest. The farmers tried to trap them in large pans of tin coated in tar."

Wheat and corn were the Lunden's primary crops.

- During recurring national recessions over the 1870s, the family experienced little change. "The country had no banks and no business establishments larger than small stores. There could be no failures where there was nothing to fail."
- When prices dropped and money was hard to get, some men stole away from their debt-burdened farms by night, taking their mortgage chattels with them. From Forest City, as from Decorah, "the Minnesota border was not more than a dozen or 15 miles away, and when the line was crossed, the fugitives were reasonably safe from the agents of the law."
- The 1880 census shows that 24 percent of Iowa farmers were tenants; the percentage of tenant farmers was growing.
- Barbed wire, the invention of Joseph F. Glidden, was a boon to homesteaders, reducing the expense of fencing in an almost timberless country; by 1883 Glidden's company produced 600 miles of new barbed wire per day.

Life in the Community: Winnebago County, Iowa
- Winnebago County was in the northeastern corner of Iowa, near the Mississippi River.
- As elsewhere in the United States, early immigrants to northeastern Iowa played a key role in attracting relatives and friends to the region.
- Beginning in 1877 the new U.S. Postal money order system transferred an average of $2.3 million to Europe annually. Approximately 44 percent of the money was used for prepaid passage tickets to America.
- Most of the settlers to Winnebago County came across the ocean on steamers, which carried as many as 300 passengers in the cabin class and 1,500 in steerage; steerage was the level most immigrants could afford.
- Immigration was encouraged by steamship lines, which employed agents in the major European cities to promote travel to the United States. Agents were paid according to the number of tickets sold.

- Many Norwegians found Winnebago County, Iowa, cold and trying, even though most had come from farms in Norway that were 1,200 miles closer to the North Pole; the severity of the winters in Iowa was a disappointment to some.
- In the 1870s the assurances of the real-estate agents, officers of land-grant railroads, state officials, and immigration agents that "rain will follow the plow" were borne out; by the 1880s, however, the cruel variability of the grassland climate was clearly evident.
- Norwegians who quickly took on American ways were often called "Norwegian Yankees."
- Most of the immigrant farmers remained desperately poor; their daughters often found work as domestic helpers in nearby towns.
- Native-born American parents frowned on any union with young men or women "of the invading race"; for their part, Norwegian farmers steadfastly opposed their children's marriage into a non-Norwegian American family.
- Railways helped open the agricultural West by making it profitable to market crops across the country; immigrant farmers were a source of railway revenue when they needed to ship their crops to market.
- In 1880 the Minneapolis and St. Louis Railroad completed track to Forest City, to the jubilation of local farmers, who no longer had to haul their grain long distances.
- In the United States, the Western states and railroads were eager for immigrants to fill the land; they wanted buyers for the 500,000 acres of land that the federal government granted them along their rights-of-way.
- As early as 1852, Wisconsin employed a commissioner of emigration to tout the attractions of that state.
- An 1880 story by the *New York Times* on "Opportunities for Settlers upon the Public Lands" asserted, "There is very little public land in this state unoccupied, and the character of what there is left may be learned through the United States Land-Offices at Des Moines and Sioux City. Nearly 1,000,000 acres are held by various railroads in the middle part of the western section of the state, however, these are purchasable at from $2.50 to $10 and more per acre."

Harvesting wheat, a labor intensive task for the Lundens's, became easier with the invention of the combine in the 1880s.

Proximity to the Mississippi River made it easier for settlers to arrive in northeastern Ohio.

- Because most did not speak English well, new Norwegian immigrants were very wary of being cheated on land deals or supply purchases; some immigrants were charged excessive interest-up to 55 percent-in crooked land deals.
- All farmers, regardless of nationality, took July Fourth off to celebrate Independence Day; most Norwegians did not understand the Declaration of Independence, but that did not prevent them from participating.
- Labor unions experienced phenomenal growth in the West following the Great Strike of 1877, when railroad employee wages were cut 10 percent, the third salary reduction in three years.
- Cities across the nation were affected in what became the bloodiest labor disturbance the United States had ever experienced.
- In all, 57 strikers, soldiers, and rioters died during the strike, as a result of which $3 million in railroad property and 126 locomotives were destroyed.
- The Noble Order of the Knights of Labor, which sought to gather all American workers into one big union, was approaching seven hundred thousand members. Better pay and the eight-hour day were the union rallying cries.
- In cities such as Denver and San Francisco, violent demonstrations occurred that year against Chinese labor; mobs smashed Chinese homes, cut the pigtails off Chinese men, and lynched victims.

৯৯৯৯৯৯৯৯

Norwegian Immigration Timeline

1825 The sloop *Restauration* sailed from Stavanger, Norway, with 52 passengers, considered the beginning of the movement of 900,000 Norwegians to North America; among countries in Europe, only Ireland had greater mass migration.

1833 Cleeng Peerson walked from Kendall township in New York State to Ohio, where he founded the first Norwegian settlement in the Midwest, in La Salle County in Illinois, southwest of Chicago.

1836 Two ships with 167 emigrants sailed from Stavanger, Norway, for the newly established Fox River settlement in Illinois.

1837 A Norwegian minister condemned "America fever" as a contagious disease.

Ole Nattestad wrote *Beskrivelse over en reise til Nordamerica (Description of a Journey to North America)*.

1838 Ole Rynning's emigrant guide, *True Account of America,* was published.

Ole Nattestad founded the first Norwegian settlement in Wisconsin-Jefferson Prairie in Rock County.

Bishop Neumann's pastoral letter *A Word of Admonition to the Peasants in the Diocese of Bergen who Desire to Emigrate* provoked Norwegians in America.

1840 In the 1840s Wisconsin became the main region of Norwegian settlement and remained the center of Norwegian activity until the Civil War.

1841 The first book in America printed in Norwegian, *Doctor Martin Luther's Small Catechism, with Plain Introduction for Children, and Sentences from the Word of God to Strengthen the Faith of the Meek,* was published.

1842 Lay preacher Elling Eielsen built a combined dwelling and meeting house in La Salle County called a *forsamlingshus,* an assembly house, not a church.

1844 The first Norwegian Lutheran confirmation in America was conducted.

Johan R. Reiersen published *Veiviser for Norske Emigranter til De forenede Nordamerikanske Stater og Texas (Pathfinder for Norwegian Emigrants to the United States and Texas)*.

1845 The first Norwegian church building was inaugurated in Muskego, Wisconsin.

The Muskego Manifesto, an open letter signed by 80 men, was issued in defense of the immigrants in America.

Johan R. Reiersen led a group of Norwegian peasants from Agder to land he had selected in Texas later named Normandy.

1846 The Evangelical Lutheran Church in America was founded by Elling Eielsen.

1847 The first Norwegian-American newspaper, *Nordlyset (Northern Lights),* was published in Muskego, Wisconsin.

1848 When gold was discovered in the Sacramento valley in California, many Norwegians were taken by gold fever.

1849 The repeal of the British Navigation Acts permitted Norwegian ships to transport emigrants to Québec.

1850 The first Norwegian emigrants arrived in Québec aboard Norwegian sailing ships and from there to the United States.

1851 *Kirkelig Maanedstidende* (*Church Monthly*) was launched.

The first Norwegian pioneers came to Minnesota.

1852 *Emigranten,* an important pioneer newspaper, published its first issue.

1853 The Synod of the Norwegian-Evangelical Lutheran Church in America (the Norwegian Synod) was organized.

1854 Ninety percent of the Norwegian emigrants first landed in Québec.

The first issue of *Den Norske Amerikaner* (*The Norwegian American*) was published in Madison, Wisconsin.

Norwegian settlements in Minnesota took their names from places in Norway: Vang, Toten, Eidsvold, Dovre, Sogn, and Aspelund.

1858 Minnesota became a state.

1860 About 55,000 Norwegian immigrants lived in the states of Illinois, Wisconsin, Iowa and Minnesota; 60 percent had been born in Norway.

1861 Norwegian immigrants numbering 4,100 joined the Union Army.

1862 The Homestead Act made available to every American citizen 160 acres of surveyed government land.

Dakota Indians unexpectedly attacked Norwegian settlers in the Minnesota River Valley.

1865 Emigration records showed that 77,873 Norwegians had left Norway, mainly from the fjord districts of western Norway and the mountain areas of eastern Norway.

1866 Steamships gradually replaced sailing ships, making mass emigration possible.

1868 The first illustrated periodical in Norwegian in America, *Billed-Magazin,* was published in Madison, Wisconsin.

The Norwegian Dramatic Society was established in Chicago.

1869 The first singing society, Normanna Sangerkor (Normanna Singers' Choir), was founded in La Crosse, Wisconsin.

1870 The census showed that Scandinavians were the largest foreign-born group in Minnesota.

1874 St. Olaf College was founded in Northfield, Minnesota.

1876 Skandinaven's bookstore opened in Chicago.

1879 The land boom in North Dakota was dominated by Norwegians.

1880 The Danish Thingvalla Line established the first direct passenger route by steamship between Scandinavia and the United States.

1883 Torjus and Mikkel Hemmestvedt, considered to be the best skiers of their day in Norway, became pioneer ski jumpers in America.

1884 Den norsk-amerikanske Venstreforening (The Norwegian-American Liberal Society) was formed because "our old fatherland's independence and freedom are at stake."

1885 H. A. Foss published the novel *Husmanns-Gutten* (*The Cotter's Son*).

1887   *Minneapolis Tidende* was one of the three most important newspapers in the Midwest.

The first statue of Leiv Eiriksson was unveiled in Boston.

1889   Dakota became a state and was divided into South and North Dakota.

1890   The United Church (Den forenede kirke) was organized with support from immigrants.

The newspaper *Western Viking* was established in Seattle.

1891   *Nordisk Tidende* (*Nordic Times*) was established in New York by the printer Emil Nielsen from Horten.

The Augsburg Publishing House was established by the United Norwegian Lutheran Church.

1892   Ellis Island replaced Castle Garden as a receiving and control station for immigrants.

Knute Nelson was elected governor of Minnesota.

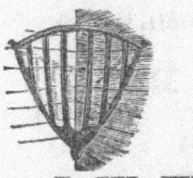  
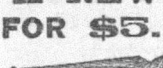

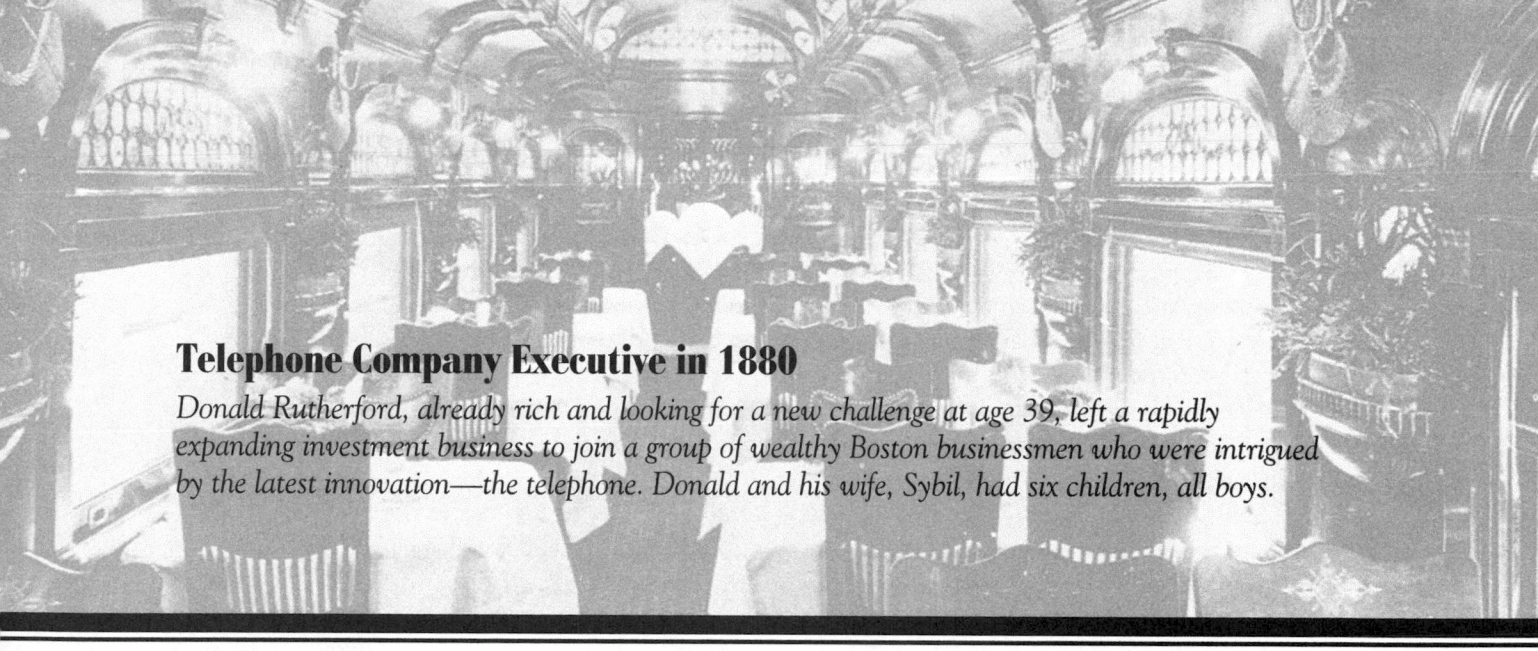

Telephone Company Executive in 1880

Donald Rutherford, already rich and looking for a new challenge at age 39, left a rapidly expanding investment business to join a group of wealthy Boston businessmen who were intrigued by the latest innovation—the telephone. Donald and his wife, Sybil, had six children, all boys.

Life at Home

- Born in 1840, Donald Rutherford grew up on his father's estate near Boston, Massachusetts; Donald's father was a wealthy merchant who had earned a fortune through trade with China.
- Donald attended Harvard, but he was expelled when a fraternity prank resulted in the injury of a watchman.
- Through his lawyers, Donald's father purchased a building that Harvard had wanted to acquire; as a result, criminal charges were not filed, but expulsion could not be avoided.
- Donald fought in the Civil War, attaining the rank of colonel for his gallantry on behalf of the Union Army.
- In 1865 he married Sybil, the daughter of a well-known writer and philosopher.
- They set up housekeeping in a cottage adjoining his father's home; an arborvitae hedge bordered their driveway, a wisteria vine spilled over the front porch, and an apple orchard could be seen in the distance.
- His father's business was so lucrative and the opportunities so great that Donald left Sybil, his wife of just one month, for nearly three years to complete a business deal.
- By the time he returned home, Donald's fortune had been made.
- Thereafter, for 20 years, Donald worked for his father's import business and invested in railroad development in the West as well as in some local development.
- He believed it was part of his Scottish heritage to make money and pass it along to his children; with six sons to provide for, he set himself ambitious goals, and met them.
- Donald no longer felt challenged by the import business, and while he remained engaged by the riskier business of western railroad development, he was looking for new business opportunities.

Donald Rutherford was a rich man by the time he was 30.

- The development of the telephone looked like a good way to renew his energy and possibly make some money.
- Over the past decade, his investments in western railroads had afforded the family economic freedom and an excuse to travel by train throughout the West.
- Everyone in the family, especially his sons, was fascinated by the sight of Indians, cowboys, and buffalo on the plains.
- Entertaining and educating his children while making money gave Donald great pleasure.
- Donald enjoyed a very prominent place in society-inherited from his father but maintained through his own abilities.
- The Rutherfords recently attended a costume ball to celebrate the end of the Christian season of Lent; newspaper stories claimed that this evening event cost $250,000, with $11,000 spent on flowers, $155,730 on costumes, and $62,270 for champagne.
- According to one newspaper story, "The season brings the flowers again and Easter brings the new bonnets, but not the bonnets alone. It brings to that unemployed, pleasure seeking society relaxation from the restraints of Lent and ushers in a round of entertainment all the more rapid in procession and delirious in excitement for the long season of fasting and self-denial which has gone before."
- Sybil's upbringing had not been lavish, but she had come to enjoy coaching-riding through the woods in a perfectly appointed coach drawn by four horses and attended by three or four coachmen.
- Donald considered the $20,000 cost of operating a coach for the season excessive, but he did not object.
- He indulged in buying objects made of ivory, mostly from China, where he still occasionally traveled on business with his father; his constant companion was a silver walking cane topped with an ornate ivory handle shaped like an elephant's head with the trunk grasping the cane as though it were a log.
- Donald made sure that the cane was prominent in a painting done of his entire family.

The Rutherford family fortune was made, in part, through investments in western railroads.

- During a visit to New York, he had learned that oil paintings of families-including grandparents-depicted against the background of an estate were very popular; for his wife's birthday, he hired a family portrait painter.
- By 1876 Donald had built a large Greek Revival-style home on the family estate.
- While it was being built, the couple's two oldest boys lived on the family yacht (along with two servants), which was anchored in the cove; they were brought ashore for meals.
- When the house was completed, it was capped with a weathervane designed and executed by a local artisan; the weathervane depicted Donald riding his prize horse.
- At his estate Donald loved to invent charades and organize costume parties.
- He and Sybil were members of a group of 20 friends known as the Game Club; the club held evening meetings at the homes of members every fortnight during the winter and spring months.
- Upon arrival at the meeting, members were presented with a slip of paper on which subjects were written; each person then wrote a poem on his or her topic, and the poems were read and discussed during dinner.
- Often the poems were humorous; Sybil recently wrote one entitled, "Few and Faint But Fearless Still," which began "Up on her tousled hair, with a lofty courage undaunted, / Lightly she balanced a structure, most marvelous and aesthetic, / Fuzzy and wide and reckless, and adorned with manifold colors; / Here lay a plume, soft and long, exactly the shade of a pickle, / When it emerges, fresh and green, from a wide-mouthed bottle. / Next to it nestled another, as red as a much-faded car seat."
- With his brother-in-law, Donald was developing a Concord grape-growing venture on his property-as a sideline.
- He insisted that his children attend church, although he rarely went himself; his family had donated the land and the money to have the chapel built.

Life at Work

- Donald Rutherford was well known for his head for figures and taste for making money and social connections-the perfect combination for a young company struggling to survive.
- In his first year on the job at the telephone company, lawsuits with Western Union and others were settled, making it possible for the company to begin focusing on cautious, deliberate expansion.
- The telephone, under Patent No. 174,465, entitled "Improvement in Telegraphy," had been approved four years earlier, on March 7, 1876.
- The explanation of an unbroken electrical current, magnets, and variable resistance in the design of the telephone made this patent potentially one of the most valuable of the day.
- The hard work of creating a commercially successful telephone company was just beginning.
- The original telephone company, created by inventor Alexander Graham Bell and his father-in-law, ran out of money in 1879, drained of nearly $100,000 by patent legal battles.
- To survive, Bell and his backers turned National Bell Telephone over to a group of Boston investors- including Donald Rutherford-to run.
- Within months of taking over the company in 1879, the Boston group ended the pitched battle with competitor Western Union in an agreement through which Western Union sold all its

A commercially successful telephone began with an unbroken electrical current and magnets.

National Bell Telephone Company reached a deal with competitor Western Union, agreeing to keep out of the telegraph business.

telephone properties; in return, Western Union would receive 20 percent of National Bell Company's license fees-the fees from district exchanges.

- In addition, Bell Company agreed to keep out of the telegraph business and to deliver to Western Union any telegraph messages it might receive for transmission.
- Bell stock, which had been unsellable at $50 a share, zoomed to $1,000 a share in November after the settlement was announced.
- Donald's job was to make Bell Telephone profitable; he did not like to take chances, believing that slow, deliberate use of capital would result in survival.
- The board, composed of his friends in Boston, agreed.
- Donald was in conflict with Bell Telephone's general manager, who was pushing to invest in higher-quality service to customers; this, Donald thought, would simply drive up costs.
- Donald held that when you owned a monopoly and had no competitors, you didn't have to provide the highest level of service to compete.
- At this stage, his priority was to control costs so that the company could return a large profit to its Boston investors-period.
- Recently the board had agreed that inventor Alexander Graham Bell was no longer providing enough service to the company to warrant his $5,000 annual wage and should be terminated.

- Now that the patent lawsuits were no longer an issue, Bell was not needed for his testimony in court cases; besides, Bell was chiefly interested in inventions for the deaf and was not living up to his contract to advance the science of the telephone.
- The legal fees of the law firm that had spent several years attempting to save Bell Telephone amounted to $50,000; the lawyers agreed to accept $20,000.
- Donald's experience investing in western railroad expansion taught him that too much activity could cause jealousy and competing factions.
- He understood that building a monopoly was dangerous and open to attack; however, he believed a monopoly was necessary if the telephone was to prosper and spread across the nation.
- For this reason he was very aggressive in defending Bell's ability to set rates and expand service.
- He publicly stated that the "complaints as to rates are often made thoughtlessly, and in ignorance of the expenses and risks which attend the business."

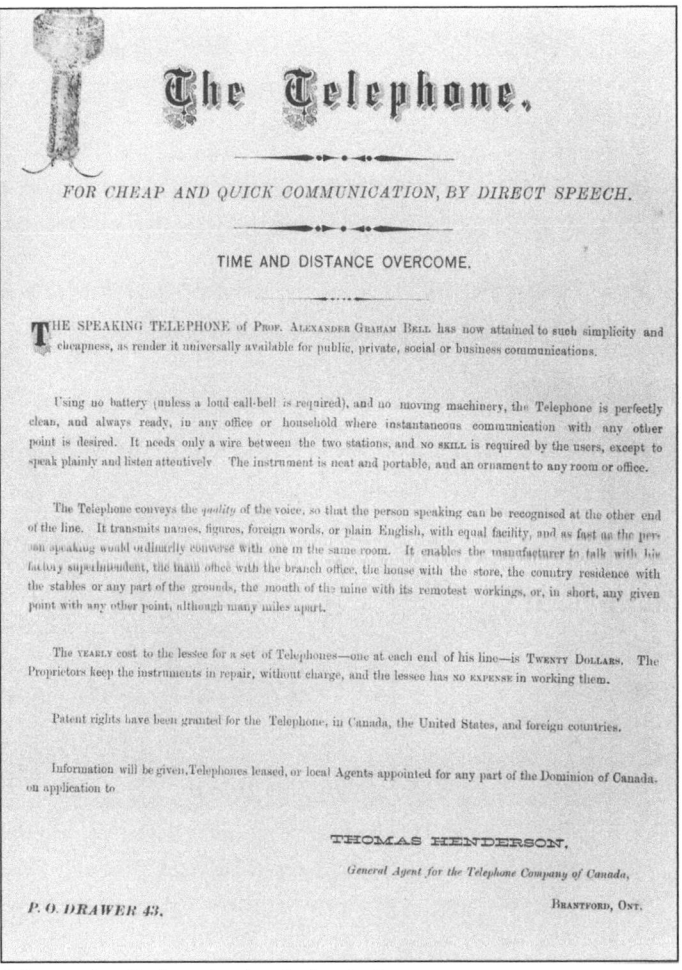

A "press release" advocating the telephone's virtues.

- Donald also opposed all regulation, saying, "No state in fairness ought to destroy that which the patent system has created," and he has warned those who wish to regulate the business that the "attack upon rates is one of the most direct methods of removing all inducement to extend telephone facilities."
- The cost of phone service varies nationally; in San Francisco, where the competing service just folded, Bell was preparing to raise its charges from $40 to $60 a year.
- The common practice was to allow unlimited calls, charging instead a flat rate for the service.
- The first phone subscribers tended to be physicians concerned about emergencies; the New York and New Jersey Telephone Company served 937 physicians and hospitals.
- Other major New York subscribers included 401 drugstores, 363 liquor stores, 315 livery stables, 162 metalworking plants, 146 lawyers, 126 contractors, and 100 print shops.
- In 1880 there were 132,692 telephones in the hands of American licensees, and only nine cities in the United States with populations of over 10,000 that did not yet have a telephone exchange.
- The rapid expansion of telephones, requiring thousands of wires strung between poles, caused political conflicts.
- Putting telephone lines underground was not economically or technically practical.
- Although various cities might prevent the expansion of telephones into residential areas, Donald was convinced that business phones were more profitable anyway; he had little desire to use capital on residential expansion.

- Bell Telephone, which opposed reduced rates for residential customers, declared, "Cheaper service will simply multiply the nuisance of wires and poles and excite political pressure to put wires underground without materially improving profits or permanently improving relations with the public."
- Net earnings of the company were more than $200,000 this year, of which $178,500 would be paid in dividends to stockholders; earnings in 1881 were expected to be even better.
- The company had only 540 stockholders; the average annual payout per stockholder in 1880 was $330.
- It was the policy of the company's Boston investors to pay out most of the profits to stockholders as dividends rather than to plow the proceeds back into the company for maintenance and expansion.

Life in the Community: Boston, Massachusetts

- Approximately 350,000 people lived within the boundaries of Boston; another 350,000 lived in the surrounding areas and suburbs of the city.
- Founded in 1630 by members of the Massachusetts Bay Colony, Boston was the capital of the state and its most populous city.
- The population was growing rapidly-about 20 percent per decade-driven by immigration and the migration of rural workers into the city looking for better-paying jobs.
- Social background exerted a profound influence upon jobs and where people live; the Boston Irish newspaper, *The Pilot*, said, "The race is not run with an equal chance; the poor man's son carries double weight."
- A center of learning and culture, Boston was visited by Charles Dickens for a reading of "A Christmas Carol," and the Old Corner Bookstore was a regular meeting place for Henry Wadsworth Longfellow, Ralph Waldo Emerson, and Oliver Wendell Holmes Sr.
- Only three years earlier, more than 100 clergymen, including Rector Phillips Brooks, had walked in procession reciting Psalm 24 with the wardens of the new Trinity Church to dedicate the structure built on land created by the filling in of Back Bay.

Horse-drawn buggies were a common sight in Boston in 1880.

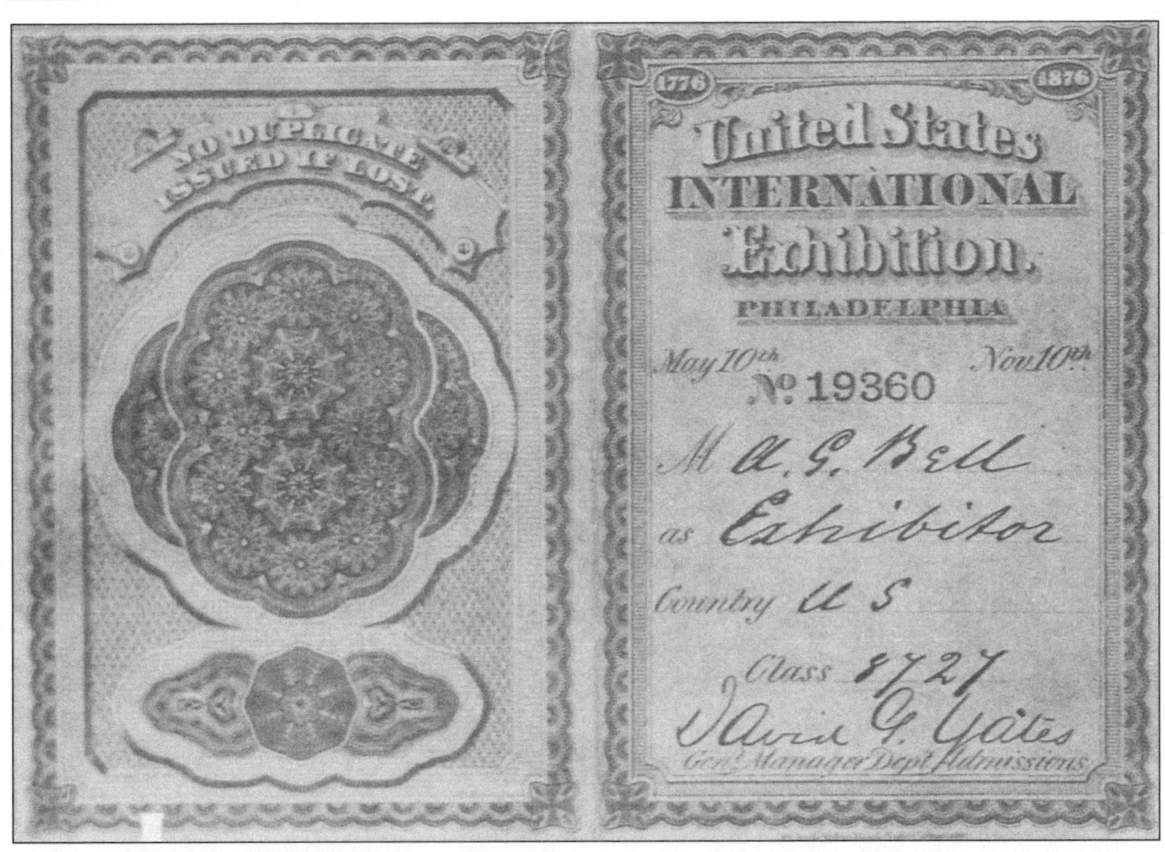

- Christian Science began in Boston, at what became the Mother Church, while King's Chapel was the birthplace of American Unitarianism.
- The city's elite still prided themselves, as the Duke of Newcastle once said of Boston, that everything about the city was "in better taste than the entertainment of the New Yorkers."
- Fashionable ladies were now sporting bustles; a bustle, called the "improver," required three great pads of horsehair, over which a cascade of silk drapery fell behind the figure.
- Wealthy Bostonians spent their summers at exclusive Newport, Rhode Island, learning lawn tennis on a court marked out like an hourglass, wide at the base lines and narrow at the net.
- Boxer John L. Sullivan was developing a reputation in Boston for hitting his opponents so hard that they accused him of "kicking like a mule."
- Sullivan had a fight booked against American champion Paddy Ryan for a purse of $5,000.

Educational Reformer and Teacher in Rural Wisconsin in 1881

With two years of college under her belt and two years of experience teaching in northern Michigan, Mary Greene was ready for the educational changes sweeping the nation.

Life at Home

- In 1881, when Mary Greene entered her tiny, one-room school in Wisconsin for the first time, she was well aware of the educational reforms reaching the prairielands.
- Industrialist Horace Mann-building on the ideas of Thomas Jefferson-had seen to that.
- A modern education required a standard curriculum, universal attendance, and graduated steps to completion; Mary was proud to be at the center of the transformation.
- In 1778 Thomas Jefferson, while still a member of the Virginia Assembly, proposed that all children be guaranteed three years of public schooling.
- It was a radical concept that he believed was essential to the perpetuation of democracy.
- "General education will enable every man to judge for himself what will secure or endanger his freedom," Jefferson said.
- "But was it necessary?" asked his fellow landowners, who already paid a fee to send their children to private "dame schools"; besides, no one was sure that field hands needed the capacity to read William Shakespeare.
- The debate raged for decades.
- Despite its professed belief that free, universal education was essential to maintaining democracy in perpetuity, by 1840 America still offered few educational opportunities to the children of its agrarian workers and its industrial workforce.
- With no state supervision, inconsistent local budgets, and a tepid commitment to instructing the masses, America's schools languished.
- Most of the schools offered an education linked to the Protestant Bible; the most common schoolbook was the *New-England Primer*-used to

Young teacher Mary Greene was ready for educational reform.

teach reading and the fundamentals of the Protestant catechism.

- The few older boys who stayed in school beyond the grammar school years studied mathematics, Latin, and philosophy.
- Mary Greene was fully aware of the role Horace Mann played in changing attitudes.
- His personal inspection of a thousand Massachusetts schools over a six-year period had demonstrated that most lacked adequate light, heat, and ventilation.
- With no standardized textbooks, pupils spent hours memorizing or reciting passages from books they brought from home, no matter how dated or irrelevant these tomes might be.
- Mann supported a new system called "common schools" that would serve all boys and girls and teach a common body of knowledge that would give each student an equal chance at life.
- "It is a free school system, it knows no distinction of rich and poor. ... Education, then, beyond all other devices of human origin, is the equalizer of the conditions of men, the great balance wheel of the social machinery."
- Mann proposed that the state both establish a taxation system adequate to meet the needs of

Horace Mann was instrumental in changing attitudes toward education.

the schools and create standards or expectations to be applied on a statewide basis.
- Additional innovations included the introduction of standardized textbooks, school desk chairs with backs, a bell to signal the time, and a blackboard large enough to be easily visible.
- Convinced that an educated citizenry benefited the entire community, Mann was also a major proponent of teacher education and universal taxation.
- Fearing any statewide control, local school boards attacked the plans vociferously-but the debate fully aired the concept that everyone in society should pay for universal education.
- In 1879 a uniform grading program was instituted in Wisconsin.
- And in 1881, for the first time, students were formally charted on their progress.
- Mary herself had been educated in Wisconsin schools that mirrored the educational process that Mann criticized.
- During Mary's school years, the role of the teacher was largely to oversee and monitor pupil behavior; there was no clear curriculum and no graduated steps to higher grades.
- Raised on a farm as one of nine children, Mary's father loved school so much that his parents agreed to extend his education to the sixth grade, whereas most of his classmates and siblings left school after three years.
- Her mother had had no formal education beyond Bible reading at home, and she desperately wanted one of her children to acquire enough education to become a preacher, a teacher, or an undertaker, since all three guaranteed paying jobs.
- Mary was taught to commit to memory words for public recitation; the student who possessed the best memory of the word list was deemed the most satisfactory pupil.
- Education experts speculated that since the object of education was to strengthen the innate properties of the mind, recitations served as the rigorous, muscle-building exercise children needed.

- Mary also became acquainted with the custom of "boarding 'round"; her teachers moved from house to house every two weeks, spending time in the home of each child who attended her school.
- Mary was thrilled when the teacher came to stay at her house; only years later did she realize that the custom was necessary because of the low wages paid to female teachers, and that few adults would wish to change their location every two weeks.

Life at Work

- Mary Greene's first challenge as a newly hired teacher was to figure out when the school year started.
- Every year the school board set the date for the start of the school year based upon the amount of school taxes that had been collected; the funds covered teacher wages and contingencies.
- Only after the numbers were in could the local school board establish the calendar for the winter and summer terms, each of which ran about four months.
- In rural areas school attendance was an erratic, seasonal activity based on the farming needs of the family, the opening day of hunting season, or the unexpected illness of a prized animal.
- In Otsego, Wisconsin, the summer term traditionally began after the spring planting of the potato crop, and the winter term started after the harvest.
- Some boys attended school only during the summer session.
- In years past men were hired as schoolteachers in the winter term, when boys were considered more obstreperous and difficult to teach; women were hired for the summer term.
- From 1867 to 1880, the one-room school in Otsego was served by 25 different teachers.
- It made for very poor continuity, and the skills of the students lagged.
- At the same time, women were beginning to dominate teaching.
- Women were considered better suited temperamentally to the teaching profession.
- Women would also work for less.
- For the first time in years, the school board had contracted with Mary to cover the entire year, telling her that they wished to break the cycle of frequently changing teachers.
- Unlike her predecessors, Mary was experienced both in teaching and in the ways of politics.
- Before the school year began, she visited the most influential families in the area to demonstrate why a child's education should take precedence over helping out with potato farming; to even better

Mary's approach to teaching included spending time outdoors.

The typical one-room schoolhouse served a variety of children.

effect, she talked about the future as a time of change when their children would need the ability to read and write effectively.

- The community listened and threw its support behind education.
- They even embraced the statewide curriculum establishing graded steps toward graduation using statewide standards-including an expectation that a child's education should last eight years.
- Using the plans distributed by the Wisconsin State Superintendent's Office and based on their abilities, pupils were to be graded or grouped into one of three levels: primary form, middle form, and upper form.
- Movement from one grade to the next was to be determined based on a system of examinations.
- The year Mary arrived, the school was transitioning from the New England Primer to the McGuffey Reader.
- McGuffey Readers, including a primer, a speller, and five readers, had been around since 1836; nearly 100 million copies had been sold.
- The readers were designed to become progressively more challenging with each volume; word repetition in the text was featured as a learning tool, helping to develop reading skills.
- Sounding-out, enunciation, and accents were emphasized, gradually introducing new words and carefully reinforcing the old.
- McGuffey's Readers also provided questions after each story to aid the teacher and assist in the statewide plan to establish grades.

- While Mary's youngest students, eager to catch up with their older brothers and sisters, loved the energy and focus of the new curriculum, the older students fought the changes.
- A year earlier, they knew exactly what was required to obtain high grades; now, everything was unfamiliar.
- So on the last day of the first week, the older students staged a strike, refusing to re-enter the classroom after recess.
- Mary simply ignored them while she taught the first graders, leaving the protesters alone.
- One by one her charges, looking very sheepish, reappeared in her classroom.
- They all expected to be paddled-a punishment Mary avoided.
- "I don't plan to tell your parents what you have done," she proclaimed at the end of the school day, adding, "I expect no more student strikes-leave that to the unions that are fighting for workers' rights."
- The next day Mary devoted the first hour of classroom time to explaining why change was taking place.
- She told her 28 charges that "what was good enough for pa is good enough for me" was no longer true.
- "The world is getting more competitive; each year hundreds of thousands of people arrive in America searching for work. They want jobs-your jobs-so that they can raise their families."
- With that out of the way, Mary got out a map of Europe to show everyone where the immigrants were coming from.
- Then she helped everyone with their arithmetic by demonstrating how many zeros were in 100,000-as in 100,000 new immigrants.
- Next she used a horseshoe to demonstrate how to measure in inches-and then she asked one of the boys to throw the horseshoe and showed how to measure in feet.
- Then a student brought in a plot of his family's property, and the next class was devoted to acres, divisions, and calculating angles.
- But when one of her quietest students brought in figures showing the shoulder height of her cows compared with their weight and asked how math could be used to determine the weight of cows in the field, Mary knew it was going to be a good year.

LUNDBORG'S PERFUMES.

Lundborg's Perfume, Edenia.
Lundborg's Perfume, Maréchal Niel Rose.
Lundborg's Perfume, Alpine Violet.
Lundborg's Perfume, Lily of the Valley.

LUNDBORG'S RHENISH COLOGNE.

The YOUNG LADY'S JOURNAL (London) says, "Edenia is one of the most delicate and agreeable perfumes; it suggests the odor of many favorites. Lundborg's perfumes are very tastefully put up in little boxes, and are suitable offerings to give to any lady."

Life in the Community: Otsego, Wisconsin

- Otsego got its start as a transportation center, functioning as a station on the Chicago, Milwaukee & St. Paul Railroad.
- Situated in the prairie region north of Madison, Wisconsin, Otsego served as the center of the regional agricultural and dairy industries; potatoes dominated the agricultural crops throughout the county.
- By 1881 Otsego had a graded school and Lutheran and Catholic churches.

- The Modern Woodmen of America and the Catholic Order of Foresters provided much of Otsego's social life.
- Wayne B. Dyer, the first settler in the area, arrived in 1844 and erected a log house in which to live and host weary travelers.
- Located on the direct route between Milwaukee and Stevens Point, Dyer's hostelry thrived; Dyer prevailed upon quite a number of travelers to settle nearby, and by December 1847 a post office was established.
- As other hotels were built, the village attained a fair degree of prosperity.
- In January 1849, the growing community was organized into a town called Otsego.
- Madison was created in 1836 when former federal judge James Duane Doty, planning to build a city on the site, purchased over a thousand acres of swamp and forest land on the isthmus between lakes Mendota and Monona.
- The Wisconsin Territory had been created earlier that year, and its legislature was tasked with choosing a permanent location for its capital.
- Doty lobbied aggressively for the legislature to select Madison as the new capital, offering buffalo robes to the freezing legislators-and promising choice Madison lots at discount prices to undecided voters.
- Doty named the city Madison for James Madison, the fourth president of the United States, who had died on June 28, 1836.
- He named the streets for the other 38 signers of the U.S. Constitution.
- Even though Madison was still a city only on paper, the territorial legislature voted on November 28 in favor of establishing Madison as the capital, largely because of its location halfway between the new and growing urban communities around Milwaukee in the east and the long-established strategic post of Prairie du Chien in the west.
- When Wisconsin became a state in 1848, Madison remained the capital, and the following year it became home to the University of Wisconsin-Madison.

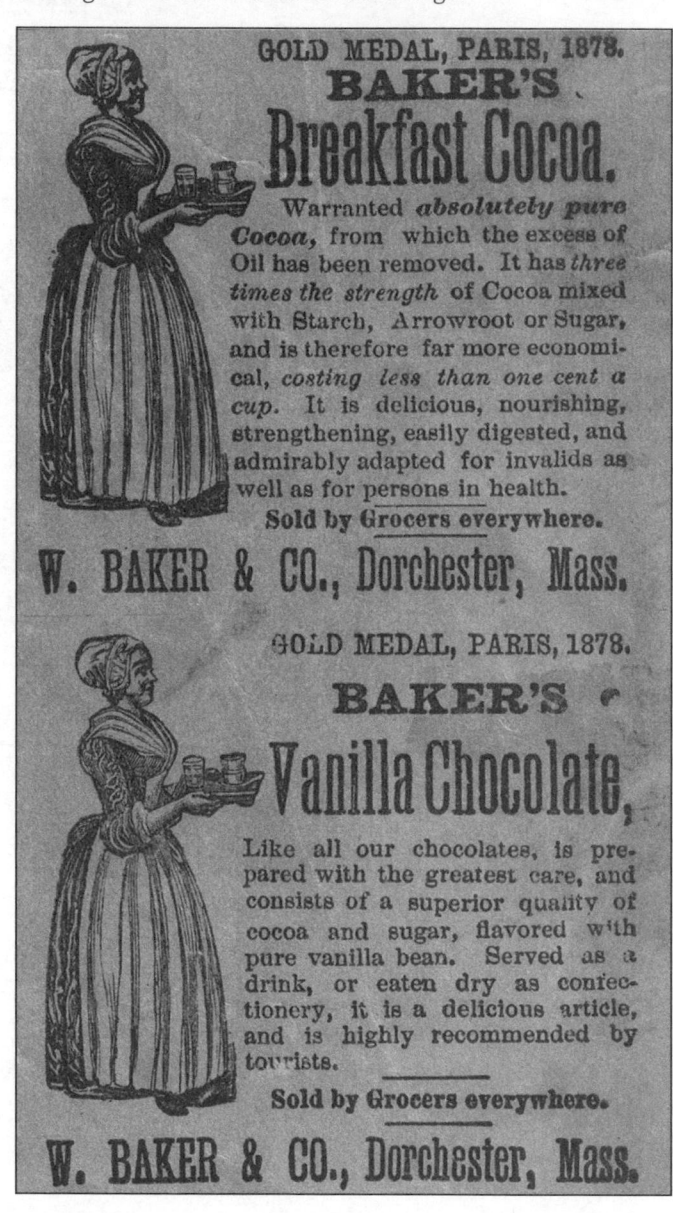

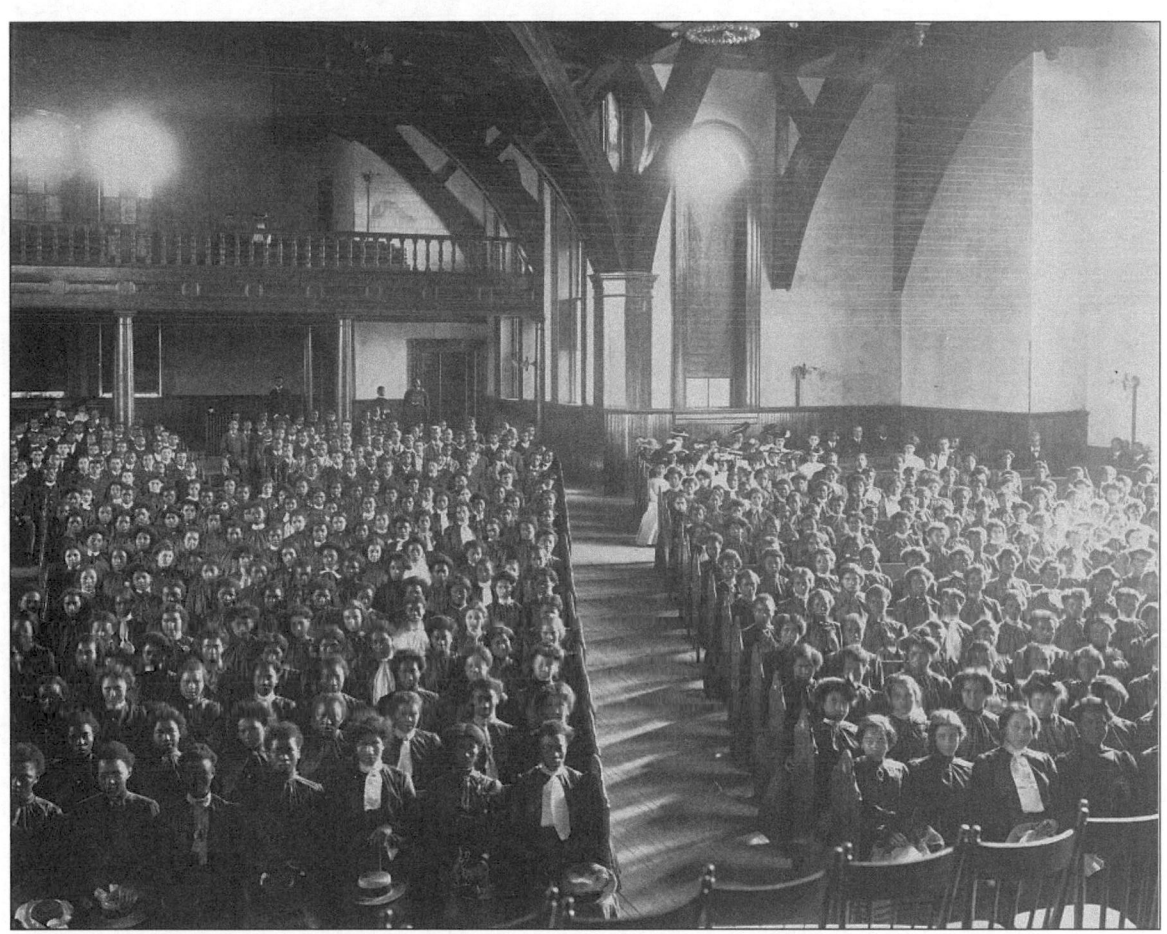

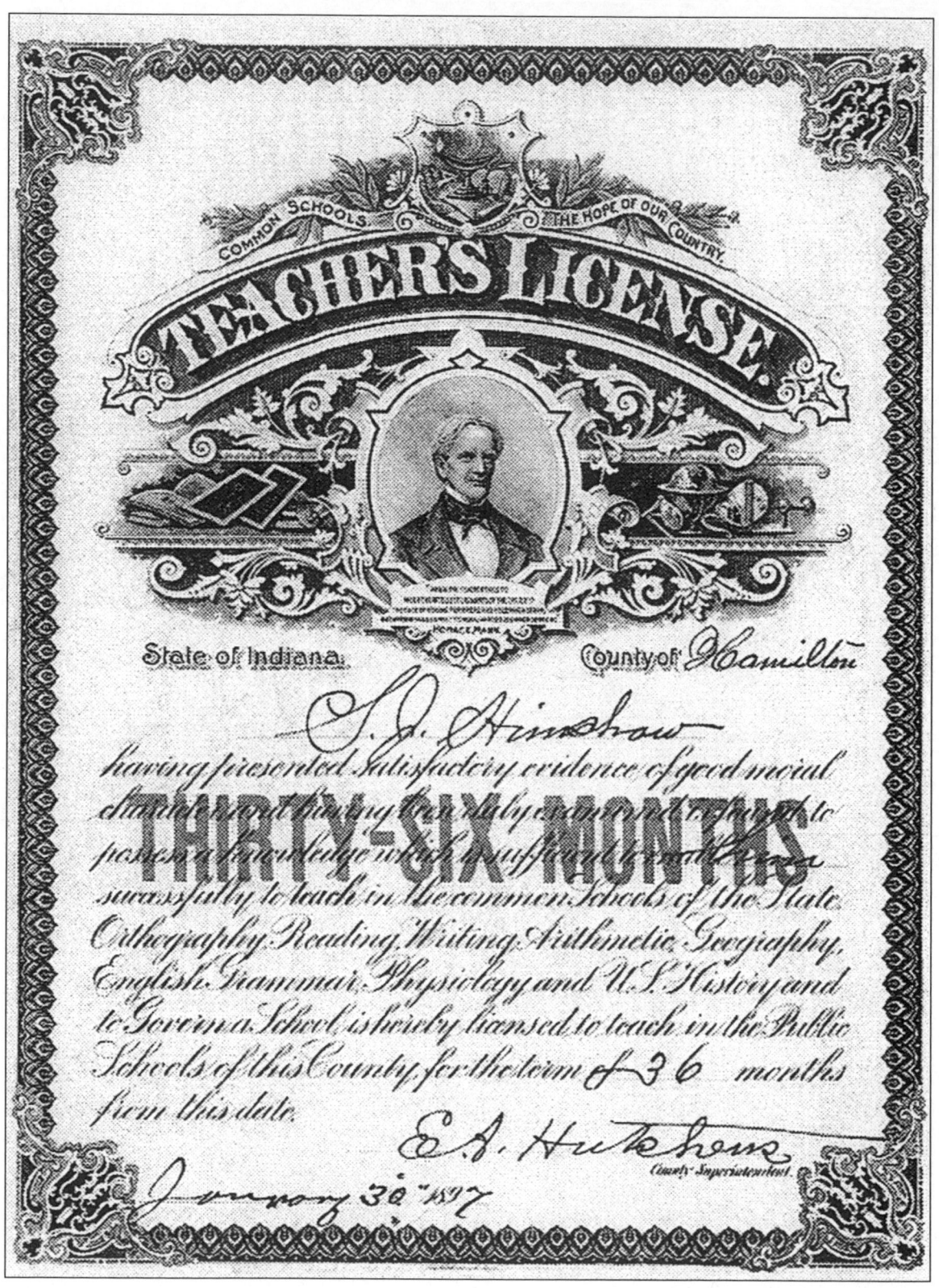

Thirteen-Year-Old Orphan in 1882

Ora McFadden and his two sisters had lost their parents and their middle-class life in 1878, when an epidemic of yellow fever swept through Memphis, Tennessee. For the past four years, the three children had lived in the Catholic Orphan Asylum.

Life at Home

- At night Ora often dreamed about the house he had lived in before he and his sisters, Iris and Rose, came to the orphanage.
- Ora had had a bedroom of his own-just up the stairs from the kitchen, from which good smells emanated.
- He had had a dog and friends and a mother who tucked him in at night and a father who loved to tell stories.
- Then the yellow fever epidemic hit Memphis, and everything changed.
- Yellow fever had already devastated Memphis four times in the 1800s, most recently in 1873, when approximately two thousand people died.
- That dreadful figure was eclipsed in 1878, when more than eight times as many people perished in Memphis of yellow fever.
- In 1878 a New Orleans steamboat deckhand was the first person to die.
- He was followed by Mrs. Kate Bionda, who operated a snack shop patronized by river men, and then by James McConnell, a policeman.
- More than 20,000 citizens-half the city-then fled Memphis in fear.
- The *Public Ledger* observed, "At no time within the history of our city has there been such a sudden or effective panic among the people of Memphis. Our community is in a state of great alarm, and all who can leave are doing so."
- When the yellow fever outbreak began, Ora's father, a bank clerk, sent the family north while he stayed behind in Memphis to provide necessary travel funds to fleeing residents.
- The family took the Louisville & Nashville train north a hundred miles to the country home of Ora's aging grandmother; Ora noticed that many additional railroad cars had been added to accommodate all the extra passengers fleeing Memphis.

Ora McFadden lost his parents during the yellow fever epidemic.

27

- It was a frightening time, and the three children clung tightly to their mother for most of the trip; no one felt the need to appear brave.
- *The Daily Appeal* said, "The ordinary courtesies of life were ignored; politeness gave way to selfishness and the desire for personal safety broke through the social amenities."
- To further assist the citizens of Memphis, Ora's father joined the Citizen's Relief Committee, which had two white members and one black member from each of the city's ten wards.
- Space was set aside in the hospital for indigents; schools were converted to hospitals.
- Of the 40,000 original residents of Memphis, only 7,000 whites and 13,000 blacks stayed in the city.
- Most of the people who remained within the city's four square miles were volunteers or were already ill, or they stayed because they thought they were immune to the disease.
- It was generally believed that African Americans had a higher resistance to yellow fever than did whites.
- Once the epidemic began, the Howard Association of New Orleans, which had been founded specifically to combat yellow fever, employed 3,000 nurses to care for the sick,

Ora's father was a bank clerk.

two-thirds of whom were males from Memphis, both black and white.
- In addition, 500 nurses came from outside the city to help-volunteers from Catholic, Protestant, and Hebrew groups-along with many who were employed by fraternal organizations such as the Odd Fellows and the Masons.
- Hundreds of nurses died caring for patients.
- During the first week of September, the city government and Board of Health ceased to function.
- That same week, Ora's father became ill with yellow fever.
- He was immediately given the "Creole treatment," consisting of small doses of castor oil or calomel to keep the bowels open, sponge baths to reduce fever, adequate covering in the event of chills, and absolute rest of mind and body.
- When Ora's mother learned that her husband was sick, she and the children's grandmother returned to Memphis.
- During the next two weeks, they all caught yellow fever, and they died within days of each other.
- Suddenly, Ora, Iris, and Rose were orphans.
- After the fever passed, the city was full of wandering, homeless children.
- African American gravediggers labored day and night for two dollars a day, but they could not keep up with the mountain of coffins.
- When Ora and his sisters returned to Memphis, as instructed by the authorities, they were placed in a Catholic Orphan Asylum, where they had remained for the past four years.
- They had not forgotten how nice their mother smelled when she tucked them in at night.

Life at School and the Orphanage

- Every evening while lying in his bed in the orphanage, Ora pulled out the ferrotype pictures taken when the family was still together.
- He remembered that the pictures had been taken on a Saturday afternoon; his father's barber had proudly set up a photography studio, complete with desks, chairs, and props.
- The McFaddens had been among his first customers.
- Ora's father and mother even got dressed up for the occasion, although the children did not.
- Pictures were taken of Ora, then aged eight, and of his sisters; there were also photographs of Ora's father, mother, and grandmother.
- It was a great afternoon of fun; Ora had been unsure that he could remain standing completely still for 30 seconds so the photograph would not be spoiled, but he managed to do it.
- Most of the photos of his mother and of his sister Iris were lost when the children were taken to the orphanage.
- Ora still liked nothing better than to look at the pictures, even when they made him sad; he was determined always to remember what his mother, father and grandmother looked like before they died.
- The orphanage was filled with other children who also lost their parents in the epidemic.
- As the oldest child, Ora had felt it was his duty to lead the children into the orphanage for the first time, although he was frightened beyond words.

- Everyone was very nice, but the house was extremely chaotic then.
- Too many children had come too quickly, and few Sisters remained to care for them.
- Later things improved, and everyone learned what was expected of them as well as what they could themselves expect.
- Before coming to the orphanage, many of the children had been living on the streets for months, begging for food from house to house.
- Until the hard winter came in January, many of the street children did not want to stay at the orphanage because so many of the nuns had died of fever during the epidemic.
- Everyone in Memphis had thought that God would make the Sisters safe.
- Many of the nuns Ora knew at the orphanage had arrived since the fever.
- Most of them believed that if they could control the influences that made up a child's life and thoughts, the child wouldn't ever be a truant or disrespectful, or run with a gang.
- Ora's English lessons were taught from the textbook *Graded Lessons in English*; his younger sisters used the McGuffey Reader, which had many delightful pictures.
- First published in 1836, the McGuffey Readers had become the basic schoolbook in 37 states; more than two million copies were sold each year.

- Little Rose loved to repeat the alphabet as she learned it from the first reader-from "A is for axe" and "B is for box" all the way to "Y is for yoke" and "Z is for zoo."
- The books were filled with pictures of boys with hoops, kites, and skates and girls happily playing with dolls, sleds, and jump-ropes.
- At the orphanage the children were also instructed in the French language.
- Girls were taught to sew, wash, iron and cook; sewing was taken in from city residents to support the institution and to encourage the industrial education of the children.
- About half of the girls were in the sewing department and half in the mending department.
- Boys were trained in breadmaking, farm work and blacksmithing.
- Ora had found great joy in the bakery, but he knew his destiny was to work on the docks, where he could make enough money to buy back his childhood home.
- The orphanage's chapel, fitted with seats of natural wood and decorated with walnut moldings, could accommodate 250 people.
- The nuns insisted that everyone attend chapel regularly; the boys were lectured on temperance and told to pledge that they would never use alcohol or tobacco.
- The cost of housing the children was generally $5 per month.
- The Catholic churches of the area provided additional support; in 1881 the churches had provided $116 for the sustenance of the 15 Sisters, while an additional $423 was donated toward the upkeep of the 125 children.

MATHEMATICS.

- The dormitories were furnished with single iron beds and straw mattresses.
- Iris had learned to iron as well as how to sew; she liked to iron because it meant she got to be around the nuns; one Sister, she had told Ora, talked just like their mother.
- Under the mattress of her bed, the only place she considered private, Iris kept her collection of trading cards advertising Soapine soap products.
- She especially liked the cards decorated with a gold rim, which depicted little girls like her.
- Mr. Anderson at the corner store, a man who had known her father and mother well, saved them for her as a special reminder of home.
- On Sunday afternoons the Sisters read aloud to the orphans, often from the newspaper, which carried features just for children, such as "How Yap Got the Slipper."
- On some nights the three children climbed together to the orphanage roof and looked toward the Mississippi River.
- Ora then imagined the day he would go to work there.
- Some nights Ora pretended he could see his father walking from his station at the bank down to the Cotton Exchange, just as he had done every day.
- Ora's father, as a bank clerk, had been heavily involved in the city's cotton business, often serving as middleman between buyer and seller and handling the financial exchange of goods; the bank received a commission for such services.
- When he turned 14, Ora would have to leave the orphanage and support himself; the girls could remain there until they were 16.
- He believed that if he could raise the money to buy back his parents' home one day, by working on the cotton docks, he and his sisters could live there again and be happy.

Life in the Community: Memphis, Tennessee

- After the yellow fever epidemic of 1878, doctors throughout the city advocated better sanitation methods to prevent another outbreak.
- In fact, yellow fever returned the following year, although with less severity.
- Even in the best of neighborhoods, the streets contained animal droppings; most homes had backyard privies, windows were unscreened against flies and mosquitoes, and water often was contaminated.
- To improve conditions, the city ordered that unconfined goats and hogs in the city be impounded.
- New regulations were created concerning the dumping of dead animals and the proper ways of emptying privies.
- An extensive sewer construction effort was under way; 30 miles of lines had been built in 1880 and 1881.
- Worldwide more than $4.5 million was donated to Southern cities hit by the fever; $1 million was donated to Memphis alone, $45,000 of which came from New York City.
- Additional contributions came from all across the United States, Europe, Asia, Australia, and South America.
- Still, the epidemic was the last economic straw for the struggling city-Memphis was bankrupt.
- When the yellow fever struck, more than a million dollars in back taxes were due, and most of it was now rendered uncollectible.
- Residents continued to leave the city, some because of their fear of a new outbreak of yellow fever, others simply because Memphis seemed to be a dying city that offered few opportunities.
- In addition, Memphis was battling a flood that had disrupted one of its key economic mainstays, the shipping of cotton on the Mississippi River.
- Since 1873 Memphis had operated a spot market for cotton through the Cotton Exchange; cotton was bought and sold on the spot.
- By contrast, in a futures market, cotton was purchased based on expectations of its value.

Lawn Tennis Player in 1883

James Raubach, who lived on a stipend from his father, continually annoyed and frustrated his parents, who wanted him to settle down, marry, and get serious about his life rather than waste his time playing lawn tennis.

Life at Home

- Twenty-seven-year-old James Raubach lived a life built around one overriding passion: lawn tennis.
- His mother wanted to know why he was not married.
- His father, Frank, was seething that his only son, instead of applying his fancy Ivy League education to the nobility of work, preferred the inconsequential silliness of play.
- James's older sister, who devoted her time to dresses and fancy balls, always inquired why she never saw him at the more fashionable balls.
- Only his younger sister noticed that he was happy only when playing tennis with his friends.
- His father had made his money through hard work in the green grocery business and had been lucky enough to pull out of the stock market one month prior to the onset of the Panic of 1873, which lasted six years.
- As a result he had had sufficient capital in hand during the panic to buy up his competitors and monopolize the wholesale food market in New England.
- But no amount of business success could entirely distract Frank Raubach from what he saw as his son's complete lack of seriousness.
- James had repeatedly told his father that he would settle down and find a girl to marry, but all Frank saw was impoverished British nobility coming to America to snap up the most eligible girls.
- Frank told his son that he might have a better chance of finding a girl if he wasn't so busy with his tennis club all the time.
- He had also hinted that unless James settled down, married, and got a job, his stipend would end sooner rather than later.
- The Raubachs were on the margins of high society, having the money but not having made it in the accepted way.

James Raubach much preferred playing lawn tennis to looking for a job.

- Frank had always envisioned that James would marry well and launch the family into full acceptance into society.
- Therefore he demanded that James attend the Vanderbilts' ball, known to attract a large number of eligible young ladies.
- James agreed, but he had little enthusiasm for his father's machinations.
- He rarely dated the women who fluttered around him.
- Several years earlier, James had bought a house in Harlem, on 116th Street, a prosperous area where he could easily live off the $800 stipend his father sent him once a month.
- Thanks to the elevated railroads, installed in Harlem in 1880, an increasing number of people were moving into the area.
- The train also allowed James to get to his club without having to hire a carriage, which made his money go much further.
- He was careful with his allowance.
- He didn't even consider trying any of Mr. Edison's new light bulbs, because the cost would force him to get a job.

James was a founding member of the National Lawn Tennis Association.

- James rarely drank, although, after matches, he did go out with his friends to the bars.
- Before lawn tennis, James's passion had been cricket.
- Now he believed tennis was far more dynamic than cricket and had a better chance of success in the United States.

Life at Work

- James Raubach was a founding member of the United States National Lawn Tennis Association, which was a merger of the New York, Boston, and Philadelphia Lawn Tennis clubs.
- The first meeting of the National Lawn Tennis Association was held at the Fifth Avenue Hotel in New York, on May 21, 1881.
- The impetus for the founding was to standardize the inconsistent rules and equipment used around the country.
- These problems were manifested in the lawn tennis tournament held on Staten Island by the Staten Island Cricket and Baseball Club on September 1, 1880.
- The *Richmond County Sentinel* wrote about the tournament, "It will no doubt furnish quite a good deal of amusement to Staten Islanders to see able-bodied men playing this silly game."
- The prize was a silver cup engraved with "The Champion Lawn-Tennis Player of America," worth about $100.
- The first problem arose over the size of the ball.
- Two members of the Beacon Park Athletic Association in Boston complained that the ball, manufactured by Ayres of England, was two-thirds the size of the ball they played with in Boston.
- The judges pointed out that the ball had "Regulation" stitched on it, and that if the two gentlemen did not wish to use the ball, they could pull out of the tournament.

- Another argument erupted about the scoring method of counting to 15, a system that had been taken from the game of rackets.
- The height of the net caused still another argument.
- Afterwards, the National Lawn Tennis Association was created in part to codify the rules of the game.
- Thirty-six delegates, representing 19 clubs directly and 16 more by proxy, gathered to inaugurate the association.
- James was a member for the Country Club of Westchester County, on 59th Street.
- The association decided to hold a national championship in Newport, Rhode Island.
- This tournament was far more successful, although-unlike the previous tournament-it was open only to club members, not to the public.
- They avoided controversy before the game, announcing that the Ayres ball would still be used.
- The singles game was won by R. D. Sears, an innovator who played the game differently than most players.

Croquet was losing popularity to lawn tennis.

- Traditionally players stood close to the net, but Sears played back near the serving line.
- This allowed him more time to reach a ball hit to him and return it.
- James said that it was the most exhausting game of tennis he had ever witnessed, and he spent much of the rest of the singles tournament studying Sears's game.
- Since then James had entered every tournament he could, though he never placed very high.
- He thought it was important to check his game against the best in the country.
- It was very hard to practice regularly in the winter because there were very few indoor tennis courts in the country.
- Some were set up in empty halls and armories, but there were almost no covered courts, as there were in England.
- James tried to convince his father to let him and his friends practice in his house, but he was never successful.
- The next tournament was played at the Newport Casino.
- There were still some rumblings about the rules, including the size of the ball and location of the tournaments.
- These issues were expected to be voted on within a few years.

Life in the Community: New York City

- New York was widely considered the premier city for high society in the nineteenth century; Boston was too insular, Philadelphia had been passed by in the commercial revolution; Washington, District of Columbia, better served its poor.
- New York had grown very quickly since 1845, when there were only 25 millionaires.
- In 1883 New York City resident John Jacob Astor was the richest man in the United States, with a personal wealth of $25 million.

Typical dress of the gentlemen who attended Mrs. Astor's New York City balls.

- Most upper-class strivers wanted to be part of "The 400": those who were seen at one of Mrs. Astor's balls.
- Supposedly 400 was the number of people who could comfortably fit into her ballroom, although twice that number were invited to certain parties.
- In 1883 the Vanderbilts put a crimp in Mrs. Astor's domination of the city's society elite in a particularly ingenious and expensive way.
- Mrs. Astor had never invited the Vanderbilt girls to any of her balls, even though Mr. Vanderbilt was one of the richest men in New York.
- They were not the right type of people for Mrs. Astor.
- Finally the Vanderbilts decided to force their way into this high society by putting on an expensive and luxurious ball of their own.

- It is rumored that the ball cost more than $250,000.
- It was to be the event of the year, expected to compare to the Prince of Wales ball in 1860.
- Mrs. Astor and her daughter were not invited.
- When Mrs. Astor's daughter inquired as to why, she was told that Mrs. Vanderbilt had not had the pleasure of meeting the young girl or her mother.
- In response a coach was immediately sent for, and the Astors raced to the Vanderbilts' home to pay their respects.
- An invitation was then sent.
- New York had More gentleman's clubs than any other city in the United States.
- Each had its own rules of behavior, and many had strict caps on the number of men who could join.
- The Manhattan Club, for members of the Democratic Party, capped the number of members at 600.
- The creation of these clubs was driven by the explosion of new money.
- When just anyone could make a million dollars, personal wealth was no longer a reliable way to tell who was worthy of being at the top of the social hierarchy.
- Seemingly, every movement of this social class was chronicled in the papers, including parties and invitation lists.
- *The Police Gazette*, taken over by Richard Kyle Fox-a man who had been described as someone who knew how to hate-served up an endless supply of upper-class gossip and titillation.
- The city was still reeling from the October 1881 revolt against the Tammany Hall political patronage machine, when the nomination process was taken out of the hands of a select group of 25 power brokers and turned over to more than 600 delegates.
- Tammany Hall had controlled New York City politics since the Civil War.
- People hoped that the corruption in New York City government might lessen now that the nomination process had changed.
- Grover Cleveland had become governor of the state in 1882, and there were whispers that he might run for president in the next election.

- The Statue of Liberty, a gift from France, was originally slated for completion in 1876-in time for the country's Centennial-but now it was not expected until sometime around 1885; some people worried that even then the base still would not be ready for it.
- The fundraising for the Statue of Liberty's base had been going so slowly that Joseph Pulitzer wrote an editorial piece in *The World* complaining that the rich were not bearing their share of the cost.
- To help raise money for the project, Emma Lazarus's poem "The New Colossus" was solicited for an auction of artwork staged by the "Art Loan Fund Exhibition in Aid of the Bartholdi Pedestal Fund for the Statue of Liberty."
- But the statue was only one of several major projects under way.
- After 13 years of construction, the $16 million Brooklyn Bridge was expected to finally connect Manhattan to Brooklyn.
- Twenty lives were lost in the construction of the great bridge, which rose 276 feet into the air.
- Its 86-foot-wide surface accommodated two outer roadways for horse-drawn vehicles, two tracks for trains, and a center walk for foot traffic.
- Showman P. T. Barnum led 21 of his elephants across the span on opening day to assure spectators of its safety-and to publicize his circus.
- Just days after the opening ceremony, 12 people were killed in a stampede on the crowded bridge when a rumor circulated that it was about to collapse.
- Electricity was becoming more common in the city, and telegraph and electrical wires between the buildings were hung so thickly that many were afraid the wires would collapse under their own weight.
- Thomas Edison had recently completed work on his filament light bulb, to delight of the city's rich.
- On September 4,1882, Edison finished his new power plant and lit 800 lamps and 50 square blocks of lower Manhattan.
- Orders poured in for Edison to electrify private houses; everyone who could possibly afford it wanted the new electric light.

Croquet and Lawn-Tennis
Indiana Weekly Messenger (Pennsylvania), January 11, 1882

Croquet has lost its popularity, and it is only in remote western towns that one can hear the click of the mallet as it strikes some ball or head or the wail of some too eager girl who has smashed her own foot. Elsewhere croquet has not been played for nearly two years. The croquet mallet has been turned into the beanpole, and the balls have been thrown at vagrant dogs, so that of the 11 million croquet sets formally in the possession of private citizens of the United States, there are now not more than 63 sets which are fit for use.

The disappearance of this pestilent game is a great gain for the cause of morality and public order. Next to horse-dealing, which, according to the Westminster Catechism, "worketh the corruption of the whole nature of him who sells horses," croquet has a far more withering and blasting effect upon what is good in human nature than any other agency. It leads to lying almost as certainly as does trout-fishing. Mr. Herbert Spencer, in his tables and social statistics, asserts that 82 per cent of all ladies who play croquet will systematically claim to have passed hoops they have not passed, and 90 per cent will insist they never stirred the ball which received the stroke of the mallet in that peculiar feat called "croqueting." Of course, those who habitually indulge in flights of the imagination to put it mildly such as those who must inevitably lose all respect for the truth. They who cheat their lovers at croquet will find it easy to deceive their husbands in the game of married life. From cheating to quarreling which in croquet is short and inevitable. In nine games out of every 10 the recording angel is compelled to take notice that Miss Smith has audibly mentioned "it is pretty sickening to see how that Brown girl cheats," and that Miss Brown has openly called Miss Robinson a "mean and hateful thing." In its latter days croquet was characterized not merely by cheating and bad language but by assassination. It was so easy for a quick-tempered and indignant girl to hit her partner over the shins as a rebuke for his bad play, or to strike a faithless lover over the head who had formed a partnership with a hated rival, and perhaps defended her from the accusation of cheating, that mallet outrages became frightfully prevalent. In England alone, in the year 1879, seven had their skulls fractured, 194 were seriously bruised, either in one or both shins, and 605 young ladies were hit in the region of the shoes by mallets thrown by other young ladies. I like to say the state of things existed about the same time in this country, but in the absence of trustworthy statistics it can only be said that all proportion of mallet outrages is as great here as in England. It was this terrible feature of the game which caused a general uprising of all good citizens against it, and led to this substitution of lawn tennis in its place.

The peculiar feature of lawn-tennis is the net which is stretched between the players with a view of preventing adversaries from assaulting one another. The players use a light ball, with which it is impossible to inflict any serious injury, and instead of clubs they play with instruments somewhat resembling the battledore of the last generation, and unfit for offensive purposes except, perhaps, in connection with very young children. The game has commended itself to parents and peaceable people by its apparent safety, and so far it has certainly been unstained by any murderous affrays. Still, it must be evident to everyone that the net commonly used is far too frail. It could be broken down by the rush of a heavy girl, and it would be easy for an agile girl to climb over it. If lawn-tennis is to maintain its reputation as a safe and peaceful game, the net should be made of wire instead of twine; it should be at least a foot higher, and the upper edge should be strewn with broken glass laid in cement or furnished with sharp iron spikes. Sooner or later some mild and imbecile player will madden his adversary to such an extent that nothing but personal violence will be any comfort to her, and she will get over or through the frail twine net with a suddenness that will dazzle the unhappy victim.

Railroad Construction Engineer in 1883

Thirty-year-old Gareth Rowlands was employed by the Pennsylvania Railroad, for which he had worked for a dozen years, primarily as a construction engineer. He and his wife, Margaret, had two small children, David and Grace.

Life at Home

- Gareth Rowlands was born in Montgomery County, Pennsylvania, on an estate that had been the home of his father's family for five generations.
- His ancestors came to Pennsylvania from Wales in the late 1600s; they were members of the Society of Friends.
- Gareth began his education at the Lower Merion Academy, and at age 15 he entered the Rensselaer Polytechnic Institute, near Albany, New York.
- After one year of postgraduate work, he completed his formal education at age 18.
- His work required that he determine the exact route of each new railroad line, a job requiring considerable construction knowledge and excellent negotiating skills.

- He married Margaret, a girl well-known to his family, when they both turned 20; the couple settled in Philadelphia.
- David arrived two years after their marriage, and Grace two years after that.
- At Margaret's insistence, they attended the local Roman Catholic Church. Nationwide there are 12 million Catholics.
- The number of immigrants flooding the city was taxing the ability of the church to care for everyone; many members of the various ethnic groups did not like worshipping together.
- Like many of their friends, Gareth and Margaret collected several etchings-by Winslow Homer, Joseph Baker, and Foxcroft Cole-displaying these prints in the parlor, where they can be seen by visitors.
- In his spare time, Gareth loved to sail and to take excursion steamers to Cape May, south of the city.
- The Rowlands especially enjoyed vacationing at the Bryn Mawr resort, now

Gareth Rowlands worked for the Pennsylvania Railroad.

connected to the city by the Pennsylvania Railroad; the development of the line was one of his projects.

- Gareth dreamed of building a summer home there, but he could not afford two houses.
- Publisher George W. Childs had just completed an enormous residence in Bryn Mawr, in the style of a Swiss chalet.
- The extension of the Pennsylvania Railroad to Chestnut Hill generated similar excitement and development.
- The Wissahickon Inn was nearing completion; its architectural form was "Old English," now in vogue for suburban hotels.
- Already recognized for his expertise at work, Gareth was being urged by many within the railroad community to become more politically active, as a way to get ahead.
- Many men were becoming rich overnight through their association with local politics.
- Gareth was asked to join a group informally called the "All-Night Poker Players," composed of powerful business and political interests-evidence that his time had come.
- He became acquainted with men who had made fortunes investing in the refining of gasoline, the creation of a telephone network, and land development.
- Gareth's expertise and responsibility for determining where railroad lines would be laid made him a potentially valuable member of the group.

The Rowlands vacationed at the Bryn Mawr Resort.

Gareth enjoyed sailing in his spare time.

- At one gathering Gareth met John Wanamaker, whose department store was the talk of Philadelphia, and listened to a talk by Edwin J. Houston, who produced the Thomson-Houston arc light.

Life at Work

- Railroading as a whole was enjoying great prosperity; despite labor problems and complaints about rates, it operated a virtual monopoly.
- Railroad men were respected members of the community-a construction engineer especially so.
- Gareth's first job on the railroad was as a rodman on an engineering corps to locate the line of Pennsylvania's Mountain Division, a particularly difficult section over the Allegheny Mountains.
- His next engineering assignment involved projecting a line from Philadelphia to Bethlehem, Pennsylvania.
- Despite continuing competition, the Pennsylvania Railroad Company continued to pay its stockholders a regular return.
- To meet customer demand, the Pennsylvania Railroad Company purchased the Philadelphia and Baltimore Central Railroad Company, which formed a back route between Philadelphia and the Susquehanna River.
- The rail line was considered a "farmers' railroad" because so much of the area through which it passed was agricultural; subscriptions from farmers paid for the road, guaranteeing that it would stop at certain farm towns.

The Pennsylvania Railroad Company purchased the Philadelphia and Baltimore Central Railroad Company.

- The Pennsylvania regularly carried oil from the western part of the state; some oil producers were so angry about freight rates that they discussed developing pipelines to ship their own oil.
- Gareth was convinced the cost was too high and the project too impractical.
- Railroading's recent history was marked by bitter labor wars, increasing competition, and continuing reductions in freight rates.
- The Great Strike of 1877 stopped railroad traffic for a week in cities as distant as Pittsburgh and Chicago.
- Most railroad men believed French and German socialists were responsible-not the recent wage cuts announced for the rail lines.
- Meanwhile many farmers blamed the railroads for luring people away from the farms and small towns into the cities.
- The Pennsylvania began double tracking their lines to provide faster travel.
- Newer and stronger locomotives were presenting challenges; their ability to travel at faster speeds made them unstable on the curves.
- Safety devices, such as the automatic couplers invented by Eli Hamilton Janney following the Civil War, were installed on all trains, and they saved lives.
- Most important was the air brake, which allowed railroads to run faster and use heavier trains.
- Gareth's company currently was installing new signals to improve efficiency; the tracks had become so congested that movement had to be controlled by space rather than time.
- Battery-operated circuit controls signaled automatically within a block, allowing multiple trains to travel safely.

Life in the Community: Philadelphia, Pennsylvania
- Philadelphia began as part of the quasi-religious utopian experiment of William Penn, who established the central area of the city in 1683.
- The grid pattern of streets and properties reflected both his aesthetic preference for order and his skill as a real estate developer.
- The city grew rapidly, and Penn prospered.
- By 1800 rowhouses had become the dominant form of residence in the city.
- They were attractive and cheap to maintain, with brick facades and attached party walls.

Trains led to the development of "bedroom suburbs," allowing workers to live distances away from their place of business.

- The success of the Pennsylvania Railroad, incorporated in 1846 to build a line from Harrisburg to Pittsburgh, was considered an economic necessity if Philadelphia was to hold its own.
- In July 1858 a Pennsylvania Railroad train made the first trip over Pennsylvania Railroad tracks all the way from Philadelphia to Pittsburgh.
- The Philadelphia Bank was a key founder of the railroad, having bought stock in the venture.
- By 1883 the United States boasted 115,000 miles of track; in the early 1880s, it cost about $40,000 per mile to lay track.
- Railroading was not simply part of the American infrastructure; in 1883 it *was* the American infrastructure.
- The ability of American railroads to move people in style promoted the nineteenth-century development of resort hotels, spas, national parks, and scenic wonderlands.
- Trains also led to the development of "bedroom suburbs," allowing workers to live farther and farther away from their place of business; after 1880 a pattern of railroad commuting to bedroom suburbs was a fixture of American urban life.
- Nearly all cities of any size, especially those in the East, developed railroad commuting; Philadelphia-like New York, Boston, and Chicago-developed a vast and complex network of commuter lines.
- In 1883 Philadelphians could choose among 13 separate passenger railways within the city, operating more than 1,200 cars pulled by more than 7,000 horses on 264 miles of track.
- The track mileage was increasing yearly, extending the horse-car lines into the suburban sections and quickening the development of rural areas and farmlands.
- In 1882 the Union line, inspired by the examples of San Francisco and Chicago, built a cable road on Columbia Avenue from Twenty-Third Street to the east entrance of Philadelphia's Fairmount Park, the city's favorite playground.
- The gross earnings of the American railway companies in 1882 totaled $752 million. Of that sum, $552 million was from freight earnings and $173 million from passenger traffic.
- Over the previous ten years, freight traffic had tripled, while passenger travel had doubled.

- These huge increases demanded major improvements and additions to keep the traffic flowing.
- Accommodating commuter traffic provided business but was not as profitable as freight, which made fewer demands, required fewer stops, and could be picked up and delivered at remote (and therefore less expensive) facilities.
- When the industrial revolution occurred in Philadelphia, most of the available land close to the city was occupied by commercial or residential activity.
- This historical development pattern spurred industrial development up and down the Delaware River.
- By 1880 the leading industry was clothing and textiles, which employed 40 percent of the city's work force.
- Other key industries included machine tools and hardware, shoe and boot manufacturing, paper and printing, iron, and steel.
- Most establishments were small; financially conservative Philadelphians preferred to operate on a cash basis instead of borrowing to finance plants, equipment, and inventories.
- Citizens of Philadelphia could choose among 36 different banks.
- With the development of the telegraph and telephone, dozens of overhead wires dangled from 4,000 poles across the city.
- Many in the city, including key railroad officials, believed the wires were a symbol of the city's progress.
- But to control the proliferation of telegraph poles, the city passed an ordinance prohibiting the erection of new poles without a city permit.
- In 1882 the Brush Electric Light Company installed lighting on Chestnut Street at its own expense to demonstrate the value of electricity.
- Philadelphia's first telephone directory, published in 1878, contained 47 names.
- Fairmount Park was visited in June 1883 by half a million people; in addition, 5,400 equestrians cantered along its bridle paths, while 95,000 horse drawn carriages paraded down its drives.
- Squat little paddle-wheel vessels made regular runs from Fairmount landing, some by moonlight.
- Six ferry lines along the Delaware connected Philadelphia with opposite points on the Jersey shore; the cost was $0.03.
- Second in size only to New York, Philadelphia in 1883 had a population of approximately 1.3 million, largely as a result of massive foreign immigration.
- Although the *Philadelphia Evening Bulletin* had the highest circulation in the city, residents had a choice of 17 newspapers, many in foreign languages and published to meet the needs of the new immigrants

Seventeen-year-old Liu Wang came to America on the promise of wealth and adventure. Fourteen years of low wages and discrimination taught him to love life as a traveling photographer's assistant.

Life at Home

- Liu Wang's "coming to America" story always included his being packed in a tiny wooden crate, traveling on a leaky ship, trying not to attract the attention of the vicious dockworkers, and suffering severe dehydration.

- The story of his 61-day trip from China to San Francisco in 1872 always solicited cheers, tears, and another round of drinks.

- Suffocating confinement in a tiny, wet box hidden in the well of a heaving ship made for a far better story than a purchased, cramped space in steerage where everyone threw up on their neighbors while wondering why the trip to "Gold Mountain" was off to such a rocky start.

- In fact Liu was 17 years old when he arrived in San Francisco, but the spirit within him always quickened when he heard-or told-a fascinating tale of adventure and cunning.

- Practically since his first week in the United States, Liu had continued to visit the docks and witness the excitement of fortune-seeking men as they clambered off clipper ships with names like *Stag-Hound, Fleet Wing,* or *Sea-witch-*all of which were capable of traversing the ocean waters southward from New York, past the tip of South America, and northward again up along the continent's west coast, docking in San Francisco in just a hundred days.

- Adventure hunters fresh from the boats were always eager to have their picture taken; after a few stiff drinks, some would even believe the photographs cost $2 a pose-twice the normal price.

- Indeed, an American photographer with a lively Chinese assistant could make good money when the docks were full.

- Since arriving in San Francisco from the desperately poor region of Suchow, China, 14 years earlier, Liu had panned for

Liu Wang arrived in San Francisco when he was 17-years-old.

47

gold, lost a wife, picked strawberries, and fallen in love with the life of a traveling photography wagon.

- Only starvation awaited Liu in China, where land ownership had become more concentrated in the hands of a wealthy few.
- Like most peasants, he could either revolt or leave.
- But he never lost his love of water or the beauty of his homeland; homesickness always hovered nearby.
- Suchow was a city on the east bank of Tai Hu Lake.
- It was one of the oldest cities in China and was prized for its delicate silk embroidery, magnificent palaces, and soaring temples; its canals and ancient bridges had earned the city its Western nickname, the "Venice of China."
- As a boy Liu had learned to fish with cormorants on the lake.
- The birds were leashed at the boats and tossed into the water to fish.
- Once the cormorant caught a fish, the bird was hauled to the boat; a ring around its throat stopped it from swallowing its catch.
- It was a grand adventure but a poor way to make a living.
- Like many in his village, Liu believed the stories told about America, where food was always plentiful.

Liu came from the city of Suchow, China, on the banks of Tai Hu Lake.

Liu's birthplace was dubbed the Venice of China for its culture and beauty.

- He told himself he would be away only a few years until he made his fortune; repeatedly, he told the same story to his new wife.
- Liu's parents warned him repeatedly to be careful of the labor traders who roamed the docks looking for customers, but didn't ask him to stay in China, knowing they could never feed nine children adequately.
- To keep his young wife safe while he made his fortune, Liu made arrangements for her to stay behind.
- Chinese women did not go to strange places willingly.
- For two years she waited faithfully, mostly without complaint.
- When she decided to continue her life with another man, she regretted that she was never taught to write so that she could express the emptiness she felt.
- Liu would not know for another two years that his wife had run off, and then he learned of it only through village gossip brought by new arrivals.
- Chinese men in America outnumbered Chinese women 20 to 1.

Life at Work

- China's closed-door policy to the rest of the world had ended in 1842, when England defeated China in the Opium Wars, forcing China to open itself to foreign trade and permit its citizens to leave the country.
- The development of a passage system then allowed poor Chinese laborers to finance the journey by agreeing to work out their debt after arrival.
- This system quickly became popular among the emigrants traveling to other parts of Asia as well as to Australia and North America.
- Arrangements were handled at the treaty ports by Chinese recruiters working for Western entrepreneurs; this kind of labor contracting was known as "pig selling."
- When Liu arrived in California in 1872, however, the resentment of native-born Americans toward immigrants was already well established.
- American feelings were deep-seated and often supported by public policy, especially toward Asians.

- The first Chinese had entered California in 1848, and within a few years, thousands more came, lured by the promise of *Gam Sann,* "Gold Mountain."
- Discriminatory laws designed to protect American jobs were quickly passed, forcing the Chinese out of the gold fields and into low-paying, menial jobs.
- The Chinese immigrants laid tracks for the Central Pacific Railroad, reclaimed swampland in the Sacramento delta, developed shrimp and abalone fisheries, and provided cheap labor wherever there was work no other group wanted or needed.
- Beginning in 1872 groups such as the Anti-Coolie Association and the Supreme Order of the Caucasians staged boycotts of Chinese labor throughout the country.
- The boycotts cost Liu his job in the gold fields shoveling slurry, and later his job picking strawberries.
- The Panic of 1873 followed; although it was caused largely by the overcapitalization of the railroads, Chinese immigrants were blamed for the lost American jobs.
- The Chinese were attacked by violent mobs during bloody riots that erupted in Chinatowns from Denver to Los Angeles.
- Anti-Chinese riots even occurred in Liu's home town of San Francisco, which had the largest and best-established Chinatown.
- A community of only nine city blocks, it housed over 30,000 people.
- "The Chinese must go!" was the official slogan of Denis Kearney of California's Workingmen's Party; to win votes, politicians echoed this cry, and labor leaders exploited the issue to encourage unionization of "real" Americans.
- Liu, however, found work with Edward Roberts, a traveling photographer, and moved from place to place helping him take pictures of the newly wealthy, the soon-to-be wealthy, and the newly arrived.
- Liu liked to tell photography customers that the Chinese came to the United States before the arrival of most Jewish, Italian, Hungarian, and Polish immigrants.
- Most ignored his comments; a minority muttered, "They can all go back now."
- Liu often wondered whether Thomas Jefferson had thought at all about the Chinese people when he wrote "all men are created equal" and that liberty was an "unalienable right."

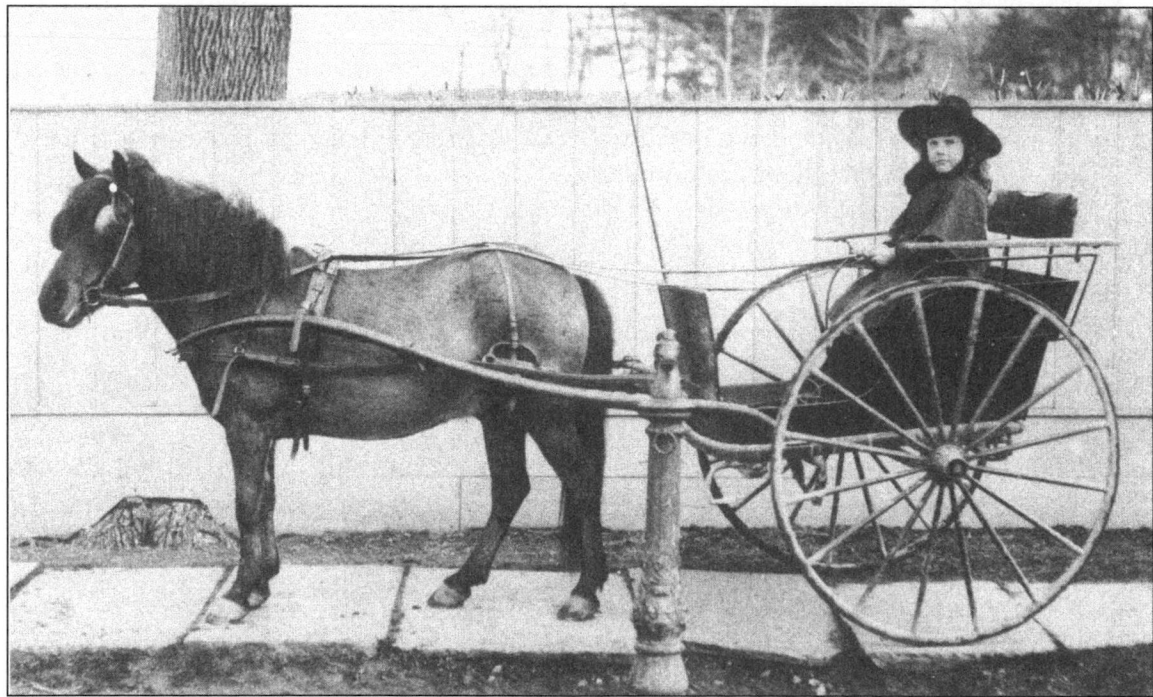

Liu worked for traveling photographer Edwards Roberts, who photographed newly arrived European immigrants, like this young woman.

- Christian missionaries saw the Chinese immigrants as the chance of a lifetime; Liu believed he'd been baptized 12 times in 10 different cities by Christian ministers-some self-proclaimed-who were eager for converts.
- Most of the time, he was rewarded with a nice dinner and new clothes.
- Often, the church people did not realize how well he spoke English and that he understood the slurs "yellow peril" and "heathen."
- Many times, especially on the long buggy rides from town to town, Liu and his boss Edward talked about why the Chinese were so hated.
- "It's pretty simple," Edward declared. "The bosses know the Chinese workers will always stick together. They hate it when a bunch of Chinese gaggle together in a group to talk; they just know that they are being plotted against."
- Chinese workers were seen as being on the side of major corporations, railroads, and large landowners, and thus against American workers and small farmers.
- "The workers resent the Chinese because they will work for less, even if it's a job the workers don't want," Edward remarked.
- In 1876 anti-Chinese sentiment was so intense that Congress launched an investigation into Chinese immigration.
- During the hearings, held in San Francisco, the committee heard 1,200 pages of testimony.

Packing, unpacking, and setting up the camera was Liu's job

- Industrialists such as Leland Stanford and Charles Crocker testified that the Chinese were industrious and dependable, and that without them the Transcontinental Railroad would not have been built.
- Farmers, dependent on Chinese labor, defended the Chinese as well, praising them for their agricultural skills.
- Yet public officials often referred to the Chinese as heathens who lived in filthy quarters.
- Labor leaders testified that the Chinese drove "decent white men" out of work, forcing their wives and children to starve.
- Before 1882 America had a free immigration policy without restrictions.
- But in 1882, reacting to the immigration laws beginning to be passed by the states, the federal government asserted its authority to control immigration and passed the first immigration law, barring "lunatics" and felons from entering the country.
- Then, in the midst of the West Coast backlash against Chinese labor, Congress passed the Chinese Exclusion Act in 1882, temporarily suspending the immigration of skilled and unskilled Chinese laborers for ten years and prohibiting the naturalization of any Chinese.
- Only officials, teachers, students, merchants, and those who "traveled for curiosity" were exempted from the act, in accordance with an 1880 treaty with China.
- The law required resident Chinese to obtain a permit to re-enter if they left the country.

- It also stated that, "hereafter no State court or court of the United States shall admit Chinese to citizenship; and all laws in conflict with this act are hereby repealed."
- Imperial China was too weak and impoverished to exert any influence to counter American policy.
- Nevertheless Liu continued learning English and traveling around California in the back of the photography wagon with Edward, the self-proclaimed "King of the Carte de Visite."
- In polite society, cartes de visite, or visiting cards, were left by visitors making formal calls on acquaintances and business associates.
- Therefore the cards, bearing the image of the visitor, were steadily in demand.
- Packing, unpacking and setting up the camera was Liu's job, along with cooking, cleaning, fixing wagon wheels and scaring unhappy customers with his long sword.
- The heavy camera itself had four lenses designed to make four small photographs, each measuring 3.25 x 2.125 inches, on a full-size plate of 6.5 x 8.5 inches.

The discovery of gold lured Chinese immigrants to San Francisco.

- These photographs could be produced cheaply, selling for half the price charged by a portrait photographer.
- The pose was stylized; usually the subject stood next to a table piled high with books or sat in a fancy highbacked chair to display a favorite rifle or other possession.
- The resulting photograph displayed the face small enough that slight movements by the subject would not cause the picture to be out of focus.
- Most of the men did not smile; instead, they stared grimly into the camera.

Life in the Community: San Francisco, California

- San Francisco was on its way to becoming a respectable town in 1848 when fate intervened in the form of gold.

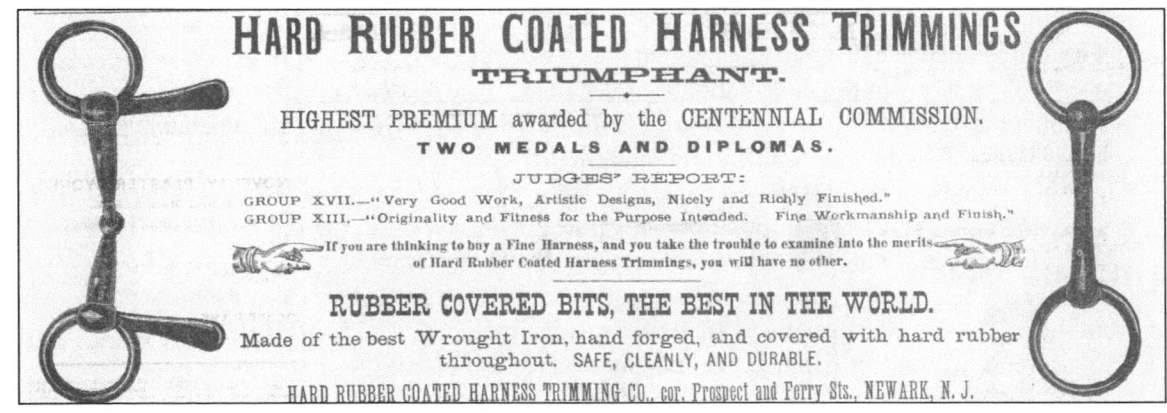

Peddlers were a familiar sight in many California towns.

- The result was the California Gold Rush, a flood of gold seekers to the West Coast from the eastern, southern, and midwestern United States as well as from China and elsewhere.
- All of the newcomers were convinced they would become rich overnight.
- The discovery of gold was a transforming event for California—and for the Chinese immigrants who responded to the lure of prospective wealth.
- Most immigrants fully expected to return to their homeland someday.
- Many knew so little about the "new world" that they were not even sure whether it rained in California.
- The Chinese were employed to build some intrastate railroads in California as early as 1858, but the first large-scale use of Chinese labor was on the Central Pacific, the western portion of the great Transcontinental Railroad, from 1865 to 1869.
- Ultimately, 12,000 Chinese carved tunnels and laid track across the Sierra Nevada; an estimated 1,200 of them were killed in the process, buried in avalanches during the severe winters or blown apart while handling explosives.
- The work required both skill and daring, including the ability to carve ledges from cliffs while hanging in baskets.
- Their speed was remarkable; when racing to meet the Union Pacific coming from the East, Chinese workers laid 10 miles of track in one day.
- The Chinese also worked on the western portion of the Southern Pacific and on portions of the Northern Pacific lines.
- By 1880, more than 105,000 Chinese were in the United States, most of them in California, where they converted the tule swamps of the Sacramento-San Joaquin River Delta into rich farmland, cultivated and harvested vineyards, and raised sugar beets, citrus fruits, and celery crops.

- Chinese farmers dominated the strawberry-growing industry in California, and they pioneered new methods of horticulture.
- In 1880 they amounted to more than a third of California's truck gardeners, and Chinese vegetable peddlers became a familiar sight in many towns.
- Chinese factory workers were also important in the California industries that had grown up during the Civil War, especially woolen mills and the cigar, shoe, and garment industries of San Francisco.
- By the early 1870s, approximately 70 percent to 80 percent of woolen-mill workers and 90 percent of the cigar makers in the city were Chinese immigrants.
- By the mid-1870s, they were a majority of the shoemakers and garment makers, producing almost all the undergarments on the market; they also manufactured brooms, slippers, and cigar boxes.
- Although never more than a tenth of the California population, they formed about a quarter of the state's labor force, because they were nearly all males of working age.
- In the 1880s the Chinese accounted for 86 percent of the work force in the salmon canneries of California and the Northwest, 80 percent of the shirtmakers in San Francisco, 70 percent to 80 percent of the work force in the wool industry, 84 percent of cigar-industry workers, and 50 percent of the fishery workers.

&〜&〜&〜&〜&〜

Chinese Immigration Timeline

1847-1850 A drought in Canton Province in China and the discovery of gold in California in 1848 ignited Chinese immigration to the United States.

1849 Three hundred twenty-five Chinese were recorded as residents of California; about 4,018 Chinese lived in the United States.

1850 Chinese were invited to march in President Zachery Taylor's funeral procession, and helped celebrate California's admission to the union later that year.

1852 California legislature reenacted the Foreign Miners' Tax law targeted at Chinese.

A monthly Alien Poll Tax charged each Chinese $2.50.

Twenty thousand Chinese arrived in America.

1854 The state of California barred any Chinese from testifying in court against a white; the courts also provided that "No Black, or Mulato person, or Indian, shall be allowed to give evidence in favor of, or against a White man."

1859 The California Superintendent of Education asked that state funds be withheld from schools that enrolled Chinese students.

1860 The census counted 34,933 Chinese.

1870 A San Francisco city ordinance prohibited the use of sidewalks against those carrying loads on a pole, aimed at the Chinese method of carrying heavy objects.

The census recorded 63,100 Chinese, an 81 percent increase from the previous decade.

1872 Chinese were forbidden to have business licenses or to own land.

1877 The California legislature appealed to Congress to limit Chinese immigration.

1879 The California legislature adopted a new constitution containing a section with punitive anti-Chinese provisions.

1880   President Hayes renegotiated the Burlingame Treaty with China, securing the right of the United States to regulate, limit, or suspend (but not prohibit) Chinese immigration.

Two years before the Chinese Exclusion Act was enacted, the census counted 105,465 Chinese, a 67 percent increase from 1870.

Talmage on the Chinese, He Takes Strong Ground in Defense of Them
New York Times, September 20, 1880

Mr. Talmage spoke yesterday morning in the Brooklyn Tabernacle on the Chinese question. The Tabernacle was crowded. His text contained these words, "Who is My Neighbor?" (Luke 10:29). The substance of the sermon will be found in the abstract which follows: "Is he brute or immortal? Will he help me or hurt me? Must he be welcomed or driven back? I am going to give the result of my summer observations in California. For many days I do not think there was a half hour in which I was not brought into the presence of the Chinese subject. The gentlemen who were my companions were, open and above-board, antagonistic to Chinese immigration. One of them was Dr. Moares, President of the Board of Health, than whom no greater enemy of Chinese immigration exists. So I saw the worst of it, and I tell you it is bad enough and filthy enough and dreadful enough, but I tell you also that the underground life of New York City is 50 percent worse. White wickedness is more brazen by far than yellow wickedness, and as for malodors, the only difference is between the malodors of whisky and opium, and the former is a thousand times worse than the latter. The crowded tenement-houses of New York are more abominable than the Chinese quarters of San Francisco. From what I saw on my recent visit and from my observations 10 years ago, of all the population that came to the United States during the past 40 years, none have been more industrious, more sober, more harmless, more honest, more genial, more courteous, more obliging than the Chinese.

"It is objected that the Chinese do not spend their money where they make it. This is false. They pay in the city of San Francisco yearly rentals amounting to $2.4 million. As a tax to the state government the Chinese pay over $4.0 million a year. All that stays in California. They pay in customs to the United States Government $9.4 million annually. All this stays in the country. It comes poorly from us to charge them with sending money out of the country when there are thousands of American and English merchants in China. Where do you suppose they send theirs to? Besides, we have been applauding for 25 or 30 years the German and Irish serving-maids for their self-denial in sending money home to the old folks, and I think what's good for one nation is good for another. It is again objected that the Chinese are pagans and wear a peculiar dress. What do the objectors refer to? To their cue? George Washington wore a cue. Benjamin Franklin wore a cue. John Hancock wore a cue. Your great-grandfathers wore cues. If this country stands it will be because the Joss house of the Chinaman, the cathedral of the Roman Catholic, the meeting-house of the pagan, and the church of the Presbyterian are protected alike. There are numerous Chinese missions in San Francisco, and I told the people of that city that the man who gives one penny toward those missions does more to settle the Chinese question than 10,000 orators speaking for 10,000 years. These Chinese make good Christians. How insignificant and contemptible will the Christians of the present day appear when it comes to be demonstrated that the Chinese were brought to this country, not by the Six Chinese Companies, but by God Almighty in order to Christianize them? Some of them are descendants of men who forgot more than we ever knew. Common school education is more widely spread in China than in America. You cannot find a Chinaman who is unable to read and write, while there are hundreds of thousands of Americans who, if called upon to sign a paper, would be obliged to affix their mark. The Chinese invented the art of printing, the mariner's compass, the manufacture of porcelain, paper-making, and many other things ages before any other nation thought them out. Five hundred years before Christ came Confucius, who anticipated the Golden Rule, and who, when asked to compress in one sentence a direction for human life, said: "Do not unto others what you would not have them do to you." I think the Chinese are God's favorite nation, from the fact that He made more of them than of any other nation on Earth.

People don't seem to understand that their right to come here implies our right to go there. It will not be many years before the cry in China may be, "Must the Americans go?" [Laughter.] The Chinese scare is the most unreasonable and unmitigated humbug ever invented. They have been coming over 25 years, and they do not number over 200,000, while other nationalities have been coming by millions. Compared with those they are as a drop of rain on a summer ocean. If they increase no faster for the next 100 years, they will be a most insignificant element in our population. Moreover, there are fewer Chinese in America today than last year, fewer than two years ago. The whole spirit of the Chinese Government is against any of its people leaving home. They are taxed for the privilege of landing on our shores, they are taxed for street-cleaning, yet not one cent is spent in the Chinese quarters. The United States Government broke its solemn treaty with them. When Americans were outraged in China, the Chinese Government cheerfully paid $500,000 compensation, but we refuse to pay a cent for the outrages on Chinamen. In the name of Almighty God, the maker of nations, He who made all of one blood, I impeach the United States Government for its perfidy against the Chinese. [Applause.] This question is a complicated and tremendous one. It is higher than your City Hall; higher than the heathen goddess on top of the Capitol at Washington; higher than your church steeples. It is so high as to be on a level with God's own throne."

Mr. Talmage said during the announcements previous to the sermon: "There is a delusion abroad that Mormonism is dying out, when it is growing hour by hour, and will overshadow the nation unless some means be taken to prevent it. Next Sunday I will discuss that question."

Traveling Salesman and Entrepreneur in 1885

After a youth spent on a farm and some years in the Union Army, Buck Blanchard wanted to direct his own success by becoming an entrepreneur, selling books and making profits from the sales of other "canvassers."

Life at Home

- Buck Blanchard met his first traveling salesman when he was eight years old.
- The peddler was from Connecticut, a distant, almost unimaginable place for a boy living in rural Ohio in 1841.
- The hawker's speech, his dress, and the way he displayed the "highest value" mantel clock he had brought all seemed impressive to young Buck.
- While strolling together on the quarter-mile run up to the farmhouse, the man asked Buck about that year's crops, the number of brothers and sisters he had, the foods his mother liked to cook, and what church they all attended.
- Buck was delighted by all the attention.
- Buck's father was not happy to see the peddler.
- Previous waves of Yankee salesmen had left farmers with mediocre goods, merchants unhappy about lost sales, and housewives suddenly discontented by their husband's stinginess, even though most farmhouse wives never knew they needed the peddler's wares until he arrived and convinced them that his products would transform their lives.
- This was especially true if the area had been worked by a traveling lightning-rod salesman; lightning-rod salesmen were notorious for frightening farmers into signing contracts filled with hidden costs and additional fees.
- Buck's newfound friend had concerns of his own: Ohio farm wives were well known for their bargaining skills.
- Bartering was a respected skill in a nation without a uniform currency in which three-quarters of the population were farmers dependent on bargaining to obtain everything from soap to wagon wheels.

Buck Blanchard was a successful traveling salesman.

- Each peddler had to calculate the exchange rates of Ohio bank-issued funds, the appropriate value of six large eggs (to be prepared in case they were they offered as part of the settlement), and the possibility of selling the clock he had on hand later in the year when the harvest was past and farmers were feeling more prosperous.
- Clock peddlers, who charged $10 or more for their product, preferred bank notes or coins-commodities in short supply in most farmhouses.
- Buck was fascinated by how the peddler talked his normally stubborn father into leaving his plow, listening to a lengthy spiel, and then walking to the farmhouse to see how a "genuine Eli Terry" clock looked on the mantel.
- Along the way, the salesman called each of the children by name, as though he were a visiting uncle, mused about the rumored rise in wheat prices and praised God for the moral leadership provided by the Methodist church where the family worshipped.
- He even mentioned the intention of their nearest neighbor to buy a clock "not nearly so fine as this one."
- In the end the salesman asked Buck's parents to do him a favor: keep the clock for a month so "I don't have to tote it" around Ohio.
- When he returned 26 days later, Buck's family had received so many compliments on being sophisticated clock owners that they begged the peddler to let them buy it.
- The experience left Buck dazzled by the power of words and the vision of being an entrepreneur free from the seasonal burdens imposed by plowing, planting, and picking.
- When Buck joined the Union Army in 1862, the clock was still one of his mother's most prized possessions, even though it had stopped working years before.
- Buck was 30 years old when he joined the Army in the hope of leaving small-town Ohio behind.
- His immediate goal was to study the way the military distributed supplies so that he could be a regional mercantile man when the war ended.

Buck longed for a way off the farm.

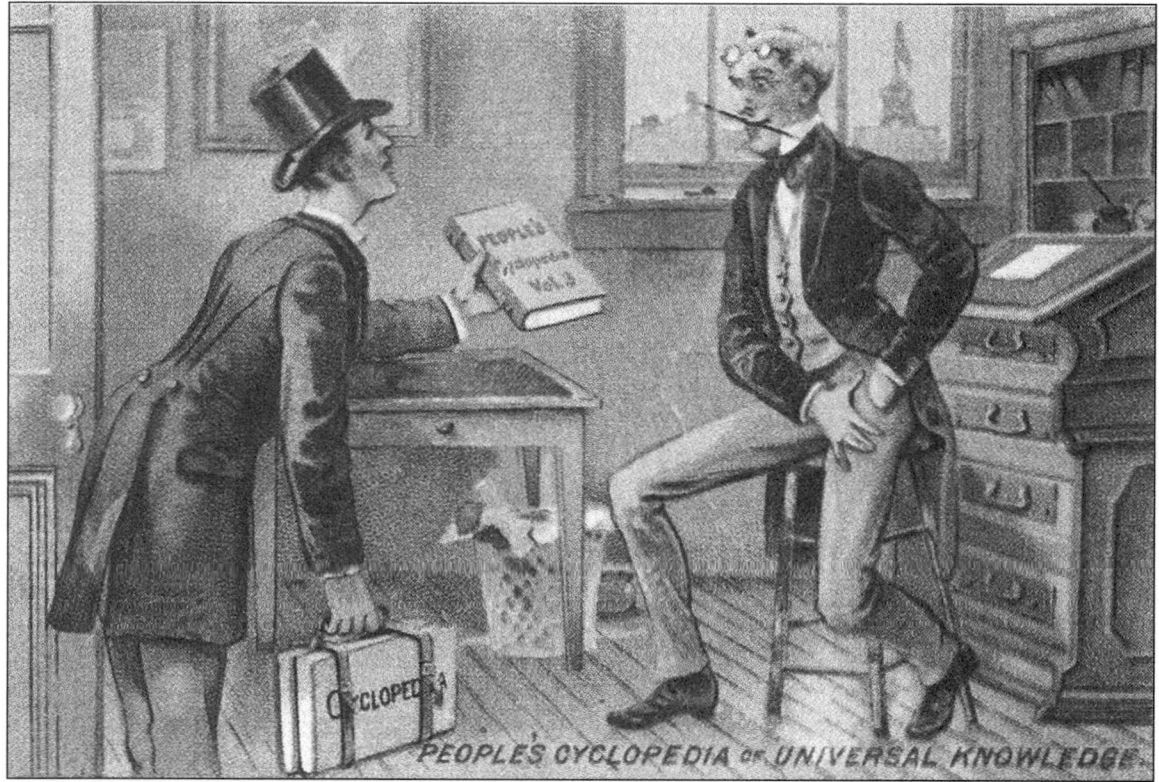

PEOPLE'S CYCLOPEDIA OF UNIVERSAL KNOWLEDGE

- After two years of service in the Quartermaster Corps, he knew a lot about mud, blood, standing around on idle days, and working like a demon on busy ones.
- He also learned to love the pomp and ceremony of the military, with all its glitz and glamour, even though Buck was disappointed by General Ulysses S. Grant's perennially rumpled look.
- Buck and Grant were both in Nashville, Tennessee, in the spring of 1864, when General Grant was asked to assume command of all the Union armies.
- By the time the war with the South ended, however, Buck had little interest in commanders, commands, or being commanded.
- He had even less interest in returning to being a farmer; after discovering how big the nation really was, he was convinced that being an entrepreneur was his destiny.
- So Buck rented an apartment in Columbus, Ohio, and then took to the road to claim his fortune selling Bibles, *Webster's American Spelling Book,* and the *Farmer's Almanac.*
- For special customers Buck discreetly carried scandalous titles such as *Memoirs of a Woman of Pleasure* (better known as *Fanny Hill*).
- Buck also read everything he could find on salesmanship, including the wryly satirical *The Clockmaker; or, The Sayings and Doings of Samuel Slick, of Slickville*; first published as a serial in Nova Scotia and soon available in the United States, it perfectly captured Sam Slick, the quintessential Yankee peddler.
- A dozen magazine and book subscription houses-most headquartered in Hartford, Connecticut-employed as many as 50,000 part-time agents per year, including disabled soldiers, retired ministers, and children.
- Book peddlers hawked 600-page volumes detailing the events of the Civil War or natural history or life in Central America.
- Most agents had to purchase the books at a discount and pay their own expenses, and they were responsible for tracking down customers to collect payments.

- Contract agents were forbidden from selling any copies to store owners.
- Materials in the canvassing kit included a sales handbook, advice for overcoming objections, calling cards, weekly report forms, posters, and strategies for closing the sale.
- American industry also provided new products to the traveling salesman: a new pie crimper, an improved apple peeler, a darning machine, or a patented farm gate.
- But Buck carefully avoided selling patent medicines, composed of curative spices liberally endowed with alcohol.
- During his first year on the road, he had met a patent medicine man whose arm was broken and face was mangled by a gang of dissatisfied customers.
- It was a lesson Buck never forgot.

Life at Work

- Buck Blanchard's big break came in 1885 when he put his Union uniform back on and became a regional distributor for the *Personal Memoirs of U. S. Grant.*
- Now 52 years old, Buck was weary of the road but still enthusiastic about becoming rich as a peddler-or "canvasser," the term he now preferred.
- During the past decade, some 53,000 salesmen had taken to the roads, often with overlapping circuits or territories.
- Buck's plan was to manage a dozen or so salespeople in the Ohio-Indiana area and receive a percentage of their sales.
- He knew that the secret of success was the ability to arouse interest in the "mystery" of the book, not necessarily in the book itself; he had even sold books to people who couldn't read but wanted the prestige conferred by a bound volume prominently displayed in the parlor.
- And this time he could become an entrepreneur in partnership with author Mark Twain and none other than General Ulysses S. Grant.
- Former General and President Grant had started writing his memoirs in the summer of 1884 after learning that he had cancer.

Buck put on a Union uniform and became a regional distributor for the Personal Memoirs of U.S. Grant.

Washington D.C. in 1885.

- As a result of a financial reversal, Grant was bankrupt.
- Desperate to avoid leaving his family destitute at his death, he announced plans to finish the two-volume project in less than a year.
- Mark Twain, eager to earn more money from his own projects and also to profit from the works of others, had recently formed his own publishing company.
- When Twain learned that Grant had first agreed to publish his memoir with the well-established Century Company but had failed to come to terms, he went to see the ailing general.
- He knew that Grant's brokerage company, Grant and Ward, had declared bankruptcy after Grant's partner Ferdinand Ward had engaged in fraud and left the former president nearly broke.
- Twain persuaded Grant to sign with his new publishing company, promising him an astounding 70 percent of the profits, even though the book was still unfinished.
- While the ailing Grant, with little assistance, handwrote his massive two-volume autobiography, Twain's company secured agents to sell the work in cities throughout the nation.
- Of particular interest were the 80,000 Union Army veterans, who were viewed as the perfect sales force-all eager retell the heroic battles that they had waged two decades earlier and to earn money as well.
- Grant frantically worked on his memoirs, sometimes compiling up to 10,000 words a day; he died on July 23, 1885, just five days after completing the manuscript.
- The anticipation that had been building up was intensified by the mourning following Grant's death.

- In total, ten thousand canvassers fanned out over the countryside, all carefully drilled in the principles set forth in the Twain company's little manual, *How to Introduce the Personal Memoirs of U.S. Grant.*
- It contained necessary arguments to help the agent deliver an effective spiel: introduce yourself by name, shake hands, keep the prospectus concealed from view in a special pocket on the inside of your coat.
- Buck fully understood this was the opportunity for which he had been waiting his entire life.
- If he could manage a dozen salespeople across Ohio, he could make a killing.
- The entire nation knew that General Grant had been fending off death for months simply to complete the memoir.
- Newspapers across the country had shown dramatic photographs of Grant's heroic exertions to complete the book that, it was opined, every American should read.
- Besides, Grant's two green-and-gold volumes would serve as the perfect accent for the marble-top center table in every civilized home and would be a fitting companion for the family Bible.

Mark Twain convinced Grant to give the rights to his memoirs to Twain's publishing company, and then wrote a manual on how to sell it.

- Buck had had little trouble recruiting a dozen men eager once again to wear their soldier's uniform, this time for the purpose of making money.
- They came from all corners of the state and possessed widely varying sales experience.
- At their first meeting, Buck talked about the glorious battles of the Civil War described in the book; he then became animated, expressing disbelief that people would deny themselves the pleasure of this tome.
- Carefully, Buck told the group that each volume would contain a facsimile of the gold medal presented by Congress to General Grant in 1863 in honor of his successes.
- Then he showed them where to find within the 600 large octavo pages a fine steel portrait of the general made from a daguerreotype taken when he was 21 years of age, plus more than a dozen maps and a steel engraving of Grant's birthplace.
- He taught them how to respond when customers said, "I can't afford a $3.50 book right now," by offering delayed payments "when times are better."
- "More orders are lost," he explained, "because the agent does not hang on long enough than because of any other one cause."
- Prospects were to be told the book was a great investment whose value would grow over time.
- "Get the prospect seated-a tree stump or fancy chair, it doesn't matter-where you can put the book right in their lap-but make sure you turn the pages and keep talking," Buck instructed, based on the recommendations in the company manual.
- Buck told his sales force never to use the word *dollars*-"three fifty is fine"-and made it clear that he expected them to make 20 exhibitions daily in towns and 15 in the country.
- He also provided financial incentives for one-third of all sales including the leather-bound edition, the prices of which ranged from $4.50 to $12.50.

- For the first three weeks, Buck traveled the state, making calls with his peddlers and offering them tips on how to close deals.
- After that, he simply waited for the letters to arrive accounting for the number of sales in each region of the state.
- Within 60 days, more than 1,000 books had been sold in Ohio, and more than 100,000 nationwide.
- The autobiography was a huge success, and women were delighted that the Grants would be well provided for upon the general's passing.
- Buck was enormously pleased: 80 percent of the sales force met their quota, and 35 percent exceeded expectations, thereby earning a bonus.
- The top salesman sold more than 800 books, collected 95 percent of the money owed on the books, and made more than $600 in four months.
- Buck's personal take after six months was equally impressive: $2,357 for directing the team salesmen.
- He truly was an entrepreneur at last, with new plans for the future.

Life in the Community: Columbus, Ohio

- The selection of Columbus as the capital of Ohio was the result of compromise, geography, and deal-making.
- After Ohio achieved statehood in 1803, political infighting among Ohio's more prominent leaders caused the state capital to be moved from Chillicothe to Zanesville and back again.
- The state legislature finally decided that a new capital city, located in the center of the state, was a necessary compromise.
- Several small towns and villages petitioned the legislature for the honor of becoming the state capital, but ultimately a coalition of land speculators made the most attractive offer.
- Named in honor of Christopher Columbus, the capital city was founded on February 14, 1812.
- Although plagued by outbreaks of cholera, the town began to boom after the National Road reached Columbus from Baltimore in 1831, complementing the city's new link to the Ohio and Erie Canal.
- A wave of immigrants from Europe brought significant numbers of Irish and German workers to the area.
- With a population of only 3,500, Columbus was officially chartered as a city on March 3, 1834.
- By 1850 the Columbus and Xenia Railroad became the first railroad to enter the city, followed by the Cleveland, Columbus and Cincinnati Railroad in 1851.

REGINA
QUEEN OF MUSIC BOXES.

Plays 1000 Tunes

Plays with more brilliancy than any other music box made. Has no delicate parts to get out of order. Plays from 20 to 30 minutes with one winding. Plays your own selection of music. Has indestructible tune discs and can be safely operated by a child. Sold by all music dealers. Boxes from $7 to $70.

THE NEW ORCHESTRAL REGINA.

A musical marvel. The largest music box made. Just the thing for hotels and public places. A big money maker. Send for catalogue. REGINA MUSIC BOX CO., Rahway, N. J.

The majority of immigrant farm workers in Columbus, Ohio were Irish and German.

- By 1875 Columbus was served by eight railroads.
- On January 7, 1857, the Ohio Statehouse finally opened to the public after 18 years of construction.
- During the Civil War, Columbus was a major base for the volunteer Union Army, housing 26,000 troops and holding up to 9,000 Confederate prisoners of war at Camp Chase.
- By virtue of the Morrill Land-Grant Colleges Act, the Ohio Agricultural and Mechanical College was founded in 1870 on the former estate of William and Hannah Neil.
- By the 1880s Columbus had become known as the "Buggy Capital of the World," thanks to the presence there of some two dozen buggy factories-most notably the Columbus Buggy Company, which was founded in 1875 by C. D. Firestone.
- The Columbus Consolidated Brewing Company also rose to prominence during this time, and it may have achieved even greater success were it not for the influence of the Anti-Saloon League, which was based in neighboring Westerville.
- In the steel industry, a forward-thinking man named Samuel P. Bush presided over the Buckeye Steel Castings Company.
- Columbus was also a known as a center of labor organization: in 1886, Samuel Gompers founded the American Federation of Labor in Druid's Hall on South Fourth Street.

Shoe Lasting Machine Inventor in 1886

Shoe manufacturing was transformed when Jan Ernst Matzeliger, the son of a Dutch engineer, invented a machine that would attach the shoe's upper to the sole, revolutionizing the shoe-making industry.

Life at Home

- Born in the Dutch colony of Dutch Guiana, or Suriname, in 1852, Jan Ernst Matzeliger was the son of a Dutch engineer who headed the government's machine works in the capital city, Paramaribo.
- Because most of the colony was located at or below sea level, the Dutch, with the labor provided by some 300,000 West African slaves, had built numerous dikes and seawalls to reclaim the land from the sea.
- Jan's mother was a slave on one of the eight hundred sugar plantations stretched across the island.
- Ethnically and culturally diverse families were common in Suriname, where slaves outnumbered the white Dutch settlers 14 to 1.
- But Jan never saw his mother after his earliest years; he spent most of his youth with his father and paternal aunt in Paramaribo.
- When he was ten years old, his father entered him in a machine apprentice program.
- There he learned to cut and shape metal on a fast-moving lathe and how to manipulate other power-operated machines.
- At age 19, Jan followed the lure of the sea, serving two years as a merchant seaman before coming ashore in Philadelphia.
- There he found his options limited by his Dutch African heritage, as well as his inability to speak more than a few words of English.
- Unfortunately, the Panic of 1873, one of the worst depressions in United States history, was also under way.
- The economic downturn was triggered by the overbuilding of railroads and speculation in the bonds that underwrote their construction.
- Nearly 90 railroad companies disappeared; more than 18,000 other businesses dependent on the railroads went bankrupt.
- Unemployment surged to 14 percent.

Jan Ernst Matzeliger invented a machine that attached together the tops and bottoms of shoes.

- Despite being a skilled machinist, Jan initially managed to find only a string of unfulfilling odd jobs, but then he managed to become an apprentice at a shoemaking shop.
- The shoe factory was stocked with the revolutionary McKay stitching machines, which helped bring automation to the shoemaking industry.
- A McKay was capable of sewing the outer soles of shoes to the inner soles; previously, this time-consuming operation had been done by hand.
- After attending a Philadelphia exhibition that showcased Lynn, Massachusetts, as the shoe-making center of America, Jan decided to move there to pursue his dream of being an inventor.

Life at Work

- By the time Jan Matzeliger was 26, he had left Philadelphia for Lynn, Massachusetts, the shoemaking capital of the world.
- Although he arrived in Lynn with few possessions, Jan had carefully charted the course he would take to realize his ambitions.
- First, he found a job operating a McKay stitching machine for the M. H. Harney Company.
- He rented a room at the West Lynn Mission on Charles Street, in the area of town populated by African Americans.
- To get on the fast track to citizenship, Jan enrolled in night school to learn English.
- To further improve himself, he purchased a set of books called *Popular Educator* and a five-volume series called *Science for All*.
- Jan then used a second-hand set of drafting instruments to draw out his mechanical innovations every night, after the grind of ten-hour work days in the shoe factory.
- For pleasure Jan painted landscapes on dishes, oils on canvas, and watercolors on paper, and he made toys for children.

Jan enrolled in night school to learn English.

Beal Brothers Shoe Company allowed Jan to work on his machine in their factory.

- Driven to excel, he spent the majority of his earnings on materials for his projects, often while neglecting basic creature comforts.
- Sometimes he denied himself proper warmth during the New England winters, proper rest and nourishment; cornmeal mush was his standard meal.
- In the 1880s, even with labor-saving innovations like the McKay, the shoe industry was still far from being fully mechanized.
- The process of fastening the shoe upper to the inner sole, or "lasting," was an intricate process that had defied the most exhaustive attempts at mechanization.
- As a result, the men who did this work, known as lasters, were the most skillful and best paid workers in the shoe industry; their detail-oriented step in the making of shoes had to be done completely by hand.
- But because most of the steps that led up to this crucial phase were mechanized and "lasting" was not, hundreds of nearly completed shoes often piled up while waiting for the laster to do his work.
- An experienced laster could process 50 or 60 pairs of shoes per day.
- Gordon McKay, who manufactured the stitching machine, had spent $120,000 in a fruitless attempt to build a machine that could form, shape, tug, pleat, hold and tack like a human laster.
- Realizing his need for more working space and access to machine tools, Jan parlayed his mechanical aptitude into a job with Beal Brothers Shoe Company, where he was given access to both space and tools.
- He scoured junkyards and factory dumps for discarded levers, pulleys, gears and cams which he reworked to his specifications.
- After two years of solitary work, he created a crude working prototype for a mechanized laster, for which he filed for a patent on January 24, 1882.

- The resulting 15-page document of text and drawings was so complex that an inspector from the U.S. Patent Office personally visited Jan to have him explain the invention.
- At this point, financing became a serious issue.
- In order to produce a model that would work under demanding factory conditions, Jan needed precision parts manufactured in a professional machine shop.
- Obtaining the necessary capital meant giving up the rights to a portion of the future profits; this was simply the first step in the long process of getting a patent.
- Thanks to his reputation as a skilled machinist, Jan obtained the financial backing he needed from Charles H. Delnow and Melville S. Nichols in return for two-thirds of all eventual profits-a substantial price to pay to see his dream fulfilled.
- His lasting machine patent was issued on March 20, 1883, with Delnow and Nichols listed as assignees.
- Jan's experimental machine took three years of hard work, soaring excitement, and deep despair to complete.
- Some days Jan was unsure he would ever be successful.
- Jan demonstrated his machine on May 29, 1885; his device flawlessly fashioned 75 pairs of shoes that day.
- The shoes were indistinguishable from handmade shoes-but were produced five times faster than a human laster could produce them.
- A hand operation that previously required highly paid, skilled workers five to six minutes per shoe could now be done by machine in one minute.
- And Jan's invention could handle all shoe styles, including women's pointed-toe shoes made of various grades of leather.

Jan's invention cut the time it took to put a shoe together from five minutes to one.

- The impossible had become a reality.
- Once a worker placed an insole and upper on Jan's last machine, it drove a tack, turned the shoe, pleated the leather, drove another tack, then turned the shoe-until the process was completed.
- In 1886 Jan sold the consolidated hand method lasting machine company all rights to his patents for more than $15,000 in stock.
- As use of the lasting machine spread, the price of shoes fell rapidly-from an average $6.00 a pair to $3.00.
- Advertisements sprouted in newspapers across the nation touting $3.00 shoes; entire companies sprang up to meet the demand for less expensive shoes.
- With his newfound wealth, Jan bought a house on the same street as his commercial backers and rented the house to the couple with whom he had boarded for years.

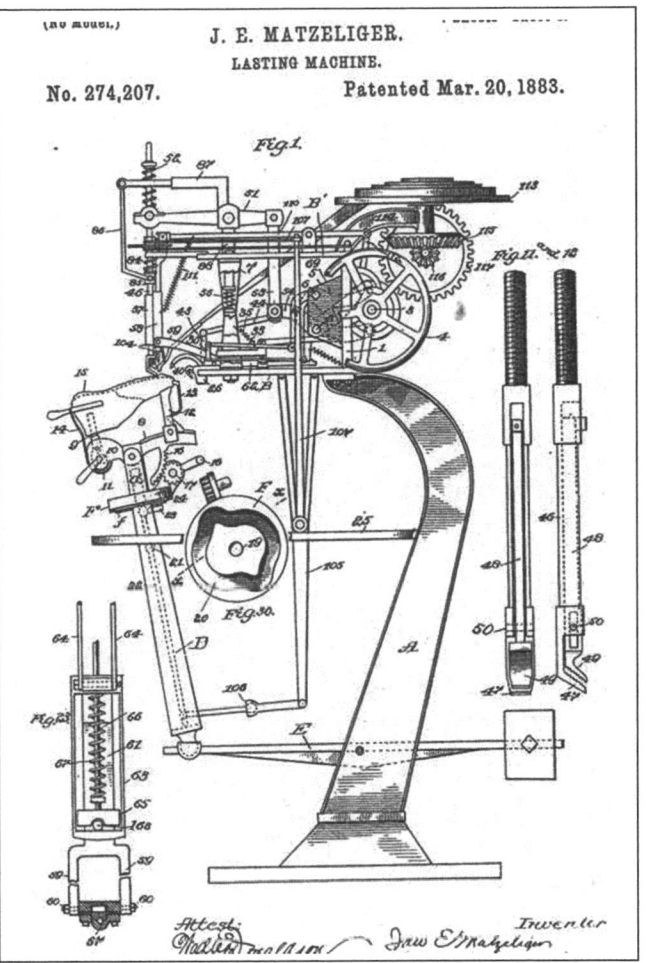

Jan's lasting machine revolutionized the shoe manufacturing industry.

Life in the Community: Paramaribo, Suriname, and Philadelphia, Pennsylvania

- Suriname, the Dutch colony where Jan Matzeliger was born, was settled by men and women from Holland's most prominent families.
- Built from bricks that had been carried as ballast in the hulls of sailing ships and topped by red-tiled roofs, the homes in Paramaribo resembled gingerbread houses.
- In fact, if not for the orange trees, royal palms, and tamarinds that lined the streets and walkways, the city looked like a piece of Amsterdam transported to the New World.
- The river docks where Jan and the other boys of Paramaribo played were filled with merchant steamships from all over the world.
- The Dutch were proud of their reputation as formidable seamen, and Jan was no different from the average young Dutchman in this respect.
- In 1871 he sailed with the Dutch East India Company for two years before landing in Philadelphia.
- In the 1870s Philadelphia was a black cultural center with a black-owned and operated hospital and black newspapers, and it was the home of the largest contingent of black entrepreneurs in the world.
- Although Philadelphia was a leading manufacturing city, Jan found his career path handicapped by his Dutch African heritage and his limited understanding of racial interaction in America.
- The black population of Philadelphia was 4 percent, the largest of any major northern city, but Jan formed no close relationships there because of the cultural differences between himself and the African Americans whom he lived among.

Jan's family in the Dutch colony of Suriname.

- Also, the Panic of 1873 and the five-year depression that followed increased black unemployment in Philadelphia to 70 percent by 1876.
- Between 1873 and 1876, 18,000 businesses failed and half a million workers lost their jobs in one of the worst financial disasters in American history.
- Frederick Douglass, the most influential black man in America and a former resident of Lynn, Massachusetts, spoke at the 1876 Centennial exhibition held in Philadelphia, which showcased Lynn as the shoe capital of the world.
- After he moved to Lynn, Jan was refused membership in three local churches, the Episcopal, Roman Catholic, and Unitarian; he never forgot the slights.
- He never attempted to join the only black church in town, the African Methodist Episcopal church, which embodied an African American culture he did not understand or relate to.

Cattle Rancher in 1888

In 1872 Karl Watson, his wife, Charlotte, and his six sons moved from Union County, South Carolina, to San Antonio, Texas, to escape the ravages of poverty and the political upheaval that followed the Civil War. The Watsons quickly established a cattle ranch that they gradually expanded to cover several thousand acres.

Life at Home

- The Watsons were refugees of the Civil War; such families were often nicknamed "GTTs" because of the "Gone to Texas" signs they left behind.
- In Union County, near the North Carolina border, the Watsons were successful cotton farmers; they owned no slaves prior to the Civil War.
- During the Civil War, Karl and one of his sons, Caleb, fought in the Confederate Army.
- After the war ended, the cost of cotton and vegetable seeds was high, labor was difficult to find, and federal troops seemed determined to charge Karl with violating the rights of freed slaves.
- Although he was not involved in violence against the former slaves, as a community leader, Karl was expected to stop it.
- Karl was well respected in the community, but in the atmosphere of postwar devastation and social, political, and economic dislocation, he had concluded that there was little he could do to control the situation.
- Moreover, it had become clear to him that the longer he stayed, the more he had to lose.
- So Karl and his family left everything behind and moved west.
- They settled in south-central Texas, purchasing a ranch outside of San Antonio.
- The small house they first built was later used by the field hands.
- The new home they built in the mid-1880s replicated the house they had left behind in South Carolina, including a spacious central hallway running the length of the house, high ceilings, and towering square columns on the wraparound porch.
- Although Karl and his sons prospered in Texas, Charlotte was not happy; she missed her family and friends and the beauty of spring in South Carolina.
- She corresponded regularly with her relatives in the East.

Karl Watson was a cattle rancher in Texas.

71

- She longed for servants who spoke English, finding Spanish trying and her halfhearted efforts to learn it far from adequate.
- Charlotte hated the Texas climate and the lack of water; when clothes were washed, the water often was so dirty that the clothes were no better off for the effort.
- Charlotte also wanted a more refined life, regularly buying perfumes and scents and waiting anxiously for the once-a-week train to get packages she has ordered from Boston, Charleston, and New York.

Life at Work

- The Watson family presided over a cattle herd of 25,000 head; last year Karl sold 5,000 animals and grossed $90,000.
- Karl used his profits to upgrade the farm, buy additional land, and upgrade his cattle.
- When the family arrived, they had little knowledge of ranching, but Karl had brought with him sufficient capital to buy good quality land and cattle.
- After hiring a few cowhands, he purchased a herd of beef cattle, instructed the hired help to round up wild cattle on the open range, and began acquiring more land.
- For the first few years, beef had brought high prices; Karl planned to double the size of the herd by allowing them to graze on public lands.
- Many of his neighbors were now financing their herd expansion with money from foreign investors-primarily from Europe-but Karl doesn't like to have partners, especially partners who provide only money and no labor.
- Karl also disliked the claims being made to attract investors; Walter Baron von Richthofen's recent book *Cattle Raising on the Plains of North America*, for example, had asserted that "there is not the slightest element of uncertainty in cattle-raising."
- James S. Brisbin claimed in *The Beef Bonanza; or How to Get Rich on the Plains* that $250,000 borrowed at 10 percent and invested in cattle would yield $810,000 in five years.

The Watsons' cattle herd numbered 25,000 head.

Karl hired mostly white cowboys, despite the fact that Mexicans worked for less.

- The cattle industry of the San Antonio area had been growing rapidly for many years; Mexican landowners gave the industry its start in the area when they abandoned their land and animals after the Mexican War, turning loose more than 300,000 beef cattle.
- Ranchers from the East and South quickly took advantage of the open lands, wild beef, and established ranches.
- For most of America's history, pork had dominated the meat supply of cities; in the 1850s, tastes shifted to beef, driving up demand.
- Chicago emerged from the Civil War as the major meat-packing center of the nation, handling cattle as well as hogs.
- In the 1870s, before refrigeration, most cattle sold in Chicago were shipped east for butchering.
- Using industrialized slaughter techniques developed for hogs, Chicago took advantage of the western expansion of the railroad network and the development of refrigeration to bring beef to the tables of America.
- Beef did especially well during the boom times of the early 1870s and the early 1880s; when the economy slumped, the cattle business slowed immediately.
- Karl and his sons quickly "learned cow" so they could expand their holdings and get the best breeding stock.
- Properly raised, a $4 yearling could turn into a $20 steer or heifer in just three years.
- Caleb, as the eldest son, was told he could keep every fourth calf born; in just two years, he accumulated 250 head.
- In Texas, if the land was good, a single cow generally needed 10 acres of grass to graze on; twice as much acreage was needed if the land was dry.
- Each cow drank up to 30 gallons of water a day, so every consideration of cattle ranching revolved around water.
- A small river ran through Karl's property; he wanted to control the headwaters so he could expand further.
- Controlling the lands bordering a stream often included the exclusive rights to a much larger area of range land lying along the stream.

- The Watsons learned to locate water by watching swallows: if the birds carried mud for nest building in their mouths, the Watsons knew that a water hole lay in the direction from which they came.
- The family learned how to recognize different grasses and to judge the freshness of a hoofprint by counting the insect tracks across it.
- The Watson family began to maximize its income through specialization; calves survived better in Texas but fattened faster in the grasslands of Nebraska.
- Their focus was now on breeding stock and shipping cattle north at two years old; a steer in Nebraska at age four weighed 1,200 pounds, while the same animal in Texas would only weigh 900 pounds at that age.
- Under this system cattle often were owned by three or four companies before being led to slaughter in Chicago.
- Specialization also meant that if a cattle glut hit the market-as had happened in 1885-it would be the Northern ranchers who were most at risk; the cattle ranchers in Texas could hold their cattle until prices went back up.
- The year 1887 had been worrisome; cattle worth $9.35 per hundredweight in 1882 brought only $1.00 for the same weight in 1887.
- Karl was also concerned about another strike; when the cowboys struck for higher wages in 1883, it required all the cattle ranchers working together to break the strike.
- Karl employed mostly white cowboys, but he was reconsidering this practice after being told that Mexican cowboys would work at half the pay of Anglos.
- Karl's ranch hands were forbidden to gamble, drink, or carry six-shooters in their off hours; Karl believed that liquor, gambling, and guns were a formula for serious trouble.
- After losing hundreds of cattle on the drive north in 1887, Karl considered shipping his herd by rail; several ranchers in the association were also talking about ending the risky and time-consuming cattle drives.
- But rail rates were still very high, and in addition, the American Humane Society had established a series of rules concerning the shipment of cattle by rail.
- On balance the ranchers were inclined to think that train shipment was more trouble than it was worth.
- Between drives, the cowboys on Karl's ranch spent much of their time stringing barbed wire along the property line; the wire controlled the cattle, cut labor costs, and protected the cows from inferior, free-roaming bulls.
- In some parts of Texas, the smaller cattle ranchers vociferously objected to barbed wire fences, believing that the larger rangers were cutting them off from public lands.
- Even President Grover Cleveland got involved, issuing a federal order that illegal fencers using barbed wire to control public lands would be prosecuted.

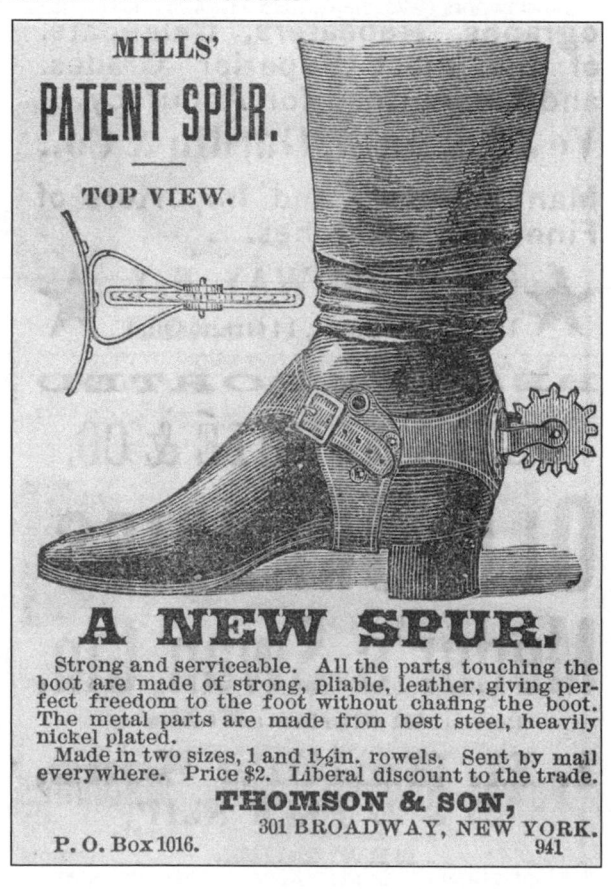

MILLS'
PATENT SPUR.
—
TOP VIEW.

A NEW SPUR.

Strong and serviceable. All the parts touching the boot are made of strong, pliable, leather, giving perfect freedom to the foot without chafing the boot. The metal parts are made from best steel, heavily nickel plated.
Made in two sizes, 1 and 1½in. rowels. Sent by mail everywhere. Price $2. Liberal discount to the trade.
THOMSON & SON,
301 BROADWAY, NEW YORK.
P. O. Box 1016.
941

Caleb, Karl's oldest son, was allowed to keep every fourth calf born.

- After the cowboys' strike, Watson and most of the other ranchers in his area joined a regional cattlemen's organization.
- Working together, the association held round-ups in the spring to gather and brand newborn calves, helped establish registry of brands, and hired detectives to track down cattle thieves.
- The association was working to persuade England to drop its embargo on American beef; the ban was designed to prevent pleuropneumonia, a fever prevalent in Texas, from reaching Europe.

Life in the Community: San Antonio, Texas

- Founded as a Spanish mission in 1700, San Antonio by 1862 had lived under the flags of six countries: Spain, France, Mexico, the Republic of Texas, the Confederate States of America, and the United States.
- The town's best-known landmarks were the Alamo, where 185 men died in 1836 defending the city against a Spanish army for two weeks, and the Spanish Governor's Palace.
- Just after Texas gained independence, the economy of San Antonio was in ruins.
- Within ten years, however, the economy began to improve, thanks to the distribution of finished goods from the Northeast to the newly established ranches and farms of central and south Texas-and to large-scale smuggling across the Mexican border.
- Real prosperity came following the end of the Civil War; mercantile stores, trolley companies, water systems, and breweries all developed quickly, along with a barbed-wire manufacturing company.
- By 1881 gas lights, which had flickered in the streets since 1866, were found in the houses of the most prosperous.
- Rail transportation came to San Antonio in the 1870s, connecting the city to Galveston, Texas, and the Gulf of Mexico, followed in the 1880s by new rail lines running north to ship cattle and south into Mexico.

- As the cattle were shipped out, tourists were shipped in by rail.
- In the 20 years following the Civil War, the city's population increased 208 percent, to 37,600.
- By 1882 the telephone exchange boasted 200 subscribers.
- Unlike in many Southern cities, where the aftermath of the Civil War drove wedges between different groups of people, San Antonio's German, French, Spanish, and Anglo populations tended to work together.
- For example, the city's Easiest Street Car Company, organized in 1874, was jointly owned by a number of influential Germans and Anglos.
- Range ranching had become very big business in Texas; in the northern range and Texas alone, no fewer than 11 million cattle were pastured.
- Buffalo once filled the continent; throughout Texas, they were common.
- The Plains Indians measured the world in terms of the buffalo: the Crow measured big trees as one-robe, two-robe, or three-robe trees, depicting the number needed to stretch around the trunk; to explain size, others spoke of tepees as 12-robe or 15-robe tepees.
- The activities of buffalo changed the western landscape; they often denuded grasslands, since a single buffalo consumed the same amount as would four deer.
- They also destroyed cornfields, stopped trains, and knocked down tepees.
- In the nineteenth century, buffalo came under increasing pressure owing to predation, competition with horses and then cattle for grazing lands, and, especially by mid-century, drought.
- By 1833 buffalo were extinct east of the Mississippi River.
- Mass slaughter by settlers and commercial hunters once the West was opened by the railroad led to the rapid demise of the buffalo in the West.
- By the mid-1880s, the buffalo had virtually vanished from the plains.

Key Dates in Texas History

1519 Alonso Alvarez de Pineda of Spain mapped Texas coast

1532 Hernando de Soto's expedition explored part of northeast Texas

1541 Francisco Vasquez de Coronado traveled across part of west Texas

1682 Spanish missionaries built two missions in Texas, near present-day El Paso

1685 Robert Cavelier, Sieur de La Salle, founded Fort St. Louis, a French settlement on Texas coast

1718 Spaniards established missions and fort on site of present-day San Antonio

1821 Texas became part of new Empire of Mexico; Americans led by Stephen F. Austin settled in Texas

1835 Texas began revolution against Mexico

1836 Independence from Mexico declared; Mexican forces overwhelmed and defeated American defenders at Alamo; Sam Houston defeated Mexicans in Battle of San Jacinto; Texas won its independence and became Republic of Texas

1845 Texas admitted to Union, becoming 28th state

1861 Texas seceded from Union and joined Confederacy

1870 Texas readmitted to the Union

Professional Baseball Player in 1888

Mike Kelly's Irish immigrant parents both died before he was 13-years-old. His baseball career began with the Cincinnati Red Stockings.

Life at Home

- Mike Kelly's birth on New Year's Eve 1857 coincided with the formation of the first legitimate baseball league, the National Association of Base Ball Players.
- For Mike it proved to be a good omen.
- The time saw the beginning of a cult of masculinity in America, when men learned new codes of sexuality and competitive sports.
- Mike's parents, Michael Kelly Sr. and Catherine Kelly, were part of the exodus of nearly one million people from Ireland fleeing the Great Famine and looking for a fresh start in the New World.
- Like the more than 550,000 Irish immigrants before them, they endured the laughter of Americans when they first stepped off a ship wearing clothes considered in America to be 20 years out of fashion.
- The couple settled in Troy, New York, near other Irish families; their son was born in Troy.
- Unlike many immigrants of other nationalities who came to America seeking farmland and open spaces, the Irish tended to cluster in cities, attempting to re-create the close-knit communities they cherished back in Ireland.
- When Mike could barely walk, his father-along with 140,000 other Irish-born men-joined the Union Army in the Civil War and fought until the war's conclusion in 1865.
- During the war years, the family moved to Washington, District of Columbia, so Mike could attend school; there Mike first played baseball.
- After the war was over, Mike's father fell ill, and he moved the family to Paterson, New Jersey, when Mike was 11 years old.
- Mike Senior hoped that the climate of New Jersey, coupled with better work in the thriving town, would help speed his recovery.

Mike "King" Kelly

Outfielder/Catcher/Manager

Mike Kelly was the son of Irish immigrants.

- But he never truly recovered, and he died a little over a year after moving to Paterson; Catherine became sick as well, and she died less than a year after her husband.
- Orphaned, Mike worked during the summers and stayed with a family friend so he could continue attending school and playing baseball.
- Often the baseballs themselves were made from shreds of India rubber wrapped with yarn from a stocking and covered with pieces of an ordinary glove; ready-made baseballs were scarce and much cherished when they could be found.
- A store-bought Willow Wand bat with the words "Home Run" printed in red letters cost $0.15 and was used by both teams.
- No one wore gloves, not even the catcher.
- To support himself, Mike took a job in a textile mill carrying baskets of coal to the top floor for the foreman; Mike could complete the work in a morning and still earn a day's wages.
- He could then spend the rest of his time on the ball field, catching bare-handed and honing his skills.
- That summer, Mike got his first taste of theater when he opened up a playhouse in the cellar of a friend's home.
- A mechanical failure almost killed Mike's friend Jim McCormick, ending the adventure but not Mike's passion for the vaudeville stage.
- At age 15 Mike was good enough at baseball to be invited to play on a semiprofessional team, the Paterson Keystones, organized by his theater friend's father.
- During his time with the Keystones, Mike played as much baseball as he wanted and was paid a small wage for it, too.

Baseballs were often made from scraps of rubber.

- He didn't quit his morning job carrying coal until he was 20 years old, when he was signed to the Cincinnati Red Stockings, the first professional team to pay all of its players.
- Baseball was well rooted into the American culture by 1877.

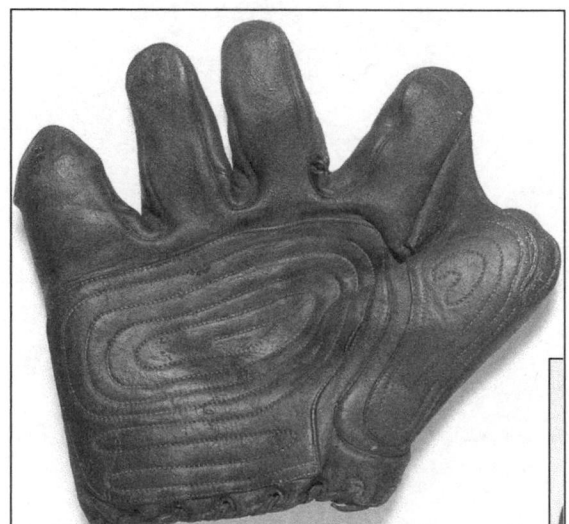

An early catcher's glove from about 1870.

- Most fans believed that baseball had been invented by General Abner Doubleday in 1839, but in reality it was the culmination of several different games dating back to the 1700s.
- A similar game, rounders, was played at roughly the same time in America; in rounders the ball was bowled, not pitched, and the batter had to carry the bat while rounding the bases or he was out.
- Baseball was one of the few spectator sports-besides boxing and horse racing-regularly attended by factory workers; the society elite leaned toward lawn tennis, croquet, and archery.
- A family-friendly sport, unlike boxing, baseball was attended en masse by many Americans on leisurely Saturday afternoons.

- Its popularity was sufficient to elicit sermons in Protestant churches nationwide, condemning the playing or watching of baseball on Sundays.
- For America's Catholics, baseball was less of an issue, and games often followed Sunday Mass.
- Due to the simplicity of the equipment, baseball was just as accessible to the poor as to the rich; it differed from such sports as tennis or golf, which required special equipment that needed to be purchased.
- Any boy could make a bat out of a decent-sized branch; finding twine and tape for a ball was fairly easy as well.
- Friends would gather in any open field or city street, and a ball game would begin.
- Such was the popularity of baseball that occasionally a shopkeeper might leave the store for an hour to watch the game down the street.
- Even the police were known to take time off their beat to view a good match.
- The winners of a professional game were treated like heroes in their home town and afforded respect by the citizens of other towns and cities.
- During his first years playing in Cincinnati, Ohio, Mike developed his catching skills, which would earn him a reputation as an innovative player-as well as a handsome paycheck.

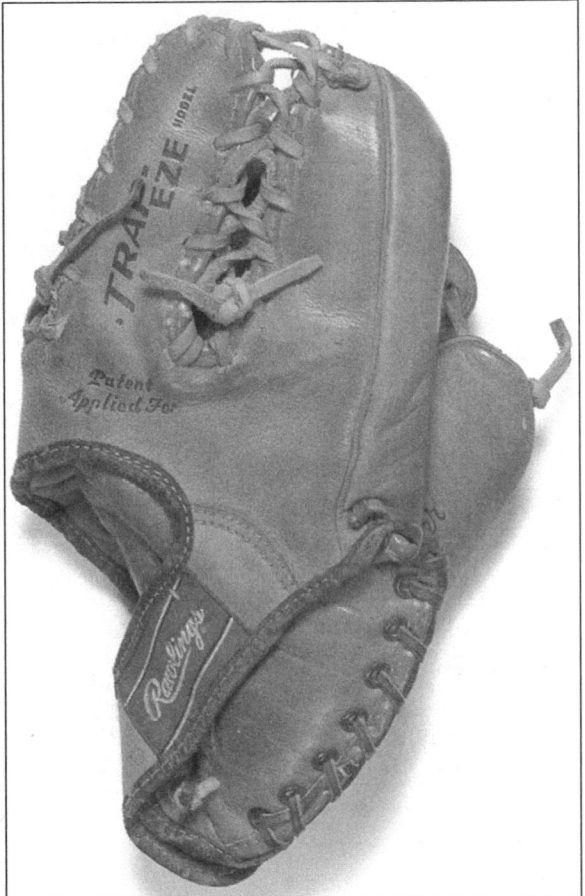

A modern day catcher's mitt.

- The rules of baseball never really concerned Mike, who bent and even broke the rules to gain the upper hand.
- He paid even less attention to the unwritten rules, and was always waiting for the umpire to turn his back.
- He was skilled at reading the opposing pitcher, which allowed him to steal bases with deft efficiency.
- Occasionally he would even steal third base from first base without ever even touching second, and then challenge the umpire to show him the rule that prohibited the maneuver.
- His base-stealing repertoire also included taking a base by force, sliding high toward an opposing baseman with one leg in an attacking position.
- This slide became one of Kelly's trademarks.

Life at Work

- As a member of the Cincinnati Red Stockings, Mike Kelly was able to play the game he loved, rent his own place for the first time, and pursue acting again.
- Life was good, and he did well.
- After a few years in Cincinnati, Cap Anson recruited Mike to play for the game's acknowledged powerhouse team, the Chicago White Stockings.
- After Mike reported for the season on April 1, 1880, Anson taught him the value of training well and remaining in shape.
- Mike tried to teach Anson the value of a day's leisure and a healthy pint of ale, without success.

- Nevertheless, they developed a close friendship, and in his autobiography, Mike had no criticism of Anson, just respectful memories of Anson's honesty and hardworking nature.
- Anson, too, was a baseball innovator, introducing baseball fundamentals such as using a third-base coach, having one fielder back up another, signaling batters, and rotating two star pitchers to rest their arms.
- Aided by speedy players like Mike Kelly, Anson taught his players to aggressively run the bases, forcing the opposition to make errors.
- Anson was among the first to institute spring training and send his club to warmer climates in the South to prepare for the season.
- During his time as a catcher with the White Stockings, Mike set up a series of "signals" with the pitcher, communicated by gestures he made with his hands; the system proved quite effective and caught on with other pitchers in the league.
- He also arranged a similar system with the outfielders, signaling them to move in on their respective base; he would then throw over the baseman's head, right into the hands of the outfielder.
- The runner, believing the ball had been poorly thrown, would then try to steal the next base, where the outfielder would then relay the ball for an easy out.
- During his final season with the White Stockings, after an away game versus the

A typical baseball uniform at the turn of the 20th century.

Washington Olympics, Mike joined his team on a trip to the White House to meet President Grover Cleveland.
- Later he described it as one of the highest honors he had ever received.
- That year, 1886, he earned another honor, the distinction of being the best at bat in the National League.
- In Chicago Mike sought out the gaudiest hotel in the city, the Palmer House-dubbed fireproof by its owners and an eyesore by its competitors.
- Mike spent his money effortlessly, buying the best of everything.
- Despite having married Agnes Hedifen in October 1881, he ate at expensive restaurants and went to some lengths to impress the ladies.
- His clothes reflected the latest fashions: Italian leather shoes, ascots with weighty brooches, suits made of the finest materials.
- One journalist wrote that Mike "whirled his cane around like he owned the city."
- His salary was not exorbitant; he only made enough to push him into the upper middle class, but Mike spent his money as if he had millions.
- He drank in expensive bars and rubbed shoulders with the high society of Chicago, who often attended grand balls thrown for the White Stockings after key victories.

- His drinking came to the attention of his team's owner, A. G. Spalding, who hired the Pinkerton Detective Agency to tail Mike off the field and keep tabs on his late-night drinking sprees.
- When confronted by a detective who accused him of drinking lemonade with his friends at three in the morning, Mike indignantly replied, "It was straight whiskey! I've never had a lemonade at that hour in my life!"
- Mike was often the subject of the tabloids' hottest stories, which related his late-night escapades in the company of many young women.
- Agnes didn't mind the tabloids' claims, she said, even if there was some truth to them.
- Mike was a famous man in Chicago, and he brought home good money, to which she was not at all opposed.
- In 1887 he was traded to the Boston Beaneaters for a record $10,000, after which he was known as the Ten Thousand Dollar Beauty.
- In Boston Mike was paid a record salary for the professional leagues: $5,000 a year-$2,000 for playing on the team and $3,000 for the use of his picture in team advertisements.
- The advertisement fee was an innovation used to bypass the $2,000 salary cap that the National League had put on its players.
- Bostonians were overjoyed to have "stolen" this fantastic and sly catcher and presented him with a pair of white stallions and a carriage to convey him from his complimentary house to the ball field to show their gratitude to him for switching teams.
- The mayor himself held a special banquet for Mike and presented him with a gold watch and chain, among other gifts.
- Mike was unaccustomed to this kind of treatment; in Chicago he had been grateful to receive a regular salary.
- In Boston Mike trained hard every day, but he still spent his nights in bars and saloons.
- When asked by a reporter if he drank during a game, he replied, "It depends on the length of the game."
- For one season he successfully captained the Beaneaters, but he felt that the game's best captain would always be Cap Anson.
- In his autobiography Mike said that if he captained half as well as Anson did, it would be a success in his eyes.
- But that did not diminish a friendly rivalry between the Chicago White Stockings and the Boston Beaneaters, fueled by Boston's acquisition of Mike, whom the White Stockings had considered to be their star player.
- It seemed the entire community would turn out for a game between the two teams, who would play more fiercely than usual.

- The home team was spurred by crowd noise to greater heights of courage; the visiting team was ignited by spit from the stands.
- While playing with Boston, Mike continued to look for new ways to take advantage of a play or rule.
- During a game against Philadelphia, knowing the rules stated that a player may enter the game on "notice" to the umpire, Mike jumped out from the dugout, yelled to the umpire, "Kelly catching for Boston," and caught the ball for an out.
- Baseball substitution rules were changed as a result.
- Mike played various positions but made a name for himself as a catcher; when he began, a rubber mouthpiece was the only protection the catcher had against the fastballs heading his way from the pitching mound, just 45 feet from the batter.
- By the time Mike arrived in Boston, a catcher's mask had been developed by a player from Harvard to reduce the chances of "disfigurement," and chest protectors were becoming more common.
- During the off-season, Mike often took jobs on vaudeville stages, acting in short bits and reciting poetry.
- After it first appeared in 1888, the poems included his favorite, "Casey at the Bat," thought to have been inspired by Kelly himself.
- Audiences loved his recitation and many fans imagined Mike as the cocky protagonist of the poem.
- Occasionally, to the delight of the audience, he would replace the names in the poem with his own name and other team names, making the irony and exaggeration in the poem even funnier .
- He loved the laughter of the wintertime theater crowd, which felt different from the whoops and cheers he heard from the baseball grandstands.

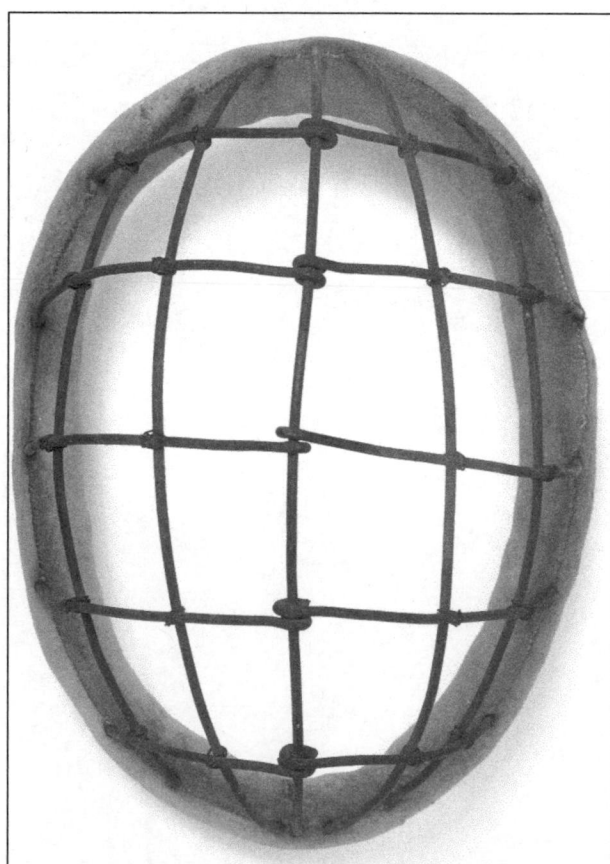

A catcher's mask was developed by a player from Harvard.

- The popularity of both baseball and vaudeville theater were on the rise; cheap productions had very little need for elaborate sets or costumes, so shows could go on at any time.
- That kept the cost of admission to a vaudeville production low, and the humor correspondingly lowbrow.
- Several tobacco companies, such as Old Gold Cigarettes, began marketing their product using tradable cards depicting baseball players; Mike carried the Allen and Ginter version of himself around for weeks, showing it to everyone.
- The small, sepia-toned photographs were glued onto thick cardboard mounts and distributed widely; over 500 subjects were included-especially the major stars like Mike Kelly, Cap Anson, Connie Mack, and Charles Comiskey.
- To further enhance his fame, Mike published his autobiography, the first to be written by a professional athlete.
- Entitled *Play Ball!: Stories of the Ball Field*, the book was introduced and assembled by *Boston Globe* columnist John J. Drohan and was published by Emery & Hughes.

- It sold for $0.25 and was published just prior to the 1888 baseball season.
- In the book, Mike retold some of his favorite moments from both baseball and theater, and gave his personal opinion on many of the famous players and managers of the day, most notably Cap Anson.
- He also said that while baseball was an important part of any boy's upbringing, he felt that children ought to stay in school; a good education was the secret to earning a better salary.

Life in the Community: Boston, Massachusetts

- Boston was a thriving city of 350,000 when Mike Kelly was traded from Chicago and became the Ten Thousand Dollar Beauty.
- Boston had a rich culture melded from the culture of many different nationalities and ethnicities.
- Visitors to America always sought out Boston, either first or last, in their quest to get to know the new world of the United States.
- Still, Boston's many cultural groups were often at odds with each other, fighting over politics, religion, and territorial bounds in the city.
- Conflict between the Catholics and the Protestants, left behind when they set sail for America, sparked again, this time between neighbors.
- The Irish featured prominently among the Catholic groups.
- The Great Famine of the 1840s and 1850s was still fresh in the minds of many.
- In 1872 a fire wiped out approximately 776 buildings in the city, destroying countless homes and businesses and leaving 20 people dead and many others wounded.
- This tragedy affected the Irish community more than most; many Irish-owned businesses were destroyed, putting hundreds of Irish out of work as well as displacing them from their homes.
- Intense adherence to the Catholic faith had helped them through times of need while adapting to the New World.
- Their mistrust of Protestants, fueled by their extreme sense of national pride, had caused them to turn to their church for answers.
- The church provided a stern set of rules to be strictly followed, no matter the cost.
- The church also presented them with openings for acting out pent-up aggression: through sports.
- The churches would organize baseball and football teams, constituting the first amateur league set up for boys.
- Many Irish neighborhoods had their own baseball teams by the middle of the 1870s.
- Priests encouraged youths to play sports because sports instilled a sense of hard work, fair play, and teamwork.

- Sports also allowed for heroism, a sense a self-worth, and a pride in their culture.
- Neighborhood teams staged friendly contests, and often would go to watch the Beaneaters take on challengers from across the country.
- Young Irish boys who came to these games were thrilled by the sly moves and often daring tricks of the catcher, Mike Kelly, whom they saw as an idol.
- Despite their newfound love of baseball, Boston's Irishmen were becoming increasingly restive about the discriminatory treatment they often received, and they desired to be further integrated into American society.
- Signs reading "No Irish Need Apply" had once been a common sight in Boston, especially during the pre-Civil War era.
- As the Irish gained respect and political power, these signs gradually disappeared, until in 1888 there were barely any left in the city.
- Boston elected its first Irish mayor, Hugh O'Brien, in 1884.
- He was elected again in 1885, and again in 1886 and 1887, when he presented Mike Kelly with a new gold watch and chain, among other presents from the people of Boston.

SPEAKER, BOSTON AMER.

Red Sox baseball was popular with mostly everyone in the city of Boston.

Letter to Mike Kelly from A.G. Spalding, from
Play Ball: Stories of the Diamond Field

Chicago, Feb. 19, 1887.

M. J. Kelly, Hyde Park, N. Y.

Dear Sir—I am in receipt of your picture, in costume and batting position, and the same has been handed to our engraver, with instructions to get out as good a cut as possible for the forthcoming Guide.

I congratulate you on the magnificent salary that I understand you will receive from the Boston club next season, and I hope you will not disappoint them, but will make yourself not only worthy of the amount that you will receive from them, but also of the very large bonus that they have paid the Chicago club for your release. I am just in receipt of a letter from Mr. Billings, from which I quote as follows

"Kelly did not say a word against you; said the Chicago club was a good one to get money of, when wanted. Anson worked him pretty hard sometimes, when not in condition, and there is where the trouble lies, I think."

I am very glad to know that you have no personal feeling towards me, for I certainly have none towards you, and I do not believe you can truthfully say that either myself or the Chicago club have taken any advantage of you, but have always treated you right and fair. I have placed no credence in the rumors and alleged interviews that have been published in the New York papers, from time to time, knowing, from my own experience, how these interviews are manufactured. As you will, no doubt, be captain of the Boston nine, you will find it necessary, or at least it will be advisable, to set examples to your men in the way of habits and deportment, that will be an incentive for them to follow…

Wishing you every prosperity and success in your new position, I am,

Yours truly,

G. Spalding.

Baseball Timeline

1700s Baseball was created by combining rules from other ball games in colonial America.

1791 In Pittsfield, Massachusetts, to promote the safety of the exterior of the newly built meeting house, particularly the windows, a by-law barred "any game of wicket, cricket, baseball, batball, football, cats, fives, or any other game played with ball" within eighty yards of the structure -the first instance of the game of *baseball* being referred to by that name on the North American continent.

1823 A letter in the *National Advocate*, a New York newspaper, refers to "the manly and athletic game of 'base ball'"—16 years before its supposed invention by Abner Doubleday.

1839 Abner Doubleday was credited (falsely) with inventing baseball in Cooperstown, New York.

1856 The New York *Mercury* coined the phrase "the National Pastime."

1857 The National Association of Base Ball Players (NABBP) was formed.

1867 Candy Cummings threw the first curve-ball in baseball.

1869 The Cincinnati Red Stockings became the first officially fully professional baseball club; the following year, with a profit of $1.35, the team disbanded.

1870 The earliest documented use of a glove by a catcher was recorded.

1874 The baseball batter's box was officially adopted.

1876 The National League was established, with William Hulbert as president.

1877 The catcher's mask was first used in a baseball game by James Tyng of Harvard.

1879 Professional baseball adopted the reserve clause, giving teams the right to automatically renew a player's contract at the end of each season.

1882 The American Baseball Association was founded.

1884 The Louisville Slugger, a popular bat, was introduced.

1885 The official rules governing the making and materials of a baseball were written, never to be changed.

1887 Michael "King" Kelly was traded to the Boston Beaneaters from Chicago for a record $10,000

New Teacher for the Dakota Sioux in 1888

Although at first Corabelle Fellows did not know the language or customs of the Sioux peoples, she trekked from Washington, District of Columbia, to the Dakotas to teach Sioux children nearly everything from arithmetic and reading to sewing and geography.

Life at Home

- When Corabelle Fellows began her journey to the Dakotas in 1884, she had never met a Native American, taught in a school, or gleaned any understanding of the Sioux peoples she intended to help.
- The headstrong, well-educated teen was determined to punish her Washington society parents for breaking up her potential love affair with an older man.
- Going to a place she had never seen to teach people she didn't know seemed to be a good idea, despite everyone's concerns for her safety.
- Only eight years earlier, the nation had been shocked to learn of "Custer's Last Stand" at the Battle of the Little Bighorn.
- That day in late June, the 7th Cavalry Regiment of the U.S. Army lost 278 soldiers in the most famous action of the Great Sioux War of 1876.
- It was an overwhelming victory for the Lakota Sioux, Northern Cheyenne, and Arapaho, who were led by several major war leaders-including Crazy Horse and Gall-inspired by the visions of Sitting Bull (Th?ath?á ka Íyotake).
- The "massacre," as it was immediately labeled, resurrected latent fears of random and unprovoked Indian attacks, even though Little Big Horn was neither.
- When Europeans arrived in the New World, more than two hundred distinctly different Native American cultures existed on the North American continent.
- The various tribal groups spoke mutually unintelligible languages, and their hunting, housing, and living customs varied widely.
- Despite their distinctiveness, they were habitually lumped together in popular culture and by the Eastern press.

With little experience, Corabelle Fellows moved West to teach Sioux children.

- Despite receiving a good education, Corabelle had formed only hazy notions about Native American cultures, for the most part acquiring these ideas from the popular press.
- Since the 1860s a flood of dime novels from the presses of New York City and Boston had presented stereotyped or highly romanticized depictions of Indian cultures; almost always, the Indian characters were simply foils for the white heroes.
- Growing up in Glens Falls, New York; several Missouri communities; and Washington, District of Columbia, Corabelle loved playing with her dolls, dressing the family cat in the latest fashions, and watching her father, a photographer, employ his craft.
- As a child in Washington, she played on the steps of the U.S. Capitol building when Congress was in session and her father served as doorman.
- She fell in love with the Corcoran Art Gallery and borrowed books from the Congressional library.
- Her mother had been educated in music, French, needlework, and fine cookery; when no schools were available for Corabelle and her sister Marian, their mother taught them

Corabelle married Samuel Campbell.

herself-six days a week-in the finer points of writing, reading, arithmetic, geography, physiology and sewing.
- "Always when we least expected it, mother would call us to her and demand the spelling of words, the boundaries of a state, the multiplication tables, or the poem she had set us to learn, or ask us to write a paragraph on the circulation of the blood," Corabelle later recalled in a memoir.
- The two girls sewed an hour each day and also routinely learned their catechism for Sunday.
- When her mother finally accepted Corabelle's decision to move West to teach Indians, she gave her a flatiron in the hope that "even in that outlandish place, you will remember to keep your clothes pressed."
- Her mother staged an elaborate going-away party and arranged for Corabelle to attend the inaugural ball of President James A. Garfield-to remind her of what she would be missing.
- Corabelle made the journey westward in late November 1884, traveling to take up her post at a school affiliated with the American Board of Commissioners for Foreign Missions, which had begun among the Dakota people in 1834.
- Corabelle found herself crying frightened tears throughout most of the train ride from Washington to Springfield, Dakota Territory; "As we neared the end of the journey, I gradually achieved a calmer mind and a less swollen face," she later admitted.
- The trip featured bruising bumps, sleepless nights, and swollen rivers that defied crossing; Corabelle was miserable.
- When she arrived at the Santee Reservation on the day before Thanksgiving, she stepped into the "most penetrating cold I had ever experienced."

Corabelle's first assignment was teaching Indian girls to sew.

- After years of work, the reservation's Normal School consisted of 18 buildings on 480 acres and accommodated 206 students.
- The boarding school was at the heart of the mission-emphasizing religious instruction and industrial vocational training.
- School courses included farming, carpentry, printing, and blacksmithing for boys, and sewing, cooking, and housekeeping for girls.
- The school provided training in the reading and writing of the Dakota language, a path developed by white missionaries focused on Bible reading; at other times of the day, only English was permitted to be spoken.
- When the federal government insisted that only English be taught, the Missionary Society balked, saying the rules were "illegal, unscientific, and irreligious."

Life at Work
- Shortly after the five-foot-one, 100-pound Corabelle Fellows arrived at the Dakota reservation, she was given a new, Indian name.
- Even though "Corabelle" meant "beautiful girl," the Indian girls looked into her eyes and rendered a separate verdict: in Lakota, her name would be Wichipitowan, or Blue Star.
- Everyone, it seemed, pronounced the rechristening appropriate; "You want a name of good meaning," she was told.
- Her first class among the Sioux comprised 15 Indian girls aged five to seven; Corabelle's assignment was to teach them how to sew.
- "They knew but little English. I knew no Sioux. But I could show them how. ... I took each docile brown hand in mine and guided it to set fine hemming stitches in the squares of purple, orange, blue, and scarlet calico which they held. They sat on the circle upon little chairs and turned their large, bright black eyes on me unblinkingly. There was not a sound."
- Soon she was introduced to more students and taught classes in a variety of subjects: arithmetic, reading, etiquette.

- At night at her home, she received visitors, always in twos and threes; the Sioux, she learned, rarely went anywhere alone.
- "Blame and praise are thus equally divided, especially blame."
- The girls came for help with their lessons; the boys usually wanted to play dominoes.
- The girls also loved to finger her clothing-particularly silk or cotton dresses-drink coffee, and listen to stories about what a city was like.
- The boys were fascinated by geography and quite readily grasped the relationship of one area to another; when she displayed several maps of the United States as they related to a world map, she was pronounced most knowledgeable and clearly had earned the admiration of the boys.
- Corabelle had assumed that the wisdom of replacing the culture of the Indian students with her own was self-evident.
- She gave children English first names and used their fathers' names as their last names, ignoring indigenous naming practices.
- She came to learn that her pupils were incorrigible gum chewers-in and out of the classroom.
- Gum was manufactured from the juice of the purple coneflower, which they sliced and dripped into a pottery bowl.
- When the liquid was boiled down, the residue was a fine, rubberlike substance that could be chewed constantly.
- The boys chewed with much noise and swagger; the girls were experts at snapping.

- After seven months of successful teaching, Corabelle was asked to take on a new assignment-among the "rougher Indians, who spoke a different dialect of Sioux."
- Six other teachers-unable to endure the cold, the food, the language, or the odors-had failed to make a success of this assignment.
- At the next reservation school site in Oahe, on the Missouri River near Fort Sully, Corabelle learned the rhythms and customs of Native American life: why each tepee was set up exactly the same way, the process making of pottery, how to properly scrape an animal skin, the art of lassoing an animal.
- One day she was invited to go hunting for beans with the women of the village.
- The children showed her how to find among the grasses handfuls of beans carefully stored by the prairie mice.
- When they returned, each woman carried approximately three pounds of purloined beans.
- After two years among the Indians, Corabelle was invited to a new Indian Center at the Cheyenne River Reservation in Nebraska.
- By this time her parents were proud of the path she had taken and repeatedly said so during a round of Washington parties given in her honor.
- Language continued to be a major issue: instruction was in English only at the government schools, while the vernacular was permitted at the schools in which Corabelle taught.

Corabelle's mother accepted her decision reluctantly.

- But the tide had firmly turned: Indians would only be successful in American society when they abandoned their old ways.
- When she arrived in Nebraska, Corabelle was met by a platform filled with cowboys and Indians eager to get a glimpse of "the new schoolmarm."
- "The fellow bowed with his hand over his heart and offered me an elbow. As I reached to take it, thinking he had been sent to meet me, he fired a pistol above my head. At this signal, the mob swirled about the end of the coach, pistols popping, war whoops ringing."
- The Indians were reluctant to attend school because scalp locks and painted faces were not permitted, so Corabelle taught three teens-Dog Bear, Gray Bear, and White Owl-at night when others were not around.
- They were asked not to wear frightful paint because Corabelle thought it was ugly.
- In addition she had to fight off a marriage proposal-and virtual kidnapping-which she accidently encouraged because she didn't understand the traditional rituals.
- "The white blanket is worn by the Cheyenne man who seeks a mate. I had spoken to him; therefore, I approved of him. I left my house alone, and after sunset-final proof of my approval and interest-and he'd been in his own right to attempt to carry me off. I retraced his trail the next day. He had carried me to within possibly 200 feet of his tepee.
- "Had he once entered it with me, by the law of the Cheyenne, I would have been his lawful squaw property from that hour forward."

- Corabelle's time as a teacher drew to a close after she worked briefly at a boarding school at Fort Benning, Georgia, where she met Samuel Campbell, the son of a trader and a Sioux woman who was raised by an Episcopal priest.
- On March 15, 1888, Corabelle Fellows married Samuel Campbell, ending her teaching career-but not her time in the West.

Life in the Community: The Dakotas

- Prior to Corabelle Fellows's arrival, the Lakota people had lost most of their land in Minnesota through treaties signed in 1837, 1851, and 1858.
- The terms of the Treaty of Fort Laramie in 1868 granted the Lakota a single large reservation that covered parts of North Dakota, South Dakota, and four other states.
- After the conclusion of the Indian Wars in the 1870s, the U.S. government confiscated about one-half of this reservation; the Great Sioux Reservation was reduced from 60 million acres to less than 22 million acres.
- Reservation treaties sometimes included food and supply stipend agreements, in which the federal government would grant a certain amount of goods to a tribe yearly.
- The implementation of the policy was erratic, however, and in many cases the stipend goods were not delivered.
- These treaties were often established by executive order and rarely pleased anyone.
- All the while, missionaries were urging the Indians to abandon traditional ways and adopt the white culture.
- Progress among the Dakota peoples was defined as "interest in speaking the English language, monogamy replacing polygamy, houses that incorporated windows and doors, and an interest in agriculture."

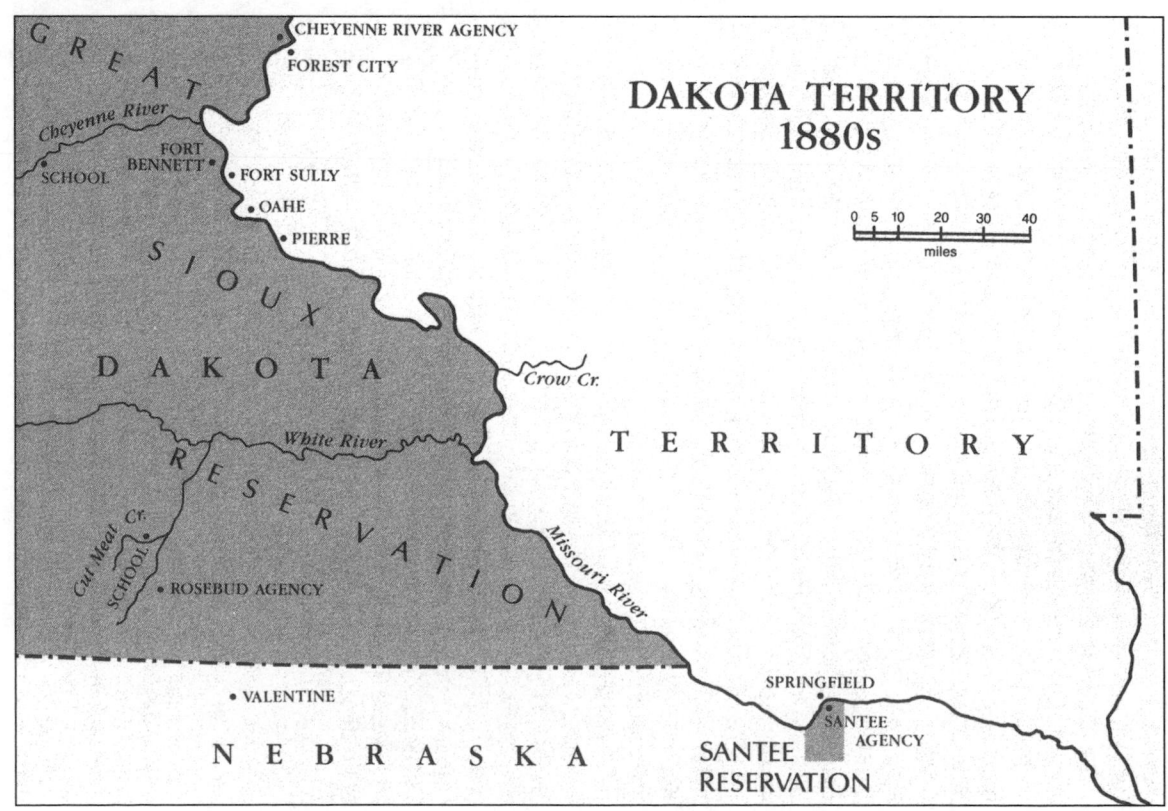

White missionaries urged Indians to abandon their traditional ways.

- The creation of American Indian reservations began in earnest during the administration (1845-1849) of President James K. Polk, who believed in the establishment of "colonies" for the Native Americans in the region beyond the Mississippi River.
- The establishment of reservations, or "permanent" Indian frontiers, was also indelibly tied to the policy of Indian removal from lands east of the Mississippi now desired by white settlers.
- In most cases the West's reservation policy either reduced the homeland of the native people or required that they move to a new location where they would have less land that needed to be protected from white immigrants flooding the area.
- In 1851 Congress passed the Indian Appropriations Act, which authorized the creation of Indian reservations in modern-day Oklahoma.
- Relations between settlers and natives continued to deteriorate as the settlers encroached on Indian territory and consumed the natural resources in the West.
- By the late 1860s, President Ulysses S. Grant pursued a stated "peace policy" as a possible solution to the conflict.
- The policy included a reorganization of the Indian Service, with the goal of relocating various tribes from their ancestral homes to parcels of land established specifically for their habitation.
- The policy called for the replacement of government officials by religious men, nominated by churches, to oversee the Indian agencies on reservations, in order to teach Christianity to the native tribes.
- The Quakers were especially active in this philosophy for reservations; their "civilization" policy was aimed at eventually preparing the tribes for citizenship.
- White settlers objected to the size of land parcels; various reports submitted to Congress found widespread corruption among the federal Native American agencies, and many tribes who ignored the relocation orders were then forced onto their limited land parcels.
- Enforcement of the policy required the U.S. Army to restrict the movements of various tribes by force, leading to a number of Native American massacres and some wars.

- The most well-known conflict was the Sioux War on the northern Great Plains, between 1876 and 1881, which included the Battle of Little Bighorn.
- By the 1880s government officials, military officers, and congressional leaders were unanimous in their agreement that allowing tribal landholdings and promoting tribal culture should end.
- They also believed that reservations should disappear along with Indian identity.
- In 1887 Congress undertook a significant change in reservation policy with the passage of the Dawes Act, which began the policy of granting small parcels of land to individuals, not tribes as a whole.
- The government's policy continued to assume that the road to salvation followed the white road to the church, school, and farm.
- This belief remained firm even when the dry Plains proved difficult or even impossible to farm.

Textile Mill Worker in 1890

John McGloin, a third-generation Scots-Irishman, lived in Atlanta, Georgia, with his wife, Amelia, and their four-year-old son, Charles. John was a 49-year-old card grinder in a textile mill and a Civil War veteran. His wife, age 30, worked at home, sewing and knitting for her neighbors. The family also took in a boarder to help make ends meet.

Life at Home

- The McGloin family rented a two-room apartment, paying $21.00 annually, or $1.75 a month; the boarder-Amelia's cousin-paid $10.00 a year, or about $0.93 per month.
- The apartment was heated by a woodstove; wood cost the McGloins $35.00 a year.
- Oil lamps provided the lighting. The family used 13 gallons of oil during the year, at a cost of $1.95.
- The McGloins' home was comfortably furnished, and Amelia had a sewing machine, as was duly noted in a government survey. The survey did not mention rugs, although rugs were noted as among the possessions of some of their neighbors.
- John was a veteran of the Confederate Army.
- The 19-year difference in John's age and Amelia's was not uncommon because of the number of men killed in the war and the low birthrate in the South during Reconstruction.
- The Scots-Irish began immigrating to the United States in the 1840s; many settled in the American South.
- The Protestant Irish immigrants began to call themselves Scots-Irish to distinguish themselves from the predominantly Catholic Irish immigrants who arrived later.
- Many of the newcomers had no skills except farming, but most lacked the financial resources to become homesteaders.
- Over the past year, John had spent $20.00 on clothing; Amelia spent $20.00 on herself, and $6.00 was used for Charles, mostly for shoes.
- Amelia sewed much of the family's clothing at home, purchasing the cloth in bulk and using Clark's Spool Cotton, the most popular thread of the time.
- Clark's not only provided a quality product but fed the imagination of isolated women by

Both John and Amelia worked to make ends meet.

presenting the product with elegant color pictures of faraway places.

- In 1890 the McGloins spent $26.90 on furniture. In that year a drop-head sewing machine in a five-drawer oak cabinet cost $9.85, a chifforobe in solid oak was $11.00, and a washstand sold for $4.85.
- Woodmen of the World's burial insurance became available in 1890; the family spent $2.60 on a policy. That year they gave $3.00 to the Baptist Church and $0.50 to other charities.
- John, like many men his age, was proud of his association with the Woodmen and with other fraternal organizations.
- To supplement their diet and cash flow, the McGloins raised vegetables and chickens alongside the house they lived in.
- Amelia, an excellent seamstress, was in demand among her neighbors to make and repair shirts and dresses. In addition, she crocheted a version of the popular "four-in-hand" scarf.
- Roundworms were a problem throughout the South in 1890; Dill's Worm Syrup, an "elegant preparation for Round and Pin worms," was advertised as "pleasant to take-the Children like it."

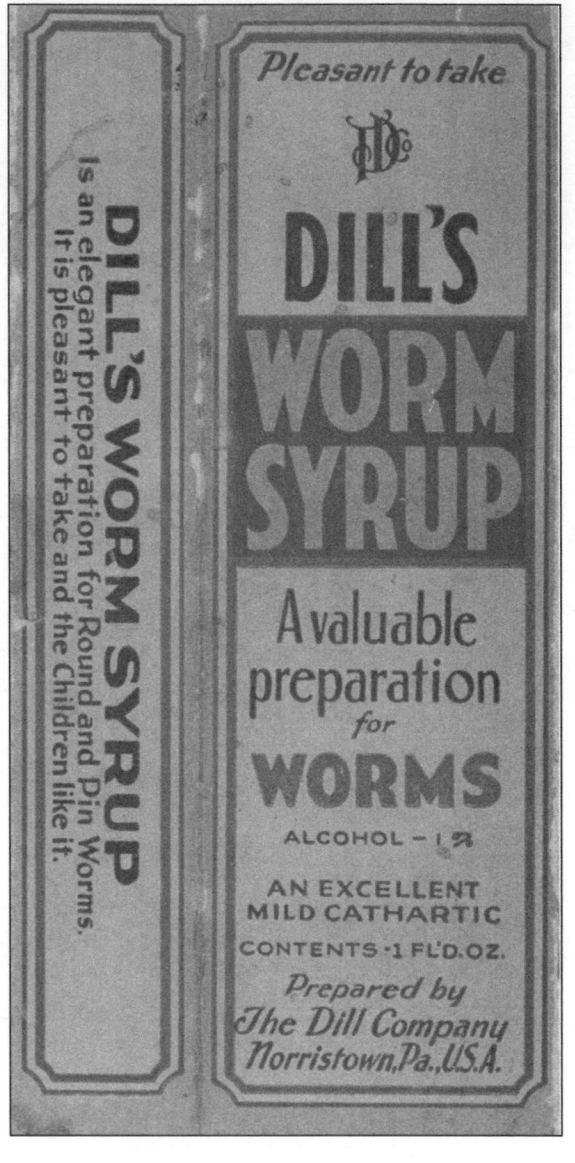

Life at Work

- As agricultural conditions worsened in the 1880s and 1890s, many small farmers were forced to seek other kinds of work.
- Meanwhile, merchants tightened credit, causing even greater economic hardship among farmers.
- John grew up on a farm in southern Georgia, but after the Civil War, he found that he had to leave the farm behind.
- He was enticed into mill work by promises of higher pay.
- To attract workers recruiters distributed fliers, known as "dodgers," that offered social events such as fairs and circuses in addition to train fare and company housing.
- The recruiters often focused on large rural families, which often could supply three or four additional workers in addition to the man of the house.
- Mill managers quickly learned that the "best operatives will not go where the tenements are bad."
- Most manufacturers viewed the company town as an extension of the factory itself.
- Placing the houses near mills reduced travel time and tardiness; in many communities, it was a status symbol to live in the shadow of the factory walls.
- Generally the mill managers expected a family to supply as many mill workers as there were rooms in the company house.
- John and Amelia's family was too small as yet to qualify for a house in the company town.
- John was wary of being drawn into the cycle of indebtedness to the company for housing and expenditures at the company store that entrapped so many of his co-workers.

- The mill's location in a rapidly growing urban area meant that there was a steady supply of worker streaming in, keeping wages low.
- John was determined to avoid the system of family labor that, by keeping the husband's wages low, made it necessary for whole families to work at the mill to make ends meet.
- The factory refused to hire black workers, who were available and capable.
- Labor costs consumed about 55 percent of a textile mill's expenses in 1890. Daily wages were $1.00 a day for laborers and varied from $1.25 and $3.50 a day for skilled workers.
- Women, who were the majority of the work force at the textile mill, earned from about $1.50 to $6.00 per week.
- A work week ran 6 days and averaged 11 hours per day.
- John worked from 6 a.m. to 6 p.m.; he was allowed short breaks.
- Card grinding was skilled labor, requiring mechanical aptitude, patience, good hearing, and the habit of precision.
- John was a steady worker, and for that reason and because of his technical ability and experience, he was a valuable worker.
- Like many textile workers, John not only maintained close connections to farming but remained knowledgeable about agricultural prices and farm equipment.

Life in the Community: Atlanta, Georgia

- From 1860 to 1890, Atlanta's population grew from 9,554 to 65,533, of whom more than 37,000 were categorized as white and more than 28,000 as black.
- Recent immigration had had a strong impact on Northern cities, but 90 percent of Atlanta's residents were from the South; only 3.8 percent were foreign-born.
- In 1887 the city began converting from gas to electric streetlamps; three years later it had 167 "arc lights" and 436 "series lights" in use.
- In 1890 the chief sanitary inspector reported that about two-thirds of the city's privies were served by night-soil carts, of which there were 12.
- More than 40 miles of water pipe were laid in 1890, and 3,759 residential and commercial subscribers were recorded in the tap book.
- Few working-class whites and even fewer blacks lived near water mains.
- Atlanta's desire to become a manufacturing center was hampered by the lack of concentrated urban markets in the South.
- In addition, Southern industry was effectively penalized by the freight rates Southern manufacturers were charged to; rail rates going north were higher than rates going south, making all goods made in the South more expensive.
- By the late nineteenth century, the centers of fastest urban growth in the South were the industrial cities of the interior-the Southern Piedmont-rather than the coastal cities. In 1860 the region's ten largest cities were ports, but by the 1890s two inland cities-Atlanta and Nashville-had become the South's largest.
- Department stores in Atlanta had begun using an innovation known as the "fixed price method" so that housewives would know what each item cost before going to the counter to make their purchases.
- The telephone and pneumatic tube were now being used to move cash and receipts around the store.
- Department stores provided housewives with a new freedom-the right to look around the store without the obligation to make a purchase.
- This meant that the humblest wife of a mill hand could rub shoulders with the city's elite while shopping for handkerchiefs.

"STUDY."—J. H. SHARP.

IRECTIONS FOR

CROCHETING

"FOUR-IN-HAND SCARFS."

WITH

BELDING BROS. & CO.'S

PURE · DYE · CROCHET · AND · KNITTING · SILK.

Joshua Hamilton was a merchant who ran a general store in Cinncinati, Ohio. He was enamored with the idea of being part of a barbershop quartet, with its unaccompanied four-part harmonies and ringing chords.

Life at Home

- When Joshua Hamilton turned 35 years old, he discovered a new love that haunted him day and night.
- Married with four children-all girls-Joshua found himself humming late in the afternoons as he considered ways to satisfy his new obsession.
- His wife thought his preoccupation was crazy; nevertheless, she did not object when he discovered his need to be away every Tuesday night and many a Sunday afternoon.
- But she still could not understand how or why being a member of a barbershop quartet had captured his soul.
- Joshua had sung in the church choir most of his life-his baritone voice was prized by every preacher who had traveled through Cincinnati, Ohio but without being able to explain, he insisted that being a member of a barbershop quartet was different.
- Born in 1856, prior to the war that divided and devastated the nation, Joshua grew up the son of a merchant whose every expectation was that his biblically named son would follow in his footsteps.
- Not that Joshua objected-he was good at math, found peace in the often meticulous process of stocking shelves, and was happy to flirt with the girls who came into the store to buy candy and cloth.
- In fact, he met his future wife in the store; he assisted her mother in the purchase of whale-bone corsets and other unmentionables that ladies seemed to require.
- As was the custom at all stores, no prices were shown on the merchandise, which allowed him to offer her mother great deals.
- Despite her embarrassment at the nature of the transactions, she knew that his intention was to

Joshua Hamilton was obsessed with his barbershop quartet.

signal to her that she was the reason he was aiming to please her mother.

- He courted her around her father's piano, where his rich singing voice set him apart from other suitors; during Sunday night family "sings" around the piano, he was always the star.

- Nearly half the homes in middle-class Cincinnati had pianos for family song sessions; when friends gathered, group singing was often expected.

- Thomas Edison's phonograph machine, invented a decade earlier, was still not in wide distribution, so live music still dominated.

- The Hamilton clan had moved to Ohio from Pennsylvania in the 1840s to elude the onslaught of German and Welsh immigrants arriving from Europe.

- Grandpa Hamilton concluded Pennsylvania was just getting too crowded and it was time to move.

Joshua grew up with a large extended family, and singing was usually part of family gatherings.

- He established a new store in the countryside outside Cincinnati and then watched in amazement as America's population explosion flowed westward to crowd around him once again.

- By the 1870s the Cincinnati store was practically within the city and no longer stocked steel plows or harnesses for a brace of oxen.

- Times had changed: For every farmer moving to the area, there were 20 men looking for factory jobs, which paid steadily and required less risk.

- But supplies for horses and mules still dominated one corner of the store despite the epizootic of 1872, when four million horses-nearly one-fourth of the nation's stock-died of the disease, bringing

Joshua courted his future wife by singing at her piano.

the nation to a virtual standstill for three months before the winter weather killed the mosquitoes that transmitted the virus.

- The outbreak was blamed on unrestricted immigrant microbes; similarly, the Panic of 1873 was blamed on an excessive supply of unskilled labor, despite compelling evidence to the contrary.
- In 1882 a $0.50 head tax was imposed on any immigrant entering the country by water, but it did little to slow down the flood of immigrants seeking opportunity in America.
- Most arrived saying they planned to return to their native land once they had made their fortune; one quarter did return, and many more crossed back and forth on an annual basis.
- Immigrants also arrived in Cincinnati as children, wards of the New York Children's Aid Society, whose "orphan trains" annually moved thousands of abandoned and orphaned children from East Coast cities to new homes in the West.
- Joshua was four when he first witnessed the spectacle of dozens of children-many of whom couldn't speak English-lined up at the railroad depot station.
- Couples desiring a child would then pick one or two children from the group and take them home for adoption.
- The rest would be loaded onto trains and taken to the next city where they would be picked over by the next set of adults.
- In all, 90,000 children found shelter in this manner-sometimes purely as unpaid labor, more often as members of the family.
- The New York Children's Aid Society brought Joshua's best friend, Wayne, to Dayton; Wayne became the town mortician and a fellow member of the barbershop quartet.

- Wayne was born Gert Derkondoeff, but his new adoptive family didn't think that name sounded American; they told him at breakfast on his third day in Ohio that he was to call himself Wayne, and that was that.
- Wayne's new father was a conductor on the railroad who often returned home after weeks away with wonderful tales of colorful Indians, smelly stockyards in Chicago, and famous people who had ridden on his train.
- During the summers Wayne's family went to the cool atmosphere of a lakeside resort, and Joshua was often invited to go along.
- Wayne's father would join them every other weekend.
- One night, when the boys were 14 or 15, the evening's entertainment was a barbershop quartet known for its sweet harmonies.
- The boys were mesmerized by what they heard and practiced for weeks without achieving a satisfactory sound.
- But when school began in the fall, they set the experience aside.
- Only many years later, perhaps prompted by recordings played on Thomas Edison's phonograph machine, did they return to their early passion for barbershop quartet singing and seek out the other members of their quartet.

Life at Work

- Surprisingly, along with Joshua Hamilton's newfound interest in barbershop quartet singing came a renewed excitement about the store.

Joshua's family all worked in the store.

- For the first time in years, Joshua took great pleasure in constructing the elaborate chromolithographed W. A. Burpee Seed display, arranging the Merrick's Six Cord Soft Finish Spool Cotton display cabinet, and selling nickel packs of firecrackers to the neighborhood boys.
- Joshua was having fun again.
- The cooperation, the teamwork, the harmonizing sound, and the applause all pleased him.
- And just ahead was an opportunity to demonstrate their skills at a fundraiser for the children's school; each of his four girls was sewing a new dress for the big event.
- Admission was priced at the popular sum of five cents.
- Since 1883, when the Treasury Department issued a five-cent coin composed of one part nickel and three parts copper, merchants had been competing for the coin bearing the American Indian profile.
- In Joshua's establishment, customers ordered "a nickel's worth" of cheese; a handful of crackers pulled from the cracker barrel cost a nickel, as did a draft beer down the street.
- Even the "dime" novels sold for a nickel.
- Dr. Will Zimmer, the tenor in Joshua's quartet, often joked that he would be happy to receive a nickel for his medical services: "It would be more than I'm receiving now."

Downtown Cincinnati, Ohio.

- The fourth member of the quartet, R. H. Long, came from a long line of theater people and often took the initiative to obtain singing dates and promote the events.
- Barbershop music, with its close, unaccompanied four-part harmonies and ringing chords, was believed to be a uniquely American tradition.
- Joshua believed it had evolved from numerous musical styles featuring uncomplicated melodies that could be harmonized with a variety of four-part chords when sung *a cappella*.
- Barbershop harmony's four voice parts required a tenor, lead, baritone and bass to be effective; the melody was sung by the lead voice while the first tenor harmonized in a lighter voice above it.
- The bass sang the roots and fifth of the chord, while the baritone filled in the chord sometimes below the lead, sometimes above it.
- It was a glorious way to spend an evening with friends-especially when the harmonies were solid and produced the "fifth ring."
- The defining characteristic of the barbershop style for Joshua was the ringing chord-also called the angel's voice or the fifth voice.
- Barbershop arrangements stressed chords and chord progressions that favored "ringing" at the expense of suspended and diminished chords.
- Wayne talked about the physical impact on him personally: "a tingling of the spine, the raising of the hairs on the back of the neck, the spontaneous arrival of gooseflesh on the forearm."

- Will often described the effect as an addiction, a great big chord that gets people "hooked."
- Achieving the effect produced in Joshua the emotional impact of rapture.

Life in the Community: Cincinnati, Ohio

- Chartered as a village in 1803, Cincinnati experienced significant growth in 1811 with the introduction of steam navigation on the Ohio River.
- Thanks to the Ohio River, opportunities abounded: hotels, restaurants, and taverns opened to meet the needs of settlers traveling westward; steamboats were manufactured and repaired in the city; and farmers brought their fresh-grown crops to the city for transport down the Ohio and Mississippi rivers to New Orleans, one of Ohio's major markets.
- At the same time, the availability of the Miami and Erie Canal reduced the cost of traveling from western Ohio to Cincinnati, allowing the city to develop into an important meatpacking center.
- Farmers brought their livestock-especially pigs-to the city, where they were slaughtered, processed, sold to Western settlers, or shipped to various markets.
- This earned the city the tag "Porkopolis" of the United States.
- The first mass migration of Germans in 1830 and then of the Irish a decade later swelled Cincinnati's population to close to 50,000 people.
- With the introduction of lager beer in the 1830s, German brewers became the predominant force in the industry, and the number of breweries in the city increased from eight in 1840 to 36 in 1860.
- William Holmes McGuffey first published his *Eclectic Reader* for school children in Cincinnati in 1836; the reader eventually 122 million copies.

Traveling in style.

- Harriet Beecher Stowe-the author of *Uncle Tom's Cabin*-called Cincinnati home for 18 years, while the city itself, located directly across the Ohio River from Kentucky, a slaveholding state, was a hotbed of abolitionist activity.
- Abolitionists taking part in the Underground Railroad began to secretly smuggle runaway slaves across the Ohio River to potential freedom in Ohio.
- Many in the city opposed the abolitionists, fearing that if slavery ended, they would face competition from the freed African-Americans.
- With the outbreak of the Civil War, George B. McClellan, a prominent Cincinnati resident and the commander of Ohio's State Militia, selected a site near the city for the recruitment and training of 50,000 Union soldiers.
- By the 1880s Cincinnati boasted a population of 300,000 and the honor of being the largest city in Ohio.
- During this period Cincinnati's major cultural institutions began to take shape, including the art museum and art academy, the conservatory of music, the public library, the zoo, and Cincinnati Music Hall.
- In response to the decline of riverboat trade in the 1870s, the city built its own Southern rail line-the only Ohio city to make such a move-at a cost of $20 million.
- By 1890 more than 15 railroads connected Cincinnati and its industry to other parts of the United States: iron production, meat packing, cloth production, and woodworking.
- In 1887 Cincinnati's industries employed 103,325 people and produced more than $200 million in goods.

Popular Barbershop Quartet Songs

"Down by the Old Mill Stream"

"Down Our Way"

"Honey/Li'l Lize Medley"

"Let Me Call You Sweetheart"

"Mister Jefferson Lord, Play That Barbershop Chord" (referenced above)

"My Wild Irish Rose"

"Shine on Me"

"The Story of the Rose" ("Heart of My Heart")

"Sweet Adeline"

"Sweet and Lovely"

"Sweet, Sweet Roses of Morn"

"Wait 'Til the Sun Shines, Nellie"

"You Tell Me Your Dream (I'll Tell You Mine)"

"From the First Hello"

"Goodbye, My Coney Island Baby"

West Point Graduate on the Frontier in 1891

As the Indian Wars came to an end, Second Lieutenant Eddie Rausch, an Ohio native, was assigned the unrewarding task of patrolling the windswept lands of North Dakota, while reliving the Battle of Pine Ridge in his memory and praying for a warmer assignment.

Life at Home

- Edwin "Eddie" Rausch grew up in a small community in northeastern Ohio, equidistant from Cleveland and Lake Erie.
- His childhood was filled with tales of military adventures frequently and robustly recounted by his great-uncles and loosely based on their Civil War exploits.
- Rausch men, he was told repeatedly, were born to fight, ever since Johann Rausch was conscripted to serve his German princeling and found himself rented out to fight for the British against the American colonists.
- After the Revolutionary War, Johann stayed in America, settled in the middle of the vast new nation, and produced a long line of soldiers, farmers and merchants.
- Eddie Rausch was destined to be a soldier, his uncles averred.
- The third son in a family of seven, Eddie proved to be an average student but a superb horseman who loved the outdoors.
- His father, a prosperous farmer and shopkeeper, used his political connections to wangle Eddie an appointment to West Point.
- After a lifetime of dime-store war novels and family battle stories, Eddie envisioned himself in the midst of historic cavalry assaults.
- Instead his first major clash was with the Corps' stringent engineering curriculum, with Eddie ending up on the losing side.
- At graduation, postings were determined by a student's class rank; Eddie Rausch, horse-lover and man of the outdoors, was not in the top half of the class of 1889, and as a result he was the last officer chosen for the cavalry.
- His assignment was the unpopular role of leading the 9th Cavalry Regiment, one of two all-black cavalry units in the army, now stationed in the West.

Second Lieutenant Eddie Rausch was assigned work in North Dakota.

Eddie's fellow comrades were a diverse bunch.

- Although Second Lieutenant Rausch was happy to be out of school and back in the saddle, he was uncertain about this assignment.
- No blacks lived in his section of Ohio, and he had known few in his entire life; it was widely believed in the military that blacks made good soldiers-if led by a strong and resourceful white officer.
- When he arrived at Fort Robinson, Nebraska, Eddie was immediately impressed with the quality of his troops, finding the Negroes to be excellent soldiers.
- While many in K-Troop were planning to make a career of the military and acted accordingly, many of the white men at Fort Robinson considered soldiering a temporary position and consequently were lazy and undisciplined.
- Months later, emergency orders arrived for K-Troop to move out immediately to Fort Buford in the Dakota Territory. Eddie was elated-a chance to engage the enemy at last!
- While some officers studied the Indians' customs, background, weapons, and tools, Eddie used his ample quiet time to study the military mission of each Western fort, including Fort Buford.
- Not only was it well known as the place where Chief Sitting Bull surrendered but it also played a significant role in keeping the Native Americans in check so settlers and railroads could continue westward.
- A call for additional troops could mean only one thing-an Indian uprising.

Life at Work
- The urgent telegram arrived on November 19, 1890, at Fort Robinson, Nebraska.
- "Move out as soon as possible with the troop of cavalry at your post; bring all the wagon transportation you can spare, pack-mules and saddles; extra ammunition and rations will be provided when you reach the railroad.-By order of the Department Commander."

- The soldiers of Second Lieutenant Eddie Rausch's K-Troop-nicknamed "Buffalo Soldiers" by the Indians-were needed: it was time to move out.
- At the railroad station, word came that the Sioux of the Dakota Territory were on the warpath and had murdered settlers.
- The rumors meshed with stories Eddie had heard about a new Native American religious movement.
- Zealots of the Ghost Shirt movement believed that soon the buffalo would return and all white men would be swallowed by the land; they also had come to believe that the special shirts they wore into battle would make them impervious to bullets.
- Perceptive about the ways of the world, Eddie understood that the Ghost Shirt religion had sprung forth out of desperation.
- For months he had been hearing stories that the once-proud Sioux, the former overlords of the Northern Plains, were starving on the reservations of North Dakota and South Dakota.
- It was well known that many Indian agents had been stealing the majority of food supplies sent to the reservations and selling the provisions to white travelers.
- As a result many Indians were willing to listen intently to stories told by a Paiute Indian named Wovoka, who claimed that the ghosts would return in the spring, bringing with them the buffalo and all other game the whites had slaughtered.
- Although agents in the Pine Ridge, Rosebud, Cheyenne River, and Standing Rock reservations attempted to ignore the Ghost Dancers, thousands of Native Americans were now in a state of religious frenzy.

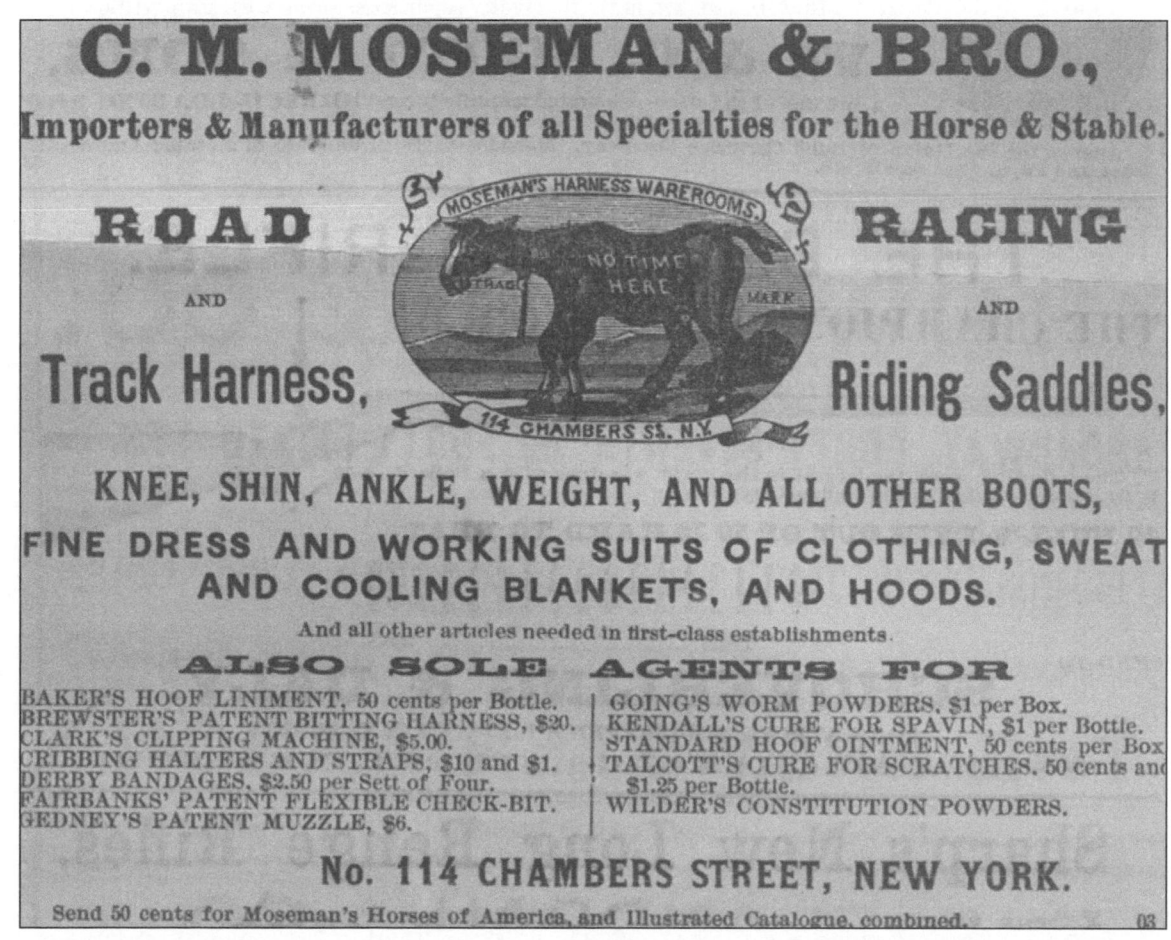

Additional troops on their way to manage the Indian uprising.

- When a new, inexperienced Indian agent at the Pine Ridge Reservation in South Dakota grew terrified of the Ghost Dancers and their threats, he desperately wired for assistance.
- Troops from the 1st, 2nd, 5th, 6th, 7th, 8th and 9th cavalry regiments, along with supporting infantry, were sent in support.
- The show of force was needed to calm the situation, the agent said; others saw the troop movement as the perfect opportunity to arrest aging Chief Sitting Bull, whom many blamed for the tension.
- Matters only became worse when the arrest of Sitting Bull was so badly botched that the famous warrior chief was killed.
- In response troops from the 7th Cavalry, accompanied by an artillery unit with two Hotchkiss machine guns, were called out to control a potential Native American uprising.
- When they arrived at Wounded Knee and attempted to disarm a band of Miniconjou Sioux under the leadership of Chief Big Foot, a bloodbath ensued.
- More than two hundred Native American men, women, and children, including Big Foot, were killed, and 26 soldiers died-many when they were caught in the crossfire from their own side.
- The Battle of Wounded Knee, better known as a massacre, prompted both hostile and friendly Sioux factions to unite for battle near Pine Ridge-requiring the men of Eddie Rausch's K-Troop.
- More than four thousand angry Indians had gathered.
- Eddie learned his troops were needed only after a 50-mile scouting trip through the Badlands.
- The men immediately struck camp and set out through the snowy night, arriving at Pine Ridge at 5:30 in the morning, having traveled 100 miles in a single day.
- No sooner had they dismounted than word came that the unit's supply wagons were under attack four miles away.
- The soldiers remounted, rode rapidly to the scene and dispersed the Sioux with one concentrated charge; one Buffalo Soldier was lost.
- Shortly after returning to camp, word came that the exhausted K-Troop and most of the 9th Cavalry were needed once more.
- To give the men a few hours' sleep before setting out again, the 7th Cavalry was sent instead.
- While K-Troop slept, the 7th Cavalry was lured into a trap; after chasing a band of Indians caught burning a small building, they found themselves cornered in a canyon.
- The 7th Cavalry realized it was surrounded; the Indians controlled the bluffs and could fire down on them with impunity.

- Out of options, the 7th Cavalry took cover and hoped that reinforcements would arrive soon.
- Upon learning of their plight, the 9th Cavalry, including K-Troop, was awakened and directed to the canyon, thundering into the area at 1:30 in the afternoon.
- While the Ghost Dance cult had preached that the whites would be swallowed up, nothing had been said about black men.
- Uncertainty spread throughout the Sioux, with many awestruck by the sight of K-Troop.
- Quickly, the deadly Hotchkiss machine gun was set up and used to sweep the top of the canyon, after which the troops dismounted and were told to attack.
- With six officers leading 170 men, Eddie and his units ferociously charged the right canyon wall.
- A few shots were fired by the Indians, but the sight of the massed soldiers in full charge quickly scattered the Sioux.
- When the battle was won without the 9th Cavalry losing a man, the soldiers' fear before the charge was replaced with joy, pride, and relief.
- The trapped soldiers of the 7th rushed from their hiding places and unselfconsciously hugged their rescuers.
- Eddie was proud-very proud indeed; his first battle, and both he and his men had done well.
- That sense of pride grew when Commanding General Miles, Department of Missouri, held a parade to review all the troops involved in the Battle of Pine Ridge.
- It was thrilling for Eddie to join his soldiers, who were covered in thick coats and hats of beaver fur, riding in triumph across the snowy field for review.
- Just as his men rode by the reviewing stand, Eddie and the black troops of K-Troop, 9th Cavalry, received the ultimate compliment-General Miles raised his gloved hand in a show of respect.
- Thus was their triumph in battle acknowledged.
- Having played a role in quashing the revolt gave Eddie something to think about during the long, lonely patrols that now dominated his life.
- Almost immediately after K-Troop's return to Fort Robinson, Major Henry began lobbying for the regiment to be transferred to Fort Myer, Virginia, for ceremonial duty-considered one of the most prestigious postings in the army.
- In April the Secretary of War ordered Major Henry to take command at Fort Myer, and to take one troop of the 9th with him.
- Henry chose K-Troop, ordering them to prepare to embark for the nation's capital.

Typical soldier housing in North Dakota.

- Eddie could not believe his luck.
- After a hard, exhausting winter, this duty was exactly what he needed.
- Unfortunately, as he prepared to leave with his troops, Eddie was informed that although the Buffalo Soldiers of K-Troop were leaving, the white officers were not.
- Second Lieutenant Rausch learned he was to be replaced by a cousin of the Army's commanding general, who had been on recruiting duty in New York for the past two years.
- Even worse, he was to be permanently transferred to the infantry at Fort Buford-he was going back to the Dakotas.
- The change from cavalry to infantry also meant a reduction in pay, from $1,500 a year to $1,400.
- So much for being a hero.
- After six months of endless patrols on the Great Plains, watching for Indians and drinking cups of bad coffee, Eddie's greatest fear was not hostile Indians, but boredom.

Life in the Community: Fort Buford, North Dakota

- Unwilling to cope with Indian depredations along the Bozeman Trail, the Army had begun in 1866 to establish a chain of forts along the Missouri River, a major route to the newly discovered Montana gold fields.
- Fort Buford was created near the confluence of the Yellowstone River and the Missouri River, in hostile Indian territory.

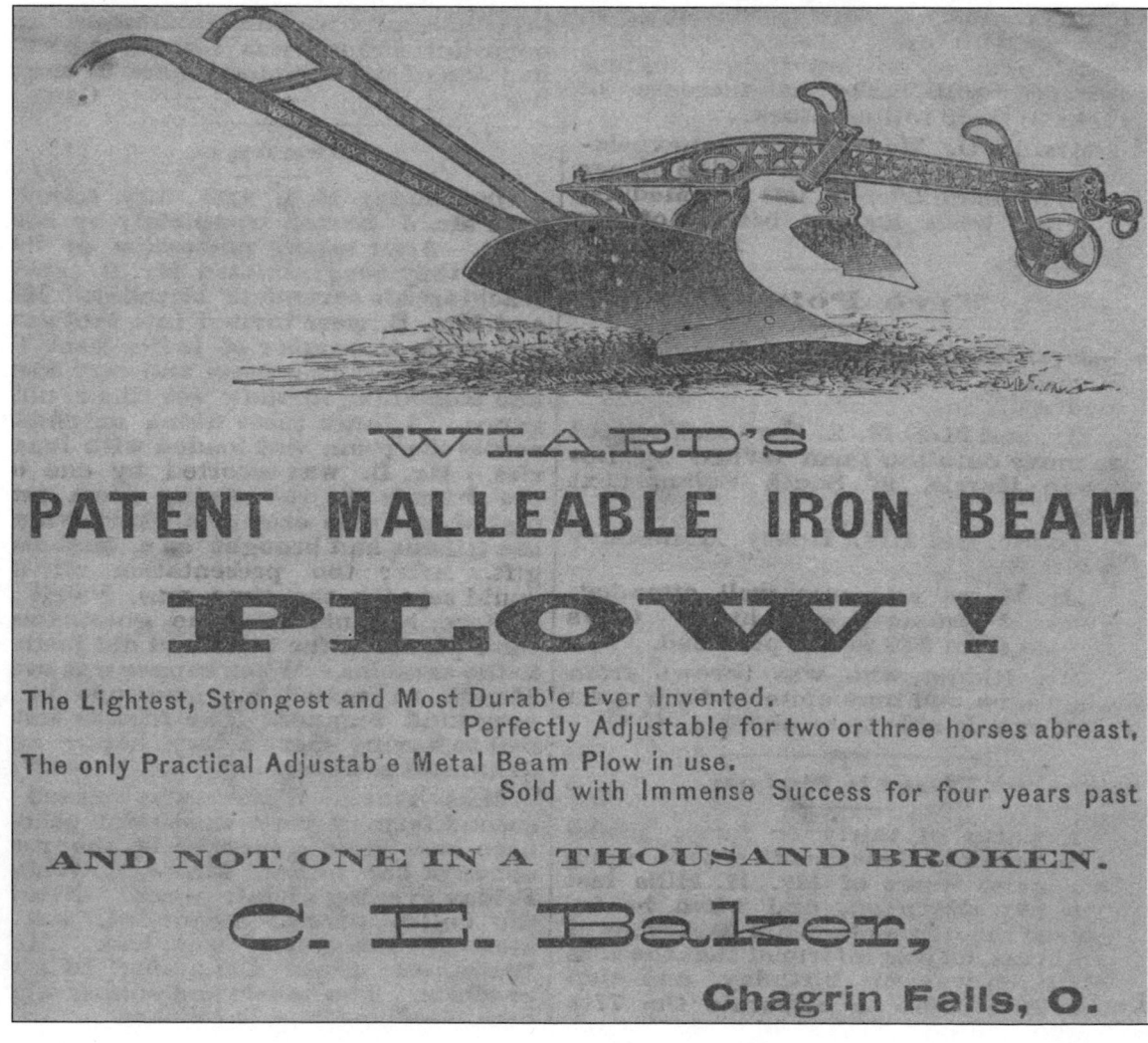

- Its principal role was to protect land and river routes used by immigrants settling the West in the 1860s and 1870s.
- Shortly after construction, Fort Buford became known for having the most intolerable weather of any post in the U.S. Army.
- Its location on the plains near the Canadian border guaranteed that its summers were hot and dry and its winters long and brutally cold; for many, a posting to Fort Buford was comparable to being sent to Siberia.
- The fort was named for Major General John Buford, a hero of the Battle of Gettysburg during the Civil War.
- Construction of the fort in the Dakota Territory began in June 1866, under the command of Brevet Lieutenant Colonel William G. Rankin.
- By November the finished fort consisted of a 30-foot-square stockade, enclosing log and adobe buildings constructed to house a single company garrison.
- The building of the fort and survey activities by the Northern Pacific Railway in 1871 invited attacks by the Sioux and their leader, Chief Sitting Bull, who believed that the expeditions violated the Treaty of 1868.
- By 1875, to meet the growing demands of Indian retaliation, the post had been expanded numerous times; it housed six companies.
- The new facilities often were constructed of locally made clay bricks and wood.
- In 1875 the secretary of the interior asked the secretary of war to force the Indians onto their respective reservations.
- This prompted the Sioux Wars of 1876-1879, during which the defeat of Gen. George Custer at the Battle of Little Big Horn and Chief Sitting Bull's flight to Canada occurred.
- Sitting Bull's trek into Canada was an attempt to maintain his independence, but a lack of natural game for hunting and the desire of his people to be with their relatives led him to return to the Dakota Territory.
- Thirty-five families-187 people in all-traveled with Sitting Bull in July 1881 to Fort Buford, where the Sioux chief surrendered his Winchester .44 caliber carbine to Fort Buford's commander, Major D. H. Brotherton.
- For most of the succeeding decade, the role of the Army at Fort Buford was to protect survey and construction crews of the Great Northern Railway, prevent Native Americans from crossing the international boundary from Canada, and police the area against outlaws.
- Troops posted at Fort Buford were also called upon to protect the weaker tribes of the area-the Assiniboine, Mandan, Hidatsa, and Arikira-from attack by the more powerful Sioux.
- The fort was manned by the four companies of the 25th Infantry, one of two black infantry regiments.
- Physically the post was a collection of wooden buildings loosely grouped around a parade ground.
- These buildings included a large, 20-room house for the commanding officer, smaller cottages for the other married officers, barracks for the enlisted men, a dining hall and kitchen, stables, a hospital, an ammunition magazine, storehouses, and laundresses' quarters.

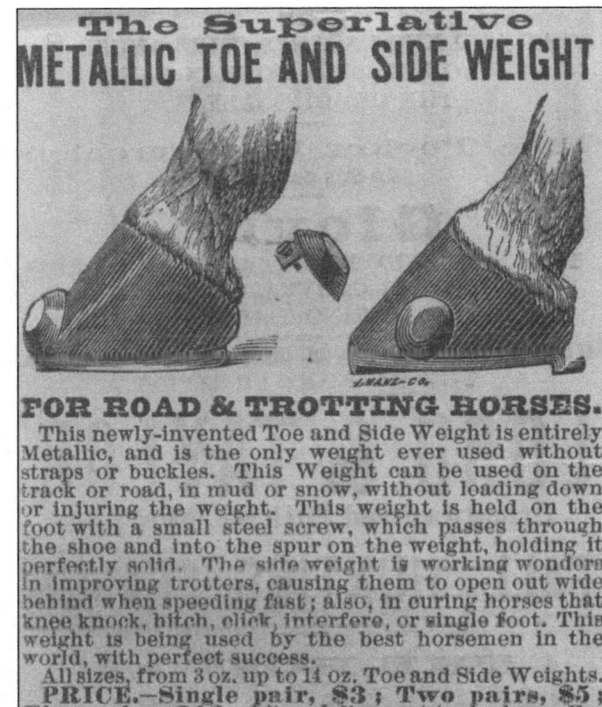

- Money for maintenance was in short supply, and the buildings, although neat, look shabby.
- During the warmer months, one company of soldiers handled border duty, while a second kept the peace between the Indian reservations and the mining camps across the Montana border—a constant and increasingly difficult problem.
- Native Americans described the long lines of infantrymen marching across the Dakota winter prairie as "walk-a-heaps" because the men's bodies, horses, and long fur coats combined into one large mass.
- The long lines often include mules, the workhorses of the West.
- Packing a mule required considerable experience but was worth the effort; a mule—said to be the only animal Noah didn't take on the Ark—could carry up to 300 pounds of supplies over rough country 30 miles a day.
- In addition to being hardier than horses, mules needed less food.

Mules were the workhorses of the West.

Monthly Pay of Army Enlisted Men
in Active Service, 1890

Company Grade	First Year	Fifth Year
Private (Artillery, Cavalry and Infantry)	$13	$16
Private, Second Class (Engineers and Ordnance	13	16
Musician (Engineers, Artillery and Infantry)	13	16
Trumpeter (Cavalry)	13	16
Wagoner	14	14
Artificer	15	15
Corporal (Artillery, Cavalry and Infantry)	15	18
Blacksmith and Furrier	15	18
Saddler (Cavalry)	15	18
Sergeant (Artillery, Cavalry and Infantry)	17	20
Private, First Class (Engineers and Ordnance)	17	20
Corporal (Engineers and Ordnance)	20	23
First Sergeant (Artillery, Cavalry and Infantry)	22	25
Sergeant (Engineers, Ordnance and Signal Corps)	34	37
Sergeants, First Class (Signal Corps)	45	48

Yearly and Monthly Pay of Army Officers
in Active Service, 1890

Grade	Yearly	Monthly	After 10 Years of Service
Major General	$7,500	$625	$0
Brigadier General	5,500	458	0
Colonel	3,500	291	350
Lieutenant Colonel	3,000	250	300
Major	2,500	208	250
Captain, Mounted	2,000	166	200
Captain, Not Mounted	1,800	150	180
Regimental Adjutant	1,800	150	180
Regimental Quartermaster	1,800	150	180
First Lieutenant, Mounted	1,600	133	160
First Lieutenant, Not Mounted	1,500	125	150
Second Lieutenant, Mounted	1,500	125	150
Second Lieutenant, Not Mounted	1,400	116	140
Chaplain	1,500	125	150

Mining Company Owner in 1892

Silver mining built the town of Leadville, Colorado—and John Gustin's fortune. John was convinced that America would always need silver, even if the government repealed the Sherman Silver Purchase Plan. He and his wife, Lucille, had no children.

Life at Home

- Born in Pennsylvania, John Gustin migrated west following the advice of newspaper publisher Horace Greeley in 1877: "Go West, Young Man."
- John and Lucille had the means to live in a 13-bedroom mansion built by craftsmen imported from England and Scotland; most of the materials were also brought from England to ensure authenticity.
- John was very proud of Leadville, which became a bustling city almost overnight; he despised the Eastern press for dwelling on the brothels and bars that come with a mining town.
- Mining had brought so much wealth to Leadville and Denver that down on Main Street, at stores such as Zaitz Mercantile and the surrounding shops, John had his choice of the best of everything.
- He liked to boast to snobbish East Coast friends, "I can buy anything I desire, from a buggy to a hat to smoked meat to a cocktail-anything you have in New York."
- He sent them articles from the newspapers of Leadville to prove his point; the city has seven newspapers, all eager to describe in full the annual balls and frequent dinners and the elaborate wedding dresses of the city's brides.
- John was urging Lucille to return to playing the piano; to encourage her, he had recently ordered a Baldwin piano to be shipped from the East.
- He planned to put the piano in the music room; perhaps then he would succeed in getting rid of the Turkish leather couch Lucille had bought in England.
- At a recent party, several of their neighbors had bragged about going into the wilderness for a camping trip-complete with servants.
- Lucille enjoyed hearing her friends talk about the joys of "roughing it" in a tent, but she had no plans to follow their example; she was happy to continue sleeping on her soft, feather-stuffed mattress.

John Gustin migrated from Pennsylvania to Colorado.

With a fortune made from silver mining, the Gustin's built an extravagant home.

- John loved his work; Lucille loved to travel, particularly to Paris, where she frequently shopped in the finest stores.
- To fit in with French society, she was intensively studying the French language, despite her distinct American accent; in France, she poured money into the Blérancourt Museum, with its great art collection and Franco-American historical documents.
- During her many trips abroad, Lucille socialized with the rich and famous, including, in England, Sir Thomas Lipton, the tea millionaire.
- She was also able to attend a play starring the famous actor Johnston Forbes-Robertson as Romeo.
- At home, the better ladies of Leadville were promoting Valentine's Day celebrations; all of the women ordered elaborate valentines from New York and Germany, competing with each other for the grandest design.
- The men were reluctantly going along.
- Lucille selected a three-dimensional valentine featuring a hot air balloon.
- Her energy and her husband's fortune had significantly swelled the building fund of the Cathedral of the Immaculate Conception.
- The Catholic Church was a well-organized focus of social programs and power within the community.

Life at Work

- John decided to go West because he wanted to "grow up with the country."
- He had tried farming in Nebraska and working in the quartz mines of the Deadwood gulch; finally, at the time of the big miners' strike, he made his way to Leadville.

- During his early years in Colorado, he staked a claim to several mines, but he was forced to abandon them because of financial difficulties.
- While serving as superintendent to the Smith and Moffat mines, he discovered a new silver vein, and he received part ownership as a reward.
- John subsequently became the largest owner of the Ibex Mining Company and a minority stockholder in several other mines in the area.
- His honesty attracted capital when others were wanting; many men of wealth liked to be associated with him.
- He loaned money to more than one western miner who was in need; repayment often came in the form of silver stock certificates.
- John completed several deals at the elegant New York Club, which served as something of a gentleman's gambling parlor.
- Unconcerned about the federal government's efforts to reduce its silver consumption, John believed that the nation would always need silver.
- In 1889 the price of silver had dipped to $0.93 an ounce, but the price climbed again in 1890 when Congress doubled the amount of silver purchased by the federal government.

John was known as a friend to the miners, helping them and their families.

- The Silver Purchase Act required the Department of the Treasury to purchase 4.5 million ounces of silver at market prices every month.
- Farmers and others in debt believed that an unlimited amount of cheap silver in the monetary system would help solve their economic woes.
- Many East Coast financiers were more wedded to the gold standard, considering the Sherman Silver Purchase Plan a colossal waste of money.
- After John came West, he often voted for the Republican ticket, but later he shifted his politics and supported the Populists.
- He believed that many of the tenets of the newly formed Populist Party were so sound that they would survive even if the party did not.
- The Populist platform called for a national currency-safe, sound, and flexible-issued by the general government only; a graduated income tax; government ownership of railroads and telegraph lines; and the abolition of land monopolies.
- To attract the labor vote, the Populists were also calling for the eight-hour day and restrictive immigration laws.
- John was known as the miner's friend; he had often come to the aid of injured miners or their families when he became aware of their needs.

- In Leadville mining camps were divided ethnically. The Cornish, who learned the skill of smelting in England, lived in Jacktown, near the smelters; the Finns all clustered to the East.
- Only men of English origin were hired at Horace Tabor's Little Pittsburgh and Chrysolite mines.
- Many of the men also supported families back East or in their country of origin; this year, the Leadville post office processed 13,352 U.S. money orders, totaling $201,346, and 2,195 international money orders, valued at $59,724.

Life in the Community: Leadville, Colorado

- Gold was discovered in 1858 along the banks of the Cherry Creek, near Denver.
- Within months, more than ten thousand men descended on the area to pan for gold, which was difficult to mine because of an abundance of black sand.
- In 1875 two men sent a sample of this sand for mineral content tests, which showed it was 40 percent lead and contained up to 40 ounces of silver per ton.
- By 1877 Leadville was in the midst of a silver boom.
- Set in the upper Arkansas River Valley, in the center of Colorado, Leadville had an elevation of 10,200 feet, giving it the distinction of being the highest incorporated city in the United States.
- To the east stood the Mosquito Range, and to the west, the Sawatch, home of the two highest peaks in the state.
- Winter arrived in mid-October and stayed until May; in between, in a typical year, more than 200 inches of snow fell.
- The town of Leadville was incorporated in 1880 and named for the secondary metal in which the silver was found, but it was nicknamed the "Magic City" and "Silver City" for the metal that provided its wealth.
- From 1880 the railroad connected Leadville to the rest of the world; as a result, businesses such as the Delaware Hotel were booming.
- The city directory of 1879 read, "The city of Leadville is one of the marvels of the present age. Two years ago it had no existence, while today it has long streets and broad avenues many miles in

Mining made Leadville, Colorado, a booming town.

extent, with large and handsome buildings on every side. As recently as August 1877, only six rude log cabins were to be found where today, well-designed edifices can be counted by the thousand."

- The same directory listed an array of businesses in the town: four assay offices, three bakeries, five boardinghouses, two booksellers and stationers, seven boot- and shoe merchants, three carpenters, three carpet dealers, eight civil- and mining engineering offices, nine clothing stores, 18 law firms, five meat markets, 10 physicians, 25 saloons, one scenic painter, one undertaker and three theaters.

- A visitor recently noted, "We can look up its length possibly two miles. It was a crawling mass of horses, mules, wagons and men. It looked impossible to get through, but we made it in about two hours."

- The quality of the city's opera house attracted excellent Eastern acts entertaining throughout the West, thanks to the management's habit of paying the actors in silver.

Leadville boasted a variety of modern buildings and homes.

- Gas lighting, installed in 1879, was also a draw, giving the opera house and the streets of the city a soft glow.

- The city's population of 30,000 was just a few thousand shy of rival Denver's.

- Many of the silver mine owners believed that the brothels and bars along State Street provided a safe place for their miners to let off steam, although they were concerned that too many prostitutes on the streets would hurt the city's reputation.

- The climate of Leadville was blamed for "an uncontrollable desire for mountain dew," or liquid refreshment, in the city.

- The *Leadville Chronicle* opined that, "Other localities have their vegetarians, but Leadville has her whisketarians. It requires no more self-control for total abstinence here than elsewhere, provided people care to exert it, but a general spirit of recklessness pervades the air and few care to combat it."

- Leadville had three hospitals; St. Vincent's, the most prominent, was opened in 1879 by a band of Sisters of Charity from Leavenworth, Kansas.

- St. Vincent's recently added a new operating room that was bright and cheery, "being tiled most artistically while the walls have an enamel finish."

- The hospital was operated by three doctors and eight sisters; according to its records, it had served 5,667 Catholics and 3,122 non-Catholics; nationalities represented included 2,677 Irish, 2,133 Americans, 713 Germans, 478 English, 169 Austrians, 69 Polish, 60 Welsh, 409 French Canadians, 62 Bohemians, 454 Swedes, 402 Italians, 361 Scots, 89 Norwegians, 68 Russians, and 61 Swiss.

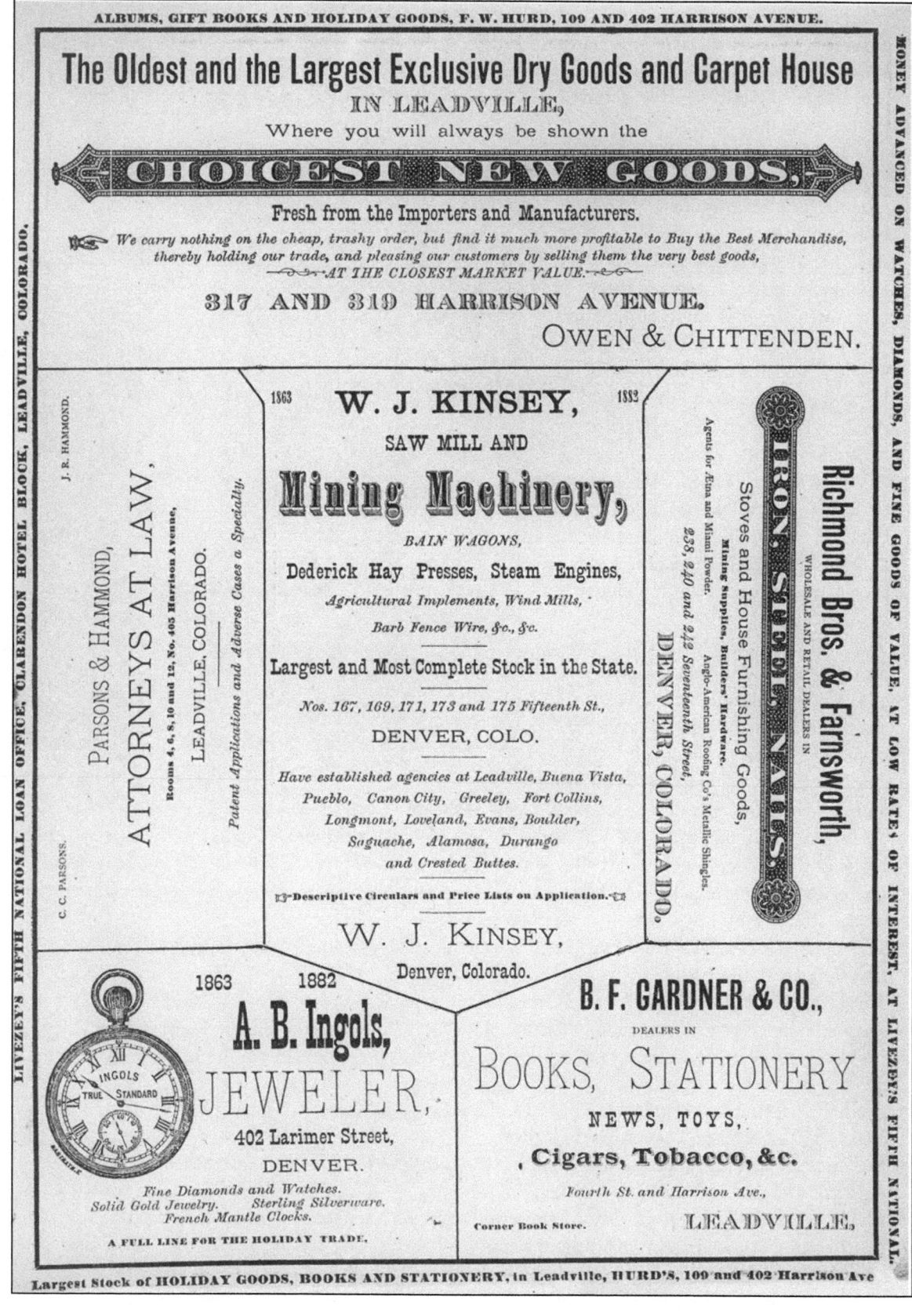

Sweet-Potato Farmer in 1892

João Soares, a second-generation Portuguese American farmer, lived in Northern California. Like most farmers in their community of Portuguese immigrants, the Soares family grew sweet potatoes, and like many of their neighbors, they were tenant farmers. João and his wife, María, had three children, two boys and one girl.

Life at Home

- The Soares family lived in a rented three-room house; they were saving their money to buy a neighboring farm, which had a farmhouse in good repair.
- María saw to the cleanliness and neatness of the family's home, despite the tight quarters.
- She took great pride in her thriftiness and had already begun teaching her young daughter, Teresa, the importance of thrift in managing a household.
- Meals typically centered around fish stew, fava beans cooked in tomato sauce with onions and bacalau.
- The family was Catholic; the church was a link to the past and the old country.
- Much of the family's social life revolved around religious festivals and holy days.
- Festivals were important to Portuguese workers and featured mountains of food; Portuguese immigrants considered it humiliating not to provide a "good table" or to run out of food during a party.
- Foods associated with the Festas do Espiritu Santoestas-religious festivals honoring the Holy Ghost-included sweet bread, *linguiça* (Portuguese sausage), and *sopas*, a roast beef, bread, and gravy soup made in huge quantities and distributed to all.
- The two sons in the family, António and Carlito, were old enough to help on the farm, and João was seeing to it that they learned not only the best methods of cultivating the sweet potato but the many skills necessary to operate a farm effectively.
- As João well knew and carefully explained, an inefficient farm would not prosper, and when times were good, it was necessary to prepare for the leaner times that might follow.

João Soares was a second-generation Portuguese American farmer.

María was teaching her daughter and her friend how to manage a household.

- Teresa was not yet old enough for school, and neither of her parents considered school to be a high priority for her.
- María expected to keep Teresa at home and teach her what she would need to know to manage a household when she was grown.
- Both João and María Soares were able to read *Uniao Portuguesa*, a Portuguese-language newspaper published in San Francisco.

Life at Work

- The Portuguese farmers of the Atwater area, the Soares family among them, tended to come from other parts of California, not directly from the Azores.
- Nearly all Portuguese immigrants to California arrived "poor in circumstances albeit rich in enterprise, and they acquired land on installment payments."
- The sweet potato plants were started in hotbeds and then planted in the fields.
- Cultivation of sweet potatoes was labor-intensive.
- In California sweet potatoes were cured in the ground before harvest.
- In the beginning many food brokers were skeptical that there would be a market for sweet potatoes, and farmers had to sell on consignment.
- Shipping sweet potatoes to market was made more difficult because the train schedule was unpredictable.
- Farmers were forced to spend hours waiting by the tracks to flag down the train so that their produce could be taken to market.
- The freight rate from Atwater to San Francisco was $0.44 per hundred pounds.

João planned to add dairy cows to the family's sweet potato farm.

- To remain competitive the Portuguese farmers formed cooperatives and partnerships, allowing them to ship more cheaply and buy supplies less expensively.
- Encouraged by María, João became active in the local cooperative.
- He was skilled at negotiating, and his abilities were respected by the other members of the cooperative.
- By 1892 sweet potatoes from the area were known as "Atwaters" and commanded a higher price than sweet potatoes grown in the Sacramento delta area.
- Once they acquired their own farm, the Soares family planned to add dairy farming to their sweet potato farm operations.

Life in the Community: Northern California
- Prior to 1888 land in the Atwater and Buhach area of Merced County was used for dry grain farming.
- The Crocker-Huffman irrigation system made it possible to grow irrigated crops such as sweet potatoes in the region.
- The first Portuguese farmers arrived in Northern California in 1883.
- In that year John B. Ávila, born on São Jorge, Azores, bought (with his brother) irrigated land in the Atwater area and planted it with sweet potatoes from the Azores.
- Ávila and other Portuguese farmers were credited with making the sweet potato a major commercial crop in California.
- Most of the crop was shipped to San Francisco.
- Farmers could purchase small tracks of land, approximately 20 acres, which sold for $100 an acre, plus water rights, which cost $1 a year per acre.

- Irrigation was critical to the production of sweet potatoes.
- In 1889 California irrigated a million acres of land.
- Prior to 1890, according to census records, 36,342 Portuguese immigrated to the United States, settling primarily in Massachusetts or California.
- By 1892 Oakland was the unofficial Portuguese capital of California, with some four thousand Portuguese residents.
- The farmers formed fraternal societies to provide insurance and assistance to members who became sick or to their widows and surviving children.
- At the death of a member, the surviving members were assessed the sum of $1; the money was given to the widow and children of the deceased.
- These societies also raised money to assist other countries, especially Latin or Catholic, that had suffered tragedies such as hurricanes or earthquakes.
- In California Portuguese immigrants were also involved in salmon fishing, sheep herding, the dairy industry, and canning-factory work; Portuguese farmers also grew asparagus.

Farming was hard work.

- As with most foreign-speaking groups in America, a short-lived newspaper in the language of the old country was created.
- Considerable anti-Catholic feeling was growing nationwide, causing problems and tension in the community.
- More newcomers from the East had begun to arrive in the area; in a rate war between the Southern Pacific and the Santa Fe railroad, the Southern Pacific offered a passenger rate of $1 for persons traveling from Kansas City to Los Angeles.
- Wheat cultivation dominated many parts of California because of the climate and ease of transportation of dry grains to the East Coast.
- Many California growers depended on markets outside the state, requiring cooperation and sophisticated marketing programs to sell their product.
- In the 1880s California growers adopted trade names as a marketing ploy to sell more of their produce.
- It was estimated that in 1885 the cost of planting a 10-acre citrus orchard in Los Angeles County and bringing it to bearing fruit was $230 per acre.
- In 1890 California produced 1.5 million cases of canned goods, valued at $6 million.
- California's dried fruit and canning industry was growing; preserving the produce in these ways helped ensure that "seasonal glut" did not drive prices down.
- The introduction of the refrigerated railway car, which appeared in 1889, had a revolutionary impact on the marketing of fresh fruits to the East Coast.
- The Southern Pacific Railroad offered special rates to growers who supplied 15 cars of produce daily.
- Cheap labor, provided by Chinese workers, was critical to the success of Northern California fruit growers.
- "At the present prices of fruit, we could not grow it without Chinese labor," the Reverend William Brier, a fruit grower, told a U.S. Senate Committee investigating Chinese immigration.
- Smaller farmers typically hired Chinese labor, paying them less than non-Chinese workers; the average agricultural wage for non-Chinese was $1.90 per day.
- After 1886 the Chinese were prohibited from owning land in California.

Yale University Oarsman in 1893

Chet Taylor couldn't wait for the day he could compete as a Yale University student in the Yale-Harvard Regatta, an event held annually since 1859. He made the team in his sophomore year.

Life at Home

- Yale sophomore Chet Taylor was sure of one thing: of all the collegiate sports, rowing made the most stringent demands upon a gentleman's unselfish devotion to his task.
- In baseball and football, there was the stimulus and excitement of frequent, almost daily, games.
- For track athletes there were plenty of brushes with friends or an occasional outside contest to fortify their interest in running, jumping, and throwing.
- But in boating, although there were many days of enjoyment, the thrill of competition was a one-day event.
- A rower labored for six months, day after day, preparing for a contest that was all over in a brief 20 minutes.
- To be prepared for that day and be fit to represent the university, a man had to be willing to go through months of training and hard work without the encouragement of enthusiastic admirers applauding the effort.
- When the weather posed a twisted vindictiveness against an oarsman, then a show of character and spirit was especially required.
- Chet loved being on the water, the feel of the oars, the muscle strain in his shoulders, and the satisfying sounds of water against the bow.
- He believed that only men of strong character, men in whom perseverance and patience were marked traits, could with sincerity call themselves collegiate oarsmen.
- His father had been an oarsman, and he had taught Chet well.
- Chet grew up learning how to maintain his oars and care for his boats as though they were cherished heirlooms.

Yale sophomore Chet Taylor and his younger sister.

The Taylor family.

- His mother and three older sisters praised him mightily throughout his boyhood whenever he rowed past the family home, racing against himself.
- But despite all the family support, he fully understood that an oarsman was a self-made man.
- A good coach might correct a fault, even an ingrained one, but it was the athlete who got up early, stayed late, and gave his all on the day of the race.
- Chet also felt very lucky to be at Yale University.
- After Chet's years of dreaming about college, a reversal of fortunes (possibly a bad investment; his father would not discuss it) threatened to shipwreck his college plans.
- But then his Uncle Clarence stepped in with the needed financial support.
- Uncle Clarence, a Yale man, owned more than 250 buildings in the heart of New York's commercial district.
- He was a director of the Chemical Bank and the Metropolitan Opera House, and he lived in a New York City mansion envied by all.
- He didn't have a son who could row for Yale in the annual race against Harvard, so Chet became the lucky substitute son.
- So when he left his home in Pittsburgh, Pennsylvania, Yale-bound Chet knew his college years would include rowing and the opportunity to repay his uncle in the only currency he might have: a win over Harvard.

Life at Work

- When Chet Taylor first arrived at Yale his freshman year, he assumed that he would soon be crewing on an eight-oared shell.
- Nothing was more elegant and poetic than the rhythmic swaying of eight bodies dipping eight perfectly balanced oars into the water to propel an exquisitely designed boat to its destination.
- Chet was sure he would win a spot quickly, although, as he was told, rowing eight-oared shells was a privilege rarely extended to freshmen.
- Chet, a 5'5" freshman, had primarily raced singles and fours.
- In the view of his elders, Chet found, racing in singles, while an excellent sport, rarely prepared a man to be a member of the synchronized crew.
- After his hurt feelings healed, Chet came to realize that at Yale, at least, paying your dues, waiting your turn, and serving the needs of others was considered part of the education of the gentleman boater.
- So during Chet's first year at Yale, he could regularly be found wiping down the boats inside and out when they came out of the water or preparing the varsity boat by rubbing it with pumice, smoothing it with soapstone, and greasing it with oil and paraffin.
- This was not easy work.
- The eight-oared shell was made of cedar and weighed from 230 to 275 pounds.
- Boat lengths ranged from 59 to 61 feet.
- They averaged 9 inches deep from gunwale to keel, with a 4-inch washboard above the gunwale.
- The middle breadth was typically 20 to 25 inches, narrowing to 16 or 18 inches at the end of the cockpit.
- Oars weighed approximately 7.5 pounds and were 8.5 feet long.
- Early on, Chet knew that he would not participate in sport as a professional, for money.
- He would play only for victory.
- The Harvard-Yale Regatta first took place in 1852 and had been an annual event since 1859.
- The first prize was a pair of black-walnut, silver-inscribed trophy oars dating back to the inaugural event.

Although not an oarsman as a freshman, Chet maintained the boats and supported the team.

Crew was also popular among women.

- Originally a three-mile race, the regatta changed into a four-mile sprint on the Thames River, in New London, Connecticut, in 1876.
- Two years before Chet arrived, Harvard had won in an upstream time of 21 minutes, 23 seconds-34 seconds ahead of Yale.
- Yale avenged that loss during Chet's freshman year.
- Having earned his spot, Chet became an oarsman in his sophomore year.
- The 1893 race was scheduled for June 30; as it had been the year before, the race was to be downstream.
- A crowd of 40,000 turned out along the four-mile route to witness the race; the weather that day was capricious, with intense headwinds and rough water.
- As starting time approached, conditions grew even worse-a gale kicked up white caps on the river.
- When it came time to take his place in the shell, Chet was calm, energized, and silent.
- Now was the time, the seniors insisted, when character and training would emerge.
- Harvard jumped out to an early lead with strong and confident strokes in the choppy water.
- The second mile was all Yale, and no one wanted victory more than Chet.

- During the third mile, his shoulders screamed and his arms ached; a strong headwind made for a slow time and exhausted rowers.
- In the fourth mile, Chet achieved excellent positioning to maintain the Yale lead.
- Until he crossed the finish line, he didn't hear a single sound from the crowd of 40,000.
- Once Yale won, however, he was engulfed in noise.
- Every whistle in town, on the river, and in the harbor blended with blasts from the railroads and factories and cheers from the exuberant Yale supporters, creating triumphant pandemonium.
- Experts declared it the hardest race a Yale crew had rowed in years.
- Afterwards the eight were put on a train to New Haven, where they were greeted with a reception followed by a banquet marked by victory toasts.
- Chet went to bed that night with the sounds of firecrackers and tin horns filling the streets.

Life in the Community: New Haven, Connecticut

- Yale University was experiencing growth in 1893; five buildings were under construction, and the university's endowment fund exceeded $4 million for the first time.
- Enrollment surpassed two thousand; many feared the university was becoming too big.
- Yale traced its beginnings to "An Act for Liberty to Erect a Collegiate School," passed by the General Court of the Colony of Connecticut on October 9, 1701, in an effort to create an institution to train ministers.
- Originally called the Collegiate School, it opened in the home of its first rector, Abraham Pierson, in Killingworth; after several moves, the college moved in 1716 to New Haven, Connecticut.
- In 1718 Elihu Yale, who had made a fortune in India as a representative of the East India Company, donated to the school nine bales of goods that were sold for more than £560, a substantial sum at the time.

A typical scene in New Haven, Connecticut, home of Yale University.

- When Yale donated 417 books and a portrait of King George I, the school changed its name to Yale College in gratitude to its benefactor-and perhaps in the hope that he would give the college another large donation or bequest.
- In July 1779 hostile British forces occupying New Haven threatened to raze the college; Yale graduate Edmund Fanning, secretary to the British General in command of the occupation, interceded, and the college was spared.
- Yale gradually expanded to include the Yale School of Medicine (1810), Yale Divinity School (1822), Yale Law School (1824), Yale Graduate School of Arts and Sciences (1847), the Sheffield Scientific School (1847), and Yale School of Fine Arts (1869).
- Yale Divinity School was founded by Congregationalists who felt that the Harvard Divinity School had become too liberal.
- In 1887, as the college continued to grow during the presidency of Timothy Dwight V, Yale College was renamed Yale University.

Rowing
Walter Camp's Book of College Sports, 1893

A coach may correct a fault, but faults in rowing are apt to be like the formed habits of mature life, almost ingrained, and to eradicate them requires the steadily fixed and unflagging attention of the individual himself. At first it is a distinct effort at every stroke for him to avoid a lapse into his old or natural way. For days, and it may be weeks, he feels that he must think every time; but then there comes a day when it is more natural and easy to do it the right way than the old way, and his lesson is learned. But this is only one fault, and lucky indeed would be the oarsman who found he had but one fault to correct. In fact, it is a wonder that more men did not become discouraged in their early attempts; but the man who goes in for this sport, and sticks doggedly at it, putting his whole thought and attention upon the instructions he is receiving, reaps in the end the reward for all his labors. To some men, rowing, so far as eventually securing a seat in the varsity boat, is as much out of the question as becoming a varsity ballplayer. There is a knack about rowing as about any other game of skill, but patience and perseverance have made more boatman out of some terribly unpromising material so that one can hardly feel justified in saying to any man, "You'll never be an oarsman." Some of the best men in Harvard and Yale boats have been men who during their first year, yes, even their second year, have been looked upon by the coaches as decidedly doubtful. Besides the monotony of the rowers' training, there must also be considered the fact that in a great final contest, the oarsman does not come into actual contact with his opponent; and so there is lacking the usual stimulus to outdo that so marked in foot-ball, and present to a less extent in the other sports. It is here that the result of the dogged determination is seen; and the same earnest patience which makes the oarsman take kindly to the coach's severest criticisms and put his whole mind into correcting the trivial fault, drives him on when every stroke is a pain and his whole strength seems exhausted… Thus, it is seen that many components-strength, skill, quickness, perseverance, and bulldog pluck, with a cheerful acquiescence to hardships and sacrifices-must be nicely balanced in the oarsman; and the selecting of their men to answer these requirements is the most difficult task of captains and coaches.

Under the Elms, Sketches of Yale Life

Edited by John Addison Porter, 1885

Groups under the elm trees! Groups under the elms just after dinner, when everyone prefers a pipe and a comfortable sprawl in the grass, to climbing up four flights of stairs and translating *Undine*, or cramming for Biennial! Under the elms these hot days, where so carelessly, so lazily and so deliciously cool we lie, reading, joking, laughing, smoking, peeping out at times from the thick shade, at the old iron pointers, which spasmodically twitch along towards recitation time and quickly drawing back our heads with the gratifying assurance that we've a half hour yet before beginning the old, old fight with books, the flesh and the Devil!

Under the elms five minutes before the clanging of the remorseless old sentinel and Lyceum belfry! What a fluttering and sometimes cutting of leaves! What a racing through the whole lesson to get some clue which will enable colloquial men to save an inglorious fizzle, and philosophicals to make a triumphant rush! What varied expressions of countenance! Here smiling complacently, there scowls; this man whistles, that one swears; here the serenity of indifference, there the serenity of despair. Now the bell begins to ring. What slow and toilsome ascent up the narrow stairs! What a sudden bolting into the recitation room as the last stroke dies away, and the door closes with a slam behind the last loiterer, and upon a division meekly expectant of the hour's worse contingencies.

❧❦❧❦❧❦❧❦

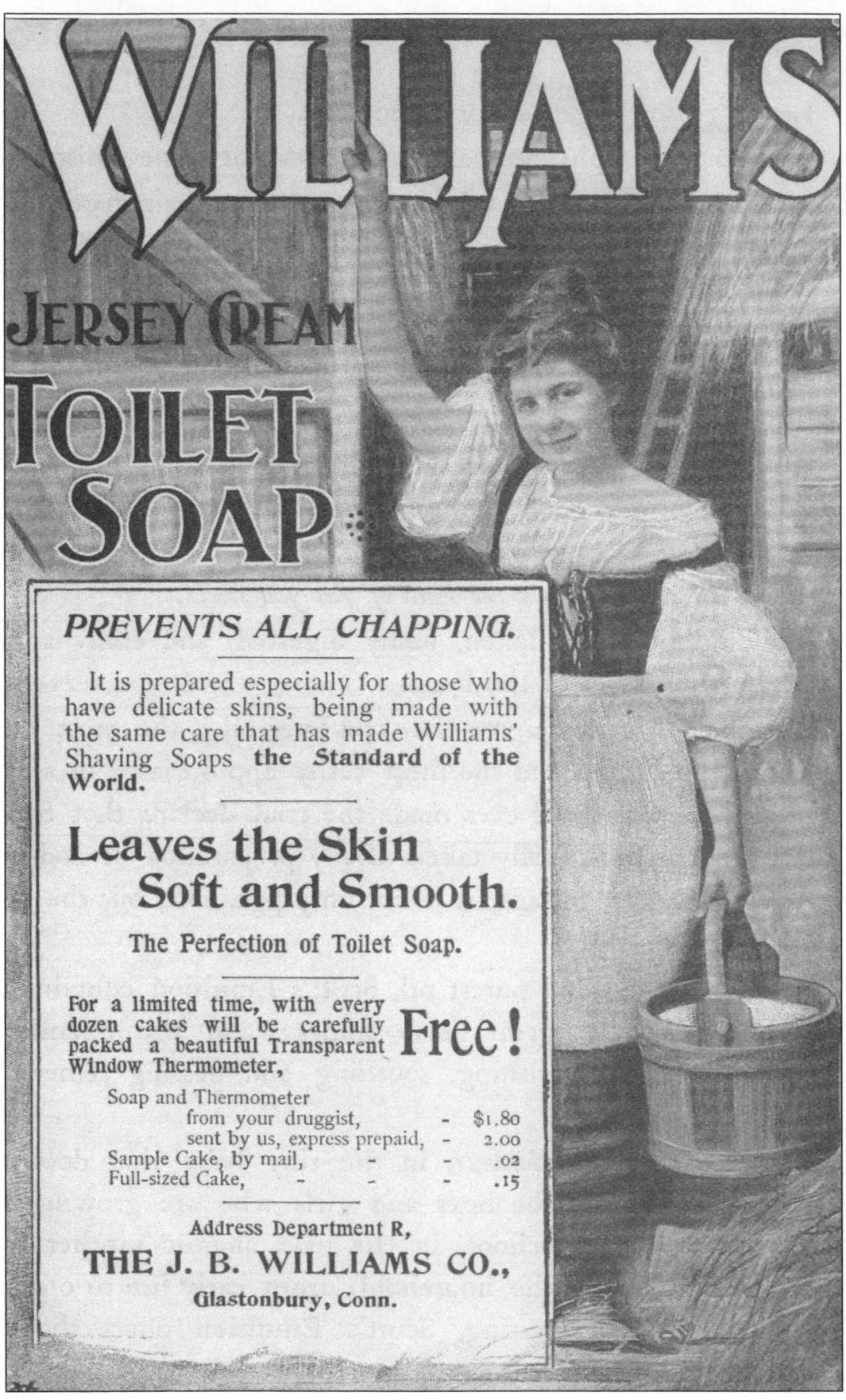

Children's Aid Society Agent in 1894

Otis Sandusky used his experience as a foundling sent west on an "orphan train" to make the experience smoother and less frightening for other orphans arriving in Dysart, Iowa.

Life at Home

- Otis Sandusky liked to think of himself as a crusader for children, although he would never actually say that aloud.
- Since he started acting as a part-time agent for the Children's Aid Society, he had felt as though he was rescuing children from a life of crime or worse.
- After all, he had done well after being shipped out of New York City into the healthy air of the Midwest; why shouldn't more homeless children be saved from urban blight?
- When he was three years old, after a five-day ride on the orphan train, Otis Sandusky was taken in by a farm family and named after his new father.
- It was his first real name.
- He had simply been called "Baby Boy" by the Sisters of Charity, who operated the Foundling Asylum and coordinated adoptions through the Children's Aid Society.
- The first recorded appearance of Baby Boy was as a day-old baby abandoned in a basket provided by the Founding Asylum of New York City.
- The note pinned to his shirt and probably written by his mother said simply, "Care for my baby boy. I can't."
- The unnamed child was one of seven children left at the Foundling Asylum that week.
- At three years old, Baby Boy was placed on an orphan train with 39 other two- and three-year-olds being sent for adoption in the West.
- When the orphan train stopped at a depot station in Indiana, Baby Boy and the other

"Baby Boy" was taken in from the orphan train at three years old, by the Sanduskys.

The Sanduskys were farmers in Iowa.

children-a wriggling mass of tired, hungry, cold toddlers from the streets of New York-were lined up on the platform.

- Baby Boy began to cry.
- The nine families who had gathered to choose a child all passed him by without a look.
- Within an hour, 11 children had been picked out by the farm families and loaded into horse-drawn wagons to be taken to their new homes.
- The children who were not picked were marched back onto the train for inspection at the next designated depot station-in Illinois or Iowa or Texas.
- Baby Boy cried at the next stop, and the next.
- When the orphan train stopped in Dysart, Iowa, it was down to six children-five girls and Baby Boy, who couldn't stop crying.
- That's where the Sandusky family found a child and Otis got a name, a home, and a future.
- Baby Boy Otis was named after Otis and Celestine Sandusky's first child, who had died of cholera.
- Otis's new father, Big Otis, was not sure this tiny, red-faced crybaby would be much of a farm hand, but over time he was pleasantly surprised.
- At the constant urging of Celestine, the Sanduskys formally adopted Otis on his fifth birthday-the age of the first Otis Sandusky when he died.
- Over time, the Sanduskys would adopt three more orphan train children-two boys and then a girl named Pearl.

Otis and Celestine Sandusky named "Baby Boy" after their son, who died of cholera.

- When Otis turned 17, he began helping out whenever an orphan train came near, serving as agent, scout, and recruiter for adoptive families in Iowa.
- Otis was even made a member of the screening committee, which included the town doctor, a clergyman, the newspaper editor, a store owner, and a teacher-all men, of course.
- The committee helped to select potential parents for the children.
- Otis was persuaded to tell his personal story in church to encourage other families to adopt.
- His little brothers made faces at him from the balcony, but Pearl, who was very polite and attentive, simply smiled throughout the talk.
- Otis's primary job was farm work, especially at planting and harvesting times, but he cherished his designation as agent, which brought with it a little extra cash and the chance to see children who had started life just as he had.

Life at Work

- On a wintry day in 1894, Father Anton Erdman, pastor of the St. Benedict's Catholic Church in Sexton, Iowa, and "Little" Otis Sandusky were both at the depot when the orphan train arrived in Dysart with a baker's dozen of very young children.
- By long tradition and habit, all the frightened children would have been unceremoniously herded off the train and ushered into the town hall to be adopted by anyone who would have them-just as Otis himself had been.
- As always before, the children who were not selected by a family would have been put back on the train to try again in another town along the route.
- The rejection would be a terrible feeling for scared, homesick little children, as Otis well knew.
- Still, this procedure had been followed for decades.
- Since 1857 the Children's Aid Society had transferred 26,000 homeless, abused, or unwanted children from the urban squalor of New York City to a healthy environment in the countryside.
- This time, however-thanks to Otis's intervention-within minutes of their arrival, the children were loaded into Father Erdman's surrey for a ride to the rectory of St. Benedict.

- It was there, Otis had convinced the committee, that families could meet the frightened orphans and more easily decide to take them home.
- The rectory felt more like a home than did a bare, impersonal train station.
- The blistering winter weather chapped the children's faces and elicited runny noses, making them look less healthy and attractive to prospective parents.
- For days the children had been in the care of only the conductor and one agent; most of the children possessed only the clothes they wore.
- Many thought they had been placed on the train and sent away because they did something wrong.
- Nuns had sewn the names of the children in the dress or shirt they wore, their only identification or connection with their New York City homes.
- Most had no birth certificate nor contact with anyone who could tell them about their past.
- Many had been baptized as Catholics regardless of their birth mother's religion.
- The children were not even aware that they had dirty, coal-streaked faces when they arrived in Dysart to meet their prospective parents.
- Otis tried to clean up the children, knowing that the sickly and those who were crying were picked last in this rough land of hard work and bitter cold.

As a teenager, Otis helped the children on the orphan train be less frightened.

- The rectory was warm, but for all his scrubbing and good intentions, Otis couldn't help but upset the sensitive ones even more.
- Then the couples arrived; many of them had requested a child, often designating gender and eye or hair color.
- The orphan train had not stopped in 13 months, and many families were eager for a chance to adopt.
- Several of the women had been at the church service at which Otis spoke about his early life aboard the orphan train.
- He hated it when the women talked about the "crybaby" part, and he vowed not to mention that again.
- Thanks to a country fiddler who was sympathetic to the orphan train children, the rectory felt festive, just as Otis had hoped, and children began to look a little less scared.
- Slowly, the farmers and their wives walked from child to child, attempting in barely more than an instant to make a lifetime decision.
- Most of the couples already had children but wanted more.

- Childbirth was a dangerous experience on the prairie, and farmers could always use another hand.
- One by one, the children were selected and went to stand beside their new parents.
- But when the rectory party was over, one little blond boy remained.
- The Merrills had planned to adopt only one of the 13 children, but after Father Erdman talked quietly with Elmer Merrill, the family ended up with two children.
- To Otis's great relief, all of the children had been adopted.

Life in the Community: Dysart, Iowa

- The Children's Aid Society of New York and the Foundling Hospital (as the Founding Asylum was renamed in 1880) required no legal adoption process, but adopting families had to promise to provide the children with some schooling and to report to the institution about the child on a yearly basis.
- Children were taken on trains in groups of 10 to 40, under the supervision of at least one "Western" agent, to selected stops along the route.
- Railroads were the least expensive way to move children westward from the poverty of inner city homes, orphanages, and poorhouses; sometimes children were taken on board right from the streets.
- In the open air of the West and Midwest, it was believed, solid, God-fearing homes could be found for the children.
- The Sisters of Charity worked tirelessly to save lives and help both the young, unwed mothers and the children, but they rarely gathered information on the parents of a child.
- Often a child was left at the Foundling Hospital with no information; the baby was simply placed in a basket on a turntable, and a sister inside the building would turn it to bring the baby inside without the adult ever being seen.
- This device made it possible for people to save the babies while remaining anonymous.
- As the program developed, the sisters requested that unwed pregnant women stay at the Foundling Hospital to have their babies and then nurse their own child plus another one for a time.
- At the end of the agreed-upon time, the mothers could leave with no further restrictions placed on them.
- Nevertheless, the goal was to bond mother and child so the mothers would seek a way to keep their children.
- While at the Foundling, many women were taught a craft or skill that would help them find work and raise their children, with a little help.

MRS. WINSLOW'S SOOTHING SYRUP, FOR CHILDREN TEETHING.

Wherever these Receipt Books are distributed, Mrs. Winslow's Soothing Syrup will be found at some Store in the vicinity.

Mrs. Winslow's Soothing Syrup.

This valuable preparation has been used with never-failing success in thousands of cases.

It not only relieves the child from pain, but invigorates the stomach and bowels, corrects acidity, and gives tone and vigor to the whole system.

It will almost instantly relieve griping in the bowels.

We believe it the best and surest remedy in the world, in all cases of

Dysentery and Diarrhœa in Children,

whether it arises from teething or from any other cause.

Look well for the genuine article, with fac-simile of *CURTIS & PERKINS, New York*, on the outside wrapper, without which none is genuine.

Mrs. Winslow's Soothing Syrup is sold by all Druggists throughout the United States.

- The women learned safe and sanitary cooking and housekeeping methods.
- As a result of exceptionally high immigration into America's port cities, the problem of homeless or abused children grew rapidly.
- Children as young as six years old worked to help support the family.
- Working conditions were generally unregulated, and many men were killed in accidents at work.
- This left women and children to make their own living as best they could, even though few jobs were open to women with children.
- Infectious diseases spread rapidly in unsanitary living quarters, leading to the early deaths of overworked mothers.
- In nearly all the East Coast port cities, orphanages were rapidly built to care for as many children as could possibly be taken.
- To place the children, priests and ministers throughout the Midwest and the West would make an announcement to the congregation, asking for volunteers to take the children.
- Couples could sign up for a male or female child, specifying the hair and eye color they preferred.
- The priest would then notify the Children's Aid Society or the Foundling Hospital that the community could take a specific number of children with blond hair and blue eyes; brown hair and brown eyes; black hair and blue eyes; or a certain skin complexion.
- One such request was for a boy with red hair, because the farmer had five red-haired daughters and no sons.
- Everyone agreed that if a family got a child who "fit in," the child and the community would do better.
- Older children were also placed.
- Boys over 16 years of age were to be retained as members of the family for one year, after which a mutual arrangement would be made concerning their future.
- Parties taking these boys agreed to write to the Children's Aid Society at least once a year, or to have the boys do so.
- If for any reason a child had to be removed from the household, the Children's Aid Society did so at their own expense.
- Most children began their new lives legally classified as indentured; thus, they were ineligible to inherit unless the family adopted them or a will specified that they were to be given an inheritance.

꧁꧂꧁꧂꧁꧂꧁꧂

Children's Day at the Circus, More Than Five Thousand of Them Have an Afternoon of Pleasure
New York Times, April 13, 1894

Yesterday was a great day for the children of the institutions of the city, when more than 5,000 of the youngsters attended Barnum & Bailey's great show, at Madison Square Garden. Great was the rejoicing of the children when they saw the elephants, the lions, tigers, and all sorts of animals from the four quarters of the globe.

The masterful doings of the men, women, and horses in the circus rings were likewise a wonder to the little visitors, who have infrequent experiences in the amusement world. They cheered lustily at the brilliant equestrian and acrobatic feats of the performers. The following is a partial list of the institutions represented at the show: St. Joseph's Asylum, Children's Aid Society, Avenue B School, New-York Infant Asylum, Children's Fold, Hebrew Sheltering Guardian, Neighborhood Guild, Protestant Half Orphans' Asylum, Duane Industrial School, Asylum of the Sacred Heart, St. Barnabas, Charities and Correction, Phelps School, Sisters of Mercy, God's Providence and St. Barnabas, Hospital for Cripples, Dominican Convent of Our Lady of the Rosary, Mission of the Immaculate Virgin, Protestant Episcopal Orphan Asylum, Italian Mission, Hebrew Institute, West Side Italian School, Industrial School of United Hebrews, Lady Deborah's Mission, St. Michael's Home, Home industrial School, St. Monica's Little Mother's Aid, University Settlement, and St. Vincent's Orphan Asylum.

❧❧❧❧❧❧❧❧

Festivities for Foundlings, Six Hundred Little Ones Have Turkey and Cranberry Sauce
New York Times, November 30, 1894

The New-York Foundling Hospital, at Sixty-eighth Street and Lexington Avenue, was the scene yesterday of joyful festivities, which will long dwell in the memories of the 600 little tots who are tenderly cared for in that institution.

For weeks they had heard tales of roast turkey and cranberry sauce, until they even dreamed of the feast to come.

Promptly at 12 o'clock the doors of the long playroom were thrown open, and the tables were quickly surrounded by 300 mothers and the older children.

In addition to this, the seven nurseries, each of which is 90 feet long and 30 feet wide, were fitted with tables, and at these were placed the 600 babies and "run-arounds," the latter being the children old enough to get into mischief.

Sister Irene, who is at the head of the hospital staff, and her 34 assistants, all decked out in their pretty costumes of blue with white aprons, white sleeves, and white Swiss cap, managed the dinner in perfect style.

"We do not often give them turkey," said one of the sisters, "because roast beef is more wholesome, and there is danger with the bones in eating fowl." The sisters were constantly called upon yesterday to extract stray turkey bones from little throats.

"Our children," continued the sister, "range in ages from one day to six years, the great majority of them being under two years old. They receive a training here that is intended to fit them for adoption by the best families. Since the founding of the hospital 24 years ago, we have cared for 26,000 infants, 10,000 of whom have been placed in permanent homes.

"Five thousand needy and homeless mothers have also shared the charitable shelter of the Foundling Hospital, and our outdoor department gives constant employment to 1,100 respectable women, who nurse the little foundlings in their own homes."

Cash Register Inventor and Company Founder in 1895

Saloon owner James Ritty, tired of being robbed by employees dipping into the cash drawer or pocketing customers' money for themselves, decided to create a machine that prevented such thefts from happening. The National Cash Register Company arose from his invention.

Life at Home

- It was retirement day for James Jacob "Jake" Ritty, and Jake thought his felt like a life well lived.
- His restaurant, Ritty's Pony House, had been visited by the world's most famous actors and athletes; he was acknowledged as a supportive member of the Dayton, Ohio, community; and he was an inventor.
- Even the success of the National Cash Register Company did not diminish his contentment-he had been paid well for his idea, even though others had profited more from it.
- History would record that he was the inventor of the cash register.
- Born in 1836 in Dayton, Ohio, the son of French immigrants Dr. Leger Ritty and his wife, Mary, Jake briefly attended medical school, and he was listed as a physician in the 1860 census.
- When the Civil War broke out in 1861, 25-year-old Jake enlisted in the 4th Ohio Cavalry, where he was promoted from first lieutenant to captain during his three years of service.
- Jake called himself a "Dealer in Pure Whiskeys, Fine Wines, and Cigars" when he opened his first saloon in 1871.
- The Pony House first opened its doors in 1882, when beer was a nickel a stein and $0.15 a bucket.
- The building on South Jefferson Street where the Pony House was established had previously been a school for teaching French and English to young ladies.
- To make the saloon attractive and unique, Jake commissioned woodcarvers from the Barney and Smith Car Company to convert 5,400 pounds of Honduras mahogany into a huge bar.
- The result was a wooden bar both tall and wide, a style reminiscent of the interior of a passenger rail car; the initials JR were carved into the center peak and the left and right sections.

James Ritty created a cash machine that prevented employee theft.

- To accompany the drinks, a free lunch was offered-open to all-consisting of boiled eggs, sardines, blind robins (smoked herring), cold meats, pigs' feet, pickles, pretzels, crackers, and bread.
- It wasn't the only free lunch.
- Despite a booming business, the Pony House was losing money every year into the pockets of cashiers and bartenders who took the customers' dinner and bar payments but did not deposit them into the company cash box.
- Jake had no way to determine how much he was losing or how to stop the thefts.
- It was a problem that plagued every merchant-how to keep the profits from walking out the door in the pockets of employees.
- In 1878, while on a steamboat trip to Europe, Jake became intrigued by a mechanism that counted the number of times the ship's propeller went around.

Early attempts at theft-proof cash machines were not successful.

- A number of recent inventions, such as the screw propeller and the triple expansion engine, had recently made transoceanic shipping economically viable, ushering in an era of cheap and safe travel and trade around the world.
- Jake wondered if something like this could be made to record the cash transactions in his restaurant and saloon.
- When he returned to Dayton, Jake and his brother John, a skilled mechanic, began designing a device for counting cash.
- The first two attempts were dismal failures.

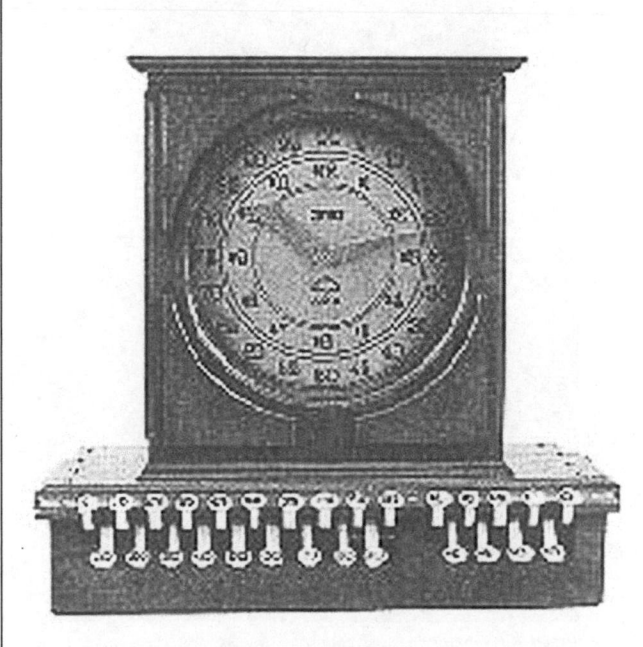

Ritty's Incorruptible Cashier was patented in 1879.

- Their third design operated by pressing a key that represented a specific amount of money.
- It recorded the amount of each transaction.
- They had invented a way to reconcile the nightly cash with the sales receipts: their machine would keep everyone honest.
- Jake was delighted.
- Both the honest and dishonest cashiers disliked this intrusion into "their" affairs.
- Jake and his brother called the design, patented in 1879, "Ritty's Incorruptible Cashier."
- It consisted of two rows of keys attached to a dial that looked like a large clock face which together kept a running total of the amount deposited.

- A bell-later advertised as the "bell heard round the world"-rang when the register was opened.
- The register also had a totaling feature that summed all the cash values for the keys pressed during the day.
- The 22" x 14" x 20" machine looked like a clock mounted on a board.
- To the Ritty brothers, it looked like the way to make a fortune.
- But the patent was simply a right to do business, not a ticket to success.

Life at Work

- Upon reflection, James Ritty recognized that he was unprepared for the amount of work required to set up a manufacturing plant and sell his new invention, the cash register.
- Restaurants and bars he understood; manufacturing and distribution of a product as heavy as a cash register were an entirely different proposition.
- Four long, frustrating years after they received a patent in 1883, Jake and his brother started the National Manufacturing Company with high expectations.
- They quickly discovered that businessmen were reluctant to buy expensive machines that they had done without before.
- And Jake didn't have time or inclination to manufacture his machine and travel from place to place to sell it while continuing to run his saloon.
- So Jake and John sold the patent to a group of Ohio investors, including John Henry Patterson, who believed they could fulfill Jake's dream of commercializing his invention and thereby making a fortune.

Outskirts of Dayton, Ohio.

- The investor group paid $6,500 for the rights to the "Incorruptible Cashier."
- Soon thereafter, Patterson bought out the other investors and changed the firm's name to the National Cash Register Company.
- John Patterson had also grown up in Dayton, Ohio, where he attended public schools and worked in his father's saw and gristmills.
- Patterson graduated from Dartmouth College in 1867 and worked as a collector of tolls on the Miami and Erie Canal for three years before entering the coal industry, serving as manager of the Southern Ohio Coal and Iron Company.
- His coal distribution business had been losing revenues to pilfering, so he bought two of the cash registers, sight unseen.
- Within six months, he reduced his debt from $16,000 to $3,000 and became convinced that every businessman needed a cash register.
- After Patterson bought the patent rights to Ritty's invention, he improved its operation by adding spare rolls to reconcile the day's transactions in each price range.

The National Cash Register's redesign of Ritty's machine.

- This was accomplished by building a hole puncher into each cash register that created holes to represent the amount of the purchase.
- If the paper had two holes punched in the dollars column, for example, and 50 holes punched in the cents column, the total would be $2.50.
- At the end of a transaction, a bell rang on the cash register and recorded the amount received on a large dial on the front of the machine.
- At the end of the day, the merchant could add up the holes and, therefore, his daily cash.
- As head of the National Cash Register Company (NCR), Patterson quickly expanded the factory's workforce and the number of salesmen.
- He also persuaded salesmen who sold registers part-time to become full fledged national agents and devote all of their energy to his product.
- Under his system, agents were shipped cash-rich consignments with a retail price of $150 to $200.
- Salesmen were entitled to a 50 percent discount on the purchase price, and many became wealthy overnight.
- During its first decade of operation, NCR produced 16,000 registers and brought dozens of lawsuits against its competitors.
- As department stores proliferated and retailers nationwide recognized the value of a good on-site accounting system, 86 companies began manufacturing different types of cash registers.
- In 1888 NCR had agents working in 34 U.S. cities, from Pensacola, Florida, to Portland, Oregon.
- Patterson also dreamed of creating an international sales organization such as the Singer Manufacturing Company had established for selling its sewing machines.

- Since other organizations such as McCormick and Kodak had proved that Europeans would buy American goods, Patterson wanted to add NCR to that list.
- In 1893 the company sold 100 registers per month in Germany.
- By 1895 about 23 percent of total sales were made outside the United States and Canada, with Great Britain representing 9 percent and South Africa 2 percent.
- Early advertisements shouted in bold headlines "Stop the Leaks," showing shop owners how they were being ruined by clerks who stole from unmonitored cash drawers.
- NCR even hired detectives to watch as unsupervised employees pilfered from their employers, thus creating testimonials for the NCR machine.
- NCR also used advertisements to highlight an owner's fear of losing profits from sloppy recordkeeping.
- By 1895 one-fourth of the company's registers were in saloons, while 17 percent had been sold to general merchants and 11 percent to drugstores.

Life in the Community: Dayton, Ohio

- Dayton, Ohio, was not only a manufacturing center for cash registers: it was an employee laboratory.
- Dayton was home to a wide variety of manufacturing firms-the National Cash Register Company among them-very much interested in ways to reduce the cost of making its products in a era when extensive efforts were under way to accurately measure productivity.
- The National Cash Register Company experimented with its lighting and discovered that brightly lit factories resulted in better productivity.
- To reward loyalty NCR also provided for its workers a cafeteria, hospital, library, and recreational facility.
- The company showed movies and hosted lectures for employees during lunchtime-all innovations for a city known for its manufacturing skills.
- After Ohio became a state in 1803, Dayton became the seat of Montgomery County, but growth was slow until the War of 1812.
- During the War of 1812, Dayton served as a mobilization point for American attacks on Canada and against British troops in the northwestern part of the United States.
- After the war, a tobacco factory, two banks, textile mills, and several other businesses were launched.

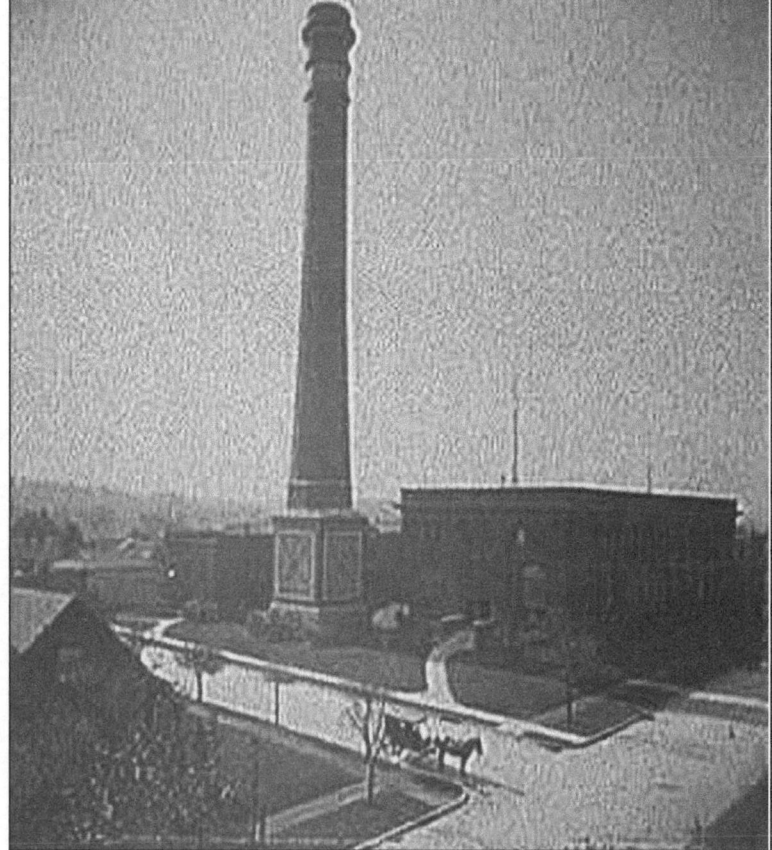

Downtown Dayton, Ohio.

- With the completion of the Miami and Erie Canal in 1829, Dayton was linked to Cincinnati, promoting growth.
- Nine turnpikes connected Dayton to other areas of the state.
- By the 1840s, Dayton was one of the largest and wealthiest communities in Ohio.
- By the late 1800s, the community supported a growing publishing industry, offering publications that focused either on religious issues-such as *Christian World*, *Young Catholic Messenger*, *Ohio Bible Teacher*-or agricultural interests-such as *Farmer's Home*, the *Ohio Swine Journal*, and the *Ohio Poultry Journal*.
- There were also German newspapers for the area's German settlers.
- A number of companies in Dayton manufactured farm implements, including the Buckeye Mower and Reaper Company.

Anti-Corset Campaigner in 1896

Cora Gaillard, the wife of a doctor in Bridgeport, Connecticut, and a mother of three daughters, was concerned about the health risks associated with wearing corsets, and made her opinions public.

Life at Home

- For years Cora Gaillard had been hearing attacks on the wearing of corsets.
- At times it seemed that every bellicose speaker who could spell MD had found an opportunity to condemn the sturdy undergarment, revered for its ability to fashion an hourglass figure.
- Some doctors blamed tightly laced corsets for weak stomach muscles in girls, fainting spells, numbness of the legs-even infertility.
- Others emphasized the impact on women's respiratory system, which was widely understood to be different from that of men.
- And cartoonists and stereographic card manufacturers loved to show sisters pulling the lacing so tight on one another that the process required one sister's foot to be braced on the back of the other.
- The conversion of Cora Gaillard began with her three teenage daughters and was supported by her husband, a medical doctor in Bridgeport, Connecticut.
- After several years of hearing complaints from her husband's patients, Cora became convinced the corset made the marriage bed uncomfortable and generally led to reduced sexual relations between husband and wife.
- Fashion dictated, and vanity demanded, that corsets must create continuous and severe constriction.
- Even waists that naturally measured 25 inches could be cinched back to 19 inches with a French-designed back-fastening corset with a long steel busk down the front.
- Cora remembered well the sacrifices she had made as a teenager to achieve a tiny waist, using a modern steam-molded, spoon-busk corset with enough boning and cording to create a perfect hourglass shape.

Cora Gaillard was convinced that wearing corsets caused health risks.

- Whenever she rebelled against the confining garment, her mother invariably reminded her that wearing a corset was a "hallmark of virtue" and that "an uncorseted woman reeked of license."
- But Cora now had healthy teenage daughters nearing marriageable age, and she was motivated to protest by her desire for numerous healthy grandchildren.
- She was concerned that fainting, poor circulation, and lethargy in women were all a result of tightly laced corsets.
- Cora had begun dressing her girls in corsets when each reached the age of nine.
- The two oldest, Florence and Lucca, willingly accepted the confining strictures as a symbol of growing up.
- The youngest, Carolina-the tomboy-hated corsets and more than once abandoned the undergarment behind the rosebush hedge.

- Maybe it was a sign: The two oldest girls had been named for the Italian hometowns of their great-grandparents, Florence and Lucca, to honor the first Proiettis to come to America.
- They were conservative, conscientious, and religious.
- Carolina had been named for the home state of her paternal grandmother, who was from the undisciplined city of Charleston, South Carolina-where liquor drinking, horse races, and cockfights went on openly, even on Sundays.
- Despite her tussles with Carolina, Cora secretly came to agree with her that tight corsets deformed young women and restricted their movement-something that Carolina could not tolerate.
- Although Cora herself intended to continue wearing a corset, she bought bust girdles for her daughters instead so that they could at least make full use of their lungs.
- She hoped the bust girdle would help them avoid the many complaints common to corset-wearing women.

Life at Work

- For most of her married life, Cora Gaillard had assisted in her husband's medical practice; she was nurse, office manager, counselor, and substitute doctor.
- Despite her husband's fancy diplomas and advanced education, Cora was convinced that she knew as much about medicine as he did, especially when it came to women's health.
- Day after day she cared for women who were in pain because of the clothing they wore, although their menfolk all agreed that women just liked to complain.
- That's why she had finally written a letter to the editor that stirred up quite a lot of trouble.
- She had not shown it to her husband before sending it, because she knew he would object.
- Still, she hadn't expected as much of a reaction as she got.

- What was done was done, she decided, and she was going to accept the Bridgeport Women's Club's invitation to speak about corsets the following month.
- Someone needed to speak out about how fashion, vanity, tradition-and the preferences of men-affected women's health.
- Cora was riled up about the tendency of women to faint because of excessive constriction, and about the disgusting way that tight corsets rearranged vital organs.
- Corsets had even been known to break women's ribs.
- Women were prevented from doing normal household tasks because they could not bend over.
- And in her letter Cora hadn't even addressed the burden of multiple petticoats that hung off the waist or the tyranny of tight garters that cut off circulation to the legs.
- Cora had even read somewhere that Susan B. Anthony had said, "I can see no business avocation in which woman in her present dress can possibly earn equal wages with man."
- But Cora was in enough trouble with her husband without her quoting the words of a feminist like Susan B. Anthony.
- That would only invite accusations that she supported both equality and free love, like the radicals.
- Already she was being accused of trying to de-sex women.
- Cora had heard that some people were comparing her to Washington's Dr. Mary E. Walker, who advocated that men and women were so similar in anatomy that the sexes should dress identically.

Fashion dictated women's appearance and activities.

- In fact, all because of that one letter to the editor, Cora encountered criticism from every corner claiming that she wanted the sexes to be equal, when all she wanted was for women to enjoy good health.
- To many, Cora's corset protest was bad for the community; some of her husband's patients were employed by a Bridgeport corset maker.
- Her own embarrassed daughters-even free-spirited Carolina-wanted nothing to do with their mother's anti-corset campaign.
- How radical, really, was one-piece flannel underwear in place of a confining corset?
- Moreover, Cora detested women's long skirts, which dragged on the ground, picking up all sorts of filth; why couldn't women wear skirts four inches off the floor so they could walk without stumbling?

- Anyway, it was obvious, Cora thought, that the freedom offered by the modern bicycle was going to propel changes in courting, dress, and women's health.
- Her girls were going to be part of the future, no matter what anyone said.
- Secretly, she believed that any town that would elect P. T. Barnum as its mayor should not take itself so seriously.
- Meanwhile, the elder two girls were hardly speaking to her, and Carolina insisted on sitting separately at church.

Life in the Community: Bridgeport, Connecticut

- The city of Bridgeport, Connecticut, had long seen itself as a business town; it was proud of its manufacturing tradition, including the production of gun cartridges, brass goods-and corsets.
- Beginning in the 1830s, the invention of the metal eyelet and its use in corsets allowed greater force to be exerted when lacing tightly.
- About the same time, the medical attacks on corsets began, especially as more women attempted to attain the wasplike figure then in vogue.
- Corsets were commonly worn 14 hours per day; some women also employed nightstays to ensure that the waist was retrained to the smaller size.
- Complaints associated with tight lacing included nervous disorders, hysterical fits of crying and insomnia, constipation, indigestion, headache, backache, curvature of the spine, respiratory problems and fainting, apoplexy, apathy, soured temper, lack of appetite, starvation, displacement of the liver, effects on the secretion of bile, anemia, chlorosis, neurasthenia, hernias, imperfect circulation, dyspepsia, nausea, vomiting, pressure on the breasts, inflamed nipples, displacement of the uterus, and lack of sexual desire.
- Elizabeth Stuart Phelps was unequivocal about the corset, saying in 1874: "Make a bonfire of the cruel steels that have lorded over your thorax and abdomen for so many years and heave a sigh of relief, for your emancipation, I assure you, from this moment has begun."
- Doctors, too, railed that the contraption was harmful, documenting that corsets put up to 80 pounds of pressure on every square inch of a woman's torso, squeezing her rib cage in while pressing on her internal organs.
- Two doctors, brothers Lucien and Ira De Ver Warner, were among the critics; having become aware that women were not about to flout fashion and stop wearing corsets, Dr. Lucien Warner designed an alternative corset, which the brothers brought to market in 1873 after Dr. De Ver Warner's wife tested and approved it.
- Dr. Warner's Coraline Health Corsets, made from "Coraline" plant fiber and engineered to achieve the desirable hourglass shape without creating the health hazards, were manufactured by the Warner brothers in Bridgeport from 1876.
- "Coraline," the company's literature explained, "is manufactured from ixtle, a

Slim waists were preferred at all costs.

plant which grows in Mexico and some parts of South America. In general appearance, it resembles somewhat the American aloe or century plant, but its leaves are longer and more slender."

- "Scattered through the centre of these pulpy leaves are a number of round, tough, elastic fibres like bristles, which average about two feet in length." The processed fibers were wound in thread and sewn into the corset.

- The corset was then "tempered" by being passed through heated dies, creating a durable and flexible corset.

- The Warner factory at Atlantic and Lafayette street employed some 1,200 women.

- Many of the women were immigrants, for whom the Warners provided an innovative settlement-house-like institute to ease their integration into American society.

- The company's brochures described the factory: "It occupies a floor space of over two acres, is four stories high, and has a frontage on three streets of 536 feet. The upper part of the building overlooks Long Island Sound, which is less than half a mile distant. All the rooms are heated by steam, and are abundantly supplied with light and air."

- The Warners were phenomenally successful, becoming the largest corset manufacturer in the United States.

- The medical community was far from united, however: While some said tight lacing reduced fertility, others claimed that the weaker sex needed corsets to support their frail bodies.

- According to outspoken feminist Frances Willard, "Niggardly waists and niggardly brains go together. A ligature around the vital organs at the smallest diameter of the womanly figure means an impoverished blood supply to the brain, and may explain why women scream when they see a mouse."

- Yet a flood of advertisements pitched a corset for every activity, including leisure, sleeping, riding, and bicycling; there were even pregnancy and nursing corsets.

- By the 1890s more than four hundred brands were being manufactured as they became more affordable and accessible to working-class women.

Timeline of Corsets and Ladies' Undergarments

Early 1700s Corsets were a must for bourgeois and noble women in Europe, eager to separate themselves from the popular classes, who could not afford the specialized garment.

Working class women adopted a "little corset" which laced up the front, rather than the back, and was more affordable.

Mid-1700s An anti-corset campaign raged across Europe by doctors concerned that corsets deformed women's bodies.

Frenchman Jacques Bonnaud wrote a pamphlet about the effect of corsets on women entitled, "The Degradation of the Human Race Through the Use of the Whalebone Corset: A Work in Which One Demonstrates That It Is to Go Against the Laws of Nature, To Increase Depopulation and Bastardize Man, So to Speak, When One Submits Him to Torture from the First Moments of His Existence, Under the Pretext of Forming Him."

Corset manufacturers asserted that corsetwearing city girls had better bodies than country girls because of the corset.

1795 Following the French revolution, the corset was exiled temporarily.

1804 The corset reappeared in France in support of the empire waist style that emphasized a high waist to accentuate a woman's breasts.

1830s Swiss industrialist Jean Werly built the first corset factory to mass produce affordable corsets.

Corset advertisements began appearing in European magazines, while expensive American magazines such as *Godey's Lady's Book* would not show them for another 30 years.

1840s New-style corsets emerged, made from white twill cotton that used vertical rows of whalebone shaped to the natural body.

1850s Major innovations in undergarment production included eyelet holes strengthened with metal rings, while India rubber and elastic were alternatives to whalebone.

Women corset-makers began to dominate in England, France, and Germany, all of which supplied the United States market.

1860 The number of corsetières working in Paris totaled 3,772, while stay manufacturing in London employed 10,000 workers.

1868 Britain produced three million corsets a year for its own use and imported two million more corsets from France and Germany.

1874 Mary J. Safford-Blake, M.D., lectured against the immovable bondage of the corset, while Carolina E. Hastings called the corset "an instrument of human torture" and blamed the deterioration of the thoracic muscles on its wearing.

1880 The popularity of ready-to-wear corsets encouraged manufacturers to expand the line of corsets using different varieties of materials, colors, sizes, and fits; brightly colored corsets also became more acceptable.

1881 *The New York Times* predicted that all women would be wearing trousers within two or three years.

1886 Bustles returned and in a more exaggerated form than before; they sometimes jutted out at right angles from the center back of the body.

Steel strips were attached to the insides of dresses to exaggerate the backward curve of the bustle.

1890s To promote better health, Dr Gustave Jaeger marketed a range of woolen underwear including "Sanitary Woolen Corsets" for women.

Manufacturers interested in selling health-supporting corsets advertised the electric corset, to emphasize the metallic composition of the garment.

1896 The Sears, Roebuck catalogue featured 20 types of corsets; the most popular was Dr. Warner's Health Corset, which featured straps over the shoulders and light boning.

❧❧❧❧❧❧❧❧❧

Fresh Censure of the Corset, Prominent Medical Testimony Against Any Use of Stays
New York Times, February 12, 1893

An Englishwoman's periodical is carrying on a crusade against tight lacing. In this evil, a serious obstacle is the Pharisaical element. As in temperance, it is the "moderate drinker" who is the most hard to reform, and in religion, the "moral man" most difficult to convert, so of corsets it is the woman who "does not lace" who perhaps is chiefly responsible for a failure to abolish entirely the use of stays. She wears them, oh, yes, but "so loose they cannot possibly do any harm." And her abhorrence of wasp waists equals that of the most active reformer. These lukewarm impediments will do well to read what an English medical expert says about any use of the corset

"This apparatus is, per se, an unscientific appliance, and many women suffer from its use who do not in any way 'pull in.' Strip a man to the waist and you will see no markings of the skin; similarly examine the waist of a woman who has been wearing a corset however loosely applied, and the skin is found marked by pressure, pinched up, and corrugated. While the skirts are suspended from the waist, some protection from pressure in the way afforded by the corset, even if modified, is necessary, and it seems, therefore, that the fundamental error of dress in women is suspension from the waist, entailing pressure on important organs, instead of from the shoulders, as in men."

The corset should be discarded; but if it must be retained…it should be made without whalebone or steel springs, and should be held up by a band over the shoulder… Nothing ought to interfere with the action of the abdominal muscles and the diaphragm.

—Lecture by Arvilla B. Haynes, M.D., 1874

Salmon Cannery Cooperative Manager in 1896

Seamus Cavanagh managed a salmon cannery cooperative in Alaska, established to streamline the operations of all salmon fisheries and to improve profits. Seamus and his wife, Eileen, had four children and divided their time between San Francisco and Sitka, Alaska.

Life at Home

- Seamus was born in New Jersey, the son of Irish immigrants.
- In the 1860s his parents brought the family westward to California, one of America's leading fishing states.
- His father created a company in San Francisco that specialized in fishing supplies; offices were established in Vancouver, British Columbia; Seattle; and Astoria, Oregon.
- Eileen was the daughter of a Canadian salmon cannery operator; Seamus met her during his extensive travels throughout the Pacific Coast region serving as a drummer, or salesman, for his father's fishing- supply concern.
- Now aged 46, Seamus owned a home in San Francisco and another home in Sitka, Alaska; the home in Alaska was designed using plans developed from looking at a picture in a magazine.
- During the salmon season, Seamus lived in Alaska; seven months out of the year, he operated out of San Francisco, where he had many vendor and other business connections.
- Eileen had come to love the social amenities of a big city, and she often dreaded the trips into the wilderness each year.
- Her youngest child had died of measles in Sitka and was buried there; returning to the grave each year was difficult.
- Eileen was involved with charity work at the Salvation Army in San Francisco.
- The Stevenson Street Women's Shelter and Receiving Home had recently opened; homeless women could get a bed there for a nickel.
- Each year Eileen organized a shoe-and-stocking fund drive for poor children through the Salvation Army, hoping that a supply of shoes would improve school attendance among the poor.

Seamus Cavanagh managed a salmon cannery in Alaska.

- The Salvation Army also started a fund to help discharged convicts; the wealthy of the city were placing offering boxes on their dining tables so guests could contribute.
- When her husband was in Alaska on business, Eileen enjoyed attending lectures. Recently she had heard the Rev. Anna Shaw, who "shares with Miss Susan B. Anthony the distinction of leading the female suffrage agitation in this country," according to the *San Francisco Examiner*.
- The Christmas season was special for the Cavanaghs; Eileen made a great effort to mail fancy, German-made Christmas cards to her childhood friends in British Columbia, Seamus's family in New Jersey, and their friends in San Francisco and Sitka.
- She also followed the latest fashions, often hiring a Chinese seamstress to copy the elegant designs that appeared in magazines such as *The Delineator*.
- Seamus was closely watching the presidential election, which pitted Republican William McKinley against Democrat populist William Jennings Bryan.

Seamus's youngest child died of the measles.

- Bryan's plans to print silver in a ratio of 16 silver coins to every gold dollar and thus create more money in circulation appeared to Seamus to be an excellent way of wresting financial control away from the East by creating inflation; he thought that the gold standard had outlived its usefulness.
- Bryan appeared to be gaining support throughout the West, building momentum "like a prairie fire."
- Thanks to an invention making the manufacture of political campaign buttons inexpensive, thousands of buttons depicting the candidates were arriving, even in remote Alaska.
- The Cavanagh boys, Michael, William, and Desmond, loved anything related to the sea, shipping, and conquering the water.
- With their grandfather's help, they were building a small boat and imagining a trip across the harbor.

Life at Work

- After several years of running a canning company for his father-in-law, Seamus organized a group of Alaskan canners in a single association.
- His plan was to improve profits for all Alaskan canners in the association by reducing competition among them; this would allow them to control the price of salmon, even during the peak years.
- The structure he created relied on centralized control and volume buying, abandoning the high-risk owner-managed cannery for a corporation operated by salaried executives.
- He thought that the rapid expansion of the canneries in the early 1890s was creating suicidal competition.

- Many canneries were cutting prices so drastically that they could not repay their bank loans or purchase the netting, supplies, and canning materials they needed.
- Following the consolidation, Seamus was asked to manage the 24 canneries that formed the new corporation; each of the former owner-managers was now a director of the association.
- Within this structure, Seamus succeeded in reducing the cost of operations; he could also control the quantity and price of raw fish available to each cannery as well as the market for canned salmon.
- Most of all, the corporate structure eliminated internal competition for fish and seasonal labor.
- This configuration ensured that all salmon canneries would share in the profits of the region; when salmon runs were light in one area, they could be supported by heavy runs in another.
- Cooperative buying also proved to be possible; the association was able cut the cost of canning and netting supplies.
- Alaska's 42 salmon canneries pack 1.5 million cases annually.
- Competition had been driving production costs up and increasing the price of the final product.
- The association arrangement allowed the cannery managers to clear their operations of debt and to finance improvements; several subsequently expanded.
- Seamus also used his leverage to close less efficient canneries, improving the profits of the collective as a whole.
- To change the corporate structure of the canneries required that bankers raise more than $1 million to finance the merger.
- Seamus received a fee of $25,000 in common stock for putting together the deal.
- One area the association did not control was the cost of shipping.
- Steamships were the lifeline of coastal Alaska; residents of the territory often heaped their wrath and their scorn upon the steamship lines.

Seamus and Eileen organized social outings.

- Most residents of Alaska resented their dependence on the carriers, which were headquartered in Massachusetts.
- They also complained that the carriers' exorbitant rates had hamstrung the development of Alaska.
- It was agreed that the carriers' service quality ranged from poor to indifferent.

Life in the Community: Sitka, Alaska

- Prior to the formation of the salmon-canning industry, traders, businessmen, and entrepreneurs had come to Alaska in search of sea otter pelts (early 1800s), to hunt whales (1830s), to mine gold (1849), and to export ice, fur, and coal (1850s).
- Russian Orthodox missionaries formed many churches throughout Alaska, especially among the Native populations.
- Inspired by the philosophy of "manifest destiny," American leaders debated the acquisition of Alaska as early as the 1840s; Americans had been maritime traders, primarily for furs, for more than 50 years.
- The onset of the Civil War put a temporary halt to American ambitions.
- Following the Civil War, the Russians were willing to negotiate, fearing they could not defend the land if the United States or Britain started a war.
- In the spring of 1867, Russia and the United States agreed on a treaty to transfer Alaska to American control.
- The purchase price was $7.2 million; the Alaska acquisition was often referred to as "Seward's Folly," after William Seward, President Abraham Lincoln's secretary of state, who actively promoted the treaty.

- When the treaty was taken to the U.S. Senate, however, it received a near-unanimous vote; only two senators voted against it.
- On October 18, 1867, Alaska officially became part of the United States.
- By terms of the treaty, the Russian Orthodox Church members owned all Russian churches in Alaska and the Russian Orthodox Church remained an active presence there; Russians had the option of returning to Russia or becoming U.S. citizens.
- The treaty specified that "uncivilized tribes" would be subject to whatever laws the United States adopted toward them.

ᎧᏍᏋᏍᎧᏍᏋᏍᎧᏍᏋᏍ

The Salmon King of Oregon, Rogue River Salmon, by Gordon Dodds

"(R.D.) Hume's empire depended on his success in catching the Chinook salmon. If the salmon were taken successfully, he could speculate and develop other enterprises. The fishermen he employed used two techniques for catching salmon. The older of the two was seining. This operation took place as soon as the tide began to recede and, naturally, took place only on the tidelands. When the tide turned, the men waded out on the sand and placed one end of the seine in a large boat; the other end was fastened to a small dory. At a signal, the boat pulling the seine circled around against the current so as to trap the fish heading upstream. The men in the dory hurried to the bar with the shore end of the net, trying to get it in as soon as possible in order to prevent the escape of the salmon around the shore end. After this was done, the outer line was brought in to shore by the seine boat. Up to this point in the process the seining operations were standard on the Sacramento and on the Columbia. Hume, however, patented an invention in 1895 that made use of a windlass. Instead of hauling the seine in from the shore manually, he employed horses to pull the hawser, attached to the seine, around a windlass so that the net could be brought in with greater speed and less labor than under the old method."

Socially Prominent Bon Vivant in 1897

Roger Fairmont and his wife, Vivian, were each left millions by their parents in stocks, bonds, and real estate. Roger Fairmont had not needed to hold a job in years. He and Vivian enjoyed good wine, trips to Europe, and ten-course dinners with friends in their Fifth Avenue home in New York City.

Life at Home

- The Fairmont home was always well-stocked with rare French wines; it was Roger Fairmont's claim to fame that he knew his wines and served only the best.
- One of the couple's greatest pleasures was giving elaborate dinners, which were served on gold plates in a room that looked like a forest of roses and orchids.
- Dinners at the Fairmonts' began at the continental hour of eight; all menus for the ten-course meals were in French.
- Roger and Vivian particularly liked to begin the feast with terrapin soup-matched, of course, with the perfect French wine.
- Succeeding courses included such dishes as beef larded with truffles, a confection of sweetbreads, paté de foie gras, and canvasback duck as well as imported asparagus, mushrooms, and artichokes; a sorbet would then be served to refresh the palate before a serving of French cheeses and desserts.
- For these events the Fairmonts hired additional servants; Roger believed it to be unseemly to have more than 20 servants on permanent staff at any one time.
- During dinner, the discussion always turned to Europe, giving the Fairmonts the opportunity to mention their "latest discovery."
- They collected European oil paintings and highly ornate French furniture; they considered little in America to be distinguished enough to be worth owning.
- Vivian had, however, recently acquired a lovely silver urn because she admired its engravings, even though it was a "local piece" made by a New York City silversmith about 1850.
- Rarely did the Fairmonts acknowledge that they employed three men to scour Europe

Roger Fairmont inherited his family's fortune.

looking for the finest paintings, furniture, and jewelry available for purchase, preferably before they actually came on the market; when a desirable item was identified, the men were authorized to serve as the Fairmonts' business agents and make the purchase.

- The Fairmont residence was perfectly situated to observe Fifth Avenue parades and celebrations.
- The couple lived close enough to Central Park to enjoy an afternoon of ice skating, provided there were not too many people around.
- Roger was increasingly uncomfortable with the "new wealth" coming into the neighborhood
- He was especially disturbed that the home of patent-medicine king "Sarsaparilla Townsend" had recently been demolished to build an Italian mansion made mostly of marble; the building was too extravagant for words.
- Vivian had even heard people brag that they had bought a painting because it was the right size for their

The Fairmont home was filled with expensive pieces.

room rather than because it was the best possible painting to acquire.
- Some families seemed happy to buy American art from artists of the so-called Hudson River School.
- The Fairmonts often escaped the city to spend time on their yacht, which had a full crew year-round; they spent approximately $75,000 a year on the vessel's care and upkeep.
- Their teenage children were living in Paris, developing a taste for exquisitely designed clothing and French champagne.
- Their 17-year-old daughter Marietta fell in love with cycling and now owned half a dozen bicycles and dozens of riding outfits.
- When they sent Marietta to France, Vivian and Roger were hoping she would fall in love with a count or duke; a European title certainly would add prestige to their wealth.
- Roger, however, was not sure he was ready-financially-for his daughter to marry; after all, at Consuelo Vanderbilt's wedding to the Duke of Marlborough, the bride had received from her mother a set of pearls that had once belonged to Catherine the Great, and from her father more than $2.5 million in railroad stock.
- In addition to their usual tours of Europe, the Fairmonts in recent years had visited Africa, wanting to see for themselves the magnificent animals there.
- Vivian wore coats made from exotic furs rarely seen in New York.
- Roger was considering devoting one of the rooms in their home to the display of mounted rare specimens of African wildlife; these would certainly provide topics of conversation for his guests.

The Fairmonts visited Africa to see the exotic wildlife.

- Because of their interest in African wildlife, the Fairmonts were thinking about making a major contribution to the New York Botanical Gardens, which sponsored scientific expeditions on the continent.
- This year, however, they were planning to visit the wilds of North Carolina for a stay at Biltmore, the home of George Vanderbilt; the 30,000-acre estate boasted gardens designed by Frederick Law Olmstead.
- Biltmore was considered the most astonishing American home of the day.
- Roger had recently ordered a 12-gauge hammerless gun with 30-inch Whitworth steel barrels made by the Parker Company so he can shoot birds with the Vanderbilts while he was there.
- Each year, for their traditional 16-foot Christmas tree, Vivian ordered one-of-a-kind, German-made Christmas ornaments, always including several with figures designed to look like their children.
- This year the Fairmonts were debating whether to choose a new decorating theme.
- Vivian was considering a display of stained-glass ornaments to commemorate the 22-foot tall Tiffany windows she and her sisters gave to St. Michael's Church in honor of their parents.

Life at Work

- Vivian's grandfather had established the family's extraordinary wealth through his early entry into the fur trade.
- From there he expanded into silks, spices, and tea, eventually gaining near-monopolistic control of natural resources as diverse as the sandalwood forests of Hawaii and the otter population in Alaska.
- Much of his early income was then invested in New York real estate and the creation of a food business.
- His New York holdings and financial clout were sufficient to persuade city officials to expand roads and services to his property.

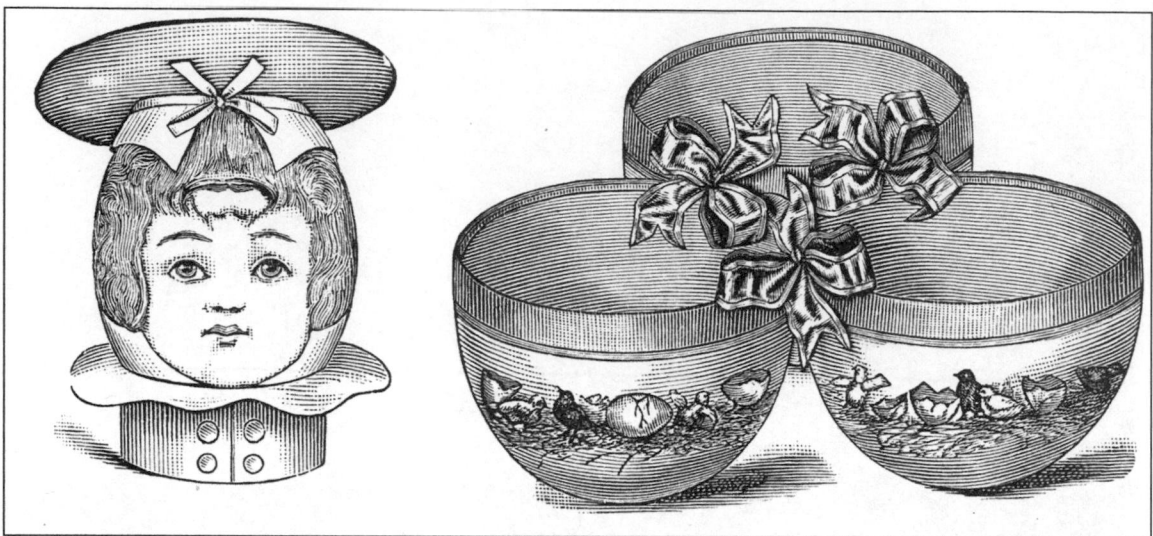

- Roger's family's money had more recent origin, dating from the early days of the Civil War, when his father secured government contracts to supply clothing, food, and supplies to the army.
- Within two years the elder Fairmont's factories had been completely converted to manufacturing materials for the Union Army; he garnered millions from his ability to respond quickly to the government's demands.
- Much of the couple's yearly income was derived from ownership of tenements in the Bowery district and along the lower edges of the East River, where Vivian's family had purchased land years before.
- The dramatic rise in immigration made every building valuable; some of the houses have been cut into ten units accommodating up to ten people per room.
- During the summers overcrowding and unsanitary conditions gave rise to cholera and yellow fever outbreaks.
- Roger placed a corporation in charge of managing his wife's tenant houses to maintain the properties and collect the rents.
- The couple considered most of the newly arrived immigrants to be uncivilized savages.
- The extensive renovations demanded by the city and progressive reformers, in Roger's view, would only result in more vandalism, making the improvements a waste of time.
- Years before, through a longtime connection to William Tweed, Vivian's father had been a member of the city's tenement housing committee; he had helped see to it that little legislation was passed.
- Unlike his father-in-law, Roger avoided all such civic and political activities, convinced that no good could come from them.
- The obsession of the poor with "millionaire watching" made him uneasy; he wanted to avoid publicity.
- To make his family less conspicuous, he had asked the coachman to stop using the red carpet when his carriage arrived at restaurants and the theater.
- Vivian agreed with her mother that a woman's name should only appear in the newspaper twice in her lifetime-when she married and when she died.
- Still, Vivian sent a servant out to buy *Truth* magazine every week so she could see the elegant pictures and read stories about New York's more prominent "400."
- She loved the new, graceful illustrations being drawn by Rose O'Neill.
- Nevertheless, some issues were getting too serious for her.

- Roger was appalled that the women's rights movement seemed to be gaining steam among New York's intellectuals; its leaders were female pests, "simply loathsome dealers in clack," he believed.
- Roger was once again investing in the stock market, thanks to tips from friends.
- Only through timely information had he been able to sell all of his stock in the Philadelphia and Reading Railroad before its failure helped trigger the "Panic of 1893," which actually lasted several years.
- During the panic more than 15,000 businesses failed, including 158 national banks.
- Fearing that the unemployment lines, soup kitchens, crop failures, and widespread anger at trusts would turn to violence, the family spent most of 1894 and early 1895 in Europe.

Life in the Community: New York City

- New York was fascinated by its wealthy, who were growing more willing to flaunt their wealth.
- In 1894 P. F. Collier's *Once A Week* magazine began photographing and running stories on the homes of New York's 400 wealthiest citizens, featuring one each week; the series proved to be extremely popular.
- Some newspapers were offering photographers up to $100 for pictures of the city's wealthiest residents.
- *Munsey's Magazine* called the number of weddings of wealthy American heiresses to titled Englishmen an "epidemic," accusing the newly wealthy of cravenly seeking respectability.
- Early each morning the servants of the city's elite lined up along the docks near West Washington Market to buy oysters for the "the lady's breakfast."
- The New York Telephone Company operated 12 telephone exchanges, each with operators lined up at 250-foot-long switchboards; the women were referred to as "Hello Girls."
- Delmonico's, one of New York's finest restaurants, had ten locations, including one on Fifth Avenue and Forty-fourth Street, near the Fairmonts' home.
- The homes of the Astors and the Vanderbilts set the standard for the city.
- A race to bigger and fancier homes was under way in New York; some costing more than $3 million to build.

Fifth Avenue, New York City.

- For some, the real place to subtly establish wealth was Newport, Rhode Island, where old money was safe from the nouveau riche-people whose money came from patent medicines, chewing gum, copper, and tobacco.
- The Vanderbilts' cottage in Newport had 110 rooms, 45 bathrooms, and a garage that could accommodate a hundred cars.
- The home also afforded elaborate stables for the family's horses, which slept in linens embroidered with the house crest.

The elaborate furnishings of the Fairmonts' apartment.

Housemaid in 1898

Gwen Shanklin, a 16-year-old Welsh girl, worked as a maid for a wealthy Philadelphia family. The lady of the house was trying hard to copy many of the manners and routines of the English.

Life at Home

- Originally from Bethesda, Wales, a region known for the quality of its quarries, Gwen Shanklin loved working in America, where there was plenty of food to eat and the homes were heated.
- In Wales her father had often treated her like a servant, demanding that she take care of him, especially after her mother died when she was 13 years old.
- Finally, when she was 14, Gwen was sent to London, where she was employed as a servant girl for a wealthy family.
- In London Gwen learned the rules of a grand house and how to handle the needs of a large family.
- Still, Gwen wanted to better herself, and she saw little opportunity to do that in her London situation.
- Answering a newspaper advertisement, she immigrated to Philadelphia, escaping the dampness of London for the promise of America.
- She found Philadelphia to have a pervasive brownness, thanks to innumerable furnaces burning the soft coal of Pennsylvania.
- But she was pleased by her new position.
- A child in this wealthy American household could be said to be living in paradise; her employer's five daughters seemed to get whatever they asked of their father, Mr. Pfannebecker-from new dresses to carriage rides.
- Permission for the girls to travel or attend social functions and parties, however, was left entirely to the discretion of Mrs. Pfannebecker.
- When Gwen had first arrived, she had found the smells coming from the kitchen so enticing that she felt she could eat the air.
- Like most large Philadelphia homes, the Pfannebeckers' house was constructed of dark red brick with white marble steps, and the red brick was accented with white mantels and

Welsh-born Gwen Shanklin was a maid in Philadelphia.

Gwen worked for a wealthy family with five daughters.

shutters on the first floor and green on the second.
- Even though the house, with 24 bedrooms, was massive, Gwen felt comfortable following her regular routine.
- Like many wealthy Philadelphians, her employers prized the interior quality of their home above its outward appearance.
- Accordingly the house contained many beautiful objects, including many made in England.
- A matching pair of china doorstops in the main living room particularly fascinated Gwen.
- One doorstop featured a cat dressed as a woman holding a parasol and wearing a fancy hat with a red band tied under its chin and a frilly blue dress and apron; the second doorstop depicted a dog dressed as a man carrying a walking stick in one paw and wearing a tan suit with a green waistcoat, a watch chain, and gold buttons. The dog sported a tall hat on his head.
- Seeing them in the early morning light always made Gwen smile.
- The head of the household, Mr. Pfannebecker, was very different from her father; when possible and appropriate, she watched him closely.
- He was very rich and a staunch Republican, and he was not nearly so mean as the newspapers reported.
- He was German and a mill owner-both characteristics she had been warned to be wary of-yet he was kind to his daughters and did not molest the servants.
- The second daughter, Louise, who was the same age as Gwen, owned a beautiful music box bearing 12 musicians who danced to the music while bowing a violin, hitting the drum, or blowing a horn.
- Gwen loved to watch the musicians dance to the music.
- Each of the daughters had a distinct personality.

- Louise was a bookworm, and her father loved to brag that her memory was astounding and her brains the best in the family.
- The third daughter had the style in the family; she cared about clothes, and her sashes and hair ribbons were always tied better and were more chic than those of her sisters.
- The youngest child had developed a habit of going from mother to father and from one sister to the next until she got what she wanted; Gwen thought she was terribly spoiled but said nothing about this to the other servants, some of whom could be terrible gossips.
- For most of her early life, Gwen had worn her hair free around her shoulders; once employed she was instructed always to have her hair braided while at work.
- Another maid, who came from Scotland, helped her fix her hair in braids and pin them to the back of her head.
- Recently Gwen had decided to have her hair cut short in preparation for having a studio picture of herself taken.
- She loved the new look and wanted to send the picture home to show everyone that she was doing well.
- Gwen frequently was delighted by the foods available to the servants once the household had been served.
- She often dined on a combination of chicken salad and fried oysters (one of Mr. Pfannebecker's favorite dishes), oyster croquettes, fresh shad, soft-shell crabs, Philadelphia ice cream, cream cheese, and terrapin and snapper soup.

The Pfannebecker's house had 24 bedrooms, and the family loved to entertain.

- European wines were often served to the family with dinner but were rarely included in the servants' meals.
- Despite all the good food available, Gwen was cautious about what she ate.
- She knew for a fact, for example, that swallowing grape seeds caused appendicitis; that had actually happened to a friend of hers.

Life at Work

- Having worked for a time in London, Gwen was grateful that American houses were well-heated, and she had few regrets about leaving behind the cold-water discipline of the English upper classes.
- The most difficult part of her 17-hour day was the morning.
- As a maid, she began work at 5:30 a.m., when she cleaned the kitchen floors and heated water.
- By 6:30 a.m. she woke the more senior staff and helped lay and relight the fires in the 12 fireplaces located throughout the house.
- After that she helped start the other servants' breakfast and delivered breakfast to the upstairs maid, who worked in the nursery.

The Pfannebecker daughters' childhood was very different from Gwen's.

- At 7:30 a.m., dressed in a print dress, she went upstairs with jugs of fresh water and tea trays to wake the five girls; at the same time, she took away the chamber pots and emptied their contents.
- The chamber pots were emptied and replaced three or four times during the day; in addition, some of the senior servants had their own chamber pots.
- Most, however, used an outhouse located 28 steps from the back kitchen.
- The only flushing water closet in the house was off the master's bedroom.
- Mrs. Pfannebecker insisted that everyone, including servants, participate in morning prayer services in the parlor three days a week.
- At noon the servants ate lunch, and at 1 p.m., Gwen helped to serve the family's lunch, having changed into a black dress with a white lace cap and a white apron.
- She made her dresses herself and always ensured that they were clean and well-starched.
- By 2:30 lunch ended; Gwen often took a nap before the 4:30 p.m. tea time for the household.
- Before Mrs. Pfannebecker toured England, the family had rarely observed afternoon tea; now, convinced that high tea was the epitome of civilized life, she insisted that all work cease at 4:30 p.m. for tea.
- Some foods were restricted in the house; Mrs. Pfannebecker banned all soft drinks, declaring them to be "common" -despite the pleas of her daughters

- By 6 p.m. Gwen had helped set the banquet table for dinner; as part of the preparations for dinner, she and one other maid arranged the table linen, which was very heavy and beautifully monogrammed.
- At each plate Gwen carefully laid oversized table napkins measuring 30 inches square; afterward she helped serve or assisted in the kitchen until the meal ended.
- The family usually dressed formally for the multicourse dinner.
- Once it was over, cleanup normally took until 9 p.m., when Gwen and the other servants ate dinner before retiring at 10 p.m.
- Until recently, maids had had no days off; Gwen was allowed most Sunday afternoons free unless guests were expected at the home.
- Her biggest breaks took place in the summer, when the family went by rail to their country estate a few miles outside the city.
- When the family went away, they took only ten servants with them, so Gwen took on different duties, such as washing the walk each Saturday, polishing silver, or receiving supplies for the kitchen.
- At these times she was allowed to take long walks, since the demands of the house were fewer.
- On one such trip, she discovered Fairmount Park, which looked like a 12-mile-long valley in the center of the city.
- While out, Gwen often bought shaved ice at one of the numerous apothecary stores and went window-shopping, strolling past the many fine stores.
- On a recent trip, a handsome young man had spoken to her favorably; she often thought about that encounter but had not seen him since, even though she often walked the same route.
- Mrs. Pfannebecker insisted that the household follow English customs, and for that reason she hired only servants from the British Isles.
- Following Mrs. Pfannebecker's most recent trip to Britain, the madam's friends whispered, "She is more English than the English."
- Her fascination with England did not end with work routines and observing afternoon tea; she also loved to serve English foods.

Setting the table for lavish dinners were part of Gwen's duties.

- It was now obligatory to offer every guest a piece of Callard & Bowser's Butter-Scotch Candy out of the tin box Mrs. Pfannebecker bought in England.
- The box features a hen and her chicks, and Gwen took great care never to mention that normally in Britain, this particular design was reserved for the nursery or the sickroom.
- Nor did she snicker when the madam talked about the aristocracy of Philadelphia-meaning the very rich, not the titled, as in Europe.
- Coffee came to the house in large canvas sacks, one sack of mocha, the other of Java; the beans were parched in the kitchen, one panful at a time, and a single day's supply was then ground in a hand-mill.
- Gwen was impressed when a merchant brought around a mandarin orange, which he called "the kid glove orange" because it could be peeled without removing one's gloves.
- Last Christmas the fruiterer who supplied the house year-round sent a handsome basket of fruit as a gift, including oranges, both red and yellow apples, bananas, assorted nuts, and Malaga grapes.
- The whole basket was dripping with gold and silver tinsel; tucked in the corners were firecrackers, a box of candy, and balloons for the children.
- On Christmas Day Gwen received a gift of cloth for a new dress from the family, and she joined the entire staff for an afternoon of singing Christmas carols in the parlor.
- The household was buzzing about a new invention that could protect them from illness; Mr. Pfannebecker purchased a Ralston new-process water-still that sterilized water with heat to destroy bacteria and then re-aerated the water with sterilized air.
- Everyone in the house felt safer from invading microbes now, although the fear of yellow fever and other diseases always lingered in Philadelphia; this was one of the reasons the family maintained its own garden, especially for the cultivation of healthful vegetables.

- Work in the massive garden was often done by three men and a mule; the tools used included small steel plows, hand tools, and a horse-driven Zephaniah Breed Weeder and Cultivator, which proved invaluable in bettering crop production.
- One afternoon most of the staff was allowed to stop work to watch a hot-air balloon ascend to the sky.
- Gwen joined the five sisters on the third-floor balcony, where they could see the balloon being inflated with gas and then witness a man climbing into a large woven basket.
- As the ropes were untied, he waved his arms wildly to acknowledge the crowd and then slowly floated upward and out of sight.
- Another joy of city life was the ice cream cart; several times a week, the ice cream vendors peddled ice cream blocks in push carts.
- Ringing a large dinner bell, they wended their way down the streets selling blocks of vanilla, chocolate, pineapple and lemon ice cream, each block wrapped in wax paper; the price is $0.05.
- Gwen looked forward to a lemon ice-cream break, especially in the afternoons.

Life in the Community: Philadelphia, Pennsylvania

- Philadelphia's principal boulevards were wide; Broad Street, especially its northern portion, was wider than the great boulevards of Paris or the Ringstrassen of Central Europe.
- With about 1.3 million residents, Philadelphia was the third-largest American city and one of the ten largest cities in the world.
- In all, it encompassed 130 square miles-making it larger than London-thanks to the Consolidation Act of 1854.
- Because so much property was included in the city limits under this act, people still went fox hunting within the city's municipal boundaries.
- Although Philadelphia had experienced significant growth over the 1890s, the percentage of foreign-born residents, at 23 percent, was lower in 1898 than New York's, at 38 percent, and Boston's, at 35 percent.
- The Jewish population is growing rapidly owing to immigration from Russia and Rumania.
- Unlike New York, the streets of which appeared to be constantly in motion, Philadelphia gave the appearance of lacking the fierce energy of many other American cities.
- Philadelphia had few landmarks recognizable to people who are not from the city, and even fewer renowned vistas.
- The solitary exception was City Hall, with the enormous statue of William Penn topping its tower.
- There, 547 feet above the street, visitors could obtain a view of the city; tourists even used a Kodak camera to capture the scene.
- Some consider the statue, constructed by Alexander Milne Calder in 1894, a Philadelphian Statue of Liberty.

HALL'S Vegetable Sicilian HAIR RENEWER

Beautifies and restores Gray Hair to its original color and vitality ; prevents baldness ; cures itching and dandruff. A fine hair dressing.

R. P. HALL & CO., Props., Nashua, N. H.

SOLD BY ALL DRUGGISTS.

- Real-estate prices were reasonable compared with those of other urban areas; a middle-class house containing seven rooms could be rented for $15 a month.
- Between 1886 and 1893, approximately 50,000 houses were built in western and northern Philadelphia, most of them financed by the 450 neighborhood savings-and-loan associations.
- More people owned their homes in Philadelphia than in any other city in the world.
- The city also enjoyed a sense of spaciousness; typically, 100 houses in Philadelphia accommodated an average of 550 people, while in New York, the same number of houses harbored 1,650 inhabitants, according to census figures.
- Philadelphia was known for its shops and local wares: Dexter's for cakes, Margerum's for beef, Fluke's for dainties, Dreka's for stationery, Sautter's for ice cream, Jones's for oysters and Leary's for books.

Gardeners for the Pfannebeckers used the Zephaniah Breed Weeder and Cultivator.

- Leary's, owned by Mayor Edwin S. Stuart, was considered one of the finest bookshops in the United States.
- A cherished tradition of the city, especially among the more élite families, was for the men to be involved in cooking special dishes; wealthy businessmen were often seen at the market selecting meat, and many took great pride in their ability to make mayonnaise.

African American Wood Turner in 1898

George Patterson, an African American wood turner who made a living creating handsome and durable plow handles, lived in Farmville, a central Virginia community where the chief economic activities were tobacco farming and tobacco processing. George's wife, Anna, worked as a stemmer in a tobacco factory, along with Sarah, the eldest of their three children.

Life at Home

- The Pattersons rented a two-room home; the living room was on the first floor and the kitchen on the second. The staircase was open. The monthly rent was $3.00.
- George and Anna hoped to buy a lot near their home for $50.00 and build a three-room house, which would cost $300.00 to $500.00, depending upon how much work the family was able to do itself.
- George had applied to a building association in Farmville comprising white and black shareholders for assistance with financing the home; George had an excellent employment record, and so the association had agreed to help.
- George maintained a large vegetable garden to supplement the family diet and bring in a little extra cash during the summertime, when he was able to sell some of the produce.
- The foundry where George worked operated only when there were orders waiting; usually George worked 32 weeks a year.
- The other 20 weeks each year, while laid off, he fished, hunted, and tended the garden.
- The family kept chickens for eggs and meat; the children had the responsibility of caring for the chickens.
- Anna's mother had died when Anna was only two years old, so her father had raised her. As she recalled, "I had to work."
- "I learnt how to cook when I wasn't big enough to reach the stove. When I was little, my father used to carry me to the field with him and put me in a basket and sit me under a tree while he worked."
- The Patterson children, like all children in the community, had grown up working with their parents or else on a neighboring farm, where they were especially needed at planting time and at the harvest.

George Patterson made plow handles in Virginia.

- The surveyor of Farmville found that many residents, including the Pattersons, could not answer the question "age at nearest birthday," because few vital records had been kept.
- The children attended school for approximately 109 days a year.
- None of the Patterson children-all of whom were under the age of 16, although Sarah was close-had yet married, breaking a pattern of early marriages or cohabitation set during slavery days and among the first generation of freedmen.
- In the Farmville community, about 42 percent of the people could read and write, 17.5 percent could read but not write, and 40 percent were "wholly illiterate." The literacy status of a small segment of the community was unknown.
- The Pattersons enjoyed reading *Demorest's Family Magazine*; Anna removed many of the color prints from the magazine and mounted them on the walls of their home.
- She also liked *The Ladies' Home Journal*, which was very popular in the community because of its sewing and fashion tips.

The Pattersons enjoyed magazines and their colorful prints.

- Black dolls for children had been manufactured in Germany since the early 1890s; they were widely available through advertisements in *Youth's Companion Magazine*.

Life at Work

- The woodworking foundry where George was employed was chiefly concerned with the turning of plow handles.
- The plow handles were turned on a mechanical lathe that required George to stand all day.
- The foundry employed ten black and four white mechanics, paying them from $0.75 to $1.00 a day "without discrimination."
- Anna worked as a stemmer in the tobacco sheds, where Sarah had recently joined her after leaving school.
- The manufacture of tobacco strips required separating the dry tobacco leaf from its woody stem.
- Loose tobacco was taken to the factory and placed on the floor according to grade, style, and quality.
- Once enough of a certain grade or style had been gathered into a "hogshead of strips," it was taken to another room and sprinkled and steamed, a little at a time.
- The bundles were stemmed once the leaves became supple and pliant.
- Women and young men drew out the stems, and children then tied the strips of tobacco into uniform bundles.

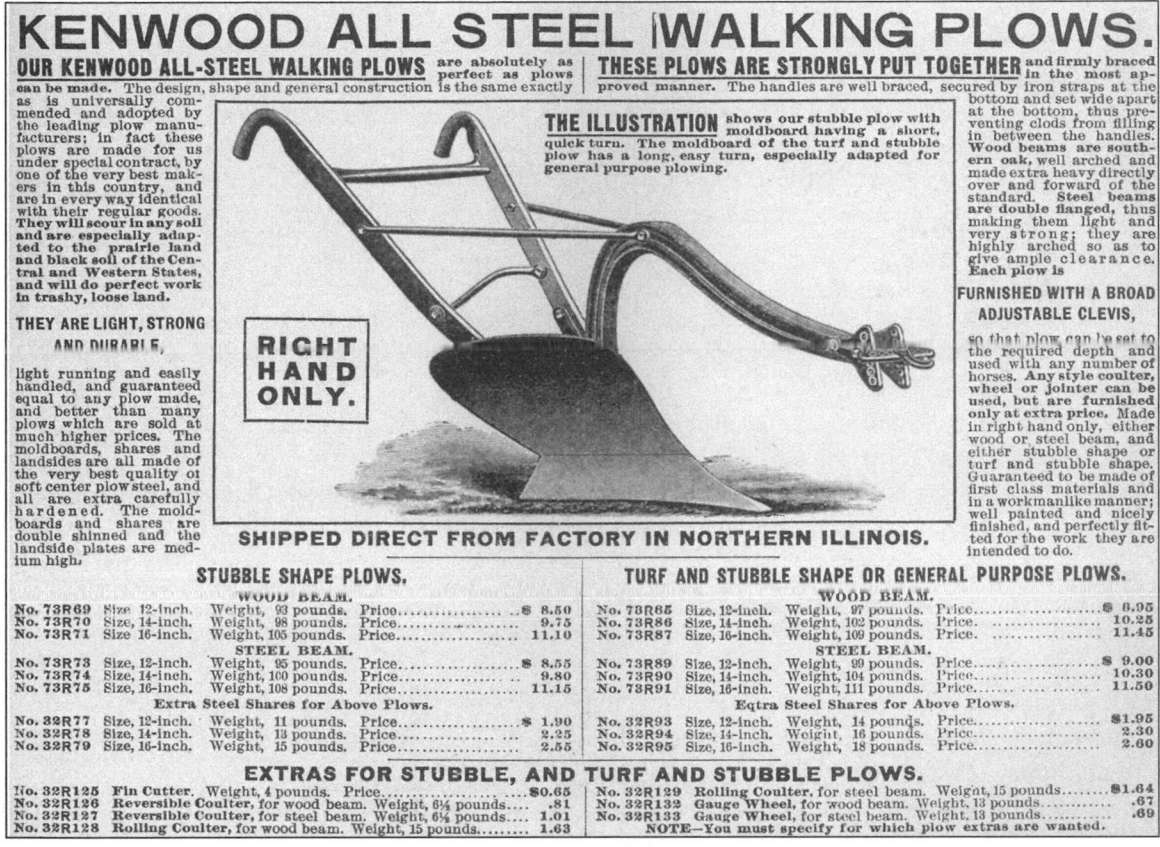

- These bundles were weighed, stretched on sticks, and hung up in the drying room for eight to ten hours.
- When thoroughly dried and cooled, the tobacco was again steamed as it hung and then cooled for two days. Finally, it was steamed a third time, in a steam box; straightened; and packed into a container known as a hogshead.
- Women who stemmed the tobacco were paid $0.50 for every hundred pounds of stemmed tobacco; with the aid of children, they could stem from 100 to 300 pounds a day.
- Anna made $6.00 a week for stemming about 200 pounds per day over a six-day week; Sarah, being relatively new to the task, was not yet as deft as her mother.
- Other women laborers received $0.35 to $0.40 a day.
- Children were often kept out of school for all or part of the harvest time to help with the factory work.
- Men who steamed and "prized" tobacco (packed the tobacco into hogsheads) received from $0.75 to $1.00 a day.

Life in the Community: Farmville, Virginia

- Farmville, Virginia, was located within Prince Edward County, near the center of Virginia. It produced seven-eighths of the tobacco crop of the state.
- Farmville, the county seat, was a market town of 2,500 inhabitants on the upper waters of the Appomattox.
- Agriculture dominated the economy of the county, tobacco being the leading crop, followed by corn, wheat, oats, and potatoes.

- More than 70 percent of the farms in the county were cultivated by their owners; 31 percent of the farms were fewer than 50 acres in size.
- The county's population in 1890 was more than 14,000; of that total, more than 9,000 were black and 5,000 white. At the time of the Civil War, the slave property of the county was valued at $2.5 million.
- The town was three-fifths African American; that fraction had been growing since 1850.
- An emerging African American middle class played a key economic role in the life of the community.
- After 1890, however, the black population had begun to decline because of the "Great Migration" of African Americans to the cities-principally Richmond, Norfolk, Baltimore, and New York.
- As a result of this emigration, Farmville's population included fewer persons aged 20 to 30 than might have been expected.
- The town's public buildings included an opera house, a normal school (teachers' college) for white girls, a courthouse and a jail, a bank, and a depot.
- The only school for black children was a large frame building with five rooms. The school term extended to six months, from September 15 to April 1.
- A teacher's salary averaged $30.00 a month, which restricted the competition for this job to residents of the town.
- Between the ages of 5 and 15 years, boys and girls attended school in the same proportions. After that, however, the boys generally dropped out to go to work.
- Of the 205 children who attended the school in 1896-1897, only 52 percent attended the full term of six months. Thirty-three percent attended half the term. Eleven percent stayed in school for less than three months.
- The Farmville area was described as having "good" air and an "abundance of lithia and sulphur waters, which now and then attract visitors."
- Farmville was the trading center for six counties; on Saturday, the regular market day, the town population swelled to nearly twice its normal size, "from the influx of county people-mostly Negroes-some in carriages, wagons, and ox carts, and some on foot."

A former slave owned the area's brickmaking business.

- Of the 459 African American working men in Farmville, 128 worked in the tobacco factory, 58 were laborers, 17 were porters, 14 worked for the canning factory, 10 worked in wood turning, 6 were coopers (barrel makers), five were barbers, and three peddled candy.
- The women were largely confined to jobs as domestic servants, teachers, day laborers, or tobacco and canning factory employees.
- Domestic servants ordinarily received $4.00 per month, a cook made $5.00 per month.
- Farmville's African Americans conducted some business enterprises entirely on their own, including a brickyard, groceries, barbershops, restaurants, a lumberyard, a whipmaking shop, a steam laundry, a hotel, and farms.
- The brickmaking business of Farmville was owned by a former slave who bought his own and his family's freedom, purchased his former master's estate, and eventually hired his former master to work for him. He owned a thousand acres of land in the county and a considerable number of buildings.
- In his brickyard this very successful African American entrepreneur employed about 15 hands, mostly boys from 16 to 20 years of age. The brickyard ran five or six months a year,

Anna Patterson worked as a stemmer in a tobacco factory.

making 200,000 to 300,000 bricks. The employees received $12.00 a month and extra pay for extra work.
- More than half of the brick homes in the area were made with bricks from this establishment, and this entrepreneur repeatedly drove white competitors out of business.
- The next-wealthiest African American in the town was a barber who reportedly was worth about ten thousand dollars. There were five barbershops in the community-three for whites and two for blacks-and all were run by African Americans.
- In the years after Emancipation, many former slaves who had been house servants turned to barbering and restaurant management.
- The income of a barber varied from $5.00 to $15.00 a week.
- The position of preacher was the most influential of all positions in the community; of the two leading preachers in town, one was paid $480.00 a year plus house rent; the other made $600.00 a year.
- The economic importance of Farmville's African American population had brought many white men to call the preachers and teachers "mister" and to raise their hats to their wives.
- The African American town jailer was also a wood merchant, a whipmaker, and a farmer. His younger daughters were being educated at the Virginia Seminary in Lynchburg, a coeducational Baptist school for African American students.
- Many in the Farmville community were sharecroppers. Sharecropping, which grew out of conditions in the post-Civil War period, made it possible for planters to obtain labor without paying wages and for landless farmers to get soil without buying it or paying rent in cash.

- The lack of capital still impacted growth in Farmville, as well as elsewhere throughout the South.
- Only 47 national banks existed in the ten "cotton states" of the South, and many counties in Virginia had no banking facilities at all.
- The highly risky business of agriculture entailed competing for what little money was available.
- The unique credit institution that emerged to fill the gap was the country store: the country store merchant performed the functions of the banker for large and small farm owners.
- Sharecroppers' landlords had to furnish teams, tools, food, clothing, and shelter; the tenants produced the crops.
- The landowner seldom had sufficient cash on hand to cover these costs; cash was provided by the merchant, normally using the planter's share of the crop as a security pledge.
- Merchants often demanded that the sharecroppers grow "cash crops" such as cotton or tobacco-not vegetables-to improve their chances of being repaid.

Businessman in 1898

For 66-year-old Jerome Arbutney, the decision of the U.S. Army during the Spanish-American War to launch its invasion against Cuba from his beloved city of Tampa, Florida, was both a golden opportunity and a nightmare.

Life at Home

- A native of Hartford, Connecticut, businessman Jerome Arbutney had moved to Tampa in 1884 to seek his fortune, just as the town was taking off.
- When Jerome arrived at Florida's West Coast community on the Gulf of Mexico, the town had some 800 residents.
- Jerome's business operations thrived, but the past two months had been the busiest of his life.
- Since the beginning of the year, Jerome had been attempting to use his political clout in support of a war against Spain-and to help his beloved Tampa.
- In telegram after telegram to his congressman and the Secretary of War, Jerome had asserted that chasing Spain from the Caribbean would not only make the United States more secure but would allow American companies to establish highly profitable trade opportunities with Cuba.
- In Jerome's view Spain had, viciously and deliberately, started a war through the sinking of the battleship *Maine*.
- The sinking of the *Maine* took place on February 15, 1898; although the explosion was of unknown origin, Americans insisted the Spanish were responsible.
- The best way to respond to this outrage, Jerome claimed, was to launch an invasion of Spanish-held Cuba-through Port Tampa.
- Jerome knew a lot about trade and making money; thanks to an extensive line of steamships, he was a major importer and exporter of goods to and from Cuba.
- It happened that Jerome owned the only rail line linking the city of Tampa with its busy port.
- The United States was quick to launch the Spanish-American War, yet the nation was, in fact, unprepared for war.

Jerome Arbutney owned the only rail line linking Tampa's city and port.

America found itself in need of an army at the start of the Spanish-American War.

- An army had to be raised, war taxes created, plans drawn up, and countless other decisions made.
- On numerous occasions President William McKinley had emphasized that there was a "humanitarian object to be obtained."
- According to press reports, McKinley was concerned that the condition of the starving masses in Cuba "undoubtedly" had been "aggravated by the outbreak of hostilities."
- It took nearly two months for Tampa to be chosen as the supply base for operations in Cuba and one of the principal mobilization points for U.S. troops.
- Now that Washington had recognized Jerome's wisdom and selected Tampa as the place from which to dispatch troops, much work needed to be done.
- Then, within 45 days, 20,000 troops were shipped into the community and stationed in seven camps in and around Tampa.
- Jerome's city, his business, and his life plunged into turmoil.
- Some local merchants made a fortune in sales to the Army, while others struggled to get any supplies at all to sell.
- Jerome was prepared; in addition to charging the military for the use of his rails and steamships, one of his smaller companies was asked to supply food-particularly fish-to the Army.
- Jerome was also the principal supplier of fresh water.

Life at Work

- Port Tampa, where supplies arrived and troops departed, was situated at the end of a narrow, nine-mile-long peninsula, and it was connected to Tampa by a single wagon road and a railroad line.
- Shortly after Tampa was selected as the army's point of embarkation, several thousand railway cars were sent south, only to be caught in a massive traffic jam extending more than 500 miles up the East Coast.

- Supply trains as far away as Columbia, South Carolina, were unable to leave their stations because of the backup.
- No single authority was in charge of coordinating supplies, troops, and equipment as America mobilized for war.
- Worse, no system for loading and unloading supplies in Tampa had been established by the military; dozens of individual military units spent entire days searching for supplies and loading and unloading boxes from the railway cars whenever they spotted materials they needed.
- Some supplies were unloaded the day they arrived, only to be left unclaimed or pilfered, while railcars-including some carrying food-were sidetracked for weeks in the hot Florida sun.
- Major General Nelson Miles complained, "There were over 300 [box]cars loaded with war materiel along the [rail]roads about Tampa. ... Fifteen cars loaded with uniforms were sidetracked 25 miles away from Tampa."
- Five thousand rifles were missing, while the ammunition for them had been found scattered among dozens of cars on the sidetracks of the railroads.
- The quartermaster general in Washington thought it unnecessary to label the railcars in advance.
- Entire regiments were then assigned the task of guarding the supplies that did arrive.
- In late April the national media predicted the immediate invasion of Cuba; when June arrived, the pressure was building.
- Unfortunately, the hastily organized embarkation suffered a variety of other problems; several of the volunteer regiments arrived without uniforms, while others came without weapons, blankets, tents, or camp equipment.
- In addition, thousands of wives, girlfriends, and mothers of newly inducted soldiers showed skill and unrelenting enthusiasm managing to make the trip to Tampa to see their men off.
- Some women who had the money to pay for a first-class ticket found that they were given priority over troop trains and supply shipments.
- Women were not the only camp followers in the city.

Troops leaving Tampa caused major congestion.

Tampa was overrun with troops waiting for orders.

- To control the thieves and cutthroats flooding Tampa, Jerome and other businessmen hired teams of men-mostly from the docks-to patrol the streets and "encourage" the riff-raff to leave the city.
- Since Jerome's rail line was the only one running from Tampa to Port Tampa, he repeatedly stated that he should decide what boxcars moved and when, but the Army disagreed.
- Although Jerome was still angry at the military for threatening to take control of the railway unless he stepped aside, he worked hard to be a good host to the military, staging an elaborate gala at the grand Tampa Bay Hotel shortly after the troops arrived.
- The 511-room Moorish-style structure, which cost $2.5 million to build and $500,000 to furnish, was the perfect setting for entertaining, since all of the general officers were already lodged there.
- In fact, so many officers attended the event, it was deemed the largest assembly of regular Army officers since the end of the Civil War in 1865.
- News reports also claimed the gathering included representatives of every West Point class since 1850.
- The parties were magnets for the plethora of colonels produced by the volunteer armies.
- Overnight, according to press reports, everyday businessmen were instantly "transmuted by a gubernatorial word into colonels-nothing less than colonels."
- As a result the city was overrun with stars, bars, and epaulets-all bestowed on the wearers whether or not they had ever fired a rifle or executed a single military maneuver.
- The hotel was also the temporary home of war correspondents, including Stephen Crane and Richard Harding Davis; military attachés of foreign powers; and luminaries such as Clara Barton of the American Red Cross.
- All the while, officials in Washington were growing anxious, knowing the U.S. Navy's blockade of Santiago Harbor could not last forever.
- The troops needed to be in Cuba, not Tampa.

- Then, on June 13, almost without warning, Army Commander Miles issued orders for the hot, tired men to board the troop ships. The invasion was about to begin.
- Because of the limited number of ships available, volunteers, horses, and many supplies had to be left behind.
- In all, 35 transports carrying 20,000 men left for Cuba, along with 14 warships, which served as escorts.
- Overnight Tampa became a veritable ghost town.
- Jerome could now relax, briefly.
- He would soon have to turn his attention to the tourists-some 35,000 of them-who would shortly be heading south.

Life in the Community: Tampa, Florida

- The settlement that became Tampa grew up around Fort Brooke, a U.S. Army outpost established on Tampa Bay in 1824 near the mouth of the Hillsborough River, which had been given its name by British surveyors in 1769.
- The village was incorporated as Tampa in 1849 and reincorporated as a town in 1855, but it grew slowly, owing to hostilities with the Seminole and repeated outbreaks of yellow fever.

Tampa grew up around a U.S. army outpost.

- Despite serving as a port, Tampa had poor transportation links until Henry Brady Plant's South Florida Railway opened the area to greater commerce in the mid-1880s.
- The railroad finally connected with Tampa in August 1885.
- Despite record low temperatures in 1886, another outbreak of yellow fever in 1887, and the disastrous freeze of 1895, Tampa in 1898 had a population of approximately 26,000.
- The state of Florida comprised roughly 400,000 people, 80 percent of whom lived outside the cities and towns.
- Growth was driven by several major industries: phosphate processing, used in fertilizer; tourism during the months of January, February, and March; and the rapid evolution of Tampa as a center of U.S. cigar-making.
- River pebble phosphate was first discovered in 1888 along the Peace River south of Tampa, and within a few years it was a major export product.
- Tampa's cigar-making community was centered in Ybor City.
- Beginning in the 1880s, the cigar industry had shifted to Ybor City from Key West.
- Most of Key West's cigar manufacturers were Spanish or Cuban; they employed thousands of Cubans who had fled Cuba after a civil war broke out there in 1868.
- The manufacturers were unsettled by a disastrous Key West labor strike in 1885, and they sought a new location where labor was not organized.
- Don Vicente Martinez Ybor had been forced to shut down a cigar factory in New York City because of labor unrest.
- In Tampa most workers in the industry had come from Cuba, Italy, and Greece.
- Ybor and his associates also recognized that Plant's South Florida Railroad would give Tampa a more strategic location for market distribution.
- Ybor planned a community outside Tampa where workers would be provided with a good living and working environment so that they would not be motivated to organize or strike.
- Ybor also actively courted other owners to attract them to the area, and it began to grow rapidly.
- The leaders of Tampa soon decided to annex the new community, and despite Ybor's opposition, Ybor City was incorporated into the City of Tampa in June 1887.
- Ybor City nevertheless retained its ethnic identity and traditions.
- By 1890 Tampa, including Ybor City, had a population of approximately six thousand.
- Tampa's role in cigar production was so significant that José Marti, called the George Washington of Cuba, visited the city several times before his death in 1895.

The port of Tampa, Florida.

College Professor in 1898

Jarrett Winston grew up in Atlanta, Georgia, committed to entering the ministry. After an accident at age 16, he had to relinquish this dream. Uncertain about his future, he considered becoming a teacher.

Life at Home

- Even though Jarrett Winston had shared the stress that permeated his household during important religious holidays, at times of great conflict in the church, or at the death of a beloved parishioner, he accepted his calling at an early age.
- The third of eight children, he was called "little preacher man" by the time he was seven, thanks to an impromptu religious service he conducted one morning among the hens.
- History will record that none of the chickens sought conversion at the end of his talk, but the rooster remained to the end of the service.
- Jarrett's long-planned career in the ministry was literally crushed when he was 16; a wagon fully loaded with grain rolled over his legs, rendering them unusable.
- As he recovered, he grew more and more despondent; convinced that no one would want a cripple, as he thought of himself, he even contemplated suicide.
- In his darkest hour, it was his mother, not his father, who shone a light on a possible future.
- On the front page of the *Atlanta Journal* was a two-column picture of a legless Civil War veteran teaching a college class in biology.
- "Here," his mother said, "is a profession that focuses only on the mind and not on the body." "With two years of college," she continued, "you could become a college professor."
- He could even use his position in the front of the class, she whispered conspiratorially, to pick out his wife.
- It was the first time he had laughed out loud since the accident.
- His timing tuned out to be excellent.
- As the nineteenth century drew to a close, the increasing role of the United States as a world power bolstered its confidence; one result was a sharp improvement in the status

Jarrett Winston gave up his dream of becoming a minister and focused on teaching.

191

Jarrett's mother encouraged her children to focus on learning and education.

of professionals in an increasingly industrialized world.

- College professors were among those whose prestige was rising, coupled with the emergence of the modern university.
- In addition to the numerous existing traditional denominational colleges and large universities, libraries, laboratories, and endowments were increasingly important features of American education.
- With these advances came professional schools, higher salaries and increased prestige.
- At the same time, the clergy were losing ground as molders of opinion; as more farmers became city dwellers and factory workers, multigenerational ties to a particular church faded.
- Despite the constant pain in his back and legs, Jarrett shifted his focus to the study of math-a subject he had always enjoyed but had shunned as being unimportant to a minister.
- As his mother predicted-and helped orchestrate-Jarrett was admitted to Emory College, located in remote Oxford, Georgia.

- Conceived in 1836, Emory had been named in honor of Rev. John Emory, an American Methodist bishop whose broad vision for education incorporated the development of the character as well as the mind.
- The college's motto was *Cor prudentis possidebit scientiam*, "The wise heart seeks knowledge."
- In 1891-1892, Jarrett's first year at Emory, the college catalogue banned students from attending any ball, theater production, horserace, or cockfight; from imbibing intoxicating drinks, playing cards, and playing any game for stakes; from keeping a firearm or any other deadly weapon or a horse, a dog, or a servant; from engaging in anything forbidden by the faculty; from associating with persons of known bad character; from visiting points beyond the limits of Oxford without permission from some member of the faculty and visiting points more distant without written permission from parents or guardians as well as permission of the president of the college; from visiting any place of ill repute or at which gaming was practiced or intoxicating liquors were sold; from engaging in any "match game" or "intercollegiate" game of football, baseball, and so on.

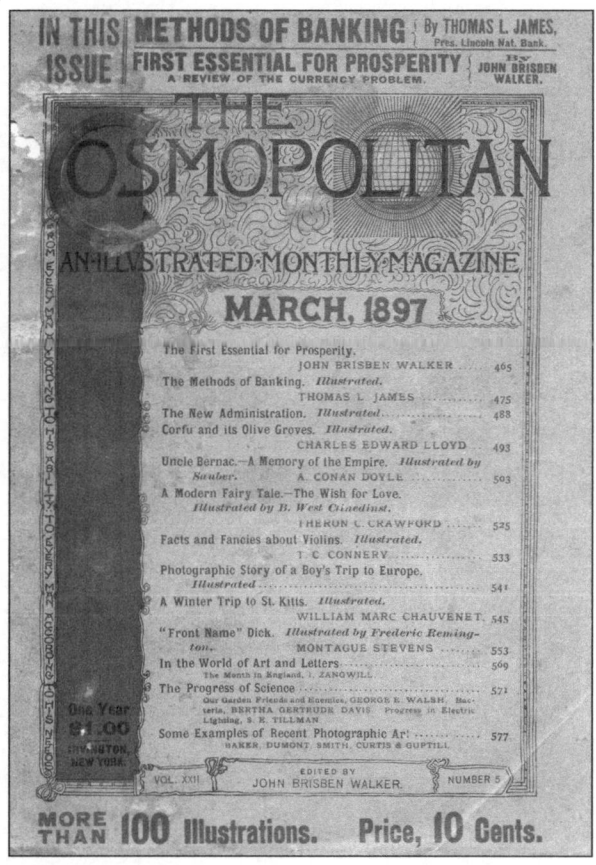

- Jarrett blossomed in the intellectually challenging atmosphere of Emory.
- He also found romance with Naomi Arthur, a student at nearby Covington Female Academy, and they married after graduation.
- Both of them found jobs as teachers in a school outside Atlanta: Jarrett taught 23 children, aged 11 to 14; Naomi was assigned 33 first graders.
- Despite being at the top of his class academically at Emory, Jarrett found instructing 11- to 14-year-olds intimidating and unfulfilling.
- Once the students had become accustomed to Jarrett's crutches and no longer asked inappropriately personal questions, they began to take advantage of his lack of mobility.
- One overly large 14-year-old farm boy walked out of class and dared Jarrett to do something about it; math lessons were sometimes lost in the wake of classroom turmoil.
- Jarrett lasted a year, by the end of which he was more than ready to give up on teaching.
- Then he received a letter from Rev. Samuel Lander inviting him to interview for a math professor's job at Williamston Female College, located in Williamston, South Carolina.
- Jarrett was offered the position in 1896.

Life at Work

- After the two-day buggy ride from Atlanta to Williamston, South Carolina, Jarrett Winston was ready to take up his new position.
- Reverend Samuel Lander met with Jarrett to explain the school's innovative educational method.
- "The leading peculiarity of our plan," Lander said, "is that we do not give a pupil three or four difficult studies at once, as is usual in other institutions. We devote special attention, though not

quite exclusive, to one principal subject for five weeks, then lay that one down and take up another in the same way for five weeks more."

- Jarrett was impressed with the seriousness of the college's intentions and the industry of its students.

- Williamston Female College had been created through a joint stock company formed by friends of education, mostly citizens of Williamston.

- Its published objective was to "furnish young ladies, at low rates, a thorough education as far as its course extends, giving them opportunity, encouragement, and help, to lay deep and well the foundation, and erect there and on, with care and patience, the beauteous superstructure of accurate scholarship, combined in symmetrical proportions with physical vigor, cultivated manners, and sanctified affections."

- Founded in February 1872 by Reverend Lander, Williamston Female College and its founder had much to offer Jarrett.

- Samuel Lander was also the son of a Methodist minister, and education had been an important part of his upbringing.

- As important, Reverend Lander embraced Jarrett's physical handicap and even made plans for several of the female students to assist him to and from class.

Williamston Female College took pride in educating young ladies.

- Jarrett's wife Naomi swiftly put an end to that scheme, declaring that she would be her husband's legs.

- By 1898, the year the upstart college had gained the support of the South Carolina Conference of the Methodist Episcopal Church, South, Jarrett and Naomi were a familiar sight at the college's hotel-turned-classroom.

- Jarrett, still endowed with a religious zeal, wanted to devote his energy to training young women to be teachers.

- Even though important steps were being taken to provide college opportunities for teachers, South Carolina student funding was scant.

- By 1896 the per-pupil spending for whites stood at $3.11, while spending on black pupils was $1.05.

- As a result, the teachers assigned to educate children were often fresh from the schoolroom themselves-quite often town girls with a high-school education who taught for diversion and a $75.00-a-month salary.

- Jarrett had come to believe that if teaching was to attain the distinction of a profession, raising the quality of the personnel in the classroom was essential.

- South Carolina's English settlers in the 1700s brought with them the belief that education was a private, voluntary matter.

- Families of the upper and middle classes were expected to pay for the education of their children, most of whom attended private or church schools or were taught by tutors.
- Public support for education was reserved for orphans and pauper children "in limited numbers and a limited time."
- Early educational efforts were focused on spreading rudimentary learning among the population, both for humanitarian reasons and to foster civilized behavior among the working class.
- Following the American Revolution, a new philosophy emerged, based on the belief that a democratic government could not succeed if the masses were denied an education.
- This outlook-which was embraced by some of the progressive thinkers among the aristocracy-eventually led, in 1811, to a new school law.
- The bill to Establish Free Schools throughout the State was aimed at placing at least one public school in each of the state's 44 election districts.
- From a budget standpoint, each district received $300 per state representative.
- The legislature gave no consideration to the number of students who might attend a school, nor to the need for more schools in thinly populated areas.
- Lowcountry leaders were generally wealthy, with enough education to value learning, and with a greater willingness to support the government through taxes.
- With the advent of universal male suffrage (for whites) in 1810, many Lowcountry leaders felt it imperative to improve the education of the Upcountry majority.
- Although the law allowed any white child to attend the free schools, it gave first preference to the poor, so most working families were too proud to participate in the "pauper schools" and kept their children at home.
- The South Carolina College Faculty presented a report that cited two school deficiencies: physical and moral.
- The physical deficiency was the sparseness of the program.
- The moral shortcoming was explained as: the carelessness of the poor about the education of their children; the selfishness that led them to prefer their children's labors to their children's improvement; and the foolish pride that prevented them from receiving as a bounty that which they could not procure in any better way.
- It was also reported that "the attendance of each individual is short, irregular and inadequate to secure proficiency."
- Some pupils attended no more than a few days; at best, some attended a few weeks of the year.
- In the Upcountry, many districts had no free schools at all, spending the meager aid instead on private tuition for a select few.
- The law also failed to appropriate state aid according to the needs of each area.
- Despite population shifts toward the Piedmont, the Upcountry, the law's system of distribution tended to favor wealthier counties in the Lowcountry-establishing a lasting pattern of unequal school finance.
- The school terms were seasonal-in session only when the children could be spared from farm work.
- Despite the structural gaps in South Carolina, Jarrett began to make progress-firmly supported by Reverend Lander's working philosophy on the college's standard scholarship.
- "We are frequently asked by anxious parents when their daughters will graduate. This we can never answer, for one might be disappointed on the work of one "section," even the last one in her course," Rev. Lander wrote to his students.
- "We carefully avoid mere surface work. By frequent reviews, by extra problems and exercises, independent investigations, actual use of apparatus, and written examinations, in short, by every means in our reach, we enjoy a credible acquaintance with each subject as the essential condition of advancement."

- Indeed, Jarrett found that his pupils embraced the arithmetic courses he taught with enthusiasm; many stayed after class to ask questions and listen to his ideas-occasionally remaining long enough to elicit a remark from his wife.
- Jarrett was encouraged to demand high quality from his students and to be a tough grader.
- Three of his four math classes rose artfully to the challenge; in response, respect replaced sympathy in Jarrett's mind-several of his students had the potential to be great teachers.
- As Reverend Lander had said, "We point with pride to the small number of our alumnae; our object is not to graduate young ladies, but to conduct their education as well as we can for the time they remain in our care; we dwell on these facts, not in the spirit of boasting, but principally to prevent misunderstandings and dissatisfaction."
- To make its goals perfectly clear, Williamston Female College began running a notice within its bulletin stating, "Young ladies sometimes attend boarding school merely for the sake of spending a few months in pleasant circumstances, and of referring to their school days in afterlife.
- We kindly warn all such they would not be pleased within our school."

Annie Oakley, in the late 1890s. It was not unusual for young ladies to be proficient marksmen.

Life in the Community: Williamston, South Carolina

- The founding of the town of Williamston made the fortune of West Allen Williams, whose discovery of a mineral spring with healing properties on his land turned the tiny farming town near Anderson, South Carolina, into a tourist attraction.
- As news of the medicinal waters spread, the town grew more and more rapidly-especially after the railroads arrived in 1851.
- Some local promoters even dubbed the community the "Saratoga of the South"-a reference to the famous Saratoga spa in upstate New York, which had been a major tourist attraction for decades.
- To accommodate the influx of newcomers, the Mammoth Hotel was built near the spring; it was the largest building in the state at that time, featuring 150 rooms plus a bowling alley and several ballrooms.
- Initially the town was known as Mineral Springs, but in 1852, when the town received its charter, the name was changed to Williamston to honor the town's founder.
- West Allen Williams had set aside property not only to preserve the spring but to provide sites for schools and churches.
- In 1872 Reverend Samuel Lander established a girls' school in Williamston; the first-term enrollment was 36 students, but by the end of the first academic year, 60 young women were enrolled.

Area mill owners encouraged entire families to work in the mills.

- Within a decade the school boasted 159 students: 71 from Williamston, 73 from other parts of South Carolina, and the remainder from six additional states.
- Reverend Lander exerted his influence to have the sale of liquor prohibited in Williamston-anticipating the passage of the Eighteenth Amendment decades later.
- As the end of the century approached, cotton mills were established in the area; the mills played a major role in shaping the local communities.
- Farmers, eager or forced to abandon the uneven economy of Southern agriculture, flocked to the industrial mills for the opportunity to be paid regularly.
- Mill owners actively recruited entire families to work in the textile mills-believing that education was not a necessity for farm children, whose future was in the mills.
- The settlers of the area were mostly Scots-Irish and came from Virginia and Pennsylvania to farm corn and raise hogs; later, they planted cotton.
- By the late nineteenth century, the Anderson County area had numerous textile mills.
- Thanks to the innovations of Anderson engineer William Whitner, electricity could be conducted by wire to mills throughout the county.
- In 1894 Whitner leased a plant in a grist and flour mill at High Shoals on the Rocky River, about six miles southeast of Anderson, where he established his Anderson Water, Light & Power Company.
- At High Shoals he installed an experimental alternating current generator in order to generate electric power and transmit it to the city's water system pump.

- Whitner's water-powered generator supplied enough power to light the city as well as to operate several small businesses in Anderson.
- Anderson thereby became the first city in the United States to have a continuous supply of electric power.
- Local historians bragged that the first cotton gin in the world to be operated by electricity was built in Anderson County in 1897; as a result, Anderson became known as the "Electric City."

Teenage Garment Industry Labor Organizer in 1898

Harry Gladstone was five-years-old when his family arrived in New York City from Poland. At 15, he organized the boys and girls in the clothing trade to fight for better wages and working conditions.

Life at Home

- Harry Gladstone's first impression of America was formed at the Immigration Station at Castle Island, New York.
- There, five-year-old Harry was examined, poked, and peered at by an officious man who spoke no Yiddish and didn't appear to like those who did.
- It was one of Harry's earliest memories.
- In 1888, Harry, his sisters, and parents were among a flood of Jewish immigrants seeking opportunity in America.
- The family fled Poland when the wave of attacks against Jews in the Pale of Settlement accelerated; the family was desperate when they finally found help from the Alliance Israelite Universelle, which provided them with clothing, medical care, and enough money for passage to the United States.
- Steerage accommodations were spartan but inexpensive; Harry's father said often, "Don't complain if you are still alive."
- Two-thirds of the ocean liners carrying immigrants docked in New York Harbor.
- To five-year-old Harry, it seemed that most of the world's "tired and poor" were unloaded the day he arrived.
- In accordance with dictates to keep undesirables from entering the United States, every new immigrant was thoroughly examined with the often-stated threat that the ill or unemployable would be sent back to Europe.
- Tired, scared, and enormously wary of people in uniforms, Harry was driven to be extra friendly.
- No one responded to a single comment he made, no matter how hard he tried.
- Then a woman attached to the Hebrew Immigrant Aid Society stepped forward to translate Harry's Yiddish into English.
- The immigration officer became no more friendly, but at least he stopped staring at Harry in a mean way.

Harry Gladstone went from poor immigrant to labor leader.

Immigrant peddlers were a common sight in New York City.

- By the time Harry's family arrived in New York City, "all the gold had already been raked from the streets," his father said.
- The promise of instant prosperity dissipated; noise, people, poverty, and problems were everywhere.
- To support the family, Harry's father became a fruit peddler, pushing a handcart up and down the streets of New York City.
- On the Lower East Side alone, 150,000 peddlers sold their wares.
- Harry's father knew he could make more money if he left the city, but travel was costly and the risks high.
- When he struck out to explore Pennsylvania and the opportunities that lay west, he promised to return soon.
- That day was the last time Harry saw his father, the last day he attended school, the last time he considered himself a child.
- Harry had only spent three years in the Chrystie Street Grammar School before he was needed, at age nine, to go to work to support his family.
- At first he stayed in the peddler's game, like his father, but he soon realized that he could make more money in the clothing industry, the needlecrafts, if he was willing to work long enough hours.
- Ready-to-wear clothing had been growing in popularity, made possible by new, heavy sewing machines, steam presses, and millions of immigrants willing to work 16 hours a day sewing garments.
- It didn't take Harry long to figure out that the cards were stacked in favor of the factory owners; few workers got ahead.

Students in a New York City public school, photographed by Jacob A. Riis. Harry spent three years in school before leaving, at age nine, to work.

- Men earned between $6 and $10 a week, women and girls between $4 and $5.
- The factory owners employed skilled cutters who cut out the garment pieces from fabric and then sent bundles of cuttings to the contractors, who hired workers to do the basting, sewing, pressing, and finishing.
- A garment was usually made by a team of three: the cutting machine operator, the baster, and the finisher.

Life at Work

- The past week had been the most exhilarating of Harry Gladstone's young life.
- He was only 15, but he was now the leader of a labor union that had defeated the bosses.
- The strike settlement was signed at the same hour as the peace protocol settling the Spanish-American War was approved by the representatives of the United States and Spain.
- A month ago he was just Harry Gladstone, a machine tender or basting puller in a jacketmaker's sweatshop.
- Now he was being triumphantly called the "boy agitator of the East Side" by the New York newspapers.
- Thanks to a quick mind and hard work, he spoke English fluently enough, and even preferred that tongue to his native Yiddish when addressing the boys, whom he is fond of referring to as his "fellow workmen."
- His prominence in the children's jacketmakers' strike was due to the initiative he took in organizing the boys and girls in the trade.
- The union he founded to fight the needlecraft bosses had 75 members, both boys and girls.

Harry and other children worked long hours in a clothing factory.

- The youngest boy was 12 years old; he was unsure of the youngest girl's age, because girls wouldn't tell their correct ages.
- The strike was over wages and the way the workers' wages were measured.
- The average machine tender, or turner, made $2 to $3 a week.
- "While the operators are working on them jackets, we must keep turning the sleeves and flaps and the collars," Harry said. "Sometimes three or four operators commence to holler at us, so that we get mixed up and nearly go crazy trying to attend to them all.
- "But the boss don't care, he paid us the same."
- The children's jacketmakers' strikers demanded that they be paid $1 per machine and that the work day be limited to 9 hours, down from 12.
- When the strike ended, Harry wanted to continue making speeches.
- But the workers were not much interested; it was time to tend to bread-and-butter issues like feeding their families.
- Throughout the strike, Harry believed it was his job to help hold the union together by telling them to "think about your poor fathers and mothers you have got to support."
- Harry also reminded his fellow workers that they could be attending school and getting an education if the bosses did not demand 12-hour days-or longer-"in a pesthole, pulling bastings, turning collars and sleeves, and running around as if they were crazy."
- Harry firmly believed in the philosophy, "If you don't look out for yourselves, who will?"
- Besides, these are children, he said to reporters, who were being asked to work long hours: children who "have not had time to grow up, to get strength for work," and must spend their "dearest days in the sweatshop."
- To his fellow strikers, Harry said, "The only way to get good wages is to stick together, so let us be true to our union."

Life in the Community: Lower East Side, New York City

- The growing economy of the United States attracted millions of eager newcomers after the Civil War.
- Twelve million people boarded ships to come to America between 1865 and 1900.

- About half were Germans and Irish, and nearly a million were British, many of whom had industrial experience.
- The number of machinists exploded from 55,000 in 1870 to nearly 300,000 just 30 years later.
- The expansion of machine-made manufacturing allowed the country's industrial output to outstrip that of England by 1885.
- During the 1880s, American steamship and railroad agents combed southeastern Europe to entice workers with promises of abundance and opportunity around every corner.
- As the nineteenth century came to a close, immigrants continued to pour into America; the second-largest single group, next to the Italians, was the Jews from Eastern Europe.
- They came from Romania and the Austrian province of Galicia, but especially from the Jewish Pale of Settlement in Poland-part of the Russian empire-to escape the violent pogroms there.
- Most found abundance in lesser quantities than had been reported.
- Often entire families were forced to work to make ends meet.
- Most re-formed themselves into ethnic communities based upon old customs, religions, and language.
- Although the many nationalities mingled at work, intermarriage was rare.
- At their houses of worship, immigrants found religious leaders who knew the familiar liturgy, the language, and news from their communities back home.
- To further strengthen ethnic ties, fraternal associations were created that provided mutual insurance against illness or took charge of the burial arrangements when someone in the community died.
- Yet despite differences in language and culture, the union movement often reached across ethnic lines to create a unified organization.
- The expanded size of factories and the cost of machinery concentrated industrial power into fewer hands, making employers more aggressive and determined to control costs-including wages.
- The continuing flood of immigrants made negotiating for wage increases difficult.
- Within the clothing industry, union organization was impacted by the number of tailors who worked beside their wives and daughters in tiny apartments.

[Form 21-1901]

STATE OF NEW YORK — Book 1 Page 363

Department of Labor

Bureau of Factory Inspection

ALBANY, FEB 17 1905

DEAR *Gentlemen*

Please inform this Department whether the following requirements specified in the notification sent you *11-3-04*, have been complied with:

Guard all set screws on collars of shafting.

Yours respectfully,

Jno. M. MacPin
Commissioner of Labor

John Williams
First Deputy Commissioner of Labor.

PLEASE RETURN THIS CARD WITH REPLY.

a7679

- In the 1890s approximately 18,000 tailors worked in New York City alone.
- Most were themselves employed by fellow tailors.
- Tailors were paid by the piece and often worked 12-hour days in poorly lit rooms.
- By the last decade of the 1800s, unions and strikes were proliferating, even though the workers themselves often doubted the union's ability to help them.
- The labor union movement was further bolstered when skilled workers such as locomotive engineers and craftsmen embraced it.
- During the depression of 1893-1897, unemployment topped 16 percent.
- Long hours and unpredictable, unpaid layoffs were the rule, and safety and working conditions were largely unregulated.
- The upper class and the emerging middle class of America discounted demands for better living conditions.
- Most industrial towns financed their municipal improvements by levies on the residents who would benefit directly from them; thus, working class areas were excluded from sewer systems, decent water supplies, lighting, and paved roads.
- Children of workers tended to drop out of school earlier to aid the family, often jeopardizing the next generation's opportunity for prosperity.

How the Other Half Lives
by Jacob A. Riis, 1890

Turning the corner into Hester Street, we stumble upon a nest of cloakmakers in the busy season. Six months of the year the cloakmaker is idle, or nearly so. Now is his harvest. Seventy-five cents a cloak, all complete, is the price in this shop. The cloak is of cheap plush, and might sell for eight or nine dollars over the store counter.

Seven dollars is the weekly wages of this man with wife and two children, and $9.50 rent to pay per month. A boarder pays about a third of it. There was a time when he made $10.00 a week and thought himself rich. But wages have come down fearfully in the last two years. Think of it: "come down" to this.

The other cloakmakers aver that they can make as much as $12.00 a week, when they are employed, by taking their work home and sewing till midnight. One exhibits his account-book with a Ludlow Street sweater. It shows that he and his partner, working on first-class garments for a Broadway house in the four busiest weeks of the season, made together from $15.15 to $19.20 a week by striving from 6 a.m. to 11 p.m., that is to say, from $7.58 to $9.60 each.

The sweater in this work probably made as much as 50 percent, at least on their labor. Not far away is a factory in a rear yard where the factory inspector reports teams of tailors making men's coats at an average of $0.27 a coat, all complete except buttons and buttonholes.

Labor History Timeline

1840 President Martin Van Buren signed an executive order that established a 10-hour workday without a decrease in pay.

1842 The Massachusetts Supreme Court ruled that unions were legal organizations and had the right to organize and strike.

1849 The carpenters in San Francisco and Sacramento struck for a pay of $16 a day, and agreed to $14 a day.

1851 Two railroad strikers were killed and others injured by the state militia in Portgage, New York.

1860 In Lynn, Massachusetts, 800 women operatives and 4,000 workmen marched during a shoemaker's strike.

The Union movement comprised two million members.

1866 The National Labor Union was formed by printers, machinists, and stonecutters.

1867 Massachusetts established the first factory inspections focused on safety standards.

1869 The Knights of Labor was formed.

1874 Unemployed workers were beaten in New York's Tompkins Square Park by a detachment of mounted police who charged into the crowd, striking men, women, and children indiscriminately with billy clubs.

1877 U.S. railroad workers began strikes to protest wage cuts that halted the movement of U.S. railroads and resulted in federal troops being called out to force an end to the nationwide strike.

Ten protesting miners were hanged in Pennsylvania.

A general strike called by members of the Chicago German Furniture Workers Union resulted in battles with federal troops, who killed 30 workers and wounded over 100.

1881 Samuel Gompers established the Federation of Trades and Labor Unions.

1882 Thirty thousand workers marched in the first Labor Day parade in New York City "to show the strength and esprit de corps of the trade and labor organizations."

1884 The Federation of Organized Trades and Labor unions passed a resolution demanding that "8 hours shall constitute a legal day's work."

1886 Two hundred thousand workers nationwide went on strike to demand the universal adoption of the eight-hour day.

The size and influence of the Knights of Labor grew as hundreds of thousands of American workers joined.

About 16,000 workers, dominated by Poles, walked off their jobs in Milwaukee, Wisconsin, angrily denouncing the 10-hour workday; as protesters chanted for the eight-hour day, the militia fired into the crowd, killing seven.

The Haymarket Riot in Chicago erupted, the origin of international May Day observances.

1887 The Louisiana militia shot 35 unarmed Black sugar workers striking to gain a dollar-per-day wage, and lynched two strike leaders.

Congress passed labor relations acts pertaining to arbitration rights of railroad workers.

1890   New York garment workers won the right to unionize after a seven-month strike.

Los Angeles Times owner locked out striking typographers and declared war on the labor movement.

The Sherman Anti-trust Act passed to combat industrial abuses.

1892   The homestead strike at the Carnegie steel mill in Homestead, Pennsylvania, resulted in the deaths of seven Pinkerton guards and 11 strikers.

Striking miners in Coeur D'Alene, Idaho, dynamited the Frisco Mill, leaving it in ruins.

1893   The Pullman Palace Car Company strike resulted in the burning of seven buildings within the 1892 World's Columbian Exposition in Chicago's Jackson Park; 14,000 federal and state troops were required to put down the strike, which was sparked by a reduction in wages.

Congress passed legislation requiring safety equipment on railroad engines.

1894   Attempting to break a strike, federal troops killed 34 American Railway Union members, who were led by Eugene Debs against the Pullman Company in the Chicago area.

The American Federation of Labor called for the organization of women into trade unions.

1896   The state militia was sent to Leadville, Colorado, to break a miner's strike.

1897   Nineteen unarmed striking coal miners and mine workers were killed and 36 wounded by a posse in the Lattimer Massacre for refusing to disperse near Hazleton, Pennsylvania.

1898   The Erdman Act, which made it a criminal offense for railroads to dismiss employees based on their union activities, was declared invalid by the United States Supreme Court.

Clarinetist in John Philip Sousa's Band in 1899

Albert Gustoff was 31 when he was hired to play clarinet for John Philip Sousa's band. After working for 7 band leaders in 13 years, he still couldn't imagine a better job.

Life at Home

- The song "Stars and Stripes Forever" had recently been added to the repertoire of John Philip Sousa's band, and clarinetist Albert Gustoff got goose bumps just from the opening notes.
- He almost wept with joy the first time he witnessed the crowd's reaction to the marching tune; he was convinced that his boss, "The King of March" had captured the essence of America's spirit-energy, strength, and beauty.
- Born in California to a serial entrepreneur, Albert had learned early that homelessness was often only one bad decision away.
- Several of the relocations were highly opportunistic-coming in the middle of the night with less than ten minutes to pack.
- In fact, one of his father's elaborate schemes was responsible for Albert's interest in music, and specifically in the clarinet.
- To promote a saloon he was helping to open, Albert's father, Smiley Gustoff, had formed a small band to play out front and attract attention.
- When several of the band members failed to show, six-year-old Albert was presented with a clarinet and pressed into service.
- The little boy was barely able to coax a coherent note from the instrument, but he loved the attention it garnered and enjoyed the way it felt in his hands.
- With sufficient begging and a promise to carry his father's beer bucket back to the boarding house, Albert got lessons from a semitalented, occasionally sober musician from back East whose reasons for heading West involved a married woman, her powerful husband, shots fired in the darkness, and a posse hunting for him in three states.

Albert Gustoff played clarinet in John Philip Sousa's band.

- Originally from Pennsylvania, Albert's father moved West during the 1849 Gold Rush.
- Gold turned out to be difficult to find and backbreaking to recover, so Smiley Gustoff began selling wheelbarrows to miners-a more profitable business that required minimal sweat.
- Wheelbarrows were owned by the successful and unsuccessful alike; an optimistic newcomer could be sold two.
- Albert's mother left her second husband in 1867 to follow Smiley into Texas, where defeated and defiant Southerners were migrating to start a new life.
- Smiley was there to sell them land he didn't actually own, along with farm equipment they couldn't actually use.
- Like many of Smiley's entrepreneurial adventures, the Texas land business had a short life once the sheriff began informing the newcomers they were farming on someone else's land.

St. Louis was a bustling city.

- Albert was born in 1868 at midnight; he was the only sober person in the motel room.
- He quickly came to find comfort in the sounds of dance hall music pounded out on the piano below; if there was dancing under way, he knew where to find his mother.
- Albert's school met only when a teacher was available, but money could be made day or night by a clever child able to play five instruments for tips.
- Despite the adulation that came from playing a peppy tune on the trumpet or piano, Albert never forgot the joy of blowing through a clarinet.
- But it was not until he visited St. Louis in the early 1890s that he fully understood that there were various types of clarinets, including octave, sopranino, soprano, alto, tenor, baritone, and bass.

Life at Work

- Albert Gustoff had just completed a long night of entertaining the party crowd in one of St. Louis's more high-class dance halls when he was approached by a sober man in a black suit.
- To Albert he would have looked like trouble if his enthusiasm had not been obvious from his face.
- The man was a talent scout for John Philip Sousa, the legendary leader of the Marine Corps Band.
- "Mr. Sousa wants you to try out for his touring band," the man said. "He thinks you may be the B-flat clarinetist he has been seeking."
- Albert was stunned.
- The John Philip Sousa Band, established in 1892, was a living symbol of America's emerging power in the world.
- The band toured across the United States and Europe to heavy applause and packed audiences; its musicians represented the cream of the world's musical crop.

- The players hailed from outstanding schools such as the Paris Conservatory and the Leipzig Conservatory; many had previously been employed by premier orchestras such as the Boston Symphony Orchestra, the New York City Ballet Orchestra, and the Grand Opera House in London.
- What an honor for an itinerant musician with no formal musical training!
- To be accepted as a clarinetist at that level was a particular honor.
- Thanks to Sousa and Patrick Gilmore, the clarinet had reached a high level of appreciation as a woodwind of special warmth and flexibility.
- The clarinet's introduction in American musical culture came largely through military bands; more than 80 British regiments serving in America between 1755 and 1783 had their own bands featuring clarinets, oboes, bassoons, horns, and trumpets.
- By the late nineteenth century, approximately 10,000 amateur and professional concert bands (of varying quality) had spread throughout the United States.
- One of the most successful and influential American bandleaders was Patrick Gilmore, who first organized his own military band in 1859.
- By 1875 Gilmore had organized a military band in New York made up of the finest musicians available; the band toured across the United States performing concerts and dramatically popularizing military music.
- Aspiring musician and violinist John Philip Sousa was but one of many inspired by the concerts.
- Unlike most American bandleaders at the time, Gilmore used a large woodwind section to balance the sound of the brass instruments.
- Five years later, the 26-year-old Sousa, who had served two tours with the U.S. Marine Corps Band as an apprentice musician and had been playing the violin professionally and composing for several years, accepted leadership of the Marine Band.
- He grew a robust black beard to give his appearance more authority.
- In 1891 Sousa led the Marine Band on a concert tour lasting five weeks.
- This tour-the first in the band's history-included eight or nine concerts a week, and the band traveled through 12 states.
- It was an exhausting experience.
- Shortly thereafter, Sousa left the Marine Corps to direct his own band-and Albert was given an opportunity of a lifetime.
- For Sousa, after 12 years of service to the Marine Corps Band, organizing his own band was a chance to earn $6,000 a year plus 20 percent of the new band's profits; for Albert, it was an opportunity to play music with some of the finest instrumentalists in the world.
- A teacher in St. Louis had alerted Sousa to a raw talent he needed to hire.

John Philip Sousa let the U.S. Marine Band before forming his own band.

- Albert was ready, and by 1899 he was an occasional soloist.
- His fellow clarinetists hailed from Italy, France, and Spain, and they were demanding.
- Sometimes Albert's lack of formal training showed; this only increased his anxiety and sense of inferiority over never having gone abroad to study music, as was the usual practice for serious musicians.
- One frustrating day was spent trying to make a permanent "record" of the band's powerful but subtle sound.
- Despite being known for its "marching music," the John Philip Sousa Band rarely marched in a row playing music.
- Most concerts were staged affairs in grand halls before a seated audience.
- The concerts always started on time-precisely on time-often opening with the William Tell Overture played so smoothly and with such subtlety it sounded like the work of a great symphony orchestra.
- This would be followed by a march drawn from Sousa's operetta *El Capitan* and another march, "The High School Cadets"-all performed to thunderous applause.
- Then Albert would step to the front of the stage to play "Bride of the Waves," written by his bandmate Herbert L. Clarke.
- When Clarke played the solo, his sweet, crystal tones brought even stolid older women to tears.
- Albert was always intimidated when he was assigned the solo.

Life in the Community: St. Louis, Missouri

- St. Louis, Missouri, was the nation's fourth-largest city when Albert Gustoff was discovered there.

St. Louis and the Mississippi River.

- Located at the confluence of the Mississippi and Missouri river, St. Louis was dubbed the "Gateway City" because it was the city thousands of settlers passed through on their way West.
- St. Louis was also a melting pot for dozens of musical ideas and movements, including the blues and ragtime.
- The city was the center for ragtime music, a syncopated sound symbolized by musician Scott Joplin's famous song "Maple Leaf Rag."
- This ragtime piano tradition, plus a wealth of raucous clubs throughout the city, also led to the birth of the blues.
- The dynamic flow of people through the city allowed for various styles to combine; the folk music traditions of the river community meshed with the highly formalized classical sounds from the big cities.
- The rough nature of the city also contributed songs to the lexicon of American music.
- "Frankie and Johnny" depicted the murder on Targee Street of 17-year-old Allen Britt by a 22-year-old St. Louis dancer, Frankie Baker; "Stagger Lee" described a December 1895 shootout between "Stack" Lee Shelton and William "Billy" Lyons in a saloon at 11th and Morgan street.
- St. Louis was also a budding center of innovation.
- In 1893, after a few entrepreneurs formed several automobile companies, the first "horseless carriages" appeared on the streets of St. Louis.
- Some companies lasted only long enough to produce a handful of cars; others lasted for years and manufactured thousands of vehicles.

⊱⊰⊱⊰⊱⊰⊱⊰

Development of the Clarinet

During the late 1600s, before the clarinet existed, the chalumeau, considered the first true reed instrument, was used by musicians.

Johann Christoph Denner and his son Jacob improved the chalumeau by inventing the speaker key, which gave the instrument a greater register and Johann Christoph Denner recognition as the inventor of the clarinet.

Unlike other woodwind instruments, the clarinet has a cylindrical bore giving it its distinct sound.

During the late 1700s, the clarinet was improved through the shape of the tone holes; keys were also altered, including the development of the 13-keyed model.

In the mid-1800s, the fingering system developed by Theobald Boehm for the flute was adapted to the clarinet by Hyacinthe Klose and Auguste Buffet.

Wolfgang Amadeus Mozart, Johannes Brahms, Carl Maria von Weber and Hector Berlioz all wrote music for the clarinet.

The cylindrical bore is primarily responsible for the clarinet's distinctive timbre, which varies among its three main registers, known as the chalumeau, clarino, and altissimo; the tone quality can vary greatly with the musician, the music, the instrument, the mouthpiece, and the reed.

Clarinets have the largest pitch range of common woodwinds, thanks to the intricate key organization.

John Philip Sousa Quotations

- America can well expect to develop a goodly amount of composers, for she has a goodly number of people.

- American teachers have one indisputable advantage over foreign ones; they understand the American temperament and can judge its unevenness, its lights and its shadows.

- Any composer who is gloriously conscious that he is a composer must believe that he receives his inspiration from a source higher than himself.

- Anybody can write music of a sort. But touching the public heart is quite another thing.

- Composers are the only people who can hear good music above bad sounds.

- From childhood I was passionately fond of music and wanted to be a musician. I have no recollection of any real desire ever to be anything else.

- Governmental aid is a drawback rather than an assistance, as, although it may facilitate in the routine of artistic production, it is an impediment to the development of true artistic genius.

- Grand opera is the most powerful of stage appeals, and that almost entirely through the beauty of music.

- I can almost always write music; at any hour of the 24, if I put pencil to paper, music comes.

- I firmly believe that we have more latent musical talent in America than there is in any other country. But to dig it out, there must be good music throughout the land-a lot of it.

- Everyone must hear it, and such a process takes time.

- I have always believed that 98 percent of a student's progress is due to his own efforts, and 2 percent to his teacher.

- I still feel the impulse to give young writers a hearing, and I believe I have played more unpublished compositions than any other band leader in the country.

- I think that the quality of all bands is steadily improving, and it is a pleasant thought to me that perhaps the efforts of Sousa's Band have quickened that interest and improved that quality.

- Jazz will endure just as long people hear it through their feet instead of their brains.

- No nation as young as America can be expected to become immediately a power in the arts.

SECTION TWO: HISTORICAL SNAPSHOTS

The years leading up to the twentieth century were shaped by major change. Electricity and the telephone swept the nation. Women's rights were being recognized and fashions were changing. Immigrants from many countries called America home and changed the landscape forever. These Historical Snapshots highlight significant firsts and milestones from 1880 to 1899, as the Washington Monument opened to the public, Literary Digest began publication, and Chicago's first elevated rail line opened, forming the now-famous Loop.

Early 1880s

- Singer sold 539,000 sewing machines, up from 250,000 in 1875
- The census declared that the United States now had 100 millionaires
- A&P operated 95 grocery stores from Boston to Milwaukee
- The plush Del Monte Hotel in Monterey, California, opened
- Halftone photographic illustrations appeared in newspapers for the first time
- Writer Mark Twain produced the first piece of telephone fiction, in which he described his reaction to listening to only one end of a telephone conversation
- To make the invention of the electric light bulb practical, Thomas Edison opened his own factory staffed by 133 men, turning out 1,000 lamps a day
- According to fashion magazines, the "waist ideal" for women was 18 inches; well-dressed ladies wore corsets supported by whalebones to attain the standard
- *Scientific American* lauded the telegraph for having promoted "a kinship of humanity"
- The Supreme Court ruled that the 1862 federal income tax law was unconstitutional
- The Diamond Match Company was created
- The Southern Pacific Railway linked New Orleans with San Francisco
- The Barnum and Bailey Circus was formed
- Marshall, Fields & Co. stores were created through a reorganization
- Chicago meatpacker Gustavus F. Swift perfected the refrigerator car, allowing Chicago dressed meat to be shipped to the East Coast
- The national population was increasing by one million people per year, due to immigration
- Two percent of New York homes had running water
- New York's Brooklyn Bridge was under construction
- Thomas Edison and Alexander Graham Bell formed the Oriental Telephone Company
- The city of Phoenix, Arizona, was incorporated
- Kansas became the first state to prohibit all alcoholic beverages
- Black colleges Spelman College in Georgia and the Tuskegee Institute in Alabama opened
- The University of Connecticut was founded as the Storrs Agricultural School
- Clara Barton established the American Red Cross
- The USS *Jeannette* was crushed in an Arctic Ocean ice pack
- President James Garfield was shot by Charles Julius Guiteau and died 11 weeks later

- Vice President Chester Arthur became the nation's twenty-first president
- Sheriff Pat Garrett shot and killed outlaw William Henry McCarty, Jr.-widely known as Billy the Kid-outside Fort Sumner, New Mexico
- Sioux Chief Sitting Bull led the last of his fugitive people in surrender to U.S. troops at Fort Buford in Montana
- Atlanta, Georgia hosted the International Cotton Exposition
- In London, Richard D'Oyly Carte opened the Savoy Theatre, the world's first public building to be fully lit by electricity, using Joseph Swan's incandescent light bulbs
- The Gunfight at the O.K. Corral in Tombstone, Arizona, captured nationwide media attention
- The magazine *Judge* was first published
- New York City's first independent school for girls, Convent of the Sacred Heart, was founded
- The United States National Lawn Tennis Association and The United States Tennis Association were established, and the first U.S. Tennis Championships were played
- An internal combustion engine powered by gasoline was invented by German engineer Gottlieb Daimler
- In Chicago, electric cable cars were installed, travelling 20 blocks and averaging a speed of less than two miles per hour
- The Andrew Jergens Company was founded to produce soaps, cosmetics and lotions
- Canadian Club whiskey was introduced by the Hiram Walker Distillery
- Van Camp Packing Company produced six million cans of pork and beans for shipment to Europe and U.S. markets
- The Brooklyn Bridge opened
- *Ladies' Home Journal* began publication, with Cyrus H. K. Curtis as its publisher
- The first malted milk was produced in Racine, Wisconsin
- The first peapodder machine was installed in Owasco, New York, replacing 600 cannery workers
- The American Baseball Association was established
- The United States banned Chinese immigration for 10 years
- Robert Lewis Stevenson's *Treasure Island* was first published
- Boxer John L. Sullivan defeated Paddy Ryan to win the heavyweight boxing crown
- The first skyscraper was built in Chicago, topping out at 10 stories
- Robert Koch described a method of preventative inoculation against anthrax
- The Pendleton Civil Service Reform Act established a merit system, including examinations, and the Civil Service Commission worked to end federal employment abuses
- Former Confederate Vice President Alexander H. Stephens was elected governor of Georgia
- The U.S. Supreme Court ruled that the Fourteenth Amendment barred discriminatory action by the states, not by private individuals, rendering two sections of the Civil Rights Act of 1875 unconstitutional
- Abolitionist Sojourner Truth died at Battle Creek, Michigan, at age 86
- Oregon newspaper publisher Abigail Duniway persuaded the state legislature to approve a constitutional amendment providing for woman suffrage, but voters rejected the measure
- U.S. clergymen and liberals organized The Friends of the Indian and held their first conference at the Mohonk Mountain House in New York's Shawangunk Mountains
- New Jersey became the first state to legalize labor unions
- George Westinghouse pioneered control systems for long-distance natural gas pipelines and gas-distribution networks

- John D. Rockefeller's Standard Oil Trust monopoly absorbed Tidewater Pipe, bringing the trust's holdings to 20,000 wells, employing 100,000 people
- The Brooklyn Elevated Railroad brought railway service to America's second-largest city
- The Northern Pacific Railroad was completed with a ceremony at Gold Creek in Montana Territory after 13 years of work
- Chicago meatpacker Philip D. Armour created Armour Car Lines
- U.S. railroads adopted standard time beginning at noon, November 18, as telegraph lines transmitted time signals to all major cities, which eliminated more than 100 local time zones
- California-born engineer John Montgomery built a gull-winged glider and made a controlled flight in a heavier-than-air craft
- A machine patented by Massachusetts inventor Jan Matzeliger allowed the upper portions of shoes to be shaped mechanically rather than by hand
- Engineer Hiram S. Maxim patented the first fully automatic machine gun
- *Science* magazine began publication with the backing of Alexander Graham Bell and his father-in-law, Gardiner G. Hubbard
- The first direct telegraphic service between the United States and Brazil began
- Thomas Edison pioneered the radio tube by passing electricity from a filament to a plate of metal inside an incandescent light globe
- Joseph Pulitzer of the *St. Louis Post-Dispatch* acquired the *New York World* from Jay Gould
- More than 3,000 Remington typewriters were sold, up from about 2,350 the previous year

Late 1880s/Early 1890s

- The National Geographic Society was founded
- Inventor Eadweard Muybridge met with Thomas Edison to discuss the concept of sound film
- The Football League was formed
- Brazil abolished the last remnants of slavery
- Handel's *Israel in Egypt* was recorded onto wax cylinder at The Crystal Palace, the first recording of classical music
- The British Parliament permitted bicycles on public roads on condition that they were equipped with a bell to be rung while on the carriageway
- Berta Benz drove 40 miles in a car manufactured by her husband Karl Benz, the first "long-distance" automobile drive
- George Eastman registered the trademark Kodak and received a patent for his camera, which used roll film
- Charles Turner became the first cricket bowler to take 250 wickets in an English season
- The Washington Monument officially opened to the general public

Put a Kodak In your Pocket.

The Folding Pocket Kodak is only 1½ inches in thickness, so shaped as to slip readily into the pocket and so light as to be no trouble when there, yet is capable of making pictures 2¼ x 3¼ inches of the finest quality.

Uses our light-proof film cartridges and

LOADS IN DAYLIGHT.

Price Folding Pocket Kodak, with achromatic lens, - $10.00
Light-proof Film Cartridge, 12 exposures 2¼ x 3¼, - .40

KODAKS $5.00 to $25.

Catalogues free at agencies or by mail.

No Camera is a KODAK unless manufactured by the Eastman Kodak Co.

EASTMAN KODAK CO.
ROCHESTER, N. Y.

- Incumbent U.S. President Grover Cleveland won the popular vote, but lost the Electoral College vote to Republican challenger Benjamin Harrison, therefore losing the election
- During a bout of mental illness, Dutch painter Vincent van Gogh cut off the lower part of his left ear
- John Robert Gregg first published *Gregg Shorthand*
- Susan B. Anthony organized a Congress for Women's Rights in Washington, DC
- U.S. President Grover Cleveland declared the Chinese "impossible of assimilation with our people and dangerous to our peace and welfare"
- The 91-centimeter telescope was first used at Lick Observatory
- In January, blizzards hit the Dakota Territory, as well as Montana, Minnesota, Nebraska, Kansas, and Texas, leaving 235 dead
- The Agriculture College of Utah was founded in Logan, Utah
- The Brighton Beach Hotel in Coney Island was moved 520 feet using six steam locomotives by civil engineer B.C. Miller to save it from ocean storms

- Congress established the Fort Belknap Indian Reservation, covering 1,014,064 square miles in north central Montana
- "Casey at the Bat," a baseball poem written by Ernest Thayer, was published in *The San Francisco Examiner*
- The Republican Convention in Chicago selected Benjamin Harrison and Levi Morton as its nominees for president and vice president, respectively
- Richard Wetherill and his brother-in-law discovered the ancient Indian ruins of Mesa Verde in southwestern Colorado
- The gramophone was invented
- Benjamin Harrison was elected president of the United States
- The alternating-current electric motor was developed
- Anti-Chinese riots erupted in Seattle
- *National Geographic Magazine* began publication
- The first typewriter stencil was introduced
- Parker Pen Company was started in Janesville, Wisconsin
- Tobacco merchant Washington B. Duke produced 744 million cigarettes
- The Ponce de Leon Hotel was opened in St. Augustine, Florida
- The Oklahoma Territory lands, formerly reserved for Indians, were opened to white settlers
- Safety Bicycle was introduced; more than one million would be sold in the next four years
- Electric lights were installed in the White House

- Aunt Jemima pancake flour was invented at St. Joseph, Missouri
- Calumet baking powder was created in Chicago
- "Jack the Ripper" murdered six women in London
- J.P. Dunlop invented the pneumatic tire
- Heinrich Hertz and Oliver Lodge independently identified radio waves as belonging to the same family as light waves
- Two-thirds of the nation's 62.9 million people still lived in rural areas; 32.7 percent were immigrants or the children of at least one immigrant parent
- The census showed that 53.5 percent of the farms in the United States were fewer than 100 acres
- The first commercial dry cell battery was invented
- Three percent of Americans, age 18 to 21, now attended college
- *Literary Digest* began publication
- Restrictive anti-Black "Jim Crow" laws were enacted throughout the South
- Thousands of Kansas farmers were bankrupted by the tight money conditions
- The $3 million Tampa Bay Hotel was completed in Florida
- The population of Los Angeles reached 50,000, up 40,000 in 10 years
- The 1890 census showed that 53.5 percent of the farms in the United States comprised fewer than 100 acres
- "American Express Travelers Cheques" was copyrighted
- Thousands of Kansas farmers were bankrupted by the tight money conditions
- Restrictive "Jim Crow" laws were being enacted throughout the South
- The first electric oven for commercial sale was introduced in St. Paul, Minnesota
- America claimed 4,000 millionaires
- George A. Hormel & Co. introduced the packaged food Spam
- The penalty kick was introduced into soccer
- The International Brotherhood of Electrical Workers was organized
- New Scotland Yard became the headquarters of the London Metropolitan Police
- Eugene Dubois discovered *Homo erectus* fossils in the Dutch colony of Java
- Bicycle designer Charles Duryea, 29, and his toolmaker brother James designed a gasoline engine capable of powering a road vehicle
- Edouard Michelin obtained a patent for a "removable" bicycle tire that could be repaired quickly in the event of puncture
- The Jarvis winch, patented by Glasgow-born Scottish shipmaster John C. B. Jarvis, enabled ships to be manned by far fewer men and permitted the development of the windjammer
- Rice and Stanford Universities were chartered
- John T. Smith patented corkboard, using a process of heat and pressure, for insulation
- Commercial bromine was produced electrolytically by Herbert H. Dow's Midland Chemical Company in Michigan
- Bacteriologist Anna Williams obtained her M.D. from the Women's Medical College of New York and began work in America's first diagnostic laboratory, part of the city's Health Department
- Chicago's Provident Hospital became the first interracial hospital in America
- The lapidary encyclical "Of New Things" by Pope Leo XIII declared that employers have the moral duty as members of the possessing class to improve the "terrible conditions of the new and often violent process of industrialization"

- Educator William Rainey Harper became president of the new University of Chicago with funding from merchant Marshall Field and oilman John D. Rockefeller
- Irene Coit became the first woman admitted to Yale University
- The electric self-starter for automobiles was patented
- The Automatic Electric Company was founded to promote a dial telephone patented by Kansas City undertaker Almon B. Strowger, who was convinced that his phone calls were being diverted to a rival embalmer
- *Tess of the d'Urbervilles* by Thomas Hardy; *The Light That Failed* by Rudyard Kipling; *The Picture of Dorian Gray* by Oscar Wilde, and *Tales of Soldiers and Civilians* by Ambrose Bierce were published
- The first issue of the *Afro American* newspaper was published in Baltimore, Maryland
- Fire seriously damaged New York City's original Metropolitan Opera House
- The *Moravia*, a passenger ship arriving from Germany, brought cholera to the United States
- The first heavyweight-title boxing match fought with gloves ended when James J. Corbett, "Gentleman Jim," knocked out John L. Sullivan in the twenty-first round
- An early version of "The Pledge of Allegiance" appeared in *The Youth's Companion*
- John Philip Sousa's band made its first appearance
- The University of Chicago opened
- The federal government convinced the Crow Indians to give up 1.8 million acres of their reservation in the mountainous area of Montana for $0.50 per acre
- The first long-distance telephone line between Chicago and New York was formally opened
- Chicago dedicated the World's Columbian Exposition
- Former President Cleveland beat incumbent Benjamin Harrison and became the first president to win non-consecutive terms in the White House
- The pneumatic automobile tire was patented in Syracuse, New York
- The U.S. Immigration Service opened Ellis Island in New York Harbor for processing immigrants, replacing Castle Garden, which was closed cue to overcrowding and corruption
- In Springfield, Massachusetts, the rules of basketball were published for the first time
- Former president Abraham Lincoln's birthday was declared a national holiday
- New York State unveiled the new mechanical lever, automatic ballot voting machine
- General Electric Co., formed by the merger of the Edison Electric Light Co. and other firms, was incorporated
- The prototype of the first commercially successful American automobile was completed in Springfield, Massachusetts, by brothers Frank and Charles E. Duryea
- Congress passed the Geary Chinese Exclusion Act, which required Chinese in the United States to be registered or face deportation
- Charles Brady King of Detroit invented the pneumatic hammer
- The Sierra Club was organized in San Francisco by John Muir
- Andrew Beard received a patent for the rotary engine
- New York City boss Richard Croker's fortune is estimated to be $8 million
- An improved carburetor for automobiles was invented
- The first successful gasoline tractor was produced by a farmer in Waterloo, Iowa
- Chicago's first elevated railway went into operation, forming the famous Loop
- The $1 Ingersoll pocket watch was introduced, bringing affordable timepieces to the masses
- The General Electric Company was created through a merger
- Pineapples were canned for the first time

- Diesel patented his internal combustion engine
- The Census Bureau announced that for the first time in America's history, a frontier line was no longer discernible; all unsettled areas had been invaded
- The first automatic telephone switchboard was activated
- Cream of Wheat was introduced by Diamond Mill of Grand Forks, North Dakota
- New York's 13-story Waldorf Hotel was opened
- The first Ford motorcar was road tested
- The Philadelphia and Reading Railroad went into receivership
- Wrigley's Spearmint and Juicy Fruit chewing gum were introduced by William Wrigley, Jr.

Late 1890s

- Mail Pouch tobacco was introduced
- Continental Casualty Company was founded
- Radical Emma Goldman, advocate of free love, birth control, homosexual rights and "freedom for both sexes," was arrested
- The Presbyterian Assembly condemned the growing bicycling fad for enticing parishioners away from church
- Motorcar production reached nearly 1,000 vehicles
- Nearly 150 Yiddish periodicals were being published, advocating radical labor reform
- Wheat prices rose to $1.09 per bushel
- Republican William McKinley was sworn into office as America's 25th president
- Boston's H.P. Hill used glass bottles to distribute milk
- Jell-O was introduced by Pearl B. Wait
- The Winton Motor Carriage Company was organized
- Dow Chemical Company was incorporated
- "Happy Birthday to You," originally composed by sisters Mildred and Patty Hill in 1893 as "Good Morning to All," became popular
- The "grandfather clause" marched across the South, ushering in widespread use of Jim Crow laws and restricting most blacks from voting
- Pepsi-Cola was introduced in New Bern, North Carolina, by pharmacist Caleb Bradham
- J.P. Stevens & Company was founded in New York
- Toothpaste in collapsible metal tubes was invented by Connecticut dentist Lucius Sheffield
- The trolley replaced horsedrawn cars in Boston
- Wesson Oil was introduced
- *The New York Times* dropped its price from $0.03 to $0.01, tripling circulation
- The Union Carbide Company was formed
- The creation of the crown bottle cap was credited with extending the shelf life of beer
- America boasted more than 300 bicycle manufacturing companies
- Cellophane was invented by Charles F. Cross and Edward J. Bevan
- Uneeda Biscuit Company was created
- The consolidation of Greater New York City was created through the merger of Brooklyn and Manhattan
- Henry James published "The Turn of the Screw"

- The Travelers Insurance Company of Hartford, Connecticut, issued the first automobile insurance policy which cost $11.25 to purchase $5,000 in liability coverage
- The Supreme Court ruled that a child born in the United States to Chinese immigrants was a U.S. citizen, and therefore could not be deported under the Chinese Exclusion Act
- Postcards were first authorized by the Post Office
- The battleship *Maine* was destroyed in Havana harbor, Cuba, killing 260 of its crew, triggering the Spanish-American, War
- Admiral George Dewey's fleet attacked Spain's holdings in Manila Bay, the Philippines conquering the nation for America
- The boll weevil began its destructive spread through the cotton fields of the South
- H.G. Wells published the classic "War of the Worlds," about an invasion of Earth by Martians
- Buddy Bolden, cornetist and New Orleans brass band leader, practiced what would later be called jazz
- Giraud Foster used the money earned from the invention of closure snaps for clothing to build a $2.5 million estate on 400 acres in Lee, Massachusetts
- America's first forestry school was founded in the Pisgah National Forest in North Carolina
- A telephone excise tax was created to help finance the Spanish-American War
- The Reverend Charles Lutwidge Dodgson, better known as Lewis Carroll, author of *Alice in Wonderland, Through the Looking-Glass*, and other classic works of children's literature, died of pneumonia at age 65
- Robert Allison of Port Carbon, Pennsylvania, became the first person to buy an American built automobile
- Annie Oakley promoted the service of women in combat situations with the United States military, offering "the services of a company of 50 lady sharpshooters' who would provide their own arms and ammunition should war break out with Spain"
- In the Battle of Manila Bay, Commodore Dewey destroyed the Spanish squadron, leading to the American capture of the Philippines
- The Trans-Mississippi Exposition World's Fair opened in Omaha, Nebraska
- Marie and Pierre Curie discovered radium
- John Jacob Abel isolated epinephrine (adrenaline)
- Goodyear Tire and Rubber Company was founded
- Shiga Kiyoshi, a Japanese bacteriologist, discovered the Shigella bacillus, responsible for dysentery
- The United Mine Workers of America was founded
- The first concrete grain elevator was erected near Minneapolis
- The Spanish-American War formally ended with a peace treaty between the United States and Spain
- Voting machines were approved by the U.S. Congress for use in federal elections
- Mount Rainier National Park was established in Washington State
- Felix Hoffmann patented aspirin and Bayer registered the drug as a trademark
- At Sing Sing Penitentiary, Martha M. Place became the first woman executed in an electric chair
- Students at the University of California, Berkeley, stole the Stanford Axe from Stanford University "yell leaders," thus establishing the Axe as a symbol of the rivalry between the schools
- The First Hague Peace Conference was opened in The Hague by Willem de Beaufort, Minister of Foreign Affairs of The Netherlands
- The paper clip was patented by Norwegian Johan Vaaler

- Mile-a-Minute Murphy earned his famous nickname after he rode a bicycle for one mile in under a minute on Long Island
- America's first juvenile court was established in Chicago
- The White Star Line's transatlantic ocean liner RMS Oceanic sailed on its maiden voyage
- The Second Boer War erupted in South Africa between the United Kingdom and the Boers of the Transvaal and Orange Free State
- The Alpha Sigma Tau Sorority was founded in Ypsilanti, Michigan
- The Bronx Zoo opened in New York City
- David Hilbert created the modern concept of geometry with the publication of his book Grundlagen der Geometrie
- Gold was discovered in Nome, Alaska

Annual Income, Standard Jobs

The numbers below are annual income for standard jobs across America in the years 1883, 1890, and 1898.

Category	1883	1890	1898
Blacksmiths	$1.50/day/60 hr week	$2.27/day/60 hr week	$3.14/day/60 hr week
Bricklayers	$3.23/day/60 hr week	$3.55/day/55 hr week	$3.41/day/48 hr week
Carpenters and Joiners	$2.57/day/60 hr week	n/a	n/a
Cigar Makers	$2.54/day/58 hr week	$4.50/day/n.a hr week	$6.13/day/48 hr week
Engineers, Stationary	$2.24/day/64 hr week	n/a	$3.17/day/60 hr week
Farm Labor	$1.25/day/63 hr week	$1.49/day/63 hr week	n/a
Firemen	$1.50/day/60 hr week	n/a	n/a
Glassblowers (bottle)	$4.23/day/51 hr week	$3.80/day/51 hr week	$3.97/day/54 hr week
Hod Carriers (bricks)	$1.94/day/60 hr week	$1.80/day/57 hr week	$1.97/day/48 hr week
Horseshoers	$1.68/day/60 hr week	$2.14/day/n.a hr week	$2.35/day/59 hr week
Marble Cutters	$2.69/day/60 hr week	$3.21/day/54 hr week	$4.22/day/48 hr week
Painters	$3.25/day/58 hr week	$2.61/day/55 hr week	$2.47/day/50 hr week
Plasterers	$2.98/day/59 hr week	$3.50/day/54 hr week	n/a
Plumbers	$3.50/day/58 hr week	$2.94/day/48 hr week	$3.74/day/48 hr week
Shoemakers	$1.67/day/60 hr week	$2.00/day/n.a hr week	$3.00/day/60 hr week
Silk Weavers	$2.07/day/60 hr week	$2.37/day/60 hr week	n/a
Stonemasons	$3.31/day/60 hr week	$3.39/day/50 hr week	$3.67/day/48 hr week

Selected Prices

1883

Alfred Peats Wallpaper, per Roll	$0.15
Anti-Skeet Pesticide	$0.10
Baby Educator Crackers, Six to a Box	$0.20
Bicycle, Columbia	$75.00
Boudoir Safe	$100.00
Chromo Business Cards	$0.05
Dental Fee, Silver Filling	$0.50
Featherbone Corset	$0.18
Hall Typewriter	$40.00
Horse Muzzle	$2.50
Illinois Central Railroad Round-Trip	$0.25
Keep's Collar for Men	$0.15
Kenton Baking Powder	$0.20
Lemonoide Furniture Polish	$0.50
Lottery Ticket, $30,000 Prize	$2.00
Metcalf Writing Paper, 72 Sheets	$0.75
Milson's Patent Ozone Disinfectant, Small	$8.00
Mother's Friend Liniment	$1.00
New Hygeia Bust Form	$0.50
Oil Paint, Tube	$0.05
Pistol	$20.00
Royal Argard Burner and Chimney	$1.25
Sun Parasol for Women	$0.50
The Great American Aquarium Ticket, Adult	$0.50
Tooth Extraction	$0.25
Tuition, Law School, Two Years	$200.00
Tuition, West Branch Boarding School, per Year	$225.00
Van Camp's Pork & Beans	$0.06
Wamsutta Muslin Shirt	$1.00
Williams Shaving Soap, Six Round Cakes	$0.40

1890

Castoria Medicine for Infants	$0.35
Cigar	$0.05
Coffee, 11 Pounds Parched	$1.00
Cupid Snap Waist For Children	$1.00
Dominola Card Game	$0.20
Gillespies' Patent Horse Muzzle	$2.50
Grapevines, Three Sample Vines	$0.15
Hall Typewriter	$40.00
Henderson Flexo Girdle	$1.25
J. Bride & Co. Pocket Watch	$12.00
Lemonoide Furniture Polish	$0.50
Linene Collars or Cuffs	$0.25
Lowney's Chocolate Bon-Bons	$0.60
Music Box, Self Playing, Eight Tunes	$15.00
Oil Heater, No Coal, No Ashes	$12.00
Printing Press, Self Inker	$5.00
Rice, Fancy White Rice, 240-Pound Sack	$0.04

Standard Shirt. $1.50
Twilled Lace Thread, 500 Yards $0.10
White Label Soup, Two Dozen Pint Cans $2.00

1898

Artificial Leg $75.00
Blush, for Lips and Face $1.00
Carriage, Wire or Wooden Wheels. $12.35
Chocolate, Pound $0.20
Cloth, Shirting Percale $0.13
Coffee, Pound $0.25
Dinner Set, English Porcelain, 100 Pieces $14.00
Dinner, New York City $1.25
Doilies, Nine Linen. $0.10
Face Powder $0.25
Flour, Half Barrel. $2.50
Folding Bed $15.00
Fountain Pen. $4.00
Gloves, Man's Kid $1.50
Hair Curler $1.00
Hotel Room, Columbia, SC $2.50
Insecticide, Quart $1.00
Magazine, *Ladies' Home Journal* $0.10
Man's Shirt $1.50
Music Box $6.00
Pesticide, Mosquito, Six Wafers $0.10
Piano Lessons, 24 . . . .$8.00
Piano, Steinway. $200.00
Pocket Watch $12.00
Sarsparilla, Bottle $1.00
Shirt, Man's. $1.50
Tea, Breakfast $0.65
Tooth Extraction. $0.25
Watch, Woman's $5.00
Woman's Bicycle Costume $7.50

The Value of a Dollar, 1860-2014

Composite Consumer Price Index; 1860=1

Year	Amount	Year	Amount	Year	Amount	Year	Amount
1860	$1.00	1899	$1.00	1938	$1.70	1977	$7.30
1861	$1.06	1900	$1.01	1939	$1.67	1978	$7.85
1862	$1.22	1901	$1.02	1940	$1.69	1979	$8.74
1863	$1.52	1902	$1.04	1941	$1.77	1980	$9.97
1864	$1.89	1903	$1.06	1942	$1.96	1981	$10.94
1865	$1.96	1904	$1.07	1943	$2.08	1982	$11.62
1866	$1.92	1905	$1.06	1944	$2.12	1983	$11.99
1867	$1.78	1906	$1.08	1945	$2.17	1984	$12.50
1868	$1.71	1907	$1.13	1946	$2.35	1985	$12.95
1869	$1.64	1908	$1.11	1947	$2.68	1986	$13.20
1870	$1.58	1909	$1.10	1948	$2.90	1987	$13.67
1871	$1.47	1910	$1.14	1949	$2.87	1988	$14.24
1872	$1.47	1911	$1.14	1950	$2.90	1989	$14.92
1873	$1.45	1912	$1.17	1951	$3.13	1990	$15.72
1874	$1.37	1913	$1.19	1952	$3.19	1991	$16.38
1875	$1.32	1914	$1.20	1953	$3.22	1992	$16.88
1876	$1.29	1915	$1.22	1954	$3.24	1993	$17.38
1877	$1.26	1916	$1.31	1955	$3.23	1994	$17.83
1878	$1.20	1917	$1.54	1956	$3.28	1995	$18.33
1879	$1.20	1918	$1.82	1957	$3.39	1996	$18.88
1880	$1.23	1919	$2.08	1958	$3.48	1997	$19.32
1881	$1.23	1920	$2.41	1959	$3.50	1998	$19.63
1882	$1.23	1921	$2.16	1960	$3.56	1999	$20.06
1883	$1.22	1922	$2.02	1961	$3.60	2000	$20.74
1884	$1.18	1923	$2.06	1962	$3.64	2001	$21.32
1885	$1.17	1924	$2.06	1963	$3.68	2002	$21.66
1886	$1.13	1925	$2.11	1964	$3.73	2003	$22.16
1887	$1.14	1926	$2.13	1965	$3.79	2004	$22.76
1888	$1.14	1927	$2.09	1966	$3.90	2005	$23.53
1889	$1.11	1928	$2.06	1967	$4.02	2006	$24.29
1890	$1.09	1929	$2.06	1968	$4.19	2007	$24.97
1891	$1.09	1930	$2.01	1969	$4.42	2008	$25.91
1892	$1.09	1931	$1.83	1970	$4.67	2009	$25.81
1893	$1.08	1932	$1.65	1971	$4.88	2010	$26.22
1894	$1.04	1933	$1.57	1972	$5.03	2011	$27.06
1895	$1.01	1934	$1.61	1973	$5.35	2012	$27.63
1896	$1.01	1935	$1.65	1974	$5.93	2013	$28.05
1897	$1.00	1936	$1.67	1975	$6.47	2014	$28.49
1898	$1.00	1937	$1.73	1976	$6.85		

SECTION FOUR: ALL AROUND US

This section offers a ringside seat to the issues and attitudes that formed American thoughts and actions from 1880 to 1899. These 86 documents, listed in chronological order below, from popular newspapers and magazines of the time, are generally reprinted in their entirety. They show how Americans' changing ideas on music, education, movies, fashion, shopping, politics, and women's work were shaped. Read about home remedies, immigration, social moires, and the political climate as the country raced toward the twentieth century.

༺≈ঙ≈ঙ≈ঙ≈ঙ≈ঙ༻

Early American Home Remedies
advertisement from the 1880s

"The best cure for wounds from rusty nails, pitchforks, etc., is beef-gall. Take a pint bottle to your butcher, get him to fill it with the fresh gall, cork tightly and set away in the cellar. It will become somewhat offensive, but will promptly cure the worse case of injuries from the above cases after all doctor's remedies have failed. Bathe the wound and adjoining parts freely, and keep on a bandage wet with it."

༺≈ঙ≈ঙ≈ঙ≈ঙ≈ঙ༻

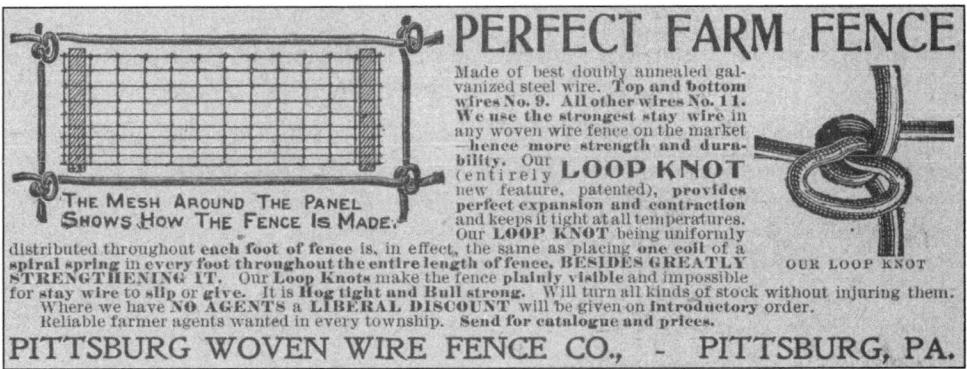

Clubs for the Coyote Country's Gentry
American Heritage, 1880

"No institution better symbolized the rise and power of the cattle barons than the extraordinary Cheyenne Club that Wyoming ranchmen built in 1880 to give themselves the comforts befitting their status. The three-story mansardroofed, brick-and-wood building had wine vaults, two grand staircases, a smoking room, a reading room, a dining room, hardwood floors, and plush carpets.

Limited by charter to only 200 hand-picked members, the Cheyenne Club claimed, with some reason, to have the finest steward in America. And its deft servants were recruited by founding President Philip Dater in Canada, where, under the British flag, the tradition of genteel service still flourished. 'No wonder they like the club at Cheyenne,' wrote Western buff Owen Wister, who was himself a Philadelphia clubman. 'It's the pearl of the prairies…'

Inside, members dressed for dinner on gala evenings in white tie and tails, which an old Nebraska member nicknamed 'Herefords' in honor of the white-chested, red-coated cattle. At dinner the members could savor such viands as caviar, pickled eels, French peas, and Roquefort cheese, together with liberal quantities of suitable drink and tobacco… Members were strictly accountable for their behavior: they were permitted no profanity, no drunkenness, no cheating at cards, no drinking in the reading room. And when Harry Oelrichs kicked a servant down the stairs the club kicked out Oelrichs. 'Ah, yes,' exclaimed a reminiscing English member, 'cow punching, as seen from the veranda of the Cheyenne Club, was a most attractive proposition.' "

༺≈ঙ≈ঙ≈ঙ≈ঙ≈ঙ༻

Excerpt from Gen. James A. Garfield's letter accepting the Republican nomination for the presidency, 1880

"The material interests of this country, the tradition of its settlement, and the sentiment of our people, have led the Government to offer the widest hospitality to emigrants who seek our shores for new and happier homes, willing to share the burdens as well as the benefits of our society, and intending that their posterity shall become an undistinguishable part of our population. The recent movement of the Chinese to our Pacific coast partakes but little of the qualifies of such an immigration, either in its purposes or result. It is too much like an importation to be welcomed without restriction; too much like an invasion to be looked upon without solicitude. We cannot consent to allow any form of servile labor to be introduced among us under the guise of immigration."

A Losing Book Concern, The American Book Exchange in a Receivers Hands
New York Times, November 27, 1881

During the past two or three months rumors have been current in business circles of the financial unsoundness of the American Book Exchange, and yesterday the truthfulness of the rumors was demonstrated by the appointment of a receiver for the company. The exact amount of the liabilities is not stated, and there are conflicting reports as to the ability of the managers of the company to extricate themselves from this financial embarrassment. It is conceded by those who are in a position to know all the facts that the Exchange has, since its organization, been doing a very large business on comparatively small capital, and the fact that all of its numerous publications have been put upon the market at extraordinarily low prices has not only aroused the animosity of many rival publishers, but has given rise to quite a general belief that no money is being made by the company.

Other Business Troubles

Dispatches were received in this city yesterday announcing the failure of the well-known house of Dumas and Allen, dealers in cotton and guano, at Forsythe, Georgia. The house was established many years ago, and they did a very large business. They owned a warehouse and real estate valued at $80,000. They owe considerably more in New York, but the full amount of the liabilities is not definitely known.

Reports from St. Louis state that the Missouri Zinc Company had been placed in the hands of Lucian Eaton as receiver. The company was incorporated in 1809 with a capital of $100,000 and eventually was controlled by Messrs. Eaton and Thomas T. Richards, who became the principal owners. Since the suicide of Thomas T. Richards in May, the affairs of the concern have been in bad shape and culminated in the appointment of a receiver.

Letter to the Editor
Philadelphia Public Ledger, August 1882

"No resident west of Broad Street desires the electric light. Would any one of the editors or owners of the daily paper like one in front of his private dwelling?

Would Mayor King or any members of Council be delighted with one in front of his sleeping chamber? There is no city in the world where it would be tolerated in a street occupied almost entirely by private residences as West Chestnut Street is. Do you admire the six red poles in each square?"

How Yap Got the Slipper
The Knoxville Tennessee Chronicle, March 22, 1882

Molly was so happy playing with her doll baby that she had no time to notice Yap.

That little dog was jealous. He barked yap! yap! very loudly, and now sat looking at Molly out of the corners of his eyes, wondering what mischief he could get into, and so worry her into playing with him. Suddenly he trotted off, his mind quite made up as to what to do.

"Molly, Molly," called mamma.

"Mamma, don't call so loud," whispered Molly. "My little doll baby is sleeping."

"Molly," called mamma again, "make haste and see what Yap is after. I am sure he is in my room."

"Oh, what a bad doggie," sighed Molly, with her face in a pucker, but she put her baby down, and went to see after the dog.

There he was on the staircase, with mamma's slipper in his mouth. When he saw Molly he dropped the slipper, and ran past her, looking very much as if he was laughing.

Molly shook her finger at him, and laughing, too, picked up the slipper and carried it to mamma.

But Yap was too smart to be cheated out of his fun in that way. So he ran into the yard and began to bark furiously at Puss. Mrs. Puss cared little for his barking, and soon he stopped. Then Molly looked out of the window and said, "Yap and Puss look as if they were talking to each other, mamma." And so they were.

"Oh, you beautiful darling," said Molly, taking her baby against her, and hugging it tight; "Come and let us take a walk." Then she sat down to put on the doll's best clothes, and while she was very busy and almost ready for the walk, she thought she heard a sound, tip tip, on the staircase, and ran to see what was the matter.

"Mamma," she screamed, "come here—oh, do come!" and mamma hurried out to see Pussy bringing the slipper down to Yap, who was waiting at the foot of the stairs.

How they laughed when Pussy dropped the slipper under Yap's nose, and he trotted off in a grand way!

Molly ran after him, and found him ready to bury it with some other treasures at the end of the yard.

"Mamma," said Molly, when she returned to the house with the second slipper, "do you think dogs and cats can talk? I do."

And Molly thinks so to this day.

Wayside Gatherings, sayings from
The Yorkville Enquirer, 1882

- A cremated body leaves a residuum of only ounces; all besides is stored in the gaseous Elements

- A deacon in Indiana has four boys, the youngest of whom is named Doxology, because he's the last of the hims

- The microscopists say that a mosquito has 22 teeth in the end of its bill, 11 above and the same number below

- It is said that of the total working expenses of the railroads, over 60 percent goes in various ways to the wage-earners

- If one's hands perspire easily when doing delicate work, they should be bathed in a few drops of cologne occasionally

- It would take 40 years for all the water in the great lakes to pour over Niagara at the rate of one million cubic feet a second

- The expressions "Hallelujah" and "Amen" are said to have been introduced into Christian worship by St. Jerome, about A.D. 390

- Instantaneous photography has revealed the fact that the former method of representing electricity as a fiery zigzag was entirely false

- The tensile strength of a wet rope is only one third the strength of the rope when dry, while a rope saturated with grease or soap is weaker still

Wayside Gatherings.

- The eve of a great event—Mother Eve when she ate the apple.
- Thirty-four pounds of raw sugar make twenty-one of refined.
- To accumulate dollars, my son, you must have sense to begin with.
- Napoleon the Great was a Mason. He was raised at Malta, 1798.
- Prudence is a plume dropped from the wing of some past folly.
- Good sense is the best friend a man can have in an emergency.
- A false friend and a shadow attend only when the sun shines.
- Churches built in the United States in 1891 numbered over eighty-five hundred.
- It is the hardest thing in the world to make a Christian out of selfish people.
- When a pickpocket pulls at your watch, tell him plainly that you have no time to spare.
- The Methodist church needs 1,000 new preachers every year to keep its pulpits supplied.
- When a boy is smart, there is a question whether he got it from her folks or his people.
- Women of today are on the average two inches taller than they were twenty-five years ago.
- Those who occupy the highest stations often think with regret of some pleasanter one they left below.
- The wife of a poor manafacturer, living in Ashley county, Tenn., recently gave birth to six children, all boys.

Recent Inventions
Scientific American, July 22, 1882

Improved Button: Mr. William H. Ward, of Topeka, Kansas, has patented an improved button. This button consists of a fastening made of a strip of thin flexible metal having angular slots cut in one end and rolled into a cylindrical shape, an eyelet in which the fastening is secured, and a back. The back is a central perforation through which the high eyelet and clasp are passed and secured by spreading their inner ends. The face of the button is secured in the back in the usual manner, and is constructed with a depression which fits into the end of the eyelet and fastening, and assists in forming a firm and compact button. The eyelet forming the stem of the button is made so as to allow the face of the button to rotate. Mr. Ward has also recently patented improved pliers for attaching the buttons to garments.

Spark Arrester: An efficient and durable spark arrester, that is easily attached to and detached from the smokestack of a locomotive, has recently been patented by Mr. John L. Kantner, of South Easton, Pennsylvania. Inside the smokestack is placed a concavo-convex grate, formed of parallel bars attached at their ends to a rim. This grate fits into the outer part of an outer rim, and has guide pins which enter vertical slots in the rim. The rim is fitted into the smokestack and rests against the rim of the lower grate.... With this construction, the incandescent pieces that are carried up the smokestack will be broken, by striking against the grate bars, into such small pieces as to be rendered incapable of doing damage.

Show Card Holder: A novel device for holding price and show cards has recently been patented by Mr. Will. C. Rood, of Quincy, Illinois. A frame is provided on its front side, at its lower age and ends, with grooved flanges, behind which a sign or show card can be passed and retained. At the rear side, near its bottom edge, the frame has a socket for receiving the upper end of the standard, the lower end of which fits in an aperture in the top of the base. At the upper edge of the rear side, a ring is attached by which the frame may be suspended from a nail.

Phantom Lights at Sea
Scientific American, July 22, 1882

Fulton Market fish dealer gives the following explanation of some of the strange lights, phantom vessels, and other mysterious appearances that puzzle seamen:

"Two years ago I went menhaden fishing, and one day as we were going up the Sound, one of the hands said he hoped we are not going off the Point, meaning Montauk. I asked him why. He seemed kind of offish, but at last he let out that he had seen ships sailing about in the dead of night in a dead calm. I laughed at him, but two nights later we came to anchor at Gardiner's Bay, and it is a hot night we stretched out on deck. In the middle of the night I was awakened by someone giving me a tremendous jerk, and when I found myself on my feet, my mate, shaking like a leaf, was pointing over the rail. I looked, and sure enough, there was a big schooner about an eighth of a mile away, bearing down on us. There wasn't a breath of wind in the bay, but on she came at a 10-knot rate, headed right for us. 'Sing out to the skipper,' I said. 'It's no use,' said my mate, hanging on to me. 'It's no vessel.' But there she was, within 100 yards of us. Shaking him off, I swung into the rigging, and yelled 'Schooner ahoy!' And shouted to her to bear away, but in a second the white sails were right aboard of us. I yelled to the hands, and made ready to jump, when, like a flash, she disappeared, and the skipper came on deck with all hands and wanted to know if we had the jimjams. I'd have sworn that I had seen the *Flying Dutchman* but for one thing. We saw the same thing about a week afterwards. The light passed around us and went up the bay. I got out the men and seine [a large net] and followed in the path of the phantom schooner, and as sure as you are alive, we made the greatest single haul of menhaden on record. The light, to my mind, was nothing more or less than the phosphorescence that hovered over the big shoal. The oil from so many millions of fish moving along was enough to produce a light; but you will find men all along the shores of Long Island who believe there is a regular phantom craft that comes in on and off—similar to a coaster in the spirit trade. I saw an account of something like this in the Portland papers sometime after, and I thought it was very remarkable; for wherever you find menhaden you may look for queer lights on the water—phantom ships and the like."

"Men who began life as bargaining for small wares will invariably become sharpers. The commanding aim of every such man will soon be to make a good bargain, and he will soon speedily consider every gainful bargain as a good one. The tricks of fraud will assume in his mind the same place which commercial skill and an honorable system of dealing hold in the mind of merchant."

—*Timothy Dwight, president of Yale College*

The Authentic Life of Billy the Kid
by Pat Garrett, 1882

(On the night of July 14, 1881, Sheriff Pat Garrett and his two deputies were hunting for the outlaw Billy the Kid. The residents of that section of New Mexico were sympathetic to the Kid and the lawmen could extract little information. Garrett decided to seek out an old friend, Peter Maxwell, who might tell him the Kid's whereabouts. As chance would have it, the Kid stumbled right into the Sheriff's hands. Garrett published his account of the incident a year after it happened.)

I then concluded to go and have a talk with Peter Maxwell, Esq., in whom I felt sure I could rely. We had ridden to within a short distance of Maxwell's grounds when we found a man in camp and stopped. To Poe's great surprise, he recognized in the camper an old friend and former partner, in Texas, named Jacobs. We unsaddled here, got some coffee, and, on foot, entered an orchard which runs from this point down to a row of old buildings, some of them occupied by Mexicans, not more than 60 yards from Maxwell's house. We approached these houses cautiously, and when within earshot, heard the sound of voices conversing in Spanish. We concealed ourselves quickly and listened; but the distance was too great to hear words, or even distinguish voices. Soon a man arose from the ground, in full view, but too far away to recognize. He wore a broad-brimmed hat, a dark vest and pants, and was in his shirtsleeves. With a few words, which fell like a murmur on our ears, he went to the fence, jumped it, and walked down towards Maxwell's house.

Little as we then suspected it, this man was the Kid. We learned, subsequently, that, when he left his companions that night, he went to the house of a Mexican friend, pulled off his hat and boots, threw himself on a bed, and commenced reading a newspaper. He soon, however, hailed his friend, who was sleeping in the room, told him to get up and make some coffee, adding: "Give me a butcher knife and I will go over to Pete's and get some beef; I'm hungry." The Mexican arose, handed him the knife, and the Kid, hatless and in his stocking-feet, started to Maxwell's, which was but a few steps distant.

When the Kid, by me unrecognized, left the orchard, I motioned to my companions, and we cautiously retreated a short distance, and, to avoid the persons whom we had heard at the houses, took another route, approaching Maxwell's house from the opposite direction. When we reached the porch in front of the building, I left Poe and McKinney at the end of the porch, about 20 feet from the door of Pete's room, and went in. It was near midnight and Pete was in bed. I walked to the head of the bed and sat down on it, beside him, near the pillow. I asked him as to the whereabouts of the Kid. He said that the Kid had certainly been about, but he did not know whether he had left or not. At that moment a man sprang quickly into the door, looking back, and called twice in Spanish, "Who comes there?" No one replied and he came on in. He was bareheaded. From his step I could perceive he was either barefooted or in his stocking-feet, and held a revolver in his right hand and a butcher knife in his left. He came directly towards me. Before he reached the bed, I whispered: "Who is it, Pete?" but received no reply for a moment. It struck me that it might be Pete's brother-in-law, Manuel Abreu, who had seen Poe and McKinney, and wanted to know their business. The intruder came close to me, leaned both hands on the bed, his right hand almost touching my knee, and asked, in a low tone: "Who are they, Pete?" at the same instant Maxwell whispered to me, "That's him!" Simultaneously, the Kid must have seen, or felt, the presence of a third person at the head of the bed. He raised quickly his pistol, a self-cocker, within a foot of my breast. Retreating rapidly across the room he cried: "Quien es? Quien es?" ("Who's that? Who's that?") All this occurred in a moment. Quickly as possible I drew my revolver and fired, threw my body aside, and fired again. The second shot was useless; the Kid fell dead. He never spoke. A struggle or two, a little strangling sound as he gasped for breath, and the Kid was with his many victims.

Mirror Fashions, New Designs for Spring
Demorest's Monthly Magazine, 1883

"Among the features of the new designs for the spring and summer season are neatness and perfect practicability. The novelty is less striking than the beauty and simplicity, which is shown in the elegance of form and the absence of superfluous puffery.

The over-garments for suits exhibit particular evidence of this fact. The first one to which we shall call attention is the 'Helena' polonaise. A very ladylike garment, suited to cashmere, poplin, silk, or any kind of washing goods or grenadine, it is especially becoming in black grenadine, and may be trimmed with fine 'yak' or guipure lace.

The skirt worn with this polonaise may be trimmed with graduated flounces or kilt-plaiting. If the latter, the front breadth should be composed wholly of the plaiting laid lengthwise from the top to the bottom, the sides and back being arranged to form plaited flounces. If gathered flounces are required, as for grenadine, then the flounces upon the front breadth must be extended to the waist."

ॐ৯৯৯৯৯৯৯৯

The Greatest Medical Discovery since the Creation of Man, or since the Commencement of the Christian Era advertisement, 1883

"There never has been a time when the healing of so many different diseases has been caused by outward application as the present. It is an undisputed fact that over half of the entire population of the globe resorts to the use of ordinary plasters.

Dr. Melvin's Capsicum Porous Plasters are acknowledged by all who have used them to act quicker than any other plaster they ever before tried, and that one of these plasters will do more real service than a hundred of the ordinary kind. All other plasters are slow to action, and require to be worn continually to effect a cure; but with these it is entirely different: the instant one is applied the patient will feel its effect.

Physicians in all ages have thoroughly tested and well know the effect of Capsicum; and it has always been more or less used as a medical agent for an outward application, but it is only of very recent date that its advantages in a porous plaster have been discovered. Being, however, convinced of the wonderful cures effected by Dr. Melvin's Capsicum Porous Plasters and their superiority over all other plasters, they now actually prescribe them, in their practice, for such diseases as rheumatism, pain in the side and back, and all such cases as have required the use of plasters or liniments. After you have tried other plasters or liniments, and they have failed, and you want a certain cure, ask your druggist for Dr. Melvin's Capsicum Porous Plaster, and take no other; or on receipt of $0.25 for one, $1.00 for five, or $2.00 for a dozen, they will be mailed, post paid, to any address in the United States or Canada. Novelty Plaster Works, Lowell, Mass, U.S.A."

ॐ৯৯৯৯৯৯৯৯

Caught in the Act, The curiosities of pictures of the movements of men and animals
New York Times, June 10, 1883

Eadweard Muybridge spoke last evening of the "romance and reality of animals and locomotion" to a large and enthusiastic audience in the hall of Union League Club. The lecture was illustrated by stereopticon and zoopraxiscope pictures thrown on a screen and representing horses in motion while trotting, running, and leaping, and oxen, deer, dogs, hounds, and other animals taken while in motion. Similar pictures of men boxing, wrestling, fencing, tumbling, and engaging in various athletic sports were also shown. The practical value of the pictures was shown by the zoopraxiscope, by which the series of pictures instantaneously taken actually reproduced on canvas the gaits of various animals and the movements of men while boxing, jumping, and tumbling.

৯~৫৯~৫৯~৫৯~৫৯~৫

Sporting Shot from Iron
The Cedar Rapids Evening Gazette, (Iowa) January 12, 1883

A company has been formed in Iowa for the purpose of manufacturing sporting shot from iron. It is stated that the trials which have been made of the shot have proven it to be fully equal and in some respects superior to lead shot. No tower is required, as the shot is made by the process with less than three feet drop. The company is nearly ready to put the new manufacture into the market, and, as it can be sold at a much lower price than lead shot, the demand will probably soon assume large proportions. It is stated that the iron shot looks well and cannot be distinguished from lead shot by inspection.

৯~৫৯~৫৯~৫৯~৫৯~৫

Mrs. W. K. Vanderbilt's Great Fancy Dress Ball
New York Times, March 27, 1883

The Vanderbilt ball has agitated New York society more than any social event that has occurred here in many years. Since the announcement that it would take place, which was made about a week before the beginning of Lent, scarcely anything else has been talked about. It has been on every tongue and a fixed idea in every head. It has disturbed the sleep and occupied the waking hours of social butterflies, both male and female, for over six weeks, and has even, perhaps, interfered to some extent with that rigid observance of Lenten devotions which the Church exacts. Amid the rush and excitement of business, men have found their minds haunted by uncontrollable thoughts as to whether they should appear as Robert le Diable, Cardinal Richelieu, Otho the barbarian, or the Count of Monte Cristo, while the ladies have been driven to the verge of distraction in the effort to settle the comparative advantages of ancient, medieval, and modern costumes, or the relative superiority, from an effective point of view, of such characters and symbolic representations as Princess de Croy, Rachel, Mary Stuart, Marie Antoinette, the Four Seasons, Night, Morning, Innocence, and the Electric Light. Invitations have, of course, been in great demand, and in all about 1,200 were issued.

As Lent drew to a close, everybody having decided what he or she was going to wear, the attention of the select few turned from the question of costumes to the settlement of the details of the ball itself and the practicing of the parts assigned to them in the various fancy quadrilles decided on to make the most conspicuous features of the entertainment. The drilling in these quadrilles has been going on assiduously in Mrs. William Astor's and other private residences for more than a week, while prospective guests not so favored as to be able to witness these preliminary entertainments have had to content themselves with recounting such items of information as could be extracted from the initiated. As early as 7 o'clock last evening, although the ball was not to begin until 11, gentlemen returning from the hair-dressers' with profusely powdered heads were to be seen alighting from coupes along Fifth Avenue, and hurrying up the steps of their residences to complete their toilets. About the same time the passage up the avenue of an express wagon containing the horses for the hobbyhorse quadrille attracted a great deal of attention. By 8 o'clock a large crowd of inquisitive loungers was collected in Fifth Avenue and Fifty-second Street watching Mr. Vanderbilt's brilliantly illuminated residence and a group of workmen putting up the awning before the entrance. Inside, long before the ball commenced, the house was in a blaze of light, which shown upon profuse decorations of flowers. These, which were by Klunder, were at once novel and imposing. They were confined chiefly to the second floor, although throughout the hall and parlors on the first floor, were distributed in vases and gilded baskets filled with natural roses of extraordinary size, such as the dark crimson Jacqueminot, the deep pink Glorie de Paris, the pale pink Baroness de Rothschild and Adolphe de Rothschild, the King of Morocco; the Duchess of Kent and the new and beautiful Marie Louise Vassey, but a delightful surprise

greeted the guests upon the second floor, as they reached the head of the grand stairway. Grouped around the clustered columns which ornament either side of the stately hall were tall palms overtopping a dense mass of ferns and ornamental grasses, while suspended between the capitals of the columns were strings of variegated Japanese lanterns. Entered through this hall is the gymnasium, a spacious apartment, where supper was served on numerous small tables. But it had not the appearance of an apartment last night; it was like a garden in a tropical forest. The walls were nowhere to be seen, but in their places an impenetrable thicket of fern above fern and palm above palm, while from the branches of the palms hung a profusion of lovely orchids, displaying a rich variety of color and an almost endless variation of fantastic forms. In the centre of the room was a gigantic palm, upon whose umbrageous head rested a thick cluster of that beautiful Cuban vine, vougen villa, which trailed from the dome in the centre of the ceiling.

To make the resemblance to a garden more complete, two beautiful fountains played in opposite corners of the apartment. The doors of the apartment, thrown back against the walls, were completely covered with roses and lilies of the valley.

The scene outside the brilliantly lighted mansion, as the guests began to arrive, was novel and interesting. Early in the evening a squad of police officers arrived to keep the expected crowd of sightseers in order and to direct the movements of drivers and cabmen. Before 10 o'clock men and women were wandering about the streets outside of the house and glancing at the windows, or peering under the double canopies which led up to the door. They took up positions on the steps of the houses opposite or stood on the adjacent corners waiting for the carriages to arrive, and then all who could obtain room on the sidewalks crowded at the outsides of the canopies and gazed curiously and enviously at the gorgeously costumed gentlemen and ladies whom the ushers assisted to alight. Carriages containing the more youthful and impatient of the maskers drove past the mansion before 10:30 o'clock, the occupant peering surreptitiously under the curtain to see if others were arriving as he rolled by.

Carriages drove slowly by while the ladies and gentlemen in them, who were not in costume, gazed out of the windows and at the crowds about the house, indicating that curiosity was not confined to the humble walks of life entirely. At 11 o'clock the maskers began to arrive in numbers, and the eager lookers-on in the street were able to catch glimpses through the windows of flashing sword hilts, gay costumes, beautiful flowers, and excited faces. Handsome women and dignified men were assisted from the carriages in their fanciful costumes, over which were thrown shawls, Ulster's and light wraps. Pretty and excited girls and young men, who made desperate efforts to appear blasé, were seen to descend and run up the steps into the brilliantly lighted hall. Club men who looked bored arrived singly and in pairs and quartets, in hired cabs, and whole families drove up in elegant equipages with liveried coachmen and footmen. A great many ladies were accompanied by their maids, who were not allowed to leave the carriages, whereat there was some grumbling. Gentlemen's valets were treated in the same manner, and the ushers insisted that these orders were imperative. At 11:30 o'clock the throng of carriages before the mansion and waiting at the corners was so great that the utmost efforts of the police were necessary to keep the line in order, and many gentlemen left their carriages in adjacent streets and walked up to the canopy which was the entrance to the fairyland. Most of the gentlemen gave orders to their coachmen to call for them at 3 o'clock. Others made the hour as late as 4, and some of the more seasoned and wiser party-goers ordered their carriages as early as 1 and 2 o'clock.

The guests had all arrived, save a few stragglers, at midnight, and the crowd began to disperse. A few still remained to wander about in the vicinity of the house, or to gaze into the area windows or up to the more brilliant plate-glass in the stories above. At 1 the police were the sole occupants of the street before the house, with the exception of an occasional wandering belated pedestrian. The guests on arriving found themselves in a grand hall about 65 feet long, 16 feet in height, and 20 feet in width. Under foot was a floor of polished and luminous Echallion stone, and above them a ceiling richly paneled in oak. Over a high wainscoting of Caen stone, richly carved, are antique Italian tapestries, beautifully worked by hand. Out of this hall to the right rises the grand stairway, which is not only the finest piece of work of its kind in this country, but one of the finest in the world. The stairway occupies a space 30 feet square, the whole structure of the stairway being of the finest Caen stone, carved with wonderful delicacy and vigor. It climbs by ample easy stages to a height of 50 feet, ending in a pendentive dome. Another stairway, also in Caen stone, leading from the second to the third story, is seen through a rampant arch, with an effect which recalls the unique and glorious stairway of the Chateau of Chambord. In the gymnasium, on the third floor, a most beautiful apartment, 50 feet in length by 35 in width, the members of the six organized quadrilles of the evening gradually assembled before 11 o'clock. Lots were drawn Saturday last by the ladies in charge of those quadrilles to decide the order in which they should be danced, it being previously agreed that the ball should be opened by the "Hobby-horse Quadrille," a fantastic set, under the leadership of Mrs. S.S. Howland and Mr. James V. Parker, to which by common consent the privilege was assigned of filling the scene for five minutes and no more.

The first place among the more picturesque quadrilles was drawn by the "Mother Goose Quadrille," under the leadership of Mrs. Lawrence Perkins. At a little after 11 o'clock, to the strains of Gilmore's Band, the six quadrilles, comprising in all nearly a hundred ladies and gentlemen, were formed in order in the gymnasium and began to move in a glittering processional pageant down the grand stairway and through the hall.

Winding through the motley crowd of princes, monks, cavaliers, highlanders, queens, kings, dairymaids, bull-fighters, knights, brigands, and nobles, the procession passed down the grand stairway and through the hall into a noble room on the front of the house in the style of Francois Premier, 25 feet in width by 40 in length, wainscoted richly and heavily in carved French walnut and hung in dark red plush. Vast carved cabinets and an immense, deep fire-place give an air of antique grandeur to this room, from which the procession passed into a bright and charming salon of the style of Louis XV, 30 feet in width by 35 in length, wainscoted in oak and enriched with carved work and gilding. The whole wainscoting of this beautiful apartment was brought from a chateau in France. On the walls hang three French-Gobelin tapestries a century old, but in the brilliance and freshness of their coloring seemingly the work of yesterday, and over the chimney-piece hangs a superb portrait of Mrs. Vanderbilt by Madrazo, full of spirit, character, and grace…

❧❧❧❧❧❧❧

The Macnicol Case
The Fitchburg Sentinel (Massachusetts), January 1883

The approaching trial of a Kentucky school teacher for various offenses of dress will decide the important question whether there is any particular style of dress which a schoolteacher must adopt, and whether certain peculiarities of dress are in themselves sufficiently immoral to justify the offenders removal from all connection with the great work of educating Kentucky's small boys.

It appears that Mr. Macnicol, of the Norville School District, has been charged by the ladies of his district with "official misconduct." The specifications are four in number. It is alleged that he does not wear a coat; that his trousers are so ragged as to expose portions of his body; that he wears only one suspender, and that he never puts on a pair of stockings. The charge and specifications are to be investigated by a School Commissioner, and the results of the investigation are awaited with intense anxiety.

There seems a strong possibility that the four specifications above cited will be sustained by sufficient evidence. It is said that witnesses without number may be made to testify to the condition of Mr. Macnicol's trousers and suspenders, and to his habitual rejection of coat and stockings. It does not follow, however, that the charge of official misconduct will be sustained. Whether a schoolteacher who is guilty of ragged trousers, of one suspender, and a dislike of coat and a dislike of wearing stockings is also necessarily guilty of "official misconduct" is a question of law rather than of fact.

There are many pleas which Mr. Macnicol can urge in defence of his conduct. He may insist that the so-called ragged condition of his trousers is due to an excessive love of neatness. What his indiscriminating accusers regarded as rents may be simply holes made by cutting out pieces of cloth that have become accidentally stained with ink. Or he may take the broad general ground that his trousers have been worn out in the cause of education and that the alleged rags are the glorious scars sustained while endeavoring to instill the multiplication table into the system of a boy peculiarly impervious to clubs and reason. There is no particular pattern of trousers prescribed by any school regulation which has yet been brought to his knowledge, and he can claim the same right to wear openwork trousers that his fair accusers claim for themselves in connection with open work stockings.

As to Mr. Macnicol's failure to wear a coat, it is merely an evidence of his zeal in the cause of education. How can a Kentucky schoolteacher hope to teach half-grown Kentucky boys with his coat on? If he "means business," and proposes to accomplish any real good, he must take off his coat. Does not the Kentucky preacher take off not merely his coat, but his collar, whenever he means to preach a really eloquent sermon? And did anyone ever hear of a Kentucky political orator or barroom debater who either spoke or argued with his coat on? Mr. Macnicol, if he is wise, will confess to teaching without a coat and glory in it. The ladies of the Norville School District are doubtless admirable women, but they know very little about teaching Kentucky boys if they fancy it can be done with a coat on. No coat ever yet made would last a Kentucky teacher for a single week if he did not take it off before grasping his cane and summoning a boy to come to him and acquire the first principles of arithmetic....

It is to be hoped that Mr. Macnicol will be triumphantly acquitted. If he is found guilty of official misconduct, no schoolteacher will be safe who does not obtain written instructions from the ladies of the district as to which articles of clothing he must wear and who does not habitually dress in the presence of witnesses. And if women can dictate how the male schoolteacher shall clothe himself, men will have the right to say what clothes a female teacher must wear. From such a state of things, the acquittal of Mr. Macnicol alone can save us.

ॐ॰ॐ॰ॐ॰ॐ॰ॐ

Young Ladies And Dress
The Naiad, Williamston, South Carolina, December 1884

A lady who had taught for over 30 years once gave the writer some very interesting information. "When a new scholar was introduced," she said, "I always look first at her dress. If it was plain, neat, and tidy, I was pretty confident that I had good material to work with. For the first two or three years of my teaching, I was in the habit of scrutinizing the features, and the formation of the heads, but these came at last to be quite secondary considerations. One school was so expensive that none but the daughters of the wealthy could possibly enter it; so when a young lady came to the classroom in a plain dress, I was sure that it was on account of her idea of the fitness of things.

This argued common sense. Common sense is always in direct antagonism to vanity, and, where there is no vanity, there is seldom self-consciousness. So, you see, a plain dress came to mean a great deal to me. I learned never to expect anything from a girl whose school dress was silk or velvet. I shall always retain the impression made upon me by a quiet little body in a blue flannel dress, and plain trimmings. She came from one of the first families in wealth and culture, and was the most unobtrusive child I ever knew, as well as the most brilliant. When she told me on graduation day that she had decided to study for a physician, I was not in the least surprised, and I was sure she would succeed, and she certainly has the most marvelous manner. She carried off every honor, and, though the girls in 'purple and fine linen' sneered at her plain attire, and lack of style, there was not one who could ever compete with her."

Certainly, on the whole, the deductions of this teacher are correct. It takes time to array oneself in elaborate garments, and the girl whose mind is occupied with loops and trimming and general furbelows cannot, for philosophical reason, have room for much else. Then there is the reason deeper than this, even. The girl whose tastes are in the line of dress and display has not an intellectual development. She may be imitative and intuitive to a degree, but she will generally be superficial in her learning and shallow in character.

A very good story in this connection is told of a prominent musician in New York. A young lady went to him for a course of "finishing off" lessons. "Let's see what you can do," said the teacher, and placed before her a simple aria of Mozart's. She played a few measures, and was interrupted. "Take off your rings," said the great man. A few measures more, and another interruption. "Take off your bracelets." A little further on, she was stopped again. "Your sleeves are too long. I cannot see your wrists." She stopped and penned up her sleeves with a face on fire. At last she succeeded in finishing the selection.

"Do you want me to teach you?" the instructor asked, as she took her hands from the keys.

"Yes, sir."

"Very well. Come tomorrow at this hour, without any jewelry, and in some sort of a dress you can breathe in. I don't know at all how you have played this aria, because of the rattling gew-gaws, and the distracting noise you make in getting your breath.

I am afraid you haven't the instinct of a musician. A musician thinks first of his art, and the last of his appearances; but it seems to me you think first, last, and always of how you look."

Now this may seem to some rough and very uncalled for, but he was an honest soul and a grand musician. His words prove true. This young lady had not the musical instinct, and, after a fair trial, was dismissed. Her teacher proved that her practice had been superficial, and all that she had done had been spoiled by vanity and self-consciousness.

A schoolgirl who dressed very plainly, but in good taste, was once asked why she did not "rig up" more.

"Because," she said, "I haven't time to fuss about clothes, and learn, too, and then I should like to have something new to wear when I was older. Velvets and brocades, and diamonds and pearls, and all those fine things will be new to me by and by, and there's nothing left for you girls to anticipate."

࿆࿆࿆࿆࿆࿆࿆

Manual: How to Introduce the Personal Memoirs of U.S. Grant, 1885

Canvassing in Towns

Make a thorough canvas. See every family from whom there is a possibility of obtaining an order, on each street before leaving it, even if you have to call several times at some residences. It is not policy to canvas one whole side of a street before canvassing the other; you should canvas one side of the street until you reach a crossing, then cross over and canvas the other side. The object in doing this is to keep within the influence of your names. Only a systematic, careful canvas pays and permits the agent to canvas a long time in a place.

What Door to Enter

Always go in at the front door; it shows that you have respect for yourself and your business. Entering back or kitchen doors advertises a salesman's work as fit only for the less honorable parts of the house. Advertise your work as fit for the sitting room, library, or the parlor, by seeking to enter and sit there; show that you are a gentleman, and at home in the most honorable part of the house.

While on the steps of the house, soliciting admission, keep the hat on the head, merely touching it to the lady, until invited to cross the threshold. Upon entering the house, remove your hat as soon as you are inside. Be very easy and agreeable in your manners, but do not go to the extreme of making yourself too agreeable.

How to Leave the House

In leaving the house, be careful not to turn your back to the family; retire sideways, keeping your eye on the good people, and let your last glance be full of sunshine.

Salesmen did not receive an order by saying "good day" and immediately turning their backs to the family. This will never do. It is not retreating in good order, with colors flying. The proper way is to retire backwards or sideways saying: "I think you will yet conclude to order a copy, and when you do, you can drop me a line in the post office." While doing this, shower smiles on the people as bountiful as though you had received an order for 10 copies—then walk off treading the ground as though victory sat enthroned upon your brow; to do this will require much effort on your part at first, but practice will make perfect, and it must be done. Though some hours, or even days, may prove financially fruitless, yet time will show all to be well at the close of the week, if you push steadily on.

Lee's Surrender at Appomattox Court House
Personal Memoirs of U.S. Grant, Volume II, 1886

I had known General Lee in the old army, and had served with him in the Mexican War; but did not suppose, owing to the difference in our age and rank, that he would remember me, while I would more naturally remember him distinctly, because he was the chief of staff of General Scott in the Mexican War. When I had left camp that morning I had not expected so soon the result that was then taking place, and consequently was in rough garb. I was without a sword, as I usually was when on horseback on the field, and wore a soldier's blouse for a coat, with the shoulder straps of my rank to indicate to the army who I was. When I went into the house I found General Lee. We greeted each other, and after shaking hands, took our seats. I had my staff with me, a good portion of whom were in the room during the whole of the interview. What General Lee's feelings were I do not know. As he was a man of much dignity, with an impassible face, it was impossible to say whether he felt inwardly glad that the end had finally come, or felt sad over the result, and was too manly to show it. Whatever his feelings, they were entirely concealed from my observation; but my own feelings, which had been quite jubilant on the receipt of his letter, were sad and depressed. I felt like anything rather than rejoicing at the downfall of a foe who had fought so long and valiantly, and had suffered so much for a cause, though that cause was, I believe, one of the worst for which a people ever fought, and one for which there was the least excuse. I do not question, however, the sincerity of the great mass of those who were opposed to us. General Lee was dressed in a full uniform which was entirely new, and was wearing a sword of considerable value, very likely the sword which had been presented by the State of Virginia; at all events, it was an entirely different sword from the one that would ordinarily be worn in the field. In my rough traveling suit, the uniform of a private with the straps of a lieutenant-general, I must have contrasted very strangely with a man so handsomely dressed, six feet high and of faultless form. But this was not a matter that I thought of until afterwards. We soon fell into a conversation about old army times. He remarked that he remembered me very well in the old army; and I told him that as a matter of course I remembered him perfectly, but from the difference in our rank and years (there being about sixteen years' difference in our ages), I had thought it very likely that I had not attracted his attention sufficiently to be remembered by him after such a long interval. Our conversation grew so pleasant that I almost forgot the object of our meeting. After the conversation had run on in this style for some time, General Lee called my attention to the object of our meeting, and said that he had asked for this interview for the purpose of getting from me the terms I proposed to give his army. I said that I meant merely that his army should lay down their arms, not to take them up again during the continuance of the war unless duly and properly exchanged. He said that he had so understood my letter. Then we gradually fell off again into conversation about matters foreign to the subject which had brought us together. This continued for some little time, when General Lee again interrupted the course of the conversation by suggesting that the terms I proposed to give his army ought to be written out.

Editor's Drawer, from a Western correspondent
Harper's New Monthly Magazine, **May 1886**

I recently listened to a debate in one of the school lyceums of this city upon the momentous question of "woman suffrage."

The debater upon the "anti-women" side was doubtless engaged in his first effort, and this fact, together with a slight impediment of speech and a most original series of arguments, combined to produce one of the funniest and most unanswerable speeches I've ever heard. Here it is, almost in full:

"Ladies and gentlemen, the first thing to find out is w-w-what man was m-made for, and what w-w-woman was made for. God created Adam first, and put him in the Garden of Eden. T-then he made Eve, and p-put her there, too. If he hadn't created Eve, there never would have been all the s-s-sin there is now in this w-world. If He hadn't made Eve, she never would have p-p-picked the apple and eaten it. N-n-no she never would have picked it and g-given it to Adam to eat. Paul in his epistles said woman should k-k-keep still. And besides, ladies and gentlemen, women couldn't fill the offices. I d-d-defy you to p-point to a woman in this city or c-country that could be sheriff. Would a woman turn out in the dead of night to track and arrest a m-m-murderer? I say n-no! Ten to one she would elope w-w-with him!" And amid thunders of applause and laughter, the gallant defender of men's rights triumphantly took his seat.

A student of "Squire" Farley, a distinguished lawyer of Groton Massachusetts, says to the Squire one day, "I cannot understand how circumstantial evidence can be stronger than positive testimony."

"I will illustrate it," said the Squire. "My milkman brings a can of milk, and says, 'Squire, I know that this is pure milk, for I have milked it from the cow, washed the can thoroughly, strained it into the can, and nobody else has handled it.' Now when I take the stopper from the can, out leaps a bullfrog. Surely the frog is stronger evidence than the man."

⤜⤛⤜⤛⤜⤛⤜⤛

Editor's Study
Harper's New Monthly Magazine, **May 1886**

Mr. Robert Louis Stevenson, in his new romance, *The Strange Case of Dr. Jekyll and Mr. Hyde*, follows the lines explored by Mr. Edward Bellamy in this romance of Miss Ludington's sister. But the Patent Office abounds in simultaneously invented machinery, and, at any rate, Mr. Stevenson may claim an improvement upon the apparatus of Mr. Bellamy. The American writer supposed several selves in each human being, capable of meeting one another in a different state of existence. Mr. Stevenson immensely simplifies the supposition by reducing the selves to the number two—a moral self and an unmoral self. The moral self of Dr. Jekyll, who, by the use of a certain drug, liberated Mr. Hyde, his unmoral self or evil principle, went about wreaking all his bad passions without the inconvenience of substantial remorse; all he had to do was take the infusion of that potent salt and become Dr. Jekyll again. The trouble in the end was that Mr. Hyde, from being at first smaller and feebler than Dr. Jekyll, outgrew him and formed the habit of coming forth without the use of the salt. Dr. Jekyll was obliged to kill them both.

The romancer cannot often be taken very seriously, we suppose. He seems commonly to be working out a puzzle, and at last we have produced an intellectual toy; but Mr. Stevenson, who is inevitably a charming and sympathetic writer, and whom we first knew as the author of certain poems of deep meaning and sincerity, does something more than this in his romance.

He not only fascinates, he impresses upon the reader the fact that if we indulge the evil in us, it outgrows the good. The lesson is not quite new, and in enforcing it he becomes dangerously near the verge of allegory, for it is one of the hard conditions of romance that his personages starting with a *parti pris* can rarely be characters with a living growth, but are apt to be types, limited to the expression of one principle, simple, elemental, lacking the God-given complexity of motive which we find in all the human beings we know.

Child Life, Curiosity and Other Matters
Ballou's Monthly Magazine, July 1886

Many a child goes astray, not because there is a want of prayer or virtue at home, but simply because the home lacks sunshine. A child needs smiles as much as flowers need sunbeams. Children look little beyond the present moment. If a thing pleases, they are apt to seek; if it displaces, they are apt to avoid it. If home is the place where faces are sour, and words harsh, and fault finding is ever in the ascendant, they will spend as many hours as possible elsewhere.

Things Pleasant and Otherwise
Ballou's Monthly Magazine, July 1886

DAVID Key, of Tennessee, told a good story of a man in the mountain region of his state, who was a stereotyped candidate for local offices of all descriptions, but who would never give a decided opinion upon any question. On one occasion when he was a candidate for the position of Sheriff, there was great excitement on the enforcement of the school tax. He addressed quite a gathering at a muster, but evaded the only question the audience wanted to hear about, and just as he was closing a fellow shouted

"Tell us about your school tax. Are you for it or are you not?"

The crowd cheered, and the orator, thus pressed for a declaration of opinion, said

"Gentlemen, you have a right to ask for an answer. I have no concealment to make. I am a frank man, and to you I say in all frankness, if it is a good thing I am for it, if it is a bad thing I am against it."

Among the Wild Indians, Corabelle Fellows
The Word Carrier, January 1886

The sight that grieves me most is to see women doing work that is much too hard for them, when they have children that need their care and strength. It is hard to sit by and see the men allow their wives to bring great heavy wood upon their backs, while they (the men) idle their time away, generally preparing for a dance in the evening, with paint, ornaments, and feathers. I hope the day will come when these heathen customs will be done away with, and the man will learn that his first Christian duty is to his wife and children; to shield them from these things, and be noble enough to do the hard work. The women will have to learn to be more cleanly, and out of scanty material have their homes pleasant and neat. Oh, how much there is for most of them to learn.

The Indian children were all most anxious to be noticed. "He Mye" ("This is I") was their constant phrase. It was their way of showing they could answer the question, that they wanted to be invited to my room, that they were standing at my desk and wanted me to acknowledge their value and presence. The smallest girls were a constant delight. I marveled at their patience and ability in sewing. Before the year was out, they were making all manner of undergarments.

இ~இ~இ~இ~இ~இ~இ~இ

The Road to Renown, Indicated by an event in the Illinois Metropolis
Logansport Daily Pharos, June 25, 1887

Chicago, June 25—The fuss and feathers kicked up over the presence of the Boston "$10,000 beauty," Mike Kelly, the base ballist, in this city Friday could not have been surpassed had he been some distinguished statesman or philanthropist, and to say that baseball circles were greatly worked up on the occasion is putting it mildly. The noted "all rounder" put up at the Leland, the most "recherché" hotel in the city, and was waited upon as soon after his arrival as could be thought of by a host of admirers of himself and the national game. Reporters in squads hung on his remarks regarding the momentous question as to who would carry off the pennant this year, and other kindred subjects, with ears wide open and pencils poised to catch the full significance of what he said and fix it indelibly on the pages of history as recorded in the daily paper, while a number of the more enthusiastic citizens went to a great expense in procuring a floral offering which was seven feet high and proportionately wide and thick, of the choicest flowers to present to him at the ball park.

As the day wore on, a crowd gathered at the Leland Hotel, where the visitors were stopping. There were four singers in somber raiment in the throng and they sang a meaningless but highly complimentary song to Kelly. Then a cry came for a speech, but the ball player could not speak, owing to a lame leg. The four men in somber raiment sang another song, and then the crowd surged upon the ballplayer and shook his great brown hands. The spectacle was affecting, sublime. A great man was among his friends again. The noon hour had passed when the Chicago players were driven up in front of the hotel to escort Kelly and his colleagues to the park. Flint, Baldwin, Burns and Williamson were in the first carriage. The second vehicle was occupied by Clarkson, Sunday, Darling, and Ryan, and the third by Geiss, Sullivan, Pfeiffer, and Daly. Then came the carriage in which only Mike and Anson were to ride. It was drawn by four bay horses and a long, cadaverous looking man in a funeral plug-hat was on the box.

It was a little after 1 o'clock when the tall drum major in front of Austin's band and all of the carriages slung his staff high into the air. There was an explosion of triumphant melody and the march began amid a roar of cheers. No exalted soldier, fresh from the shot and shell river cities of his enemy, need ask for greater homage than was paid to Mr. Kelly by the baseball cranks of Chicago. A howling, surging mass of humanity swayed against the big banger's barouche, and above the din and uproar of the rabble were exultant shrieks of jeweled cornets and tuneful grunts of tuba and trombone. Anson and Kelly dipped their caps whenever people were wildly demonstrative, and once or twice the man from Boston waved his hand to someone familiar in the crowd. The procession moved west on Madison as far as Throop Street. Crowds lined the sidewalks the entire distance, and at times the cheering was so great as to be almost deafening. It was 2:50 o'clock when the carriages swung into the park from the Throop Street entrance. As the procession, still headed by the puffing musicians, marched towards the diamond over the green turf, a roar of cheers burst from the 12,000 people packed in the stands and encircling the grounds proper. The tumult grew deafening as Kelly's familiar face came nearer the plate, and when he stepped upon the turf near home plate the cheering could have been heard five blocks away.

And after all, the first break of the phenomenon when play opened was to muff an easy fly that one of the Chicago boys sent right into his hands. The game was a batter's game from the start. Both clubs put their crack pitchers in the box—Clarkson for Chicago and Radburne for Boston—and Flint and Daly kept watch behind the bat. But the clubs had no respect for the ball tossers, and the fielders were kept busy hunting leather through the game, as the score shows—Chicago: 15, Boston: 18. But Mike was troubled with "Charley-horses."

Hornung was the first man to bat for Boston. The great left fielder hit the ball along the third base line, and Burns juggled it so long that the batsman reached first in safety. Then came only Mike. He hobbled up to the plate and was getting into position when two ushers from the grand stand loped up to the plate with a big floral diamond, across the face of which was the word in immortelles: "Kelly." The piece was surmounted by flags, and was held in place, easel fashion, by two bats. A jockey's cap, made of red, white, and blue silk, accompanied the floral present, which was from the player's friends. The crowd cheered and compelled Kelly to wear his flashy new bonnet. Whether the spectacle Kelly presented boodooed Clarkson will never be known, but it is certain that the Chicago pitcher couldn't place the balls anywhere near the plate, and the batsman was sent to his base. While Kelly was waiting for a ball he could reach, Hornung started out to steal second. Flint hoisted the ball over Pfeiffer's head, and before it could be returned to the diamond the left fielder was on third. Kelly now attempted to duplicate Hornung's performance, but his dickey legs could not carry him to second ahead of Flint's sharp throw to Pfeiffer, and he returned to his bench with an unutterable look of disgust. Flint neither laughed nor smiled. His weather beaten face fell apart from the apex of his nose and slid around the back of his ears. It was the greatest exhibition of facial expression ever seen on a ball field. Wise's foul tip was squeezed by Flint and then Nash reached first on five bad balls and stole second with a rush. With two men on the bases, Morrill popped up a fly which Sullivan pulled down with both hands. For Chicago, Sunday hit sharply to Nash and was thrown out at first. Ryan burled the bat Dunlap gave him against one of Radburne's curves and sent the ball spinning out into left field. The young man then tried to steal second, and was nipped by Daily to Kelly. Sullivan struck out. Just as the Champions were going into the field, Lionel Adams of New Orleans presented Anson with a floral basket inscribed in immortelles: "Old Man."

Since about 1872 efforts had been put forth by every agent to make agriculturalists of these Indians, but the soil and the climate will not allow it.... It may be said that the Indian has been furnished with an occupation to employ his time; but I see no good in keeping these Indians employed at what they cannot make a living in this country.

—United States Office of Indian Affairs, Annual Report, 1887

Casey at the Bat, by Ernest Thayer, 1888

The Outlook wasn't brilliant for the Mudville nine that day

The score stood four to two, with but one inning more to play.

And then when Cooney died at first, and Barrows did the same,

A sickly silence fell upon the patrons of the game.

A straggling few got up to go in deep despair. The rest

Clung to that hope which springs eternal in the human breast;

They thought, if only Casey could get but a whack at that,

We'd put up even money, now, with Casey at the bat.

But Flynn preceded Casey, as did also Jimmy Blake,

And the former was a lulu and the latter was a cake;

So upon that stricken multitude grim melancholy sat,

For there seemed but little chance of Casey's getting to the bat.

But Flynn let drive a single, to the wonderment of all,

And Blake, the much despised, tore the cover off the ball;

And when the dust had lifted, and the men saw what had occurred,

There was Jimmy safe at second and Flynn a-hugging third.

Then from 5,000 throats and more there rose a lusty yell;

It rumbled throuh the valley, it rattled in the dell;

It knocked upon the mountain and recoiled upon the flat,

For Casey, mighty Casey, was advancing to the bat.

There was ease in Casey's manner as he stepped into his place;

There was pride in Casey's bearing and a smile on Casey's face.

And when, responding to the cheers, he lightly doffed his hat,

No stranger in the crowd could doubt 'twas Casey at the bat.

Ten thousand eyes were on him as he rubbed his hands with dirt;

Five thousand tongues applauded when he wiped them on his shirt.

Then while the writhing pitcher ground the ball into his hip,

Defiance gleamed in Casey's eye, a sneer curled Casey's lip.

And now the leather-covered sphere came hurtling through the air,

And Casey stood a-watching it in haughty grandeur there.

Close by the sturdy batsman the ball unheeded sped,

"That ain't my style," said Casey. "Strike one," the umpire said.

From the benches, black with people, there went up a muffled roar,

Like the beating of the storm-waves on a stern and distant shore.

"Kill him! Kill the umpire!" shouted someone on the stand;

And it's likely they'd a-killed him had not Casey raised his hand.

With a smile of Christian charity great Casey's visage shone;

He stilled the rising tumult; he bade the game go on;

He signaled to the pitcher, and once more the spheroid flew;

But Casey still ignored it, and the umpire said, "Strike two."

"Fraud!" cried the maddened thousands, and echo answered fraud;

But one scornful look from Casey and the audience was awed.

They saw his face grow stern and cold, they saw his muscles strain,

And they knew that Casey wouldn't let that ball go by again.

The sneer is gone from Casey's lip, his teeth are clenched in hate;

He pounds with cruel violence his bat upon the plate.

And now the pitcher holds the ball, and now he lets it go,

And now the air is shattered by the force of Casey's blow.

Oh, somewhere in this favored land the sun is shining bright;

The band is playing somewhere, and somewhere hearts are light,

And somewhere men are laughing, and somewhere children shout;

But there is no joy in Mudville—mighty Casey has struck out.

ॐ❄ॐ❄ॐ❄ॐ❄

The Ghost Dance, *Chronicle of Indian Wars*, 1889

In 1889, the [Ghost Dance] movement was suddenly revived when another Northern Paiute, Wovoka (1856-1932), was stricken with fever during a total eclipse of the sun. He recovered and reported that, during his illness, he had been transported to the afterworld, where he had seen legions of dead Indians happily at work and play, and where the Supreme Being had told him to return to his people, to tell them to love one another, to work, and to live in peace

with whites. The Supreme Being promised that, if they followed these injunctions faithfully, they would be reunited with the dead, death would cease to exist, and the white race would vanish…

Although Wovoka's message was explicitly specific, Teton Sioux leaders of the Pine Ridge Reservation suppressed the injunction to live peacefully and used the Ghost Dance deliberately to foment an uprising. At Pine Ridge and elsewhere, special "ghost shirts" were fashioned of white muslin and decorated with the sun, moon, stars and eagles or sage hens. The shirts, it was declared, offered protection against many dangers, especially bullets.

Sweet Tooters
Elyria Democrat (Ohio), December 19, 1889

The Marine band this is smallest national band in the world, yet one the most deservedly famous. Until 1878, the band was composed of 76 pieces, but Secretary of the Navy Hon. Richard Thompson reduced the number to 38, and it so remains until this day. At the Paris Exposition of 1888, a prize was competed for by nine national bands, in the presence of 30,000 spectators. It was one of the grandest musical carnivals in the history of civilization. In the Austrian band, there were 70 pieces, the Prussian, 87; Bavarian, 52; Baden, 54; Belgian, 59; Holland, 56; French, 62; Spanish, 64, and Russian, 71. The prize was awarded to the Bavarian Band. The British and American national bands did not compete. The above facts were communicated to me by Mr. John Philip Sousa, the leader of the Marine Band. He added: "The German national band is now composed of 47 pieces; the Austrian has from 70 to 90; and the British band has 60 to 75 pieces. You can see, therefore, that the Marine Band of only 38 pieces is comparatively a small band; what we lack numerically we tried make up in quality. When it comes to supplying volume of harmony, we managed to make ourselves heard."

Yes, and during the recent conclave of Sir Knights Templar in this city, the people of Washington were led to look with greater pride than ever upon the Marine Band, for by contrast with the celebrated bands of other cities, the Marine Band demonstrated its great superiority. Accustomed as we were to hear the great orchestra, for it is such, our people have come to take it as a matter of course that the Marine Band shall always play well, but the recent parade participated in by 20,000 plumed Knights and about 100 bands from every city in the nation awakened local pride and stirred enthusiasm to fevered heat. When the red-coated musicians, with their unpretentious leader, marched by, steadily, carefully, methodically, as one great organ fingered by a master, it seemed as though the very air was filled with the "sound of a great Amen," and that the lost chord had been found. Mr. Sousa, on the following evening, said: "Yes, the band played well, never better, in fact; I am proud of them. In fact, we are all proud of each other; we are really a band of brothers now, in the sense that there's an esprit du corps such as was never before developed in the band. Every man is proud of his own part, does it well and conscientiously, and all together are proud of their work and perfectly confident so that we do not falter nor question whether we are doing well or not."

Where the Pistol Toters Live
Atlanta Constitution, May 2, 1890

"A close reading of the new columns of the Northern dailies convinced us long ago that, despite the talk about the hip pocket in the South, there is a much larger percentage of pistol toters in the North than in this region. If the newspapers tell the truth, young men, boys, and even women in the North carry pistols much more generally than was ever the custom in the South. In this section our laws against carrying concealed weapons are very strict, and they are rigidly enforced. Up North, whatever the laws may be on the subject, they do not appear to be respected. *The New York Tribune* ought to be a good authority on this matter. It says that a very fair percentage of the men one meets on the streets of New York have revolvers stored away somewhere about their persons. It thinks that this percentage is larger on Broadway than on the less pretentious streets, and says that if a mad dog should take a turn around Union Square the spectator would be astonished to see the number of men who would draw pistols."

❧❧❧❧❧❧❧

Diseases Incident to the Season
Demorest's Family Magazine, April 1890

"During the winter and spring months, the fat babies—with more adipose than muscle, more loose, flabby tissue than good vital development—will be having the croup. A little exposure will bring it on.

The 'depurators' are not all doing faithful work: the liver is sluggish and skin is torpid, and very little chilling on the surface will send the debris of the system into the wrong direction. Instead of being carried off through the natural outlets, and the system purified from day to day, it will remain in the blood; and the first check that is given to the skin depuration will turn all this waste in on the mucous surfaces. If the bowels should chance to be the weakest part, we shall have a case of diarrhea or dysentery; if the lungs should incline to be weak, then beware of an attack of pneumonia: though with the general conditions before referred to, it will be in all probability the croup.

The child may have had these croupy attacks before. If so, the mother will at once understand the situation: the wheezy breathing will give her a note of warning, and the doctor will be immediately summoned, for this is a disease which you cannot afford to trifle with. Often a few hours will develop symptoms and conditions that are necessarily fatal. But supposing it to be a first attack: the mother may not be made aware of the fact that the child is seriously ailing, and when at last she concludes to send for the physician, he will know, the moment he enters the room, that it will be a struggle between life and death. The sharp 'crowing' sound that is made as the child tries to get his breath tells that the 'false membrane' is already formed or forming, and that the chances are already against the patient."

❧❧❧❧❧❧❧

This report, written in 1908 by William Leiserson, detailed the struggles of the Jewish labor movement in New York in the 1890s

"In February 1890, the cloakmakers began to rebel against the reduction in wages and the bad treatment to which they were subjected at the hands of the contractors. Shop after shop went on strike, and they called upon the United Hebrew Trades to conduct the strikes for them. That body sent a committee of three, among them Joseph Barondess, a delegate from the

Knee Pants Makers, to 92 Hester Street, where most of the strikers were assembled. The committee found the men from each shop conducting separate meetings in different rooms. To each of the meetings they repeated their plan of uniting all the strikers in one strong union. It was hailed with joy, and Barondess was elected to lead the united strikers.

The strike lasted six weeks, and ended with a complete victory for the union. Even Meyer Jonasson, the most prominent cloak manufacturer in New York, was forced to come to the basement at 92 Hester Street, the striker's headquarters, to sign the union agreement. All together, 3,500 cloakmakers had been out, but many went back to work within three weeks when some employers began to concede to the demands.

As a result of the victory the Cloakmakers' Union became very strong. Immediately after the settlement it had 2,800 members divided into nine branches, one for each cloak manufacturing house. This form of organization was found unsatisfactory and the executive committee decided to divide the union into branches of 300 members each. By May 1, 1890, the union had grown to eleven branches with over 3,000 members. It had good control of the trade, and the employers were afraid of it. For a short time there was peace. Toward the end of May, however, ten manufacturers suddenly locked out all their cloakmakers. They refused to employ any more union men.

The struggle was most bitter. At first it seems as if the union would be defeated, but Barondess got the cutters and the contractors to join the operators against the manufacturers. On June 16, 1890, Operators and Cloakmakers Union No. 1, Cloak and Suit Cutters' Union, and the Contractors' Union, entered into an agreement to combine their strength against the manufacturers' association until the unions were recognized. The united force held a mass meeting in Cooper Union, where addresses were delivered in Yiddish and English. Six thousand people were present at the meeting.

The sympathy of the press during this strike was with the strikers. Many New York papers opened subscription lists to help them. The suffering of starving cloakmakers fighting for a chance to live they described in great headlines. When, after striking for two months some of the men became violent and attacked the scabs, the papers said they had been driven to desperation by hunger.

The public helped the strikers in many ways. A Jewish congregation offered dinners at 5 cents a piece to cloakmakers with union cards. Collections for their benefit were taken up in churches, department stores, and bank houses. A certain Professor Garside, of whom very little was known except that he was an eloquent speaker, became prominent in this strike as a friend of the cloakmakers. He brought to the union every day sacks full of money which he had gathered by collections throughout the city.

The lockout had lasted nine weeks when the manufacturers asked the union to send a committee to settle all offences. The joy of the strikers was unbounded. A monster mass meeting was held in Cooper Union to celebrate the victory. The large auditorium was packed and many were turned away.

The negotiations of the committee with the manufacturers lasted three days. Then an agreement was brought to the Union, signed by the manufacturers. It was written in English. Since few cloakmakers could understand the language, the strike committee decided to take the agreement to Abraham Cahan to find out whether it was a good settlement or not. Cahan read it and was astounded. 'It was the worse settlement that could have been made,' he declared, and advised them to call a mass meeting immediately, and there he read the agreement to the audience in their own language.

That mass meeting will be remembered by those who attended it as long as they live. Cahan read the agreement point by point and there arose cries of 'Treachery! Villainy! Let us continue the strike!'

A vote was taken by ballot on the question of remaining on strike. The affirmative received 1,536 votes, while 20 voted against striking. Then came the question of getting funds. All the old sources were exhausted. But hundreds of men and women took off their rings, watches, and earrings. With tears in their eyes they took them to the chairman on the platform and told him to sell or pawn their jewelry, only that they may have money to continue the strike. In a quarter of an hour there was thrown on the chairman's table over $10,000 worth of jewelry.

This meeting was fully described in the newspapers the next day. The manufacturers saw that the strikers were bound to hold out for a long time. In two weeks an agreement was signed granting all the demands of the union. The important difference between the agreements was that the first one submitted made no mention of a price list. It had left the employers free to lower wages."

ଈଶଈଶଈଶଈଶଈଶ

Leadville Construction Projects
The Western Architect and Building News, June 1890

"For M. Myman: two-story brick block, 40x110; cost $10,000. H.C. Dimick, architect. Contract not let.

For Harrison Reduction Works: two ore houses, 40x80; cost $1,500. H.C. Dimick, contractor.

For Maid of Erin mine: assay office; cost $1,300, H.C. Dimick, architect. Contract not let.

For D.A. Sullivan: one-story frame store, 25x44; cost $3,000. W.W. Bragg, carpenter; day work.

Mr. George Thomas is having a frame dwelling built on East Twelfth Street, cost $1,000. Jon B. Pott is the carpenter; day work."

"Government should not support the people," President Grover Cleveland said, after vetoing a congressional appropriation of $10,000 in seeds for Texas farmers. "I do not believe that the power and duty of the general government ought to be extended to the relief of individual suffering which is in no manner properly related to the public service or benefit… The lesson should constantly be enforced that though the people support the government, government should not support the people."

Gilbert and Sullivan
Sandusky Daily Register (Ohio), January 2, 1890

That famous comic opera-literary-musical co-partnership acting under the firm name of Gilbert & Sullivan has scored another success in their latest production the *Gondoliers, or the King of Barataria*. It was produced at the Savoy Theatre, in London, early in December. The piece, both as to music and play, has been very favorably criticized. Doubtless it will soon be produced in America.

When Gilbert and Sullivan appeared before the public as claimants for attention as comic opera writers, Offenbach was the zenith star. He produced a great number of burlesques. Mme. Aimee was the great medium through which Offenbach's operas became familiar to the American people. The operas were French and so was Aimee. The two went well together. As the dialogue was in a language that few Americans can understand, the operas were not very objectionable. At any rate they took amazingly.

But there was nothing either English or American in Offenbach's operas. The public had become, in a measure, saturated with them when a little cloud, no bigger than a man's hand, appeared which was destined to obscure Offenbach and drive him out of America altogether. *Her Majesty's Ship Pinafore*, a new comic opera, was put on the boards. It was written by Arthur Sullivan and W.S. Gilbert, the latter having published some time before. The work, which showed considerable ability in the comic line, *Pinafore* was English to the core. The music, the words, the action were remarkable and together produced a gem. Besides, there was in it a most delightful satire on the chief lord of the admiralty of the British Navy.

There was something prairie fire-like in the way *Pinafore* took. To have heard it once was nothing. Almost everyone heard it half a dozen times. And many people can say they had listened to from ten to fifteen representations of it. It was the beginning of a new school, and so excellent in all parts that it seemed the public would never grow tired of it.

Then came *The Pirates of Penzance* from the same brains. The novelty was not there, of course; that was all in *Pinafore*, but the public was ready for more, and *The Pirates* was a success. Oscar Wilde was at that time exciting the tension of the people of London, and the next opera Gilbert and Sullivan produced was *Patience*, a satire on Wilde and his followers. It contained a great number of very pretty airs and the music, though not as inspiring as that of *Pinafore*, was very refined. It had an excellent run.

Since then the partners have been bringing out operas almost without limit. *Princess Ida* was based on Tennyson's poem "The Princess," which, something of a satire in itself, gave a favorable opportunity for Gilbert and Sullivan. Since *Princess* there has come out *The Mikado*, *Ruddygore*, *The Golden Legend* and others.

Costly Gifts for a Bride, Nuptials of
John Jacob Astor and Miss Ava Dowle Willing, 1891

United Press, February 18, 1891

"PHILADELPHIA, Feb. 17—Miss Ava Dowle Willing, daughter of Mr. and Mrs. Edward Shippen Willing, was married to Mr. John Jacob Astor, of New York, at 1 o'clock this afternoon.

The wedding ceremony, which was witnessed by about 150 of the immediate relatives and close friends of the Astor and Willing families, was performed by the Rev. William Nelson McVickar, rector of the fashionable Episcopal Church of the Holy Trinity, at the beautiful home of the bride's parents on South Broad Street.

The fact that the wedding was celebrated in Lent was not allowed to detract from the brilliance of the occasion.

At the wedding breakfast the bridal table was set with 18 covers. The dining room itself was ornamented with whole chimes of wedding bells. Everything about the table was in pure white, only white bride's roses, white orchids and white violets being used.

A reception was held from 3 to 5 o'clock, and between those hours the house was filled with representative society people of Philadelphia, New York, Boston, Washington, Baltimore and other leading cities.

No Philadelphia bride ever received presents as magnificent as those sent to Miss Willing. Their aggregate runs high up in the hundreds of thousands of dollars. The groom's gift was a tiara of diamonds, possibly unsurpassed by any in America. His father gave a double bowknot of diamonds, from which hangs a pendant of huge brilliance about the size of a nickel. He also gave a diamond necklace and crescent of diamonds and sapphires some four inches in length.

The principal gifts of Mrs. Astor were five diamond stars, each as large as a silver half-dollar. These jewels were enclosed in a massive box of solid silver. Mrs. Astor also gave eight silver dishes, each about three feet in length.

Mr. and Mrs. Orme Wilson sent a pair of magnificent silver candelabra over a yard long. Mr. and Mrs. J. Coleman Drayton's presents were two silver dishes of exquisite open work. Mr. and Mrs. Roosevelt sent a large centerpiece of silver. Altogether, there were upwards of 300 presents.

The wedding tour consists of a trip South, the bride and groom keeping their immediate destination secret. On March 23 they will sail for Europe."

How Cartridges Are Made
Harper's Weekly, January 24, 1891

In no other branch of industry are more ingenuity and human skill employed than in the making of instruments and materials to take life. The Patent Office is full of models of firearms and devices for the speedy changing of men from tall to long, and the number is being increased from day to day. The inventive genius of America, upon which the optimistic of coast defense rely for the protection of American ports from foreign foes in case of sudden war, is not idle. It is always busy, and just as ready to sell its product to the foreign foe as to anybody else.

If any foreign power harbored a secret design to make war upon the United States next year, it could contract today with the great rifle and ammunition manufacturers of this country for weapons and cartridges enough to equip all its soldiers and leave the United States unarmed, except with a lot of heavy, clumsy, single-shot rifles and a few tons of spoiled ammunition.

In the matter of weapons, this country would be at a great disadvantage if called upon to engage in conflict with a European power, because the machinery and tools for turning out rifles of a new model cannot be made in a day, but it would not take the great cartridge factories long to fill the belts of the largest army that was ever mustered.

The most extensive plant for the making of cartridges is in Bridgeport, Connecticut, and its capacity is two million cartridges of all kinds per day. The machinery adapted to military ammunition of the pattern now in use can turn out 750,000 loaded shells in a working day, certainly enough to carry on any ordinary single engagement.

❦❧❦❧❦❧❦❧❦

Electro-Plating
The Youth's Companion, February 19, 1891

Whenever a current of electricity passes through a liquid which contains metallic salt in solution, the metal of the salt would be deposited upon the place where the current leaves the liquid. The ends of the wires which bring and carry away the current are called electrodes. The electrode which is connected with the zinc and the battery is the one which receives the deposit.

This principle lies at the foundation in the process of electro-plating, by means of which any cheap sheet metal is covered with a thin coating of a dearer metal.

To experiment with electro-plating you will need three things—a battery, a plating bath and a means of cleaning the article which is to be plated.

For a battery, three cells of any of the batteries hitherto described will suffice. Connect the zinc of No. 1 to the copper or carbon of No. 2, the zinc of No. 2 to the carbon of No. 3 and the remaining terminals of No. 1 and No. 3 are connected with the bath.

As a receptacle for the solution, use a pint bowl—a cheap finger bowl, or bread and milk bowl with wide bottom, will do. Across the top of this, place two bright copper or brass wires, an eighth of an inch in diameter. Connect the ends of these with a terminal of the battery.

To plate with copper, fill the bowl with a solution made by dissolving two ounces of blue vitriol in a pint of boiling water.

To plate with silver, use a solution of 70 grains each silver cyanide and potassium cyanide in a little less than a pint of water. These salts are poisonous, and the hand should not be brought to the mouth after handling them.

Upon the wire, which is connected with the zinc of the battery, hang, by means of an S-shaped hook of bright copper wire, the article to be plated. Upon the other wire suspend in the same manner a piece of sheet copper, about the same size as the article.

In order that the article may receive an even coating of metal, it must be thoroughly cleaned.... After this it should not be touched by the hands, but must be handled with tissue paper. The perspiration from the hands would prevent the deposit from adhering. In some cases it is necessary to dip the article, for a few minutes, in nitric acid, and then thoroughly rinse with water.

After the articles have received a sufficiently thick coating, they may be removed from the bath and washed in an abundance of water. The copper needs no further attention; but silver-plated articles appear dull, and will need to be polished. This can be done with a chamois skin and any ordinary polishing powder.

࿙࿚࿙࿚࿙࿚࿙࿚

An Ermine by Flash-Light
The Youth's Companion, February 19, 1891

A subscriber has recently sent us a photograph of a very large and beautiful ermine, in its white winter pelage, taken under somewhat peculiar circumstances.

Our correspondence family consists of two daughters, young ladies, 16 and 18 years of age, who last summer became much interested in photography. Their home is in one of the extreme Northern states of the country, where they have a farm, and what is more to the point of our story, a large hennery.

One morning about the middle of December, it was discovered that three fine "Plymouth Rock" chickens lay on the floor beneath their roost, dead—the brain of each having been very cleverly and cleanly removed through a small hole near the base of the skull.

Immediately on observing this peculiarity in the marauder's manner of attack, our friend fancied that a weasel had levied upon him, but after noting the distance which the animal had been obliged to leap, laterally, to reach the roost, he came to the conclusion that it could hardly have been a common weasel, and must have been the weasel's larger and less frequently seen congener, the stoat, or ermine.

He understood the habits of this little epicure among the mustelidae sufficiently well to note that it would, in all probability, return for the brains of three more chickens the following night, and continue the process indefinitely, unless its career was summarily cut short.

The hennery building is a large one, not easily closed to the entry of so small and insidious a robber, and he could think of no better way of procedure than to post himself, with a bull's-eye lantern and a small shot-gun, just within the doorway, leading from a passage into the hennery, at about level with the chicken roost.

Sitting quietly here, he thought, at first sounds of commotion from the chickens, he might be able to turn the line relied upon the rooster, and shoot the ferocious little disturber.

They had no sooner broached this plan at the breakfast table, than his daughters proposed an amendment.

"Let us watch with you!" they exclaimed, "With our camera and flashlight, we'll get a picture of the rascal! We will flash the lights and get a photograph, and you may do the shooting. We will see whether you can shoot quicker than we can take a picture!"

As they were quite enthusiastic, the plan was adopted. During the day the camera was prepared for instantaneous photography, also the little alcohol lamp along with the rubber bulb for puffing a pinch of magnesia powder into the flame, to produce the kind of light necessary for securing a picture. The camera was focused as accurately as possible, in advance, and all made ready for quick work.

The party began the vigil at nine in the evening, well wrapped in blankets and robes, for the mercury was almost down to zero.

They had long to wait. It was after one o'clock in the morning before the ermine was heard, effecting an entrance at a small crevice beneath the eaves of the building.

A minute or two later, they heard it leap down upon the roost. A sudden outcry from one of the fowls succeeded, immediately. One of the girls then flashed the lights; then they all plainly saw the white, slim creature on the back of one of the speckled chickens, in the very act of turning his neck to bite into the brain.

A perfect picture was secured. And, meantime, paterfamilias blazed away with his gun, and riddled both the ermine and the chicken with shot. He was too late to get his part of the performance into the photograph.

Ta-ra-ra-boom-dee-ay,
attributed to Henry Sayers, 1891

I'm not extraordinarily shy,

And when a nice young man is nigh,

For his heart I have a try,

And faint away with tearful cry!

When the good young man in haste,

Will support me 'round the waist,

I don't come to while thus embraced,

Till of my lips he steals a taste!

Washington
The Youth's Companion, February 19, 1891

Ninety-one years have rolled away since the death of George Washington. During that long period, many brilliant reputations have shone upon us for a while, only to fade away and collapse into oblivion. His name retains all its interest for us, and probably more people have been particularly occupied of late with his career, its relics and its records than ever before.

At the great sale of Washington mementos, held a few weeks ago in Philadelphia, the prices paid even for trifling objects once possessed by the great man and his family were extraordinary.

A legal document related to the execution of his will, which his hand had never touched, brought $50, and an autographed letter $85.

A list of his slaves, written and signed by his own hand, brought $440. Two of his memorandum books brought $800. His family Bible was sold for $760, and books from his library, containing his signature or that of his wife, commanded prices varying from $60 to $150 each.

Pieces of piano music, which had been played by Miss Custis, brought considerable sums, and a dinner invitation was sold for $18.

The sale attracted universal attention, and everyone lamented that the whole collection had not been bought by Congress and deposited at Mount Vernon, where it could have been seen by every pilgrim to that sacred site.

There is a special reason for this vivid survival of his celebrity, apart from his services to this country; it is his singularly interesting career.

From his boyhood to the last week of his life, he was a prolific writer. As soon as he could write well enough, he kept a book into which he copied anything that pleased or impressed him in his reading, and carefully entered his early cipherings and surveys in a book that is preserved to the present day.

Twenty-Five Years of Change in San Antonio
history and guide of 1892

"Where stood the old adobe huts, magnificent iron, stone, and brick buildings are to be seen. Instead of the yell of the Comanche you hear the scream of the locomotive all round the city. Where the unsightly Mexican cart met the gaze, you see now the beautiful and convenient street cars, with their sleek, fat mules and their jingling bells. In the place of the mesquite thicket, where the coyote held his nightly revels, you see fine, broad avenues, lined on either side with beautiful and stately residences, surrounded with magnificent groves of shade trees and lovely gardens of flowers. Tall spires, piercing the skies, now mark the places where pious people assemble to worship God. The same spot was then occupied by the ravenous wolves that made the night hideous with their weird howls… The cobblestone sidewalks have given place to the beautiful, broad, smooth artificial stone, and the rough cobblestones of the streets have been crushed and filled until they are as smooth as the shell streets of Galveston."

The Celebration of the 350th Anniversary of Portuguese
Explorer Juan R. Cabrilho's Landing in California in 1542
Uniao Portuguesa, September 4, 1892

"On the 29th all business places closed as hundreds poured into the city…at 10:00 the representative of Governor Markham arrived…anchored offshore was the reproduction of the 'San Salvador,' built by the commission…and flying the Spanish flag. All the crew, a total of nine, was composed of Portuguese in honor of the great navigator…. Carrying a Spanish flag and cross 'Cabrilho disembarked while local Indians (taking part in the drama) knelt. Cabrilho then lifted his sword high reenacting the first claim to California…. It is difficult to describe the solemn feeling of that moment.'"

The Oakland Tribune, February 23, 1892

"On Sunday morning the new Catholic church on Chestnut Street, north of Seventh, recently built for the Portuguese members of that denomination, was dedicated to St. Joseph with appropriate ceremonies by His Grace the Right Reverend Patrick W. Riordan, Archbishop of the Diocese. The opening of the new edifice ends a long struggle for the natives of Portugal in Oakland, who have worked earnestly for a great many years to secure for themselves a place of worship where they can perform their religious duties in their native tongue. There are many hundreds of these Portuguese families in this city, and very few of them know much of the English language. In fact much difficulty was experienced at the confessional and during church ceremonies because of this fact, which ultimately led to the establishment of a Portuguese church in St. Mary's parish."

Life in Leadville
Leadville Chronicle Annual, 1892

"The correspondents of eastern papers are accustomed to representing that Sunday is a carnival day in Leadville; that the stores are open; that the saloons, the gambling houses and the questionable places of amusement flourish as on no other day; that inebriety staggers along the streets, and that sensuality parades in gorgeous apparel through all the thoroughfares. Through such assumptions and misrepresentations, with the amplifications of a readily resourceful imagination and the colorings of a gorgeous fancy, the correspondents are able to manufacture wonderfully entertaining letters that exactly suit the preconceived ideas and notions of the great mass of eastern readers. The fact is, however, that the Sabbath is well-observed in Leadville as in any other western city of life and push. The truth of the matter is that in all the great cities of the West, and especially the New West, the pushing impulses of enterprise, emulation and ambition are so strong and untiring that they scarcely permit men to stop for one day in the seven. They indeed almost push the people out of the restraining hold and beyond the controlling power of early teachings, early associations and early impressions. However, it is no uncommon thing to hear a rough, muscular miner retort to a blasphemous, arguing infidel: "See here, mister, my mother used to believe the Bible, and I'll be damned if I'll hear it abused."

H.C. Merwin
Atlantic Monthly, 1892

"The upper class, with notable exceptions, is without high aims, without sympathy, without civic pride of feeling. It has not even the personal dignity of a real aristocracy. Its sense of honor is very crude. And as this is devoted to selfish spending, so the business class is devoted to the remorseless getting, of money."

A Rich Man's Grievance
The Naiad, A Monthly Journal of Christian Education, December 1892

"The people who have the most trouble in selecting and buying holiday presents are those who have the most money. Nearly all of their friends are rich, and no present can surprise or gratify simply because it is costly. It must be unique and exquisitely beautiful, to provoke more than languid thanks. A rich man thus unburdens his mind of what he calls a grievance:

'Here I am worth $200,000; my friend Jones is worth a million; Smith counts his property at half a million; my neighbor Robinson pays taxes on $300,000. All of them have all the conveniences and luxuries that money can buy. Their wives and children are supplied with everything they need or wish. It is folly for me to buy a Christmas present, expecting by it to give them any special pleasure. They will thank me kindly, and next year would no doubt send me a present that costs twice as much as mine.

'What possible pleasure can I feel when Jones sends me for a holiday gift a volume of Shakespeare that costs $100? Or how much self-denial does it cost me to buy my wife the handsomest gold watch to be found at the jewelers?

'I have gone into the shops during Christmas week, and watched the poor people who are getting little gifts that cost $0.25 or a dollar, and I have actually envied them, knowing how much pleasure such a gift would bring to both giver and receiver.

'There are some things that riches cannot buy. One is the keen delight that comes from the exercise of self-denial in giving. That is the property of the poor. The rich know nothing of it. If there is any time in the year when I heartily wish that I were a poorer man, it is during the holidays, when so many other people are wishing they had more money.'

There is truth in this, and poor people with small purses but big hearts ought to be encouraged by it. That pair of mittens that you are knitting in the few minutes snatched from household work and drudgery, done at night when you are tired from the day's duties, will give more pleasure to you and your son than if they cost nothing more than the money expended in a mere purchase.

That simple toy, bought with hard-earned wages, will gratify your child. The children of the wealthy are not gratified by the most elaborate inventions.

Gifts that are made by loving hands are always more prized than gifts purchased with money; and the rare pleasure experienced by the poor in the presents they receive is born of the relish that comes because presents are few. And the highest joy of Christmas time does not come from the power to give costly presents, but from that loving self-denial which makes the poor rich in warm hearts and generous feelings, and in the keen realization of that spirit of which the Savior Himself spoke, when He said, "It is more blessed to give than to receive."

ॐॐॐॐॐॐॐॐ

Poverty Is Expensive
The Yorkville Enquirer, Yorkville, South Carolina, October 26, 1892

"There is nothing so expensive as poverty," says a Washington housewife. It seems paradoxical to put it so, but no poor man can afford not to be a few dollars ahead in the world. The extreme case is that of the very poor, who must pay for coal double the price charged the rich, because they have to get it by the bushel or scuttle full, and so with everything else.

The poor woman must pay $50 for a sewing machine on installments, though she could buy it for $35 cash down. Her lack of the ready cash costs her $15, that is, whereas it is the poor who ought to get everything cheaper; they have always to pay enormously more than the rich for the same things, merely because they are poor.

In extremity they must seek the pawnbroker, who again preys upon their slender resources because they have so little. Credit for anything always costs money, and the poor are those who must pay for it. "Our means are very moderate and the only reason that we get along so comfortably as we do is that we never owe for anything.

"Years ago we were always in debt, and the struggle was severe to get along, without counting the distress and annoyance incidental to owing tradesmen money. Finally, we found out what the matter was, and got square with the world through a long effort of self-denial. Our income is no greater now than it was then, but it produces at least one-third more because we have no bills. Depend upon it; a poor man cannot afford to be somewhat ahead of the world, otherwise the world will very soon get so far ahead of him that life will be a burden."

ം∕ം∕ം∕ം∕ം∕ം∕ം∕ം∕

Railroads and Immigrants, Westbound Passengers Must Have Clean Bills of Health
New York Times, September 13, 1892

All the railroads have refused to carry immigrants West unless each has a certificate from a surgeon in the employ the federal government. This action was due to the firm stand taken by the Illinois State Board of Health.

Last week Chairman IP Farmer of the Truck Line Commission received a circular from F. W. Reilly, Secretary of Illinois State Board of Health, saying that no Immigrants would be allowed to pass through the state or enter it over any road unless each was provided with a certificate signed by the physician of the Marine Hospital Service stating that he had been under inspection for a certain length of time, all danger of cholera had past, and there was no danger of smallpox.

The circular further stated that if the passengers of the road bringing them into the state had not such certificates, they would be quarantined, and at the expense of the road which carried them…

On Saturday a large number of immigrants bound West were stopped at the Grand Central Station and the New York, Ontario and Western Station. They were sent back to Ellis Island, on Sunday were sent West over the Pennsylvania.

ം∕ം∕ം∕ം∕ം∕ം∕ം∕ം∕

The Limitations of the Cash Drawer Advertisement
National Cash Register Company, 1892

I am the oldest criminal in history.

I have acted in my present capacity for many thousands of years.

I have been trusted with millions of dollars.

I have lost a great deal of this money.

I have constantly held temptation before those who have come in contact with me.

I have placed a burden upon the strong, and broken down the weak.

I have caused the downfall of many honest and ambitious young people.

I have ruined many business men who deserved success.

I have betrayed the trust of those who have depended upon me.

I am a thing of the past, a dead issue.

I am a failure.

I am the Open Cash Drawer.

"We were obliged to be away from the store most of the time so we employed a superintendent. At the end of three years, although we had sold annually about $50,000 worth of goods on which there was a large margin, we found ourselves worse off than nothing. We were in debt, and we could not account for it, because we lost nothing by bad debt and no goods had been stolen. But one day I found several bread tickets lying around loose, and discovered that our oldest clerk was favoring his friends by selling below the regular prices. Another day I noticed a certain credit customer buying groceries. At night, on looking over the blotter, I found that the clerk had forgotten to make any entry of it. This set me to thinking that the goods might often go out of the store in this way—without our ever getting a cent for them. One day we received a circular from someone in Dayton, Ohio, advertising a machine which recorded money and sales in retail stores. The price was $100. We telegraphed for two of them, and when we saw them we were astonished at the cost. They were made mostly of wood, had no cash drawer, and were very crude. But we put them in the store, and, in spite of their deficiencies, at the end of 12 months we cleared $6,000."

—John Patterson, President of the National Cash Register Company

Circular Letter

The National Cash Register Company
Dayton, Ohio, U.S.A.,
February 4, 1892

To All Managers:

We send you under separate cover devices for beating the Simplex Cash Register which consists of a lead bullet with a common horse hair attached. We want you to have your agents call on the parties who are using the Simplex Register, in your territory, and explain how easy it is to beat them. (But do not show them how to do it.)

You can easily ask the proprietor to step away about 20 feet from the machine, and then, by concealing the bullet in your hand, register any amount you want by simply dropping the bullet in the small hole directly under the amount you wish to register.

In all cases, be sure and withdraw the bullet from the machine at the same time that you open the cash drawer (that is, providing you can get the combination of the lock), which can be easily done.

Of course, if you do not want to open the cash drawer, you can step away from the machine and the proprietor (unless he has an eagle eye) cannot discover the horse hair protruding from the machine. Be particularly careful to cut the horse hair off so that it will protrude only about one inch from the opening. We think agents will have little trouble in using the above simple device effectively and impressing users that they have a machine which can easily be beaten and is worthless.

Kindly let us know what success you have in using the above device.

Side Talks with Girls, by Ruth Ashmore
The Ladies' Home Journal, December 1893

"In signing a letter to a young man I would not put just my Christian name, but, instead, would write my name out in full."

"It is not necessary to put on the deepest mourning for a mother-in-law; a nun's veiling would be in perfectly good taste."

"Massage given with olive oil will tend to develop the bust, neck, and arms, but if one has a tendency toward superfluous hair the oil will be apt to increase its growth."

Preamble of the National Populist Party Platform, 1893

"The national power to create money is appropriated to enrich bondholders; a vast public debt payable in legal-tender currency has been funded into gold-bearing bonds, thereby adding millions to the burdens of the people.

Silver, which has been accepted as coin since the dawn of history, has been demonetized to add to the purchasing power of gold by decreasing the value of all forms of property as well as human labor, and the supply of currency is purposely abridged to fatten usurers, bankrupt enterprise and enslave industry. A vast conspiracy against mankind has been organized on two continents, and it is rapidly taking possession of the world. If not met and overthrown at once, it forebodes terrible social convulsions, the destruction of civilization and the establishment of an absolute despotism."

The Panic of 1893

Wall Street stock prices experienced a sudden drop on May 5, 1893; the market collapsed in a panic June 27.

During the ensuing turmoil, 600 banks closed their doors; more than 15,000 businesses failed.

Seventy-four railroads went into receivership; the recession continued for four years.

The 1880s had been a period of remarkable economic expansion in the United States, propelled by the building of railroads.

The overbuilding of railroads and related bankruptcies dragged down the U.S. economy, which worsened when European investors withdrew funds and businesses were starved for capital.

Many companies tried to take over other firms, seriously endangering their own stability; at the same time silver, mined using rail connections, began to flood the market.

An early sign of trouble was the bankruptcy of the Philadelphia and Reading Railroad, which had greatly overextended itself, on February 23, 1893.

The average U.S. worker earned $9.42 per week; new immigrants often received less than $1 per day.

Millions of unemployed workers roamed the streets, begging for help, and children were abandoned.

As the economy worsened, people rushed to withdraw their money from banks.

European investors began to take payment only in gold, depleting U.S. gold reserves and threatening the value of the U.S. dollar, which was backed by gold.

A series of failures followed, including the Northern Pacific Railway, the Union Pacific Railroad and the Atchison, Topeka & Santa Fe Railroad.

17-19 percent of the workforce was unemployed at the Panic's peak, which when, combined with the loss of life savings by failed banks, meant that once secure middle class families could not meet their mortgage obligations.

Many walked away from recently built homes.

Economic conditions forced U.S. railroads to reduce their orders for sleeping cars; the Pullman Palace Car Company reduced wages by one-fourth, while charging full rents in company housing.

George M. Pullman and his executives continued to draw full salaries.

The American Railway Union was founded by socialist Eugene V. Debs.

Lithuanian-born anarchist Emma Goldman urged striking clockmakers to steal bread if they could not afford to buy food for their families.

Congress repealed the 1890 Sherman Silver Purchase Act; the United States returned to the gold standard.

Gentlemen
Walter Camp's Book College Sports, **1893**

A gentleman against a gentleman always plays to win. There is a tacit agreement between them that each shall do his best, and the best man shall win. A gentleman does not make his living, however, from his athletic prowess. He does not earn anything from his victories except glory and satisfaction. Perhaps the first falling off in this respect began when the laurel wreath became a mug. So long as the mug was but the emblem, and valueless otherwise, there was no harm. There is still no harm where the mug or trophy hanging in the room of the winner is indicative of his skill; but if the silver mug becomes a solid dollar, either at the hands of the winner or the donor, let us have the laurel back again.

A gentleman never competes for money, directly or indirectly. Make no mistake about this. No matter how winding the road may be that eventually brings the sovereign into the pocket, it is the price of what should be dearer to you than anything else, your honor. It is quite the fashion to say "sentimental bosh" to anyone who preaches such an old-fashioned thing as honor; but among true gentlemen, my boy, it is just as real an article as ever, and it is one of the few things that never rings false.

Announcement
The Algona Courier (Iowa), 1894

Father Schemel Bancroft (Iowa) has of late found good homes for 10 children which were sent him from an orphan asylum in New York which shelters 2,000 waifs. Father Eckert of Wesley has also found good homes for several and we understand that in the vicinity of the Prairie Church fifteen of the homeless children have of late been placed in comfortable homes. One day last week a number of the little waifs from the same place arrived in Algona over the Northwestern Road. All have been placed with good families…

Festivities for Foundlings, Six Hundred Little Ones Have Turkey and Cranberry Sauce
New York Times, November 30, 1894

The New York Foundling Hospital, at Sixty-eighth Street and Lexington Avenue, was the scene yesterday of joyful festivities, which will long dwell in the memories of the 600 little tots who are tenderly cared for in that institution.

For weeks they had heard tales of roast turkey and cranberry sauce, until they even dreamed of the feast to come.

Promptly at 12 o'clock the doors of the long playroom were thrown open, and the tables were quickly surrounded by 300 mothers and the older children.

In addition to this, the seven nurseries, each of which is 90 feet long and 30 feet wide, were fitted with tables, and at these were placed the 600 babies and "run-arounds," the latter being the children old enough to get into mischief.

Sister Irene, who is at the head of the hospital staff, and her 34 assistants, all decked out in their pretty costumes of blue with white aprons, white sleeves, and white Swiss cap, managed the dinner in perfect style.

"We do not often give them turkey," said one of the sisters, "because roast beef is more wholesome, and there is danger with the bones in eating fowl." The sisters were constantly called upon yesterday to extract stray turkey bones from little throats.

"Our children," continued the sister, "range in ages from one day to six years, the great majority of them being under two years old. They receive a training here that is intended to fit them for adoption by the best families. Since the founding of the hospital 24 years ago, we have cared for 26,000 infants, 10,000 of whom have been placed in permanent homes.

"Five thousand needy and homeless mothers have also shared the charitable shelter of the Foundling Hospital, and our outdoor department gives constant employment to 1,100 respectable women, who nurse the little foundlings in their own homes."

Her Point of View
New York Times, February 25, 1894

The dress reform symposiums which have been held at the Madison Square Garden through the week have evidently driven the wedge of sensible dress a little further in. It is still apparently a case of St. Anthony preaching to the fishes, "Much delighted were they, but preferred the old way."

But in point of fact there is a large class of women who are convinced that they are miserably clothed, and who are only waiting for custom to pave the way for a change in their garments.

It is a melancholy truth that men who rail at women's slavery to fashion and foolish notions of dress are among the chief obstacles in the way. They talk and inveigh, but when it comes to the women's—their women's-acting, they prove the stumbling blocks. When physicians who urge their patients to doff corsets, wear untrammeling gowns and broad-soled boots, are not able or willing to insist that their wives and daughters shall reapthe benefits of this advice, it militates against its usefulness. And the lay husbands and fathers are no better. "You women are geese to dress as you do," is a kind of stock phrase with them, but they are tremendously tenacious that their womenkind shall be counted in with the flock.

"Nice woman, that Mrs. So-and-So," a man says, "but a little odd, you know. Affects thick waists, short skirts, and that sort of thing." And the same man will look over his wife's gown and comment, with a little mournful philosophy: "My dear, I'm afraid you're growing stout. Where is that slender sylph I married?"

Men have got a distinct office in this dress reform movement. They have got to accord their individual support as well as to indulge in abstract theorizing. A happy destiny has emancipated them in a great degree. But they did not achieve this greatness; it was thrust upon them. There is abundant evidence to prove that men are as devoted to dress and custom as women, have about as many vanities concerning their personal appearance, and are as willing, many of them, to sacrifice personal comfort to accomplish them.

Aside from the men, however, it is of course undeniable that woman is her own worst foe in the matter. She is learning though, slowly, but surely, and her emancipation is not far away.

Conservative women do not look for or desire the radical changes that are offered by many reformers. A skirt that clears the ankles is a sensible and convenient length, possessing for walking all the advantages that one of knee length does. Many women wear the former now and are unnoticed.

The chief points that should be insisted upon are the suspension of the garments from the shoulders, the doing away of stiff boning and heavy cumbersome trimmings and methods of cut. This Mrs. Jenness Miller and others have shown that it is possible to accomplish, and yet accommodate the gown in general features to the prevailing mode. Nor is a variety of fabric and design to be frowned upon. It must follow that different tastes and purses will dictate different choosings.

Any reform must come gradually. The physical culture movement is doing its work, even though the women lace themselves into corsets after their hour of exercise. Pretty soon the operation will be too difficult and the corset will be discarded. Many corset-wearing mothers are keeping them from their growing daughters. This is the way for the work to go on, slowly and without a startling innovation. It will not be done in a day or a month or a year, but 50 years from now women will study with amazement the fashion plates of today and wonder that their sisters could have lived in such clothing.

A View of the Pullman Strike
The Wall Street Journal, July 5, 1894

An executive officer of one of the corporations which had considerable trouble during the last year with the labor element, said Tuesday: "I believe that this Pullman boycott will be a good thing for the people. It is bound to terminate in the complete defeat of the strikers. And such being the case, it is better to have it in a radical form than to have sporadic cases from month to month and year to year. The discontent of labor has become more and more assertive month by month since last summer. It can be liked to poison in the human system, and it is better (to carry out the simile) that the poison cause prostration and be thrown off by Nature through a fit of sickness than to remain in the system, manifesting its deadly effect for an unlimited time."

❧❧❧❧❧❧❧❧

An Indian Murder; Donald Austin, an Alaska Chief of Police,
Killed in a Chinaman's Saloon
San Francisco Examiner, December 1895

"The steamer *City of Topeka,* which arrived from Alaska this morning, brought the news of the brutal murder at Sitka on December 21 of Donald Austin, the Indian Chief of Police. The murder was committed in a saloon run by Chum Long. As a result Herbert Mills, the principal in the tragedy, was held over by Justice Delaney on a charge of murder. Long was held for manslaughter, and two sailors from the revenue cutter *Wolcott* for assault. While they were in the saloon the two sailors assaulted Austin, knocking him down. As soon as he rose, Mills struck him from behind and knocked him down again. Then they pounced on him and pounded his head on the hard floor. Long threw the unconscious Indian into a back room and later, when other Indians began to make inquiries for Austin, Long tossed his lifeless body out into the street, where it was found a few hours later."

❧❧❧❧❧❧❧❧

What Women May Wear, Not Corsets, of All Things,
Said Mrs. M. S. Lawrence
New York Times, May 22, 1895

A large and interested audience of girls was gathered in the Teachers College, at Morningside Heights, yesterday afternoon, when Mrs. Margaret Stanton Lawrence, the physical director of the college, gave a lecture upon dress, with all the necessary illustrative accompaniments.

A skeleton, revealed by the open door of a little portable closet, rattled his bones rather cheerfully than otherwise against the narrow walls of his abiding place. The Venus of Milo, hanging complacently by the side of an abnormally ugly specimen of the wasp-waisted woman, the interior of the human structure in various natural and unnatural conditions on charts, and the figure of the modern woman, as she appears occasionally in a comparatively healthy condition, were exhibited.

There was to be seen a bicycle gown, a part of a rainy day dress, and sundry mysterious packages which revealed in time the few hygienic garments the woman who considers herself properly clad wears beneath her gowns, bicycle or otherwise.

The lecture was particularly intended for the mothers of the college girls, but owing to the weather they did not appear. Mrs. Elizabeth Cady Stanton, Mrs. Lawrence's mother, was the guest of honor, and was heartily applauded by the girls as she came into the room with her daughter.

The corset is the bête noire against which Mrs. Lawrence contends with every principle of theory and practice, and it was the basis of all her remarks yesterday. The organs contained in the thorax were illustrated by a cheerful-looking artificial set of cheese cloths made to measurement by Dr. Eliza Mosher of Brooklyn, under whom Mrs. Lawrence studied. The heart was a dainty pincushion affair of red and blue, and other bodily organs were represented in a like manner. The lungs were such a commodious breathing apparatus that every girl present wondered if it could be possible that there was space enough in her chest to contain such an amount of delicate mechanism.

"I have been asked," said Mrs. Lawrence, "if the various organs were colored in this way, but they are not. The colors merely indicate the different organs.

"The development of women is most important, for it depends upon their condition whether those who come after will be well or ill able to stand the tremendous strain that comes upon the people of the nineteenth and twentieth centuries.

"It is because of the corset that one of the toasts at all medical dinners is, 'Woman, God's Best Gift to Man and the Support of the Doctors.' The corsets are pretty machines, often trimmed with gay ribbon and lace, but the loosest corset causes a pressure of 40 pounds on the most sensitive part of the body, and a tight corset a pressure equal to 70 or 80 pounds. 'Armorsides, warranted not to break,' I have seen on some of the corset advertisements, and it is a very good name, I think."

Then Mrs. Lawrence showed her pretty cheesecloth organs in their proper places and how they all suffered from pressure upon any one of them. It was about this time that a gentle ripple of laughter started at one side of the room, and gradually spread over it. It was only an innocent and unsuspecting young man, who with notebook in hand had mistakenly wandered into a woman's dress convocation.

"Has that man gone?" said Mrs. Lawrence, as she made her way back to the charts. He had gone very quickly, and every one laughed again.

"A man and a woman breathe exactly alike when properly dressed," went on Mrs. Lawrence. "It is necessary to have plenty of oxygen, and that is only obtained by deep breathing. Dr. Austin Flint says that after they are grown, women do not breathe as men do, but that is not so. He has experimented with fashionable women only. Dr. Mosher has made experiments with men. Without a corset, breathing is low down, and with a corset, merely in the chest."

❧❧❧❧❧❧❧❧

Miss Armstrong Exonerated, the Teacher Freed of Horsewhipping Charges, But Complainant Is Bitter Against School Trustees
New York Times, May 17, 1895

WHITESTONE, L.I.—At a meeting of the Board of Education held here tonight, the committee appointed at the request of Miss Edith Armstrong, a teacher in the public school, to investigate the horsewhipping charge made against her by William Joyce, rendered a report exonerating the teacher.

In his complaint, Mr. Joyce alleged that his son, William, and Edward Gleason were severely horsewhipped by Miss Armstrong, and were held during a part of such whipping by Principal William M. Peck, that the teacher was in the habit of flogging the pupils before the classes, and that on numerous occasions she had thrown the boys on the floor, and, holding them by placing her knee on their chests, pounded them with books.

Miss Armstrong admitted having whipped the boys, but claims that the whipping was not unduly severe, and says that she only struck them on the necks and bodies when they attempted to disarm her.

Trustee Robert S. Munson, chairman of the committee made to investigate the charges, and Principal Peck reported that they and trustee L.W. Ensign had made a preliminary examination in Mr. Joyce's presence, and they were agreed that the charges were without foundation and that no public investigation was necessary. The report was accepted and the committee discharged.

William Joyce this evening said he was far from satisfied with the investigation made by the committee appointed by the Board of Education. He said he was hastily summoned to the school a few days ago, and arrived as the session was over. He alleges that Mr. Peck conducts the school in the most undignified manner. Mr. Joyce says he will demand an examination into the charges specific to his complaint. He will use other means, he said, to have the facts of the case brought out that the school trustees refused to properly investigate.

Tea around the Table: Handkerchiefs
The Delineator, A Journal of Fashion, Culture and Fine Arts
by the Butterick Publishing Company, 1896

"Take my word for it, my dears, no part of feminine belongings so truly shows the refined gentlewoman as does the handkerchief. Heavy with embroidery or drawn—work it need not be—indeed, any aggressive decoration is in bad taste; but dainty and fine it must be, the finer the better. Who has not seen the toilette of an otherwise well-dressed woman quite spoiled by a coarse, common handkerchief! A *mouchoir* with a colored border may look smart when tucked into a jacket front, but such an extreme better befits Mrs. Dashaway than it does Mme. Juste-Milieu. A frock may be very elegant, but it is the little things that confirm the wearer's claim to being a well-dressed woman. Even if a gown or jacket shows wear, the fresh and well-fitted shoes and gloves, the pretty veil, and fine handkerchief redeem the whole."

Millions Shipped East, Gold Coin Sent from
California in a Baggage Car
San Francisco Examiner, January 1, 1896

"The gold in the sub-treasury was increased on Tuesday by the arrival of $1 million in $20 pieces from the mint in San Francisco. The rush on the part of some of the financiers at the beginning of the Venezuelan discussion to draw gold from the sub-treasury for foreign shipment caused the authorities to draw on the San Francisco mint, and during the past month $20 million in gold has been shipped East. The last shipment, which included besides the gold almost two tons of silver bullion, left San Francisco in an ordinary baggage car. The car was guarded by two messengers armed with revolvers and rifles, but as it was not generally known that the gold was being shipped, no trouble was expected from outlaws."

Will Penetrate Wood, A New Light That Is Being Used in Photography
San Francisco Examiner, January 8, 1896

"The noise of war's alarms should not distract attention from a marvelous triumph of science which is reported from Vienna. It is announced Professor Routhen of Wurzburg University has discovered light which, for the purpose of photography, will penetrate wood, flesh, and most other organic substances. The Professor has succeeded in photographing metal weights which were in a closed wooden case, also a man's hand which shows only the bones, the flesh being invisible."

❧❧❧❧❧❧❧❧

An Essay on the Present Distribution of Wealth in the United States
by Charles B. Spahr, 1896

The Rich and the Poor in 1890

Estates by Annual Income	Number of Families	Aggregate Wealth	Average per Family
Wealth Classes $50,000 and over	125,000	$33 billion	$264,000
Well-to-Do Classes $5,000 to $50,000	1,375,000	$23 billion	$16,000
Middle Classes $500 to $5,000	5,500,000	$8.2 billion	$1,500
Poorer Classes Under $500	5,500,000	$0.8 billion	$150

❧❧❧❧❧❧❧❧

Bicycling and Its Attire
The Delineator, April 1896

Bicycling is an evolution. For several years merely a branch of athletics, indulged in as a pastime by the ultra, it has developed into a serious factor in fin de siècle progress. Its merits are many and its pleasures incalculable. No other mode of travel, save, perhaps horseback riding, is capable of giving such thorough enjoyment as the wheel, so exhilarating is the ease and rapidity of its motion, and none is more conductive to health and symmetrical bodily development. Many for whom outdoor exercises have heretofore possessed no attraction and whose habits were sluggish for the lack of them, are fascinated by the wheel, claiming it is without rival, its influence being felt mentally as well as physically. Distances are rapidly and easily covered; varied prospects are successfully presented, and new ideas and trains of thought are engendered.

The hygienic value of wheeling appeals to every admirer of vigorous and healthy manhood and womanhood. While certain muscles are brought more into action than others, all are benefited by the exercise. The power of the respiratory organs is strengthened by the large quantities of pure air taken into the lungs, creating a more perfect oxygenation of the blood and invigorating the entire system, a tonic far pleasanter than any yet compounded by chemist. Physicians now generally concede the value of the wheel in the treatment of invalids and convalescents able to take a form of exercise requiring so much physical exertion...

The best dress for wheeling is still a mooted question, opinion being divided between the short skirt and the bloomer costume. Whichever is adopted, it should be as light in weight as possible and so fashioned that it will in no wise hamper the movements of the rider. In long full skirts there lurks danger; they become easily entangled in the chain or pedals and thus bring about disaster. Wool sweaters with large sleeves are fashionable, but are objected to by some on the score of their snug fit, which sharply defines the figure. They absorb perspiration, however, and are for that reason particularly desirable for warm weather wear. Fashion provides numerous other waists as smart as they are convenient. If a corset is insisted upon (the rider will be far more comfortable without one), a short, lightly boned affair that ends above the hips and is made without steels in front, should be chosen.

☙❧☙❧☙❧☙❧

Progress in Electric Lighting, by S.E. Tillman
The Cosmopolitan Magazine, March 1897

"Both arc and incandescent electric lighting are so well established and so fully developed that any very great or radical improvement can scarcely be expected to come suddenly, yet in both systems, steady, if slow, progress toward perfection is being made.

In arc lighting the 'short arc' with heavy current and low voltage or pressure has been succeeded by the 'long arc' with smaller current and higher voltage. At the same time a larger number of lights have been placed upon the same circuit, and the leading wires diminished in size. Ten years ago 25 lights in one circuit was a large number, whereas now circuits include from 75 to 150; then the total voltage on one circuit amounted to 1,200 or 1,500, and now it runs up to 6,000 or 7,000 volts. Notwithstanding the great increase in pressure employed, the wires have been successfully placed underground; an achievement which the electrical companies in this country were not inclined to admit as economically practicable. The most distinct recent step in arc lighting has been the inclosing [sic] of the carbons in an airtight receptacle, by which they last from 125 to 150 hours without renewal. In these inclosed lights the arc is made longer, the current smaller, and the voltage for a single lamp greater than in any other form. These lamps are giving very satisfactory results and are coming into competition with incandescent lamps for the general illumination of stores, hotel corridors, etc. The standard inclosed arc only requires three or five amperes, and they can run from the ordinary incandescent circuit of 110 volts.

Improvements in the mechanical details of arc lamps have kept pace with the modifications in their principles of construction; indeed, the improved details have made the better lights possible; thus the inclosed lamp only became possible with the production of the refined carbons of the past few years.

In incandescent electric lighting, distinct advantages toward cheaper and better lights have been made. The principal agents tending to this result have been two—first the great reduction in the first cost of the lamps; second the improved efficiency of the lamps. Since incandescent lighting became a success the cost of the lamps has been reduced over one-half, and at the same time the efficiency of the lamps has been nearly doubled. Formerly it required the expenditure of one horsepower of current energy to each seven or eight lamps of 16 candlepower each; now the same amount of energy supplies 15 lamps. It is probable that the efficiency of the lamps will yet be considerably increased, but the limit in cost of production would seem to be nearly reached.

The development of electric lighting has caused greater progress in gas lighting in the past 12 years than had been made in the previous 60. The light-giving power of gas has been trebled and the cost of gas production reduced. The rapid, enormous, and permanent development of incandescent electric lighting is shown by a recent statement in the *Electrical Engineer* that there are now invested in this industry $600 million of capital."

The King's Daughters, Edited by Mrs. Margaret Bottome
The Ladies' Home Journal, June 1897

"I heard yesterday of a dainty little lady who was standing on the dock by the side of a distinguished-looking gentleman, and their attention was attracted to the trouble of a woman with a child in her arms, who would not pass on as she was commanded to do. No one could understand a word the woman said. One after another, of different nationalities, went up to her, but she did not understand either French or German any better than she did English. The officer became impatient, and was about to lay hands on her when the beautiful little lady bounded away from her escort and in a moment stood by the side of the woman, and the face that had shown such terror and anguish was soon wreathed in smiles. After a few moments' conversation with her, the little lady turned to the crowd and said, 'She is from Honolulu. Her husband was to meet her at this steamer. She hasn't a cent with her and she feared to move till her husband came.' A young man with the badge of the Salvation Army said, 'Come lads, let us all give ten cents apiece to the poor woman,' and hands went into pockets and more than ten cents came from a good many, and the poor woman was comforted, and felt less friendless and alone."

⇛⇛⇛⇛⇛⇛⇛⇛

The Luxury of Ocean Travel, Advertising Supplement
The Cosmopolitan, March 1897

"There is a favorite saying, particularly among the good, old-fashioned people, that they do not intend to go to Europe until there is a bridge built across the Atlantic. There probably will never be an opportunity to cross the ocean this way, but the trip has, in these modern days, been made so easy, so comfortable and so short, that it has become a pleasure instead of a trial, a matter of recreation instead of a hardship.

Ships of immense size, constructed of iron and steel, propelled by enormous horsepower and furnished luxuriously, ply back and forth between New York and Europe with the regularity of express trains, and, the records show, with much less danger to life and limb.

This is particularly true of the service maintained by the *North German Lloyd*, the largest steamship in the world, and the one that has for many years carried more passengers between New York and Europe than any other line.

The ships employed in what is known as the North Express Service of the *North German Lloyd*, the *Havel*, the *Spree*, the *Lahn*, the *Trave*, the *Aller* and the *Saale*, are veritable floating hotels of the magnificent type. Structurally, they stand for the highest science attained by modern shipbuilding. Mechanically, they represent the most improved types of marine engineering skill, and as regards accommodations for passengers, they are unsurpassed by any ships floating.

Several of them, notably the *Saale* and the *Trave*, have recently undergone extensive improvements. New and more powerful engines and boilers of greater capacity have been added, increasing their speed very materially. Wooden awning decks have been built over the promenade decks, so that there should be a complete protection from the sun, rain and flying spindrift. The lifeboats have been elevated, leaving the long and wide promenade deck unobstructed from end to end. Changes have also been made in the interior arrangements, which have materially increased the size of the smoking rooms, and the ladies' and the dining saloons. Similar changes will be made before the opening of the tourist season in the *Lahn*, so that the entire fleet will be in excellent condition to meet the demands upon it during the coming spring, summer and autumn.

The *North German Lloyd* maintains a double weekly Express Service between New York and Bremen, in addition to its popular all-the-year round line to Genoa, via Gibraltar and Naples. It is, therefore, the only line that offers travelers the much-appreciated opportunity of going to Europe by one route and returning by another, thus avoiding the necessity of retracing one's steps to the point of landing. This plan enables the tourist to enjoy a much wider view of Europe without increasing the cost of ocean transportation....

The Express steams of the *North German Lloyd* sailing from New York on Saturdays touch first at Cherbourg, France, proceeding from there directly to Bremerhaven. This service is maintained for the convenience of travelers desiring to reach Paris or points in Switzerland and Central Europe in the quickest possible time and by the shortest route. It avoids the necessity of crossing the often vexatious English Channel in small steamers, and shortens the time between New York and the French capital about 12 hours. At Cherbourg, the *North German Lloyd* drops anchor in the beautiful harbor, and passengers and baggage are transferred to the quay upon the company's commodious tender. Special trains meet each steamer, reaching Paris in six hours. Passengers desiring to visit Germany or points in the northern central portion of Europe find Bremen a convenient point from which to begin their travels. It is one of the chief cities of Germany and railroads radiate in every direction. It is also one of the most interesting cities in Europe, farfamed for its handsome public buildings, its historical associations and beautiful park."

❧❧❧❧❧❧❧❧

Bacteria, the Progress of Science, by Bertha Gerneaux Davis
The Cosmopolitan, March 1897

Zoologists and botanists alike laid claim to the bacteria until comparatively recent years, but the zoologists were forced to yield to their botanical brethren, and the curious little organisms popularly known as "microbes" are now classified, almost without question, among the simplest of the plant forms, and as near relatives of algae. The common form of bacteria is rod-shaped, though others are spiral, spherical and egg-shaped. In size they vary considerably. Some of the larger forms are 20/25,000 of an inch in length, while one of the smallest is about 1/50,000 of an inch. To give a rather more definite idea of the minuteness of some of these organisms, imagine 1,500 placed end to end, hardly reaching across a pinhead. Extremely powerful lenses must consequently

be brought to bear upon them before they will yield up the secret of their life history and workings; and, as the little bodies are almost transparent, the microscopist is obliged to stain them with some dye to render them anything but shadowy and indistinct.

❧❧❧❧❧❧❧❧

Narcotics and Improper Dress
New York Times, October 14, 1897

First in importance, because of its widespread character and of the profound mischief which it works in the human organism, must be mentioned the narcotic habit. Whatever may be the particular poison to which the individual may be addicted, whether alcohol, tobacco, opium, cocaine, tea or coffee, chloral, absinthe, or hasheesh, the vice is one and the same. The recent studies of Andriesen, Tuke, Hodge, and others have shown how these drugs destroy man, soul and body, by producing degeneration of the delicate fibres by means of which nerve cells communicate with one another, thus isolating the individual units of the cerebrum, and so destroying memory, coordination, will, and judgment, and wrecking the individual physically, mentally, and morally.

Next in the category of destructive forces, I must enumerate the slavery to conventional dress. A careful study of this subject has convinced me that, aside from the liquor and tobacco habits, there is no deteriorating force which deals such destructive blows against the constitution of the race as the wrong, unphysiological customs in dress which prevail among civilized American women.

Scarcely a woman can be found who has reached the age of 25 or 30, and who has worn the conventional dress, who is not suffering from dislocation of the stomach, the kidneys, the bowels, or some other important internal organ. The present outlook is, however, somewhat hopeful. The bicycle has forever delivered women from the thralldom of long skirts, and gives encouragement that the necessity for breathing capacity may yet banish the corset and its accompanying tight bands.

$\wp\!\!\prec\!\!\wp\!\!\prec\!\!\wp\!\!\prec\!\!\wp\!\!\prec\!\!\wp\!\!\prec\!\!\wp\!\!\prec$

New Information Notes
Self Culture, A Magazine of Knowledge, April, 1897

A fruitful cause of collisions at sea during fogs is to be found in the difficulty experienced in locating the position of all foghorns, sirens and other such sonorous signals. One of the devices lately brought out for removing this danger consists of two microphones, one in the bow and the other in the stern of the vessel. The bow microphone is connected with the telephone placed at the right ear, and the stern microphone with another at the left ear of the operator, who otherwise is isolated from the sound of the signal. Taking the speed of the sound and the time it takes to travel the length of the ship, the observer can estimate the direction of the fog signal. When both sounds are simultaneous, the signal is at right angles to the vessel.

****

Superintendent Knoll, at the Hudson Street Hospital, New York City, recently completed an x-ray photograph clearly outlining the brachial artery of the right arm of an adult. This is said to be the first time such a feat has been accomplished. The patient was 60 years old and had been suffering from an affection of the arm. The physicians were unable to tell exactly what was the matter. The photograph clearly shows deposits of lime salts in the blood, which has hardened the artery. The treatment of the case was governed accordingly.

****

What is the most expensive product of the world? It is charcoal thread (filament de charbon), which is employed for incandescent lamps. It is, for the most part, manufactured at Paris and comes from the hands of an artist who desires his name to remain unknown in order to better protect the secret of manufacture. It is by the gramme (15 1/2 grains) that this product is sold at wholesale. In reducing its price to the basis of pounds, it is easily found out that the filaments for the lamps of 20 candles are worth $8,000 per pound, and for lamps of 30 candles they are worth $12,000 per pound.

****

In an article entitled "Made in Japan," a contemporary describes how manufacturing nations have always encroached upon each other's domains. The Dutch, importing English clay, made good profit out of imitations of Chinese porcelain, and after a while the Dutch product became firmly established in the markets of the world as Delft ware. English potters copied the Dutch pattern, sold it a good deal cheaper, and the North of England became the headquarters for Delft china. Lately the Japanese, having acquainted themselves with the patterns best liked in England, encroach upon the domain long monopolized by the English potter. The Japanese product is much finer and stronger, and above all much cheaper than the best English ware, and thus Japan is providing the markets with goods which were originally regarded as a Chinese monopoly.

❦❧❦❧❦❧❦❧

Household Helps and New Ideas
Ladies' Home Journal, April 1898

The deep cutting in fine glass requires special care to keep it clean and brilliant. A brush is now sold for polishing and drying cut glass. It is made of the finest Russian bristles and does the work speedily and well.

❦❧❦❧❦❧❦❧

Risks of Modern Life
The Youth's Companion, February 17, 1898

Most of the appliances of modern civilization bring risks as well as advantages. The people who lived a hundred years ago could not travel so rapidly nor communicate with each other across great distances so conveniently as we do; but on the other hand, they were strangers to some perils which are familiar nowadays.

Their journeys were slow and serious affairs; but they were in no danger of being blown up on a steamboat, or tumbled over a railway embankment, or even of being run over by a trolley car or a "scorching" wheelman. Their houses were not lighted by electricity or by gas; but they were not burned up by reason of badly insulated wires or asphyxiated in their beds. They knew nothing of 15-story buildings, but they also knew nothing of elevator accidents.

Nevertheless, it is doubtful if more lives are lost by accident in travel, in proportion to the number of people travelling, than was the case a century ago.

Hundreds of people travel by water now than did so then; but ocean travel has been made relatively more safe, as well as more swift and comfortable, by modern appliances. There are still possibilities of collision or of striking a reef in a fog, but it almost never happens that a modern, seaworthy vessel founders through stress of weather. One steamship company which has sent its steamers back and forth across the Atlantic for more than 50 years is able to boast that it has never lost the life of a passenger in the service.

As to the railways, in 1896, 181 passengers were killed on the railways of the United States, and nearly 2,900 were injured. When these figures are compared with the amount of passenger traffic, it appears that the railways carried nearly three million passengers for every one who was killed and about 180,000 passengers for every passenger injured.

A famous humorist once compared the number of people killed in railway accidents with the number dying in their beds, and reached the conclusion that it was several thousand times more risky to lie in bed than to travel on a railway.

It was a playful exaggeration; but it is true that, if modern discovery and invention have resulted in new hazards to human life, they have also supplied new safeguards and preventives.

Fruits as Foods and Fruits as Poisons, by S. T. Rorer
Ladies' Home Journal, June 1898

Fruits Which I Allow on My Table

It may be interesting to know that the fruits allowed on my table are fresh figs, dried ones carefully cooked, guavas canned without sugar, guava jelly, orange marmalade made by special home recipe, dates both raw and cooked with almonds, persimmons, bananas cooked, and an occasional dish of prunes with the skins removed, blackberries and dewberries, slightly cooked, strained and made into flummery. The objection to the latter [sic] fruit, however, is the addition of starch and sugar, which is prone to fermentation. All fruits, whether cooked or raw, should be used without sugar. It must be remembered that sugar in no way neutralizes an acid; for this an alkali must be used. Sugar sprinkled over an acid fruit masks the objectionable and severe acid until it slips by the "guard-keeper," the palate. Once in the stomach, however, it regains its own position and grants the same to the irritating acid.

Acid Fruits Have No Food Value

Acid fruits are used by the great majority to stimulate the appetite, that they must eat what is called "breakfast," miscalled, however, for really there is no fast to break. It is well to observe that the person who eats a heavy luncheon at or near midnight is the same who eats one or two good-sized oranges or a dish of strawberries to give him an appetite the next morning.

Another fact of no small importance is that starches are digested and sugars converted only in an alkaline medium. What, then, becomes of the bowl of cereals taken immediately after these acid fruits for breakfast, taking no account of the sugar that is usually sprinkled over it? The intestinal tract must sooner or later become irritated by these fermenting foods. The blood loses its alkalinity, and a train of diseases, already only too well-established in the system, follows such a diet.

Fruits and bread and butter are very common mixtures for those who have at the end of the day a supper. One can see at a glance that such combinations are not wise.

Protection from Flies
Southern Poultry and Stockman's Guide, September 1898

An old, tried-and-true remedy for flies is pine tar and grease, says the Progressive Farmer. Many a fisherman has found this a welcome protection to his own person whilst pursuing his art destructive to the finny tribe. For our cows can be found no more effective remedy for the attack of flies and probably no cheaper one than pine tar one part and crude cottonseed oil two parts. If too thick add more oil, but the more expensive and less dirty it makes the cows. We have used two parts of oil to one of tar, being careful to brush it on with a piece of coarse burlap and not use enough to make the hair very sticky, but enough so about two applications per week will keep flies looking elsewhere than on cattle thus smeared for a free lunch.

The best protection against flies yet tried at the Experimental Farm has been clutches of chickens used in combination with care to clean up the cow yard regularly. All droppings are brought daily to the manure pit, and near this the chicks have had their homes, so they find fruitful scratching ground and grow fat on fly larvae.

The Evolution of the Colored Soldier
by W. Thorton Parker, M.D., 1898

Late A. A. Surgeon, U.S. Army
North American Review, February 1898

When colored troops were enrolled, soon after the close of the War of the Rebellion, the Southern states were in a chaotic condition. Troops occupied the strategic centres, and "carpet bag" politicians and adventurers swarmed into the conquered territory, their thirst for money making them willing to risk safety in order to arrive early upon the field to reap the harvest that cruel war had placed within their reach. The Negroes, freed from slavery and intoxicated with the license which they knew not how to use reasonably, were ready for almost anything except wage labor.

The war being at an end, the profession of arms, with the showy uniform and military pomp, offered them a temping experience. To recruit a colored regiment was, therefore, not a very difficult undertaking, especially when ignorance and savagery were no bar to acceptance by the recruiting officers. Hundreds of freed Negroes flocked to the recruiting stations and were quickly transformed into recruits for the U.S. colored regiments. The fiat had gone forth that the freed men were no longer to be merely enrolled as soldiers to do duty as teamsters for the quartermaster's department, but that they were to appear as soldiers, drill and do guard duty, with equal rights with the white veterans of the late war. In compliance with this idea, an expedition assembled and marched westward from Fort Leavenworth, Kansas, in the early spring of 1867, over the Santa Fe Trail, through the "Great Deserts," which were then occupied by the active and warlike Indians. Their advent astonished everyone. The frontiersmen looked upon them as a military caricature, the fruit of some political deal, unexplained and unreasonable. The officers detailed to serve with them were half ashamed to have it known. The white soldiers who came in contact with these recent slaves, now wearing their uniform of the regular army, felt insulted and injured. Their redskin adversaries heaped derision upon the Negroes by taunts and jests, loudly called them "Buffalo soldiers," and declared them "heap bad medicine" because they could not and would not scalp them. Such was the very unpromising advent of colored troops to do service as soldiers on equal terms with regular troops...

❧❧❧❧❧❧❧❧

How We Live at a Frontier Fort, by Maria Brace Kimball
The Outlook, February 5, 1898

The soldier's day begins at sunrise. As the light breaks through the pines on the eastern horizon, the deep vibrations of the morning gun are followed by the lively march of Reveille. That halfheard, ghostly music always stirs me with awe at the thought of another day begun, and with pleasure in the lingering dream that keeps back the actualities of the day...

Work in the frontier post includes all the trades from sawing of logs to mending of shoes, for the soldier is no specialist, but an all-round character, who must dig and plant, cook and scrub, as well as ride, shoot and saber...

From Reveille to Retreat the day is occupied with saber practice, gymnastics and horse exercise in winter, with drills, sham battles and target practice in summer. The leisure hours of the enlisted men are also well provided for. Outdoors, he has football and baseball, hunting and fishing. Indoors, he has a reading room and library as well as concerts and balls.

In the Officers' Row the days are not less busy than in the barracks opposite. Though the average military man is not deeply interested in general literature, upon his own subjects he is well-read. He often studies, too, topics related to the comparatively unknown regions of our country which he inhabits, and becomes an expert in natural history, archaeology and Indian folklore. The officer's wife also has tactics to master in this land of no shops, no markets, no dressmakers. The daily meals require careful foresight when butter and eggs must be bought in Kansas, vegetables and fruit in California. The Thanksgiving turkey and celery and cranberries are bespoken by letter before the president has issued his proclamation. Baby's dolls and toys are ordered from catalogues two months before Christmas. The sewing is done by the mother's skillful fingers, aided by patterns and fashion plates. With all these industries she finds time to play the piano, to read, to visit and to teach the children their earliest lessons.

In the clubroom, tales of stirring Indian campaigns are told and retold by the veterans; surely those who have made the peace of the Plains should be permitted to fight their battles o'er again in the quiet of the garrison. These heroes of our Indian wars form a naïve and unworldly type—that of an American who is unruffled by the cares of the voter, the competition of the trades, or the rivalries of civil professions…

Public opinion in America frowns upon the professional soldier. The man of books regards him as a medieval heguman, born out of his time; the man of affairs looks upon him as an accessory of government, useful on occasion, yet a costly and troublesome piece of machinery. A strong military power is popularly considered a menace to liberty and free institutions. A standing army, on the contrary, fosters that military spirit which tends not to destroy, but to uphold and protect government.

ॐॐॐॐॐॐ

Evangelists Going to Cuba
New York Times, May 16, 1898

When the United States troops at Tampa embark for Cuba, they may be followed soon after by some of the famous evangelists in the United States. Gen. O. O. Howard, retired, now an evangelist, arrived at Tampa today, accompanied by Major D. W. Whipple.

A movement was recently inaugurated by D. D. Moody, having for its object the sending of noted speakers to the various rendezvous of the soldiers, and to hold meetings for their spiritual instruction. Gen. Howard and Major Whipple have visited Chickamauga, Atlanta and Mobile. As most of the regiments are without chaplains, the sending to Cuba of several noted divines to work among the soldiers is contemplated.

It is hardly probable that they will accompany the soldiers when the expedition moves out, but once the army is settled in Cuba and the campaign against the Spanish forces is fairly on, the evangelical work will be actively begun. Gen. Howard and Major Whipple spoke at the Tampa Heights Camp Grounds tonight.

ॐॐॐॐॐॐ

Hot Weather at Tampa, Soldiers Suffering in the Sun and Daily Drills Are Cut Short, Military Fever Also Burns
New York Times, May 25, 1898

Despite the fact that sunstroke is unknown under the fierce blaze of the tropical sun in this part of Florida, many of the unseasoned volunteers are suffering discomforts from excessive heat and the piercing glare of the sand. One walks here between two fires. From the cloudless sky the sun pours a flood of light as brilliant and burning as molten brass, and from the waste of sand, white and gleaming, comes a heating glare as dazzling as if each grain of sand were a refracting mirror. The skin tingles and burns in this double heat, and the brain becomes dazed.

To the young volunteers from the Northern states, the heat and glare are a severe trial. They have never before experienced such powerful sunlight, and many of them have come here from places where the snow was still lingering in the valleys and on the sides of the hills. To withstand the effects of such a sudden change from snow to fire, one must have what few of these young volunteers have, an iron frame. Even the troops from this state, accustomed to exposure in such sun, are affected by the intense heat, and the hardened soldiers, who have been seasoned by years of baking and broiling in the alkali deserts, suffer from exhaustion. The glare pains the eyes also, and produces headache and soreness of the lids, until one is driven to the awful refuge of smoked glasses.

There have been no fatal results from the heat, however, and the officers are now looking with keen solicitude after the comfort and health of the troops. The hours of drilling have been shortened, from three and four a day to an hour and a half, and all exercises are confined to the early morning or late afternoon. For the rest of the day, lounging or sleeping in the tents, and for the night, freedom to roam over the little city and explore its half dozen points of interest; a turn about the big hotel and its flower-burdened grounds; a glance at the queer mixture of fashionable and martial life that war has thrown together here in its crucible—and then more lounging and sleep under the white tents.

⊰⊱⊰⊱⊰⊱⊰⊱⊰⊱

Breaking Camp at Tampa, Great Confusion Follows the Orders for the Troops to Board the Transports. Roads and Railways Blocked. Chaotic Scenes All the Way from Camp to Dock
New York Times, June 14, 1898

After nearly two months of somewhat theatric bustle and noise, and the movement of troops hither and thither, and after a dozen orders from Washington and elsewhere to be ready to start at once, which orders were countermanded as rapidly as they were made, the army of invasion has got itself into a fleet of transports and has moved a few feet out into the bay.

The troops had been concentrated at Tampa for weeks. Their white tents lay like a pigmy city, squat amid the glaring sand waste. The heat and the labor of drilling in the soft sand were enervating them, and their spirits were sinking under the depressing toll and heat and mysterious delay. Were they getting ready? Were those who have charge of the army preparing it for the campaign, and for the kind of campaign it was expected to conduct? A single night revealed the true condition of affairs to the army itself, to the government, and to the enemy.

Tuesday, there was in the air that unnamed feeling that something was to be done or attempted soon. Before night, troops were moving.

They knew not where or why, but instantly everyone was convinced that the long-expected advance on Cuba had begun. Later there was a general rush for Port Tampa and the transports. The army was certainly on the march.

A Scene of Confusion
At once there was indescribable confusion. It was not the mere stir and bustle that must accompany even the most exact movements of an army, and which may readily be mistaken for confusion. It was confusion, unmistakable confusion.

There is one railway and one wagon road between Tampa and Port Tampa. The distance is short, not more than nine miles; but they are nine miles of sand, and the wagons sink a foot and more in the clogging white powder that has been ground beneath wheels and hoofs for weeks. The railway was blocked despite the fact that only military trains were run. Cars filled with soldiers or supplies, ammunition, and guns, stood on every sidetrack, and it was almost impossible to get even an engine through the confused mass. Trains fared worse, and only a few troops got through, although it had been estimated that at least 2,500 could be carried to the port every hour. In this emergency the sand road was used by the soldiers and by the wagon and pack trains. It was soon blocked as tight as the railway, and the nine miles lengthened to as many leagues. Wagons broke down under their heavy loads in the deep sandbeds; jaded horses and worn-out pack-mules stumbled on and on and fell by the roadside, in the way of the tolling rear. The port that seemed so near at sunset seemed as far away as the pole before midnight.

The army had been suddenly set to a task that it had not prepared for and could not perform. It began the inevitable abandonment of all impediments. The first thing to be left behind was the recruit; the next was the untrained volunteer. Then the larger tents were abandoned, and only the shelter tent was allowed the soldier. The recruit and the untrained volunteer were left to the enjoyment of the big tents and the spreading sand wastes and the drill sergeant. Rations were limited to the 14 days' regular and 10 days' travel ration; and officers' baggage was cut down from 250 to 80 pounds. Even the horses of the officers were left, and only six were allowed to each regiment. The larger part of the cavalry was dismounted, and even the "Rough Riders" of Theodore Roosevelt—inglorious without their steeds—were ordered to go to the front on foot. Lt. Col. Roosevelt said, very gallantly, that he would gladly go to the front if he had to go on "all fours."

With all this cutting down and stripping, the army was immobile. It was apparently without sufficient guidance at this critical moment, just as it had been for weeks, apparently without a supreme head that could direct and provide. Even the regular army, so small that one would be justified in believing that it could have been handled as readily and as effectively as a missile weapon, was found to be cumbersome. It had not been supplied with light clothing, and the soldiers sweltered in their heavy winter uniforms. They had not sufficient wagon transportation and, consequently, the drivers were overworked and wearied out. Midnight Tuesday I found hundreds of them, heavy with fatigue, lying in the sand by the side of their wagons. The mules stood panting in their traces. In spite of the hurry and fever of preparation, only a few troops had reached the transports by daylight. The order had been issued that all should be ready to sail before sunrise.

᏶᏶᏶᏶᏶᏶᏶᏶

Scenes in the City of Tampa, by W. J. Rouse
The New York Times Illustrated Magazine, May 15, 1898

Dwellers in Northern cities at this time of excitement on the Southern coast have little or no idea of the excitement that prevails in the Florida cities, and particularly in those that are centres of military operations.

What a huge thing the army is when it is brought together, yet how small is it when compared to the standing army of other nations! The vast expanse of ground covered by the camps, the limitless number of horses, wagons and men needed to move an army, or even a regiment, can better be described by photographs than by mere words. To a civilian who has never been in an army camp, the bivouac of four or five regiments looks as if countless thousands of soldiers were quartered there. To the experienced eye of the general, however, the smallness of the real force and the magnitude of paraphernalia necessary to its use are more readily apparent.

In Tampa, in Port Tampa, and in Port Tampa City, during the last two or three weeks, everything has been of warlike character. Throngs of people surround the headquarters of the officers, eager for any item or atom of news that may be overheard or dropped. At the newspaper offices other crowds gather to discuss the meager bulletins set forth on glaring sheets of colored paper. Other crowds content themselves with reading telegrams pasted in a frame, which was once a deck skylight of the lamented battleship *Maine.* Dark scowls lurk upon the faces of American men as Spanish is heard spoken all around them. Whether by Cuban or Spanish refugee, even the musical language is hated. A mere suspicion that a man may be a Spanish spy would be enough to cause his life to end suddenly here, for this is a cosmopolitan city, where men of all classes meet, and where only one political or national feeling is permitted to exist—a love for the Stars and Stripes…

The city of Tampa proper has a population of about 5,000 souls. It is the centre of the cigar manufacturing industry, which has been constantly moving from Key West for several years. It is poor in architecture, poor in population, and worse as regards streets and highways than any city I have yet seen. It is impossible to drive half a mile out of town in a carriage. The wheels will simply mire in the soft, white sea sand. It is almost unlighted at night, and its business houses, with only a few notable exceptions, are far below what one would expect to see in a city of its size.

There are two military camps, one on the "heights," where none but infantry are encamped, and the camp on Picnic Island, at the very shores of Tampa Bay, nine miles from the town. There are quartered all the light batteries of artillery in the army, one or two entire regiments of cavalry, and several regiments of infantry…. They have far the advantage of the soldiers on the "heights," for they have the finest bathing facilities imaginable and, of course, take the fullest advantage of them. In the artillery camp, which is nearest the railroad tracks, long lines of frowning, slim-bodied rifles gleam in the sunlight, or in the late afternoon cast wavering shadows athwart the forms of lounging men, whose faces, lighted now and again by the wavy scintillations of the rippling water, show tanned and bronzed from service on the frontier and exposure on the sandy plains of Florida. They are a grim, Herculean lot of men, who have seen service and who are in love with their vocation….

At the farther side of this encampment from the tracks is a row of single tents, in which Col. Randolph and his staff have their temporary homes. The side walls are elevated to allow the cool breeze from the bay to play through, and everything is as neat and in perfect order as in the quarters of an officer in one of the permanent garrisons. A little table, improvised from a box lid, a camp cot with its army bedding, a stand, a folding table, a water basin set on three tent pegs to form a stand, a folding table, a candle stuck in a bottle, a sabre, an old service blouse, and a spare campaign hat complete his furnishings…

Still farther from the railroad tracks lies the cavalry camp. Its duty is more diversified than that of the artillery, for theirs is a more active arm of the service. Their drills have a continuous dash and vim seen nowhere else. If one is fortunate enough to be in camp when an inspecting officer comes around, he will see an entire regiment turn out, in heavy marching order, with everything on the man and horse that is to be carried when the cavalry take the field. The vastness of an army of cavalry is then apparent. Over the broad, sandy beach for almost a mile, they spread and stand at attention until the inspection is finished. Then, with a dash and a jump, they wheel by troops and gallop off to camp, glad that the necessary trial is over. The little groups around the mess tents, the cooking outfits, the conical wall tents of the men, their songs, their jokes with each other, their sports and pastimes, their clowns, their acrobats and their story tellers—all these have a place in the camp and are a part of it…

When off duty, the enlisted man, no matter what arm of the service he be in, fraternizes with his friends in other branches, and goes to town with them for a good time. With the call to arms widely wished for, the stentorian cries of "On to Cuba" mingled with "Remember the *Maine*" echo through the streets.

East Side Saloon Men Protest, Talk of Fighting the Brewers' Position on the Beer Tax
New York Tribune, July 1, 1898

A lively meeting of the members of the East Side Liquor Dealers' Association was held yesterday in Liberty Hall, No. 257 East Houston Street. The association was formed last Monday, and its primary object is to fight the beer brewers in the stand which the latter have taken in relation to the war tax on beer. Speeches were made in English and German, and it was stated that the East Side saloonkeepers would suffer more from being compelled by the brewers to pay all the war tax of $1 a barrel on beer than their brethren in more favored sections of the city because they have to give big schooners and pints. They also have to compete with many cheap places where beer is sold for $0.03 a glass. The fact that the brewers charged the whole of the $1 tax on the saloonkeepers, when the government allows a rebate to the brewers of $0.07 for leakage, was also brought out…

An Irishman, who was one of the speakers, advised his hearers to shorten their pints. He declared that a good way to measure a pint was to turn on the spigot and let it run until the dealer counted eight. He acknowledged that many of his customers objected to his new method of measuring, but he said he told them if they did not like it, to drink ice water.

Letter to the Editor: Troops with Springfield Rifles, Reasons Why They Are Put at a Disadvantage with Obsolete Weapons and Powder
New York Tribune, July 1, 1898

Sir: As a regular subscriber to our valued journal, I trust you will spare me space for a few remarks relative to a subject which I look upon as of the utmost importance to us at the present time. I refer to a statement said to emanate from the War Department, and relating to small arms for our volunteer forces. The statement is that "the question of the armament of the troops with proper rifles cannot be discussed."

If this decision is final, it means sending our boys into action armed with the Springfield rifle, an obsolete weapon, and far inferior in every respect to that with which our foe is supplied. The Spanish regular arm is the Mauser magazine small-bore rifle, using smokeless powder ammunition, and having a range vastly superior to the Springfield, which is a single-shot rifle, using black powder, giving slow velocity and high trajectory. Our men will be subject to annihilation by an enemy they cannot see, and owing to the absence of smoke, could not even approximately locate, while each puff from the Springfield would betray the shooter and be a well-defined target for concentrated fire, almost inevitably resulting in a casualty on our side.

This would be a severe test, even for veterans, one to which our boys should never be subjected, and I feel sure your attention has only to be called to the matter in order that it may receive a thorough ventilation, which will compel a reconsideration.

I ask your aid in the interest of those who have friends and relatives in the ranks, and also in the interest of the boys themselves, who, as volunteers, form the bulk of our forces, and upon whom the success of our arms will largely depend.

—F.A. Ilion, New York

Troubles of Ladies' Tailors
New York Times, June 13, 1898

Ladies' tailoring is becoming an important branch of industry in this city, and the 1,500 and odd union ladies' tailors are complaining that their employers have taken advantage of the dull season to try and break up their organization.

In this trade, the men have been encroaching upon the domain of the female dressmaker, and men's tailor-made suits have, it is said, been steadily becoming more fashionable, and many men who were formally employed in the male tailor's trade have become ladies' tailors because they can earn more money. They earn between $18 and $20 per week.

With the return of the summer, the dull season for ladies' tailors begins. Fashionable girls and women hurry off to the summer resorts, where, the men say, gauze and muslin and other light clothing are the general rule, and the women are not so particular as to the exact fit of these outdoor summer garments as they are about their city dresses. Consequently, the demand for fine dresses has greatly fallen off, and that for fashionable evening dresses does not cut much of a figure.

The men say that the employers have taken advantage of all this, and are urging them to sign statements that they will not join any union while in their employ, and if they are already members of unions, to state that fact.

Thomas & Co. Close Down
New York Times, February 6, 1898

As a result of the strike among the employees, the firm of Thomas & Co., shoe manufacturers at Hewes and South Fifth Streets, Brooklyn, yesterday shut down its large plant, and it is not known how long it will be closed.

There were nearly 500 employees, among them Dennis Ward. He is regarded by the union men as a "scab." They requested the superintendent, Charles Turner, to discharge him. The superintendent refused, and on Tuesday, 250 men went on strike. Two days later the strikers were joined by 100 more employees. It was said that the shutdown was necessary because the boilers needed an overhauling.

The strikers denied this last night, and said the firm could not go on with work while the strike is in progress. The strikers declare they will not yield until Ward is discharged. The firm, it is said, will not discharge Ward, but would not object should he voluntarily withdraw.

৵৵৵৵৵৵৵

Small Riot of Shop Girls
New York Times, January 22, 1898

There was a small riot of shop girls in Sixth Avenue last night, resulting from the arrest of one of their escorts.

A large number of young men have been in the habit of gathering about the employees' entrance of the Siegel-Cooper Company's store in the evening at the time for the hundreds of girls who are employed there to leave and go to their homes. The authorities of the store instructed Detective Bernard and Special Policeman John Leonard, whom they employ, to disperse the gathering.

Last evening, the young men as they assembled were warned to keep away. They defied the officers and maintained that they had the right to stand or walk in the street as long as they were peaceful. George Wallun of 410 East Twenty-third Street, who said he was in the habit of calling to escort a young woman to whom he is engaged, mounted a box and proceeded to make a speech. Bernard arrested him, and Leonard was leading him away when the girls began to swarm out like hornets. They surrounded the policeman and the prisoner and made Leonard's face burn with their sarcasms.

The young woman for whom Wallun had called fainted when she heard he was under arrest. She was promptly carried away by her friends, but the incident increased the indignation of the other girls who gathered 500 strong on the sidewalk and said they would strike if the order against escorts was not rescinded.

This section begins with six state-by-state ranking tables from the 1880, 1900, and 2010 Census, designed to help define the times during which the families profiled in Section One lived. Table topics are listed below. Following the state-by-state tables are reprints from the 1890 Census of Population, including Progress of the Nation: 1790 to 1890. This data is portrayed by maps, tables, graphs, charts and narrative, helping to visualize the environment at that time. Note that the reprints show two page numbers: the number at the top of the page is from the original Census document.

State-by-State Comparative Tables: 1880, 1900 and 2010

Eleventh Census of the United States: 1890

Population of the United States, Part I

Total Population

Area	Population			1880		1900		2010	
	1880	1900	2010	Area	Rank	Area	Rank	Area	Rank
Alabama	1,262,505	1,828,697	4,779,736	New York	1	New York	1	California	1
Alaska	n/a	n/a	710,231	Pennsylvania	2	Pennsylvania	2	Texas	2
Arizona	40,440	122,931	6,392,017	Ohio	3	Illinois	3	New York	3
Arkansas	802,525	1,311,564	2,915,918	Illinois	4	Ohio	4	Florida	4
California	864,694	1,485,053	37,253,956	Missouri	5	Missouri	5	Illinois	5
Colorado	194,327	539,700	5,029,196	Indiana	6	Texas	6	Pennsylvania	6
Connecticut	622,700	908,420	3,574,097	Massachusetts	7	Massachusetts	7	Ohio	7
D.C.	177,624	278,718	601,723	Kentucky	8	Indiana	8	Michigan	8
Delaware	146,608	184,735	897,934	Michigan	9	Michigan	9	Georgia	9
Florida	269,493	528,542	18,801,310	Iowa	10	Iowa	10	North Carolina	10
Georgia	1,542,180	2,216,331	9,687,653	Texas	11	Georgia	11	New Jersey	11
Hawaii	n/a	n/a	1,360,301	Tennessee	12	Kentucky	12	Virginia	12
Idaho	32,610	161,772	1,567,582	Georgia	13	Wisconsin	13	Washington	13
Illinois	3,077,871	4,821,550	12,830,632	Virginia	14	Tennessee	14	Massachusetts	14
Indiana	1,978,301	2,516,462	6,483,802	North Carolina	15	North Carolina	15	Indiana	15
Iowa	1,624,615	2,231,853	3,046,355	Wisconsin	16	New Jersey	16	Arizona	16
Kansas	996,096	1,470,495	2,853,118	Alabama	17	Virginia	17	Tennessee	17
Kentucky	1,648,690	2,147,174	4,339,367	Mississippi	18	Alabama	18	Missouri	18
Louisiana	939,946	1,381,625	4,533,372	New Jersey	19	Minnesota	19	Maryland	19
Maine	648,936	694,466	1,328,361	Kansas	20	Mississippi	20	Wisconsin	20
Maryland	934,943	1,188,044	5,773,552	South Carolina	21	California	21	Minnesota	21
Massachusetts	1,783,085	2,805,346	6,547,629	Louisiana	22	Kansas	22	Colorado	22
Michigan	1,636,937	2,420,982	9,883,640	Maryland	23	Louisiana	23	Alabama	23
Minnesota	780,773	1,751,394	5,303,925	California	24	South Carolina	24	South Carolina	24
Mississippi	1,131,597	1,551,270	2,967,297	Arkansas	25	Arkansas	25	Louisiana	25
Missouri	2,168,380	3,106,665	5,988,927	Minnesota	26	Maryland	26	Kentucky	26
Montana	39,159	243,329	989,415	Maine	27	Nebraska	27	Oregon	27
Nebraska	452,402	1,066,300	1,826,341	Connecticut	28	West Virginia	28	Oklahoma	28
Nevada	62,266	42,335	2,700,551	West Virginia	29	Connecticut	29	Connecticut	29
New Hampshire	346,991	411,588	1,316,470	Nebraska	30	Oklahoma	30	Iowa	30
New Jersey	1,131,116	1,883,669	8,791,894	New Hampshire	31	Maine	31	Mississippi	31
New Mexico	119,565	195,310	2,059,179	Vermont	32	Colorado	32	Arkansas	32
New York	5,082,871	7,268,894	19,378,102	Rhode Island	33	Florida	33	Kansas	33
North Carolina	1,399,750	1,893,810	9,535,483	Florida	34	Washington	34	Utah	34
North Dakota	36,909	319,146	672,591	Colorado	35	Rhode Island	35	Nevada	35
Ohio	3,198,062	4,157,545	11,536,504	D.C.	36	Oregon	36	New Mexico	36
Oklahoma	n/a	790,391	3,751,351	Oregon	37	New Hampshire	37	West Virginia	37
Oregon	174,768	413,536	3,831,074	Delaware	38	South Dakota	38	Nebraska	38
Pennsylvania	4,282,891	6,302,115	12,702,379	Utah	39	Vermont	39	Idaho	39
Rhode Island	276,531	428,556	1,052,567	New Mexico	40	North Dakota	40	Hawaii	40
South Carolina	995,577	1,340,316	4,625,364	South Dakota	41	D.C.	41	Maine	41
South Dakota	98,268	401,570	814,180	Washington	42	Utah	42	New Hampshire	42
Tennessee	1,542,359	2,020,616	6,346,105	Nevada	43	Montana	43	Rhode Island	43
Texas	1,591,749	3,048,710	25,145,561	Arizona	44	New Mexico	44	Montana	44
Utah	143,963	276,749	2,763,885	Montana	45	Delaware	45	Delaware	45
Vermont	332,286	343,641	625,741	North Dakota	46	Idaho	46	South Dakota	46
Virginia	1,512,565	1,854,184	8,001,024	Idaho	47	Arizona	47	Alaska	47
Washington	75,116	518,103	6,724,540	Wyoming	48	Wyoming	48	North Dakota	48
West Virginia	618,457	958,800	1,852,994	Hawaii	n/a	Nevada	49	Vermont	49
Wisconsin	1,315,497	2,069,042	5,686,986	Oklahoma	n/a	Hawaii	n/a	D.C.	50
Wyoming	20,789	92,531	563,626	Alaska	n/a	Alaska	n/a	Wyoming	51
United States	50,155,783	75,994,575	308,745,538	United States	–	United States	–	United States	–

Note: The following states were technically territories during the 1880 Census: North and South Dakota (Dakota Territory); Montana; Washington; Idaho; Wyoming; Utah; Oklahoma; New Mexico; and Arizona. The following states were technically territories during the 1900 Census: Oklahoma; New Mexico; and Arizona.
Source: U.S. Census Bureau, 1880 Census of Population; U.S. Census Bureau, 1900 Census of Population; U.S. Census Bureau, Census 2010

White Population

Area	Percent of Population			1880		1900		2010	
	1880	1900	2010	Area	Rank	Area	Rank	Area	Rank
Alabama	52.45	54.75	68.53	New Hampshire	1	New Hampshire	1	Vermont	1
Alaska	n/a	n/a	66.68	Vermont	2	Vermont	2	Maine	2
Arizona	86.94	75.57	73.01	Maine	2	Maine	3	West Virginia	3
Arkansas	73.71	72.02	77.00	Wisconsin	4	Wisconsin	4	New Hampshire	4
California	88.72	94.46	57.59	Minnesota	5	Iowa	5	Iowa	5
Colorado	98.35	98.03	81.31	Nebraska	6	Minnesota	6	Wyoming	6
Connecticut	98.08	98.24	77.57	Iowa	7	Nebraska	7	North Dakota	7
D.C.	66.44	68.72	38.47	Utah	8	Michigan	8	Montana	8
Delaware	81.96	83.35	68.89	Massachusetts	9	Massachusetts	9	Idaho	9
Florida	52.92	56.26	75.04	New York	10	New York	10	Kentucky	10
Georgia	52.97	53.30	59.74	South Dakota	11	Utah	11	Wisconsin	11
Hawaii	n/a	n/a	24.74	Michigan	12	Connecticut	12	Nebraska	12
Idaho	88.97	95.50	89.09	Illinois	13	Illinois	13	Utah	13
Illinois	98.48	98.20	71.53	Colorado	14	Colorado	14	South Dakota	14
Indiana	98.00	97.70	84.33	Connecticut	15	Rhode Island	15	Minnesota	15
Iowa	99.38	99.41	91.31	North Dakota	16	Indiana	16	Indiana	16
Kansas	95.59	96.32	83.80	Indiana	17	North Dakota	17	Kansas	17
Kentucky	83.53	86.73	87.79	Pennsylvania	18	Ohio	18	Oregon	18
Louisiana	48.40	52.81	62.56	Rhode Island	19	Pennsylvania	19	Missouri	19
Maine	99.68	99.68	95.23	Ohio	20	Kansas	20	Ohio	20
Maryland	77.51	80.17	58.18	New Jersey	21	Wyoming	21	Pennsylvania	21
Massachusetts	98.92	98.73	80.41	West Virginia	22	New Jersey	22	Rhode Island	22
Michigan	98.63	99.07	78.95	Kansas	23	Washington	23	Colorado	23
Minnesota	99.50	99.18	85.30	Wyoming	24	Idaho	24	Massachusetts	24
Mississippi	42.36	41.33	59.13	Oregon	25	West Virginia	25	Michigan	25
Missouri	93.29	94.79	82.80	Missouri	26	Oregon	26	Connecticut	26
Montana	90.36	92.99	89.44	New Mexico	27	South Dakota	27	Tennessee	27
Nebraska	99.42	99.08	86.12	Montana	28	Missouri	28	Washington	28
Nevada	86.01	83.63	66.16	Washington	29	California	29	Arkansas	29
New Hampshire	99.78	99.81	93.89	Idaho	30	Montana	30	Florida	30
New Jersey	96.54	96.21	68.58	California	31	New Mexico	31	Arizona	31
New Mexico	90.93	92.27	68.37	Arizona	32	Kentucky	32	Oklahoma	32
New York	98.68	98.46	65.75	Nevada	33	Oklahoma	33	Illinois	33
North Carolina	61.96	66.72	68.47	Kentucky	34	Nevada	34	Texas	34
North Dakota	98.06	97.67	90.02	Delaware	35	Delaware	35	Delaware	35
Ohio	97.49	97.66	82.69	Maryland	36	Maryland	36	New Jersey	36
Oklahoma	n/a	84.79	72.16	Texas	37	Texas	37	Virginia	36
Oregon	93.31	95.42	83.65	Tennessee	38	Tennessee	38	Alabama	38
Pennsylvania	97.99	97.45	81.92	Arkansas	39	Arizona	39	North Carolina	39
Rhode Island	97.62	97.78	81.41	D.C.	40	Arkansas	40	New Mexico	40
South Carolina	39.28	41.62	66.16	North Carolina	41	D.C.	41	Alaska	41
South Dakota	98.66	94.81	85.90	Virginia	42	North Carolina	42	Nevada	42
Tennessee	73.84	76.22	77.56	Georgia	43	Virginia	43	South Carolina	42
Texas	75.22	79.60	70.40	Florida	44	Florida	44	New York	44
Utah	98.93	98.45	86.09	Alabama	45	Alabama	45	Louisiana	45
Vermont	99.68	99.75	95.29	Louisiana	46	Georgia	46	Georgia	46
Virginia	58.24	64.33	68.58	Mississippi	47	Louisiana	47	Mississippi	47
Washington	89.46	95.79	77.27	South Carolina	48	South Carolina	48	Maryland	48
West Virginia	95.81	95.46	93.90	Hawaii	n/a	Mississippi	49	California	49
Wisconsin	99.55	99.46	86.20	Oklahoma	n/a	Hawaii	n/a	D.C.	50
Wyoming	93.50	96.24	90.71	Alaska	n/a	Alaska	n/a	Hawaii	51
United States	86.54	87.91	72.41	United States	–	United States	–	United States	–

Note: The following states were technically territories during the 1880 Census: North and South Dakota (Dakota Territory); Montana; Washington; Idaho; Wyoming; Utah; Oklahoma; New Mexico; and Arizona. The following states were technically territories during the 1900 Census: Oklahoma; New Mexico; and Arizona.
Source: U.S. Census Bureau, 1880 Census of Population; U.S. Census Bureau, 1900 Census of Population; U.S. Census Bureau, Census 2010

Black Population

Area	Percent of Population			1880		1900		2010	
	1880	1900	2010	Area	Rank	Area	Rank	Area	Rank
Alabama	47.53	45.24	26.18	South Carolina	1	Mississippi	1	D.C.	1
Alaska	n/a	n/a	3.28	Mississippi	2	South Carolina	2	Mississippi	2
Arizona	0.38	1.50	4.05	Louisiana	3	Louisiana	3	Louisiana	3
Arkansas	26.25	27.97	15.43	Alabama	4	Georgia	4	Georgia	4
California	0.70	0.74	6.17	Georgia	5	Alabama	5	Maryland	5
Colorado	1.25	1.59	4.01	Florida	6	Florida	6	South Carolina	6
Connecticut	1.85	1.68	10.14	Virginia	7	Virginia	7	Alabama	7
D.C.	33.55	31.11	50.71	North Carolina	8	North Carolina	8	North Carolina	8
Delaware	18.04	16.62	21.36	D.C.	9	D.C.	9	Delaware	9
Florida	47.01	43.65	15.96	Arkansas	10	Arkansas	10	Virginia	10
Georgia	47.02	46.69	30.46	Tennessee	11	Tennessee	11	Tennessee	11
Hawaii	n/a	n/a	1.57	Texas	12	Texas	12	Florida	12
Idaho	0.16	0.18	0.63	Maryland	13	Maryland	13	New York	13
Illinois	1.51	1.76	14.55	Delaware	14	Delaware	14	Arkansas	14
Indiana	1.98	2.29	9.12	Kentucky	15	Kentucky	15	Illinois	15
Iowa	0.59	0.57	2.93	Missouri	16	Oklahoma	16	Michigan	16
Kansas	4.33	3.54	5.88	Kansas	17	Missouri	17	New Jersey	17
Kentucky	16.46	13.26	7.78	West Virginia	18	West Virginia	18	Ohio	18
Louisiana	51.46	47.10	32.04	New Jersey	19	New Jersey	19	Texas	19
Maine	0.22	0.19	1.18	Ohio	20	Kansas	20	Missouri	20
Maryland	22.49	19.79	29.45	Rhode Island	21	Pennsylvania	21	Pennsylvania	21
Massachusetts	1.05	1.14	6.63	Pennsylvania	22	Ohio	22	Connecticut	22
Michigan	0.92	0.65	14.17	Indiana	23	Indiana	23	Indiana	23
Minnesota	0.20	0.28	5.17	Connecticut	24	Rhode Island	24	Nevada	24
Mississippi	57.47	58.51	37.02	Illinois	25	Illinois	25	Kentucky	25
Missouri	6.70	5.19	11.58	Wyoming	26	Connecticut	26	Oklahoma	26
Montana	0.88	0.63	0.41	New York	27	Colorado	27	Massachusetts	27
Nebraska	0.53	0.59	4.54	Colorado	28	Arizona	28	Wisconsin	28
Nevada	0.78	0.32	8.10	Massachusetts	29	New York	29	California	29
New Hampshire	0.20	0.16	1.14	Michigan	30	Massachusetts	30	Kansas	30
New Jersey	3.43	3.71	13.70	Montana	31	Wyoming	31	Rhode Island	31
New Mexico	0.85	0.82	2.07	New Mexico	32	New Mexico	32	Minnesota	32
New York	1.28	1.37	15.86	Nevada	33	California	33	Nebraska	33
North Carolina	37.96	32.97	21.48	California	34	Michigan	34	Arizona	34
North Dakota	0.31	0.09	1.18	Iowa	35	Montana	35	Colorado	35
Ohio	2.50	2.33	12.20	Nebraska	36	Nebraska	36	Washington	36
Oklahoma	n/a	7.05	7.40	Washington	37	Iowa	37	West Virginia	37
Oregon	0.28	0.27	1.81	Arizona	38	Washington	38	Alaska	38
Pennsylvania	2.00	2.49	10.85	Vermont	39	Nevada	39	Iowa	39
Rhode Island	2.35	2.12	5.72	North Dakota	40	Minnesota	40	New Mexico	40
South Carolina	60.70	58.37	27.90	South Dakota	41	Oregon	41	Oregon	41
South Dakota	0.29	0.12	1.25	Oregon	42	Utah	42	Hawaii	42
Tennessee	26.14	23.77	16.66	Maine	43	Vermont	42	South Dakota	43
Texas	24.71	20.36	11.85	Wisconsin	44	Maine	44	Maine	44
Utah	0.16	0.24	1.06	Minnesota	45	Idaho	45	North Dakota	44
Vermont	0.32	0.24	1.00	New Hampshire	45	New Hampshire	46	New Hampshire	46
Virginia	41.76	35.63	19.39	Utah	47	Wisconsin	47	Utah	47
Washington	0.43	0.49	3.57	Idaho	47	South Dakota	47	Vermont	48
West Virginia	4.19	4.54	3.41	Hawaii	n/a	North Dakota	49	Wyoming	49
Wisconsin	0.21	0.12	6.32	Oklahoma	n/a	Hawaii	n/a	Idaho	50
Wyoming	1.43	1.02	0.84	Alaska	n/a	Alaska	n/a	Montana	51
United States	13.12	11.62	12.61	United States	–	United States	–	United States	–

Note: The following states were technically territories during the 1880 Census: North and South Dakota (Dakota Territory); Montana; Washington; Idaho; Wyoming; Utah; Oklahoma; New Mexico; and Arizona. The following states were technically territories during the 1900 Census: Oklahoma; New Mexico; and Arizona.
Source: U.S. Census Bureau, 1880 Census of Population; U.S. Census Bureau, 1900 Census of Population; U.S. Census Bureau, Census 2010

American Indian/Alaska Native Population

Area	Percent of Population 1880	1900	2010	1880 Area	Rank	1900 Area	Rank	2010 Area	Rank
Alabama	0.02	0.01	0.59	Arizona	1	Arizona	1	Alaska	1
Alaska	n/a	n/a	14.77	New Mexico	2	Nevada	2	New Mexico	2
Arizona	8.64	21.54	4.64	Washington	3	Oklahoma	3	South Dakota	3
Arkansas	0.02	0.01	0.76	Nevada	4	New Mexico	4	Oklahoma	4
California	1.88	1.04	0.97	Montana	5	South Dakota	5	Montana	5
Colorado	0.08	0.27	1.11	California	6	Montana	6	North Dakota	6
Connecticut	0.04	0.02	0.31	North Dakota	7	Idaho	7	Arizona	7
D.C.	0.00	0.01	0.35	Oregon	8	North Dakota	8	Wyoming	8
Delaware	0.00	0.00	0.47	South Dakota	9	Washington	9	Washington	9
Florida	0.07	0.07	0.38	Wyoming	10	Wyoming	10	Oregon	10
Georgia	0.01	0.00	0.33	Utah	11	Oregon	11	Idaho	11
Hawaii	n/a	n/a	0.31	Idaho	12	California	12	North Carolina	12
Idaho	0.51	2.61	1.37	Michigan	13	Utah	13	Nevada	13
Illinois	0.00	0.00	0.34	Minnesota	14	Minnesota	14	Utah	13
Indiana	0.01	0.01	0.28	Wisconsin	15	Wisconsin	15	Minnesota	15
Iowa	0.03	0.02	0.36	Mississippi	16	Nebraska	16	Colorado	16
Kansas	0.08	0.14	0.99	Maine	17	North Carolina	17	Nebraska	17
Kentucky	0.00	0.00	0.23	North Carolina	18	Colorado	18	Kansas	18
Louisiana	0.09	0.04	0.67	Louisiana	18	Michigan	19	California	19
Maine	0.10	0.11	0.65	Colorado	20	Mississippi	20	Wisconsin	20
Maryland	0.00	0.00	0.35	Kansas	20	Kansas	20	Arkansas	21
Massachusetts	0.02	0.02	0.29	Florida	22	Maine	22	Texas	22
Michigan	0.44	0.26	0.63	Texas	23	New York	23	Louisiana	23
Minnesota	0.29	0.52	1.15	Nebraska	24	Florida	23	Maine	24
Mississippi	0.16	0.14	0.51	Connecticut	25	Louisiana	25	Michigan	25
Missouri	0.01	0.00	0.46	Rhode Island	26	Pennsylvania	26	Alabama	26
Montana	4.25	4.66	6.32	Iowa	26	Virginia	27	Rhode Island	27
Nebraska	0.05	0.31	1.01	Tennessee	28	Connecticut	27	New York	28
Nevada	4.50	12.32	1.19	Arkansas	28	Texas	27	Mississippi	29
New Hampshire	0.02	0.01	0.24	Alabama	28	Iowa	27	Delaware	30
New Jersey	0.01	0.00	0.33	Massachusetts	28	Massachusetts	27	Missouri	31
New Mexico	8.17	6.73	9.38	New York	28	Indiana	32	South Carolina	32
New York	0.02	0.07	0.55	New Hampshire	28	South Carolina	32	Florida	33
North Carolina	0.09	0.30	1.28	Missouri	34	New Hampshire	32	Virginia	34
North Dakota	1.61	2.18	5.44	Georgia	34	Alabama	32	Iowa	35
Ohio	0.00	0.00	0.22	Virginia	34	Tennessee	32	Maryland	36
Oklahoma	n/a	8.15	8.58	South Carolina	34	D.C.	32	D.C.	36
Oregon	0.97	1.20	1.39	Indiana	34	Rhode Island	32	Vermont	36
Pennsylvania	0.00	0.03	0.21	New Jersey	34	Arkansas	32	Illinois	39
Rhode Island	0.03	0.01	0.58	Maryland	40	Missouri	40	New Jersey	40
South Carolina	0.01	0.01	0.42	Ohio	40	Illinois	40	Georgia	40
South Dakota	0.81	5.04	8.82	Pennsylvania	40	Ohio	40	Tennessee	42
Tennessee	0.02	0.01	0.32	Vermont	40	New Jersey	40	Hawaii	43
Texas	0.06	0.02	0.68	Kentucky	40	Delaware	40	Connecticut	43
Utah	0.56	0.95	1.19	Delaware	40	Georgia	40	Massachusetts	45
Vermont	0.00	0.00	0.35	D.C.	40	Kentucky	40	Indiana	46
Virginia	0.01	0.02	0.37	West Virginia	40	Maryland	40	New Hampshire	47
Washington	5.86	1.94	1.54	Illinois	40	West Virginia	40	Kentucky	48
West Virginia	0.00	0.00	0.20	Alaska	n/a	Vermont	40	Ohio	49
Wisconsin	0.24	0.40	0.96	Hawaii	n/a	Alaska	n/a	Pennsylvania	50
Wyoming	0.67	1.82	2.37	Oklahoma	n/a	Hawaii	n/a	West Virginia	51
United States	0.13	0.31	0.95	United States	–	United States	–	United States	–

Note: The following states were technically territories during the 1880 Census: North and South Dakota (Dakota Territory); Montana; Washington; Idaho; Wyoming; Utah; Oklahoma; New Mexico; and Arizona. The following states were technically territories during the 1900 Census: Oklahoma; New Mexico; and Arizona.

Source: U.S. Census Bureau, 1880 Census of Population; U.S. Census Bureau, 1900 Census of Population; U.S. Census Bureau, Census 2010

Asian Population

Area	Percent of Population			1880		1900		2010	
	1880	1900	2010	Area	Rank	Area	Rank	Area	Rank
Alabama	0.00	0.00	1.12	Idaho	1	California	1	Hawaii	1
Alaska	n/a	n/a	5.37	California	2	Nevada	2	California	2
Arizona	4.04	1.38	2.76	Nevada	2	Oregon	3	New Jersey	3
Arkansas	0.02	0.00	1.24	Oregon	4	Washington	4	New York	4
California	8.70	3.76	13.05	Montana	5	Montana	5	Nevada	5
Colorado	0.31	0.12	2.76	Wyoming	6	Idaho	6	Washington	6
Connecticut	0.02	0.07	3.79	Washington	7	Arizona	7	Maryland	7
D.C.	0.01	0.17	3.50	Arizona	8	Wyoming	8	Virginia	8
Delaware	0.00	0.03	3.18	Utah	9	Utah	9	Alaska	9
Florida	0.01	0.02	2.42	Colorado	10	New Mexico	10	Massachusetts	10
Georgia	0.00	0.01	3.25	South Dakota	11	D.C.	11	Illinois	11
Hawaii	n/a	n/a	38.60	New Mexico	12	Colorado	12	Minnesota	12
Idaho	10.36	1.70	1.22	Louisiana	12	Massachusetts	13	Texas	13
Illinois	0.01	0.03	4.57	Arkansas	14	New York	14	Connecticut	14
Indiana	0.00	0.01	1.58	Connecticut	14	Rhode Island	15	Oregon	15
Iowa	0.00	0.00	1.74	North Dakota	14	New Jersey	16	D.C.	16
Kansas	0.00	0.00	2.38	New Jersey	14	Connecticut	17	Georgia	17
Kentucky	0.00	0.00	1.13	New York	14	North Dakota	18	Delaware	18
Louisiana	0.05	0.04	1.55	Texas	19	Maryland	19	Rhode Island	19
Maine	0.00	0.02	1.02	Florida	19	Louisiana	20	Arizona	20
Maryland	0.00	0.05	5.52	Rhode Island	19	South Dakota	20	Colorado	20
Massachusetts	0.01	0.11	5.34	Massachusetts	19	Pennsylvania	22	Pennsylvania	22
Michigan	0.00	0.01	2.41	Illinois	19	New Hampshire	22	Florida	23
Minnesota	0.00	0.01	4.04	D.C.	19	Delaware	22	Michigan	24
Mississippi	0.00	0.02	0.87	Missouri	25	Texas	22	Kansas	25
Missouri	0.00	0.01	1.64	Tennessee	25	Illinois	22	Wisconsin	26
Montana	4.51	1.72	0.63	Minnesota	25	Mississippi	27	North Carolina	27
Nebraska	0.00	0.02	1.77	New Hampshire	25	Nebraska	27	New Hampshire	28
Nevada	8.70	3.73	7.24	Wisconsin	25	Maine	27	Utah	29
New Hampshire	0.00	0.03	2.16	Mississippi	25	Florida	27	Nebraska	30
New Jersey	0.02	0.08	8.25	Georgia	25	Virginia	31	Iowa	31
New Mexico	0.05	0.18	1.37	Ohio	25	Missouri	31	Oklahoma	32
New York	0.02	0.10	7.33	Pennsylvania	25	Indiana	31	Ohio	33
North Carolina	0.00	0.00	2.19	Virginia	25	Wisconsin	31	Missouri	34
North Dakota	0.02	0.06	1.03	Michigan	25	Ohio	31	Indiana	35
Ohio	0.00	0.01	1.67	Vermont	25	Michigan	31	Louisiana	36
Oklahoma	n/a	0.01	1.73	Kentucky	25	Oklahoma	31	Tennessee	37
Oregon	5.44	3.12	3.69	Delaware	25	Minnesota	31	New Mexico	38
Pennsylvania	0.00	0.03	2.75	Alabama	25	Georgia	31	South Carolina	39
Rhode Island	0.01	0.09	2.89	Iowa	25	West Virginia	31	Vermont	40
South Carolina	0.00	0.00	1.28	South Carolina	25	Vermont	31	Arkansas	41
South Dakota	0.23	0.04	0.93	Kansas	25	Arkansas	42	Idaho	42
Tennessee	0.00	0.00	1.44	West Virginia	25	South Carolina	42	Kentucky	43
Texas	0.01	0.03	3.84	Nebraska	25	Alabama	42	Alabama	44
Utah	0.35	0.36	2.00	Indiana	25	North Carolina	42	North Dakota	45
Vermont	0.00	0.01	1.27	North Carolina	25	Tennessee	42	Maine	46
Virginia	0.00	0.01	5.50	Maine	25	Kansas	42	South Dakota	47
Washington	4.24	1.78	7.15	Maryland	25	Kentucky	42	Mississippi	48
West Virginia	0.00	0.01	0.67	Alaska	n/a	Iowa	42	Wyoming	49
Wisconsin	0.00	0.01	2.27	Hawaii	n/a	Alaska	n/a	West Virginia	50
Wyoming	4.40	0.92	0.79	Oklahoma	n/a	Hawaii	n/a	Montana	51
United States	0.21	0.15	4.75	United States	–	United States	–	United States	–

Note: The following states were technically territories during the 1880 Census: North and South Dakota (Dakota Territory); Montana; Washington; Idaho; Wyoming; Utah; Oklahoma; New Mexico; and Arizona. The following states were technically territories during the 1900 Census: Oklahoma; New Mexico; and Arizona.
Source: U.S. Census Bureau, 1880 Census of Population; U.S. Census Bureau, 1900 Census of Population; U.S. Census Bureau, Census 2010

Homeownership

Area	Percent of Population			1880		1900		2010	
	1880	1900	2010	Area	Rank	Area	Rank	Area	Rank
Alabama	n/a	34.4	69.7	Alabama	n/a	North Dakota	1	West Virginia	1
Alaska	n/a	n/a	63.1	Alaska	n/a	Idaho	2	Minnesota	2
Arizona	n/a	57.5	66.0	Arizona	n/a	South Dakota	3	Michigan	3
Arkansas	n/a	47.7	66.9	Arkansas	n/a	New Mexico	4	Iowa	3
California	n/a	46.3	56.0	California	n/a	Utah	5	Delaware	5
Colorado	n/a	46.6	65.5	Colorado	n/a	Wisconsin	6	Maine	6
Connecticut	n/a	39.0	67.5	Connecticut	n/a	Nevada	7	New Hampshire	7
D.C.	n/a	24.0	42.0	D.C.	n/a	Maine	8	Vermont	8
Delaware	n/a	36.3	72.0	Delaware	n/a	Minnesota	9	Utah	9
Florida	n/a	46.8	67.3	Florida	n/a	Michigan	10	Idaho	10
Georgia	n/a	30.6	65.7	Georgia	n/a	Iowa	11	Indiana	11
Hawaii	n/a	n/a	57.7	Hawaii	n/a	Vermont	12	Alabama	12
Idaho	n/a	71.6	69.9	Idaho	n/a	Kansas	13	Pennsylvania	13
Illinois	n/a	45.0	67.4	Illinois	n/a	Oregon	14	Mississippi	13
Indiana	n/a	56.1	69.8	Indiana	n/a	Arizona	15	South Carolina	15
Iowa	n/a	60.5	72.1	Iowa	n/a	Nebraska	16	Wyoming	15
Kansas	n/a	59.1	67.7	Kansas	n/a	Montana	17	Missouri	17
Kentucky	n/a	51.5	68.7	Kentucky	n/a	Indiana	18	Kentucky	18
Louisiana	n/a	31.4	67.3	Louisiana	n/a	Wyoming	19	New Mexico	19
Maine	n/a	64.8	71.3	Maine	n/a	West Virginia	20	Tennessee	20
Maryland	n/a	40.0	67.5	Maryland	n/a	Washington	21	Wisconsin	21
Massachusetts	n/a	35.0	62.3	Massachusetts	n/a	Oklahoma	22	South Dakota	21
Michigan	n/a	62.3	72.1	Michigan	n/a	New Hampshire	23	Montana	23
Minnesota	n/a	63.5	73.1	Minnesota	n/a	Ohio	24	Kansas	24
Mississippi	n/a	34.5	69.6	Mississippi	n/a	Kentucky	25	Ohio	25
Missouri	n/a	50.9	68.8	Missouri	n/a	Missouri	26	Maryland	26
Montana	n/a	56.6	68.0	Montana	n/a	Virginia	27	Connecticut	26
Nebraska	n/a	56.8	67.2	Nebraska	n/a	Arkansas	28	Illinois	28
Nevada	n/a	66.2	58.8	Nevada	n/a	Florida	29	Florida	29
New Hampshire	n/a	53.9	70.9	New Hampshire	n/a	Colorado	30	Oklahoma	29
New Jersey	n/a	34.3	65.4	New Jersey	n/a	North Carolina	30	Louisiana	29
New Mexico	n/a	68.5	68.5	New Mexico	n/a	Texas	32	Virginia	32
New York	n/a	33.2	53.3	New York	n/a	California	33	Nebraska	32
North Carolina	n/a	46.6	66.7	North Carolina	n/a	Tennessee	33	Arkansas	34
North Dakota	n/a	80.0	65.4	North Dakota	n/a	Illinois	35	North Carolina	35
Ohio	n/a	52.5	67.6	Ohio	n/a	Pennsylvania	36	Arizona	36
Oklahoma	n/a	54.2	67.3	Oklahoma	n/a	Maryland	37	Georgia	37
Oregon	n/a	58.7	62.1	Oregon	n/a	Connecticut	38	Colorado	38
Pennsylvania	n/a	41.2	69.6	Pennsylvania	n/a	Delaware	39	New Jersey	39
Rhode Island	n/a	28.6	60.7	Rhode Island	n/a	Massachusetts	40	North Dakota	39
South Carolina	n/a	30.6	69.3	South Carolina	n/a	Mississippi	41	Washington	41
South Dakota	n/a	71.2	68.1	South Dakota	n/a	Alabama	42	Texas	42
Tennessee	n/a	46.3	68.2	Tennessee	n/a	New Jersey	43	Alaska	43
Texas	n/a	46.5	63.7	Texas	n/a	New York	44	Massachusetts	44
Utah	n/a	67.8	70.5	Utah	n/a	Louisiana	45	Oregon	45
Vermont	n/a	60.4	70.7	Vermont	n/a	South Carolina	46	Rhode Island	46
Virginia	n/a	48.8	67.2	Virginia	n/a	Georgia	46	Nevada	47
Washington	n/a	54.5	63.9	Washington	n/a	Rhode Island	48	Hawaii	48
West Virginia	n/a	54.6	73.4	West Virginia	n/a	D.C.	49	California	49
Wisconsin	n/a	66.4	68.1	Wisconsin	n/a	Hawaii	n/a	New York	50
Wyoming	n/a	55.2	69.3	Wyoming	n/a	Alaska	n/a	D.C.	51
United States	n/a	46.5	65.1	United States	–	United States	–	United States	–

Note: The following states were technically territories during the 1880 Census: North and South Dakota (Dakota Territory); Montana; Washington; Idaho; Wyoming; Utah; Oklahoma; New Mexico; and Arizona. The following states were technically territories during the 1900 Census: Oklahoma; New Mexico; and Arizona.

Source: U.S. Census Bureau, 1880 Census of Population; U.S. Census Bureau, 1900 Census of Population; U.S. Census Bureau, Census 2010

DEPARTMENT OF THE INTERIOR,
CENSUS OFFICE.

ROBERT P. PORTER,
Superintendent.
Appointed April 20, 1889; resigned July 31, 1893.

CARROLL D. WRIGHT,
Commissioner of Labor in charge.
Appointed October 5, 1893.

REPORT

ON

POPULATION OF THE UNITED STATES

AT THE

ELEVENTH CENSUS: 1890.

PART I.

WASHINGTON, D. C.:
GOVERNMENT PRINTING OFFICE.
1895.

PROGRESS OF THE NATION

1790 TO 1890.

BY ROBERT P. PORTER, HENRY GANNETT, AND WILLIAM C. HUNT.

PROGRESS OF THE NATION.

AGGREGATE POPULATION.

The following table shows the aggregate population of the United States at each census from 1790 to 1890, together with the per cent of increase during each decade:

CENSUS YEARS.	Aggregate population.	Per cent of increase.
1790	3,929,214	....
1800	5,308,483	35.10
1810	7,239,881	36.38
1820	9,633,822	33.07
1830	12,866,020	33.55
1840	17,069,453	32.67
1850	23,191,876	35.87
1860	31,443,321	35.58
1870	38,558,371	22.63
1880	50,155,783	30.08
1890	62,622,250	24.86

The population of the United States on June 1, 1890, as shown by the general enumeration for all the states and organized territories, was 62,622,250; including 325,464 Indians and other persons in the Indian territory and on Indian reservations and 32,052 persons in Alaska, specially enumerated under the law, the entire population of the country was 62,979,766. In 1880 the population of the United States, exclusive of the population of the Indian territory, Indian reservations, and Alaska, was 50,155,783. The absolute increase of the population in the ten years intervening was 12,466,467, and the percentage of increase was 24.86. In 1870 the population was stated as 38,558,371. According to these figures the absolute increase in the decade between 1870 and 1880 was 11,597,412, and the percentage of increase was 30.08.

Upon their face these figures show that the population increased 869,055 more between 1880 and 1890 than between 1870 and 1880, while the rate of increase apparently diminished from 30.08 to 24.86 per cent. If these figures were derived from correct data, they would be disappointing. Such a reduction in the rate of increase, in the face of the heavy immigration during the past ten years, would argue a diminution in the fecundity of the population, or a corresponding increase in its death rate. These figures are, however, easily explained when the character of the data used is understood. It is well known, the fact having been demonstrated by extensive and thorough investigation, that the census of 1870 was grossly deficient in the southern states, so much so as not only to give an exaggerated rate of increase of the population between 1870 and 1880 in these states, but to affect materially the rate of increase in the country at large.

These omissions were not the fault of the Census Office nor within its control. The census of 1870 was taken under a law which the Superintendent, Francis A. Walker, characterized as "clumsy, antiquated, and barbarous". The Census Office had no power over its enumerators save a barren protest, and even this right was questioned in some quarters. In referring to these omissions the Superintendent of the Tenth Census (1880) said in his report in relation to the taking of the census in South Carolina: "It follows, as a conclusion of the highest authority, either that the census of 1870 was grossly defective in regard to the whole of the state or some considerable parts thereof, or else that the census of 1880 was fraudulent". Those therefore who believe in the accuracy and honesty of the Tenth Census—and that was thoroughly established—must accept the alternative offered by Superintendent Walker, namely, that the Ninth Census was "grossly defective". What was true of South Carolina was also true, in greater or less degree, of all the southern states.

xii   PROGRESS OF THE NATION.

There are, of course, no means of ascertaining accurately the extent of these omissions, but an approximation to it may be obtained by the following method:

It is fair to assume that the rates of increase in population of the southern states between 1860 and 1870 and between 1870 and 1880 were related to one another in a proportion similar to the corresponding rates in the northern states during the same periods. In the term " southern states " is here included the two Virginias, the two Carolinas, Georgia, Florida, Alabama, Mississippi, Louisiana, Texas, Arkansas, Tennessee, and Kentucky. The census of 1870 is known or is suspected to have been deficient in all these states. In the other states and territories there is no suspicion of incompleteness.

The population of the southern states in 1860, 1870, and 1880 was as follows:

1860	10,259,016
1870	11,250,411
1880	15,257,393

The population of the other states and territories in 1860, 1870, and 1880 was as follows:

1860	21,184,305
1870	27,307,960
1880	34,898,390

The rate of increase in these other states and territories was 28.91 per cent between 1860 and 1870, and 27.80 per cent between 1870 and 1880. These two rates are so nearly equal that in extending them to the southern states they may be regarded as identical; in other words, it may be assumed that the rate of increase in the southern states between 1860 and 1870 and between 1870 and 1880 was the same.

Classified as white and negro, the population of the southern states was as follows:

CENSUS YEARS.	White.	Negro. (a)
1860	6,366,703	3,890,037
1870	7,067,213	4,179,222
1880	9,592,568	5,657,635

a Includes all persons of negro descent.

The increase of the white population between 1860 and 1880 was 50.67 per cent, or at a uniform rate for each ten years of 22.75 per cent. The increase of the negro population between 1860 and 1880 was 45.44 per cent, or at the rate of 20.60 per cent for each ten years. Applying these rates of increase respectively to the white and negro population in 1860, the white population in 1870 was approximately 7,815,128 and the negro 4,691,385. These results are in excess of the figures as returned by the census of 1870, in the case of the white 747,915, and in the case of the negro 512,163, a total of 1,260,078, which may be assumed as approximately the extent of the omissions by the faulty census of 1870. The total population in 1870 was, therefore, approximately 39,818,449 instead of 38,558,371.

Assuming these figures to represent approximately the true population in 1870, the rates of increase would stand as follows:

	PER CENT.
1860 to 1870	26.64
1870 to 1880	25.96
1880 to 1890	24.86

Omitting from consideration those states in which the census of 1870 is known or is presumed to have been faulty, the rate of increase between 1870 and 1880 in the remaining states has been very nearly maintained in the decade from 1880 to 1890. The census of 1870 is known or is presumed to have been deficient in nearly all the states of the South Atlantic and South Central divisions, while in the North Atlantic, North Central, and Western divisions no evidence of incompleteness has been detected. The population of these three last named divisions in 1870, 1880, and 1890, with the numerical increase and the percentage of increase for the two decades, is set forth in the following table:

CENSUS YEARS.	Population.	INCREASE.	
		Number.	Per cent.
1870	26,270,351		
1880	33,639,215	7,368,864	28.05
1890	42,791,437	9,152,222	27.21

It will be seen that the numerical increase between 1880 and 1890 exceeded that between 1870 and 1880 by 1,783,358, and that the proportional increase was only 0.84 per cent less.

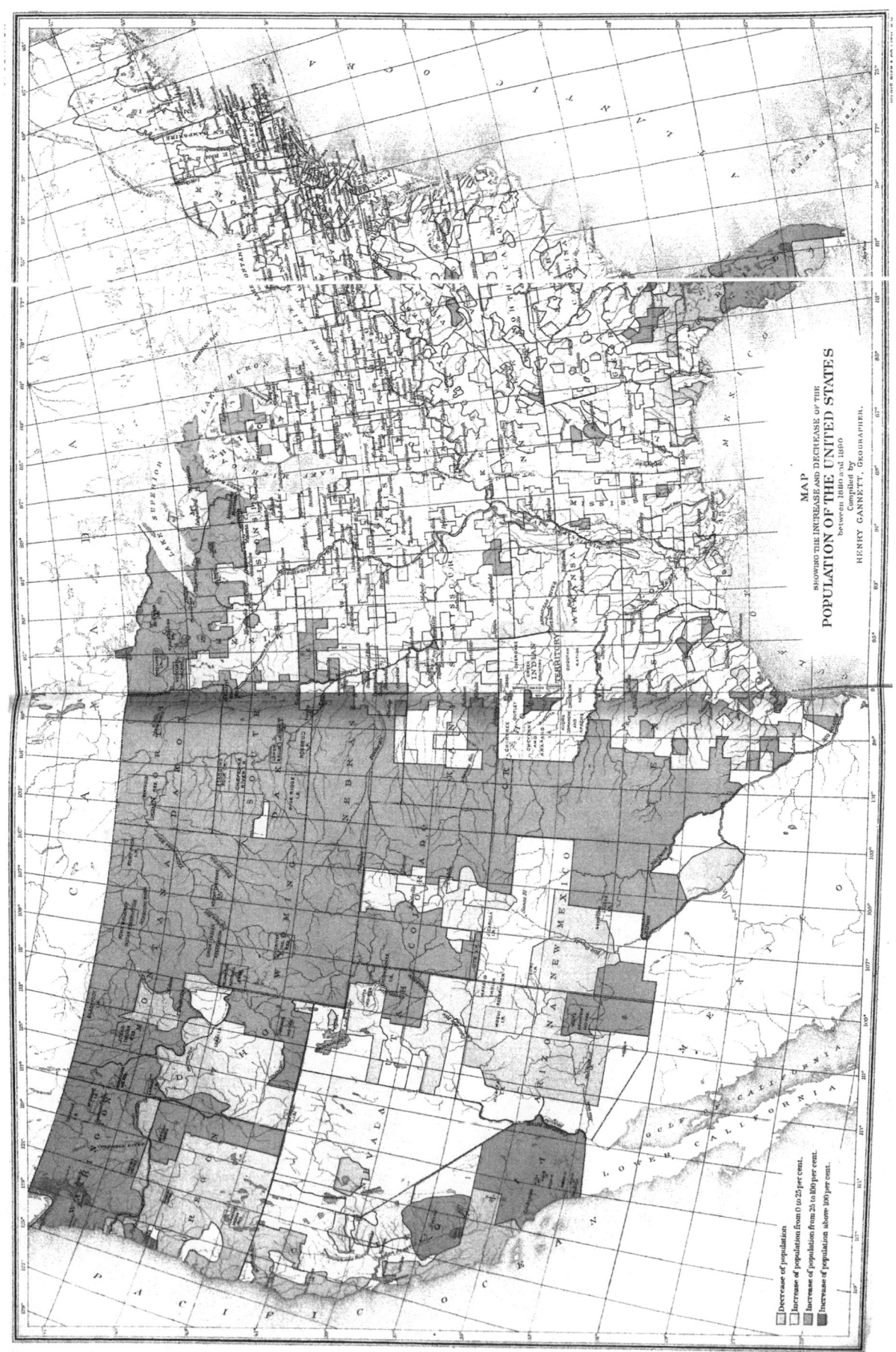

AGGREGATE POPULATION. xiii

The following table shows the percentage of increase in total population for each decade since 1790, derived from Table 2, pages 4 and 5, post:

PERCENTAGE OF INCREASE IN TOTAL POPULATION: 1790 TO 1890.

STATES AND TERRITORIES.	1880 to 1890	1870 to 1880	1860 to 1870	1850 to 1860	1840 to 1850	1830 to 1840	1820 to 1830	1810 to 1820	1800 to 1810	1790 to 1800
The United States	24.86	30.08	22.63	35.58	35.87	32.67	33.55	33.07	36.38	35.10
North Atlantic division	19.95	17.96	16.09	22.81	27.00	21.00	27.22	24.95	32.29	33.92
Maine	1.87	3.51	a0.22	7.74	16.22	25.62	33.92	30.42	50.74	57.16
New Hampshire	8.51	9.01	a2.38	2.55	11.74	5.66	10.37	13.78	16.64	29.58
Vermont	0.04	0.52	4.90	0.31	7.59	4.02	18.94	8.20	41.06	80.82
Massachusetts	25.57	22.35	18.38	23.79	34.81	20.85	16.68	10.83	11.63	11.69
Rhode Island	24.94	27.23	24.47	18.35	35.57	11.97	17.09	7.91	11.30	0.43
Connecticut	19.84	15.86	16.80	24.10	19.62	4.13	8.10	5.04	4.36	5.49
New York	18.00	15.97	12.94	25.29	27.52	20.60	39.83	43.07	62.81	73.19
New Jersey	27.74	24.83	34.83	37.27	31.14	16.36	15.64	12.08	16.30	14.67
Pennsylvania	22.77	21.61	21.19	25.71	34.09	27.87	28.71	29.31	34.49	38.67
South Atlantic division	16.59	29.79	9.11	14.65	19.20	7.67	19.11	14.43	16.99	23.47
Delaware	14.93	17.27	11.41	22.60	17.22	1.74	5.50	0.10	13.07	8.76
Maryland	11.49	19.73	13.66	17.84	24.04	5.14	9.74	7.04	11.42	6.82
District of Columbia	29.71	34.87	75.41	45.26	18.24	9.74	20.57	37.53	70.46	....
Virginia	9.48	23.40	b23.25	12.29	14.67	2.34	13.73	9.20	10.72	17.74
West Virginia	23.34	39.92	....							
North Carolina	15.59	30.65	7.03	14.22	15.35	2.00	15.52	15.00	16.19	21.42
South Carolina	15.63	41.10	0.27	5.27	12.47	2.27	15.60	21.11	20.12	38.75
Georgia	19.14	30.24	12.00	16.69	31.07	33.78	51.57	35.08	55.17	97.08
Florida	45.24	43.54	33.70	60.59	60.52	56.86	....			
North Central division	28.78	33.76	42.70	68.35	81.23	108.11	87.49	102.99	474.77	
Ohio	14.83	19.99	13.92	18.14	30.33	62.01	61.35	151.90	408.07	
Indiana	10.82	17.71	24.45	36.63	44.13	99.04	133.07	500.24	334.07	
Illinois	24.32	21.18	48.36	101.06	78.81	202.44	185.42	349.13		
Michigan	27.92	38.25	58.06	88.38	87.34	570.90	200.97	84.06		
Wisconsin	28.23	24.73	35.93	154.06	886.88					
Minnesota	66.74	77.57	155.61	2,730.72						
Iowa	17.68	36.96	76.91	251.13	345.85					
Missouri	23.56	25.97	45.62	73.30	77.75	173.19	111.03	210.29		
North Dakota.. } South Dakota.. }	c278.41	d853.23	d193.18							
Nebraska	134.06	267.83	326.45							
Kansas	43.27	173.35	239.91							
South Central division	23.02	38.62	11.54	34.05	42.24	46.72	51.91	72.89	134.09	206.08
Kentucky	12.73	24.81	14.31	17.64	25.98	13.36	21.94	38.77	83.98	199.90
Tennessee	14.60	22.55	13.40	10.68	20.92	21.60	61.20	61.53	147.81	105.88
Alabama	19.84	26.63	3.40	24.96	30.62	90.86	142.01			
Mississippi	13.96	36.68	4.63	30.47	61.46	174.96	81.08	86.07	355.95	
Louisiana	19.01	29.31	2.67	36.74	46.92	63.35	41.08	99.75		
Texas	40.44	94.45	35.48	184.21						
Oklahoma										
Arkansas	40.58	65.05	11.20	107.46	115.12	221.00	113.17			
Western division	71.27	78.46	60.02	246.15						
Montana	237.49	90.14	....							
Wyoming	192.01	128.00								
Colorado	112.12	387.47	16.30							
New Mexico	28.40	30.14	a1.76	51.94						
Arizona	47.43	318.72								
Utah	44.42	65.88	115.49	253.89						
Nevada	a26.51	46.54	519.67							
Idaho	158.77	117.41								
Washington	365.13	213.57	106.62							
Oregon	79.53	92.22	73.30	204.65						
California	39.72	54.34	47.44	310.37						

a Decrease.

b Decrease; due to loss of territory, West Virginia having been set off from Virginia December 31, 1862.

c North Dakota and South Dakota combined. Apportioning the population of Dakota territory in 1880, North Dakota increased 395.05 per cent, and South Dakota increased 214.60 per cent.

d Dakota territory.

xiv   PROGRESS OF THE NATION.

The thirteen original states, which comprise practically the North Atlantic and South Atlantic divisions, were, to a great extent, settled communities at the time of the First Census, in 1790, and their rate of increase in the early decades, though in certain cases considerable, was in no case excessive. In certain cases, indeed, it was very small, as in Rhode Island, Connecticut, Delaware, and Maryland.

These two groups of states, from the time of the earliest records, have been the sources of supply for a great westward migration. Their children have peopled the great interior valley and the mountains of the west. They have swarmed from the Atlantic coast to the prairies, plains, mountains, and deserts by millions during the last century. The extent of this movement can not be estimated, but some idea of it may be obtained from the fact that in 1880, out of 22,000,000 persons born in the Atlantic states, over 3,000,000 were found living in other states entirely to the westward.

In the North Atlantic division this draft has been in great part made good, especially during the past forty years, by foreign immigration, which has thus replaced to a great extent the original stock. Such is not the case, however, with the South Atlantic states, which, owing in part to climatic conditions and in part to the presence of the negro race, have received insignificant foreign immigration.

In the North Central, South Central, and Western divisions the rate of increase was at first very large, and gradually diminished as the population increased in number and approximated settled conditions.

The general law governing the increase of population is that, when not disturbed by extraneous causes, such as wars, pestilences, immigration, emigration, etc., increase of population goes on at a continually diminishing rate. The operation of this law in this country has been disturbed in recent years by the civil war, which, besides the destruction of a vast number of lives, decreased the birth rate materially during its progress. It was followed by an increased birth rate, as is invariably the case under similar circumstances. The normal rate of increase has been, and is, greatly disturbed also by immigration, and it is difficult to estimate the effect of this upon our rate of increase.

Throughout the whole table, in nearly every state, there is distinctly traceable the result of the late civil war upon the rate of increase between 1860 and 1870. It is, however, much more marked in the southern than in the northern states, showing how much more severely these states were strained by the conflict.

The table on the preceding page, showing the percentages of increase in population by states and territories from 1790 to 1890, is supplemented in the case of a few states and territories by the following table, in which are given, in addition to the results of the United States censuses of 1880 and 1890, the results of state censuses taken in 1885, with the exception of Michigan, the census of that state having been taken in 1884:

STATES AND TERRITORIES.	POPULATION.			INCREASE.		PER CENT OF INCREASE.	
	1890	1885	1880	1885 to 1890	1880 to 1885	1885 to 1890	1880 to 1885
Colorado	412,198	243,910	194,327	168,288	49,583	69.00	25.52
Dakota (a)	511,527	415,610	135,177	95,917	280,433	23.08	207.46
Florida	391,422	342,551	269,493	48,871	73,058	14.27	27.11
Iowa	1,911,896	1,753,980	1,624,615	157,916	129,365	9.00	7.96
Kansas	1,427,096	1,268,530	996,096	158,566	272,434	12.50	27.35
Massachusetts	2,238,943	1,942,141	1,783,085	296,802	159,056	15.28	8.92
Michigan	2,093,889	1,853,658	1,636,937	240,231	216,721	12.96	13.24
Minnesota	1,301,826	1,117,798	780,773	184,028	337,025	16.46	43.17
Nebraska	1,058,910	740,645	452,402	318,265	288,243	42.97	63.71
New Jersey	1,444,033	1,278,033	1,131,116	166,900	146,917	13.06	12.99
New Mexico	153,593	134,141	119,565	19,452	14,576	14.50	12.19
Oregon	313,767	194,150	174,768	119,617	19,382	61.61	11.09
Rhode Island	345,506	304,284	276,531	41,222	27,753	13.55	10.04
Washington	349,390	129,438	75,116	219,952	54,322	169.93	72.32
Wisconsin	1,686,880	1,563,413	1,315,497	123,467	247,916	7.90	18.85

a North Dakota and South Dakota combined for 1890; Dakota territory in 1880 and 1885.

In comparing the results of these state censuses with those of the United States censuses, it must be understood that the state censuses were taken under different authority, by different machinery, and by different methods from those employed in the United States censuses.

In the state of Kansas the course of the population can be traced even more closely than in the other states represented in the preceding table. Since 1885 this state has taken a census each year, the results of which are shown in the accompanying statement, together with the United States censuses of 1880 and 1890:

1880. United States census		996,096
1885. State census		1,268,530
1886. State census		1,406,738
1887. State census		1,514,578
1888. State census		1,518,552
1889. State census		1,464,914
1890. United States census		1,427,096

AGGREGATE POPULATION.

In the principal tables the states and territories are grouped as North Atlantic, South Atlantic, North Central, South Central, and Western divisions. This grouping is a natural one, and by the aid of it certain characteristic features in the development of the states are brought out. The North Atlantic division is primarily a manufacturing section. As a necessary result of the predominance of manufacturing, there is a great development of urban population. Indeed, more than half of the inhabitants are grouped in cities.

The predominant industry of the North Central division is agriculture, although in many of these states manufactures are now acquiring prominence. The industries of the South Atlantic and South Central divisions are still almost entirely agricultural, while in the Western division the leading industries are agriculture, mining, and grazing.

In the course of the settlement and development of a country the industries commonly follow one another in a certain order. After the hunter, trapper, and prospector, who are commonly the pioneers, the herdsman follows, and for a time the raising of cattle is the leading industry. As settlement becomes less sparse, this is followed by agriculture, which in its turn, as the population becomes more dense, is succeeded by manufactures, and, as a consequence, the aggregation of the people in cities. All stages of this progress are seen in this country.

In Maine, New Hampshire, and Vermont the rate of increase between 1870 and 1880 was not quite maintained during the past decade, probably due to a large migration of the farming population to the far west, while manufactures had not assumed great prominence. In Vermont there has been only a trifling increase of population.

In the other states of this division, with the exception of Rhode Island, viz, Massachusetts, Connecticut, New York, New Jersey, and Pennsylvania, manufactures have assumed so great prominence that they have not only sufficed to maintain the former rate of increase but even to increase it. The rate in Massachusetts has increased from 22.35 to 25.57 per cent; in Connecticut from 15.86 to 19.84; in New York from 15.97 to 18.00; in New Jersey from 24.83 to 27.74, and in Pennsylvania from 21.61 to 22.77. It will be seen, furthermore, that this augmentation of the rate of increase is greater in the more easterly states than in the three westerly ones above mentioned, owing to the relatively greater development of manufacturing industries.

Turning to the table on the preceding page, showing the results of the state censuses, it appears that during the first half of the last decade the rate of increase in Massachusetts was below the average of the decade, being only 8.92 per cent, while in the last half it was much greater, or 15.28 per cent. The case is somewhat similar in Rhode Island, although not in so marked a degree, the rates of increase between 1880 and 1885 and between 1885 and 18'0 being, respectively, 10.04 and 13.55 per cent. In New Jersey the rate of increase seems to have been maintained quite uniformly throughout the decade.

In the North Central group of states various conditions prevail. In Ohio, Indiana, Iowa, and Missouri, and in Illinois, if the city of Chicago be dropped from consideration, the rate of increase has declined decidedly. In Ohio it has fallen from 19.99 to 14.83 per cent; in Indiana from 17.71 to 10.82; in Iowa from 36.06 to 17.68; in Missouri from 25.97 to 23.56 per cent, in spite of the rapid growth of St. Louis and Kansas city, and in Illinois, dropping Chicago from consideration, from 14.89 to 5.90 per cent. In these states the agricultural industry, which is still the prominent one, has begun to decline, owing to the sharp competition of western farms. The farming population has migrated westward, and the growth of manufactures is not yet sufficiently rapid to repair these losses. The southern portions of Michigan, Wisconsin, and Minnesota are under similar conditions, but the northern parts of these states, lying upon the frontier of settlement, have filled up with sufficient rapidity to repair wholly or in part the losses of the southern parts. Michigan increased at the rate of 38.25 per cent between 1870 and 1880, while between 1880 and 1890 the rate was but 27.92 per cent. The increase between 1880 and 1890 was cut into unequal parts by the state census taken in 1884. In the first four years of the decade the increase was 13.24 per cent, while in the last six years it was 12.96 per cent. As the rate of increase in this state is declining, the state census taken in 1884 corroborates the United States census of 1890. In Wisconsin the last decade shows an increase of 28.23 per cent, as against an increase of 24.73 per cent in the decade from 1870 to 1880. The state census of Wisconsin, taken in 1885, cuts the decade into two equal parts, and shows an increase during the first half of 18.85 per cent and during the second half of but 7.90 per cent.

Minnesota increased 77.57 per cent between 1870 and 1880 and 66.74 per cent between 1880 and 1890, the numerical increase being over half a million in the past decade. The state census, taken in 1885, shows that the bulk of this increase occurred between 1880 and 1885. The numerical increase during the first five years was 337,025, and the rate of increase 43.17 per cent, while during the last half of the decade the numerical increase was 184,028, and the rate of increase 16.46 per cent.

During the past ten years the population of Dakota, considering the two states of North Dakota and South Dakota together, has increased from 135,177 to 511,527, or 278.41 per cent; Nebraska from 452,402 to 1,058,910, or 134.06 per cent, and Kansas from 996,096 to 1,427,096, or 43.27 per cent. This increase has not, however, continued uniformly throughout the decade. In 1885 Dakota contained 415,610 inhabitants, or more than four-fifths of its present population. Nebraska contained 740,645 inhabitants in the same year, thus dividing the numerical increase quite equally between the two halves of the decade, but leaving the greater percentage of increase in the first half. In the same year Kansas by its state census had 1,268,530 inhabitants, showing that nearly two-thirds of

PROGRESS OF THE NATION.

xvi

the numerical gain was acquired during the first half of the decade. The industries of these states are almost purely agricultural, and are largely dependent on the supply of moisture, either in the form of rain or by irrigation. Through these states passes what is known as the sub-humid belt, a strip of country several degrees in width, in which during rainy years there is an abundance of moisture for the needs of crops, while in the years when the rainfall is below the average the supply is deficient. In this region little provision has been made for artificial irrigation, the settlers having thus far been content to depend upon rainfall. Into this region settlers flocked in large numbers in the early years of the decade, drawn thither by the fertility of the land and by the fact that for a few years the rainfall had been sufficient for the needs of agriculture. During the past two or three years, however, the conditions of rainfall have materially changed. It has fallen decidedly below the normal, and the settlers have thereby been forced to emigrate. Thousands of families have abandoned this region and gone to Oklahoma and the Rocky Mountain region. This migration is well shown in the progress of Kansas, as indicated by its annual censuses. These censuses show a rapid increase in population from 1880 up to 1887; 1888 shows but a slight increase over 1887, while 1889 shows a reduction in the population, leading up to the further reduction shown by the United States census in 1890.

Throughout the South Atlantic and South Central states the rate of increase has diminished, and in most of these states it has diminished materially. A certain reduction in the percentage of increase, especially in the eastern part of this region, was to have been expected, due not only to the operation of general laws but also to the fact that there has been considerable migration from the states east of the Mississippi river to the westward, and but little immigration. Taken together, however, these two causes by no means account for the reduction in the rate of increase in these states. The real cause is to be found, as was stated early in this discussion, in the imperfections of the census of 1870. These imperfections resulted in giving a comparatively low rate of increase between 1860 and 1870, and an exaggerated increase between 1870 and 1880. The following table, showing the rates of increase during the last three decades in these states, illustrates the imperfections of the census of 1870:

STATES.	PER CENT OF INCREASE.		
	1860 to 1870	1870 to 1880	1880 to 1890
Virginia	a4.44	23.46	9.48
North Carolina	7.93	30.65	15.59
South Carolina	0.27	41.10	15.03
Georgia	12.60	30.24	19.14
Alabama	3.40	26.63	19.84
Mississippi	4.63	36.68	13.96
Louisiana	2.67	29.31	10.01
Kentucky	14.31	24.81	12.73
Tennessee	13.40	22.55	14.60

a Of Virginia and West Virginia together.

It is but reasonable to suppose that in these states, which were ravaged by war from 1861 to 1865, the rate of increase in the decade which includes the war period should be less than a normal one. Of all these states Virginia, whose soil was the principal theater of the war, must have suffered most severely, and during the period in question it increased at the rate of but 4.44 per cent. Next to Virginia, Tennessee suffered most severely, and yet it increased 13.40 per cent. On the other hand, North Carolina, which suffered less severely, gained but 7.93 per cent, and South Carolina, which suffered less in comparison with Virginia, apparently remained at a standstill as regards population. Georgia gained 12 per cent, while Alabama gained but 3.40 per cent, Louisiana 2.67 per cent, and Mississippi 4.63 per cent, although they were comparatively remote from active operations, and suffered relatively little from the ravages of war. On the other hand, those states which suffered the most severely from the war made during the decade from 1870 to 1880 the smallest proportion of gain of the southern states, whereas the reverse should have been the case. Thus Virginia gained 23.46 per cent, Kentucky 24.81, and Tennessee 22.55, while the states that were farther removed from active operations were North Carolina, which gained 30.65; South Carolina, 41.10; Georgia, 30.24; Alabama, 26.63; Mississippi, 36.68, and Louisiana, 29.31 per cent. These startling discrepancies were due, first, to the imperfections of the census of 1870, which, as has been demonstrated, were greatest in South Carolina, Mississippi, Louisiana, Alabama, Georgia, and North Carolina, although they were not by any means wanting in Virginia, Kentucky, and Tennessee; and, second, in part, to migration of the negro population from South Carolina and other recent slave states.

The industries of these two sections are almost purely agricultural. During the past ten years manufactures have obtained a slight footing and mining has made considerable growth in the mountain regions, but these causes have thus far produced but a comparatively trifling movement of population. The urban population, although great in proportion to that which existed formerly, is very small in proportion to the rural population of the region.

AGGREGATE POPULATION.   xvii

During the first half of the last decade Florida had a rapid growth. The population between 1880 and 1885 increased 73,058, or at the rate of 27.11 per cent. This rapid growth, however, received a serious check in 1887 and 1888 by an epidemic of yellow fever and by severe frosts. The growth since 1885 has, therefore, been comparatively slow.

Arkansas has continued to grow at a rapid rate, having increased 40.58 per cent in the last ten years. Texas also has increased with great rapidity, the numerical increase of its population being 643,774, or 40.44 per cent.

In the Western division the conditions of growth have been varied. In the earlier years of the decade the discovery of valuable silver and copper mines in the mountains of Montana, in the neighborhood of Butte, drew to that state a large immigration, which engaged not only in mining, but in developing the agricultural resources. Wyoming has continued to grow with accelerated rapidity.

The census of Colorado in 1880 was taken on the top wave of a mining excitement, which had filled its mountains with miners, prospectors, and speculators, increasing its population enormously, especially in the mountainous country. The census of the state taken in 1885 was, on a superficial view, very surprising. It showed that most of the mining counties had lost population during the five years preceding. This loss was, however, more than made up by the growth of its cities and its agricultural counties. The census of 1890 shows still further reduction of population in the mining regions of the state, and on the other hand an extraordinary development of its urban population and its farming element. New Mexico, Arizona, and Utah show rates of increase which are small when the sparsely settled condition of these territories is considered, while Nevada shows an absolute diminution in population of 16,505, or 26.51 per cent, leaving it with a population less than that of any other state. This condition of things is a natural result of the failure of the Comstock and other mines, work upon which has practically ceased. Idaho has increased its population 158.77 per cent. Its prosperity is mainly due to its mines, although people are now turning to agriculture in considerable numbers.

The growth of Washington has been phenomenal, the population in 1890 being nearly five times that of 1880. As is shown by the state census taken in 1885, this growth has been almost entirely during the last five years of the decade. The inducements which have attracted settlers are in the main its fertile soil and ample rainfall, which enable farming to be carried on without irrigation over almost the entire state. The growth of Oregon, though less rapid, has been at a rate of 79.53 per cent during the past decade. The numerical increase has been 138,999, of which over four-fifths have been acquired during the past five years. The additions to its population are mainly in the valleys of the Columbia and Willamette rivers.

California, which increased 54.34 per cent during the decade from 1870 to 1880, has maintained during the past decade a rate of increase of 39.72 per cent. This increase, though widespread throughout the state, has been most marked in its great cities and in the southern part.

The following table shows the relative rank in population of the states and territories in 1890 and in 1880:

1890	1880	1890	1880
1 New York.	1 New York.	26 Nebraska.	26 Minnesota.
2 Pennsylvania.	2 Pennsylvania.	27 Maryland.	27 Maine.
3 Illinois.	3 Ohio.	28 West Virginia.	28 Connecticut.
4 Ohio.	4 Illinois.	29 Connecticut.	29 West Virginia.
5 Missouri.	5 Missouri.	30 Maine.	30 Nebraska.
6 Massachusetts.	6 Indiana.	31 Colorado.	31 New Hampshire.
7 Texas.	7 Massachusetts.	32 Florida.	32 Vermont.
8 Indiana.	8 Kentucky.	33 New Hampshire.	33 Rhode Island.
9 Michigan.	9 Michigan.	34 Washington.	34 Florida.
10 Iowa.	10 Iowa.	35 Rhode Island.	35 Colorado.
11 Kentucky.	11 Texas.	36 Vermont.	36 District of Columbia.
12 Georgia.	12 Tennessee.	37 South Dakota.	37 Oregon.
13 Tennessee.	13 Georgia.	38 Oregon.	38 Delaware.
14 Wisconsin.	14 Virginia.	39 District of Columbia.	39 Utah.
15 Virginia.	15 North Carolina.	40 Utah.	40 Dakota.
16 North Carolina.	16 Wisconsin.	41 North Dakota.	41 New Mexico.
17 Alabama.	17 Alabama.	42 Delaware.	42 Washington.
18 New Jersey.	18 Mississippi.	43 New Mexico.	43 Nevada.
19 Kansas.	19 New Jersey.	44 Montana.	44 Arizona.
20 Minnesota.	20 Kansas.	45 Idaho.	45 Montana.
21 Mississippi.	21 South Carolina.	46 Oklahoma.	46 Idaho.
22 California.	22 Louisiana.	47 Wyoming.	47 Wyoming.
23 South Carolina.	23 Maryland.	48 Arizona.	
24 Arkansas.	24 California.	49 Nevada.	
25 Louisiana.	25 Arkansas.		

POP——2

xviii   PROGRESS OF THE NATION.

It will be seen that, as in 1880, New York still heads the list, and is followed by Pennsylvania. Ohio and Illinois have exchanged places. Of the other changes in the list the most marked are those of Texas, which rises from No. 11 to No. 7; Kentucky, which drops from 8 to 11; Minnesota, which rises from 26 to 20; Nebraska, which rises from 30 to 26; Maryland, which drops from 23 to 27; Colorado, which rises from 35 to 31; Vermont, which drops from 32 to 36; Washington, which rises from 42 to 34; Delaware, which drops from 38 to 42; Nevada, which drops from 43 to 49, and Arizona, which drops from 44 to 48. The average change in rank is 2.2 places.

PROGRESS OF THE NATION: 1790 TO 1890.

The accompanying series of maps of the United States, showing the density of the population, is intended to exhibit the increase and the movement of population from the date of the First Census, in 1790, through ten decades, to 1890. Of these maps, the first nine, up to and including that of 1870, are reproductions from the "Statistical Atlas of the United States", published in 1874. The earlier ones are on the same scale as those of the atlas; the later ones are reduced in scale.

The method by which these maps have been constructed is that used for the atlas above referred to, and is explained in that work. This explanation is here reproduced, with such changes and modifications as appear to be necessary.

These maps, one for each census, show the density of population, that is, the number of individuals to a square mile, arranged within certain groups.

The general method of preparing these maps has been uniform, and is as follows: the county has been taken, in general, as a unit. Its population, at the period to which the map refers, having been ascertained, the population of all cities of 8,000 inhabitants or more, existing within it, has been deducted therefrom, the population of such cities being represented by circles of solid color, separate from the other population, which latter has been regarded, for the purposes of illustration, as rural population uniformly spread over the surface of the county. The rural population has been divided by the area of the county in square miles, the quotient representing the average density of settlement.

In cases, however, where the county was of unusual extent, or there was reason to believe that its density differed greatly in different parts, the county has been no longer taken entire, but has been examined by sections, even sections as small as its townships or other civil divisions. The number of counties thus broken up for the purpose of comparison would naturally vary greatly. In some census years, as in the case of the later ones, it would amount to several hundred; in others, particularly the earlier ones, to scarcely as many score.

The average density of each county, or part of a county, having been thus ascertained, the sections so taken have been grouped according to five degrees of density, as explained in the legends accompanying the maps. The general plan of grouping has been to make as many large groups as could be made without merging any appreciable proportion in groups of a markedly different grade: thus, if a single county of small extent belonging to group 3, should be surrounded by many counties of group 4 or of group 2, it would not be preserved distinct, but would take the shading of its general section, either 2 or 4, as the case might be. If, however, a county of group 4 or 5 should appear among counties of group 1 or 2, the distinction would be regarded of sufficient importance to be maintained. Again, a county whose average density brought it within group 4 might be found with counties of group 3 on one side and of group 5 on the other, appearing thus to belong to a group distinct from both, yet an examination into the density of its constituent townships might, and generally would, develop the fact that those parts of the county which bordered on group 3 were really of that grade, while the parts bordering on group 5 belonged in that class. In such a case, the division of the county by a central line, and the throwing of parts on the one side and on the other, into the adjacent groups, would not only dispense with the necessity for preserving a small separate group upon the map, but would even more correctly represent the facts of the case than would be done by representing the entire county as of group 4. Again, a tier of counties along a river or a railroad might yield a quotient showing an average population of only 30 to a square mile, and thus appear to belong in group 3, whereas an examination of the townships composing the county might show that, for a few miles back from the river, the density was much greater; while in the portion farthest away from the river the density was much less than the average, thus splitting the county, perhaps, into two groups, viz, 4 and 2.

The county, and, in some cases, the township, has been adopted as a unit, not with a view to representing separately each such subdivision, for this the scale of the map would not permit, but for the sake of more definitely determining the true line of demarcation between large groups.

Such being the system and the scope of the illustrations under consideration, it is proposed briefly to discuss the increase and movement of population from 1790 to 1890. It should be remembered throughout that the maps do not profess to exhibit settlements which do not reach an average of 2 to the square mile for a tract large enough to be clearly shown to the eye on the scale employed. It follows that the outside line of color indicates the limits of population of 2 or more to the square mile, the petty population that lies beyond being made up of the solitary ranchman, trapper, or fisherman, or of mining parties, lumber camps, and the like. This line, which limits the average density of 2 to a square mile, is considered as the limit of settlement—the frontier line of population.

Eleventh Census of the United States
Robert P. Porter, Superintendent.

1790

POPULATION.

MAP

SHOWING IN FIVE DEGREES OF DENSITY THE DISTRIBUTION
WITHIN THE TERRITORY EAST OF THE 100TH MERIDIAN
OF THE

POPULATION OF THE UNITED STATES

excluding Indians not taxed.

Compiled from the Returns of Population at the First Census 1790.

NOTE

✳ Center of Population.   39°16.5′N.
76°11.2′W.

LEGEND.

Under 2 inhab to the Sq Mile.
2..6   I
6..18   II
18..45   III
45..90   IV
90 and over   V

Cities over 8000 inhabitants in solid color
in circles proportionate to population.

LITH. A. HOEN & CO. BALTIMORE.

PROGRESS FROM 1790 TO 1890.

An inspection of the maps relating to the earlier census years will show that the progress of population westward across the Appalachian system has taken place, in the main, along four lines. The northernmost of these, which was the first to be developed, runs through central New York, following up, generally, the Mohawk river. This line has, throughout our history, been one of the principal courses of population in its westward flow. The second crosses southern Pennsylvania, western Maryland, and northern Virginia, parallel to and along the course of the upper Potomac. The third runs through Virginia, passing southwestward down the great Appalachian valley, crossing thence over into Kentucky and Tennessee. South of this, the principal movement westward has been around the end of the Appalachian chain, through Georgia and Alabama.

Let us consider the results of measurement and computations as to the extent of this line of settlement, and as to the space which it incloses on the different maps.

1790.

The First Census of the United States, taken as of the first Monday in August, 1790, under the provisions of the second section of the first article of the Constitution, shows the population of the thirteen states now existing and of the unorganized territory to be, in the aggregate, 3,929,214.

This population is distributed almost entirely on the Atlantic seaboard, extending from the eastern boundary of Maine nearly to Florida, and in the region known as the Atlantic plain. Only a very small proportion of the inhabitants of the United States, not, indeed, more than 5 per cent, is found west of the system of the Appalachian mountains. The average depth of settlement, in a direction at right angles to the coast, is 255 miles. The densest settlement is found in eastern Massachusetts, Rhode Island, and Connecticut, and about New York city, whence population has extended northward up the Hudson, and is already quite dense as far as Albany. The settlements in Pennsylvania, which started from Philadelphia, on the Delaware, have extended northeastward, and form a solid body of occupation from New York, through Philadelphia, down to the upper part of Delaware.

The Atlantic coast, as far back as the limits of tide water, is well settled at this time from Casco bay southward to the northern border of North Carolina. In what is now the "district of Maine", sparse settlement extends along the whole seaboard. The southern two-thirds of New Hampshire and nearly all of Vermont are covered by population. In New York, branching off from the Hudson at the mouth of the Mohawk, the line of population follows up a broad gap between the Adirondacks and the Catskills, and even reaches beyond the center of the state, occupying the whole of the Mohawk valley and the country about the interior New York lakes. In Pennsylvania population has spread northwestward, occupying not only the Atlantic plain, but, with sparse settlements, the region traversed by the numerous parallel ridges of the eastern portion of the Appalachians. The general limit of settlement is, at this time, the southeastern edge of the Allegheny plateau, but beyond this, at the junction of the Allegheny and Monongahela rivers, a point early occupied for military purposes, considerable settlements exist which were established prior to the war of the Revolution. In Virginia settlements have extended westward beyond the Blue Ridge, and on the western slope of the Allegheny mountains, though very sparsely. From Virginia, also, a narrow tongue of settlement penetrates into the "Kentucky country", which is almost as populous as Vermont or Georgia, and down to the head of the Tennessee river in the great Appalachian valley, where the "state of Franklin" has been for four years a political unit. In North Carolina the settlements are abruptly limited by the base of the Appalachians. The state is occupied with remarkable uniformity, except in its southern and central portion, where population is comparatively sparse. In South Carolina, on the other hand, there is evidence of much natural selection, apparently with reference to the character of the soil. Charleston is now a city of considerable magnitude, and about it is grouped a comparatively dense population; but all along a belt running southwestward across the state, near its central part, the settlement is very sparse. This area of sparse settlement joins that of central North Carolina, and runs eastward to the coast, near the junction of the two states. Further westward, in the "up country" of South Carolina, the density of settlement is noticeable, due to the improvement in soil. At this date settlements are almost entirely agricultural, and the causes for variation in their density are general ones. The movements of population at this epoch may be traced in almost every case to the character of the soil, and to facility of transportation to the seaboard; and, as the inhabitants are dependent mainly upon water transportation, we find the settlements also conforming themselves very largely to the navigable streams.

Outside the area of continuous settlement, which we have attempted to sketch, is found a number of smaller settlements of greater or less extent. The principal of these lies in the northern part of what is now known as the "territory south of the river Ohio", and comprises an area of 10,900 square miles. Another, in western Virginia, lies upon the Ohio and Kanawha rivers, and comprises 750 square miles. A third, in the southern part of the "territory south of the river Ohio", upon the Cumberland river, embraces 1,200 square miles.

In addition to these, there is a score or more of small posts, or incipient settlements, scattered over what is an almost untrodden wilderness, such as Detroit, Vincennes, Kaskaskia, Prairie du Chien, Mackinac, and Green Bay, beside the humble beginnings of Elmira and Binghamton, in New York, which, even at this time, lie outside the body of continuous settlement and embrace about 1,000 square miles.

Following the line which limits this great body of settlement in all its undulations, we find its length to be 3,200 miles. In this measurement no account has been made of slight irregularities, such as those in the ordinary

PROGRESS OF THE NATION.

xx

meanderings of a river which forms the boundary line of population; but we have traced all the ins and outs of this frontier line, which seem to indicate a distinct change in the settlement of the country for any cause, whether of progression or of retrogression. Thus the area of settlement is the area embraced between the frontier line and the coast, diminished by such unsettled areas as may lie within it, and increased by such settled areas as lie without it. These are not susceptible of very accurate determination, owing to the fact that our best maps are, to a certain extent, incorrect in boundaries and areas; but all the accuracy required for our present purpose can be secured. The settled area of 1790, as indicated by the line traced, is 226,085 square miles. The entire body of continuously settled area lies between 31° and 45° north latitude and 67° and 83° west longitude.

Outside of this body of continuous settlement are the smaller areas mentioned above, which, added to the main body of settled area, give as a total 239,935 square miles, the aggregate population being 3,929,214, and the average density of settlement 16.38 to the square mile.

The "district of Maine" belongs to Massachusetts. Georgia extends to the Mississippi river. Kentucky and Tennessee are known as the "territory south of the river Ohio", and Ohio, Indiana, Illinois, Michigan, Wisconsin, and a part of Minnesota, as the "territory northwest of the river Ohio". Spain claims possession of Florida, with a strip along the southern border of Georgia, and all of the region west of the Mississippi river.

1800.

At the Second Census, that of 1800, the frontier line, as it appears on the map, has been rectified, so that while it embraces 282,208 square miles, it describes a course, when measured in the same manner as that of 1790, of only 2,800 lineal miles. The advancement of this line has taken place in every direction, though in some parts of the country much more markedly than in others.

In Maine and New Hampshire there is apparent only a slight northward movement of settlement; in Vermont, on the other hand, while the settled area has not decidedly increased, its density has become greater. Massachusetts shows but little change, but in Connecticut the settlements along the lower course of the Connecticut river have appreciably increased.

In New York settlement has poured up the Hudson to the mouth of the Mohawk, and thence, through the great natural roadway, westward. The narrow tongue, which before extended out beyond the middle of the state, has now widened until it spreads from the southern border of the state to Lake Ontario. A narrow belt of settlement even stretches down the St. Lawrence, and along all the northern border of the state, to Lake Champlain, completely surrounding what may be characteristically defined as the Adirondack region.

In Pennsylvania settlements have extended up the Susquehanna and joined the New York groups, leaving, as yet, an unsettled space in the northeast corner of the state, which comprises a body of rugged mountain country. With the exception of a little strip along the western border of Pennsylvania, the northern part of the state, west of the Susquehanna, is as yet entirely without inhabitants. Population has streamed across the southern half of the state, and settled in a dense body about the forks of the Ohio river, where we note the beginning of Pittsburg, and thence extended slightly into the "territory northwest of the river Ohio".

In Virginia we note but little change, although there is a general extension of settlement, with an increase in density, especially along the coast. North Carolina is now almost entirely covered with population; the mountain region has, generally speaking, been nearly all reclaimed to the service of man. In South Carolina there is a general increase in density of settlement, while the southwestern border has been carried down, until now the Altamaha river is its limit. The settlements in northern Kentucky have spread southward across the state, and even into Tennessee, forming a junction with the little settlement, noted at the date of the last census, on the Cumberland river. The group thus formed has extended down the Ohio, nearly to its junction with the Tennessee and the Cumberland, and across the Ohio river, where we note the beginning of Cincinnati. Other infant settlements appear at this date. On the east side of the Mississippi river is a strip of settlement along the bluffs below the Yazoo bottom. Above this, on the west side, we note the beginning of St. Louis, not at this time within the United States, and across the river an adjacent settlement in what is now known as Indiana territory, while all the pioneer settlements previously noted have grown to a greater or less extent.

From the region embraced between the frontier line and the Atlantic must be deducted the Adirondack tract, in northern New York, and the unsettled region in northern Pennsylvania, already referred to; so that the actual area of settlement, bounded by a continuous line, is to be taken at 271,908 square miles. All this lies between 30° 45' and 45° 15' north latitude, and 67° and 88° west longitude.

To this should be added the aggregate extent of all settlements lying outside of the frontier line, which collectively amount to 33,800 square miles, making a total area of settlement of 305,708 square miles. As the aggregate population is 5,308,483, the average density of settlement is 17.36.

The infant settlements of this period have been much retarded at many points by the opposition of the Indian tribes; but in the neighborhood of the more densely settled portions of the northern part of the country these obstacles have been of less magnitude than farther south. In Georgia, especially, the large and powerful tribes of Creeks and Cherokees have stubbornly opposed the progress of population.

PROGRESS FROM 1790 TO 1890.   xxi

During the decade Vermont, formed from a part of New York, has been admitted to the Union; also Kentucky and Tennessee, formed from the "territory south of the river Ohio"; Mississippi territory has been organized, having, however, very different boundaries from what is known later as the state of that name; while the "territory northwest of the river Ohio" has been divided and Indiana territory organized from the western portion.

1810.

In the decade from 1800 to 1810 we note great changes, especially the extension of the sparse settlements of the interior. The hills of western New York have become almost entirely covered with population, which has spread along the south shore of Lake Erie well over into Ohio, and has effected a junction with the previously existing body of population about the forks of the Ohio river, leaving unsettled an included heart-shaped area in northern Pennsylvania, which comprises the rugged country of the Appalachian plateau. The occupation of the Ohio river has now become complete, from its head to its mouth, with the exception of small gaps below the mouth of the Tennessee. Spreading in every direction from the "dark and bloody ground" of Kentucky, settlement covers almost the entire state, while the southern border line has been extended to the Tennessee river, in what is now known as Mississippi territory. In Georgia settlements are still held back by the Creek and the Cherokee Indians, although in 1802 a treaty with the former tribe relieved the southwestern portion of the state of their presence, and left the ground open for occupancy by the whites. In Ohio settlements, starting from the Ohio river and from southwestern Pennsylvania, have worked northward and westward, until they cover two-thirds of the area of the state. Michigan and Indiana are still virgin territory, with the exception of a little strip about Detroit, in the former, and two small areas in the latter, one in the southeastern part of the territory extending along the Ohio river, and one in the southwestern part extending up the Wabash from its mouth to and including the settlement at Vincennes. St. Louis, from a fur-trading post, has become an important center of settlement, population having spread northward above the mouth of the Missouri and southward along the Mississippi to the mouth of the Ohio. On the Arkansas, near the mouth, is a similar body of settlement. The transfer of the territory of Louisiana to our jurisdiction, which was effected in 1803, has brought into the country a large body of population, which stretches along the Mississippi river from its mouth nearly up to the northern limit of what is now known as the "territory of Orleans" and up the Red and Washita rivers, in general occupying the alluvial regions. The incipient settlements noted on the last map in Mississippi have effected a junction with those of Louisiana, while in what is now the lower part of Mississippi territory a similar patch appears upon the Mobile river.

In this decade large additions have been made to the territory of the United States, and many changes have been effected in the lines of interior division. The purchase of Louisiana has added 1,124,685 square miles, an empire in itself, to the United States, and has given to us absolute control of the Mississippi and its navigable branches. Georgia, during the same period, has ceded to the United States about two-thirds of her territory. The state of Ohio has been formed from a portion of what previously was known as the "territory northwest of the river Ohio". Michigan territory has been erected, comprising at this time the peninsula north of Ohio and the lower part of Indiana territory and south of the straits. Indiana territory has become restricted in its limits to the following boundaries: Lake Michigan and Michigan on the north, Ohio on the east, the Ohio river on the south, and Illinois on the west, with a detached area on Lake Superior. Illinois territory comprises all territory west of Lake Michigan and Indiana, north of the Ohio, and east of the Mississippi. The "territory of Orleans", which lies west of the Mississippi, has been carved out of the Louisiana purchase. The remainder of the territory acquired from France is known by the name of "Louisiana territory".

At this date the frontier line is 2,900 miles long, and includes between itself and the Atlantic 408,895 square miles. From this must be deducted several large areas of unsettled land: first, the area in northern New York, now somewhat smaller than ten years before, but still by no means inconsiderable in extent; second, the heart-shaped area in northwestern Pennsylvania, embracing part of the Allegheny plateau, in size about equal to the unsettled area in New York; third, a strip along the western part of Virginia, extending from the Potomac, southward, taking in a part of eastern Kentucky and southwestern Virginia, and extending nearly to the border line of Tennessee; fourth, a comparatively small area in northern Tennessee, upon the Cumberland plateau. These tracts together comprise 26,050 square miles, making the actual area of settlement included within the frontier line 382,845 square miles. All this lies between latitude 29° 30' and 45° 15' north, and between the meridians of 67° and 88° 30' west.

Beyond the frontier there are, in addition to the steadily increasing number of outposts and minor settlements, several considerable bodies of population, which have been above noted. The aggregate extent of these, and of the numerous small patches of population scattered over the west and south, may be estimated at 25,100 square miles, making the total area of settlement in 1810, 407,945 square miles, the aggregate population being 7,239,881, and the average density of settlement 17.75 to the square mile.

Between 1800 and 1810 the principal territorial changes have been as follows: Ohio has been admitted, and the territories of Illinois and Michigan have been formed, the former from part of Indiana territory and the latter from parts of Indiana territory and the "territory northwest of the river Ohio".

xxii

PROGRESS OF THE NATION.

1820.

The decade from 1810 to 1820 has witnessed several territorial changes. Florida at this date (1820) is a blank upon the map. The treaty with Spain to transfer Florida to the United States is signed, but the delivery has not yet taken place. Alabama and Mississippi, made from Mississippi territory, have been organized and admitted as states. Indiana and Illinois appear as states, with restricted limits. The "territory of Orleans", with somewhat enlarged boundaries, has been admitted as a state and is known as Louisiana. The "district of Maine" has also been erected into a state. Arkansas territory has been cut from the southern portion of the territory of Louisiana. The Indian territory has been constituted to serve as a reservation for the Indian tribes. Michigan territory includes all territory east of the Mississippi and north of Illinois, Indiana, and Ohio. That part of the old Louisiana territory remaining, after cutting out Arkansas and the Indian territory, has received the name of "Missouri territory".

Again, in 1820, we note a great change in regard to the frontier line. It has become vastly more involved and complex, extending from southeastern Michigan, on Lake St. Clair, southwestward into Missouri territory; thence, making a great semicircle to the eastward, it sweeps west again around a body of population in Louisiana, and ends on the Gulf coast in that state. The area included by it has immensely increased, but much of this increase is balanced by the great extent of unsettled land included within it.

Taking up the changes in detail, we note, first, the great increase in the population of central New York, a belt of increased settlement having swept up the Mohawk valley to Lake Ontario, and along its shore nearly to the Niagara river. A similar increase is seen about the forks of the Ohio river, while in northern Pennsylvania the unsettled region on the Appalachian plateau has sensibly decreased in size. The unsettled area in western Virginia and eastern Kentucky has very greatly diminished, population having extended almost entirely over the Allegheny region in these states. The little settlements about Detroit have extended and spread along the shore of Lake Erie, until they have joined those in Ohio. The frontier line in Ohio has crept northward and westward, leaving only the northwestern corner of the state unoccupied. Population has spread northward from Kentucky and westward from Ohio into southern Indiana, covering sparsely the lower third of that state. The groups of population around St. Louis, which at the time of the previous census were enjoying a rapid growth, have extended widely, making a junction with the settlements of Kentucky and Tennessee, along a broad belt in southern Illinois; following the main water courses, population has gone many scores of miles up the Mississippi and the Missouri rivers. The settlements in Alabama, which, up to this time, had been very much retarded by the Creeks, have been rapidly reinforced and extended, in consequence of the victory of General Jackson over this tribe and the subsequent cession of portions of this territory. Immigration to Alabama has already become considerable, indicating that in a short time the whole central portion of the state, embracing a large part of the region drained by the Mobile river and its branches, will be covered by settlements, to extend northward and effect a junction with the Tennessee and Kentucky settlements, and westward across the lower part of Mississippi, until they meet the Louisiana settlements. In Georgia the Cherokees and the Creeks still hold settlement back along the line of the Altamaha river. There are, however, scattered bodies of population in various parts of the state, though of small extent. In Louisiana we note a gradual increase of the extent of redeemed territory, which appears to have been limited almost exactly by the borders of the alluvial region. In Arkansas the settlements, which we saw in 1810 near the mouth of the Arkansas river, have extended up the bottom lands of that river, forming a body of population of considerable size. Beside these, a small body is found in the southern central part of the state, at the southeastern base of the hill region, and another in the prairie region in the northern part.

The frontier line now has a length of 4,100 miles, embracing an area, after taking out all the unsettled regions included between it, the Atlantic, and the Gulf, of 504,517 square miles, all lying between 29° 30′ and 45° 30′ north latitude, and between 67° and 93° 45′ west longitude. Outside the frontier line are some bodies of population on the Arkansas, White, and Washita rivers, in Arkansas, as before noted, as well as some small bodies in the northwest. Computing these at 4,200 square miles in the aggregate, we have a total settled area of 508,717 square miles, the aggregate population being 9,633,822, and the average density of settlement 18.94 to the square mile.

1830.

In the decade from 1820 to 1830 other territorial changes have occurred. In the early part of the decade the final transfer of Florida from Spanish jurisdiction was effected, and it became a territory of the United States. Missouri has been carved from the southeastern part of the old Missouri territory, and admitted as a state. Otherwise the states and territories have remained nearly as before. Settlement during the decade has again spread greatly. The westward extension of the frontier does not appear to have been so great as in some former periods, the energies of the people being mainly given to filling up the included areas. In other words, the decade from 1810 to 1820 seems to have been one of blocking out work which the succeeding decade has been largely occupied in completing.

During this period the Indians, especially in the south, have still delayed settlement to a great extent. The Creeks and the Cherokees in Georgia and Alabama, and the Choctaws and the Chickasaws in Mississippi, occupy

Eleventh Census of the United States
Robert P. Porter, Superintendent.

1830

POPULATION.

LEGEND.

Under 2 inhab. to the Sq. Mile

2 - 6.

6 - 18.

18 - 45.

45 - 90.

90 and over

Cities over 8000 inhabitants in solid color
in circles proportionate to population.

MAP
SHOWING IN FIVE DEGREES OF DENSITY THE DISTRIBUTION
WITHIN THE TERRITORY EAST OF THE 100TH MERIDIAN
OF THE
POPULATION OF THE UNITED STATES
excluding Indians not taxed.
Compiled from the Returns of Population at the Fifth Census 1830.

NOTE
Center of Population.   38°57.9'W.
29°16.8'W.

LITH. A.HOEN & CO. BALTIMORE.

PROGRESS FROM 1790 TO 1890.   xxiii

large areas of the best portions of those states, and successfully resist encroachment upon their territory. Georgia, however, has witnessed a large increase in settlement during the decade. The settlements which have heretofore been staid on the line of the Altamaha have spread westward across the central portion of the state to its western boundary, where they have struck against the barrier of the Creek territory. Stopped at this point, they have moved southward down into the southwest corner, and over into Florida, extending even to the Gulf coast. Westward they have stretched across the southern part of Alabama, and joined that body of settlement which was previously formed in the drainage basin of the Mobile river. The Louisiana settlements have but slightly increased, and no great change appears to have taken place in Mississippi, owing largely to the cause above noted, viz, the occupancy of the soil by Indians. In Arkansas the spread of settlement has been in a strange and fragmentary way. A line reaches from Louisiana to the Arkansas river and up that river to the state line, where it is stopped abruptly by the boundary of the Indian territory. It extends up the Mississippi, and joins the great body of population in Tennessee. A branch extends northeastward from near Little Rock to the northern portion of the state. All these settlements within Arkansas territory are as yet very sparse. In Missouri the principal extension of settlement has been in a broad belt up the Missouri river, reaching to the state line, at the mouth of the Kansas river, where quite a dense body of population appears. Settlement has progressed in Illinois, from the Mississippi river eastward and northward, covering more than half of the state. In Indiana it has followed up the Wabash river, and thence has spread until it reaches nearly to the north line of the state. But little of Ohio remains unsettled. The sparse settlements about Detroit, in Michigan territory, have broadened out, extending toward the interior of the lower peninsula, while isolated patches have appeared in various other localities.

Turning to the more densely settled parts of the country, we find that settlement is slowly making its way northward in Maine, although discouraged by the poverty of the soil and the severity of the climate. The unsettled tract in northern New York is decreasing, but very slowly, as is also the case with the unsettled area in northern Pennsylvania. In western Virginia the unsettled tracts are reduced to almost nothing, while the vacant region in eastern Tennessee, on the Cumberland plateau, is rapidly diminishing.

At this date, 1830, the frontier line has a length of 5,300 miles, and the aggregate area now embraced between the ocean, the Gulf, and the frontier line is 725,406 square miles. Of this, however, not less than 97,389 square miles are comprised within the included vacant tracts, leaving only 628,017 square miles as the settled area within the frontier line, all of which lies between latitude 29° 15' and 46° 15' north, and between longitude 67° and 95° west.

Outside the body of continuous settlement are no longer found large groups, but several small patches of population appear in the states of Ohio, Indiana, and Illinois, and in Michigan territory, aggregating 4,700 square miles, making a total settled area, in 1830, of 632,717 square miles. As the aggregate population is 12,866,020, the average density of settlement is 20.33 to the square mile.

1840.

During the decade ending in 1840 the territory of Michigan has been divided; that part east of Lake Michigan and north of Ohio and Indiana, together with the greater part of the peninsula between Lakes Superior and Michigan, has been created into the state of Michigan, the remainder being known as Wisconsin territory. Iowa territory has been created out of that part of Missouri territory lying north of the Missouri state line and east of the Missouri river, and Arkansas has been admitted to the Union.

In 1840 we find, by examining the map of population, that the process of filling up and completing the work blocked out between 1810 and 1820 has been carried still further. From Georgia, Alabama, and Mississippi the Cherokee, Creek, Choctaw, and Chickasaw Indians, who, at the time of the previous census, occupied large areas in these states, and formed a very serious obstacle to settlement, have been removed to the Indian territory, and their country has been opened up to settlement. Within the two or three years which have elapsed since the removal of these Indians the lands relinquished by them have been entirely taken up, and the country has been covered with a comparatively dense settlement. In northern Illinois, the Sac and Fox and Pottawatomie tribes having been removed to the Indian territory, their country has been promptly taken up, and we now find settlements carried over nearly the whole extent of Indiana and Illinois, and across Michigan and Wisconsin as far north as the forty-third parallel. Population has crossed the Mississippi river into Iowa territory, and occupies a broad belt up and down that stream. In Missouri the settlements have spread northward from the Missouri river nearly to the boundary of the state, and southward till they cover most of the southern portion, and make connection in two places with the settlements of Arkansas. The unsettled area found in southern Missouri, together with that in northwestern Arkansas, is due to the hilly and rugged nature of the country, and to the poverty of the soil, as compared with the rich prairie lands all around. In Arkansas the settlements remain sparse, but have spread widely away from the streams, covering much of the prairie parts of the state. There is, beside the area in northwestern Arkansas just mentioned, a large area in the northeastern part of the state, comprised almost entirely within the alluvial regions of the St. Francis river, and also one in the southern portion, extending over into northern Louisiana, which is entirely in the fertile prairie section. The fourth unsettled region lies in the southwestern part of the state.

xxiv   PROGRESS OF THE NATION.

In the older states we note a gradual decrease in the unsettled areas, as in Maine and New York. In northern Pennsylvania the unsettled section has nearly disappeared. A small portion of the unsettled patch on the Cumberland plateau still remains. In southern Georgia the Okefenokee swamp and the pine barrens adjacent have thus far repelled settlement, although population has increased in Florida, passing entirely around this area to the south. The greater part of Florida, however, including nearly all the peninsula and several large areas along the Gulf coast, still remains without settlement. This is due in part to the nature of the country, being alternately swamp and hummock, and in part to the hostility of the Seminole Indians, who still occupy nearly all of the peninsula.

The frontier line in 1840 has a length of 3,300 miles. This shrinking in its length is due to its rectification on the northwest and southwest, owing to the filling out of the entire interior. It incloses an area of 900,658 square miles, all lying between latitude 29° and 46° 30′ north, and longitude 67° and 95° 30′ west. The vacant tracts have, as noted above, decreased, although they are still quite considerable in Missouri and Arkansas. The total area of the vacant tracts is 95,516 square miles. The settled area outside the frontier line is notably small, and amounts, in the aggregate, to only 2,150 square miles, making the entire settled area 807,292 square miles in 1840. The aggregate population being 17,069,453, the average density is 21.14 to the square mile.

1850.

Between 1840 and 1850 the limits of our country have been further extended by the annexation of the state of Texas and of territory acquired from Mexico by the treaty of Guadalupe Hidalgo. The states of Iowa, Wisconsin, and Florida have been admitted to the Union, and the territories of Minnesota and Oregon have been created. An examination of the map shows that the frontier line has changed very little during this decade. At the western border of Arkansas the extension of settlement is peremptorily limited by the boundary of the Indian territory; but, curiously enough also, the western boundary of Missouri puts almost a complete stop to all settlement, notwithstanding that some of the most densely populated portions of the state lie directly on that boundary.

In Iowa settlements have made some advance, moving up the Missouri, the Des Moines, and other rivers. The settlements in Minnesota at and about St. Paul, which appeared in 1840, have greatly extended up and down the Mississippi river, while other scattering bodies of population appear in northern Wisconsin. In the southern part of the state settlement has made considerable advance, especially in a northeasterly direction, toward Green Bay. In Michigan the change has been very slight.

Turning to the southwest we find Texas, for the first time on the map of the United States, with a considerable extent of settlement; in general, however, it is very sparse, most of it lying in the eastern part of the state, and being largely dependent upon the grazing industry.

The included unsettled areas now are very small and few in number. There still remains one in southern Missouri, in the hilly country; a small one in northeastern Arkansas, in the swampy and alluvial region; and one in the similar country in the Yazoo bottom lands in western Mississippi. Along the coast of Florida are found two patches of considerable size, which are confined to the swampy coast regions. The same is the case along the coast of Louisiana. The sparse settlements of Texas are also interspersed with several patches devoid of settlement. In southern Georgia the large vacant space heretofore noted, extending also into northern Florida, has disappeared, and the Florida settlements have already reached southward to a considerable distance in the peninsula, being now free to extend without fear of hostile Seminoles, the greater part of whom have been removed to the Indian territory.

The frontier line, which now extends around a considerable part of Texas and issues on the Gulf coast at the mouth of the Nueces river, is 4,500 miles in length. The aggregate area included by it is 1,005,213 square miles, from which deduction is to be made for vacant spaces, in all, 64,339 square miles. The isolated settlements lying outside this body in the western part of the country amount to 4,775 square miles.

It is no longer by a frontier line drawn around from the St. Croix river to the Gulf of Mexico that we embrace all the population of the United States, excepting only a few outlying posts and small settlements. We may now, from the Pacific, run a line around 80,000 miners and adventurers, the pioneers of more than one state of the Union soon to arise on that coast. This body of settlement has been formed, in the main, since the acquisition of the territory by the United States, and, it might even be said, within the last year (1849–1850), dating from the discovery of gold in California. These settlements may be computed rudely at 33,600 square miles, making a total area of settlement of 979,249 square miles, the aggregate population being 23,191,876, and the average density of settlement 23.68 to the square mile.

1860.

Between 1850 and 1860 the territorial changes noted are as follows: the territory of New Mexico has been created, and the territory south of the Gila river, which has been acquired from Mexico by the Gadsden purchase (1853), has been added to it; Minnesota has been admitted as a state; Kansas and Nebraska territories have been formed from parts of Missouri territory; California and Oregon have been admitted as states, while in the unsettled parts of the Cordilleran region two new territories (Utah and Washington) have been formed out of parts of that terra incognita which we bought from France as a part of Louisiana, and of that which we acquired by conquest

Eleventh Census of the United States
Robert P. Porter, Superintendent.

1860

POPULATION.

LEGEND.

Under 2 inhab to the Sq Mile

2 _ 6 I

6 _ 18 II

18 _ 45 III

45 _ 90 IV

90 and over V

Cities over 8000 inhabitants in solid color
in circles proportionate to population.

MAP
SHOWING IN FIVE DEGREES OF DENSITY THE DISTRIBUTION
WITHIN THE TERRITORY EAST OF THE 100ᵀᴴ MERIDIAN
OF THE
POPULATION OF THE UNITED STATES
excluding Indians not taxed.
Compiled from the Returns of Population at the Eighth Census 1860.

NOTE
✳ Centre of Population   39° 00.4′ N.
                          82° 48.6′ W.

PROGRESS FROM 1790 TO 1890.

from Mexico. At this date we note the first extension of settlements beyond the line of the Missouri river. The march of settlement up the slope of the Great Plains has begun. In Kansas and Nebraska population is now found beyond the ninety-seventh meridian. Texas has filled up even more rapidly, its extreme settlements reaching to the one hundredth meridian, while the gaps noted at the date of the last census have all been filled by population. The incipient settlements about St. Paul in Minnesota, have grown like Jonah's gourd, spreading in all directions, and forming a broad band of union with the main body of settlement down the line of the Mississippi river. In Iowa settlements have crept steadily northwestward along the course of the drainage, until the state is nearly covered. Following up the Missouri population has reached out beyond the northern border of Nebraska territory. In Wisconsin the settlements have moved at least one degree farther north, while in the lower peninsula of Michigan they have spread up the lake shores, nearly encircling it on the side next Lake Michigan. On the upper peninsula the little settlements which appeared in 1850 in the copper region on Keweenaw point have extended and increased greatly in density as that mining interest has developed in value. In northern New York there is apparently no change in the unsettled area. In northern Maine we note, for the first time, a decided movement toward the settlement of its unoccupied territory in the extension of the settlements on its eastern and northern border up the St. John river. The unsettled regions in southern Missouri, northeastern Arkansas, and northwestern Mississippi have become sparsely covered by population. Along the gulf coast there is little or no change. There is to be noted a slight extension of settlement southward in the peninsula of Florida.

The frontier line now measures 5,300 miles, and embraces 1,126,518 square miles, lying between latitude 28° 30′ and 47° 30′ north, and between longitude 67° and 99° 30′ west. From this deduction should be made on account of vacant spaces, amounting to 39,139 square miles, found mainly in New York and along the Gulf coast. The outlying settlements beyond the one hundredth meridian are now numerous. They include, among others, a strip extending far up the Rio Grande in Texas, embracing 7,475 square miles (a region given over to the raising of sheep), while the Pacific settlements, now comprising two sovereign states, are nearly three times as extensive as at 1850, embracing 99,900 square miles. The total area of settlement in 1860 is thus 1,194,754 square miles, the aggregate population being 31,443,321 and the average density of settlement 26.32 to the square mile.

1870.

During the decade from 1860 to 1870 a number of territorial changes have been effected in the extreme west. A great tract stretching into Arctic regions and containing few people was purchased in 1867 from Russia and is called Alaska. Arizona, Colorado, Dakota, Idaho, Montana, Nevada, and Wyoming have been organized as territories. Kansas, Nebraska, and Nevada have been admitted as states. West Virginia has been cut off from the mother commonwealth and made a separate state.

In 1870 we note a gradual and steady extension of the frontier line westward over the great plains. The unsettled areas in Maine, New York, and Florida have not greatly diminished, but in Michigan the extension of the lumber interests northward and inward from the lake shore has reduced considerably the unsettled portion. On the upper peninsula the settlements have increased somewhat, owing to the discovery of the rich iron deposits destined to play so important a part in the manufacturing industry of the country.

Settlement has spread westward to the boundary of the state in southern Minnesota, and up the Big Sioux river in southeastern Dakota. Iowa is entirely reclaimed, excepting a small area of perhaps 1,000 square miles in its northwestern corner. Through Kansas and Nebraska the frontier line has moved steadily westward, following in general the courses of the larger streams and of the newly constructed railroads. The frontier in Texas has changed but little, that little consisting of a general westward movement. In the Cordilleran region settlements have extended but slowly. Those upon the Pacific coast show little change, either in extent or in density. In short, we see everywhere the effects of the war in the partial arrest of the progress of development.

The settlements in the west, beyond the frontier line, have arranged themselves mainly in three belts. The most eastern of these is located in central Colorado, New Mexico, and Wyoming, along the eastern base of and among the Rocky mountains. To this region settlement was first attracted in 1859 and 1860 by the discovery of mineral deposits, and has been retained by the richness of the soil and by the abundance of water for irrigation, which have promoted the agricultural industry.

The second belt of settlement is that of Utah, settled in 1847 by the Mormons fleeing from Illinois. This community then differed, and still differs, radically from that of the Rocky mountains, being essentially agricultural, mining having been discountenanced from the first by the church authorities, as tending to fill the "Promised land" with Gentile adventurers, and thereby imperil Mormon institutions. The settlements of this group, as seen on the map for 1870, extend from southern Idaho southward through central Utah, and along the eastern base of the Wahsatch range to the Arizona line. They consist mainly of scattered hamlets and small towns, about which are grouped the farms of the communities.

The third strip is that in the Pacific states and territories, extending from Washington territory southward to southern California and eastward to the system of "sinks", in western Nevada. This group of population owes its existence to the mining industry. Originated in 1849 by a great immigration movement, it has grown by successive impulses as new fields for rapid money getting have been developed. Latterly, however, the value of this region to the agriculturist has been recognized, and the character of the occupations of the people is undergoing a marked change.

PROGRESS OF THE NATION.

xxvi

These three great western groups comprise nine-tenths of the population west of the frontier line. The remainder is scattered about in the valleys and the mountains of Montana, Idaho, and Arizona, at military posts, isolated mining camps, and on cattle ranches.

The frontier line in 1870 embraces 1,178,068 square miles, all between 27° 15′ and 47° 30′ north latitude, and between 67° and 99° 45′ west longitude. From this, however, deduction is to be made of 37,739 square miles on account of interior spaces containing no population. To what remains we must add 11,810 square miles on account of settled tracts east of the one hundredth meridian, lying outside of the frontier line, and 120,100 square miles on account of settlements in the Cordilleran region and on the Pacific coast, making the total area of settlement for 1870 not less than 1,272,239 square miles, the aggregate population being 38,558,371, and the average density of settlement 30.31 to the square mile.

1880.

In 1880 we find that during the decade Colorado has been added to the sisterhood of states. The first point that strikes us in examining the map showing the areas of settlement at this date, as compared with previous ones, is the great extent of territory which has been brought under occupation during the past ten years. Not only has settlement spread westward over large areas in Dakota, Nebraska, Kansas, and Texas, thus moving the frontier line of the main body of settlement westward many scores of miles, but the isolated settlements of the Cordilleran region and of the Pacific coast show enormous accessions of occupied territory.

The migration of farming population to the northeastern part of Maine has widened the settled area to a marked extent, probably more than has been done during any previous decade. The vacant space in the Adirondack region of northern New York has been lessened in size, and its limits have been reduced practically to the actual mountain tract. The most notable change, however, in New England and the middle states, including Ohio and Indiana, has been the increase in density of population and the migration to cities, with the consequent increase of the urban population, as indicated by the number and the size of the spots representing these cities upon the map. Throughout the southern states there is to be noted, not only a general increase in the density of population and a decrease of unsettled areas, but a greater approach to uniformity of settlement throughout the whole region. The unsettled area of the peninsula of Florida has decreased decidedly, while the vacant spaces heretofore seen along the upper coast of Florida and Louisiana have entirely disappeared. Although the Appalachian Mountain system is still distinctly outlined by its general lighter color on the map, its density of population more nearly approaches that of the country on the east and on the west. In Michigan there is seen a very decided increase of the settled region. Settlements have not only surrounded the head of the lower peninsula, but they leave only a very small body of unsettled country in the interior. In the upper peninsula the copper and the iron interests, and the railroads which subserve them, have peopled quite a large extent of territory. In Wisconsin the unsettled area is rapidly decreasing as railroads stretch their arms out over the vacant tracts. In Minnesota and in eastern Dakota the building of railroads, and the development of the latent capabilities of this region in the cultivation of wheat, have caused a rapid flow of settlement, and now the frontier line of population, instead of returning to Lake Michigan, as it did ten years ago, meets the boundary line of the British possessions west of the ninety-seventh meridian. The settlements in Kansas and Nebraska have made great strides over the plains, reaching at several points the boundary of the humid region, so that their westward extension beyond this point is to be governed hereafter by the supply of water in the streams. As a natural result, we see settlements following these streams in long ribbons of population. In Nebraska these narrow belts have reached the western boundary of the state at two points: one upon the South Platte and the other upon the Republican river. In Kansas, too, the settlements have followed the Kansas river and its branches and the Arkansas nearly to the western boundary of the state. Texas also has made great strides, both in the extension of the frontier line of settlement and in the increase in the density of population, due both to the building of railroads and to the development of the cattle, sheep, and agricultural interests. The heavy population in the prairie portions of the state is explained by the railroads which now traverse them. In Dakota, beside the agricultural region, in the eastern part of the territory, we note the formation of a body of settlement in the Black Hills, in the southwest corner, which, in 1870, was a part of the reservation of the Sioux Indians. This settlement is the result of the discovery of valuable gold deposits. In Montana there appears a great extension of the settled area, which, as it is mainly due to agricultural interests, is found chiefly along the courses of the streams. Mining has, however, played not a small part in this increase in settlement. Idaho, too, shows a decided growth from the same causes. The small settlements which, in 1870, were located about Boise city, and near the mouth of the Clearwater, have now extended their areas to many hundreds of square miles. The settlement in the southeastern corner of the territory is almost purely of Mormons, and has not made a marked increase.

Of all the states and territories of the Cordilleran region Colorado has made the greatest stride during the decade. From a narrow strip of settlement, extending along the immediate base of the Rocky mountains, the belt has increased so that it comprises the whole mountain region, beside a great extension outward upon the plains. This increase is the result of the discovery of very extensive and very rich mineral deposits about Leadville, producing a "stampede" second only to that of 1849 and 1850 to California. Miners have spread over the whole

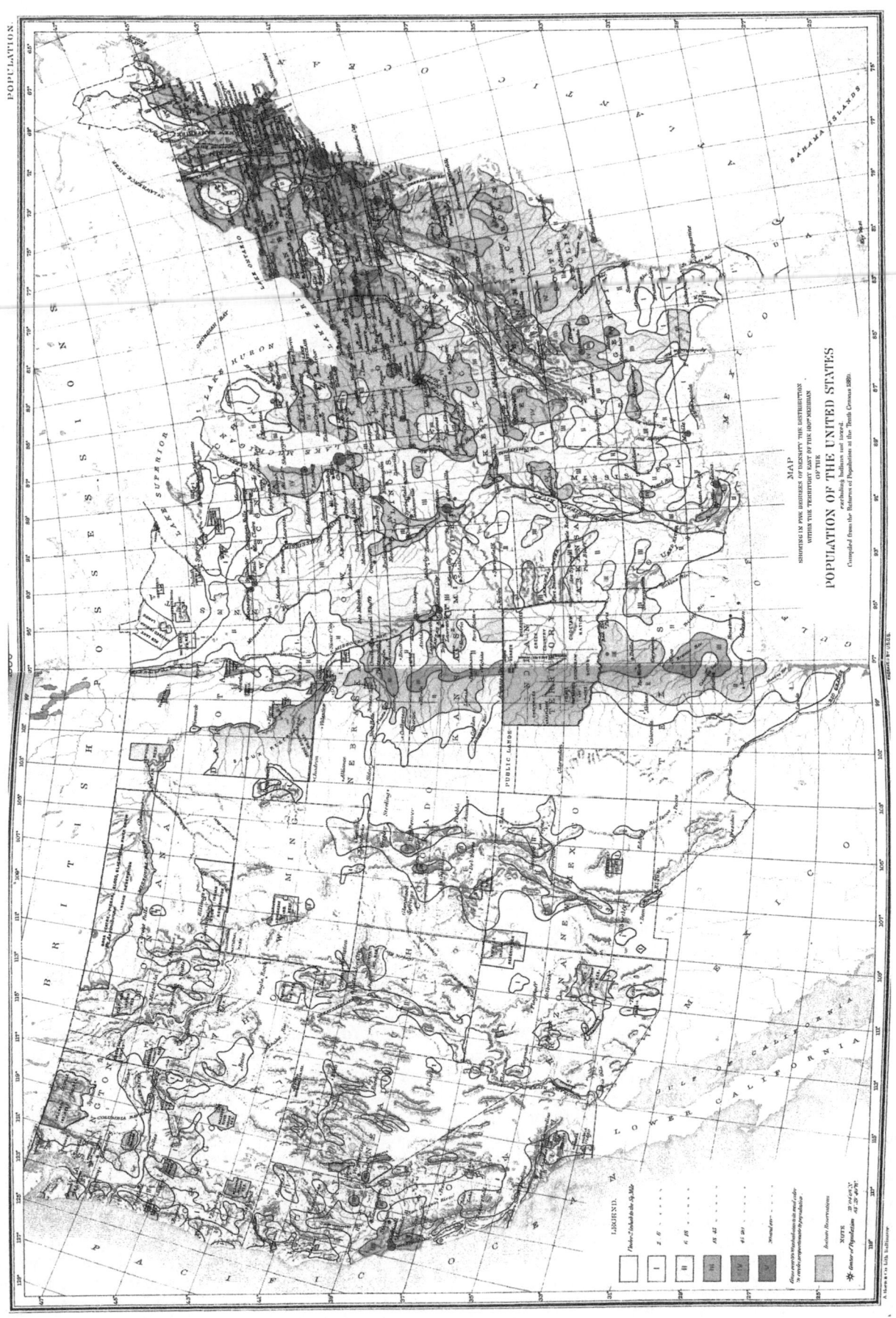

PROGRESS FROM 1790 TO 1890.

mountain region, till every range and ridge swarms with them. New Mexico shows but little change, although the recent extension of railroads in the territory and the opening up of mineral resources promise in the near future to add largely to its population. Arizona, too, although its extent of settlement has increased somewhat, is but just commencing to enjoy a period of rapid development, owing to the extension of railroads and to the suppression of hostile Indians. Utah presents us with a case dissimilar to any other of the territories—a case of steady, regular growth, due almost entirely to its agricultural capabilities, as was noted previously. This is due to the policy of the Mormon church, which has steadily discountenanced mining and speculation in all forms, and has encouraged in every way agricultural pursuits. Nevada shows a slight extension of settlement due mainly to the gradual increase in the agricultural interest. The mining industry is probably not more flourishing at present in this state than it was ten years ago, and the population dependent upon it is, if anything, less in number. In California, as the attention of the people has become devoted more and more to agricultural pursuits, at the expense of the mining and cattle industries, we note a tendency to a more even distribution of the inhabitants. The population in some of the mining regions has decreased, while over the area of the great valley, and in the fertile valleys of the coast ranges it has increased. In Oregon the increase has been mainly in the section east of the Cascade range, a region drained by the Des Chutes and the John Day rivers, and by the smaller tributaries of the Snake, a region which, with the corresponding section in Washington territory, is now coming to the front as a wheat producing district. In most of the settled portions here spoken of irrigation is not necessary for the cultivation of crops, and consequently the possibilities of the region in the direction of agricultural development are very great. In Washington territory, which in 1870 had been scarcely touched by immigration, we find the valley west of the Cascade mountains tolerably well settled throughout, while the stream of settlement has poured up the Columbia into the valleys of the Wallawalla and the Snake rivers and the great plain of the Columbia, induced thither by the facilities for raising cattle and by the great profits of wheat cultivation.

The length of the frontier line in 1880 is 3,337 miles. The area included between the frontier line, the Atlantic and the Gulf coast, and the northern boundary is 1,398,940 square miles, lying between 26° and 49° north latitude and 67° and 102° west longitude. From this must be deducted, for unsettled areas, as follows:

	SQUARE MILES.
Maine	12,000
New York	2,200
Michigan	10,200
Wisconsin	10,200
Minnesota	34,000
Florida	20,800

making a total of 89,400 square miles, leaving 1,309,540 square miles.

To this must be added the isolated areas of settlement in the Cordilleran region and the extent of settlement on the Pacific coast, which amount, in the aggregate, to 260,025 square miles, making a total settled area of 1,569,565 square miles. The population is 50,155,783, and the average density of settlement 31.96 to the square mile.

1890.

This census completes the history of a century; a century of progress and achievement unequaled in the world's history. A hundred years ago there were groups of feeble settlements sparsely covering an area of 239,935 square miles, and numbering less than 4,000,000. The century has witnessed our development into a great and powerful nation; it has witnessed the spread of settlement across the continent until not less than 1,947,280 square miles have been redeemed from the wilderness and brought into the service of man, while the population has increased and multiplied by its own increase and by additions from abroad until it numbers 62,622,250.

During the decade just past a trifling change has been made in the boundary between Nebraska and Dakota by which the area of Nebraska has been slightly increased. Dakota territory has been cut in two and the states of North Dakota and South Dakota admitted. Montana, Wyoming, Idaho, and Washington have also been added to the sisterhood of states. The territory of Oklahoma has been created out of the western half of the Indian territory, and to it has been added the strip of public land lying north of the panhandle of Texas.

The most striking fact connected with the extension of settlement during the past decade is the numerous additions which have been made to the settled area within the Cordilleran region. Settlements have spread westward up the slope of the plains until they have joined the bodies formerly isolated in Colorado, forming a continuous body of settlement from the east to the Rocky mountains. Practically the whole of Kansas has become a settled region, and the unsettled area of Nebraska has been reduced in dimensions to a third of what it was ten years ago. What was a sparsely settled region in Texas in 1880 is now the most populous part of the state, while settlements have spread westward to the escarpment of the Staked Plains. The unsettled regions of North Dakota and South Dakota have been reduced to half their former dimensions. Settlements in Montana have spread until they now occupy one-third of the state. In New Mexico, Idaho, and Wyoming considerable extensions of area are to be noted. In Colorado, in spite of the decline of the mining industry and the depopulation of its mining regions, settlement has spread, and two-thirds of the state are now under the dominion of man. Oregon and Washington

xxviii   PROGRESS OF THE NATION.

show equally rapid progress, and California, although its mining regions have suffered, has made great inroads upon its unsettled regions, especially in the south. Of all the western states and territories Nevada alone is at a standstill in this respect, its settled area remaining practically the same as in 1880. When it is remembered that the state has lost one-third of its population during the past ten years, the fact that it has held its own in settled area is surprising until it is understood that the state has undergone a material change in occupations during the decade, and that the inhabitants, instead of being closely grouped and engaged in mining pursuits, have become scattered along its streams and have engaged in agriculture.

Settlement is spreading with some rapidity in Maine, its unsettled area having dwindled from 12,000 to about 4,000 square miles. The unsettled portion of the Adirondack region in New York has also diminished, there being now but 1,000 square miles remaining. The frontier has been pushed still farther southward in Florida, and the unsettled area has been reduced from 20,800 to 13,000 square miles.

Lumbering and mining interests have practically obliterated the wilderness of Michigan and have reduced that of Wisconsin to less than one-half of its former area. In Minnesota the area of the wild northern forests has been reduced from 34,000 to 23,000 square miles. The population is 62,622,250, and the average density of settlement 32.16 to the square mile.

VACANT SPACES ON THE DENSITY MAP.

Within the settled portions of the United States are several areas which, for various reasons, have thus far remained unsettled. There are also areas which, though long ago, perhaps early in our history, were occupied by inhabitants, and which now remain sparsely settled, notwithstanding the vast increase of population in the general regions in which they are situated. The former have been enumerated above. It may be instructive to glance at them in detail, in order to discover the reasons why settlement has passed them by.

The northern portion of Maine, comprising 4,000 square miles, is practically without settlement. The only inhabitants of this region are the occupants of logging camps, who remain there only in the winter, and a handful of enterprising summer tourists. The country is a dense forest, mainly level, but diversified here and there by hills, which in a few instances rise to the dignity of mountains. It is traversed by numerous small streams, strung upon which are many lakes and lakelets, the whole forming a most complicated system of water communication, navigable, however, only by canoes, owing to numerous falls and rapids.

The climate is severe, and this, added to the poverty of the soil and the labor involved in clearing it for agriculture, has prevented its occupation, while rich farming lands can be obtained under liberal homestead laws in the west. Another, and slightly more remote, cause has operated, to a considerable extent, in preventing the spread of settlement in this state. This is the decline in shipbuilding, especially of wooden vessels—a business in which this state was largely interested. This has not only checked the general prosperity of the state, but has injured the lumber business greatly. During recent years there has been a slight movement into this region. A line of settlement has extended up the eastern border of the state, and this is now spreading very gradually westward. It is safe to predict, however, that not until all that part of the prairie country which lies east of the limit of the arid region shall have been settled will population move decidedly toward this section.

A second section which has thus far defied settlement is the Adirondack region. This presents very serious obstacles to settlement—so serious that the central portion of it remains today without inhabitants. It consists of scattered groups of mountains, standing in short ranges or ridges. These mountains rise to heights of 4,000 to 5,000 feet, a few peaks exceeding the latter figures. The valleys are all at a considerable elevation. On the east the mountains descend abruptly to Lakes George and Champlain; on the west, they fall off into a sort of plateau, extending toward the St. Lawrence and Lake Ontario. On the north and south the ridges fall off gradually to the lower country. The whole region is densely covered with forests. It is watered by numerous mountain torrents, while the valleys and the plateau on the west are dotted with numberless lakes and ponds. The elevation and the consequently severe climate of the valleys, and the country immediately adjacent, are such as to discourage, if not to preclude, agriculture.

Elsewhere in the Appalachian region there are no unsettled areas of sufficient magnitude to be represented on our map, although in many localities the population is very sparse. In Pennsylvania the narrow ridges of this system are covered with coal and iron miners; in Virginia the grain fields extend to and over their summits; in North Carolina and Tennessee the high mountains are without settlements, owing to their rugged character and their great elevation. But these areas, although large in the aggregate, are severally very small.

In northern Wisconsin the case is not dissimilar to that of northern Maine. This is a region of heavy forest, lying far to the north, under a severe climate. Settlement has, to a certain extent, passed it by, following westward the belt of open, fertile prairie. But, on the other hand, immigration to this state is still going on; the lumber business, which is here the pioneer of settlement, is being actively prosecuted, and every year settlement is closing in upon this vacant space, and its area is constantly and rapidly diminishing.

The unsettled portion of Minnesota is under conditions somewhat similar. The prairie portion of the state is now occupied, and settlements have encroached heavily upon the region of forests. The northern part of this unsettled region, unlike Wisconsin, is not occupied by forests, but is covered with a scrubby growth of hackmatack and other brush. A large proportion of the surface is occupied by lakes and swamps.

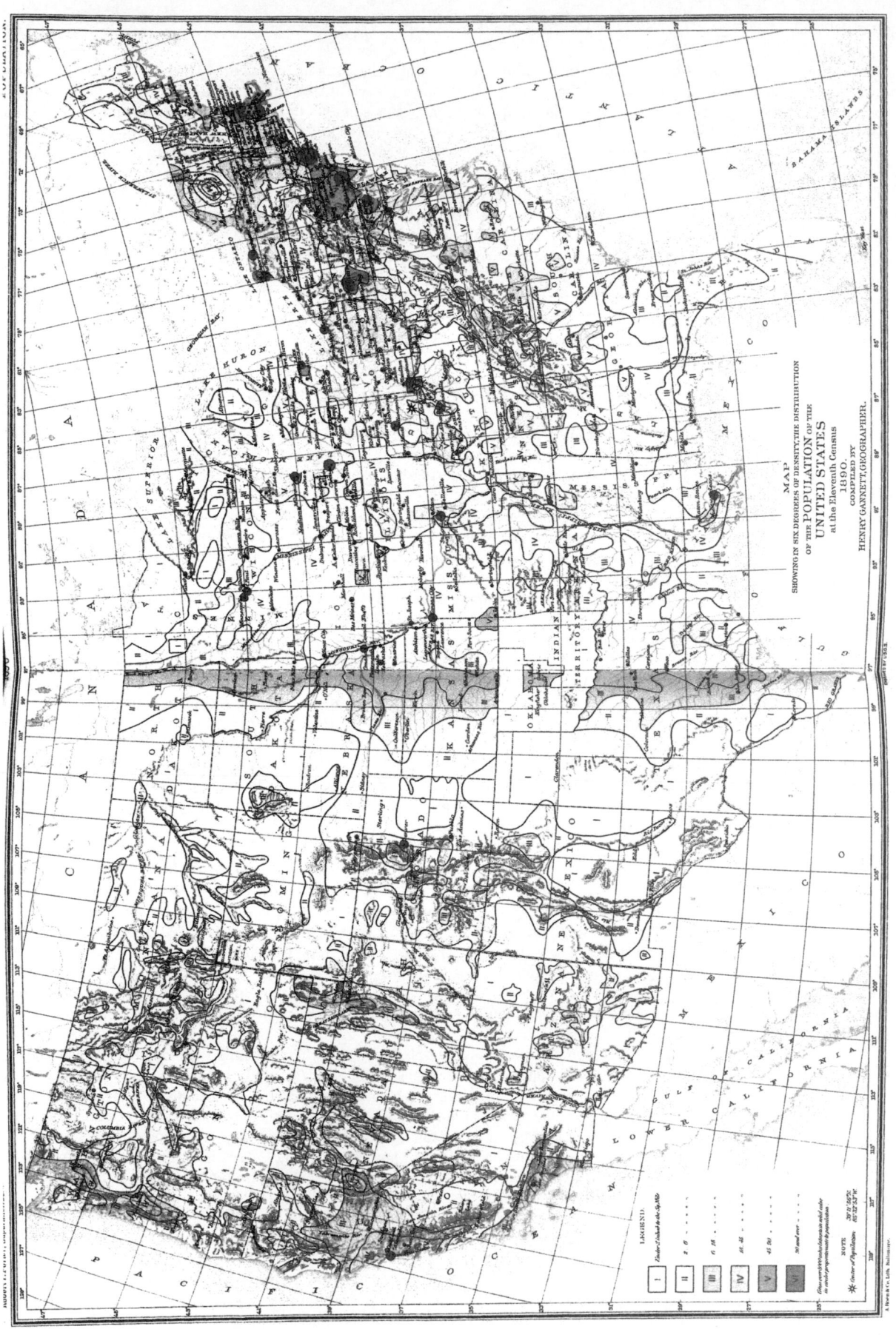

VACANT SPACES ON THE DENSITY MAP.   xxix

A large proportion of the area of the peninsula of Florida is practically without settlement. This appears to be due in part to the direction of the general movement of population, which has been westward from Georgia and the Carolinas; in part to the want of good harbors, and other inducements to settle upon the coast, and thus to create starting points for the settlement of the interior; but also, and very largely, to the fact that a considerable portion of the area is swampy and difficult of access, and, consequently, remote from markets.

The peninsula is underlaid mainly by a limestone formation, geologically very recent. Its surface consists largely of hummocks and ridges, alternating with belts and patches of swamp and myriads of swampy lakes. The Everglades, which occupy an immense area in the southern portion of the peninsula, seem to be a culmination of the general characteristics of the peninsula, and the following description of them, from the pen of Professor E. A. Smith, illustrates the extreme of these characteristics:

The Everglades, which form so singular and unique a feature of Florida, may be described, in general terms, as consisting of a shallow lake of vast extent, occupying a basin or depression in the limestone of the country. From surveys recently made, it is known that the whole bed of the Everglades has considerable elevation above the sea, so that the draining of this area is merely a question of time and expense. All the streams which flow from the Everglades are interrupted by falls or rapids. The Caloosahatchee is navigable by steamers to within 10 miles of Lake Okeechobee, where the rapids begin.

The water over the Everglades varies in depth from 6 inches to as many feet, and teems with aquatic and semi-aquatic grasses and other plants. From this maze of water and vegetation rise innumerable islands, containing from 1 to 100 acres of land. These islands are covered with a growth of cypress, sweet bay, crab wood, mastic, cocoa palms, cabbage palmetto, and live and water oaks, beneath which bloom flowers in almost endless variety. Notwithstanding the shallowness of the water in the Everglades, and the profuseness of the vegetation growing in it, it is comparatively pure and clear, and abounds in fish, turtles, and alligators. Bears, panthers, wild-cats, and deer inhabit the islands.

Lake Okeechobee is about 50 miles long from northwest to southeast, and about 20 miles broad, and from 8 to 20 feet deep. Its northeastern and eastern shores are skirted with a low hummock of red bay, live oak, water oak, and other timber; its western and southwestern shore with a dense growth of saw grass.

The lake has no visible outlet, except as its waters soak through the Everglades, and the lands around the lake can never be made available till the waters are lowered by artificial canals.

Having thus gone through the successive census years, tracing the course of the outside line of population and estimating the settled area inclosed between this line and the ocean, let us now go back to 1790, and follow out the movement of population along the several degrees of latitude, to note the relative rapidity and steadiness of advance within each belt of territory. Owing to the difficulty of locating with precision the numerous small patches of population in the Pacific states and territories up to and including 1870, the computations shown in the following table are restricted to the country east of the one hundredth meridian up to that period. The figures for 1880 and 1890 are for the whole country.

Before the results of such computations can be satisfactorily stated, an explanation must be given of the method followed.

First. The successive parallels are taken as the central lines of zones half a degree wide; and where any parallel passes through vacant spaces, any body of population lying within a quarter degree, upon either side thereof, is referred thereto, after being reduced to the width of half a degree in latitude. Where a solid body of population lies close up against a parallel on one side, however, no reduction is made on account of the absence of population on the other side. The only important exception to the rule is in the case of the thirty-fourth parallel, where, after crossing the ninety-fourth meridian, it runs through the southern portion of the Indian territory, shortly above the northern line of Texas. As the absence of population as known to the census (Indians in tribal relations not being recognized by the census law) from the line of this parallel in this part of its course is the result of express exclusion by treaty stipulations the population just below is not referred to it.

Second. The starting point on the coast is taken, not from the extreme end of any cape or promontory upon which the parallel may chance to emerge from the Atlantic, but from the average projection of the coast line in the general neighborhood of the parallel. In the case of Long Island, the eastern half was taken to fill up the western end of the sound, and the forty-first parallel was assumed, for the purposes of these computations, to begin with 73° west longitude.

Third. The northern lakes and all considerable bays were omitted from consideration, as also the British possessions when crossed by the parallels under measurement.

Fourth. All spaces vacant of population were skipped, the same rule being adopted for measuring and referring to parallels spaces which are not directly upon any parallel, as in the case of the populated areas lying above or below a parallel when passing through vacant spaces.

XXX   PROGRESS OF THE NATION.

The result of the application of these rules to our measurements is to give the populated areas along each parallel either in one continuous body or in several groups, as population is broken by foreign territory, by lakes or bays, or by large vacant spaces. Consolidating all such, however, and reducing all the populated spaces on each parallel to a continuous line, we have the following as the breadth of the settled area in miles along the successive parallels at each census from 1790 to 1890:

EXTENT OF SETTLED AREA: 1790 TO 1890.

[Miles.]

DEGREE OF NORTH LATITUDE.	1790	1800	1810	1820	1830	1840	1850	1860	1870	1880	1890
49										37	270
48										56	600
47							79	131	209	291	940
46					15	20	50	125	230	385	1,300
45	30	317	392	392	392	421	437	521	858	940	1,568
44	226	252	279	279	299	308	404	731	777	874	1,450
43	339	355	425	425	485	792	816	1,001	1,137	1,156	1,428
42	234	375	568	581	691	963	984	1,143	1,248	1,316	1,785
41	258	396	471	548	663	1,013	1,107	1,277	1,325	1,375	2,080
40	358	371	584	613	912	1,134	1,140	1,220	1,252	1,376	2,120
39	270	456	595	888	1,038	1,043	1,043	1,168	1,224	1,397	2,100
38	425	566	707	831	871	1,020	1,032	1,141	1,193	1,278	2,035
37	344	606	706	746	797	902	1,018	1,018	1,134	1,260	1,910
36	462	533	682	751	878	1,034	1,057	1,057	1,057	1,057	1,456
35	384	395	391	575	961	976	1,030	1,030	1,030	1,030	1,425
34	302	327	302	610	707	916	938	938	938	938	1,310
33	175	192	230	328	554	815	989	1,105	1,055	1,156	1,450
32	30	114	227	597	742	763	929	1,023	1,008	1,109	1,357
31	10	25	240	357	634	678	860	983	991	1,053	1,062
30			150	180	323	373	725	785	785	799	840
29						30	255	372	372	414	427
28						20	83	102	140	188	244
27								25	25	47	186
26								65	65	65	65

In all this discussion regarding the population and the area of the United States, Alaska is intentionally omitted.

THE SETTLED AREA IN 1890.

In the following tables are presented the results of computations relating to the density of the rural, as distinguished from the urban, population at the census of 1890, in comparison with the corresponding results of previous enumerations. In this discussion it is to be understood that all cities of 8,000 inhabitants or more are taken out of consideration, and, as explained previously, in connection with the density maps, the deduction of the population of cities sometimes brings the county into a lower population group than at the preceding census, notwithstanding the actual increase of population in both rural and urban parts. Thus we may suppose a county, with an area of 400 square miles, to have had in 1880 a population of 20,000, and its county town 6,500 inhabitants. The county would therefore, if treated as a whole, fall into group 4; that is, the group having a density 45 to 90 to the square mile. In 1890, however, we will suppose the population to have increased to 24,000, of which 8,500 are now found in the county town, which thereupon becomes a city within our definition, and is therefore excluded from the mass of population. The county then sinks into class 3; that is, the group having between 18 and 45 inhabitants to the square mile. Such cases are, of course, few in number. The lowest grade of settlement taken for this discussion is that which contains a population of 2 to the square mile. All the region outside this line may be regarded as practically unsettled territory, peopled, if at all, by a few scattering graziers, wandering prospectors, lumbermen, or hunters.

For purposes of discussion this region may be divided, according to density of population, into five groups corresponding to those upon the general density maps. These groups are as follows:

1. A population of from 2 to 6 to a square mile.
2. A population of from 6 to 18 to a square mile.
3. A population of from 18 to 45 to a square mile.
4. A population of from 45 to 90 to a square mile.
5. A population of 90 or more to a square mile.

Of these groups of population of different density, as they may be called, the first three indicate a predominantly agricultural condition. Speaking broadly, agriculture in the United States is not carried to such a point as to afford employment and support to a population in excess of 45 to a square mile; and, consequently, the fourth and fifth groups do not appear with us, except as trade and manufactures arise and the classes rendering personal and professional services are multiplied.

THE SETTLED AREA IN 1890.   xxxi

Of the agricultural groups, the first represents a very sparse population, such as in our western country might be sustained by the grazing industry, without any cultivation of the soil; and accordingly we find this group at the present time mainly represented in the states and territories of the far west. The poorest tillage regions also sink into this group, and hence we find not inconsiderable portions of some of the older states in this class. In 1790, however, No. 1 was the largest single group in what is now Maine, in New York, Pennsylvania, South Carolina, and in what is now the state of West Virginia.

The second group—6 to 18 inhabitants to the square mile—indicates almost universally the existence of defined farms or plantations and the systematic cultivation of the ground, but this either in an early stage of settlement or upon more or less rugged soil. Thus we find this group still large in many of the western and southwestern states and in the mountainous regions of the Atlantic slope. In 1790, however, this group far exceeded in area Nos. 3, 4, and 5 combined.

The third group—18 to 45 inhabitants to the square mile—almost universally indicates a highly successful agriculture. Here and there the presence of petty mechanical industries raises a difficult farming or planting region into this group, but in general, where manufactures exist at all, they induce a population of 45 or more to the square mile.

We should therefore expect to find, as is the case, No. 3 the predominant group in northern New England, in the southern states, and, of the northern central states, Illinois, Michigan, Wisconsin, Iowa, Missouri, and Kansas. In 1790, No. 3 was the largest single group in Delaware, Maryland, Massachusetts, New Hampshire, New Jersey, and Virginia (exclusive of what is now West Virginia).

The fourth group almost universally indicates the existence of commercial and manufacturing industry and the multiplication of personal and professional services. Massachusetts, Connecticut, New York, New Jersey, Pennsylvania, Delaware, Maryland, Ohio, and Indiana are the states in which this group is found in excess of any other. In none of these states was this group in excess in 1790. Two of them, Ohio and Indiana, can scarcely be said to have been settled at all (Marietta, Ohio, having been founded in 1788, while in Indiana there were but two or three small settlements, the remains of French occupation). In New York and Pennsylvania, at that date, group 1 was predominant.

The fifth group represents a very advanced condition of industry, as this degree of settlement is only reached where manufacturing and trading cities are numerous. At the First Census only a few counties, and even at the Eleventh Census less than 25,000 square miles, were found populated to this extent. In Rhode Island and the District of Columbia alone is this degree of density found in excess of every other.

Having thus sought to give a general, but necessarily somewhat vague, impression of the meaning of these groups of population, the following tables are presented with a view of illustrating the present status of our population in regard to extent and density of settlement.

The following table presents the areas in square miles of the total settled area and of the different groups of settlement at the date of each census:

CENSUS YEARS.	Total area of settlement: 2 or more to the square mile.	GROUP 1. 2 to 6 to the square mile.	GROUP 2. 6 to 18 to the square mile.	GROUP 3. 18 to 45 to the square mile.	GROUP 4. 45 to 90 to the square mile.	GROUP 5. 90 or more to the square mile.
1790	239,935	83,436	83,346	59,282	13,051	820
1800	305,708	81,010	123,267	82,504	17,734	1,193
1810	407,945	116,629	154,410	108,155	27,490	1,243
1820	508,717	140,827	177,153	150,390	39,004	1,343
1830	632,717	151,460	225,894	186,503	65,446	3,414
1840	807,292	183,607	291,819	241,587	84,451	5,828
1850	979,249	233,697	294,698	338,796	100,794	11,264
1860	1,194,754	260,866	353,341	431,601	134,722	14,224
1870	1,272,239	245,897	363,475	470,529	174,036	18,302
1880	1,569,565	384,820	373,890	554,300	231,410	25,145
1890	1,947,280	592,037	393,943	701,845	235,148	24,307

PROGRESS OF THE NATION.

Notwithstanding the constant passage of territory from lower into higher groups by reason of increase in the number of inhabitants, the lower groups have been so rapidly increased by settlement of new territory that they have increased in every case, except that in 1800 and 1870 slight diminutions are noted in group 1. In 1890 a trifling reduction is seen in the highest group. This is doubtless an indirect result of the rapid development of cities in the territory falling into this group, as each city, upon reaching a population of 8,000, is subtracted from the population of its county, thereby materially reducing the apparent density of the population of the county. To a certain extent the case is similar in the next group, that of 45 to 90 inhabitants to a square mile, which during the past decade increased in area but 3,738 square miles.

It will be noted that the settled area has constantly and rapidly increased, but by no means at a uniform rate or at rates proportional to the increase of population. The following table shows the rates of increase of the settled area and of the population placed in juxtaposition:

CENSUS YEARS.	Settled area.	Population.	PER CENT OF INCREASE.	
			Settled area	Population
1790	239,935	3,929,214		
1800	305,708	5,308,483	27.41	35.10
1810	407,945	7,239,881	33.44	36.38
1820	508,717	9,633,822	24.70	33.07
1830	632,717	12,866,020	24.38	33.55
1840	807,292	17,069,453	27.59	32.67
1850	979,249	23,191,876	21.30	35.87
1860	1,194,754	31,443,321	22.01	35.58
1870	1,272,239	38,558,371	6.49	22.63
1880	1,569,565	50,155,783	23.37	30.08
1890	1,947,280	62,622,250	24.06	24.86

In 1890 the population was nearly 16 times as great as in 1790, while during the century the settled area was increased only about eightfold. In general, the increase of population has gone on at a much more rapid rate than that of settled area.

During the decade from 1880 to 1890 the inroads upon the unsettled region have been unprecedented in amount, not less than 377,715 square miles having been redeemed, exceeding by 80,389 square miles the area settled between 1870 and 1880.

The following table shows the percentage of the area of each group of population of the total area of settlement at each census. The total for each census year equals 100 per cent in all cases.

CENSUS YEARS.	GROUP 1.	GROUP 2.	GROUP 3.	GROUP 4.	GROUP 5.
1790	34.77	34.74	24.71	5.44	0.34
1800	26.50	40.32	26.99	5.80	0.39
1810	28.59	37.85	26.51	6.74	0.31
1820	27.08	34.82	20.56	7.27	0.27
1830	23.94	35.70	29.48	10.34	0.54
1840	22.74	36.15	29.83	10.46	0.72
1850	23.87	30.09	34.00	10.29	1.15
1860	21.83	29.57	36.13	11.28	1.16
1870	19.33	28.57	36.98	13.68	1.44
1880	24.52	23.82	35.32	14.74	1.60
1890	30.40	26.23	36.04	12.08	1.25

THE SETTLED AREA IN 1890.   xxxiii

The following table presents in detailed form, by states and territories, the extent of settled area and the area in each of the density groups:

AREAS IN SQUARE MILES OF THE DIFFERENT GROUPS OF SETTLEMENT IN 1890.

STATES AND TERRITORIES.	Total area of settlement: 2 or more to the square mile.	GROUP 1. 2 to 6 to the square mile.	GROUP 2. 6 to 18 to the square mile.	GROUP 3. 18 to 45 to the square mile.	GROUP 4. 45 to 90 to the square mile.	GROUP 5. 90 or more to the square mile.
The United States	1,947,990	599,097	353,543	701,845	235,148	24,367
North Atlantic division	156,682	11,759	10,099	45,733	69,267	19,824
Maine	25,720	9,624	6,596	6,703	2,806	....
New Hampshire	8,828	708	886	5,245	1,989	....
Vermont	9,135	....	730	7,487	918	....
Massachusetts	8,040	....	....	959	4,149	2,932
Rhode Island	1,085	....	....	....	320	765
Connecticut	4,845	....	....	....	4,072	773
New York	46,580	1,427	1,887	13,172	28,266	1,828
New Jersey	7,455	....	....	1,550	3,055	2,850
Pennsylvania	44,985	....	....	10,617	23,602	10,676
South Atlantic division	255,450	19,854	55,585	143,962	35,152	897
Delaware	1,960	....	....	810	1,150	....
Maryland	9,860	....	....	2,906	6,123	887
District of Columbia	60	....	....	....	....	60
Virginia	40,125	....	3,109	29,895	7,121	....
West Virginia	24,645	....	9,190	11,766	3,689	....
North Carolina	48,580	....	6,313	38,060	4,207	....
South Carolina	30,170	....	369	23,560	6,241	....
Georgia	58,980	1,166	16,153	35,040	6,621	....
Florida	41,070	18,688	20,451	1,931	....	....
North Central division	636,570	119,520	144,736	270,084	99,589	2,632
Ohio	40,760	....	....	1,616	37,744	1,400
Indiana	35,910	....	....	12,484	23,426	....
Illinois	56,000	....	....	41,890	14,110	....
Michigan	57,430	12,349	13,651	16,844	13,806	780
Wisconsin	51,148	8,410	14,360	20,672	7,302	404
Minnesota	56,259	9,871	25,766	20,622	....	....
Iowa	55,475	....	4,246	50,167	1,062	....
Missouri	68,735	....	14,892	52,705	1,030	48
North Dakota	26,973	17,835	9,138	....	....	....
South Dakota	43,848	19,343	23,150	1,355	....	....
Nebraska	63,061	26,801	17,040	19,220	....	....
Kansas	80,971	24,920	22,493	32,440	1,109	....
South Central division	431,795	67,863	107,251	225,137	31,140	904
Kentucky	40,000	....	1,643	25,149	12,491	717
Tennessee	41,750	....	4,114	24,985	12,651	....
Alabama	51,540	....	9,472	37,717	4,351	....
Mississippi	46,340	....	10,007	35,502	831	....
Louisiana	45,420	7,608	18,490	18,319	816	187
Texas	150,810	59,755	40,313	50,742	....	....
Oklahoma	2,890	....	....	2,890	....	....
Arkansas	53,045	....	23,212	29,833	....	....
Western division	466,783	373,532	76,272	16,929	....	50
Montana	46,796	45,941	855	....	....	....
Wyoming	22,852	22,852	....	....	....	....
Colorado	68,492	57,810	9,430	1,248	....	....
New Mexico	45,580	35,625	9,964	....	....	....
Arizona	24,645	24,645	....	....	....	....
Utah	27,580	20,421	5,701	1,458	....	....
Nevada	11,948	10,022	1,208	718	....	....
Idaho	39,143	37,233	1,910	....	....	....
Washington	36,945	22,202	13,461	1,282	....	....
Oregon	46,189	39,124	5,018	2,047	....	....
California	96,604	57,657	28,716	10,181	....	50

PROGRESS OF THE NATION.

xxxiv

Up to and including 1880 the country had a frontier of settlement, but at present the unsettled area has been so broken into by isolated bodies of settlement that there can hardly be said to be a frontier line. In the discussion of its extent and its westward movement it can not, therefore, any longer have a place in the census reports.

DENSITY OF POPULATION.

The following statement shows the gross area (land and water surface) which the country, exclusive of Alaska, had at the date of each census, from 1790 to 1890:

	SQUARE MILES.		SQUARE MILES.
1790	827,844	1850	2,980,959
1800	827,844	1860	3,025,600
1810	1,999,775	1870	3,025,600
1820	1,999,775	1880	3,025,600
1830	2,059,043	1890	3,025,600
1840	2,059,043		

At the time of the first two censuses the United States comprised only the territory between the Atlantic ocean and the Mississippi river. In 1803 the enormous area of the Louisiana purchase was added, which, as it was entirely unsettled at that time, reduced the number of inhabitants to the square mile to a little more than one-half what it was previously. In 1821 the purchase of the Floridas from Spain increased our territory by nearly 60,000 square miles. Between 1840 and 1850 the acquisition of territory from Mexico under the treaty of Guadalupe Hidalgo, and in 1853 by the Gadsden purchase, made a vast increase of territory, which again reduced the average number of inhabitants to the square mile. The last acquisition of territory, that of Alaska, containing nearly 600,000 square miles, was made in 1867.

Notwithstanding these great acquisitions of territory (excluding Alaska), which have increased our domain from 827,844 to 3,025,600 square miles, the density of population (see page xxxv) has increased from 4.80 to 21.31 inhabitants to the square mile within the century.

The following table shows for 1890 the gross areas (land and water surface) of states and territories in square miles:

STATES AND TERRITORIES.	Gross area.	Water surface.	Land surface.	STATES AND TERRITORIES.	Gross area.	Water surface.	Land surface.
Total	3,025,600	55,600	2,970,000	Nebraska	77,510	670	76,840
				Nevada	110,700	860	109,740
Alabama	52,250	710	51,540	New Hampshire	9,305	300	9,005
Arizona	113,020	100	112,920	New Jersey	7,815	360	7,455
Arkansas	53,850	805	53,045	New Mexico	122,580	120	122,460
California	158,360	2,380	155,980	New York	49,170	1,550	47,620
Colorado	103,925	280	103,645	North Carolina	52,250	3,670	48,580
Connecticut	4,990	145	4,845	North Dakota	70,795	600	70,195
Delaware	2,050	90	1,960	Ohio	41,060	300	40,760
District of Columbia	70	10	60	Oklahoma (a)	39,030	200	38,830
Florida	58,680	4,440	54,240	Oregon	96,030	1,470	94,560
Georgia	59,475	495	58,980	Pennsylvania	45,215	230	44,985
Idaho	84,800	510	84,290	Rhode Island	1,250	165	1,085
Illinois	56,650	650	56,000	South Carolina	30,570	400	30,170
Indiana	36,350	440	35,910	South Dakota	77,650	800	76,850
Indian territory	31,400	400	31,000	Tennessee	42,050	300	41,750
Iowa	56,025	550	55,475	Texas	265,780	3,490	262,290
Kansas	82,080	380	81,700	Utah	84,970	2,780	82,190
Kentucky	40,400	400	40,000	Vermont	9,565	430	9,135
Louisiana	48,720	3,300	45,420	Virginia	42,450	2,325	40,125
Maine	33,040	3,145	29,895	Washington	69,180	2,300	66,880
Maryland	12,210	2,350	9,860	West Virginia	24,780	135	24,645
Massachusetts	8,315	275	8,040	Wisconsin	56,040	1,590	54,450
Michigan	58,915	1,485	57,430	Wyoming	97,890	315	97,575
Minnesota	83,365	4,160	79,205				
Mississippi	46,810	470	46,340	Delaware bay	620	620	
Missouri	69,415	680	68,735	Raritan bay and lower New York bay.	100	100	
Montana	146,080	770	145,310				

a Including Cherokee country and No Man's Land.

DENSITY OF POPULATION. XXXV

The following table shows the density of population, or number of inhabitants per square mile (land surface only), of each state and territory at each census. The areas and the population of Alaska and the Indian territory are not considered in computing density.

DENSITY OF POPULATION AT EACH CENSUS: 1790 TO 1890.

STATES AND TERRITORIES.	1890	1880	1870	1860	1850	1840	1830	1820	1810	1800	1790
The United States........	21.31	17.29	13.30	10.84	7.93	8.43	6.35	4.91	3.69	6.61	4.89
North Atlantic division	107.37	89.52	75.89	55.37	53.23	41.72	34.20	26.88	21.51	16.26	12.14
Maine	22.11	21.71	20.97	21.02	19.51	16.79	13.36	9.98	7.65	5.08	3.23
New Hampshire............	41.81	38.53	35.35	36.21	35.31	31.60	29.91	27.10	23.82	20.42	15.76
Vermont..................	36.39	36.38	36.19	34.49	34.30	31.96	30.72	25.83	23.85	16.91	9.35
Massachusetts.............	278.48	221.78	181.26	153.12	123.70	91.75	75.92	65.07	58.71	52.59	47.11
Rhode Island	318.44	254.87	200.33	160.94	135.99	100.30	89.58	76.51	70.90	63.71	63.43
Connecticut	154.03	128.52	110.93	94.97	76.53	63.98	61.44	56.70	54.06	51.81	49.11
New York	125.95	106.74	92.04	81.49	65.04	51.01	40.29	28.81	20.14	12.37	7.14
New Jersey...............	193.82	151.73	121.54	90.15	65.67	50.07	43.93	37.21	32.94	28.32	24.70
Pennsylvania.............	116.88	95.21	78.20	64.60	51.39	38.32	29.97	23.29	18.01	13.30	9.06
South Atlantic division.........	32.98	28.28	21.79	19.97	17.42	14.61	13.57	14.28	12.48	10.66	8.64
Delaware.................	85.97	74.80	63.78	57.25	46.70	39.84	39.16	37.12	37.08	32.79	30.15
Maryland.................	105.72	94.82	79.20	69.08	59.13	47.67	45.34	41.31	38.50	34.64	32.23
District of Columbia........	3,839.87	2,960.40	2,195.00	1,251.33	861.45	485.69	442.60	367.10	266.92	156.59	....
Virginia..................	41.27	37.70	30.53	24.95	21.95	19.14	18.70	16.44	15.05	13.59	11.54
West Virginia.............	30.95	25.09	17.04	....	....	....	....	....	....	....	....
North Carolina...........	33.30	28.81	22.05	20.43	17.89	15.51	15.19	13.15	11.43	9.84	8.11
South Carolina	38.16	33.00	23.39	23.32	22.16	19.70	19.26	16.66	13.76	11.45	8.26
Georgia..................	31.15	26.15	20.08	17.93	15.36	11.72	8.76	5.78	4.28	2.76	1.40
Florida	7.22	4.97	3.46	2.59	1.61	1.00	0.64	....	....	....	....
North Central division	29.68	23.04	17.23	12.07	7.17	4.45	2.14	1.14	0.39	0.20	....
Ohio.....................	90.10	78.46	65.39	57.40	48.59	37.28	23.01	14.26	5.66	1.11	....
Indiana..................	61.05	55.09	46.80	37.61	27.52	19.10	9.55	4.10	0.68	0.03	....
Illinois..................	68.33	54.96	45.36	30.57	15.20	8.50	2.81	0.90	0.09	....	....
Michigan.................	36.46	28.50	20.62	13.04	6.92	3.70	0.23	0.06	0.10	....	....
Wisconsin	30.08	24.16	19.37	14.25	5.61	0.51	....	....	....	....	....
Minnesota	16.44	9.86	5.55	2.17	0.04	....	....	....	....	....	....
Iowa....................	34.46	29.29	21.52	12.17	3.46	0.21	....	....	....	....	....
Missouri.................	38.98	31.55	25.04	17.20	9.92	5.58	2.13	1.01	0.32	....	....
North Dakota	2.60 }	a0.92	a0.10	a0.06	....	....	....	....	....	....	....
South Dakota............	4.28 }										
Nebraska	13.78	5.94	1.61	0.08	....	....	....	....	....	....	....
Kansas	17.47	12.19	4.46	0.85	....	....	....	....	....	....	....
South Central division..........	18.94	16.51	11.91	10.08	7.65	8.00	5.93	3.97	2.30	1.94	0.63
Kentucky	46.47	41.22	33.03	28.80	24.56	19.50	17.20	14.10	10.16	5.52	1.84
Tennessee	42.34	36.94	30.14	26.58	24.02	19.86	16.33	10.13	6.27	2.53	0.85
Alabama.................	29.30	24.50	19.34	18.71	14.97	11.46	6.01	2.48	....	....	....
Mississippi...............	27.83	24.42	17.87	17.08	13.00	8.11	2.95	1.63	0.43	0.24	....
Louisiana................	24.63	20.69	16.00	15.59	11.40	7.76	4.75	3.37	1.69	....	....
Texas....................	8.52	6.07	3.12	2.30	0.81	....	....	....	....	....	....
Oklahoma	1.59	....	....	....	....	....	....	....	....	....	....
Arkansas................	21.27	15.13	9.13	8.21	3.96	1.84	0.57	0.27	....	....	....
Western division	2.58	1.50	0.84	0.53	0.16	....	....	....	....	....	....
Montana.................	0.91	0.27	0.14	....	....	....	....	....	....	....	....
Wyoming.................	0.62	0.21	0.09	....	....	....	....	....	....	....	....
Colorado.................	3.98	1.87	0.38	0.33	....	....	....	....	....	....	....
New Mexico..............	1.25	0.98	0.75	0.36	0.29	....	....	....	....	....	....
Arizona	0.53	0.36	0.09	....	....	....	....	....	....	....	....
Utah	2.53	1.75	1.06	0.18	0.05	....	....	....	....	....	....
Nevada..................	0.42	0.57	0.39	0.06	....	....	....	....	....	....	....
Idaho....................	1.00	0.39	0.18	....	....	....	....	....	....	....	....
Washington..............	5.22	1.12	0.36	0.06	....	....	....	....	....	....	....
Oregon..................	3.32	1.85	0.96	0.55	0.05	....	....	....	....	....	....
California	7.75	5.54	3.59	2.44	0.59	....	....	....	....	....	....

a Dakota territory.

The above table shows that, with the exception of the District of Columbia, which is in effect a municipality, the most densely settled state is Rhode Island, and next to that Massachusetts. In these states the density of population is as great as in many of the most densely settled European states. Indeed the entire North Atlantic

PROGRESS OF THE NATION.

division of states, which is pre-eminently the manufacturing section of the country, contains an average of over 100 inhabitants to the square mile. The South Atlantic and South Central divisions, which are pre-eminently farming regions, are much less densely peopled. The scattered character of the population of the western states and territories is illustrated by the low density of population.

CENTER OF POPULATION.

By the Eleventh Census the center of population in 1890 was in the following position:

Latitude	39°	11'	56"
Longitude	85	32	53

In ten years the center of population has moved westward 53' 13", or about 48 miles, and northward 7' 48", or about 9 miles. It rests now in southern Indiana, at a point a little west of south of Greensburg, the county seat of Decatur county, and 20 miles east of Columbus, Indiana.

The closeness with which the center of population, through such rapid westward movement as has been recorded, has clung to the parallel of 39° of latitude can not fail to be noticed. The most northern point reached was at the start in 1790; the most southern point was in 1830, the preceding decade having witnessed a rapid development of population in the southwest, Alabama, Arkansas, Mississippi, and Louisiana having been admitted as states and Florida annexed and organized as a territory. The extreme variation in latitude has been less than 19 minutes, while the hundred years of record have accomplished a movement of longitude of over 9 degrees. Assuming the westward movement to have been uniformly along the parallel of 39° of latitude, the westward movement of the several decades has been as follows: 1790–1800, 41 miles; 1800–1810, 36 miles; 1810–1820, 50 miles; 1820–1830, 39 miles; 1830–1840, 55 miles; 1840–1850, 55 miles; 1850–1860, 81 miles; 1860–1870, 42 miles; 1870–1880, 58 miles, and 1880–1890, 48 miles, a total westward movement of 505 miles. The sudden acceleration of movement between 1850 and 1860 was due to the transfer of a considerable body of population from the Atlantic to the Pacific coast, 12 individuals in San Francisco exerting as much pressure at the then pivotal point, viz, the crossing of the eighty-third meridian and the thirty-ninth parallel, as 40 individuals at Boston.

The center of population is the center of gravity of the population of the country, each individual being assumed to have the same weight. The method of determination used, in order that the result might be comparable with that obtained in 1880, was in brief as follows:

The population of the country was first distributed by "square degrees", as the area included between consecutive parallels and meridians has been designated. A point was then assumed tentatively as the center, and corrections in latitude and longitude to this tentative position were computed. In this case the center was assumed to be at the intersection of the parallel of 39° with the meridian of 86° west of Greenwich. The population of each square degree was assumed to be located at the center of that square degree, except in cases where it was manifest that this assumption would be untrue, as, for instance, where a part of the square degree was occupied by the sea or other large body of water, or where it contained a city of considerable magnitude which was situated "off center". In these cases the position of the center of the population of the square degree was estimated as nearly as possible. The distance of each such center of population of a square degree, whether assumed to be at the center of the square degree or at a distance from the center, from the assumed parallel and from the assumed meridian, was then computed. The population of each square degree was then multiplied by its distance from the assumed parallel of latitude, and the sums of the products, or moments, north and south of that parallel were made up. Their difference, divided by the total population of the country, gave a correction to the latitude. In a similar manner the east and west moments were made up, and from them a correction in longitude was obtained.

In 1790 the center of population was at 39° 16.5' north latitude and 76° 11.2' west longitude, which a comparison of the best maps available would seem to place about 23 miles east of Baltimore. During the decade from 1790 to 1800 it appears to have moved almost due west to a point about 18 miles west of the same city, being in latitude 39° 16.1' and longitude 76° 56.5'.

From 1800 to 1810 it moved westward and slightly southward to a point about 40 miles northwest by west of Washington, being in latitude 39° 11.5' and longitude 77° 37.2'. The southward movement during this decade appears to have been due to the annexation of the territory of Louisiana, which contained quite extensive settlements.

From 1810 to 1820 it moved westward and again slightly southward to a point about 16 miles north of Woodstock, Virginia, being in latitude 39° 5.7' and longitude 78° 33'. This second southward movement appears to have been due to the extension of settlements in Mississippi, Alabama, and eastern Georgia.

From 1820 to 1830 it moved still westward and southward to a point about 19 miles southwest of Moorefield, in the present state of West Virginia, being in latitude 38° 57.9' and longitude 79° 16.9'. This is the most decided southward movement that it has made during any decade. It appears to have been due in part to the addition of Florida to our territory and in part to the great extension of settlements in Alabama, Louisiana, Mississippi, and Arkansas, or generally, it may be said, in the southwest.

xxxvi   PROGRESS OF THE NATION.

division of states, which is pre-eminently the manufacturing section of the country, contains an average of over 100 inhabitants to the square mile. The South Atlantic and South Central divisions, which are pre-eminently farming regions, are much less densely peopled. The scattered character of the population of the western states and territories is illustrated by the low density of population.

CENTER OF POPULATION.

By the Eleventh Census the center of population in 1890 was in the following position:

Latitude	39°	11′	56″
Longitude	85	32	53

In ten years the center of population has moved westward 53′ 13″, or about 48 miles, and northward 7′ 48″, or about 9 miles. It rests now in southern Indiana, at a point a little west of south of Greensburg, the county seat of Decatur county, and 20 miles east of Columbus, Indiana.

The closeness with which the center of population, through such rapid westward movement as has been recorded, has clung to the parallel of 39° of latitude can not fail to be noticed. The most northern point reached was at the start in 1790; the most southern point was in 1830, the preceding decade having witnessed a rapid development of population in the southwest, Alabama, Arkansas, Mississippi, and Louisiana having been admitted as states and Florida annexed and organized as a territory. The extreme variation in latitude has been less than 19 minutes, while the hundred years of record have accomplished a movement of longitude of over 9 degrees. Assuming the westward movement to have been uniformly along the parallel of 39° of latitude, the westward movement of the several decades has been as follows: 1790–1800, 41 miles; 1800–1810, 36 miles; 1810–1820, 50 miles; 1820–1830, 39 miles; 1830–1840, 55 miles; 1840–1850, 55 miles; 1850–1860, 81 miles; 1860–1870, 42 miles; 1870–1880, 58 miles, and 1880–1890, 48 miles, a total westward movement of 505 miles. The sudden acceleration of movement between 1850 and 1860 was due to the transfer of a considerable body of population from the Atlantic to the Pacific coast, 12 individuals in San Francisco exerting as much pressure at the then pivotal point, viz, the crossing of the eighty-third meridian and the thirty-ninth parallel, as 40 individuals at Boston.

The center of population is the center of gravity of the population of the country, each individual being assumed to have the same weight. The method of determination used, in order that the result might be comparable with that obtained in 1880, was in brief as follows:

The population of the country was first distributed by "square degrees", as the area included between consecutive parallels and meridians has been designated. A point was then assumed tentatively as the center, and corrections in latitude and longitude to this tentative position were computed. In this case the center was assumed to be at the intersection of the parallel of 39° with the meridian of 86° west of Greenwich. The population of each square degree was assumed to be located at the center of that square degree, except in cases where it was manifest that this assumption would be untrue, as, for instance, where a part of the square degree was occupied by the sea or other large body of water, or where it contained a city of considerable magnitude which was situated "off center". In these cases the position of the center of the population of the square degree was estimated as nearly as possible. The distance of each such center of population of a square degree, whether assumed to be at the center of the square degree or at a distance from the center, from the assumed parallel and from the assumed meridian, was then computed. The population of each square degree was then multiplied by its distance from the assumed parallel of latitude, and the sums of the products, or moments, north and south of that parallel were made up. Their difference, divided by the total population of the country, gave a correction to the latitude. In a similar manner the east and west moments were made up, and from them a correction in longitude was obtained.

In 1790 the center of population was at 39° 16.5′ north latitude and 76° 11.2′ west longitude, which a comparison of the best maps available would seem to place about 23 miles east of Baltimore. During the decade from 1790 to 1800 it appears to have moved almost due west to a point about 18 miles west of the same city, being in latitude 39° 16.1′ and longitude 76° 56.5′.

From 1800 to 1810 it moved westward and slightly southward to a point about 40 miles northwest by west of Washington, being in latitude 39° 11.5′ and longitude 77° 37.2′. The southward movement during this decade appears to have been due to the annexation of the territory of Louisiana, which contained quite extensive settlements.

From 1810 to 1820 it moved westward and again slightly southward to a point about 16 miles north of Woodstock, Virginia, being in latitude 39° 5.7′ and longitude 78° 33′. This second southward movement appears to have been due to the extension of settlements in Mississippi, Alabama, and eastern Georgia.

From 1820 to 1830 it moved still westward and southward to a point about 19 miles southwest of Moorefield, in the present state of West Virginia, being in latitude 38° 57.9′ and longitude 79° 16.9′. This is the most decided southward movement that it has made during any decade. It appears to have been due in part to the addition of Florida to our territory and in part to the great extension of settlements in Alabama, Louisiana, Mississippi, and Arkansas, or generally, it may be said, in the southwest.

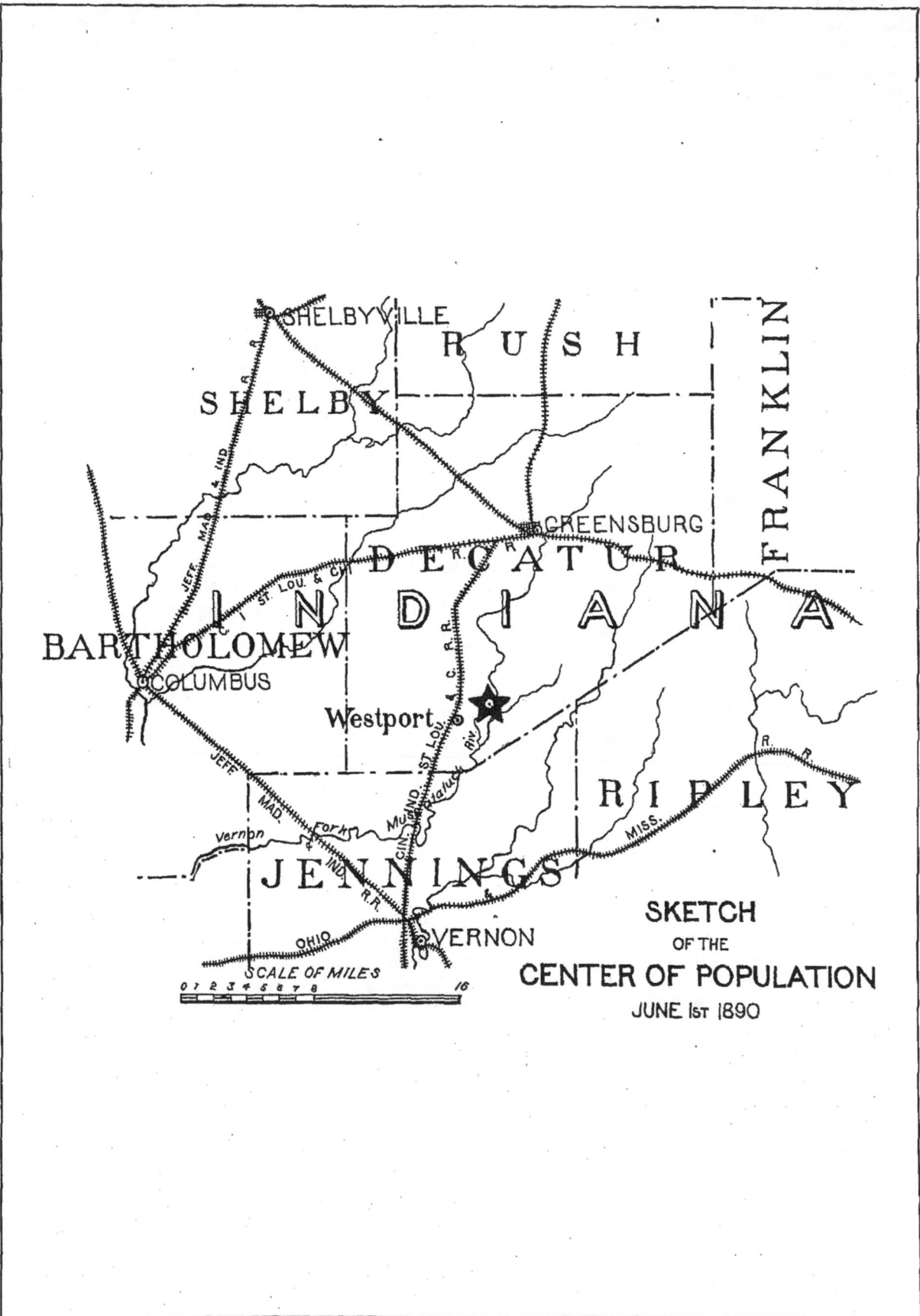

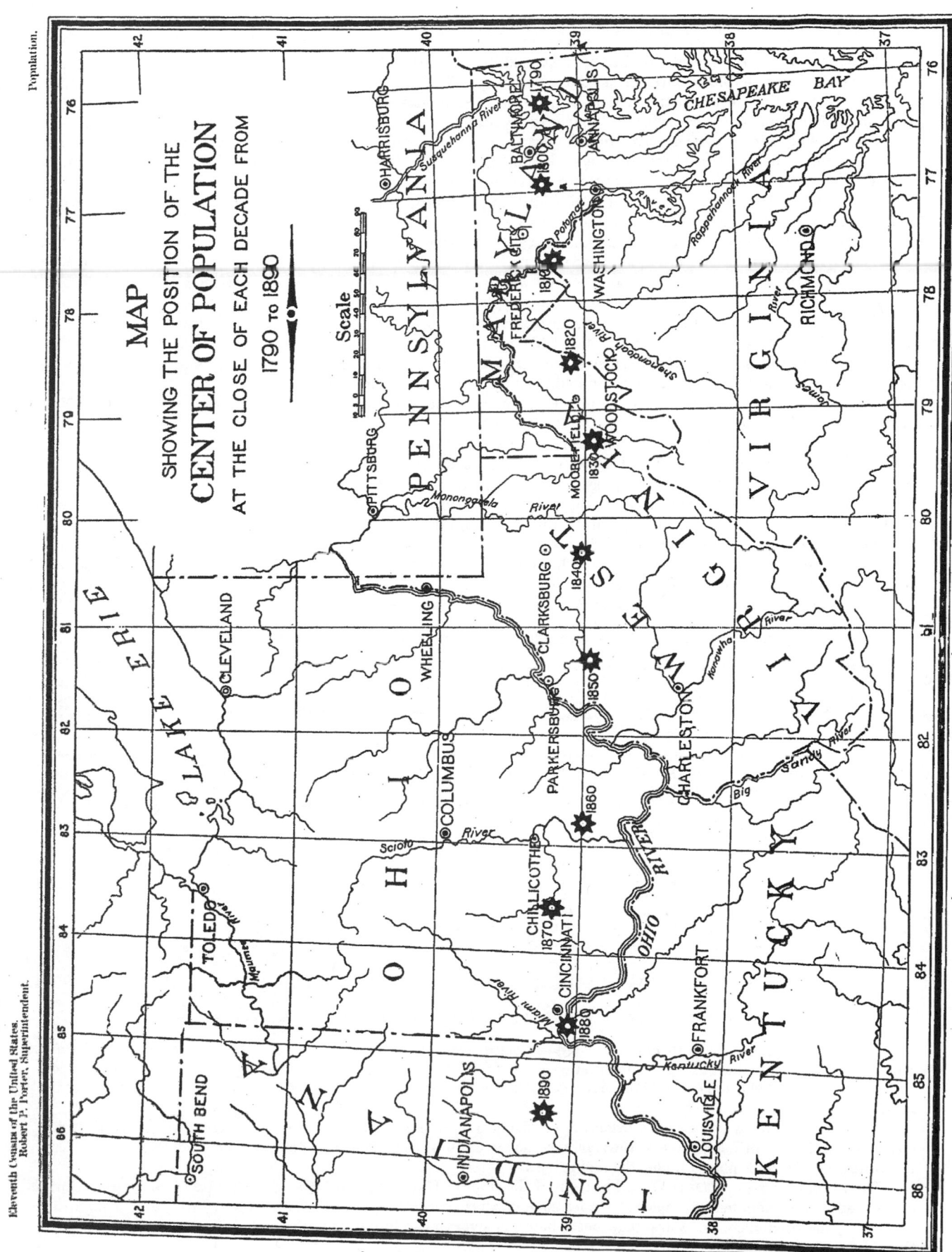

CENTER OF POPULATION.

From 1830 to 1840 it moved still farther westward, but slightly changed its direction northward, reaching a point 16 miles south of Clarksburg, in the present state of West Virginia, being in latitude 39° 2′ and longitude 80° 18′. During this decade settlement had made decided advances in the prairie states and in the southern portions of Michigan and Wisconsin, the balance of increased settlement evidently being in favor of the northwest.

From 1840 to 1850 it moved westward and slightly southward again, reaching a point about 23 miles southeast of Parkersburg, in the present state of West Virginia, in latitude 38° 59′ and longitude 81° 19′, the change of direction southward being largely due to the annexation of Texas.

From 1850 to 1860 it moved westward and slightly northward, reaching a point 20 miles south of Chillicothe, Ohio, this being in latitude 39° 0.4′, longitude 82° 48.8′.

From 1860 to 1870 it moved westward and sharply northward, reaching a point about 48 miles east by north of Cincinnati, Ohio, in latitude 39° 12′, longitude 83° 35.7′. This northward movement was due in part to waste and destruction in the south consequent upon the civil war, and in part probably to the fact that the census of 1870 was defective in its enumeration of the southern people, especially of the newly enfranchised negro population.

In 1880 the center of population had returned southward to nearly the same latitude which it had in 1860, being in latitude 39° 4.1′, longitude 84° 39.7′. This southward movement was due only in part to an imperfect enumeration at the south in 1870. During the decade from 1870 to 1880 the southern states made a large positive increase, both from natural growth and from immigration southward.

During the past decade the center of population has moved northward into practically the same latitude which it occupied in 1870. It has moved westward 53′ 13″, or 48 miles, being less by 10 miles than its movement during the preceding decade, 6 miles greater than the movement between 1860 and 1870, and slightly less than the average westward movement since the First Census, its present position being in latitude 39° 11′ 56″ and longitude 85° 32′ 53″. The most salient point of its progress during the past decade is the northing which has been made, which is largely due to the great development in the cities of the northwest and in the state of Washington, and also in no small degree to the increase of population in New England.

The center of the area of the United States, excluding Alaska, is in northern Kansas in approximate latitude 39° 55′ and approximate longitude 98° 50′. The center of population is therefore about three-fourths of a degree south and more than 13 degrees east of the center of area.

The following table shows the movement of the center of population since 1790:

POSITION OF THE CENTER OF POPULATION: 1790 TO 1890.

CENSUS YEARS.	North latitude.	West longitude.	Approximate location by important towns.	Westward movement in miles during preceding decade.
1790	39° 16. 5′	76° 11. 2′	23 miles east of Baltimore, Maryland	
1800	39 16. 1	76 56. 5	18 miles west of Baltimore, Maryland	41
1810	39 11. 5	77 37. 2	40 miles northwest by west of Washington, District of Columbia	36
1820	39 5. 7	78 33. 0	16 miles north of Woodstock, Virginia	50
1830	38 57. 9	79 16. 9	19 miles west-southwest of Moorefield, in the present state of West Virginia	39
1840	39 2. 0	80 18. 0	16 miles south of Clarksburg, in the present state of West Virginia	55
1850	38 59. 0	81 19. 0	23 miles southeast of Parkersburg, in the present state of West Virginia	55
1860	39 0. 4	82 48. 8	20 miles south of Chillicothe, Ohio	81
1870	39 12. 0	83 35. 7	48 miles east by north of Cincinnati, Ohio	42
1880	39 4. 1	84 39. 7	8 miles west by south of Cincinnati, Ohio	58
1890	39 11. 9	85 32. 9	20 miles east of Columbus, Indiana	48

GEOGRAPHICAL DISTRIBUTION OF POPULATION.

DISTRIBUTION OF POPULATION ACCORDING TO DRAINAGE BASINS.

In the tables appended are given the approximate area of each drainage basin in square miles (land and water surface), and the aggregate population, foreign born population, and negro population, of each such drainage basin in 1890, 1880, and 1870, together with the number of inhabitants of each such class to the square mile.

The drainage areas are classified primarily by the two oceans and the Great Basin; second, by sections of the coast; third, by the principal rivers, the rivers of each section of the coast being arranged under that section, and the branches of a river placed under the main river.

The primary divisions are set at the margin of the page. Under each primary division its secondary divisions are placed, being indented one space. Under each of these secondary divisions the tertiary divisions are placed, and so on, the subdivisions of a drainage basin being in every case indented within that of the stream comprising them.

xxxviii   PROGRESS OF THE NATION.

The New England coast comprises the area and population of the basins of the several rivers given beneath it, and, in addition to these, the area and population of the minor streams and of the immediate coast from the eastern border of Maine to the Hudson river.

The Middle Atlantic coast comprises, besides the basin of the rivers under it, in like manner the basins of the minor streams and of the coast itself as far as the mouth of the Potomac, including that stream.

The South Atlantic coast, in like manner, comprises the country from the Potomac southward to Florida.

The Gulf of Mexico, commencing with the peninsula of Florida, embraces the coast and the whole Mississippi valley to the mouth of the Rio Grande, including the latter stream.

The population of the various subdivisions was obtained by using the county as a unit, and subdividing the counties into tenths in cases where they lie partly in one basin and partly in another. Of course, in making these divisions of counties, population and not area was considered.

The areas of the different river basins were measured approximately from maps, and were finally adjusted to suit a total area of the United States of 3,025,600 square miles, exclusive of Alaska.

From the first table it appears that 96.16 per cent of the inhabitants live in the country which is drained to the Atlantic ocean; that 52.69 per cent of the population live in the region drained by the Gulf of Mexico, and that 43.77 per cent of the entire population of the country are congregated in the drainage area of the Mississippi river; that only 0.41 per cent live in the Great Basin, and 3.43 per cent on the Pacific coast. It shows, further, that the proportion living within the region drained to the Atlantic is steadily diminishing, while of this region the part drained to the Gulf of Mexico is becoming relatively more populous, as is the case in a still more marked degree in the region drained to the Pacific.

From the second of these tables it appears that of the foreign born population nearly 93 per cent live within the Atlantic drainage basin; that three-fourths of 1 per cent live in the Great Basin, and a little over 6 per cent upon the Pacific slope. The proportion living in the region drained by the Atlantic is slowly diminishing, while that upon the Pacific slope is increasing. In the region draining to the Gulf of Mexico there are about 37 per cent, and in the Mississippi basin 34.50 per cent.

The third table shows the distribution of the population of pure and mixed negro blood. It appears that 99.76 per cent, or 9,976 persons out of every 10,000, live within the Atlantic drainage basin, leaving only the most trifling number for the Great Basin and the Pacific slope. It appears also that in the region draining into the Gulf of Mexico there are 61 per cent or a little over three-fifths of the entire negro element, while in the Mississippi basin there is one-third of this entire element.

DISTRIBUTION OF THE AGGREGATE POPULATION ACCORDING TO DRAINAGE BASINS: 1870 TO 1890.

DRAINAGE BASINS.	Approximate area in square miles.	1890		1880		1870	
		Total population.	Population per square mile.	Total population.	Population per square mile.	Total population.	Population per square mile.
Atlantic ocean	2,178,210	60,220,763	27.65	48,707,352	22.36	37,706,410	17.31
New England coast	61,830	4,486,813	72.57	3,811,102	61.64	3,286,410	53.15
St. John river	7,890	53,381	6.77	46,615	5.91	37,544	4.76
Penobscot river	8,934	113,179	12.67	111,050	12.43	112,326	12.57
Kennebec river	10,102	236,553	23.42	231,345	22.90	224,365	22.21
Merrimac river	4,864	616,594	126.77	500,978	103.00	436,238	89.69
Connecticut river	11,269	782,216	69.41	692,803	61.48	618,171	54.86
Housatonic river	1,933	251,701	130.21	208,920	108.08	182,738	94.54
Middle Atlantic coast	83,020	11,482,411	138.31	9,646,057	116.19	8,038,651	96.83
Hudson river	13,366	1,094,126	81.86	1,009,082	75.50	959,376	71.78
Delaware river	12,012	2,561,113	213.21	2,175,800	181.14	1,834,009	152.68
Susquehanna river	27,655	1,965,184	71.06	1,673,847	60.53	1,445,902	52.28
Potomac river	14,479	870,135	60.10	791,007	54.63	657,644	45.42
South Atlantic coast	132,040	4,248,466	32.18	3,705,807	28.07	2,799,126	21.20
James river	9,684	495,910	51.21	448,891	46.35	365,913	37.79
Cape Fear river	8,310	239,399	28.81	212,904	25.62	164,994	19.85
Neuse river	5,299	216,933	40.94	197,552	37.28	149,761	28.26
Pedee river	17,098	600,277	35.11	505,252	29.55	367,785	21.51
Roanoke river	9,237	404,281	43.77	364,160	39.42	276,289	29.91
Santee river	14,606	607,098	41.31	507,205	34.51	373,380	25.41
Savannah river	11,402	446,569	39.17	384,739	33.74	280,783	24.63
Altamaha river	14,109	473,967	33.59	401,789	28.48	301,091	21.34
Great Lakes	135,763	6,762,321	49.81	5,307,026	39.09	4,223,236	31.11
St. Lawrence river	13,636	474,158	34.77	469,554	34.43	458,834	33.65
Lake Ontario	12,387	1,006,668	81.27	926,128	74.77	853,486	68.90
Lake Erie	17,207	2,179,269	126.65	1,720,712	100.00	1,372,848	79.78
Lake Huron	18,839	439,393	23.32	313,255	16.63	176,914	9.39
Lake Michigan	45,876	2,507,562	54.66	1,820,534	39.81	1,327,417	28.93
Lake Superior	17,830	155,271	8.71	50,843	2.85	33,737	1.89
Red River of the North	39,577	247,518	6.25	69,993	1.77	3,361	0.08

GEOGRAPHICAL DISTRIBUTION OF POPULATION. xxxix

DISTRIBUTION OF THE AGGREGATE POPULATION ACCORDING TO DRAINAGE BASINS: 1870 TO 1890—Continued.

DRAINAGE BASINS.	Approximate area in square miles.	1890		1880		1870	
		Total population.	Population per square mile.	Total population.	Population per square mile.	Total population.	Population per square mile.
Atlantic ocean—Continued.							
Gulf of Mexico	1,725,980	32,993,234	19.12	26,167,367	15.16	19,355,620	11.21
Apalachicola river	18,918	699,713	36.99	608,057	32.14	486,296	25.71
Mobile river	43,436	1,425,649	32.82	1,207,680	27.80	938,242	21.60
Tombigbee river	18,896	611,338	32.35	499,882	26.45	383,763	20.31
Alabama river	23,820	784,099	32.92	679,170	28.51	520,821	22.12
Pascagoula river	8,980	129,084	14.37	98,800	11.00	68,476	7.63
Pearl river	8,670	175,698	20.27	148,635	17.14	114,588	13.22
Sabine river	20,440	172,656	8.45	134,860	6.60	85,413	4.18
Trinity river	17,960	449,718	25.04	315,220	17.55	128,244	7.14
Brazos river	59,646	512,621	8.59	363,892	6.10	165,986	2.78
Colorado river	41,220	183,524	4.45	125,860	3.05	55,004	1.33
Nueces river	18,944	41,633	2.20	27,635	1.46	11,204	0.59
San Antonio river	16,352	169,847	10.39	122,413	7.49	72,137	4.41
Rio Grande	128,792	156,150	1.21	115,517	0.90	79,370	0.62
Mississippi river	1,240,039	27,411,522	22.11	21,776,479	17.56	16,333,045	13.17
Yazoo river	12,794	415,400	32.47	366,502	28.65	259,563	20.29
Illinois river	29,013	1,867,935	64.38	1,474,337	50.82	1,206,706	41.59
Rock river	9,792	532,117	54.34	506,835	51.76	497,302	50.79
Wisconsin river	12,280	259,778	21.15	208,180	16.95	167,361	13.63
Chippewa river	8,892	141,529	15.92	84,240	9.47	43,022	4.84
St. Croix river	7,576	92,854	12.26	59,892	7.90	30,664	4.05
Minnesota river	16,000	327,852	20.49	231,065	14.44	119,847	7.49
Cedar river	12,492	393,021	31.46	372,556	29.82	290,884	23.29
Des Moines river	14,652	423,128	28.88	328,746	22.44	224,993	15.36
Ohio river	201,720	10,986,877	54.47	9,588,303	47.53	7,839,424	38.86
Tennessee river	43,897	1,384,733	31.55	1,177,144	26.82	927,054	21.12
Cumberland river	18,573	720,012	38.77	643,819	34.66	529,088	28.49
Kentucky river	7,425	291,022	39.19	253,890	34.19	203,230	27.37
Green river	9,065	358,804	39.58	332,056	36.63	262,874	29.00
Licking river	3,658	221,478	60.55	200,207	54.76	161,132	44.05
Kanawha river	16,690	334,795	20.06	263,947	15.81	182,131	10.91
Monongahela river	7,625	495,636	65.00	375,939	49.30	292,320	38.34
Allegheny river	11,437	970,869	84.89	809,026	70.82	645,752	56.46
Miami river	5,400	469,596	86.96	413,592	76.59	351,370	65.07
Scioto river	6,480	444,124	68.54	400,856	61.86	337,914	52.15
Muskingum river	7,740	541,378	69.95	505,106	65.27	445,934	57.61
Wabash river	33,725	1,915,790	56.81	1,727,214	51.21	1,455,300	43.15
Big Sandy river	4,050	190,283	46.98	154,012	38.03	109,886	27.13
Missouri river	527,155	4,560,561	8.65	2,841,451	5.39	1,604,465	3.04
Big Sioux river	7,880	119,337	15.14	51,241	6.50	5,290	0.67
Yellowstone river	69,683	21,574	0.31	3,184	0.05	241	0.00
Platte river	90,011	647,104	7.19	267,230	2.97	68,471	0.76
Kansas river	59,256	985,524	16.63	623,621	10.52	176,308	2.98
Osage river	15,444	508,291	32.91	385,848	24.98	273,444	17.71
Arkansas river	185,671	1,771,312	9.54	1,141,007	6.15	533,831	2.88
Cimarron river	17,360	55,690	3.21	4,203	0.24	1,693	0.10
Canadian river	42,710	54,766	1.28	24,850	0.58	18,887	0.44
White river	27,925	338,395	12.11	244,455	8.75	147,979	5.30
Red river (Louisiana)	89,970	955,757	10.62	705,806	7.84	445,366	4.95
Washita river	19,138	360,506	18.84	281,582	14.71	187,385	9.79
St. Francis river	7,884	162,897	20.66	118,108	14.99	78,428	9.95
Great Basin	228,150	256,130	1.12	210,908	0.92	125,384	0.55
Great Salt Lake	32,400	156,150	4.82	104,621	3.23	65,627	2.03
Humboldt river	32,148	38,119	1.19	49,864	1.55	29,592	0.92
Pacific ocean	619,240	2,145,357	3.46	1,237,433	2.00	726,577	1.17
Colorado river	225,049	208,643	0.93	109,188	0.49	39,495	0.18
Green river	47,222	27,494	0.58	10,709	0.23	4,800	0.10
Grand river	26,472	47,349	1.79	14,795	0.56	165	0.01
Little Colorado river	29,208	3,821	0.13	3,644	0.12	428	0.01
Gila river	68,623	45,917	0.67	28,348	0.41	6,954	0.10
Sacramento river	58,824	378,402	6.43	324,308	5.51	240,246	4.08
San Joaquin river	29,952	134,206	4.48	88,902	2.97	67,450	2.25
Klamath river	14,660	18,199	1.24	14,627	1.00	10,000	0.68
Columbia river	216,537	393,415	1.82	222,737	1.03	104,882	0.48
Willamette river	11,700	129,782	11.00	78,326	6.69	50,271	4.30
Snake river	103,835	142,091	1.37	55,256	0.53	21,530	0.21
Clarke Fork	63,291	46,067	0.73	12,274	0.19	7,215	0.11

xl

PROGRESS OF THE NATION.

DISTRIBUTION OF THE FOREIGN BORN POPULATION ACCORDING TO DRAINAGE BASINS: 1870 TO 1890.

DRAINAGE BASINS.	Approximate area in square miles.	1890		1880		1870	
		Foreign born population.	Foreign born population per square mile.	Foreign born population.	Foreign born population per square mile.	Foreign born population.	Foreign born population per square mile.
Atlantic ocean	2,178,210	8,595,004	3.95	6,232,764	2.86	5,272,190	2.42
New England coast	61,830	1,111,989	17.98	764,982	12.37	611,859	9.90
St. John river	7,890	10,515	1.33	8,358	1.06	7,011	0.89
Penobscot river	8,934	11,954	1.34	8,561	0.96	8,910	1.00
Kennebec river	10,103	20,630	2.04	17,306	1.71	10,655	1.05
Merrimac river	4,864	165,257	33.98	106,888	21.98	82,936	17.05
Connecticut river	11,269	179,132	15.90	130,173	11.55	110,274	9.79
Housatonic river	1,933	58,669	30.35	40,867	21.14	37,487	19.39
Middle Atlantic coast	83,020	2,248,320	27.08	1,670,184	20.12	1,542,297	18.58
Hudson river	13,366	195,543	14.63	169,041	12.65	190,244	14.23
Delaware river	12,012	450,770	37.53	345,284	28.74	325,959	27.14
Susquehanna river	27,655	224,389	8.11	153,775	5.56	151,030	5.49
Potomac river	14,479	32,905	2.27	34,018	2.35	34,856	2.41
South Atlantic coast	132,040	31,116	0.24	29,537	0.22	29,066	0.22
James river	9,684	9,139	0.94	7,492	0.77	7,318	0.76
Cape Fear river	8,310	687	0.08	800	0.10	797	0.10
Neuse river	5,290	471	0.09	592	0.11	544	0.10
Pedee river	17,098	903	0.05	973	0.06	851	0.05
Roanoke river	9,237	1,462	0.16	1,290	0.14	757	0.08
Santee river	14,696	1,844	0.13	2,093	0.14	2,055	0.14
Savannah river	11,402	4,039	0.35	4,176	0.37	4,450	0.39
Altamaha river	14,109	1,841	0.13	1,549	0.11	1,566	0.11
Great Lakes	135,763	1,689,541	12.44	1,205,852	8.88	1,007,071	7.42
St. Lawrence river	13,636	71,488	5.24	74,903	5.49	89,185	6.54
Lake Ontario	12,387	185,159	14.95	160,789	12.98	161,581	13.04
Lake Erie	17,207	496,548	28.86	365,940	21.27	312,219	18.14
Lake Huron	18,839	133,641	7.09	98,156	5.21	52,149	2.77
Lake Michigan	45,876	724,774	15.80	482,118	10.51	373,581	8.14
Lake Superior	17,830	77,940	4.37	23,946	1.34	18,356	1.03
Red River of the North	39,577	114,124	2.88	33,530	0.85	1,539	0.04
Gulf of Mexico	1,725,980	3,399,914	1.97	2,528,670	1.47	2,080,358	1.21
Apalachicola river	18,918	3,703	0.20	2,958	0.16	2,892	0.15
Mobile river	43,436	12,547	0.29	7,492	0.17	7,509	0.17
Tombigbee river	18,896	6,732	0.36	2,732	0.14	2,008	0.11
Alabama river	23,820	4,316	0.18	2,693	0.11	2,826	0.12
Pascagoula river	8,980	799	0.09	680	0.08	685	0.08
Pearl river	8,670	929	0.11	1,078	0.12	1,203	0.14
Sabine river	20,440	1,218	0.06	1,099	0.05	387	0.02
Trinity river	17,960	12,001	0.67	7,238	0.40	1,005	0.06
Brazos river	59,646	23,132	0.39	14,908	0.25	7,005	0.12
Colorado river	41,220	16,777	0.41	12,695	0.31	6,872	0.17
Nueces river	18,944	9,093	0.48	7,683	0.41	2,086	0.16
San Antonio river	16,352	25,337	1.55	18,635	1.14	12,969	0.79
Rio Grande	128,792	31,023	0.24	22,107	0.17	12,470	0.10
Mississippi river	1,240,030	3,190,805	2.57	2,377,454	1.92	1,985,936	1.60
Yazoo river	12,794	2,113	0.17	2,541	0.20	3,539	0.28
Illinois river	29,013	455,514	15.70	308,104	10.62	265,878	9.16
Rock river	9,792	127,524	13.02	118,385	12.09	133,561	13.64
Wisconsin river	12,280	68,054	5.54	53,185	4.33	46,891	3.82
Chippewa river	8,892	47,906	5.39	26,969	3.03	14,643	1.65
St. Croix river	7,576	36,805	4.87	22,969	3.03	12,507	1.65
Minnesota river	16,000	111,336	6.96	80,171	5.01	44,727	2.80
Cedar river	12,492	73,113	5.85	66,682	5.34	51,408	4.12
Des Moines river	14,652	64,958	4.43	44,622	3.05	25,975	1.77
Ohio river	201,720	746,785	3.70	634,499	3.15	619,550	3.07
Tennessee river	43,897	10,571	0.24	6,544	0.15	5,331	0.12
Cumberland river	18,573	8,246	0.44	6,362	0.34	6,796	0.37
Kentucky river	7,425	3,965	0.53	3,627	0.49	3,664	0.49
Green river	9,065	2,621	0.29	2,773	0.31	2,948	0.33
Licking river	3,658	16,280	4.45	16,812	4.60	17,223	4.71
Kanawha river	16,690	3,892	0.23	2,778	0.17	2,144	0.13
Monongahela river	7,625	68,789	9.02	37,737	4.95	30,694	4.03
Allegheny river	11,437	142,265	12.44	100,734	8.81	90,225	7.89
Miami river	5,400	56,400	10.44	54,727	10.13	56,647	10.49
Scioto river	6,480	28,160	4.35	27,674	4.27	28,367	4.38
Muskingum river	7,740	38,979	5.04	36,079	4.66	37,246	4.81
Wabash river	33,725	99,167	2.94	98,958	2.93	95,585	2.83
Big Sandy river	4,050	4,192	1.04	4,437	1.10	4,413	1.09

GEOGRAPHICAL DISTRIBUTION OF POPULATION.

xli

.rRIBUTION OF THE FOREIGN BORN POPULATION ACCORDING TO DRAINAGE BASINS: 1870 TO 1890—Continued.

DRAINAGE BASINS.	Approximate area in square miles.	1890		1880		1870	
		Foreign born population.	Foreign born population per square mile.	Foreign born population.	Foreign born population per square mile.	Foreign born population.	Foreign born population per square mile.
Atlantic ocean—Continued.							
Gulf of Mexico—Continued.							
Mississippi river—Continued.							
Missouri river	527,155	664,663	1.26	359,369	0.68	207,224	0.39
Big Sioux river	7,880	33,906	4.30	14,704	1.87	2,194	0.28
Yellowstone river	69,683	4,333	0.06	821	0.01	54	0.00
Platte river	90,011	138,101	1.53	66,103	0.73	20,924	0.23
Kansas river	59,256	143,014	2.41	93,353	1.58	31,820	0.54
Osage river	15,444	24,599	1.59	18,605	1.20	15,284	0.99
Arkansas river	185,671	91,595	0.49	59,442	0.32	14,778	0.08
Cimarron river	17,360	3,304	0.19	345	0.02	144	0.01
Canadian river	42,710	2,617	0.06	756	0.02	593	0.01
White river	27,925	2,679	0.10	1,931	0.07	752	0.03
Red river (Louisiana)	89,970	8,754	0.10	7,454	0.08	4,073	0.05
Washita river	19,138	2,531	0.13	2,518	0.13	1,336	0.07
St. Francis river	7,884	3,160	0.40	3,406	0.43	3,288	0.41
Great Basin	228,150	68,071	0.30	71,679	0.31	48,804	0.21
Great Salt Lake	32,400	42,307	1.31	33,430	1.03	24,098	0.74
Humboldt river	32,148	12,027	0.37	19,777	0.62	13,321	0.41
Pacific ocean	619,240	585,872	0.95	375,500	0.61	246,235	0.40
Colorado river	225,049	49,435	0.22	29,835	0.13	11,214	0.05
Green river	47,222	7,723	0.16	3,566	0.08	1,845	0.04
Grand river	26,472	10,620	0.40	2,965	0.11	41	0.00
Little Colorado river	29,208	542	0.02	656	0.02	187	0.01
Gila river	68,623	16,229	0.24	13,235	0.19	4,504	0.07
Sacramento river	58,824	90,702	1.60	100,884	1.72	84,520	1.44
San Joaquin river	29,952	32,975	1.10	25,399	0.85	21,975	0.73
Klamath river	14,660	4,493	0.31	5,153	0.35	4,529	0.31
Columbia river	216,537	108,138	0.50	45,370	0.21	21,417	0.10
Willamette river	11,700	22,321	1.91	10,086	0.86	3,677	0.31
Snake river	103,835	23,461	0.23	12,820	0.12	8,829	0.09
Clarke Fork	63,291	16,620	0.26	4,499	0.07	3,439	0.05

PROGRESS OF THE NATION.

xlii

DISTRIBUTION OF THE NEGRO(a) POPULATION ACCORDING TO DRAINAGE BASINS: 1870 TO 1890.

DRAINAGE BASINS.	Approximate area in square miles.	1890		1880		1870	
		Negro population.	Negro population per square mile.	Negro population.	Negro population per square mile.	Negro population.	Negro population per square mile.
Atlantic ocean	2,178,210	7,451,871	3.42	6,572,708	3.02	4,874,543	2.24
New England coast	61,830	44,185	0.71	39,520	0.64	31,395	0.51
St. John river	7,890	42	0.01	46	0.01	68	0.01
Penobscot river	8,934	123	0.01	137	0.02	185	0.02
Kennebec river	10,102	361	0.04	408	0.04	429	0.04
Merrimac river	4,864	3,390	0.70	2,741	0.56	1,916	0.39
Connecticut river	11,269	5,815	0.52	5,789	0.51	4,947	0.44
Housatonic river	1,933	4,274	2.21	4,355	2.25	3,921	2.03
Middle Atlantic coast	83,020	573,996	6.91	526,728	6.34	425,443	5.12
Hudson river	13,366	14,375	1.08	14,770	1.11	13,962	1.04
Delaware river	12,012	82,152	6.84	68,238	5.68	53,029	4.41
Susquehanna river	27,655	22,513	0.81	20,102	0.73	17,865	0.65
Potomac river	14,479	183,505	12.67	178,368	12.32	144,208	9.96
South Atlantic coast	132,040	2,267,088	17.17	2,079,086	15.75	1,546,387	11.71
James river	9,684	221,238	22.85	216,770	22.38	177,701	18.36
Cape Fear river	8,310	87,364	10.51	83,557	10.05	60,766	7.31
Neuse river	5,299	95,407	18.00	95,887	18.10	68,862	13.00
Pedee river	17,098	246,341	14.41	215,786	12.62	147,671	8.64
Roanoke river	9,237	187,900	20.34	183,433	19.86	137,622	14.90
Santee river	14,696	280,793	19.11	240,908	16.39	168,564	11.47
Savannah river	11,402	239,622	21.02	209,924	18.41	148,772	13.05
Altamaha river	14,109	248,253	17.60	212,447	15.06	156,556	11.10
Great Lakes	135,763	44,408	0.33	38,870	0.29	30,102	0.22
St. Lawrence river	13,636	1,310	0.10	1,456	0.11	1,275	0.09
Lake Ontario	12,387	5,570	0.45	6,126	0.49	5,623	0.45
Lake Erie	17,207	17,226	1.00	16,727	0.97	13,289	0.77
Lake Huron	18,839	2,082	0.11	1,346	0.07	744	0.04
Lake Michigan	45,870	17,397	0.38	13,103	0.29	9,075	0.20
Lake Superior	17,830	823	0.05	112	0.01	96	0.01
Red River of the North	39,577	272	0.01	98	0.00	1	0.00
Gulf of Mexico	1,725,080	4,521,022	2.62	3,888,406	2.25	2,841,215	1.65
Apalachicola river	18,918	361,573	19.11	312,731	16.53	244,519	12.93
Mobile river	43,436	643,206	14.81	573,463	13.20	443,560	10.21
Tombigbee river	18,896	298,767	15.81	260,408	13.78	199,351	10.55
Alabama river	23,820	331,405	13.91	300,497	12.62	232,234	9.75
Pascagoula river	8,980	49,717	5.54	39,291	4.38	24,895	2.77
Pearl river	8,670	78,591	9.06	66,749	7.70	49,355	5.69
Sabine river	20,440	54,348	2.66	45,615	2.23	30,275	1.48
Trinity river	17,960	71,937	4.01	53,488	2.98	31,483	1.75
Brazos river	59,646	115,364	1.93	91,253	1.53	59,281	0.99
Colorado river	41,220	33,618	0.82	29,102	0.71	18,067	0.44
Nueces river	18,944	1,378	0.07	1,287	0.07	813	0.04
San Antonio river	16,352	33,583	2.05	26,956	1.65	18,190	1.11
Rio Grande	128,792	1,785	0.01	1,778	0.01	1,312	0.01
Mississippi river	1,240,030	2,474,778	2.00	2,157,007	1.74	1,556,404	1.26
Yazoo river	12,704	262,434	20.51	218,619	17.09	135,174	10.57
Illinois river	29,013	10,152	0.66	13,681	0.47	7,929	0.27
Rock river	9,792	1,279	0.13	1,592	0.16	1,207	0.12
Wisconsin river	12,280	316	0.03	208	0.02	266	0.02
Chippewa river	8,892	99	0.01	70	0.01	61	0.01
St. Croix river	7,576	130	0.02	76	0.01	50	0.01
Minnesota river	16,000	269	0.02	168	0.01	83	0.01
Cedar river	12,492	847	0.07	953	0.08	585	0.05
Des Moines river	14,652	3,209	0.22	2,315	0.16	1,295	0.09
Ohio river	201,720	790,956	3.92	753,744	3.74	600,190	2.98
Tennessee river	43,897	225,737	5.14	213,011	4.85	167,350	3.81
Cumberland river	18,573	152,602	8.22	151,814	8.17	130,246	7.01
Kentucky river	7,425	61,894	8.34	63,393	8.54	54,827	7.38
Green river	9,065	52,468	5.79	56,084	6.19	44,427	4.90
Licking river	3,658	18,241	4.99	20,002	5.48	17,212	4.71
Kanawha river	16,600	27,065	1.62	22,501	1.35	15,226	0.91
Monongahela river	7,625	11,092	1.57	9,151	1.20	6,595	0.86
Allegheny river	11,437	8,239	0.72	6,358	0.56	4,334	0.38
Miami river	5,400	15,385	2.85	13,016	2.41	9,885	1.83
Scioto river	6,480	17,887	2.76	16,550	2.55	13,640	2.10
Muskingum river	7,740	5,749	0.74	5,469	0.71	4,321	0.56
Wabash river	33,725	30,902	0.92	27,014	0.80	15,374	0.46
Big Sandy river	4,050	6,509	1.61	5,300	1.31	3,902	0.96

a Includes all persons of negro descent.

GEOGRAPHICAL DISTRIBUTION OF POPULATION.

xliii

DISTRIBUTION OF THE NEGRO (a) POPULATION ACCORDING TO DRAINAGE BASINS: 1870 TO 1890—Continued.

DRAINAGE BASINS.	Approximate area in square miles.	1890		1880		1870	
		Negro population.	Negro population per square mile.	Negro population.	Negro population per square mile.	Negro population.	Negro population per square mile.
Atlantic ocean—Continued.							
Gulf of Mexico—Continued.							
Mississippi river—Continued.							
Missouri river	527, 155	137, 272	0. 26	121, 777	0. 23	87, 240	0. 17
Big Sioux river	7, 880	102	0. 01	40	0. 01	41	0. 01
Yellowstone river	69, 683	382	0. 01	42	0. 00	2	0. 00
Platte river	90, 011	6, 159	0. 07	2, 348	0. 03	633	0. 01
Kansas river	59, 256	25, 998	0. 44	22, 183	0. 37	9, 572	0. 16
Osage river	15, 444	17, 309	1. 12	15, 554	1. 01	9, 632	0. 62
Arkansas river	185, 671	156, 888	0. 84	98, 927	0. 53	56, 108	0. 30
Cimarron river	17, 360	2, 047	0. 12	25	0. 00	18	0. 00
Canadian river	42, 710	1, 585	0. 04	307	0. 01	34	0. 00
White river	27, 925	54, 808	1. 97	37, 158	1. 33	21, 657	0. 78
Red river (Louisiana)	89, 970	377, 756	4. 20	299, 632	3. 33	195, 364	2. 17
Washita river	19, 138	161, 992	8. 46	126, 726	6. 62	80, 301	4. 20
St. Francis river	7, 884	31, 316	3. 97	19, 137	2. 43	9, 322	1. 18
Great Basin	228, 150	863	0. 00	738	0. 00	477	0. 00
Great Salt Lake	32, 400	414	0. 01	186	0. 01	109	0. 00
Humboldt river	32, 148	225	0. 01	336	0. 01	258	0. 01
Pacific ocean	619, 240	17, 306	0. 03	7, 347	0. 01	4, 989	0. 01
Colorado river	225, 049	2, 950	0. 01	352	0. 00	101	0. 00
Green river	47, 222	157	0. 00	19	0. 00	27	0. 00
Grand river	26, 472	339	0. 01	71	0. 00	2	0. 00
Little Colorado river	29, 208	178	0. 01	8	0. 00	2	0. 00
Gila river	68, 623	969	0. 01	113	0. 00	14	0. 00
Sacramento river	58, 824	3, 867	0. 07	2, 813	0. 05	2, 224	0. 04
San Joaquin river	29, 952	1, 464	0. 05	740	0. 02	513	0. 02
Klamath river	14, 660	126	0. 01	87	0. 01	43	0. 00
Columbia river	216, 537	2, 275	0. 01	575	0. 00	414	0. 00
Willamette river	11, 700	430	0. 04	168	0. 01	108	0. 01
Snake river	103, 835	286	0. 00	84	0. 00	66	0. 00
Clarke Fork	63, 291	498	0. 01	66	0. 00	26	0. 00

a Includes all persons of negro descent.

The following table, which is a condensation of the table that appears on pages xxxviii and xxxix, shows the percentage of the total population of the principal drainage basins of the country as it existed in the three decades mentioned:

DIVISIONS.	1890	1880	1870
	Per cent.	Per cent.	Per cent.
The United States	100. 00	100. 00	100. 00
Atlantic ocean	96. 16	97. 11	97. 79
New England coast	7. 16	7. 60	8. 52
Middle Atlantic coast	18. 34	19. 23	20. 85
South Atlantic coast	6. 78	7. 39	7. 26
Great Lakes	10. 80	10. 58	10. 95
Red River of the North	0. 39	0. 14	.0. 01
Gulf of Mexico	52. 69	52. 17	50. 20
Great Basin	0. 41	0. 42	0. 33
Pacific ocean	3. 43	2. 47	1. 88

Of the percentages given in the preceding table for the drainage basin of the Gulf of Mexico, the tertiary division of the Mississippi river embraces 43.77 per cent for 1890, 43.42 for 1880, and 42.36 for 1870.

DISTRIBUTION OF POPULATION IN ACCORDANCE WITH TOPOGRAPHIC FEATURES.

Considering the surface of the United States broadly, it is seen to contain two great elevated areas. The eastern, known as the Appalachian Mountain system, is separated from the Atlantic by a broad plain sloping gently eastward. The western, known as the Cordilleran Mountain system, is many times as broad as the eastern system, more than twice as high, and the mountain ranges which crown it are vastly greater in number and more complex. It extends westward to the Pacific coast.

Between these two systems lies a broad valley, most of which is drained by the Mississippi river to the Gulf of Mexico. The northeastern part is drained by the St. Lawrence river and the system of the Great Lakes to the Gulf of St. Lawrence, while along the gulf coast are considerable areas drained by other streams.

PROGRESS OF THE NATION.

xliv

The country thus broadly outlined contains every variety of surface found upon the globe. The various effects due to differences in slope, elevation, and climate are all represented.

An attempt has been made in the table shown on page xlvi to subdivide the country into areas differing in the character of their surface, their products, and their climate, and to classify the population in accordance therewith. These subdivisions are briefly characterized as follows:

COAST SWAMPS.—These swamps are found along the South Atlantic and Gulf coasts, extending inland to varying distances, in some places as much as 100 miles. They have the greatest breadth in North Carolina and Louisiana, but border the coast nearly all the way from southeast Virginia to the mouth of the Rio Grande, Texas. Upon the Atlantic coast the surface of these swamps, while exceedingly level, has ample slope for drainage, and accordingly as the land becomes valuable their borders are being drained and converted into farms. In the Carolinas a considerable area of them is utilized for rice plantations. In the main they are well timbered, principally with cypress and juniper, among which is a luxuriant growth of cane. The population of this region is mainly of the negro race, the climate being very unhealthy for the white race.

ATLANTIC PLAIN.—The Atlantic plain comprises the strip of land lying between the Coast swamps and the fall line throughout the Atlantic states south of New York and the Gulf states as far as the Mississippi river. It is characterized by a level surface, a low elevation, scarcely reaching 200 feet above the sea, is underlaid by recent sedimentary rocks, and, except where they have been removed by the hand of man, is covered with pine forests.

PIEDMONT REGION.—This region comprises a strip of country extending from Maine to Alabama, lying between the fall line on the east and the Blue Ridge on the west. It is underlaid by metamorphic rocks and forested with a mixed growth of broad and narrow leaf trees. The lower portion is comparatively level, being broken only by the beds of streams, but in the neighborhood of the Blue Ridge and throughout New England it is hilly.

NEW ENGLAND HILLS.—This name has been applied to the hill country in the upper part of New England, including all of the upper part of Maine, the White mountains of New Hampshire, the Green mountains of Vermont, and the Adirondacks of New York, all of which is a broken, mountainous country, ranging in elevation from 1,000 to 6,000 feet, and covered with forests.

APPALACHIAN MOUNTAIN REGION.—This region includes the Blue Ridge and the Appalachian valley lying immediately north and west of it, and extends from New Jersey to Georgia and Alabama. The Blue Ridge consisting of a single range throughout Pennsylvania, Maryland, and Virginia, expands in North Carolina into a very complex mass of mountains, and there reaches its maximum elevation, namely, 6,700 feet.

The Appalachian valley is drained in New Jersey and Pennsylvania by the Delaware and Susquehanna rivers, in Virginia by the Potomac, James, and Kanawha rivers, and in Tennessee mainly by the Tennessee river. It is traversed by numerous ranges, some of them assuming the dignity of separate mountain ranges, and all of them running closely parallel to one another and to the general direction of the valley.

CUMBERLAND-ALLEGHENY PLATEAU.—Rising from the northwest border of the Appalachian valley is an escarpment extending more or less continuously from northeastern Pennsylvania down through Maryland, Virginia, and Tennessee into Alabama. From the summit of this escarpment a plateau stretches with a general northwestern slope. This plateau is everywhere deeply scored by streams with a general northwesterly direction. These streams have cut the plateau into a mass of very irregular ridges and gorges, making it one of the most intricate mountain regions on the globe. The entire region is densely covered with forests, the hand of man having removed but a very small part of them.

INTERIOR TIMBERED REGION.—This region comprises southern Ohio and Indiana, the western half of Kentucky and Tennessee, and the northeastern part of Mississippi, together with small areas in adjoining states. It possesses no characteristic features beyond the fact that, except in the settled regions, it is covered with forests.

LAKE REGION.—A narrow strip of country bordering on the Great Lakes has been segregated under this name. It includes small parts of New York, Pennsylvania, and Ohio, and most of Michigan, Wisconsin, and northern Minnesota. Owing to the proximity of large bodies of water this region has many of the characteristics of a coast climate. The atmosphere being moist, the winters are abnormally warm and the summers abnormally cool. This region contains great pine forests, which are still serving as a main source of supply of that timber.

OZARK MOUNTAIN REGION.—This region is located in northwest Arkansas, southwest Missouri, and the eastern part of the Indian territory. In Arkansas it is made up of a succession of narrow ranges 2,000 to 3,000 feet high, having a generally east and west trend, separated by somewhat broad valleys. Farther to the northeast, in Missouri, the hills become merely a confused mass, without order or system.

ALLUVIAL REGION OF THE MISSISSIPPI.—This region extends in a rapidly widening strip from Cairo, at the mouth of the Ohio, to the coast swamps in Louisiana, into which it merges without any sharp line of demarcation. It includes parts of the states of Missouri, Arkansas, Mississippi, and Louisiana, besides a trifling area in Kentucky and Tennessee. Much the larger portion of it is marshy, and is below the level of the water in the rivers. The dry land lies mainly along the immediate banks of the streams, having been formed by deposition from overflows. With the exception of the cultivated land, this region is entirely covered with forests. The soil is of the highest

GEOGRAPHICAL DISTRIBUTION OF POPULATION.

degree of fertility, but the climate is hostile to the white race, and by far the larger proportion of its inhabitants is of the negro race.

PRAIRIE REGION.—This region comprises a small portion of western Indiana, most of Illinois and Iowa, southern Wisconsin and Minnesota, northern Missouri, and eastern North Dakota, South Dakota, Kansas, and Nebraska, and extends in a broad belt down through the Indian territory and Texas.

On the east it merges by insensible degrees into the forest-clad regions, and on the west by equally insensible degrees into the Great Plains. It is a region of transition from the one to the other. Its climate is such that without protection forests can not thrive.

Its surface is level or slightly undulating, and was, in its natural state, covered with luxuriant grasses, but timber growth was scarce, and was confined almost entirely to the bluffs and the borders of streams. With the protection afforded by man, the growth of forests has increased in this region, until now it presents a landscape diversified by a tree growth the extent of which is constantly increasing. It is the granary of the country.

GREAT PLAINS.—Merging with the prairie region by insensible degrees are the Great Plains, extending from approximate longitude 99° to the foot of the Rocky mountains, and from the Canadian border to the Rio Grande. It is a region devoid of timber, except in the narrowest strips along certain streams, but sparsely covered with bunch grass, changing in the more arid regions to sage, artemisia, cactus, and yucca. Its surface is a monotonous, billowy expanse, broken only here and there by lines of cliffs and buttes.

Throughout this region the rainfall is insufficient for the needs of agriculture, and irrigation is necessary for the cultivation of the soil. The supply of water in the flowing streams is sufficient to irrigate only a small part of the land, and the extent to which settlement is possible will in the future become, therefore, a question of the abundance of water and not of land.

CORDILLERAN REGION.—The Cordilleran region is naturally subdivided into districts which differ from one another in certain features and have other features in common. Except in the extreme northwest, in Washington, western Oregon, and northwest California, the climate is arid and the rainfall is insufficient for agriculture. This aridity of climate and deficiency of rainfall increase southward and reach a maximum in southern Nevada, California, and Arizona. The prevalence of forests accompanies the rainfall. Upon the northwest coast and inland as far as the Cascade range in Oregon and Washington the country is densely covered with forests of great trees. This forest belt extends inland through northern Washington and Idaho into the mountainous region of Montana, and thence southeastward, accompanying the mountain ranges into the Yellowstone Park. Elsewhere no forests are found except upon the mountains, and in the more arid regions of the south even the mountains are bare to their summits. The valleys produce only the vegetation characteristic of an arid region. Where the rainfall is abundant bunch grass is found, but as the rainfall diminishes and the dryness of the atmosphere increases, the vegetation of the valleys changes to artemisia, cactus, yucca, and other desert plants.

ROCKY MOUNTAIN REGION.—This region, including the easternmost portion of the Cordilleran system, comprising western Montana, eastern Idaho, western Wyoming, central Colorado, and New Mexico, with a little of Texas, is composed of a series of ranges separated by valleys of greater or less breadth, trending parallel to one another a little west of north and east of south. It is naturally subdivided into two parts. The northern part extends from Canada southeastward into central Wyoming; thence for a distance of 100 miles or thereabout the mountain ranges disappear, leaving in their place only broad plateaus. The ranges reappear in southern Wyoming and extend thence southward. In the northern part the mountains range in altitude from 9,000 to 13,000 feet or more, rising from a base of 4,000 or 5,000 feet. In the southern part the base is much higher, rising in Colorado to 6,000 or 8,000 feet, with high mountain valleys reaching 10,000 feet above the sea, while many of the ranges exceed 14,000 feet in altitude. Both the general level of the country and the mountain ranges diminish in altitude southward.

PLATEAU REGION.—This region comprises most of the drainage basin of the Colorado river above the mouth of the Virgin, in southern Nevada. It is a region of great plateaus, whose surfaces are level or slightly inclined, and which terminate with great lines of cliffs, in some cases thousands of feet in height. From the mountains which border this range on the east, north, and west these plateaus descend by a succession of gigantic steps from an elevation of 12,000 feet down to 1,000 or 2,000 feet above the sea. Every stream is in a canyon, and as the rainfall is light and spasmodic a great majority of these canyons are dry during the greater part of the year. In many regions these canyons are so abundant as to have reduced the plateau to a mere skeleton, or the process of erosion may have gone still further, so that nothing is left of the upper plateau but fragments in the form of mesas and buttes.

The higher plateaus in the neighborhood of the mountains are green and forested from the abundant rainfall. The lower plateaus, on the other hand, have only the sparsest vegetation or are absolutely sterile.

BASIN REGION.—In the interior of the Cordilleran region is an area comprising practically all of Nevada, western Utah, part of eastern California, and southern Oregon, which has no drainage to the sea. It is a closed basin. The only discharge of its waters is by sinking into the thirsty soil or by evaporation into the thirsty atmosphere. This is the most desert part of the country, with the exception of the course of the lower Colorado and Gila rivers. The rainfall is scanty, even upon the mountains; so scanty, indeed, that there are but two or three running streams of any magnitude within it. Its surface is diversified by many ranges of mountains having a general parallel trend

xlvi   PROGRESS OF THE NATION.

rising from flat valleys filled with alluvium. These ranges divide the basin into numerous minor basins, in each of which water collects and sinks. In the eastern part the largest basin is that known as the Great Salt Lake, into which several small streams flow from the Wasatch mountains. In the western part the principal basin is that of the Humboldt river. The elevation of the floor of the basin ranges from 6,000 feet near its middle line, downward, reaching in Death valley, in eastern California, an elevation of 200 feet below the level of the sea.

COLUMBIAN MESAS.—The drainage basin of the Snake river, in Idaho, Oregon, and Washington, together with a part of the basin of the Columbia, in the latter state, has been in great part covered by eruptions of basalt, which, bursting out of the soil at various points, has spread over the country, forming a table land.

SIERRA NEVADA.—Separating the Great Basin from the California valley, in eastern California, is a broad, heavy, forest-covered range of mountains with long slopes to the west and an abrupt ascent to the east.

PACIFIC VALLEY.—West of the Cascade range and the Sierra Nevada and stretching from Puget sound to southern California is a valley drained in Oregon by the Willamette and in California by the Sacramento and San Joaquin rivers. In its southern part, south of the latitude of the bay of San Francisco, the climate is such that irrigation is necessary, while north of it the rainfall is sufficient, and in Oregon and Washington is more than sufficient, for the farmers' needs. Where the rainfall is insufficient this valley is treeless, but farther north, and especially in Oregon and Washington, it is covered with dense forests.

CASCADE RANGE.—Stretching northward in line with the Sierra Nevada, but distinguished sharply from it by the character of its formation, is the Cascade range. It is a series of extinct volcanoes, rising from a high plateau of volcanic rock. This range is densely forested.

COAST RANGES.—Separating this valley from the Pacific is a succession of ranges trending parallel with the coast, and known as the Coast ranges. In southern California the valleys among these ranges are of the highest degree of fertility, and produce grapes and tropical fruits in profusion. Farther north the country is but little settled or even explored.

The following tables show, for each of the subdivisions characterized above, the aggregate population, foreign born population, and negro population, in thousands at each of the last three censuses, namely, 1890, 1880, and 1870. They show also the numerical increase expressed in even thousands, the per cent of increase, the number in each 100,000 of the total population, the density or the population per square mile and, finally, the increase per square mile in each subdivision.

Grouping these subdivisions, it will be seen from the first table that in the swamp regions of the country, including in that term the coast marshes and the alluvial region of the Mississippi river, there are 2,694,000 inhabitants, or 4.30 per cent of the total population. This, as was previously stated, consists mainly of the negro race. In the desert and semi-desert regions of the country in 1890 there are found 1,469,000, or 2.35 per cent of the population. In the mountain region of the west there are found 1,535,000 people, or about 2.45 per cent, and in the eastern mountain region 10,888,000 people, or about one-sixth of the entire population.

DISTRIBUTION OF THE AGGREGATE POPULATION IN ACCORDANCE WITH TOPOGRAPHIC FEATURES: 1870 TO 1890.

TOPOGRAPHIC DIVISIONS.	POPULATION IN THOUSANDS.			INCREASE IN THOUSANDS.				NUMBER IN EACH 100,000 OF TOTAL POPULATION.			POPULATION PER SQUARE MILE.			INCREASE PER SQUARE MILE.	
				1880 to 1890		1870 to 1880								1880 to 1890	1870 to 1880
	1890	1880	1870	Number.	Per cent.	Number.	Per cent.	1890	1880	1870	1890	1880	1870		
Coast swamps	1,809	1,569	1,284	240	15.30	285	22.20	2,889	3,128	3,330	21.24	18.42	15.08	2.82	3.34
Atlantic plain	8,784	7,113	5,546	1,671	23.49	1,567	28.25	14,027	14,182	14,384	75.15	60.85	47.45	14.30	13.40
Piedmont region	7,858	6,660	5,468	1,198	17.99	1,192	21.80	12,548	13,279	14,181	65.88	55.84	45.84	10.04	10.00
New England hills	2,290	2,171	1,995	119	5.48	176	8.82	3,657	4,329	5,174	40.69	38.57	35.44	2.12	3.13
Appalachian Mountain region	2,849	2,386	1,959	463	19.40	427	21.80	4,550	4,757	5,081	49.83	41.73	34.26	8.10	7.47
Cumberland-Allegheny plateau	5,740	4,787	3,940	962	20.10	847	21.50	9,180	9,544	10,218	59.33	49.41	40.66	9.92	8.75
Interior timbered region	11,292	9,891	7,976	1,401	14.16	1,915	24.01	18,032	19,720	20,686	44.32	38.82	31.31	5.50	7.51
Lake region	3,578	2,507	1,722	1,071	42.72	785	45.50	5,714	4,998	4,466	25.12	17.60	12.09	7.52	5.51
Ozark Mountain region	1,041	734	473	307	41.83	261	55.18	1,662	1,463	1,227	22.76	16.05	10.34	6.71	5.71
Alluvial region of the Mississippi	885	683	460	202	29.58	223	48.48	1,413	1,362	1,193	23.55	18.18	12.24	5.37	5.94
Prairie region	13,048	9,777	6,715	3,271	33.46	3,062	45.60	20,836	19,493	17,415	28.79	21.57	14.82	7.22	6.75
Great Plains	737	222	73	515	231.98	149	204.11	1,177	443	189	1.53	0.46	0.15	1.07	0.31
North Rocky Mountain region	153	50	29	103	206.00	21	72.41	244	100	75	1.13	0.37	0.21	0.76	0.16
South Rocky Mountain region	247	192	78	55	28.65	114	146.15	394	383	202	2.11	1.64	0.67	0.47	0.97
Plateau region	110	81	29	29	35.80	52	179.31	176	162	75	0.60	0.49	0.17	0.17	0.32
Basin region	403	252	149	151	59.92	103	69.13	644	502	386	1.37	0.86	0.51	0.51	0.35
Columbian mesas	219	91	27	128	140.66	64	237.04	350	181	70	1.95	0.81	0.24	1.14	0.57
Sierra Nevada	146	136	111	10	7.35	25	22.52	233	271	288	4.90	4.57	3.73	0.33	0.84
Pacific valley	435	248	166	187	75.40	82	49.40	695	494	431	9.11	5.19	3.48	3.92	1.71
Cascade range	179	54	30	125	231.48	24	80.00	286	108	78	5.50	1.66	0.92	3.84	0.74
Coast ranges	810	552	328	258	46.74	224	68.29	1,293	1,101	851	14.32	9.76	5.80	4.56	3.96

GEOGRAPHICAL DISTRIBUTION OF POPULATION.

The following table relating to the distribution of the foreign born shows that more than one-fourth of this element is found in the prairie region. The next most populous regions are the Atlantic plain, with its great cities, and the lake region. These three areas taken together include more than one-half of the entire foreign born element. A notable proportion of this element is also found in the subdivisions of the western Cordilleran region. On the other hand, the low coast swamps, the alluvial region of the Mississippi and the Ozark mountains contain very few of this element.

DISTRIBUTION OF THE FOREIGN BORN POPULATION IN ACCORDANCE WITH TOPOGRAPHIC FEATURES: 1870 TO 1890.

| TOPOGRAPHIC DIVISIONS. | FOREIGN BORN POPULATION IN THOUSANDS. | | | INCREASE IN THOUSANDS. | | | | NUMBER IN EACH 100,000 OF TOTAL FOREIGN BORN POPULATION. | | | FOREIGN BORN POPULATION PER SQUARE MILE. | | | INCREASE PER SQUARE MILE. | |
| | | | | 1880 to 1890 | | 1870 to 1880 | | | | | | | | | |
	1890	1880	1870	Number.	Per cent.	Number.	Per cent.	1890	1880	1870	1890	1880	1870	1880 to 1890	1870 to 1880
Coast swamps	141	118	116	23	10.49	2	1.72	1,524	1,766	2,084	1.66	1.39	1.36	0.27	0.03
Atlantic plain	1,655	1,213	1,053	442	36.44	160	15.19	17,892	18,159	18,915	14.16	10.38	9.01	3.78	1.37
Piedmont region	1,002	686	585	316	46.06	101	17.26	10,833	10,264	10,508	8.40	5.75	4.91	2.65	0.84
New England hills	417	348	339	69	19.83	9	2.65	4,508	5,210	6,089	7.41	6.18	6.02	1.23	0.16
Appalachian Mountain region	178	131	140	47	35.88	a9	a6.43	1,924	1,961	2,515	3.11	2.29	2.45	0.82	a0.16
Cumberland-Allegheny plateau	780	566	531	214	37.81	35	6.59	8,433	8,473	9,538	8.05	5.84	5.48	2.21	0.36
Interior timbered region	734	665	638	69	10.38	27	4.23	7,935	9,955	11,460	2.88	2.61	2.50	0.27	0.11
Lake region	1,066	684	471	382	55.85	213	45.22	11,524	10,240	8,461	7.48	4.80	3.31	2.68	1.49
Ozark Mountain region	22	15	9	7	46.67	6	66.67	238	225	162	0.48	0.33	0.20	0.15	0.13
Alluvial region of the Mississippi	12	12	12	......	......	......	......	130	180	216	0.32	0.32	0.32	......	......
Prairie region	2,393	1,702	1,344	691	40.60	358	26.64	25,870	25,479	24,142	5.28	3.76	2.97	1.52	0.79
Great Plains	141	57	21	84	147.37	36	171.43	1,524	853	377	0.29	0.12	0.04	0.17	0.08
North Rocky Mountain region	46	16	14	30	187.50	2	14.29	497	239	251	0.34	0.12	0.10	0.22	0.02
South Rocky Mountain region	42	33	9	9	27.27	24	266.67	454	494	162	0.36	0.28	0.08	0.08	0.20
Plateau region	20	11	5	9	81.82	6	120.00	216	165	90	0.12	0.07	0.03	0.05	0.04
Basin region	106	91	57	15	16.48	34	59.65	1,146	1,362	1,024	0.36	0.31	0.19	0.05	0.12
Columbian mesas	35	17	6	18	105.88	11	183.33	378	254	108	0.31	0.15	0.05	0.16	0.10
Sierra Nevada	38	48	47	a10	a20.83	1	2.13	411	719	844	1.28	1.61	1.58	a0.33	0.03
Pacific valley	109	61	41	48	78.69	20	48.78	1,179	913	737	2.28	1.28	0.86	1.00	0.42
Cascade range	46	10	4	36	360.00	6	150.00	497	150	72	1.41	0.31	0.12	1.10	0.19
Coast ranges	267	196	125	71	36.22	71	56.80	2,887	2,934	2,245	4.72	3.46	2.21	1.26	1.25

a Decrease.

The following table showing the distribution of the negro element is sharply contrasted with that of the foreign born element. The interior timbered region contains more than one-fourth of the negro element of the country, and the Atlantic plain another fourth. The coast swamps and the alluvial region of the Mississippi contain large proportions. Indeed, these regions, together with the Piedmont region, contain nearly nine-tenths of the negro population.

DISTRIBUTION OF THE NEGRO (a) POPULATION IN ACCORDANCE WITH TOPOGRAPHIC FEATURES: 1870 TO 1890.

| TOPOGRAPHIC DIVISIONS. | NEGRO POPULATION IN THOUSANDS. | | | INCREASE IN THOUSANDS. | | | | NUMBER IN EACH 100,000 OF TOTAL NEGRO POPULATION. | | | NEGRO POPULATION PER SQUARE MILE. | | | INCREASE PER SQUARE MILE. | |
| | | | | 1880 to 1890 | | 1870 to 1880 | | | | | | | | | |
	1890	1880	1870	Number.	Per cent.	Number.	Per cent.	1890	1880	1870	1890	1880	1870	1880 to 1890	1870 to 1880
Coast swamps	774	702	570	72	10.26	132	23.16	10,361	10,667	11,080	9.09	8.24	6.69	0.85	1.55
Atlantic plain	1,861	1,632	1,218	229	14.03	414	33.90	24,913	24,799	24,959	15.92	13.96	10.42	1.96	3.54
Piedmont region	1,504	1,369	1,037	135	9.86	332	32.02	20,134	20,802	21,250	12.61	11.48	8.69	1.13	2.79
New England hills	13	15	14	b2	b13.33	1	7.14	174	228	287	0.23	0.27	0.25	b0.04	0.02
Appalachian Mountain region	201	178	134	23	12.92	44	32.84	2,691	2,705	2,746	3.52	3.11	2.34	0.41	0.77
Cumberland-Allegheny plateau	161	149	119	12	8.05	30	25.21	2,155	2,264	2,439	1.66	1.54	1.23	0.12	0.31
Interior timbered region	1,897	1,718	1,267	179	10.42	451	35.60	25,395	26,105	25,963	7.45	6.74	4.97	0.71	1.77
Lake region	19	17	13	2	11.76	4	30.77	254	258	266	0.13	0.12	0.09	0.01	0.03
Ozark Mountain region	53	37	23	16	43.24	14	60.87	710	562	471	1.16	0.81	0.50	0.35	0.31
Alluvial region of the Mississippi	537	408	252	129	31.62	156	61.90	7,189	6,200	5,164	14.29	10.86	6.71	3.43	4.15
Prairie region	416	342	225	74	21.64	117	52.00	5,569	5,197	4,611	0.92	0.75	0.50	0.17	0.25
Great Plains	13	5	2	8	160.00	3	150.00	174	76	41	0.03	0.01	0.00	0.02	0.01
Cordilleran region	21	9	6	12	133.33	3	50.00	281	137	123	0.02	0.01	0.01	0.01	......

a Includes all persons of negro descent.

b Decrease.

xlviii   PROGRESS OF THE NATION.

DISTRIBUTION OF POPULATION IN ACCORDANCE WITH ALTITUDE.

During recent years the active prosecution of topographic surveys by the United States Geological Survey and the extension of railroads into remote regions have added greatly to our knowledge of the relief of the country, and greatly increased the material available for making a contour map of the country. This material has been compiled in the office of the United States Geological Survey, and among other uses to which it has been put a map has been prepared from it on a scale of 1: 2,500,000, or about 40 miles to 1 inch, showing approximate contour lines at 100 feet, 500 feet, 1,000 feet, 1,500 feet, 2,000 feet, and thence by intervals of 1,000 feet up to 12,000 feet above sea level. This map has been used in the distribution of population herewith presented. From it the counties falling between the different contour lines have been drawn off and tabulated. In cases where a contour divides a county, the portions upon each side of the contour have been estimated to the nearest tenths of counties, having due regard in each case to the distribution of population within the county. The population in 1870, 1880, and 1890 was then classified in accordance with the tabulated list of counties.

The following table shows the distribution of the aggregate population in accordance with altitude:

DISTRIBUTION OF THE AGGREGATE POPULATION IN ACCORDANCE WITH ALTITUDE: 1870 TO 1890.

ALTITUDE IN FEET.	POPULATION IN THOUSANDS.			NUMBER IN EACH 100,000 OF TOTAL POPULATION WITHIN EACH GIVEN ALTITUDE.			CHANGE IN NUMBER IN EACH 100,000.		NUMBER IN EACH 100,000 OF TOTAL POPULATION BELOW EACH ALTITUDE.			POPULATION PER SQUARE MILE.			INCREASE PER SQUARE MILE.	
	1890	1880	1870	1890	1880	1870	1880 to 1890	1870 to 1880	1890	1880	1870	1890	1880	1870	1880 to 1890	1870 to 1880
0 to 100	10,387	8,273	6,441	16,587	16,495	16,705	+92	−210	16,587	16,495	16,705	51.84	41.29	32.15	10.55	9.14
100 to 500	13,838	11,054	9,240	22,098	23,235	23,064	−1,137	−720	38,685	39,730	40,609	35.65	30.02	23.80	5.63	6.22
500 to 1,000	23,947	19,813	15,914	38,240	39,503	41,273	−1,263	−1,770	76,925	79,233	81,942	43.85	36.28	29.14	7.57	7.14
1,000 to 1,500	9,431	7,256	5,136	15,060	14,467	13,320	+593	+1,147	91,985	93,700	95,262	23.84	18.34	12.98	5.50	5.36
1,500 to 2,000	2,354	1,597	978	3,759	3,184	2,536	+575	+648	95,744	96,884	97,798	9.84	6.68	4.09	3.16	2.59
2,000 to 3,000	1,154	723	405	1,843	1,441	1,050	+402	+391	97,587	98,325	98,848	4.37	2.74	1.53	1.63	1.21
3,000 to 4,000	381	185	124	608	360	322	+239	+47	98,195	98,694	99,170	2.14	1.04	0.70	1.10	0.34
4,000 to 5,000	296	135	75	473	269	195	+204	+74	98,668	98,963	99,365	1.14	0.52	0.29	0.62	0.23
5,000 to 6,000	487	270	137	778	538	355	+240	+183	99,446	99,501	99,720	2.21	1.23	0.62	0.98	0.61
6,000 to 7,000	161	98	56	257	195	145	+62	+50	99,703	99,696	99,865	0.98	0.60	0.34	0.38	0.26
7,000 to 8,000	94	59	33	150	118	86	+32	+32	99,853	99,814	99,951	1.03	0.64	0.36	0.39	0.28
8,000 to 9,000	43	39	14	69	78	36	−9	+42	99,922	99,892	99,987	1.05	0.95	0.84	0.10	0.61
9,000 to 10,000	39	45	3	62	90	8	−28	+82	99,984	99,982	99,995	2.03	2.34	0.16	a0.31	2.18
10,000 and over	10	9	2	16	18	5	−2	+13	100,000	100,000	100,000	0.54	0.49	0.11	0.05	0.38

a Decrease.

The figures of distribution in 1870 and 1880, herewith presented, have been obtained by the use of a much more elaborate map than that used in 1880, and therefore differ somewhat from those published in the report of the Tenth Census.

It is seen by the table and diagram accompanying that about one-sixth of the people of the country live less than 100 feet above sea level, namely, along the immediate seaboard and in the swampy and alluvial regions of the south, and that more than three-fourths live below 1,000 feet, while below 5,000 feet are found nearly 99 per cent of the inhabitants. At great altitudes there is found only the most trifling proportion.

In the area below 500 feet is included nearly all that part of the population which is engaged in manufacturing and in the foreign commerce of the country and most of that engaged in the culture of cotton, rice, and sugar.

The interval between the 500 feet and 1,500 feet contours comprises the greater part of the prairie states and the grain-producing states of the northwest.

East of the ninety-eighth meridian the contour of 1,500 feet is practically the upper limit of population, all the country lying above that elevation being mountainous.

The population between 2,000 and 5,000 feet is found mainly on the slope of the great western plains. In this region the belt between 2,000 and 3,000 feet is almost everywhere the debatable ground between the arid region of the Cordilleran plateau and the humid region of the Mississippi valley. Above 3,000 feet irrigation is almost universally necessary for success in agricultural operations.

Between 4,000 and 5,000 feet, and more markedly between 5,000 and 6,000 feet, it will be noticed that the population is decidedly in excess of the grade or grades below it. This is mainly due to the fact that the densest settlement at high altitudes in the Cordilleran region is at the eastern base of the Rocky mountains and in the valleys about Great Salt Lake, which regions lie between 4,000 and 6,000 feet. Of these the extensive settlements at the base of the mountains in Colorado are mainly between 5,000 and 6,000 feet.

Above 6,000 feet the population, which is confined, of course, to the Cordilleran region, is almost entirely engaged in the pursuit of mining, and the greater part of it is located in Colorado, New Mexico, Nevada, and California.

GEOGRAPHICAL DISTRIBUTION OF POPULATION. xlix

While the population is increasing numerically in all altitudes, its relative movement is decidedly toward the region of greater altitudes, and is most marked in the country lying between 1,000 and 6,000 feet above the sea.

The density of population is greatest near sea level in the narrow strip along the seaboard which contains our great seaports. The density diminishes gradually and rather uniformly up to 2,000 feet, where the population becomes quite sparse.

The average elevation of the country, excluding Alaska, is about 2,500 feet. The average elevation at which the inhabitants lived, taking cognizance of their distribution, in 1870 was 687 feet; in 1880 it had increased to 739 feet, and in 1890 to 788 feet.

The following table shows the distribution of the foreign born element in altitude above sea level:

DISTRIBUTION OF THE FOREIGN BORN POPULATION IN ACCORDANCE WITH ALTITUDE: 1870 TO 1890.

ALTITUDE IN FEET.	FOREIGN BORN POPULATION IN THOUSANDS.			NUMBER IN EACH 100,000 OF TOTAL FOREIGN BORN POPULATION WITHIN EACH GIVEN ALTITUDE.			CHANGE IN NUMBER IN EACH 100,000.		NUMBER IN EACH 100,000 OF TOTAL FOREIGN BORN POPULATION BELOW EACH ALTITUDE.			FOREIGN BORN POPULATION PER SQUARE MILE.			INCREASE PER SQUARE MILE.	
	1890	1880	1870	1890	1880	1870	1880 to 1890	1870 to 1880	1890	1880	1870	1890	1880	1870	1880 to 1890	1870 to 1880
0 to 100	2,320	1,682	1,431	25,081	25,180	25,705	−99	−525	25,081	25,180	25,705	11.58	8.40	7.14	3.18	1.26
100 to 500	1,321	1,043	938	14,281	15,614	16,849	−1,333	−1,235	39,362	40,794	42,554	3.40	2.69	2.42	0.71	0.27
500 to 1,000	3,500	2,587	2,278	37,838	38,727	40,920	−889	−2,193	77,200	79,521	83,474	6.41	4.74	4.17	1.67	0.57
1,000 to 1,500	1,380	956	690	14,919	14,311	12,394	+608	+1,917	92,119	93,832	95,868	3.49	2.42	1.74	1.07	0.68
1,500 to 2,000	318	166	93	3,438	2,485	1,671	+953	+814	95,557	96,317	97,539	1.33	0.69	0.39	0.64	0.30
2,000 to 3,000	119	65	33	1,287	973	593	+314	+380	96,844	97,290	98,132	0.45	0.25	0.13	0.20	0.12
3,000 to 4,000	48	26	21	519	389	377	+130	+12	97,363	97,679	98,509	0.27	0.15	0.12	0.12	0.03
4,000 to 5,000	57	30	19	616	449	341	+167	+108	97,979	98,128	98,850	0.22	0.12	0.07	0.10	0.05
5,000 to 6,000	114	74	46	1,232	1,108	826	+124	+282	99,211	99,236	99,676	0.52	0.34	0.21	0.18	0.13
6,000 to 7,000	34	19	11	368	284	198	+84	+86	99,579	99,520	99,874	0.21	0.12	0.07	0.09	0.05
7,000 to 8,000	17	10	4	184	150	72	+34	+78	99,763	99,670	99,946	0.19	0.11	0.04	0.08	0.07
8,000 to 9,000	9	7	2	97	105	36	−8	+69	99,860	99,775	99,982	0.22	0.17	0.05	0.05	0.12
9,000 to 10,000	10	12	1	108	180	18	−72	+162	99,968	99,955	100,000	0.52	0.63	0.05	a0.11	0.58
10,000 and over	3	3	......	32	45	......	−13	+45	100,000	100,000	100,000	0.16	0.16	......	......	0.16

a Decrease.

It is seen that about one-fourth of all the foreign born live at an altitude less than 100 feet above the sea, that more than three-fourths live at an altitude less than 1,000 feet, and 99 per cent live below the contour of 6,000 feet. A larger proportion live at low altitudes than is the case with the total population, which is doubtless due to the fact that many of this element live in our large cities, which are mainly upon the seaboard. On the other hand, at great altitudes there are found a larger proportion than of the total population.

The direction of spread of the foreign born element is toward the regions of great altitude. There has been during the past twenty years a diminution in the proportion living below the contour of 1,000 feet and a general increase in the number at great elevations.

The average altitude at which the foreign born element lived in 1890 is 800 feet, which is decidedly greater than that of the total population.

The table on the following page shows the distribution of the negro population in accordance with altitude. From this it is seen that not quite one-fourth of this element live at less than 100 feet, being a smaller proportion than in the case of the foreign born element, but a larger proportion than is the case with the total population. About 70 per cent live at a less altitude than 500 feet, which is a vastly greater proportion than in the case either of the total population or of the foreign born element, while below 1,000 feet we find 94.5 per cent, and below 2,000 feet are found 99 out of every 100 of the negro inhabitants.

No decided movement of the negro population in altitude is perceptible.

The average elevation at which the negro element was living in this country in 1890 is 427 feet. It will be noted that this is greatly below that of the total population and the foreign born element. Indeed, these results emphasize the tendency of the negro element toward low and hot parts of the country.

PROGRESS OF THE NATION.

DISTRIBUTION OF THE NEGRO (*a*) POPULATION IN ACCORDANCE WITH ALTITUDE: 1870 TO 1890.

ALTITUDE IN FEET.	NEGRO POPULATION IN THOUSANDS.			NUMBER IN EACH 100,000 OF TOTAL NEGRO POPULATION.			CHANGE IN NUMBER IN EACH 100,000.		NUMBER IN EACH 100,000 OF TOTAL NEGRO POPULATION BELOW EACH ALTITUDE.			NEGRO POPULATION PER SQUARE MILE.			INCREASE PER SQUARE MILE.	
	1890	1880	1870	1890	1880	1870	1880 to 1890	1870 to 1880	1890	1880	1870	1890	1880	1870	1880 to 1890	1870 to 1880
0 to 100	1,708	1,499	1,144	22,865	22,778	23,443	+87	−665	22,865	22,778	23,443	8.53	7.48	5.71	1.05	1.77
100 to 500	3,536	3,070	2,231	47,336	46,650	45,717	+686	+933	70,201	69,428	69,160	9.11	7.91	5.75	1.20	2.16
500 to 1,000	1,816	1,668	1,962	24,211	25,340	25,881	1,006	592	94,510	94,771	95,041	0.00	0.05	0.01	0.28	0.74
1,000 to 1,500	279	242	169	3,735	3,677	3,463	+58	+214	98,247	98,451	98,504	0.71	0.61	0.43	0.10	0.18
1,500 to 2,000	60	50	38	803	760	779	+43	−19	99,050	99,211	99,283	0.25	0.21	0.16	0.04	0.05
2,000 to 3,000	43	38	27	576	577	554	−1	+23	99,626	99,788	99,837	0.16	0.14	0.10	0.02	0.04
3,000 to 4,000	15	9	6	201	137	123	+64	+14	99,827	99,925	99,960	0.08	0.05	0.03	0.03	0.02
4,000 to 5,000	4	2	1	53	30	20	+23	+10	99,880	99,955	99,980	0.02	0.01	0.00	0.01	0.01
5,000 to 6,000	6	2	1	80	30	20	+50	+10	99,960	99,985	100,000	0.03	0.01	0.00	0.02	0.01
6,000 to 7,000	2	1	....	27	15	....	+12	+15	99,987	100,000	100,000	0.01	0.01	....	....	0.01
7,000 to 8,000	1	....	....	13	....	....	+13	....	100,000	100,000	100,000	0.01	....	....	0.01	....

a Includes all persons of negro descent.

DISTRIBUTION OF POPULATION IN ACCORDANCE WITH MEAN ANNUAL TEMPERATURE.

The great increase in the amount of data concerning the distribution of temperature in the country during the past ten years, produced by the extension of State Weather Services, rendered it advisable to collect material and prepare a new map showing the distribution of the isothermals, and to make therefrom a recomputation of the distribution of population in 1870 and 1880. The necessary data have been freely contributed by the Chief Signal Officer of the Army, General A. W. Greely, and by the several directors of the State Weather Services, to whom this office is under great obligations. The information collected from these various sources has been placed upon a map of the United States, and isothermals have been drawn in accordance with their indications, combined with a knowledge of the relief of the country and the influence of the relief upon temperature. The counties falling between the different isothermal lines have been drawn from the maps in tabular form and the population classified in accordance therewith.

The following table is presented as embracing the results of this investigation. In this table the first column shows the degrees of temperature; the second, third, and fourth columns show a distribution of population in thousands in accordance with the isothermal lines; the fifth, sixth, and seventh columns show the number in each 100,000 of the total population, at the date designated, living between the various isothermal lines; the eighth and ninth columns show the change in the number from census to census under the assumption that the entire population was 100,000; the tenth, eleventh, and twelfth columns show the number of inhabitants, the total population being assumed as 100,000, living under temperature conditions below each of the several grades; the thirteenth, fourteenth, and fifteenth columns show the density of population, that is, the number of inhabitants per square mile in each of the several grades, while the last two columns show the increase in density.

DISTRIBUTION OF THE AGGREGATE POPULATION IN ACCORDANCE WITH MEAN ANNUAL TEMPERATURE: 1870 TO 1890.

DEGREES OF TEMPERATURE.	POPULATION IN THOUSANDS.			NUMBER IN EACH 100,000 OF TOTAL POPULATION WITHIN EACH GRADE.			CHANGE IN NUMBER IN EACH 100,000.		NUMBER IN EACH 100,000 OF TOTAL POPULATION BELOW EACH GRADE.			POPULATION PER SQUARE MILE.			INCREASE PER SQUARE MILE.	
	1890	1880	1870	1890	1880	1870	1880 to 1890	1870 to 1880	1890	1880	1870	1890	1880	1870	1880 to 1890	1870 to 1880
Below 40	1,035	579	354	1,653	1,154	918	+499	+236	1,653	1,154	918	4.70	2.64	1.61	2.06	1.03
40 to 45	5,122	3,718	2,745	8,170	7,413	7,119	+766	+294	9,832	8,567	8,037	12.52	9.11	6.72	3.41	2.39
45 to 50	17,173	13,705	11,177	27,423	27,325	28,986	+98	−1,663	37,255	35,892	37,025	28.61	22.87	18.65	5.74	4.22
50 to 55	19,778	16,248	12,794	31,583	32,395	33,181	−812	−786	68,838	68,287	70,206	31.02	25.55	20.11	5.47	5.44
55 to 60	8,626	7,137	5,291	13,775	14,230	13,722	−455	+508	82,613	82,517	83,928	22.78	18.80	14.01	3.89	4.88
60 to 65	6,178	5,007	3,529	9,866	9,983	9,152	−117	+831	92,479	92,500	93,080	17.80	14.53	10.24	3.36	4.29
65 to 70	3,932	3,141	2,183	6,279	6,262	5,662	+17	+600	98,758	98,762	98,742	14.16	11.33	7.88	2.83	3.45
70 to 75	758	610	479	1,210	1,216	1,242	−6	−26	99,968	99,978	99,984	7.49	6.02	4.72	1.47	1.30
75 and over	20	11	6	32	22	16	+10	+6	100,000	100,000	100,000	3.60	2.01	1.03	1.59	0.98

GEOGRAPHICAL DISTRIBUTION OF POPULATION.

li

A glance at the table will show that in 1870, 1880, and 1890 more than half the population was living under a temperature between 45 and 55 degrees, and that between 45 and 60 degrees were found from 70 to 75 per cent of the inhabitants. Only a trifle over 1 per cent were living where the temperature was greater than 70 degrees, while in the region where the mean annual temperature was above 75 degrees the number of inhabitants was trifling. The number of inhabitants to the square mile not only expresses the density of population, but also gives a comparative measure of the absolute number and the increase in absolute number. The greatest density has been, since 1870, where the temperature ranges from 50 to 55 degrees. From this as a maximum it diminishes rapidly both with an increase and decrease in temperature. The most rapid proportional increase in population has taken place at the two extremes, where it has trebled during the twenty years intervening between 1870 and 1890, while in the same time it has increased but about 50 per cent in the most densely settled group.

The average annual temperature of the territory of the United States, excluding Alaska from consideration, is 53 degrees. The average annual temperature under which the people of the country live, taking into account the density of settlement, is practically the same.

The following table, when contrasted with that showing the distribution of the total population in accordance with mean annual temperature, develops the fact that, as a whole, the foreign born live under temperature conditions considerably lower than the total population. These differences may be summarized in the statement that while the average temperature under which the total population lives is 53 degrees, that of the foreign born is 48 degrees. Nearly 41 per cent live where the temperature ranges from 45 to 50 degrees, while between 40 and 55 degrees of temperature are found more than 86 per cent of the entire foreign born.

DISTRIBUTION OF THE FOREIGN BORN POPULATION IN ACCORDANCE WITH MEAN ANNUAL TEMPERATURE: 1870 TO 1890.

DEGREES OF TEMPERATURE.	FOREIGN BORN POPULATION IN THOUSANDS.			NUMBER IN EACH 100,000 OF TOTAL FOREIGN BORN POPULATION WITHIN EACH GRADE.			CHANGE IN NUMBER IN EACH 100,000.		NUMBER IN EACH 100,000 OF TOTAL FOREIGN BORN POPULATION BELOW EACH GRADE.			FOREIGN BORN POPULATION PER SQUARE MILE.			INCREASE PER SQUARE MILE.	
	1890	1880	1870	1890	1880	1870	1880 to 1890	1870 to 1880	1890	1880	1870	1890	1880	1870	1880 to 1890	1870 to 1880
Below 40	317	137	66	3,427	2,051	1,186	+1,376	+865	3,427	2,051	1,186	1.44	0.62	0.30	0.82	0.32
40 to 45	1,335	886	625	14,432	13,263	11,227	+1,169	+2,036	17,859	15,314	12,413	3.27	2.17	1.53	1.10	0.64
45 to 50	3,787	2,680	2,298	40,941	40,120	41,279	+821	—1,159	58,800	55,434	53,692	6.32	4.47	3.83	1.85	0.64
50 to 55	2,891	2,209	1,982	31,254	33,069	35,603	—1,815	—2,534	90,054	88,503	89,295	4.43	3.38	3.04	1.05	0.34
55 to 60	559	478	371	6,043	7,156	6,664	—1,113	+492	96,097	95,659	95,959	1.54	1.32	1.02	0.22	0.30
60 to 65	117	88	68	1,265	1,317	1,221	—52	+96	97,362	96,976	97,180	0.37	0.28	0.22	0.09	0.06
65 to 70	138	102	70	1,492	1,527	1,257	—35	+270	98,854	98,503	98,437	0.50	0.37	0.25	0.13	0.12
70 to 75	95	94	84	1,027	1,407	1,509	—380	—102	99,881	99,910	99,946	0.04	0.03	0.83	0.01	0.10
75 and over	11	6	3	119	90	54	+29	+36	100,000	100,000	100,000	2.00	1.09	0.54	0.91	0.55

The following table, showing the distribution of the negro element in accordance with the mean annual temperature, presents a sharp contrast to both the preceding tables, and especially to that showing the distribution of the foreign born population. The average temperature under which the negro element exists in this country, namely, 61 degrees, is no less that 8 degrees higher than that of the total population and 13 degrees higher than that of the foreign born population.

DISTRIBUTION OF THE NEGRO (a) POPULATION IN ACCORDANCE WITH MEAN ANNUAL TEMPERATURE: 1870 TO 1890.

DEGREES OF TEMPERATURE.	NEGRO POPULATION IN THOUSANDS.			NUMBER IN EACH 100,000 OF TOTAL NEGRO POPULATION WITHIN EACH GRADE.			CHANGE IN NUMBER IN EACH 100,000.		NUMBER IN EACH 100,000 OF TOTAL NEGRO POPULATION BELOW EACH GRADE.			NEGRO POPULATION PER SQUARE MILE.			INCREASE PER SQUARE MILE.	
	1890	1880	1870	1890	1880	1870	1880 to 1890	1870 to 1880	1890	1880	1870	1890	1880	1870	1880 to 1890	1870 to 1880
Below 40	3	2	1	40	30	20	+10	+10	40	30	20	0.01	0.01	0.00	....	0.01
40 to 45	16	13	10	214	198	205	+16	—7	254	228	225	0.04	0.03	0.02	0.01	0.01
45 to 50	161	136	106	2,155	2,067	2,172	+88	—105	2,409	2,295	2,397	0.27	0.23	0.18	0.04	0.05
50 to 55	702	692	533	10,201	10,515	10,922	—314	—407	12,610	12,810	13,319	1.17	1.06	0.82	0.11	0.24
55 to 60	1,805	1,703	1,331	24,163	25,877	27,275	—1,714	—1,398	36,773	38,687	40,594	4.98	4.70	3.67	0.28	1.03
60 to 65	2,721	2,318	1,614	36,426	35,223	33,074	+1,203	+2,149	73,199	73,910	73,668	8.71	7.42	5.17	1.29	2.25
65 to 70	1,761	1,512	1,113	23,574	22,975	22,808	+599	+167	96,773	96,885	96,476	6.36	5.46	4.02	0.90	1.44
70 to 75	235	202	171	3,146	3,069	3,504	+77	—435	99,919	99,954	99,980	2.32	1.99	1.69	0.33	0.30
75 and over	6	3	1	81	46	20	+35	+26	100,000	100,000	100,000	1.09	0.54	0.18	0.55	0.36

a Includes all persons of negro descent.

lii   PROGRESS OF THE NATION.

The negro population is the most numerous in that region which has a mean annual temperature between 60 and 65 degrees, where there are found 36 per cent of their whole number; between 55 and 60 degrees there are found 24 per cent, and between 65 and 70 degrees there are 24 per cent of the total number. Thus between 55 and 70 degrees there are living 84 per cent of the entire negro element.

DISTRIBUTION OF POPULATION IN ACCORDANCE WITH MEAN ANNUAL RAINFALL.

Through the courtesy of the Chief Signal Officer of the Army, General A. W. Greely, and of the directors of the Weather Services of the various states, the latest and most reliable data regarding the rainfall of the country have been placed at the disposal of this office. In addition to this, a compilation has been made of all other accessible material, including the Smithsonian collections and the records of the state engineer of California. From these various sources data from nearly 2,000 stations have been obtained, platted upon a map of the United States, and the curves of mean annual rainfall, at intervals of 10 inches, sketched in accordance with their indications, supplemented by our knowledge of the relief of the country and its known influence upon rainfall.

From the map thus prepared the counties falling between the different curves of mean annual rainfall were drawn off in lists. In cases where the county was cut in parts by a curve, due weight was given in the partition of the county to any inequality in distribution of population. The population was then distributed by counties, in accordance with the lists. The result is shown in the table appended:

DISTRIBUTION OF THE AGGREGATE POPULATION IN ACCORDANCE WITH MEAN ANNUAL RAINFALL: 1870 TO 1890.

INCHES OF RAINFALL.	POPULATION IN THOUSANDS.			NUMBER IN EACH 100,000 OF TOTAL POPULATION WITHIN EACH GRADE.			CHANGE IN NUMBER IN EACH 100,000.		NUMBER IN EACH 100,000 OF TOTAL POPULATION BELOW EACH GRADE.			POPULATION PER SQUARE MILE.			INCREASE PER SQUARE MILE.	
	1890	1880	1870	1890	1880	1870	1880 to 1890	1870 to 1880	1890	1880	1870	1890	1880	1870	1880 to 1890	1870 to 1880
Below 10	188	139	74	300	277	192	+23	+85	300	277	192	0.76	0.56	0.30	0.20	0.26
10 to 20	1,636	695	386	2,613	1,386	949	+1,227	+437	2,913	1,663	1,141	1.84	0.78	0.41	1.06	0.37
20 to 30	3,781	2,178	736	6,038	4,342	1,909	+1,696	+2,433	8,951	6,005	3,050	8.16	4.70	1.59	3.46	3.11
30 to 40	21,353	17,539	14,129	34,098	34,969	36,643	−871	−1,674	43,049	40,974	39,693	43.19	35.47	28.58	7.72	6.89
40 to 50	24,710	20,556	16,472	39,459	40,984	42,720	−1,525	−1,736	82,508	81,958	82,413	59.08	49.15	39.39	9.93	9.76
50 to 60	10,122	8,303	6,251	16,164	16,734	16,212	−570	+522	98,672	98,692	98,625	25.10	20.87	15.54	4.29	5.33
60 to 70	798	638	524	1,274	1,272	1,359	+2	−87	99,946	99,964	99,984	18.20	14.55	11.95	3.65	2.60
70 and over	34	18	6	54	36	16	+18	+20	100,000	100,000	100,000	3.98	2.11	0.70	1.87	1.41

In this table the first column shows the grades, expressed in inches of rainfall; the second, third, and fourth columns show the population in thousands found in each grade in 1890, 1880, and 1870; the fifth, sixth, and seventh columns show the number in each 100,000 of the population in each of these grades at the periods under consideration; the eighth and ninth columns show the increase or decrease in number; the tenth, eleventh, and twelfth columns show the number of inhabitants in each 100,000 below each grade, and therefore are cumulative columns; the thirteenth, fourteenth, and fifteenth columns show the population per square mile in each grade in 1890, 1880, and 1870, and the last two columns show the increase in population per square mile.

It will be noticed that the main body of the population of the country inhabits the region in which the annual rainfall is between 30 and 50 inches, nearly three-fourths of the inhabitants being found there. On either side, as the rainfall increases or diminishes, the population diminishes rapidly. It will be seen further that the arid region of the west, where the rainfall is less than 20 inches, a region which comprises two-fifths of the entire area of the country, contains at present less than 3 per cent of the population.

The greatest density of population is in the area enjoying from 40 to 50 inches of annual rainfall, the average of this region being 59.08 inhabitants to the square mile. Next to that is the area having from 30 to 40 inches, where the density is 43.19. The density of population has increased rapidly in these regions. It is apparent, however, that the most rapid increase, as expressed by density of population, is where the rainfall ranges from 20 to 30 inches; that is, in the eastern portion of the Great Plains ranging from Texas to Dakota, where the density has increased in twenty years from 1.59 to 8.16.

The average annual rainfall upon the surface of the United States, as deduced from the map previously mentioned, is 29.6 inches. The average annual rainfall with relation to the population, deduced by giving weight to each area of country in proportion to the number of its inhabitants, was, in 1870, 42.5 inches; in 1880 it had diminished to 42 inches, and in 1890 to 41.4 inches, the diminution being caused mainly by the settlement of the Great Plains and the arid regions of the west.

GEOGRAPHICAL DISTRIBUTION OF POPULATION. liii

The following table shows the distribution of the foreign born element with reference to rainfall in 1890, 1880, and 1870:

DISTRIBUTION OF THE FOREIGN BORN POPULATION IN ACCORDANCE WITH MEAN ANNUAL RAINFALL: 1870 TO 1890.

INCHES OF RAINFALL.	FOREIGN BORN POPULATION IN THOUSANDS.			NUMBER IN EACH 100,000 OF TOTAL FOREIGN BORN POPULATION WITHIN EACH GRADE.			CHANGE IN NUMBER IN EACH 100,000.		NUMBER IN EACH 100,000 OF TOTAL FOREIGN BORN POPULATION BELOW EACH GRADE.			FOREIGN BORN POPULATION PER SQUARE MILE.			INCREASE PER SQUARE MILE.	
	1890	1880	1870	1890	1880	1870	1880 to 1890	1870 to 1880	1890	1880	1870	1890	1880	1870	1880 to 1890	1870 to 1880
Below 10	51	49	28	551	734	503	−183	+231	551	734	503	0.21	0.20	0.11	0.01	0.09
10 to 20	368	164	95	3,979	2,455	1,706	+1,524	+749	4,530	3,189	2,209	0.41	0.18	0.11	0.23	0.07
20 to 30	955	596	265	10,324	8,922	4,760	+1,402	+4,162	14,854	12,111	6,969	2.13	1.33	0.59	0.80	0.74
30 to 40	3,852	2,904	2,577	41,643	43,473	46,291	−1,830	−2,818	56,497	55,584	53,260	8.04	6.06	5.38	1.98	0.68
40 to 50	3,800	2,807	2,455	41,081	42,021	44,099	−940	−2,078	97,578	97,605	97,359	9.09	6.71	5.87	2.38	0.84
50 to 60	144	96	82	1,557	1,437	1,473	+120	−36	99,135	99,042	98,832	0.36	0.24	0.20	0.12	0.04
60 to 70	69	58	64	746	868	1,150	−122	−282	99,881	99,910	99,982	1.57	1.32	1.46	0.25	a0.14
70 and over	11	6	1	119	90	18	+29	+72	100,000	100,000	100,000	1.29	0.70	0.12	0.59	0.58

a Decrease.

It will be seen that by far the greater proportion of the foreign born population lives where the rainfall ranges from 30 to 50 inches annually, the proportion ranging from 90 per cent in 1870 down to about 83 per cent in 1890. As to the proportion of the foreign born living within these limits in recent years, it has not increased in the regions where the rainfall is greater, but where it is less, that is, in the western states and territories. The proportion of the foreign born living under a rainfall of 20 to 30 inches has increased in twenty years from less than 5 per cent up to more than 10 per cent. It has increased in approximately the same proportion in those regions where the rainfall is still less, that is, between 10 and 20 inches.

The following table shows the distribution of the negro element in respect to mean annual rainfall:

DISTRIBUTION OF THE NEGRO (a) POPULATION IN ACCORDANCE WITH MEAN ANNUAL RAINFALL: 1870 TO 1890.

INCHES OF RAINFALL.	NEGRO POPULATION IN THOUSANDS.			NUMBER IN EACH 100,000 OF TOTAL NEGRO POPULATION WITHIN EACH GRADE.			CHANGE IN NUMBER IN EACH 100,000.		NUMBER IN EACH 100,000 OF TOTAL NEGRO POPULATION BELOW EACH GRADE.			NEGRO POPULATION PER SQUARE MILE.			INCREASE PER SQUARE MILE.	
	1890	1880	1870	1890	1880	1870	1880 to 1890	1870 to 1880	1890	1880	1870	1890	1880	1870	1880 to 1890	1870 to 1880
Below 10	2	1	......	27	15	......	+12	+15	27	15	......	0.01	0.00	......	0.01	......
10 to 20	17	7	3	227	107	62	+120	+45	254	122	62	0.02	0.01	0.00	0.01	0.01
20 to 30	29	16	7	388	243	143	+145	+100	642	365	205	0.06	0.04	0.02	0.02	0.02
30 to 40	385	344	252	5,154	5,227	5,164	−73	+63	5,796	5,592	5,369	0.80	0.72	0.53	0.08	0.19
40 to 50	2,352	2,168	1,676	31,486	32,043	34,344	−1,457	−1,401	37,282	38,535	39,713	5.62	5.18	4.01	0.44	1.17
50 to 60	4,481	3,855	2,780	59,987	58,578	56,967	+1,409	+1,611	97,269	97,113	96,680	11.14	9.58	6.91	1.56	2.67
60 and over	204	190	162	2,731	2,887	3,320	−150	−433	100,000	100,000	100,000	3.90	3.63	3.09	0.27	0.54

a Includes all persons of negro descent.

The above table shows that the vast majority of the negro race, more than nine-tenths of their whole number, live where the rainfall ranges from 40 to 60 inches, and that no less than 60 per cent live where the rainfall is between 50 and 60 inches. Their habitat is thus again strongly contrasted with that of the inhabitants of foreign birth.

While there is little movement of this race perceptible in the above table, what little thus appears is in the direction of a region of greater rainfall. Thus in twenty years the negro element living where the rainfall was between 40 and 50 inches has materially diminished, while it has materially increased in the region having between 50 and 60 inches.

PROGRESS OF THE NATION.

liv

DISTRIBUTION OF POPULATION IN ACCORDANCE WITH MEAN RELATIVE HUMIDITY OF THE ATMOSPHERE.

The atmosphere along the Atlantic, Gulf, and Lake coasts, and the entire Pacific coast is heavily charged with moisture. It is especially so upon the coast of Oregon and Washington, where the atmosphere is more highly charged with moisture than elsewhere within our territory. The high mountain regions of the Appalachian and to a considerable extent those of the Rocky mountain ranges also have a moist atmosphere. The moisture is less in the Piedmont region east of the Appalachians and in the Upper Mississippi valley. Passing across the prairies and the Great Plains, the amount of moisture in the atmosphere diminishes still more, while the minimum is reached in the Great Basin, in Utah, Nevada, southern Arizona, and southeastern California. In a general way, the amount of moisture in the atmosphere increases and decreases with the rainfall, but this is not always the case. The upper lake region, with an atmosphere as moist as that of Washington city, has a much smaller rainfall. The coast of southern California, with a deficient rainfall, has as moist an atmosphere as the Atlantic coast.

In the following table, showing this distribution, the population is given to the nearest thousands, as the results aimed at are merely general relations. The first column defines the groups, expressed in percentages of saturation; the second, third, and fourth columns, the absolute number of inhabitants in thousands in the various groups at the Eleventh, Tenth, and Ninth censuses; the fifth, sixth, and seventh columns, the number in each 100,000 of the total population within each group; the eighth and ninth columns, the change in number in each 100,000 of the total population; the tenth, eleventh, and twelfth columns, the number in each 100,000 of the total population below each group; the thirteenth, fourteenth, and fifteenth columns show the density of population, that is, the number of inhabitants per square mile, while the last two columns show the increase in density.

DISTRIBUTION OF THE AGGREGATE POPULATION IN ACCORDANCE WITH MEAN RELATIVE HUMIDITY: 1870 TO 1890.

PERCENTAGE OF SATURATION.	POPULATION IN THOUSANDS.			NUMBER IN EACH 100,000 OF TOTAL POPULATION WITHIN EACH GROUP.			CHANGE IN NUMBER IN EACH 100,000.		NUMBER IN EACH 100,000 OF TOTAL POPULATION BELOW EACH GROUP.			POPULATION PER SQUARE MILE.			INCREASE PER SQUARE MILE.	
	1890	1880	1870	1890	1880	1870	1880 to 1890	1870 to 1880	1890	1880	1870	1890	1880	1870	1880 to 1890	1870 to 1880
Below 50.........	309	219	137	493	437	355	+56	+82	493	437	355	1.14	0.81	0.50	0.33	0.31
50 to 55	433	202	91	692	403	236	+289	+167	1,185	840	591	1.67	0.78	0.35	0.89	0.43
55 to 60	291	134	61	465	267	158	+198	+109	1,650	1,107	749	1.12	0.52	0.24	0.60	0.28
60 to 65	868	439	136	1,386	875	353	+511	+522	3,036	1,982	1,102	3.29	1.66	0.52	1.63	1.14
65 to 70	22,969	19,279	14,388	36,679	38,438	37,315	−1,759	+1,123	39,715	40,420	38,417	31.18	26.17	19.53	5.01	6.64
70 to 75	34,067	27,280	21,885	54,401	54,390	56,759	+11	−2,369	94,116	94,810	95,176	39.63	31.73	25.46	7.90	6.27
75 to 80	3,341	2,403	1,730	5,335	4,791	4,487	+544	+304	99,451	99,601	99,663	14.76	10.61	7.64	4.15	2.97
80 and over......	344	200	130	549	399	337	+150	+62	100,000	100,000	100,000	5.53	3.21	2.00	2.32	1.12

A glance at this table shows that nearly all the population breathe an atmosphere containing 65 to 75 per cent of its full capacity of moisture; that is, the atmosphere is from two-thirds to three-fourths saturated. In 1890, 57,036,000 out of 62,622,250 were found in this region; in 1880, 46,559,000 out of 50,155,783, and in 1870, 36,273,000 out of 38,558,371. The number of inhabitants living in a drier atmosphere was at each census comparatively trifling, numbering in 1870 less than 500,000, and in 1890 less than 2,000,000. In the moister atmosphere were found larger numbers scattered along the Gulf coast and the shores of Washington and Oregon.

The most rapid increase is found near the top and bottom of the scale, and particularly in the more arid region, where the population has nearly doubled during each of the last two periods.

GEOGRAPHICAL DISTRIBUTION OF POPULATION.   lv

The following table shows that with the persons of foreign birth nearly two-thirds breathe an atmosphere which has a relative humidity between 70 and 75 per cent, and that nearly one-fourth of them are found where the atmosphere is charged to the extent of 65 to 70 per cent, the proportion of this element of the population being trifling elsewhere:

DISTRIBUTION OF THE FOREIGN BORN POPULATION IN ACCORDANCE WITH MEAN RELATIVE HUMIDITY: 1870 TO 1890.

PERCENTAGE OF SATURATION.	FOREIGN BORN POPULATION IN THOUSANDS.			NUMBER IN EACH 100,000 OF TOTAL FOREIGN BORN POPULATION WITHIN EACH GROUP.			CHANGE IN NUMBER IN EACH 100,000.		NUMBER IN EACH 100,000 OF TOTAL FOREIGN BORN POPULATION BELOW EACH GROUP.			FOREIGN BORN POPULATION PER SQUARE MILE.			INCREASE PER SQUARE MILE.	
	1890	1880	1870	1890	1880	1870	1880 to 1890	1870 to 1880	1890	1880	1870	1890	1880	1870	1880 to 1890	1870 to 1880
Below 50	82	72	47	887	1,078	844	−191	+234	887	1,078	844	0.30	0.27	0.17	0.03	0.10
50 to 55	72	30	14	778	449	251	+329	+198	1,665	1,527	1,095	0.28	0.12	0.05	0.16	0.07
55 to 60	72	30	14	778	449	251	+329	+198	2,443	1,976	1,346	0.28	0.12	0.05	0.16	0.07
60 to 65	132	81	40	1,427	1,213	719	+214	+494	3,870	3,189	2,065	0.50	0.31	0.15	0.19	0.16
65 to 70	2,183	1,820	1,464	23,000	27,246	26,298	−3,646	+948	27,470	30,435	28,363	2.90	2.47	1.90	0.43	0.48
70 to 75	5,897	4,135	3,624	63,752	61,901	65,098	+1,851	−3,197	91,222	92,336	93,461	6.86	4.81	4.22	2.05	0.59
75 to 80	718	452	321	7,762	6,766	5,766	+996	+1,000	98,984	99,102	99,227	3.17	2.00	1.42	1.17	0.58
80 and over	94	60	43	1,016	898	773	+118	+125	100,000	100,000	100,000	1.51	0.96	0.69	0.55	0.27

The following table, showing the distribution of the negro population in respect to atmospheric moisture, develops the fact that no less than 95 per cent, or nineteen-twentieths, live where the relative humidity is between 65 and 75 per cent, the proportion elsewhere being trifling:

DISTRIBUTION OF THE NEGRO(a) POPULATION IN ACCORDANCE WITH MEAN RELATIVE HUMIDITY: 1870 TO 1890.

PERCENTAGE OF SATURATION.	NEGRO POPULATION IN THOUSANDS.			NUMBER IN EACH 100,000 OF TOTAL NEGRO POPULATION WITHIN EACH GROUP.			CHANGE IN NUMBER IN EACH 100,000.		NUMBER IN EACH 100,000 OF TOTAL NEGRO POPULATION BELOW EACH GROUP.			NEGRO POPULATION PER SQUARE MILE.			INCREASE PER SQUARE MILE.	
	1890	1880	1870	1890	1880	1870	1880 to 1890	1870 to 1880	1890	1880	1870	1890	1880	1870	1880 to 1890	1870 to 1880
Below 50	3	2	1	40	30	20	+10	+10	40	30	20	0.01	0.01	0.00	......	0.01
50 to 55	8	4	2	107	61	41	+46	+20	147	91	61	0.03	0.02	0.01	0.01	0.01
55 to 60	8	4	2	107	61	41	+46	+20	254	152	102	0.03	0.02	0.01	0.01	0.01
60 to 65	9	5	2	121	76	41	+45	+35	375	228	143	0.03	0.02	0.01	0.01	0.01
65 to 70	2,993	2,779	2,054	40,007	42,228	42,091	−2,161	+137	40,442	42,456	42,234	4.06	3.77	2.79	0.29	0.98
70 to 75	4,152	3,537	2,619	55,582	53,746	53,668	+1,836	+78	96,024	96,202	95,902	4.83	4.11	3.05	0.72	1.06
75 to 80	295	249	199	3,949	3,783	4,078	+166	−295	99,973	99,985	99,980	1.30	1.10	0.88	0.20	0.22
80 and over	2	1	1	27	15	20	+12	−5	100,000	100,000	100,000	0.03	0.02	0.02	0.01	......

a Includes all persons of negro descent.

DISTRIBUTION OF POPULATION IN ACCORDANCE WITH LATITUDE AND LONGITUDE.

Three tables are given on the following pages, the first showing the population of the country in 1890 by thousands, distributed by square degrees; that is, by areas included between consecutive parallels and consecutive meridians. It is in effect a population map of the country, showing not only the total population of each square degree, but an approximation to the relative density of population in each square degree. The magnitude of the numbers betrays the whereabouts of the great centers of population, as New York, Chicago, etc., while on the other hand, the sparseness of population upon the Cordilleran plateau is shown in an equally forcible manner.

The second and third tables are abstracts from the first table. The second table shows the distribution of the population in accordance with latitude, giving first the absolute population in thousands between each two consecutive parallels across the country in 1890, 1880, and 1870; the percentages of increase in population between each two parallels; the number of inhabitants in each group, upon the assumption that the total population was 100,000 at each of these three censuses; the number in 100,000 north of each parallel of latitude; the number of inhabitants per square mile; and the increase or decrease in the density of population.

The third table presents similar facts regarding the distribution of population in accordance with longitude, arranged in a similar manner.

PROGRESS OF THE NATION.

lvi

POPULATION IN EACH SQUARE DEGREE

DEGREES OF LONGITUDE.	DEGREES OF LATITUDE.											
	48-49	47-48	46-47	45-46	44-45	43-44	42-43	41-42	40-41	39-40	38-39	37-38
Total	144	388	547	1,064	2,134	3,235	6,655	7,506	9,832	7,284	4,606	3,528
67- 68		5	5	27	22							
68- 69		5	24	47	69							
69- 70		5	13	25	126	33		3				
70- 71			3	20	91	153	460	124				
71- 72				9	92	162	1,233	915				
72- 73					123	120	345	455	31			
73- 74					111	150	373	465	2,573			
74- 75					75	72	273	311	1,080	196	1	
75- 76					75	216	200	354	554	1,414	141	38
76- 77					21	155	309	252	543	727	118	114
77- 78						223	207	153	198	249	366	242
78- 79						130	426	142	244	138	129	137
79- 80						12	101	209	539	141	63	156
80- 81							8	288	602	172	73	100
81- 82								448	291	219	140	78
82- 83					3	65	60	122	231	252	207	83
83- 84			1	11	34	161	395	305	237	256	170	91
84- 85			12	30	24	161	197	217	268	671	303	181
85- 86			8	13	62	169	210	217	252	222	374	140
86- 87			9	7	29	63	60	105	232	286	158	143
87- 88		1	37	49	73	156	384	950	134	209	235	186
88- 89		16	37	27	141	201	311	218	150	165	150	152
89- 90			16	28	80	113	182	135	180	184	184	155
90- 91			22	18	72	98	150	217	156	162	615	77
91- 92	5	6	14	42	101	115	121	134	187	138	92	57
92- 93	10	22	19	56	124	105	107	142	122	134	112	74
93- 94		1	10	212	275	79	92	173	116	151	121	140
94- 95		1	19	71	82	55	84	114	124	348	150	167
95- 96	4	17	42	50	45	53	90	185	118	168	139	123
96- 97	13	32	32	29	35	61	88	241	167	83	61	79
97- 98	31	31	25	19	30	48	41	80	105	90	95	107
98- 99	18	12	12	25	22	26	21	41	94	67	54	52
99-100	6	4	6	14	11	5	11	32	52	40	24	17
100-101	5	3	5	3	6		6	10	30	20	12	11
101-102	2	1	3				3	5	20	19	9	6
102-103			2		2	1	14	6	8	42	2	3
103-104	1		1	1	18	11	13	8	7	41	4	10
104-105			1	1	1	2	4	8	10	58	42	19
105-106			1	1	1	2	5	9	16	29	17	11
106-107			1	1	2	1	2	4	5	25	9	10
107-108			1		1	1	1	2	1	9	12	7
108-109	1	1	2		1		1	2	1	4	8	5
109-110	1	1	3	2			1	2	2	1	1	
110-111			3	4	5	1	2	2	2	7	2	3	1
111-112			7	7	6	3	4	8	47	55	21	7	2
112-113			12	17	22	3	4	7	2	27	4	4	2
113-114	2	4	8	7	1	3	2	5	2	3	3	5
114-115	1	1	2	2	1	3	3	1	1			
115-116	1	4	2	1	2	3	1	1	1	1		
116-117	2	3	13	1	5	8	1	1	2	2		
117-118	2	44	25	9	5	1	1	1	1	1		1
118-119	2	10	14	15	6	1	1	1	1	1	1	5
119-120		3	2	6	4	2	1	3	3	17	4	10
120-121	3	6	4	10	2	1	1	4	4	30	30	17
121-122	23	53	15	25	5	1	1	5	7	36	82	146
122-123	9	56	27	96	34	8	11	8	13	22	62	350
123-124	1	14	20	25	20	11	9	11	12	14	12	
124-125	1	4	1		2	5	2	3	7			

GEOGRAPHICAL DISTRIBUTION OF POPULATION.

lvii

IN 1890 TO THE NEAREST THOUSAND.

					DEGREES OF LATITUDE—continued.								DEGREES OF LONGITUDE.
36–37	35–36	34–35	33–34	32–33	31–32	30–31	29–30	28–29	27–28	26–27	25–26	24–25	
2,660	2,490	2,239	2,503	2,282	1,362	1,101	844	109	61	22	7	10	
													67– 68
													68– 69
													69– 70
													70– 71
													71– 72
													72– 73
													73– 74
													74– 75
8	5												75– 76
178	57	16											76– 77
136	135	62	1										77– 78
170	149	70	10										78– 79
174	115	136	90	65									79– 80
143	184	144	142	64				4	2	1			80– 81
122	153	170	140	102	74	43	38	25	9	2		19	81– 82
164	133	100	154	71	40	39	47	19	12				82– 83
170	103	136	175	146	48	84	4						83– 84
90	122	122	271	153	102	71	2						84– 85
117	132	145	166	146	123	28	1						85– 86
205	187	137	152	158	65	10							86– 87
141	111	102	96	164	65	32							87– 88
153	131	104	156	113	48	61							88– 89
115	237	129	118	101	53	31	17						89– 90
79	76	116	120	144	121	83	313						90– 91
72	83	95	68	85	95	148	57						91– 92
56	75	103	65	79	57	67	12						92– 93
95	88	58	84	105	49	26	3						93– 94
77	70	20	74	96	53	29	24						94– 95
			112	87	76	64	69	3					95– 96
5			132	154	100	119	74	10					96– 97
11	32		75	114	88	107	82	23	11	7	7		97– 98
5		2	25	46	51	30	80	11	13	11			98– 99
	1	10	10	18	17	13	12	10	14	1			99–100
2	2	3	2	8	6	2	6	4					100–101
1	2	1	1	2	3	1	1						101–102
1	1				1	1							102–103
6	7	6	1	1	1	1	1						103–104
6	7	6	1	1	6	3	1						104–105
13	16	5	2	3	5	2							105–106
7	10	5	3	3	2								106–107
6	7	3	3	5	2								107–108
1	5	3	4	4	2								108–109
1	1	1	3	4	3								109–110
				4	3	2							110–111
1	2	2	3	4	3								111–112
1	2	2	4	5	1								112–113
		1	2	3									113–114
1	1	3	1	4									114–115
	3	5	3										115–116
1	5	5	3	3									116–117
1	4	23	17	18									117–118
14	6	76	10										118–119
16	8	14											119–120
15	17	8											120–121
20	5												121–122
													122–123
													123–124
													124–125

lviii   PROGRESS OF THE NATION.

DISTRIBUTION OF THE AGGREGATE POPULATION IN ACCORDANCE WITH LATITUDE: 1870 TO 1890.

DEGREES OF LATITUDE.	POPULATION IN THOUSANDS.			PER CENT OF INCREASE.		NUMBER IN EACH 100,000 OF TOTAL POPULATION WITHIN THE PARALLELS.			NUMBER IN EACH 100,000 OF TOTAL POPULATION NORTH OF EACH PARALLEL.			POPULATION PER SQUARE MILE.			INCREASE PER SQUARE MILE.	
	1890	1880	1870	1880 to 1890	1870 to 1880	1890	1880	1870	1890	1880	1870	1890	1880	1870	1880 to 1890	1870 to 1880
48–49	144	17	6	747.06	183.33	230	34	15	230	34	15	1.51	0.18	0.06	1.33	0.12
47–48	388	79	30	391.14	163.33	620	157	78	850	191	93	3.49	0.71	0.27	2.78	0.44
46–47	547	215	84	154.42	155.95	874	429	218	1,724	620	311	4.15	1.63	0.64	2.52	0.99
45–46	1,064	483	249	120.29	93.98	1,699	963	646	3,423	1,583	957	7.66	3.48	1.79	4.18	1.69
44–45	2,134	1,768	1,354	20.70	30.58	3,408	3,525	3,512	6,831	5,108	4,469	13.27	10.99	8.42	2.28	2.57
43–44	3,235	2,678	2,197	20.80	21.89	5,166	5,339	5,698	11,997	10,447	10,167	19.79	16.38	13.44	3.41	2.94
42–43	6,655	5,358	4,485	24.21	19.46	10,627	10,683	11,632	22,624	21,130	21,799	38.71	31.17	26.09	7.54	5.08
41–42	7,506	5,938	4,716	26.41	25.91	11,986	11,839	12,231	34,610	32,969	34,030	40.79	32.27	25.63	8.52	6.64
40–41	9,832	7,803	6,177	25.04	27.29	15,701	15,677	16,020	50,311	48,646	50,050	53.36	42.67	33.52	10.69	9.15
39–40	7,284	6,265	4,994	16.26	25.45	11,632	12,491	12,952	61,943	61,137	63,002	39.96	34.37	27.30	5.59	6.98
38–39	4,606	3,996	3,129	15.27	27.71	7,355	7,967	8,115	69,298	69,104	71,117	25.58	22.20	17.38	3.38	4.82
37–38	3,528	2,831	2,017	24.62	40.36	5,634	5,644	5,231	74,932	74,748	76,348	19.01	15.97	11.38	3.04	4.59
36–37	2,660	2,170	1,644	22.58	32.00	4,248	4,326	4,264	79,180	79,074	80,612	15.08	12.30	9.32	2.78	2.98
35–36	2,490	2,078	1,594	19.83	30.36	3,976	4,143	4,134	83,156	83,217	84,746	14.10	11.77	9.03	2.33	2.74
34–35	2,239	1,805	1,282	24.04	40.80	3,575	3,599	3,325	86,731	86,816	88,071	13.29	10.71	7.61	2.58	3.10
33–34	2,503	1,940	1,291	29.02	50.27	3,997	3,868	3,348	90,728	90,684	91,419	10.15	12.52	8.33	3.63	4.19
32–33	2,282	1,939	1,383	17.69	40.20	3,644	3,866	3,587	94,372	94,550	95,006	10.18	13.75	9.81	2.43	3.94
31–32	1,362	1,060	747	28.49	41.90	2,175	2,113	1,937	96,547	96,663	96,943	12.03	9.36	6.60	2.67	2.76
30–31	1,101	865	595	27.28	45.38	1,758	1,725	1,543	98,305	98,388	98,486	11.05	9.30	6.46	2.56	2.93
29–30	844	673	505	25.41	33.27	1,348	1,342	1,310	99,653	99,730	99,796	15.35	12.24	9.18	3.11	3.06
28–29	109	61	39	78.69	56.41	174	122	101	99,827	99,852	99,897	4.10	2.30	1.47	1.80	0.83
27–28	61	36	18	69.44	100.00	97	72	47	99,924	99,924	99,944	3.03	1.70	0.80	1.24	0.90
26–27	22	21	12	4.76	75.00	35	42	31	99,959	99,966	99,975	1.44	1.38	0.79	0.06	0.59
25–26	7	7	6	....	16.67	11	14	15	99,970	99,980	99,990	1.74	1.74	1.49	....	0.25
24–25	19	10	4	90.00	150.00	30	20	10	100,000	100,000	100,000	234.57	123.46	49.38	111.11	74.08

GEOGRAPHICAL DISTRIBUTION OF POPULATION.

lix

DISTRIBUTION OF THE AGGREGATE POPULATION IN ACCORDANCE WITH LONGITUDE: 1870 TO 1890.

DEGREES OF LONGITUDE.	POPULATION IN THOUSANDS.			PER CENT OF INCREASE.		NUMBER IN EACH 100,000 OF TOTAL POPULATION WITHIN THE MERIDIANS.			NUMBER IN EACH 100,000 OF TOTAL POPULATION EAST OF EACH MERIDIAN.			POPULATION PER SQUARE MILE.			INCREASE PER SQUARE MILE.	
	1890	1880	1870	1880 to 1890	1870 to 1880	1890	1880	1870	1890	1880	1870	1890	1880	1870	1880 to 1890	1870 to 1880
67- 68.............	59	53	49	11.32	8.16	94	106	127	94	106	127	15.40	13.89	12.84	1.57	1.05
68- 69.............	145	130	125	11.54	4.00	232	259	324	326	365	451	14.54	13.04	12.54	1.50	0.50
69- 70.............	205	202	201	1.49	0.50	327	403	521	653	768	972	18.58	18.30	18.21	0.28	0.09
70- 71.............	851	606	547	40.43	10.79	1,359	1,208	1,419	2,012	1,976	2,391	83.01	59.11	53.36	23.90	5.75
71- 72.............	1,907	1,703	1,434	11.57	22.94	3,141	3,515	3,719	5,153	5,491	6,110	151.32	135.63	110.32	15.69	25.31
72- 73.............	1,074	921	824	16.61	11.77	1,715	1,836	2,137	6,868	7,327	8,247	78.83	67.60	60.48	11.23	7.12
73- 74.............	3,672	3,037	2,404	20.91	26.33	5,864	6,055	6,235	12,732	13,382	14,482	245.55	203.09	160.76	42.46	42.33
74- 75.............	2,008	1,604	1,454	25.19	10.32	3,206	3,198	3,771	15,938	16,580	18,253	100.16	80.01	72.53	20.15	7.48
75- 76.............	3,005	2,591	2,196	15.98	17.99	4,799	5,166	5,695	20,737	21,746	23,948	110.82	95.56	80.99	15.26	14.57
76- 77.............	2,490	2,220	1,902	12.16	16.72	3,976	4,426	4,933	24,713	26,172	28,881	76.41	68.12	58.37	8.29	9.75
77- 78.............	1,972	1,761	1,488	11.98	18.35	3,149	3,511	3,859	27,862	29,683	32,740	59.50	53.13	44.89	6.37	8.24
78- 79.:...........	1,745	1,376	1,103	26.82	24.75	2,787	2,743	2,861	30,649	32,426	35,601	49.31	38.88	31.17	10.43	7.71
79- 80.............	1,801	1,670	1,308	7.84	27.68	2,876	3,330	3,392	33,525	35,756	38,993	50.73	47.04	36.84	3.69	10.20
80- 81.............	1,936	1,559	1,213	24.18	28.52	3,092	3,108	3,146	36,617	38,864	42,139	40.24	32.40	25.21	7.84	7.19
81- 82.............	2,073	1,683	1,277	23.17	31.79	3,310	3,356	3,312	39,927	42,220	45,451	34.65	28.13	21.34	6.52	6.79
82- 83.............	1,802	1,572	1,239	20.36	26.88	3,021	3,134	3,213	42,948	45,354	48,664	33.08	27.48	21.66	5.60	5.82
83- 84.............	2,527	2,049	1,583	23.33	29.44	4,035	4,085	4,105	46,983	49,439	52,769	44.81	36.34	28.07	8.47	8.27
84- 85.............	2,997	2,578	2,054	16.25	25.51	4,786	5,140	5,327	51,769	54,579	58,096	49.16	42.29	33.69	6.87	8.60
85- 86.............	2,525	2,181	1,762	15.77	23.78	4,032	4,348	4,570	55,801	58,927	62,666	42.26	36.51	29.49	5.75	7.02
86- 87.............	2,126	1,831	1,484	16.11	23.38	3,395	3,651	3,849	59,196	62,578	66,515	42.10	36.26	29.39	5.84	6.87
87- 88.............	3,125	2,258	1,664	38.40	35.70	4,990	4,502	4,316	64,186	67,080	70,831	59.91	43.29	31.90	16.62	11.39
88- 89.............	2,334	2,052	1,712	13.74	19.86	3,727	4,091	4,440	67,913	71,171	75,271	37.23	32.73	27.31	4.50	5.42
89- 90.............	2,007	1,855	1,597	11.43	16.16	3,301	3,698	4,142	71,214	74,869	79,413	32.10	28.80	24.80	3.30	4.00
90- 91.............	2,648	2,296	1,852	18.43	20.73	4,229	4,458	4,803	75,443	79,327	84,216	39.11	33.03	27.36	6.08	5.67
91- 92.............	1,715	1,480	1,195	15.88	23.85	2,739	2,951	3,099	78,182	82,278	87,315	25.10	21.66	17.49	3.44	4.17
92- 93.............	1,541	1,264	967	21.91	30.71	2,461	2,520	2,508	80,643	84,798	89,823	22.26	18.26	13.97	4.00	4.29
93- 94.............	1,878	1,401	946	34.05	48.10	2,999	2,793	2,453	83,642	87,591	92,276	27.07	20.10	13.63	6.88	6.56
94- 95.............	1,667	1,261	807	32.20	56.26	2,662	2,514	2,093	86,304	90,105	94,369	23.41	17.71	11.33	5.70	6.38
95- 96.............	1,399	995	516	40.60	92.83	2,234	1,984	1,338	88,538	92,089	95,707	18.77	13.35	6.92	5.42	6.43
96- 97.............	1,515	900	375	68.33	140.00	2,419	1,794	973	90,957	93,883	96,680	19.72	11.71	4.88	8.01	6.83
97- 98.............	1,259	722	207	74.38	248.79	2,010	1,440	537	92,967	95,323	97,217	14.90	8.55	2.45	6.35	6.10
98- 99.............	724	367	59	97.28	522.03	1,156	732	153	94,123	96,055	97,370	8.46	4.29	0.69	4.17	3.60
99-100.............	328	127	13	158.27	876.92	524	253	34	94,647	96,308	97,404	4.05	1.57	0.16	2.48	1.41
100-101.............	146	48	5	204.17	860.00	233	96	13	94,880	96,404	97,417	1.95	0.64	0.07	1.31	0.57
101-102.............	80	5	1	1,500.00	400.00	128	10	3	95,008	96,414	97,420	1.13	0.07	0.01	1.06	0.06
102-103.............	84	11	2	663.64	450.00	134	22	5	95,142	96,436	97,425	1.18	0.15	0.03	1.03	0.12
103-104.............	139	33	8	321.21	312.50	222	66	21	95,364	96,502	97,446	1.89	0.45	0.11	1.44	0.34
104-105.............	177	86	31	105.81	177.42	283	171	80	95,647	96,673	97,526	2.51	1.22	0.44	1.29	0.78
105-106.............	138	107	44	28.97	143.18	220	213	114	95,867	96,886	97,640	2.10	1.63	0.67	0.47	0.96
106-107.............	90	85	39	5.88	117.95	144	170	101	96,011	97,056	97,741	1.43	1.35	0.62	0.08	0.73
107-108.............	61	26	13	134.62	100.00	97	52	34	96,108	97,108	97,775	0.98	0.42	0.21	0.56	0.21
108-109.............	43	16	8	168.75	100.00	69	32	21	96,177	97,140	97,796	0.67	0.25	0.13	0.42	0.12
109-110.............	27	13	2	107.69	550.00	43	26	5	96,220	97,166	97,801	0.42	0.20	0.03	0.22	0.17
110-111.............	41	24	6	70.83	300.00	65	48	16	96,285	97,214	97,817	0.64	0.37	0.09	0.27	0.28
111-112.............	182	119	70	52.94	70.00	291	237	182	96,576	97,451	97,999	2.86	1.87	1.10	0.99	0.77
112-113.............	119	56	27	112.50	107.41	190	112	70	96,766	97,563	98,069	1.91	0.90	0.43	1.01	0.47
113-114.............	51	21	12	142.86	75.00	81	42	31	96,847	97,605	98,100	0.83	0.34	0.20	0.49	0.14
114-115.............	25	11	10	127.27	10.00	40	22	26	96,887	97,627	98,126	0.42	0.18	0.17	0.24	0.01
115-116.............	28	13	12	115.38	8.33	45	26	31	96,932	97,653	98,157	0.48	0.22	0.20	0.26	0.02
116-117.............	55	24	10	129.17	140.00	88	48	26	97,020	97,701	98,183	0.93	0.41	0.17	0.52	0.24
117-118.............	154	59	24	161.02	145.83	246	118	62	97,266	97,819	98,245	2.71	1.04	0.42	1.67	0.62
118-119.............	164	58	22	182.76	163.64	262	116	57	97,528	97,935	98,302	3.04	1.07	0.41	1.97	0.66
119-120.............	93	71	41	30.99	73.17	148	142	106	97,676	98,077	98,408	1.77	1.35	0.78	0.42	0.57
120-121.............	152	119	88	27.73	35.23	243	237	228	97,919	98,314	98,636	3.01	2.35	1.74	0.66	0.61
121-122.............	424	258	178	64.34	44.94	677	514	462	98,596	98,828	99,098	9.30	5.66	3.91	3.64	1.75
122-123.............	705	475	285	48.42	66.67	1,126	947	739	99,722	99,775	99,837	18.09	12.19	7.31	5.90	4.88
123-124.............	149	96	56	55.21	71.43	238	191	145	99,960	99,966	99,982	4.70	3.03	1.76	1.67	1.27
124-125.............	25	17	7	47.06	142.86	40	34	18	100,000	100,000	100,000	4.38	2.98	1.23	1.40	1.75

lx

PROGRESS OF THE NATION.

Naturally the greater density of population in a square degree is governed by the location of the larger cities. Thus the two square degrees between latitudes 40° and 41° and longitudes 73° and 75°, comprising New York, Brooklyn, Jersey city, and other large cities, contain 3,653,000 inhabitants. The square degree between latitudes 42° and 43° and longitudes 71° and 72°, comprising Boston and its suburbs, has 1,233,000 inhabitants; that between latitudes 39° and 40° and longitudes 75° and 76°, which comprises most of Philadelphia, has 1,414,000, while that between latitudes 41° and 42° and longitudes 87° and 88°, in which is situated most of Chicago, contains 950,000 people.

The following diagrams show graphically the distribution of the aggregate population in accordance with latitude and longitude at each of the three censuses under consideration:

POPULATION BY MILLIONS.

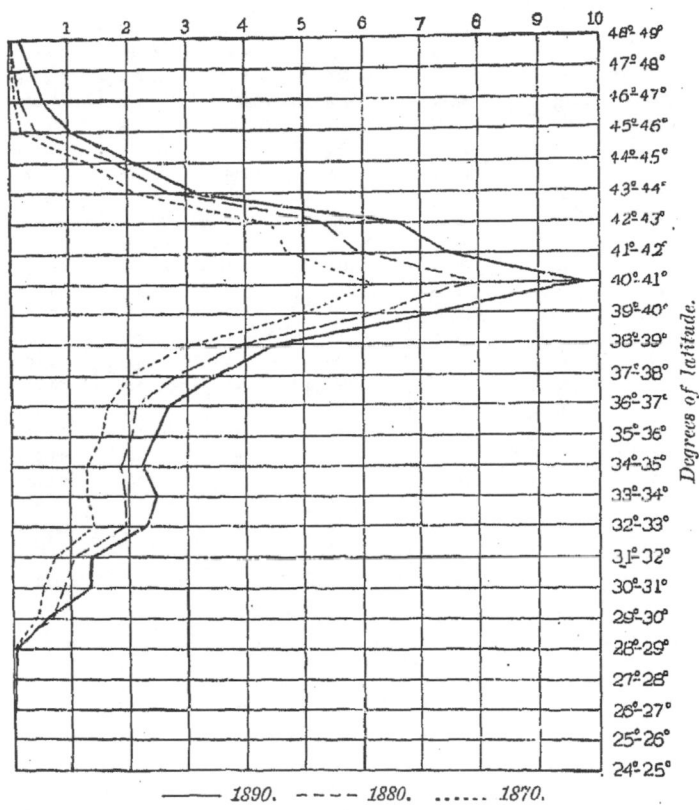

——— 1890.   – – – – 1880.   ...... 1870.

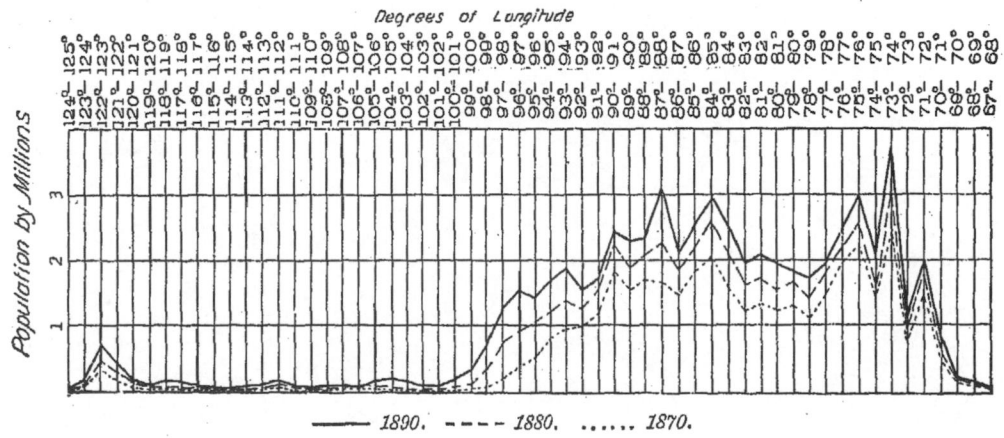

——— 1890.   – – – – 1880.   ...... 1870.

GEOGRAPHICAL DISTRIBUTION OF POPULATION.

The following tables show the distribution of the foreign born population in accordance with latitude and longitude:

DISTRIBUTION OF THE FOREIGN BORN POPULATION IN ACCORDANCE WITH LATITUDE: 1880 AND 1890.

DEGREES OF LATITUDE.	FOREIGN BORN POPULATION IN THOUSANDS.		PER CENT OF INCREASE.	NUMBER IN EACH 100,000 OF TOTAL FOREIGN BORN POPULATION WITHIN THE PARALLELS.		NUMBER IN EACH 100,000 OF TOTAL FOREIGN BORN POPULATION NORTH OF EACH PARALLEL.		FOREIGN BORN POPULATION PER SQUARE MILE.		INCREASE PER SQUARE MILE.
	1890	1880	1880 to 1890	1890	1880	1890	1880	1890	1880	1880 to 1890
48–49	66	6	1,000.00	714	90	714	90	0.69	0.06	0.63
47–48	137	32	328.13	1,481	470	2,195	560	1.23	0.29	0.94
46–47	193	74	160.81	2,086	1,108	4,281	1,677	1.46	0.56	0.90
45–46	331	140	136.43	3,578	2,096	7,859	3,773	2.38	1.01	1.37
44–45	522	406	28.57	5,643	6,078	13,502	9,851	3.25	2.52	0.73
43–44	742	507	21.29	8,022	8,937	21,524	18,788	4.54	3.65	0.89
42–43	1,596	1,127	41.61	17,254	16,871	38,778	35,659	9.28	6.56	2.72
41–42	1,682	1,174	43.27	18,184	17,575	56,962	53,234	9.14	6.38	2.76
40–41	1,949	1,426	36.68	21,070	21,347	78,032	74,581	10.58	7.74	2.84
39–40	883	731	20.79	9,546	10,943	87,578	85,524	4.84	4.01	0.83
38–39	448	433	3.46	4,843	6,482	92,421	92,006	2.40	2.41	0.08
37–38	286	233	22.75	3,092	3,488	95,513	95,494	1.61	1.31	0.30
36–37	38	24	58.33	411	359	95,924	95,853	0.22	0.14	0.08
35–36	37	23	60.87	400	344	96,324	96,197	0.21	0.13	0.08
34–35	45	22	104.55	487	329	96,811	96,526	0.27	0.13	0.14
33–34	33	22	50.00	357	329	97,168	96,855	0.21	0.14	0.07
32–33	42	36	16.67	454	539	97,622	97,394	0.30	0.26	0.04
31–32	25	14	78.57	270	210	97,892	97,604	0.22	0.12	0.10
30–31	45	30	50.00	487	449	98,379	98,053	0.49	0.33	0.16
29–30	96	91	5.49	1,038	1,362	99,417	99,415	1.75	1.66	0.09
28–29	12	7	71.43	130	105	99,547	99,520	0.45	0.26	0.10
27–28	19	13	46.15	205	195	99,752	99,715	0.94	0.65	0.29
26–27	9	11	a18.18	97	165	99,849	99,880	0.59	0.72	a0.13
25–26	3	3	....	32	45	99,881	99,925	0.75	0.75	....
24–25	11	5	120.00	119	75	100,000	100,000	135.80	61.73	74.07

a Decrease.

PROGRESS OF THE NATION.

lxii

DISTRIBUTION OF THE FOREIGN BORN POPULATION IN ACCORDANCE WITH LONGITUDE: 1880 AND 1890.

DEGREES OF LONGITUDE.	FOREIGN BORN POPULATION IN THOUSANDS.		PER CENT OF INCREASE.	NUMBER IN EACH 100,000 OF TOTAL FOREIGN BORN POPULATION WITHIN THE MERIDIANS.		NUMBER IN EACH 100,000 OF TOTAL FOREIGN BORN POPULATION EAST OF EACH MERIDIAN.		FOREIGN BORN POPULATION PER SQUARE MILE.		INCREASE PER SQUARE MILE.
	1890	1880	1880 to 1890	1890	1880	1890	1880	1890	1880	1880 to 1890
67– 68	10	9	11.11	108	135	108	135	2.02	2.36	0.26
68– 69	15	12	25.00	162	180	270	315	1.50	1.20	0.30
69– 70	18	10	80.00	195	150	465	465	1.69	0.91	0.75
70– 71	202	88	129.55	2,184	1,317	2,649	1,782	10.70	8.58	11.12
71– 72	572	441	29.71	6,184	6,602	8,833	8,384	44.00	33.93	10.07
72– 73	238	169	40.83	2,573	2,530	11,406	10,914	17.47	12.40	5.07
73– 74	1,183	899	31.59	12,789	13,458	24,195	24,372	79.11	60.12	18.99
74– 75	422	295	43.05	4,562	4,416	28,757	28,788	21.05	14.71	6.34
75– 76	513	406	26.35	5,546	6,078	34,303	34,866	18.92	14.97	3.95
76– 77	261	198	31.82	2,822	2,964	37,125	37,830	8.01	6.08	1.93
77– 78	128	102	25.49	1,384	1,527	38,509	39,357	3.86	3.08	0.78
78– 79	201	109	84.40	2,173	1,632	40,682	40,989	5.68	3.08	2.60
79– 80	165	157	5.10	1,784	2,350	42,466	43,339	4.65	4.42	0.23
80– 81	160	102	56.86	1,730	1,527	44,196	44,866	3.33	2.12	1.21
81– 82	188	129	45.74	2,032	1,931	46,228	46,797	3.14	2.16	0.98
82– 83	108	107	0.93	1,167	1,602	47,395	48,399	1.89	1.87	0.02
83– 84	272	211	28.91	2,940	3,159	50,335	51,558	4.82	3.74	1.08
84– 85	260	229	13.54	2,811	3,428	53,146	54,986	4.27	3.76	0.51
85– 86	174	145	20.00	1,881	2,171	55,027	57,157	2.91	2.43	0.48
86– 87	118	94	25.53	1,276	1,407	56,303	58,564	2.34	1.86	0.48
87– 88	692	410	68.78	7,481	6,138	63,784	64,702	13.27	7.86	5.41
88– 89	337	291	15.81	3,643	4,356	67,427	69,058	5.38	4.64	0.74
89– 90	234	191	22.51	2,530	2,859	69,957	71,917	3.63	2.97	0.66
90– 91	362	342	5.85	3,913	5,120	73,870	77,037	5.35	5.05	0.30
91– 92	184	167	10.18	1,989	2,500	75,859	79,537	2.69	2.44	0.25
92– 93	175	137	27.74	1,892	2,051	77,751	81,588	2.53	1.98	0.55
93– 94	264	154	71.43	2,854	2,305	80,605	83,893	3.80	2.22	1.58
94– 95	175	125	40.00	1,892	1,871	82,497	85,764	2.40	1.70	0.70
95– 96	182	117	55.56	1,968	1,751	84,465	87,515	2.44	1.57	0.87
96– 97	239	129	85.27	2,584	1,931	87,049	89,446	3.11	1.68	1.43
97– 98	197	108	82.41	2,130	1,617	89,179	91,063	2.33	1.28	1.05
98– 99	114	58	96.55	1,232	868	90,411	91,931	1.33	0.68	0.65
99–100	55	20	175.00	595	299	91,006	92,230	0.68	0.25	0.43
100–101	23	9	155.56	249	135	91,255	92,365	0.31	0.12	0.19
101–102	12	1	1,100.00	130	15	91,385	92,380	0.17	0.01	0.16
102–103	17	3	466.67	184	45	91,569	92,425	0.24	0.04	0.20
103–104	26	8	225.00	281	120	91,850	92,545	0.35	0.11	0.24
104–105	33	14	135.71	357	210	92,207	92,755	0.47	0.20	0.27
105–106	24	16	50.00	259	239	92,466	92,994	0.36	0.24	0.12
106–107	16	15	6.67	173	224	92,639	93,218	0.25	0.24	0.01
107–108	10	4	150.00	108	60	92,747	93,278	0.16	0.06	0.10
108–109	8	3	166.67	86	45	92,833	93,323	0.13	0.05	0.08
109–110	7	4	75.00	76	60	92,909	93,383	0.11	0.06	0.05
110–111	12	10	20.00	130	150	93,039	93,533	0.10	0.16	0.03
111–112	49	38	28.95	530	569	93,569	94,102	0.77	0.60	0.17
112–113	38	17	123.53	411	254	93,980	94,356	0.61	0.27	0.34
113–114	15	6	150.00	162	90	94,142	94,446	0.25	0.10	0.15
114–115	6	3	100.00	65	45	94,207	94,491	0.10	0.05	0.05
115–116	8	5	60.00	86	75	94,293	94,566	0.14	0.08	0.06
116–117	11	9	22.22	119	135	94,412	94,701	0.19	0.15	0.04
117–118	29	11	163.64	313	165	94,725	94,866	0.51	0.19	0.32
118–119	34	14	142.86	367	210	95,092	95,076	0.63	0.26	0.37
119–120	21	22	a4.55	227	329	95,319	95,405	0.40	0.42	a0.02
120–121	37	36	2.78	400	539	95,719	95,944	0.73	0.71	0.02
121–122	124	81	53.09	1,340	1,212	97,059	97,156	2.72	1.78	0.94
122–123	233	169	37.87	2,519	2,530	99,578	99,686	5.98	4.34	1.64
123–124	33	19	73.68	357	284	99,935	99,970	1.04	0.60	0.44
124–125	6	2	200.00	65	30	100,000	100,000	1.05	0.35	0.70

a Decrease.

GEOGRAPHICAL DISTRIBUTION OF POPULATION.

lxiii

The following tables show the distribution of the negro population in accordance with latitude and longitude:

DISTRIBUTION OF THE NEGRO (a) POPULATION IN ACCORDANCE WITH LATITUDE: 1880 AND 1890.

DEGREES OF LATITUDE.	NEGRO POPULATION IN THOUSANDS.		PER CENT OF INCREASE.	NUMBER IN EACH 100,000 OF TOTAL NEGRO POPULATION WITHIN THE PARALLELS.		NUMBER IN EACH 100,000 OF TOTAL NEGRO POPULATION NORTH OF EACH PARALLEL.		NEGRO POPULATION PER SQUARE MILE.		INCREASE PER SQUARE MILE.
	1890	1880	1880 to 1890	1890	1880	1890	1880	1890	1880	1880 to 1890
48–49										
47–48	2			27		27		0.02		0.02
46–47	1	1		13	15	40	15	0.01	0.01	
45–46	3	2	50.00	40	30	80	45	0.02	0.01	0.01
44–45	5	4	25.00	67	61	147	106	0.03	0.02	0.01
43–44	10	10		134	152	281	258	0.06	0.06	
42–43	51	43	18.60	683	653	964	911	0.30	0.25	0.05
41–42	78	65	20.00	1,044	988	2,008	1,899	0.42	0.35	0.07
40–41	154	125	23.20	2,062	1,899	4,070	3,798	0.84	0.68	0.16
39–40	421	382	10.21	5,636	5,805	9,706	9,603	2.31	2.10	0.21
38–39	485	474	2.32	6,493	7,203	16,199	16,806	2.69	2.63	0.06
37–38	512	492	4.07	6,854	7,476	23,053	24,282	2.89	2.78	0.11
36–37	593	565	4.96	7,938	8,585	30,991	32,867	3.36	3.20	0.16
35–36	658	588	11.90	8,809	8,935	39,800	41,802	3.73	3.33	0.40
34–35	828	722	14.68	11,084	10,971	50,884	52,773	4.91	4.28	0.63
33–34	1,112	884	25.79	14,886	13,433	65,770	66,206	7.18	5.71	1.47
32–33	1,197	1,090	9.82	16,024	16,563	81,794	82,769	8.49	7.73	0.76
31–32	564	474	18.99	7,550	7,203	89,344	89,972	4.98	4.19	0.79
30–31	480	405	18.52	6,426	6,154	95,770	96,126	5.21	4.40	0.81
29–30	283	235	20.43	3,788	3,571	99,558	99,697	5.15	4.27	0.88
28–29	23	14	64.29	308	213	99,866	99,910	0.87	0.53	0.34
27–28	4	2	100.00	54	30	99,920	99,940	0.20	0.10	0.10
26–27		1	b100.00		15	99,920	99,955		0.07	b0.07
25–26						99,920	99,955			
24–25	6	3	100.00	80	45	100,000	100,000	74.07	37.04	37.03

a Includes all persons of negro descent.   b Decrease.

lxiv

PROGRESS OF THE NATION.

DISTRIBUTION OF THE NEGRO (a) POPULATION IN ACCORDANCE WITH LONGITUDE: 1880 AND 1890.

DEGREES OF LONGITUDE.	NEGRO POPULATION IN THOUSANDS.		PER CENT OF INCREASE.	NUMBER IN EACH 100,000 OF TOTAL NEGRO POPULATION WITHIN THE MERIDIANS.		NUMBER IN EACH 100,000 OF TOTAL NEGRO POPULATION EAST OF EACH MERIDIAN.		NEGRO POPULATION PER SQUARE MILE.		INCREASE PER SQUARE MILE.
	1890	1880	1880 to 1890	1890	1880	1890	1880	1890	1880	1880 to 1890
67- 68										
68- 69										
69- 70										
70- 71	7	4	75.00	94	61	94	61	0.08	0.30	0.20
71- 72	21	20	5.00	281	304	375	365	1.62	1.54	0.08
72- 73	11	10	10.00	147	152	522	517	0.81	0.73	0.08
73- 74	56	49	14.29	750	745	1,272	1,262	3.74	3.28	0.46
74- 75	49	40	22.50	656	608	1,928	1,870	2.44	2.00	0.44
75- 76	156	149	4.70	2,088	2,264	4,016	4,134	5.75	5.50	0.25
76- 77	358	357	0.28	4,793	5,425	8,809	9,559	10.99	10.95	0.04
77- 78	467	458	1.97	6,252	6,959	15,061	16,518	14.09	13.82	0.27
78- 79	302	302	....	4,043	4,589	19,104	21,107	8.53	8.53	....
79- 80	362	338	7.10	4,846	5,136	23,950	26,243	10.20	9.52	0.68
80- 81	356	298	19.46	4,766	4,528	28,716	30,771	7.40	6.10	1.21
81- 82	407	348	16.95	5,449	5,288	34,165	36,059	6.80	5.82	0.98
82- 83	332	243	36.63	4,445	3,692	38,610	39,751	5.80	4.25	1.55
83- 84	352	301	16.94	4,712	4,574	43,322	44,325	6.24	5.34	0.90
84- 85	467	423	10.40	6,252	6,428	49,574	50,753	7.66	6.94	0.72
85- 86	342	307	11.40	4,578	4,665	54,152	55,418	5.72	5.14	0.58
86- 87	377	336	12.20	5,047	5,106	59,199	60,524	7.47	6.65	0.82
87- 88	369	348	6.03	4,940	5,288	64,139	65,812	7.07	6.67	0.40
88- 89	315	301	4.65	4,217	4,574	68,356	70,386	5.02	4.80	0.22
89- 90	374	355	5.35	5,007	5,394	73,363	75,780	5.81	5.51	0.30
90- 91	587	470	24.89	7,858	7,142	81,221	82,922	8.67	6.94	1.73
91- 92	410	329	24.62	5,489	4,999	86,710	87,921	6.00	4.81	1.19
92- 93	201	168	19.64	2,691	2,553	89,401	90,474	2.90	2.43	0.47
93- 94	177	150	18.00	2,370	2,279	91,771	92,753	2.55	2.16	0.39
94- 95	155	137	13.14	2,075	2,082	93,846	94,835	2.18	1.92	0.26
95- 96	166	141	17.73	2,222	2,143	96,068	96,978	2.23	1.89	0.34
96- 97	163	119	36.97	2,182	1,808	98,250	98,786	2.12	1.55	0.57
97- 98	82	57	43.86	1,098	866	99,348	99,652	0.97	0.67	0.30
98- 99	16	9	77.78	214	137	99,562	99,789	0.19	0.11	0.08
99-100	3	2	50.00	40	30	99,602	99,819	0.04	0.02	0.02
100-101	1	1	....	13	15	99,615	99,834	0.01	0.01	....
101-102	1	....	....	13	....	99,628	99,834	0.01	....	0.01
102-103	1	....	....	13	....	99,641	99,834	0.01	....	0.01
103-104	2	1	100.00	27	15	99,668	99,849	0.03	0.01	0.02
104-105	4	1	300.00	54	15	99,722	99,864	0.06	0.01	0.05
105-106	1	1	....	13	15	99,735	99,879	0.02	0.02	....
106-107	1	1	....	13	15	99,748	99,894	0.02	0.02	....
107-108	1	....	....	13	....	99,761	99,894	0.02	....	0.02
108-109	1	....	....	13	....	99,774	99,894	0.02	....	0.02
109-110	1	....	....	13	....	99,787	99,894	0.02	....	0.02
110-111	1	....	....	13	....	99,800	99,894	0.02	....	0.02
111-112	1	....	....	13	....	99,813	99,894	0.02	....	0.02
112-113	1	....	....	13	....	99,826	99,894	0.02	....	0.02
113-114	....	....	....	....	....	99,826	99,894	....	....	....
114-115	....	....	....	....	....	99,826	99,894	....	....	....
115-116	....	....	....	....	....	99,826	99,894	....	....	....
116-117	....	....	....	....	....	99,826	99,894	....	....	....
117-118	1	....	....	13	....	99,839	99,894	0.02	....	....
118-119	2	....	....	27	....	99,866	99,894	0.04	....	0.02
119-120	1	....	....	13	....	99,879	99,894	0.02	....	0.04
120-121	1	....	....	13	....	99,892	99,894	0.02	....	0.02
121-122	4	2	100.00	54	30	99,946	99,924	0.02	....	0.02
122-123	4	4	....	54	61	100,000	99,985	0.09	0.04	0.05
123-124	....	1	....	....	15	100,000	100,000	0.10	0.10	....
124-125	....	....	....	....	....	100,000	100,000	....	0.03	b0.03

a Includes all persons of negro descent.

b Decrease.

369

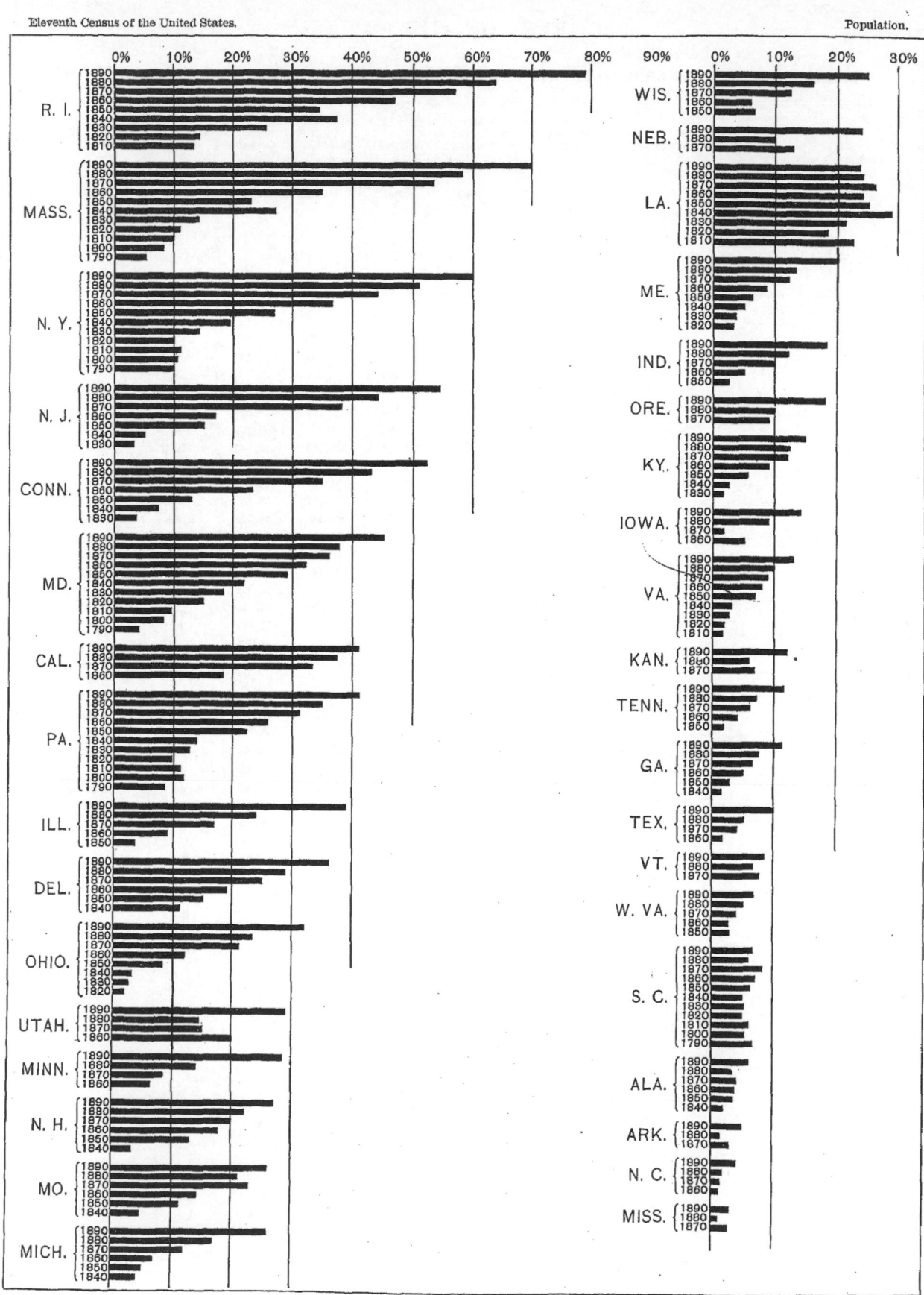

PROPORTION OF URBAN TO TOTAL POPULATION, BY STATES AND TERRITORIES—HISTORICAL.

NOTE.—Colorado, Nevada, and Florida are not shown, because these states had urban population in 1880 and 1890 only.

URBAN POPULATION.   lxv

URBAN POPULATION.

In the published records of former censuses urban population has been defined as that element living in cities, or other closely aggregated bodies of population, containing 8,000 inhabitants or more. This definition of the urban element, although a somewhat arbitrary one, is used in the present discussion of the results of the Eleventh Census in order that they may be compared directly with those of earlier censuses.

Throughout the United States, with the exception of the New England states, there is no difficulty or uncertainty in carrying out the above definition of urban population. Excepting in these states, municipal charters are generally granted only to dense bodies of population, and all such bodies are incorporated and their limits sharply defined by the acts of incorporation. In the New England states, on the contrary, the general practice is to subdivide the counties into towns, which are, so far as area and distribution of population are concerned, similar as political divisions to the townships of the states of the Upper Mississippi valley. When certain conditions of population are fulfilled these towns are chartered bodily as cities. Thus these cities may contain considerable numbers of rural population, and, conversely, certain towns may contain dense bodies of population of magnitude sufficient to be classed as urban. It is therefore possible in these states to make only an approximate separation of the urban and rural elements. According to this definition the urban population of the country was 18,284,385 in 1890, the total population being 62,622,250. The urban population in 1890 constituted 29.20 per cent of the total population. Corresponding figures for the several censuses are given in the following table:

CENSUS YEARS.	Population of the United States.	Population of cities having 8,000 inhabitants or more.	Inhabitants of specified cities in each 100 of the total population.
1790	3,929,214	131,472	3.35
1800	5,308,483	210,873	3.97
1810	7,239,881	356,920	4.93
1820	9,633,822	475,135	4.93
1830	12,866,020	864,509	6.72
1840	17,069,453	1,453,994	8.52
1850	23,191,876	2,897,586	12.49
1860	31,443,321	5,072,256	16.13
1870	38,558,371	8,071,875	20.93
1880	50,155,783	11,318,547	22.57
1890	62,622,250	18,284,385	29.20

It will be seen that the proportion of urban population has increased gradually during the past century from 3.35 up to 29.20 per cent, or from one-thirtieth up to nearly one-third of the total population. The increase has been quite regular from the beginning up to 1880, while from 1880 to 1890 it has made a leap from 22.57 up to 29.20 per cent, thus illustrating in a forcible manner the accelerated tendency of our population toward urban life. The number of cities having a population of 8,000 or more increased from 6 in 1790 to 286 in 1880, whence it has leaped to 448 in 1890.

The urban element in 1890 is distributed very unequally over the country, as is shown below by geographical divisions:

GEOGRAPHICAL DIVISIONS.	Urban population.	Per cent of entire urban population.
The United States	18,284,385	100.00
North Atlantic	9,015,383	49.31
South Atlantic	1,419,904	7.76
North Central	5,793,896	31.69
South Central	1,147,089	6.27
Western	908,053	4.97

The North Atlantic division contains nearly one-half the urban population of the country, while the North Atlantic and North Central divisions together contain nearly five-sixths.

In the North Atlantic division 51.81 per cent, or more than one-half the entire population, is contained in cities of 8,000 inhabitants or more. During the past ten years the urban element in this division has increased 44.15 per cent, while the total population has increased but 19.95 per cent. This relative increase is well distributed among the several states of this division, with the single exception of Vermont, whose urban element has increased but little. In Maine, Vermont, Massachusetts, Rhode Island, and New York the numerical increase in the urban element is greater than the increase of the total population, so that in these states the rural population has actually diminished in number. This rapid increase in the urban element of the North Atlantic division is due to the equally rapid extension of manufactures and commerce, requiring the aggregation of the inhabitants into compact bodies.

lxvi
PROGRESS OF THE NATION.

In the North Central division 25.91 per cent, or a trifle more than one-fourth of the inhabitants, are classed as urban. In the past ten years the number of the urban element has nearly doubled, while the total population has increased but 28.78 per cent. The number of cities has increased from 95 in 1880 to 152 in 1890. The increase in number of urban population, viz, 2,769,217, is comprised mainly in a few large cities; thus the total increase in the 11 largest cities, comprising a trifle more than one-half of the urban population of this section, is 1,446,089, or more than half the entire gain in urban population in this division.

In the South Atlantic and South Central divisions the proportion of urban population is comparatively small, being in the first named but 16.03 per cent of the entire population, or less than one-sixth, and in the second but 10.45 per cent, the proportion of urban to the total population in all the southern states being less than 13 per cent. The industries of these states are mainly agricultural, and while manufactures and mining are making some progress they are still in their infancy. The progress in these branches of industry may be measured roughly by the growth of the urban element. In 1880 this element numbered 1,616,095, and constituted less than 10 per cent of the population. In 1890 it numbered 2,567,053, having increased 58.84 per cent, while the total population had increased but 20.07 per cent.

In certain of these states the proportion of urban population is still trifling; thus, in Mississippi it constitutes but 2.64, in North Carolina but 3.87, and in Arkansas but 4.89 per cent of the total population.

Mining, commerce, and manufactures in the western states and territories are in a much more advanced stage, as is shown by the greater proportion of the urban element. Considered as a whole, the urban element in the Western division in 1890 constituted 29.99 per cent of the whole population, while in 1880 it constituted 23.97 per cent. It has therefore gained much more rapidly than the total population.

In 1880 there was but 1 city, New York, which had a population in excess of a million. In 1890 there were 3, New York, Chicago, and Philadelphia.

In 1870 there were but 14 cities each containing more than 100,000 inhabitants. In 1880 this number had increased to 20, and in 1890 to 28.

The relative rank of the cities having a population of 100,000 or more at the date of each of these censuses is set forth in the following table:

RANK.	1890	1880	1870
1	New York, N. Y.	New York, N. Y.	New York, N. Y.
2	Chicago, Ill.	Philadelphia, Pa.	Philadelphia, Pa.
3	Philadelphia, Pa.	Brooklyn, N. Y.	Brooklyn, N. Y.
4	Brooklyn, N. Y.	Chicago, Ill.	St. Louis, Mo.
5	St. Louis, Mo.	Boston, Mass.	Chicago, Ill.
6	Boston, Mass.	St. Louis, Mo.	Baltimore, Md.
7	Baltimore, Md.	Baltimore, Md.	Boston, Mass.
8	San Francisco, Cal.	Cincinnati, Ohio.	Cincinnati, Ohio.
9	Cincinnati, Ohio.	San Francisco, Cal.	New Orleans, La.
10	Cleveland, Ohio.	New Orleans, La.	San Francisco, Cal.
11	Buffalo, N. Y.	Cleveland, Ohio.	Buffalo, N. Y.
12	New Orleans, La.	Pittsburg, Pa.	Washington, D. C.
13	Pittsburg, Pa.	Buffalo, N. Y.	Newark, N. J.
14	Washington, D. C.	Washington, D. C.	Louisville, Ky.
15	Detroit, Mich.	Newark, N. J.	
16	Milwaukee, Wis.	Louisville, Ky.	
17	Newark, N. J.	Jersey city, N. J.	
18	Minneapolis, Minn.	Detroit, Mich.	
19	Jersey city, N. J.	Milwaukee, Wis.	
20	Louisville, Ky.	Providence, R. I.	
21	Omaha, Neb.		
22	Rochester, N. Y.		
23	St. Paul, Minn.		
24	Kansas city, Mo.		
25	Providence, R. I.		
26	Denver, Colo.		
27	Indianapolis, Ind.		
28	Allegheny, Pa.		

URBAN POPULATION. lxvii

The following table shows the 50 principal cities of the United States in the order of their rank, giving the population in 1890 and 1880, and the increase from 1880 to 1890:

POPULATION OF THE FIFTY PRINCIPAL CITIES IN 1890 IN THE ORDER OF THEIR RANK.

CITIES.	POPULATION. 1890	POPULATION. 1880	INCREASE. Number.	INCREASE. Per cent.	CITIES.	POPULATION. 1890	POPULATION. 1880	INCREASE. Number.	INCREASE. Per cent.
New York, N. Y	1,515,301	1,206,299	309,002	25.62	Denver, Colo	106,713	35,629	71,084	199.51
Chicago, Ill	1,099,850	503,185	596,665	118.58	Indianapolis, Ind	105,436	75,056	30,380	40.48
Philadelphia, Pa	1,046,964	847,170	199,794	23.58	Allegheny, Pa	105,287	78,682	26,605	33.81
Brooklyn, N. Y	806,343	566,663	239,680	42.30	Albany, N. Y	94,923	90,758	4,165	4.59
St. Louis, Mo	451,770	350,518	101,252	28.89	Columbus, Ohio	88,150	51,647	36,503	70.68
Boston, Mass	448,477	362,839	85,638	23.60	Syracuse, N. Y	88,143	51,792	36,351	70.19
Baltimore, Md	434,439	332,313	102,126	30.73	Worcester, Mass	84,655	58,291	26,364	45.23
San Francisco, Cal	298,997	233,959	65,038	27.80	Toledo, Ohio	81,434	50,137	31,297	62.42
Cincinnati, Ohio	296,908	255,139	41,769	16.37	Richmond, Va	81,388	63,600	17,788	27.97
Cleveland, Ohio	261,353	160,146	101,207	63.20	New Haven, Conn	81,298	62,882	18,416	29.29
Buffalo, N. Y	255,664	155,134	100,530	64.80	Paterson, N. J	78,347	51,031	27,316	53.53
New Orleans, La	242,039	216,090	25,949	12.01	Lowell, Mass	77,696	59,475	18,221	30.64
Pittsburg, Pa	238,617	156,389	82,228	52.58	Nashville, Tenn	76,168	43,350	32,818	75.70
Washington, D. C	230,392	177,624	52,768	29.71	Scranton, Pa	75,215	45,850	29,365	64.05
Detroit, Mich	205,876	116,340	89,536	76.96	Fall River, Mass	74,398	48,961	25,437	51.95
Milwaukee, Wis	204,468	115,587	88,881	76.90	Cambridge, Mass	70,028	52,669	17,359	32.96
Newark, N. J	181,830	136,508	45,322	33.20	Atlanta, Ga	65,533	37,409	28,124	75.18
Minneapolis, Minn	164,738	46,887	117,851	251.35	Memphis, Tenn	64,495	33,592	30,903	92.00
Jersey city, N. J	163,003	120,722	42,281	35.02	Wilmington, Del	61,431	42,478	18,953	44.62
Louisville, Ky	161,129	123,758	37,371	30.20	Dayton, Ohio	61,220	38,678	22,542	58.28
Omaha, Neb	140,452	30,518	109,934	360.23	Troy, N. Y	60,956	56,747	4,209	7.42
Rochester, N. Y	133,896	89,366	44,530	49.83	Grand Rapids, Mich	60,278	32,016	28,262	88.27
St. Paul, Minn	133,156	41,473	91,683	221.07	Reading, Pa	58,661	43,278	15,383	35.54
Kansas city, Mo	a132,716	55,785	76,931	137.91	Camden, N. J	58,313	41,659	16,654	39.98
Providence, R. I	132,146	104,857	27,289	26.02	Trenton, N. J	57,458	29,910	27,548	92.10

a Includes a population of 13,048 for territory which, by decision of the supreme court of the state, is now outside the limits of Kansas city.

The following table shows the number of cities classified according to population at the date of each census:

NUMBER OF CITIES CLASSIFIED ACCORDING TO POPULATION: 1790 TO 1890.

CENSUS YEARS.	Total.	8,000 to 12,000.	12,000 to 20,000.	20,000 to 40,000.	40,000 to 75,000.	75,000 to 125,000.	125,000 to 250,000.	250,000 to 500,000.	500,000 to 1,000,000.	1,000,000 and over.
1790	6	1	3	1	1					
1800	6	1		3	2					
1810	11	4	2	3		2				
1820	13	3	4	2	2	2				
1830	26	12	7	3	1	1	2			
1840	44	17	11	10	1	3	1	1		
1850	85	36	20	14	7	3	3	1	1	
1860	141	62	34	23	12	2	5	1	2	
1870	226	92	63	39	14	8	3	5	2	
1880	286	110	76	55	21	9	7	4	3	1
1890	448	170	107	91	35	14	14	7	1	3

lxviii   PROGRESS OF THE NATION.

The following table shows, by states and groups of states, the total population in 1880 and 1890, the urban population in the same years, the number of cities, and the proportion which the urban population bears to the total population:

URBAN POPULATION: 1880 AND 1890.

STATES AND TERRITORIES.	TOTAL POPULATION.		URBAN POPULATION.		NUMBER OF CITIES AND PER CENT OF URBAN OF TOTAL POPULATION.			
					1890		1880	
	1890	1880	1890	1880	Number.	Per cent.	Number.	Per cent.
The United States	62,622,250	50,155,783	18,284,385	11,318,547	448	29.20	286	22.57
North Atlantic division	17,401,545	14,507,407	9,015,383	6,254,096	199	51.81	137	43.11
Maine	661,086	648,936	130,346	87,100	8	19.72	5	13.42
New Hampshire	376,530	346,991	103,058	76,200	5	27.37	5	21.96
Vermont	332,422	332,286	26,350	21,500	2	7.93	2	6.47
Massachusetts	2,238,943	1,783,085	1,564,931	1,042,039	47	69.90	33	58.44
Rhode Island	345,506	276,531	272,571	175,500	10	78.89	6	63.46
Connecticut	746,258	622,700	385,287	266,100	17	51.63	13	42.73
New York	5,997,853	5,082,871	3,599,877	2,591,267	46	60.02	33	50.98
New Jersey	1,444,933	1,131,116	780,912	495,650	20	54.04	12	43.82
Pennsylvania	5,258,014	4,282,891	2,152,051	1,498,740	44	40.93	28	34.99
South Atlantic division	8,857,920	7,597,197	1,419,964	942,387	36	16.03	23	12.40
Delaware	168,493	146,608	61,431	42,478	1	36.46	1	28.97
Maryland	1,042,390	934,943	465,479	351,665	4	44.65	3	37.61
District of Columbia	230,392	177,624	230,392	159,871	1	100.00	2	90.01
Virginia	1,655,980	1,512,565	221,965	148,230	9	13.40	6	9.80
West Virginia	762,794	618,457	53,038	30,737	3	6.95	1	4.97
North Carolina	1,617,947	1,399,750	62,544	26,615	5	3.87	2	1.90
South Carolina	1,151,149	995,577	78,915	60,020	3	6.86	2	6.03
Georgia	1,837,353	1,542,180	199,169	112,881	7	10.84	5	7.32
Florida	391,422	269,493	47,031	9,890	3	12.02	1	3.67
North Central division	22,362,279	17,364,111	5,793,896	3,024,679	152	25.91	95	17.42
Ohio	3,672,316	3,198,062	1,159,342	745,894	29	31.57	20	23.32
Indiana	2,192,404	1,978,301	400,566	244,063	18	18.27	11	12.34
Illinois	3,826,351	3,077,871	1,485,955	732,021	24	38.83	18	23.78
Michigan	2,093,889	1,636,937	546,095	271,566	20	26.08	12	16.59
Wisconsin	1,686,880	1,315,497	424,546	212,431	17	25.17	9	16.15
Minnesota	1,301,826	780,773	309,315	107,623	8	28.37	4	13.78
Iowa	1,911,896	1,624,615	269,230	152,578	12	14.08	10	9.30
Missouri	2,679,184	2,168,380	703,743	459,309	8	26.27	5	21.18
North Dakota	182,719	a36,909						
South Dakota	328,808	a98,268	10,177		1	3.10		
Nebraska	1,058,910	452,402	259,048	43,521	8	24.46	2	9.62
Kansas	1,427,096	996,096	165,879	55,613	9	11.62	4	5.58
South Central division	10,972,893	8,919,371	1,147,089	673,708	37	10.45	20	7.55
Kentucky	1,858,635	1,648,690	276,454	198,603	7	14.87	5	12.05
Tennessee	1,767,518	1,542,359	202,337	99,527	5	11.45	4	6.45
Alabama	1,513,017	1,262,505	89,135	45,845	4	5.89	2	3.63
Mississippi	1,289,600	1,131,597	34,098	11,814	3	2.64	1	1.04
Louisiana	1,118,587	939,946	261,496	224,090	3	23.05	2	23.84
Texas	2,235,523	1,591,749	225,346	80,682	11	10.08	5	5.07
Oklahoma	61,834							
Arkansas	1,128,179	802,525	55,223	13,138	4	4.89	1	1.64
Western division	3,027,613	1,767,697	908,053	423,677	24	29.99	11	23.97
Montana	132,159	39,159	24,557		2	18.58		
Wyoming	60,705	20,789	11,690		1	19.26		
Colorado	412,198	194,327	152,795	50,449	4	37.07	2	25.96
New Mexico	153,593	119,565						
Arizona	59,620	40,440						
Utah	207,905	143,963	59,732	20,768	2	28.73	1	14.43
Nevada	45,761	62,266	8,511	10,917	1	18.60	1	17.53
Idaho	84,385	32,610						
Washington	349,390	75,116	98,765		3	28.27		
Oregon	313,767	174,768	56,917	17,577	2	18.14	1	10.06
California	1,208,130	864,694	495,086	323,966	9	40.98	6	37.47

a Population of Dakota in 1880 apportioned according to the present limits of North Dakota and South Dakota.

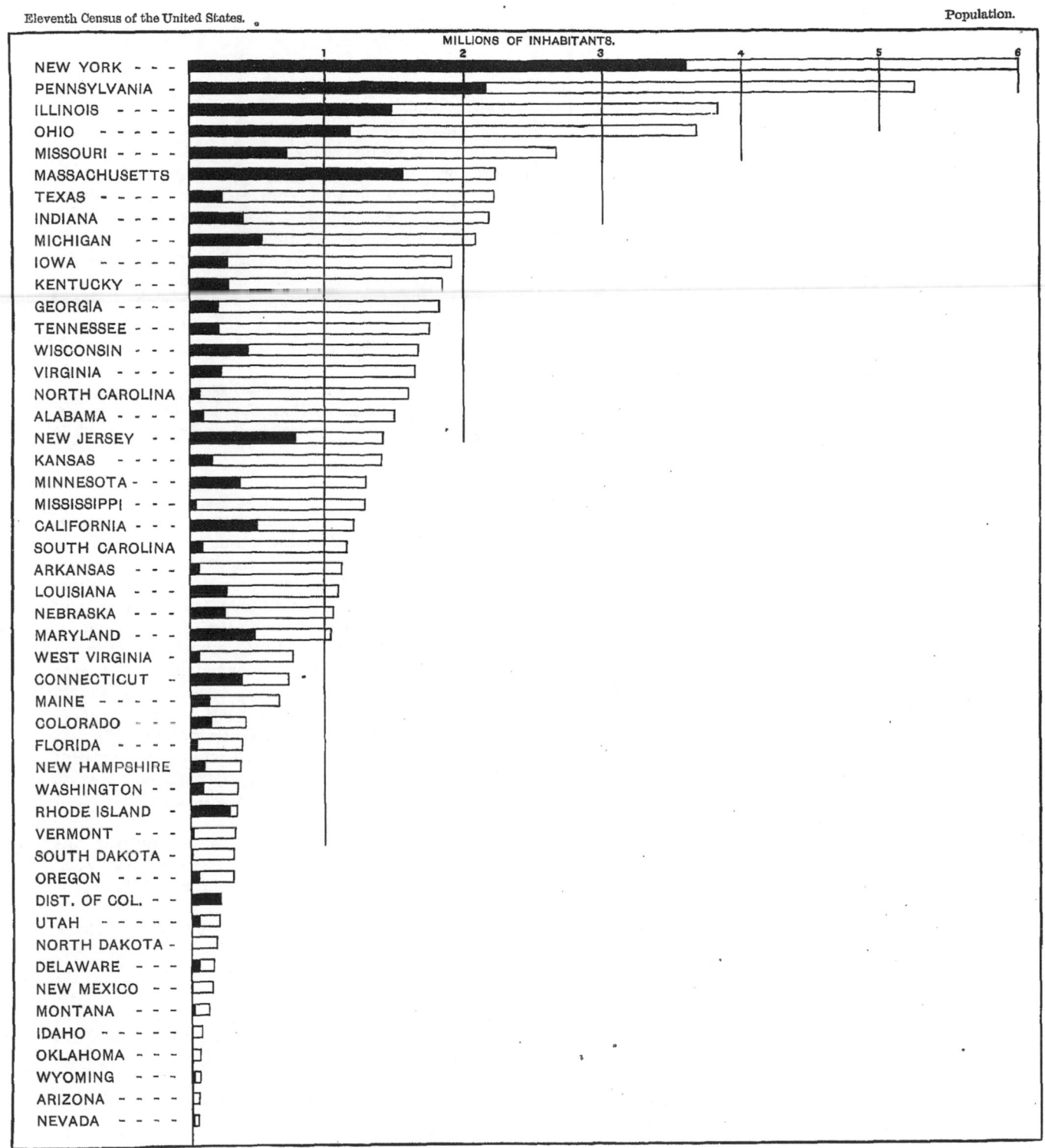

Eleventh Census of the United States.   Population.

MILLIONS OF INHABITANTS.

URBAN AND TOTAL POPULATION, BY STATES AND TERRITORIES: 1890.

NOTE.—The total length of each column represents the aggregate population of the state or territory, while the black part of the column represents the urban element, that is, the proportion contained in cities having 8,000 inhabitants or more.

RURAL POPULATION.

lxix

In defining what constitutes a city, in each case the Census Office has consistently maintained the policy of including only such population as lives within the charter limits, because no other defined limits exist. In many cases, however, this does not give to the city all the population which naturally belongs to it. There may be populous suburbs, which are to all intents and purposes parts of the city, whose inhabitants transact business within the city, who may be served by the same post office, but who, living without the charter limits, are not included in the city's population. Of this our greatest city, New York, is a forcible example. Within a radius of 15 miles of the city hall, on Manhattan island, the people are in effect citizens of New York, so far as their business and social interests go, although politically they live in different cities, counties, and states. This body of population contains considerably in excess of 3,000,000 persons, or two-thirds the number in London, which is, similarly, a congeries of municipalities. Next to London, New York and its suburbs form the largest city of the globe. Other cases are those of St. Paul and Minneapolis, whose corporate limits join one another, and Bristol, Tennessee, and Bristol, Virginia, two corporations whose line of division follows the middle of the main street of the city, and which have a joint population of 6,226. Texarkana, Texas, and Texarkana, Arkansas, form a similar case. Knoxville, Tennessee, has large suburbs immediately adjoining, whose population would, if added, increase it to very nearly 40,000 inhabitants.

The rate of growth of many of these cities, especially those situated west of the Mississippi river, has been amazing. Chicago has added over half a million to her inhabitants, thus more than doubling her size in ten years. Minneapolis, St. Paul, Omaha, and Denver have expanded to triple or quadruple their former size, while all over the west smaller cities have sprung up as if by magic.

RURAL POPULATION.

During the last decade the rural population has diminished in numbers over a considerable part of the country, especially in the eastern and north central states. The areas over which this diminution has occurred are represented on the accompanying map, which has been prepared upon the following basis: from the total population of each county in 1890 has been subtracted the population of all cities or other compact bodies of population which number 1,000 or more. From the population of the same counties in 1880 has been subtracted the population of the same places at that time, and the remainders, which are assumed to be the rural population, are compared for increase or decrease. This process presents no difficulties or uncertainties in any part of the country except in the New England states, where the town system prevails, and where, as a rule, no smaller political units exist than these towns. The towns contain in most cases both urban and rural population in varying proportions, and unless one has personal acquaintance with them he has no basis for obtaining the relative proportion of these elements in any town except as indicated by the total population of the town. If the town be large the presumption is that it contains a considerable urban population, while if it is small it is probably all or nearly all rural. In the case of these towns the elimination of the urban element has been largely a matter of personal acquaintance, an estimate based thereon being guided to some extent by the population of the town, a population in excess of 2,500 indicating that a considerable proportion of the people were living under urban conditions.

The first table on the following page shows the proportion which the areas in which the rural population has diminished bears to the total areas of the states. This was prepared by footing up the counties in which such diminution had taken place and comparing the totals with the areas of the states. It shows that upon 16 per cent of the area of the country the rural population has diminished; that this diminution has been much greater in the North Atlantic division than elsewhere and least in the South Central division. It is greatest in New York state, where nearly five-sixths of the area has lost rural population; in Vermont, where more than three-fourths has lost; in Maine and New Hampshire, where nearly two-thirds has lost. It is surprisingly low in Massachusetts, but here it should be added as a qualification of the figures that the majority of the counties of that state have gained only a trifling amount; have barely held their own in this respect. In the North Central division the states of Illinois, Ohio, Indiana, and Iowa, together with southern Michigan and Wisconsin, have diminished in rural population over great areas. These areas in Illinois and Ohio comprise over three-fifths of the state and in Indiana and Iowa more than two-fifths.

Among the southern states Maryland has lost over the greatest territory, an area which exceeds half that of the state, while in Virginia much of the country lying east of the Blue Ridge has lost in rural population. The cotton states as a rule have lost very little.

Among the western states Nevada has lost rural population over nine-tenths of its area, and Utah, California, and Colorado have lost over areas which are notable because they occur in these newly settled states. The losses in these states are doubtless due not to a reduction in farming area, for they are not of strictly rural population, but to a reduction in the scattered mining population of those states.

Out of a total increase of population in the United States of 12,466,467 the rural population has increased 4,078,422, as is seen from the second table on the following page; in other words, about one-third of the total increase of the country during the past decade has been in its rural element. This increase has been distributed among the states in a most irregular manner. The North Atlantic division has suffered a decrease of rural population to the extent of 37,941. In all the other divisions of the country there has been an increase, but this increase has been in no way proportional to the total increase of population.

lxx

PROGRESS OF THE NATION.

PERCENTAGE OF TOTAL AREA SHOWING LOSS IN RURAL POPULATION: 1890.

STATES AND TERRITORIES.	Per cent.	STATES AND TERRITORIES.	Per cent.
The United States	16.25	North Central division—Continued.	
		Minnesota	8.21
North Atlantic division	58.96	Iowa	43.26
		Missouri	15.99
Maine	64.96	North Dakota	
New Hampshire	63.10	South Dakota	
Vermont	77.20	Nebraska	
Massachusetts	18.92	Kansas	7.24
Rhode Island	28.11		
Connecticut	60.85		
New York	82.00	South Central division	9.10
New Jersey	28.06	Kentucky	22.79
Pennsylvania	38.20	Tennessee	28.71
		Alabama	12.24
South Atlantic division	16.65	Mississippi	13.61
		Louisiana	4.34
Delaware	32.14	Texas	5.21
Maryland	54.11	Oklahoma	
District of Columbia		Arkansas	
Virginia	41.57		
West Virginia	1.79	Western division	12.22
North Carolina	13.12		
South Carolina	4.56	Montana	
Georgia	14.11	Wyoming	
Florida	10.25	Colorado	8.78
		New Mexico	
		Arizona	
North Central division	20.10	Utah	14.75
		Nevada	90.50
Ohio	61.39	Idaho	
Indiana	47.39	Washington	
Illinois	65.73	Oregon	1.54
Michigan	26.61	California	13.96
Wisconsin	18.25		

The following table shows the net numerical increase or decrease in rural population in the United States, groups of states, and the several states and territories:

INCREASE OR DECREASE IN RURAL POPULATION: 1880 TO 1890.

STATES AND TERRITORIES.	Increase.	Decrease.	STATES AND TERRITORIES.	Increase.	Decrease.
The United States	4,078,422		North Central division—Continued.		
			Iowa	121,709	
North Atlantic division		37,941	Missouri	176,171	
			North Dakota }	332,330	
Maine		24,391	South Dakota }		
New Hampshire		8,575	Nebraska	346,834	
Vermont		18,944	Kansas	229,823	
Massachusetts		6,522			
Rhode Island		508	South Central division	1,314,973	
Connecticut		11,964			
New York		163,176	Kentucky	98,087	
New Jersey	31,316		Tennessee	77,985	
Pennsylvania	164,823		Alabama	168,227	
			Mississippi	124,914	
South Atlantic division	664,346		Louisiana	120,255	
			Texas	396,846	
Delaware	40		Oklahoma	51,620	
Maryland		17,220	Arkansas	267,139	
District of Columbia (a)					
Virginia	45,035		Western division	587,280	
West Virginia	114,943				
North Carolina	156,909		Montana	52,485	
South Carolina	108,780		Wyoming	20,268	
Georgia	183,761		Colorado	87,518	
Florida	72,008		New Mexico	20,547	
			Arizona	14,882	
North Central division	1,549,764		Utah	22,542	
			Nevada		13,085
Ohio		13,274	Idaho	50,735	
Indiana	8,073		Washington	136,715	
Illinois		66,741	Oregon	79,773	
Michigan	104,877		California	114,900	
Wisconsin	103,206				
Minnesota	206,756				

a No rural population.

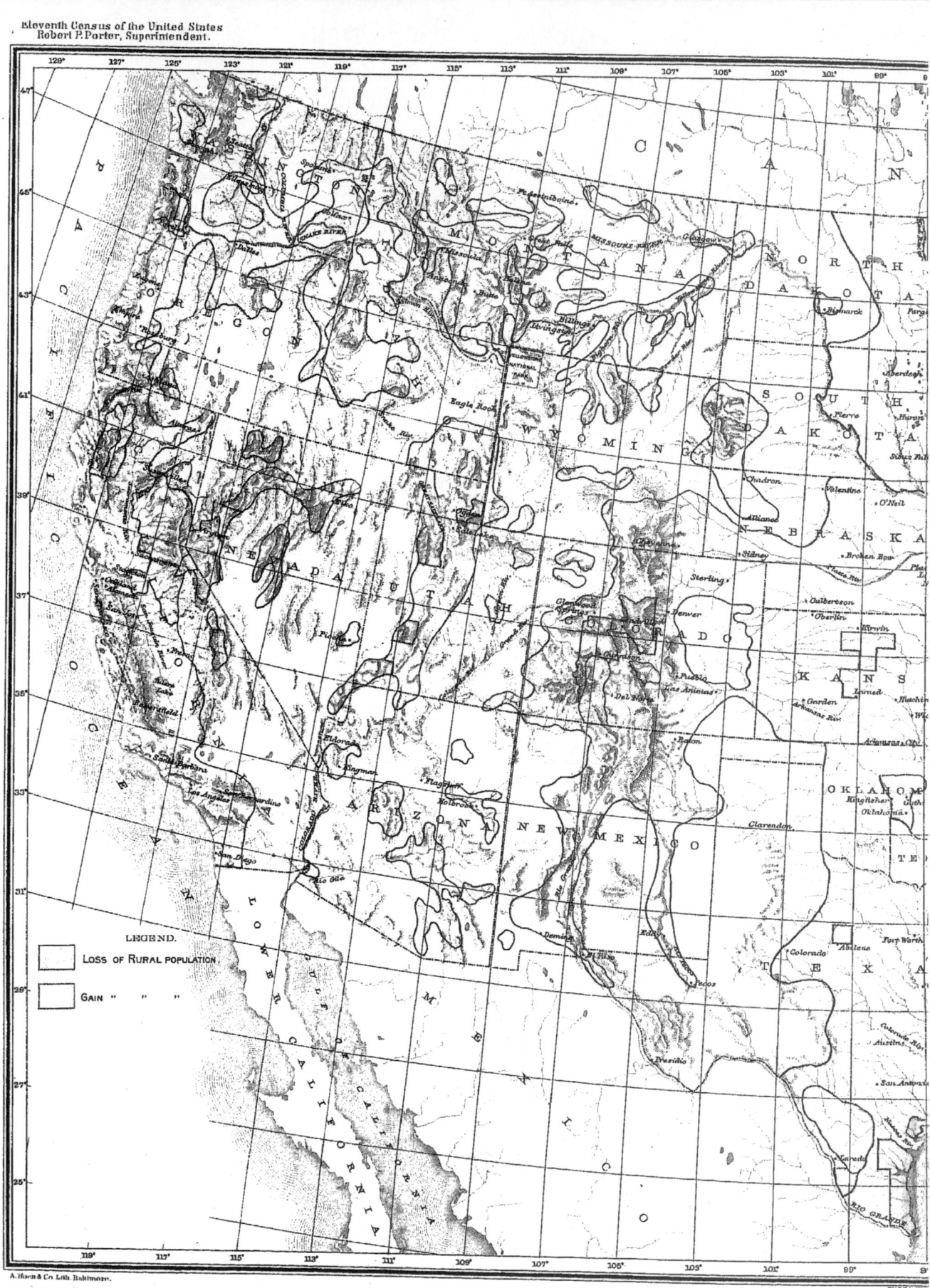

Eleventh Census of the United States
Robert P. Porter, Superintendent.

LEGEND.

Loss of Rural population

Gain " " "

A. Hoen & Co. Lith. Baltimore.

ENGRAVED

POPULATION.

MAP
SHOWING
GAIN OR LOSS
OF RURAL POPULATION
BETWEEN 1880 AND 1890.
COMPILED BY
HENRY GANNETT, GEOGRAPHER.

SEX.

Among the states in the North Atlantic division there has been a loss of rural population throughout New England and New York, the only states of this division in which the rural population has increased being New Jersey and Pennsylvania.

In the South Atlantic division the only state which has suffered a loss is Maryland, although Delaware has but a small gain. Virginia has lost heavily in certain parts, but the net result for the state has been a gain. In the other states of this division most of the increase in population has consisted in an increase of this element.

In the North Central division there has been a loss of rural population in Ohio and Illinois, while in Indiana the gain is trifling. In the other states of this division the gain in rural population has been substantial, especially in those upon the plains.

In every state of the South Central division there has been a considerable gain in the rural population. The same is true also of the states and territories comprising the Western division, with the exception of Nevada, which, with its great loss in total population, has suffered a corresponding loss in the rural element.

SEX.

The aggregate population on June 1, 1890, was 62,622,250. Of this number 32,067,880 were males and 30,554,370 were females. The following table shows for the United States as a whole the proportion which the number of each sex bears to the total population at each census from 1850 to 1890:

CENSUS YEARS.	Males.	Females.
	Per cent.	Per cent.
1850	51.04	48.96
1860	51.16	48.84
1870	50.56	49.44
1880	50.88	49.12
1890	51.21	48.79

From the above table it is apparent that for 1890 in the United States males were in excess of females in the proportion of 51.21 and 48.79. This excess of males is to be expected in this case, owing to the effects of immigration. Where natural increase is not interfered with either by immigration or emigration, wars or pestilence, the proportion of the sexes is nearly equal, females being slightly in excess of males. This is shown (but rather imperfectly, on account of the effect of emigration) in the following table, which presents the proportions of the sexes in certain European countries:

COUNTRIES.	Males.	Females.
	Per cent.	Per cent.
United Kingdom	48.54	51.46
Austria	48.92	51.08
Denmark	48.76	51.24
Germany	49.03	50.97
Netherlands	49.42	50.58
Spain	49.04	50.96
Sweden	48.43	51.57
Norway	47.87	52.13

In every one of these countries, without exception, females are in excess, constituting from 50.58 to 52.13 per cent of the whole population. In the United Kingdom, Denmark, Germany, Sweden, and Norway it may be accounted for by emigration, but in the cases of Austria, Netherlands, and Spain there is little emigration, and the figures are practically those of undisturbed natural increase. Judging, therefore, from these cases, it would appear that under undisturbed conditions the female sex outnumbers the male sex nearly in the proportion of 51 to 49.

The effect of emigration upon the population of the other countries is roughly measured by the fact that the average proportion of females to males in them is about 51.5 to 48.5. In the case of the United States, however, normal conditions are modified by immigration. Among the immigrants to this country males are in excess of females in the proportion of 3 to 2, and to this fact, coupled with the excessive immigration during the past decade, is to be attributed the large proportion of males.

If the history of the distribution of the population by sex from 1850 to 1890 is examined it is seen that males have always been in excess of females; that between 1850 and 1860 the proportion increased slightly, while between 1860 and 1870 it diminished by six-tenths of 1 per cent, which in such a matter as this is a very large reduction. This was doubtless due in great measure to the mortality of the civil war, the ravages of which were confined to the male sex, and in which probably not far from a million of our citizens lost their lives. Between 1870 and 1880 and 1880 and 1890 the proportion of males had again increased, reaching at the latter date a proportion slightly in excess of that which was shown in 1860.

PROGRESS OF THE NATION.

lxxii

The following table shows the proportion of males and females in each state and territory in 1890, 1880, 1870, 1860, and 1850:

PERCENTAGE OF MALES AND FEMALES OF TOTAL POPULATION: 1850 TO 1890.

STATES AND TERRITORIES.	1890		1880		1870		1860		1850	
	Males.	Females.	Males.	Females.	Males.	Females.	Males.	Females.	Males.	Females.
The United States	51.21	48.79	50.88	49.12	50.56	49.44	51.16	48.84	51.04	48.96
North Atlantic division	49.87	50.13	49.36	50.64	49.43	50.57	49.70	50.30	50.30	49.70
Maine	50.71	49.00	49.04	50.86	45.94	50.66	50.49	49.51	51.01	48.99
New Hampshire	49.55	50.45	49.14	50.86	48.90	51.10	49.01	50.99	49.13	50.87
Vermont	50.94	49.06	50.22	49.78	50.13	49.87	50.39	49.61	50.95	49.05
Massachusetts	48.58	51.42	48.14	51.86	48.29	51.71	48.47	51.53	49.12	50.88
Rhode Island	48.63	51.37	48.11	51.89	48.20	51.80	48.18	51.82	48.85	51.15
Connecticut	49.52	50.48	49.11	50.89	49.36	50.64	49.11	50.89	49.54	50.46
New York	49.63	50.37	49.29	50.71	49.36	50.64	49.82	50.18	50.62	49.38
New Jersey	49.89	50.11	49.50	50.50	49.63	50.37	49.86	50.14	50.12	49.88
Pennsylvania	50.71	49.29	49.89	50.11	49.93	50.07	50.05	49.95	50.53	49.47
South Atlantic division	49.88	50.12	49.46	50.54	48.96	51.04	50.09	49.91	50.08	49.92
Delaware	50.79	49.21	50.55	49.45	50.10	49.90	50.52	49.48	50.21	49.79
Maryland	49.47	50.53	49.43	50.57	49.30	50.70	49.62	50.38	50.14	49.86
District of Columbia	47.56	52.44	47.05	52.95	47.22	52.78	47.28	52.72	46.75	53.25
Virginia	49.78	50.22	49.29	50.71	48.73	51.27	50.50	49.50	50.49	49.51
West Virginia	51.17	48.83	50.85	49.15	50.42	49.58				
North Carolina	49.30	50.61	49.15	50.85	48.42	51.58	49.93	50.07	49.58	50.42
South Carolina	49.72	50.28	49.26	50.74	48.74	51.26	49.36	50.64	49.31	50.69
Georgia	50.07	49.93	49.47	50.53	48.89	51.11	50.31	49.69	50.37	49.63
Florida	51.59	48.41	50.63	49.37	50.36	49.64	51.94	48.06	52.52	47.48
North Central division	51.85	48.15	51.92	48.08	51.72	48.28	52.14	47.86	52.08	47.92
Ohio	50.53	49.47	50.47	49.53	50.18	49.82	50.87	49.13	51.35	48.65
Indiana	51.01	48.99	51.07	48.93	51.05	48.95	51.78	48.22	51.79	48.21
Illinois	51.55	48.45	51.55	48.45	51.83	48.17	52.73	47.27	52.65	47.35
Michigan	52.14	47.86	52.68	47.32	52.17	47.83	52.69	47.31	52.78	47.22
Wisconsin	51.87	48.13	51.70	48.30	51.66	48.34	52.51	47.49	53.94	46.06
Minnesota	53.41	46.59	53.68	46.32	53.51	46.49	54.11	45.89	61.15	38.85
Iowa	52.01	47.99	52.21	47.79	52.42	47.58	52.52	47.48	52.57	47.43
Missouri	51.70	48.30	51.98	48.02	52.07	47.93	52.64	47.36	52.46	47.54
North Dakota	55.60	44.40	a60.88	a39.12	a62.60	a37.40	a57.83	a42.17		
South Dakota	54.82	45.18								
Nebraska	54.10	45.90	55.09	44.91	57.26	42.74	58.11	41.89		
Kansas	52.70	47.30	53.88	46.12	55.50	44.50	55.20	44.80		
South Central division	50.98	49.02	50.62	49.38	50.12	49.88	51.45	48.55	51.33	48.67
Kentucky	50.72	49.28	50.50	49.50	50.39	49.61	51.25	48.75	51.17	48.83
Tennessee	50.44	49.56	49.88	50.12	49.53	50.47	50.70	49.30	50.28	49.72
Alabama	50.06	49.94	49.32	50.68	49.02	50.98	50.75	49.25	50.85	49.15
Mississippi	50.38	49.62	50.12	49.88	49.93	50.07	51.30	48.70	51.39	48.61
Louisiana	50.01	49.99	49.87	50.13	49.82	50.18	52.26	47.74	53.04	46.96
Texas	52.45	47.55	52.64	47.36	51.74	48.26	52.99	47.01	53.52	46.48
Oklahoma	56.17	43.83								
Arkansas	51.92	48.08	51.87	48.13	51.24	48.76	52.30	47.70	52.33	47.67
Western division	58.88	41.12	60.53	39.47	61.50	38.50	68.10	31.90	73.61	26.39
Montana	66.50	33.50	71.96	28.04	81.43	18.57				
Wyoming	64.81	35.19	68.07	31.93	79.17	20.83				
Colorado	59.50	40.50	66.45	33.55	62.26	37.74	95.37	4.63		
New Mexico	54.07	45.93	53.94	46.06	51.30	48.70	52.49	47.51	51.57	48.43
Arizona	61.34	38.66	69.74	30.26	71.31	28.69				
Utah	53.13	46.87	51.76	48.24	50.84	49.16	50.29	49.71	53.13	46.87
Nevada	63.84	36.16	67.48	32.52	76.20	23.80	89.50	10.50		
Idaho	60.78	39.22	66.91	33.09	81.23	18.77				
Washington	62.27	37.73	61.20	38.80	62.58	37.42	72.85	27.15		
Oregon	57.95	42.05	59.15	40.85	58.44	41.56	60.21	39.79	62.12	37.88
California	57.95	42.05	59.93	40.07	62.38	37.62	71.93	28.07	92.42	7.58

a Dakota territory.

The above table shows the wide range among the states and territories in the proportion which the sexes bear to each other. The extreme on one side is the District of Columbia, where no less than 52.44 per cent of the

SEX.   lxxiii

total population are females. This is followed at some distance by Massachusetts, where women form 51.42 per cent of the whole number. On the other hand are the newer states and territories of the far west, where we find Montana, with a population made up of 2 parts male to 1 female, and Wyoming, where but 35.19 per cent of the population are females. In both the North Atlantic and South Atlantic divisions females are slightly in excess of males. In the South Central division males are slightly in excess, and in the North Central division they are in excess to a much larger extent, while in the Western division nearly three-fifths of the population are males.

These differences are easy of explanation. The Atlantic divisions form an old settled region whence naturally for many decades a stream of emigration has flowed westward. This emigration has consisted in considerable proportion of the male element. In this way the eastern communities have been depleted. It is true that in the northeastern states the place of these emigrants has been filled to some extent by foreign immigration from Europe, otherwise its effect would be vastly more marked. The manufacturing centers of the northeastern states have attracted not only males from among the immigrants but to a large extent females also, especially of Irish and French-Canadian extraction, who form the bulk of the factory operatives. The same cause which has reduced the proportion of males in the Atlantic states has increased it in the central and western states. In the North Central division and in the Western division to this cause is to be added foreign immigration, which, consisting largely of males, increases still further the proportion of that sex.

Glancing at the history unfolded by this table, it is seen that in the North Atlantic division females have been in excess at each census since 1850; that this excess reached its maximum in 1880, and is now diminishing, as the effect of immigration from Europe overcomes that of emigration to the west. In each of the states composing this division this proportionate increase of the female element can be traced, reaching its maximum in 1870 or 1880, and thereafter diminishing. The effect of the civil war upon the elements of the population of these states is scarcely perceptible.

In the South Atlantic division different conditions prevail. Immigration to these states is but slight, and not sufficient to affect the constitution of the population as regards sex. These states are found to be almost equally divided between the sexes in 1850 and 1860. In 1870 the proportion of males has diminished 1.13 per cent, the effect undoubtedly of the civil war. Since then the proportion of males has increased, and the numbers of the sexes are nearly equal in 1890. Among the various states composing this division there is considerable variety as regards sex. In Delaware, Maryland, and the District of Columbia there is little evidence of the effect of the civil war, while in the other states that effect is very strongly marked. Indeed, in North Carolina and Georgia there is a reduction in the proportion of males due to this cause of about 1.5 per cent, which in most cases has been recovered during the past twenty years.

In the North Central division still different conditions have prevailed. In 1850 many of these states were upon the frontier, and in the forty years that have elapsed the frontier has moved away beyond them and they have assumed the conditions of old settled communities. There has been as a rule comparatively little emigration from these states. On the other hand, there has been a vast amount of immigration to them, both from states farther east and from Europe, and of course it is understood that this immigration is disproportionately male. Starting then in 1850, this division of the states comprised a considerable excess of the male element. This element diminished appreciably by 1870, and since then has somewhat more than held its own. The influence of the war was probably slight, but, whether large or small, it can not be distinguished from the effect of other causes, to which it must be secondary. Among the various states considerable diversity exists, since this division stretches from Ohio, which in 1850 was an old settled community, to Kansas, Nebraska, North Dakota, and South Dakota, which even at present are sparsely settled on their western borders.

The South Central division comprises a group of states extending from Alabama, a well settled state even in 1850, on the east, to Texas, which in 1845 was admitted to the Union, on the west. It is a section which has received little foreign immigration, but which has been filled up by immigration from the South Atlantic states and by natural increase. In 1850 this section contained a considerable excess of the male element. In 1860 this had increased a little, and in 1870 had decidedly diminished, owing, doubtless, to the ravages of the civil war. Between 1870 and 1880 these losses were being repaired.

The Western division comprises states and territories some of which were not known by name in 1850, and others which at that date contained but a few thousand white inhabitants. Even now, without exception, they are sparsely settled. In 1850 this division was peopled with 3 males to 1 female. In 1860 the proportion had declined to 2 to 1; in 1870 and 1880 more than 6 out of 10 were males, and in 1890 the proportion of males was a little smaller. Indeed, in 1890 the least proportion of males in all these states and territories was in Utah, where 53.13 per cent were of that sex, and the largest proportion of males was in Montana, where they outnumbered the females in the proportion of 2 to 1. Considering these states and territories as regards extreme cases of disproportion between the sexes, it is seen that the population of Colorado in 1860 was composed of 95.37 per cent of males; that the population of Nevada in the same year was composed of 89.50 per cent of males, and that California in 1850, in the height of the gold excitement, contained only 7.58 per cent of women.

For the United States as a whole there are for every 100,000 males 95,280 females in 1890. In 1880 there were 96,544 females to every 100,000 males, while in 1870 there were 97,801 females to every 100,000 males.

lxxiv   PROGRESS OF THE NATION.

The following table gives, by states and territories, arranged geographically, the whole number of males and females as returned under the census of 1890, and the number of females to each 100,000 males for the censuses of 1890, 1880, and 1870:

RELATIVE PROPORTIONS OF FEMALES TO MALES: 1870 TO 1890.

STATES AND TERRITORIES.	MALES.	FEMALES.	NUMBER OF FEMALES TO EACH 100,000 MALES.		
	1890	1890	1890	1880	1870
The United States	32,067,880	30,554,370	95,280	96,544	97,801
North Atlantic division	8,677,798	8,723,747	100,530	102,600	102,293
Maine	332,590	328,496	98,769	100,253	100,226
New Hampshire	186,566	189,964	101,821	103,483	104,510
Vermont	169,327	163,095	96,320	99,108	99,462
Massachusetts	1,087,709	1,151,234	105,840	107,712	107,075
Rhode Island	168,025	177,481	105,628	107,871	107,485
Connecticut	369,538	376,720	101,944	103,642	102,606
New York	2,976,893	3,020,960	101,480	102,883	102,603
New Jersey	720,819	724,114	100,457	102,013	101,502
Pennsylvania	2,666,331	2,591,683	97,200	100,448	100,282
South Atlantic division	4,418,769	4,439,151	100,461	102,177	104,256
Delaware	85,573	82,920	96,900	97,830	99,615
Maryland	515,691	526,699	102,135	102,287	102,838
District of Columbia	109,584	120,808	110,242	112,525	111,764
Virginia	824,278	831,702	100,901	102,868	105,500
West Virginia	390,285	372,509	95,445	96,651	98,552
North Carolina	799,149	818,798	102,459	103,479	106,546
South Carolina	572,337	578,812	101,131	103,010	105,176
Georgia	919,925	917,428	99,729	102,126	104,525
Florida	201,947	189,475	93,824	97,512	98,574
North Central division	11,594,910	10,767,369	92,863	92,594	93,350
Ohio	1,855,736	1,816,580	97,890	98,153	99,264
Indiana	1,118,347	1,074,057	96,040	95,801	95,880
Illinois	1,972,308	1,854,043	94,004	94,001	92,922
Michigan	1,091,780	1,002,100	91,787	89,822	91,674
Wisconsin	874,951	811,929	92,797	93,436	93,558
Minnesota	695,321	606,505	87,227	86,276	80,871
Iowa	994,453	917,443	92,256	91,551	90,763
Missouri	1,385,238	1,293,946	93,410	92,371	92,034
North Dakota	101,590	81,129	79,859 }	a64,257	a59,732
South Dakota	180,250	148,558	82,418 }		
Nebraska	572,824	486,086	84,858	81,512	74,644
Kansas	752,112	674,984	89,745	85,608	80,196
South Central division	5,593,877	5,379,016	96,159	97,570	99,506
Kentucky	942,758	915,877	97,149	98,019	98,447
Tennessee	891,585	875,933	98,244	100,495	101,897
Alabama	757,456	755,561	99,750	102,770	103,993
Mississippi	649,687	639,913	98,496	99,514	100,261
Louisiana	559,350	559,237	99,980	100,520	100,714
Texas	1,172,553	1,062,970	90,654	89,982	93,263
Oklahoma	34,733	27,101	78,027	....	....
Arkansas	585,755	542,424	92,608	92,785	95,146
Western division	1,782,526	1,245,087	69,850	65,200	62,614
Montana	87,882	44,277	50,382	38,075	22,801
Wyoming	39,343	21,362	54,297	46,898	26,306
Colorado	245,247	166,951	68,075	50,488	60,612
New Mexico	83,055	70,538	84,929	85,384	94,917
Arizona	36,571	23,049	63,025	43,394	40,235
Utah	110,463	97,442	88,212	93,216	96,700
Nevada	29,214	16,547	56,641	48,185	31,230
Idaho	51,290	33,095	64,525	49,464	23,104
Washington	217,562	131,828	60,593	63,392	59,807
Oregon	181,840	131,927	72,551	69,052	71,130
California	700,059	508,071	72,575	66,873	60,309

a Dakota territory.

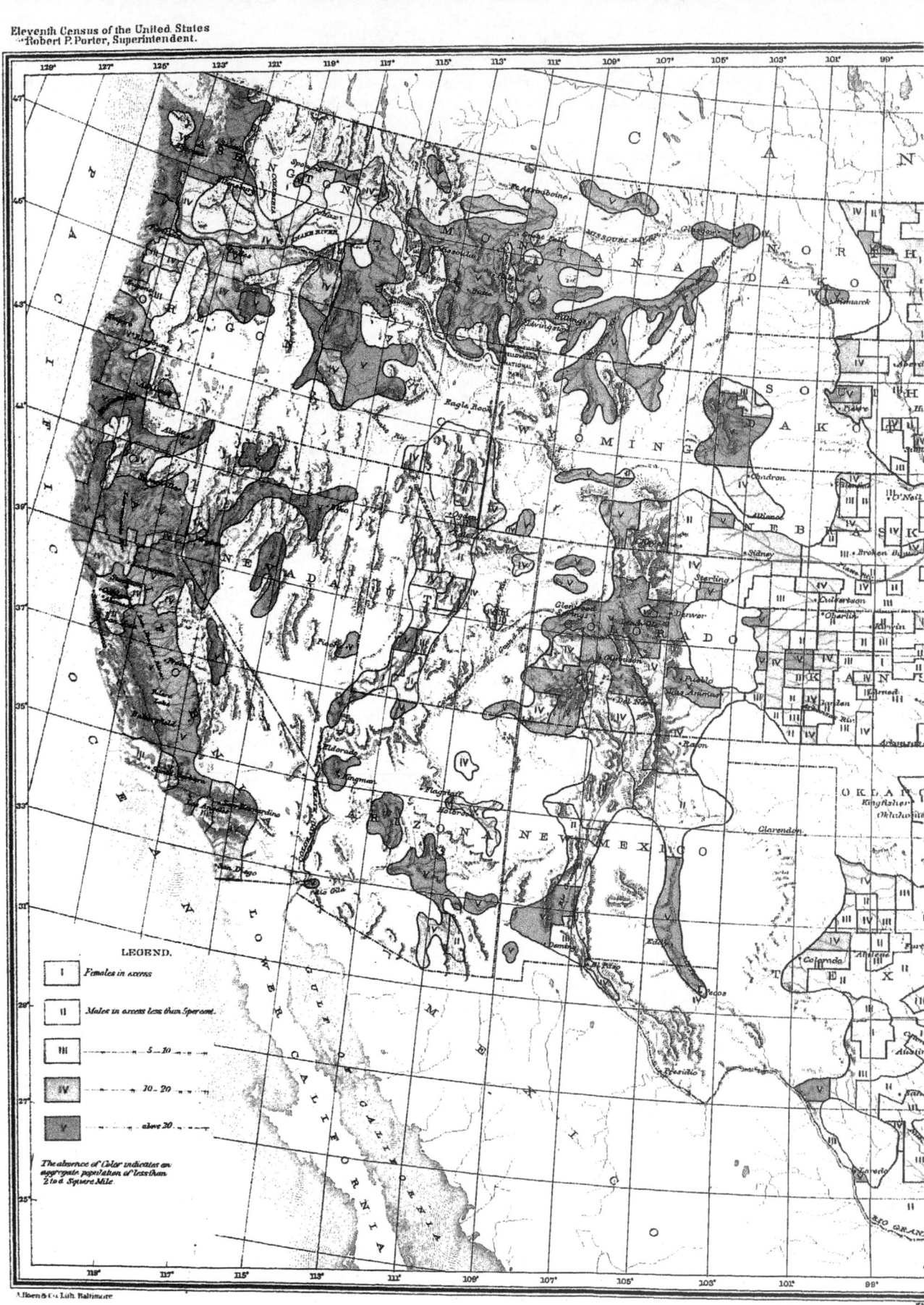

Eleventh Census of the United States
Robert P. Porter, Superintendent.

LEGEND.

I	Females in excess
II	Males in excess less than 5 per cent.
III	5 – 10
IV	10 – 20
V	above 20

The absence of Color indicates an
aggregate population of less than
2 to a Square Mile.

A.Hoen & Co. Lith.Baltimore.

POPULATION.

MAP
SHOWING
THE PREDOMINATING SEX
at the Eleventh Census,
COMPILED BY
HENRY GANNETT, GEOGRAPHER.

SEX.

lxxv

The greatest preponderance of females in 1890 is found in the District of Columbia, or 110,242 females to every 100,000 males. In 1880 also the District of Columbia contained the highest proportion of females to males, or 112,525 females to every 100,000 males. In Massachusetts, the state having the next greatest excess of females over males in 1890, there are 105,840 females to every 100,000 males, while in Rhode Island, the state showing the third largest excess of females over males, there are 105,628 females to every 100,000 males. In 1880 Rhode Island was second as to the excess of females, with 107,871 females to every 100,000 males, and Massachusetts third, with 107,712 females to every 100,000 males.

Grouping the states with reference to the proportion of the sexes, it is seen that, besides the District of Columbia, there are 10 states, namely, Connecticut, Maryland, Massachusetts, New Hampshire, New Jersey, New York, North Carolina, Rhode Island, South Carolina, and Virginia, in which females are in excess. Every one of these, it will be noticed, is in one of the two Atlantic divisions.

In the remaining states males are in excess. Of these there are 13, namely, Alabama, Delaware, Georgia, Indiana, Kentucky, Louisiana, Maine, Mississippi, Ohio, Pennsylvania, Tennessee, Vermont, and West Virginia, in which the whole number of females represents 95 per cent or more of the whole number of males.

In 14 states and territories the number of females is between 80 and 95 per cent of the number of males. These are as follows: Arkansas, Florida, Illinois, Iowa, Kansas, Michigan, Minnesota, Missouri, Nebraska, New Mexico, South Dakota, Texas, Utah, and Wisconsin. In the remaining states and territories the whole number of females represents from 50 to 80 per cent of the whole number of males. These are Arizona, California, Colorado, Idaho, Montana, Nevada, North Dakota, Oklahoma, Oregon, Washington, and Wyoming.

The constitution of the population of many of the states with regard to sex has changed materially since 1880, while throughout the country at large there has been an increase in the proportion of males.

The increase of the male element in the country at large has resulted in transferring from the list of states in which females were in excess in 1880 to those in which males are in excess no fewer than 6 states, namely, Alabama, Georgia, Louisiana, Maine, Pennsylvania, and Tennessee. In general, it has increased the proportion of males in the northern and southern central states. On the other hand, the development of settled conditions in the group of western states and territories has reduced the proportion of males among them.

The whole number of states and territories where the females exceed the males in 1890 is 11 as against 17 in 1880. All of the states and territories showing an excess of females over males in 1890 are found in the North Atlantic and South Atlantic divisions, as was also true of the states and territories having an excess of females over males in 1880, with the exception of Alabama, Louisiana, and Tennessee, in the South Central division.

In 1880 there were 5 states and territories in which the number of females was less than 50 per cent of the number of males, namely, Arizona, Idaho, Montana, Nevada, and Wyoming, while in 1890 there is no state or territory where the number of females is not at least 50 per cent of the number of males.

In 1890 there are 11 states and territories, mainly in the Western division, in which the number of females is from 50 to 80 per cent of the number of males as against 5 states and territories in 1880.

For the remaining states and territories the number of females is over 80 per cent but less than 100 per cent of the number of males.

The females as compared with the males have lost relatively since 1880 in the United States as a whole, the numerical loss being 1,264 females to each 100,000 males as against a relative loss in 1880 of 1,257 females to each 100,000 males. There has been a relative loss during the decade of 2,070 females to each 100,000 males in the North Atlantic division; of 1,716 females to each 100,000 males in the South Atlantic division, and 1,411 females to each 100,000 males in the South Central division. There has been a slight increase relatively, on the other hand, of 269 females to each 100,000 males in the North Central division, and 4,650 females to each 100,000 males in the Western division. In 19 states and territories there has been a relative increase of females to each 100,000 males, while in 29 states and territories there has been a relative decrease of females to each 100,000 males, as is shown by the following table, giving in addition to the increase or decrease in 1890, on the assumed basis of 100,000 males, the increase or decrease as shown by the census of 1880 as compared with 1870:

RELATIVE INCREASE OF FEMALES TO EACH 100,000 MALES.

STATES AND TERRITORIES.	Increase since 1880.	Increase or decrease from 1870 to 1880.	STATES AND TERRITORIES.	Increase since 1880.	Increase or decrease from 1870 to 1880.
Arizona	19,631	+3,159	Oregon	3,499	−2,078
Colorado	17,587	−10,124	Nebraska	3,346	+6,868
Dakota (a)	17,230	+4,525	Michigan	1,965	−1,852
Idaho	15,061	+26,360	Missouri	1,039	+337
Montana	11,407	+16,174	Minnesota	951	−595
Nevada	8,456	+16,955	Iowa	795	+788
Wyoming	7,399	+20,592	Texas	672	−3,281
California	5,702	+6,564	Indiana	239	−79
Kansas	4,137	+5,412	Illinois	3	+1,079

a North Dakota and South Dakota combined.

lxxvi

PROGRESS OF THE NATION.

RELATIVE DECREASE OF FEMALES TO EACH 100,000 MALES.

STATES AND TERRITORIES.	Decrease since 1880.	Increase or decrease from 1870 to 1880.	STATES AND TERRITORIES.	Decrease since 1880.	Increase or decrease from 1870 to 1880.
Utah	5,004	—3,484	New Jersey	1,556	+511
Florida	3,688	—1,062	Maine	1,484	+27
Pennsylvania	3,248	+166	New York	1,403	+280
Alabama	3,020	—1,223	West Virginia	1,206	—1,701
Washington	2,799	+3,585	North Carolina	1,020	—3,067
Vermont	2,788	—354	Mississippi	1,018	—747
Georgia	2,397	—2,399	Delaware	930	—1,785
District of Columbia	2,283	+761	Kentucky	870	—428
Tennessee	2,251	—1,402	Wisconsin	639	—122
Rhode Island	2,243	+386	Louisiana	540	—104
Virginia	1,967	—2,332	New Mexico	455	—9,533
South Carolina	1,879	—2,166	Ohio	203	—1,111
Massachusetts	1,872	+637	Arkansas	182	—2,361
Connecticut	1,698	+1,036	Maryland	152	—551
New Hampshire	1,662	—1,027			

The increase of females since 1880 for North Dakota and South Dakota is for these 2 states combined as compared with Dakota territory in 1880 and 1870.

In all the states and territories comprising the North Atlantic and South Atlantic divisions the females have decreased relatively as compared with males. This is also largely true of the South Central division, the females having decreased relatively in all the states and territories, with the exception of Texas. In Oklahoma in 1890 there are 78,027 females to each 100,000 males. The females have increased relatively as compared with males in all the states comprising the North Central division, with the exception of Ohio and Wisconsin. The females have also increased relatively as compared with the males in the states and territories comprising the Western division, with the exception of New Mexico, Utah, and Washington.

SEX.

The following table shows, by states and territories, the numerical increase in males and females for each decade since 1850:

INCREASE IN MALES AND FEMALES: 1850 TO 1890.

STATES AND TERRITORIES.	INCREASE IN MALES.				INCREASE IN FEMALES.			
	1880 to 1890	1870 to 1880	1860 to 1870	1850 to 1860	1880 to 1890	1870 to 1880	1860 to 1870	1850 to 1860
The United States	6,549,000	6,025,255	3,408,361	4,247,544	5,917,407	5,572,157	3,706,689	4,003,901
North Atlantic division	1,517,176	1,080,953	814,036	926,220	1,376,962	1,127,724	890,426	1,041,197
Maine	8,532	10,955	a4,086	19,718	3,618	11,066	2,722	25,392
New Hampshire	16,040	14,886	a4,176	3,506	13,499	13,805	a3,597	4,501
Vermont	2,440	1,166	6,035	a1,247	* a2,304	569	8,518	2,225
Massachusetts	229,260	154,661	107,066	108,196	226,589	171,073	119,210	128,356
Rhode Island	34,995	28,274	20,623	12,055	33,080	30,904	22,110	15,020
Connecticut	63,756	40,512	39,276	42,290	50,802	44,734	38,031	47,065
New York	471,571	342,093	229,097	365,591	443,411	358,019	272,327	417,750
New Jersey	160,807	110,250	114,021	89,705	152,920	114,770	119,440	92,775
Pennsylvania	529,676	378,156	304,080	286,316	445,447	382,784	311,056	308,113
South Atlantic division	661,071	891,884	178,816	343,762	599,652	851,703	310,001	341,851
Delaware	11,465	11,480	5,030	10,734	10,420	10,113	6,860	9,956
Maryland	53,504	77,203	44,086	48,575	53,943	76,846	49,750	55,440
District of Columbia	26,006	21,386	26,693	11,335	26,762	24,538	20,027	12,058
Virginia	78,689	148,531	b209,043	88,237	64,726	138,871	b162,112	86,420
West Virginia	75,790	91,652	222,843	....	68,547	84,791	219,171	....
North Carolina	111,241	169,204	23,088	64,712	106,950	159,185	55,651	58,871
South Carolina	81,929	146,506	a3,418	17,686	73,643	143,465	5,316	17,515
Georgia	156,944	184,026	47,010	75,480	138,229	174,045	79,813	75,621
Florida	65,503	41,896	21,618	27,003	56,420	39,849	25,706	25,076
North Central division	2,578,960	2,302,118	1,970,963	1,928,605	2,419,178	2,080,882	1,913,432	1,764,516
Ohio	241,800	276,386	147,388	178,354	232,454	256,416	178,361	185,828
Indiana	107,986	152,367	158,734	187,367	106,117	145,297	171,475	174,645
Illinois	385,785	269,986	413,776	454,440	362,805	287,994	414,164	406,041
Michigan	229,425	244,610	223,051	184,798	227,527	208,268	211,895	166,661
Wisconsin	194,882	135,183	137,487	242,733	176,501	125,644	141,352	227,757
Minnesota	276,172	183,850	142,215	•89,368	244,881	157,217	125,468	76,578
Iowa	146,317	222,219	271,424	253,441	140,064	208,376	247,083	229,258
Missouri	258,051	230,840	274,146	264,369	252,753	216,245	265,137	235,599
North Dakota.. South Dakota..	c199,544	d73,418	d6,081	d2,707	c176,806	d47,578	d3,263	d2,040
Nebraska	323,583	178,816	53,005	16,760	282,025	150,593	40,487	12,081
Kansas	215,445	334,443	143,046	50,178	215,553	297,254	114,147	48,028
South Central division	1,070,331	1,289,382	256,978	759,035	974,191	1,195,570	408,774	706,101
Kentucky	110,108	166,915	73,354	89,501	99,777	160,764	91,073	81,688
Tennessee	122,308	145,930	60,629	58,586	102,851	137,000	88,090	48,498
Alabama	134,827	133,891	a553	96,948	115,685	131,622	33,344	95,630
Mississippi	82,510	153,756	7,473	94,224	75,403	149,910	20,144	91,555
Louisiana	90,596	106,589	a7,829	95,308	88,045	106,442	26,742	94,842
Texas	334,713	414,283	103,390	206,387	309,061	358,887	110,974	185,236
Oklahoma	34,733	....	....	....	27,101	....	....	....
Arkansas	160,476	168,018	20,514	117,901	156,178	150,030	28,507	107,652
Western division	712,492	400,918	187,568	280,922	547,424	316,209	183,966	150,236
Montana	59,705	11,406	16,771	....	33,295	7,158	3,824	....
Wyoming	25,191	6,933	7,219	....	14,725	4,738	1,890	....
Colorado	116,116	104,311	a7,871	32,691	101,755	59,152	13,458	1,586
New Mexico	18,559	17,361	a1,956	17,340	15,460	10,330	314	14,620
Arizona	8,369	21,315	6,887	....	10,811	9,467	2,771	....
Utah	35,954	30,388	23,866	14,209	27,988	26,789	22,647	14,684
Nevada	a12,805	9,640	26,242	6,137	a3,700	10,135	9,392	720
Idaho	29,472	9,634	12,184	....	22,303	7,977	2,815	....
Washington	171,589	30,983	6,544	8,446	102,085	20,178	5,817	3,148
Oregon	78,450	50,250	21,540	23,333	60,540	33,595	16,918	15,838
California	181,883	168,697	76,142	187,757	161,553	135,750	104,111	99,640

a Decrease.
b Decrease; due to loss of territory, West Virginia having been set off from Virginia December 31, 1862.
c North Dakota and South Dakota combined.
d Dakota territory.

lxxviii   PROGRESS OF THE NATION.

The following table shows, by states and territories, the percentage of increase in males and females for each decade since 1850:

PERCENTAGE OF INCREASE IN MALES AND FEMALES: 1850 TO 1890.

STATES AND TERRITORIES.	PER CENT OF INCREASE IN MALES.				PER CENT OF INCREASE IN FEMALES.			
	1880 to 1890	1870 to 1880	1860 to 1870	1850 to 1860	1880 to 1890	1870 to 1880	1860 to 1870	1850 to 1860
The United States	25.66	30.01	21.19	35.88	24.02	29.23	24.14	35.26
North Atlantic division	21.19	17.78	15.46	21.34	18.74	18.13	16.71	24.28
Maine	2.63	3.50	a1.29	6.63	1.11	3.53	0.87	8.89
New Hampshire	9.41	9.56	a2.61	2.30	7.65	8.49	a2.16	2.78
Vermont	1.46	0.70	4.37	a0.78	a1.39	0.35	5.45	1.44
Massachusetts	26.71	21.98	17.94	22.15	24.51	22.70	18.79	25.37
Rhode Island	26.31	26.99	24.51	16.72	23.68	27.45	24.43	19.90
Connecticut	20.85	15.27	17.38	23.02	18.87	16.44	16.34	25.16
New York	18.82	15.81	11.88	23.32	17.20	16.13	13.99	27.31
New Jersey	28.74	24.52	34.21	36.56	26.77	25.15	35.44	37.99
Pennsylvania	24.79	21.50	20.91	24.51	20.75	21.71	21.47	26.94
South Atlantic division	17.59	31.12	6.65	14.67	15.62	28.51	11.58	14.63
Delaware	15.47	18.33	10.48	23.36	14.37	16.21	12.35	21.83
Maryland	11.58	20.05	12.93	16.62	11.41	19.41	14.37	19.07
District of Columbia	31.12	34.39	75.19	46.91	28.46	35.30	75.61	43.81
Virginia	10.55	24.88	b25.93	12.20	8.44	22.11	b20.51	12.28
West Virginia	24.10	41.13			22.55	38.69		
North Carolina	16.17	32.62	4.66	15.02	15.03	28.80	11.20	13.44
South Carolina	16.71	42.00	a0.98	5.37	14.58	39.66	1.49	5.17
Georgia	20.57	31.79	8.84	16.54	17.74	28.76	15.19	16.82
Florida	48.01	44.31	29.64	58.80	42.41	42.76	38.09	62.57
North Central division	28.60	34.20	41.56	68.53	28.98	33.20	43.95	68.14
Ohio	14.98	20.66	12.38	17.05	14.67	19.31	15.52	19.29
Indiana	10.69	17.76	22.70	36.60	10.96	17.66	26.83	36.65
Illinois	24.32	20.51	45.83	101.36	24.32	21.91	51.18	100.72
Michigan	26.60	39.00	50.51	88.04	29.37	36.78	50.79	88.70
Wisconsin	28.66	24.81	33.73	147.36	27.78	24.65	38.37	161.90
Minnesota	65.89	78.13	152.78	2,404.95	67.72	76.91	158.94	3,243.46
Iowa	17.25	35.50	76.57	250.80	18.15	36.08	77.30	251.48
Missouri	22.89	25.75	44.06	73.88	24.28	26.21	47.36	72.07
North Dakota ⎫ South Dakota ⎬	c242.47	d826.67	d217.41		c334.35	d897.19	d159.95	
Nebraska	129.83	253.91	320.20		139.26	286.47	335.13	
Kansas	40.15	165.38	241.72		46.92	183.29	237.67	
South Central division	23.91	39.98	8.66	34.36	22.12	37.25	14.60	33.71
Kentucky	13.23	25.07	12.38	17.82	12.23	24.53	16.33	17.45
Tennessee	15.90	23.41	10.77	11.62	13.30	21.71	16.10	9.73
Alabama	21.65	27.40	a0.11	24.71	18.08	25.90	7.02	25.21
Mississippi	14.55	37.19	1.84	30.23	13.38	36.17	7.56	30.72
Louisiana	19.33	29.43	a2.12	34.74	18.69	29.18	7.91	39.00
Texas	39.95	97.81	32.29	181.39	40.99	90.85	39.07	187.46
Oklahoma								
Arkansas	40.71	67.68	9.01	107.33	40.43	63.52	13.72	107.60
Western division	66.59	75.67	44.50	220.26	78.47	82.92	93.18	318.35
Montana	211.89	68.01			303.18	187.19		
Wyoming	178.00	96.04			221.86	249.50		
Colorado	89.92	420.27	a24.08		156.08	333.37	848.55	
New Mexico	28.78	36.83	a3.98	54.66	28.09	23.09	0.71	49.05
Arizona	29.68	309.50			88.34	341.65		
Utah	48.25	68.87	117.83	235.01	40.30	62.79	113.13	275.29
Nevada	a30.47	29.77	427.60		a18.27	100.23	1,304.44	
Idaho	135.08	79.07			206.66	283.37		
Washington	373.24	206.69	77.48		352.35	225.08	184.78	
Oregon	75.89	94.58	68.18	282.55	84.81	88.89	81.05	314.50
California	35.10	48.27	27.86	219.39	46.62	64.41	97.61	1,419.98

a Decrease.
b Decrease; due to loss of territory, West Virginia having been set off from Virginia December 31, 1862.
c North Dakota and South Dakota combined.
d Dakota territory.

389

SEX, GENERAL NATIVITY, AND COLOR.

TABLE 9.—POPULATION BY SEX, GENERAL NATIVITY, AND COLOR, BY STATES AND TERRITORIES: 1890.

TABLE 10.—COLORED POPULATION CLASSIFIED AS NEGROES, MULATTOES, QUADROONS, OCTOROONS, CHINESE, JAPANESE, AND CIVILIZED INDIANS, BY STATES AND TERRITORIES: 1890.

TABLE 11.—MALE AND FEMALE POPULATION, BY STATES AND TERRITORIES: 1850 TO 1890.

TABLE 12.—NATIVE AND FOREIGN BORN POPULATION, BY STATES AND TERRITORIES: 1850 TO 1890.

TABLE 13.—WHITE AND NEGRO POPULATION, BY STATES AND TERRITORIES: 1850 TO 1890.

TABLE 14.—CHINESE, JAPANESE, AND CIVILIZED INDIAN POPULATION, BY STATES AND TERRITORIES: 1860 TO 1890.

TABLE 15.—NATIVE AND FOREIGN BORN AND WHITE AND NEGRO POPULATION, BY COUNTIES: 1870 TO 1890.

TABLE 16.—CHINESE POPULATION, BY COUNTIES: 1870 TO 1890.

TABLE 17.—JAPANESE POPULATION, BY COUNTIES: 1870 TO 1890.

TABLE 18.—CIVILIZED INDIAN POPULATION, BY COUNTIES: 1870 TO 1890.

TABLE 19.—POPULATION, BY SEX, GENERAL NATIVITY, AND COLOR, OF PLACES HAVING 2,500 INHABITANTS OR MORE: 1890.

TABLE 20.—NATIVE AND FOREIGN BORN AND WHITE AND COLORED POPULATION, CLASSIFIED BY SEX, BY STATES AND TERRITORIES: 1890.

TABLE 21.—NEGRO, CHINESE, JAPANESE, AND CIVILIZED INDIAN POPULATION, CLASSIFIED BY SEX, BY STATES AND TERRITORIES: 1890.

TABLE 22.—NATIVE AND FOREIGN BORN AND WHITE AND COLORED POPULATION, CLASSIFIED BY SEX, BY COUNTIES: 1890.

TABLE 23.—NATIVE AND FOREIGN BORN AND WHITE AND COLORED POPULATION, CLASSIFIED BY SEX, OF PLACES HAVING 2,500 INHABITANTS OR MORE: 1890.

390

THE TOTAL POPULATION
AND ITS
ELEMENTS AT EACH CENSUS.

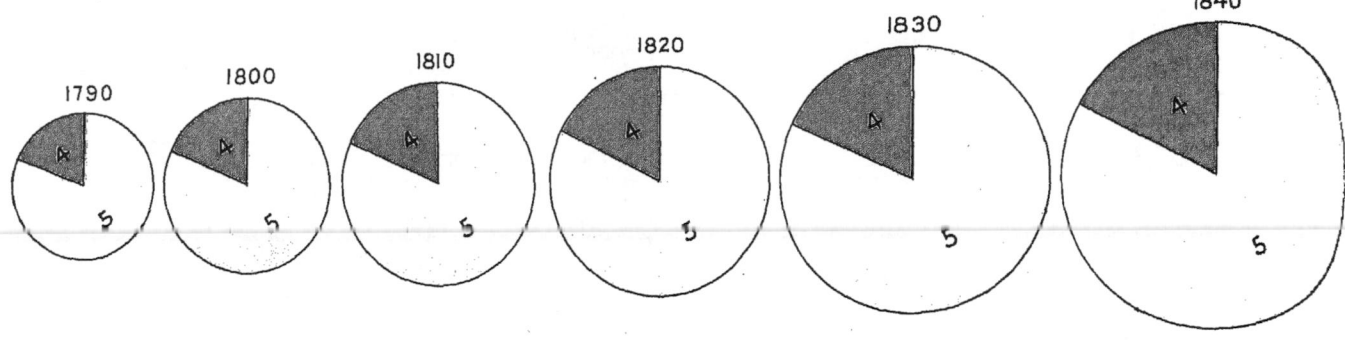

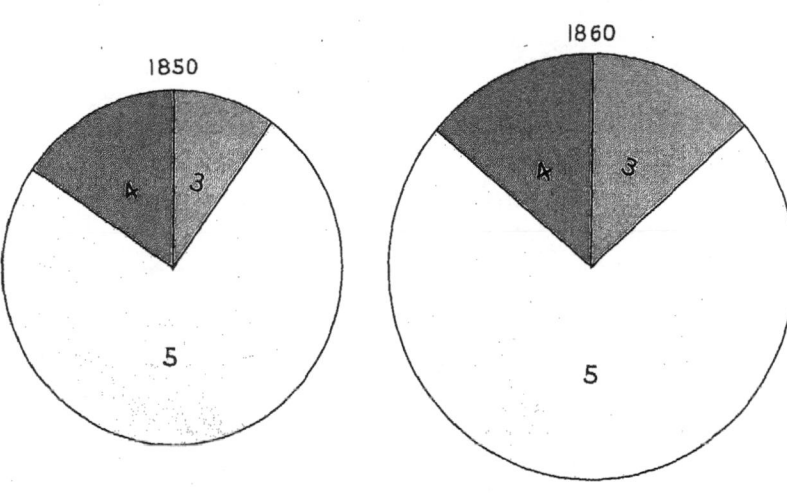

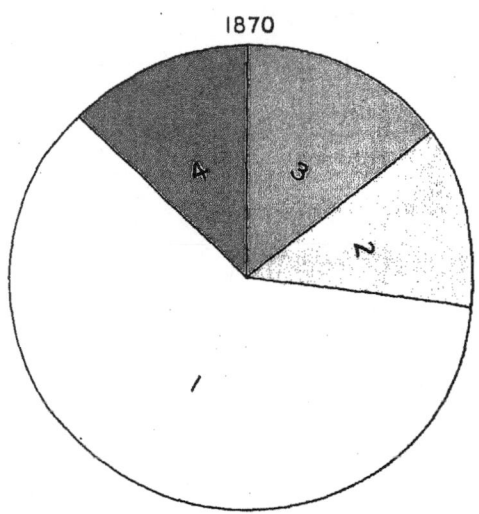

LEGEND.

NATIVE OF NATIVE PARENTS __ 1

NATIVE OF FOREIGN PARENTS _ 2

FOREIGN BORN _____ 3

COLORED _____ 4

ALL WHITES 1790 TO 1840 ___ 5
NATIVE WHITES 1850 AND 1860

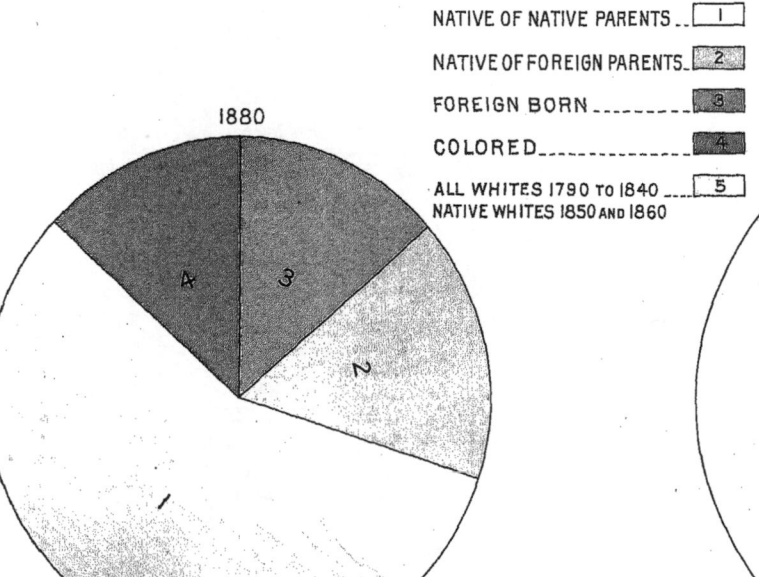

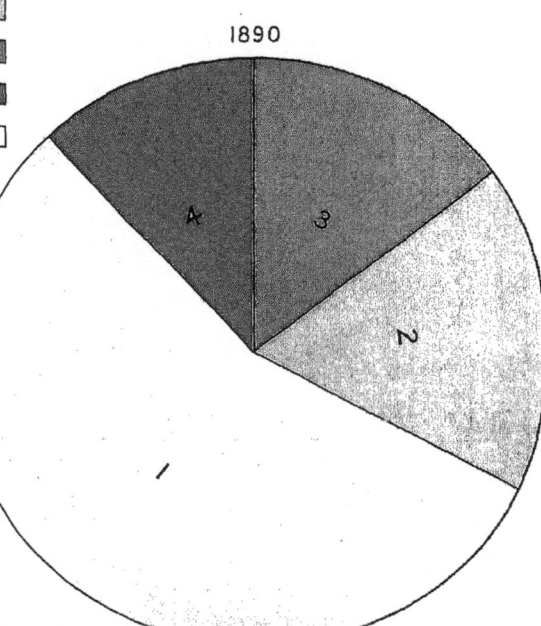

SEX, GENERAL NATIVITY, AND COLOR. 395

TABLE **9.**—POPULATION BY SEX, GENERAL NATIVITY, AND COLOR, BY STATES AND TERRITORIES: 1890.

STATES AND TERRITORIES.	Total population.	SEX.		NATIVE AND FOREIGN BORN.	
		Male.	Female.	Native.	Foreign.
The United States	62,622,250	32,067,880	30,554,370	53,372,703	9,249,547
North Atlantic division	17,401,545	8,677,798	8,723,747	13,513,368	3,888,177
Maine	661,086	332,590	328,496	582,125	78,961
New Hampshire	376,530	186,566	189,964	304,190	72,340
Vermont	332,422	169,327	163,095	288,334	44,088
Massachusetts	2,238,943	1,087,709	1,151,234	1,581,806	657,137
Rhode Island	345,506	168,025	177,481	239,201	106,305
Connecticut	746,258	369,538	376,720	562,657	183,601
New York	5,997,853	2,976,893	3,020,960	4,426,803	1,571,050
New Jersey	1,444,933	720,819	724,114	1,115,958	328,975
Pennsylvania	5,258,014	2,666,331	2,591,683	4,412,294	845,720
South Atlantic division	8,857,920	4,418,769	4,439,151	8,649,395	208,525
Delaware	168,493	85,573	82,920	155,332	13,161
Maryland	1,042,390	515,691	526,699	948,094	94,296
District of Columbia	230,392	109,584	120,808	211,622	18,770
Virginia	1,655,980	824,278	831,702	1,637,606	18,374
West Virginia	762,794	390,285	372,509	743,911	18,883
North Carolina	1,617,947	799,149	818,798	1,614,245	3,702
South Carolina	1,151,149	572,337	578,812	1,144,879	6,270
Georgia	1,837,353	919,925	917,428	1,825,216	12,137
Florida	391,422	201,947	189,475	368,400	22,032
North Central division	22,362,279	11,594,910	10,767,369	18,302,165	4,060,114
Ohio	3,672,316	1,855,736	1,816,580	3,213,023	459,293
Indiana	2,192,404	1,118,347	1,074,057	2,046,199	146,205
Illinois	3,826,351	1,972,308	1,854,043	2,984,004	842,347
Michigan	2,093,889	1,091,780	1,002,109	1,550,009	543,880
Wisconsin	1,686,880	874,951	811,929	1,167,681	519,199
Minnesota	1,301,826	695,321	606,505	834,470	467,356
Iowa	1,911,896	994,453	917,443	1,587,827	324,069
Missouri	2,679,184	1,385,238	1,293,946	2,444,315	234,869
North Dakota	182,719	101,590	81,129	101,258	81,461
South Dakota	328,808	180,250	148,558	237,753	91,055
Nebraska	1,058,910	572,824	486,086	856,368	202,542
Kansas	1,427,096	752,112	674,984	1,279,258	147,838
South Central division	10,972,893	5,593,877	5,379,016	10,651,072	321,821
Kentucky	1,858,635	942,758	915,877	1,799,279	59,356
Tennessee	1,767,518	891,585	875,933	1,747,489	20,029
Alabama	1,513,017	757,456	755,561	1,498,240	14,777
Mississippi	1,289,600	649,687	639,913	1,281,648	7,952
Louisiana	1,118,587	559,350	559,237	1,068,840	49,747
Texas	2,235,523	1,172,553	1,062,970	2,082,567	152,956
Oklahoma	61,834	34,733	27,101	59,094	2,740
Arkansas	1,128,179	585,755	542,424	1,113,915	14,264
Western division	3,027,613	1,782,526	1,245,087	2,256,703	770,910
Montana	132,159	87,882	44,277	89,063	43,096
Wyoming	60,705	39,343	21,362	45,792	14,913
Colorado	412,198	245,247	166,951	328,208	83,990
New Mexico	153,593	83,055	70,538	142,334	11,259
Arizona	59,620	36,571	23,049	40,825	18,795
Utah	207,905	110,463	97,442	154,841	53,064
Nevada	45,761	29,214	16,547	31,055	14,706
Idaho	84,385	51,290	33,095	66,929	17,456
Washington	349,390	217,562	131,828	259,385	90,005
Oregon	313,767	181,840	131,927	256,450	57,317
California	1,208,130	700,059	508,071	841,821	366,309

396   STATISTICS OF POPULATION.

TABLE **9.**—POPULATION BY SEX, GENERAL NATIVITY, AND COLOR, BY STATES AND TERRITORIES: 1890—Continued.

STATES AND TERRITORIES.	Aggregate white.	NATIVE WHITE.			Foreign white.	Total colored. (a)
		Total.	Native parents.	Foreign parents.		
The United States	54,983,890	45,862,023	34,358,348	11,503,675	9,121,807	7,038,360
North Atlantic division	17,121,981	13,247,115	8,891,405	4,355,710	3,874,866	270,504
Maine	659,263	580,508	506,703	73,805	78,695	1,823
New Hampshire	375,840	303,644	253,690	50,015	72,196	690
Vermont	331,418	287,394	225,245	62,149	44,024	1,004
Massachusetts	2,215,373	1,561,870	955,430	606,440	653,503	23,570
Rhode Island	337,859	231,832	137,550	94,282	106,027	7,647
Connecticut	733,438	550,283	357,235	193,048	183,155	12,820
New York	5,923,952	4,358,260	2,520,807	1,837,453	1,565,692	73,901
New Jersey	1,396,581	1,068,596	696,718	371,878	327,985	48,352
Pennsylvania	5,148,257	4,304,668	3,238,088	1,066,580	843,589	100,757
South Atlantic division	5,592,149	5,389,833	5,067,379	322,454	202,316	3,265,771
Delaware	140,066	126,970	109,355	17,615	13,096	28,427
Maryland	826,493	732,706	576,285	156,421	93,787	215,897
District of Columbia	154,695	136,178	107,309	28,869	18,517	75,697
Virginia	1,020,122	1,001,933	976,758	25,175	18,189	635,858
West Virginia	730,077	711,225	670,214	41,011	18,852	32,717
North Carolina	1,055,382	1,051,720	1,044,483	7,237	3,662	562,565
South Carolina	462,008	455,865	445,195	10,670	6,143	689,141
Georgia	978,357	966,465	946,782	19,683	11,892	858,996
Florida	224,949	206,771	190,998	15,773	18,178	166,473
North Central division	21,911,927	17,858,470	12,250,155	5,608,315	4,053,457	450,352
Ohio	3,584,805	3,126,252	2,334,517	791,735	458,553	87,511
Indiana	2,146,736	2,000,733	1,697,998	302,735	146,003	45,008
Illinois	3,768,472	2,927,497	1,882,693	1,044,804	840,975	57,879
Michigan	2,072,884	1,531,283	917,693	613,590	541,601	21,005
Wisconsin	1,680,473	1,161,484	434,649	726,835	518,989	6,407
Minnesota	1,296,159	829,102	310,951	518,151	467,057	5,667
Iowa	1,901,086	1,577,154	1,063,967	513,187	323,932	10,810
Missouri	2,528,458	2,294,176	1,856,477	437,699	234,282	150,720
North Dakota	182,123	100,775	37,428	63,347	81,348	590
South Dakota	327,290	236,447	127,232	109,215	90,843	1,518
Nebraska	1,046,888	844,644	594,224	250,420	202,244	12,022
Kansas	1,376,553	1,228,923	992,326	236,597	147,630	50,543
South Central division	7,487,576	7,168,997	6,661,648	507,349	318,579	3,485,317
Kentucky	1,590,462	1,531,222	1,406,918	124,304	59,240	268,173
Tennessee	1,336,637	1,316,738	1,283,481	33,257	19,899	430,681
Alabama	833,718	819,114	796,421	22,693	14,604	679,299
Mississippi	544,851	537,127	520,354	16,773	7,724	744,749
Louisiana	558,395	509,555	413,090	96,465	48,840	560,192
Texas	1,745,935	1,594,406	1,408,880	185,586	151,469	489,588
Oklahoma	58,826	56,117	51,554	4,563	2,709	3,008
Arkansas	818,752	804,658	780,950	23,708	14,094	309,427
Western division	2,870,257	2,197,608	1,487,761	709,847	672,649	157,356
Montana	127,271	86,941	55,982	30,959	40,330	4,888
Wyoming	59,275	44,845	30,325	14,520	14,430	1,430
Colorado	404,468	321,962	242,148	79,814	82,506	7,730
New Mexico	142,719	131,859	119,320	12,539	10,860	10,874
Arizona	55,580	38,117	24,090	14,027	17,463	4,040
Utah	205,899	153,766	68,452	85,314	52,133	2,006
Nevada	39,084	27,190	14,784	12,406	11,894	6,677
Idaho	82,018	66,554	45,400	21,154	15,464	2,367
Washington	340,513	254,319	185,562	68,757	86,194	8,877
Oregon	301,758	253,936	203,969	49,967	47,822	12,069
California	1,111,672	818,119	497,729	320,390	293,553	96,458

a Persons of negro descent, Chinese, Japanese, and civilized Indians.

SEX, GENERAL NATIVITY, AND COLOR. 397

TABLE **10.**—COLORED POPULATION CLASSIFIED AS NEGROES, MULATTOES, QUADROONS, OCTOROONS, CHINESE, JAPANESE, AND CIVILIZED INDIANS, BY STATES AND TERRITORIES: 1890.

| STATES AND TERRITORIES. | Total colored. | PERSONS OF NEGRO DESCENT. | | | | | Chinese. | Japanese. | Civilized Indians. |
		Total.	Negroes.	Mulattoes.	Quadroons.	Octoroons.			
The United States	7,638,360	7,470,040	6,337,980	956,989	105,135	69,936	107,475	2,039	58,806
North Atlantic division	279,564	269,906	207,175	51,492	6,240	4,999	6,177	247	3,234
Maine	1,823	1,190	507	462	107	114	73	1	559
New Hampshire	690	614	248	183	70	113	58	2	16
Vermont	1,004	937	521	328	51	37	32	1	34
Massachusetts	23,570	22,144	14,108	6,815	728	493	984	18	424
Rhode Island	7,047	7,393	5,396	1,679	226	92	69	5	180
Connecticut	12,820	12,302	9,221	2,453	367	261	272	18	228
New York	73,901	70,092	54,852	12,469	1,622	1,149	2,935	148	726
New Jersey	48,352	47,638	40,436	6,123	701	378	608	22	84
Pennsylvania	100,757	107,596	81,886	20,980	2,368	2,362	1,140	32	983
South Atlantic division	3,265,771	3,262,690	2,823,905	374,765	38,946	25,074	669	55	2,357
Delaware	28,427	28,386	24,837	3,213	197	139	37	....	4
Maryland	215,897	215,657	181,296	31,094	2,078	1,189	189	7	44
District of Columbia	75,697	75,572	55,736	17,989	1,126	721	91	9	25
Virginia	635,858	635,438	512,997	107,217	9,772	5,452	55	16	349
West Virginia	32,717	32,690	23,336	7,583	758	1,013	15	3	9
North Carolina	562,565	561,018	483,817	65,687	5,897	5,617	32	1	1,514
South Carolina	689,141	688,934	621,781	53,400	8,120	5,633	34	....	173
Georgia	858,996	858,815	773,682	72,072	8,795	4,266	108	5	68
Florida	166,473	166,180	146,423	16,510	2,203	1,044	108	14	171
North Central division	450,352	431,112	297,331	107,701	15,092	10,988	2,351	117	16,772
Ohio	87,511	87,113	50,078	29,191	4,112	3,732	183	22	193
Indiana	45,668	45,215	31,557	10,970	1,526	1,162	92	18	343
Illinois	57,870	57,028	40,346	13,583	1,862	1,237	740	14	97
Michigan	21,005	15,223	7,036	5,589	1,376	1,222	120	38	5,621
Wisconsin	6,407	2,444	1,007	782	290	365	119	9	3,835
Minnesota	5,667	3,683	1,981	1,166	310	226	94	2	1,888
Iowa	10,810	10,685	7,503	2,318	585	279	64	1	60
Missouri	150,726	150,191	114,739	30,966	2,932	1,547	400	6	127
North Dakota	596	373	153	109	70	41	28	1	194
South Dakota	1,518	541	310	164	44	23	195	....	782
Nebraska	12,022	8,913	6,091	2,155	405	262	214	2	2,893
Kansas	50,543	49,710	36,530	10,708	1,580	892	93	4	736
South Central division	3,485,317	3,479,251	2,993,692	416,411	43,068	26,080	1,434	61	4,571
Kentucky	268,173	268,071	216,085	46,152	3,577	2,257	28	3	71
Tennessee	430,881	430,678	356,215	65,222	5,485	3,756	51	6	146
Alabama	679,299	678,489	601,069	65,993	7,040	4,387	48	3	759
Mississippi	744,749	742,559	657,393	72,945	8,039	4,182	147	7	2,036
Louisiana	560,192	559,193	468,240	76,840	8,597	5,516	333	39	627
Texas	489,588	488,171	422,447	55,319	6,219	4,186	710	3	704
Oklahoma	3,008	2,973	2,156	688	77	52	25	....	10
Arkansas	309,427	309,117	269,487	33,252	4,034	2,344	92	....	218
Western division	157,356	27,681	16,477	6,620	1,789	2,795	96,844	1,559	31,872
Montana	4,888	1,490	1,086	257	93	54	2,532	6	860
Wyoming	1,430	922	671	195	37	19	465	....	43
Colorado	7,730	6,215	4,056	1,778	229	152	1,398	10	107
New Mexico	10,874	1,956	970	419	236	331	361	3	8,554
Arizona	4,040	1,357	932	390	20	15	1,170	1	1,512
Utah	2,006	588	379	145	29	35	806	4	608
Nevada	6,677	242	140	77	12	13	2,833	3	3,599
Idaho	2,367	201	100	53	30	18	2,007	....	159
Washington	8,877	1,602	1,044	371	101	86	3,260	360	3,655
Oregon	12,000	1,186	557	287	134	208	9,540	25	1,258
California	96,458	11,322	6,542	2,848	868	1,264	72,472	1,147	11,517

STATISTICS OF POPULATION.

398

TABLE 11.—MALE AND FEMALE POPULATION, BY STATES AND TERRITORIES: 1850 TO 1890.

STATES AND TERRITORIES.	MALES.					FEMALES.				
	1890	1880	1870	1860	1850	1890	1880	1870	1860	1850
The United States	32,067,880	25,518,820	19,493,565	16,085,204	11,837,660	30,554,370	24,636,963	19,064,806	15,358,117	11,354,216
North Atlantic division	8,677,798	7,160,622	6,079,069	5,265,633	4,339,413	8,723,747	7,346,785	6,219,061	5,328,035	4,287,438
Maine	332,590	324,058	313,103	317,189	297,471	328,496	324,878	313,812	311,090	285,698
New Hampshire	186,566	170,526	155,640	159,816	156,220	189,964	176,465	162,660	166,257	161,756
Vermont	166,027	166,857	165,721	155,786	160,668	166,085	165,555	164,830	156,312	154,087
Massachusetts	1,087,709	858,440	703,779	596,713	488,517	1,151,234	924,645	753,572	634,353	505,997
Rhode Island	168,025	133,030	104,756	84,133	72,078	177,481	143,501	112,597	90,487	75,467
Connecticut	369,538	305,782	265,270	225,994	183,704	376,720	316,918	272,184	234,153	187,088
New York	2,976,893	2,505,322	2,163,229	1,933,532	1,567,041	3,020,960	2,577,549	2,219,530	1,947,203	1,529,453
New Jersey	720,810	559,922	449,672	335,051	245,346	724,114	571,194	456,424	336,984	244,209
Pennsylvania	2,666,331	2,136,055	1,758,499	1,454,419	1,168,103	2,591,683	2,146,236	1,763,452	1,451,796	1,143,083
South Atlantic division	4,418,760	3,757,698	2,865,814	2,686,998	2,343,236	4,439,151	3,839,499	2,987,796	2,677,705	2,335,854
Delaware	85,573	74,108	62,628	56,689	45,955	82,920	72,500	62,387	55,527	45,577
Maryland	515,691	462,187	384,984	340,898	292,323	526,699	472,756	395,910	346,151	290,711
District of Columbia	109,584	83,578	62,192	35,490	24,104	120,808	94,046	69,508	39,581	27,523
Virginia	824,278	745,589	597,058	806,101	717,864	831,702	766,976	628,105	790,217	703,797
West Virginia	390,285	314,495	222,843	....	....	372,509	303,962	219,171	....	....
North Carolina	790,149	687,908	518,704	495,616	430,904	818,798	711,842	552,657	497,006	438,135
South Carolina	572,337	490,408	343,902	347,320	329,634	578,812	505,169	361,704	356,388	338,873
Georgia	919,925	762,981	578,955	531,945	456,465	917,428	779,199	605,154	525,341	449,720
Florida	201,947	136,444	94,548	72,930	45,927	189,475	133,049	93,200	67,494	41,518
North Central division	11,594,910	9,015,920	6,713,802	4,742,839	2,814,234	10,767,369	8,348,191	6,207,309	4,353,877	2,589,301
Ohio	1,855,736	1,613,936	1,337,550	1,190,162	1,016,808	1,816,580	1,584,126	1,327,710	1,149,349	963,521
Indiana	1,118,347	1,010,361	857,994	699,260	511,893	1,074,057	967,940	822,643	651,168	476,523
Illinois	1,972,308	1,586,523	1,316,537	902,761	448,321	1,854,043	1,491,318	1,223,351	800,190	403,140
Michigan	1,091,780	862,855	617,745	394,694	209,896	1,002,109	774,582	566,314	354,419	187,758
Wisconsin	874,951	680,660	544,886	407,449	164,716	811,929	635,428	509,784	368,432	140,075
Minnesota	695,321	419,149	235,299	93,084	3,710	606,505	361,624	204,407	78,939	2,361
Iowa	994,453	848,136	625,917	354,493	101,052	917,443	776,479	568,103	320,420	91,103
Missouri	1,385,238	1,127,187	896,347	622,201	357,832	1,293,946	1,041,193	824,948	559,811	324,212
North Dakota	101,590	} a82,296	a8,878	a2,797	....	81,129	} a52,881	a5,803	a2,040	....
South Dakota	180,250					148,558				
Nebraska	572,824	249,241	70,425	16,760	....	486,086	203,161	52,568	12,081	....
Kansas	752,112	536,667	202,224	59,178	....	674,984	459,429	162,175	48,028	....
South Central division	5,503,877	4,514,546	3,225,164	2,968,186	2,209,151	5,379,016	4,404,825	3,209,246	2,800,472	2,004,371
Kentucky	942,758	832,590	665,675	592,321	502,730	915,877	816,100	655,336	563,363	479,675
Tennessee	891,585	769,277	623,347	562,718	504,132	875,933	773,082	635,173	547,083	498,585
Alabama	757,456	622,620	488,738	480,291	392,343	755,501	639,870	508,254	474,910	379,283
Mississippi	649,687	567,177	413,421	405,948	311,724	639,013	564,420	414,501	385,357	204,892
Louisiana	559,350	468,754	302,165	369,994	274,596	559,237	471,192	364,750	338,008	243,166
Texas	1,172,553	837,840	423,557	320,167	113,780	1,002,970	753,909	395,022	284,048	98,812
Oklahoma	34,733	....	....	....	....	27,101	....	....	....	....
Arkansas	585,755	416,279	248,261	227,747	109,846	542,424	386,246	236,210	207,703	100,051
Western division	1,782,526	1,070,034	609,116	421,548	131,626	1,245,087	697,663	381,394	197,428	47,192
Montana	87,882	28,177	16,771	....	....	44,277	10,982	3,824	....	....
Wyoming	39,343	14,152	7,219	....	....	21,362	6,637	1,899	....	....
Colorado	245,247	129,131	24,820	32,691	....	166,951	65,196	15,044	1,586	....
New Mexico	83,055	64,496	47,135	49,091	31,742	70,538	55,069	44,739	44,425	29,805
Arizona	36,571	28,202	6,887	....	....	23,049	12,238	2,771	....	....
Utah	110,463	74,509	44,121	20,255	6,046	97,442	69,454	42,665	20,018	5,334
Nevada	29,214	42,019	32,379	6,137	....	16,547	20,247	10,112	720	....
Idaho	51,290	21,818	12,184	....	....	33,095	10,792	2,815	....	....
Washington	217,562	45,973	14,990	8,446	....	131,828	29,143	8,905	3,148	....
Oregon	181,840	103,381	53,131	31,591	8,258	131,927	71,387	37,792	20,874	5,036
California	700,059	518,176	349,479	273,337	85,580	508,071	346,518	210,768	106,657	7,017

a Dakota territory.

SEX, GENERAL NATIVITY, AND COLOR.

399

TABLE **12.**—NATIVE AND FOREIGN BORN POPULATION, BY STATES AND TERRITORIES: 1850 TO 1890.

STATES AND TERRITORIES.	NATIVE BORN.					FOREIGN BORN.				
	1890	1880	1870	1860	1850	1890	1880	1870	1860	1850
The United States	53,372,703	43,475,840	32,991,142	27,304,624	20,947,274	9,249,547	6,679,943	5,567,229	4,138,697	2,244,002
North Atlantic division	13,513,368	11,692,887	9,778,124	8,570,363	7,301,308	3,888,177	2,814,520	2,520,600	2,023,905	1,325,543
Maine	582,125	590,053	578,034	590,826	551,344	78,961	58,883	48,881	37,453	31,825
New Hampshire	304,190	300,697	288,689	305,135	303,711	72,340	46,294	29,611	20,938	14,265
Vermont	288,334	291,327	283,396	282,355	280,405	44,088	40,959	47,155	32,743	33,715
Massachusetts	1,581,806	1,339,594	1,104,032	970,960	830,490	657,137	443,491	353,319	260,106	164,024
Rhode Island	230,201	202,538	161,957	137,226	123,643	106,305	73,993	55,396	37,394	23,902
Connecticut	562,657	492,708	423,815	379,451	332,274	183,601	129,992	113,639	80,696	38,518
New York	4,426,803	3,871,492	3,244,406	2,879,455	2,441,465	1,571,050	1,211,379	1,138,353	1,001,280	655,929
New Jersey	1,115,958	909,416	717,153	549,245	429,607	328,975	221,700	188,943	122,790	59,948
Pennsylvania	4,412,294	3,695,002	2,976,642	2,475,710	2,008,309	845,720	587,829	545,309	430,505	303,417
South Atlantic division	8,649,395	7,422,939	5,686,766	5,202,203	4,574,180	208,525	174,258	166,844	162,500	104,010
Delaware	155,332	137,140	115,879	103,051	86,279	13,101	9,468	9,136	9,165	5,253
Maryland	948,094	852,137	697,482	600,520	531,825	94,296	82,806	83,412	77,529	51,209
District of Columbia	211,622	160,502	115,446	62,596	46,709	18,770	17,122	16,254	12,484	4,918
Virginia	1,637,606	1,497,869	1,211,409	1,561,260	1,398,676	18,374	14,696	13,754	35,058	22,985
West Virginia	743,911	600,192	424,923	....	....	18,883	18,265	17,091	....	....
North Carolina	1,614,245	1,396,008	1,068,332	989,324	866,458	3,702	3,742	3,029	3,298	2,581
South Carolina	1,144,879	987,891	697,532	693,722	659,800	6,270	7,686	8,074	9,986	8,707
Georgia	1,825,216	1,531,016	1,172,982	1,045,615	899,697	12,137	10,564	11,127	11,671	6,488
Florida	368,490	259,584	182,781	137,115	84,676	22,932	9,909	4,967	3,309	2,769
North Central division	18,302,105	14,447,282	10,647,826	7,553,358	4,753,220	4,060,114	2,916,829	2,333,285	1,543,358	650,375
Ohio	3,213,023	2,803,119	2,292,767	2,011,262	1,762,136	459,293	394,943	372,493	328,249	218,193
Indiana	2,046,199	1,834,123	1,539,163	1,232,144	932,844	146,205	144,178	141,474	118,284	55,572
Illinois	2,984,004	2,494,295	2,024,693	1,387,308	739,578	842,347	583,576	515,198	324,643	111,892
Michigan	1,550,009	1,248,429	916,049	600,020	342,951	543,880	388,508	268,010	149,093	54,703
Wisconsin	1,167,681	910,072	690,171	498,954	194,914	519,199	405,425	364,499	276,927	110,477
Minnesota	834,470	513,097	279,009	113,295	4,100	467,356	267,676	160,697	58,728	1,977
Iowa	1,587,827	1,302,965	989,328	568,836	171,245	324,069	261,650	204,692	106,077	20,969
Missouri	2,444,315	1,956,802	1,490,028	1,021,471	605,452	234,869	211,578	222,267	160,541	76,592
North Dakota	101,258	} a83,382	} a9,366	a3,063	....	{ 81,461	} a51,795	} a4,815	a1,774	....
South Dakota	237,753					91,055				
Nebraska	856,368	354,988	92,245	22,490	....	202,542	97,414	30,748	6,351	....
Kansas	1,279,258	886,010	316,007	94,515	....	147,838	110,086	48,392	12,691	....
South Central division	10,651,072	8,645,097	6,201,279	5,538,726	4,166,767	321,821	274,274	233,131	229,932	136,755
Kentucky	1,799,279	1,589,173	1,257,613	1,095,885	950,985	59,356	59,517	63,398	59,799	31,420
Tennessee	1,747,489	1,525,657	1,239,204	1,088,575	997,064	20,029	16,702	19,316	21,226	5,653
Alabama	1,498,240	1,252,771	987,030	951,849	764,114	14,777	9,734	9,962	12,352	7,509
Mississippi	1,281,648	1,122,388	816,731	782,747	601,738	7,952	9,209	11,191	8,558	4,788
Louisiana	1,068,840	885,800	665,088	627,027	449,529	49,747	54,146	61,827	80,975	68,233
Texas	2,082,567	1,477,133	750,168	560,793	194,911	152,956	114,616	62,411	43,422	17,681
Oklahoma	59,094	....	....	....	....	2,740	....	....	....	....
Arkansas	1,113,915	792,175	470,445	431,850	208,426	14,204	10,350	5,026	3,600	1,471
Western division	2,256,703	1,267,635	677,147	489,974	151,799	770,910	500,062	313,363	179,602	27,019
Montana	89,063	27,638	12,616	....	....	43,096	11,521	7,979	....	....
Wyoming	45,792	14,939	5,605	....	....	14,913	5,850	3,513	....	....
Colorado	328,208	154,537	33,265	31,611	....	83,990	39,790	6,599	2,666	....
New Mexico	142,334	111,514	86,254	86,798	59,396	11,259	8,051	5,620	6,723	2,151
Arizona	40,825	24,391	3,849	....	....	18,795	16,049	5,809	....	....
Utah	154,841	99,969	56,084	27,519	9,336	53,064	43,994	30,702	12,754	2,044
Nevada	31,055	36,613	23,690	4,793	....	14,706	25,653	18,801	2,064	....
Idaho	66,929	22,636	7,114	....	....	17,456	9,974	7,885	....	....
Washington	259,385	59,313	18,931	8,450	....	90,005	15,803	5,024	3,144	....
Oregon	256,450	144,265	79,323	47,342	12,272	57,317	30,503	11,600	5,123	1,022
California	841,821	571,820	350,416	233,466	70,795	366,309	292,874	209,831	146,528	21,802
										17,798

a Dakota territory.

STATISTICS OF POPULATION.

TABLE 13.—WHITE AND NEGRO POPULATION, BY STATES AND TERRITORIES: 1850 TO 1890.

STATES AND TERRITORIES.	WHITE.					NEGRO. (a)				
	1890	1880	1870	1860	1850	1890	1880	1870	1860	1850
The United States	54,983,890	43,402,970	33,589,377	26,922,537	19,553,068	7,470,040	6,580,793	4,880,009	4,441,830	3,638,803
North Atlantic division	17,121,981	14,273,844	12,117,269	10,438,028	8,477,089	269,906	229,417	179,738	156,001	149,762
Maine	659,263	646,852	624,809	626,947	581,813	1,190	1,451	1,606	1,327	1,356
New Hampshire	375,840	346,229	317,697	325,579	317,456	614	685	580	494	520
Vermont	331,410	331,218	329,613	314,369	313,402	937	1,057	924	709	718
Massachusetts	2,215,373	1,763,782	1,443,156	1,221,432	985,450	22,144	18,697	13,947	9,602	9,064
Rhode Island	337,859	269,939	212,219	170,649	143,875	7,393	6,488	4,980	3,952	3,670
Connecticut	733,438	610,769	527,549	451,504	363,099	12,302	11,547	9,668	8,627	7,693
New York	5,923,952	5,016,022	4,330,210	3,831,590	3,048,325	70,092	65,104	52,081	49,005	49,069
New Jersey	1,396,581	1,092,017	875,407	646,699	465,509	47,638	38,853	30,658	25,336	24,046
Pennsylvania	5,148,257	4,197,016	3,456,609	2,849,259	2,258,160	107,596	85,535	65,294	56,949	53,626
South Atlantic division	5,502,149	4,654,112	3,635,238	3,305,107	2,818,219	3,262,690	2,941,202	2,216,705	2,058,198	1,860,871
Delaware	140,066	120,160	102,221	90,589	71,169	28,386	26,442	22,794	21,627	20,363
Maryland	826,493	724,693	605,497	515,918	417,943	215,657	210,230	175,391	171,131	165,091
District of Columbia	154,695	118,006	88,278	60,763	37,941	75,572	59,596	43,404	14,316	13,746
Virginia	1,020,122	880,858	712,089	1,047,299	894,800	635,438	631,616	512,841	548,907	526,861
West Virginia	730,077	592,537	424,033	....	....	32,690	25,886	17,980	....	....
North Carolina	1,055,382	867,242	678,470	629,942	553,028	561,018	531,277	391,650	361,522	316,011
South Carolina	462,008	391,105	289,667	291,300	274,563	688,934	604,332	415,814	412,320	393,944
Georgia	978,357	816,906	638,926	591,550	521,572	858,815	725,133	545,142	465,698	384,613
Florida	224,949	142,605	96,057	77,746	47,203	166,180	126,690	91,689	62,677	40,242
North Central division	21,911,927	16,961,423	12,698,503	8,899,969	5,267,988	431,112	385,621	273,080	184,239	135,607
Ohio	3,584,805	3,117,920	2,601,946	2,302,808	1,955,050	87,113	79,900	63,213	36,673	25,279
Indiana	2,146,736	1,938,798	1,655,837	1,338,710	977,154	45,215	39,228	24,560	11,428	11,262
Illinois	3,768,472	3,031,151	2,511,096	1,704,291	846,034	57,028	46,368	28,762	7,628	5,436
Michigan	2,072,884	1,614,560	1,167,282	736,142	395,071	15,223	15,100	11,849	6,799	2,583
Wisconsin	1,680,473	1,309,618	1,051,351	773,693	304,756	2,444	2,702	2,113	1,171	635
Minnesota	1,296,159	776,884	438,257	169,395	6,038	3,683	1,564	759	259	39
Iowa	1,901,086	1,614,600	1,188,207	673,779	191,881	10,685	9,516	5,762	1,069	333
Missouri	2,528,458	2,022,826	1,603,146	1,063,489	592,004	150,184	145,350	118,071	118,508	90,040
North Dakota	182,123	} b153,147	b12,887	b2,576	....	373	} b401	b94	....	....
South Dakota	327,290					541				
Nebraska	1,046,888	449,764	122,117	28,696	....	8,913	2,385	789	82	....
Kansas	1,376,553	952,155	346,377	106,390	....	49,710	43,107	17,108	627	....
South Central division	7,487,576	5,961,315	4,227,971	3,728,866	2,812,195	3,479,251	3,012,701	2,204,106	2,038,913	1,491,327
Kentucky	1,590,462	1,377,179	1,098,692	919,484	761,413	268,071	271,451	222,210	236,167	220,992
Tennessee	1,336,637	1,138,831	936,119	826,722	756,836	430,678	403,151	322,331	283,019	245,881
Alabama	833,718	662,185	521,384	526,271	426,514	678,489	600,103	475,510	437,770	345,109
Mississippi	544,851	479,398	382,896	353,899	295,718	742,559	650,291	444,201	437,404	310,808
Louisiana	558,395	454,954	362,065	357,456	255,491	559,193	483,655	364,210	350,373	262,271
Texas	1,745,935	1,197,237	564,700	420,891	154,034	488,171	393,384	253,475	182,921	58,558
Oklahoma	58,826	....	....	....	....	2,973	....	....	....	....
Arkansas	818,752	591,531	362,115	324,143	162,189	309,117	210,666	122,169	111,259	47,708
Western division	2,870,257	1,612,276	910,396	550,567	177,577	27,081	11,852	6,380	4,479	1,241
Montana	127,271	35,385	18,306	....	....	1,490	346	183	....	....
Wyoming	59,275	19,437	8,726	....	....	922	298	183	....	....
Colorado	404,468	191,126	39,221	34,231	....	6,215	2,435	456	46	....
New Mexico	142,719	108,721	90,393	82,924	61,525	1,956	1,015	172	85	22
Arizona	55,580	35,160	9,581	....	....	1,357	155	26	....	....
Utah	205,899	142,423	86,044	40,125	11,330	588	232	118	59	50
Nevada	39,084	53,556	38,959	6,812	....	242	488	357	45	....
....	82,018	29,013	10,618	....	....	201	53	60	....	....
...ton	340,513	67,199	22,195	11,138	....	1,602	325	207	30	....
....	301,758	163,075	86,929	52,160	13,087	1,186	487	346	128	207
....	1,111,672	767,181	499,424	323,177	91,635	11,322	6,018	4,272	4,086	962

a Includes all persons of negro descent.   b Dakota territory.

SEX, GENERAL NATIVITY, AND COLOR.

401

TABLE 14.—CHINESE, JAPANESE, AND CIVILIZED INDIAN POPULATION, BY STATES AND TERRITORIES: 1860 TO 1890.

[No Chinese, Japanese, or civilized Indians shown in the Census Report for 1850.]

STATES AND TERRITORIES.	CHINESE.				JAPANESE.				CIVILIZED INDIANS.			
	1890	1880	1870	1860	1890	1880	1870	1860	1890	1880	1870	1860
The United States	107,475	105,465	63,199	34,933	2,039	148	55	....	58,806	66,407	25,731	44,021
North Atlantic division	6,177	1,028	137	....	247	41	21	....	3,234	2,477	1,565	239
Maine	73	8	1	....	1	....	....	....	559	625	499	5
New Hampshire	58	14	....	....	2	....	....	....	16	63	23	....
Vermont	32	....	....	....	1	....	....	....	34	11	14	20
Massachusetts	984	229	87	....	18	8	10	....	424	369	151	32
Rhode Island	60	27	....	....	5	....	....	....	180	77	154	19
Connecticut	272	123	2	....	18	6	....	....	228	255	235	16
New York	2,935	909	29	....	148	17	....	....	726	819	439	140
New Jersey	608	170	5	....	22	2	10	....	84	74	16	....
Pennsylvania	1,146	148	13	....	32	8	1	....	983	184	34	7
South Atlantic division	669	74	11	....	55	5	....	....	2,357	1,804	1,656	1,398
Delaware	37	1	....	....	....	....	....	....	4	5	....	....
Maryland	189	5	2	....	7	....	....	....	44	15	4	....
District of Columbia	91	13	3	....	9	4	....	....	25	5	15	1
Virginia	55	6	4	....	16	....	....	....	349	85	229	112
West Virginia	15	5	....	....	3	....	....	....	9	20	1	....
North Carolina	32	....	....	....	1	1	....	....	1,514	1,230	1,241	1,158
South Carolina	34	9	1	....	....	....	....	....	173	131	124	88
Georgia	108	17	1	....	5	....	....	....	68	124	40	38
Florida	108	18	....	....	14	....	....	....	171	180	2	1
North Central division	2,351	813	9	....	117	8	1	....	16,772	10,246	9,518	12,508
Ohio	183	109	1	....	22	3	....	....	193	130	100	30
Indiana	92	29	....	....	18	....	....	....	343	246	240	290
Illinois	740	209	1	....	14	3	....	....	97	140	32	32
Michigan	120	27	1	....	38	1	1	....	5,624	7,240	4,926	6,172
Wisconsin	119	16	....	....	9	....	....	....	3,835	3,161	1,206	1,017
Minnesota	94	24	....	....	2	1	....	....	1,888	2,300	690	2,369
Iowa	64	33	3	....	1	....	....	....	60	466	48	65
Missouri	409	91	3	....	6	....	....	....	127	113	75	20
North Dakota	28	} a238	....	....	{ 1	}			{ 194	} a1,391	a1,200	a2,261
South Dakota	195								782			
Nebraska	214	18	....	....	2	....	....	....	2,893	235	87	63
Kansas	93	19	....	....	4	....	....	....	736	815	914	180
South Central division	1,434	848	211	....	61	....	....	....	4,571	4,507	2,122	879
Kentucky	28	10	1	....	3	....	....	....	71	50	108	33
Tennessee	51	25	....	....	6	....	....	....	146	352	70	60
Alabama	48	4	....	....	3	....	....	....	759	213	98	160
Mississippi	147	51	16	....	7	....	....	....	2,036	1,857	809	2
Louisiana	333	489	71	....	30	....	....	....	627	848	569	173
Texas	710	136	25	....	3	....	....	....	704	992	379	403
Oklahoma	25	....	....	....	....	....	....	....	10	....	....	....
Arkansas	92	133	98	....	....	....	....	....	218	195	89	48
Western division	96,844	102,102	62,831	34,933	1,559	94	33	....	31,872	41,373	10,870	28,997
Montana	2,532	1,765	1,949	....	6	....	....	....	800	1,663	157	....
Wyoming	465	914	143	....	....	....	....	....	43	140	66	....
Colorado	1,398	612	7	....	10	....	....	....	107	154	180	....
New Mexico	361	57	....	....	3	....	....	....	8,554	9,772	1,300	10,507
Arizona	1,170	1,630	20	....	1	2	....	....	1,512	3,493	31	....
Utah	806	501	445	....	4	....	....	....	608	807	179	89
Nevada	2,833	5,416	3,152	....	3	3	....	....	3,590	2,803	23	....
Idaho	2,007	3,379	4,274	....	....	....	....	....	150	165	47	....
Washington	3,260	3,186	234	....	360	1	....	....	3,655	4,405	1,319	426
Oregon	9,540	9,510	3,330	....	25	2	....	....	1,258	1,094	318	177
California	72,472	75,132	49,277	34,933	1,147	86	33	....	11,517	16,277	7,241	17,798

a Dakota territory.

STATE OR TERRITORY OF BIRTH.

560

STATISTICS OF POPULATION.

TABLE **24.**—NATIVE POPULATION, DISTRIBUTED ACCORDING TO STATE

	STATES AND TERRITORIES.	Number living in each state or territory.	Maine.	New Hampshire.	Vermont.	Massachusetts.	Rhode Island.	Connecticut.	New York.	New Jersey.	Pennsylvania.	Delaware.	Maryland.
1	The United States..	53,372,703	764,210	364,694	422,359	1,531,148	231,716	583,876	5,224,662	1,046,694	4,906,050	166,497	1,050,800
2	North Atlantic division	13,513,368	677,421	328,184	336,153	1,403,571	218,127	530,138	4,336,113	968,686	4,207,301	27,233	65,146
3	Maine	582,125	553,962	7,640	1,575	10,386	659	540	2,307	287	631	23	115
4	New Hampshire.......	304,190	14,876	240,174	15,419	21,311	850	1,023	5,620	337	613	20	104
5	Vermont............	288,334	1,667	9,503	249,590	7,244	341	999	14,964	228	430	13	49
6	Massachusetts.........	1,581,806	86,988	57,745	34,393	1,256,408	21,044	25,403	48,383	4,597	7,785	360	2,150
7	Rhode Island	239,201	3,716	2,056	2,073	25,574	179,108	9,281	7,864	1,164	1,708	98	668
8	Connecticut	562,657	3,037	2,449	4,194	25,810	7,589	448,804	46,299	5,610	4,231	220	879
9	New York............	4,426,803	7,837	5,955	24,801	39,331	5,610	32,471	3,991,033	55,481	73,202	1,527	8,043
10	New Jersey	1,115,958	2,086	1,210	1,370	7,899	1,345	6,483	122,578	857,547	67,303	5,572	6,914
11	Pennsylvania...........	4,412,294	3,252	1,452	2,732	9,608	1,581	5,134	97,065	43,435	4,051,398	19,391	45,015
12	South Atlantic division	8,649,395	4,117	2,072	2,144	8,461	1,264	4,147	32,563	9,904	77,154	129,686	912,121
13	Delaware..........	155,332	222	347	90	258	93	212	1,672	2,347	12,843	119,917	14,035
14	Maryland..........	948,094	693	182	216	1,486	221	654	6,017	2,303	27,497	8,071	846,329
15	District of Columbia....	211,622	933	565	565	2,113	275	890	8,101	1,434	7,263	514	31,766
16	Virginia............	1,637,606	435	187	232	972	141	480	5,641	1,593	7,533	713	8,976
17	West Virginia.........	743,911	246	52	92	445	43	128	1,512	448	17,143	138	7,425
18	North Carolina	1,614,245	163	69	92	387	38	226	1,090	290	998	93	834
19	South Carolina	1,144,879	134	48	44	309	65	106	837	171	358	30	414
20	Georgia.............	1,825,216	392	171	296	813	191	489	2,941	587	1,343	111	1,259
21	Florida	368,490	899	451	517	1,678	197	902	4,743	731	2,176	99	880
22	North Central division	18,302,165	49,281	25,872	68,701	79,256	8,099	37,945	706,275	53,804	521,435	7,258	57,285
23	Ohio.........	3,213,023	2,111	2,007	4,720	9,178	745	6,332	57,210	8,121	121,324	1,177	15,480
24	Indiana..........	2,046,190	1,075	699	1,478	2,640	306	1,315	20,923	4,000	40,491	1,042	5,808
25	Illinois..........	2,984,004	6,445	5,019	11,354	18,893	1,811	7,654	110,220	12,044	76,723	1,429	11,343
26	Michigan..........	1,550,000	4,332	2,514	9,452	8,141	740	4,532	193,111	6,391	32,947	410	1,493
27	Wisconsin.........	1,167,681	6,656	2,775	9,397	6,756	722	3,078	70,259	2,470	17,067	218	954
28	Minnesota.........	834,470	12,847	3,452	7,083	8,507	772	2,688	48,307	2,261	16,601	228	1,280
29	Iowa	1,587,827	4,539	3,524	9,301	7,420	819	3,634	66,623	5,069	63,084	709	4,707
30	Missouri..........	2,444,315	2,048	1,184	2,431	4,780	542	2,043	30,689	3,414	37,622	743	6,844
31	North Dakota..........	101,258	959	345	965	884	88	205	6,785	432	3,090	36	177
32	South Dakota..........	237,753	1,752	813	2,418	1,597	183	685	17,168	779	7,435	77	457
33	Nebraska..........	856,368	3,477	1,805	4,974	5,901	714	3,323	44,345	4,200	42,387	616	3,419
34	Kansas	1,279,258	3,040	1,735	4,528	4,999	657	2,366	40,635	4,617	62,064	573	5,224
35	South Central division......	10,651,072	2,451	1,122	1,922	5,036	602	2,111	26,804	3,250	25,468	740	18,302
36	Kentucky	1,799,270	274	145	194	787	79	296	3,843	581	5,453	112	1,622
37	Tennessee	1,747,489	307	206	301	779	112	364	3,949	420	4,319	93	1,358
38	Alabama	1,498,240	270	120	204	543	55	298	2,086	327	2,318	80	1,483
39	Mississippi............	1,281,648	100	46	87	202	32	83	1,074	141	758	45	1,771
40	Louisiana............	1,068,840	283	94	154	563	55	202	2,706	245	1,245	83	2,788
41	Texas	2,082,567	795	351	622	1,592	184	641	8,783	1,022	6,437	238	2,866
42	Oklahoma	59,094	83	28	128	111	18	56	1,324	127	1,405	21	153
43	Arkansas............	1,113,915	279	132	232	459	67	171	3,039	387	3,533	68	1,261
44	Western division..........	2,256,703	30,940	7,444	13,439	34,824	3,624	9,535	122,907	11,050	74,692	1,580	8,052
45	Montana.............	89,063	1,722	317	716	1,345	110	371	6,283	636	4,871	77	532
46	Wyoming............	45,792	418	206	485	750	100	246	3,183	271	2,938	43	357
47	Colorado............	328,208	3,192	1,072	2,378	5,099	568	1,889	23,964	2,299	20,005	381	1,815
48	New Mexico	142,334	231	89	189	323	49	116	1,610	137	1,518	33	207
49	Arizona	40,825	367	112	146	447	36	105	1,755	201	1,023	30	308
50	Utah	154,841	489	185	373	856	78	302	3,611	463	2,432	76	276
51	Nevada.............	31,055	721	115	289	523	47	139	1,736	220	881	19	148
52	Idaho.............	66,929	663	120	290	449	50	185	2,574	211	1,986	28	161
53	Washington	259,385	5,585	872	1,748	3,443	370	972	16,065	1,307	11,122	194	1,029
54	Oregon	256,450	1,929	463	1,012	1,851	196	611	9,450	798	6,599	117	727
55	California	841,821	15,623	3,893	5,813	19,738	2,020	4,599	52,676	4,507	21,317	582	3,897

STATE OR TERRITORY OF BIRTH.   561

OR TERRITORY OF BIRTH, BY STATES AND TERRITORIES: 1890.

STATE OR TERRITORY OF BIRTH, ARRANGED GEOGRAPHICALLY—continued.

South Atlantic division—Continued.							North Central division.									
District of Columbia.	Virginia.	West Virginia.	North Carolina.	South Carolina.	Georgia.	Florida.	Ohio.	Indiana.	Illinois.	Michigan.	Wisconsin.	Minnesota.	Iowa.	Missouri.	North Dakota.	
127,866	2,167,087	644,711	1,854,873	1,318,555	2,003,167	277,310	3,826,514	2,179,507	3,014,005	1,321,490	1,254,925	653,685	1,397,438	2,076,462	54,986	1
8,724	70,142	11,209	10,254	6,343	5,740	2,213	68,748	8,455	20,803	17,648	8,656	3,665	6,855	6,878	307	2
67	223	17	62	42	66	44	243	67	235	153	231	150	117	55	4	3
51	177	17	52	27	57	26	344	43	364	238	200	142	148	88	28	4
28	133	17	25	15	42	18	367	61	396	256	261	93	179	65	7	5
869	5,775	156	1,630	757	779	324	3,347	780	3,013	1,663	1,223	647	888	721	68	6
285	1,457	52	229	150	150	91	428	90	319	174	213	87	94	72	11	7
360	2,336	111	680	263	358	144	1,591	292	1,095	612	431	170	287	278	25	8
3,085	18,334	638	3,621	3,101	2,685	909	15,966	3,046	8,664	10,557	4,157	1,421	2,564	2,711	212	9
963	10,013	232	1,487	694	675	365	3,222	720	1,779	911	598	193	428	629	27	10
3,016	31,694	9,969	2,468	1,294	934	292	34,240	3,336	4,938	3,084	1,742	757	2,134	2,059	125	11
110,623	1,761,364	578,529	1,650,086	1,199,914	1,720,955	262,546	43,718	5,260	5,497	3,157	1,609	820	2,102	3,717	145	12
151	1,385	49	171	135	44	14	282	81	117	66	29	19	20	63	3	13
5,140	30,507	4,375	1,659	619	590	130	2,274	468	731	310	209	64	189	521	11	14
102,639	37,184	789	1,576	854	722	161	2,932	1,111	1,155	653	325	233	414	587	24	15
1,948	1,557,033	3,034	29,242	1,299	789	199	2,133	424	500	635	322	84	205	557	58	16
226	100,051	569,873	1,696	147	155	20	31,601	875	545	144	79	69	424	502	8	17
123	17,578	104	1,561,460	16,072	3,307	216	376	281	146	144	53	15	57	136	6	18
55	2,694	27	16,324	1,112,769	6,795	378	164	53	57	37	10	5	24	50	......	19
211	10,577	112	31,195	49,972	1,671,981	7,250	1,517	608	613	366	146	87	175	377	15	20
124	3,755	166	6,754	18,047	36,572	254,178	2,439	1,350	1,633	802	436	244	594	834	20	21
4,950	171,948	44,904	47,754	8,006	11,946	1,403	3,556,123	2,051,361	2,813,596	1,254,591	1,196,779	620,707	1,294,341	1,860,976	50,963	22
804	41,710	18,710	3,273	842	1,307	173	2,772,013	35,525	12,090	17,210	3,308	953	4,433	4,089	99	23
294	17,898	2,755	13,553	1,350	1,196	97	104,174	1,614,600	31,116	11,844	2,119	719	4,539	6,128	80	24
1,300	21,873	3,807	6,550	1,631	1,924	284	126,040	96,349	2,196,288	21,321	31,911	4,143	24,522	40,984	537	25
245	2,719	608	646	186	224	97	80,147	22,015	11,843	1,123,978	17,547	1,704	3,584	2,026	261	26
138	1,247	314	198	123	181	64	19,034	6,609	19,424	11,618	953,273	10,870	6,986	2,310	878	27
299	2,068	700	373	143	258	67	18,408	10,038	25,373	11,782	59,369	554,535	20,841	3,532	2,533	28
247	12,779	2,901	2,850	386	434	68	102,734	51,008	114,471	10,315	41,629	8,074	999,453	22,311	1,314	29
788	45,320	5,134	12,670	2,095	3,995	300	84,907	70,563	135,585	7,805	8,787	2,291	37,312	1,662,556	233	30
32	277	169	46	19	28	6	3,192	1,384	3,084	3,973	9,869	13,052	4,559	805	43,783	31
85	872	289	158	43	95	11	8,994	4,867	17,851	7,078	28,146	15,433	26,128	2,969	116	32
345	8,194	2,821	1,612	314	705	104	59,803	40,250	107,802	13,886	26,696	5,483	95,886	28,590	774	33
364	16,982	6,627	5,825	874	1,599	132	116,671	98,138	137,903	13,775	14,125	3,441	66,148	84,016	355	34
1,474	143,970	5,599	138,828	101,836	258,760	10,424	72,009	61,294	63,703	8,969	5,400	2,367	13,009	107,097	352	35
198	27,794	2,708	6,793	1,026	2,031	142	31,949	22,701	6,784	802	432	155	571	5,339	34	36
172	20,943	439	32,033	8,396	23,085	427	10,064	5,851	4,537	1,763	838	434	833	4,377	71	37
199	16,002	230	15,491	24,355	95,875	3,969	3,764	1,741	1,374	561	267	131	324	861	31	38
148	18,629	97	23,313	19,088	20,245	710	1,254	852	1,218	350	171	77	226	1,965	7	39
251	13,682	154	10,625	7,262	12,517	1,301	1,599	1,015	1,313	406	352	146	846	2,438	31	40
362	25,053	1,199	24,837	20,452	66,739	3,325	10,391	11,429	22,590	2,641	1,811	763	3,967	46,685	72	41
7	917	257	495	132	551	27	3,734	4,090	5,347	696	592	226	3,013	7,421	55	42
137	11,950	515	24,641	21,125	37,726	523	9,254	13,615	20,540	1,750	946	435	3,229	38,011	51	43
2,095	19,663	4,470	7,951	2,456	5,751	724	94,916	53,157	110,406	37,125	42,072	26,131	81,147	97,994	3,019	44
122	1,149	243	266	165	214	31	5,017	2,406	5,138	3,335	3,924	3,411	4,792	6,105	491	45
47	618	169	131	60	152	62	2,858	1,371	3,430	947	1,409	441	3,636	2,615	102	46
271	3,679	1,200	1,532	357	1,501	138	23,806	12,596	28,196	6,844	7,051	1,952	20,008	21,952	211	47
52	548	105	191	80	246	34	1,604	900	1,804	423	393	103	795	2,326	19	48
71	584	69	191	117	256	30	1,234	661	1,328	386	331	84	617	1,781	16	49
71	650	107	281	98	325	19	2,058	1,140	3,333	860	716	343	2,402	1,872	41	50
33	241	46	58	16	41	11	1,031	381	959	403	869	41	507	897	2	51
69	666	187	392	60	157	10	2,426	1,675	3,363	914	1,348	912	2,938	3,909	128	52
225	2,452	641	1,244	236	641	118	13,882	8,965	17,053	8,737	11,443	11,040	14,512	12,359	1,219	53
300	2,384	564	1,167	165	420	47	11,551	8,322	14,043	4,067	5,519	3,482	12,478	15,329	443	54
834	6,692	1,109	2,498	1,102	1,798	224	28,849	14,731	31,159	10,209	9,560	4,322	18,372	28,849	347	55

STATISTICS OF POPULATION.

TABLE **24.**—NATIVE POPULATION, DISTRIBUTED ACCORDING TO STATE

	STATES AND TERRITORIES.	North Central division—Continued.			South Central division.								
		South Dakota.	Nebraska.	Kansas.	Kentucky.	Tennessee.	Alabama.	Mississippi.	Louisiana.	Texas.	Indian territory.	Oklahoma.	Arkansas.
1	The United States..	92,790	362,084	624,679	2,095,834	2,014,431	1,579,994	1,288,344	1,023,132	1,445,772	8,941	1,515	762,875
2	North Atlantic division	335	1,468	3,242	6,658	3,509	2,058	1,359	4,295	2,157	275	30	622
3	Maine	5	34	50	42	35	17	24	42	23	1	....	18
4	New Hampshire........	14	38	50	56	20	29	21	29	15	8	2	6
5	Vermont..............	9	39	67	29	20	17	13	22	31	5	....	8
6	Massachusetts..........	26	202	373	595	349	261	148	482	249	16	1	84
7	Rhode Island	4	19	45	74	42	37	17	50	37	1	....	7
8	Connecticut...........	6	80	120	205	114	118	50	192	192	6	1	21
9	New York............	132	486	1,183	2,588	1,296	949	602	2,330	931	39	8	208
10	New Jersey	15	101	209	619	268	214	134	442	209	22	5	52
11	Pennsylvania.........	124	463	1,145	2,450	1,356	416	344	706	470	177	13	218
12	South Atlantic division	72	460	1,340	13,690	23,706	35,182	5,070	3,243	2,732	140	35	1,396
13	Delaware..............	4	6	17	51	23	6	9	18	8	4	....	2
14	Maryland..............	15	53	130	507	292	223	177	353	150	13	26	52
15	District of Columbia ...	15	71	190	737	734	400	350	366	252	27	....	98
16	Virginia..............	7	111	147	2,808	4,921	552	365	371	326	44	3	151
17	West Virginia	10	58	293	5,368	752	90	79	99	103	4	1	57
18	North Carolina	2	17	68	390	4,810	581	400	131	239	10	2	155
19	South Carolina.........	4	3	8	181	554	774	361	101	123	5	....	76
20	Georgia..............	2	39	97	1,499	9,782	19,451	1,576	667	836	25	3	530
21	Florida	13	102	390	2,149	1,832	16,105	1,753	1,137	695	8	....	275
22	North Central division	89,565	338,791	557,953	326,031	141,595	13,337	14,700	12,637	15,312	2,926	130	25,525
23	Ohio.................	88	621	2,475	38,766	4,459	1,025	1,065	1,234	556	401	7	446
24	Indiana..............	93	657	3,458	66,284	9,891	961	741	718	633	89	2	688
25	Illinois..............	377	2,812	7,961	54,815	30,804	3,013	2,967	2,814	1,812	135	21	2,343
26	Michigan.............	228	757	1,741	1,977	831	214	213	276	313	35	2	154
27	Wisconsin............	613	790	1,028	1,332	635	172	162	219	151	17	1	117
28	Minnesota............	1,607	801	988	2,812	764	241	357	360	264	77	4	195
29	Iowa	1,733	6,708	7,015	10,388	4,026	358	515	482	463	48	19	494
30	Missouri.............	216	4,705	32,074	99,945	67,501	5,029	5,101	4,402	6,269	890	20	17,075
31	North Dakota	273	182	197	307	113	28	39	50	61	11	2	27
32	South Dakota	83,246	2,384	1,141	877	396	104	98	90	252	14	1	117
33	Nebraska.............	847	307,237	12,782	8,745	3,522	585	708	565	788	68	24	673
34	Kansas	244	11,128	487,093	39,783	17,963	1,667	2,644	1,367	3,750	1,132	27	3,196
35	South Central division	244	2,422	20,230	1,721,585	1,825,116	1,521,643	1,262,605	997,110	1,405,976	4,635	1,294	725,358
36	Kentucky	14	105	569	1,609,001	49,752	1,995	1,817	1,236	961	30	3	1,150
37	Tennessee............	39	135	484	27,527	1,516,797	22,045	24,850	1,901	2,034	64	4	4,807
38	Alabama.............	13	48	191	3,983	25,185	1,267,906	15,009	2,286	1,822	45	....	1,094
39	Mississippi..........	2	53	137	5,847	23,715	63,650	1,063,666	17,194	2,201	34	....	4,558
40	Louisiana	38	128	341	4,914	4,541	21,481	34,771	922,885	8,712	86	5	4,551
41	Texas	64	607	4,044	44,655	106,678	100,763	70,273	38,898	1,370,243	1,880	10	47,705
42	Oklahoma............	23	672	10,048	2,895	2,507	538	700	294	5,381	1,045	1,271	1,538
43	Arkansas.............	51	614	4,416	22,703	95,941	43,265	51,510	12,416	14,622	1,451	1	659,955
44	Western division	2,574	18,943	41,914	27,870	20,505	4,774	4,610	5,847	19,595	965	26	9,974
45	Montana.............	383	665	1,306	1,515	662	150	127	184	418	51	4	187
46	Wyoming............	216	2,030	1,385	656	374	114	113	96	595	42	1	217
47	Colorado.............	132	5,601	13,265	6,049	3,290	970	872	910	2,035	270	4	1,315
48	New Mexico..........	6	170	1,170	803	708	324	288	214	4,835	96	....	545
49	Arizona	6	77	450	700	579	279	221	184	1,682	58	1	441
50	Utah	42	717	694	714	588	237	188	115	285	19	....	90
51	Nevada..............	4	73	130	319	182	48	27	88	60	3	....	60
52	Idaho...............	62	631	1,649	809	663	135	134	425	487	44	....	708
53	Washington...........	1,057	3,238	8,160	3,267	3,003	436	455	359	2,806	142	3	1,514
54	Oregon..............	368	2,662	5,930	3,399	3,351	290	326	309	1,164	77	3	1,574
55	California	298	3,019	7,775	9,549	7,015	1,782	1,859	2,963	5,719	163	10	3,323

STATE OR TERRITORY OF BIRTH.　　563

OR TERRITORY OF BIRTH, BY STATES AND TERRITORIES: 1890—Continued.

Montana	Wyoming	Colorado	New Mexico	Arizona	Utah	Nevada	Idaho	Washington	Oregon	California	Alaska	Born in the United States (state not specified)	Born at sea under United States flag	American citizens born abroad	
26,045	12,076	95,876	130,244	17,768	140,270	23,466	24,089	61,896	138,559	523,746	322	396,652	1,463	8,547	1
257	100	1,001	115	117	200	151	78	637	452	5,382	45	129,401	519	2,131	2
11	2	22	8	3	6	24	5	17	14	271	1	1,400	37	112	3
4	2	23	3	1	2	9	3	4	4	125	....	1,220	5	138	4
2	5	23	2	1	3	7	1	5	5	79	1	761	9	179	5
42	31	176	32	7	32	71	24	78	139	1,038	6	9,000	104	335	6
....	1	23	48	3	6	2	2	20	5	107	1	1,071	21	46	7
6	3	49	17	3	5	11	....	28	25	278	3	2,845	34	69	8
74	73	389	172	28	89	80	27	246	140	2,351	10	83,465	154	891	9
23	10	80	41	10	21	31	7	31	33	437	11	9,537	47	106	10
191	33	280	122	61	41	56	9	228	67	696	12	20,102	108	261	11
75	43	216	70	34	38	46	30	504	102	782	11	23,519	66	118	12
2	....	3	2	2	1	....	1	10	....	30	....	455	8	5	13
12	7	47	13	8	4	12	5	138	22	158	4	3,959	17	25	14
26	16	45	22	13	20	6	16	257	28	256	....	1,864	10	25	15
6	7	27	7	1	2	5	1	62	15	93	1	2,185	5	24	16
8	2	14	4	1	2	8	1	7	6	49	....	2,105	6	7	17
2	1	15	3	....	3	2	1	1	4	34	....	2,990	3	3	18
3	5	4	3	2	....	....	....	3	....	8	....	635	4	4	19
5	1	36	6	3	2	1	5	8	10	84	4	6,736	5	8	20
11	4	25	10	4	4	12	....	18	17	70	2	2,590	8	17	21
1,583	1,191	6,790	989	283	1,287	814	515	968	1,804	8,416	44	127,698	661	5,061	22
35	32	229	111	18	45	30	40	87	93	672	5	14,039	80	190	23
31	17	152	28	5	16	20	5	82	80	318	2	8,953	28	49	24
208	64	744	114	30	110	109	33	155	210	1,545	7	28,292	230	365	25
62	24	276	52	15	55	53	15	46	110	604	....	8,651	56	1,846	26
79	36	177	28	2	32	53	17	34	57	371	1	7,561	55	304	27
186	40	185	30	4	38	26	24	88	93	442	2	9,736	40	113	28
135	125	593	50	17	290	92	77	106	260	854	5	10,906	27	348	29
300	101	1,265	207	51	206	173	82	154	299	1,513	9	22,500	82	1,288	30
83	13	38	17	3	9	5	4	8	16	89	....	497	10	182	31
79	119	287	26	45	51	45	20	40	66	181	....	1,540	3	32	32
138	564	1,229	94	45	298	86	107	96	229	891	8	7,254	18	170	33
247	116	1,615	232	48	137	122	91	122	292	936	5	7,760	23	165	34
199	96	926	835	421	130	118	139	178	370	2,305	39	78,663	80	330	35
15	10	54	18	1	6	10	1	15	25	173	....	9,374	17	22	36
29	8	70	19	5	13	9	4	22	37	178	2	10,257	1	8	37
4	5	27	22	321	2	5	3	12	24	107	3	7,144	7	13	38
1	5	21	7	2	4	....	4	....	10	53	9	7,773	4	9	39
4	2	37	27	1	7	11	4	14	15	107	6	3,742	27	27	40
96	46	413	651	81	78	56	57	82	177	1,413	17	27,538	23	112	41
25	5	154	65	5	3	6	31	16	32	109	....	714	1	2	42
25	15	150	26	5	17	21	35	17	59	255	2	12,121	9	137	43
23,825	10,586	86,879	127,905	16,913	138,009	22,197	23,327	59,589	135,842	506,771	183	87,871	128	907	44
21,618	112	286	23	8	769	392	218	63	1,958	1,126	....	2,983	6	51	45
120	8,476	1,163	136	33	1,573	93	272	27	118	282	....	596	3	16	46
168	400	70,486	9,331	85	1,124	210	91	60	541	1,155	5	6,538	15	90	47
9	30	1,371	116,254	234	272	44	30	17	30	470	....	263	2	6	48
26	45	200	1,274	15,466	2,836	251	168	42	164	3,142	1	228	2	16	49
193	518	772	81	199	119,781	607	706	44	101	800	3	3,181	5	14	50
35	32	67	13	31	785	14,531	72	28	123	3,182	1	1,185	3	5	51
351	260	370	27	42	9,028	413	19,819	820	2,189	1,308	1	570	5	18	52
533	227	1,001	130	77	551	608	848	54,227	12,803	9,043	36	6,907	15	125	53
326	183	663	54	47	481	599	716	3,222	111,850	10,330	17	4,418	12	155	54
456	263	1,440	582	691	1,400	4,449	387	1,039	5,956	475,843	119	10,412	60	411	55

STATISTICS OF POPULATION.

564

TABLE 25.—NATIVE WHITE POPULATION, DISTRIBUTED ACCORDING TO

| | STATES AND TERRITORIES. | Number living in each state or territory. | STATE OR TERRITORY OF BIRTH, ARRANGED GEOGRAPHICALLY. | | | | | | | | | | |
| | | | North Atlantic division. | | | | | | | | | South Atlantic division. | |
			Maine.	New Hampshire.	Vermont.	Massachusetts.	Rhode Island.	Connecticut.	New York.	New Jersey.	Pennsylvania.	Delaware.	Maryland.
1	The United States..	45,862,023	762,335	364,155	421,310	1,518,979	227,333	574,910	5,176,133	1,014,956	4,835,812	135,503	809,743
2	North Atlantic division	13,247,115	675,769	327,731	335,224	1,392,506	213,908	521,578	4,291,042	937,725	4,143,370	19,723	46,029
3	Maine	580,568	552,674	7,631	1,575	10,362	656	539	2,282	286	625	22	100
4	New Hampshire	303,644	14,862	239,895	15,407	21,265	848	1,020	5,605	333	612	10	87
5	Vermont	287,394	1,664	9,486	248,968	7,179	340	995	14,808	225	424	13	45
6	Massachusetts	1,561,870	86,745	57,641	34,296	1,246,953	20,781	25,019	47,720	4,428	7,360	279	1,428
7	Rhode Island	231,832	3,696	2,049	2,006	25,254	175,585	9,027	7,547	1,072	1,533	37	270
8	Connecticut	550,283	3,022	2,444	4,163	25,415	7,486	441,746	45,235	5,377	4,079	172	563
9	New York	4,358,260	7,793	5,936	24,670	38,869	5,480	31,858	3,950,856	53,682	71,662	1,168	6,503
10	New Jersey	1,068,596	2,074	1,202	1,370	7,798	1,203	6,308	120,755	830,673	64,358	3,473	4,220
11	Pennsylvania	4,304,668	3,239	1,447	2,709	9,411	1,529	5,006	96,174	41,649	3,992,717	14,540	32,813
12	South Atlantic division	5,389,833	4,045	2,027	2,122	8,109	1,185	3,981	31,709	9,483	74,691	106,571	694,377
13	Delaware	126,970	219	317	90	252	90	203	1,624	2,207	12,184	97,401	10,008
14	Maryland	732,706	681	180	211	1,417	206	622	5,857	2,208	26,646	7,505	650,454
15	District of Columbia....	136,178	915	563	560	2,014	237	835	7,773	1,344	6,857	460	16,751
16	Virginia	1,001,933	430	185	227	914	132	448	5,408	1,546	7,377	675	7,662
17	West Virginia	711,225	242	52	92	439	43	127	1,501	445	16,965	137	7,135
18	North Carolina	1,051,720	161	69	88	366	37	223	1,069	277	948	84	606
19	South Carolina	455,865	127	46	44	290	61	157	806	166	310	26	272
20	Georgia	966,465	382	171	296	771	189	476	2,903	573	1,293	96	727
21	Florida	206,771	888	444	514	1,646	190	890	4,678	717	2,102	91	612
22	North Central division	17,858,470	49,215	25,854	68,649	78,884	8,060	37,808	704,442	53,590	518,876	7,087	54,670
23	Ohio	3,120,252	2,102	2,004	4,711	9,035	741	6,284	56,027	8,086	120,243	1,146	14,712
24	Indiana	2,000,733	1,072	699	1,477	2,622	306	1,307	20,870	3,989	40,384	1,032	5,603
25	Illinois	2,927,497	6,435	5,014	11,343	18,317	1,797	7,628	109,851	11,901	76,200	1,415	10,838
26	Michigan	1,531,283	4,322	2,514	9,449	8,108	738	4,522	102,721	6,340	32,023	334	1,354
27	Wisconsin	1,161,484	6,655	2,773	9,391	6,751	717	3,075	60,928	2,467	17,036	214	930
28	Minnesota	829,102	12,838	3,450	7,681	8,488	769	2,074	48,208	2,257	16,543	224	1,227
29	Iowa	1,577,154	4,538	3,522	9,292	7,411	815	3,631	66,508	5,060	63,639	700	4,730
30	Missouri	2,294,176	2,037	1,181	2,428	4,746	540	2,031	30,602	3,401	37,381	732	6,329
31	North Dakota	100,775	959	345	965	883	88	294	6,776	431	3,082	36	172
32	South Dakota	236,447	1,751	813	2,418	1,591	183	685	17,153	770	7,428	77	448
33	Nebraska	844,644	3,472	1,804	4,968	5,946	711	3,317	44,283	4,102	42,302	611	3,237
34	Kansas	1,228,923	3,034	1,735	4,526	4,986	655	2,360	40,555	4,597	61,025	566	5,000
35	South Central division	7,168,997	2,403	1,104	1,886	4,835	573	2,059	26,432	3,179	24,641	633	6,418
36	Kentucky	1,531,222	272	145	193	776	76	294	3,807	574	5,350	109	1,443
37	Tennessee	1,316,738	365	200	296	755	108	358	3,911	415	4,209	82	904
38	Alabama	819,114	265	119	194	523	55	200	2,044	310	2,250	65	685
39	Mississippi	537,127	95	44	82	183	30	78	1,020	135	624	27	291
40	Louisiana	509,555	265	91	146	508	50	184	2,615	220	1,120	53	480
41	Texas	1,594,466	784	341	617	1,554	175	632	8,703	1,007	6,295	230	1,915
42	Oklahoma	56,117	83	28	128	110	17	56	1,820	127	1,383	10	130
43	Arkansas	804,658	274	130	230	426	62	167	3,012	379	3,305	58	555
44	Western division	2,197,608	30,903	7,439	13,429	34,045	3,607	9,484	122,508	10,979	74,225	1,489	8,240
45	Montana	86,941	1,722	317	716	1,340	110	368	6,260	630	4,819	75	447
46	Wyoming	44,845	418	206	484	749	100	244	3,173	269	2,922	41	312
47	Colorado	321,962	3,184	1,072	2,376	5,056	567	1,884	23,913	2,288	19,935	334	1,743
48	New Mexico	131,859	231	89	189	320	48	115	1,602	134	1,495	31	159
49	Arizona	38,117	364	111	146	444	35	103	1,736	191	972	25	150
50	Utah	153,766	485	185	372	855	76	300	3,605	461	2,424	75	242
51	Nevada	27,190	720	115	289	522	46	138	1,732	210	879	18	133
52	Idaho	66,554	662	120	290	448	50	185	2,571	210	1,970	28	158
53	Washington	254,319	5,584	872	1,747	3,427	369	902	16,024	1,302	11,003	192	990
54	Oregon	253,936	1,928	462	1,012	1,840	194	608	9,419	796	6,575	113	705
55	California	818,119	15,605	3,800	5,808	19,644	2,012	4,577	52,473	4,479	21,132	557	3,201

STATE OR TERRITORY OF BIRTH.

STATE OR TERRITORY OF BIRTH, BY STATES AND TERRITORIES: 1890.

STATE OR TERRITORY OF BIRTH, ARRANGED GEOGRAPHICALLY—continued.

	South Atlantic division—Continued.						North Central division.									
District of Columbia.	Virginia.	West Virginia.	North Carolina.	South Carolina.	Georgia.	Florida.	Ohio.	Indiana.	Illinois.	Michigan.	Wisconsin.	Minnesota.	Iowa.	Missouri.	North Dakota.	
90,001	1,334,985	622,063	1,192,833	551,199	1,104,904	147,729	3,766,458	2,153,102	2,984,471	1,307,022	1,248,684	650,209	1,391,166	1,934,102	54,407	1
5,554	90,805	10,800	9,751	8,357	5,870	1,855	58,680	8,335	20,608	17,438	8,935	3,619	6,808	6,400	467	2
61	131	16	44	32	50	38	243	67	238	153	231	150	114	55	4	3
46	106	12	33	22	43	21	344	41	364	238	200	142	148	88	28	4
24	63	17	20	11	31	16	366	60	396	256	261	93	179	64	7	5
507	1,470	124	424	305	480	222	3,299	770	3,000	1,647	1,218	642	886	707	62	6
102	231	47	71	57	106	54	417	80	310	174	213	87	92	68	11	7
202	728	60	232	156	261	111	1,578	287	1,093	611	420	170	285	268	25	8
2,008	6,097	509	1,377	1,975	1,819	660	15,772	3,020	8,612	10,489	4,138	1,421	2,556	2,645	210	9
659	2,388	183	444	448	452	262	3,171	708	1,767	900	591	192	426	614	26	10
1,885	11,821	9,131	1,106	741	613	199	33,499	3,203	4,893	2,970	1,654	722	2,122	1,891	94	11
77,507	1,076,385	559,483	1,063,878	483,024	903,910	136,824	42,778	5,129	5,381	3,106	1,555	790	2,085	3,494	102	12
124	652	36	124	89	32	12	275	80	114	65	29	18	20	59	3	13
4,269	17,345	3,952	956	419	442	98	2,194	400	713	306	199	58	186	484	8	14
70,943	13,181	626	656	463	402	110	2,774	1,059	1,115	631	322	230	408	552	24	15
1,624	940,520	2,844	15,057	807	566	143	2,037	409	490	632	286	81	200	537	18	16
193	88,275	551,684	1,249	104	115	16	31,154	870	540	138	79	69	422	581	8	17
90	10,645	89	1,015,829	9,087	2,845	170	338	275	145	141	51	15	57	123	6	18
35	892	19	10,860	435,594	3,683	215	146	47	51	36	10	3	24	34	......	19
137	3,274	81	15,895	20,195	873,234	4,052	1,475	587	601	358	143	83	175	331	15	20
92	1,601	152	3,243	7,206	22,591	132,008	2,385	1,342	1,612	790	436	242	503	793	20	21
4,285	145,619	42,838	40,825	6,054	9,256	1,150	3,500,404	2,026,540	2,780,347	1,240,643	1,190,927	617,720	1,289,111	1,729,570	50,555	22
622	30,504	17,073	1,287	442	833	128	2,721,445	34,723	12,542	16,899	3,285	926	4,413	4,484	98	23
266	16,587	2,686	11,558	1,168	1,003	91	163,018	1,503,394	30,642	11,603	2,102	700	4,518	5,023	80	24
1,122	18,836	3,722	5,844	1,252	1,368	223	124,727	95,205	2,172,851	20,917	31,080	4,110	24,250	35,838	534	25
190	1,932	623	297	114	173	87	70,023	21,291	11,202	1,111,425	17,387	1,087	3,517	1,938	260	26
128	1,118	308	164	107	154	56	18,965	6,578	19,363	11,539	948,550	10,814	6,966	2,235	878	27
265	1,805	690	321	102	196	63	18,260	9,944	25,243	11,714	59,187	552,320	20,732	3,218	2,422	28
228	11,133	2,850	2,684	324	314	61	102,010	50,021	114,063	10,272	41,556	8,654	905,624	28,210	1,314	29
726	39,523	5,063	11,954	1,703	3,410	237	84,444	70,309	133,949	7,735	8,724	2,263	37,073	1,548,627	229	30
30	252	167	42	15	23	0	3,168	1,384	3,073	3,970	9,864	13,021	4,555	843	43,536	31
81	848	285	153	36	79	11	8,975	4,859	17,838	7,073	28,128	15,383	26,108	2,872	112	32
294	7,652	2,791	1,456	266	584	95	59,644	40,138	107,587	13,854	26,408	5,056	95,325	20,201	738	33
332	15,339	6,580	5,065	525	1,119	101	110,176	97,794	137,394	13,642	14,058	3,424	66,030	77,091	354	34
773	72,196	5,227	77,538	56,277	182,892	7,510	70,166	60,148	62,195	8,812	5,284	2,257	12,831	98,541	343	35
160	22,699	2,626	6,006	785	1,607	110	31,458	22,190	6,455	776	422	148	556	4,845	31	36
113	19,535	394	25,010	4,925	13,189	305	9,793	5,716	4,328	1,742	817	420	814	3,596	67	37
80	4,007	197	7,971	15,574	71,319	3,144	3,658	1,693	1,339	551	205	122	322	723	30	38
42	2,751	60	6,728	9,286	9,489	380	1,037	760	1,055	326	140	59	192	850	7	39
60	1,302	90	1,181	2,632	6,492	590	1,390	953	1,179	391	326	137	834	1,364	31	40
245	15,674	1,141	17,325	14,594	54,597	2,710	10,147	11,274	22,340	2,614	1,792	749	3,916	43,814	72	41
7	796	255	408	89	483	21	3,714	4,075	5,309	693	591	220	3,009	7,267	55	42
66	5,342	464	12,900	8,392	25,716	259	8,969	13,487	20,100	1,719	931	396	3,188	36,082	50	43
1,882	17,750	4,416	6,841	2,007	4,976	644	94,421	52,950	100,880	37,023	41,983	25,808	80,331	96,097	2,940	44
98	947	236	215	117	176	25	4,959	2,380	5,114	3,325	3,919	3,386	4,778	5,969	452	45
41	450	166	111	39	131	54	2,810	1,364	3,413	945	1,403	437	3,026	2,500	102	46
253	3,503	1,277	1,349	291	1,216	122	23,085	12,497	27,951	6,814	7,012	1,090	19,301	21,312	177	47
39	426	102	145	57	208	33	1,578	900	1,790	419	300	100	786	2,219	19	48
44	344	67	150	59	210	23	1,206	647	1,310	383	329	82	612	1,727	16	49
62	610	107	270	93	316	18	2,650	1,136	3,329	854	711	343	2,400	1,831	41	50
28	219	46	52	12	40	11	1,024	379	952	400	368	38	596	881	2	51
66	654	187	383	57	150	10	2,420	1,672	3,359	900	1,347	910	2,934	8,897	126	52
198	2,183	633	1,183	215	597	108	13,826	8,942	17,592	8,725	11,436	11,028	14,504	12,270	1,217	53
293	2,337	502	1,145	144	388	43	11,519	8,315	14,013	4,057	5,516	3,476	12,474	15,267	443	54
760	6,077	1,093	1,838	923	1,544	197	28,744	14,709	31,057	10,192	9,552	4,318	18,320	28,224	345	55

566 STATISTICS OF POPULATION.

TABLE 25.—NATIVE WHITE POPULATION, DISTRIBUTED ACCORDING TO STATE

	STATES AND TERRITORIES.	North Central division—Continued.			South Central division.								
		South Dakota.	Nebraska.	Kansas.	Kentucky.	Tennessee.	Alabama.	Mississippi.	Louisiana.	Texas.	Indian territory.	Oklahoma.	Arkansas.
1	The United States	91,774	358,454	603,423	1,772,308	1,563,992	875,362	583,004	510,305	1,053,080	6,826	1,440	566,700
2	North Atlantic division	235	1,370	3,205	5,891	2,930	1,667	1,135	3,824	1,947	106	24	541
3	Maine	5	34	50	38	33	15	24	32	21	1	......	17
4	New Hampshire	14	38	50	47	28	28	20	28	15	5	2	6
5	Vermont	9	39	67	26	17	16	12	10	31	5	......	8
6	Massachusetts	24	202	371	530	309	213	119	419	235	12	1	77
7	Rhode Island	3	19	45	65	33	24	13	40	20	1	......	7
8	Connecticut	6	84	120	182	95	91	48	150	91	4	1	18
9	New York	132	485	1,167	2,262	1,072	814	525	2,147	801	20	7	177
10	New Jersey	14	99	208	546	219	161	101	309	195	9	5	47
11	Pennsylvania	28	370	1,127	2,195	1,124	305	273	590	439	40	8	184
12	South Atlantic division	72	434	1,298	12,707	21,274	24,972	3,507	2,544	2,489	95	32	1,280
13	Delaware	4	6	17	46	14	3	6	14	7	......	......	1
14	Maryland	15	52	130	431	240	160	137	295	113	9	24	42
15	District of Columbia	15	66	182	617	580	234	211	250	216	21	......	84
16	Virginia	7	92	127	2,659	4,518	415	255	315	306	30	3	140
17	West Virginia	10	58	292	5,200	687	65	55	83	90	4	1	53
18	North Carolina	2	17	66	358	4,523	404	253	101	224	5	2	144
19	South Carolina	4	3	6	148	447	551	231	72	104	3	......	73
20	Georgia	2	38	91	1,261	8,726	12,731	951	523	757	17	2	493
21	Florida	13	102	387	1,987	1,539	10,400	1,408	891	663	6	......	256
22	North Central division	88,609	335,414	538,297	272,952	119,371	9,546	8,096	9,266	12,758	2,008	110	23,234
23	Ohio	88	616	2,452	26,331	2,751	573	619	991	490	212	7	302
24	Indiana	85	651	3,434	51,604	7,787	686	523	618	590	56	2	645
25	Illinois	375	2,786	7,855	47,574	25,398	2,068	1,604	2,108	1,680	105	17	1,093
26	Michigan	227	755	1,724	1,229	611	160	164	237	304	22	2	145
27	Wisconsin	613	798	1,027	1,204	528	128	125	206	148	15	......	110
28	Minnesota	1,561	788	970	2,492	549	159	257	314	246	73	3	148
29	Iowa	1,728	6,679	6,960	9,757	4,272	256	355	442	450	47	17	432
30	Missouri	216	4,646	30,745	91,129	62,143	4,105	2,834	3,212	5,042	785	17	16,020
31	North Dakota	273	182	197	280	101	23	32	40	58	9	2	26
32	South Dakota	82,545	2,367	1,130	850	359	66	82	84	233	13	1	110
33	Nebraska	758	304,130	12,135	7,849	3,144	448	637	424	732	58	24	613
34	Kansas	200	11,016	469,608	32,563	11,728	814	864	521	2,185	613	27	2,624
35	South Central division	241	2,343	19,300	1,454,381	1,401,008	835,087	566,107	480,262	1,017,319	3,741	1,250	531,029
36	Kentucky	14	100	545	1,362,836	41,313	1,493	1,279	1,017	881	22	3	1,050
37	Tennessee	30	133	455	21,637	1,153,739	14,319	11,221	1,210	1,735	41	2	3,456
38	Alabama	13	48	189	3,252	20,293	660,848	9,261	1,738	1,570	39	......	969
39	Mississippi	2	40	101	2,217	12,241	33,431	440,070	6,850	1,551	20	......	1,708
40	Louisiana	35	107	309	1,819	1,914	10,668	15,774	444,230	5,129	49	......	2,782
41	Texas	64	643	3,908	40,609	97,348	83,144	59,982	28,387	989,908	1,363	10	43,018
42	Oklahoma	23	667	9,449	2,524	1,864	458	468	160	5,225	1,034	1,234	1,472
43	Arkansas	51	605	4,344	19,487	72,296	30,726	27,452	5,670	11,311	1,173	1	477,414
44	Western division	2,557	18,893	41,323	26,377	19,409	4,090	4,159	5,409	18,576	876	24	9,710
45	Montana	368	658	1,286	1,401	569	132	101	157	390	47	3	175
46	Wyoming	216	2,016	1,343	582	307	91	95	82	570	39	1	207
47	Colorado	132	5,652	12,943	5,574	3,035	628	720	812	1,918	243	4	1,234
48	New Mexico	6	167	1,133	673	615	301	266	187	4,741	70	......	525
49	Arizona	6	75	443	564	468	255	203	159	1,607	40	1	434
50	Utah	41	716	689	675	566	218	182	104	267	16	......	85
51	Nevada	4	73	126	310	176	42	25	84	64	3	......	56
52	Idaho	62	630	1,647	884	656	129	129	422	486	43	......	700
53	Washington	1,057	3,233	8,147	3,157	3,033	416	399	323	2,279	139	3	1,504
54	Oregon	308	2,661	5,916	3,369	3,318	272	320	294	1,154	76	3	1,570
55	California	297	3,012	7,650	9,188	6,666	1,606	1,719	2,785	5,100	154	9	3,214

STATE OR TERRITORY OF BIRTH, ARRANGED GEOGRAPHICALLY—continued.

STATE OR TERRITORY OF BIRTH.   567

OR TERRITORY OF BIRTH, BY STATES AND TERRITORIES: 1890—Continued.

Montana.	Wyoming.	Colorado.	New Mexico.	Arizona.	Utah.	Nevada.	Idaho.	Washington.	Oregon.	California.	Alaska.	Born in the United States (state not specified).	Born at sea under United States flag.	American citizens born abroad.	
25,174	11,923	94,803	120,526	16,064	139,507	20,788	23,872	58,136	136,914	506,233	279	337,071	1,381	8,162	1
906	150	1,059	070	61	204	287	77	460	426	5,307	42	125,313	497	2,073	2
11	1	22	8	3	6	24	5	16	14	271	1	1,384	37	112	3
4	2	23	3	1	3	9	3	4	4	124	....	1,211	5	188	4
1	5	23	2	1	3	7	1	5	5	79	1	753	9	170	5
41	31	173	31	7	32	70	24	41	139	1,029	5	8,788	99	330	6
....	1	22	48	3	6	2	2	6	5	104	1	1,024	19	45	7
6	3	49	15	3	5	11	....	21	25	274	3	2,678	33	69	8
71	73	385	168	24	89	79	27	167	137	2,320	10	82,150	147	860	9
18	8	80	34	7	21	30	7	25	32	430	11	9,027	46	92	10
54	32	276	67	12	39	55	8	175	65	676	10	18,298	102	248	11
72	41	212	59	31	34	45	29	337	90	740	11	13,520	50	103	12
2	....	3	2	2	1	....	1	8	....	28		315	8	5	13
12	5	46	11	7	3	11	5	123	11	150	4	2,546	16	23	14
25	10	42	21	12	20	6	16	122	28	241	....	1,309	8	25	15
5	7	27	6	1	2	5	1	50	15	90	1	1,480	5	17	16
8	2	14	4	1	2	8	1	7	6	48		1,831	6	5	17
1	1	15	2	....	3	2	1	1	4	30		1,632	3	2	18
3	5	4	....	1	....			3		5		226	2	2	19
5	1	36	5	3	1	1	4	8	10	80	4	3,190	4	8	20
11	4	25	8	4	2	12	....	15	16	68	2	982	7	16	21
1,518	1,167	6,679	950	277	1,281	802	506	933	1,785	8,310	40	119,962	624	4,912	22
34	32	229	110	18	45	30	38	80	88	656	5	13,360	79	162	23
30	11	145	28	4	16	20	5	32	80	311	2	8,404	28	47	24
205	64	736	107	20	109	109	32	145	209	1,523	7	26,643	230	328	25
62	24	275	50	15	55	57	15	46	99	594	....	8,396	56	1,792	26
79	36	173	28	2	32	53	17	33	57	370	1	7,486	55	300	27
181	36	185	30	4	38	26	24	80	92	408	2	9,445	49	112	28
129	125	588	48	17	290	92	77	106	260	850	5	10,079	27	342	29
297	101	1,233	196	51	205	163	82	149	299	1,492	5	19,643	47	1,282	30
83	13	36	17	3	9	4	4	8	16	88	....	490	10	182	31
77	116	284	26	45	51	45	19	39	66	180	....	1,501	3	32	32
132	496	1,206	82	42	295	86	107	95	229	884	8	6,816	18	176	33
209	113	1,589	228	47	136	121	86	120	290	924	5	7,090	22	157	34
191	94	885	796	98	114	112	125	152	357	2,310	38	44,331	75	189	35
14	10	50	15	1	6	10	1	13	23	167	....	6,399	17	21	36
28	7	63	16	5	11	7	4	20	35	165	2	5,998	1	7	37
3	5	25	15	2	2	5	3	6	19	96	3	2,884	5	11	38
1	5	13	7	1	4	....	2	....	6	48	9	2,358	3	8	39
4	2	35	23	....	3	7	2	3	13	95	6	1,712	24	18	40
91	45	404	631	80	70	56	52	78	170	1,383	16	17,637	21	-101	41
25	5	153	65	5	3	6	30	16	32	106	....	681	1	1	42
25	15	142	24	4	15	21	31	16	59	248	2	6,662	3	22	43
23,187	10,465	85,974	118,345	15,597	137,874	19,542	23,135	56,254	134,256	489,566	148	38,945	126	885	44
20,989	107	282	23	8	767	390	213	60	1,952	1,114	....	2,787	6	47	45
119	8,384	1,154	127	32	1,573	93	271	26	118	281	....	589	3	16	46
165	481	78,659	9,265	82	1,117	209	91	60	533	1,095	5	6,400	15	88	47
9	28	1,349	106,824	225	270	43	30	12	39	467		241	2	6	48
26	45	200	1,260	14,160	2,835	249	168	42	164	2,971	1	219	2	16	49
193	512	785	80	198	119,107	587	701	44	101	889	3	3,157	5	14	50
35	32	67	13	31	784	12,015	70	28	120	3,091	1	74	3	4	51
345	258	369	27	41	9,001	410	19,675	802	2,172	1,297	1	557	5	18	52
530	225	1,056	125	77	547	606	834	50,967	12,748	8,990	17	6,552	15	121	53
323	133	661	54	46	476	578	695	3,179	110,436	10,170	16	4,100	12	152	54
453	260	1,412	547	688	1,397	4,362	387	1,034	5,873	459,201	104	9,209	58	403	55

568

STATISTICS OF POPULATION.

TABLE **26.**—NATIVE WHITE POPULATION OF NATIVE PARENTAGE, DISTRIBUTED

	STATES AND TERRITORIES.	Number living in each state or territory.	STATE OR TERRITORY OF BIRTH, ARRANGED GEOGRAPHICALLY.										
			North Atlantic division.									South Atlantic division.	
			Maine.	New Hampshire.	Vermont.	Massachusetts.	Rhode Island.	Connecticut.	New York.	New Jersey.	Pennsylvania.	Delaware.	Maryland.
1	The United States..	34,358,348	608,306	313,010	339,083	902,110	139,074	383,463	3,118,874	681,484	3,063,376	117,242	636,706
2	North Atlantic division....	8,891,405	592,917	279,765	263,809	810,168	129,451	340,013	2,466,532	623,197	3,112,239	16,434	35,363
3	Maine	506,703	483,660	6,837	1,293	8,353	472	439	1,622	216	433	17	87
4	New Hampshire	253,629	13,509	201,720	12,818	16,092	540	770	3,754	244	431	16	64
5	Vermont	225,245	1,439	8,543	194,531	5,866	249	840	10,635	153	279	9	36
6	Massachusetts	955,430	77,752	51,665	27,447	707,512	13,858	18,247	28,833	2,625	4,358	206	1,014
7	Rhode Island	137,550	3,006	1,482	1,085	15,281	102,826	6,148	3,822	515	812	27	183
8	Connecticut	357,235	2,566	1,973	3,105	17,517	5,827	280,694	31,340	3,284	2,553	135	414
9	New York	2,520,807	6,558	5,245	20,210	27,554	3,975	24,605	2,252,562	34,769	50,109	924	4,362
10	New Jersey	696,718	1,819	1,066	1,077	5,231	740	4,576	65,135	548,587	45,508	3,112	3,321
11	Pennsylvania	3,238,088	2,608	1,234	2,243	6,162	964	3,694	68,829	32,824	3,007,666	11,088	25,882
12	South Atlantic division	5,067,379	3,667	1,837	1,926	6,432	903	3,340	21,785	7,776	60,992	93,195	546,004
13	Delaware	109,355	195	245	76	179	68	155	1,103	1,903	9,527	84,630	9,412
14	Maryland	576,285	595	167	181	953	144	470	3,263	1,683	21,950	7,141	508,854
15	District of Columbia	107,309	858	543	510	1,717	202	714	5,730	1,129	5,638	420	14,375
16	Virginia	976,758	393	164	214	676	80	357	3,993	1,813	5,825	622	6,799
17	West Virginia	670,214	213	43	73	343	21	109	991	351	14,390	112	5,720
18	North Carolina	1,044,483	150	65	79	321	31	189	791	225	783	79	604
19	South Carolina	445,195	112	44	39	248	56	139	470	122	229	25	225
20	Georgia	946,782	348	150	268	613	131	412	1,827	461	935	80	600
21	Florida	190,908	803	416	486	1,382	161	786	3,617	580	1,607	71	405
22	North Central division	12,250,155	42,825	23,727	60,317	58,813	5,774	31,152	532,526	41,071	419,377	5,904	43,457
23	Ohio	2,334,517	1,837	1,877	4,280	7,205	587	5,500	40,805	6,557	96,689	681	12,326
24	Indiana	1,697,998	961	641	1,300	2,044	237	1,056	15,274	3,316	34,222	952	4,850
25	Illinois	1,882,693	5,742	4,693	10,117	13,623	1,315	6,051	76,560	9,137	60,928	1,109	8,534
26	Michigan	917,693	3,649	2,240	8,263	6,441	541	3,920	157,605	5,058	27,142	270	937
27	Wisconsin	434,649	5,640	2,514	8,171	4,567	419	2,421	52,587	1,500	12,171	126	413
28	Minnesota	310,951	10,840	3,105	6,496	5,796	411	2,052	34,443	1,446	11,570	150	727
29	Iowa	1,063,967	4,108	3,288	8,298	5,584	601	3,061	51,972	3,855	52,238	553	3,637
30	Missouri	1,856,477	1,775	1,064	2,118	3,450	385	1,574	20,495	2,438	20,186	644	5,039
31	North Dakota	37,428	838	271	788	483	43	233	4,856	319	2,433	25	123
32	South Dakota	127,232	1,537	760	2,088	1,106	122	511	13,069	539	5,912	52	299
33	Nebraska	594,224	3,115	1,677	4,417	4,587	549	2,782	33,660	3,206	34,501	512	2,541
34	Kansas	902,326	2,783	1,588	3,981	3,927	534	1,982	31,694	3,700	52,825	512	4,031
35	South Central division	6,661,648	2,095	992	1,642	3,517	420	1,628	17,143	2,344	17,853	520	5,073
36	Kentucky	1,406,918	232	130	153	519	48	205	2,033	404	3,503	85	996
37	Tennessee	1,283,481	315	185	257	612	88	297	2,759	341	3,136	64	715
38	Alabama	796,421	242	106	171	415	37	247	1,358	216	1,430	52	519
39	Mississippi	520,354	76	40	67	139	21	62	629	108	460	22	240
40	Louisiana	413,090	226	84	137	382	34	149	1,632	163	813	44	428
41	Texas	1,408,880	673	302	533	1,064	142	492	5,545	717	4,558	104	1,508
42	Oklahoma	51,554	75	25	122	82	15	49	991	99	1,108	15	108
43	Arkansas	780,950	256	120	202	304	35	127	2,196	296	2,755	53	460
44	Western division	1,487,761	26,802	6,689	11,389	23,180	2,526	7,380	80,888	7,096	52,915	1,180	5,870
45	Montana	55,982	1,389	257	516	780	58	252	3,891	356	3,075	63	321
46	Wyoming	30,325	309	187	364	531	87	164	2,072	177	1,995	34	198
47	Colorado	242,148	2,775	980	1,961	3,733	410	1,502	16,317	1,404	14,187	277	1,232
48	New Mexico	119,320	200	82	149	216	33	82	1,025	94	962	27	114
49	Arizona	24,090	318	103	123	300	26	85	1,170	134	738	19	123
50	Utah	68,452	429	160	315	630	52	250	2,417	328	1,671	57	179
51	Nevada	14,784	593	98	238	296	32	94	1,034	113	549	10	77
52	Idaho	45,490	556	98	234	289	34	143	1,672	135	1,416	22	95
53	Washington	185,562	4,610	757	1,495	2,441	256	769	11,310	950	8,292	151	730
54	Oregon	203,969	1,708	426	907	1,372	141	502	6,959	586	5,200	88	553
55	California	497,729	13,906	3,561	5,087	12,592	1,417	3,487	33,021	2,729	14,830	432	2,257

STATE OR TERRITORY OF BIRTH.   569

ACCORDING TO STATE OR TERRITORY OF BIRTH, BY STATES AND TERRITORIES: 1890.

STATE OR TERRITORY OF BIRTH, ARRANGED GEOGRAPHICALLY—continued.

South Atlantic division—Continued.							North Central division.									
District of Columbia.	Virginia.	West Virginia.	North Carolina.	South Carolina.	Georgia.	Florida.	Ohio.	Indiana.	Illinois.	Michigan.	Wisconsin.	Minnesota.	Iowa.	Missouri.	North Dakota.	
64,954	1,293,509	584,822	1,182,744	535,209	1,084,803	136,033	2,877,992	1,840,818	1,882,776	714,962	430,777	194,596	912,667	1,540,618	14,493	1
3,811	18,923	8,155	3,012	2,539	2,692	1,063	40,573	6,069	13,476	11,892	5,719	2,441	5,092	3,885	311	2
51	112	13	38	28	47	31	195	58	189	95	199	124	103	40	4	3
39	88	9	32	20	39	17	277	35	282	142	146	107	126	73	14	4
19	42	10	19	8	24	13	297	54	342	191	204	69	162	49	7	5
371	1,102	84	369	292	377	167	2,415	597	2,091	1,007	749	434	668	502	34	6
63	184	18	61	43	72	41	256	53	173	74	93	34	60	38	2	7
144	605	49	208	111	206	94	1,220	228	794	430	287	124	219	189	14	8
1,371	4,818	381	1,083	1,214	1,171	444	10,360	2,112	5,285	7,362	2,688	990	1,820	1,451	152	9
468	2,003	135	360	304	325	119	2,196	520	1,125	578	323	114	301	336	16	10
1,285	9,909	7,456	842	510	431	137	23,357	2,412	3,195	2,007	1,030	445	1,615	1,187	68	11
50,742	1,051,874	529,992	1,057,292	471,795	888,705	126,593	36,907	4,500	4,271	2,288	1,048	577	1,750	2,957	75	12
88	592	27	117	81	24	10	214	68	78	41	16	13	18	45	2	13
3,222	15,657	3,390	864	306	349	70	1,620	339	478	193	116	39	113	355	5	14
51,705	11,970	514	618	399	361	86	2,434	972	924	407	225	176	375	447	21	15
1,311	922,153	2,719	14,854	756	522	131	1,785	362	387	423	177	58	175	488	6	16
140	85,654	523,019	1,215	85	102	13	27,188	772	442	100	55	62	380	524	8	17
69	10,415	86	1,010,159	8,842	2,801	150	271	254	125	92	45	12	50	112	6	18
80	836	19	10,096	426,110	3,497	198	121	44	42	30	7	1	22	30	......	19
103	3,103	74	15,641	28,232	858,819	3,866	1,212	485	480	277	102	65	136	277	14	20
74	1,494	138	3,128	6,984	22,230	122,069	2,002	1,204	1,315	635	305	151	481	670	13	21
2,592	136,743	37,873	39,627	5,147	8,279	836	2,673,813	1,732,516	1,727,481	670,174	397,544	176,592	831,506	1,358,729	12,370	22
428	28,410	14,250	1,198	359	675	95	2,016,098	26,044	9,428	11,503	2,056	618	3,626	3,198	78	23
186	15,834	2,488	11,399	1,075	936	74	188,752	1,350,907	23,622	8,928	1,245	511	3,933	4,808	62	24
580	17,448	3,320	5,042	1,014	1,177	163	104,400	81,810	1,291,464	12,862	13,928	2,082	16,440	23,104	310	25
129	1,650	535	237	80	126	44	64,102	17,822	6,305	585,461	6,938	909	2,510	1,298	154	26
64	893	232	137	59	105	37	14,392	5,110	9,645	5,204	289,227	4,508	4,058	1,027	447	27
168	1,522	564	274	73	141	39	13,089	7,572	11,574	5,757	21,429	140,995	9,687	1,625	678	28
148	10,305	2,634	2,591	259	250	40	89,606	46,983	73,470	7,397	20,088	4,276	613,043	16,571	830	29
401	37,949	4,678	11,670	1,518	3,239	190	71,178	64,303	104,834	5,627	5,239	1,478	31,295	1,215,955	151	30
24	205	151	33	8	17	5	2,415	1,097	2,230	3,000	3,297	1,572	609	8,687		31
50	770	250	142	18	62	7	7,488	3,081	10,764	4,176	12,281	6,377	14,741	2,252	43	32
199	7,236	2,635	1,377	232	495	70	51,177	36,064	74,062	10,368	13,715	3,203	73,741	22,111	456	33
206	14,521	6,136	4,927	452	1,056	72	101,116	90,724	109,483	10,372	8,398	2,248	56,860	66,171	174	34
576	69,861	4,876	76,348	54,096	180,581	7,065	50,007	51,090	54,654	6,511	3,286	1,617	10,785	91,901	241	35
117	22,039	2,481	5,925	733	1,525	88	18,401	16,661	5,534	525	198	105	389	4,258	22	36
83	19,021	366	24,706	4,717	12,883	264	7,786	4,931	3,714	1,318	509	309	649	3,125	44	37
60	3,786	153	7,789	15,178	70,484	3,000	2,583	1,370	937	420	102	75	210	561	21	38
29	2,663	51	6,624	9,012	9,340	351	813	648	836	237	100	52	143	666	5	39
50	1,281	70	1,151	2,059	6,366	526	1,124	784	907	291	219	99	659	930	22	40
170	15,122	1,000	17,023	14,140	53,986	2,585	8,336	10,279	19,554	1,872	1,042	509	3,238	41,221	51	41
3	769	244	405	86	476	16	3,344	3,844	4,794	569	398	165	2,044	6,889	35	42
55	5,180	442	12,725	8,171	25,521	235	7,620	12,573	18,378	1,279	598	303	2,853	34,251	41	43
1,233	16,168	3,926	6,465	1,632	4,546	476	76,692	46,643	82,894	24,097	23,180	13,369	63,534	83,166	1,496	44
54	837	188	191	92	158	16	3,858	1,977	3,463	1,475	1,976	1,623	3,466	5,124	201	45
28	395	139	100	30	105	35	2,196	1,176	2,386	602	817	256	2,813	2,035	65	46
163	3,207	1,165	1,288	245	1,132	99	18,961	10,959	20,991	4,621	4,070	1,154	15,229	17,877	119	47
29	388	91	142	49	198	24	1,237	772	1,291	268	222	54	614	1,803	10	48
33	315	63	141	50	200	19	970	566	1,040	258	207	62	540	1,496	7	49
46	567	95	258	87	303	13	2,142	1,000	2,463	517	416	176	1,770	1,291	29	50
15	193	41	48	10	32	5	820	327	696	261	178	18	464	744	2	51
51	588	161	373	51	140	5	1,995	1,522	2,650	606	729	377	2,420	3,505	74	52
124	2,017	563	1,147	175	542	81	11,230	7,968	18,134	5,339	5,970	5,273	11,200	10,891	585	53
207	2,200	460	1,109	130	363	32	9,842	7,549	11,548	2,853	2,873	1,859	10,363	13,970	198	54
483	5,461	960	1,668	718	1,373	147	23,441	12,827	28,205	7,297	5,722	2,517	14,655	24,350	206	55

570 STATISTICS OF POPULATION.

TABLE **26.**—NATIVE WHITE POPULATION OF NATIVE PARENTAGE, DISTRIBUTED ACCORDING

	STATES AND TERRITORIES.	STATE OR TERRITORY OF BIRTH, ARRANGED GEOGRAPHICALLY—continued.											
		North Central division—Continued.			South Central division.								
		South Dakota.	Nebraska.	Kansas.	Kentucky.	Tennessee.	Alabama.	Missis- sippi.	Louisiana.	Texas.	Indian terri- tory.	Okla- homa.	Arkan- sas.
1	The United States..	37,679	213,353	456,388	1,645,362	1,530,127	855,197	565,650	404,315	891,301	6,153	1,263	553,175
2	North Atlantic division	164	1,030	2,441	3,924	2,104	1,193	821	2,054	1,205	78	13	373
3	Maine................	5	26	49	32	24	15	22	24	18	1	....	14
4	New Hampshire........	9	23	43	35	25	10	15	24	14	5	1	5
5	Vermont...........	7	35	56	24	16	15	9	12	27	4	....	6
6	Massachusetts........	15	151	297	357	249	106	95	265	158	9	1	45
7	Rhode Island..........	2	13	33	45	22	18	9	26	15	1	....	3
8	Connecticut	3	62	86	142	63	79	35	95	68	4	1	14
9	New York..........	90	358	889	1,543	718	536	348	1,048	496	18	6	118
10	New Jersey	10	66	138	359	136	120	78	209	129	7	1	33
11	Pennsylvania..........	23	296	850	1,387	851	225	210	351	280	29	3	135
12	South Atlantic division	51	329	1,095	11,964	20,648	24,253	3,316	1,836	2,260	85	19	1,233
13	Delaware.............	2	6	8	38	10	2	6	7	4	....	....	1
14	Maryland.............	11	38	93	318	186	137	109	200	87	7	13	38
15	District of Columbia....	9	49	155	553	524	207	197	193	187	17	....	70
16	Virginia.............	3	54	85	2,591	4,430	389	237	238	288	27	3	130
17	West Virginia.........	10	52	277	4,962	650	58	43	58	76	3	1	49
18	North Carolina	2	16	66	346	4,481	382	248	90	220	5	....	144
19	South Carolina	3	3	5	137	423	534	223	61	98	3	....	73
20	Georgia	2	36	76	1,148	8,469	12,480	902	435	729	17	2	480
21	Florida.............	9	75	330	1,871	1,475	10,058	1,351	554	571	6	....	242
22	North Central division	35,980	196,850	402,380	250,273	114,056	8,407	6,541	4,372	10,407	1,716	76	21,784
23	Ohio................	60	507	2,006	19,600	2,037	398	447	435	334	152	5	258
24	Indiana.............	70	567	3,143	46,734	7,209	593	440	287	477	55	2	578
25	Illinois.............	250	2,048	6,362	44,488	24,393	1,791	1,256	967	1,267	81	11	1,782
26	Michigan...........	131	530	1,315	925	453	130	108	137	184	17	1	109
27	Wisconsin...........	369	493	650	885	381	97	73	87	68	7	....	66
28	Minnesota...........	765	448	589	1,901	405	108	151	143	118	58	2	101
29	Iowa	1,105	5,141	5,998	8,001	3,043	194	253	183	338	41	9	380
30	Missouri............	179	3,808	26,251	87,586	60,531	3,895	2,407	1,512	4,973	722	16	15,473
31	North Dakota	70	96	129	243	78	21	28	18	44	3	....	15
32	South Dakota	32,386	1,514	821	608	294	52	66	34	169	9	....	85
33	Nebraska...........	475	173,224	10,613	7,202	2,943	403	541	265	584	50	8	524
34	Kansas	120	8,474	345,033	31,011	11,209	725	771	304	1,851	521	22	2,412
35	South Central division	171	1,876	17,261	1,355,410	1,375,127	817,743	551,326	393,105	861,343	3,514	1,143	520,627
36	Kentucky	11	84	459	1,267,335	40,358	1,308	1,168	584	834	19	3	1,008
37	Tennessee	20	106	415	20,636	1,132,256	13,924	10,741	901	1,666	38	1	3,323
38	Alabama	11	39	103	2,791	19,613	646,710	8,917	1,209	1,484	32	....	942
39	Mississippi	1	36	87	2,064	11,910	32,717	429,328	5,217	1,462	10	....	1,708
40	Louisiana	21	81	243	1,562	1,779	10,201	14,692	354,830	4,590	44	....	2,680
41	Texas	48	542	3,368	39,579	96,095	81,997	58,976	24,802	835,280	1,278	8	42,435
42	Oklahoma	18	494	8,008	2,438	1,833	444	454	143	5,057	990	1,130	1,441
43	Arkansas...........	41	494	3,978	19,005	71,283	30,442	27,050	5,359	10,970	1,094	1	467,095
44	Western division...........	1,304	13,268	33,211	23,791	18,192	3,601	3,646	2,948	16,086	760	12	9,158
45	Montana...........	159	415	996	1,268	508	110	84	99	338	31	1	155
46	Wyoming	143	1,398	1,091	506	272	75	87	58	490	31	1	190
47	Colorado...........	82	4,057	10,358	5,005	2,777	561	610	559	1,623	212	2	1,149
48	New Mexico...........	6	117	860	615	560	284	228	120	4,256	66	....	490
49	Arizona	3	50	375	514	441	245	190	115	1,428	37	1	424
50	Utah	17	447	530	599	534	209	166	60	234	14	....	71
51	Nevada..............	....	51	95	274	158	29	24	31	50	2	....	51
52	Idaho..............	30	441	1,415	811	635	114	115	178	446	42	....	679
53	Washington	500	2,228	6,521	2,879	2,866	360	349	202	1,970	125	1	1,401
54	Oregon	177	1,931	4,829	3,145	3,219	253	271	196	1,031	72	....	1,509
55	California...........	187	2,133	6,123	8,175	6,222	1,361	1,522	1,321	4,220	128	6	3,033

STATE OR TERRITORY OF BIRTH. · 571

TO STATE OR TERRITORY OF BIRTH, BY STATES AND TERRITORIES: 1890—Continued.

STATE OR TERRITORY OF BIRTH, ARRANGED GEOGRAPHICALLY—continued.

Western division.

Montana.	Wyoming.	Colorado.	New Mexico.	Arizona.	Utah.	Nevada.	Idaho.	Washington.	Oregon.	California.	Alaska.	Born in the United States (state not specified).	Born at sea under United States flag.	American citizens born abroad.	
14,081	5,765	62,923	111,180	6,945	53,039	9,011	14,197	38,659	109,805	256,160	180	256,713	396	4,701	1
141	108	774	167	42	127	172	53	302	238	3,118	37	69,547	127	1,531	2
7	....	19	6	2	4	17	5	13	13	222	1	1,312	21	75	3
3	2	17	1	....	3	7	3	4	4	103	....	1,153	2	105	4
1	4	20	2	1	1	5	1	5	4	60	....	692	2	146	5
36	23	145	27	5	19	47	17	36	51	679	5	7,473	36	247	6
....	1	11	....	3	2	1	2	5	3	61	1	781	4	27	7
3	3	38	5	3	3	5	....	8	19	168	3	1,952	12	45	8
43	53	284	76	17	50	50	16	98	75	1,253	9	38,373	32	626	9
9	4	55	14	4	17	10	4	17	22	211	11	5,491	5	73	10
39	18	185	36	7	28	30	5	116	47	361	7	12,320	13	187	11
61	33	179	43	25	23	24	24	223	77	523	5	12,741	18	78	12
....	....	1	2	2	1	....	1	7	....	17	....	298	2	4	13
8	5	35	7	4	1	5	5	102	8	93	....	2,218	3	13	14
25	10	40	15	11	14	2	13	51	24	166	....	1,185	4	22	15
5	7	22	6	....	2	1	1	37	14	70	....	1,434	1	15	16
5	1	12	3	1	1	4	1	5	6	41	....	1,753	4	4	17
1	1	13	2	....	3	....	....	1	2	28	....	1,623	2	1	18
3	5	2	....	1	....	....	....	2	....	3	....	222	....	2	19
5	....	33	5	3	....	....	3	5	7	56	4	3,161	1	6	20
9	4	21	3	3	1	12	....	13	16	49	1	847	1	11	21
1,041	501	4,851	647	204	605	523	373	626	1,394	5,688	27	101,405	203	2,361	22
28	20	173	80	11	19	27	28	59	77	436	4	10,696	7	126	23
27	9	121	21	4	11	15	2	23	60	223	2	7,579	6	37	24
139	34	472	68	20	50	75	23	97	156	945	4	21,971	144	237	25
38	15	152	23	14	32	27	8	34	66	389	....	7,377	12	1,073	26
42	8	118	11	2	18	21	8	19	30	186	....	4,927	7	213	27
91	16	101	23	3	17	14	14	35	46	227	2	6,946	8	77	28
80	64	430	26	11	126	15	57	81	205	628	4	9,790	5	234	29
250	67	979	141	36	99	133	73	101	273	1,160	4	17,779	3	63	30
42	4	18	9	2	7	1	3	6	13	54	....	365	4	54	31
41	39	183	20	39	29	26	11	21	52	81	....	1,137	....	27	32
85	240	881	66	26	126	59	81	54	170	657	3	6,072	2	107	33
169	75	1,223	159	36	71	80	65	98	237	702	4	6,766	5	113	34
151	64	706	501	68	91	89	116	129	325	1,858	32	41,990	15	136	35
10	5	40	10	1	4	10	1	9	20	130	....	6,182	2	19	36
23	6	54	14	5	8	4	3	15	32	144	2	5,885	1	4	37
3	4	20	7	2	1	3	3	6	16	71	2	2,841	....	9	38
1	4	5	5	1	3	....	2	....	5	41	9	2,281	....	5	39
3	1	25	16	....	1	6	2	1	11	52	2	1,590	3	15	40
67	27	316	371	51	59	40	49	69	158	1,107	15	15,994	8	66	41
24	5	125	56	5	2	5	29	14	28	89	....	661	1	1	42
20	12	121	22	3	13	21	27	15	55	224	2	6,556	1	17	43
12,687	4,969	56,413	109,831	6,606	52,193	8,203	13,631	37,379	107,771	244,973	79	31,030	33	595	44
11,292	2	....	1	....	7	....	....	1	1,825	592	....	2,446	3	35	45
82	4,008	843	104	22	547	72	151	20	95	205	....	563	....	15	46
93	236	51,512	8,845	49	561	100	60	34	481	736	3	6,239	2	65	47
8	16	1,076	99,326	150	191	32	24	7	31	338	....	223	....	6	48
18	20	153	977	5,786	1,787	126	106	30	136	1,827	....	186	....	9	49
119	104	493	63	117	43,306	252	352	23	74	538	3	2,854	1	12	50
22	10	36	10	18	403	4,783	42	16	94	1,521	1	72	1	2	51
241	112	271	14	25	4,204	235	11,521	715	1,876	802	....	528	2	7	52
278	116	707	84	45	248	302	612	33,362	10,634	5,560	15	6,103	6	80	53
251	101	483	41	30	240	369	540	2,507	87,783	7,007	5	3,877	4	100	54
283	154	839	366	304	699	1,923	223	664	4,742	225,838	52	8,439	14	264	55

572

STATISTICS OF POPULATION.

TABLE 27.—NATIVE WHITE POPULATION OF FOREIGN PARENTAGE, DISTRIBUTED

	STATES AND TERRITORIES.	Number living in each state or territory.	North Atlantic division.									South Atlantic division.	
			Maine.	New Hampshire.	Vermont.	Massachusetts.	Rhode Island.	Connecticut.	New York.	New Jersey.	Pennsylvania.	Delaware.	Maryland.
1	The United States..	11,503,675	94,029	51,145	82,227	616,869	88,259	191,447	2,057,259	333,472	1,172,436	18,261	172,077
2	North Atlantic division	4,355,710	82,852	47,966	71,415	582,338	84,457	181,505	1,824,510	314,528	1,031,140	3,289	10,666
3	Maine	73,865	69,014	794	282	2,009	184	100	660	70	192	5	13
4	New Hampshire........	50,015	1,353	38,175	2,589	4,573	308	250	1,851	80	181	3	23
5	Vermont..............	62,149	225	943	54,437	1,313	91	155	4,233	72	145	4	9
6	Massachusetts..........	606,440	8,993	5,976	6,849	539,441	6,923	6,772	18,887	1,803	3,011	73	414
7	Rhode Island..........	94,282	690	567	981	9,973	72,759	2,879	3,725	557	721	10	87
8	Connecticut	193,048	456	471	1,058	7,808	1,659	161,052	13,895	2,113	1,526	37	149
9	New York............	1,837,453	1,235	691	4,460	11,315	1,505	7,253	1,698,294	18,913	21,553	244	2,141
10	New Jersey............	371,878	255	136	293	2,567	463	1,792	55,620	282,086	18,760	301	890
11	Pennsylvania..........	1,066,580	631	213	466	3,249	565	1,312	27,345	8,825	985,051	2,552	6,931
12	South Atlantic division	322,454	378	190	196	1,677	282	641	9,924	1,707	13,099	13,376	147,383
13	Delaware..............	17,615	24	72	14	73	22	48	521	304	2,657	12,852	656
14	Maryland..............	156,421	86	13	30	464	62	143	2,504	525	4,687	364	141,000
15	District of Columbia....	28,869	57	20	50	297	35	121	2,043	215	1,219	40	2,376
16	Virginia	25,175	37	21	13	238	43	91	1,505	233	1,552	53	953
17	West Virginia..........	41,011	29	9	19	96	22	18	510	94	2,506	25	1,415
18	North Carolina	7,237	11	4	9	45	6	34	278	52	165	5	92
19	South Carolina	10,670	15	2	5	42	5	18	336	44	90	1	47
20	Georgia	19,083	34	21	28	158	58	64	1,076	112	358	16	127
21	Florida	15,773	85	28	28	264	29	104	1,061	128	405	20	117
22	North Central division	5,608,315	6,390	2,127	8,332	20,071	2,286	6,056	171,916	12,519	90,499	1,183	11,213
23	Ohio................	791,735	265	127	431	1,830	154	784	10,622	1,529	23,554	165	2,386
24	Indiana..............	302,735	111	58	177	578	69	251	5,596	673	6,162	80	843
25	Illinois..............	1,044,804	693	321	1,226	4,694	482	1,577	33,291	2,854	15,362	306	2,304
26	Michigan..............	613,590	673	265	1,186	1,667	197	593	35,116	1,282	5,481	55	417
27	Wisconsin..............	726,835	1,015	259	1,220	2,184	298	654	17,341	967	4,865	88	517
28	Minnesota..............	518,151	1,998	345	1,185	2,692	328	622	13,705	811	4,973	65	500
29	Iowa	513,187	430	234	994	1,827	214	570	14,506	1,205	11,401	147	1,603
30	Missouri..............	437,699	262	117	310	1,296	155	457	10,107	963	8,195	88	1,290
31	North Dakota	63,347	121	74	177	400	45	61	1,920	112	649	11	40
32	South Dakota	109,215	214	53	330	485	61	174	4,084	240	1,516	25	140
33	Nebraska..............	250,420	357	127	551	1,359	162	535	10,017	980	7,741	90	606
34	Kansas..............	236,597	251	147	545	1,059	121	378	8,801	807	9,000	54	909
35	South Central division......	507,349	308	112	244	1,318	153	431	9,280	835	6,788	104	1,345
36	Kentucky	124,304	40	15	40	257	28	89	1,774	170	1,856	24	447
37	Tennessee............	33,257	50	21	39	143	20	61	1,152	74	1,073	18	189
38	Alabama	22,693	23	13	23	108	18	43	686	100	820	13	106
39	Mississippi............	16,773	19	4	15	44	8	16	391	27	104	5	42
40	Louisiana............	96,465	39	7	9	126	16	35	983	63	313	9	58
41	Texas	185,586	111	39	84	490	33	140	3,158	290	1,737	26	317
42	Oklahoma	4,563	8	3	6	28	2	7	329	28	185	4	31
43	Arkansas............	23,708	18	10	28	122	27	40	816	83	640	5	95
44	Western division	709,847	4,101	750	2,040	11,465	1,081	2,154	41,620	3,883	21,310	300	2,370
45	Montana..............	30,959	338	60	200	560	52	116	2,309	274	1,744	12	126
46	Wyoming..............	14,520	109	19	120	218	33	80	1,101	92	927	7	114
47	Colorado..............	79,814	409	112	415	1,323	157	382	7,596	794	5,748	57	511
48	New Mexico..........	12,539	31	7	40	104	15	33	577	40	533	4	45
49	Arizona	14,027	46	8	23	144	9	18	566	57	234	6	36
50	Utah................	85,314	56	25	57	225	24	50	1,188	133	753	18	63
51	Nevada..............	12,406	127	17	51	226	14	44	698	106	330	8	56
52	Idaho................	21,154	108	22	56	159	16	42	899	75	563	6	63
53	Washington	68,757	965	115	252	980	113	193	4,714	352	2,801	41	260
54	Oregon	49,967	220	36	105	468	53	106	2,460	210	1,875	25	152
55	California............	320,390	1,699	329	721	7,052	595	1,090	19,452	1,750	6,302	125	944

STATE OR TERRITORY OF BIRTH.

573

ACCORDING TO STATE OR TERRITORY OF BIRTH, BY STATES AND TERRITORIES: 1890.

	STATE OR TERRITORY OF BIRTH, ARRANGED GEOGRAPHICALLY—continued.															
	South Atlantic division—Continued.						North Central division.									
District of Columbia.	Virginia.	West Virginia.	North Carolina.	South Carolina.	Georgia.	Florida.	Ohio.	Indiana.	Illinois.	Michigan.	Wisconsin.	Minnesota.	Iowa.	Missouri.	North Dakota.	
25,047	41,416	37,241	10,089	15,990	20,101	11,690	888,466	312,284	1,101,695	592,060	817,907	455,613	478,499	393,484	39,914	1
1,143	4,112	1,944	739	1,298	1,178	520	18,116	2,266	7,192	5,546	3,216	1,178	1,716	2,535	156	2
10	19	3	6	4	12	7	48	9	44	58	32	26	11	15	....	3
7	18	3	1	2	4	4	67	6	82	96	54	35	22	15	14	4
5	21	7	1	3	7	3	69	6	54	65	57	24	17	15	....	5
136	368	40	55	103	109	55	884	173	909	640	469	208	218	205	28	6
30	47	29	10	14	34	13	161	36	137	100	120	53	23	30	9	7
58	123	11	24	45	55	17	358	59	299	175	142	46	66	79	11	8
697	1,279	128	294	761	648	216	5,412	908	3,327	3,127	1,450	431	727	1,194	58	9
191	385	48	84	144	127	143	975	188	642	322	268	78	125	278	10	10
600	1,852	1,675	264	222	182	62	10,142	881	1,698	963	624	277	507	704	26	11
20,765	24,511	29,401	6,586	11,229	15,205	10,231	5,871	629	1,110	818	507	222	335	537	27	12
36	60	9	7	8	8	2	61	12	36	24	13	5	2	14	1	13
1,047	1,688	556	92	113	93	28	574	121	235	118	83	19	73	129	3	14
19,238	1,211	112	38	64	41	24	340	87	191	134	97	54	38	105	3	15
313	18,367	125	203	51	44	12	252	47	103	209	109	23	25	49	12	16
53	2,621	28,065	34	19	13	3	3,966	98	98	38	24	7	42	57	....	17
21	230	3	5,670	245	44	20	67	21	20	40	6	3	7	11	....	18
5	50	....	173	9,484	186	17	25	3	9	6	3	2	2	4	....	19
34	171	7	254	963	14,415	186	263	102	121	81	41	18	39	54	1	20
18	107	14	115	282	361	9,939	323	138	297	164	131	91	112	114	7	21
1,693	8,876	4,965	1,198	907	977	323	820,591	294,024	1,058,866	570,469	793,383	441,134	457,605	370,841	38,185	22
194	2,184	2,823	89	83	158	33	705,347	8,679	3,114	5,306	1,229	308	787	1,286	20	23
80	753	108	159	93	67	17	24,260	242,487	7,020	2,675	857	198	585	1,115	18	24
533	1,388	402	202	238	191	60	20,327	13,395	881,387	8,055	17,752	2,028	7,810	12,734	224	25
61	282	88	60	34	47	43	14,921	3,469	4,897	525,964	10,449	778	1,007	640	106	26
64	225	76	27	48	49	19	4,573	1,450	9,718	6,245	659,323	6,216	2,908	1,208	431	27
98	283	126	47	29	55	24	5,120	2,372	13,669	5,957	37,758	405,334	11,045	1,593	1,444	28
80	828	210	93	65	64	21	13,004	3,938	40,593	2,875	21,468	3,778	382,581	3,639	484	29
325	1,574	385	284	185	171	47	13,266	5,916	29,115	2,108	3,485	785	5,778	332,072	78	30
6	47	16	9	7	6	1	753	287	1,443	1,631	6,864	9,724	2,983	234	34,840	31
31	78	35	11	18	17	4	1,487	878	7,074	2,897	15,847	8,950	11,367	620	69	32
95	416	156	70	34	89	25	8,467	4,074	32,925	3,486	12,001	1,853	21,584	4,180	282	33
126	818	444	138	73	63	29	15,000	7,070	27,911	3,270	5,660	1,176	9,170	10,920	180	34
197	2,335	351	1,190	2,181	2,311	454	20,159	9,058	7,541	2,301	1,998	640	2,046	6,640	102	35
43	660	145	81	52	82	22	13,057	5,529	921	251	224	43	167	587	9	36
30	514	28	313	208	306	41	2,007	785	614	424	248	111	165	471	23	37
20	221	44	182	396	835	144	1,075	323	402	131	103	47	112	102	9	38
13	88	9	104	274	149	29	224	112	219	89	40	7	49	184	2	39
10	111	11	30	573	126	64	266	109	273	100	107	38	175	434	9	40
66	552	81	302	454	611	125	1,811	995	2,786	742	750	240	678	2,593	21	41
4	27	11	3	3	7	5	370	231	515	124	193	61	365	378	20	42
11	162	22	175	221	195	24	1,349	914	1,812	440	333	93	335	1,831	9	43
649	1,582	490	376	375	430	168	17,729	6,307	26,986	12,926	18,803	12,439	16,797	12,931	1,444	44
44	110	48	24	25	18	9	1,101	412	1,604	1,850	1,943	1,763	1,312	845	251	45
13	55	27	11	9	26	19	614	188	1,047	343	586	181	813	465	37	46
90	296	112	61	46	84	23	4,724	1,538	6,960	2,193	2,042	536	4,072	3,435	58	47
10	38	11	3	8	10	9	341	128	499	151	168	46	172	326	9	48
11	29	4	9	9	10	4	236	81	270	125	122	20	72	231	9	49
16	43	12	12	6	13	5	508	136	866	337	295	167	630	540	12	50
13	26	5	4	2	8	6	204	52	256	139	190	20	132	137	....	51
15	66	26	10	6	10	5	425	150	709	303	618	533	514	392	52	52
74	166	70	36	40	55	27	2,596	974	4,458	3,386	5,466	5,755	3,304	1,389	632	53
86	137	42	36	14	25	11	1,677	766	2,465	1,204	2,643	1,617	2,111	1,297	245	54
277	616	133	170	210	171	50	5,303	1,882	7,762	2,895	3,830	1,891	3,665	3,874	139	55

574

STATISTICS OF POPULATION.

TABLE 27.—NATIVE WHITE POPULATION OF FOREIGN PARENTAGE, DISTRIBUTED ACCORDING

STATE OR TERRITORY OF BIRTH, ARRANGED GEOGRAPHICALLY—continued.

	STATES AND TERRITORIES.	North Central division—Continued.			South Central division.								
		South Dakota.	Nebraska.	Kansas.	Kentucky.	Tennessee.	Alabama.	Mississippi.	Louisiana.	Texas.	Indian territory.	Oklahoma.	Arkansas.
1	The United States..	54,095	145,101	147,035	126,946	33,865	20,165	17,354	105,990	161,788	673	186	13,525
2	North Atlantic division	71	340	764	1,967	826	474	314	1,770	742	28	11	108
3	Maine	....	8	1	6	9	....	2	8	3	....	....	3
4	New Hampshire	5	15	7	12	3	9	5	4	1	....	1	1
5	Vermont	2	4	11	2	1	1	3	7	4	1	....	2
6	Massachusetts	9	51	74	173	60	47	24	154	77	3	....	32
7	Rhode Island	1	6	12	20	11	6	4	14	14	....	....	4
8	Connecticut	3	22	34	40	32	12	13	55	23	....	....	4
9	New York	42	127	278	719	354	278	177	1,090	395	11	1	59
10	New Jersey	4	33	70	187	83	41	23	100	66	2	4	14
11	Pennsylvania	5	74	277	808	273	80	63	239	150	11	5	40
12	South Atlantic division....	21	105	203	743	626	719	191	708	220	10	13	53
13	Delaware	2	....	9	8	4	1	....	7	3	....	....	....
14	Maryland	4	14	37	113	54	32	28	95	26	2	11	4
15	District of Columbia	6	17	27	64	56	27	14	57	20	4	....	14
16	Virginia	4	38	42	68	88	26	18	77	18	3	....	4
17	West Virginia	....	6	15	238	37	7	12	25	23	1	....	4
18	North Carolina	....	1	....	12	42	22	5	11	4	....	2	....
19	South Carolina	1	....	1	11	24	17	8	11	6	....	....	....
20	Georgia	....	2	15	113	257	245	49	88	23	....	....	13
21	Florida	4	27	57	116	64	342	57	337	92	....	....	14
22	North Central division	52,680	138,564	135,917	22,679	5,315	1,139	1,555	4,804	2,351	202	43	1,450
23	Ohio	28	109	356	6,632	714	175	172	556	156	60	2	104
24	Indiana	15	84	291	4,960	488	93	83	331	113	1	....	67
25	Illinois	125	738	1,493	3,086	1,005	277	348	1,201	413	24	6	211
26	Michigan	96	225	409	304	158	30	56	100	120	5	1	30
27	Wisconsin	244	305	377	319	147	31	52	110	80	8	....	44
28	Minnesota	796	340	401	591	144	51	106	171	128	15	1	47
29	Iowa	623	1,538	962	856	329	62	102	259	112	6	8	52
30	Missouri	37	838	4,494	3,543	1,612	270	427	1,700	609	63	1	547
31	North Dakota	203	86	68	37	23	2	4	31	14	6	2	11
32	South Dakota	50,159	853	309	152	65	14	16	50	64	4	1	30
33	Nebraska	283	130,906	2,122	647	201	45	96	159	148	8	16	89
34	Kansas	71	2,542	124,635	1,552	429	89	93	217	334	2	5	212
35	South Central division	70	467	2,039	98,971	25,881	17,344	14,781	96,157	155,976	227	107	11,302
36	Kentucky	3	16	86	95,501	955	185	111	433	47	3	....	47
37	Tennessee	19	27	40	1,001	21,483	395	480	309	60	3	1	133
38	Alabama	2	9	86	461	680	14,138	344	526	95	3	....	27
39	Mississippi	1	4	14	153	331	714	11,342	1,633	89	7	....	60
40	Louisiana	14	26	66	257	135	467	1,082	89,400	530	1	....	102
41	Texas	16	101	540	1,030	1,253	1,147	1,006	3,525	154,628	85	2	583
42	Oklahoma	5	173	841	86	31	14	14	17	168	44	104	31
43	Arkansas	10	111	366	482	1,013	284	402	311	341	70	....	10,319
44	Western division	1,253	5,625	8,112	2,586	1,217	489	513	2,461	2,490	116	12	552
45	Montana	209	243	290	133	61	22	17	58	52	16	2	20
46	Wyoming	73	618	252	76	35	16	8	24	80	8	....	17
47	Colorado	50	1,595	2,585	569	258	67	110	253	295	31	2	85
48	New Mexico	....	50	264	58	55	17	38	58	485	10	....	29
49	Arizona	3	25	68	50	27	10	13	44	170	3	....	10
50	Utah	24	269	150	76	32	9	16	44	33	2	....	14
51	Nevada	4	22	31	36	18	13	1	53	14	1	....	5
52	Idaho	32	189	232	73	21	15	14	244	40	1	....	27
53	Washington	557	1,005	1,626	278	167	56	50	121	309	14	2	103
54	Oregon	191	730	1,087	224	99	19	49	98	123	4	3	181
55	California	110	879	1,527	1,013	444	245	197	1,464	880	26	3	61

STATE OR TERRITORY OF BIRTH.   575

TO STATE OR TERRITORY OF BIRTH, BY STATES AND TERRITORIES: 1890—Continued.

STATE OR TERRITORY OF BIRTH, ARRANGED GEOGRAPHICALLY—continued. / Western division.

Montana.	Wyoming.	Colorado.	New Mexico.	Arizona.	Utah.	Nevada.	Idaho.	Washington.	Oregon.	California.	Alaska.	Born in the United States (state not specified).	Born at sea under United States flag.	American citizens born abroad.	
11,093	6,158	31,880	9,337	9,119	86,468	11,777	9,675	19,477	27,109	250,073	99	80,358	985	3,461	1
65	48	270	200	19	77	115	24	158	188	2,189	5	55,766	370	542	2
4	1	3	2	1	2	7		3	1	49		72	16	37	3
1		6	2	1		2				21		58	3	33	4
	1	3			2	2			1	19	1	61	7	33	5
5	8	28	4	2	13	23	7	5	88	350		1,315	63	83	6
		11	48		4	1		1	2	43		243	15	18	7
3		11	10		2	6		13	6	106		726	21	24	8
28	20	101	92	7	30	29	11	69	62	1,007	1	43,777	115	234	9
9	4	25	20	3	4	20	3	8	10	219		3,536	41	19	10
15	14	91	31	5	11	25	3	59	18	315	3	5,978	80	61	11
11	8	33	16	6	11	21	5	114	13	217	6	779	41	25	12
2		2						1		11		17	6	1	13
4		11	4	3	2	6		21	3	57	4	328	13	10	14
	6	2	6	1	6	4	3	71	4	75		124	4	3	15
		5		1		4		13	1	20	1	55	4	2	16
3	1	2	1		1	4		2		7		78	2	1	17
		2				2	1		2	2		9	1	1	18
		2						1		2		4	2		19
	1	3			1	1	1	3	3	24		29	3	2	20
2		4	5	1	1			2		19	1	135	6	5	21
477	570	1,828	303	73	676	279	133	307	391	2,622	13	18,557	421	2,551	22
6	12	56	30	7	28	3	10	21	11	220	1	2,673	72	36	23
3	2	24	7		5	5	3	9	20	88		825	22	10	24
66	30	264	39	9	59	34	9	48	53	578	3	4,072	86	91	25
24	9	123	27	1	23	26	7	12	33	205		1,019	44	719	26
37	28	55	17		14	32	9	14	27	184	1	2,559	48	87	27
90	20	84	7	1	21	12	10	45	46	211		2,409	41	95	28
40	61	158	22	6	164	47	20	25	55	222	1	889	22	108	29
47	34	254	55	15	106	30	9	48	26	332	1	1,804	44	1,219	30
41	9	18	8	1	2	3	1	2	3	34		125	6	128	31
36	77	101	6	6	22	19	8	18	14	99		384	3	5	32
47	256	325	16	16	169	27	26	41	50	227	5	744	16	60	33
40	38	306	69	11	65	41	21	24	53	222	1	324	17	44	34
40	30	179	295	30	23	23	9	23	32	452	6	2,341	60	53	35
4	5	10	5		2			4	3	37		217	15	2	36
5	1	9	2		3	3	1	5	3	21		113		3	37
		1	5	8		1	2		3	25	1	43	5	2	38
		1	8	2		1			1	7		77	3	3	39
1	1	10	7		2	1		2	2	43	4	122	21	3	40
24	18	88	260	29	11	16	3	9	12	276	1	1,643	13	35	41
1		28	9		1	1	1	2	4	19		20	1		42
5	3	21	2	1	2		4	1	4	24		106	2	5	43
10,500	5,496	29,561	8,514	8,991	85,631	11,339	9,504	18,875	26,485	244,593	69	2,915	93	290	44
6,697	105	282	22	8	760	390	213	50	127	522		341	3	12	45
37	4,376	311	23	10	1,026	21	120	6	23	76		26	3	1	46
72	245	27,147	420	33	550	100	31	26	52	359	2	161	13	23	47
1	12	273	7,498	75	79	11	6	5	8	129		18	2		48
8	25	47	283	8,383	1,048	123	62	12	28	1,144	1	33	2	7	49
74	318	272	17	81	75,801	335	349	21	27	351		803	4	2	50
13	22	31	3	13	381	7,232	28	12	26	1,570		2	2	2	51
104	146	98	13	16	4,797	175	8,154	87	296	495	1	29	3	11	52
252	109	349	41	32	299	304	222	17,005	2,114	3,421	2	449	9	41	53
72	32	178	13	16	236	209	155	672	22,653	3,163	11	223	8	52	54
170	106	573	181	324	698	2,439	164	270	1,131	233,363	52	830	44	139	55

576

STATISTICS OF POPULATION.

TABLE **28.**—NATIVE COLORED (*a*) POPULATION, DISTRIBUTED ACCORDING

| | Number living in each state or territory. | STATE OR TERRITORY OF BIRTH, ARRANGED GEOGRAPHICALLY. | | | | | | | | | | |
| STATES AND TERRITORIES. | | North Atlantic division. | | | | | | | | | South Atlantic division. | |
		Maine.	New Hampshire.	Vermont.	Massachusetts.	Rhode Island.	Connecticut.	New York.	New Jersey.	Pennsylvania.	Delaware.	Maryland.
1	The United States..	7,510,680	1,875	539	1,049	12,189	4,383	8,960	48,529	31,738	70,238	30,994	247,063
2	North Atlantic division....	266,253	1,652	453	929	11,065	4,219	8,560	45,071	30,961	63,922	7,510	19,117
3	Maine	1,557	1,288	9	....	24	3	1	25	1	6	1	15
4	New Hampshire	546	14	279	12	46	2	3	15	4	1	1	17
5	Vermont	940	3	17	822	65	1	4	96	3	6	....	4
6	Massachusetts	19,936	243	104	97	9,455	263	384	663	169	416	81	731
7	Rhode Island	7,369	20	7	7	320	3,523	254	317	92	175	61	698
8	Connecticut	12,374	15	5	31	395	103	7,058	1,064	233	152	57	310
9	New York	68,543	44	19	131	462	130	613	40,177	1,790	1,540	350	2,440
10	New Jersey	47,362	12	8	6	101	142	115	1,823	26,874	2,045	2,099	2,004
11	Pennsylvania	107,626	13	5	23	197	52	128	891	1,786	58,681	4,851	12,202
12	South Atlantic division	3,259,562	72	45	22	352	79	166	854	421	2,463	23,115	217,744
13	Delaware	28,362	3	30	....	6	3	9	48	140	659	22,426	3,967
14	Maryland	215,388	12	2	5	69	15	32	160	95	851	566	196,075
15	District of Columbia....	75,444	18	2	5	90	38	55	328	90	406	48	15,015
16	Virginia	635,673	5	2	5	58	9	32	143	47	156	38	1,308
17	West Virginia	32,686	4	....	....	6	....	1	11	3	178	1	290
18	North Carolina	562,525	2	....	4	21	1	3	30	13	50	9	138
19	South Carolina	689,014	7	2	....	19	4	9	31	5	39	4	142
20	Georgia	858,751	10	....	....	42	2	13	38	14	50	15	532
21	Florida	161,719	11	7	3	32	7	12	65	14	74	8	277
22	North Central division	443,695	66	18	52	372	39	137	1,833	214	2,559	171	2,615
23	Ohio	86,771	9	3	9	143	4	48	283	35	1,081	31	777
24	Indiana	45,466	3	....	1	18	....	8	53	11	107	10	115
25	Illinois	56,507	10	5	11	76	14	26	369	53	433	14	505
26	Michigan	18,726	10	....	3	33	2	10	390	51	324	76	139
27	Wisconsin	6,197	1	2	6	5	5	3	331	3	31	4	24
28	Minnesota	5,368	9	2	2	19	3	14	99	4	58	4	53
29	Iowa	10,673	1	2	9	9	4	3	55	9	45	9	67
30	Missouri	150,139	11	3	3	34	2	12	87	13	241	11	515
31	North Dakota	483	....	....	....	1	....	1	9	1	8	....	5
32	South Dakota	1,306	1	....	....	6	....	....	15	....	7	....	9
33	Nebraska	11,724	5	1	6	15	3	6	62	14	85	5	182
34	Kansas	50,395	6	....	2	13	2	6	80	20	139	7	224
35	South Central division	3,482,075	48	18	36	201	29	52	372	71	827	107	6,884
36	Kentucky	268,057	2	....	1	11	3	2	36	7	94	3	179
37	Tennessee	430,751	2	....	5	24	4	6	38	5	110	11	454
38	Alabama	679,126	5	1	10	20	....	8	42	11	68	15	798
39	Mississippi	744,521	5	2	5	19	2	5	54	6	134	18	1,480
40	Louisiana	559,285	18	3	8	55	5	18	91	19	119	30	2,302
41	Texas	488,101	11	10	5	38	9	9	80	15	142	18	951
42	Oklahoma	2,977	....	....	....	1	1	....	4	....	22	2	14
43	Arkansas	309,257	5	2	2	33	5	4	27	8	138	10	706
44	Western division	59,095	37	5	10	179	17	51	399	71	467	91	703
45	Montana	2,122	....	....	....	5	....	3	23	6	52	2	85
46	Wyoming	947	....	....	1	1	....	2	10	2	16	2	45
47	Colorado	6,246	8	....	2	43	1	5	51	11	70	47	72
48	New Mexico	10,475	....	....	....	3	1	1	8	3	23	2	48
49	Arizona	2,708	3	1	....	3	1	2	19	10	51	5	149
50	Utah	1,075	4	....	1	1	2	2	6	2	8	1	34
51	Nevada	3,865	1	....	....	1	1	1	4	1	2	1	10
52	Idaho	375	1	....	....	1	....	....	3	1	7	....	3
53	Washington	5,066	1	....	1	16	1	10	41	5	29	2	39
54	Oregon	2,514	1	1	....	11	2	3	31	2	24	4	22
55	California	23,702	18	3	5	94	8	22	203	28	185	25	196

a Persons of negro descent, Chinese, Japanese, and civilized Indians.

STATE OR TERRITORY OF BIRTH.

TO STATE OR TERRITORY OF BIRTH, BY STATES AND TERRITORIES: 1890.

	District of Columbia.	Virginia.	West Virginia.	North Carolina.	South Carolina.	Georgia.	Florida.	Ohio.	Indiana.	Illinois.	Michigan.	Wisconsin.	Minnesota.	Iowa.	Missouri.	North Dakota.	
	South Atlantic division—Continued.							**North Central division.**									
1	37,805	832,102	22,648	662,040	767,356	898,263	129,581	60,056	26,405	29,534	14,468	6,241	3,476	6,272	142,360	579	1
2	3,170	47,101	1,110	6,503	2,506	1,876	630	1,059	100	135	210	121	41	31	278	40	2
3	6	92	1	18	10	7	6	....	....	2	....	....	....	3	....	....	3
4	5	71	5	19	5	14	5	....	2	....	....	....	....	....	....	....	4
5	4	70	....	5	4	11	2	1	1	....	....	....	....	....	1	....	5
6	362	4,305	32	1,206	362	293	102	48	10	13	16	5	5	2	14	6	6
7	183	1,226	5	158	93	44	37	11	1	9	....	....	2	2	4	....	7
8	158	1,008	51	448	107	97	33	13	5	2	1	2	....	2	10	....	8
9	1,017	12,237	129	2,244	1,126	806	249	194	26	52	68	19	....	8	66	2	9
10	304	7,025	40	1,043	240	223	103	51	12	12	11	7	1	2	15	1	10
11	1,131	19,873	838	1,302	553	321	93	741	43	45	114	88	35	12	168	31	11
12	33,116	684,970	19,046	586,208	716,890	817,045	125,722	940	131	116	51	54	21	17	223	43	12
13	27	733	13	47	46	12	2	7	1	3	1	....	1	....	4	....	13
14	877	13,162	423	703	200	148	32	80	8	18	4	10	6	3	37	3	14
15	31,696	24,003	163	920	391	320	51	158	52	40	22	3	3	6	35	....	15
16	324	616,513	190	14,185	492	223	56	96	15	10	5	36	3	5	20	40	16
17	33	12,376	18,189	447	43	40	4	447	5	5	6	....	....	2	11	....	17
18	33	6,933	15	545,640	6,985	462	46	38	6	1	3	2	....	....	13	....	18
19	20	1,802	8	5,455	677,175	3,112	103	18	6	6	1	....	2	....	16	....	19
20	74	7,303	31	15,300	20,777	798,747	3,198	42	21	12	8	3	4	....	46	....	20
21	32	2,154	14	3,511	10,781	13,981	122,170	54	17	21	3	....	2	1	41	....	21
22	665	26,329	2,066	6,929	1,952	2,690	244	55,719	24,821	27,249	18,948	5,852	2,981	5,230	131,406	408	22
23	182	11,116	1,646	1,986	400	474	45	50,508	802	154	317	23	27	20	205	1	23
24	28	1,311	69	1,095	182	103	6	1,156	21,215	474	241	17	10	21	205	....	24
25	187	3,037	85	706	379	556	61	1,319	1,144	23,437	404	231	33	272	5,146	3	25
26	55	787	45	349	72	51	10	1,124	724	141	12,553	100	17	17	88	1	26
27	10	129	6	34	16	27	8	69	31	61	79	4,723	65	20	75	....	27
28	33	203	10	52	41	62	4	199	94	130	68	182	2,206	109	314	111	28
29	10	1,046	51	166	62	120	7	124	87	408	43	73	20	3,829	2,101	....	29
30	62	5,806	71	716	302	585	63	463	254	1,636	70	63	28	239	113,920	4	30
31	2	25	2	4	4	5	....	24	....	11	3	5	31	4	22	247	31
32	4	24	4	5	7	16	....	19	8	13	5	18	100	20	97	4	32
33	51	542	30	156	48	121	9	159	118	275	32	290	427	561	2,299	36	33
34	32	1,648	47	760	340	480	31	495	344	509	133	67	17	118	6,925	1	34
35	701	71,774	372	61,290	45,559	75,877	2,905	1,843	1,146	1,508	157	125	110	178	8,556	9	35
36	38	5,095	82	787	241	424	32	401	511	329	26	10	7	15	494	3	36
37	59	10,408	45	7,614	3,471	9,806	122	271	135	209	21	21	14	19	781	4	37
38	119	11,905	33	7,520	8,781	24,556	825	106	48	35	10	2	9	2	138	1	38
39	106	15,878	37	16,585	9,802	10,756	330	217	92	163	24	31	18	34	1,115	....	39
40	191	12,290	64	9,444	4,630	6,025	711	209	62	134	15	26	9	12	1,074	....	40
41	117	9,379	58	7,512	5,858	12,142	615	244	155	250	27	19	14	51	2,871	....	41
42	....	121	2	87	43	68	6	20	15	38	3	1	....	4	154	....	42
43	71	6,608	51	11,741	12,733	12,010	264	285	128	350	31	15	39	41	1,929	1	43
44	213	1,913	54	1,110	449	775	80	495	207	526	102	89	323	816	1,897	70	44
45	24	202	7	51	48	38	6	58	17	24	10	5	25	14	136	30	45
46	6	168	3	20	21	21	8	48	7	17	2	6	4	10	115	....	46
47	18	176	13	183	66	285	16	121	99	245	30	39	262	707	640	34	47
48	13	122	3	46	23	38	1	26	9	14	4	3	3	9	107	....	48
49	27	240	2	44	58	46	7	28	14	18	3	2	2	5	54	....	49
50	9	40	....	11	5	9	1	8	4	4	6	5	....	2	41	....	50
51	5	22	....	6	4	1	....	7	2	7	3	1	3	1	16	....	51
52	3	12	....	9	3	7	....	6	3	4	5	1	2	4	12	2	52
53	27	260	8	61	21	44	10	56	23	61	12	7	12	8	89	2	53
54	7	47	2	22	21	32	4	32	7	30	10	3	6	4	62	....	54
55	74	615	16	660	179	254	27	105	22	102	17	17	4	52	625	2	55

578

STATISTICS OF POPULATION.

TABLE **28.**—NATIVE COLORED (*a*) POPULATION, DISTRIBUTED ACCORDING TO

STATE OR TERRITORY OF BIRTH, ARRANGED GEOGRAPHICALLY—continued.

	STATES AND TERRITORIES.	North Central division—Continued.			South Central division.								
		South Dakota.	Nebraska.	Kansas.	Kentucky.	Tennessee.	Alabama.	Mississippi.	Louisiana.	Texas.	Indian territory.	Oklahoma.	Arkansas.
1	The United States..	1,016	3,630	21,256	323,526	450,439	704,632	705,340	512,827	392,083	2,115	66	196,175
2	North Atlantic division	100	98	37	767	579	391	224	471	210	169	0	81
3	Maine	......	......	......	4	2	2	......	10	2	......	......	1
4	New Hampshire.......	......	......	......	9	1	1	1	1	......	3	......	......
5	Vermont....	......	......	......	3	3	1	1	3	......	......	......	......
6	Massachusetts.........	2	......	2	65	40	48	29	63	14	4	......	7
7	Rhode Island	1	......	......	9	9	13	4	10	8	......	......	......
8	Connecticut	......	2	......	23	19	27	8	42	101	2	......	3
9	New York	......	1	16	326	224	135	77	183	40	10	1	31
10	New Jersey	1	2	1	73	49	53	33	43·	14	13	......	5
11	Pennsylvania..........	96	93	18	255	232	111	71	116	31	137	5	34
12	South Atlantic division	......	26	42	983	2,432	13.210	1,563	699	243	45	3	110
13	Delaware	......	......	......	5	9	3	3	4	1	4	......	1
14	Maryland.......	......	1	......	76	52	54	40	58	37	4	2	10
15	District of Columbia....	......	5	8	120	154	166	139	116	36	6	......	14
16	Virginia	......	19	20	149	403	137	110	56	20	14	......	11
17	West Virginia.......	......	......	1	168	65	25	24	16	4	......	......	4
18	North Carolina	......	......	2	32	293	177	147	30	15	5	......	11
19	South Carolina	......	......	2	33	107	223	130	20	19	2	......	3
20	Georgia	......	1	6	238	1,056	6,720	625	144	79	8	1	37
21	Florida	......	......	3	162	293	5,705	345	246	32	2	......	19
22	North Central division	896	3,377	19,656	53,079	22,224	3,791	6,604	3,371	2,554	918	11	2,291
23	Ohio.....	......	5	23	12,435	1,708	452	446	243	66	180	......	84
24	Indiana.....	8	6	24	14,590	2,104	275	218	100	43	33	......	43
25	Illinois	2	26	106	7,241	5,406	945	1,363	646	132	30	4	350
26	Michigan.....	1	2	17	748	220	54	49	39	9	13	......	9
27	Wisconsin.....	......	1	1	128	107	44	37	13	3	2	1	7
28	Minnesota.....	46	13	18	320	215	82	100	40	18	4	1	47
29	Iowa	5	29	55	631	354	102	160	·40	13	1	2	62
30	Missouri	......	50	1,329	8,816	5,448	864	2,267	1,250	627	114	3	1,955
31	North Dakota	......	......	......	27	12	5	7	1	3	2	......	1
32	South Dakota	701	17	11	27	37	38	16	6	19	1	......	1
33	Nebraska.....	89	3,107	647	896	378	137	161	141	56	10	......	60
34	Kansas.....	44	112	17,425	7,220	6,235	793	1,780	840	1,565	519	......	572
35	South Central division	3	70	930	267,204	424,108	686,556	696,498	507,848	388,657	894	44	193,420
36	Kentucky	......	5	24	246,225	8,439	502	538	219	.80	8	......	100
37	Tennessee.....	......	2	29	5,890	363,058	7,726	13,638	691	299	23	2	1,851
38	Alabama	......	......	2	731	4,892	607,058	5,748	548	243	6	......	125
39	Mississippi.....	......	13	36	3,630	11,474	30,219	622,996	10,344	650	14	......	2,790
40	Louisiana	3	21	32	3,095	2,627	10,813	18,997	478,655	3,583	87	5	1,769
41	Texas	......	24	136	4,046	9,330	17,610	10,291	10,511	380,335	517	......	4,687
42	Oklahoma	......	5	599	371	643	80	232	134	156	11	37	66
43	Arkansas.....	......	9	72	3,216	23,645	12,539	24,058	6,746	3,811	278	......	182,541
44	Western division	17	50	591	1,493	1,096	684	451	438	1,019	89	2	264
45	Montana.....	15	7	20	114	93	27	26	27	28	4	1	12
46	Wyoming	......	14	42	74	67	23	18	14	25	3	......	10
47	Colorado.....	0	......	322	475	255	342	152	98	117	27	......	81
48	New Mexico.....	......	3	37	130	93	23	22	27	94	20	......	20
49	Arizona	......	2	7	136	111	24	18	25	75	18	......	7
50	Utah.....	1	1	5	39	22	19	6	11	18	8	......	5
51	Nevada.....	......	......	4	9	6	6	2	4	5	......	......	4
52	Idaho.....	......	1	2	15	7	6	5	3	1	1	......	2
53	Washington.....	......	5	13	110	60	20	56	36	27	3	......	10
54	Oregon.....	......	1	14	30	33	18	6	15	10	1	......	4
55	California	1	7	125	361	349	176	140	178	619	9	1	100

a Persons of negro descent, Chinese, Japanese, and civilized Indians.

STATE OR TERRITORY OF BIRTH.

579

STATE OR TERRITORY OF BIRTH, BY STATES AND TERRITORIES: 1890—Continued.

STATE OR TERRITORY OF BIRTH, ARRANGED GEOGRAPHICALLY—continued.

Western division.

Montana.	Wyoming.	Colorado.	New Mexico.	Arizona.	Utah.	Nevada.	Idaho.	Washington.	Oregon.	California.	Alaska.	Born in the United States (state not specified).	Born at sea under United States flag.	American citizens born abroad.	
871	153	1,073	9,718	1,704	763	2,678	217	3,760	1,645	17,513	43	59,581	82	385	1
147	4	12	69	56	2	4	1	197	6	75	9	4,000	22	68	2
....	1	....	....	....	....	....	....	1	....	....	....	16	....	....	3
....	....	....	....	....	....	....	....	....	....	1	....	9	....	....	4
1	....	....	....	....	....	....	....	....	....	....	....	8	....	....	5
1	....	3	1	....	....	1	....	37	....	9	1	212	5	5	6
....	....	1	....	....	....	....	....	14	....	3	....	47	2	1	7
....	....	2	....	....	....	....	....	7	....	4	....	167	1	....	8
3	....	4	4	4	....	1	....	79	3	31	....	1,315	7	31	9
5	2	....	7	3	....	1	....	6	1	7	....	510	1	8	10
137	1	4	55	49	2	1	1	53	2	20	2	1,804	6	13	11
3	2	4	11	3	4	1	1	167	12	42	....	9,000	7	15	12
....	....	....	....	....	....	....	....	2	....	2	....	140	....	....	13
....	2	1	2	1	1	1	....	15	11	8	....	1,413	1	2	14
1	....	3	1	1	....	....	....	135	....	15	....	555	2	....	15
1	....	....	1	....	....	....	....	12	....	3	....	600	....	7	16
....	....	....	....	....	....	....	....	....	....	1	....	274	....	2	17
1	....	....	1	....	....	....	....	....	....	4	....	1,358	....	1	18
....	....	....	3	1	....	....	....	....	....	8	....	400	2	2	19
....	....	....	1	....	1	....	1	....	....	4	....	3,546	1	....	20
....	....	....	2	....	2	....	....	3	1	2	....	1,608	1	1	21
65	24	111	39	6	6	12	9	35	19	106	4	7,730	37	149	22
1	....	....	1	....	....	....	2	7	5	16	....	670	1	28	23
1	6	7	....	1	....	....	....	....	....	7	....	549	....	2	24
3	....	8	7	1	1	....	1	10	1	22	....	1,640	....	37	25
....	....	1	2	....	....	....	....	....	11	10	....	255	....	54	26
....	....	4	....	....	....	....	....	1	....	1	....	75	....	4	27
5	4	....	....	....	....	....	....	8	....	4	....	291	....	1	28
6	....	5	2	....	....	....	....	....	....	4	....	227	....	6	29
3	....	32	11	....	....	1	10	....	5	21	4	2,866	35	6	30
....	....	2	....	....	....	....	1	....	....	1	....	7	....	....	31
2	3	3	....	....	....	....	1	1	....	1	....	39	....	....	32
6	8	23	12	3	3	....	....	1	....	7	....	438	....	3	33
38	3	26	4	1	1	1	5	2	2	12	....	670	1	8	34
8	2	41	39	323	16	6	14	26	22	85	1	34,332	14	141	35
1	....	4	3	....	....	....	....	2	2	6	....	2,975	....	1	36
1	1	7	3	....	2	2	....	2	2	13	....	4,250	....	1	37
1	....	2	7	319	....	....	....	6	5	11	....	4,260	2	2	38
....	....	8	....	....	1	....	2	....	4	5	....	5,415	1	1	39
....	....	2	4	1	4	4	2	11	2	12	....	2,030	3	9	40
5	1	9	20	1	8	....	5	4	7	30	1	9,901	2	11	41
....	....	1	....	....	....	....	1	....	....	1	....	33	....	1	42
....	....	8	2	1	2	....	4	1	....	7	....	5,459	6	115	43
648	121	905	9,560	1,316	735	2,655	192	3,335	1,586	17,205	35	3,426	2	22	44
629	5	4	....	....	2	2	5	3	6	12	....	196	....	4	45
1	92	9	9	1	....	....	1	1	....	1	....	7	....	....	46
3	9	827	66	3	7	1	....	....	8	60	....	138	....	2	47
....	2	22	9,430	9	2	1	....	5	....	3	....	22	....	....	48
....	....	....	14	1,297	1	2	....	....	....	171	....	9	....	....	49
....	6	7	1	1	674	20	5	....	....	1	....	24	....	....	50
....	....	....	....	....	1	2,516	2	....	3	91	....	1,111	....	1	51
6	2	1	....	1	27	3	144	18	17	11	....	13	....	....	52
3	2	5	5	....	4	2	14	3,260	55	53	19	445	....	4	53
3	....	2	....	1	5	21	21	43	1,414	160	1	318	....	3	54
3	3	28	35	3	12	87	....	5	83	16,642	15	1,143	2	8	55

COUNTRY OF BIRTH.

TABLE 32.—FOREIGN BORN POPULATION, DISTRIBUTED ACCORDING TO COUNTRY OF BIRTH, BY STATES AND TERRITORIES: 1890.

TABLE 33.—FOREIGN BORN POPULATION, DISTRIBUTED ACCORDING TO COUNTRY OF BIRTH, BY COUNTIES: 1890.

TABLE 34.—FOREIGN BORN POPULATION, DISTRIBUTED ACCORDING TO COUNTRY OF BIRTH, FOR CITIES HAVING 25,000 INHABITANTS OR MORE: 1890.

STATISTICS OF POPULATION.

TABLE **32.**—FOREIGN BORN POPULATION. DISTRIBUTED ACCORDING

	STATES AND TERRITORIES.	Total foreign born.	NORTH AND SOUTH AMERICANS.					GREAT BRITAIN AND IRELAND.		
			Canada and New-foundland.	Mexico.	Central America.	South America.	Cuba and West Indies.	England.	Scotland.	Wales.
1	The United States	9,249,547	980,938	77,853	1,192	5,006	23,256	908,141	242,231	100,079
2	North Atlantic division	3,888,177	490,229	651	437	1,793	7,235	446,353	119,382	51,081
3	Maine	78,961	52,076	8	15	22	93	7,976	2,745	410
4	New Hampshire	72,340	46,321	9	4	12	19	4,759	1,906	79
5	Vermont	44,088	25,004	10	1	7	14	3,518	1,730	650
6	Massachusetts	657,137	207,601	94	61	252	1,103	76,400	21,909	1,527
7	Rhode Island	106,305	27,934	8	9	32	119	20,901	4,984	104
8	Connecticut	183,601	21,231	12	10	65	200	20,572	5,992	620
9	New York	1,571,050	93,193	330	237	921	4,065	144,060	35,332	8,108
10	New Jersey	328,975	4,698	66	43	211	578	43,778	13,163	1,060
11	Pennsylvania	845,720	12,171	114	57	271	1,047	125,080	32,081	38,391
12	South Atlantic division	208,525	5,412	207	56	479	12,978	21,474	7,144	1,787
13	Delaware	13,101	309	3	2	5	30	1,901	432	61
14	Maryland	94,296	1,020	22	22	99	263	5,590	2,323	781
15	District of Columbia	18,770	655	24	16	34	102	2,126	578	71
16	Virginia	18,374	780	25	3	52	88	3,342	1,034	300
17	West Virginia	18,883	374	6		8	10	2,700	914	398
18	North Carolina	3,702	355	8	2	7	28	882	381	24
19	South Carolina	6,270	159	2	2	24	56	504	293	7
20	Georgia	12,137	609	18		32	119	1,585	619	108
21	Florida	22,932	1,151	99	9	218	12,282	2,754	570	56
22	North Central division	4,060,114	401,660	685	147	709	1,036	312,153	81,619	34,401
23	Ohio	459,293	18,515	65	23	112	128	50,947	10,275	12,005
24	Indiana	146,205	4,954	39	13	17	32	11,196	2,948	888
25	Illinois	842,347	39,525	143	31	170	278	70,473	20,465	4,138
26	Michigan	543,880	181,416	89	14	75	138	55,854	12,068	709
27	Wisconsin	519,199	33,163	20	10	36	52	23,628	5,494	4,207
28	Minnesota	467,356	43,580	31	6	62	61	14,730	5,315	1,470
29	Iowa	324,069	17,465	41	16	26	91	26,205	7,701	3,601
30	Missouri	234,869	8,525	130	19	90	148	18,648	4,601	1,802
31	North Dakota	81,461	23,045	6	3	6	5	3,309	1,788	108
32	South Dakota	91,055	9,493	19	1	10	15	5,111	1,579	605
33	Nebraska	202,542	12,105	34	1	43	29	14,472	3,830	1,182
34	Kansas	147,838	11,874	68	10	62	59	18,080	5,540	2,488
35	South Central division	321,821	8,153	52,129	180	357	1,105	24,588	6,493	1,088
36	Kentucky	50,356	1,173	28	7	12	25	4,162	1,010	380
37	Tennessee	20,029	1,020	35	12	57	35	2,852	704	620
38	Alabama	14,777	620	34	4	20	69	2,934	1,391	308
39	Mississippi	7,952	345	31	11	8	39	884	203	21
40	Louisiana	49,747	762	404	100	78	648	2,456	465	60
41	Texas	152,956	2,866	51,559	52	103	262	9,441	2,172	321
42	Oklahoma	2,740	420	11	1	1	2	290	118	10
43	Arkansas	14,264	947	27	2	18	25	1,569	430	130
44	Western division	770,010	75,484	24,181	363	1,668	902	103,573	27,593	10,820
45	Montana	43,096	9,040	49	13	13	11	6,480	1,588	710
46	Wyoming	14,913	1,314	23	1	1	8	3,147	1,380	533
47	Colorado	83,990	9,142	607	3	42	57	14,406	4,339	2,082
48	New Mexico	11,259	681	4,504	1	10	16	1,258	436	123
49	Arizona	18,795	732	11,534	11	33	14	1,117	318	85
50	Utah	53,064	1,222	19	5	15	9	20,899	3,474	2,387
51	Nevada	14,706	1,662	121	1	31	14	2,140	360	212
52	Idaho	17,456	1,791	30		6	7	3,138	643	770
53	Washington	90,005	17,412	81	10	93	65	9,854	3,514	1,070
54	Oregon	57,317	6,460	49	9	58	31	5,668	2,242	374
55	California	366,309	26,028	7,164	309	1,366	670	35,457	9,299	1,800

a Not specified.

COUNTRY OF BIRTH. 607

TO COUNTRY OF BIRTH, BY STATES AND TERRITORIES: 1890.

GREAT BRITAIN AND IRELAND—continued.		GERMANIC NATIONS.						SCANDINAVIAN NATIONS.			
Great Britain. (a)	Ireland.	Germany.	Austria.	Holland.	Belgium.	Luxemburg.	Switzerland.	Norway.	Sweden.	Denmark.	
951	1,871,509	2,784,894	123,271	81,828	22,639	2,882	104,069	322,665	478,041	132,543	1
568	1,241,116	898,321	61,549	17,759	5,783	100	24,208	16,084	87,750	15,197	2
10	11,444	1,104	58	16	21	....	29	311	1,704	696	3
4	14,800	1,631	96	10	7	....	62	251	1,210	64	4
1	9,810	877	59	17	12	....	70	38	870	58	5
113	259,902	28,034	1,148	609	295	6	1,052	2,510	18,624	1,512	6
12	38,920	3,200	177	44	147	....	133	285	3,392	154	7
3	77,880	28,176	1,187	121	165	2	998	523	10,021	1,474	8
362	483,375	498,602	33,145	8,366	1,342	65	11,557	8,002	28,430	6,238	9
7	101,059	106,181	4,641	7,924	645	8	4,158	1,317	4,159	2,991	10
56	243,836	230,516	21,038	652	3,149	19	6,149	2,238	19,346	2,010	11
46	48,003	81,449	2,154	341	220	8	1,815	660	1,797	623	12
16	6,121	2,409	49	12	5	....	52	14	246	41	13
1	18,735	52,436	1,388	122	60	6	300	164	305	130	14
2	7,224	5,778	130	32	24	....	211	70	128	72	15
13	4,578	4,361	109	68	22	1	200	102	215	108	16
....	4,709	7,292	221	22	36	....	610	7	72	44	17
....	451	1,077	15	7	3	....	82	13	51	26	18
3	1,665	2,502	75	7	11	....	47	23	60	36	19
....	3,374	3,079	101	29	31	1	178	88	191	61	20
11	1,056	1,855	66	42	28	....	185	179	529	105	21
245	433,719	1,570,112	39,175	61,309	14,874	2,707	54,415	283,847	335,871	89,633	22
80	70,127	235,608	5,115	1,514	870	28	11,070	511	2,742	956	23
4	20,819	84,900	544	1,157	733	25	3,478	285	4,512	718	24
37	124,498	338,382	8,087	8,762	2,001	279	8,115	30,339	86,514	12,044	25
34	39,065	135,509	3,639	20,410	2,232	54	2,562	7,795	27,366	6,335	26
5	33,300	259,819	4,856	6,252	4,567	325	7,181	65,696	20,157	13,885	27
15	28,011	116,955	5,108	1,796	910	670	3,745	101,109	99,913	14,133	28
23	37,353	127,246	1,715	7,941	384	953	4,310	27,078	30,276	15,519	29
27	40,966	120,461	2,660	740	766	55	6,765	526	5,602	1,333	30
12	2,967	8,943	300	288	58	7	256	25,773	5,583	2,860	31
2	4,774	18,188	675	1,428	183	128	571	19,257	7,740	4,309	32
....	15,963	72,618	4,032	1,149	262	151	2,542	3,032	28,364	14,345	33
6	15,870	46,423	2,384	872	808	32	3,820	1,786	17,096	3,136	34
23	43,198	114,645	10,410	532	688	15	6,093	1,807	4,720	1,388	35
....	13,926	32,620	314	135	97	1	1,892	120	184	92	36
5	5,016	5,304	180	47	21	5	1,027	41	332	92	37
11	2,604	3,945	202	26	31	1	169	47	294	71	38
3	1,865	2,284	144	25	14	1	111	54	305	90	39
1	9,236	14,625	571	76	275	2	521	136	328	232	40
2	8,201	48,843	8,758	130	216	3	1,711	1,313	2,806	640	41
....	329	739	56	6	5	....	54	36	138	37	42
1	2,021	6,225	185	87	29	2	608	60	333	125	43
69	105,473	120,367	9,983	1,887	1,574	52	17,538	20,267	47,897	25,702	44
1	6,048	5,600	939	103	64	2	408	1,957	3,771	683	45
1	1,900	2,037	232	17	19	....	106	345	1,357	630	46
1	12,352	15,151	2,700	192	136	3	1,255	893	9,659	1,050	47
....	960	1,413	172	46	35	2	122	42	149	54	48
....	1,171	1,188	105	17	17	....	144	59	168	180	49
6	2,045	2,121	109	254	13	....	1,386	1,854	5,886	9,023	50
....	2,646	1,563	135	4	12	....	429	69	814	332	51
....	1,917	1,939	130	23	41	1	528	741	1,524	1,241	52
3	7,799	15,390	1,110	227	313	16	1,324	8,334	10,272	2,807	53
11	4,891	12,475	664	244	201	4	2,083	2,271	3,774	1,288	54
46	63,138	61,472	3,687	760	663	24	9,743	3,702	10,923	7,764	55

608   STATISTICS OF POPULATION.

TABLE **32.**—FOREIGN BORN POPULATION, DISTRIBUTED ACCORDING TO

	STATES AND TERRITORIES.	SLAV NATIONS.				LATIN NATIONS.				
		Russia.	Hungary.	Bohemia.	Poland.	France.	Italy.	Spain.	Portugal.	Greece.
1	The United States	182,644	62,435	118,106	147,440	113,174	182,580	6,185	15,996	1,887
2	North Atlantic division	92,896	45,540	12,254	56,694	40,809	118,621	2,404	4,674	604
3	Maine	420	16	3	54	441	253	53	70	2
4	New Hampshire	188	19	3	30	222	312	8	25	
5	Vermont	153	35	10	59	175	445	13	30	1
6	Massachusetts	7,325	389	581	3,341	3,273	8,066	304	3,051	53
7	Rhode Island	682	19	14	182	460	2,468	17	833	10
8	Connecticut	3,027	1,140	177	1,501	2,048	5,285	45	230	5
9	New York	58,466	15,598	9,129	22,718	20,443	64,141	1,603	284	413
10	New Jersey	5,320	3,417	306	3,615	4,714	12,980	145	20	27
11	Pennsylvania	17,315	24,901	2,031	25,191	9,033	24,662	216	131	81
12	South Atlantic division	5,900	1,153	1,708	2,471	2,509	4,894	621	151	167
13	Delaware	197	114	3	337	183	450	4	1	1
14	Maryland	4,258	207	1,554	1,797	623	1,416	53	27	16
15	District of Columbia	244	41	10	65	385	467	44	9	5
16	Virginia	407	448	73	67	331	1,219	36	47	18
17	West Virginia	126	236	0	69	213	632	3		4
18	North Carolina	86	3	11	9	55	28	2	11	1
19	South Carolina	178	13	11	63	138	106	25	7	37
20	Georgia	282	62	35	38	306	150	65	14	49
21	Florida	122	29	5	26	275	408	389	35	36
22	North Central division	69,907	13,850	99,514	81,104	38,615	21,837	706	515	404
23	Ohio	4,576	5,431	11,009	5,937	7,171	3,857	61	86	59
24	Indiana	576	436	288	3,114	3,297	408	20	25	16
25	Illinois	8,407	3,126	26,627	28,878	8,540	8,035	152	255	254
26	Michigan	11,883	637	2,311	15,669	5,182	3,088	61	26	10
27	Wisconsin	2,279	486	11,999	17,000	2,060	1,123	23	15	19
28	Minnesota	7,293	1,256	9,055	7,503	1,869	828	36	22	11
29	Iowa	782	213	10,928	453	2,327	399	189	7	1
30	Missouri	2,414	582	3,855	1,651	4,175	2,416	78	38	10
31	North Dakota	4,098	192	1,129	237	203	21	14	1	
32	South Dakota	12,398	321	2,488	276	350	269	7	11	1
33	Nebraska	5,454	449	16,893	2,332	1,256	717	26	14	10
34	Kansas	9,801	721	3,022	394	2,236	616	39	15	4
35	South Central division	2,713	866	3,687	2,458	14,376	12,314	1,314	236	267
36	Kentucky	390	67	58	176	1,108	707	31	10	4
37	Tennessee	463	257	13	182	490	788	17	4	8
38	Alabama	274	150	25	54	592	322	52	8	55
39	Mississippi	120	41	6	74	440	425	61	5	9
40	Louisiana	345	66	14	100	8,437	7,707	880	112	44
41	Texas	977	228	3,215	1,591	2,730	2,107	250	80	145
42	Oklahoma	57	22	250	4	82	11	1	1	1
43	Arkansas	87	35	97	277	428	187	4	7	1
44	Western division	11,228	1,026	943	1,713	16,865	24,914	1,140	10,420	445
45	Montana	719	48	98	93	478	734	6	25	11
46	Wyoming	794	17	31	18	127	259	8	7	1
47	Colorado	1,306	350	212	272	1,328	3,882	50	28	27
48	New Mexico	73	9	8	24	284	355	23	14	1
49	Arizona	53	9	3	13	206	207	21	19	7
50	Utah	290	23	8	20	205	347	12	26	3
51	Nevada	39	6	11	39	226	1,120	97	197	7
52	Idaho	113	9	11	15	178	500	18	20	4
53	Washington	2,118	104	239	200	1,046	1,408	45	110	47
54	Oregon	2,583	73	79	96	842	580	24	115	78
55	California	3,140	369	243	914	11,855	15,495	836	9,859	250

a Not specified.

COUNTRY OF BIRTH.

COUNTRY OF BIRTH, BY STATES AND TERRITORIES: 1890—Continued.

	ASIATIC NATIONS.				ALL OTHERS.								
Asia. (a)	China.	Japan.	India.	Africa.	Atlantic islands.	Australia.	Europe. (a)	Pacific islands.	Sandwich Islands.	Turkey.	Born at sea.	Other countries.	
2,260	100,688	2,202	2,143	2,207	9,739	5,984	12,579	2,065	1,304	1,839	5,533	479	1
1,048	6,086	393	918	802	6,381	1,600	6,705	399	186	1,122	1,596	243	2
9	76	4	22	11	17	25	28	10	2	3	60	....	3
14	74	8	17	6	11	13	1	6	2	22	21	4	4
2	39	1	7	11	5	6	1	3	1	11	22	3	5
319	1,124	65	206	153	4,973	212	106	123	104	310	280	12	6
59	75	8	20	25	547	23	38	33	5	63	28	30	7
33	298	22	48	21	183	86	39	15	13	49	60	6	8
358	3,135	209	349	299	490	683	5,147	112	45	427	585	80	9
59	657	31	100	159	71	112	266	31	6	71	144	21	10
195	1,208	45	140	117	78	440	1,079	66	8	166	396	81	11
120	641	54	120	228	184	139	471	73	22	53	168	25	12
....	38	....	....	14	1	18	8	1	....	5	7	....	13
16	205	7	9	22	43	31	120	29	3	9	86	18	14
11	95	18	11	21	3	12	25	2	5	7	12	1	15
60	57	13	35	16	16	22	68	15	4	10	11	....	16
1	23	....	3	7	6	7	12	....	....	4	17	1	17
2	13	....	12	11	8	9	13	6	....	3	7	1	18
6	23	....	5	30	5	....	44	1	....	1	7	4	19
13	82	1	9	57	10	14	94	1	2	3	9	....	20
11	105	15	36	50	83	26	87	18	8	11	12	....	21
651	2,525	149	613	365	416	1,310	2,974	461	81	323	2,818	157	22
119	211	26	68	60	11	168	350	19	6	77	329	11	23
33	91	25	12	17	2	61	253	15	5	3	172	14	24
152	778	24	121	78	272	326	836	53	25	52	441	34	25
73	140	39	70	37	27	122	116	24	7	10	409	9	26
45	136	9	26	33	19	77	98	27	8	4	354	1	27
57	106	3	71	30	18	111	428	30	3	45	245	53	28
36	70	6	40	24	7	112	230	20	8	12	251	1	29
58	425	6	85	29	14	106	232	23	10	58	265	9	30
2	28	....	10	6	5	19	104	4	....	24	46	....	31
19	202	....	9	5	6	38	123	203	3	2	79	1	32
20	216	8	42	17	17	74	143	18	3	31	97	23	33
27	113	3	59	29	18	96	61	25	3	5	130	1	34
168	1,359	31	160	472	77	254	1,908	123	11	92	323	31	35
17	27	1	25	10	5	27	384	2	....	13	54	2	36
11	54	4	13	34	7	19	158	8	2	6	23	3	37
61	42	3	18	69	3	35	113	7	....	....	18	5	38
3	106	1	13	48	....	7	122	2	....	....	21	1	39
9	334	10	15	82	27	36	270	73	6	16	50	12	40
60	695	3	72	201	33	100	782	26	3	53	111	8	41
2	24	....	1	3	....	3	3	....	....	....	4	....	42
5	77	....	3	25	2	27	136	5	....	4	33	....	43
273	95,477	1,665	332	340	2,681	2,681	461	1,009	1,004	249	628	23	44
5	2,564	7	13	11	4	47	16	19	1	9	20	1	45
8	474	....	9	9	1	15	7	2	3	7	15	....	46
30	1,447	13	29	24	12	101	82	20	2	14	82	....	47
7	369	4	7	5	2	12	5	14	....	1	13	....	48
....	1,199	3	3	10	2	38	4	6	3	....	6	....	49
12	808	5	15	77	8	118	20	78	156	2	53	1	50
1	2,792	3	8	1	21	39	9	12	2	2	11	....	51
2	2,018	....	2	16	8	24	....	16	2	2	18	1	52
14	3,275	377	24	28	17	237	58	114	120	6	79	12	53
30	9,465	29	20	20	19	145	66	106	32	4	45	....	54
164	71,066	1,224	202	139	2,587	1,905	194	622	674	202	277	8	55

FOREIGN PARENTAGE.

BY STATES AND TERRITORIES: 1890.

TABLE 35.—AGGREGATE, WHITE, AND COLORED POPULATION, DISTRIBUTED ACCORDING TO NATIVE OR FOREIGN PARENTAGE.

TABLE 36.—WHITE PERSONS HAVING EITHER FOREIGN FATHERS AND FOREIGN MOTHERS, FOREIGN FATHERS AND NATIVE MOTHERS, OR FOREIGN MOTHERS AND NATIVE FATHERS.

TABLE 37.—WHITE PERSONS HAVING BOTH PARENTS BORN IN SPECIFIED COUNTRIES, OR OF MIXED FOREIGN PARENTAGE.

TABLE 38.—NATIVE WHITE PERSONS HAVING BOTH PARENTS BORN IN SPECIFIED COUNTRIES, OR OF MIXED FOREIGN PARENTAGE.

TABLE 39.—FOREIGN WHITE PERSONS HAVING BOTH PARENTS BORN IN SPECIFIED COUNTRIES, OR OF MIXED FOREIGN PARENTAGE.

TABLE 40.—WHITE PERSONS HAVING FATHERS BORN IN SPECIFIED COUNTRIES AND NATIVE MOTHERS.

TABLE 41.—NATIVE WHITE PERSONS HAVING FATHERS BORN IN SPECIFIED COUNTRIES AND NATIVE MOTHERS.

TABLE 42.—FOREIGN WHITE PERSONS HAVING FATHERS BORN IN SPECIFIED COUNTRIES AND NATIVE MOTHERS.

TABLE 43.—WHITE PERSONS HAVING MOTHERS BORN IN SPECIFIED COUNTRIES AND NATIVE FATHERS.

TABLE 44.—NATIVE WHITE PERSONS HAVING MOTHERS BORN IN SPECIFIED COUNTRIES AND NATIVE FATHERS.

TABLE 45.—FOREIGN WHITE PERSONS HAVING MOTHERS BORN IN SPECIFIED COUNTRIES AND NATIVE FATHERS.

TABLE 46.—WHITE PERSONS HAVING FATHERS BORN IN SPECIFIED COUNTRIES AND MOTHERS BORN IN SOME OTHER FOREIGN COUNTRY.

TABLE 47.—WHITE PERSONS HAVING MOTHERS BORN IN SPECIFIED COUNTRIES AND FATHERS BORN IN SOME OTHER FOREIGN COUNTRY.

TABLE 48.—WHITE PERSONS OF MIXED FOREIGN PARENTAGE, CLASSIFIED ACCORDING TO PRINCIPAL COMBINATIONS OF PARENTAGE.

TABLE 49.—WHITE PERSONS HAVING EITHER FATHERS OR MOTHERS BORN IN SPECIFIED COUNTRIES.

FOR CITIES HAVING 25,000 INHABITANTS OR MORE: 1890.

TABLE 50.—AGGREGATE, WHITE, AND COLORED POPULATION, DISTRIBUTED ACCORDING TO NATIVE OR FOREIGN PARENTAGE.

TABLE 51.—WHITE PERSONS HAVING EITHER FOREIGN FATHERS AND FOREIGN MOTHERS, FOREIGN FATHERS AND NATIVE MOTHERS, OR FOREIGN MOTHERS AND NATIVE FATHERS.

TABLE 52.—WHITE PERSONS HAVING BOTH PARENTS BORN IN SPECIFIED COUNTRIES, OR OF MIXED FOREIGN PARENTAGE.

TABLE 53.—NATIVE WHITE PERSONS HAVING BOTH PARENTS BORN IN SPECIFIED COUNTRIES, OR OF MIXED FOREIGN PARENTAGE.

TABLE 54.—FOREIGN WHITE PERSONS HAVING BOTH PARENTS BORN IN SPECIFIED COUNTRIES, OR OF MIXED FOREIGN PARENTAGE.

TABLE 55.—WHITE PERSONS HAVING FATHERS BORN IN SPECIFIED COUNTRIES AND NATIVE MOTHERS.

TABLE 56.—NATIVE WHITE PERSONS HAVING FATHERS BORN IN SPECIFIED COUNTRIES AND NATIVE MOTHERS.

TABLE 57.—FOREIGN WHITE PERSONS HAVING FATHERS BORN IN SPECIFIED COUNTRIES AND NATIVE MOTHERS.

TABLE 58.—WHITE PERSONS HAVING MOTHERS BORN IN SPECIFIED COUNTRIES AND NATIVE FATHERS.

TABLE 59.—NATIVE WHITE PERSONS HAVING MOTHERS BORN IN SPECIFIED COUNTRIES AND NATIVE FATHERS.

TABLE 60.—FOREIGN WHITE PERSONS HAVING MOTHERS BORN IN SPECIFIED COUNTRIES AND NATIVE FATHERS.

TABLE 61.—WHITE PERSONS HAVING FATHERS BORN IN SPECIFIED COUNTRIES AND MOTHERS BORN IN SOME OTHER FOREIGN COUNTRY.

TABLE 62.—WHITE PERSONS HAVING MOTHERS BORN IN SPECIFIED COUNTRIES AND FATHERS BORN IN SOME OTHER FOREIGN COUNTRY.

FOREIGN PARENTAGE.

681

TABLE **35.**—AGGREGATE, WHITE, AND COLORED POPULATION, DISTRIBUTED ACCORDING TO NATIVE OR FOREIGN PARENTAGE, BY STATES AND TERRITORIES: 1890.

[Under the designation of "foreign parentage" are included all persons, whether of native or foreign birth, who have either foreign fathers and foreign mothers, foreign fathers and native mothers, or foreign mothers and native fathers. All other persons, that is, those having both parents native born, one parent native and one parent unknown, or both parents unknown, are considered as being of native parentage.]

STATES AND TERRITORIES.	AGGREGATE POPULATION.			WHITE POPULATION.			COLORED POPULATION. (a)		
	Total.	Of native parentage.	Of foreign parentage.	Total.	Of native parentage.	Of foreign parentage.	Total.	Of native parentage.	Of foreign parentage.
The United States.........	62,622,250	41,946,204	20,676,046	54,983,890	34,464,247	20,519,643	7,638,360	7,481,957	156,403
North Atlantic division.............	17,401,545	9,185,707	8,215,838	17,121,981	8,925,304	8,196,677	279,564	260,403	19,161
Maine......	661,086	509,928	151,158	659,263	508,550	150,713	1,823	1,378	445
New Hampshire.............	376,530	255,237	121,293	375,840	254,739	121,101	690	498	192
Vermont.................	332,422	227,945	104,477	331,418	227,081	104,337	1,004	864	140
Massachusetts..........	2,238,943	979,822	1,259,121	2,215,373	961,447	1,253,926	23,570	18,375	5,195
Rhode Island.............	345,506	145,054	200,452	337,859	137,890	199,969	7,647	7,164	483
Connecticut.............	746,258	370,770	375,488	733,438	358,724	374,714	12,820	12,046	774
New York.............	5,997,853	2,599,887	3,397,966	5,923,952	2,533,402	3,390,550	73,901	66,485	7,416
New Jersey.............	1,444,933	746,751	698,182	1,396,581	699,835	696,746	48,352	46,916	1,436
Pennsylvania.............	5,258,014	3,350,313	1,907,701	5,148,257	3,243,636	1,904,621	109,757	106,677	3,080
South Atlantic division.............	8,857,920	8,324,540	533,380	5,592,149	5,070,499	521,650	3,265,771	3,254,041	11,730
Delaware	168,493	137,790	30,703	140,066	109,460	30,606	28,427	28,330	97
Maryland	1,042,390	792,011	250,379	826,493	577,023	249,470	215,897	214,988	909
District of Columbia.	230,392	183,462	46,930	154,695	108,262	46,433	75,697	75,200	497
Virginia.	1,655,980	1,612,415	43,565	1,020,122	977,069	43,053	635,858	635,346	512
West Virginia.	762,794	703,144	59,650	730,077	670,506	59,571	32,717	32,638	79
North Carolina.	1,617,947	1,606,691	11,256	1,055,382	1,044,577	10,805	562,565	562,114	451
South Carolina.............	1,151,149	1,133,546	17,603	462,008	445,314	16,694	689,141	688,232	909
Georgia	1,837,353	1,804,669	32,684	978,357	947,037	31,320	858,996	857,632	1,364
Florida	391,422	350,812	40,610	224,949	191,251	33,698	166,473	159,561	6,912
North Central division	22,362,279	12,741,925	9,620,354	21,911,927	12,302,086	9,609,841	450,352	439,839	10,513
Ohio......	3,672,316	2,425,143	1,247,173	3,584,805	2,338,863	1,245,942	87,511	86,280	1,231
Indiana	2,192,404	1,745,183	447,221	2,146,736	1,699,843	446,893	45,668	45,340	328
Illinois	3,826,351	1,949,125	1,877,226	3,768,472	1,893,145	1,875,327	57,879	55,980	1,899
Michigan	2,093,889	948,062	1,145,827	2,072,884	930,131	1,142,753	21,005	17,931	3,074
Wisconsin	1,686,880	443,871	1,243,009	1,680,473	438,074	1,242,399	6,407	5,797	610
Minnesota	1,301,826	320,043	981,783	1,296,159	315,029	981,130	5,667	5,014	653
Iowa	1,911,896	1,078,708	833,188	1,901,086	1,068,159	832,927	10,810	10,549	261
Missouri	2,679,184	2,009,873	669,311	2,528,458	1,860,232	668,226	150,726	149,641	1,085
North Dakota	182,719	38,414	144,305	182,123	38,008	144,115	596	406	190
South Dakota	328,808	129,521	199,287	327,290	128,337	198,953	1,518	1,184	334
Nebraska	1,058,910	609,050	449,860	1,046,888	597,403	449,485	12,022	11,647	375
Kansas	1,427,096	1,044,932	382,164	1,376,553	994,862	381,691	50,543	50,070	473
South Central division.............	10,972,893	10,139,855	833,038	7,487,576	6,666,797	820,779	3,485,317	3,473,058	12,259
Kentucky	1,858,635	1,675,255	183,380	1,590,462	1,407,417	183,045	268,173	267,838	335
Tennessee	1,767,518	1,714,160	53,358	1,336,637	1,284,016	52,621	430,881	430,144	737
Alabama	1,513,017	1,475,133	37,884	833,718	796,801	36,917	679,299	678,332	967
Mississippi	1,289,600	1,263,871	25,729	544,851	520,531	24,320	744,749	743,340	1,409
Louisiana	1,118,587	969,372	149,215	558,395	413,669	144,726	560,192	555,703	4,489
Texas ...	2,235,523	1,897,350	338,173	1,745,935	1,411,390	334,545	489,588	485,960	3,628
Oklahoma	61,834	54,607	7,227	58,826	51,647	7,179	3,008	2,960	48
Arkansas	1,128,179	1,090,107	38,072	818,752	781,326	37,426	309,427	308,781	646
Western division	3,027,613	1,554,177	1,473,436	2,870,257	1,499,561	1,370,696	157,356	54,616	102,740
Montana	132,159	58,498	73,661	127,271	56,578	70,693	4,888	1,920	2,968
Wyoming	60,705	31,388	29,317	59,275	30,469	28,806	1,430	919	511
Colorado	412,198	249,285	162,913	404,468	243,166	161,302	7,730	6,119	1,611
New Mexico	153,593	129,873	23,720	142,710	119,487	23,232	10,874	10,386	488
Arizona	59,620	26,799	32,821	55,580	24,236	31,344	4,040	2,563	1,477
Utah	207,905	70,107	137,798	205,899	69,088	136,811	2,006	1,019	987
Nevada	45,761	18,750	27,011	39,084	14,958	24,126	6,677	3,792	2,885
Idaho	84,385	45,897	38,488	82,018	45,566	36,452	2,367	331	2,036
Washington	349,390	193,264	156,126	340,513	188,523	151,990	8,877	4,741	4,136
Oregon	313,767	207,492	106,275	301,758	205,329	96,429	12,009	2,163	9,846
California	1,208,130	522,824	685,306	1,111,672	502,161	609,511	96,458	20,663	75,795

a Persons of negro descent, Chinese, Japanese, and civilized Indians.

682   STATISTICS OF POPULATION.

TABLE **36.**—WHITE PERSONS HAVING EITHER FOREIGN FATHERS AND FOREIGN MOTHERS, FOREIGN FATHERS

	STATES AND TERRITORIES.	WHITE PERSONS OF FOREIGN PARENTAGE.			
		Total.	Having foreign fathers and foreign mothers.	Having foreign fathers and native mothers.	Having foreign mothers and native fathers.
1	The United States	20,519,643	17,011,781	2,424,693	1,083,159
2	North Atlantic division	8,196,677	6,980,995	794,892	420,790
3	Maine	150,713	116,584	19,230	14,899
4	New Hampshire	121,101	104,556	9,121	7,424
5	Vermont	104,337	76,219	17,394	10,724
6	Massachusetts	1,253,926	1,103,303	83,944	66,679
7	Rhode Island	199,969	178,139	11,863	9,967
8	Connecticut	374,714	331,769	25,993	16,952
9	New York	3,390,550	2,907,109	321,323	162,118
10	New Jersey	696,746	597,435	66,358	32,953
11	Pennsylvania	1,904,621	1,565,881	239,666	99,074
12	South Atlantic division	521,650	397,135	92,109	32,406
13	Delaware	30,606	24,971	3,741	1,894
14	Maryland	249,470	198,916	36,668	13,886
15	District of Columbia	46,433	35,448	7,386	3,599
16	Virginia	43,053	30,996	9,506	2,551
17	West Virginia	59,571	41,981	13,292	4,298
18	North Carolina	10,805	6,042	3,581	1,182
19	South Carolina	16,694	11,629	4,009	1,056
20	Georgia	31,320	21,225	8,209	1,886
21	Florida	33,698	26,017	5,627	2,054
22	North Central division	9,609,841	7,888,916	1,216,790	504,135
23	Ohio	1,245,942	981,084	192,385	72,473
24	Indiana	446,893	332,320	86,205	28,368
25	Illinois	1,875,327	1,592,371	202,979	79,977
26	Michigan	1,142,753	915,667	142,105	84,981
27	Wisconsin	1,242,399	1,067,186	124,608	50,605
28	Minnesota	981,130	865,866	78,794	36,470
29	Iowa	832,927	664,524	119,712	48,691
30	Missouri	668,226	513,651	118,993	35,582
31	North Dakota	144,115	129,610	9,036	5,469
32	South Dakota	198,953	167,929	20,289	10,735
33	Nebraska	440,485	373,185	52,418	23,882
34	Kansas	381,691	285,523	69,206	26,962
35	South Central division	820,779	625,558	152,688	42,533
36	Kentucky	183,045	140,849	32,946	9,250
37	Tennessee	52,621	36,849	12,304	3,468
38	Alabama	36,917	26,195	8,522	2,200
39	Mississippi	24,320	14,857	7,944	1,519
40	Louisiana	144,726	107,574	20,394	7,758
41	Texas	334,545	269,940	49,470	15,135
42	Oklahoma	7,179	4,887	1,628	664
43	Arkansas	37,426	24,413	10,480	2,533
44	Western division	1,370,696	1,119,177	168,214	83,305
45	Montana	70,693	60,016	7,260	3,417
46	Wyoming	28,806	23,751	3,109	1,940
47	Colorado	161,302	132,972	19,282	9,048
48	New Mexico	23,232	17,559	3,947	1,726
49	Arizona	31,344	26,316	2,747	2,281
50	Utah	136,811	107,130	16,889	12,792
51	Nevada	24,126	19,989	2,621	1,516
52	Idaho	36,452	27,902	5,480	3,070
53	Washington	151,990	125,019	18,389	8,582
54	Oregon	96,429	74,966	15,521	5,942
55	California	609,511	503,557	72,969	32,985

FOREIGN PARENTAGE. 683

AND NATIVE MOTHERS, OR FOREIGN MOTHERS AND NATIVE FATHERS, BY STATES AND TERRITORIES: 1890.

NATIVE WHITE PERSONS OF FOREIGN PARENTAGE.				FOREIGN WHITE PERSONS OF FOREIGN PARENTAGE.				
Total.	Having foreign fathers and foreign mothers.	Having foreign fathers and native mothers.	Having foreign mothers and native fathers.	Total.	Having foreign fathers and foreign mothers.	Having foreign fathers and native mothers.	Having foreign mothers and native fathers.	
11,503,675	8,085,019	2,378,729	1,039,927	9,015,968	8,926,762	45,964	43,242	1
4,355,710	3,171,242	778,339	406,129	3,840,967	3,809,753	16,553	14,661	2
73,865	42,561	18,020	13,284	76,848	74,023	1,210	1,015	3
50,015	34,700	8,488	6,827	71,086	69,856	633	597	4
62,149	36,193	16,296	9,660	42,188	40,026	1,098	1,064	5
606,440	462,493	80,536	63,411	647,486	640,810	3,408	3,208	6
94,282	73,030	11,555	9,697	105,687	105,109	308	270	7
193,048	150,952	25,487	16,609	181,666	180,817	506	343	8
1,837,453	1,365,744	315,002	156,707	1,553,097	1,541,365	6,321	5,411	9
371,878	274,064	65,433	32,381	324,808	323,371	925	572	10
1,066,580	731,505	237,522	97,553	838,041	834,376	2,144	1,521	11
322,454	199,532	91,317	31,605	199,196	197,603	792	801	12
17,615	12,063	3,700	1,852	12,991	12,908	41	42	13
156,421	106,346	36,434	13,641	93,049	92,570	234	245	14
28,869	18,116	7,293	3,460	17,504	17,332	93	139	15
25,175	13,244	9,467	2,464	17,878	17,662	129	87	16
41,011	23,506	13,250	4,255	18,560	18,475	42	43	17
7,297	2,536	3,547	1,154	3,568	3,506	34	28	18
10,670	5,659	3,973	1,038	6,024	5,970	36	18	19
19,683	9,719	8,145	1,819	11,637	11,506	64	67	20
15,773	8,343	5,508	1,922	17,625	17,674	110	132	21
5,608,315	3,932,693	1,194,079	481,543	4,001,526	3,956,223	22,711	22,592	22
791,735	529,548	190,917	71,270	454,207	451,536	1,468	1,203	23
302,735	189,226	85,642	27,867	144,158	143,094	563	501	24
1,044,804	767,377	199,082	77,445	830,523	824,994	2,997	2,532	25
613,590	404,448	133,783	75,359	529,163	511,219	8,322	9,622	26
726,835	555,113	122,851	48,871	515,564	512,073	1,757	1,734	27
518,151	406,808	76,761	34,582	462,979	459,058	2,033	1,888	28
513,187	347,780	118,105	47,242	319,740	318,744	1,547	1,449	29
437,699	284,845	116,072	34,782	230,527	228,806	921	800	30
63,347	50,108	8,363	4,876	80,768	79,502	673	593	31
109,215	79,344	19,742	10,129	89,738	88,585	547	606	32
250,420	175,942	51,433	23,045	199,065	197,243	985	837	33
236,507	142,154	68,368	26,075	145,094	143,369	898	827	34
507,349	315,062	151,005	41,282	313,430	310,496	1,683	1,251	35
124,304	82,422	22,772	9,110	58,741	58,421	174	146	36
33,257	17,710	12,156	3,391	19,364	19,139	148	77	37
22,693	12,113	8,429	2,151	14,224	14,082	93	49	38
16,773	7,396	7,884	1,493	7,547	7,461	60	26	39
96,465	59,696	29,158	7,611	48,261	47,878	236	147	40
185,586	122,540	48,624	14,422	148,959	147,400	846	713	41
4,563	2,325	1,607	631	2,616	2,562	21	33	42
23,708	10,860	10,375	2,473	13,718	13,553	105	60	43
709,847	466,490	163,989	79,368	660,849	652,687	4,225	3,937	44
30,959	20,781	7,026	3,152	39,734	39,235	234	265	45
14,520	9,612	3,029	1,879	14,286	14,139	80	67	46
79,814	52,370	18,804	8,640	81,488	80,602	478	408	47
12,539	7,054	3,857	1,628	10,693	10,505	90	98	48
14,027	9,208	2,655	2,164	17,317	17,108	92	117	49
85,314	55,922	16,747	12,645	51,497	51,208	142	147	50
12,406	8,387	2,569	1,450	11,720	11,602	52	66	51
21,154	12,761	5,412	2,981	15,298	15,141	68	89	52
68,757	43,183	17,653	7,921	83,233	81,836	736	661	53
49,967	29,233	15,119	5,615	46,462	45,733	402	327	54
320,890	217,979	71,118	31,293	280,121	285,578	1,851	1,692	55

684

STATISTICS OF POPULATION.

TABLE 37.—WHITE PERSONS HAVING BOTH PARENTS BORN IN SPECIFIED COUNTRIES,

[Under the term "mixed foreign parentage" are included all persons whose parents are both foreign born but of different nationalities, as father born in Ireland
combinations of mixed foreign parentage are given by states and

	STATES AND TERRITORIES.	Total.	BOTH PARENTS BORN IN SPECIFIED COUNTRIES.					
			Ireland.	Germany.	England.	Scotland.	Wales.	Canada (English).
1	The United States	17,011,781	4,142,199	5,776,186	1,330,123	393,158	169,832	503,209
2	North Atlantic division	6,980,995	2,654,816	1,754,744	599,817	174,138	82,106	216,489
3	Maine	110,584	26,874	1,679	9,799	3,520	338	27,809
4	New Hampshire	104,556	30,010	2,428	6,288	2,642	68	10,907
5	Vermont	76,219	24,524	1,339	5,341	2,918	1,394	10,100
6	Massachusetts	1,103,303	546,390	49,500	94,942	32,564	1,436	100,651
7	Rhode Island	178,139	80,980	5,461	26,737	6,656	175	4,680
8	Connecticut	331,769	108,226	49,187	28,643	8,738	699	5,539
9	New York	2,907,109	1,029,539	972,603	201,230	56,260	13,905	47,800
10	New Jersey	597,435	211,100	200,124	59,445	17,641	1,457	2,807
11	Pennsylvania	1,565,881	537,173	472,423	167,386	43,100	62,634	6,240
12	South Atlantic division	397,135	105,385	177,736	29,561	11,841	2,858	2,874
13	Delaware	24,971	13,422	4,673	2,685	577	84	181
14	Maryland	198,916	42,482	117,612	8,207	4,263	1,410	465
15	District of Columbia	35,448	14,653	11,824	2,788	904	99	294
16	Virginia	30,906	9,109	8,768	4,304	1,629	404	434
17	West Virginia	41,981	12,300	18,151	4,165	1,505	667	174
18	North Carolina	6,042	848	1,932	1,246	760	15	105
19	South Carolina	11,629	3,517	4,842	780	499	17	74
20	Georgia	21,225	7,161	6,686	2,035	893	109	336
21	Florida	26,017	1,893	3,248	3,351	811	53	721
22	North Central division	7,888,916	1,068,878	3,372,581	504,406	149,021	64,404	234,570
23	Ohio	981,084	160,451	541,507	78,615	16,552	25,224	8,107
24	Indiana	332,320	49,483	207,188	18,070	5,286	1,433	3,023
25	Illinois	1,592,371	284,740	690,588	108,182	33,672	6,562	22,075
26	Michigan	915,667	100,998	276,258	92,462	26,031	1,104	107,518
27	Wisconsin	1,067,186	92,904	551,834	43,607	11,387	9,258	19,077
28	Minnesota	865,866	75,967	244,634	22,397	10,516	2,848	24,459
29	Iowa	664,524	99,595	269,603	45,252	14,521	6,547	11,203
30	Missouri	513,651	95,098	297,095	28,590	7,793	3,264	4,578
31	North Dakota	129,610	8,553	17,541	5,226	4,354	212	13,079
32	South Dakota	167,929	13,685	38,566	8,727	3,077	1,454	6,040
33	Nebraska	373,185	40,267	140,301	24,573	7,180	2,222	7,925
34	Kansas	285,523	38,137	97,466	28,750	9,552	4,276	6,597
35	South Central division	625,558	96,740	256,619	33,720	10,164	2,992	4,216
36	Kentucky	140,843	34,680	82,095	6,427	1,705	652	507
37	Tennessee	36,840	10,821	10,685	3,902	1,115	972	554
38	Alabama	26,195	5,545	7,779	3,868	1,059	548	314
39	Mississippi	14,857	3,863	4,688	1,248	407	23	203
40	Louisiana	107,574	22,003	37,857	3,726	831	128	448
41	Texas	269,940	15,169	100,865	11,835	3,264	400	1,406
42	Oklahoma	4,887	764	1,420	521	215	30	246
43	Arkansas	24,413	3,895	11,230	2,173	668	221	478
44	Western division	1,119,177	216,380	214,506	162,559	47,094	17,472	45,108
45	Montana	60,016	13,577	9,519	8,746	2,901	1,003	4,624
46	Wyoming	23,751	4,267	3,558	4,748	2,230	803	930
47	Colorado	132,972	25,759	28,148	21,073	6,764	3,122	5,748
48	New Mexico	17,559	1,947	2,367	1,636	655	158	301
49	Arizona	26,316	2,160	1,783	1,641	507	123	380
50	Utah	107,130	3,959	3,406	42,121	6,554	4,116	853
51	Nevada	19,989	5,402	2,799	3,409	729	396	1,109
52	Idaho	27,902	3,773	3,451	5,885	1,257	1,671	1,149
53	Washington	125,019	16,096	26,177	18,743	6,127	2,492	9,854
54	Oregon	74,966	9,251	22,239	8,283	3,796	580	8,541
55	California	503,557	130,183	111,059	51,274	15,574	2,978	16,511

FOREIGN PARENTAGE. 685

OR OF MIXED FOREIGN PARENTAGE, BY STATES AND TERRITORIES: 1890.

and mother born in England, father born in England and mother born in Ireland, father born in Germany and mother born in France, and so on. The principal territories for the total number of white persons in Table 48, pages 698–701.]

Canada (French).	Sweden.	Norway.	Denmark.	Bohemia.	France.	Hungary.	Italy.	Russia.	Other countries.	Of mixed foreign parentage.	
442,041	690,401	550,227	194,449	205,365	177,007	69,761	236,008	248,165	961,325	922,268	1
331,253	114,904	15,976	18,313	17,592	58,481	51,306	150,721	125,752	268,650	350,937	2
32,925	2,325	368	1,004	1	655	9	308	542	497	7,841	3
44,853	1,354	329	61	3	319	20	346	212	361	4,295	4
23,521	924	35	71	12	343	29	472	190	555	4,142	5
136,412	23,693	2,841	1,770	949	4,557	340	10,613	9,796	22,379	64,470	6
32,235	4,080	274	130	20	540	17	2,978	860	3,081	9,235	7
22,592	13,048	499	1,916	193	2,827	1,191	6,379	3,751	6,053	12,288	8
37,521	37,713	8,958	7,115	13,249	29,787	18,673	83,263	81,755	124,163	143,554	9
519	5,290	1,415	3,957	423	6,331	3,909	16,248	6,731	30,576	29,662	10
675	26,477	1,257	2,289	2,742	13,122	27,118	30,114	21,906	75,985	75,150	11
224	2,257	694	653	2,638	3,281	1,225	5,912	7,793	23,402	18,801	12
3	326	11	43	4	251	138	553	224	637	1,159	13
41	370	205	143	2,383	857	184	1,841	5,686	5,847	6,920	14
37	162	58	73	9	403	46	614	323	789	2,372	15
16	226	105	89	119	436	485	1,441	561	909	1,871	16
20	113	2	40	51	290	252	596	150	1,408	2,079	17
6	62	12	27	11	63	3	43	123	224	472	18
20	84	16	39	18	101	14	143	252	492	631	19
41	233	93	65	39	431	74	208	333	923	1,565	20
31	681	192	134	4	350	29	473	141	12,173	1,732	21
102,723	505,043	503,912	133,728	178,013	67,978	15,259	28,767	97,318	442,660	418,686	22
1,504	4,075	550	1,262	18,640	13,723	6,167	5,055	6,349	40,398	43,905	23
472	7,066	383	1,022	561	6,467	478	537	824	15,938	14,083	24
10,136	126,742	44,860	15,039	43,755	14,277	3,288	10,918	12,030	92,665	71,947	25
45,799	36,809	10,844	9,519	3,732	8,470	489	3,881	14,103	92,413	85,147	26
14,142	28,741	120,665	22,350	23,815	3,643	418	1,324	2,649	77,230	43,233	27
18,382	150,016	182,775	21,177	18,220	3,303	1,417	1,016	9,722	35,958	42,453	28
1,257	48,784	53,820	23,745	21,812	4,114	262	582	1,051	29,210	33,216	29
531	8,351	709	1,895	6,028	7,158	627	3,505	3,291	19,509	25,571	30
4,251	7,650	44,698	3,915	2,103	352	256	26	5,130	1,990	10,274	31
1,732	11,710	35,647	6,853	4,908	579	424	310	18,363	6,223	9,022	32
1,132	45,155	6,097	21,279	28,928	2,146	528	886	7,875	17,521	19,170	33
3,385	29,304	2,864	4,763	5,505	3,746	910	718	15,931	13,545	20,065	34
344	6,639	2,553	1,750	5,833	24,435	887	17,158	3,550	122,425	35,524	35
52	370	36	125	71	2,026	52	1,065	503	4,504	5,073	36
17	439	50	110	12	742	282	1,170	620	2,842	2,516	37
29	319	43	86	32	806	181	376	341	1,442	2,417	38
6	400	59	120	8	721	48	604	132	925	1,402	39
114	427	149	304	18	15,002	63	10,937	467	5,650	9,450	40
99	4,089	2,077	825	5,091	4,242	197	2,730	1,301	104,820	11,461	41
8	194	82	47	457	139	30	9	64	194	452	42
19	401	57	142	144	667	28	267	122	2,048	1,853	43
7,497	61,558	27,092	39,996	1,289	22,832	1,084	33,450	13,752	109,188	98,320	44
2,589	4,298	2,526	891	109	637	59	775	791	2,228	4,653	45
100	1,799	485	960	36	170	3	293	884	582	1,885	46
640	12,307	1,184	2,310	330	1,887	435	4,649	1,618	6,980	9,928	47
23	197	58	67	8	378	10	390	89	8,103	1,082	48
24	200	63	271	3	328	7	224	53	17,262	1,203	49
41	9,184	2,775	16,858	15	282	17	414	303	2,873	13,350	50
278	367	73	480	20	300	6	1,360	39	1,398	1,884	51
121	2,101	1,137	2,232	14	231	4	532	114	1,183	3,047	52
1,827	12,252	11,073	3,525	325	1,420	94	1,554	2,660	4,753	11,047	53
458	4,811	2,998	1,076	131	1,163	77	659	3,308	5,419	6,576	54
1,396	13,943	4,720	10,726	298	16,027	372	22,600	3,893	58,407	43,596	55

686

STATISTICS OF POPULATION.

TABLE 38.—NATIVE WHITE PERSONS HAVING BOTH PARENTS BORN IN SPECIFIED

[Under the term "mixed foreign parentage" are included all persons whose parents are both foreign born but of different nationalities, as father born in Ireland
combinations of mixed foreign parentage are given by states and

	STATES AND TERRITORIES.	Total.	BOTH PARENTS BORN IN SPECIFIED COUNTRIES.					
			Ireland.	Germany.	England.	Scotland.	Wales.	Canada (English).
1	The United States	8,085,019	2,164,397	3,006,342	488,661	134,243	75,375	183,602
2	North Atlantic division	3,171,242	1,358,707	861,535	205,497	58,051	34,618	65,012
3	Maine	42,561	13,340	598	2,956	733	123	8,988
4	New Hampshire	34,700	13,627	818	1,814	658	11	3,252
5	Vermont	36,193	13,749	474	1,640	806	522	4,025
6	Massachusetts	462,493	271,263	21,324	28,236	8,578	374	24,800
7	Rhode Island	73,030	39,663	2,286	8,211	1,979	50	1,424
8	Connecticut	150,952	89,008	21,236	9,677	2,998	185	1,773
9	New York	1,365,744	530,445	475,943	73,117	20,554	6,109	17,515
10	New Jersey	274,064	107,555	94,817	20,673	5,737	522	693
11	Pennsylvania	731,505	280,057	244,039	59,173	15,948	26,722	1,942
12	South Atlantic division	199,532	57,108	97,449	10,098	4,841	1,245	680
13	Delaware	12,063	7,199	2,218	968	180	32	38
14	Maryland	106,346	23,562	65,701	3,278	2,089	718	121
15	District of Columbia	18,116	7,686	6,369	932	324	43	85
16	Virginia	13,244	4,492	4,481	1,245	553	105	96
17	West Virginia	23,506	7,383	10,936	1,661	665	304	40
18	North Carolina	2,536	377	864	411	356	4	70
19	South Carolina	5,659	1,878	2,368	247	206	9	10
20	Georgia	9,719	3,724	3,085	626	259	17	78
21	Florida	8,343	807	1,427	730	200	13	142
22	North Central division	3,932,693	591,732	1,808,233	190,997	53,083	31,244	102,196
23	Ohio	529,548	95,320	307,454	30,015	6,657	12,670	3,103
24	Indiana	189,226	28,248	122,889	7,016	2,310	648	1,300
25	Illinois	767,377	154,231	355,381	41,934	12,693	2,634	8,392
26	Michigan	404,448	46,156	137,844	32,888	6,330	422	47,524
27	Wisconsin	555,113	55,481	293,039	20,754	4,702	4,940	9,398
28	Minnesota	406,808	43,583	128,277	8,147	3,168	1,509	10,478
29	Iowa	347,780	60,301	143,421	19,751	5,980	3,092	5,703
30	Missouri	284,845	53,155	173,243	11,411	2,943	1,502	1,777
31	North Dakota	50,108	2,938	8,036	1,340	621	105	5,220
32	South Dakota	79,344	8,007	19,696	3,526	1,017	745	2,615
33	Nebraska	175,942	23,092	68,301	10,558	2,909	1,115	8,600
34	Kansas	142,154	21,211	50,652	11,457	3,679	1,853	3,077
35	South Central division	315,062	52,913	143,672	11,191	3,607	1,104	1,285
36	Kentucky	82,422	20,479	40,676	2,607	691	292	157
37	Tennessee	17,710	5,781	5,439	1,290	408	380	151
38	Alabama	12,113	2,879	3,916	1,140	648	167	81
39	Mississippi	7,396	2,012	2,467	421	196	5	58
40	Louisiana	59,696	12,822	23,454	1,565	342	31	146
41	Texas	122,540	6,719	52,909	3,153	997	125	435
42	Oklahoma	2,325	403	695	210	76	21	108
43	Arkansas	10,860	1,818	5,116	715	249	83	149
44	Western division	466,490	103,937	95,453	61,878	14,661	7,164	14,425
45	Montana	20,781	6,049	3,981	2,502	725	433	1,217
46	Wyoming	9,612	2,246	1,535	1,762	771	250	415
47	Colorado	52,370	12,283	13,026	7,113	2,152	1,129	1,671
48	New Mexico	7,054	884	994	443	214	55	112
49	Arizona	9,208	908	631	588	132	34	101
50	Utah	55,922	1,769	1,296	21,816	3,094	1,939	402
51	Nevada	8,387	2,639	1,230	1,294	241	142	330
52	Idaho	12,761	1,607	1,519	2,823	506	943	375
53	Washington	43,183	6,942	11,315	3,911	1,361	857	2,956
54	Oregon	29,233	4,006	9,813	2,563	1,073	232	1,258
55	California	217,979	64,604	50,113	17,063	4,392	1,150	5,577

FOREIGN PARENTAGE.

687

COUNTRIES, OR OF MIXED FOREIGN PARENTAGE, BY STATES AND TERRITORIES: 1890.

and mother born in England, father born in England and mother born in Ireland, father born in Germany and mother born in France, and so on. The principal territories for the total number of white persons in Table 48, pages 698–701.]

				BOTH PARENTS BORN IN SPECIFIED COUNTRIES—continued.						Of mixed foreign parentage.	
Canada (French).	Sweden.	Norway.	Denmark.	Bohemia.	France.	Hungary.	Italy.	Russia.	Other countries.		
157,104	217,217	238,679	66,196	90,195	68,572	13,048	54,742	69,802	342,574	714,270	1
110,797	28,029	3,138	4,195	5,941	19,701	8,516	32,181	31,934	71,283	272,107	2
9,721	650	70	319	1	212	1	62	121	92	4,574	3
11,517	192	84	10	....	72	3	39	30	58	2,515	4
11,132	123	2	22	2	124	3	58	47	120	2,684	5
43,355	5,147	569	308	360	1,216	67	2,799	2,262	7,068	44,707	6
9,882	921	52	17	5	101	2	547	180	811	6,899	7
7,852	3,042	137	476	40	851	184	1,115	731	1,442	10,199	8
16,997	9,482	1,766	1,422	4,561	10,400	4,141	19,306	22,402	35,993	115,591	9
122	1,208	245	1,046	124	1,989	580	3,548	1,420	9,170	24,606	10
219	7,264	213	515	842	4,736	3,535	4,707	4,732	16,529	60,332	11
58	486	106	113	928	1,067	169	1,180	1,888	6,720	15,381	12
....	70	....	5	1	69	19	98	29	150	969	13
12	87	51	27	854	326	45	435	1,389	1,705	5,886	14
9	33	13	8	1	87	12	202	105	233	1,974	15
4	24	6	14	48	143	45	211	145	237	1,395	16
15	18	....	6	7	100	21	31	19	479	1,821	17
2	14	....	4	3	12	2	19	20	46	317	18
7	33	....	10	7	72	2	42	75	162	531	19
5	44	8	12	7	100	19	50	71	272	1,282	20
4	154	28	27	....	98	4	92	26	3,385	1,206	21
44,123	172,095	227,102	46,647	30,464	30,086	3,925	7,181	32,176	180,521	321,288	22
569	1,154	110	351	48,001	6,883	1,350	1,339	1,903	15,062	36,989	23
225	2,545	130	389	276	3,275	87	124	277	6,738	12,160	24
5,028	41,619	16,909	4,661	17,004	6,100	965	3,042	3,616	33,732	58,837	25
17,800	9,896	3,462	3,318	1,582	3,576	120	665	2,642	38,120	51,998	26
6,256	8,748	56,071	8,706	12,052	1,584	108	264	528	36,325	36,097	27
8,431	50,857	83,182	17,441	8,896	1,378	407	219	2,982	14,835	33,018	28
637	18,802	27,272	8,474	11,023	1,839	80	81	301	13,217	27,737	29
198	2,671	242	586	2,837	3,189	150	1,075	932	7,036	21,898	30
1,506	2,087	19,258	945	908	105	71	7	1,255	723	4,824	31
842	4,030	16,672	2,540	2,464	238	122	59	7,250	2,662	6,850	32
512	17,299	2,648	7,554	12,164	884	169	182	2,845	6,921	15,189	33
1,939	12,318	1,155	1,702	2,597	1,626	287	124	7,045	5,141	15,691	34
88	1,961	920	444	2,390	10,660	200	5,116	933	48,014	30,558	35
17	97	13	39	28	943	13	348	121	1,561	5,250	36
5	88	14	27	2	290	85	441	155	1,082	2,072	37
2	86	3	17	9	338	43	85	71	634	1,994	38
....	105	5	30	3	298	10	187	24	342	1,233	39
32	97	32	92	8	6,794	7	3,309	127	2,090	8,748	40
25	1,344	801	205	2,091	1,682	25	651	377	41,519	9,482	41
2	59	48	14	198	57	14	2	16	65	337	42
5	85	4	20	51	264	3	93	42	721	1,442	43
2,038	14,646	7,413	14,797	472	6,452	238	9,084	2,871	36,027	74,936	44
630	607	565	238	24	178	14	68	97	401	8,057	45
31	469	149	267	9	45	....	20	106	146	1,391	46
206	2,865	316	671	129	628	111	799	358	1,670	7,243	47
2	51	22	15	1	87	1	53	15	3,310	795	48
5	54	10	101	1	65	1	18	9	5,596	954	49
18	3,238	1,015	8,043	7	96	3	78	24	1,111	11,973	50
53	67	12	155	9	70	1	252	5	303	1,566	51
17	596	415	1,029	4	77	....	20	6	353	2,471	52
542	2,340	2,982	786	126	411	11	133	580	1,127	6,794	53
134	1,178	794	418	60	359	23	114	772	1,658	4,778	54
400	3,181	1,133	3,079	102	4,427	73	7,529	890	20,352	33,914	55

688 STATISTICS OF POPULATION.

TABLE 39.—FOREIGN WHITE PERSONS HAVING BOTH PARENTS BORN IN SPECIFIED

[Under the term "mixed foreign parentage" are included all persons whose parents are both foreign born but of different nationalities, as father born in Ireland
combinations of mixed foreign parentage are given by states and

	STATES AND TERRITORIES.	Total.	BOTH PARENTS BORN IN SPECIFIED COUNTRIES.					
			Ireland.	Germany.	England.	Scotland.	Wales.	Canada (English).
1	The United States	8,926,762	1,977,802	2,769,844	841,462	258,915	94,457	319,064
2	North Atlantic division	3,809,753	1,296,109	893,209	394,320	116,087	47,488	151,477
3	Maine	74,023	13,534	1,081	6,843	2,787	215	18,911
4	New Hampshire	69,856	16,383	1,610	4,474	1,984	57	7,715
5	Vermont	40,026	10,775	865	3,701	2,052	872	5,475
6	Massachusetts	640,810	275,127	28,176	66,706	23,986	1,062	75,851
7	Rhode Island	105,109	41,317	3,175	18,526	4,677	125	3,250
8	Connecticut	180,817	79,218	27,951	18,966	5,740	514	3,766
9	New York	1,541,365	499,094	496,660	128,119	35,715	7,796	30,291
10	New Jersey	323,371	103,545	105,307	38,772	11,904	935	1,914
11	Pennsylvania	834,376	257,116	228,384	108,213	27,242	35,912	4,298
12	South Atlantic division	197,603	48,277	80,287	19,463	7,000	1,613	2,188
13	Delaware	12,908	6,223	2,455	1,717	388	52	143
14	Maryland	92,570	18,920	51,911	4,929	2,174	692	344
15	District of Columbia	17,332	6,967	5,455	1,856	580	56	209
16	Virginia	17,662	4,617	4,287	3,059	1,076	209	338
17	West Virginia	18,475	4,917	7,215	2,504	840	363	134
18	North Carolina	3,506	471	1,068	835	404	11	119
19	South Carolina	5,970	1,630	2,474	533	293	8	64
20	Georgia	11,506	3,437	3,601	1,409	634	92	258
21	Florida	17,674	1,086	1,821	2,621	611	40	579
22	North Central division	3,956,223	477,146	1,564,348	304,460	96,838	33,100	132,383
23	Ohio	451,536	74,122	234,053	48,000	9,895	12,545	5,004
24	Indiana	143,094	21,235	84,290	10,460	2,967	785	1,723
25	Illinois	824,094	130,509	335,207	66,248	20,980	3,928	13,683
26	Michigan	511,219	54,842	138,414	59,574	19,005	682	59,994
27	Wisconsin	512,073	37,423	258,795	22,853	6,025	4,318	10,579
28	Minnesota	459,058	32,384	116,357	14,250	7,348	1,339	13,981
29	Iowa	310,744	39,204	126,182	25,501	8,541	3,455	5,500
30	Missouri	228,806	41,943	123,852	17,173	4,850	1,762	2,700
31	North Dakota	79,502	5,615	9,505	3,886	3,733	107	7,850
32	South Dakota	88,585	5,678	18,870	5,201	2,060	709	3,425
33	Nebraska	197,243	17,175	72,000	14,015	4,271	1,107	4,325
34	Kansas	143,369	16,926	46,814	17,302	5,873	2,423	3,520
35	South Central division	310,496	43,827	112,947	22,520	6,557	1,888	2,931
36	Kentucky	58,421	14,201	32,419	3,730	1,014	360	350
37	Tennessee	19,139	5,040	5,246	2,612	707	592	403
38	Alabama	14,082	2,666	3,863	2,748	1,311	381	233
39	Mississippi	7,461	1,851	2,221	827	211	18	145
40	Louisiana	47,878	9,181	14,403	2,161	489	97	302
41	Texas	147,400	8,450	47,956	8,082	2,267	284	1,031
42	Oklahoma	2,562	361	725	311	139	18	138
43	Arkansas	13,553	2,077	6,114	1,458	419	138	329
44	Western division	652,687	112,443	119,053	100,681	32,433	10,308	30,685
45	Montana	39,235	7,528	5,538	6,244	2,176	660	3,407
46	Wyoming	14,139	2,021	2,023	2,986	1,459	553	604
47	Colorado	80,602	13,476	15,122	13,960	4,612	1,993	4,074
48	New Mexico	10,505	1,063	1,373	1,193	441	103	270
49	Arizona	17,108	1,258	1,152	1,053	375	89	288
50	Utah	51,208	2,190	2,110	20,805	3,460	2,177	451
51	Nevada	11,602	2,763	1,569	2,115	488	194	770
52	Idaho	15,141	2,166	1,932	3,062	751	728	774
53	Washington	81,836	9,154	14,862	9,832	4,766	1,635	6,898
54	Oregon	45,733	5,245	12,426	5,720	2,723	348	2,283
55	California	285,578	65,579	60,946	34,211	11,182	1,828	10,934

FOREIGN PARENTAGE.

COUNTRIES, OR OF MIXED FOREIGN PARENTAGE, BY STATES AND TERRITORIES: 1890.

[and mother born in England, father born in England and mother born in Ireland, father born in Germany and mother born in France, and so on. The principal territories for the total number of white persons in Table 48, pages 698-701.]

Canada (French).	Sweden.	Norway.	Denmark.	Bohemia.	France.	Hungary.	Italy.	Russia.	Other countries.	Of mixed foreign parentage.	
284,937	473,184	311,548	128,253	115,170	108,435	56,713	181,266	178,363	618,751	207,998	1
220,456	86,875	12,838	14,118	11,651	38,780	42,790	118,540	93,818	192,367	78,830	2
23,204	1,675	298	685	....	443	8	246	421	405	3,267	3
33,336	1,102	245	51	3	247	17	307	182	303	1,780	4
12,389	801	33	49	10	219	26	414	152	435	1,758	5
93,057	18,546	2,272	1,402	580	3,341	273	7,814	7,534	15,311	19,763	6
22,353	3,159	222	113	15	439	15	2,431	680	2,270	2,336	7
14,740	10,006	362	1,440	147	1,976	1,007	5,264	3,020	4,611	2,089	8
20,524	28,231	7,192	5,693	8,688	19,387	14,532	63,957	59,353	88,170	27,963	9
397	4,082	1,170	2,911	209	4,342	3,329	12,700	5,302	21,406	5,056	10
456	19,213	1,044	1,774	1,900	8,386	23,583	25,407	17,174	59,456	14,818	11
166	1,771	588	540	1,710	2,214	1,056	4,732	5,905	16,673	3,420	12
3	247	11	38	3	182	119	455	195	487	190	13
29	283	154	116	1,529	531	139	1,406	4,297	4,082	1,034	14
28	129	45	65	8	316	34	412	218	556	398	15
12	202	99	75	71	293	440	1,230	416	672	476	16
14	95	2	34	44	199	231	565	131	929	258	17
4	48	12	23	8	51	1	24	94	178	155	18
13	51	16	29	11	119	12	101	177	330	100	19
36	189	85	53	32	271	55	158	202	651	283	20
27	527	164	107	4	252	25	381	115	8,788	526	21
58,000	332,948	276,810	87,081	97,549	37,292	11,334	21,586	65,142	262,130	97,398	22.
935	2,921	440	911	10,630	6,840	4,817	3,716	4,446	25,336	6,916	23
247	4,521	253	653	285	3,192	301	413	547	9,200	1,923	24
5,108	85,123	27,960	11,278	26,151	8,168	2,318	7,876	8,414	58,933	13,110	25
27,909	27,003	7,382	6,201	2,150	4,894	369	3,216	11,461	54,284	33,149	26
7,886	19,993	64,594	13,653	11,763	2,059	310	1,060	2,121	40,905	7,136	27
9,951	99,759	99,593	13,736	9,330	1,925	1,010	797	6,740	21,123	9,435	28
620	23,872	26,548	15,271	10,789	2,275	173	501	750	15,993	5,479	29
333	5,680	467	1,309	3,191	3,969	477	2,430	2,359	12,533	3,073	30
2,055	5,563	25,440	2,970	1,135	247	185	19	3,875	1,267	5,450	31
890	7,671	18,975	4,313	2,444	341	302	260	11,113	3,561	2,772	32
620	27,856	3,449	13,725	16,764	1,262	359	704	5,030	10,600	3,981	33
1,440	16,986	1,709	3,061	2,908	2,120	623	594	8,286	8,404	4,374	34
256	4,078	1,033	1,315	3,443	13,769	687	12,042	2,617	74,411	4,966	35
35	273	23	86	43	1,083	39	717	382	2,943	723	36
12	351	36	83	10	452	197	729	405	1,760	444	37
27	233	40	60	23	558	138	291	270	808	423	38
6	295	54	90	5	423	38	417	108	583	169	39
82	330	117	212	10	8,208	56	7,628	340	3,560	702	40
74	2,745	1,276	620	3,000	2,560	172	2,079	924	63,301	1,079	41
6	135	34	33	250	82	22	7	48	129	115	42
14	316	53	122	93	403	25	174	80	1,327	411	43
5,459	46,912	19,679	25,199	817	16,380	846	24,366	10,881	73,161	23,384	44
1,959	3,691	1,961	658	85	459	45	707	604	1,827	1,598	45
60	1,330	336	695	27	134	3	273	778	436	494	46
434	9,532	868	1,639	201	1,259	324	3,850	1,260	5,310	2,085	47
21	146	36	52	7	291	9	337	74	4,793	287	48
19	155	53	170	2	263	6	206	44	11,066	309	49
23	5,946	1,760	8,815	8	186	14	336	279	1,762	1,386	50
225	300	61	325	11	221	5	1,108	34	1,095	818	51
104	1,505	722	1,203	10	154	4	512	108	830	576	52
1,285	9,912	8,091	2,739	199	1,009	83	1,421	2,071	3,026	4,253	53
324	3,633	2,204	1,258	71	804	54	545	2,536	3,761	1,798	54
996	10,762	3,587	7,647	196	11,600	299	15,071	3,003	38,055	9,682	55

690   STATISTICS OF POPULATION.

TABLE **40.**—WHITE PERSONS HAVING FATHERS BORN IN SPECIFIED COUNTRIES AND NATIVE MOTHERS, BY STATES AND TERRITORIES : 1890.

STATES AND TERRITORIES.	Total.	Ireland.	Germany.	England.	Scotland.	Wales.	Canada (English).	Canada (French).	Sweden.	Norway.	Denmark.	Bohemia.	France.	Hungary.	Italy.	Russia.	Other countries.
United States..	2,424,693	508,734	833,261	394,168	100,710	35,211	243,087	44,465	24,227	30,405	13,888	6,853	62,055	1,437	11,337	5,140	109,715
North Atlantic division.	794,892	236,901	218,704	139,052	34,734	14,465	73,206	27,153	3,796	953	2,060	418	15,243	502	3,542	2,169	21,904
Maine	19,230	2,792	433	3,000	771	106	8,583	2,600	138	54	81	......	213	5	62	20	372
New Hampshire...	9,121	1,764	261	1,514	445	10	3,090	1,702	31	16	20	6	97	......	37	17	111
Vermont	17,304	3,040	252	1,584	874	127	6,175	4,000	21	2	8	7	175	3	10	9	139
Massachusetts	83,944	29,044	5,208	14,824	3,776	712	17,489	7,595	641	206	257	7	1,081	11	450	164	2,479
Rhode Island	11,863	4,410	714	2,961	759	26	1,206	1,097	88	22	9	......	146	......	80	10	335
Connecticut	25,993	10,582	3,865	5,621	1,301	154	1,730	1,024	184	34	92	7	530	9	98	72	690
New York	321,323	90,895	100,071	54,849	13,611	3,177	27,671	7,626	1,406	357	928	301	6,758	320	1,549	1,265	9,030
New Jersey	66,358	17,950	22,642	14,975	3,240	382	1,666	139	324	93	331	22	1,474	32	310	171	2,607
Pennsylvania	239,666	76,424	84,658	39,724	9,957	9,771	5,596	402	963	169	334	68	4,709	116	946	438	5,331
South Atlantic division.	92,109	23,555	36,260	14,689	5,338	946	2,282	144	583	196	316	89	2,098	37	1,035	269	4,272
Delaware	3,741	1,510	759	960	147	27	71	6	44	5	10	......	102	1	26	12	61
Maryland	36,668	7,808	20,046	4,331	1,500	423	475	42	100	44	84	46	638	14	155	102	851
Dist. of Columbia..	7,386	2,170	2,300	1,413	430	52	253	22	37	12	53	......	169	8	166	14	287
Virginia	9,596	2,661	2,692	1,968	663	97	302	24	71	33	32	15	287	2	231	34	484
West Virginia	13,292	4,228	5,053	2,065	582	232	281	15	21	1	7	4	271	7	88	8	429
North Carolina	3,581	774	1,026	745	559	5	130	2	23	3	18	......	86	......	34	4	163
South Carolina	4,009	1,172	1,295	561	379	6	78	5	48	12	27	13	93	1	61	41	217
Georgia	8,209	2,461	2,096	1,486	653	66	322	15	86	15	43	9	289	1	105	33	529
Florida	5,627	771	993	1,160	425	38	361	13	144	71	42	2	163	3	169	21	1,251
North Central division.	1,216,790	192,058	491,375	181,762	44,156	15,500	138,756	15,452	15,684	27,063	6,922	5,984	27,388	624	1,906	1,658	50,442
Ohio	192,385	32,030	100,527	25,907	5,765	4,792	7,539	686	605	58	198	300	5,594	135	367	230	7,637
Indiana	86,205	12,524	47,626	10,544	2,676	560	3,677	334	635	58	161	14	3,164	22	145	96	3,971
Illinois	202,979	38,176	85,761	33,759	8,134	1,606	14,041	1,706	3,400	2,051	1,878	856	5,008	111	458	300	6,734
Michigan	142,105	15,077	29,635	27,289	5,799	556	46,584	5,098	704	392	475	173	2,549	40	156	211	6,407
Wisconsin	124,608	14,869	55,678	13,868	3,541	1,877	14,556	2,385	862	6,004	1,154	1,370	1,244	65	70	95	6,370
Minnesota	78,704	11,166	24,672	7,459	2,222	782	13,131	2,424	2,810	8,603	720	686	1,013	43	73	137	2,853
Iowa	119,712	23,106	39,831	19,611	5,259	1,831	13,257	584	2,343	4,152	1,128	1,040	2,209	40	96	100	5,125
Missouri	118,993	19,084	62,283	14,773	3,468	870	5,788	472	955	157	482	452	3,609	84	437	185	5,294
North Dakota	9,036	1,022	1,621	936	347	41	2,015	365	205	1,988	73	105	82	7	......	7	222
South Dakota	20,289	2,913	4,753	3,029	820	339	4,022	351	308	2,095	273	132	286	18	29	52	869
Nebraska	52,418	8,452	17,693	9,879	2,437	1,075	6,368	258	1,376	480	717	584	898	17	52	132	2,000
Kansas	69,260	12,133	21,295	14,708	3,688	1,171	7,778	789	1,481	427	663	263	1,732	42	83	113	2,900
South Central division.	152,688	28,773	55,365	19,495	6,089	913	5,442	344	1,279	582	857	272	12,521	147	2,632	466	17,511
Kentucky	32,946	7,366	17,164	3,779	1,058	217	819	43	90	6	30	14	998	14	219	30	1,099
Tennessee	12,304	3,654	3,282	2,152	728	166	651	18	123	21	42	10	411	31	214	28	773
Alabama	8,522	2,384	2,199	1,548	699	122	279	8	91	28	54	11	395	18	98	34	554
Mississippi	7,944	2,305	1,886	1,226	435	16	266	8	106	49	58	5	569	5	211	27	772
Louisiana	29,394	4,085	7,955	2,578	616	78	617	125	252	79	211	6	7,769	11	1,398	88	3,526
Texas	49,470	6,519	18,805	5,909	1,873	221	1,893	110	444	352	369	215	1,877	60	393	205	10,105
Oklahoma	1,628	265	471	306	118	14	274	3	17	10	12	8	38	1	2	9	80
Arkansas	10,480	2,195	3,543	1,937	562	79	643	29	156	37	81	3	464	7	97	45	602
Western division....	168,214	27,447	31,557	39,170	10,393	3,387	23,401	1,372	2,885	1,611	3,733	90	4,805	127	2,162	578	15,406
Montana	7,260	1,635	1,470	1,394	440	152	1,380	149	80	74	67	14	155	7	11	20	203
Wyoming	3,100	595	522	868	240	98	432	19	79	17	58	......	65	......	4	......	112
Colorado	10,282	3,958	4,276	4,214	1,234	538	2,897	141	295	73	130	10	520	18	114	48	821
New Mexico	8,947	501	675	429	139	27	328	24	10	12	16	5	177	5	42	10	1,547
Arizona	2,747	302	345	553	149	33	230	13	21	7	75	......	103	4	18	5	889
Utah	16,889	849	583	9,090	1,512	835	965	26	567	271	1,510	......	124	7	61	8	481
Nevada	2,621	640	380	508	171	59	511	20	21	17	50	6	60	1	21	9	147
Idaho	5,480	681	696	1,932	396	333	660	27	92	121	253	1	88	......	11	20	169
Washington	18,389	2,674	3,692	3,602	1,382	351	4,007	419	437	278	366	8	847	10	82	76	658
Oregon	15,521	2,081	3,922	3,376	1,013	183	2,670	134	315	207	241	3	357	10	55	80	874
California	72,969	13,531	14,906	13,204	3,708	778	9,321	400	968	534	967	43	2,809	65	1,743	307	9,595

FOREIGN PARENTAGE.

691

TABLE **41.**—NATIVE WHITE PERSONS HAVING FATHERS BORN IN SPECIFIED COUNTRIES AND NATIVE MOTHERS, BY STATES AND TERRITORIES: 1890.

STATES AND TERRITORIES.	Total.	Ireland.	Germany.	England.	Scotland.	Wales.	Canada (English).	Canada (French).	Sweden.	Norway.	Denmark.	Bohemia.	France.	Hungary.	Italy.	Russia.	Other countries.
United States..	2,378,729	502,155	827,823	386,711	97,661	34,863	227,144	42,356	23,810	29,883	13,077	6,744	61,187	1,390	11,096	4,962	107,267
North Atlantic division.	778,339	234,252	217,100	136,340	33,753	14,315	67,466	25,776	3,713	940	2,038	410	14,964	476	3,426	2,088	21,282
Maine	18,020	2,703	426	2,862	721	105	7,821	2,455	136	53	80	....	205	5	61	20	307
New Hampshire...	8,488	1,713	255	1,442	412	10	2,782	1,559	31	16	10	4	91	......	34	14	106
Vermont..........	16,206	2,944	251	1,484	824	126	5,591	4,717	21	2	8	7	165	3	10	9	134
Massachusetts.....	80,536	28,615	5,139	14,306	3,576	708	15,875	7,172	621	203	254	6	1,057	11	483	152	2,408
Rhode Island	11,555	4,302	711	2,918	728	25	1,112	1,032	86	22	9	......	140	.....	77	10	323
Connecticut	25,487	10,485	3,827	5,522	1,276	150	1,618	947	160	33	92	7	524	7	94	68	608
New York	315,002	89,766	99,872	53,737	13,209	3,147	25,739	7,366	1,382	352	916	296	6,001	310	1,490	1,225	6,504
New Jersey........	65,433	17,762	22,430	14,772	3,181	375	1,556	134	321	90	327	22	1,449	29	305	170	2,510
Pennsylvania......	237,522	75,902	84,189	39,297	9,826	9,669	5,372	394	946	169	333	68	4,732	111	922	420	5,172
South Atlantic division.	91,317	23,412	36,106	14,514	5,277	941	2,165	136	582	194	313	88	2,076	36	1,022	258	4,107
Delaware	3,700	1,497	754	951	144	27	63	4	44	5	10	.....	101	1	20	12	61
Maryland.........	36,434	7,759	19,977	4,283	1,491	423	456	41	100	44	84	45	633	14	150	94	831
Dist. of Columbia..	7,293	2,147	2,280	1,397	422	51	243	22	37	12	53	.....	164	8	163	13	281
Virginia	9,467	2,635	2,674	1,931	657	96	282	22	70	33	32	15	283	2	231	33	471
West Virginia.....	13,250	4,222	5,043	2,059	575	231	272	15	21	1	7	4	260	6	88	8	429
North Carolina	3,547	771	1,023	732	555	5	131	....	23	3	18	......	85	.....	34	4	109
South Carolina	3,973	1,164	1,285	556	373	6	78	5	48	11	24	13	93	1	61	41	214
Georgia..........	8,145	2,455	2,084	1,470	642	65	311	14	86	15	43	9	287	1	105	32	526
Florida	5,508	762	986	1,135	418	37	329	13	144	70	42	2	161	3	164	21	1,221
North Central division.	1,194,070	189,042	488,347	178,227	42,648	15,352	130,249	14,787	15,403	26,580	6,774	5,902	27,022	611	1,917	1,594	49,624
Ohio.............	190,917	31,820	100,149	25,672	5,654	4,770	7,213	664	600	57	197	308	5,589	132	356	221	7,535
Indiana..........	85,642	12,427	47,491	10,444	2,641	556	3,556	327	628	56	160	14	3,145	21	141	95	3,046
Illinois...........	199,982	37,608	85,157	33,246	7,003	1,584	13,354	1,654	3,334	1,944	849	842	4,958	110	447	203	6,579
Michigan.........	133,783	14,985	29,202	25,891	5,257	523	42,364	4,755	692	378	457	106	2,444	37	148	206	6,278
Wisconsin........	122,851	14,082	55,343	13,675	3,445	1,865	13,990	2,332	843	6,467	1,144	1,857	1,223	65	69	61	6,254
Minnesota........	76,761	10,930	24,401	7,235	2,077	770	12,414	2,331	2,725	8,487	704	663	973	42	72	120	2,811
Iowa.............	118,165	22,900	30,802	19,388	5,158	1,811	12,752	565	2,296	4,095	1,077	1,035	2,180	38	96	98	5,074
Missouri..........	118,072	19,550	62,030	14,612	3,410	863	5,609	455	949	156	470	450	3,576	84	430	182	5,237
North Dakota	8,363	908	1,585	853	284	58	1,683	341	204	1,981	72	105	78	7	....	7	217
South Dakota......	19,742	2,835	4,713	2,961	763	335	3,795	341	307	2,061	271	129	284	16	28	45	858
Nebraska........	51,433	8,335	17,484	9,716	2,387	1,070	6,048	249	1,353	474	706	573	875	17	48	127	1,971
Kansas	68,368	12,002	21,190	14,534	3,609	1,161	7,465	773	1,472	424	658	260	1,717	42	82	100	2,870
South Central division.	151,005	28,573	55,055	19,274	6,010	898	5,233	337	1,274	575	850	266	12,408	147	2,610	459	17,030
Kentucky	32,772	7,330	17,115	3,744	1,046	216	789	41	90	6	30	14	994	14	218	30	1,005
Tennessee	12,156	3,620	3,263	2,121	721	106	608	18	121	21	41	10	406	31	212	28	708
Alabama	8,429	2,363	2,189	1,527	692	118	264	8	91	27	54	11	391	18	97	34	515
Mississippi........	7,884	2,205	1,879	1,214	430	16	258	8	106	49	58	5	502	5	208	26	705
Louisiana.........	29,158	4,055	7,921	2,551	611	78	603	125	252	77	208	6	7,710	11	1,390	86	3,474
Texas	48,624	6,466	18,695	5,895	1,839	214	1,826	110	442	348	366	209	1,849	60	386	203	9,716
Oklahoma	1,607	261	468	305	117	14	264	3	17	10	12	8	38	1	2	0	78
Arkansas.........	10,375	2,183	3,525	1,917	554	76	621	24	155	37	81	3	458	7	97	43	594
Western division	163,989	26,876	31,215	38,356	9,973	3,357	22,031	1,320	2,838	1,594	3,702	78	4,717	120	2,121	563	15,128
Montana	7,026	1,585	1,457	1,354	410	149	1,309	143	80	72	67	14	150	7	11	20	198
Wyoming.........	3,029	582	513	854	231	97	402	17	79	17	58	......	65	......	4	....	110
Colorado..........	18,804	3,901	4,236	4,140	1,185	533	2,698	135	290	73	129	10	509	18	110	40	797
New Mexico.......	3,857	489	672	413	137	27	311	23	10	12	16	5	177	5	41	10	1,509
Arizona	2,655	295	343	544	142	33	217	13	21	7	74	......	98	4	18	5	841
Utah	16,747	841	575	9,039	1,503	831	928	24	564	269	1,409	......	123	7	59	8	477
Nevada	2,569	635	377	500	163	59	493	20	20	17	50	6	59	1	10	9	141
Idaho............	5,412	671	693	1,914	390	333	634	27	91	120	253	......	88	......	11	10	108
Washington	17,658	2,579	3,365	3,463	1,295	345	3,693	404	426	274	365	6	333	9	77	76	643
Oregon	15,119	2,017	3,886	3,305	970	182	2,537	129	308	205	237	3	347	10	55	75	853
California	71,118	13,281	14,798	12,830	3,547	768	8,809	385	949	528	954	34	2,708	59	1,716	301	9,391

692   STATISTICS OF POPULATION.

TABLE **42.**—FOREIGN WHITE PERSONS HAVING FATHERS BORN IN SPECIFIED COUNTRIES AND NATIVE MOTHERS, BY STATES AND TERRITORIES: 1890.

STATES AND TERRITORIES.	Total.	Ireland.	Germany.	England.	Scotland.	Wales.	Canada (English).	Canada (French).	Sweden.	Norway.	Denmark.	Bohemia.	France.	Hungary.	Italy.	Russia.	Other countries.
United States..	45,964	6,579	5,438	7,457	3,049	348	15,943	2,109	417	522	211	109	868	47	241	178	2,448
North Atlantic division.	16,553	2,649	1,604	2,712	981	150	5,740	1,377	83	13	22	8	279	26	116	81	712
Maine	1,210	89	7	138	50	1	762	145	2	1	1	......	8	......	1	......	5
New Hampshire	000	51	6	72	33	......	308	143	......	1	2	......	6	......	3	3	5
Vermont	1,098	96	1	100	50	1	584	251	......	......	......	......	10	......	......	......	5
Massachusetts	3,408	429	69	518	200	4	1,614	423	20	3	3	1	24	......	17	12	71
Rhode Island	308	48	3	43	31	1	94	65	2	......	......	......	6	......	3	......	12
Connecticut	506	97	38	99	25	4	112	77	15	1	......	......	6	2	4	4	22
New York	6,321	1,129	799	1,112	402	30	1,932	260	24	5	12	5	157	16	59	43	336
New Jersey	925	188	212	203	59	7	110	5	3	3	4	......	25	3	5	1	97
Pennsylvania	2,144	522	469	427	131	102	224	8	17	......	1	......	37	5	24	18	159
South Atlantic division.	792	143	154	175	61	5	117	8	1	2	3	1	22	1	13	11	75
Delaware	41	13	5	9	3	......	8	2	......	......	......	......	1	......	......	......	......
Maryland	234	49	69	48	9	......	19	1	......	......	......	1	5	......	5	8	20
Dist. of Columbia	93	23	20	16	8	1	10	......	......	......	......	......	5	......	3	1	6
Virginia	129	26	18	37	6	1	20	2	1	......	......	......	4	......	......	1	13
West Virginia	42	6	10	6	7	1	9	......	......	......	......	......	2	1	......	......	......
North Carolina	34	3	3	13	4	......	8	2	......	......	......	......	1	......	......	......	......
South Carolina	36	8	10	5	6	......	......	......	1	3	......	......	......	......	......	......	3
Georgia	64	6	12	16	11	1	11	1	......	......	......	......	2	......	......	1	3
Florida	110	9	7	25	7	1	32	......	......	1	......	......	2	......	5	......	30
North Central division.	22,711	3,016	3,028	3,535	1,508	148	8,507	665	281	483	148	82	366	13	49	64	818
Ohio	1,468	216	378	235	111	22	326	22	5	1	1	1	25	3	11	9	102
Indiana	563	97	135	100	35	4	121	7	7	......	1	......	19	1	4	1	31
Illinois	2,997	508	604	513	171	22	687	52	66	107	29	14	50	1	11	7	155
Michigan	8,322	992	483	1,308	542	33	4,220	343	12	14	18	7	105	3	8	5	189
Wisconsin	1,757	187	335	193	96	12	560	53	19	137	10	13	21	......	1	4	116
Minnesota	2,033	236	271	224	145	6	717	93	85	116	16	23	40	1	1	17	42
Iowa	1,547	206	229	223	101	20	505	10	47	57	51	5	29	2	......	2	51
Missouri	921	134	253	161	58	7	179	17	6	1	3	2	33	......	7	3	57
North Dakota	673	114	36	83	63	3	332	24	1	7	1	......	4	......	......	......	5
South Dakota	547	78	40	68	57	4	227	10	1	84	2	3	2	2	1	7	11
Nebraska	985	117	209	163	50	5	320	9	23	6	11	11	23	......	4	5	29
Kansas	808	131	105	174	79	10	313	16	9	3	5	3	15	......	1	4	30
South Central division.	1,683	200	310	221	79	15	209	7	5	7	7	6	113	......	22	7	475
Kentucky	174	36	49	35	12	1	30	2	......	......	......	......	4	......	1	......	4
Tennessee	148	34	19	31	7	......	43	......	2	......	1	......	5	......	2	......	4
Alabama	93	21	10	21	7	4	15	......	......	1	......	......	4	......	1	......	9
Mississippi	60	10	7	12	5	......	8	......	......	......	......	......	7	......	3	1	7
Louisiana	236	30	34	27	5	......	14	......	......	2	3	......	50	......	8	2	52
Texas	846	53	170	74	34	7	67	......	2	4	3	6	28	......	7	2	389
Oklahoma	21	4	3	1	1	......	10	......	......	......	......	......	......	......	......	......	2
Arkansas	105	12	18	20	8	3	22	5	1	......	......	......	6	......	......	2	8
Western division	4,225	571	342	814	420	30	1,370	52	47	17	31	12	88	7	41	15	308
Montana	234	50	13	40	39	3	71	6	......	2	......	......	5	......	......	......	5
Wyoming	80	13	9	14	9	1	30	2	......	......	......	......	5	......	......	......	2
Colorado	478	57	40	74	49	5	109	6	5	......	1	......	11	......	4	3	24
New Mexico	90	12	3	16	2	......	17	1	......	......	......	......	5	......	1	......	38
Arizona	92	7	2	9	7	......	13	......	......	......	1	......	5	......	......	......	48
Utah	142	8	8	51	9	4	37	2	3	2	11	......	1	......	2	......	4
Nevada	52	5	3	8	8	......	18	......	1	......	......	......	1	......	2	......	6
Idaho	68	10	3	18	6	......	26	......	1	1	......	1	......	......	......	1	1
Washington	736	95	27	139	87	6	314	15	11	4	1	2	14	1	5	......	15
Oregon	402	64	36	71	43	1	133	5	7	2	4	......	10	......	......	5	21
California	1,851	250	198	374	161	10	512	15	19	6	13	9	41	6	27	6	204

FOREIGN PARENTAGE. 693

TABLE 43.—WHITE PERSONS HAVING MOTHERS BORN IN SPECIFIED COUNTRIES AND NATIVE FATHERS, BY STATES AND TERRITORIES: 1890.

STATES AND TERRITORIES.	Total.	Ireland.	Germany.	England.	Scotland.	Wales.	Canada (English).	Canada (French).	Sweden.	Norway.	Denmark.	Bohemia.	France.	Hungary.	Italy.	Russia.	Other countries.
United States..	1,083,169	262,305	242,117	198,347	46,911	15,497	193,393	26,922	11,802	15,499	4,699	3,296	16,426	321	1,256	1,330	43,048
North Atlantic division.	420,790	148,558	62,713	78,714	19,175	6,855	68,576	18,120	1,827	264	302	149	4,727	140	438	433	9,700
Maine	14,899	1,644	94	1,686	298	20	8,596	2,251	83	11	14	8	48	2	3	2	130
New Hampshire...	7,424	1,458	111	1,011	297	12	3,156	1,164	33	10	1	....	20	5	4	3	130
Vermont	10,724	1,707	67	705	321	22	4,896	2,854	2	1	....	4	35	1	2	3	104
Massachusetts	66,679	23,889	1,418	10,262	2,698	232	20,439	5,039	330	35	30	8	355	1	60	20	1,857
Rhode Island	9,967	4,354	228	2,281	626	42	1,187	893	59	14	3	....	40	1	4	13	222
Connecticut	16,952	8,004	1,277	3,903	977	73	1,285	721	146	10	10	5	130	2	26	8	306
New York	162,118	57,930	28,092	30,484	6,656	1,429	23,910	4,981	649	129	130	95	2,377	109	216	281	3,741
New Jersey	32,953	13,098	6,541	7,834	1,860	240	1,149	76	125	22	51	6	461	7	49	26	1,408
Pennsylvania	99,074	36,474	23,985	20,488	5,442	4,785	3,958	141	400	32	54	23	1,252	12	74	71	1,883
South Atlantic division.	32,406	10,529	9,930	5,782	1,959	311	1,356	65	96	40	41	21	483	6	78	48	1,711
Delaware	1,804	1,018	159	452	97	12	66	2	18	....	5	....	19	....	1	3	42
Maryland	13,886	3,896	6,256	2,054	615	144	352	25	17	4	3	15	151	1	16	20	317
Dist. of Columbia..	3,599	1,503	760	669	160	20	194	18	16	12	11	....	58	....	12	....	160
Virginia	2,551	787	468	697	221	14	158	1	2	1	8	1	66	1	15	1	110
West Virginia	4,298	1,463	1,273	774	340	79	136	6	3	6	3	....	63	....	4	0	130
North Carolina	1,182	398	181	223	193	12	88	1	3	....	....	....	11	....	7	2	63
South Carolina	1,056	480	243	126	95	....	22	1	11	1	5	....	15	4	0	3	100
Georgia	1,886	682	352	368	126	19	131	5	18	7	3	4	59	....	0	3	100
Florida	2,054	302	238	369	112	11	209	6	8	9	3	1	41	....	7	2	736
North Central division.	504,135	78,254	147,261	85,221	18,945	6,066	106,728	8,029	7,772	14,190	2,160	2,975	7,890	136	264	637	17,607
Ohio	72,473	14,108	30,410	12,292	2,555	2,161	5,470	335	195	51	27	94	1,808	17	32	70	2,890
Indiana	28,368	4,810	13,371	4,290	1,006	160	2,310	167	209	39	17	11	748	6	20	80	1,174
Illinois	79,977	16,934	25,225	14,730	3,239	619	10,756	928	1,824	1,180	273	374	1,361	7	66	100	2,952
Michigan	84,881	8,510	10,864	13,916	2,858	234	40,042	3,110	338	215	186	99	1,039	15	15	60	2,502
Wisconsin	50,605	5,576	18,518	7,241	1,436	663	8,920	949	390	3,468	369	542	385	11	27	27	2,083
Minnesota	36,470	4,424	8,757	3,923	994	285	8,794	1,089	1,663	4,386	285	422	290	12	7	74	1,095
Iowa	48,691	8,137	11,529	9,151	2,418	720	10,190	300	1,094	1,850	367	509	610	8	18	26	1,698
Missouri	35,532	6,677	14,488	6,078	1,272	346	3,530	183	231	82	93	174	835	27	53	56	1,467
North Dakota	5,469	453	667	539	189	19	1,840	210	119	1,191	44	68	25	4	1	1	90
South Dakota	10,735	1,260	1,854	1,605	497	176	3,128	196	215	1,155	73	73	95	5	5	45	353
Nebraska	23,882	3,298	5,681	5,192	1,000	264	5,224	185	787	420	271	410	279	3	14	40	805
Kansas	26,902	4,058	5,897	6,255	1,481	419	5,609	377	707	153	155	139	415	21	6	81	1,120
South Central division.	42,533	9,350	13,178	6,150	1,711	318	2,201	61	257	133	80	122	2,078	22	237	95	6,631
Kentucky	9,256	2,491	3,963	1,347	374	82	335	8	17	1	7	4	264	1	17	15	330
Tennessee	3,468	1,190	710	642	165	79	265	1	29	5	7	....	89	3	30	7	237
Alabama	2,200	661	438	438	220	22	112	8	13	5	3	10	88	7	10	0	150
Mississippi	1,519	527	248	326	100	1	75	....	20	5	6	....	100	....	0	8	94
Louisiana	7,758	2,166	2,435	672	174	12	189	16	19	12	21	2	1,000	1	98	13	628
Texas	15,135	1,650	4,645	1,702	498	73	774	21	122	97	22	90	441	10	43	28	4,910
Oklahoma	664	130	113	139	42	5	158	2	8	....	8	11	6	....	....	7	85
Arkansas	2,533	535	626	584	138	44	293	5	29	8	6	5	90	....	24	8	138
Western division	83,305	15,605	9,035	22,530	5,121	1,947	14,532	647	1,850	872	2,116	29	1,248	17	239	117	7,400
Montana	3,417	662	402	708	238	90	871	89	87	62	56	11	38	....	2	4	97
Wyoming	1,946	315	231	573	165	80	340	17	62	17	56	3	23	....	1	....	67
Colorado	9,048	1,875	1,287	2,082	616	197	1,953	77	283	42	75	3	184	3	39	12	320
New Mexico	1,726	165	153	233	53	15	170	3	8	1	10	....	16	....	1	....	808
Arizona	2,281	190	81	496	72	22	163	4	43	23	65	....	13	....	3	1	1,105
Utah	12,792	814	226	7,299	1,061	691	595	30	570	201	1,368	....	46	3	45	1	342
Nevada	1,516	423	165	318	119	57	261	13	33	2	28	....	15	....	5	....	77
Idaho	3,070	249	221	1,205	218	259	407	23	139	55	180	....	25	....	4	....	85
Washington	8,582	1,273	1,241	1,726	486	152	2,613	113	179	240	58	8	135	....	4	21	333
Oregon	5,042	811	1,105	1,308	394	80	1,464	63	109	62	50	2	85	3	5	11	300
California	32,985	9,332	3,923	6,582	1,699	304	5,605	215	337	167	170	2	668	8	130	67	3,086

694

STATISTICS OF POPULATION.

TABLE **44.**—NATIVE WHITE PERSONS HAVING MOTHERS BORN IN SPECIFIED COUNTRIES AND NATIVE FATHERS, BY STATES AND TERRITORIES: 1890.

STATES AND TERRITORIES.	Total.	Ireland.	Germany.	England.	Scotland.	Wales.	Canada (English).	Canada (French).	Sweden.	Norway.	Denmark.	Bohemia.	France.	Hungary.	Italy.	Russia.	Other countries.
United States..	1,039,927	257,620	238,170	193,131	45,117	15,265	171,883	24,978	11,591	15,089	4,579	3,233	15,986	248	1,126	1,175	40,826
North Atlantic division.	406,129	146,718	61,741	76,763	18,635	6,743	61,633	16,927	1,781	251	295	147	4,563	77	387	352	9,116
Maine	13,284	1,570	88	1,535	255	20	7,414	2,123	81	10	14	8	44	2	3	1	116
New Hampshire ...	6,827	1,417	109	971	284	12	2,798	1,036	30	10	1	....	17	5	4	3	130
Vermont............	9,090	1,640	64	916	301	22	4,175	2,683	2	1	....	4	31	1	2	3	102
Massachusetts.....	63,411	23,594	1,384	9,872	2,581	226	18,506	4,634	326	34	30	8	321	1	53	22	1,729
Rhode Island	9,697	4,314	220	2,244	614	41	1,115	825	57	14	3	....	35	1	3	11	200
Connecticut	16,609	7,932	1,256	3,902	958	70	1,203	666	144	10	10	5	136	1	25	6	285
New York.........	156,707	57,147	28,531	29,690	6,451	1,404	21,559	4,755	634	120	133	93	2,308	52	193	224	3,413
New Jersey.......	32,381	12,956	6,442	7,712	1,825	236	1,057	70	124	22	50	6	447	7	46	24	1,357
Pennsylvania......	97,553	36,145	23,047	20,211	5,366	4,712	3,710	135	383	30	54	23	1,224	7	58	58	1,784
South Atlantic division.	31,605	10,407	9,777	5,581	1,916	301	1,178	58	93	39	39	20	465	6	67	46	1,612
Delaware	1,852	1,011	157	443	94	12	52	1	17	....	4	....	18	....	1	3	39
Maryland........	13,641	3,853	6,101	2,010	600	144	308	22	17	4	3	15	143	1	15	19	206
Dist. of Columbia..	3,400	1,470	720	648	152	18	173	17	16	12	11	....	54	....	9	....	100
Virginia..........	2,464	774	454	675	216	14	137	1	1	1	8	1	66	1	14	1	100
West Virginia.....	4,255	1,454	1,262	767	339	75	129	5	3	6	3	....	62	....	3	9	138
North Carolina	1,154	397	179	217	192	12	81	....	3	....	....	....	10	....	2	2	59
South Carolina	1,038	478	237	123	92	....	19	1	11	1	5	....	15	4	7	7	38
Georgia..........	1,819	673	344	355	123	19	112	5	17	6	2	3	56	....	9	3	92
Florida...........	1,922	297	233	343	108	7	167	6	8	9	3	1	41	....	7	2	690
North Central division.	481,543	76,063	144,897	82,817	18,023	5,983	94,221	7,367	7,552	13,809	2,066	2,918	7,720	128	240	579	17,160
Ohio	71,270	13,957	30,128	12,088	2,503	2,141	5,065	309	192	51	27	93	1,788	12	30	77	2,809
Indiana...........	27,867	4,743	13,249	4,298	990	150	2,107	161	207	36	17	11	736	6	20	30	1,101
Illinois	77,445	16,594	24,712	14,446	3,129	608	9,848	880	1,741	1,103	251	562	1,343	7	58	88	2,275
Michigan	75,359	7,721	10,579	12,944	2,481	222	34,260	2,770	920	212	182	64	986	14	11	64	2,484
Wisconsin	48,871	5,422	18,193	7,073	1,387	657	8,161	888	382	3,304	362	536	379	11	25	28	2,085
Minnesota.........	34,582	4,258	8,544	3,759	919	282	7,874	1,014	1,602	4,271	272	405	282	11	7	57	1,025
Iowa	47,242	7,995	11,378	8,983	2,363	708	9,422	283	1,074	1,810	333	564	601	8	17	25	1,678
Missouri..........	34,782	6,574	14,308	5,983	1,237	340	3,254	167	225	82	89	173	814	27	48	49	1,412
North Dakota......	4,876	385	652	503	147	19	1,468	175	117	1,185	44	68	24	4	1	1	83
South Dakota......	10,129	1,195	1,818	1,566	469	173	2,762	185	215	1,126	71	73	91	5	5	34	341
Nebraska.........	23,045	3,230	5,530	5,103	959	259	4,808	173	774	416	264	401	272	3	13	48	792
Kansas	26,075	3,980	5,812	6,131	1,469	415	5,192	353	697	153	154	138	402	20	5	80	1,095
South Central division.	41,282	9,237	12,897	6,034	1,668	317	2,027	60	255	130	79	119	2,039	22	217	90	6,091
Kentucky	9,110	2,448	3,916	1,331	362	82	319	8	17	1	7	4	260	1	16	15	323
Tennessee	3,391	1,183	693	631	157	78	255	....	20	5	7	....	89	3	30	7	224
Alabama	2,151	652	431	432	216	22	97	8	13	5	3	10	86	7	10	5	144
Mississippi	1,493	520	246	323	97	1	73	....	20	4	6	....	95	....	9	8	91
Louisiana.........	7,611	2,149	2,390	951	172	12	175	16	18	12	21	2	976	1	92	13	602
Texas	14,422	1,628	4,494	1,653	486	73	700	21	121	95	21	88	438	10	30	25	4,539
Oklahoma	631	126	108	136	42	5	139	2	8	....	8	11	6	....	....	5	35
Arkansas.........	2,473	531	610	577	136	44	269	5	29	8	6	4	89	....	24	8	133
Western division....	79,368	15,195	8,858	21,936	4,875	1,921	12,824	566	1,820	800	2,100	29	1,199	15	215	108	6,847
Montana..........	3,152	620	386	680	219	84	758	61	85	62	56	11	37	....	2	4	87
Wyoming.........	1,879	305	228	561	158	79	312	15	61	16	56	3	22	....	1	....	62
Colorado..........	8,640	1,826	1,271	2,026	598	194	1,732	70	278	42	72	3	178	2	34	11	303
New Mexico	1,628	160	148	219	51	15	151	3	8	1	10	....	16	....	....	....	846
Arizona...........	2,164	186	80	485	69	22	140	4	43	23	63	....	12	....	3	1	1,024
Utah.............	12,645	302	222	7,245	1,049	688	559	26	563	109	1,366	....	45	3	45	1	332
Nevada	1,450	418	164	309	113	56	226	15	33	2	28	....	15	....	3	....	70
Idaho	2,081	242	220	1,184	213	259	356	23	137	55	180	....	24	....	4	....	84
Washington	7,921	1,202	1,222	1,617	447	148	2,252	102	177	234	58	8	130	....	1	18	305
Oregon...........	5,615	783	1,088	1,256	360	79	1,315	54	107	60	48	2	80	3	4	9	367
California.........	31,293	9,151	3,829	6,354	1,598	297	5,014	195	328	166	163	2	640	7	118	64	3,367

FOREIGN PARENTAGE.

695

TABLE 45.—FOREIGN WHITE PERSONS HAVING MOTHERS BORN IN SPECIFIED COUNTRIES AND NATIVE FATHERS, BY STATES AND TERRITORIES: 1890.

STATES AND TERRITORIES.	Total.	Ireland.	Germany.	England.	Scotland.	Wales.	Canada (English).	Canada (French).	Sweden.	Norway.	Denmark.	Bohemia.	France.	Hungary.	Italy.	Russia.	Other countries.
United States	43,242	4,685	3,947	5,216	1,794	232	21,510	1,944	301	410	120	63	440	73	130	155	2,222
North Atlantic division.	14,661	1,840	972	1,951	540	112	6,943	1,193	46	13	7	2	164	63	51	81	683
Maine	1,615	74	6	151	43		1,182	128	2	1			4			1	23
New Hampshire	597	41	2	40	17		358	128	3				3				9
Vermont	1,064	64	3	79	20		721	171					4				2
Massachusetts	3,268	295	34	390	117	6	1,843	405	4	1			34		7	4	128
Rhode Island	270	40	8	37	12	1	72	68	2				5		1	2	22
Connecticut	343	72	21	64	10	3	82	55	2				3	1	1	2	21
New York	5,411	783	461	794	205	25	2,351	226	15	9	6	2	69	37	23	57	328
New Jersey	572	142	90	122	35	4	92	6	1		1		14		3	2	51
Pennsylvania	1,521	329	358	277	76	73	242	6	17	2			28	5	16	13	90
South Atlantic division.	801	122	153	151	43	10	178	7	3	1	2	1	18		11	2	99
Delaware	42	7	2	3	3		14	1	1		1		1				3
Maryland	245	43	65	44	15		44	3					8		1	1	21
Dist. of Columbia	139	33	40	21	8	2	21	1					4		3		6
Virginia	87	13	14	22	5		21		1						1		10
West Virginia	43	9	11	7	1	4	7	1					1		1		1
North Carolina	28	1	2	6	1		7	1					1		5		4
South Carolina	18	2	6	3	3		3									1	
Georgia	67	9	8	13	3		19		1	1	1	1	3				8
Florida	132	5	5	26	4	4	42										46
North Central division.	22,592	2,191	2,364	2,404	922	83	12,507	662	220	381	94	57	170	8	24	58	447
Ohio	1,20?	151	282	204	52	20	405	26	3			1	20	5	2	2	30
Indiana	561	67	128	52	16	1	203	6	2	3			10				13
Illinois	2,532	340	513	293	110	11	908	48	83	77	22	12	18		8	12	77
Michigan	9,622	798	285	972	377	12	6,882	331	12	3	4	5	53	1	4	5	78
Wisconsin	1,734	154	325	168	49	6	759	61	8	104	7	6	6		2	1	78
Minnesota	1,888	166	213	164	75	3	920	75	61	115	13	17	8	1		17	40
Iowa	1,440	142	151	168	55	12	774	17	20	40	34	5	9		1	1	20
Missouri	800	103	180	95	35	6	276	16	6		4	1	21		5	7	45
North Dakota	593	68	15	36	42		381	35	2	6			1				7
South Dakota	606	65	36	39	28	3	366	11		29	2		4			11	12
Nebraska	837	68	151	89	41	5	416	12	13	4	7	0	7		1	1	13
Kansas	827	69	85	124	42	4	417	24	10		1	1	13	1	1	1	34
South Central division.	1,251	122	281	116	43	1	174	1	2	3	1	3	39		20	5	440
Kentucky	146	43	47	16	12		16						4		1		7
Tennessee	77	16	17	11	8	1	10	1									13
Alabama	49	9	7	6	4		15						2				6
Mississippi	26	7	2	3	3		2			1			5				3
Louisiana	147	17	36	21	2		14		1				24		6		26
Texas	713	22	151	49	12		74		1	2	1	2	3		13	3	380
Oklahoma	33	4	5	3			10									2	
Arkansas	60	4	16	7	2		24					1	1				5
Western division	3,937	410	177	594	246	26	1,708	81	30	12	16		49	2	24	9	553
Montana	265	42	16	28	19	6	113	28	2				1				10
Wyoming	67	6	3	12	7	1	28	2	1	1			1				5
Colorado	408	49	18	56	18	3	221	7	5		3		6	1	5	1	17
New Mexico	98	5	5	14	2		19						1				52
Arizona	117	4	1	11	3		14				2		1				81
Utah	147	12	4	54	12	3	36	4	7	2	2		1				10
Nevada	66	5	1	9	6	1	35								2		7
Idaho	89	7	1	21	5		51		2				1				1
Washington	661	71	19	109	39	4	361	11	2	6			5		3	3	28
Oregon	327	28	17	52	34	1	149	9	2	2	2		5		1	2	23
California	1,692	181	94	228	101	7	681	20	9	1	7		28	1	12	3	319

696   STATISTICS OF POPULATION.

TABLE **46.**—WHITE PERSONS HAVING FATHERS BORN IN SPECIFIED COUNTRIES AND MOTHERS BORN IN SOME OTHER FOREIGN COUNTRY, BY STATES AND TERRITORIES: 1890.

[This table gives the number of white persons of mixed foreign parentage, as shown in the last column of Table 37 (pages 685 and 687), having fathers born in specified countries, without regard to the nationality of the mother. The principal combinations of mixed foreign parentage are given by states and territories for the total number of white persons in Table 48, pages 698–701.]

STATES AND TERRITORIES.	Total.	Ireland.	Germany.	England.	Scotland.	Wales.	Canada (English).	Canada (French).	Sweden.	Norway.	Denmark.	Bohemia.	France.	Hungary.	Italy.	Russia.	Other countries.
United States..	922,268	175,312	150,443	186,475	95,317	17,425	78,881	11,144	27,038	15,555	19,480	3,435	48,351	2,733	7,210	13,579	69,881
North Atlantic division.	350,937	81,495	49,934	81,933	36,684	7,406	26,978	4,963	5,051	2,230	3,520	739	16,486	1,275	3,021	6,748	22,474
Maine	7,841	2,220	237	1,781	944	41	1,736	200	124	67	77	17	157	4	29	28	179
New Hampshire	4,295	1,129	123	1,108	461	20	791	374	36	16	9	9	129	2	5	5	78
Vermont	4,442	1,038	117	1,054	478	43	899	442	37	11	9	2	195	4	13	8	92
Massachusetts	64,470	17,061	3,631	16,318	8,094	622	9,822	1,906	923	511	533	67	1,614	61	384	560	2,357
Rhode Island	9,235	2,755	605	2,839	1,154	71	773	196	57	28	38	3	226	15	123	42	310
Connecticut	12,288	2,697	2,002	2,948	1,248	99	847	261	277	104	190	30	533	15	112	160	765
New York	143,554	28,665	25,832	30,866	13,284	1,793	9,428	1,309	2,204	1,089	1,659	458	8,199	823	1,457	4,554	11,930
New Jersey	29,662	5,270	6,836	6,764	3,138	306	698	85	512	171	551	65	1,685	91	393	360	2,668
Pennsylvania	75,150	20,647	10,551	18,255	7,883	4,351	984	190	881	233	454	88	3,748	260	505	1,010	4,104
South Atlantic division.	18,801	3,563	3,460	3,867	2,218	362	674	72	319	152	219	36	1,150	56	343	457	1,847
Delaware	1,159	293	171	280	123	21	40	7	11	9	5	......	95	17	15	10	62
Maryland	6,920	1,379	1,411	1,331	753	158	233	26	123	61	74	25	389	13	85	214	645
Dist. of Columbia	2,372	435	411	529	247	13	69	8	32	4	26	1	126	13	86	84	288
Virginia	1,871	315	282	412	271	50	80	2	25	10	19	......	135	3	46	43	178
West Virginia	2,079	551	473	361	229	89	41	8	13	......	13	1	98	4	16	11	171
North Carolina	472	72	87	111	80	2	26	1	12	11	5	......	28	......	2	5	30
South Carolina	631	73	111	91	88	......	14	4	19	8	20	......	37	......	27	34	103
Georgia	1,565	244	299	314	177	16	82	8	31	22	14	9	120	4	32	27	157
Florida	1,732	201	215	438	250	13	89	8	53	27	43	......	119	2	34	29	211
North Central division.	418,686	71,599	75,575	73,692	40,773	6,505	41,846	5,255	17,278	10,684	10,769	2,240	21,353	1,008	1,448	4,384	34,277
Ohio	43,005	8,268	9,255	8,588	3,840	1,618	2,180	269	446	63	212	200	3,717	182	214	449	1,398
Indiana	14,083	2,098	3,814	2,045	1,194	227	624	102	266	67	95	26	1,749	10	58	121	1,087
Illinois	71,947	12,673	18,852	13,148	6,857	1,008	5,046	525	2,997	1,751	2,089	414	3,896	258	372	803	6,051
Michigan	85,147	16,445	9,371	19,548	10,798	537	15,877	2,153	1,292	918	835	100	2,698	72	195	807	3,895
Wisconsin	43,233	6,143	8,411	6,150	3,100	634	4,100	722	2,057	1,888	1,649	552	1,798	84	125	245	4,000
Minnesota	42,453	6,326	6,673	4,711	3,067	328	4,591	644	5,030	3,508	2,067	243	1,494	107	76	400	3,008
Iowa	33,216	5,992	9,401	5,784	3,344	674	2,649	142	1,258	724	1,406	174	1,531	78	44	124	2,001
Missouri	25,571	3,987	6,601	4,042	2,215	369	1,147	127	518	101	296	144	2,095	93	198	895	3,163
North Dakota	10,274	2,134	862	1,598	1,596	29	1,850	161	720	488	215	22	165	14	4	104	912
South Dakota	9,622	1,428	1,636	1,446	955	152	1,005	111	715	503	381	60	303	12	19	207	904
Nebraska	19,170	2,944	4,149	3,096	1,750	409	1,333	146	934	397	1,054	248	876	47	32	210	1,545
Kansas	20,065	3,176	4,490	3,535	2,048	410	1,438	153	445	276	477	51	1,031	51	111	440	1,924
South Central division.	35,524	4,537	8,222	5,375	2,656	425	1,026	128	756	276	641	260	4,933	190	994	715	4,380
Kentucky	5,973	976	1,694	940	438	108	195	20	54	12	30	3	769	19	65	62	588
Tennessee	2,516	415	509	463	301	37	96	2	41	5	20	1	149	46	62	59	250
Alabama	2,417	361	412	513	285	73	57	8	72	23	64	3	221	12	53	25	235
Mississippi	1,402	177	279	222	113	16	52	4	36	14	16	4	208	7	50	37	167
Louisiana	9,450	802	1,896	1,228	470	51	145	47	209	68	197	21	2,283	23	537	181	1,292
Texas	11,461	1,389	2,859	1,554	857	99	333	41	310	139	298	223	1,133	75	204	322	1,625
Oklahoma	452	80	76	99	43	5	52	3	7	7	3	2	33	......	6	5	31
Arkansas	1,853	337	437	356	149	36	96	3	27	8	13	3	137	8	17	24	202
Western division	98,320	14,118	13,252	21,608	12,986	2,727	8,357	726	3,634	2,213	4,340	160	4,423	204	1,404	1,275	6,893
Montana	4,653	983	691	879	591	141	567	87	118	94	85	7	186	11	42	47	214
Wyoming	1,885	268	183	470	351	115	161	27	60	18	55	6	74	......	9	14	74
Colorado	9,928	1,842	1,266	2,113	1,390	355	883	80	231	193	234	14	445	29	100	181	662
New Mexico	1,082	186	146	249	158	37	75	1	26	10	28	......	89	1	27	18	50
Arizona	1,263	162	240	242	142	22	102	4	32	13	28	......	132	1	40	28	75
Utah	13,359	809	798	4,081	2,137	901	572	37	1,029	546	1,712	1	173	11	73	32	447
Nevada	1,884	332	252	457	225	39	182	31	53	30	61	1	75	6	30	11	90
Idaho	3,047	391	274	774	435	172	216	17	170	98	284	1	95	......	7	11	102
Washington	11,047	1,963	1,072	2,205	1,633	171	1,544	118	485	373	296	7	439	10	46	164	521
Oregon	6,576	937	1,042	1,278	832	71	620	33	278	226	183	18	243	3	62	177	579
California	43,596	6,245	7,378	8,860	5,092	703	3,435	291	1,152	672	1,402	105	2,472	132	968	642	4,047

FOREIGN PARENTAGE.

TABLE 47.—WHITE PERSONS HAVING MOTHERS BORN IN SPECIFIED COUNTRIES AND FATHERS BORN IN SOME OTHER FOREIGN COUNTRY, BY STATES AND TERRITORIES: 1890.

[This table gives the number of white persons of mixed foreign parentage, as shown in the last column of Table 37 (pages 685 and 687), having mothers born in specified countries, without regard to the nationality of the father. The principal combinations of mixed foreign parentage are given by states and territories for the total number of white persons in Table 48, pages 698–701.]

STATES AND TERRITORIES.	Total.	Ireland.	Germany.	England.	Scotland.	Wales.	Canada (English).	Canada (French).	Sweden.	Norway.	Denmark.	Bohemia.	France.	Hungary.	Italy.	Russia.	Other countries.
United States..	922,268	204,329	127,952	158,897	79,261	21,071	145,018	12,726	24,431	22,254	10,950	6,424	36,423	1,961	2,078	6,614	61,879
North Atlantic division.	350,937	105,448	38,296	71,880	33,724	9,353	47,933	6,091	3,805	1,186	1,351	715	11,527	970	688	1,899	16,062
Maine	7,841	1,887	98	1,005	647	32	3,166	580	70	29	37	13	60	......	9	8	110
New Hampshire...	4,295	1,196	81	734	455	22	1,217	377	39	20	4	3	73	5	2	......	67
Vermont..........	4,442	1,239	67	566	353	37	1,449	506	28	14	8	......	80	1	8	5	81
Massachusetts.....	64,470	20,485	1,956	12,014	6,181	620	17,783	1,939	649	216	93	52	894	29	70	171	1,318
Rhode Island	9,235	3,168	242	2,286	1,205	116	1,267	354	87	28	17	3	120	2	19	30	231
Connecticut	12,288	4,577	1,172	2,476	1,484	159	900	223	234	50	81	14	312	19	26	73	538
New York	143,554	43,583	20,957	27,838	10,738	1,535	17,150	1,873	1,725	566	660	469	6,058	636	311	1,077	8,378
New Jersey	29,662	9,884	4,278	6,344	3,078	452	1,369	71	349	129	257	32	1,257	43	70	159	1,884
Pennsylvania......	75,150	19,429	9,445	18,536	9,573	6,380	3,632	168	624	134	194	129	2,673	235	167	376	3,455
South Atlantic division.	18,801	4,864	3,383	3,832	1,992	472	1,154	89	186	36	99	42	884	55	92	151	1,470
Delaware	1,159	474	114	237	161	26	42	2	14	......	4	3	33	7	4	6	32
Maryland.........	6,920	1,779	1,550	1,335	773	199	297	27	54	18	27	29	207	14	20	80	421
Dist. of Columbia..	2,372	775	442	456	188	30	142	15	22	2	2	4	90	12	13	15	164
Virginia..........	1,871	467	260	442	173	52	154	1	12	4	16	......	112	6	18	4	150
West Virginia.....	2,079	382	369	461	298	99	99	6	13	......	14	1	100	2	6	5	224
North Carolina	472	88	59	112	47	9	83	1	2	......	3	......	33	......	1	2	41
South Carolina	631	166	143	122	44	8	24	9	5	......	1	......	37	5	2	12	53
Georgia...........	1,505	404	208	331	138	35	111	5	26	2	15	......	101	8	7	13	101
Florida...........	1,732	329	187	336	170	14	202	23	38	10	17	5	81	1	21	14	284
North Central division.	418,686	67,247	67,212	59,068	31,674	7,515	81,085	5,709	15,825	18,318	5,699	5,095	16,827	748	569	3,719	31,776
Ohio.............	43,905	8,099	9,311	8,110	3,529	2,125	4,387	262	341	57	64	237	2,823	136	81	209	4,125
Indiana..........	14,083	2,393	3,067	2,115	1,021	297	1,181	101	246	48	66	22	1,259	17	22	58	1,570
Illinois..........	71,947	13,753	12,620	12,005	5,377	1,305	9,296	736	3,274	2,650	992	684	3,359	143	154	372	5,218
Michigan.........	85,147	14,104	7,404	12,143	7,478	667	32,449	2,217	1,313	984	428	239	1,947	42	36	389	3,307
Wisconsin........	43,233	6,162	8,854	5,026	2,459	706	6,306	665	1,546	3,772	839	1,197	1,216	42	33	182	4,228
Minnesota........	42,453	5,338	5,536	3,703	2,205	261	7,547	712	4,557	6,291	936	532	983	141	58	472	3,121
Iowa	33,216	5,034	5,503	4,871	2,764	804	5,741	279	1,343	1,414	758	540	1,392	25	20	95	2,633
Missouri.........	25,571	4,373	6,110	3,976	1,677	372	2,327	151	453	112	201	347	1,954	82	112	156	3,168
North Dakota.....	10,274	1,336	562	993	1,059	33	3,855	153	492	1,009	165	62	112	6	2	164	280
South Dakota.....	9,022	1,238	4,200	1,080	702	110	1,937	94	494	986	232	192	216	21	12	494	509
Nebraska.........	19,170	2,542	2,941	2,712	1,479	316	3,072	182	1,008	686	765	855	653	46	12	281	1,620
Kansas	20,065	2,875	3,489	2,016	1,864	519	2,987	157	758	318	253	188	913	47	27	847	1,907
South Central division.	35,524	7,630	8,890	4,628	2,217	464	1,804	116	463	218	182	405	3,620	93	237	320	4,237
Kentucky	5,073	1,424	1,488	922	396	112	370	32	76	7	8	18	573	5	24	23	495
Tennessee	2,516	499	466	432	243	74	229	12	19	5	16	1	189	17	13	26	275
Alabama	2,417	630	380	399	309	88	120	17	22	10	9	7	219	16	13	17	161
Mississippi	1,402	390	380	143	91	4	55	3	12	5	16	1	168	7	7	3	128
Louisiana.........	9,450	2,711	2,823	948	231	36	162	19	99	19	15	3	1,435	10	122	46	771
Texas	11,461	1,562	2,957	1,452	684	104	573	22	210	157	109	349	857	28	54	180	2,163
Oklahoma	452	99	56	38	55	14	103	2	3	8	2	6	32	4	1	10	19
Arkansas.........	1,853	315	351	294	208	32	192	9	22	7	7	20	147	6	3	15	225
Western division	98,320	19,140	10,171	18,880	9,654	3,267	13,042	721	4,152	2,496	3,619	107	3,565	95	492	525	8,334
Montana..........	4,653	826	379	833	619	169	870	85	180	132	62	27	174	5	10	30	252
Wyoming.........	1,885	306	159	435	265	136	244	9	72	41	61	2	57	1	20	8	89
Colorado.........	9,028	1,640	1,249	2,014	1,132	350	1,408	121	404	168	173	42	470	13	36	55	593
New Mexico......	1,082	222	130	170	116	31	113	3	15	13	10	1	63	4	3	10	178
Arizona	1,263	197	108	174	101	30	99	3	23	31	48	1	60	......	5	5	378
Utah	13,350	496	384	3,898	1,561	1,235	411	15	1,508	829	2,039	2	125	9	47	3	797
Nevada	1,884	470	208	300	225	71	246	12	40	15	63	......	55	1	9	10	159
Idaho............	3,047	274	187	718	334	317	316	13	225	141	301	7	62	1	11	2	138
Washington	11,047	1,820	974	1,864	1,271	229	2,557	158	483	519	150	28	296	3	22	87	586
Oregon	6,576	1,045	940	990	641	125	1,226	74	314	227	111	17	261	15	13	79	498
California.........	43,596	11,844	5,453	7,484	3,389	574	5,492	228	888	380	601	40	1,942	43	316	236	4,686

SCHOOL, MILITIA, AND VOTING AGES.

SCHOOL, MILITIA, AND VOTING AGES.

733

TABLE **63.**—PERSONS OF SCHOOL AGE, 5 TO 17 YEARS, INCLUSIVE, BY GENERAL NATIVITY AND COLOR, BY STATES AND TERRITORIES: 1890.

STATES AND TERRITORIES.	All classes.	Native born.	Foreign born.	Aggregate white.	NATIVE WHITE.			Foreign white.	Total colored.
					Total.	Native parents.	Foreign parents.		
The United States	18,543,201	17,621,692	921,509	15,864,465	14,946,990	10,546,885	4,400,105	917,475	2,678,736
North Atlantic division	4,418,313	4,023,060	395,253	4,354,188	3,959,766	2,361,587	1,598,179	394,422	64,125
Maine	162,646	149,781	12,865	162,217	149,380	121,720	27,660	12,837	429
New Hampshire	83,914	71,342	12,572	83,734	71,190	51,591	19,599	12,544	180
Vermont	81,957	77,146	4,811	81,687	76,876	54,419	22,457	4,811	270
Massachusetts	511,991	439,942	72,049	507,011	435,327	200,191	235,136	71,684	4,980
Rhode Island	84,229	69,788	14,441	82,519	68,090	30,984	37,106	14,429	1,710
Connecticut	175,644	157,167	18,477	172,628	154,166	78,418	75,748	18,462	3,016
New York	1,473,876	1,333,666	140,210	1,458,256	1,318,305	659,219	659,086	139,951	15,620
New Jersey	376,238	343,891	32,347	364,551	332,248	188,583	143,665	32,303	11,687
Pennsylvania	1,467,818	1,380,337	87,481	1,441,585	1,354,184	976,462	377,722	87,401	26,233
South Atlantic division	3,015,176	2,998,694	16,482	1,816,495	1,800,929	1,696,617	104,312	15,566	1,198,681
Delaware	47,491	46,351	1,140	38,755	37,618	32,034	5,584	1,137	8,736
Maryland	305,197	297,861	7,336	236,890	229,568	178,981	50,587	7,322	68,307
District of Columbia	58,484	57,715	769	37,730	36,967	27,813	9,154	763	20,754
Virginia	565,619	564,456	1,163	330,490	329,339	321,250	8,089	1,151	235,129
West Virginia	256,490	255,123	1,367	246,333	244,968	231,822	13,146	1,365	10,157
North Carolina	572,004	571,709	295	357,593	357,303	355,043	2,260	290	214,411
South Carolina	427,499	427,214	285	159,629	159,353	155,986	3,367	276	267,870
Georgia	652,342	651,579	763	336,525	335,771	329,471	6,300	754	315,817
Florida	130,050	126,686	3,364	72,550	70,042	64,208	5,834	2,508	57,500
North Central division	6,559,316	6,127,349	431,967	6,425,261	5,994,021	3,761,665	2,232,356	431,240	134,055
Ohio	1,041,900	1,003,765	38,135	1,017,425	979,360	708,321	271,039	38,065	24,475
Indiana	647,606	637,882	9,724	634,334	624,620	521,567	103,053	9,714	13,272
Illinois	1,081,397	994,243	87,154	1,065,717	978,025	564,694	413,931	87,092	15,680
Michigan	581,399	510,087	71,312	575,670	504,783	252,645	252,138	70,887	5,729
Wisconsin	504,094	449,963	54,131	502,017	447,900	138,439	309,461	54,117	2,077
Minnesota	376,678	320,076	56,602	375,148	318,607	88,488	230,119	56,541	1,530
Iowa	576,834	545,662	31,172	573,805	542,638	329,472	213,166	31,167	3,029
Missouri	833,435	818,334	15,101	785,627	770,540	608,779	161,761	15,087	47,808
North Dakota	49,881	35,453	14,428	49,714	35,311	9,782	25,529	14,403	167
South Dakota	96,302	83,532	12,770	95,904	83,143	37,239	45,904	12,761	398
Nebraska	318,908	293,193	25,715	315,821	290,124	182,727	107,397	25,697	3,087
Kansas	450,882	435,159	15,723	434,079	418,370	319,512	98,858	15,709	16,803
South Central division	3,813,848	3,783,985	29,863	2,548,593	2,518,858	2,328,800	189,980	29,735	1,265,255
Kentucky	608,846	605,779	3,067	519,810	516,750	474,332	42,418	3,060	89,036
Tennessee	604,927	603,466	1,461	452,302	450,849	439,251	11,598	1,453	152,625
Alabama	540,226	538,679	1,547	290,935	289,392	281,681	7,711	1,543	249,291
Mississippi	473,206	472,962	244	192,622	192,382	186,653	5,729	240	280,584
Louisiana	380,796	378,360	2,436	184,394	181,989	151,493	30,496	2,405	196,402
Texas	784,594	765,106	19,488	600,646	581,218	499,360	81,858	19,428	183,948
Oklahoma	18,664	18,424	240	17,767	17,529	16,054	1,475	238	897
Arkansas	402,589	401,209	1,380	290,117	288,749	280,045	8,704	1,368	112,472
Western division	736,548	688,604	47,944	719,928	673,416	398,147	275,269	46,512	16,620
Montana	23,870	21,334	2,536	23,456	20,990	11,862	9,128	2,466	414
Wyoming	12,950	11,548	1,402	12,816	11,418	6,764	4,654	1,398	134
Colorado	90,703	84,353	6,350	89,526	83,184	57,017	26,167	6,342	1,177
New Mexico	43,107	42,225	882	40,094	39,219	34,818	4,401	875	3,013
Arizona	15,153	12,666	2,487	14,465	12,028	6,210	5,818	2,437	688
Utah	67,465	62,463	5,002	67,201	62,243	22,431	39,812	4,958	264
Nevada	10,009	9,679	330	9,166	8,851	3,593	5,258	315	843
Idaho	22,839	21,725	1,114	22,717	21,618	13,382	8,236	1,099	122
Washington	79,287	72,395	6,892	77,913	71,106	47,314	23,792	6,807	1,374
Oregon	84,588	80,799	3,789	83,826	80,082	60,467	19,615	3,744	762
California	286,577	269,417	17,160	278,748	262,677	134,289	128,388	16,071	7,829

734

STATISTICS OF POPULATION.

TABLE **64.**—PERSONS OF SCHOOL AGE, 18 TO 20 YEARS, INCLUSIVE, BY GENERAL NATIVITY AND COLOR, BY STATES AND TERRITORIES: 1890.

STATES AND TERRITORIES.	All classes.	Native born.	Foreign born.	Aggregate white.	NATIVE WHITE.			Foreign white.	Total colored.
					Total.	Native parents.	Foreign parents.		
The United States	3,904,191	3,481,661	422,530	3,386,100	2,971,030	2,057,665	913,365	415,070	518,091
North Atlantic division	1,062,892	864,910	197,982	1,043,882	846,885	495,392	351,493	196,997	19,010
Maine	39,205	33,697	5,508	39,094	33,609	28,194	5,415	5,485	111
New Hampshire	22,697	16,549	6,148	22,646	16,515	12,830	3,685	6,131	51
Vermont	19,500	17,495	2,005	19,433	17,435	12,446	4,989	1,998	67
Massachusetts	138,879	98,032	40,847	137,393	96,827	47,803	49,024	40,566	1,486
Rhode Island	21,305	14,719	6,586	20,874	14,311	6,729	7,582	6,563	431
Connecticut	45,601	35,667	9,934	44,788	34,877	18,346	16,531	9,911	813
New York	363,059	289,822	73,237	358,233	285,361	134,632	150,732	72,869	4,826
New Jersey	88,754	73,566	15,188	85,246	70,148	39,399	30,749	15,098	3,508
Pennsylvania	323,892	285,363	38,529	316,175	277,799	195,013	82,786	38,376	7,717
South Atlantic division	566,337	558,807	7,530	344,875	337,848	311,962	25,886	7,027	221,462
Delaware	10,005	9,483	522	8,180	7,668	6,248	1,420	518	1,819
Maryland	65,695	62,442	3,253	51,347	48,132	35,436	12,696	3,215	14,348
District of Columbia	15,692	15,155	537	9,827	9,308	6,739	2,569	519	5,805
Virginia	106,160	105,594	566	63,842	63,291	61,330	1,961	551	42,318
West Virginia	49,179	48,652	527	46,487	45,964	42,530	3,434	523	2,692
North Carolina	101,401	101,245	156	63,304	63,149	62,693	456	155	38,097
South Carolina	73,894	73,694	200	28,515	28,322	27,498	824	193	45,379
Georgia	118,685	118,306	379	59,950	59,579	58,047	1,532	371	58,735
Florida	25,626	24,236	1,390	13,417	12,435	11,441	994	982	12,209
North Central division	1,390,017	1,217,048	172,969	1,359,602	1,187,136	746,412	440,724	172,466	30,415
Ohio	229,131	213,649	15,482	223,398	207,959	143,232	64,727	15,439	5,738
Indiana	137,566	133,551	4,015	134,291	130,286	104,971	25,315	4,005	3,275
Illinois	241,633	204,206	37,427	237,832	200,504	115,372	85,132	37,328	3,801
Michigan	122,285	96,340	25,936	121,008	95,265	51,689	43,576	25,743	1,277
Wisconsin	99,752	80,754	18,998	99,373	80,395	21,766	58,629	18,978	379
Minnesota	78,126	55,094	23,032	77,749	54,735	16,679	38,056	23,014	377
Iowa	124,348	110,660	13,688	123,611	109,937	66,583	43,354	13,674	737
Missouri	175,500	168,413	7,087	165,252	158,216	119,138	39,078	7,036	10,248
North Dakota	9,443	4,604	4,839	9,407	4,576	1,777	2,799	4,831	36
South Dakota	17,598	12,884	4,714	17,503	12,795	6,587	6,208	4,708	95
Nebraska	65,347	53,879	11,468	64,473	53,026	36,375	16,651	11,447	874
Kansas	89,288	83,005	6,283	85,705	79,442	62,243	17,199	6,263	3,583
South Central division	709,883	697,719	12,164	472,137	460,089	419,083	41,006	12,048	237,746
Kentucky	118,215	116,918	1,297	100,334	99,041	87,807	11,234	1,293	17,881
Tennessee	115,945	115,324	621	86,059	85,445	82,595	2,850	614	29,886
Alabama	99,268	98,766	502	51,806	51,308	49,600	1,708	498	47,462
Mississippi	85,895	85,716	179	34,442	34,267	32,946	1,321	175	51,453
Louisiana	74,438	73,352	1,086	36,907	35,835	26,632	9,203	1,072	37,531
Texas	139,548	131,665	7,883	107,182	99,371	86,528	12,843	7,811	32,366
Oklahoma	2,978	2,913	65	2,829	2,768	2,561	207	61	149
Arkansas	73,596	73,065	531	52,578	52,054	50,414	1,640	524	21,018
Western division	175,062	143,177	31,885	165,604	139,072	84,816	54,256	26,532	9,458
Montana	6,370	4,562	1,808	6,089	4,467	2,696	1,771	1,622	281
Wyoming	3,341	2,648	693	3,267	2,588	1,681	907	679	74
Colorado	22,447	18,992	3,455	21,937	18,569	13,725	4,844	3,368	510
New Mexico	9,436	9,003	433	8,564	8,149	7,321	828	415	872
Arizona	3,131	2,140	991	2,924	1,998	1,229	769	926	207
Utah	12,472	10,519	1,953	12,374	10,470	3,402	7,068	1,904	98
Nevada	2,382	1,989	393	2,025	1,701	755	946	324	357
Idaho	4,418	3,828	590	4,339	3,805	2,382	1,423	534	79
Washington	18,576	14,376	4,200	17,906	14,071	10,020	4,051	3,835	670
Oregon	18,777	16,409	2,368	18,220	16,204	12,578	3,626	2,016	557
California	73,712	58,711	15,001	67,959	57,050	29,027	28,023	10,909	5,753

SCHOOL, MILITIA, AND VOTING AGES.

735

TABLE **65.**—PERSONS OF SCHOOL AGE, 5 TO 20 YEARS, INCLUSIVE, BY GENERAL NATIVITY AND COLOR, BY STATES AND TERRITORIES: 1890.

STATES AND TERRITORIES.	All classes.	Native born.	Foreign born.	Aggregate white.	NATIVE WHITE. Total.	NATIVE WHITE. Native parents.	NATIVE WHITE. Foreign parents.	Foreign white.	Total colored.
The United States	22,447,392	21,103,353	1,344,039	19,250,565	17,918,020	12,604,550	5,313,470	1,332,545	3,196,827
North Atlantic division	5,481,205	4,887,970	593,235	5,398,070	4,806,651	2,856,979	1,949,672	591,419	83,135
Maine	201,851	183,478	18,373	201,311	182,989	149,914	33,075	18,322	540
New Hampshire	106,611	87,891	18,720	106,380	87,705	64,421	23,284	18,675	231
Vermont	101,457	94,641	6,816	101,120	94,311	66,865	27,446	6,809	337
Massachusetts	650,870	537,974	112,896	644,404	532,154	247,994	284,160	112,250	6,466
Rhode Island	105,594	84,507	21,027	103,393	82,401	37,713	44,688	20,992	2,141
Connecticut	221,245	192,834	28,411	217,416	189,043	96,764	92,279	28,373	3,829
New York	1,826,935	1,623,488	213,447	1,816,489	1,603,669	793,851	809,818	212,820	20,446
New Jersey	464,992	417,457	47,535	449,797	402,396	227,982	174,414	47,401	15,195
Pennsylvania	1,791,710	1,665,700	126,010	1,757,760	1,631,983	1,171,475	460,508	125,777	33,950
South Atlantic division	3,581,513	3,557,501	24,012	2,161,370	2,138,777	2,008,579	130,198	22,593	1,420,143
Delaware	57,496	55,834	1,662	46,941	45,286	38,282	7,004	1,655	10,555
Maryland	370,892	360,303	10,589	288,237	277,700	214,417	63,283	10,537	82,655
District of Columbia	74,176	72,870	1,306	47,557	46,275	34,552	11,723	1,282	26,619
Virginia	671,779	670,050	1,729	394,332	392,630	382,589	10,041	1,702	277,447
West Virginia	305,669	303,775	1,894	292,820	290,932	274,352	16,580	1,888	12,849
North Carolina	673,405	672,954	451	420,897	420,452	417,736	2,716	445	252,508
South Carolina	501,393	500,908	485	188,144	187,675	183,484	4,191	469	313,249
Georgia	771,027	769,885	1,142	396,475	395,350	387,518	7,832	1,125	374,552
Florida	155,676	150,922	4,754	85,967	82,477	75,649	6,828	3,490	69,709
North Central division	7,949,333	7,344,397	604,936	7,784,863	7,181,157	4,508,077	2,673,080	603,706	164,470
Ohio	1,271,031	1,217,414	53,617	1,240,828	1,187,319	851,553	335,766	53,504	30,208
Indiana	785,172	771,433	13,739	768,625	754,906	626,538	128,368	13,719	16,547
Illinois	1,323,030	1,198,449	124,581	1,303,549	1,179,129	680,066	499,003	124,420	19,481
Michigan	703,684	606,436	97,248	696,678	600,048	304,334	295,714	96,630	7,006
Wisconsin	603,846	530,717	73,129	601,390	528,295	160,205	368,090	73,095	2,456
Minnesota	454,804	375,170	79,634	452,897	373,342	105,167	268,175	79,555	1,907
Iowa	701,182	656,322	44,860	697,416	652,575	396,055	256,520	44,841	3,766
Missouri	1,008,935	986,747	22,188	950,879	928,756	727,917	200,839	22,123	58,056
North Dakota	59,324	40,057	19,267	59,121	39,887	11,559	28,328	19,234	203
South Dakota	113,900	96,416	17,484	113,407	95,938	43,826	52,112	17,469	493
Nebraska	384,255	347,072	37,183	380,294	343,150	219,102	124,048	37,144	3,961
Kansas	540,170	518,164	22,006	519,784	497,812	381,755	116,057	21,972	20,386
South Central division	4,523,731	4,481,704	42,027	3,020,730	2,978,947	2,747,952	230,995	41,783	1,503,001
Kentucky	727,061	722,697	4,364	620,144	615,791	562,139	53,652	4,353	106,917
Tennessee	720,872	718,790	2,082	538,361	536,294	521,846	14,448	2,067	182,511
Alabama	639,494	637,445	2,049	342,741	340,700	331,281	9,419	2,041	296,753
Mississippi	559,101	558,678	423	227,064	226,649	219,599	7,050	415	332,037
Louisiana	455,234	451,712	3,522	221,301	217,824	178,125	39,699	3,477	233,933
Texas	924,142	896,771	27,371	707,828	680,589	585,888	94,701	27,239	216,314
Oklahoma	21,642	21,337	305	20,596	20,297	18,615	1,682	299	1,046
Arkansas	476,185	474,274	1,911	342,695	340,803	330,459	10,344	1,892	133,490
Western division	911,610	831,781	79,829	885,532	812,488	482,963	329,525	73,044	26,078
Montana	30,240	25,896	4,344	29,545	25,457	14,558	10,899	4,088	695
Wyoming	16,291	14,196	2,095	16,083	14,006	8,445	5,561	2,077	208
Colorado	113,150	103,345	9,805	111,463	101,753	70,742	31,011	9,710	1,687
New Mexico	52,543	51,228	1,315	48,658	47,368	42,139	5,229	1,290	3,885
Arizona	18,284	14,806	3,478	17,389	14,026	7,439	6,587	3,363	895
Utah	79,937	72,982	6,955	79,575	72,718	25,833	46,880	6,802	362
Nevada	12,391	11,668	723	11,191	10,552	4,348	6,204	639	1,200
Idaho	27,257	25,553	1,704	27,056	25,423	15,764	9,659	1,633	201
Washington	97,863	86,771	11,092	95,819	85,177	57,334	27,843	10,642	2,044
Oregon	103,365	97,208	6,157	102,046	96,286	73,045	23,241	5,760	1,319
California	360,289	328,128	32,161	346,707	319,727	163,316	156,411	26,980	13,582

736   STATISTICS OF POPULATION.

TABLE **66.**—MALES OF SCHOOL AGE, 5 TO 17 YEARS, INCLUSIVE, BY GENERAL NATIVITY AND COLOR, BY STATES AND TERRITORIES: 1890.

STATES AND TERRITORIES.	All classes.	Native born.	Foreign born.	Aggregate white.	NATIVE WHITE.			Foreign white.	Total colored.
					Total.	Native parents.	Foreign parents.		
The United States	9,358,198	8,892,262	465,936	8,012,347	7,548,913	5,338,825	2,210,088	463,434	1,345,851
North Atlantic division	2,215,991	2,018,949	197,042	2,184,886	1,988,301	1,187,694	800,607	196,585	31,105
Maine	82,181	75,898	6,283	81,959	75,694	61,619	14,075	6,265	222
New Hampshire	42,004	36,035	5,969	41,908	35,953	26,062	9,891	5,955	96
Vermont	42,251	39,789	2,462	42,120	39,658	28,015	11,643	2,462	131
Massachusetts	255,123	219,956	35,167	252,716	217,746	100,152	117,594	34,970	2,407
Rhode Island	41,926	34,866	7,060	41,141	34,089	15,578	18,511	7,052	785
Connecticut	88,249	79,012	9,237	86,834	77,604	39,359	38,245	9,230	1,415
New York	736,230	666,826	69,404	728,604	659,342	330,537	328,805	69,262	7,626
New Jersey	188,476	172,213	16,263	182,836	166,594	94,972	71,622	16,242	5,040
Pennsylvania	739,551	694,354	45,197	726,768	681,021	491,400	190,221	45,147	12,783
South Atlantic division	1,520,419	1,511,998	8,421	919,534	911,561	859,302	52,259	7,973	600,885
Delaware	24,071	23,476	595	19,654	19,061	16,240	2,821	593	4,417
Maryland	153,135	149,411	3,694	119,011	115,323	90,002	25,321	3,688	34,124
District of Columbia	28,398	28,016	382	18,548	18,169	13,716	4,453	379	9,850
Virginia	285,128	284,501	627	167,599	166,978	162,844	4,134	621	117,529
West Virginia	129,674	129,014	660	124,507	123,849	117,175	6,674	658	5,167
North Carolina	289,064	288,903	161	181,343	181,185	180,030	1,155	158	107,721
South Carolina	215,799	215,646	153	81,313	81,166	79,485	1,681	147	134,486
Georgia	329,899	329,491	408	170,367	169,966	166,839	3,127	401	159,532
Florida	65,251	63,510	1,741	37,192	35,864	32,971	2,893	1,328	28,059
North Central division	3,316,543	3,096,221	220,322	3,249,018	3,029,069	1,906,299	1,122,770	219,949	67,525
Ohio	526,940	507,616	19,324	514,514	495,224	359,271	135,953	19,290	12,426
Indiana	326,704	321,633	5,071	320,097	315,084	263,211	51,823	5,063	6,607
Illinois	544,389	500,438	43,951	536,494	492,577	285,005	207,572	43,917	7,895
Michigan	293,166	257,156	36,010	290,295	254,480	127,001	120,798	35,806	2,871
Wisconsin	253,934	226,175	27,759	252,842	225,092	69,857	155,235	27,750	1,092
Minnesota	190,142	161,225	28,917	189,408	160,528	44,940	115,588	28,880	734
Iowa	292,978	276,855	16,123	291,453	275,333	167,759	107,574	16,120	1,525
Missouri	420,472	412,874	7,598	396,409	388,817	307,925	80,892	7,592	24,063
North Dakota	25,775	18,301	7,474	25,684	18,222	5,029	13,193	7,462	91
South Dakota	49,268	42,565	6,703	49,054	42,358	19,037	23,321	6,696	214
Nebraska	162,912	149,637	13,275	161,316	148,052	93,464	54,588	13,264	1,596
Kansas	229,863	221,746	8,117	221,452	213,343	163,110	50,233	8,109	8,411
South Central division	1,931,815	1,916,607	15,208	1,294,678	1,279,544	1,184,139	95,405	15,134	637,137
Kentucky	307,635	306,062	1,573	263,167	261,598	240,471	21,127	1,569	44,468
Tennessee	307,833	307,068	765	230,917	230,160	224,305	5,855	757	76,916
Alabama	273,812	273,604	808	148,318	147,514	143,658	3,856	804	125,494
Mississippi	240,271	240,145	126	98,015	97,891	95,055	2,836	124	142,256
Louisiana	191,243	189,970	1,273	92,770	91,515	76,448	15,067	1,255	98,473
Texas	397,071	387,218	9,853	304,932	295,113	253,602	41,511	9,810	92,139
Oklahoma	9,654	9,530	124	9,188	9,066	8,335	731	122	466
Arkansas	204,296	205,010	686	147,371	146,687	142,265	4,422	684	56,925
Western division	373,430	348,487	24,943	364,231	340,438	201,391	139,047	23,793	9,199
Montana	12,059	10,791	1,268	11,834	10,613	5,947	4,666	1,221	225
Wyoming	6,706	6,002	704	6,635	5,935	3,535	2,400	700	71
Colorado	45,863	42,579	3,284	45,286	42,008	28,941	13,067	3,278	577
New Mexico	22,014	21,538	476	20,390	19,920	17,634	2,286	470	1,624
Arizona	7,656	6,422	1,234	7,276	6,076	3,165	2,911	1,200	380
Utah	34,131	31,687	2,444	33,983	31,560	11,318	20,242	2,423	148
Nevada	5,078	4,901	177	4,625	4,462	1,790	2,672	163	453
Idaho	11,746	11,153	593	11,674	11,096	6,921	4,175	578	72
Washington	40,594	36,988	3,606	39,853	36,311	24,176	12,135	3,542	741
Oregon	42,734	40,780	1,954	42,309	40,393	30,538	9,855	1,916	425
California	144,849	135,646	9,203	140,366	132,064	67,426	64,638	8,302	4,483

SCHOOL, MILITIA, AND VOTING AGES. 737

TABLE 67.—FEMALES OF SCHOOL AGE, 5 TO 17 YEARS, INCLUSIVE, BY GENERAL NATIVITY AND COLOR, BY STATES AND TERRITORIES: 1890.

STATES AND TERRITORIES.	All classes.	Native born.	Foreign born.	Aggregate white.	NATIVE WHITE.			Foreign white.	Total colored.
					Total.	Native parents.	Foreign parents.		
The United States	9,185,003	8,729,430	455,573	7,852,118	7,398,077	5,208,060	2,190,017	454,041	1,332,885
North Atlantic division	2,202,322	2,004,111	198,211	2,169,302	1,971,465	1,173,893	797,572	197,837	33,020
Maine	80,465	73,883	6,582	80,258	73,686	60,101	13,585	6,572	207
New Hampshire	41,910	35,307	6,603	41,826	35,237	25,529	9,708	6,589	84
Vermont	39,706	37,357	2,349	39,567	37,218	26,404	10,814	2,349	139
Massachusetts	256,868	219,986	36,882	254,295	217,581	100,039	117,542	36,714	2,573
Rhode Island	42,303	34,922	7,381	41,378	34,001	15,406	18,595	7,377	925
Connecticut	87,395	78,155	9,240	85,794	76,562	39,059	37,503	9,232	1,601
New York	737,646	666,840	70,806	729,652	658,963	328,682	330,281	70,689	7,994
New Jersey	187,762	171,678	16,084	181,715	165,654	93,611	72,043	16,061	6,047
Pennsylvania	728,267	685,983	42,284	714,817	672,563	485,062	187,501	42,254	13,450
South Atlantic division	1,494,757	1,486,696	8,061	896,961	889,368	837,315	52,053	7,593	597,796
Delaware	23,420	22,875	545	19,101	18,557	15,794	2,763	544	4,319
Maryland	152,062	148,420	3,642	117,879	114,245	88,979	25,266	3,634	34,183
District of Columbia	30,086	29,699	387	19,182	18,798	14,097	4,701	384	10,904
Virginia	280,491	279,955	536	162,891	162,361	158,415	3,946	530	117,600
West Virginia	126,816	126,109	707	121,826	121,119	114,647	6,472	707	4,990
North Carolina	282,940	282,806	134	176,250	176,118	175,013	1,105	132	106,690
South Carolina	211,700	211,568	132	78,316	78,187	76,501	1,686	129	133,384
Georgia	322,443	322,088	355	166,158	165,805	162,632	3,173	353	156,285
Florida	64,799	63,176	1,623	35,358	34,178	31,237	2,941	1,180	29,441
North Central division	3,242,773	3,031,128	211,645	3,176,243	2,964,952	1,855,366	1,109,586	211,291	66,530
Ohio	514,960	496,149	18,811	502,011	484,136	349,050	135,086	18,775	12,049
Indiana	320,902	316,249	4,653	314,237	309,586	258,356	51,230	4,651	6,665
Illinois	537,008	493,805	43,203	529,223	486,048	279,689	206,359	43,175	7,785
Michigan	288,233	252,931	35,302	285,375	250,294	124,954	125,340	35,081	2,858
Wisconsin	250,160	223,788	26,372	249,175	222,808	68,582	154,226	26,367	985
Minnesota	186,536	158,851	27,685	185,740	158,079	43,548	114,531	27,661	796
Iowa	283,856	268,807	15,049	282,352	267,305	161,713	105,592	15,047	1,504
Missouri	412,963	405,460	7,503	389,218	381,723	300,854	80,869	7,495	23,745
North Dakota	24,106	17,152	6,954	24,030	17,089	4,753	12,336	6,941	76
South Dakota	47,034	40,967	6,067	46,850	40,785	18,202	22,583	6,065	184
Nebraska	155,996	143,556	12,440	154,505	142,072	89,263	52,809	12,433	1,491
Kansas	221,019	213,413	7,606	212,627	205,027	156,402	48,625	7,600	8,392
South Central division	1,882,033	1,867,378	14,655	1,253,915	1,239,314	1,144,730	94,584	14,601	628,118
Kentucky	301,211	299,717	1,494	256,643	255,152	233,861	21,291	1,491	44,568
Tennessee	297,094	296,398	696	221,385	220,689	214,946	5,743	696	75,709
Alabama	266,414	265,675	739	142,617	141,878	138,023	3,855	739	123,797
Mississippi	232,935	232,817	118	94,607	94,491	91,598	2,893	116	138,328
Louisiana	189,553	188,390	1,163	91,624	90,474	75,045	15,429	1,150	97,929
Texas	387,523	377,888	9,635	295,714	286,105	245,758	40,347	9,600	91,809
Oklahoma	9,010	8,894	116	8,579	8,463	7,719	744	116	431
Arkansas	198,293	197,599	694	142,746	142,062	137,780	4,282	684	55,547
Western division	363,118	340,117	23,001	355,697	332,978	196,756	136,222	22,719	7,421
Montana	11,811	10,543	1,268	11,622	10,377	5,915	4,462	1,245	189
Wyoming	6,244	5,546	698	6,181	5,483	3,229	2,254	698	63
Colorado	44,840	41,774	3,066	44,240	41,176	28,076	13,100	3,064	600
New Mexico	21,093	20,687	406	19,704	19,299	17,184	2,115	405	1,389
Arizona	7,497	6,244	1,253	7,189	5,952	3,045	2,907	1,237	308
Utah	33,334	30,776	2,558	33,218	30,683	11,113	19,570	2,535	116
Nevada	4,931	4,778	153	4,541	4,389	1,803	2,586	152	390
Idaho	11,093	10,572	521	11,043	10,522	6,461	4,061	521	50
Washington	38,693	35,407	3,286	38,060	34,795	23,138	11,657	3,265	633
Oregon	41,854	40,019	1,835	41,517	39,689	29,929	9,760	1,828	337
California	141,728	133,771	7,957	138,382	130,613	66,863	63,750	7,769	3,316

738

STATISTICS OF POPULATION.

TABLE 68.—MALES OF SCHOOL AGE, 18 TO 20 YEARS, INCLUSIVE, BY GENERAL NATIVITY AND COLOR, BY STATES AND TERRITORIES: 1890.

STATES AND TERRITORIES.	All classes.	Native born.	Foreign born.	Aggregate white.	NATIVE WHITE.			Foreign white.	Total colored.
					Total.	Native parents.	Foreign parents.		
The United States	1,884,502	1,676,028	208,474	1,643,025	1,441,001	1,002,922	438,079	202,024	241,477
North Atlantic division	505,358	415,923	89,435	496,436	407,775	240,426	167,349	88,661	8,922
Maine	19,519	16,916	2,603	19,462	16,878	14,140	2,738	2,584	57
New Hampshire	11,975	9,090	2,852	11,247	8,306	6,470	1,836	2,941	28
Vermont	10,089	8,894	1,195	10,053	8,865	6,330	2,535	1,188	36
Massachusetts	65,034	47,496	17,538	64,297	46,952	23,313	23,639	17,345	737
Rhode Island	10,052	7,043	3,009	9,861	6,872	3,269	3,603	2,989	191
Connecticut	22,220	17,629	4,591	21,849	17,278	9,309	7,969	4,571	371
New York	167,872	136,973	30,899	165,672	135,069	64,514	70,555	30,603	2,200
New Jersey	41,349	34,603	6,746	39,697	33,036	18,510	14,526	6,661	1,652
Pennsylvania	157,948	138,046	19,902	154,298	134,519	94,571	39,948	19,779	3,650
South Atlantic division	268,068	265,032	3,036	166,507	163,121	150,950	12,171	3,386	102,101
Delaware	4,909	4,682	227	4,003	3,778	3,113	665	225	906
Maryland	30,527	29,134	1,393	24,055	22,696	16,756	5,940	1,359	6,472
District of Columbia	6,528	6,317	211	4,295	4,095	2,982	1,113	200	2,233
Virginia	50,718	50,365	353	31,100	30,757	29,778	979	343	19,618
West Virginia	24,636	24,322	314	22,965	22,653	20,968	1,685	312	1,671
North Carolina	48,449	48,359	90	31,127	31,037	30,792	245	90	17,322
South Carolina	34,268	34,153	115	13,690	13,579	13,217	362	111	20,578
Georgia	55,889	55,673	216	28,676	28,466	27,760	706	210	27,213
Florida	12,744	12,027	717	6,596	6,060	5,584	476	536	6,148
North Central division	679,008	590,517	88,491	664,270	576,116	363,878	212,238	88,154	14,738
Ohio	109,241	101,844	7,397	106,581	99,206	68,708	30,498	7,375	2,660
Indiana	66,871	64,748	2,123	65,226	63,108	50,848	12,260	2,118	1,645
Illinois	116,120	98,019	18,101	114,192	96,173	55,956	40,217	18,010	1,928
Michigan	60,334	47,034	13,300	59,712	46,509	25,053	21,456	13,203	622
Wisconsin	49,420	39,394	10,026	49,209	39,201	10,761	28,440	10,008	211
Minnesota	38,995	26,989	12,006	38,783	26,790	8,227	18,563	11,993	212
Iowa	62,061	54,374	7,687	61,693	54,017	32,699	21,318	7,676	368
Missouri	84,410	81,077	3,333	79,663	76,371	58,007	18,364	3,292	4,747
North Dakota	4,832	2,293	2,539	4,805	2,273	936	1,337	2,532	27
South Dakota	9,174	6,531	2,643	9,119	6,481	3,366	3,115	2,638	55
Nebraska	33,163	27,196	5,967	32,658	26,709	18,464	8,245	5,949	505
Kansas	44,387	41,018	3,369	42,629	39,278	30,853	8,425	3,351	1,758
South Central division	338,222	332,040	6,182	229,734	223,629	204,185	19,494	6,105	108,488
Kentucky	57,289	56,607	682	48,817	48,137	42,717	5,420	680	8,472
Tennessee	55,846	55,505	341	42,044	41,706	40,366	1,340	338	13,802
Alabama	46,852	46,559	293	25,037	24,746	23,925	821	291	21,815
Mississippi	39,987	39,882	105	16,544	16,443	15,842	601	101	23,443
Louisiana	34,221	33,625	596	17,436	16,849	12,603	4,246	587	16,785
Texas	67,433	63,560	3,873	52,956	49,130	42,937	6,193	3,826	14,477
Oklahoma	1,355	1,323	32	1,285	1,257	1,161	96	28	70
Arkansas	35,239	34,979	260	25,615	25,361	24,584	777	254	9,624
Western division	93,246	72,516	20,730	86,078	70,360	43,533	26,827	15,718	7,168
Montana	3,685	2,468	1,217	3,472	2,422	1,506	916	1,050	213
Wyoming	2,070	1,615	455	2,025	1,583	1,066	517	442	45
Colorado	11,937	10,006	1,931	11,641	9,790	7,393	2,397	1,851	296
New Mexico	4,674	4,422	252	4,244	4,008	3,575	433	236	430
Arizona	1,739	1,160	579	1,587	1,072	667	405	515	152
Utah	6,367	5,398	969	6,294	5,368	1,765	3,603	926	73
Nevada	1,300	1,016	284	1,089	873	409	464	216	211
Idaho	2,411	2,014	397	2,344	2,003	1,281	722	341	67
Washington	10,556	7,719	2,837	10,076	7,557	5,358	2,199	2,519	480
Oregon	9,771	8,314	1,457	9,327	8,191	6,357	1,834	1,136	444
California	38,736	28,384	10,352	33,979	27,493	14,156	13,837	6,486	4,757

449

SCHOOL, MILITIA, AND VOTING AGES.

739

TABLE **69.**—FEMALES OF SCHOOL AGE, 18 TO 20 YEARS, INCLUSIVE, BY GENERAL NATIVITY AND COLOR, BY STATES AND TERRITORIES: 1890.

STATES AND TERRITORIES.	All classes.	Native born.	Foreign born.	Aggregate white.	NATIVE WHITE.			Foreign white.	Total colored.
					Total.	Native parents.	Foreign parents.		
The United States...	2,019,689	1,805,633	214,056	1,743,075	1,530,029	1,054,743	475,286	213,046	276,614
North Atlantic division	557,534	448,987	108,547	547,446	439,110	254,966	184,144	108,336	10,088
Maine	19,686	16,781	2,905	19,632	16,731	14,054	2,677	2,901	54
New Hampshire	11,422	8,226	3,196	11,399	8,209	6,360	1,849	3,190	23
Vermont	9,411	8,601	810	9,380	8,570	6,116	2,454	810	31
Massachusetts	73,845	50,536	23,309	73,096	49,875	24,490	25,385	23,221	749
Rhode Island	11,253	7,676	3,577	11,013	7,439	3,460	3,979	3,574	240
Connecticut	23,381	18,038	5,343	22,939	17,599	9,037	8,562	5,340	442
New York	195,187	152,849	42,338	192,561	150,295	70,118	80,177	42,266	2,626
New Jersey	47,405	38,963	8,442	45,540	37,112	20,889	16,223	8,437	1,856
Pennsylvania	165,944	147,317	18,627	161,877	143,280	100,442	42,838	18,597	4,067
South Atlantic division	297,669	293,775	3,894	178,368	174,727	161,012	13,715	3,641	119,301
Delaware	5,096	4,801	295	4,183	3,890	3,135	755	293	913
Maryland	35,168	33,308	1,860	27,292	25,436	18,680	6,756	1,856	7,876
District of Columbia	9,164	8,838	326	5,532	5,213	3,757	1,456	319	3,632
Virginia	55,442	55,229	213	32,742	32,534	31,552	982	208	22,700
West Virginia	24,543	24,330	213	23,522	23,311	21,562	1,749	211	1,021
North Carolina	52,952	52,886	66	32,177	32,112	31,901	211	65	20,775
South Carolina	39,626	39,541	85	14,825	14,743	14,281	462	82	24,801
Georgia	62,796	62,633	163	31,274	31,113	30,287	826	161	31,522
Florida	12,882	12,209	673	6,821	6,375	5,857	518	446	6,061
North Central division	711,009	626,531	84,478	695,332	611,020	382,534	228,486	84,312	15,677
Ohio	119,890	111,805	8,085	116,817	108,753	74,524	34,229	8,064	3,073
Indiana	70,695	68,803	1,892	69,065	67,178	54,123	13,055	1,887	1,630
Illinois	125,513	106,187	19,326	123,640	104,331	59,416	44,915	19,309	1,873
Michigan	61,951	49,315	12,636	61,296	48,756	26,636	22,120	12,540	655
Wisconsin	50,332	41,360	8,972	50,164	41,194	11,005	30,189	8,970	168
Minnesota	39,131	28,105	11,026	38,966	27,945	8,452	19,493	11,021	165
Iowa	62,287	56,286	6,001	61,918	55,920	33,884	22,036	5,998	369
Missouri	91,090	87,336	3,754	85,589	81,845	61,131	20,714	3,744	5,501
North Dakota	4,611	2,311	2,300	4,602	2,303	841	1,462	2,299	9
South Dakota	8,424	6,353	2,071	8,384	6,314	3,221	3,093	2,070	40
Nebraska	32,184	26,683	5,501	31,815	26,317	17,911	8,406	5,498	369
Kansas	44,901	41,987	2,914	43,076	40,164	31,390	8,774	2,912	1,825
South Central division	371,661	365,679	5,982	242,403	236,460	214,948	21,512	5,943	129,258
Kentucky	60,926	60,311	615	51,517	50,904	45,090	5,814	613	9,409
Tennessee	60,099	59,819	280	44,015	43,739	42,229	1,510	276	16,084
Alabama	52,416	52,207	209	26,769	26,562	25,675	887	207	25,647
Mississippi	45,908	45,834	74	17,898	17,824	17,104	720	74	28,010
Louisiana	40,217	39,727	490	19,471	18,986	14,029	4,957	485	20,746
Texas	72,115	68,105	4,010	54,226	50,241	43,591	6,650	3,985	17,889
Oklahoma	1,623	1,590	33	1,544	1,511	1,400	111	33	79
Arkansas	38,357	38,086	271	26,963	26,693	25,830	863	270	11,394
Western division	81,816	70,661	11,155	79,526	68,712	41,283	27,429	10,814	2,290
Montana	2,685	2,094	591	2,617	2,045	1,190	855	572	68
Wyoming	1,271	1,033	238	1,242	1,005	615	390	237	29
Colorado	10,510	8,986	1,524	10,296	8,779	6,332	2,447	1,517	214
New Mexico	4,762	4,581	181	4,320	4,141	3,746	395	179	442
Arizona	1,392	980	412	1,337	926	562	364	411	55
Utah	6,105	5,121	984	6,080	5,102	1,637	3,465	978	25
Nevada	1,082	973	109	936	828	346	482	108	146
Idaho	2,007	1,814	193	1,995	1,802	1,101	701	193	12
Washington	8,020	6,657	1,363	7,830	6,514	4,662	1,852	1,316	190
Oregon	9,006	8,095	911	8,893	8,013	6,221	1,792	880	113
California	34,976	30,327	4,649	33,980	29,557	14,871	14,686	4,423	996

740

STATISTICS OF POPULATION.

TABLE **70.**—MALES OF SCHOOL AGE, 5 TO 20 YEARS, INCLUSIVE, BY GENERAL NATIVITY AND COLOR, BY STATES AND TERRITORIES: 1890.

STATES AND TERRITORIES.	All classes.	Native born.	Foreign born.	Aggregate white.	NATIVE WHITE.			Foreign white.	Total colored.
					Total.	Native parents.	Foreign parents.		
The United States	11,242,700	10,568,290	674,410	9,655,372	8,989,914	6,341,747	2,648,167	665,458	1,587,328
North Atlantic division	2,721,349	2,434,872	286,477	2,681,322	2,396,076	1,428,120	967,956	285,246	40,027
Maine	101,700	92,814	8,886	101,421	92,572	75,759	16,813	8,849	279
New Hampshire	53,270	44,358	8,921	53,156	44,259	32,532	11,727	8,856	114
Vermont	52,340	48,683	3,657	52,173	48,523	34,345	14,178	3,650	167
Massachusetts	320,157	267,452	52,705	317,013	264,698	123,465	141,233	52,315	3,144
Rhode Island	51,978	41,909	10,069	51,002	40,961	18,847	22,114	10,041	976
Connecticut	110,469	96,641	13,828	108,683	94,882	48,668	46,214	13,801	1,786
New York	904,102	803,799	100,303	894,276	794,411	395,051	399,360	99,865	9,826
New Jersey	229,825	206,816	23,009	222,533	199,630	113,482	86,148	22,903	7,292
Pennsylvania	897,499	832,400	65,099	881,066	816,140	585,971	230,169	64,926	16,433
South Atlantic division	1,789,087	1,777,030	12,057	1,086,041	1,074,682	1,010,252	64,430	11,359	703,046
Delaware	28,980	28,158	822	23,657	22,839	19,353	3,486	818	5,323
Maryland	183,662	178,575	5,087	143,066	138,019	106,758	31,261	5,047	40,596
District of Columbia	34,926	34,333	593	22,843	22,264	16,698	5,566	579	12,083
Virginia	335,846	334,866	980	198,699	197,735	192,622	5,113	964	137,147
West Virginia	154,310	153,336	974	147,472	146,502	138,143	8,359	970	6,838
North Carolina	337,513	337,262	251	212,470	212,222	210,822	1,400	248	125,043
South Carolina	250,067	249,799	268	95,003	94,745	92,702	2,043	258	155,004
Georgia	385,788	385,164	624	199,043	198,432	194,599	3,833	611	186,745
Florida	77,995	75,537	2,458	43,788	41,924	38,555	3,369	1,864	34,207
North Central division	3,995,551	3,686,738	308,813	3,913,288	3,605,185	2,270,177	1,335,008	308,103	82,263
Ohio	636,181	609,460	26,721	621,095	594,430	427,979	166,451	26,665	15,086
Indiana	393,575	386,381	7,194	385,323	378,142	314,059	64,083	7,181	8,252
Illinois	660,509	598,457	62,052	650,686	588,750	340,961	247,789	61,936	9,823
Michigan	353,500	304,190	49,310	350,007	300,998	152,744	148,254	49,009	3,493
Wisconsin	303,354	265,569	37,785	302,051	264,293	80,618	183,675	37,758	1,303
Minnesota	229,137	188,214	40,923	228,191	187,318	53,167	134,151	40,873	946
Iowa	355,039	331,229	23,810	353,140	329,350	200,458	128,892	23,790	1,893
Missouri	504,882	493,951	10,931	476,072	465,188	365,932	99,256	10,884	28,810
North Dakota	30,607	20,594	10,013	30,489	20,495	5,965	14,530	9,094	118
South Dakota	58,442	49,096	9,346	58,173	48,839	22,403	26,436	9,334	269
Nebraska	196,075	176,833	19,242	193,974	174,761	111,928	62,833	19,213	2,101
Kansas	274,250	262,764	11,486	264,081	252,621	193,963	58,658	11,460	10,160
South Central division	2,270,037	2,248,647	21,390	1,524,412	1,503,173	1,388,274	114,899	21,239	745,625
Kentucky	364,924	362,669	2,255	311,984	309,735	283,188	26,547	2,249	52,940
Tennessee	363,679	362,573	1,106	272,961	271,866	264,671	7,195	1,095	90,718
Alabama	320,664	319,563	1,101	173,355	172,260	167,583	4,677	1,095	147,309
Mississippi	280,258	280,027	231	114,559	114,334	110,897	3,437	225	165,699
Louisiana	225,464	223,595	1,869	110,206	108,364	89,051	19,313	1,842	115,258
Texas	464,504	450,778	13,726	357,888	344,243	296,539	47,704	13,645	106,616
Oklahoma	11,009	10,852	156	10,473	10,323	9,496	827	150	536
Arkansas	239,535	238,589	946	172,986	172,048	166,849	5,199	938	66,549
Western division	466,676	421,003	45,673	450,309	410,798	244,924	165,874	39,511	16,367
Montana	15,744	13,259	2,485	15,306	13,035	7,453	5,582	2,271	438
Wyoming	8,776	7,617	1,159	8,660	7,518	4,601	2,917	1,142	116
Colorado	57,800	52,585	5,215	56,927	51,798	36,334	15,464	5,129	873
New Mexico	26,688	25,960	728	24,634	23,928	21,209	2,719	706	2,054
Arizona	9,395	7,582	1,813	8,863	7,148	3,832	3,316	1,715	532
Utah	40,498	37,085	3,413	40,277	36,928	13,083	23,845	3,349	221
Nevada	6,378	5,917	461	5,714	5,335	2,199	3,136	379	664
Idaho	14,157	13,167	990	14,018	13,099	8,202	4,897	919	139
Washington	51,150	44,707	6,443	49,929	43,868	29,534	14,334	6,061	1,221
Oregon	52,505	49,094	3,411	51,636	48,584	36,895	11,689	3,052	869
California	183,585	164,030	19,555	174,345	159,557	81,582	77,975	14,788	9,240

SCHOOL, MILITIA, AND VOTING AGES.

741

TABLE **71.**—FEMALES OF SCHOOL AGE, 5 TO 20 YEARS, INCLUSIVE, BY GENERAL NATIVITY AND COLOR, BY STATES AND TERRITORIES: 1890.

STATES AND TERRITORIES.	All classes.	Native born.	Foreign born.	Aggregate white.	NATIVE WHITE.			Foreign white.	Total colored.
					Total.	Native parents.	Foreign parents.		
The United States	11,204,692	10,535,063	669,629	9,595,193	8,928,106	6,262,803	2,665,303	667,087	1,609,499
North Atlantic division	2,759,856	2,453,098	306,758	2,716,748	2,410,575	1,428,859	981,716	306,173	43,108
Maine	100,151	90,664	9,487	99,890	90,417	74,155	16,262	9,473	261
New Hampshire	53,332	43,533	9,799	53,225	43,446	31,889	11,557	9,779	107
Vermont	49,117	45,958	3,159	48,947	45,788	32,520	13,268	3,159	170
Massachusetts	330,713	270,522	60,191	327,391	267,456	124,529	142,927	59,935	3,322
Rhode Island	53,556	42,598	10,958	52,391	41,440	18,866	22,574	10,951	1,165
Connecticut	110,776	96,193	14,583	108,733	94,161	48,096	46,065	14,572	2,043
New York	932,833	819,689	113,144	922,213	809,258	398,800	410,458	112,955	10,620
New Jersey	235,167	210,641	24,526	227,264	202,766	114,500	88,266	24,498	7,903
Pennsylvania	894,211	833,300	60,911	876,694	815,843	585,504	230,339	60,851	17,517
South Atlantic division	1,792,426	1,780,471	11,955	1,075,329	1,064,095	998,327	65,768	11,234	717,097
Delaware	28,516	27,676	840	23,284	22,447	18,929	3,518	837	5,232
Maryland	187,230	181,728	5,502	145,171	139,681	107,659	32,022	5,490	42,059
District of Columbia	39,250	38,537	713	24,714	24,011	17,854	6,157	703	14,536
Virginia	335,933	335,184	749	195,633	194,895	189,967	4,928	738	140,300
West Virginia	151,359	150,439	920	145,348	144,430	136,209	8,221	918	6,011
North Carolina	335,892	335,692	200	208,427	208,230	206,914	1,316	197	127,465
South Carolina	251,326	251,109	217	93,141	92,930	90,782	2,148	211	158,185
Georgia	385,239	384,721	518	197,432	196,918	192,919	3,999	514	187,807
Florida	77,681	75,385	2,296	42,179	40,553	37,094	3,459	1,626	35,502
North Central division	3,953,782	3,657,659	296,123	3,871,575	3,575,972	2,237,900	1,338,072	295,603	82,207
Ohio	634,850	607,954	26,896	619,728	592,889	423,574	169,315	26,839	15,122
Indiana	391,597	385,052	6,545	383,302	376,764	312,479	64,285	6,538	8,295
Illinois	662,521	599,992	62,529	652,863	590,379	339,105	251,274	62,484	9,658
Michigan	350,184	302,246	47,938	346,671	299,050	151,590	147,460	47,621	3,513
Wisconsin	300,492	265,148	35,344	299,339	264,002	79,587	184,415	35,337	1,153
Minnesota	225,667	186,956	38,711	224,706	186,024	52,000	134,024	38,682	961
Iowa	346,143	325,093	21,050	344,270	323,225	195,597	127,628	21,045	1,873
Missouri	504,053	492,796	11,257	474,807	463,508	361,985	101,583	11,239	29,246
North Dakota	28,717	19,463	9,254	28,632	19,392	5,594	13,798	9,240	85
South Dakota	55,458	47,320	8,138	55,234	47,099	21,423	25,676	8,135	224
Nebraska	188,180	170,239	17,941	186,320	168,389	107,174	61,215	17,931	1,860
Kansas	265,920	255,400	10,520	255,703	245,191	187,792	57,399	10,512	10,217
South Central division	2,253,694	2,233,057	20,637	1,496,318	1,475,774	1,359,678	116,096	20,544	757,376
Kentucky	362,137	360,028	2,109	308,160	306,056	278,951	27,105	2,104	53,977
Tennessee	357,193	356,217	976	265,400	264,428	257,175	7,253	972	91,793
Alabama	318,830	317,882	948	169,386	168,440	163,698	4,742	946	149,444
Mississippi	278,843	278,651	192	112,505	112,315	108,702	3,613	190	166,338
Louisiana	229,770	228,117	1,653	111,095	109,460	89,074	20,386	1,635	118,675
Texas	459,638	445,993	13,645	349,940	336,346	289,349	46,997	13,594	109,698
Oklahoma	10,633	10,484	149	10,123	9,974	9,119	855	149	510
Arkansas	236,650	235,685	965	169,709	168,755	163,610	5,145	954	66,941
Western division	444,934	410,778	34,156	435,223	401,690	238,039	163,651	33,533	9,711
Montana	14,496	12,637	1,859	14,239	12,422	7,105	5,317	1,817	257
Wyoming	7,515	6,579	936	7,423	6,488	3,844	2,644	935	92
Colorado	55,350	50,760	4,590	54,536	49,955	34,408	15,547	4,581	814
New Mexico	25,855	25,268	587	24,024	23,440	20,930	2,510	584	1,831
Arizona	8,889	7,224	1,665	8,526	6,878	3,607	3,271	1,648	363
Utah	39,439	35,897	3,542	39,298	35,785	12,750	23,035	3,513	141
Nevada	6,013	5,751	262	5,477	5,217	2,149	3,068	260	536
Idaho	13,100	12,386	714	13,038	12,324	7,562	4,762	714	62
Washington	46,713	42,064	4,649	45,890	41,309	27,800	13,509	4,581	823
Oregon	50,860	48,114	2,746	50,410	47,702	36,150	11,552	2,708	450
California	176,704	164,098	12,606	172,362	160,170	81,734	78,436	12,192	4,342

CONJUGAL CONDITION.

TABLE 81.—CONJUGAL CONDITION OF THE AGGREGATE POPULATION, CLASSIFIED BY SEX, BY STATES AND TERRITORIES: 1890.

TABLE 82.—CONJUGAL CONDITION OF THE AGGREGATE POPULATION OF THE UNITED STATES, CLASSIFIED BY SEX, GENERAL NATIVITY, COLOR, AND AGE PERIODS: 1890.

TABLE 83.—CONJUGAL CONDITION OF THE AGGREGATE POPULATION, CLASSIFIED BY SEX, GENERAL NATIVITY, COLOR, AND AGE PERIODS, BY STATES AND TERRITORIES: 1890.

TABLE 84.—CONJUGAL CONDITION OF THE AGGREGATE POPULATION, CLASSIFIED BY SEX, FOR CITIES HAVING 25,000 INHABITANTS OR MORE: 1890.

TABLE 85.—CONJUGAL CONDITION OF THE AGGREGATE POPULATION, CLASSIFIED BY SEX, GENERAL NATIVITY, COLOR, AND AGE PERIODS, FOR CITIES HAVING 100,000 INHABITANTS OR MORE: 1890.

CONJUGAL CONDITION. 829

TABLE **81.**—CONJUGAL CONDITION OF THE AGGREGATE POPULATION, CLASSIFIED BY SEX, BY STATES AND TERRITORIES: 1890.

STATES AND TERRITORIES.	Aggregate.	MALES.						FEMALES.					
		Total.	Single.	Married.	Widowed.	Divorced.	Unknown.	Total.	Single.	Married.	Widowed.	Divorced.	Unknown.
The United States...	62,622,250	32,067,880	19,945,576	11,205,228	815,437	49,101	52,538	30,554,370	17,183,988	11,126,196	2,154,015	71,895	17,676
North Atlantic division	17,401,545	8,677,798	5,072,962	3,322,329	259,877	10,007	12,623	8,723,747	4,683,294	3,293,929	726,481	15,182	4,861
Maine	661,086	332,590	181,365	137,419	12,100	1,094	612	328,496	159,907	137,184	29,938	1,337	70
New Hampshire...	376,530	186,566	99,233	78,658	7,684	800	191	189,964	91,333	78,526	18,943	1,084	78
Vermont	332,422	169,327	91,690	70,140	6,808	584	105	163,095	77,986	69,956	14,438	677	38
Massachusetts	2,238,943	1,087,709	626,862	421,946	35,513	1,394	1,994	1,151,234	619,690	421,259	107,273	2,484	528
Rhode Island	345,506	168,025	97,152	64,852	5,488	391	142	177,481	96,256	64,838	15,556	759	72
Connecticut	746,258	369,538	212,478	144,054	11,542	846	618	376,720	197,019	143,263	34,889	1,298	251
New York	5,997,853	2,976,893	1,723,617	1,155,661	91,009	2,219	4,387	3,020,960	1,600,156	1,149,995	265,456	3,395	1,958
New Jersey	1,444,933	720,819	420,454	278,957	20,119	363	926	724,114	389,141	276,345	57,763	565	300
Pennsylvania	5,258,014	2,666,331	1,620,111	970,642	69,614	2,316	3,048	2,591,683	1,451,746	952,563	182,225	3,583	1,566
South Atlantic division	8,857,920	4,418,769	2,881,663	1,436,089	94,417	2,910	3,690	4,439,151	2,657,307	1,448,455	323,050	6,132	4,207
Delaware	168,493	85,573	52,028	31,159	2,306	40	40	82,920	45,484	31,192	6,154	70	20
Maryland	1,042,390	515,691	322,428	178,195	14,125	321	622	526,699	303,348	179,888	42,583	582	298
Dist. of Columbia..	230,392	109,584	66,084	39,639	3,376	146	339	120,808	66,775	39,675	13,929	314	115
Virginia	1,655,980	824,278	545,753	257,559	19,895	583	538	831,702	509,779	258,116	61,877	1,039	891
West Virginia	762,794	390,285	253,962	127,820	7,487	359	648	372,509	225,733	127,576	18,389	674	137
North Carolina	1,617,947	799,149	529,705	253,635	15,074	878	857	818,798	502,554	257,919	56,889	836	600
South Carolina	1,151,149	572,337	378,798	182,524	10,637	210	168	578,812	352,076	184,968	40,617	483	668
Georgia	1,837,353	919,925	603,249	298,594	16,823	579	680	917,428	543,369	302,097	69,125	1,551	1,286
Florida	391,422	201,947	129,656	66,955	4,694	344	298	189,475	108,180	67,024	13,487	583	192
North Central division	22,362,279	11,594,910	7,157,290	4,114,822	285,802	23,230	13,766	10,767,369	5,996,437	4,098,449	636,284	32,230	3,969
Ohio	3,672,316	1,855,736	1,109,172	691,197	50,200	3,567	1,501	1,816,580	991,349	689,347	129,443	5,717	724
Indiana	2,192,404	1,118,347	670,867	413,733	29,892	3,000	855	1,074,057	584,186	413,523	71,252	4,711	385
Illinois	3,826,351	1,972,308	1,221,422	697,724	47,844	3,317	2,596	1,854,043	1,035,123	694,531	119,131	4,926	332
Michigan	2,093,889	1,091,780	638,209	420,700	28,482	2,805	1,584	1,002,109	522,867	416,304	59,080	3,493	365
Wisconsin	1,686,880	874,951	545,698	304,210	22,453	1,639	951	811,929	461,884	302,850	44,085	2,179	322
Minnesota	1,301,826	695,321	451,683	226,159	14,992	1,071	1,416	606,505	354,126	223,463	27,475	1,178	263
Iowa	1,911,896	994,458	619,162	349,345	23,387	1,993	566	917,443	517,787	349,083	46,625	2,880	168
Missouri	2,679,184	1,385,238	878,806	467,600	34,569	2,231	2,032	1,293,946	739,428	467,802	82,989	3,201	436
North Dakota	182,719	101,590	67,608	31,611	2,025	129	127	81,129	47,022	31,172	2,809	106	20
South Dakota	328,808	180,250	110,151	59,647	3,818	426	208	148,558	84,778	58,290	5,120	328	42
Nebraska	1,058,910	572,824	368,994	190,318	11,140	1,296	1,076	486,086	278,987	187,579	17,995	1,394	131
Kansas	1,427,096	752,112	469,428	263,173	16,991	1,756	764	674,984	378,000	263,506	29,680	2,117	781
South Central division	10,972,893	5,593,877	3,054,943	1,702,119	130,422	6,840	9,553	5,379,016	3,174,570	1,794,653	393,548	12,800	3,385
Kentucky	1,858,635	942,758	603,227	313,436	23,092	1,200	1,143	915,877	534,740	313,880	63,997	2,461	799
Tennessee	1,767,518	891,585	577,598	290,440	21,198	1,154	1,195	875,933	515,370	291,065	65,859	2,600	370
Alabama	1,513,017	757,450	490,308	244,803	15,008	744	593	755,561	450,032	245,952	58,018	1,419	140
Mississippi	1,289,600	649,687	431,069	202,798	14,778	581	461	639,913	384,334	204,194	49,616	1,233	536
Louisiana	1,118,587	559,350	365,805	178,220	13,372	632	1,261	559,237	327,686	179,458	50,270	1,193	630
Texas	2,235,523	1,172,558	777,933	362,324	26,848	1,497	3,951	1,062,970	629,785	360,756	69,228	2,568	633
Oklahoma	61,834	34,733	21,598	12,005	996	99	85	27,101	14,888	11,244	912	49	8
Arkansas	1,128,179	585,755	381,345	188,093	14,530	873	914	542,424	317,726	187,504	35,648	1,277	269
Western division	3,027,613	1,782,526	1,178,718	530,869	44,019	6,114	12,906	1,245,087	672,380	490,710	75,252	5,491	1,254
Montana	132,159	87,882	62,445	22,772	1,706	253	706	44,277	23,341	18,766	1,906	217	47
Wyoming	60,705	39,343	27,706	10,308	859	144	326	21,362	11,634	8,777	823	105	23
Colorado	412,198	245,247	161,033	75,735	6,044	736	1,699	166,951	87,490	69,100	9,575	712	74
New Mexico	153,593	83,055	50,085	29,343	2,479	207	41	70,538	36,431	28,931	4,877	290	9
Arizona	59,620	36,571	25,972	9,536	918	104	41	23,049	12,628	8,764	1,595	62	......
Utah	207,905	110,463	74,266	33,823	1,802	214	358	97,442	57,408	33,790	5,708	492	44
Nevada	45,761	29,214	19,990	8,023	771	166	264	16,547	8,924	6,282	1,051	125	165
Idaho	84,385	51,290	35,393	14,500	1,120	191	86	33,095	18,799	12,987	1,101	111	7
Washington	349,390	217,562	146,851	63,538	5,145	761	1,267	131,828	69,902	56,380	4,986	447	113
Oregon	313,767	181,840	118,827	56,202	4,853	752	1,146	131,927	73,129	52,312	5,874	537	75
California	1,208,130	700,059	455,250	216,029	19,222	2,586	6,972	508,071	272,694	194,621	37,666	2,393	697

830 STATISTICS OF POPULATION.

TABLE **82.**—CONJUGAL CONDITION OF THE AGGREGATE POPULATION OF THE UNITED STATES, CLASSIFIED BY SEX, GENERAL NATIVITY, COLOR, AND AGE PERIODS: 1890.

MALES.

GENERAL NATIVITY, COLOR, AND CONJUGAL CONDITION.	Total.	Under 15 years.	15 to 19 years.	20 to 24 years.	25 to 29 years.	30 to 34 years.	35 to 44 years.	45 to 54 years.	55 to 64 years.	65 years and over.	Age unknown.
Aggregate	32,067,880	11,290,008	3,248,711	3,104,893	2,698,311	2,425,664	3,705,648	2,627,024	1,630,373	1,233,719	103,529
Single	19,945,576	11,289,865	3,230,835	2,505,460	1,240,797	642,827	568,511	239,928	111,144	69,100	47,109
Married	11,205,228	23	16,734	585,748	1,421,407	1,728,930	2,997,030	2,213,901	1,342,414	860,925	29,104
Widowed	815,437		187	7,610	26,601	43,777	120,796	157,920	166,686	287,583	4,327
Divorced	49,101	1	28	1,468	4,340	5,832	12,837	11,393	7,895	4,074	393
Unknown	52,538	119	966	4,607	5,166	4,298	6,474	3,882	2,301	12,137	22,596
White (total)	28,206,332	9,672,145	2,818,914	2,740,864	2,407,153	2,200,973	3,327,306	2,354,204	1,479,763	1,124,304	80,646
Single	17,404,880	9,672,048	2,805,397	2,264,012	1,144,507	590,836	500,320	216,251	101,450	62,777	38,183
Married	9,992,921	11	12,734	466,877	1,234,233	1,504,904	2,699,336	1,987,488	1,219,000	738,954	19,294
Widowed	721,971		85	5,253	20,709	36,894	102,517	137,032	149,988	266,108	3,385
Divorced	43,829		15	1,091	3,547	5,088	11,387	10,392	7,345	4,658	306
Unknown	42,731	86	683	3,631	4,007	3,251	4,806	3,041	1,881	1,807	19,478
Native white (total)	23,254,474	9,300,876	2,561,256	2,264,640	1,804,608	1,651,874	2,358,789	1,537,751	947,177	763,487	64,016
Single	15,563,710	9,300,789	2,548,614	1,860,631	829,576	426,130	339,241	129,264	60,048	39,034	30,383
Married	7,142,111	6	12,044	395,732	951,904	1,189,020	1,931,311	1,310,061	790,646	546,641	14,746
Widowed	483,646		74	4,636	17,332	30,232	75,965	88,954	90,264	173,603	2,586
Divorced	34,722		14	1,016	3,183	4,516	9,399	7,785	5,203	3,345	261
Unknown	30,285	81	510	2,625	2,613	1,976	2,873	1,687	1,016	864	16,040
Native white—native parents	17,472,903	6,592,718	1,770,908	1,604,239	1,295,025	1,229,228	1,944,905	1,374,640	883,493	718,548	59,199
Single	10,951,846	6,592,646	1,759,457	1,273,130	548,307	291,392	259,243	110,000	54,332	36,193	27,146
Married	6,030,361	6	11,008	324,224	728,285	909,155	1,611,698	1,177,114	739,602	515,609	13,530
Widowed	432,200		64	3,867	13,674	23,360	68,415	78,999	83,649	162,819	2,404
Divorced	30,182		11	855	2,604	3,595	7,941	6,951	4,865	3,114	246
Unknown	28,314	66	368	2,163	2,175	1,717	2,608	1,585	955	813	15,864
Native white—foreign parents	5,781,571	2,708,158	790,348	660,401	509,583	422,646	413,884	163,102	63,684	44,939	4,826
Single	4,611,864	2,708,143	789,157	587,501	281,269	134,738	79,998	19,264	5,716	2,841	3,237
Married	1,111,810		1,036	71,508	223,639	279,865	319,613	132,947	50,954	31,032	1,216
Widowed	51,386		10	769	3,658	6,863	12,550	9,955	6,615	10,784	182
Divorced	4,540		3	161	579	921	1,458	834	338	231	15
Unknown	1,971	15	142	462	438	259	265	102	61	51	176
Foreign white	4,951,858	371,269	257,658	476,224	602,545	549,099	968,577	816,453	532,586	360,817	16,630
Single	1,841,170	371,259	256,783	403,381	315,021	164,706	170,079	86,987	41,411	23,748	7,800
Married	2,850,810	5	690	71,145	282,329	375,884	768,025	677,427	428,444	242,313	4,548
Widowed	238,325		11	617	3,377	6,662	26,552	48,078	59,724	92,505	799
Divorced	9,107		1	75	361	572	1,988	2,607	2,142	1,313	45
Unknown	12,446	5	173	1,006	1,454	1,275	1,933	1,354	865	943	3,438
Colored (total)	3,861,548	1,617,863	429,797	364,029	291,158	224,691	378,282	272,820	150,610	109,415	22,883
Single	2,540,696	1,617,817	425,438	241,448	96,290	51,991	59,191	23,677	9,685	6,323	8,026
Married	1,212,307	12	4,012	118,871	187,174	164,026	297,694	226,413	123,324	80,971	9,810
Widowed	93,466		52	2,357	5,892	6,883	18,270	20,888	16,008	21,475	942
Divorced	5,272	1	13	377	793	744	1,450	1,001	490	316	87
Unknown	9,807	33	282	976	1,099	1,047	1,668	841	418	330	3,118
Persons of negro descent	3,725,561	1,605,840	422,258	350,392	272,044	203,361	348,858	257,301	144,701	107,311	18,435
Single	2,448,567	1,605,803	418,212	230,123	81,750	37,552	38,961	16,547	7,318	5,834	6,467
Married	1,175,525	12	3,842	117,005	183,105	157,959	284,067	218,932	120,301	79,851	9,871
Widowed	91,683		50	2,336	5,813	6,745	17,934	20,468	16,358	21,067	912
Divorced	5,213	1	13	374	782	734	1,435	993	484	311	86
Unknown	4,573	24	141	554	594	371	561	361	210	248	1,599
Chinese	103,007	1,285	3,846	10,051	16,470	19,147	31,016	13,062	4,411	747	3,572
Single	71,909	1,284	3,652	8,709	13,258	13,856	19,025	6,855	2,258	379	2,633
Married	26,720		100	1,034	2,706	4,654	10,281	5,658	1,801	289	137
Widowed	530			3	21	39	130	157	131	47	2
Divorced	13			1	1	5	1	1	2	2	
Unknown	4,435	1	94	304	484	593	979	391	159	30	1,400
Japanese	1,780	49	396	610	340	176	170	17	4	3	15
Single	1,549	49	395	582	287	112	102	9			13
Married	199		1	21	47	59	59	7	3	2	
Widowed	12				2	2	5	1	1	1	
Divorced	1						1				
Unknown	19			7	4	3	3				2
Civilized Indians	30,600	10,689	3,297	2,976	2,304	2,007	3,238	2,440	1,434	1,354	861
Single	18,671	10,681	3,179	2,034	905	471	503	266	109	110	413
Married	9,863		69	811	1,226	1,354	2,387	1,816	1,009	829	362
Widowed	1,241		2	18	56	97	210	262	208	360	28
Divorced	45			2	10	5	13	7	4	3	1
Unknown	780	8	47	111	107	80	125	89	44	52	117

CONJUGAL CONDITION.

831

TABLE 82.—CONJUGAL CONDITION OF THE AGGREGATE POPULATION OF THE UNITED STATES, CLASSIFIED BY SEX, GENERAL NATIVITY, COLOR, AND AGE PERIODS: 1890—Continued.

FEMALES.

GENERAL NATIVITY, COLOR, AND CONJUGAL CONDITION.	Total.	Under 15 years.	15 to 19 years.	20 to 24 years.	25 to 29 years.	30 to 34 years.	35 to 44 years.	45 to 54 years.	55 to 64 years.	65 years and over.	Age unknown.
Aggregate	30,554,370	10,952,192	3,308,852	3,091,783	2,529,466	2,152,966	3,346,031	2,480,878	1,499,997	1,183,569	58,636
Single	17,183,988	10,950,672	2,987,949	1,601,266	641,988	326,306	330,139	171,454	86,573	66,758	20,883
Married	11,126,196	1,411	313,083	1,444,712	1,805,064	1,717,204	2,608,266	1,790,979	905,027	418,399	24,551
Widowed	2,154,615	17	4,845	36,456	69,965	96,797	206,302	447,370	499,420	693,324	10,119
Divorced	71,895	12	1,101	6,931	10,588	11,161	18,899	13,080	6,721	3,091	311
Unknown	17,676	80	974	2,418	1,861	1,498	2,425	1,995	1,056	1,997	2,772
White (total)	26,777,558	9,372,643	2,856,433	2,707,603	2,230,534	1,943,859	2,978,212	2,185,905	1,375,006	1,077,808	49,495
Single	14,946,572	9,371,429	2,604,070	1,455,162	591,276	302,038	303,601	159,679	81,451	62,183	16,283
Married	9,925,915	1,130	248,468	1,224,572	1,591,385	1,557,516	2,423,665	1,634,516	841,087	387,660	15,916
Widowed	1,831,778	6	2,519	21,135	47,357	74,003	233,882	378,516	444,907	623,528	5,925
Divorced	61,131	6	802	5,243	8,383	9,366	16,119	11,832	6,288	2,900	192
Unknown	12,162	72	574	1,491	1,133	936	1,545	1,422	1,273	1,537	2,179
Native white (total)	22,607,549	9,012,553	2,592,796	2,266,453	1,769,840	1,550,638	2,216,243	1,505,383	904,814	756,321	32,508
Single	13,799,308	9,011,402	2,362,566	1,213,898	471,460	250,407	240,189	123,275	62,364	50,213	13,534
Married	7,490,812	1,073	226,058	1,027,994	1,250,791	1,230,807	1,793,117	1,124,412	555,225	268,303	12,432
Widowed	1,256,923	5	2,344	18,616	39,207	60,242	168,000	247,405	281,808	434,783	4,423
Divorced	52,152	6	761	4,832	7,572	8,469	13,780	9,523	4,781	2,247	172
Unknown	8,354	67	467	1,113	810	713	1,058	768	636	775	1,947
Native white—native parents	16,885,445	6,354,770	1,781,616	1,580,928	1,250,156	1,147,641	1,828,798	1,352,503	846,819	713,592	28,622
Single	9,570,885	6,353,705	1,585,623	765,762	280,866	168,777	190,310	109,949	57,750	46,051	11,192
Married	6,133,033	1,006	192,949	795,480	924,765	927,600	1,480,857	1,013,877	521,493	254,687	11,229
Widowed	1,129,964	5	2,074	14,957	29,011	43,933	135,928	219,321	262,495	409,085	4,155
Divorced	44,290	6	642	3,930	5,904	6,657	11,746	8,642	4,472	2,130	161
Unknown	7,273	48	328	799	610	584	957	714	600	739	1,885
Native white—foreign parents	5,722,104	2,657,783	811,180	685,525	519,684	402,997	387,445	152,880	57,995	42,729	3,886
Single	4,210,423	2,657,697	776,943	448,136	181,594	81,630	49,879	13,326	4,614	3,262	2,342
Married	1,357,779	67	33,709	232,514	326,026	303,117	303,260	110,535	33,732	13,616	1,203
Widowed	135,959	....	270	3,659	10,196	16,309	32,162	28,084	19,313	25,698	268
Divorced	7,862	....	119	902	1,668	1,812	2,043	881	309	117	11
Unknown	1,081	10	139	314	200	129	101	54	27	36	62
Foreign white	4,170,009	360,090	263,637	441,150	460,694	393,221	761,969	680,582	470,192	321,487	7,987
Single	1,147,264	360,027	241,504	241,204	119,816	51,631	62,812	36,404	19,087	11,970	2,749
Married	2,435,103	57	21,810	196,578	340,594	326,709	630,548	510,104	285,862	119,357	3,484
Widowed	574,855	1	175	2,519	8,150	13,761	65,792	131,111	163,099	188,745	1,502
Divorced	8,979	....	41	411	811	897	2,330	2,300	1,507	653	20
Unknown	3,808	5	107	378	323	223	487	654	637	762	232
Colored (total)	3,776,812	1,579,549	452,419	384,180	289,932	209,107	367,819	244,913	124,991	105,761	18,141
Single	2,237,416	1,579,243	383,879	146,104	50,712	24,268	27,138	11,775	5,122	4,575	4,600
Married	1,200,281	281	65,515	220,140	213,679	159,688	274,601	162,403	64,540	30,739	8,635
Widowed	322,837	11	2,326	15,321	22,908	22,794	62,420	68,854	54,513	69,796	4,194
Divorced	10,764	6	299	1,688	2,205	1,795	2,780	1,248	433	191	119
Unknown	5,514	8	400	927	728	562	880	573	383	460	593
Persons of negro descent	3,744,479	1,568,929	448,860	381,156	287,507	206,616	363,723	242,378	123,559	104,373	17,378
Single	2,220,040	1,568,632	381,090	145,011	50,223	23,801	26,693	11,570	5,041	4,495	4,300
Married	1,187,700	272	64,815	218,364	211,920	157,821	271,500	160,695	63,734	30,281	8,295
Widowed	320,295	11	2,301	15,242	22,505	22,632	61,980	68,368	54,013	69,000	4,144
Divorced	10,604	6	297	1,679	2,197	1,780	2,708	1,233	429	188	117
Unknown	4,928	8	357	860	653	492	773	512	342	409	522
Chinese	3,868	704	329	484	482	555	806	275	62	11	70
Single	1,780	703	243	182	144	124	183	61	15	....	41
Married	1,952	1	84	296	328	419	580	190	36	7	11
Widowed	85	....	1	4	8	7	32	19	10	4	....
Divorced	3	....	....	....	....	1	1	1	1	....	....
Unknown	42	....	1	2	2	4	10	4	1	....	18
Japanese	259	32	51	87	48	14	18	5	4	....	....
Single	180	31	42	67	23	7	7	2	1	....	....
Married	73	1	9	20	22	6	10	3	2	....	....
Widowed	6	....	....	....	3	....	1	....	1	....	....
Divorced	....	....	....	....	....	1	....	....	....	....	....
Unknown	....	....	....	....	....	....	....	....	....	....	....
Civilized Indians	28,200	9,704	3,179	2,453	1,895	1,922	3,272	2,255	1,366	1,377	693
Single	14,504	9,787	2,504	844	322	246	255	142	65	80	259
Married	10,550	7	607	1,460	1,400	1,442	2,511	1,575	768	451	329
Widowed	2,541	....	24	75	92	154	398	467	480	792	50
Divorced	67	....	2	9	8	14	11	14	4	3	2
Unknown	544	....	42	65	73	66	97	57	40	51	53

DWELLINGS AND FAMILIES.

DWELLINGS AND FAMILIES.

913

TABLE 86.—TOTAL DWELLINGS AND PERSONS TO A DWELLING, BY STATES AND TERRITORIES: 1850 TO 1890.

[In 1860 and 1870 the total number of dwellings includes both occupied and unoccupied dwellings, while in 1850, 1880, and 1890 the total number of occupied dwellings only is given. For 1850 and 1860 the number of dwellings is for the free population only, as at those censuses the dwellings of the slave population were not returned.]

STATES AND TERRITORIES.	NUMBER OF DWELLINGS.					PERSONS TO A DWELLING.				
	1890	1880	1870	1860	1850	1890	1880	1870	1860	1850
The United States	11,483,318	8,955,812	7,042,833	4,969,692	3,362,337	5.45	5.60	5.47	5.53	5.94
North Atlantic division	2,962,345	2,430,182	2,103,500	1,808,435	1,390,005	5.87	5.97	5.85	5.86	6.21
Maine	135,255	124,950	121,953	115,933	95,802	4.89	5.19	5.14	5.42	6.09
New Hampshire	76,665	68,381	67,046	65,908	57,330	4.91	5.07	4.75	4.94	5.55
Vermont	69,817	66,769	66,145	62,977	56,421	4.76	4.98	5.00	5.00	5.57
Massachusetts	355,280	281,188	236,473	205,319	152,835	6.30	6.34	6.16	6.00	6.51
Rhode Island	52,250	41,388	34,828	27,056	22,370	6.61	6.08	6.24	6.45	6.59
Connecticut	130,779	108,458	96,880	83,022	64,013	5.71	5.74	5.55	5.50	5.79
New York	895,593	772,512	688,559	615,888	473,936	6.70	6.58	6.37	6.30	6.54
New Jersey	247,342	190,403	155,936	116,353	81,064	5.84	5.94	5.81	5.78	6.04
Pennsylvania	999,364	776,124	635,680	515,319	386,216	5.26	5.52	5.54	5.64	5.99
South Atlantic division	1,626,372	1,383,493	1,102,778	656,074	528,596	5.45	5.49	5.31	5.37	5.71
Delaware	33,882	27,215	22,577	19,288	15,290	4.97	5.30	5.54	5.72	5.84
Maryland	184,204	155,070	129,620	106,137	81,708	5.66	6.03	6.02	5.65	6.03
District of Columbia	38,798	28,687	23,308	12,338	7,917	5.94	6.19	5.65	5.83	6.00
Virginia	292,054	265,611	224,947	207,305	165,815	5.66	5.69	5.45	5.33	5.72
West Virginia	136,378	108,349	78,854	....	....	5.59	5.71	5.61	....	....
North Carolina	301,571	264,305	202,504	129,585	104,906	5.37	5.30	5.29	5.11	5.53
South Carolina	217,195	191,914	143,485	58,220	52,642	5.30	5.19	4.92	5.18	5.39
Georgia	342,874	280,474	236,436	109,009	91,200	5.36	5.33	5.01	5.46	5.75
Florida	78,816	52,868	41,647	14,132	9,022	4.97	5.10	4.57	5.57	5.34
North Central division	4,287,480	3,172,734	2,405,626	1,688,446	911,565	5.22	5.47	5.40	5.32	5.83
Ohio	720,414	580,064	495,607	425,672	336,098	5.10	5.45	5.38	5.50	5.89
Indiana	452,043	375,225	318,469	256,946	170,178	4.85	5.27	5.28	5.26	5.81
Illinois	669,812	538,221	404,155	304,732	146,544	5.71	5.72	5.47	5.62	5.81
Michigan	434,370	321,514	237,036	150,952	71,616	4.82	5.00	5.00	4.96	5.55
Wisconsin	316,163	230,361	197,098	154,036	56,316	5.34	5.50	5.35	5.04	5.42
Minnesota	229,678	136,458	81,140	40,926	1,002	5.67	5.72	5.42	4.20	6.06
Iowa	379,318	301,507	210,840	131,663	32,902	5.04	5.39	5.44	5.13	5.83
Missouri	485,320	369,180	292,760	181,069	96,849	5.52	5.87	5.87	5.89	6.14
North Dakota	37,918 }	a29,324	a3,231	a1,361	....	{4.82}	a4.61	a4.39	a3.55	....
South Dakota	68,894 }					{4.77}				
Nebraska	201,470	85,848	25,144	7,811	....	5.26	5.27	4.89	3.69	....
Kansas	202,086	180,432	71,071	33,278	....	4.80	5.26	5.13	2.96	....
South Central division	2,007,279	1,623,664	1,197,569	668,387	490,280	5.47	5.49	5.37	5.64	5.81
Kentucky	335,990	286,000	224,960	164,161	130,769	5.53	5.75	5.87	5.67	5.90
Tennessee	323,136	276,734	224,816	147,947	120,419	5.47	5.57	5.60	5.64	5.90
Alabama	281,602	240,227	198,327	96,682	73,070	5.37	5.26	5.03	5.47	5.87
Mississippi	235,056	208,297	164,150	61,460	51,681	5.47	5.43	5.04	5.77	5.74
Louisiana	204,341	174,807	150,427	63,902	49,101	5.47	5.38	4.83	5.88	5.56
Texas	402,422	287,562	141,685	77,428	27,988	5.56	5.54	5.78	5.45	5.52
Oklahoma	14,942	....	....	....	....	4.14	....	....	....	....
Arkansas	209,190	149,377	93,195	56,717	28,252	5.39	5.37	5.20	5.72	5.76
Western division	599,836	345,739	233,860	148,350	41,891	5.05	5.11	4.24	4.17	4.27
Montana	26,934	9,205	9,450	....	....	4.91	4.25	2.18	....	....
Wyoming	11,880	4,282	2,370	....	....	5.11	4.85	3.83	....	....
Colorado	81,127	39,018	10,009	....	....	5.08	4.98	3.98	....	....
New Mexico	34,671	26,311	21,053	21,945	13,453	4.43	4.54	4.36	4.26	4.57
Arizona	13,388	9,033	2,822	....	....	4.47	4.48	3.42	....	....
Utah	37,285	26,710	18,200	10,763	2,322	5.58	5.39	4.75	3.75	4.90
Nevada	10,006	14,557	12,990	....	....	4.55	4.28	3.27	....	....
Idaho	17,852	7,700	4,622	....	....	4.73	4.24	3.25	....	....
Washington	68,893	15,512	6,066	3,037	....	5.08	4.84	3.95	3.82	....
Oregon	61,925	32,374	19,372	12,277	2,374	5.07	5.40	4.60	4.27	5.60
California	235,925	161,037	126,307	100,828	23,742	5.12	5.37	4.44	3.79	3.90

a Dakota territory.

914 STATISTICS OF POPULATION.

TABLE 87.—TOTAL FAMILIES AND PERSONS TO A FAMILY, BY STATES AND TERRITORIES: 1850 TO 1890.

[In 1850 and 1860 the number of families given is for the free population only, as at those censuses the families of the slave population were not returned.]

STATES AND TERRITORIES.	NUMBER OF FAMILIES.					PERSONS TO A FAMILY.				
	1890	1880	1870	1860	1850	1890	1880	1870	1860	1850
The United States	12,690,152	9,945,916	7,579,363	5,210,934	3,598,240	4.93	5.04	5.00	5.28	5.55
North Atlantic division	3,712,242	3,023,741	2,497,494	2,048,315	1,582,978	4.69	4.80	4.92	5.17	5.45
Maine	150,355	141,843	131,017	120,863	103,333	4.40	4.58	4.78	5.20	5.64
New Hampshire	87,348	80,286	72,144	69,018	62,287	4.31	4.32	4.41	4.72	5.15
Vermont	75,869	73,092	70,462	63,781	58,573	4.38	4.55	4.69	4.94	5.36
Massachusetts	479,790	379,710	305,534	251,287	192,875	4.67	4.70	4.77	4.90	5.16
Rhode Island	75,010	60,259	46,133	35,209	28,216	4.61	4.59	4.71	4.96	5.23
Connecticut	165,890	136,885	114,981	94,831	73,448	4.50	4.55	4.67	4.85	5.05
New York	1,308,015	1,078,905	898,772	758,420	566,869	4.59	4.71	4.88	5.12	5.40
New Jersey	308,339	232,309	183,043	130,348	89,080	4.69	4.87	4.95	5.16	5.50
Pennsylvania	1,061,026	840,452	675,408	524,558	408,497	4.95	5.10	5.21	5.34	5.60
South Atlantic division	1,687,767	1,463,361	1,132,621	652,306	537,857	5.25	5.19	5.17	5.40	5.61
Delaware	34,578	28,253	22,900	18,966	15,439	4.87	5.10	5.46	5.82	5.78
Maryland	202,179	175,318	140,078	110,278	87,384	5.16	5.33	5.57	5.44	5.64
District of Columbia	43,967	34,896	25,276	12,888	8,343	5.24	5.00	5.21	5.58	5.75
Virginia	304,673	282,355	231,574	201,523	167,580	5.44	5.36	5.29	5.49	5.67
West Virginia	140,359	111,732	78,474	....	....	5.43	5.54	5.63	....	....
North Carolina	306,952	270,994	205,970	125,090	105,451	5.27	5.17	5.20	5.20	5.50
South Carolina	222,941	202,062	151,105	58,642	52,937	5.16	4.93	4.67	5.14	5.36
Georgia	352,059	303,060	237,850	109,919	91,666	5.22	5.00	4.98	5.41	5.72
Florida	80,059	54,691	39,394	15,090	9,107	4.89	4.93	4.77	5.21	5.20
North Central division	4,598,605	3,380,017	2,480,311	1,683,190	934,873	4.86	5.12	5.23	5.34	5.69
Ohio	785,291	641,907	521,981	434,134	348,514	4.68	4.98	5.11	5.39	5.68
Indiana	467,146	391,203	320,160	248,664	171,564	4.69	5.06	5.25	5.43	5.70
Illinois	778,015	591,934	474,533	315,539	149,153	4.92	5.20	5.35	5.43	5.71
Michigan	455,004	336,973	241,006	144,761	72,611	4.60	4.86	4.91	5.17	5.48
Wisconsin	335,456	251,530	200,155	147,473	57,608	5.03	5.23	5.27	5.26	5.30
Minnesota	247,975	143,374	82,471	37,319	1,010	5.25	5.45	5.33	4.61	5.98
Iowa	388,517	310,894	222,430	124,098	33,517	4.92	5.23	5.37	5.44	5.73
Missouri	528,295	403,186	316,917	192,073	100,890	5.07	5.38	5.43	5.56	5.89
North Dakota	38,478 }	a31,202	a3,090	·a1,241	....	4.75 }	a4.33	a4.59	a3.90	....
South Dakota	70,250 }					4.68 }				
Nebraska	206,820	89,135	25,075	5,931	....	5.12	5.08	4.91	4.86	....
Kansas	297,358	197,679	72,493	31,957	....	4.80	5.04	5.03	4.43	....
South Central division	2,071,120	1,697,550	1,242,411	684,024	499,767	5.30	5.25	5.18	5.51	5.70
Kentucky	354,463	302,631	232,797	166,321	132,920	5.24	5.45	5.67	5.59	5.80
Tennessee	334,194	286,539	231,365	149,335	130,004	5.29	5.38	5.44	5.59	5.87
Alabama	287,292	248,961	202,704	96,603	73,786	5.27	5.07	4.92	5.48	5.81
Mississippi	241,148	215,055	166,828	63,015	52,107	5.35	5.26	4.96	5.63	5.69
Louisiana	214,123	192,833	158,099	74,725	54,112	5.22	4.87	4.60	5.04	5.04
Texas	411,251	297,250	154,483	76,781	28,377	5.44	5.35	5.30	5.49	5.44
Oklahoma	15,029	....	....	....	....	4.11	....	....	....	....
Arkansas	213,020	154,272	96,135	57,244	28,401	5.28	5.20	5.04	5.67	5.72
Western division	620,418	372,247	226,520	143,009	42,765	4.88	4.75	4.37	4.33	4.18
Montana	27,501	9,931	7,058	....	....	4.81	3.94	2.92	....	....
Wyoming	12,065	4,604	2,248	....	....	5.03	4.52	4.06	....	....
Colorado	84,276	41,260	9,358	....	....	4.89	4.71	4.20	....	....
New Mexico	35,504	28,255	21,440	20,881	13,502	4.33	4.23	4.28	4.48	4.50
Arizona	13,495	9,536	2,290	....	....	4.42	4.24	4.22	....	....
Utah	38,816	28,373	17,219	9,500	2,322	5.36	5.07	5.04	4.96	4.90
Nevada	10,170	15,158	9,880	....	....	4.50	4.11	4.30	....	....
Idaho	18,113	7,774	4,104	....	....	4.66	4.19	3.65	....	....
Washington	70,977	16,380	5,673	2,798	....	4.92	4.59	4.22	4.14	....
Oregon	63,791	33,408	18,504	11,063	2,374	4.92	5.22	4.91	4.74	5.00
California	245,710	177,508	128,752	98,767	24,567	4.92	4.87	4.35	3.85	3.77

a Dakota territory.

AGES.

STATISTICS OF POPULATION.

2

TABLE 1.—AGES OF THE AGGREGATE POPULATION OF THE UNITED

[For "School, militia, and voting ages", see Part I

	AGES.	ALL CLASSES.			AGGREGATE WHITE.			NATIVE WHITE.		
		Total.	Males.	Females.	Total.	Males.	Females.	Total.	Males.	Females.
1	All ages	62,622,250	32,067,880	30,554,370	54,983,890	28,206,332	26,777,558	45,862,023	23,254,474	22,607,549
2	Under 1 month	44,037	22,828	21,209	39,238	20,360	18,878	39,180	20,330	18,850
3	1 to 2 months	303,228	153,891	150,337	265,391	136,464	128,927	264,926	136,222	128,704
4	3 to 5 months	440,065	224,250	215,815	379,130	193,815	185,437	378,115	193,177	184,938
5	6 to 8 months	457,999	233,086	224,913	397,136	202,543	194,593	395,629	201,783	193,846
6	9 to 11 months	315,405	160,318	155,087	278,225	141,706	136,519	277,664	141,114	135,950
7	Under 1 year	1,566,734	799,373	767,361	1,359,120	694,766	664,354	1,354,914	692,626	662,288
8	1 year	1,077,008	549,646	527,362	922,010	470,763	451,247	915,657	467,516	448,141
9	2 years	1,729,817	881,496	848,321	1,494,150	761,469	732,681	1,476,658	752,602	724,056
10	3 years	1,631,988	822,110	809,878	1,407,725	710,352	697,373	1,381,659	697,211	684,448
11	4 years	1,629,146	832,244	796,902	1,396,613	713,754	682,839	1,364,131	697,109	667,022
12	1 to 4 years	6,067,959	3,085,496	2,982,463	5,220,528	2,656,338	2,564,190	5,138,105	2,614,438	2,523,667
13	5 years	1,549,046	782,512	766,534	1,332,983	674,166	658,817	1,296,130	655,371	640,759
14	6 years	1,610,340	811,844	798,496	1,374,361	693,906	680,455	1,332,092	672,457	659,635
15	7 years	1,513,567	767,489	746,078	1,294,689	656,959	637,730	1,246,578	632,558	614,620
16	8 years	1,520,708	767,669	753,039	1,282,569	618,030	664,539	1,225,047	618,981	606,066
17	9 years	1,380,337	700,838	679,499	1,183,575	602,931	584,644	1,124,970	571,546	553,424
18	5 to 9 years	7,573,998	3,830,352	3,743,646	6,473,163	3,276,983	3,196,185	6,224,817	3,150,913	3,073,904
19	10 years	1,507,462	773,225	734,237	1,273,463	651,774	621,689	1,195,095	612,145	582,950
20	11 years	1,275,962	644,197	631,765	1,111,215	561,151	550,064	1,038,065	524,308	513,757
21	12 years	1,502,978	763,934	739,044	1,264,959	642,489	621,469	1,170,265	599,389	570,876
22	13 years	1,328,148	670,273	657,875	1,131,083	570,708	560,375	1,056,140	532,702	523,438
23	14 years	1,418,959	723,158	695,801	1,211,653	617,936	593,717	1,127,028	574,355	552,673
24	10 to 14 years	7,033,509	3,574,787	3,458,722	5,991,972	3,044,058	2,947,914	5,595,593	2,842,899	2,752,694
25	15 years	1,288,864	644,358	644,506	1,109,434	554,511	554,923	1,026,947	512,646	514,301
26	16 years	1,387,653	679,536	708,117	1,192,901	586,824	606,077	1,099,846	540,677	559,169
27	17 years	1,259,177	629,165	630,012	1,096,990	549,971	547,019	999,787	501,778	498,009
28	18 years	1,400,253	679,280	720,973	1,203,812	584,977	618,835	1,080,531	525,772	554,759
29	19 years	1,221,616	616,372	605,244	1,072,210	542,631	529,579	946,041	480,383	466,558
30	15 to 19 years	6,557,563	3,248,711	3,308,852	5,675,247	2,818,914	2,856,433	5,154,052	2,561,256	2,592,796
31	20 years	1,282,322	588,850	693,472	1,110,078	515,417	594,661	943,558	434,846	508,712
32	21 years	1,246,876	662,919	583,957	1,103,766	585,870	517,896	949,416	504,206	445,210
33	22 years	1,275,042	634,724	640,318	1,120,487	558,477	562,010	931,210	461,367	469,843
34	23 years	1,225,888	625,558	600,330	1,082,110	554,701	527,409	886,898	451,661	435,237
35	24 years	1,166,548	592,842	573,706	1,032,026	526,399	505,627	819,081	412,530	407,451
36	20 to 24 years	6,196,676	3,104,893	3,091,783	5,448,467	2,740,864	2,707,603	4,531,093	2,264,640	2,266,453
37	25 years	1,173,842	583,737	589,605	1,004,636	504,037	500,599	768,871	376,126	392,745
38	26 years	1,041,110	530,672	510,438	925,995	474,025	451,970	707,033	352,731	354,302
39	27 years	979,887	514,915	464,972	878,349	462,343	416,006	675,765	346,513	329,252
40	28 years	1,142,216	595,513	546,703	1,023,897	534,503	489,394	785,248	398,324	386,924
41	29 years	891,222	473,474	417,748	813,810	432,245	381,565	637,531	330,914	306,617
42	25 to 29 years	5,227,777	2,698,311	2,529,466	4,646,687	2,407,153	2,239,534	3,574,448	1,804,608	1,769,840
43	30 years	1,359,566	712,834	646,732	1,177,888	622,121	554,767	884,691	451,274	433,417
44	31 years	729,771	394,163	335,608	676,869	364,881	312,088	534,886	280,674	254,212
45	32 years	908,090	478,139	429,951	833,852	438,560	395,292	644,403	328,715	315,688
46	33 years	816,613	434,335	382,278	752,982	400,764	352,218	590,542	336,969	253,573
47	34 years	764,590	406,193	358,397	703,221	373,727	329,494	547,990	284,242	263,748
48	30 to 34 years	4,578,630	2,425,664	2,152,966	4,144,832	2,200,973	1,943,859	3,202,512	1,651,874	1,550,638
49	35 years	1,013,609	543,311	470,298	868,087	469,680	398,407	614,324	338,964	395,360
50	36 years	770,655	406,462	364,193	697,665	368,617	329,048	529,110	273,104	256,006
51	37 years	673,381	358,122	315,259	610,122	324,875	285,247	463,630	242,154	221,476
52	38 years	789,875	415,485	374,390	706,204	372,401	333,803	518,420	267,989	250,431
53	39 years	618,641	327,664	290,977	557,852	295,870	261,982	413,854	215,761	199,093
54	35 to 39 years	3,866,161	2,051,044	1,815,117	3,439,930	1,831,443	1,608,487	2,569,338	1,337,972	1,231,366
55	40 years	1,037,336	536,562	500,774	877,160	460,642	416,518	588,681	299,461	289,220
56	41 years	486,853	262,302	224,551	450,151	242,500	207,651	330,645	174,692	155,953
57	42 years	630,022	328,928	301,094	580,063	303,100	276,963	407,108	297,187	190,931
58	43 years	533,183	275,087	258,096	494,592	255,593	238,999	352,589	178,776	173,813
59	44 years	498,124	251,725	246,399	463,632	234,038	229,594	326,711	160,701	166,010
60	40 to 44 years	3,185,518	1,654,604	1,530,914	2,865,648	1,495,923	1,369,725	2,005,604	1,020,817	984,877
61	45 years	779,816	406,182	373,634	671,505	353,193	318,312	437,471	221,963	215,508
62	46 years	524,565	276,809	247,756	480,250	251,975	228,275	335,493	171,564	163,869
63	47 years	468,635	244,157	224,478	430,047	222,715	207,332	299,425	150,907	148,518
64	48 years	533,040	270,383	262,657	480,177	243,013	237,164	321,474	158,129	163,345
65	49 years	425,584	220,571	205,013	387,241	200,217	187,024	267,602	135,084	132,518
66	45 to 49 years	2,731,640	1,418,102	1,313,538	2,449,220	1,271,113	1,178,107	1,661,465	837,647	823,758

a Persons of negro descent, Chinese, Japanese, and civilized Indians.

AGES.

STATES, CLASSIFIED BY SEX, GENERAL NATIVITY, AND COLOR: 1890.

of the Report on Population, pages 731–826.]

NATIVE WHITE—NATIVE PARENTS.			NATIVE WHITE—FOREIGN PARENTS.			FOREIGN WHITE.			COLORED. (a)			
Total.	Males.	Females.	Total.	Males.	Females.	Total.	Males.	Females.	Total.	Males.	Females.	
34,358,343	17,472,903	16,885,445	11,503,675	5,781,571	5,722,104	9,121,867	4,951,858	4,170,009	7,638,360	3,861,548	3,776,812	1
25,822	13,373	12,449	13,358	6,957	6,401	58	30	28	4,799	2,468	2,231	2
182,643	94,181	88,450	82,283	42,038	40,245	465	242	223	43,837	22,427	21,410	3
203,284	134,856	128,428	114,831	58,321	56,510	1,015	516	499	60,935	30,557	30,378	4
274,582	140,000	134,000	121,047	61,201	59,846	1,507	760	747	60,863	30,543	30,320	5
195,326	99,799	95,527	81,738	41,315	40,423	1,161	592	569	37,180	18,612	18,568	6
941,657	482,794	458,863	413,257	209,832	203,425	4,206	2,140	2,066	207,614	104,607	103,007	7
638,444	326,611	311,833	277,213	140,905	136,308	6,353	3,247	3,106	154,998	78,883	76,115	8
1,034,753	529,095	505,658	441,905	223,507	218,398	17,492	8,867	8,625	235,667	120,027	115,640	9
968,205	489,350	478,870	413,424	207,855	205,560	26,066	13,141	12,925	224,263	111,758	112,505	10
967,593	496,077	471,516	396,538	201,032	195,506	32,512	16,645	15,867	232,503	118,490	114,013	11
3,600,025	1,841,139	1,767,886	1,529,080	773,299	755,781	82,423	41,900	40,523	847,431	429,158	418,273	12
910,072	460,990	449,082	386,058	194,361	191,677	36,853	18,795	18,058	216,063	108,346	107,717	13
948,936	479,865	469,071	383,156	192,592	190,564	42,269	21,449	20,820	235,979	117,938	118,041	14
884,285	449,398	434,887	362,293	183,160	179,133	48,102	24,392	23,710	218,857	110,509	108,348	15
880,583	446,456	434,127	344,464	172,525	171,939	57,522	29,049	28,473	238,139	119,639	118,500	16
808,024	411,159	396,865	316,946	160,387	156,559	63,605	32,385	31,220	191,762	96,907	94,855	17
4,431,900	2,247,868	2,184,032	1,792,917	903,045	889,872	248,351	126,070	122,281	1,100,800	553,369	547,461	18
862,812	444,304	418,508	332,283	167,841	164,442	78,368	39,629	38,739	233,999	121,451	112,548	19
740,038	374,446	365,592	298,027	149,862	148,165	73,150	36,843	36,307	164,747	83,046	81,701	20
838,804	427,594	411,210	340,461	171,795	168,666	84,693	43,100	41,593	239,020	121,445	117,575	21
742,650	375,527	367,120	313,484	157,175	156,309	75,543	38,006	37,537	198,465	99,565	96,900	22
780,596	399,046	381,550	346,432	175,309	171,123	84,625	43,581	41,044	207,366	105,223	102,051	23
3,961,906	2,020,917	1,943,989	1,630,687	821,982	808,705	396,379	201,159	195,220	1,041,537	530,729	510,808	24
707,882	353,904	353,978	319,065	158,742	160,323	82,487	41,865	40,622	179,430	89,847	89,583	25
756,005	371,493	384,512	343,841	169,184	174,657	93,055	46,147	46,908	194,752	92,712	102,040	26
686,192	344,643	341,549	313,595	157,135	156,460	97,203	48,193	49,010	162,187	79,104	82,093	27
749,260	367,515	381,745	331,271	158,257	173,014	123,281	59,205	64,976	196,441	94,303	102,138	28
653,185	333,353	319,832	293,756	147,030	146,726	125,269	62,248	63,021	149,406	73,741	75,665	29
3,553,524	1,770,908	1,781,616	1,601,628	790,348	811,180	521,295	257,658	263,637	882,216	429,797	452,419	30
655,220	302,054	353,166	288,338	132,792	155,546	166,520	80,571	85,949	172,244	73,433	98,811	31
670,504	357,850	312,654	278,912	146,356	132,556	154,350	81,664	72,686	143,110	77,049	66,061	32
656,435	327,949	328,486	274,805	133,448	141,357	189,217	97,080	92,167	154,555	76,247	78,308	33
626,769	323,003	303,766	260,129	128,658	131,471	195,212	103,040	92,172	143,778	70,857	72,921	34
576,239	293,383	282,856	243,742	119,147	124,595	212,045	113,869	98,176	134,522	66,443	68,079	35
3,185,167	1,604,239	1,580,928	1,345,926	660,401	685,525	917,374	476,224	441,150	748,209	364,029	384,180	36
540,926	267,207	273,719	227,045	108,919	119,026	235,765	127,911	107,854	168,706	79,700	89,006	37
497,708	249,885	247,823	209,325	102,846	106,479	218,962	121,294	97,668	115,115	56,647	58,468	38
480,208	248,063	232,145	195,557	98,450	97,107	202,584	115,830	86,754	101,538	52,572	48,966	39
565,240	289,027	276,213	220,008	109,297	110,711	234,649	136,179	102,470	118,319	61,010	57,309	40
461,099	240,843	220,256	176,432	90,071	86,361	176,279	101,331	74,948	77,412	41,229	36,183	41
2,545,181	1,295,025	1,250,156	1,029,267	509,583	519,684	1,072,239	602,545	469,694	581,090	291,158	289,932	42
650,205	333,808	316,497	234,326	117,406	116,920	293,197	171,847	121,350	181,678	89,713	91,965	43
392,815	206,290	186,525	142,071	74,384	67,687	142,003	84,127	57,876	52,882	29,362	23,520	44
474,529	242,562	231,967	169,874	86,153	83,721	189,449	109,845	79,604	74,238	39,579	34,659	45
442,550	230,456	212,094	147,992	76,513	71,479	162,440	93,795	68,645	63,631	33,571	30,060	46
416,610	216,052	200,558	131,380	68,190	63,190	155,231	89,485	65,746	61,369	32,466	28,903	47
2,376,869	1,229,228	1,147,641	825,643	422,646	402,997	942,320	549,099	393,221	433,793	224,691	209,107	48
501,566	264,360	237,206	142,758	74,604	68,154	223,763	130,716	93,047	145,522	73,631	71,891	49
417,795	215,632	202,163	111,375	57,472	53,903	168,555	95,513	73,042	72,990	37,845	35,145	50
372,215	194,605	177,610	91,415	47,549	43,866	146,492	82,721	63,771	63,259	33,247	30,012	51
420,837	217,700	203,137	97,583	50,289	47,294	187,784	104,412	83,372	83,671	43,084	40,587	52
341,940	178,600	163,340	71,914	37,161	34,753	143,998	80,109	63,889	60,789	31,794	28,995	53
2,054,293	1,070,897	983,396	515,045	267,075	247,970	870,592	493,471	377,121	426,231	219,601	206,630	54
495,075	251,871	243,204	93,606	47,590	46,016	288,479	161,181	127,298	160,176	75,920	84,256	55
282,707	149,369	133,338	47,938	25,323	22,615	119,506	67,808	51,698	36,702	19,802	16,900	56
340,193	177,323	171,870	57,875	29,864	28,011	172,995	95,913	77,082	49,959	25,828	24,131	57
366,053	151,913	151,140	46,536	23,863	22,673	142,003	76,817	65,186	38,591	19,494	19,097	58
286,382	140,532	145,850	40,329	20,169	20,160	136,971	73,387	63,584	34,442	17,637	16,805	59
1,719,410	874,008	845,402	286,284	146,809	139,475	859,954	475,106	384,848	319,870	158,681	161,189	60
384,593	194,656	189,937	52,878	27,307	25,571	234,034	131,230	102,804	108,311	52,989	55,322	61
296,504	151,351	145,153	38,929	20,213	18,716	144,817	80,411	64,406	44,315	24,834	19,481	62
265,665	133,403	132,262	33,760	17,504	16,256	130,622	71,808	58,814	38,588	21,442	17,146	63
285,257	139,894	145,363	36,217	18,235	17,982	158,703	84,884	73,819	52,863	27,379	25,483	64
239,339	120,358	118,981	28,263	14,726	13,537	119,639	65,133	54,566	38,343	20,354	17,985	65
1,471,358	739,662	731,696	190,047	97,985	92,062	787,815	433,466	354,349	282,420	146,980	135,431	66

STATISTICS OF POPULATION.

4

TABLE 1.—AGES OF THE AGGREGATE POPULATION OF THE UNITED

	AGES.	ALL CLASSES.			AGGREGATE WHITE.			NATIVE WHITE.		
		Total.	Males.	Females.	Total.	Males.	Females.	Total.	Males.	Females.
67	50 years	776,333	390,323	386,010	656,920	332,190	324,730	404,822	198,065	206,757
68	51 years	336,202	179,425	156,777	309,499	163,793	145,706	213,803	110,553	103,250
69	52 years	440,347	233,168	207,179	405,653	212,692	192,961	273,766	140,666	133,100
70	53 years	387,734	207,237	180,497	360,395	191,151	169,244	245,792	128,489	117,303
71	54 years	385,646	198,769	186,877	358,482	183,265	175,217	243,546	122,331	121,215
72	50 to 54 years	2,326,262	1,208,922	1,117,340	2,090,949	1,083,091	1,007,858	1,381,729	700,104	681,025
73	55 years	437,032	224,290	212,742	385,225	196,948	188,277	239,561	120,878	118,683
74	56 years	375,254	196,965	178,289	345,609	179,537	166,072	229,022	116,812	112,210
75	57 years	305,830	164,204	141,626	285,040	151,761	133,279	193,558	102,244	91,314
76	58 years	313,340	160,889	152,451	290,514	148,358	142,156	191,678	96,932	94,746
77	59 years	240,830	125,315	115,565	225,271	116,697	108,574	152,709	77,950	74,759
78	55 to 59 years	1,672,336	871,663	800,673	1,531,659	793,301	738,358	1,006,528	514,816	491,712
79	60 years	502,788	252,505	250,283	424,321	213,519	210,802	247,284	122,425	124,859
80	61 years	206,016	110,144	95,872	193,276	102,829	90,447	129,702	68,096	61,696
81	62 years	261,577	138,959	122,618	246,153	129,783	116,370	162,325	81,445	77,880
82	63 years	256,730	136,570	120,160	241,188	127,286	113,902	162,073	84,256	77,817
83	64 years	230,923	120,532	110,391	218,172	113,045	105,127	143,980	73,130	70,850
84	60 to 64 years	1,458,034	753,710	699,324	1,323,110	686,462	636,648	845,463	432,361	413,102
85	65 years	310,320	159,067	151,253	268,171	137,165	131,006	168,206	84,256	83,950
86	66 years	195,990	102,628	93,362	185,589	96,296	89,293	124,501	63,793	60,708
87	67 years	183,170	97,194	85,976	171,979	90,733	81,246	115,049	59,754	55,895
88	68 years	181,546	93,609	87,937	169,035	86,801	82,234	114,477	58,044	56,433
89	69 years	139,084	73,119	65,965	130,750	68,484	62,266	91,117	46,947	44,170
90	65 to 69 years	1,010,110	525,627	484,483	925,524	479,479	446,045	613,350	312,734	301,216
91	70 years	245,007	123,049	121,958	208,938	105,827	103,111	132,781	66,198	66,583
92	71 years	110,117	59,289	50,828	104,593	56,248	48,345	74,295	39,416	34,879
93	72 years	132,706	70,058	62,648	125,182	65,983	59,399	89,472	46,416	43,056
94	73 years	113,126	59,002	54,124	107,330	55,803	51,527	77,129	39,646	37,483
95	74 years	100,795	52,244	48,551	95,708	49,464	46,244	69,268	35,285	33,983
96	70 to 74 years	701,751	363,642	338,109	641,951	333,325	308,626	442,945	226,961	215,984
97	75 years	122,098	60,962	61,136	105,369	52,886	52,483	71,303	35,149	36,154
98	76 years	85,204	43,633	41,571	80,021	40,804	39,217	57,785	29,120	28,615
99	77 years	65,702	33,354	32,348	62,792	31,731	31,061	46,823	23,325	23,498
100	78 years	71,032	36,152	34,880	66,176	33,644	32,532	48,611	24,433	24,178
101	79 years	49,026	24,992	24,034	46,467	23,643	22,824	35,138	17,569	17,569
102	75 to 79 years	393,062	199,093	193,969	360,825	182,708	178,057	259,610	129,601	130,009
103	80 years	76,472	36,171	40,301	63,171	30,529	32,642	43,518	20,950	22,568
104	81 years	34,637	17,235	17,402	32,755	16,327	16,428	25,469	12,571	12,898
105	82 years	35,831	17,700	18,131	33,834	16,704	17,130	26,025	12,610	13,415
106	83 years	29,519	14,043	15,476	27,857	13,218	14,639	21,828	10,230	11,598
107	84 years	27,392	12,713	14,679	25,678	11,870	13,808	19,602	8,944	10,658
108	80 to 84 years	203,851	97,862	105,989	183,295	88,648	94,647	136,442	65,305	71,137
109	85 years	24,914	11,168	13,746	20,937	9,489	11,448	15,268	6,754	8,514
110	86 years	17,767	8,231	9,536	16,524	7,596	8,928	12,385	5,573	6,812
111	87 years	14,662	6,833	7,829	12,844	5,667	7,177	9,720	4,188	5,532
112	88 years	10,595	4,802	5,793	9,663	4,336	5,327	7,348	3,212	4,136
113	89 years	7,902	3,629	4,273	7,047	3,217	3,830	5,369	2,383	2,986
114	85 to 89 years	75,240	34,063	41,177	67,015	30,305	36,710	50,090	22,110	27,980
115	90 years	12,446	5,192	7,254	9,029	3,899	5,130	6,226	2,654	3,572
116	91 years	3,881	1,710	2,171	3,425	1,500	1,925	2,657	1,122	1,535
117	92 years	3,067	1,250	1,817	2,678	1,078	1,600	2,013	790	1,223
118	93 years	2,429	1,002	1,427	2,092	855	1,237	1,590	628	962
119	94 years	1,822	694	1,128	1,542	588	954	1,154	418	736
120	90 to 94 years	23,645	9,848	13,797	18,766	7,920	10,846	13,640	5,612	8,028
121	95 years	2,106	773	1,333	1,298	497	801	882	318	564
122	96 years	1,227	475	752	891	344	547	602	218	384
123	97 years	838	336	502	588	228	360	403	155	248
124	98 years	964	385	579	571	230	341	372	149	223
125	99 years	513	217	296	334	147	187	218	90	128
126	95 to 99 years	5,648	2,186	3,462	3,682	1,446	2,236	2,477	930	1,547
127	100 years and over	3,981	1,398	2,583	1,054	413	641	654	234	420
128	Age unknown	162,165	103,529	58,636	121,141	80,646	40,495	96,524	64,016	32,508

a Persons of negro descent, Chinese, Japanese, and civilized Indians.

AGES.

5

STATES, CLASSIFIED BY SEX, GENERAL NATIVITY, AND COLOR: 1890—Continued.

NATIVE WHITE—NATIVE PARENTS.			NATIVE WHITE—FOREIGN PARENTS.			FOREIGN WHITE.			COLORED. (a)			
Total.	Males.	Females.	Total.	Males.	Females.	Total.	Males.	Females.	Total.	Males.	Females.	
364,032	177,654	186,378	40,790	20,411	20,379	252,098	134,125	117,973	119,413	58,133	61,280	67
194,228	100,185	94,043	19,575	10,368	9,207	95,696	53,240	42,456	26,703	15,632	11,071	68
249,243	127,733	121,510	24,523	12,933	11,590	131,887	72,026	59,861	34,694	20,476	14,218	69
224,750	117,428	107,322	21,042	11,061	9,981	114,603	62,662	51,941	27,339	16,086	11,253	70
223,541	111,987	111,554	20,005	10,344	9,661	114,936	60,934	54,002	27,164	15,504	11,660	71
1,255,794	634,987	620,807	125,935	65,117	60,818	709,220	382,987	326,233	235,313	125,831	109,482	72
221,054	111,347	109,707	18,507	9,531	8,976	145,664	76,070	69,594	51,807	27,342	24,465	73
212,190	108,023	104,167	16,832	8,789	8,043	116,587	62,725	53,862	29,645	17,428	12,217	74
180,117	94,982	85,135	13,441	7,262	6,179	91,482	49,517	41,965	20,790	12,443	8,347	75
178,530	90,169	88,361	13,148	6,763	6,385	98,836	51,426	47,410	22,826	12,531	10,295	76
143,121	72,926	70,195	9,588	5,024	4,564	72,562	38,747	33,815	15,609	8,618	6,991	77
935,012	477,447	457,565	71,516	37,369	34,147	525,131	278,485	246,646	140,677	78,362	62,315	78
231,765	114,568	117,197	15,519	7,857	7,662	177,037	91,694	85,943	78,467	38,986	39,481	79
122,270	64,077	58,193	7,522	4,019	3,503	63,484	34,733	28,751	12,740	7,315	5,425	80
152,825	79,335	73,490	9,500	5,110	4,390	83,828	45,338	38,490	15,424	9,176	6,248	81
152,807	79,317	73,490	9,266	4,939	4,327	79,115	43,030	36,085	15,542	9,284	6,258	82
135,633	68,749	66,884	8,356	4,390	3,966	74,183	39,906	34,277	12,751	7,487	5,264	83
795,300	406,046	389,254	50,163	26,315	23,848	477,647	254,101	223,546	134,924	72,248	62,676	84
158,421	79,285	79,136	9,785	4,971	4,814	99,965	52,909	47,056	42,149	21,902	20,247	85
117,485	60,027	57,458	7,016	3,706	3,310	61,088	32,563	28,525	10,401	6,342	4,059	86
109,093	56,301	52,792	6,556	3,453	3,103	56,330	30,979	25,351	11,101	6,461	4,730	87
107,898	54,680	53,218	6,579	3,364	3,215	54,558	28,757	25,801	12,511	6,808	5,703	88
85,896	44,227	41,669	5,221	2,720	2,501	39,633	21,537	18,096	8,334	4,635	3,699	89
578,793	294,520	284,273	35,157	18,214	16,943	311,574	166,745	144,829	84,586	46,148	38,438	90
125,172	62,379	62,793	7,609	3,819	3,790	76,157	39,629	36,528	36,069	17,222	18,847	91
70,124	37,127	32,997	4,171	2,289	1,882	30,298	16,832	13,466	5,524	3,041	2,483	92
84,661	43,888	40,773	4,811	2,528	2,283	35,910	19,567	16,343	7,324	4,075	3,249	93
73,003	37,435	35,568	4,126	2,211	1,915	30,201	16,157	14,044	5,796	3,199	2,597	94
65,433	33,308	32,125	3,835	1,977	1,858	26,440	14,179	12,261	5,087	2,780	2,307	95
418,393	214,137	204,256	24,552	12,824	11,728	199,006	106,364	92,642	59,800	30,317	29,483	96
67,381	33,164	34,217	3,922	1,985	1,937	34,066	17,737	16,329	16,729	8,076	8,653	97
54,404	27,398	27,006	3,331	1,722	1,609	22,286	11,684	10,602	5,183	2,829	2,354	98
44,154	21,961	22,193	2,669	1,364	1,305	15,969	8,466	7,503	2,910	1,563	1,347	99
45,592	22,839	22,753	3,019	1,599	1,420	17,565	9,206	8,359	4,856	2,508	2,348	100
33,049	16,496	16,553	2,089	1,073	1,016	11,329	6,074	5,255	2,550	1,349	1,210	101
244,580	121,858	122,722	15,030	7,743	7,287	101,215	53,167	48,048	32,237	16,325	15,912	102
40,879	19,667	21,212	2,639	1,283	1,356	19,653	9,579	10,074	13,301	5,642	7,659	103
23,969	11,843	12,126	1,500	728	772	7,286	3,530	3,716	1,882	908	974	104
24,351	11,780	12,571	1,674	830	844	7,809	4,094	3,715	1,997	996	1,001	105
20,481	9,595	10,886	1,347	635	712	6,029	2,988	3,041	1,662	825	837	106
18,316	8,333	9,983	1,286	611	675	6,076	2,926	3,150	1,714	843	871	107
127,996	61,218	66,778	8,446	4,087	4,359	46,853	23,343	23,510	20,556	9,214	11,342	108
14,303	6,304	7,999	965	450	515	5,669	2,735	2,934	3,877	1,679	2,298	109
11,567	5,184	6,383	818	389	429	4,139	2,023	2,116	1,243	635	608	110
9,099	3,909	5,190	621	279	342	3,124	1,479	1,645	1,218	566	652	111
6,859	2,987	3,872	480	225	264	2,315	1,124	1,191	932	466	466	112
5,020	2,213	2,807	349	170	179	1,678	834	844	855	412	443	113
46,848	20,597	26,251	3,242	1,513	1,729	16,925	8,195	8,730	8,225	3,758	4,467	114
5,774	2,431	3,343	452	223	229	2,803	1,245	1,558	3,417	1,293	2,124	115
2,477	1,041	1,436	180	81	99	768	378	390	456	210	246	116
1,862	722	1,140	151	68	83	665	288	377	389	172	217	117
1,478	581	897	112	47	65	502	227	275	337	147	190	118
1,071	381	690	83	37	46	388	170	218	280	106	174	119
12,662	5,156	7,506	978	456	522	5,126	2,308	2,818	4,879	1,928	2,951	120
808	293	515	74	25	49	416	179	237	808	276	532	121
561	201	360	41	17	24	289	126	163	336	131	205	122
366	141	225	37	14	23	185	73	112	250	108	142	123
343	136	207	29	13	16	199	81	118	393	155	238	124
199	83	116	19	7	12	116	57	50	179	70	109	125
2,277	854	1,423	200	76	124	1,205	516	689	1,966	740	1,226	126
591	208	383	63	26	37	400	179	221	2,927	985	1,942	127
87,812	59,190	28,622	8,712	4,826	3,886	24,617	16,630	7,987	41,024	22,883	18,141	128

SCHOOL ATTENDANCE.

BY STATES AND TERRITORIES: 1890.

TABLE 9.—TOTAL PERSONS ATTENDING SCHOOL DURING THE CENSUS YEAR, CLASSIFIED BY GENERAL NATIVITY AND COLOR.

TABLE 10.—TOTAL PERSONS ATTENDING SCHOOL DURING THE CENSUS YEAR, CLASSIFIED BY SEX AND AGE PERIODS.

TABLE 11.—WHITE PERSONS ATTENDING SCHOOL DURING THE CENSUS YEAR, CLASSIFIED BY SEX AND AGE PERIODS.

TABLE 12.—NATIVE WHITE PERSONS ATTENDING SCHOOL DURING THE CENSUS YEAR, CLASSIFIED BY SEX AND AGE PERIODS.

TABLE 13.—NATIVE WHITE PERSONS OF NATIVE PARENTAGE ATTENDING SCHOOL DURING THE CENSUS YEAR, CLASSIFIED BY SEX AND AGE PERIODS.

TABLE 14.—NATIVE WHITE PERSONS OF FOREIGN PARENTAGE ATTENDING SCHOOL DURING THE CENSUS YEAR, CLASSIFIED BY SEX AND AGE PERIODS.

TABLE 15.—FOREIGN WHITE PERSONS ATTENDING SCHOOL DURING THE CENSUS YEAR, CLASSIFIED BY SEX AND AGE PERIODS.

TABLE 16.—COLORED PERSONS ATTENDING SCHOOL DURING THE CENSUS YEAR, CLASSIFIED BY SEX AND AGE PERIODS.

TABLE 17.—NEGRO PERSONS ATTENDING SCHOOL DURING THE CENSUS YEAR, CLASSIFIED BY SEX AND AGE PERIODS.

TABLE 18.—TOTAL PERSONS ATTENDING SCHOOL DURING THE CENSUS YEAR, CLASSIFIED BY SEX, AGE PERIODS, AND MONTHS OF SCHOOL ATTENDANCE.

TABLE 19.—NATIVE WHITE PERSONS OF NATIVE PARENTAGE ATTENDING SCHOOL DURING THE CENSUS YEAR, CLASSIFIED BY SEX, AGE PERIODS, AND MONTHS OF SCHOOL ATTENDANCE.

TABLE 20.—NATIVE WHITE PERSONS OF FOREIGN PARENTAGE ATTENDING SCHOOL DURING THE CENSUS YEAR, CLASSIFIED BY SEX, AGE PERIODS, AND MONTHS OF SCHOOL ATTENDANCE.

TABLE 21.—FOREIGN WHITE PERSONS ATTENDING SCHOOL DURING THE CENSUS YEAR, CLASSIFIED BY SEX, AGE PERIODS, AND MONTHS OF SCHOOL ATTENDANCE.

TABLE 22.—COLORED PERSONS ATTENDING SCHOOL DURING THE CENSUS YEAR, CLASSIFIED BY SEX, AGE PERIODS, AND MONTHS OF SCHOOL ATTENDANCE.

TABLE 23.—NEGRO PERSONS ATTENDING SCHOOL DURING THE CENSUS YEAR, CLASSIFIED BY SEX, AGE PERIODS, AND MONTHS OF SCHOOL ATTENDANCE.

FOR THE UNITED STATES: 1890.

TABLE 24.—TOTAL PERSONS ATTENDING SCHOOL DURING THE CENSUS YEAR, CLASSIFIED BY SEX, GENERAL NATIVITY, COLOR, AGE PERIODS, AND MONTHS OF SCHOOL ATTENDANCE.

FOR CITIES HAVING 25,000 INHABITANTS OR MORE: 1890.

TABLE 25.—TOTAL PERSONS ATTENDING SCHOOL DURING THE CENSUS YEAR, CLASSIFIED BY SEX AND AGE PERIODS.

TABLE 26.—NATIVE WHITE PERSONS OF NATIVE PARENTAGE ATTENDING SCHOOL DURING THE CENSUS YEAR, CLASSIFIED BY SEX AND AGE PERIODS.

TABLE 27.—NATIVE WHITE PERSONS OF FOREIGN PARENTAGE ATTENDING SCHOOL DURING THE CENSUS YEAR, CLASSIFIED BY SEX AND AGE PERIODS.

TABLE 28.—FOREIGN WHITE PERSONS ATTENDING SCHOOL DURING THE CENSUS YEAR, CLASSIFIED BY SEX AND AGE PERIODS.

TABLE 29.—COLORED PERSONS ATTENDING SCHOOL DURING THE CENSUS YEAR, CLASSIFIED BY SEX AND AGE PERIODS.

TABLE 30.—TOTAL PERSONS ATTENDING SCHOOL DURING THE CENSUS YEAR, CLASSIFIED BY SEX, AGE PERIODS, AND MONTHS OF SCHOOL ATTENDANCE.

SCHOOL ATTENDANCE.

TABLE 9.—TOTAL PERSONS ATTENDING SCHOOL DURING THE CENSUS YEAR, CLASSIFIED BY GENERAL NATIVITY AND COLOR, BY STATES AND TERRITORIES: 1890.

STATES AND TERRITORIES.	Aggregate.	Total white.	NATIVE WHITE.			Foreign white.	COLORED.		
			Total.	Native parents.	Foreign parents.		Total.	Negro. (a)	Chinese, Japanese, and civilized Indians.
The United States	11,674,873	10,667,171	10,153,289	7,204,755	2,948,534	513,882	1,007,707	999,324	8,383
North Atlantic division	3,003,712	2,967,164	2,764,443	1,732,705	1,031,738	202,721	36,548	35,458	1,090
Maine	132,032	131,715	124,919	104,765	20,154	6,706	317	223	94
New Hampshire	61,760	61,660	56,022	42,440	13,582	5,638	100	100	....
Vermont	61,007	60,847	58,082	42,689	15,393	2,765	160	151	9
Massachusetts	378,410	374,977	334,757	165,411	169,346	40,220	3,433	3,338	95
Rhode Island	55,474	54,359	47,831	23,811	24,020	6,528	1,115	1,088	27
Connecticut	126,459	124,560	114,922	62,299	52,623	9,638	1,899	1,870	29
New York	985,625	977,221	903,872	482,828	421,044	73,349	8,404	8,295	109
New Jersey	241,844	235,673	219,452	131,514	87,938	16,221	6,171	6,144	27
Pennsylvania	961,101	946,152	904,586	676,948	227,638	41,566	14,949	14,249	700
South Atlantic division	1,451,265	1,035,058	1,027,648	964,441	63,207	7,410	416,207	415,794	413
Delaware	27,822	24,925	24,354	20,977	3,377	571	2,897	2,897	....
Maryland	168,958	142,268	138,945	110,486	28,459	3,323	26,690	26,685	5
District of Columbia	36,205	25,218	24,765	18,573	6,192	453	10,987	10,979	8
Virginia	290,965	196,788	196,224	191,061	5,163	564	94,177	94,021	156
West Virginia	163,365	158,631	157,930	149,210	8,720	701	4,734	4,731	3
North Carolina	260,125	187,000	186,859	185,465	1,394	141	73,125	72,893	232
South Carolina	161,303	78,676	78,572	76,419	2,153	104	82,627	82,621	6
Georgia	267,914	175,191	174,849	170,935	3,914	342	92,723	92,722	1
Florida	74,608	46,361	45,150	41,315	3,835	1,211	28,247	28,245	2
North Central division	4,808,762	4,727,819	4,461,693	2,895,312	1,566,381	266,126	80,943	76,988	3,955
Ohio	775,524	758,842	736,277	552,460	183,817	22,565	16,682	16,631	51
Indiana	474,750	466,459	460,636	389,894	70,742	5,823	8,291	8,160	131
Illinois	763,675	753,696	705,135	427,733	277,402	48,561	9,979	9,960	19
Michigan	422,601	419,128	374,952	199,372	175,580	44,176	3,473	2,801	672
Wisconsin	364,966	363,567	329,502	109,558	219,944	34,065	1,399	455	944
Minnesota	262,711	261,652	225,582	67,721	157,861	36,070	1,059	407	652
Iowa	469,862	467,866	446,707	277,214	169,493	21,159	1,996	1,993	3
Missouri	570,924	546,382	537,769	432,570	105,199	8,613	24,542	24,510	32
North Dakota	31,806	31,742	22,567	6,992	15,575	9,175	64	51	13
South Dakota	70,087	69,828	61,710	28,967	32,743	8,118	259	67	192
Nebraska	242,960	240,934	224,222	143,337	80,885	16,712	2,026	1,286	740
Kansas	359,896	347,723	336,634	259,494	77,140	11,089	11,173	10,667	506
South Central division	1,915,059	1,446,818	1,435,568	1,336,983	98,585	11,250	468,241	468,007	234
Kentucky	357,601	320,302	318,711	293,382	25,329	1,591	37,299	37,288	11
Tennessee	337,265	273,969	273,202	265,716	7,486	707	63,296	63,283	13
Alabama	215,895	143,215	142,582	138,353	4,229	633	72,680	72,656	24
Mississippi	251,547	127,021	126,906	123,145	3,761	115	124,526	124,453	73
Louisiana	122,206	79,341	78,625	62,336	16,289	716	42,865	42,851	14
Texas	407,167	327,305	320,717	284,938	35,779	6,588	79,862	79,775	87
Oklahoma	7,200	6,937	6,858	6,257	601	79	263	262	1
Arkansas	216,178	168,728	167,967	162,856	5,111	761	47,450	47,439	11
Western division	496,080	490,312	463,937	275,314	188,623	26,375	5,768	3,077	2,691
Montana	15,395	15,241	13,869	7,988	5,881	1,372	154	106	48
Wyoming	7,863	7,781	7,033	4,248	2,785	748	82	70	12
Colorado	60,327	59,610	55,796	38,125	17,671	3,814	717	680	37
New Mexico	20,713	20,121	19,722	17,426	2,296	399	592	223	369
Arizona	7,765	7,621	6,866	3,983	2,883	755	134	50	84
Utah	41,278	41,213	38,730	13,295	25,435	2,483	65	35	30
Nevada	7,390	7,350	7,141	2,804	4,337	209	40	15	25
Idaho	14,878	14,842	14,267	8,804	5,463	575	36	27	9
Washington	52,240	51,552	47,537	31,982	15,555	4,015	688	104	584
Oregon	62,970	62,527	60,209	46,019	14,190	2,318	443	148	295
California	205,271	202,454	192,767	100,640	92,127	9,687	2,817	1,619	1,198

¡ a Includes all persons of negro descent.

STATISTICS OF POPULATION.

138

TABLE **10.**—TOTAL PERSONS ATTENDING SCHOOL DURING THE CENSUS YEAR, CLASSIFIED BY SEX AND AGE PERIODS, BY STATES AND TERRITORIES: 1890.

STATES AND TERRITORIES.	UNDER 5 YEARS.			5 TO 9 YEARS.			10 TO 14 YEARS.			15 TO 19 YEARS.			20 YEARS AND OVER.		
	Total.	Males.	Females.	Total.	Males.	Females.	Total.	Males.	Females.	Total.	Males.	Females.	Total.	Males.	Females.
United States....	8,830	4,245	4,085	3,726,044	1,888,039	1,838,005	5,607,358	2,831,005	2,776,353	2,155,141	1,111,989	1,043,152	178,005	118,864	59,141
North Atlantic division.	3,635	1,856	1,779	1,072,526	544,345	528,181	1,439,718	724,932	714,786	446,119	222,378	223,741	41,714	27,161	14,553
Maine	480	229	251	44,658	22,718	21,940	57,678	29,471	28,207	26,928	13,888	13,040	2,288	1,558	730
New Hampshire.	79	34	45	20,954	10,582	10,372	28,677	14,607	14,070	11,161	5,713	5,448	889	518	371
Vermont.........	78	39	39	19,850	10,235	9,615	28,348	14,687	13,661	11,734	6,022	5,712	997	634	363
Massachusetts...	622	307	315	140,878	70,969	69,909	175,376	88,233	87,143	54,598	25,784	28,814	6,036	4,007	2,029
Rhode Island	100	50	50	21,729	10,974	10,755	26,056	12,924	13,132	6,973	3,459	3,514	607	407	200
Connecticut	388	188	200	47,591	24,254	23,337	58,992	29,993	28,999	16,947	8,300	8,647	2,541	1,934	607
New York	1,171	631	540	355,440	180,426	175,014	477,058	241,847	235,211	138,312	68,289	70,023	13,044	8,996	4,848
New Jersey......	92	55	37	88,132	44,851	43,281	120,854	60,743	60,111	30,635	15,164	15,471	2,131	1,606	525
Pennsylvania....	616	314	302	333,294	169,336	163,958	466,079	232,427	234,252	148,831	75,759	73,072	11,681	7,501	4,180
South Atlantic division.	623	322	301	404,577	204,467	200,110	737,774	367,693	370,081	286,011	141,033	144,978	22,280	14,781	7,499
Delaware........	10	5	5	8,963	4,503	4,460	14,231	7,224	7,007	4,205	2,210	1,995	413	331	82
Maryland........	72	40	32	52,906	26,792	26,114	89,067	44,792	44,275	24,916	13,135	11,781	1,997	1,472	525
Dist. Columbia...	24	12	12	9,253	4,618	4,635	19,248	9,342	9,906	7,069	2,901	4,168	611	346	265
Virginia.........	155	74	81	79,783	40,643	39,140	146,639	72,687	73,952	60,207	28,202	32,005	4,181	2,550	1,631
West Virginia ...	52	26	26	45,861	23,450	22,411	78,411	40,058	38,353	36,105	19,296	16,869	2,876	1,865	1,011
North Carolina ..	94	50	44	66,043	33,331	32,712	129,608	64,358	65,250	58,424	29,223	29,201	5,956	3,942	2,014
South Carolina...	66	38	28	43,534	21,796	21,738	84,717	42,066	42,651	30,721	14,520	16,201	2,265	1,553	712
Georgia..........	99	53	46	76,270	38,385	37,885	130,757	68,015	70,842	48,041	23,769	25,172	2,847	2,053	794
Florida	51	24	27	21,964	10,949	11,015	36,096	18,251	17,845	15,303	7,777	7,586	1,134	669	465
North Central division.	2,841	1,408	1,373	1,591,003	805,788	785,215	2,223,154	1,130,395	1,092,759	916,988	489,587	427,401	74,776	50,557	24,219
Ohio	280	149	131	252,097	128,348	123,749	363,062	184,638	178,424	148,305	79,073	69,232	11,780	8,243	3,537
Indiana..........	164	83	81	148,319	74,745	73,574	220,586	111,727	108,859	97,271	52,572	44,699	8,410	5,706	2,704
Illinois	364	183	181	255,208	129,324	125,884	358,882	181,587	177,295	138,022	71,902	66,120	11,199	7,488	3,711
Michigan	269	138	131	147,057	74,317	72,740	198,110	100,727	97,383	71,443	37,209	34,234	5,722	3,554	2,168
Wisconsin.......	579	310	269	134,635	67,926	66,709	170,583	86,904	83,679	54,862	29,833	25,029	4,307	2,769	1,538
Minnesota.......	166	87	79	86,597	43,962	42,635	125,841	64,208	61,633	46,222	25,655	20,567	3,885	2,691	1,194
Iowa.............	407	213	194	162,684	82,212	80,472	204,175	103,969	100,206	94,324	50,925	43,399	8,272	5,692	2,580
Missouri.........	246	130	116	172,790	87,317	85,473	269,808	136,344	133,464	119,186	62,691	56,495	8,894	6,132	2,762
North Dakota....	30	10	20	11,243	5,782	5,461	14,832	7,830	7,002	5,368	3,000	2,368	333	241	92
South Dakota....	40	20	20	21,855	11,100	10,755	31,726	16,458	15,268	14,989	8,467	6,522	1,477	1,032	445
Nebraska........	140	64	76	87,168	44,280	42,888	106,278	54,483	51,795	45,730	24,867	20,863	3,644	2,496	1,148
Kansas	156	81	75	111,350	56,475	54,875	159,271	81,520	77,751	81,266	43,393	37,873	6,853	4,513	2,340
South Central division.	906	435	471	505,599	255,727	249,872	968,202	487,331	480,871	408,488	209,282	199,206	31,864	21,509	10,355
Kentucky	168	72	96	100,633	50,933	49,700	174,886	88,702	86,184	76,019	39,352	36,667	5,895	3,791	2,104
Tennessee	212	109	103	89,799	45,660	44,139	165,072	83,615	81,457	75,548	39,468	36,080	6,634	4,392	2,242
Alabama.........	81	47	34	52,290	26,317	25,973	111,884	55,648	56,236	47,458	23,770	23,688	4,182	2,742	1,440
Mississippi......	165	81	84	72,714	36,590	36,124	120,143	59,785	60,358	54,566	27,009	27,557	3,959	2,548	1,411
Louisiana........	62	22	40	36,930	18,800	18,130	65,609	32,961	32,648	18,551	8,910	9,641	1,054	731	323
Texas	141	66	75	94,000	47,279	46,721	224,339	112,821	111,518	83,303	42,218	41,085	5,384	3,913	1,471
Oklahoma	9	5	4	2,233	1,178	1,055	3,615	1,819	1,796	1,286	622	664	57	41	16
Arkansas........	68	33	35	57,000	28,970	28,030	102,654	51,980	50,674	51,757	27,933	23,824	4,699	3,351	1,348
Western division..	325	164	161	152,390	77,712	74,627	238,510	120,654	117,856	97,535	49,709	47,826	7,371	4,856	2,515
Montana.........	15	6	9	5,406	2,726	2,680	6,994	3,518	3,476	2,766	1,403	1,363	214	149	65
Wyoming........	7	3	4	2,785	1,456	1,329	3,569	1,841	1,728	1,388	715	673	114	87	27
Colorado.........	29	18	11	19,342	9,825	9,517	28,273	14,382	13,891	11,764	6,010	5,754	919	618	301
New Mexico	9	3	6	6,029	3,231	2,798	9,856	5,320	4,536	4,435	2,665	1,770	384	303	81
Arizona..........	1	1	......	2,292	1,183	1,109	4,077	2,078	1,999	1,336	653	683	49	33	16
Utah	8	3	5	11,668	6,061	5,607	20,607	10,358	10,249	8,318	4,372	3,946	677	462	215
Nevada..........	3	1	2	2,154	1,081	1,073	3,584	1,821	1,763	1,564	725	839	85	40	45
Idaho............	1	1	......	4,811	2,464	2,347	6,939	3,580	3,359	2,952	1,616	1,336	175	131	44
Washington	37	17	20	16,725	8,397	8,328	25,133	12,739	12,394	9,623	5,087	4,536	722	515	207
Oregon	41	26	15	19,152	9,648	9,504	29,058	14,669	14,389	13,613	7,136	6,477	1,106	761	345
California	174	85	89	61,975	31,640	30,335	100,420	50,348	50,072	39,776	19,327	20,449	2,926	1,757	1,169

SCHOOL ATTENDANCE.

139

TABLE 11.—WHITE PERSONS ATTENDING SCHOOL DURING THE CENSUS YEAR, CLASSIFIED BY SEX AND AGE PERIODS, BY STATES AND TERRITORIES: 1890.

STATES AND TERRITORIES.	UNDER 5 YEARS.			5 TO 9 YEARS.			10 TO 14 YEARS.			15 TO 19 YEARS.			20 YEARS AND OVER.		
	Total.	Males.	Females.	Total.	Males.	Females.	Total.	Males.	Females.	Total.	Males.	Females.	Total.	Males.	Females.
United States....	7,918	4,051	3,867	3,459,680	1,756,349	1,703,331	5,068,809	2,566,411	2,502,398	1,965,457	1,026,065	939,392	165,307	111,537	53,770
North Atlantic division.	3,622	1,848	1,774	1,060,154	538,318	521,836	1,421,060	715,720	705,340	441,251	219,968	221,283	41,077	26,678	14,399
Maine	480	229	251	44,549	22,660	21,889	57,543	29,397	28,146	26,867	13,850	13,003	2,276	1,555	721
New Hampshire .	79	34	45	20,925	10,569	10,356	28,624	14,577	14,047	11,145	5,702	5,443	887	517	370
Vermont........	77	39	38	19,785	10,199	9,586	28,281	14,656	13,625	11,713	6,009	5,704	991	628	363
Massachusetts...	622	307	315	139,608	70,364	69,244	173,762	87,466	86,296	54,105	25,556	28,549	6,880	3,970	2,910
Rhode Island	109	59	50	21,312	10,793	10,519	25,511	12,672	12,839	6,828	3,383	3,445	599	404	195
Connecticut	386	186	200	46,885	23,924	22,961	58,043	29,538	28,505	16,725	8,186	8,539	2,521	1,921	600
New York	1,166	628	538	352,610	179,024	173,586	472,584	239,579	233,005	137,313	67,817	69,496	13,548	8,930	4,618
New Jersey......	90	55	35	86,005	43,832	42,173	117,673	59,179	58,494	29,812	14,721	15,091	2,093	1,580	513
Pennsylvania....	613	311	302	328,475	166,953	161,522	459,039	228,656	230,383	146,743	74,735	72,008	11,282	7,173	4,109
South Atlantic division.	463	246	217	294,898	150,161	144,737	511,445	257,814	253,631	210,667	108,728	101,930	17,585	12,300	5,285
Delaware........	10	5	5	8,156	4,116	4,040	12,729	6,568	6,161	3,772	1,982	1,790	258	191	67
Maryland........	72	40	32	45,238	23,056	22,182	73,712	37,158	36,554	21,536	11,436	10,100	1,710	1,346	364
Dist. Columbia...	6	3	3	6,551	3,330	3,221	13,035	6,437	6,598	5,214	2,235	2,979	412	253	159
Virginia........	126	62	64	55,256	28,352	26,904	96,026	48,368	47,658	42,373	20,933	21,440	3,007	1,942	1,065
West Virginia...	52	26	26	44,506	22,786	21,720	76,001	38,894	37,107	35,244	18,825	16,419	2,828	1,831	997
North Carolina ..	74	42	32	48,894	24,786	24,108	91,189	45,788	45,401	42,042	22,079	19,963	4,801	3,404	1,397
South Carolina...	30	18	12	21,708	10,987	10,721	39,428	19,834	19,594	16,033	8,112	7,921	1,477	1,101	376
Georgia	58	33	25	50,792	25,801	24,991	87,649	43,679	43,970	34,422	17,828	16,594	2,270	1,735	535
Florida	35	17	18	13,797	6,947	6,850	21,676	11,088	10,588	10,031	5,298	4,733	822	497	325
North Central division.	2,827	1,459	1,368	1,567,693	794,270	773,423	2,182,136	1,109,539	1,072,597	901,487	481,884	419,603	73,676	49,840	23,836
Ohio............	277	147	130	246,994	125,768	121,226	354,760	180,314	174,446	145,253	77,532	67,721	11,558	8,096	3,462
Indiana..........	162	81	81	145,814	73,497	72,317	216,348	109,618	106,730	95,838	51,894	43,944	8,297	5,638	2,659
Illinois	364	183	181	252,188	127,828	124,360	353,851	179,047	174,804	136,103	71,028	65,170	11,100	7,427	3,673
Michigan........	268	137	131	145,959	73,776	72,183	196,360	99,828	96,532	70,872	36,923	33,949	5,669	3,517	2,152
Wisconsin.......	578	309	269	134,197	67,711	66,486	169,926	86,545	83,381	54,598	29,685	24,913	4,268	2,742	1,526
Minnesota.......	166	87	79	86,291	43,824	42,467	125,342	63,966	61,376	45,982	25,540	20,442	3,871	2,681	1,190
Iowa	407	213	194	162,043	81,914	80,129	203,219	103,488	99,731	93,951	50,737	43,214	8,246	5,673	2,573
Missouri	241	127	114	166,101	84,048	82,113	256,962	129,831	127,131	114,390	60,349	54,041	8,628	5,980	2,648
North Dakota....	30	10	20	11,219	5,778	5,441	14,809	7,816	6,993	5,352	2,989	2,363	332	240	92
South Dakota....	40	20	20	21,782	11,064	10,718	31,600	16,886	15,214	14,934	8,433	6,501	1,472	1,027	445
Nebraska........	140	64	76	86,554	43,956	42,598	105,343	53,990	51,353	45,328	24,653	20,675	3,569	2,435	1,134
Kansas..........	154	81	73	108,491	55,106	53,385	153,616	78,710	74,906	78,796	42,126	36,670	6,666	4,384	2,282
South Central division.	682	335	347	386,251	196,768	189,483	718,387	364,167	354,220	315,593	166,379	149,214	25,905	18,105	7,800
Kentucky	166	72	94	90,663	46,636	44,027	155,312	79,223	76,089	68,744	36,163	32,581	5,417	3,555	1,862
Tennessee	201	104	97	74,366	38,036	36,330	131,345	67,029	64,316	62,393	33,421	28,972	5,664	3,892	1,772
Alabama	59	36	23	35,828	18,324	17,504	71,982	36,317	35,665	32,189	16,954	15,235	3,157	2,177	980
Mississippi......	43	24	19	37,965	19,336	18,629	57,431	28,698	28,733	28,993	14,771	14,222	2,589	1,724	865
Louisiana........	47	18	29	24,060	12,339	11,721	41,569	21,025	20,544	12,885	6,472	6,413	780	560	220
Texas	114	54	60	75,889	38,349	37,540	178,343	90,190	88,153	68,555	35,671	32,884	4,404	3,353	1,051
Oklahoma	8	5	3	2,171	1,142	1,029	3,473	1,748	1,725	1,229	594	635	56	41	15
Arkansas........	44	22	22	45,309	23,206	22,103	78,932	39,937	38,995	40,605	22,333	18,272	3,838	2,803	1,035
Western division..	324	163	161	150,684	76,832	73,852	235,781	119,171	116,610	96,459	49,106	47,353	7,064	4,614	2,450
Montana	15	6	9	5,355	2,707	2,648	6,919	3,483	3,436	2,742	1,393	1,349	210	147	63
Wyoming	7	3	4	2,765	1,443	1,322	3,544	1,827	1,717	1,378	712	666	87	60	27
Colorado........	29	18	11	19,109	9,717	9,392	27,909	14,208	13,701	11,645	5,963	5,682	918	618	300
New Mexico	9	3	6	5,883	3,157	2,726	9,560	5,138	4,422	4,299	2,584	1,715	370	293	77
Arizona	1	1	....	2,253	1,100	1,093	3,999	2,041	1,958	1,819	646	673	49	33	16
Utah	7	2	5	11,643	6,047	5,596	20,581	10,343	10,238	8,307	4,363	3,944	675	460	215
Nevada.........	3	1	2	2,142	1,075	1,067	3,566	1,808	1,758	1,556	719	837	83	38	45
Idaho...........	1	1	....	4,805	2,460	2,345	6,919	3,570	3,349	2,942	1,609	1,333	175	131	44
Washington	37	17	20	16,528	8,308	8,220	24,791	12,578	12,213	9,485	5,018	4,467	711	507	204
Oregon	41	26	15	19,065	9,598	9,467	28,861	14,557	14,304	13,478	7,051	6,427	1,082	742	340
California	174	85	89	61,136	31,160	29,976	99,132	49,618	49,514	39,308	19,048	20,260	2,704	1,585	1,119

STATISTICS OF POPULATION.

140

TABLE **12.**—NATIVE WHITE PERSONS ATTENDING SCHOOL DURING THE CENSUS YEAR, CLASSIFIED BY SEX AND AGE PERIODS, BY STATES AND TERRITORIES: 1890.

STATES AND TERRITORIES.	UNDER 5 YEARS.			5 TO 9 YEARS.			10 TO 14 YEARS.			15 TO 19 YEARS.			20 YEARS AND OVER.		
	Total.	Males.	Females.	Total.	Males.	Females.	Total.	Males.	Females.	Total.	Males.	Females.	Total.	Males.	Females.
United States....	7,696	3,939	3,757	3,311,921	1,080,669	1,631,252	4,771,069	2,414,508	2,356,561	1,907,261	993,085	914,176	155,342	104,112	51,230
North Atlantic division.	3,473	1,766	1,707	991,939	503,339	488,600	1,304,675	657,166	647,509	426,815	212,460	214,355	37,541	24,002	13,539
Maine	461	213	248	42,306	21,498	20,808	53,882	27,566	26,316	26,062	13,441	12,621	2,208	1,502	706
New Hampshire..	77	34	40	19,014	9,570	9,442	25,465	12,994	12,471	10,229	5,105	5,100	909	400	050
Vermont.........	75	39	36	18,888	9,722	9,166	26,791	13,898	12,893	11,394	5,835	5,559	934	590	344
Massachusetts...	597	296	301	126,428	63,683	62,745	150,471	75,759	74,712	50,077	24,024	26,953	6,284	3,564	2,720
Rhode Island....	100	55	45	18,937	9,591	9,346	21,898	10,845	11,053	6,369	3,119	3,250	527	350	177
Connecticut......	371	177	194	43,668	22,266	21,402	52,464	26,716	25,748	16,102	7,839	8,263	2,317	1,754	563
New York	1,115	600	515	328,136	166,492	161,644	430,730	218,123	212,607	132,176	65,048	67,128	11,715	7,489	4,226
New Jersey......	88	53	35	80,470	40,932	39,538	108,095	54,304	53,791	28,879	14,195	14,684	1,920	1,438	482
Pennsylvania....	589	299	290	314,092	159,583	154,509	434,879	216,961	217,918	144,223	73,524	70,704	10,798	6,827	3,971
South Atlantic division.	460	244	216	292,720	149,060	143,660	507,259	255,682	251,577	209,867	108,305	101,562	17,342	12,099	5,243
Delaware	10	5	5	7,981	4,021	3,960	12,383	6,394	5,989	3,729	1,959	1,770	251	185	66
Maryland........	72	40	32	44,248	22,559	21,689	71,765	36,160	35,605	21,311	11,303	10,008	1,549	1,207	342
Dist. Columbia...	6	3	3	6,438	3,272	3,166	12,785	6,309	6,476	5,135	2,198	2,937	401	247	154
Virginia........	126	62	64	55,127	28,286	26,841	95,738	48,221	47,517	42,246	20,865	21,381	2,987	1,925	1,062
West Virginia ...	52	26	26	44,322	22,705	21,617	75,580	38,699	36,881	35,159	18,782	16,377	2,817	1,824	993
North Carolina ..	74	42	32	48,866	24,768	24,098	91,133	45,756	45,377	41,997	22,053	19,944	4,780	3,394	1,395
South Carolina...	30	18	12	21,682	10,971	10,711	39,381	19,807	19,574	16,004	8,100	7,904	1,475	1,099	376
Georgia..........	58	33	25	50,701	25,757	24,944	87,444	43,577	43,867	34,381	17,811	16,570	2,265	1,730	535
Florida	32	15	17	13,355	6,721	6,634	21,050	10,759	10,291	9,905	5,234	4,671	808	488	320
North Central division.	2,764	1,433	1,331	1,499,471	759,416	740,055	2,026,406	1,029,246	997,160	864,716	460,044	404,672	68,336	45,875	22,461
Ohio	270	143	127	240,616	122,523	118,093	341,274	173,504	167,770	142,987	76,175	66,812	11,130	7,783	3,347
Indiana..........	150	70	80	144,362	72,767	71,595	212,790	107,823	104,967	95,106	51,520	43,670	8,129	5,521	2,608
Illinois	357	180	177	238,106	120,640	117,466	324,301	164,012	160,289	132,072	68,184	63,888	10,299	6,789	3,510
Michigan	262	135	127	134,104	67,725	66,379	170,369	86,538	83,831	65,177	33,797	31,380	5,040	3,124	1,916
Wisconsin	552	295	257	124,564	62,768	61,796	149,516	75,908	73,608	51,107	27,577	23,530	3,763	2,346	1,417
Minnesota	162	87	75	78,493	39,807	38,686	103,797	52,778	51,019	40,157	21,974	18,183	2,973	1,991	982
Iowa............	404	212	192	156,711	79,225	77,486	191,538	97,457	94,081	90,331	48,489	41,842	7,723	5,276	2,447
Missouri	241	127	114	164,043	82,979	81,064	251,775	127,185	124,590	113,381	59,800	53,581	8,329	5,751	2,578
North Dakota....	30	10	20	9,313	4,804	4,509	9,635	5,084	4,551	3,406	1,889	1,524	183	134	49
South Dakota....	40	20	20	20,291	10,283	10,008	27,313	14,079	13,234	12,876	7,147	5,729	1,190	822	368
Nebraska........	134	64	70	82,664	41,972	40,692	96,300	49,208	47,092	41,919	22,540	19,379	3,205	2,171	1,034
Kansas..........	153	81	72	106,204	53,963	52,241	147,793	75,670	72,128	76,107	40,459	35,648	6,372	4,167	2,205
South Central division.	681	335	346	383,923	195,572	188,351	711,405	360,532	350,873	313,890	165,500	148,390	25,660	17,946	7,723
Kentucky	165	72	93	90,230	45,828	44,402	154,364	78,765	75,599	68,579	36,068	32,511	5,373	3,521	1,852
Tennessee	201	104	97	74,204	37,955	36,249	130,908	66,798	64,110	62,252	33,352	28,900	5,637	3,875	1,762
Alabama	59	36	23	35,660	18,236	17,424	71,621	36,129	35,492	32,094	16,907	15,187	3,148	2,171	977
Mississippi......	43	24	19	37,927	19,319	18,608	57,382	28,670	28,712	28,967	14,756	14,211	2,587	1,724	863
Louisiana........	47	18	29	23,853	12,230	11,623	41,180	20,834	20,346	12,789	6,416	6,373	756	541	215
Texas	114	54	60	74,673	37,703	36,970	174,063	87,915	86,148	67,553	35,158	32,395	4,314	3,296	1,018
Oklahoma	8	5	3	2,161	1,138	1,023	3,420	1,719	1,701	1,213	588	625	56	41	15
Arkansas........	44	22	22	45,215	23,163	22,052	78,467	39,702	38,765	40,443	22,255	18,188	3,798	2,777	1,021
Western division...	318	161	157	143,868	73,282	70,586	221,324	111,882	109,442	91,973	46,776	45,197	6,454	4,190	2,264
Montana	15	6	9	4,908	2,513	2,455	6,168	3,126	3,042	2,541	1,295	1,246	177	119	58
Wyoming........	7	3	4	2,550	1,338	1,212	3,125	1,619	1,506	1,276	653	623	75	50	25
Colorado	28	17	11	18,181	9,214	8,967	25,784	13,110	12,674	10,978	5,616	5,362	825	548	277
New Mexico	9	3	6	5,792	3,110	2,682	9,331	5,018	4,313	4,228	2,552	1,676	362	288	74
Arizona	1	1	......	2,071	1,063	1,008	3,557	1,820	1,737	1,196	580	616	41	26	15
Utah	7	2	5	11,128	5,783	5,345	19,158	9,660	9,498	7,812	4,101	3,711	625	428	197
Nevada	3	1	2	2,115	1,060	1,055	3,465	1,756	1,709	1,488	689	799	70	31	39
Idaho...........	1	1	......	4,714	2,406	2,308	6,584	3,409	3,175	2,805	1,528	1,277	163	122	41
Washington	36	17	19	15,431	7,749	7,682	22,501	11,379	11,122	8,937	4,727	4,210	632	453	179
Oregon	41	26	15	18,487	9,297	9,190	27,634	13,925	13,709	13,032	6,812	6,220	1,015	691	324
California	170	84	86	58,431	29,749	28,682	94,017	47,060	46,957	37,680	18,223	19,457	2,469	1,434	1,035

SCHOOL ATTENDANCE.

141

TABLE **13.**—NATIVE WHITE PERSONS OF NATIVE PARENTAGE ATTENDING SCHOOL DURING THE CENSUS YEAR, CLASSIFIED BY SEX AND AGE PERIODS, BY STATES AND TERRITORIES: 1890.

STATES AND TERRITORIES.	UNDER 5 YEARS.			5 TO 9 YEARS.			10 TO 14 YEARS.			15 TO 19 YEARS.			20 YEARS AND OVER.		
	Total.	Males.	Females.	Total.	Males.	Females.	Total.	Males.	Females.	Total.	Males.	Females.	Total.	Males.	Females.
United States....	4,610	2,348	2,262	2,254,297	1,144,455	1,109,842	3,345,072	1,694,627	1,650,445	1,472,714	767,972	704,742	128,062	86,018	42,044
North Atlantic division.	1,967	994	973	594,746	301,734	293,012	797,815	403,086	394,729	308,597	155,560	153,037	29,580	18,890	10,690
Maine............	381	172	209	34,565	17,471	17,094	44,883	22,995	21,888	22,872	11,885	10,987	2,064	1,403	661
New Hampshire.	57	25	32	13,484	6,791	6,693	19,146	9,779	9,367	9,009	4,588	4,421	744	423	321
Vermont........	58	30	28	13,545	6,948	6,597	19,287	9,971	9,316	8,970	4,623	4,347	829	518	311
Massachusetts...	227	118	109	57,573	28,978	28,595	71,065	35,759	35,306	31,611	14,953	16,658	4,935	2,680	2,255
Rhode Island	54	28	26	8,630	4,396	4,234	10,738	5,334	5,404	3,986	1,918	2,068	403	273	130
Connecticut	190	87	103	22,117	11,184	10,933	27,340	13,940	13,400	10,753	5,254	5,499	1,890	1,542	348
New York	536	285	251	171,136	86,917	84,219	220,359	111,783	108,576	82,786	40,850	41,936	8,011	5,018	2,993
New Jersey.....	59	36	23	46,438	23,685	22,753	62,908	31,755	31,153	20,623	10,117	10,506	1,486	1,134	352
Pennsylvania....	405	213	192	227,258	115,364	111,894	322,080	161,770	160,310	117,987	61,372	56,615	9,218	5,899	3,319
South Atlantic division.	443	236	207	273,308	139,182	134,126	474,073	239,085	234,988	200,091	103,517	96,574	16,526	11,476	5,050
Delaware	10	5	5	6,757	3,368	3,389	10,676	5,557	5,119	3,313	1,778	1,535	221	170	51
Maryland........	62	36	26	34,873	17,823	17,050	56,403	28,362	28,041	18,054	9,576	8,478	1,094	810	284
Dist. Columbia ..	4	3	1	4,896	2,490	2,307	9,459	4,681	4,778	3,883	1,678	2,205	331	196	135
Virginia	125	61	64	53,830	27,592	26,238	92,950	46,789	46,161	41,228	20,389	20,839	2,923	1,882	1,041
West Virginia ...	51	25	26	41,796	21,416	20,380	71,196	36,499	34,697	33,464	17,927	15,537	2,703	1,751	952
North Carolina...	73	42	31	48,542	24,587	23,955	90,427	45,410	45,017	41,655	21,872	19,783	4,768	3,382	1,386
South Carolina...	30	18	12	21,048	10,647	10,401	38,397	19,374	19,023	15,485	7,804	7,681	1,459	1,088	371
Georgia.........	56	31	25	49,584	25,198	24,386	85,385	42,565	42,820	33,663	17,521	16,148	2,241	1,713	528
Florida	32	15	17	11,982	6,052	5,930	19,180	9,848	9,332	9,340	4,972	4,368	781	479	302
North Central division.	1,410	722	688	945,840	479,351	466,489	1,288,455	654,882	633,573	607,246	320,943	286,303	52,361	35,080	17,281
Ohio	207	104	103	177,123	90,443	86,680	250,725	127,477	123,248	115,069	61,568	53,501	9,336	6,510	2,826
Indiana.........	134	69	65	122,614	61,738	60,876	177,262	89,776	87,486	82,621	44,797	37,824	7,263	4,966	2,297
Illinois	190	87	103	139,689	70,861	68,828	190,722	96,543	94,179	89,280	46,553	42,727	7,852	5,215	2,637
Michigan	110	49	61	66,715	33,551	33,164	89,542	45,662	43,880	39,315	29,214	19,101	3,690	2,279	1,411
Wisconsin	90	56	34	43,059	21,669	21,390	46,322	23,425	22,897	18,422	9,425	8,997	1,665	977	688
Minnesota	44	29	15	23,249	11,806	11,443	29,395	14,966	14,429	13,516	6,950	6,566	1,517	951	566
Iowa............	234	126	108	97,320	49,458	47,862	116,283	59,304	56,979	57,959	30,516	27,443	5,418	3,654	1,764
Missouri.........	203	108	95	130,846	66,145	64,701	198,413	100,470	97,943	95,931	50,568	45,363	7,177	4,965	2,212
North Dakota....	10	2	8	2,465	1,267	1,198	3,105	1,611	1,494	1,318	683	635	94	63	31
South Dakota....	16	6	10	9,435	4,785	4,650	12,526	6,443	6,083	6,301	3,415	2,886	689	465	224
Nebraska........	57	25	32	51,793	26,178	25,615	61,122	31,233	29,889	27,999	14,835	13,164	2,366	1,577	789
Kansas	115	61	54	81,532	41,450	40,082	113,038	57,972	55,066	59,515	31,419	28,096	5,294	3,453	1,836
South Central division.	644	318	326	356,304	181,548	174,756	656,382	332,667	323,715	298,717	158,053	140,664	24,936	17,485	7,451
Kentucky	159	71	88	82,082	41,741	40,341	140,866	71,921	68,945	65,116	34,389	30,727	5,159	3,405	1,754
Tennessee	200	103	97	72,221	36,966	35,255	126,981	64,841	62,140	60,748	32,673	28,075	5,566	3,835	1,731
Alabama	56	35	21	34,443	17,661	16,782	69,384	35,023	34,361	31,352	16,528	14,824	3,118	2,152	966
Mississippi	39	21	18	36,882	18,783	18,099	55,519	27,769	27,750	28,164	14,407	13,757	2,541	1,695	846
Louisiana........	41	16	25	18,866	9,649	9,217	31,983	16,196	15,787	10,783	5,487	5,296	663	480	183
Texas...........	101	49	52	66,079	33,286	32,793	152,527	76,895	75,632	62,124	32,328	29,796	4,107	3,152	955
Oklahoma	6	3	3	1,972	1,041	931	3,128	1,575	1,553	1,101	530	571	50	36	14
Arkansas........	42	20	22	43,759	22,421	21,338	75,994	38,447	37,547	39,329	21,711	17,618	3,732	2,730	1,002
Western division..	146	78	68	84,099	42,640	41,459	128,347	64,907	63,440	58,063	29,899	28,164	4,659	3,087	1,572
Montana.........	7	4	3	2,747	1,360	1,387	3,541	1,800	1,741	1,567	792	775	126	86	40
Wyoming........	3	1	2	1,482	771	711	1,886	992	894	823	449	374	54	37	17
Colorado........	13	8	5	12,000	6,086	5,914	17,521	8,981	8,540	7,917	4,120	3,797	674	447	227
New Mexico.....	9	3	6	5,054	2,723	2,331	8,200	4,423	3,777	3,823	2,324	1,499	340	275	65
Arizona.........	......	......	......	1,249	633	616	1,947	1,015	932	752	366	386	35	25	10
Utah	2	......	2	4,357	2,256	2,101	6,260	3,137	3,123	2,490	1,285	1,205	186	137	49
Nevada	2	1	1	846	418	428	1,344	673	671	575	267	308	37	22	15
Idaho...........	......	......	......	3,048	1,564	1,484	4,004	2,081	1,923	1,661	891	770	91	67	24
Washington	15	10	5	9,832	4,858	4,974	15,254	7,720	7,534	6,387	3,373	3,014	494	359	135
Oregon	35	22	13	13,891	6,990	6,901	20,046	10,592	10,414	10,289	5,408	4,881	858	588	270
California.......	60	29	31	29,593	14,981	14,612	47,444	23,553	23,891	21,779	10,624	11,155	1,764	1,044	720

STATISTICS OF POPULATION.

142

TABLE 14.—NATIVE WHITE PERSONS OF FOREIGN PARENTAGE ATTENDING SCHOOL DURING THE CENSUS YEAR, CLASSIFIED BY SEX AND AGE PERIODS, BY STATES AND TERRITORIES: 1890.

STATES AND TERRITORIES.	UNDER 5 YEARS.			5 TO 9 YEARS.			10 TO 14 YEARS.			15 TO 19 YEARS.			20 YEARS AND OVER.		
	Total.	Males.	Females.	Total.	Males.	Females.	Total.	Males.	Females.	Total.	Males.	Females.	Total.	Males.	Females.
United States....	3,086	1,591	1,495	1,057,624	536,214	521,410	1,425,997	719,881	706,116	434,547	225,113	209,434	27,280	18,094	9,186
North Atlantic division.	1,506	772	734	397,193	201,605	195,588	506,860	254,080	252,780	118,218	56,900	61,318	7,961	5,112	2,849
Maine	80	41	39	7,741	4,027	3,714	9,000	4,571	4,429	2,190	1,556	1,634	144	99	45
New Hampshire .	20	9	11	5,530	2,781	2,749	6,319	3,215	3,104	1,619	847	772	94	65	29
Vermont.........	17	9	8	5,343	2,774	2,569	7,504	3,927	3,577	2,424	1,212	1,212	105	72	33
Massachusetts...	370	178	192	68,855	34,705	34,150	79,406	40,000	39,406	19,366	9,071	10,295	1,349	884	465
Rhode Island....	46	27	19	10,307	5,195	5,112	11,160	5,511	5,649	2,383	1,201	1,182	124	77	47
Connecticut	181	90	91	21,551	11,082	10,469	25,115	12,776	12,339	5,349	2,585	2,764	427	212	215
New York	579	315	264	157,000	79,575	77,425	210,371	106,340	104,031	49,390	24,198	25,192	3,704	2,471	1,233
New Jersey......	29	17	12	34,032	17,247	16,785	45,187	22,549	22,638	8,256	4,078	4,178	434	304	130
Pennsylvania....	184	86	98	86,834	44,219	42,615	112,799	55,191	57,608	26,241	12,152	14,089	1,580	928	652
South Atlantic division.	17	8	9	19,412	9,878	9,534	33,186	16,597	16,589	9,776	4,788	4,988	816	623	193
Delaware........				1,224	653	571	1,707	837	870	416	181	235	30	15	15
Maryland........	10	4	6	9,375	4,736	4,639	15,362	7,798	7,564	3,257	1,727	1,530	455	397	58
Dist. Columbia...	2		2	1,542	773	769	3,326	1,628	1,698	1,252	520	732	70	51	19
Virginia	1	1		1,297	694	603	2,788	1,432	1,356	1,018	476	542	59	38	21
West Virginia....	1	1		2,526	1,289	1,237	4,384	2,200	2,184	1,695	855	840	114	73	41
North Carolina...	1		1	324	181	143	706	346	360	342	181	161	21	12	9
South Carolina ..				634	324	310	984	433	551	519	296	223	16	11	5
Georgia..........	2	2		1,117	559	558	2,059	1,012	1,047	712	290	422	24	17	7
Florida..........				1,373	669	704	1,870	911	959	565	262	303	27	9	18
North Central division.	1,354	711	643	553,631	280,065	273,566	737,951	374,364	363,587	257,470	139,101	118,369	15,975	10,795	5,180
Ohio.............	63	39	24	63,493	32,080	31,413	90,549	46,027	44,522	27,918	14,607	13,311	1,794	1,273	521
Indiana..........	25	10	15	21,748	10,989	10,759	35,528	18,047	17,481	12,575	6,723	5,852	866	555	311
Illinois	167	93	74	98,417	49,779	48,638	133,579	67,469	66,110	42,792	22,131	20,661	2,447	1,574	873
Michigan........	152	86	66	67,389	34,174	33,215	80,827	40,876	39,951	25,862	13,583	12,279	1,350	845	505
Wisconsin.......	462	239	223	81,505	41,099	40,406	103,194	52,483	50,711	32,685	18,152	14,533	2,098	1,369	729
Minnesota.......	118	58	60	55,244	28,001	27,243	74,402	37,812	36,590	26,641	15,024	11,617	1,456	1,040	416
Iowa	170	86	84	59,391	29,767	29,624	75,255	38,153	37,102	32,372	17,973	14,399	2,305	1,622	683
Missouri........	38	19	19	33,197	16,834	16,363	53,362	26,715	26,647	17,450	9,232	8,218	1,152	786	366
North Dakota....	20	8	12	6,848	3,537	3,311	6,530	3,473	3,057	2,088	1,199	889	89	71	18
South Dakota....	24	14	10	10,856	5,498	5,358	14,787	7,636	7,151	6,575	3,732	2,843	501	357	144
Nebraska.......	77	39	38	30,871	15,794	15,077	35,178	17,975	17,203	13,920	7,705	6,215	839	594	245
Kansas	38	20	18	24,672	12,513	12,159	34,760	17,698	17,062	16,592	9,040	7,552	1,078	709	369
South Central division.	37	17	20	27,619	14,024	13,595	55,023	27,865	27,158	15,173	7,447	7,726	733	461	272
Kentucky	6	1	5	8,148	4,087	4,061	13,498	6,844	6,654	3,463	1,679	1,784	214	116	98
Tennessee	1	1		1,983	989	994	3,927	1,957	1,970	1,504	679	825	71	40	31
Alabama	3	1	2	1,217	575	642	2,237	1,106	1,131	742	379	363	30	19	11
Mississippi......	4	3	1	1,045	536	509	1,863	901	962	803	349	454	46	29	17
Louisiana........	6	2	4	4,987	2,581	2,406	9,197	4,638	4,559	2,006	929	1,077	93	61	32
Texas...........	13	5	8	8,594	4,417	4,177	21,536	11,020	10,516	5,429	2,830	2,599	207	144	63
Oklahoma	2	2		189	97	92	292	144	148	112	58	54	6	5	1
Arkansas........	2	2		1,456	742	714	2,473	1,255	1,218	1,114	544	570	66	47	19
Western division..	172	83	89	59,769	30,642	29,127	92,977	46,975	46,002	33,910	16,877	17,033	1,795	1,103	692
Montana.........	8	2	6	2,221	1,153	1,068	2,627	1,326	1,301	974	503	471	51	33	18
Wyoming........	4	2	2	1,068	567	501	1,239	627	612	453	204	249	21	13	8
Colorado........	15	9	6	6,181	3,128	3,053	8,263	4,129	4,134	3,061	1,496	1,565	151	101	50
New Mexico.....				738	387	351	1,131	595	536	405	228	177	22	13	9
Arizona.........	1	1		822	430	392	1,610	805	805	444	214	230	6	1	5
Utah	5	2	3	6,771	3,527	3,244	12,898	6,523	6,375	5,322	2,816	2,506	439	291	148
Nevada..........	1		1	1,269	642	627	2,121	1,083	1,038	913	422	491	33	9	24
Idaho...........	1	1		1,666	842	824	2,580	1,328	1,252	1,144	637	507	72	55	17
Washington	21	7	14	5,599	2,891	2,708	7,247	3,659	3,588	2,550	1,354	1,196	138	94	44
Oregon..........	6	4	2	4,596	2,307	2,289	6,688	3,393	3,295	2,743	1,404	1,339	157	103	54
California.......	110	55	55	28,838	14,768	14,070	46,573	23,507	23,066	15,901	7,599	8,302	705	390	315

SCHOOL ATTENDANCE.

143

TABLE 15.—FOREIGN WHITE PERSONS ATTENDING SCHOOL DURING THE CENSUS YEAR, CLASSIFIED BY SEX AND AGE PERIODS, BY STATES AND TERRITORIES: 1890.

STATES AND TERRI-TORIES.	UNDER 5 YEARS.			5 TO 9 YEARS.			10 TO 14 YEARS.			15 TO 19 YEARS.			20 YEARS AND OVER.		
	Total.	Males.	Fe-males.	Total.	Males.	Fe-males.	Total.	Males.	Fe-males.	Total.	Males.	Fe-males.	Total.	Males.	Fe-males.
United States....	222	112	110	147,759	75,680	72,079	297,740	151,903	145,837	58,196	32,980	25,216	9,965	7,425	2,540
North Atlantic division.	149	82	67	68,215	34,979	33,236	116,385	58,554	57,831	14,436	7,508	6,928	3,536	2,676	860
Maine	19	16	8	2,243	1,162	1,081	3,661	1,831	1,830	805	418	387	68	53	15
New Hampshire .	2	....	2	1,911	997	914	3,159	1,583	1,576	517	267	250	49	29	20
Vermont.........	2	....	2	897	477	420	1,490	758	732	319	174	145	57	38	19
Massachusetts...	25	11	14	13,180	6,681	6,499	23,291	11,707	11,584	3,128	1,532	1,596	596	406	190
Rhode Island	9	4	5	2,375	1,202	1,173	3,613	1,827	1,786	459	264	195	72	54	18
Connecticut	15	9	6	3,217	1,658	1,559	5,579	2,822	2,757	623	347	276	204	167	37
New York	51	28	23	24,474	12,532	11,942	41,854	21,456	20,398	5,137	2,769	2,368	1,833	1,441	392
New Jersey	2	2	....	5,535	2,900	2,635	9,578	4,875	4,703	933	526	407	173	142	31
Pennsylvania....	24	12	12	14,383	7,370	7,013	24,100	11,695	12,405	2,515	1,211	1,304	484	346	138
South Atlantic division.	3	2	1	2,178	1,101	1,077	4,186	2,132	2,054	800	423	377	243	201	42
Delaware........	....	....	....	175	95	80	346	174	172	43	23	20	7	6	1
Maryland........	....	....	....	990	497	493	1,947	998	949	225	133	92	161	139	22
Dist. Columbia..	....	....	....	113	58	55	250	128	122	79	37	42	11	6	5
Virginia	....	....	....	129	66	63	288	147	141	127	68	59	20	17	3
West Virginia....	....	....	....	184	81	103	421	195	226	85	43	42	11	7	4
North Carolina ..	....	....	....	28	18	10	56	32	24	45	26	19	12	10	2
South Carolina ..	....	....	....	26	16	10	47	27	20	29	12	17	2	2	....
Georgia.........	....	....	....	91	44	47	205	102	103	41	17	24	5	5	....
Florida	3	2	1	442	226	216	626	329	297	126	64	62	14	9	5
North Central division.	63	26	37	68,222	34,854	33,368	155,730	80,293	75,437	36,771	21,840	14,931	5,340	3,965	1,375
Ohio............	7	4	3	6,378	3,245	3,133	13,486	6,810	6,676	2,266	1,357	909	428	313	115
Indiana..........	3	2	1	1,452	770	682	3,558	1,795	1,763	642	374	268	168	117	51
Illinois	7	3	4	14,082	7,188	6,894	29,550	15,035	14,515	4,121	2,339	1,782	801	638	163
Michigan	6	2	4	11,855	6,051	5,804	25,991	13,290	12,701	5,695	3,126	2,569	629	393	236
Wisconsin	26	14	12	9,633	4,943	4,690	20,410	10,637	9,773	3,491	2,108	1,383	505	396	109
Minnesota.......	4	....	4	7,798	4,017	3,781	21,545	11,188	10,357	5,825	3,566	2,259	808	690	208
Iowa	3	1	2	5,332	2,689	2,643	11,081	6,031	5,050	3,620	2,248	1,372	523	397	126
Missouri.........	....	....	....	2,118	1,069	1,049	5,187	2,646	2,541	1,009	549	460	299	229	70
North Dakota....	....	....	....	1,906	974	932	5,174	2,732	2,442	1,946	1,107	889	149	106	43
South Dakota....	....	....	....	1,491	781	710	4,287	2,307	1,980	2,058	1,286	772	282	205	77
Nebraska........	6	....	6	3,890	1,984	1,906	9,043	4,782	4,261	3,409	2,113	1,296	364	264	100
Kansas	1	....	1	2,287	1,143	1,144	5,818	3,040	2,778	2,689	1,667	1,022	294	217	77
South Central division.	1	....	1	2,328	1,196	1,132	6,982	3,635	3,347	1,703	879	824	236	159	77
Kentucky	1	....	1	433	208	225	948	458	490	165	95	70	44	34	10
Tennessee	....	....	....	162	81	81	437	231	206	141	69	72	27	17	10
Alabama.........	....	....	....	168	88	80	361	188	173	95	47	48	9	6	3
Mississippi......	....	....	....	38	17	21	49	28	21	26	15	11	2	....	2
Louisiana	....	....	....	207	109	98	389	191	198	96	56	40	24	19	5
Texas	....	....	....	1,216	646	570	4,280	2,275	2,005	1,002	513	489	90	57	33
Oklahoma	....	....	....	10	4	6	53	29	24	16	6	10	....	....	....
Arkansas........	....	....	....	94	43	51	465	235	230	162	78	84	40	26	14
Western division ..	6	2	4	6,816	3,550	3,266	14,457	7,289	7,168	4,486	2,330	2,156	610	424	186
Montana.........	....	....	....	387	194	193	751	357	394	201	98	103	33	28	5
Wyoming........	....	....	....	215	105	110	419	208	211	102	59	43	12	10	2
Colorado........	1	1	....	928	503	425	2,125	1,098	1,027	667	347	320	93	70	23
New Mexico.....	....	....	....	91	47	44	229	120	109	71	32	39	8	5	3
Arizona	....	....	....	182	97	85	442	221	221	123	66	57	8	7	1
Utah	....	....	....	515	264	251	1,423	683	740	495	262	233	50	32	18
Nevada..........	....	....	....	27	15	12	101	52	49	68	30	38	13	7	6
Idaho...........	....	....	....	91	54	37	335	161	174	137	81	56	12	9	3
Washington	1	....	1	1,097	559	538	2,290	1,199	1,091	548	291	257	79	54	25
Oregon	....	....	....	578	301	277	1,227	632	595	446	239	207	67	51	16
California........	4	1	3	2,705	1,411	1,294	5,115	2,558	2,557	1,628	825	803	235	151	84

STATISTICS OF POPULATION.

144

TABLE **16.**—COLORED PERSONS (a) ATTENDING SCHOOL DURING THE CENSUS YEAR, CLASSIFIED BY SEX AND AGE PERIODS, BY STATES AND TERRITORIES: 1890.

STATES AND TERRITORIES.	UNDER 5 YEARS.			5 TO 9 YEARS.			10 TO 14 YEARS.			15 TO 19 YEARS.			20 YEARS AND OVER.		
	Total.	Males.	Females.	Total.	Males.	Females.	Total.	Males.	Females.	Total.	Males.	Females.	Total.	Males.	Females.
United States....	412	194	218	266,364	131,690	134,674	538,549	264,594	273,955	189,684	85,924	103,760	12,008	7,837	5,971
North Atlantic division.	13	8	5	12,372	6,027	6,345	18,658	9,212	9,446	4,868	2,410	2,458	637	483	154
Maine				109	58	51	135	74	61	61	20	32	13	1	1
New Hampshire.				29	13	16	53	30	23	16	11	5	2	1	
Vermont.........	1		1	65	36	29	67	31	36	21	13	8	6	6	
Massachusetts....				1,270	605	665	1,614	767	847	493	228	265	56	37	19
Rhode Island				417	181	236	545	252	293	145	76	60	8	3	5
Connecticut......	2	2		706	330	376	949	455	494	222	114	108	20	13	7
New York.......	5	3	2	2,830	1,402	1,428	4,474	2,268	2,206	999	472	527	96	66	30
New Jersey......	2		2	2,127	1,019	1,108	3,181	1,564	1,617	823	443	380	38	26	12
Pennsylvania....	3	3		4,819	2,383	2,436	7,640	3,771	3,869	2,088	1,024	1,064	399	328	71
South Atlantic division.	160	76	84	109,670	54,306	55,373	226,329	109,879	116,450	75,344	32,305	43,039	4,695	2,481	2,214
Delaware........				807	387	420	1,502	656	846	433	228	205	155	140	15
Maryland........				7,668	3,736	3,932	15,355	7,634	7,721	3,380	1,699	1,681	287	126	161
Dist. Columbia ..	18	9	9	2,702	1,288	1,414	6,213	2,905	3,308	1,855	666	1,189	193	93	100
Virginia.........	29	12	17	24,527	12,291	12,236	50,613	24,319	26,294	17,834	7,269	10,565	1,174	608	566
West Virginia....				1,255	664	601	2,410	1,164	1,246	921	471	450	48	34	14
North Carolina ..	20	8	12	17,149	8,545	8,604	38,419	18,570	19,849	16,382	7,144	9,238	1,155	538	617
South Carolina ..	36	20	16	21,826	10,809	11,017	45,289	22,232	23,057	14,688	6,408	8,280	788	458	330
Georgia..........	41	20	21	25,478	12,584	12,894	52,108	25,236	26,872	14,519	5,941	8,578	577	318	259
Florida	16	7	9	8,167	4,002	4,165	14,420	7,163	7,257	5,332	2,479	2,853	312	172	140
North Central division.	14	9	5	23,310	11,518	11,792	41,018	20,856	20,162	15,501	7,793	7,708	1,100	717	383
Ohio............	3	2	1	5,103	2,580	2,523	8,302	4,324	3,978	3,052	1,541	1,511	222	147	75
Indiana..........	2	2		2,505	1,248	1,257	4,238	2,109	2,129	1,433	678	755	113	68	45
Illinois..........				3,020	1,496	1,524	5,031	2,540	2,491	1,829	879	950	99	61	38
Michigan........	1	1		1,098	541	557	1,750	899	851	571	286	285	53	37	16
Wisconsin.......	1	1		438	215	223	657	359	298	284	148	116	39	27	12
Minnesota.......				306	138	168	499	242	257	240	115	125	14	10	4
Iowa............				641	298	343	956	481	475	373	188	185	26	19	7
Missouri.........	5	3	2	6,629	3,269	3,360	12,846	6,513	6,333	4,796	2,342	2,454	266	152	114
North Dakota....				24	4	20	23	14	9	16	11	5	1	1	
South Dakota....				73	36	37	126	72	54	55	34	21	5	5	
Nebraska.......				614	324	290	935	493	442	403	214	188	75	61	14
Kansas..........	2		2	2,859	1,369	1,490	5,655	2,810	2,845	2,470	1,267	1,203	187	129	58
South Central division.	224	100	124	119,348	58,959	60,389	249,815	123,164	126,651	92,895	42,903	49,992	5,959	3,404	2,555
Kentucky	2		2	9,970	4,897	5,073	19,574	9,479	10,095	7,275	3,189	4,086	478	236	242
Tennessee	11	5	6	15,433	7,624	7,809	33,727	16,586	17,141	13,155	6,047	7,108	970	500	470
Alabama.........	22	11	11	16,462	7,993	8,469	39,902	19,331	20,571	15,269	6,816	8,453	1,025	565	460
Mississippi......	122	57	65	34,749	17,254	17,495	62,712	31,087	31,625	25,573	12,238	13,335	1,370	824	546
Louisiana........	15	4	11	12,870	6,461	6,409	24,040	11,936	12,104	5,666	2,438	3,228	274	171	103
Texas	27	12	15	18,111	8,930	9,181	45,996	22,631	23,365	14,748	6,547	8,201	980	560	420
Oklahoma	1		1	62	36	26	142	71	71	57	28	20	1		1
Arkansas........	24	11	13	11,691	5,764	5,927	23,722	12,043	11,679	11,152	5,600	5,552	861	548	313
Western division..	1	1		1,655	880	775	2,720	1,483	1,246	1,076	603	473	307	242	65
Montana.........				51	19	32	75	35	40	24	10	14	4	2	2
Wyoming........				20	13	7	25	14	11	10	3	7	27	27	
Colorado........				233	108	125	364	174	190	119	47	72	1		1
New Mexico.....				146	74	72	296	182	114	136	81	55	14	10	4
Arizona				39	23	16	78	37	41	17	7	10			
Utah	1	1		25	14	11	26	15	11	11	9	2	2	2	
Nevada.........				12	6	6	18	13	5	8	6	2	2	2	
Idaho...........				6	4	2	20	10	10	10	7	3			
Washington				197	89	108	342	161	181	138	69	69	11	8	3
Oregon				87	50	37	197	112	85	135	85	50	24	19	5
California				839	480	359	1,288	730	558	468	279	189	222	172	50

a Persons of negro descent, Chinese, Japanese, and civilized Indians.

SCHOOL ATTENDANCE.

145

TABLE 17.—NEGRO PERSONS (a) ATTENDING SCHOOL DURING THE CENSUS YEAR, CLASSIFIED BY SEX AND AGE PERIODS, BY STATES AND TERRITORIES: 1890.

STATES AND TERRITORIES.	UNDER 5 YEARS.			5 TO 9 YEARS.			10 TO 14 YEARS.			15 TO 19 YEARS.			20 YEARS AND OVER.		
	Total.	Males.	Females.	Total.	Males.	Females.	Total.	Males.	Females.	Total.	Males.	Females.	Total.	Males.	Females.
United States ...	409	192	217	264,545	130,721	133,824	534,864	262,575	272,289	187,464	84,672	102,792	12,042	6,809	5,233
North Atlantic division.	13	8	5	12,237	5,957	6,280	18,264	8,996	9,268	4,454	2,192	2,262	490	370	120
Maine				73	37	36	102	55	47	36	18	18	12	3	9
New Hampshire				29	13	16	53	30	23	16	11	5	2	1	1
Vermont	1		1	61	33	28	64	30	34	21	13	8	4	4	
Massachusetts ..				1,237	583	654	1,576	742	834	477	217	260	48	29	19
Rhode Island				404	174	230	532	248	284	144	75	69	8	3	5
Connecticut	2	2		694	328	366	937	447	490	221	114	107	16	9	7
New York	5	3	2	2,809	1,393	1,416	4,416	2,237	2,179	977	460	517	88	58	30
New Jersey	2		2	2,125	1,018	1,107	3,176	1,561	1,615	811	437	374	30	22	8
Pennsylvania....	3	3		4,805	2,378	2,427	7,408	3,646	3,762	1,751	847	904	282	241	41
South Atlantic division.	160	76	84	109,595	54,263	55,332	226,177	109,800	116,377	75,212	32,228	42,984	4,650	2,448	2,202
Delaware				807	387	420	1,502	656	846	433	228	205	155	140	15
Maryland........				7,668	3,736	3,932	15,355	7,634	7,721	3,373	1,699	1,679	284	125	159
Dist. Columbia...	18	9	9	2,702	1,288	1,414	6,211	2,903	3,308	1,852	664	1,188	196	92	104
Virginia........	29	12	17	24,516	12,286	12,230	50,584	24,304	26,280	17,755	7,222	10,533	1,137	577	560
West Virginia....				1,353	664	689	2,409	1,163	1,246	921	471	450	48	34	14
North Carolina ..	20	8	12	17,081	8,508	8,573	38,302	18,511	19,791	16,337	7,118	9,219	1,153	538	615
South Carolina ..	36	20	16	21,824	10,808	11,016	45,288	22,231	23,057	14,685	6,406	8,279	788	452	336
Georgia..........	41	20	21	25,478	12,584	12,894	52,107	25,235	26,872	14,519	5,941	8,578	577	318	259
Florida..........	16	7	9	8,166	4,002	4,164	14,419	7,163	7,256	5,332	2,479	2,853	312	172	140
North Central division.	13	8	5	22,349	11,031	11,318	39,212	19,879	19,333	14,526	7,160	7,366	888	538	350
Ohio............	3	2	1	5,095	2,576	2,519	8,281	4,308	3,973	3,036	1,535	1,501	216	143	73
Indiana..........	2	2		2,477	1,231	1,246	4,191	2,088	2,103	1,387	660	727	103	65	38
Illinois				3,014	1,491	1,523	5,025	2,538	2,487	1,829	879	950	92	54	38
Michigan				912	445	467	1,396	716	680	463	239	224	30	15	15
Wisconsin	1	1		150	58	92	220	107	113	79	46	33	5	3	2
Minnesota				135	60	75	192	90	102	75	32	43	5	4	1
Iowa............				640	297	343	954	481	473	373	188	185	26	19	7
Missouri........	5	3	2	6,627	3,268	3,359	12,834	6,504	6,330	4,781	2,334	2,447	263	149	114
North Dakota....				18	2	16	17	11	6	15	10	5	1	1	
South Dakota....				18	12	6	33	21	12	13	8	5	3	3	
Nebraska........				484	260	224	615	317	298	175	75	100	12	5	7
Kansas	2		2	2,779	1,331	1,448	5,454	2,698	2,756	2,300	1,154	1,146	132	77	55
South Central division.	223	100	123	119,805	58,944	60,861	249,722	123,122	126,600	92,817	42,808	49,049	5,940	3,389	2,551
Kentucky	2		2	9,970	4,897	5,073	19,567	9,472	10,095	7,274	3,188	4,086	475	233	242
Tennessee	11	5	6	15,431	7,624	7,807	33,722	16,583	17,139	13,150	6,045	7,105	969	499	470
Alabama.........	22	11	11	16,456	7,993	8,463	39,893	19,325	20,568	15,261	6,811	8,450	1,024	564	460
Mississippi	121	57	64	34,733	17,248	17,485	62,679	31,072	31,607	25,554	12,223	13,331	1,366	821	545
Louisiana........	15	4	11	12,867	6,458	6,409	24,037	11,934	12,103	5,660	2,432	3,228	272	169	103
Texas	27	12	15	18,097	8,924	9,173	45,967	22,024	23,343	14,712	6,541	8,171	972	555	417
Oklahoma........	1		1	61	36	25	142	71	71	57	28	29	1		1
Arkansas........	24	11	13	11,690	5,764	5,926	23,715	12,041	11,674	11,149	5,600	5,549	861	548	313
Western division.				1,059	526	533	1,489	778	711	455	224	231	74	64	10
Montana........				34	11	23	52	25	27	17	5	12	3	2	1
Wyoming........				17	10	7	21	11	10	5	1	4	27	27	
Colorado........				232	108	124	341	174	167	106	47	59	1		2
New Mexico.....				99	27	72	77	51	26	43	18	25	4	2	2
Arizona.........				23	7	16	23	12	11	4	2	2			
Utah...........				15	7	8	16	8	8	4	3	1	1	1	
Nevada.........				8	3	5	2	2		4	3	1			
Idaho..........				6	4	2	14	5	9	7	4	3			
Washington.....				36	19	17	49	23	26	19	6	13	1		1
Oregon.........				57	46	11	73	40	33	17	11	6	1		1
California.......				532	284	248	821	427	394	229	124	105	37	32	5

a Includes all persons of negro descent.

146   STATISTICS OF POPULATION.

TABLE 18.—TOTAL PERSONS ATTENDING SCHOOL DURING THE CENSUS YEAR, CLASSIFIED BY SEX, AGE PERIODS, AND MONTHS OF SCHOOL ATTENDANCE, BY STATES AND TERRITORIES: 1890.

STATES, TERRITORIES, AND MONTHS OF SCHOOL ATTENDANCE.	ALL AGES.			UNDER 10 YEARS.			10 TO 14 YEARS.			15 YEARS AND OVER.		
	Total.	Males.	Females.	Total.	Males.	Females.	Total.	Males.	Females.	Total.	Males.	Females.
North Atlantic division:												
Maine	132,032	67,864	64,168	45,138	22,947	22,191	57,678	29,471	28,207	29,216	15,446	13,770
1 month or less	5,287	2,716	2,571	2,929	1,491	1,438	1,396	705	691	962	520	442
2 to 3 months	13,909	7,889	6,020	5,339	2,644	2,695	3,920	2,100	1,820	4,650	3,145	1,505
4 to 5 months	29,348	15,398	13,950	10,617	5,365	5,252	12,800	6,763	6,037	5,931	3,270	2,661
6 months or more	83,488	41,861	41,627	26,253	13,447	12,806	39,562	19,903	19,659	17,673	8,511	9,162
New Hampshire	61,760	31,454	30,306	21,033	10,616	10,417	28,677	14,607	14,070	12,050	6,231	5,819
1 month or less	3,864	1,922	1,942	1,857	921	936	1,401	700	701	606	301	305
2 to 3 months	4,253	2,397	1,856	1,887	956	931	1,242	661	581	1,124	780	344
4 to 5 months	10,793	5,531	5,262	3,771	1,885	1,886	5,140	2,075	2,405	1,882	971	911
6 months or more	42,850	21,604	21,246	13,518	6,854	6,664	20,894	10,571	10,323	8,438	4,179	4,259
Vermont	61,007	31,617	29,390	19,928	10,274	9,654	28,348	14,687	13,661	12,731	6,656	6,075
1 month or less	2,227	1,171	1,056	1,148	596	552	614	311	303	465	264	201
2 to 3 months	5,712	3,437	2,275	2,191	1,110	1,081	1,465	846	619	2,056	1,481	575
4 to 5 months	6,490	3,523	2,967	2,211	1,096	1,115	2,648	1,452	1,196	1,631	975	656
6 months or more	46,578	23,486	23,092	14,378	7,472	6,906	23,621	12,078	11,543	8,579	3,936	4,643
Massachusetts	378,410	189,300	189,110	141,500	71,276	70,224	175,376	88,233	87,143	61,534	29,791	31,743
1 month or less	19,949	10,069	9,880	9,817	4,920	4,897	6,891	3,451	3,440	3,241	1,698	1,543
2 to 3 months	8,604	4,358	4,246	5,684	2,717	2,967	1,525	747	778	1,395	894	501
4 to 5 months	7,605	3,874	3,731	3,743	1,851	1,892	2,328	1,152	1,176	1,534	871	663
6 months or more	342,252	170,999	171,253	122,256	61,788	60,468	164,632	82,883	81,749	55,364	26,328	29,036
Rhode Island	55,474	27,823	27,651	21,838	11,033	10,805	26,056	12,924	13,132	7,580	3,866	3,714
1 month or less	3,462	1,752	1,710	1,663	835	828	1,278	649	629	521	268	253
2 to 3 months	2,804	1,487	1,317	1,089	485	604	1,227	697	530	488	305	183
4 to 5 months	2,128	1,100	1,028	985	468	517	756	386	370	387	246	141
6 months or more	47,080	23,484	23,596	18,101	9,245	8,856	22,795	11,192	11,603	6,184	3,047	3,137
Connecticut	126,450	64,669	61,790	47,979	24,442	23,537	58,992	29,993	28,999	19,488	10,234	9,254
1 month or less	9,040	4,627	4,413	4,206	2,159	2,047	3,411	1,739	1,672	1,423	729	694
2 to 3 months	3,228	1,674	1,554	1,959	919	1,040	678	366	312	591	389	202
4 to 5 months	4,041	2,304	1,737	1,652	833	819	1,459	846	613	930	625	305
6 months or more	110,150	56,064	54,086	40,162	20,531	19,631	53,444	27,042	26,402	16,544	8,491	8,053
New York	985,625	500,189	485,436	356,611	181,057	175,554	477,058	241,847	235,211	151,956	77,285	74,671
1 month or less	77,013	39,916	37,097	33,973	17,263	16,710	30,975	15,658	15,317	12,065	6,995	5,070
2 to 3 months	33,976	18,470	15,506	17,253	8,356	8,897	8,080	4,460	3,620	8,643	5,654	2,989
4 to 5 months	57,394	33,565	23,829	18,603	9,073	9,530	20,137	11,812	8,325	18,654	12,680	5,974
6 months or more	817,242	408,238	409,004	286,782	146,365	140,417	417,866	209,917	207,949	112,594	51,956	60,638
New Jersey	241,844	122,419	119,425	88,224	44,906	43,318	120,854	60,743	60,111	32,766	16,770	15,996
1 month or less	20,531	10,593	9,938	8,812	4,433	4,379	8,930	4,556	4,374	2,789	1,604	1,185
2 to 3 months	7,564	4,199	3,365	3,658	1,725	1,933	2,154	1,212	942	1,752	1,262	490
4 to 5 months	9,170	5,306	3,864	3,328	1,634	1,694	3,712	2,167	1,545	2,130	1,505	625
6 months or more	204,579	102,321	102,258	72,426	37,114	35,312	106,058	52,808	53,250	26,095	12,399	13,696
Pennsylvania	961,101	485,337	475,764	333,910	169,650	164,260	466,679	232,427	234,252	160,512	83,260	77,252
1 month or less	44,474	22,370	22,104	19,964	10,011	9,953	16,941	8,404	8,537	7,569	3,955	3,614
2 to 3 months	50,742	26,976	23,766	20,175	9,678	10,497	16,036	8,328	7,708	14,531	8,970	5,561
4 to 5 months	89,368	49,315	40,053	25,892	12,842	12,990	40,214	21,729	18,485	23,322	14,744	8,578
6 months or more	776,517	386,676	389,841	267,939	137,119	130,820	393,488	193,966	199,522	115,000	55,591	59,499
South Atlantic division:												
Delaware	27,822	14,273	13,549	8,973	4,508	4,465	14,231	7,224	7,007	4,618	2,541	2,077
1 month or less	1,138	618	520	565	324	241	405	196	209	168	98	70
2 to 3 months	2,168	1,308	860	627	280	347	915	562	353	626	406	160
4 to 5 months	2,924	1,636	1,288	845	398	447	1,433	805	628	646	433	213
6 months or more	21,592	10,711	10,881	6,936	3,506	3,430	11,478	5,661	5,817	3,178	1,544	1,634
Maryland	108,958	86,231	82,727	52,078	26,832	26,146	89,067	44,792	44,275	26,913	14,607	12,306
1 month or less	6,528	3,344	3,184	2,542	1,264	1,278	2,735	1,385	1,350	1,251	695	556
2 to 3 months	9,530	5,611	3,919	3,134	1,553	1,581	3,785	2,154	1,631	2,611	1,904	707
4 to 5 months	13,350	7,452	5,898	3,607	1,865	1,742	6,637	3,652	2,985	3,106	1,935	1,171
6 months or more	139,550	69,824	69,726	43,695	22,150	21,545	75,910	37,601	38,309	19,945	10,073	9,872
District of Columbia	36,205	17,219	18,986	9,277	4,630	4,647	19,248	9,342	9,906	7,680	3,247	4,433
1 month or less	1,790	862	928	521	254	267	809	410	399	460	198	262
2 to 3 months	458	223	235	173	79	94	170	89	81	115	55	60
4 to 5 months	920	430	490	331	137	194	405	218	187	193	75	118
6 months or more	33,028	15,704	17,324	8,252	4,160	4,092	17,864	8,625	9,239	6,912	2,919	3,993
Virginia	290,965	144,156	146,809	79,938	40,717	39,221	146,639	72,687	73,952	64,388	30,752	33,636
1 month or less	14,983	7,728	7,255	5,294	2,683	2,611	6,225	3,224	3,001	3,464	1,821	1,643
2 to 3 months	37,898	20,291	17,607	11,319	5,759	5,560	17,427	9,238	8,189	9,152	5,294	3,858
4 to 5 months	138,818	68,733	70,085	38,365	19,589	18,776	71,254	35,566	35,688	29,199	13,578	15,621
6 months or more	99,266	47,404	51,862	24,960	12,686	12,274	51,733	24,659	27,074	22,573	10,059	12,514

SCHOOL ATTENDANCE.

TABLE 18.—TOTAL PERSONS ATTENDING SCHOOL DURING THE CENSUS YEAR, CLASSIFIED BY SEX, AGE PERIODS, AND MONTHS OF SCHOOL ATTENDANCE, BY STATES AND TERRITORIES: 1890—Continued.

STATES, TERRITORIES, AND MONTHS OF SCHOOL ATTENDANCE.	ALL AGES.			UNDER 10 YEARS.			10 TO 14 YEARS.			15 YEARS AND OVER.		
	Total.	Males.	Females.	Total.	Males.	Females.	Total.	Males.	Females.	Total.	Males.	Females.
South Atlantic division—Cont.												
West Virginia	103,865	84,695	78,670	45,913	23,476	22,437	78,411	40,058	38,353	39,041	21,161	17,880
1 month or less	7,713	3,983	3,730	2,843	1,388	1,455	2,948	1,517	1,431	1,922	1,078	844
2 to 3 months	27,676	14,743	12,933	8,348	4,247	4,101	12,306	6,360	5,946	7,022	4,136	2,886
4 to 5 months	82,386	43,374	39,012	21,858	11,343	10,515	40,049	20,743	19,306	20,479	11,288	9,191
6 months or more	45,590	22,595	22,995	12,864	6,498	6,366	23,108	11,438	11,670	9,618	4,659	4,959
North Carolina	260,125	130,904	129,221	66,137	33,381	32,756	129,608	64,358	65,250	64,380	33,105	31,215
1 month or less	24,584	12,788	11,796	7,165	3,597	3,568	11,121	5,614	5,507	6,298	3,577	2,721
2 to 3 months	137,807	70,678	66,629	35,137	17,872	17,265	68,673	35,204	33,469	33,497	17,602	15,895
4 to 5 months	56,443	27,840	28,603	14,258	7,141	7,117	28,781	13,994	14,787	13,404	6,705	6,699
6 months or more	41,791	19,598	22,193	9,577	4,771	4,806	21,033	9,546	11,487	11,181	5,281	5,900
South Carolina	161,303	79,973	81,330	43,600	21,834	21,766	84,717	42,066	42,651	32,986	16,073	16,913
1 month or less	11,352	5,938	5,414	3,572	1,812	1,760	5,419	2,904	2,515	2,361	1,222	1,139
2 to 3 months	73,023	36,665	36,358	19,719	9,902	9,817	39,285	19,837	19,448	14,019	6,926	7,093
4 to 5 months	31,636	15,553	16,083	8,277	4,158	4,119	17,064	8,341	8,723	6,295	3,054	3,241
6 months or more	45,292	21,817	23,475	12,032	5,962	6,070	22,949	10,984	11,965	10,311	4,871	5,440
Georgia	267,914	133,175	134,739	76,369	38,438	37,931	139,757	68,915	70,842	51,788	25,822	25,966
1 month or less	21,232	11,298	9,934	6,900	3,495	3,405	9,683	5,169	4,514	4,649	2,634	2,015
2 to 3 months	114,830	59,620	55,210	32,998	16,658	16,340	59,557	30,948	28,609	22,275	12,014	10,261
4 to 5 months	55,970	27,264	28,706	16,855	8,623	8,232	29,463	14,071	15,392	9,652	4,570	5,082
6 months or more	75,882	34,993	40,889	19,616	9,662	9,954	41,054	18,727	22,327	15,212	6,604	8,608
Florida	74,608	37,670	36,938	22,015	10,973	11,042	36,096	18,251	17,845	16,497	8,446	8,051
1 month or less	3,402	1,772	1,630	1,118	537	581	1,422	743	679	862	492	370
2 to 3 months	14,394	7,671	6,723	4,124	2,119	2,005	6,701	3,533	3,168	3,569	2,019	1,550
4 to 5 months	30,410	15,485	14,925	8,736	4,438	4,298	15,179	7,741	7,438	6,495	3,306	3,189
6 months or more	26,402	12,742	13,660	8,037	3,879	4,158	12,794	6,234	6,560	5,571	2,629	2,942
North Central division:												
Ohio	775,524	400,451	375,073	252,377	128,497	123,880	363,062	184,638	178,424	160,085	87,316	72,769
1 month or less	30,800	15,263	15,037	13,732	6,836	6,896	10,011	4,962	5,049	6,557	3,465	3,092
2 to 3 months	44,579	24,308	20,271	20,060	9,662	10,398	11,145	5,805	5,340	13,374	8,841	4,533
4 to 5 months	86,927	51,945	34,982	20,720	10,455	10,265	33,297	19,114	14,183	32,910	22,376	10,534
6 months or more	613,718	308,935	304,783	197,865	101,544	96,321	308,609	154,757	153,852	107,244	52,634	54,610
Indiana	474,750	244,833	229,917	148,483	74,828	73,655	220,586	111,727	108,859	105,681	58,278	47,403
1 month or less	16,785	8,390	8,395	7,133	3,519	3,614	5,624	2,775	2,849	4,028	2,096	1,932
2 to 3 months	35,662	19,013	16,649	14,164	6,693	7,471	11,463	5,858	5,605	10,035	6,462	3,573
4 to 5 months	112,772	61,424	51,348	31,984	16,188	15,796	51,665	27,305	24,360	29,123	17,931	11,192
6 months or more	309,531	156,006	153,525	95,202	48,428	46,774	151,834	75,789	76,045	62,495	31,789	30,706
Illinois	763,675	390,484	373,101	255,572	129,507	126,065	358,882	181,587	177,295	149,221	79,390	69,831
1 month or less	40,402	20,359	20,043	18,678	9,273	9,405	14,428	7,366	7,062	7,296	3,720	3,576
2 to 3 months	61,023	34,536	26,487	25,156	12,222	12,034	16,980	9,268	7,721	18,878	13,046	5,832
4 to 5 months	104,769	60,111	44,658	28,324	14,197	14,127	45,346	25,625	19,721	31,099	20,289	10,810
6 months or more	557,481	275,478	282,003	183,414	93,815	89,599	282,119	139,328	142,791	91,948	42,335	49,613
Michigan	422,601	215,945	206,656	147,326	74,455	72,871	198,110	100,727	97,383	77,165	40,763	36,402
1 month or less	22,206	11,239	10,967	10,800	5,429	5,371	7,956	4,113	3,843	3,450	1,697	1,753
2 to 3 months	28,824	15,763	13,061	12,924	6,875	7,049	7,716	4,276	3,440	7,184	4,612	2,572
4 to 5 months	44,399	26,931	17,468	12,015	5,884	6,131	16,895	10,141	6,754	15,489	10,906	4,583
6 months or more	327,172	162,012	165,160	110,587	56,267	54,320	165,543	82,197	83,346	51,042	23,548	27,494
Wisconsin	364,966	187,742	177,224	135,214	68,236	66,978	170,583	86,904	83,679	59,169	32,602	26,567
1 month or less	17,504	8,928	8,636	9,842	4,934	4,908	5,127	2,634	2,493	2,535	1,360	1,235
2 to 3 months	30,930	16,877	14,053	15,256	7,517	7,739	8,689	4,651	4,038	6,985	4,709	2,276
4 to 5 months	44,922	25,884	19,038	13,961	6,844	7,117	18,999	10,715	8,284	11,962	8,325	3,637
6 months or more	271,550	136,053	135,497	96,155	48,941	47,214	137,768	68,904	68,861	37,627	18,208	19,419
Minnesota	262,711	136,603	126,108	86,763	44,049	42,714	125,841	64,208	61,633	50,107	28,346	21,761
1 month or less	12,708	6,381	6,327	6,202	2,980	3,222	3,789	1,892	1,897	2,717	1,509	1,208
2 to 3 months	37,547	20,574	16,973	14,801	7,267	7,534	13,652	7,193	6,459	9,094	6,114	2,980
4 to 5 months	52,162	29,195	22,967	15,141	7,771	7,370	25,880	13,930	11,950	11,141	7,494	3,647
6 months or more	160,294	80,453	79,841	50,619	26,031	24,588	82,520	41,193	41,327	27,155	13,229	13,926
Iowa	469,862	243,011	226,851	163,091	82,425	80,666	204,175	103,909	100,266	102,596	56,617	45,979
1 month or less	18,017	9,252	8,765	9,167	4,675	4,492	4,993	2,539	2,454	3,857	2,038	1,819
2 to 3 months	44,181	26,546	17,635	18,073	8,763	9,310	10,224	6,219	4,005	15,884	11,564	4,320
4 to 5 months	65,195	41,157	24,038	16,169	8,006	8,163	24,423	15,253	9,170	24,603	17,898	6,705
6 months or more	342,469	166,056	176,413	119,682	60,981	58,701	164,535	79,958	84,577	58,252	25,117	33,135
Missouri	570,924	292,614	278,310	173,036	87,447	85,589	269,808	136,344	133,464	128,080	68,823	59,257
1 month or less	29,968	15,522	14,446	12,740	6,422	6,327	10,547	5,413	5,134	6,672	3,687	2,985
2 to 3 months	81,598	44,647	36,951	28,208	14,008	14,200	31,756	16,997	14,759	21,634	13,643	7,992
4 to 5 months	129,363	70,821	58,542	34,470	17,453	17,017	60,651	32,749	27,902	34,242	20,619	13,623
6 months or more	329,995	161,624	168,371	97,609	49,564	48,045	166,854	81,185	85,669	65,532	30,875	34,657

STATISTICS OF POPULATION.

148

TABLE 18.—TOTAL PERSONS ATTENDING SCHOOL DURING THE CENSUS YEAR, CLASSIFIED BY SEX, AGE PERIODS, AND MONTHS OF SCHOOL ATTENDANCE, BY STATES AND TERRITORIES: 1890—Continued.

STATES, TERRITORIES, AND MONTHS OF SCHOOL ATTENDANCE.	ALL AGES.			UNDER 10 YEARS.			10 TO 14 YEARS.			15 YEARS AND OVER.		
	Total.	Males.	Females.	Total.	Males.	Females.	Total.	Males.	Females.	Total.	Males.	Females.
North Central division—Cont. North Dakota	31,806	16,863	14,943	11,273	5,792	5,481	14,832	7,830	7,002	5,701	3,241	2,460
1 month or less	2,598	1,362	1,236	1,381	694	687	760	395	365	457	273	184
2 to 3 months	6,071	3,434	2,637	2,301	1,181	1,120	2,411	1,334	1,077	1,259	919	440
4 to 5 months	6,521	3,613	2,908	2,088	1,084	1,004	3,159	1,714	1,445	1,274	815	459
6 months or more	10,616	8,454	8,162	5,503	2,833	2,670	8,502	4,387	4,115	2,611	1,234	1,377
South Dakota	70,087	37,077	33,010	21,895	11,120	10,775	31,726	16,458	15,268	16,466	9,499	6,967
1 month or less	3,350	1,707	1,649	1,650	800	850	949	485	464	757	422	335
2 to 3 months	12,507	7,214	5,293	4,400	2,209	2,191	4,454	2,523	1,931	3,653	2,482	1,171
4 to 5 months	17,473	10,299	7,174	4,700	2,440	2,260	8,175	4,693	3,482	4,598	3,166	1,432
6 months or more	36,751	17,857	18,894	11,145	5,671	5,474	18,148	8,757	9,391	7,458	3,429	4,029
Nebraska	242,960	126,190	116,770	87,308	44,344	42,964	106,278	54,483	51,795	49,374	27,363	22,011
1 month or less	10,241	5,259	4,982	4,885	2,450	2,435	8,038	1,538	1,500	2,318	1,271	1,047
2 to 3 months	36,537	21,696	14,841	13,761	6,904	6,857	11,803	6,963	4,840	10,973	7,829	3,144
4 to 5 months	32,247	18,643	13,604	9,936	5,017	4,919	13,759	7,946	5,813	8,552	5,680	2,872
6 months or more	163,935	80,592	83,343	58,726	29,973	28,753	77,678	38,036	39,642	27,531	12,583	14,948
Kansas	358,896	185,982	172,914	111,506	56,556	54,950	159,271	81,520	77,751	88,119	47,906	40,213
1 month or less	12,316	6,404	5,912	5,538	2,746	2,792	3,357	1,747	1,610	3,421	1,911	1,510
2 to 3 months	42,633	25,380	17,253	15,178	7,541	7,637	12,857	7,581	5,276	14,598	10,258	4,340
4 to 5 months	64,879	37,460	27,419	18,372	9,250	9,122	27,797	16,113	11,684	18,710	12,097	6,613
6 months or more	239,068	116,738	122,330	72,418	37,019	35,399	115,260	56,079	59,181	51,390	23,640	27,750
South Central division: Kentucky	357,601	182,850	174,751	100,801	51,005	49,796	174,886	88,702	86,184	81,914	43,143	38,771
1 month or less	23,239	12,262	10,977	8,214	4,087	4,127	9,167	4,858	4,309	5,858	3,317	2,541
2 to 3 months	80,906	43,824	37,082	23,569	11,936	11,633	37,103	19,900	17,203	20,234	11,988	8,246
4 to 5 months	155,935	79,797	76,138	42,102	21,458	20,644	78,398	39,703	38,695	35,435	18,636	16,799
6 months or more	97,521	46,967	50,554	26,916	13,524	13,392	50,218	24,241	25,977	20,387	9,202	11,185
Tennessee	337,265	173,244	164,021	90,011	45,769	44,242	165,072	83,615	81,457	82,182	43,860	38,322
1 month or less	23,790	12,697	11,093	7,821	4,055	3,766	9,839	5,126	4,713	6,130	3,516	2,614
2 to 3 months	125,025	67,252	58,678	35,101	17,963	17,138	60,249	31,783	28,466	30,575	17,506	13,069
4 to 5 months	97,205	50,142	47,063	25,646	13,056	12,590	48,326	24,543	23,783	23,233	12,543	10,690
6 months or more	90,345	43,153	47,192	21,443	10,695	10,748	46,658	22,163	24,495	22,244	10,295	11,949
Alabama	215,895	108,524	107,371	52,371	26,364	26,007	111,884	55,648	56,236	51,640	26,512	25,128
1 month or less	15,890	8,510	7,380	4,497	2,270	2,227	7,293	3,896	3,397	4,100	2,344	1,756
2 to 3 months	110,453	56,865	53,588	26,441	13,393	13,048	57,572	29,379	28,193	26,440	14,093	12,347
4 to 5 months	34,497	17,263	17,234	8,524	4,289	4,235	18,230	9,006	9,224	7,743	3,968	3,775
6 months or more	55,055	25,886	29,169	12,909	6,412	6,497	28,789	13,367	15,422	13,357	6,107	7,250
Mississippi	251,547	126,013	125,534	72,879	36,671	36,208	120,143	59,785	60,358	58,525	29,557	28,968
1 month or less	19,484	10,274	9,210	6,793	3,376	3,417	8,122	4,252	3,870	4,569	2,646	1,923
2 to 3 months	73,971	38,946	35,025	21,239	10,776	10,463	34,561	18,057	16,504	18,171	10,113	8,058
4 to 5 months	113,821	56,640	57,181	33,486	16,933	16,553	56,045	27,767	28,278	24,290	11,940	12,350
6 months or more	44,271	20,153	24,118	11,361	5,586	5,775	21,415	9,709	11,706	11,495	4,858	6,637
Louisiana	122,206	61,424	60,782	36,992	18,822	18,170	65,609	32,961	32,648	19,605	9,641	9,964
1 month or less	10,441	5,306	5,135	3,628	1,792	1,836	5,114	2,608	2,506	1,699	906	793
2 to 3 months	27,603	14,259	13,344	7,992	4,112	3,880	14,160	7,341	6,819	5,451	2,806	2,645
4 to 5 months	18,447	9,355	9,092	5,801	2,986	2,815	9,800	4,944	4,856	2,846	1,425	1,421
6 months or more	65,715	32,504	33,211	19,571	9,932	9,639	36,535	18,068	18,467	9,609	4,504	5,105
Texas	407,167	206,297	200,870	94,141	47,345	46,796	224,339	112,821	111,518	88,687	46,131	42,556
1 month or less	26,829	14,468	12,361	8,821	4,419	4,402	11,844	6,448	5,396	6,164	3,601	2,563
2 to 3 months	125,370	67,257	58,113	30,358	15,386	14,972	67,094	35,707	31,387	27,918	16,164	11,754
4 to 5 months	124,891	62,941	61,950	26,994	13,646	13,348	71,836	35,839	35,997	26,061	13,456	12,605
6 months or more	130,077	61,631	68,446	27,968	13,894	14,074	73,565	34,827	38,738	28,544	12,910	15,634
Oklahoma	7,200	3,665	3,535	2,242	1,183	1,059	3,615	1,819	1,796	1,343	663	680
1 month or less	746	391	355	280	131	149	318	178	140	148	82	66
2 to 3 months	2,664	1,390	1,274	860	453	407	1,318	668	650	486	269	217
4 to 5 months	1,549	777	772	457	229	228	807	423	384	285	125	160
6 months or more	2,241	1,107	1,134	645	370	275	1,172	550	622	424	187	237
Arkansas	216,178	112,267	103,911	57,068	29,003	28,065	102,654	51,980	50,674	56,456	31,284	25,172
1 month or less	17,984	9,655	8,329	5,491	2,812	2,679	7,560	3,918	3,642	4,933	2,925	2,008
2 to 3 months	121,524	64,858	56,666	31,426	16,090	15,336	57,825	30,303	27,522	32,273	18,465	13,808
4 to 5 months	35,803	18,476	17,327	9,524	4,869	4,655	17,257	8,639	8,618	9,022	4,968	4,054
6 months or more	40,867	19,278	21,589	10,627	5,232	5,395	20,012	9,120	10,892	10,228	4,926	5,302

SCHOOL ATTENDANCE.

TABLE 18.—TOTAL PERSONS ATTENDING SCHOOL DURING THE CENSUS YEAR, CLASSIFIED BY SEX, AGE PERIODS, AND MONTHS OF SCHOOL ATTENDANCE, BY STATES AND TERRITORIES: 1890—Continued.

STATES, TERRITORIES, AND MONTHS OF SCHOOL ATTENDANCE.	ALL AGES.			UNDER 10 YEARS.			10 TO 14 YEARS.			15 YEARS AND OVER.		
	Total.	Males.	Females.	Total.	Males.	Females.	Total.	Males.	Females.	Total.	Males.	Females.
Western division:												
Montana	15,395	7,802	7,593	5,421	2,732	2,689	6,994	3,518	3,476	2,980	1,552	1,428
1 month or less	973	487	486	494	241	253	296	149	147	183	97	86
2 to 3 months	2,278	1,237	1,041	961	482	479	843	454	389	474	301	173
4 to 5 months	2,055	1,093	962	725	374	351	920	483	437	410	236	174
6 months or more	10,089	4,985	5,104	3,241	1,635	1,606	4,935	2,432	2,503	1,913	918	995
Wyoming	7,863	4,102	3,761	2,792	1,459	1,333	3,569	1,841	1,728	1,502	802	700
1 month or less	455	242	213	188	102	86	161	81	80	106	59	47
2 to 3 months	1,178	646	532	499	248	251	403	217	186	276	181	95
4 to 5 months	1,428	770	658	523	261	262	626	340	286	279	169	110
6 months or more	4,802	2,444	2,358	1,582	848	734	2,379	1,203	1,176	841	393	448
Colorado	60,327	30,853	29,474	19,371	9,843	9,528	28,273	14,382	13,891	12,683	6,628	6,055
1 month or less	2,959	1,519	1,440	1,328	685	643	998	496	502	633	338	295
2 to 3 months	6,428	3,552	2,876	2,517	1,310	1,207	2,413	1,299	1,114	1,498	943	555
4 to 5 months	7,784	4,214	3,570	2,422	1,224	1,198	3,476	1,860	1,616	1,886	1,130	756
6 months or more	43,156	21,568	21,588	13,104	6,624	6,480	21,386	10,727	10,659	8,666	4,217	4,449
New Mexico	20,713	11,522	9,191	6,038	3,234	2,804	9,856	5,320	4,536	4,819	2,968	1,851
1 month or less	1,027	542	485	448	242	206	373	180	193	206	120	86
2 to 3 months	7,809	4,561	3,248	2,402	1,299	1,103	3,401	1,932	1,469	2,006	1,330	676
4 to 5 months	4,211	2,444	1,767	1,178	662	511	2,045	1,163	882	993	619	374
6 months or more	7,666	3,975	3,691	2,015	1,031	984	4,037	2,045	1,992	1,614	899	715
Arizona	7,755	3,948	3,807	2,293	1,184	1,109	4,077	2,078	1,999	1,385	686	699
1 month or less	367	191	176	139	65	74	154	83	71	74	43	31
2 to 3 months	828	418	410	285	131	154	354	181	173	189	106	83
4 to 5 months	1,460	762	698	445	235	210	743	380	363	272	147	125
6 months or more	5,100	2,577	2,523	1,424	753	671	2,826	1,434	1,392	850	390	460
Utah	41,278	21,256	20,022	11,676	6,064	5,612	20,607	10,358	10,249	8,995	4,834	4,161
1 month or less	1,861	891	970	779	378	401	672	308	364	410	205	205
2 to 3 months	7,769	4,112	3,657	2,545	1,241	1,304	3,162	1,663	1,499	2,062	1,208	854
4 to 5 months	7,924	4,317	3,607	1,870	1,001	869	4,045	2,158	1,887	2,009	1,158	851
6 months or more	23,724	11,936	11,788	6,482	3,444	3,038	12,728	6,229	6,499	4,514	2,263	2,251
Nevada	7,390	3,668	3,722	2,157	1,082	1,075	3,584	1,821	1,763	1,649	765	884
1 month or less	267	131	136	104	51	53	97	46	51	66	34	32
2 to 3 months	324	176	148	133	59	74	109	55	54	82	62	20
4 to 5 months	404	203	201	148	68	80	153	78	75	103	57	46
6 months or more	6,395	3,158	3,237	1,772	904	868	3,225	1,642	1,583	1,398	612	786
Idaho	14,878	7,792	7,086	4,812	2,465	2,347	6,939	3,580	3,359	3,127	1,747	1,380
1 month or less	749	389	360	409	202	207	214	112	102	126	75	51
2 to 3 months	4,360	2,387	1,973	1,553	823	730	1,818	971	847	989	593	396
4 to 5 months	3,099	1,664	1,435	966	494	472	1,469	772	697	664	398	266
6 months or more	6,670	3,352	3,318	1,884	946	938	3,438	1,725	1,713	1,348	681	667
Washington	52,240	26,755	25,485	16,762	8,414	8,348	25,133	12,739	12,394	10,345	5,602	4,743
1 month or less	2,781	1,428	1,353	1,422	712	710	885	432	453	474	284	190
2 to 3 months	11,445	5,952	5,493	4,168	1,975	2,193	4,747	2,440	2,307	2,530	1,537	993
4 to 5 months	8,455	4,543	3,912	2,344	1,238	1,106	4,206	2,163	2,043	1,905	1,142	763
6 months or more	29,559	14,832	14,727	8,828	4,489	4,339	15,295	7,704	7,591	5,436	2,639	2,797
Oregon	62,970	32,240	30,730	19,193	9,674	9,519	29,058	14,669	14,389	14,719	7,897	6,822
1 month or less	3,514	1,805	1,709	1,504	766	738	1,249	628	621	761	411	350
2 to 3 months	11,413	6,086	5,327	4,259	2,106	2,153	4,144	2,165	1,979	3,010	1,825	1,185
4 to 5 months	9,821	5,201	4,620	2,923	1,491	1,432	4,397	2,256	2,141	2,501	1,454	1,047
6 months or more	38,222	19,148	19,074	10,507	5,311	5,196	19,268	9,630	9,638	8,447	4,207	4,240
California	205,271	103,157	102,114	62,149	31,725	30,424	100,420	50,348	50,072	42,702	21,084	21,618
1 month or less	11,903	6,139	5,764	4,523	2,346	2,177	4,720	2,376	2,344	2,660	1,417	1,243
2 to 3 months	6,720	3,605	3,115	2,965	1,445	1,520	2,017	1,084	933	1,738	1,076	662
4 to 5 months	9,655	5,167	4,488	3,336	1,681	1,655	3,578	1,895	1,683	2,741	1,591	1,150
6 months or more	176,993	88,246	88,747	51,325	26,253	25,072	90,105	44,993	45,112	35,563	17,000	18,563

STATISTICS OF POPULATION.

150

TABLE **19.**—NATIVE WHITE PERSONS OF NATIVE PARENTAGE ATTENDING SCHOOL DURING THE CENSUS YEAR, CLASSIFIED BY SEX, AGE PERIODS, AND MONTHS OF SCHOOL ATTENDANCE, BY STATES AND TERRITORIES: 1890.

STATES, TERRITORIES, AND MONTHS OF SCHOOL ATTENDANCE.	ALL AGES.			UNDER 10 YEARS.			10 TO 14 YEARS.			15 YEARS AND OVER.		
	Total.	Males.	Females.	Total.	Males.	Females.	Total.	Males.	Females.	Total.	Males.	Females.
North Atlantic division: Maine	104,765	53,926	50,839	34,946	17,643	17,303	44,883	22,995	21,888	24,936	13,288	11,648
1 month or less	4,003	2,059	1,944	2,216	1,122	1,094	1,016	519	497	771	418	353
2 to 3 months	11,410	6,509	4,901	4,427	2,122	2,305	2,926	1,616	1,310	4,057	2,771	1,286
4 to 5 months	25,169	13,208	11,961	8,990	4,525	4,465	10,920	5,760	5,157	5,253	2,914	2,339
6 months or more	64,183	32,150	32,033	19,313	9,874	9,405	30,015	15,091	14,924	14,855	7,185	7,670
New Hampshire	42,440	21,606	20,834	13,541	6,816	6,725	19,146	9,779	9,367	9,753	5,011	4,742
1 month or less	2,155	1,070	1,085	997	484	513	697	360	337	461	226	235
2 to 3 months	3,109	1,787	1,322	1,299	664	635	890	486	404	920	637	283
4 to 5 months	8,984	4,600	4,384	3,055	1,516	1,539	4,293	2,254	2,039	1,636	830	806
6 months or more	28,192	14,149	14,043	8,190	4,152	4,038	13,266	6,679	6,587	6,736	3,318	3,418
Vermont	42,689	22,090	20,599	13,603	6,978	6,625	19,287	9,971	9,316	9,799	5,141	4,658
1 month or less	1,548	806	742	789	409	380	405	205	200	354	192	162
2 to 3 months	4,030	2,443	1,587	1,496	746	750	973	558	415	1,561	1,139	422
4 to 5 months	4,855	2,637	2,218	1,623	803	820	1,915	1,050	865	1,317	784	533
6 months or more	32,256	16,204	16,052	9,695	5,020	4,675	15,994	8,158	7,836	6,567	3,026	3,541
Massachusetts	165,411	82,488	82,923	57,800	29,096	28,704	71,065	35,759	35,306	36,546	17,633	18,913
1 month or less	8,279	4,223	4,056	3,764	1,910	1,854	2,596	1,301	1,295	1,919	1,012	907
2 to 3 months	3,848	1,930	1,918	2,623	1,209	1,414	520	261	259	705	460	245
4 to 5 months	3,301	1,074	1,027	1,624	805	819	884	440	444	793	429	364
6 months or more	149,983	74,661	75,322	49,789	25,172	24,617	67,065	33,757	33,308	33,129	15,732	17,397
Rhode Island	23,811	11,949	11,862	8,684	4,424	4,260	10,738	5,334	5,404	4,389	2,191	2,198
1 month or less	1,197	596	601	549	287	262	394	191	203	254	118	136
2 to 3 months	803	406	397	429	178	251	220	128	92	154	100	54
4 to 5 months	941	504	437	436	213	223	299	163	136	206	128	78
6 months or more	20,870	10,443	10,427	7,270	3,746	3,524	9,825	4,852	4,973	3,775	1,845	1,930
Connecticut	62,299	32,007	30,292	22,307	11,271	11,036	27,349	13,940	13,409	12,643	6,796	5,847
1 month or less	4,087	2,026	2,061	1,836	897	939	1,434	728	706	817	401	416
2 to 3 months	1,658	864	794	1,003	459	544	283	154	129	372	251	121
4 to 5 months	2,281	1,347	934	850	428	431	819	506	313	603	413	190
6 months or more	54,273	27,770	26,503	18,609	9,487	9,122	24,813	12,552	12,261	10,851	5,731	5,120
New York	482,828	244,853	237,975	171,672	87,202	84,470	220,850	111,783	108,576	90,707	45,868	44,929
1 month or less	30,640	15,584	15,056	14,699	7,391	7,308	10,767	5,463	5,304	5,174	2,730	2,444
2 to 3 months	21,934	11,940	9,994	11,073	5,369	5,704	4,906	2,704	2,202	5,955	3,867	2,088
4 to 5 months	37,082	21,602	15,480	11,905	5,785	6,120	12,475	7,280	5,195	12,702	8,537	4,105
6 months or more	393,172	195,727	197,445	133,995	68,657	65,388	192,211	96,336	95,875	66,966	30,734	36,232
New Jersey	131,514	66,727	64,787	46,497	23,721	22,776	62,908	31,755	31,153	22,109	11,251	10,858
1 month or less	9,649	4,966	4,683	4,145	2,066	2,079	3,824	1,952	1,872	1,680	948	732
2 to 3 months	4,991	2,815	2,176	2,290	1,077	1,213	1,412	810	602	1,289	928	361
4 to 5 months	5,969	3,490	2,479	1,977	922	1,055	2,381	1,418	963	1,611	1,150	461
6 months or more	110,905	55,456	55,449	38,085	19,656	18,429	55,291	27,575	27,716	17,529	8,225	9,304
Pennsylvania	676,948	344,618	332,330	227,663	115,577	112,086	322,080	161,770	160,310	127,205	67,271	59,934
1 month or less	28,142	14,151	13,991	12,584	6,277	6,307	9,888	4,894	4,994	5,670	2,980	2,690
2 to 3 months	41,373	21,966	19,407	16,067	7,710	8,357	12,781	6,554	6,227	12,525	7,702	4,823
4 to 5 months	76,420	42,436	33,984	21,227	10,543	10,684	34,549	18,770	15,779	20,644	13,123	7,521
6 months or more	531,013	266,065	264,948	177,785	91,047	86,738	264,862	131,552	133,310	88,366	43,466	44,900
South Atlantic division: Delaware	20,977	10,878	10,099	6,767	3,373	3,394	10,676	5,557	5,119	3,534	1,948	1,586
1 month or less	851	472	379	451	264	187	282	141	141	118	67	51
2 to 3 months	1,352	848	504	434	194	240	490	331	159	428	323	105
4 to 5 months	2,100	1,220	880	619	285	334	978	581	397	503	354	149
6 months or more	16,674	8,338	8,336	5,263	2,630	2,633	8,926	4,504	4,422	2,485	1,204	1,281
Maryland	110,486	56,607	53,879	34,935	17,859	17,076	56,403	28,362	28,041	19,148	10,386	8,762
1 month or less	4,304	2,206	2,098	1,764	893	871	1,677	825	852	863	488	375
2 to 3 months	6,322	3,778	2,544	2,218	1,096	1,122	2,247	1,307	940	1,857	1,375	482
4 to 5 months	8,945	5,128	3,817	2,449	1,279	1,170	4,277	2,428	1,849	2,219	1,421	798
6 months or more	90,915	45,495	45,420	28,504	14,591	13,913	48,202	23,802	24,400	14,209	7,102	7,107
District of Columbia	18,573	9,057	9,516	4,900	2,502	2,398	9,459	4,681	4,778	4,214	1,874	2,340
1 month or less	899	444	455	263	140	123	401	196	205	235	108	127
2 to 3 months	217	108	109	91	41	50	74	39	35	52	28	24
4 to 5 months	382	167	215	139	57	82	146	72	74	97	38	59
6 months or more	17,075	8,338	8,737	4,407	2,264	2,143	8,838	4,374	4,464	3,830	1,700	2,130
Virginia	191,061	96,718	94,343	53,955	27,653	26,302	92,950	46,789	46,161	44,156	22,276	21,880
1 month or less	9,873	5,193	4,680	3,641	1,835	1,806	3,809	2,014	1,795	2,423	1,344	1,079
2 to 3 months	26,715	14,610	12,105	8,271	4,213	4,058	11,779	6,337	5,442	6,665	4,060	2,605
4 to 5 months	93,248	47,262	45,986	20,708	13,704	13,004	46,424	23,535	22,889	20,056	9,963	10,093
6 months or more	61,225	29,653	31,572	15,275	7,841	7,434	30,938	14,903	16,035	15,012	6,909	8,103

SCHOOL ATTENDANCE.

TABLE **19.**—NATIVE WHITE PERSONS OF NATIVE PARENTAGE ATTENDING SCHOOL DURING THE CENSUS YEAR, CLASSIFIED BY SEX, AGE PERIODS, AND MONTHS OF SCHOOL ATTENDANCE, BY STATES AND TERRITORIES: 1890—Continued.

STATES, TERRITORIES, AND MONTHS OF SCHOOL ATTENDANCE.	ALL AGES.			UNDER 10 YEARS.			10 TO 14 YEARS.			15 YEARS AND OVER.		
	Total.	Males.	Females.	Total.	Males.	Females.	Total.	Males.	Females.	Total.	Males.	Females.
South Atlantic division—Cont.												
West Virginia	149,210	77,618	71,592	41,847	21,441	20,406	71,196	36,499	34,697	36,167	19,678	16,489
1 month or less	7,033	3,637	3,396	2,590	1,266	1,324	2,650	1,364	1,286	1,793	1,007	786
2 to 3 months	26,341	14,032	12,309	7,973	4,063	3,910	11,754	6,087	5,667	6,614	3,882	2,732
4 to 5 months	78,485	41,386	37,099	20,864	10,847	10,017	38,152	19,796	18,356	19,469	10,743	8,726
6 months or more	37,351	18,563	18,788	10,420	5,265	5,155	18,640	9,252	9,388	8,291	4,046	4,245
North Carolina	185,465	95,293	90,172	48,615	24,629	23,986	90,427	45,410	45,017	46,423	25,254	21,169
1 month or less	15,401	8,133	7,268	4,769	2,393	2,376	6,640	3,380	3,260	3,992	2,360	1,632
2 to 3 months	96,246	50,909	45,337	25,781	13,176	12,605	47,129	24,641	22,488	23,336	13,092	10,244
4 to 5 months	41,596	20,967	20,629	10,828	5,454	5,374	20,769	10,213	10,556	9,999	5,300	4,699
6 months or more	32,222	15,284	16,938	7,237	3,606	3,631	15,889	7,176	8,713	9,096	4,502	4,594
South Carolina	76,419	38,931	37,488	21,078	10,665	10,413	38,397	19,374	19,023	16,944	8,892	8,052
1 month or less	4,607	2,518	2,089	1,536	813	723	2,046	1,131	915	1,025	574	451
2 to 3 months	29,222	15,390	13,832	8,466	4,329	4,137	14,992	7,830	7,162	5,764	3,231	2,533
4 to 5 months	14,468	7,210	7,258	4,039	2,010	2,029	7,488	3,666	3,822	2,941	1,534	1,407
6 months or more	28,122	13,813	14,309	7,037	3,513	3,524	13,871	6,747	7,124	7,214	3,553	3,661
Georgia	170,935	87,028	83,907	49,640	25,229	24,411	85,385	42,565	42,820	35,910	19,234	16,676
1 month or less	12,843	6,996	5,847	4,450	2,245	2,205	5,418	2,954	2,464	2,975	1,797	1,178
2 to 3 months	71,744	38,569	33,175	21,454	10,955	10,499	35,571	18,943	16,628	14,719	8,671	6,048
4 to 5 months	35,384	17,565	17,819	10,721	5,517	5,204	17,878	8,546	9,332	6,785	3,502	3,283
6 months or more	50,964	23,898	27,066	13,015	6,512	6,503	26,518	12,122	14,396	11,431	5,264	6,167
Florida	41,315	21,366	19,949	12,014	6,067	5,947	19,180	9,848	9,332	10,121	5,451	4,670
1 month or less	1,790	969	821	591	300	291	736	400	336	463	269	194
2 to 3 months	8,067	4,433	3,634	2,428	1,233	1,195	3,569	1,932	1,637	2,070	1,268	802
4 to 5 months	17,483	9,025	8,458	5,185	2,642	2,543	8,274	4,259	4,015	4,024	2,124	1,900
6 months or more	13,975	6,939	7,036	3,810	1,892	1,918	6,601	3,257	3,344	3,564	1,790	1,774
North Central division:												
Ohio	552,460	286,102	266,358	177,330	90,547	86,783	250,725	127,477	123,248	124,405	68,078	56,327
1 month or less	20,247	10,179	10,068	9,415	4,697	4,718	6,041	2,980	3,061	4,791	2,502	2,289
2 to 3 months	36,583	19,844	16,739	16,499	7,982	8,517	9,253	4,775	4,478	10,831	7,087	3,744
4 to 5 months	71,767	42,993	28,774	17,244	8,689	8,555	27,313	15,753	11,560	27,210	18,551	8,659
6 months or more	423,863	218,086	210,777	134,172	69,179	64,993	208,118	103,969	104,149	81,573	39,938	41,635
Indiana	389,894	201,346	188,548	122,748	61,807	60,941	177,262	89,776	87,486	89,884	49,763	40,121
1 month or less	13,607	6,778	6,829	5,972	2,932	3,040	4,309	2,123	2,186	3,326	1,723	1,603
2 to 3 months	31,706	16,793	14,913	12,604	5,982	6,712	10,284	5,200	5,084	8,778	5,611	3,167
4 to 5 months	101,058	54,948	46,110	29,058	14,709	14,349	46,121	24,266	21,855	25,879	15,973	9,906
6 months or more	243,523	122,827	120,696	75,024	38,184	36,840	116,598	58,187	58,411	51,901	26,456	25,445
Illinois	427,733	219,259	208,474	139,879	70,948	68,931	190,722	96,543	94,179	97,132	51,768	45,364
1 month or less	18,404	9,300	9,164	8,634	4,280	4,354	5,447	2,793	2,654	4,383	2,227	2,156
2 to 3 months	44,698	24,889	19,809	18,624	9,033	9,591	12,939	7,006	5,933	13,135	8,850	4,285
4 to 5 months	79,473	45,185	34,288	21,951	11,055	10,896	34,529	19,362	15,167	22,993	14,768	8,225
6 months or more	285,098	139,885	145,213	90,670	46,580	44,090	137,807	67,382	70,425	56,621	25,923	30,698
Michigan	199,372	101,755	97,617	66,825	33,600	33,225	89,542	45,662	43,880	43,005	22,493	20,512
1 month or less	8,946	4,504	4,442	4,332	2,178	2,154	2,861	1,473	1,388	1,753	853	900
2 to 3 months	14,152	7,680	6,472	7,085	3,432	3,653	3,299	1,830	1,469	3,768	2,418	1,350
4 to 5 months	22,248	13,826	8,422	5,951	2,905	3,046	7,569	4,704	2,865	8,728	6,217	2,511
6 months or more	154,026	75,745	78,281	49,457	25,085	24,372	75,813	37,655	38,158	28,756	13,005	15,751
Wisconsin	109,558	55,552	54,006	43,149	21,725	21,424	46,322	23,425	22,897	20,087	10,402	9,685
1 month or less	5,388	2,696	2,692	3,225	1,623	1,602	1,338	663	675	825	410	415
2 to 3 months	9,026	4,933	4,093	5,199	2,554	2,645	1,851	1,024	827	1,976	1,355	621
4 to 5 months	12,136	7,036	5,100	4,472	2,117	2,355	4,259	2,513	1,746	3,405	2,406	999
6 months or more	83,008	40,887	42,121	30,253	15,431	14,822	38,874	19,225	19,649	13,881	6,231	7,650
Minnesota	67,721	34,702	33,019	23,293	11,835	11,458	29,395	14,966	14,429	15,033	7,901	7,132
1 month or less	2,920	1,464	1,456	1,522	721	801	775	388	387	623	355	268
2 to 3 months	6,367	3,512	2,855	3,250	1,586	1,664	1,594	885	709	1,523	1,041	482
4 to 5 months	8,927	5,160	3,767	4,009	1,519	1,490	3,541	2,020	1,521	2,377	1,621	756
6 months or more	49,507	24,566	24,941	15,512	8,009	7,503	23,485	11,673	11,812	10,510	4,884	5,626
Iowa	277,214	143,058	134,156	97,554	49,584	47,970	116,283	59,304	56,979	63,377	34,170	29,207
1 month or less	10,546	5,457	5,089	5,448	2,815	2,633	2,842	1,455	1,387	2,256	1,187	1,069
2 to 3 months	26,527	15,966	10,561	11,492	5,594	5,898	5,719	3,591	2,128	9,316	6,781	2,535
4 to 5 months	35,371	22,291	13,080	9,721	4,766	4,955	12,195	7,768	4,427	13,455	9,757	3,698
6 months or more	204,770	99,344	105,426	70,893	36,409	34,484	95,527	46,490	49,037	38,350	16,445	21,905
Missouri	432,570	222,256	210,314	131,049	66,253	64,796	198,413	100,470	97,943	103,108	55,533	47,575
1 month or less	22,088	11,528	10,560	9,643	4,869	4,774	7,205	3,738	3,467	5,240	2,921	2,319
2 to 3 months	71,216	38,777	32,439	24,850	12,321	12,529	27,792	14,853	12,939	18,574	11,603	6,971
4 to 5 months	111,101	60,958	50,143	29,851	15,126	14,725	51,777	28,064	23,713	29,463	17,768	11,695
6 months or more	228,165	110,993	117,172	66,695	33,937	32,758	111,639	53,815	57,824	49,831	23,241	26,590

STATISTICS OF POPULATION.

TABLE 19.—NATIVE WHITE PERSONS OF NATIVE PARENTAGE ATTENDING SCHOOL DURING THE CENSUS YEAR, CLASSIFIED BY SEX, AGE PERIODS, AND MONTHS OF SCHOOL ATTENDANCE, BY STATES AND TERRITORIES: 1890—Continued.

STATES, TERRITORIES, AND MONTHS OF SCHOOL ATTENDANCE.	ALL AGES.			UNDER 10 YEARS.			10 TO 14 YEARS.			15 YEARS AND OVER.		
	Total.	Males.	Females.	Total.	Males.	Females.	Total.	Males.	Females.	Total.	Males.	Females.
North Central division—Cont.												
North Dakota	6,992	3,626	3,366	2,475	1,269	1,206	3,105	1,611	1,494	1,412	746	666
1 month or less	414	204	210	231	109	122	118	55	63	65	40	25
2 to 3 months	1,030	578	452	468	235	233	319	184	135	243	159	84
4 to 5 months	1,119	624	495	379	192	187	465	243	222	275	189	86
6 months or more	4,429	2,220	2,209	1,397	733	664	2,203	1,129	1,074	829	358	471
South Dakota	28,907	15,114	13,853	9,451	4,791	4,660	12,526	6,443	6,083	6,930	3,880	3,110
1 month or less	1,194	609	585	644	307	337	296	155	141	254	147	107
2 to 3 months	4,492	2,582	1,910	1,876	942	934	1,336	755	581	1,280	885	395
4 to 5 months	5,993	3,502	2,401	1,687	857	830	2,551	1,523	1,028	1,755	1,212	543
6 months or more	17,288	8,331	8,957	5,244	2,685	2,559	8,343	4,010	4,333	3,701	1,636	2,065
Nebraska	143,397	73,848	69,489	51,850	26,203	25,647	61,122	31,293	29,880	30,365	16,412	13,953
1 month or less	6,165	3,107	3,058	2,989	1,477	1,512	1,777	892	885	1,399	738	661
2 to 3 months	20,941	12,288	8,653	8,451	4,198	4,253	6,471	3,864	2,607	6,019	4,226	1,793
4 to 5 months	18,404	10,663	7,741	5,860	2,944	2,916	7,517	4,348	3,169	5,027	3,371	1,656
6 months or more	97,827	47,790	50,037	34,550	17,584	16,966	45,357	22,129	23,228	17,920	8,077	9,843
Kansas	259,494	134,360	125,134	81,647	41,511	40,136	113,038	57,972	55,066	64,809	34,877	29,932
1 month or less	8,722	4,525	4,197	4,058	2,003	2,055	2,250	1,173	1,077	2,414	1,349	1,065
2 to 3 months	30,674	18,145	12,529	11,459	5,709	5,750	8,878	5,219	3,659	10,337	7,217	3,120
4 to 5 months	47,318	27,516	19,802	13,637	6,888	6,749	19,817	11,676	8,141	13,864	8,952	4,012
6 months or more	172,780	84,174	88,606	52,493	26,911	25,582	82,093	39,904	42,189	38,194	17,359	20,835
South Central division:												
Kentucky	293,882	151,527	141,855	82,241	41,812	40,429	140,866	71,921	68,945	70,275	37,794	32,481
1 month or less	19,566	10,403	9,163	6,928	3,478	3,450	7,501	4,003	3,498	5,137	2,922	2,215
2 to 3 months	71,069	38,728	32,341	20,931	10,585	10,346	32,274	17,410	14,864	17,864	10,733	7,131
4 to 5 months	136,970	70,668	66,302	37,088	18,975	18,113	68,387	34,844	33,543	31,495	16,849	14,646
6 months or more	65,777	31,728	34,049	17,294	8,774	8,520	32,704	15,664	17,040	15,770	7,290	8,489
Tennessee	265,716	138,418	127,298	72,421	37,069	35,352	126,981	64,841	62,140	66,314	36,508	29,806
1 month or less	18,139	9,755	8,384	6,210	3,235	2,975	7,216	3,751	3,465	4,713	2,769	1,944
2 to 3 months	99,646	53,900	45,746	28,708	14,787	13,921	46,770	24,848	21,922	24,168	14,265	9,903
4 to 5 months	81,290	42,457	38,833	21,637	11,107	10,530	39,784	20,383	19,401	19,869	10,967	8,902
6 months or more	66,641	32,306	34,335	15,866	7,940	7,926	33,211	15,859	17,352	17,564	8,507	9,057
Alabama	188,353	71,399	66,954	84,499	17,696	16,803	69,384	35,023	34,361	34,470	18,680	15,790
1 month or less	9,947	5,445	4,502	2,993	1,543	1,450	4,373	2,381	1,992	2,581	1,521	1,060
2 to 3 months	68,187	36,183	32,004	17,093	8,765	8,328	34,596	18,014	16,582	16,498	9,404	7,094
4 to 5 months	22,366	11,661	10,705	5,694	2,936	2,758	11,410	5,783	5,627	5,262	2,942	2,320
6 months or more	37,853	18,110	19,743	8,719	4,452	4,267	19,005	8,845	10,160	10,129	4,813	5,316
Mississippi	123,145	62,675	60,470	36,021	18,804	18,117	55,519	27,769	27,750	30,705	16,102	14,603
1 month or less	8,436	4,575	3,861	3,098	1,579	1,519	3,137	1,661	1,476	2,201	1,335	866
2 to 3 months	37,914	20,556	17,358	11,764	6,024	5,740	16,742	8,913	7,829	9,408	5,619	3,789
4 to 5 months	48,666	24,793	23,873	15,086	7,716	7,320	22,735	11,418	11,317	10,895	5,659	5,236
6 months or more	28,129	12,751	15,378	7,023	3,485	3,538	12,905	5,777	7,128	8,201	3,489	4,712
Louisiana	62,336	31,828	30,508	18,907	9,665	9,242	31,983	16,196	15,787	11,446	5,967	5,479
1 month or less	5,157	2,698	2,459	1,827	904	923	2,364	1,240	1,124	966	554	412
2 to 3 months	14,573	7,829	6,744	4,301	2,276	2,025	7,166	3,801	3,365	3,106	1,752	1,354
4 to 5 months	9,199	4,724	4,475	2,874	1,481	1,393	4,677	2,360	2,317	1,648	883	765
6 months or more	33,407	16,577	16,830	9,905	5,004	4,901	17,776	8,795	8,981	5,726	2,778	2,948
Texas	284,938	145,710	139,228	66,180	33,335	32,845	152,527	76,895	75,632	66,231	35,480	30,751
1 month or less	19,118	10,394	8,724	6,556	3,296	3,260	8,043	4,394	3,649	4,519	2,704	1,815
2 to 3 months	91,870	50,219	41,651	22,669	11,479	11,190	48,152	26,018	22,134	21,049	12,722	8,327
4 to 5 months	90,826	46,125	44,701	19,632	9,931	9,701	51,107	25,600	25,597	19,997	10,594	9,403
6 months or more	83,124	38,972	44,152	17,323	8,629	8,694	45,135	20,883	24,252	20,666	9,460	11,206
Oklahoma	6,257	3,185	3,072	1,978	1,044	934	3,128	1,575	1,553	1,151	566	585
1 month or less	645	333	312	248	111	137	267	151	116	130	71	59
2 to 3 months	2,365	1,239	1,126	779	414	365	1,165	593	572	421	232	189
4 to 5 months	1,364	690	674	409	206	203	708	374	334	247	110	137
6 months or more	1,883	923	960	542	313	229	988	457	531	353	153	200
Arkansas	162,856	85,329	77,527	43,801	22,441	21,360	75,994	38,447	37,547	43,061	24,441	18,620
1 month or less	12,711	6,890	5,821	4,113	2,127	1,986	5,156	2,679	2,477	3,442	2,084	1,358
2 to 3 months	91,437	49,373	42,064	24,362	12,550	11,812	42,887	22,595	20,292	24,188	14,228	9,960
4 to 5 months	28,676	14,876	13,800	7,645	3,951	3,694	13,611	6,748	6,863	7,420	4,177	3,243
6 months or more	30,032	14,190	15,842	7,681	3,813	3,868	14,340	6,425	7,915	8,011	3,952	4,059

SCHOOL ATTENDANCE.

153

TABLE 19.—NATIVE WHITE PERSONS OF NATIVE PARENTAGE ATTENDING SCHOOL DURING THE CENSUS YEAR, CLASSIFIED BY SEX, AGE PERIODS, AND MONTHS OF SCHOOL ATTENDANCE, BY STATES AND TERRITORIES: 1890—Continued.

STATES, TERRITORIES, AND MONTHS OF SCHOOL ATTENDANCE.	ALL AGES.			UNDER 10 YEARS.			10 TO 14 YEARS.			15 YEARS AND OVER.		
	Total.	Males.	Females.	Total.	Males.	Females.	Total.	Males.	Females.	Total.	Males.	Females.
Western division:												
Montana	7,988	4,042	3,946	2,754	1,364	1,390	3,541	1,800	1,741	1,693	878	815
1 month or less	515	247	268	267	121	146	156	76	80	92	50	42
2 to 3 months	1,386	746	640	595	290	305	506	281	225	285	175	110
4 to 5 months	1,123	600	523	387	197	190	495	267	228	241	136	105
6 months or more	4,964	2,449	2,515	1,505	756	749	2,384	1,176	1,208	1,075	517	558
Wyoming	4,248	2,250	1,998	1,485	772	713	1,886	992	894	877	486	391
1 month or less	284	153	131	117	67	50	99	52	47	68	34	34
2 to 3 months	698	379	319	290	143	147	243	126	117	165	110	55
4 to 5 months	880	481	399	305	149	156	406	230	176	169	102	67
6 months or more	2,386	1,237	1,149	773	413	360	1,138	584	554	475	240	235
Colorado	38,125	19,642	18,483	12,013	6,094	5,919	17,521	8,981	8,540	8,591	4,567	4,024
1 month or less	1,871	973	898	851	448	413	610	304	306	400	221	179
2 to 3 months	4,615	2,576	2,039	1,763	913	850	1,750	956	794	1,102	707	395
4 to 5 months	5,538	3,086	2,452	1,649	854	795	2,474	1,351	1,123	1,415	881	534
6 months or more	26,101	13,007	13,094	7,740	3,879	3,861	12,687	6,370	6,317	5,674	2,758	2,916
New Mexico	17,426	9,748	7,678	5,063	2,726	2,337	8,200	4,423	3,777	4,163	2,599	1,564
1 month or less	909	475	434	398	210	188	331	161	170	180	104	76
2 to 3 months	7,178	4,208	2,970	2,212	1,208	1,004	3,099	1,755	1,344	1,867	1,245	622
4 to 5 months	3,708	2,162	1,546	1,037	588	449	1,771	1,069	702	900	565	335
6 months or more	5,631	2,903	2,728	1,416	720	696	2,999	1,498	1,501	1,216	685	531
Arizona	3,983	2,039	1,944	1,249	633	616	1,947	1,015	932	787	391	396
1 month or less	218	117	101	83	42	41	85	47	38	50	28	22
2 to 3 months	474	252	222	169	80	89	189	103	86	116	69	47
4 to 5 months	964	508	456	318	165	153	462	240	222	184	103	81
6 months or more	2,327	1,162	1,165	679	346	333	1,211	625	586	437	191	246
Utah	13,205	6,815	6,480	4,359	2,256	2,103	6,260	3,137	3,123	2,676	1,422	1,254
1 month or less	661	314	347	307	153	154	215	100	115	139	61	78
2 to 3 months	2,696	1,405	1,291	1,034	502	532	1,031	529	502	631	374	257
4 to 5 months	2,448	1,311	1,137	697	357	340	1,194	647	547	557	307	250
6 months or more	7,490	3,785	3,705	2,321	1,244	1,077	3,820	1,861	1,959	1,349	680	669
Nevada	2,804	1,381	1,423	848	419	429	1,344	673	671	612	289	323
1 month or less	109	56	53	46	25	21	42	18	24	21	13	8
2 to 3 months	169	89	80	68	28	40	58	28	30	43	33	10
4 to 5 months	183	85	98	76	28	48	66	35	31	41	22	19
6 months or more	2,343	1,151	1,192	658	338	320	1,178	592	586	507	221	286
Idaho	8,804	4,603	4,201	3,048	1,564	1,484	4,004	2,081	1,923	1,752	958	794
1 month or less	540	290	250	298	152	146	156	87	69	86	51	35
2 to 3 months	2,606	1,405	1,201	1,001	531	470	1,050	559	491	555	315	240
4 to 5 months	1,962	1,057	905	622	317	305	929	495	434	411	245	166
6 months or more	3,696	1,851	1,845	1,127	564	563	1,869	940	929	700	347	353
Washington	31,982	16,320	15,662	9,847	4,868	4,979	15,254	7,720	7,534	6,881	3,732	3,149
1 month or less	1,641	840	801	851	427	424	505	249	256	285	164	121
2 to 3 months	7,335	3,750	3,585	2,623	1,197	1,426	3,001	1,517	1,484	1,711	1,036	675
4 to 5 months	5,304	2,821	2,483	1,366	704	662	2,048	1,349	1,299	1,290	768	522
6 months or more	17,702	8,909	8,793	5,007	2,540	2,467	9,100	4,605	4,495	3,595	1,764	1,831
Oregon	45,019	23,540	22,479	18,926	7,012	6,914	20,946	10,532	10,414	11,147	5,996	5,151
1 month or less	2,376	1,231	1,145	1,064	540	524	788	390	398	524	301	223
2 to 3 months	8,909	4,753	4,156	3,337	1,661	1,676	3,185	1,653	1,532	2,387	1,439	948
4 to 5 months	7,070	4,057	3,013	2,268	1,158	1,110	3,414	1,757	1,657	1,988	1,142	846
6 months or more	27,064	13,499	13,565	7,257	3,653	3,604	13,559	6,732	6,827	6,248	3,114	3,134
California	100,640	50,231	50,409	29,653	15,010	14,643	47,444	23,553	23,891	23,543	11,668	11,875
1 month or less	5,387	2,751	2,636	2,045	1,040	1,005	1,997	991	1,006	1,345	720	625
2 to 3 months	4,221	2,244	1,977	1,818	892	926	1,277	680	597	1,126	672	454
4 to 5 months	5,073	3,056	2,617	1,902	952	950	2,064	1,085	979	1,707	1,019	688
6 months or more	85,859	42,180	43,179	23,888	12,126	11,762	42,106	20,797	21,309	19,865	9,257	10,108

154
STATISTICS OF POPULATION.

TABLE 20.—NATIVE WHITE PERSONS OF FOREIGN PARENTAGE ATTENDING SCHOOL DURING THE CENSUS YEAR, CLASSIFIED BY SEX, AGE PERIODS, AND MONTHS OF SCHOOL ATTENDANCE, BY STATES AND TERRITORIES: 1890.

STATES, TERRITORIES, AND MONTHS OF SCHOOL ATTENDANCE.	ALL AGES.			UNDER 10 YEARS.			10 TO 14 YEARS.			15 YEARS AND OVER.		
	Total.	Males.	Females.	Total.	Males.	Females.	Total.	Males.	Females.	Total.	Males.	Females.
North Atlantic division: Maine	20,154	10,294	9,860	7,821	4,068	3,753	8,999	4,571	4,428	3,334	1,655	1,679
1 month or less	900	466	434	527	277	250	227	113	114	146	76	70
2 to 3 months	1,804	1,000	804	705	410	295	657	307	350	442	283	159
4 to 5 months	3,187	1,685	1,502	1,283	674	609	1,378	738	640	526	273	253
6 months or more	14,263	7,143	7,120	5,306	2,707	2,599	6,737	3,413	3,324	2,220	1,023	1,197
New Hampshire	13,582	6,917	6,665	5,550	2,790	2,760	6,319	3,215	3,104	1,713	912	801
1 month or less	998	496	502	561	283	278	352	169	183	85	44	41
2 to 3 months	761	393	368	437	205	232	190	87	103	134	101	33
4 to 5 months	1,318	677	641	554	290	264	580	285	295	184	102	82
6 months or more	10,505	5,351	5,154	3,998	2,012	1,986	5,197	2,674	2,523	1,310	665	645
Vermont	15,393	7,994	7,399	5,360	2,783	2,577	7,504	3,927	3,577	2,529	1,284	1,245
1 month or less	525	274	251	291	145	146	153	82	71	81	47	34
2 to 3 months	1,383	827	556	577	306	271	369	219	150	437	302	135
4 to 5 months	1,359	739	620	500	248	252	598	333	265	261	158	103
6 months or more	12,126	6,154	5,972	3,992	2,084	1,908	6,384	3,293	3,091	1,750	777	973
Massachusetts	169,346	84,838	84,508	69,225	34,883	34,342	79,406	40,000	39,406	20,715	9,955	10,760
1 month or less	8,518	4,272	4,246	4,706	2,347	2,359	2,853	1,450	1,403	959	475	484
2 to 3 months	3,443	1,770	1,673	2,450	1,214	1,236	502	254	248	491	302	189
4 to 5 months	3,137	1,613	1,524	1,694	830	864	884	454	430	559	329	230
6 months or more	154,248	77,183	77,065	60,375	30,492	29,883	75,167	37,842	37,325	18,706	8,849	9,857
Rhode Island	24,020	12,011	12,009	10,353	5,222	5,131	11,160	5,511	5,649	2,507	1,278	1,229
1 month or less	1,723	865	858	871	422	449	641	331	310	211	112	99
2 to 3 months	1,210	645	565	507	237	270	503	276	227	200	132	68
4 to 5 months	827	418	409	405	194	211	293	138	155	129	86	43
6 months or more	20,260	10,083	10,177	8,570	4,369	4,201	9,723	4,766	4,957	1,967	948	1,019
Connecticut	52,623	26,745	25,878	21,732	11,172	10,560	25,115	12,776	12,339	5,776	2,797	2,979
1 month or less	3,789	1,972	1,817	1,908	1,027	881	1,451	735	716	430	210	220
2 to 3 months	1,220	629	591	810	393	417	242	131	111	168	105	63
4 to 5 months	1,389	757	632	669	344	325	450	239	211	270	174	96
6 months or more	46,225	23,387	22,838	18,345	9,408	8,937	22,972	11,671	11,301	4,908	2,308	2,600
New York	421,044	212,899	208,145	157,579	79,890	77,689	210,371	106,340	104,031	53,094	26,669	26,425
1 month or less	36,673	18,996	17,677	15,977	8,190	7,787	15,653	7,900	7,753	5,043	2,906	2,137
2 to 3 months	9,972	5,418	4,554	5,243	2,515	2,728	2,383	1,340	1,043	2,346	1,563	783
4 to 5 months	17,306	10,253	7,053	5,713	2,796	2,917	6,220	3,728	2,492	5,373	3,729	1,644
6 months or more	357,093	178,232	178,861	130,646	66,389	64,257	186,115	93,372	92,743	40,332	18,471	21,861
New Jersey	87,938	44,195	43,743	34,061	17,264	16,797	45,187	22,549	22,638	8,690	4,382	4,308
1 month or less	8,593	4,455	4,138	3,776	1,938	1,838	3,928	1,995	1,933	889	522	367
2 to 3 months	1,713	895	818	1,053	484	569	388	210	178	272	201	71
4 to 5 months	2,199	1,228	971	1,029	531	498	837	478	359	333	219	114
6 months or more	75,433	37,617	37,816	28,203	14,311	13,892	40,034	19,866	20,168	7,196	3,440	3,756
Pennsylvania	227,638	112,576	115,062	87,013	44,305	42,713	112,799	55,101	57,608	27,821	13,080	14,741
1 month or less	12,545	6,318	6,227	5,802	2,954	2,848	5,244	2,601	2,643	1,499	763	736
2 to 3 months	7,085	3,775	3,310	3,324	1,566	1,758	2,110	1,173	937	1,651	1,036	615
4 to 5 months	9,933	5,339	4,594	3,612	1,815	1,797	4,115	2,210	1,905	2,206	1,314	892
6 months or more	198,075	97,144	100,931	74,280	37,970	36,310	101,330	49,207	52,123	22,465	9,967	12,498
South Atlantic division: Delaware	3,377	1,686	1,691	1,224	653	571	1,707	837	870	446	196	250
1 month or less	125	65	60	61	33	28	44	22	22	20	10	10
2 to 3 months	81	49	32	34	13	21	24	15	9	23	21	2
4 to 5 months	76	42	34	40	26	14	18	8	10	18	8	10
6 months or more	3,095	1,530	1,565	1,089	581	508	1,621	792	829	385	157	228
Maryland	28,459	14,662	13,797	9,385	4,740	4,645	15,302	7,798	7,504	3,712	2,124	1,588
1 month or less	930	501	429	350	173	177	389	223	166	191	105	86
2 to 3 months	517	305	212	203	98	105	178	102	76	136	105	31
4 to 5 months	930	473	457	261	126	135	433	210	223	236	137	99
6 months or more	26,082	13,383	12,699	8,571	4,343	4,228	14,362	7,263	7,099	3,149	1,777	1,372
District of Columbia	6,192	2,972	3,220	1,544	773	771	3,326	1,628	1,698	1,322	571	751
1 month or less	340	174	166	116	57	59	145	84	61	79	33	46
2 to 3 months	51	24	27	22	10	12	18	10	8	11	4	7
4 to 5 months	105	45	60	41	21	20	32	14	18	32	10	22
6 months or more	5,696	2,729	2,967	1,365	685	680	3,131	1,520	1,611	1,200	524	676
Virginia	5,163	2,641	2,522	1,298	695	603	2,788	1,432	1,356	1,077	514	563
1 month or less	305	154	151	80	35	45	159	87	72	66	32	34
2 to 3 months	238	138	100	80	42	38	100	60	40	58	36	22
4 to 5 months	833	468	415	230	130	100	451	241	210	202	97	105
6 months or more	3,787	1,881	1,856	908	488	420	2,078	1,044	1,034	751	349	402

SCHOOL ATTENDANCE. 155

TABLE 20.—NATIVE WHITE PERSONS OF FOREIGN PARENTAGE ATTENDING SCHOOL DURING THE CENSUS YEAR, CLASSIFIED BY SEX, AGE PERIODS, AND MONTHS OF SCHOOL ATTENDANCE, BY STATES AND TERRITORIES: 1890—Continued.

STATES, TERRITORIES, AND MONTHS OF SCHOOL ATTENDANCE.	ALL AGES.			UNDER 10 YEARS.			10 TO 14 YEARS.			15 YEARS AND OVER.		
	Total.	Males.	Females.	Total.	Males.	Females.	Total.	Males.	Females.	Total.	Males.	Females.
South Atlantic division—Cont.												
West Virginia	8,720	4,418	4,302	2,527	1,290	1,237	4,384	2,200	2,184	1,809	928	881
1 month or less	338	182	156	123	65	58	143	78	65	72	39	33
2 to 3 months	652	349	303	193	92	101	247	131	116	212	126	86
4 to 5 months	2,214	1,140	1,074	523	260	263	1,044	529	515	647	351	296
6 months or more	5,516	2,747	2,769	1,688	873	815	2,950	1,462	1,488	878	412	466
North Carolina	1,394	720	674	325	181	144	706	346	360	363	193	170
1 month or less	59	31	28	15	9	6	23	11	12	21	11	10
2 to 3 months	227	120	107	60	31	29	111	58	53	56	31	25
4 to 5 months	193	103	90	57	28	29	89	48	41	47	27	20
6 months or more	915	466	449	193	113	80	483	229	254	239	124	115
South Carolina	2,153	1,064	1,089	634	324	310	984	433	551	535	307	228
1 month or less	62	29	33	24	13	11	32	16	16	6	....	6
2 to 3 months	138	71	67	41	16	25	67	35	32	30	20	10
4 to 5 months	149	90	59	57	37	20	62	28	34	30	25	5
6 months or more	1,804	874	930	512	258	254	823	354	469	469	262	207
Georgia	3,914	1,880	2,034	1,119	561	558	2,059	1,012	1,047	736	307	429
1 month or less	177	85	92	54	25	29	72	35	37	51	25	26
2 to 3 months	314	164	150	93	45	48	155	82	73	66	37	29
4 to 5 months	250	136	114	76	46	30	117	65	52	57	25	32
6 months or more	3,173	1,495	1,678	896	445	451	1,715	830	885	562	220	342
Florida	3,835	1,851	1,984	1,373	669	704	1,870	911	959	592	271	321
1 month or less	141	65	76	57	32	25	62	24	38	22	9	13
2 to 3 months	231	110	121	85	39	46	95	48	47	51	23	28
4 to 5 months	705	367	338	233	127	106	330	167	169	186	73	63
6 months or more	2,758	1,309	1,449	998	471	527	1,377	672	705	383	166	217
North Central division:												
Ohio	183,817	94,026	89,791	63,556	32,119	31,437	90,549	46,027	44,522	29,712	15,880	13,832
1 month or less	7,869	3,938	3,931	3,542	1,743	1,799	2,953	1,456	1,497	1,374	739	635
2 to 3 months	6,155	3,407	2,748	2,968	1,391	1,577	1,196	645	551	1,991	1,371	620
4 to 5 months	12,440	7,411	5,029	2,844	1,430	1,414	4,635	2,636	1,999	4,961	3,345	1,616
6 months or more	157,353	79,270	78,083	54,202	27,555	26,647	81,765	41,290	40,475	21,386	10,425	10,961
Indiana	70,742	36,324	34,418	21,773	10,999	10,774	35,528	18,047	17,481	13,441	7,278	6,163
1 month or less	2,534	1,298	1,236	980	502	478	993	492	501	561	304	257
2 to 3 months	3,185	1,801	1,384	1,202	577	625	929	505	424	1,054	719	335
4 to 5 months	10,264	5,702	4,562	2,560	1,296	1,270	4,766	2,644	2,122	2,932	1,762	1,170
6 months or more	54,759	27,523	27,236	17,025	8,624	8,401	28,840	14,406	14,434	8,894	4,493	4,401
Illinois	277,402	141,046	136,356	98,584	49,872	48,712	133,579	67,469	66,110	45,239	23,705	21,534
1 month or less	17,136	8,579	8,557	8,370	4,122	4,248	6,425	3,291	3,134	2,341	1,166	1,175
2 to 3 months	13,474	7,962	5,512	5,689	2,761	2,928	2,902	1,624	1,278	4,883	3,577	1,306
4 to 5 months	21,343	12,701	8,642	5,481	2,708	2,773	8,861	5,162	3,699	7,001	4,831	2,230
6 months or more	225,449	111,804	113,645	79,044	40,281	38,763	115,451	57,392	58,059	30,954	14,131	16,823
Michigan	175,580	89,564	86,016	67,541	34,200	33,281	80,827	40,876	39,951	27,212	14,428	12,784
1 month or less	10,013	5,033	4,980	5,288	2,645	2,643	3,449	1,764	1,685	1,276	624	652
2 to 3 months	11,320	6,137	5,183	5,822	2,904	2,918	2,973	1,612	1,361	2,525	1,621	904
4 to 5 months	17,380	10,357	7,023	5,062	2,480	2,582	6,785	4,012	2,773	5,533	3,865	1,668
6 months or more	136,867	68,037	68,830	51,369	26,231	25,138	67,620	33,488	34,132	17,878	8,318	9,560
Wisconsin	219,944	113,342	106,602	81,967	41,338	40,629	103,194	52,483	50,711	34,783	19,521	15,262
1 month or less	10,272	5,205	5,067	5,846	2,907	2,939	2,925	1,510	1,415	1,501	788	713
2 to 3 months	18,791	10,183	8,608	9,147	4,502	4,645	5,350	2,819	2,531	4,294	2,862	1,432
4 to 5 months	28,513	16,372	12,141	8,567	4,231	4,336	12,278	6,826	5,452	7,668	5,315	2,353
6 months or more	162,368	81,582	80,786	58,407	29,698	28,709	82,641	41,328	41,313	21,320	10,556	10,764
Minnesota	157,861	81,935	75,926	55,362	28,059	27,303	74,402	37,812	36,590	28,097	16,064	12,033
1 month or less	7,584	3,744	3,840	4,083	1,964	2,119	2,006	994	1,012	1,495	786	709
2 to 3 months	24,476	13,263	11,213	10,216	5,030	5,186	8,467	4,397	4,070	5,793	3,836	1,957
4 to 5 months	35,752	19,835	15,917	10,796	5,547	5,249	17,728	9,448	8,280	7,228	4,840	2,388
6 months or more	90,049	45,093	44,956	30,267	15,518	14,749	46,201	22,973	23,228	13,581	6,602	6,979
Iowa	169,493	87,601	81,892	59,561	29,853	29,708	75,255	38,153	37,102	34,677	19,595	15,082
1 month or less	6,372	3,235	3,137	3,362	1,686	1,676	1,697	855	842	1,313	694	619
2 to 3 months	15,199	9,018	6,181	6,093	2,928	3,165	3,538	2,083	1,455	5,568	4,007	1,561
4 to 5 months	25,901	16,416	9,485	5,861	2,949	2,912	10,171	6,271	3,900	9,869	7,196	2,673
6 months or more	122,021	58,932	63,089	44,245	22,290	21,955	59,849	28,944	30,905	17,927	7,698	10,229
Missouri	105,199	53,586	51,613	33,235	16,853	16,382	53,362	26,715	26,647	18,602	10,018	8,584
1 month or less	5,561	2,807	2,754	2,324	1,170	1,154	2,305	1,140	1,165	932	497	435
2 to 3 months	6,635	3,796	2,839	2,358	1,176	1,182	2,232	1,211	1,021	2,045	1,409	636
4 to 5 months	12,040	7,074	5,866	3,856	1,716	1,640	6,042	3,179	2,863	3,542	2,179	1,363
6 months or more	80,963	39,909	40,154	25,197	12,791	12,406	42,783	21,185	21,598	12,983	5,933	6,150

156　　STATISTICS OF POPULATION.

TABLE 20.—NATIVE WHITE PERSONS OF FOREIGN PARENTAGE ATTENDING SCHOOL DURING THE CENSUS YEAR, CLASSIFIED BY SEX, AGE PERIODS, AND MONTHS OF SCHOOL ATTENDANCE, BY STATES AND TERRITORIES: 1890—Continued.

STATES, TERRITORIES, AND MONTHS OF SCHOOL ATTENDANCE.	ALL AGES.			UNDER 10 YEARS.			10 TO 14 YEARS.			15 YEARS AND OVER.		
	Total.	Males.	Females.	Total.	Males.	Females.	Total.	Males.	Females.	Total.	Males.	Females.
North Central division—Cont.												
North Dakota	15,575	8,288	7,287	6,868	3,545	3,323	6,530	3,473	3,057	2,177	1,270	907
1 month or less	1,394	757	637	918	478	440	289	162	127	187	117	70
2 to 3 months	3,101	1,745	1,356	1,441	748	693	1,110	614	496	550	383	167
4 to 5 months	3,327	1,830	1,497	1,297	680	617	1,528	844	684	502	208	109
6 months or more	7,753	3,956	3,797	3,212	1,639	1,573	3,603	1,853	1,750	938	464	474
South Dakota	32,743	17,237	15,506	10,880	5,512	5,368	14,787	7,636	7,151	7,076	4,089	2,987
1 month or less	1,707	842	865	906	443	463	460	220	240	341	179	162
2 to 3 months	5,924	3,372	2,552	2,171	1,090	1,081	2,133	1,194	939	1,620	1,088	532
4 to 5 months	9,120	5,263	3,857	2,665	1,387	1,278	4,353	2,452	1,901	2,102	1,424	678
6 months or more	15,992	7,760	8,232	5,138	2,592	2,546	7,841	3,770	4,071	3,013	1,398	1,615
Nebraska	80,885	42,107	38,778	30,948	15,833	15,115	35,178	17,975	17,203	14,759	8,299	6,460
1 month or less	3,119	1,611	1,508	1,612	827	785	877	436	441	630	348	282
2 to 3 months	12,112	7,177	4,935	4,658	2,346	2,312	3,782	2,173	1,609	3,672	2,658	1,014
4 to 5 months	11,150	6,396	4,754	3,582	1,844	1,738	4,742	2,719	2,023	2,826	1,833	993
6 months or more	54,504	26,923	27,581	21,096	10,816	10,280	25,777	12,647	13,130	7,631	3,460	4,171
Kansas	77,140	39,980	37,160	24,710	12,533	12,177	34,760	17,698	17,062	17,670	9,749	7,921
1 month or less	2,619	1,369	1,250	1,194	621	573	719	367	352	706	381	325
2 to 3 months	8,960	5,401	3,559	3,054	1,510	1,544	2,785	1,678	1,107	3,121	2,213	908
4 to 5 months	14,191	8,036	6,155	4,036	2,018	2,018	6,296	3,507	2,789	3,859	2,511	1,348
6 months or more	51,370	25,174	26,196	16,426	8,384	8,042	24,960	12,146	12,814	9,984	4,644	5,340
South Central division:												
Kentucky	25,329	12,727	12,602	8,154	4,088	4,066	13,498	6,844	6,654	3,677	1,795	1,882
1 month or less	1,147	555	592	430	193	237	525	255	270	192	107	85
2 to 3 months	1,229	671	558	422	212	210	492	263	229	315	196	119
4 to 5 months	3,602	1,850	1,752	992	500	492	1,790	912	878	820	438	382
6 months or more	19,351	9,651	9,700	6,310	3,183	3,127	10,691	5,414	5,277	2,350	1,054	1,296
Tennessee	7,486	3,666	3,820	1,984	990	994	3,027	1,057	1,970	1,575	719	856
1 month or less	333	151	182	118	46	72	141	62	79	74	43	31
2 to 3 months	702	402	300	284	117	117	366	196	170	192	119	73
4 to 5 months	1,025	516	509	281	148	133	533	262	271	211	106	105
6 months or more	5,336	2,567	2,769	1,351	679	672	2,887	1,437	1,450	1,098	451	647
Alabama	4,229	2,080	2,149	1,220	576	644	2,237	1,106	1,131	772	398	374
1 month or less	164	79	85	66	30	36	67	32	35	31	17	14
2 to 3 months	604	313	291	191	85	106	307	161	146	106	67	39
4 to 5 months	344	176	168	107	47	60	183	95	88	54	34	20
6 months or more	3,117	1,512	1,605	856	414	442	1,680	818	862	581	280	301
Mississippi	3,761	1,818	1,943	1,049	539	510	1,863	901	962	849	378	471
1 month or less	185	94	91	70	38	32	71	36	35	44	20	24
2 to 3 months	398	215	183	106	56	50	171	91	80	121	68	53
4 to 5 months	817	418	399	255	133	122	398	196	202	164	89	75
6 months or more	2,361	1,091	1,270	618	312	306	1,223	578	645	520	201	319
Louisiana	16,289	8,211	8,078	4,993	2,583	2,410	9,197	4,638	4,559	2,099	990	1,109
1 month or less	1,162	607	555	409	209	200	602	330	272	151	68	83
2 to 3 months	527	265	262	188	93	95	258	133	125	81	39	42
4 to 5 months	693	346	347	258	123	135	329	165	164	106	58	48
6 months or more	13,907	6,993	6,914	4,138	2,158	1,980	8,008	4,010	3,998	1,761	825	936
Texas	35,770	18,416	17,363	8,607	4,422	4,185	21,536	11,020	10,516	5,636	2,974	2,662
1 month or less	1,471	759	712	510	254	256	700	370	330	261	135	126
2 to 3 months	4,402	2,432	1,970	1,183	621	562	2,373	1,288	1,085	846	523	323
4 to 5 months	7,418	3,856	3,562	1,611	831	780	4,552	2,309	2,243	1,255	716	539
6 months or more	22,488	11,369	11,119	5,303	2,716	2,587	13,911	7,053	6,858	3,274	1,600	1,674
Oklahoma	601	306	295	191	99	92	292	144	148	118	63	55
1 month or less	70	37	33	23	13	10	32	15	17	15	9	6
2 to 3 months	185	88	97	57	26	31	88	38	50	40	24	16
4 to 5 months	123	61	62	39	19	20	64	33	31	20	9	11
6 months or more	223	120	103	72	41	31	108	58	50	43	21	22
Arkansas	5,111	2,590	2,521	1,458	744	714	2,473	1,255	1,218	1,180	591	589
1 month or less	263	132	131	96	54	42	97	41	56	70	37	33
2 to 3 months	1,410	772	638	396	207	189	631	343	288	383	222	161
4 to 5 months	836	433	403	236	124	112	414	211	203	186	98	88
6 months or more	2,602	1,253	1,349	730	359	371	1,331	660	671	541	234	307

SCHOOL ATTENDANCE.

TABLE 20.—NATIVE WHITE PERSONS OF FOREIGN PARENTAGE ATTENDING SCHOOL DURING THE CENSUS YEAR, CLASSIFIED BY SEX, AGE PERIODS, AND MONTHS OF SCHOOL ATTENDANCE, BY STATES AND TERRITORIES: 1890— Continued.

STATES, TERRITORIES, AND MONTHS OF SCHOOL ATTENDANCE.	ALL AGES.			UNDER 10 YEARS.			10 TO 14 YEARS.			15 YEARS AND OVER.		
	Total.	Males.	Females.	Total.	Males.	Females.	Total.	Males.	Females.	Total.	Males.	Females.
Western division: Montana	5,881	3,017	2,864	2,229	1,155	1,074	2,627	1,326	1,301	1,025	536	489
1 month or less	352	188	164	185	102	83	100	56	44	67	30	37
2 to 3 months	705	405	300	313	172	141	255	140	115	137	93	44
4 to 5 months	728	385	343	283	151	132	310	156	154	135	78	57
6 months or more	4,096	2,039	2,057	1,448	730	718	1,962	974	988	686	335	351
Wyoming	2,785	1,413	1,372	1,072	569	503	1,239	627	612	474	217	257
1 month or less	136	64	72	60	29	31	52	23	29	24	12	12
2 to 3 months	358	187	171	171	85	86	115	61	54	72	41	31
4 to 5 months	400	211	189	177	90	87	143	73	70	80	48	32
6 months or more	1,891	951	940	664	365	299	929	470	459	298	116	182
Colorado	17,071	8,863	8,808	6,196	3,137	3,050	8,263	4,129	4,134	3,212	1,597	1,615
1 month or less	876	441	435	398	211	187	308	152	156	170	78	92
2 to 3 months	1,385	746	639	614	315	299	480	254	226	291	177	114
4 to 5 months	1,810	902	908	654	313	341	769	387	382	387	202	185
6 months or more	13,000	6,774	6,826	4,530	2,298	2,232	6,706	3,336	3,370	2,364	1,140	1,224
New Mexico	2,206	1,228	1,073	738	387	351	1,131	595	536	427	241	186
1 month or less	87	49	38	38	25	13	30	11	19	19	13	6
2 to 3 months	405	263	202	152	73	79	221	131	90	92	59	33
4 to 5 months	343	191	152	101	58	43	177	95	82	65	38	27
6 months or more	1,401	720	681	447	231	216	703	358	345	251	131	120
Arizona	2,883	1,451	1,432	823	431	392	1,610	805	805	450	215	235
1 month or less	97	44	53	45	18	27	40	18	22	12	8	4
2 to 3 months	272	129	143	95	42	53	124	60	64	53	27	26
4 to 5 months	420	217	203	108	63	45	239	118	121	73	36	37
6 months or more	2,094	1,061	1,033	575	308	267	1,207	609	598	312	144	168
Utah	25,435	13,159	12,276	6,776	3,529	3,247	12,898	6,523	6,375	5,761	3,107	2,654
1 month or less	1,043	505	538	424	199	225	386	183	203	233	123	110
2 to 3 months	4,605	2,460	2,145	1,405	688	717	1,902	1,019	883	1,298	753	545
4 to 5 months	4,952	2,716	2,236	1,081	595	486	2,542	1,342	1,200	1,329	779	550
6 months or more	14,835	7,478	7,357	3,866	2,047	1,819	8,068	3,979	4,089	2,901	1,452	1,449
Nevada	4,337	2,156	2,181	1,270	642	628	2,121	1,083	1,038	946	431	515
1 month or less	141	65	76	55	24	31	50	27	23	36	14	22
2 to 3 months	139	75	64	62	29	33	46	24	22	31	22	9
4 to 5 months	195	104	91	68	37	31	78	39	30	49	28	21
6 months or more	3,862	1,912	1,950	1,085	552	533	1,947	993	954	830	367	463
Idaho	5,463	2,863	2,600	1,667	843	824	2,580	1,328	1,252	1,216	692	524
1 month or less	193	88	105	105	46	59	51	20	31	37	22	15
2 to 3 months	1,547	869	678	525	277	248	653	355	298	369	237	132
4 to 5 months	1,046	552	494	334	170	164	472	236	236	240	146	94
6 months or more	2,677	1,354	1,323	703	350	353	1,404	717	687	570	287	283
Washington	15,555	8,005	7,550	5,620	2,898	2,722	7,247	3,659	3,588	2,688	1,448	1,240
1 month or less	814	409	405	451	225	226	249	110	139	114	74	40
2 to 3 months	3,193	1,718	1,475	1,292	649	643	1,279	678	601	622	391	231
4 to 5 months	2,570	1,404	1,166	823	445	378	1,231	649	582	516	310	206
6 months or more	8,978	4,474	4,504	3,054	1,579	1,475	4,488	2,222	2,266	1,436	673	763
Oregon	14,190	7,211	6,979	4,602	2,311	2,291	6,688	3,393	3,295	2,900	1,507	1,393
1 month or less	938	457	481	384	194	190	358	180	178	196	83	113
2 to 3 months	2,052	1,079	973	802	386	416	763	384	379	487	309	178
4 to 5 months	1,821	960	861	567	283	284	811	411	400	443	266	177
6 months or more	9,379	4,715	4,664	2,849	1,448	1,401	4,756	2,418	2,338	1,774	849	925
California	92,127	46,319	45,808	28,948	14,823	14,125	46,573	23,507	23,066	16,606	7,989	8,617
1 month or less	5,552	2,836	2,716	2,143	1,124	1,019	2,327	1,184	1,143	1,082	528	554
2 to 3 months	2,009	1,074	935	979	464	515	561	309	252	469	301	168
4 to 5 months	3,274	1,722	1,552	1,225	611	614	1,207	647	560	842	464	378
6 months or more	81,292	40,687	40,605	24,601	12,624	11,977	42,478	21,367	21,111	14,213	6,696	7,517

STATISTICS OF POPULATION.

TABLE 21.—FOREIGN WHITE PERSONS ATTENDING SCHOOL DURING THE CENSUS YEAR, CLASSIFIED BY SEX, AGE PERIODS, AND MONTHS OF SCHOOL ATTENDANCE, BY STATES AND TERRITORIES: 1890.

STATES, TERRITORIES, AND MONTHS OF SCHOOL ATTENDANCE.	ALL AGES.			UNDER 10 YEARS.			10 TO 14 YEARS.			15 YEARS AND OVER.		
	Total.	Males.	Females.	Total.	Males.	Females.	Total.	Males.	Females.	Total.	Males.	Females.
North Atlantic division: Maine	6,796	3,480	3,316	2,262	1,178	1,084	3,661	1,831	1,830	873	471	402
1 month or less	370	188	182	179	90	89	149	73	76	42	25	17
2 to 3 months	655	359	296	192	104	88	320	167	153	143	88	55
4 to 5 months	930	469	461	316	153	163	473	241	232	141	75	66
6 months or more	4,841	2,464	2,377	1,575	831	744	2,719	1,350	1,369	547	283	264
New Hampshire	5,638	2,876	2,762	1,913	997	916	3,159	1,583	1,576	566	296	270
1 month or less	706	353	353	297	153	144	349	169	180	60	31	29
2 to 3 months	364	207	157	145	85	60	154	83	71	65	39	26
4 to 5 months	472	243	229	155	76	79	258	131	127	59	36	23
6 months or more	4,096	2,073	2,023	1,316	683	633	2,398	1,200	1,198	382	190	192
Vermont	2,765	1,447	1,318	899	477	422	1,490	758	732	376	212	164
1 month or less	148	88	60	66	42	24	55	24	31	27	22	5
2 to 3 months	282	156	126	111	54	57	116	65	51	55	37	18
4 to 5 months	264	140	124	84	44	40	131	66	65	49	30	19
6 months or more	2,071	1,063	1,008	638	337	301	1,188	603	585	245	123	122
Massachusetts	40,220	20,337	19,883	13,205	6,692	6,513	23,291	11,707	11,584	3,724	1,938	1,786
1 month or less	2,947	1,475	1,472	1,251	619	632	1,364	666	698	332	190	142
2 to 3 months	1,222	613	609	557	270	287	488	229	259	177	114	63
4 to 5 months	1,072	540	532	387	199	188	513	232	281	172	109	63
6 months or more	34,979	17,709	17,270	11,010	5,604	5,406	20,926	10,580	10,346	3,043	1,525	1,518
Rhode Island	6,528	3,351	3,177	2,384	1,206	1,178	3,613	1,827	1,786	531	318	213
1 month or less	468	251	217	206	103	103	211	113	98	51	35	16
2 to 3 months	751	420	331	184	63	71	490	288	202	127	69	58
4 to 5 months	321	160	161	129	54	75	151	80	71	41	26	15
6 months or more	4,988	2,520	2,468	1,915	986	929	2,761	1,346	1,415	312	188	124
Connecticut	9,638	5,003	4,635	3,232	1,667	1,565	5,579	2,822	2,757	827	514	313
1 month or less	995	545	450	381	196	185	463	245	218	151	104	47
2 to 3 months	289	153	136	118	59	59	128	66	62	43	28	15
4 to 5 months	285	146	139	97	49	48	146	69	77	42	28	14
6 months or more	8,069	4,159	3,910	2,636	1,363	1,273	4,842	2,442	2,400	591	354	237
New York	73,349	38,226	35,123	24,525	12,560	11,965	41,854	21,456	20,398	6,970	4,210	2,700
1 month or less	8,939	4,969	3,970	3,010	1,550	1,460	4,181	2,111	2,070	1,748	1,308	440
2 to 3 months	1,738	938	800	787	403	384	661	348	313	290	187	103
4 to 5 months	2,544	1,462	1,082	838	423	415	1,222	688	534	484	351	133
6 months or more	60,128	30,857	29,271	19,890	10,184	9,706	35,790	18,300	17,481	4,448	2,364	2,084
New Jersey	16,221	8,445	7,776	5,537	2,902	2,635	9,578	4,875	4,703	1,106	668	438
1 month or less	1,783	938	845	682	345	337	946	494	452	155	99	56
2 to 3 months	431	241	190	175	97	78	190	102	88	66	42	24
4 to 5 months	527	294	233	193	107	86	254	130	124	80	57	23
6 months or more	13,480	6,972	6,508	4,487	2,353	2,134	8,188	4,149	4,039	805	470	335
Pennsylvania	41,566	20,634	20,932	14,407	7,382	7,025	24,160	11,695	12,465	2,999	1,557	1,442
1 month or less	2,792	1,410	1,382	1,162	583	579	1,345	670	675	285	157	128
2 to 3 months	1,564	845	719	539	277	262	812	420	392	213	148	65
4 to 5 months	2,038	988	1,050	709	330	379	1,075	502	573	254	156	98
6 months or more	35,172	17,391	17,781	11,997	6,192	5,805	20,928	10,103	10,825	2,247	1,096	1,151
South Atlantic division: Delaware	571	298	273	175	95	80	346	174	172	50	29	21
1 month or less	21	10	11	6	2	4	10	5	5	5	3	2
2 to 3 months	16	12	4	1	1	....	10	7	3	5	4	1
4 to 5 months	20	14	6	5	3	2	7	5	2	8	6	2
6 months or more	514	262	252	163	89	74	319	157	162	32	16	16
Maryland	3,323	1,767	1,556	990	497	493	1,947	998	949	386	272	114
1 month or less	119	59	60	39	16	23	54	27	27	26	16	10
2 to 3 months	41	25	16	11	7	4	25	14	11	5	4	1
4 to 5 months	73	37	36	16	5	11	48	27	21	9	5	4
6 months or more	3,090	1,646	1,444	924	469	455	1,820	930	890	346	247	99
District of Columbia	453	229	224	113	58	55	250	128	122	90	43	47
1 month or less	34	15	19	5	2	3	18	8	10	11	5	6
2 to 3 months	4	2	2	....	....	....	1	1	....	3	1	2
4 to 5 months	15	12	3	4	4	....	6	5	1	5	3	2
6 months or more	400	200	200	104	52	52	225	114	111	71	34	37
Virginia	564	298	266	129	66	63	288	147	141	147	85	62
1 month or less	27	13	14	5	2	3	13	6	7	9	5	4
2 to 3 months	43	23	20	8	5	3	28	12	16	7	6	1
4 to 5 months	113	65	48	28	15	13	66	41	25	19	9	10
6 months or more	381	197	184	88	44	44	181	88	93	112	65	47

SCHOOL ATTENDANCE. 159

TABLE **21.**—FOREIGN WHITE PERSONS ATTENDING SCHOOL DURING THE CENSUS YEAR, CLASSIFIED BY SEX, AGE PERIODS, AND MONTHS OF SCHOOL ATTENDANCE, BY STATES AND TERRITORIES: 1890—Continued.

STATES, TERRITORIES, AND MONTHS OF SCHOOL ATTENDANCE.	ALL AGES.			UNDER 10 YEARS.			10 TO 14 YEARS.			15 YEARS AND OVER.		
	Total.	Males.	Females.	Total.	Males.	Females.	Total.	Males.	Females.	Total.	Males.	Females.
South Atlantic division—Cont.												
West Virginia	701	326	375	184	81	103	421	195	226	96	50	46
1 month or less	42	20	22	17	7	10	19	10	9	6	3	3
2 to 3 months	60	29	31	13	5	8	33	16	17	14	8	6
4 to 5 months	128	62	66	28	13	15	74	32	42	26	17	9
6 months or more	471	215	256	126	56	70	295	137	158	50	22	28
North Carolina	141	86	55	28	18	10	56	32	24	57	36	21
1 month or less	8	6	2	2	2	......	5	3	2	1	1	......
2 to 3 months	17	12	5	1	......	1	7	5	2	9	7	2
4 to 5 months	22	13	9	1	1	......	13	6	7	8	6	2
6 months or more	94	55	39	24	15	9	31	18	13	39	22	17
South Carolina	104	57	47	26	16	10	47	27	20	31	14	17
1 month or less	6	5	1	1	......	1	4	4	......	1	1	......
2 to 3 months	14	4	10	......	......	......	9	2	7	5	2	3
4 to 5 months	16	8	8	2	1	1	9	5	4	5	2	3
6 months or more	68	40	28	23	15	8	25	16	9	20	9	11
Georgia	342	168	174	91	44	47	205	102	103	46	22	24
1 month or less	14	12	2	5	4	1	4	3	1	5	5	......
2 to 3 months	14	8	6	5	1	4	7	5	2	2	2	......
4 to 5 months	28	15	13	8	3	5	12	7	5	8	5	3
6 months or more	286	133	153	73	36	37	182	87	95	31	10	21
Florida	1,211	630	581	445	228	217	626	329	297	140	73	67
1 month or less	48	28	20	20	13	7	17	9	8	11	6	5
2 to 3 months	73	41	32	31	19	12	27	13	14	15	9	6
4 to 5 months	188	99	89	62	34	28	93	48	45	33	17	16
6 months or more	902	462	440	332	162	170	489	259	230	81	41	40
North Central division:												
Ohio	22,565	11,729	10,836	6,385	3,249	3,136	13,486	6,810	6,676	2,694	1,670	1,024
1 month or less	1,249	674	575	413	222	191	619	318	301	217	134	83
2 to 3 months	677	397	280	211	110	101	261	138	123	205	149	56
4 to 5 months	1,355	770	585	273	146	127	735	394	341	347	230	117
6 months or more	19,284	9,888	9,396	5,488	2,771	2,717	11,871	5,960	5,911	1,925	1,157	768
Indiana	5,823	3,058	2,765	1,455	772	683	3,558	1,795	1,763	810	491	319
1 month or less	272	142	130	61	28	33	155	87	68	56	27	29
2 to 3 months	239	132	107	63	29	34	101	54	47	75	49	26
4 to 5 months	528	288	240	90	49	41	325	154	171	113	85	28
6 months or more	4,784	2,496	2,288	1,241	666	575	2,977	1,500	1,477	566	330	236
Illinois	48,561	25,203	23,358	14,089	7,191	6,898	29,550	15,035	14,515	4,922	2,977	1,945
1 month or less	4,279	2,233	2,046	1,468	773	695	2,349	1,184	1,165	462	276	186
2 to 3 months	1,821	1,130	691	531	274	257	701	404	297	589	452	137
4 to 5 months	2,364	1,422	942	475	237	238	1,211	697	514	678	488	190
6 months or more	40,097	20,418	19,679	11,615	5,907	5,708	25,289	12,750	12,539	3,193	1,761	1,432
Michigan	44,176	22,862	21,314	11,861	6,053	5,808	25,991	13,290	12,701	6,324	3,519	2,805
1 month or less	2,963	1,577	1,386	1,067	555	512	1,524	819	705	372	203	169
2 to 3 months	3,030	1,757	1,273	891	474	417	1,316	753	563	823	530	293
4 to 5 months	4,317	2,486	1,831	869	430	439	2,325	1,301	1,024	1,123	755	368
6 months or more	33,866	17,042	16,824	9,034	4,594	4,440	20,826	10,417	10,409	4,006	2,031	1,975
Wisconsin	34,065	18,098	15,967	9,659	4,957	4,702	20,410	10,637	9,773	3,996	2,504	1,492
1 month or less	1,850	1,002	848	742	392	350	845	453	392	263	157	106
2 to 3 months	2,980	1,681	1,299	856	431	425	1,437	779	658	687	471	216
4 to 5 months	4,161	2,423	1,738	885	482	403	2,414	1,351	1,063	862	590	272
6 months or more	25,074	12,992	12,082	7,176	3,652	3,524	15,714	8,054	7,660	2,184	1,286	898
Minnesota	36,070	19,461	16,609	7,802	4,017	3,785	21,545	11,188	10,357	6,723	4,256	2,467
1 month or less	2,166	1,153	1,013	579	287	292	997	504	493	590	362	228
2 to 3 months	6,668	3,783	2,885	1,321	649	672	3,577	1,902	1,675	1,770	1,232	538
4 to 5 months	7,427	4,175	3,252	1,320	697	623	4,583	2,451	2,132	1,524	1,027	497
6 months or more	19,809	10,350	9,459	4,582	2,384	2,198	12,388	6,331	6,057	2,839	1,635	1,204
Iowa	21,159	11,366	9,793	5,835	2,990	2,845	11,681	6,031	5,650	3,643	2,345	1,298
1 month or less	970	505	465	313	151	162	394	203	191	263	151	112
2 to 3 months	2,349	1,506	843	440	222	218	938	528	410	971	756	215
4 to 5 months	3,783	2,372	1,411	543	273	270	2,007	1,185	822	1,233	914	319
6 months or more	14,057	6,983	7,074	4,539	2,344	1,995	8,342	4,115	4,227	1,676	824	852
Missouri	8,613	4,493	4,120	2,118	1,069	1,049	5,187	2,646	2,541	1,308	778	530
1 month or less	622	316	306	163	76	87	310	160	150	149	80	69
2 to 3 months	544	320	224	114	59	55	265	153	112	165	108	57
4 to 5 months	832	454	378	173	89	84	455	244	211	204	121	83
6 months or more	6,615	3,403	3,212	1,668	845	823	4,157	2,089	2,068	790	469	321

160   STATISTICS OF POPULATION.

TABLE **21.**—FOREIGN WHITE PERSONS ATTENDING SCHOOL DURING THE CENSUS YEAR, CLASSIFIED BY SEX, AGE PERIODS, AND MONTHS OF SCHOOL ATTENDANCE, BY STATES AND TERRITORIES: 1890—Continued.

STATES, TERRITORIES, AND MONTHS OF SCHOOL ATTENDANCE.	ALL AGES.			UNDER 10 YEARS.			10 TO 14 YEARS.			15 YEARS AND OVER.		
	Total.	Males.	Females.	Total.	Males.	Females.	Total.	Males.	Females.	Total.	Males.	Females.
North Central division—Cont.												
North Dakota	9,175	4,919	4,256	1,906	974	932	5,174	2,732	2,442	2,095	1,213	882
1 month or less	781	396	385	229	106	123	349	176	173	203	114	80
2 to 3 months	1,932	1,108	824	389	198	191	981	535	446	562	375	187
4 to 5 months	2,061	1,153	908	405	212	193	1,163	625	538	493	316	177
6 months or more	4,401	2,262	2,139	883	458	425	2,681	1,396	1,285	837	408	429
South Dakota	8,118	4,579	3,539	1,491	781	710	4,287	2,307	1,980	2,340	1,491	849
1 month or less	451	255	196	99	50	49	191	110	81	161	95	66
2 to 3 months	2,077	1,248	829	350	175	175	979	569	410	748	504	244
4 to 5 months	2,326	1,425	901	341	193	148	1,257	710	547	728	522	206
6 months or more	3,264	1,651	1,613	701	363	338	1,860	918	942	703	370	333
Nebraska	16,712	9,143	7,569	3,896	1,984	1,912	9,043	4,782	4,261	3,773	2,377	1,396
1 month or less	837	477	360	293	119	114	336	185	151	208	173	95
2 to 3 months	3,334	2,150	1,184	595	334	261	1,481	883	598	1,258	933	825
4 to 5 months	2,580	1,524	1,056	460	211	249	1,443	849	594	677	464	213
6 months or more	9,961	4,992	4,969	2,608	1,320	1,288	5,783	2,865	2,918	1,570	807	763
Kansas	11,089	6,067	5,022	2,288	1,143	1,145	5,818	3,040	2,778	2,983	1,884	1,099
1 month or less	480	264	216	113	45	68	185	103	82	182	116	66
2 to 3 months	1,860	1,204	656	303	159	144	756	445	811	801	600	201
4 to 5 months	2,093	1,209	884	375	187	188	1,070	592	478	648	430	218
6 months or more	6,656	3,390	3,266	1,497	752	745	3,807	1,900	1,907	1,352	738	614
South Central division:												
Kentucky	1,591	795	796	434	208	226	948	458	490	209	129	80
1 month or less	59	26	33	9	4	5	39	16	23	11	6	5
2 to 3 months	126	68	58	29	14	15	61	29	32	36	25	11
4 to 5 months	330	171	159	92	46	46	188	92	96	50	33	17
6 months or more	1,076	530	546	304	144	160	660	321	339	112	65	47
Tennessee	767	398	369	162	81	81	437	231	206	168	86	82
1 month or less	39	25	14	11	6	5	16	9	7	12	10	2
2 to 3 months	91	46	45	15	6	9	50	28	22	26	12	14
4 to 5 months	117	66	51	24	13	11	62	37	25	31	16	15
6 months or more	520	261	259	112	56	56	309	157	152	99	48	51
Alabama	633	329	304	168	88	80	361	188	173	104	53	51
1 month or less	23	16	7	8	6	2	10	5	5	5	5	
2 to 3 months	104	57	47	26	14	12	63	36	26	15	7	8
4 to 5 months	58	33	25	14	7	7	37	22	15	7	4	3
6 months or more	448	223	225	120	61	59	252	125	127	76	37	39
Mississippi	115	60	55	38	17	21	49	28	21	28	15	13
1 month or less	9	5	4	5	3	2	4	2	2			
2 to 3 months	13	11	2				4	2	2	9	9	
4 to 5 months	31	15	16	10	4	6	7	5	2	14	6	8
6 months or more	62	29	33	23	10	13	25	14	11	14	5	9
Louisiana	716	375	341	207	109	98	389	191	198	120	75	45
1 month or less	79	43	36	20	8	12	49	28	21	10	7	3
2 to 3 months	37	19	18	11	5	6	18	8	10	8	6	2
4 to 5 months	37	16	21	10	5	5	23	10	13	4	1	3
6 months or more	563	297	266	166	91	75	299	145	154	98	61	37
Texas	6,588	3,491	3,097	1,216	646	570	4,280	2,275	2,005	1,092	570	522
1 month or less	345	185	160	77	40	37	185	94	91	83	51	32
2 to 3 months	898	504	394	145	75	70	588	328	260	165	101	64
4 to 5 months	1,559	874	685	235	125	110	1,060	605	455	264	144	120
6 months or more	3,786	1,928	1,858	759	406	353	2,447	1,248	1,199	580	274	306
Oklahoma	79	39	40	10	4	6	53	29	24	16	6	10
1 month or less	12	6	6	2	1	1	8	4	4	2	1	1
2 to 3 months	19	10	9	2	1	1	12	8	4	5	1	4
4 to 5 months	19	9	10	1		1	14	7	7	4	2	2
6 months or more	29	14	15	5	2	3	19	10	9	5	2	3
Arkansas	761	382	379	94	43	51	465	235	230	202	104	98
1 month or less	37	18	19	3	1	2	21	8	13	13	9	4
2 to 3 months	153	81	72	18	7	11	85	49	36	50	25	25
4 to 5 months	180	89	91	21	8	13	121	55	66	38	26	12
6 months or more	391	194	197	52	27	25	238	123	115	101	44	57

SCHOOL ATTENDANCE.

TABLE **21.**—FOREIGN WHITE PERSONS ATTENDING SCHOOL DURING THE CENSUS YEAR, CLASSIFIED BY SEX, AGE PERIODS, AND MONTHS OF SCHOOL ATTENDANCE, BY STATES AND TERRITORIES: 1890—Continued.

STATES, TERRITORIES, AND MONTHS OF SCHOOL ATTENDANCE.	ALL AGES.			UNDER 10 YEARS.			10 TO 14 YEARS.			15 YEARS AND OVER.		
	Total.	Males.	Females.	Total.	Males.	Females.	Total.	Males.	Females.	Total.	Males.	Females.
Western division:												
Montana	1,372	677	695	387	194	193	751	357	394	234	126	108
1 month or less........	100	51	49	40	18	22	37	17	20	23	16	7
2 to 3 months..........	175	83	92	49	20	29	77	32	45	49	31	18
4 to 5 months..........	192	100	92	53	25	28	109	56	53	30	19	11
6 months or more......	905	443	462	245	131	114	528	252	276	132	60	72
Wyoming	748	382	366	215	105	110	419	208	211	114	69	45
1 month or less........	22	14	8	9	6	3	9	5	4	4	3	1
2 to 3 months..........	91	52	39	34	16	18	39	24	15	18	12	6
4 to 5 months..........	141	75	66	38	21	17	74	36	38	29	18	11
6 months or more......	494	241	253	134	62	72	297	143	154	63	36	27
Colorado	3,814	2,019	1,795	929	504	425	2,125	1,098	1,027	760	417	343
1 month or less........	182	96	86	52	22	30	71	36	35	59	38	21
2 to 3 months..........	390	212	178	117	70	47	175	85	90	98	57	41
4 to 5 months..........	385	204	181	93	47	46	219	114	105	73	43	30
6 months or more......	2,857	1,507	1,350	667	365	302	1,660	863	797	530	279	251
New Mexico.............	399	204	195	91	47	44	229	120	109	79	37	42
1 month or less........	18	11	7	6	5	1	8	4	4	4	2	2
2 to 3 months..........	68	38	30	17	8	9	34	17	17	17	13	4
4 to 5 months..........	59	31	28	12	6	6	35	18	17	12	7	5
6 months or more......	254	124	130	56	28	28	152	81	71	46	15	31
Arizona.................	755	391	364	182	97	85	442	221	221	131	73	58
1 month or less........	45	26	19	9	5	4	24	14	10	12	7	5
2 to 3 months..........	73	33	40	18	7	11	37	17	20	18	9	9
4 to 5 months..........	70	34	36	18	6	12	37	20	17	15	8	7
6 months or more......	567	298	269	137	79	58	344	170	174	86	49	37
Utah	2,483	1,241	1,242	515	264	251	1,423	683	740	545	294	251
1 month or less........	154	71	83	47	26	21	70	25	45	37	20	17
2 to 3 months..........	454	238	216	101	49	52	226	113	113	127	76	51
4 to 5 months..........	514	281	233	84	42	42	307	167	140	123	72	51
6 months or more......	1,361	651	710	283	147	136	820	378	442	258	126	132
Nevada	209	104	105	27	15	12	101	52	49	81	37	44
1 month or less........	16	9	7	3	2	1	5	1	4	8	6	2
2 to 3 months..........	9	6	3	....	....	....	3	1	2	6	5	1
4 to 5 months..........	20	9	11	4	3	1	6	2	4	10	4	6
6 months or more......	164	80	84	20	10	10	87	48	39	57	22	35
Idaho	575	305	270	91	54	37	335	161	174	149	90	59
1 month or less........	16	11	5	6	4	2	7	5	2	3	2	1
2 to 3 months..........	199	107	92	24	13	11	111	54	57	64	40	24
4 to 5 months..........	88	54	34	9	6	3	66	41	25	13	7	6
6 months or more......	272	133	139	52	31	21	151	61	90	69	41	28
Washington.............	4,015	2,103	1,912	1,098	559	539	2,290	1,199	1,091	627	345	282
1 month or less........	293	163	130	105	53	52	121	69	52	67	41	26
2 to 3 months..........	752	400	352	203	106	97	393	206	187	156	88	68
4 to 5 months..........	526	296	230	139	80	59	301	158	143	86	58	28
6 months or more......	2,444	1,244	1,200	651	320	331	1,475	766	709	318	158	160
Oregon	2,318	1,223	1,095	578	301	277	1,227	632	595	513	290	223
1 month or less........	179	102	77	54	30	24	85	46	39	40	26	14
2 to 3 months..........	380	208	172	101	48	53	168	98	70	111	62	49
4 to 5 months..........	288	158	130	79	43	36	150	76	74	59	39	20
6 months or more......	1,471	755	716	344	180	164	824	412	412	303	163	140
California..............	9,687	4,946	4,741	2,709	1,412	1,297	5,115	2,558	2,557	1,863	976	887
1 month or less........	730	394	336	264	148	116	318	154	164	148	92	56
2 to 3 months..........	306	162	144	113	52	61	114	59	55	79	51	28
4 to 5 months..........	467	248	219	139	76	63	206	110	96	122	62	60
6 months or more......	8,184	4,142	4,042	2,193	1,136	1,057	4,477	2,235	2,242	1,514	771	743

POP—PT 2——11

STATISTICS OF POPULATION.

162

TABLE **22.**—COLORED PERSONS (a) ATTENDING SCHOOL DURING THE CENSUS YEAR, CLASSIFIED BY SEX, AGE PERIODS, AND MONTHS OF SCHOOL ATTENDANCE, BY STATES AND TERRITORIES: 1890.

STATES, TERRITORIES, AND MONTHS OF SCHOOL ATTENDANCE.	ALL AGES.			UNDER 10 YEARS.			10 TO 14 YEARS.			15 YEARS AND OVER.		
	Total.	Males.	Females.	Total.	Males.	Females.	Total.	Males.	Females.	Total.	Males.	Females.
North Atlantic division: Maine	317	164	153	109	58	51	135	74	61	73	32	41
1 month or less	14	3	11	7	2	5	4	....	4	3	1	2
2 to 3 months	40	21	19	15	8	7	17	10	7	8	3	5
4 to 5 months	62	36	26	28	13	15	23	15	8	11	8	3
6 months or more	201	104	97	59	35	24	91	49	42	51	20	31
New Hampshire	100	55	45	29	13	16	53	30	23	18	12	6
1 month or less	5	3	2	2	1	1	3	2	1	....	....	....
2 to 3 months	19	10	9	6	2	4	8	5	3	5	3	2
4 to 5 months	19	11	8	7	3	4	9	5	4	3	3	....
6 months or more	57	31	26	14	7	7	33	18	15	10	6	4
Vermont	160	86	74	66	36	30	67	31	36	27	19	8
1 month or less	6	3	3	2	....	2	1	....	1	3	3	....
2 to 3 months	17	11	6	7	4	3	7	4	3	3	3	....
4 to 5 months	12	7	5	4	1	3	4	3	1	4	3	1
6 months or more	125	65	60	53	31	22	55	24	31	17	10	7
Massachusetts	3,433	1,637	1,796	1,270	605	665	1,614	767	847	549	265	284
1 month or less	205	99	106	96	44	52	78	34	44	31	21	10
2 to 3 months	91	45	46	54	24	30	15	3	12	22	18	4
4 to 5 months	95	47	48	38	17	21	47	26	21	10	4	6
6 months or more	3,042	1,446	1,596	1,082	520	562	1,474	704	770	486	222	264
Rhode Island	1,115	512	603	417	181	236	545	252	293	153	79	74
1 month or less	74	40	34	37	23	14	32	14	18	5	3	2
2 to 3 months	40	16	24	19	7	12	14	5	9	7	4	3
4 to 5 months	39	18	21	15	7	8	13	5	8	11	6	5
6 months or more	962	438	524	346	144	202	486	228	258	130	66	64
Connecticut	1,899	914	985	708	332	376	949	455	494	242	127	115
1 month or less	169	84	85	81	39	42	63	31	32	25	14	11
2 to 3 months	61	28	33	28	8	20	25	15	10	8	5	3
4 to 5 months	86	54	32	27	12	15	44	32	12	15	10	5
6 months or more	1,583	748	835	572	273	299	817	377	440	194	98	96
New York	8,404	4,211	4,193	2,835	1,405	1,430	4,474	2,268	2,206	1,095	538	557
1 month or less	761	367	394	287	132	155	374	184	190	100	51	49
2 to 3 months	332	174	158	150	69	81	130	68	62	52	37	15
4 to 5 months	462	248	214	147	69	78	220	116	104	95	63	32
6 months or more	6,849	3,422	3,427	2,251	1,135	1,116	3,750	1,900	1,850	848	387	461
New Jersey	6,171	3,052	3,119	2,129	1,019	1,110	3,181	1,564	1,617	861	469	392
1 month or less	506	234	272	209	84	125	232	115	117	65	35	30
2 to 3 months	429	248	181	140	67	73	164	90	74	125	91	34
4 to 5 months	475	294	181	129	74	55	240	141	99	106	79	27
6 months or more	4,761	2,276	2,485	1,651	794	857	2,545	1,218	1,327	565	264	301
Pennsylvania	14,949	7,509	7,440	4,822	2,386	2,436	7,640	3,771	3,869	2,487	1,352	1,135
1 month or less	995	491	504	416	197	210	464	239	225	115	55	60
2 to 3 months	720	390	330	245	125	120	333	181	152	142	84	58
4 to 5 months	977	552	425	284	154	130	475	247	228	218	151	67
6 months or more	12,257	6,076	6,181	3,877	1,910	1,967	6,368	3,104	3,264	2,012	1,062	950
South Atlantic division: Delaware	2,897	1,411	1,486	807	387	420	1,502	656	846	588	368	220
1 month or less	141	71	70	47	25	22	69	28	41	25	18	7
2 to 3 months	719	399	320	158	72	86	391	209	182	170	118	52
4 to 5 months	728	360	368	181	84	97	430	211	219	117	65	52
6 months or more	1,309	581	728	421	206	215	612	208	404	276	167	109
Maryland	26,690	13,195	13,495	7,668	3,736	3,932	15,355	7,634	7,721	3,667	1,825	1,842
1 month or less	1,175	578	597	389	182	207	615	310	305	171	86	85
2 to 3 months	2,650	1,503	1,147	702	352	350	1,335	731	604	613	420	193
4 to 5 months	3,402	1,814	1,588	881	455	426	1,879	987	892	642	372	270
6 months or more	19,463	9,300	10,163	5,696	2,747	2,949	11,526	5,606	5,920	2,241	947	1,294
District of Columbia	10,987	4,961	6,026	2,720	1,297	1,423	6,213	2,905	3,308	2,054	759	1,295
1 month or less	517	229	288	137	55	82	245	122	123	135	52	83
2 to 3 months	186	89	97	60	28	32	77	39	38	49	22	27
4 to 5 months	427	206	221	147	55	92	221	127	94	59	24	35
6 months or more	9,857	4,437	5,420	2,376	1,159	1,217	5,670	2,617	3,053	1,811	661	1,150
Virginia	94,177	44,499	49,678	24,556	12,303	12,253	50,613	24,319	26,294	19,008	7,877	11,131
1 month or less	4,778	2,368	2,410	1,568	811	757	2,244	1,117	1,127	966	440	526
2 to 3 months	10,902	5,520	5,382	2,960	1,499	1,461	5,520	2,829	2,691	2,422	1,192	1,230
4 to 5 months	44,574	20,938	23,636	11,339	5,680	5,659	24,313	11,749	12,564	8,922	3,509	5,413
6 months or more	33,923	15,673	18,250	8,689	4,313	4,376	18,536	8,624	9,912	6,698	2,736	3,962

a Persons of negro descent, Chinese, Japanese, and civilized Indians.

SCHOOL ATTENDANCE.

163

TABLE 22.—COLORED PERSONS (a) ATTENDING SCHOOL DURING THE CENSUS YEAR, CLASSIFIED BY SEX, AGE PERIODS, AND MONTHS OF SCHOOL ATTENDANCE, BY STATES AND TERRITORIES: 1890—Continued.

STATES, TERRITORIES, AND MONTHS OF SCHOOL ATTENDANCE.	ALL AGES.			UNDER 10 YEARS.			10 TO 14 YEARS.			15 YEARS AND OVER.		
	Total.	Males.	Females.	Total.	Males.	Females.	Total.	Males.	Females.	Total.	Males.	Females.
South Atlantic division—Cont.												
West Virginia	4,734	2,333	2,401	1,355	664	691	2,410	1,164	1,246	969	505	464
1 month or less	300	144	156	113	50	63	136	65	71	51	29	22
2 to 3 months	623	333	290	169	87	82	272	126	146	182	120	62
4 to 5 months	1,559	786	773	443	223	220	779	386	393	337	177	160
6 months or more	2,252	1,070	1,182	630	304	326	1,223	587	636	399	179	220
North Carolina	73,125	34,805	38,320	17,169	8,553	8,616	38,419	18,570	19,849	17,537	7,682	9,855
1 month or less	9,116	4,618	4,498	2,379	1,193	1,186	4,453	2,220	2,233	2,284	1,205	1,079
2 to 3 months	40,817	19,637	21,180	9,295	4,665	4,630	21,426	10,500	10,926	10,096	4,472	5,624
4 to 5 months	14,632	6,757	7,875	3,372	1,658	1,714	7,010	3,727	4,183	3,850	1,372	1,978
6 months or more	8,560	3,793	4,767	2,123	1,037	1,086	4,630	2,123	2,507	1,807	633	1,174
South Carolina	82,627	39,921	42,706	21,862	10,829	11,033	45,289	22,232	23,057	15,476	6,860	8,616
1 month or less	6,677	3,386	3,291	2,011	986	1,025	3,337	1,753	1,584	1,329	647	632
2 to 3 months	43,649	21,200	22,449	11,212	5,557	5,655	24,217	11,070	12,247	8,220	3,673	4,547
4 to 5 months	17,003	8,245	8,758	4,179	2,110	2,069	9,505	4,642	4,863	3,319	1,493	1,826
6 months or more	15,298	7,090	8,208	4,460	2,176	2,284	8,230	3,867	4,363	2,608	1,047	1,561
Georgia	92,723	44,099	48,624	25,519	12,604	12,915	52,108	25,236	26,872	15,096	6,259	8,837
1 month or less	8,198	4,205	3,993	2,391	1,221	1,170	4,189	2,177	2,012	1,618	807	811
2 to 3 months	42,758	20,879	21,870	11,446	5,657	5,789	23,824	11,918	11,906	7,488	3,304	4,184
4 to 5 months	20,308	9,548	10,700	6,050	3,057	2,993	11,456	5,453	6,003	2,802	1,038	1,764
6 months or more	21,459	9,467	11,992	5,632	2,669	2,963	12,639	5,688	6,951	3,188	1,110	2,078
Florida	28,247	13,823	14,424	8,183	4,009	4,174	14,420	7,163	7,257	5,644	2,651	2,993
1 month or less	1,423	710	713	450	192	258	607	310	297	366	208	158
2 to 3 months	6,023	3,087	2,936	1,580	828	752	3,010	1,540	1,470	1,433	719	714
4 to 5 months	12,034	5,994	6,040	3,256	1,635	1,621	6,476	3,267	3,209	2,302	1,092	1,210
6 months or more	8,767	4,032	4,735	2,897	1,354	1,543	4,327	2,046	2,281	1,543	632	911
North Central division:												
Ohio	10,682	5,594	5,088	5,106	2,582	2,524	3,302	1,324	1,978	3,274	1,688	1,586
1 month or less	935	472	463	302	174	188	308	208	190	175	90	85
2 to 3 months	1,104	660	504	382	170	203	435	247	188	347	234	113
4 to 5 months	1,365	771	594	359	190	169	614	331	283	392	250	142
6 months or more	7,218	3,691	3,527	4,003	2,039	1,964	6,855	3,538	3,317	2,360	1,114	1,246
Indiana	8,291	4,105	4,186	2,507	1,250	1,257	4,238	2,109	2,129	1,546	746	800
1 month or less	372	172	200	120	57	63	167	73	94	85	42	43
2 to 3 months	532	287	245	205	105	100	199	99	100	128	83	45
4 to 5 months	922	486	436	270	134	136	453	241	212	199	111	88
6 months or more	6,465	3,160	3,305	1,912	954	958	3,419	1,696	1,723	1,134	510	624
Illinois	9,979	4,976	5,003	3,020	1,496	1,524	5,031	2,540	2,491	1,928	940	988
1 month or less	523	247	276	206	98	108	207	98	109	110	51	59
2 to 3 months	1,030	555	475	312	154	158	447	234	213	271	167	104
4 to 5 months	1,589	803	786	417	197	220	805	404	401	367	202	165
6 months or more	6,837	3,371	3,466	2,085	1,047	1,038	3,572	1,804	1,768	1,180	520	660
Michigan	3,473	1,764	1,709	1,099	542	557	1,750	899	851	624	323	301
1 month or less	284	125	159	113	51	62	122	57	65	49	17	32
2 to 3 months	322	189	133	126	65	61	128	81	47	68	43	25
4 to 5 months	454	262	192	133	69	64	216	124	92	105	69	36
6 months or more	2,413	1,188	1,225	727	357	370	1,284	637	647	402	194	208
Wisconsin	1,399	750	649	439	216	223	657	359	298	303	175	128
1 month or less	54	25	29	29	12	17	19	8	11	6	5	1
2 to 3 months	133	80	53	54	30	24	51	29	22	28	21	7
4 to 5 months	112	53	59	37	14	23	48	25	23	27	14	13
6 months or more	1,100	592	508	319	160	159	539	297	242	242	135	107
Minnesota	1,059	505	554	306	138	168	499	242	257	254	125	129
1 month or less	38	20	18	18	8	10	11	6	5	9	6	3
2 to 3 months	36	16	20	14	2	12	14	9	5	8	5	3
4 to 5 months	56	25	31	16	8	8	28	11	17	12	6	6
6 months or more	929	444	485	258	120	138	446	216	230	225	108	117
Iowa	1,996	986	1,010	641	298	343	956	481	475	399	207	192
1 month or less	129	55	74	44	23	21	60	26	34	25	6	19
2 to 3 months	106	56	50	48	19	29	29	17	12	29	20	9
4 to 5 months	140	78	62	44	18	26	50	29	21	46	31	15
6 months or more	1,621	797	824	505	238	267	817	409	408	299	150	149
Missouri	24,542	12,279	12,263	6,634	3,272	3,362	12,846	6,513	6,333	5,062	2,494	2,568
1 month or less	1,697	871	826	619	307	312	727	375	352	351	189	162
2 to 3 months	3,203	1,754	1,449	886	452	434	1,467	780	687	850	522	328
4 to 5 months	4,490	2,335	2,155	1,080	522	558	2,377	1,262	1,115	1,033	551	482
6 months or more	15,152	7,319	7,833	4,049	1,991	2,058	8,275	4,096	4,179	2,828	1,232	1,596

a Persons of negro descent. Chinese, Japanese, and civilized Indians.

164

STATISTICS OF POPULATION.

TABLE 22.—COLORED PERSONS (a) ATTENDING SCHOOL DURING THE CENSUS YEAR, CLASSIFIED BY SEX, AGE PERIODS, AND MONTHS OF SCHOOL ATTENDANCE, BY STATES AND TERRITORIES: 1890—Continued.

STATES, TERRITORIES, AND MONTHS OF SCHOOL ATTENDANCE.	ALL AGES.			UNDER 10 YEARS.			10 TO 14 YEARS.			15 YEARS AND OVER.		
	Total.	Males.	Females.	Total.	Males.	Females.	Total.	Males.	Females.	Total.	Males.	Females.
North Central division—Cont.												
North Dakota	64	30	34	24	4	20	23	14	9	17	12	5
1 month or less	9	5	4	3	1	2	4	2	2	2	2	
2 to 3 months	8	3	5	3		3	1	1		4	2	2
4 to 5 months	14	6	8	7		7	3	2	1	4	4	
6 months or more	33	16	17	11	3	8	15	9	6	7	4	3
South Dakota	259	147	112	73	36	37	126	72	54	60	39	21
1 month or less	4	1	3	1		1	2		2	1	1	
2 to 3 months	14	12	2	3	2	1	6	5	1	5	5	
4 to 5 months	34	19	15	7	3	4	14	8	6	13	8	5
6 months or more	207	115	92	62	31	31	104	59	45	41	25	16
Nebraska	2,026	1,092	934	614	324	290	935	493	442	477	275	202
1 month or less	120	64	56	51	27	24	48	25	23	21	12	9
2 to 3 months	150	81	69	57	26	31	69	43	26	24	12	12
4 to 5 months	113	60	53	34	18	16	57	30	27	22	12	10
6 months or more	1,643	887	756	472	253	219	761	395	366	410	239	171
Kansas	11,173	5,575	5,598	2,861	1,369	1,492	5,655	2,810	2,845	2,657	1,396	1,261
1 month or less	495	246	249	173	77	96	203	104	99	119	65	54
2 to 3 months	1,139	630	509	362	163	199	438	239	199	339	228	111
4 to 5 months	1,277	699	578	324	157	167	614	338	276	339	204	135
6 months or more	8,262	4,000	4,262	2,002	972	1,030	4,400	2,129	2,271	1,860	899	961
South Central division:												
Kentucky	37,299	17,801	19,498	9,972	4,897	5,075	19,574	9,479	10,095	7,753	3,425	4,328
1 month or less	2,467	1,278	1,189	847	412	435	1,102	584	518	518	282	236
2 to 3 months	8,482	4,357	4,125	2,187	1,125	1,062	4,276	2,198	2,078	2,019	1,034	985
4 to 5 months	15,033	7,108	7,925	3,930	1,937	1,993	8,093	3,855	4,178	3,070	1,316	1,754
6 months or more	11,317	5,058	6,259	3,008	1,423	1,585	6,163	2,842	3,321	2,146	793	1,353
Tennessee	63,296	30,762	32,534	15,444	7,629	7,815	33,727	16,586	17,141	14,125	6,547	7,578
1 month or less	5,279	2,766	2,513	1,482	768	714	2,466	1,304	1,162	1,331	694	637
2 to 3 months	25,396	12,874	12,522	6,144	3,053	3,091	13,063	6,711	6,352	6,189	3,110	3,079
4 to 5 months	14,773	7,103	7,670	3,704	1,788	1,916	7,947	3,861	4,086	3,122	1,454	1,668
6 months or more	17,848	8,019	9,829	4,114	2,020	2,094	10,251	4,710	5,541	3,483	1,289	2,194
Alabama	72,680	34,716	37,964	16,484	8,004	8,480	39,992	19,331	20,571	16,204	7,381	8,813
1 month or less	5,756	2,970	2,786	1,430	691	739	2,843	1,478	1,365	1,483	801	682
2 to 3 months	41,558	20,312	21,246	9,131	4,529	4,602	22,607	11,168	11,439	9,820	4,615	5,205
4 to 5 months	11,729	5,393	6,336	2,709	1,299	1,410	6,600	3,106	3,494	2,420	988	1,432
6 months or more	13,637	6,041	7,596	3,214	1,485	1,729	7,852	3,579	4,273	2,571	977	1,594
Mississippi	124,526	61,460	63,066	34,871	17,311	17,560	62,712	31,087	31,625	26,943	13,062	13,881
1 month or less	10,854	5,600	5,254	3,620	1,756	1,864	4,910	2,553	2,357	2,324	1,291	1,033
2 to 3 months	35,646	18,164	17,482	9,369	4,696	4,673	17,641	9,048	8,593	8,636	4,420	4,216
4 to 5 months	64,807	31,414	32,893	18,185	9,080	9,105	32,899	16,146	16,753	13,723	6,188	7,035
6 months or more	13,719	6,282	7,437	3,697	1,779	1,918	7,262	3,340	3,922	2,760	1,163	1,597
Louisiana	42,865	21,010	21,855	12,885	6,465	6,420	24,040	11,936	12,104	5,940	2,609	3,331
1 month or less	4,043	1,958	2,085	1,372	671	701	2,099	1,010	1,089	572	277	295
2 to 3 months	12,466	6,146	6,320	3,492	1,738	1,754	6,718	3,399	3,319	2,256	1,009	1,247
4 to 5 months	8,518	4,269	4,249	2,659	1,377	1,282	4,771	2,409	2,362	1,088	483	605
6 months or more	17,838	8,637	9,201	5,362	2,679	2,683	10,452	5,118	5,334	2,024	840	1,184
Texas	79,862	38,680	41,182	18,138	8,942	9,196	45,996	22,631	23,365	15,728	7,107	8,621
1 month or less	5,895	3,180	2,765	1,678	829	849	2,916	1,590	1,326	1,301	711	590
2 to 3 months	28,200	14,102	14,098	6,361	3,211	3,150	15,981	8,073	7,908	5,858	2,818	3,040
4 to 5 months	25,088	12,086	13,002	5,516	2,759	2,757	15,027	7,325	7,702	4,545	2,002	2,543
6 months or more	20,679	9,362	11,317	4,583	2,143	2,440	12,072	5,643	6,429	4,024	1,576	2,448
Oklahoma	263	135	128	63	36	27	142	71	71	58	28	30
1 month or less	19	15	4	7	6	1	11	8	3	1	1	
2 to 3 months	95	53	42	22	12	10	53	29	24	20	12	8
4 to 5 months	43	17	26	8	4	4	21	9	12	14	4	10
6 months or more	106	50	56	26	14	12	57	25	32	23	11	12
Arkansas	47,450	23,966	23,484	11,715	5,775	5,940	23,722	12,043	11,679	12,013	6,148	5,865
1 month or less	4,973	2,615	2,358	1,279	630	649	2,286	1,190	1,096	1,408	795	613
2 to 3 months	28,524	14,632	13,892	6,650	3,326	3,324	14,222	7,316	6,906	7,652	3,990	3,662
4 to 5 months	6,111	3,078	3,033	1,622	786	836	3,111	1,625	1,486	1,378	667	711
6 months or more	7,842	3,641	4,201	2,164	1,033	1,131	4,103	1,912	2,191	1,575	696	879

a Persons of negro descent, Chinese, Japanese, and civilized Indians.

SCHOOL ATTENDANCE.

165

TABLE 22.—COLORED PERSONS (a) ATTENDING SCHOOL DURING THE CENSUS YEAR, CLASSIFIED BY SEX, AGE PERIODS, AND MONTHS OF SCHOOL ATTENDANCE, BY STATES AND TERRITORIES: 1890—Continued.

STATES, TERRITORIES, AND MONTHS OF SCHOOL ATTENDANCE.	ALL AGES.			UNDER 10 YEARS.			10 TO 14 YEARS.			15 YEARS AND OVER.		
	Total.	Males.	Females.	Total.	Males.	Females.	Total.	Males.	Females.	Total.	Males.	Females.
Western division: Montana	154	66	88	51	19	32	75	35	40	28	12	16
1 month or less	6	1	5	2		2	3		3	1	1	
2 to 3 months	12	3	9	4		4	5	1	4	3	2	1
4 to 5 months	12	8	4	2	1	1	6	4	2	4	3	1
6 months or more	124	54	70	43	18	25	61	30	31	20	6	14
Wyoming	82	57	25	20	13	7	25	14	11	37	30	7
1 month or less	13	11	2	2		2	1	1		10	10	
2 to 3 months	31	28	3	4	4		6	6		21	18	3
4 to 5 months	7	3	4	3	1	2	3	1	2	1	1	
6 months or more	31	15	16	11	8	3	15	6	9	5	1	4
Colorado	717	329	388	233	108	125	364	174	190	120	47	73
1 month or less	30	9	21	17	4	13	9	4	5	4	1	3
2 to 3 months	38	18	20	23	12	11	8	4	4	7	2	5
4 to 5 months	51	22	29	26	10	16	14	8	6	11	4	7
6 months or more	598	280	318	167	82	85	333	158	175	98	40	53
New Mexico	592	347	245	146	74	72	296	182	114	150	91	59
1 month or less	13	7	6	6	2	4	4	4		3	1	2
2 to 3 months	98	52	46	21	10	11	47	29	18	30	13	17
4 to 5 months	101	60	41	23	10	13	62	41	21	16	9	7
6 months or more	380	228	152	96	52	44	183	108	75	101	68	33
Arizona	134	67	67	39	23	16	78	37	41	17	7	10
1 month or less	7	4	3	2		2	5	4	1			
2 to 3 months	9	4	5	3	2	1	4	1	3	2	1	1
4 to 5 months	6	3	3	1	1		5	2	3			
6 months or more	112	56	56	33	20	13	64	30	34	15	6	9
Utah	65	41	24	26	15	11	26	15	11	13	11	2
1 month or less	3	1	2	1		1	1		1	1	1	
2 to 3 months	14	9	5	5	2	3	3	2	1	6	5	1
4 to 5 months	10	9	1	8	7	1	2	2				
6 months or more	38	22	16	12	6	6	20	11	9	6	5	1
Nevada	40	27	13	12	6	6	18	13	5	10	8	2
1 month or less	1	1								1	1	
2 to 3 months	7	6	1	3	2	1	2	2		2	2	
4 to 5 months	6	5	1				3	2	1	3	3	
6 months or more	26	15	11	9	4	5	13	9	4	4	2	2
Idaho	36	21	15	6	4	2	20	10	10	10	7	3
1 month or less												
2 to 3 months	8	6	2	3	2	1	4	3	1	1	1	
4 to 5 months	3	1	2	1	1		2		2			
6 months or more	25	14	11	2	1	1	14	7	7	9	6	3
Washington	688	327	361	197	89	108	342	161	181	149	77	72
1 month or less	33	16	17	15	7	8	10	4	6	8	5	3
2 to 3 months	165	84	81	50	23	27	74	39	35	41	22	19
4 to 5 months	55	22	33	16	9	7	26	7	19	13	6	7
6 months or more	435	205	230	116	50	66	232	111	121	87	44	43
Oregon	443	266	177	87	50	37	197	112	85	159	104	55
1 month or less	21	15	6	2	2		18	12	6	1	1	
2 to 3 months	72	46	26	19	11	8	28	20	8	25	15	10
4 to 5 months	42	26	16	9	7	2	22	12	10	11	7	4
6 months or more	308	179	129	57	30	27	129	68	61	122	81	41
California	2,817	1,661	1,156	839	480	359	1,288	730	558	690	451	239
1 month or less	234	158	76	71	34	37	78	47	31	85	77	8
2 to 3 months	184	125	59	55	37	18	65	36	29	64	52	12
4 to 5 months	241	141	100	70	42	28	101	53	48	70	46	24
6 months or more	2,158	1,237	921	643	367	276	1,044	594	450	471	276	195

a Persons of negro descent, Chinese, Japanese, and civilized Indians.

166   STATISTICS OF POPULATION.

TABLE 23.—NEGRO PERSONS (a) ATTENDING SCHOOL DURING THE CENSUS YEAR, CLASSIFIED BY SEX, AGE PERIODS, AND MONTHS OF SCHOOL ATTENDANCE, BY STATES AND TERRITORIES: 1890.

STATES, TERRITORIES, AND MONTHS OF SCHOOL ATTENDANCE.	ALL AGES.			UNDER 10 YEARS.			10 TO 14 YEARS.			15 YEARS AND OVER.		
	Total.	Males.	Females.	Total.	Males.	Females.	Total.	Males.	Females.	Total.	Males.	Females.
North Atlantic division: Maine	223	113	110	73	37	36	102	55	47	48	21	27
1 month or less	8	1	7	4	1	3	4	....	4	....	....	..
2 to 3 months	16	7	9	7	3	4	7	4	3	2	....	2
4 to 5 months	38	20	18	15	5	10	14	9	5	9	6	3
5 months or more	161	85	76	47	28	19	77	42	35	37	15	22
New Hampshire	100	55	45	29	13	16	53	30	23	18	12	6
1 month or less	5	3	2	2	1	1	3	2	1	....	....	..
2 to 3 months	19	10	9	6	2	4	8	5	3	5	3	2
4 to 5 months	19	11	8	7	3	4	9	5	4	3	3	..
6 months or more	57	31	26	14	7	7	33	18	15	10	6	4
Vermont	151	80	71	62	33	29	64	30	34	25	17	8
1 month or less	4	2	2	1	....	1	1	....	1	2	2	..
2 to 3 months	15	10	5	6	3	3	6	4	2	3	3	..
4 to 5 months	10	5	5	4	1	3	3	2	1	3	2	1
6 months or more	122	63	59	51	29	22	54	24	30	17	10	7
Massachusetts	3,338	1,571	1,767	1,237	583	654	1,576	742	834	525	246	279
1 month or less	204	99	105	95	44	51	78	34	44	31	21	10
2 to 3 months	79	37	42	46	19	27	14	3	11	19	15	4
4 to 5 months	91	43	48	38	17	21	43	22	21	10	4	6
6 months or more	2,964	1,392	1,572	1,058	503	555	1,441	683	758	465	206	259
Rhode Island	1,088	500	588	404	174	230	532	248	284	152	78	74
1 month or less	72	39	33	35	22	13	32	14	18	5	3	2
2 to 3 months	38	15	23	18	6	12	13	5	8	7	4	3
4 to 5 months	36	17	19	14	7	7	12	5	7	10	5	5
6 months or more	942	429	513	337	139	198	475	224	251	130	66	64
Connecticut	1,870	900	970	696	330	366	937	447	490	237	123	114
1 month or less	107	82	85	81	39	42	63	31	32	23	12	11
2 to 3 months	60	27	33	27	7	20	25	15	10	8	5	3
4 to 5 months	84	53	31	27	12	15	42	31	11	15	10	5
6 months or more	1,559	738	821	561	272	289	807	370	437	191	96	95
New York	8,295	4,151	4,144	2,814	1,396	1,418	4,416	2,237	2,179	1,065	518	547
1 month or less	755	363	392	284	131	153	372	182	190	99	50	40
2 to 3 months	323	169	154	148	68	80	126	66	60	49	35	14
4 to 5 months	445	240	205	146	68	78	208	111	97	91	61	30
6 months or more	6,772	3,379	3,393	2,236	1,129	1,107	3,710	1,878	1,832	826	372	454
New Jersey	6,144	3,038	3,106	2,127	1,018	1,109	3,176	1,561	1,615	841	459	382
1 month or less	502	231	271	208	83	125	232	115	117	62	33	29
2 to 3 months	425	245	180	140	67	73	164	90	74	121	88	33
4 to 5 months	465	287	178	129	74	55	236	138	98	100	75	25
6 months or more	4,752	2,275	2,477	1,650	794	856	2,544	1,218	1,326	558	263	295
Pennsylvania	14,249	7,115	7,134	4,808	2,381	2,427	7,408	3,646	3,762	2,033	1,088	945
1 month or less	994	490	504	416	197	219	463	238	225	115	55	60
2 to 3 months	719	390	329	245	125	120	333	181	152	141	84	57
4 to 5 months	911	495	416	283	153	130	463	239	224	165	103	62
6 months or more	11,625	5,740	5,885	3,864	1,906	1,958	6,149	2,988	3,161	1,612	846	766
South Atlantic division: Delaware	2,897	1,411	1,486	807	387	420	1,502	656	846	588	368	220
1 month or less	141	71	70	47	25	22	69	28	41	25	18	7
2 to 3 months	719	399	320	158	72	86	391	209	182	170	118	52
4 to 5 months	728	360	368	181	84	97	430	211	219	117	65	52
6 months or more	1,309	581	728	421	206	215	612	208	404	276	167	109
Maryland	26,685	13,194	13,491	7,668	3,736	3,932	15,355	7,634	7,721	3,662	1,824	1,838
1 month or less	1,175	578	597	389	182	207	615	310	305	171	86	85
2 to 3 months	2,649	1,503	1,146	702	352	350	1,335	731	604	612	420	192
4 to 5 months	3,402	1,814	1,588	881	455	426	1,879	987	892	642	372	270
6 months or more	19,459	9,299	10,160	5,696	2,747	2,949	11,526	5,606	5,920	2,237	946	1,291
District of Columbia	10,979	4,956	6,023	2,720	1,297	1,423	6,211	2,903	3,308	2,048	756	1,292
1 month or less	517	229	288	137	55	82	245	122	123	135	52	83
2 to 3 months	185	88	97	60	28	32	77	39	38	48	21	27
4 to 5 months	424	206	218	147	55	92	221	127	94	56	24	32
6 months or more	9,853	4,433	5,420	2,376	1,159	1,217	5,668	2,615	3,053	1,809	659	1,150
Virginia	94,021	44,401	49,620	24,545	12,298	12,247	50,584	24,304	26,280	18,892	7,799	11,093
1 month or less	4,775	2,365	2,410	1,568	811	757	2,243	1,116	1,127	964	438	526
2 to 3 months	10,897	5,518	5,379	2,959	1,499	1,460	5,517	2,827	2,690	2,421	1,192	1,229
4 to 5 months	44,565	20,931	23,634	11,337	5,679	5,658	24,308	11,744	12,564	8,920	3,508	5,413
6 months or more	33,784	15,587	18,197	8,681	4,309	4,372	18,516	8,617	9,899	6,587	2,661	3,926

a Includes all persons of negro descent.

SCHOOL ATTENDANCE.

167

TABLE **23.**—NEGRO PERSONS (a) ATTENDING SCHOOL DURING THE CENSUS YEAR, CLASSIFIED BY SEX, AGE PERIODS, AND MONTHS OF SCHOOL ATTENDANCE, BY STATES AND TERRITORIES: 1890—Continued.

STATES, TERRITORIES, AND MONTHS OF SCHOOL ATTENDANCE.	ALL AGES.			UNDER 10 YEARS.			10 TO 14 YEARS.			15 YEARS AND OVER.		
	Total.	Males.	Females.	Total.	Males.	Females.	Total.	Males.	Females.	Total.	Males.	Females.
South Atlantic division—Cont. **West Virginia**	4,731	2,832	2,899	1,353	664	689	2,400	1,163	1,246	969	505	464
1 month or less	300	144	156	113	50	63	136	65	71	51	29	22
2 to 3 months	623	333	290	169	87	82	272	126	146	182	120	62
4 to 5 months	1,559	786	773	443	223	220	779	386	393	337	177	160
6 months or more	2,249	1,069	1,180	628	304	324	1,222	586	636	399	179	220
North Carolina	72,893	34,683	38,210	17,101	8,516	8,585	38,302	18,511	19,791	17,490	7,656	9,834
1 month or less	9,102	4,608	4,494	2,375	1,190	1,185	4,448	2,217	2,231	2,279	1,201	1,078
2 to 3 months	40,788	19,625	21,163	9,288	4,661	4,627	21,413	10,495	10,918	10,087	4,469	5,618
4 to 5 months	14,609	6,749	7,860	3,369	1,656	1,713	7,897	3,725	4,172	3,343	1,368	1,975
6 months or more	8,394	3,701	4,693	2,069	1,009	1,060	4,544	2,074	2,470	1,781	618	1,163
South Carolina	82,621	39,917	42,704	21,860	10,828	11,032	45,288	22,231	23,057	15,473	6,858	8,615
1 month or less	6,677	3,386	3,291	2,011	986	1,025	3,337	1,753	1,584	1,329	647	682
2 to 3 months	43,648	21,200	22,448	11,212	5,557	5,655	24,217	11,970	12,247	8,219	3,673	4,546
4 to 5 months	17,003	8,245	8,758	4,179	2,110	2,069	9,505	4,642	4,863	3,319	1,493	1,826
6 months or more	15,293	7,086	8,207	4,458	2,175	2,283	8,229	3,806	4,363	2,606	1,045	1,561
Georgia	92,722	44,098	48,624	25,519	12,604	12,915	52,107	25,235	26,872	15,096	6,259	8,837
1 month or less	8,197	4,204	3,993	2,391	1,221	1,170	4,188	2,176	2,012	1,618	807	811
2 to 3 months	42,758	20,879	21,879	11,446	5,657	5,789	23,824	11,918	11,906	7,488	3,304	4,184
4 to 5 months	20,308	9,548	10,760	6,050	3,057	2,993	11,456	5,453	6,003	2,802	1,038	1,764
6 months or more	21,459	9,467	11,992	5,632	2,669	2,963	12,639	5,688	6,951	3,188	1,110	2,078
Florida	28,245	13,823	14,422	8,182	4,009	4,173	14,419	7,163	7,256	5,644	2,651	2,993
1 month or less	1,423	710	713	450	192	258	607	310	297	366	208	158
2 to 3 months	6,023	3,087	2,936	1,580	828	752	3,010	1,540	1,470	1,433	719	714
4 to 5 months	12,034	5,994	6,040	3,256	1,635	1,621	6,476	3,267	3,209	2,302	1,092	1,210
6 months or more	8,765	4,032	4,733	2,896	1,354	1,542	4,326	2,046	2,280	1,543	632	911
North Central division: **Ohio**	16,631	8,564	8,067	5,098	2,578	2,520	8,281	4,308	3,973	3,252	1,678	1,574
1 month or less	935	472	463	362	174	188	398	208	190	175	90	85
2 to 3 months	1,160	658	502	382	179	203	434	246	188	344	233	111
4 to 5 months	1,360	768	592	357	189	168	612	330	282	391	249	142
6 months or more	13,176	6,666	6,510	3,997	2,036	1,961	6,837	3,524	3,313	2,342	1,106	1,236
Indiana	8,100	4,046	4,114	2,479	1,233	1,246	4,191	2,088	2,103	1,490	725	765
1 month or less	371	171	200	120	57	63	166	72	94	85	42	43
2 to 3 months	524	282	242	202	102	100	197	98	99	125	82	43
4 to 5 months	910	480	430	264	131	133	448	239	209	198	110	88
6 months or more	6,355	3,113	3,242	1,893	943	950	3,380	1,679	1,701	1,082	491	591
Illinois	9,960	4,962	4,998	3,014	1,491	1,523	5,025	2,538	2,487	1,921	933	988
1 month or less	522	246	276	206	98	108	206	97	109	110	51	59
2 to 3 months	1,029	554	475	311	153	158	447	234	213	271	167	104
4 to 5 months	1,588	802	786	417	197	220	805	404	401	366	201	165
6 months or more	6,821	3,360	3,461	2,080	1,043	1,037	3,567	1,803	1,764	1,174	514	660
Michigan	2,801	1,415	1,386	912	445	467	1,396	716	680	493	254	239
1 month or less	236	106	130	92	44	48	101	48	53	43	14	29
2 to 3 months	215	129	86	87	44	43	77	51	26	51	34	17
4 to 5 months	344	208	136	104	54	50	155	93	62	85	61	24
6 months or more	2,006	972	1,034	629	303	326	1,063	524	539	314	145	169
Wisconsin	455	215	240	151	59	92	220	107	113	84	49	35
1 month or less	22	9	13	11	4	7	9	3	6	2	2	....
2 to 3 months	55	35	20	25	13	12	18	12	6	12	10	2
4 to 5 months	51	26	25	13	5	8	25	14	11	13	7	6
6 months or more	327	145	182	102	37	65	168	78	90	57	30	27
Minnesota	407	186	221	135	60	75	192	90	102	80	36	44
1 month or less	32	16	16	14	5	9	11	6	5	7	5	2
2 to 3 months	19	9	10	10	2	8	5	5	....	4	2	2
4 to 5 months	27	16	11	10	6	4	13	7	6	4	3	1
6 months or more	329	145	184	101	47	54	163	72	91	65	26	39
Iowa	1,993	985	1,008	640	297	343	954	481	473	399	207	192
1 month or less	129	55	74	44	23	21	60	26	34	25	6	19
2 to 3 months	106	56	50	48	19	29	29	17	12	29	20	9
4 to 5 months	140	78	62	44	18	26	50	29	21	46	31	15
6 months or more	1,618	796	822	504	237	267	815	409	406	299	150	149
Missouri	24,510	12,258	12,252	6,632	3,271	3,361	12,834	6,504	6,330	5,044	2,483	2,561
1 month or less	1,693	870	823	619	307	312	727	375	352	347	188	159
2 to 3 months	3,199	1,750	1,449	886	452	434	1,463	776	687	850	522	328
4 to 5 months	4,485	2,332	2,153	1,078	521	557	2,375	1,261	1,114	1,032	550	482
6 months or more	15,133	7,306	7,827	4,049	1,991	2,058	8,269	4,092	4,177	2,815	1,223	1,592

a Includes all persons of negro descent.

168 STATISTICS OF POPULATION.

TABLE 23.—NEGRO PERSONS (a) ATTENDING SCHOOL DURING THE CENSUS YEAR, CLASSIFIED BY SEX, AGE PERIODS, AND MONTHS OF SCHOOL ATTENDANCE, BY STATES AND TERRITORIES: 1890—Continued.

STATES, TERRITORIES, AND MONTHS OF SCHOOL ATTENDANCE.	ALL AGES.			UNDER 10 YEARS.			10 TO 14 YEARS.			15 YEARS AND OVER.		
	Total.	Males.	Females.	Total.	Males.	Females.	Total.	Males.	Females.	Total.	Males.	Females.
North Central division—Cont.												
North Dakota	51	24	27	18	2	16	17	11	6	16	11	5
1 month or less	6	3	3	2	1	1	3	1	2	1	1	....
2 to 3 months	7	3	4	2	....	2	1	1	....	4	2	2
4 to 5 months	13	6	7	6	....	6	3	2	1	4	4	....
6 months or more	25	12	13	8	1	7	10	7	3	7	4	3
South Dakota	67	44	23	18	12	6	33	21	12	16	11	5
1 month or less	3	1	2	1	....	1	1	....	1	1	1	....
2 to 3 months	11	9	2	3	2	1	5	4	1	3	3	....
4 to 5 months	11	5	6	4	2	2	2	1	1	5	2	3
6 months or more	42	29	13	10	8	2	25	16	9	7	5	2
Nebraska	1,286	657	629	484	260	224	615	317	298	187	80	107
1 month or less	100	51	49	45	24	21	41	20	21	14	7	7
2 to 3 months	104	60	44	47	24	23	40	29	11	17	7	10
4 to 5 months	68	34	34	30	16	14	30	14	16	8	4	4
6 months or more	1,014	512	502	362	196	166	504	254	250	148	62	86
Kansas	10,667	5,260	5,407	2,781	1,331	1,450	5,454	2,698	2,756	2,432	1,231	1,201
1 month or less	487	239	248	172	76	96	199	101	98	116	62	54
2 to 3 months	1,119	614	505	360	162	198	429	231	198	330	221	109
4 to 5 months	1,262	692	570	320	155	165	606	335	271	336	202	134
6 months or more	7,799	3,715	4,084	1,929	938	991	4,220	2,031	2,189	1,650	746	904
South Central division:												
Kentucky	37,288	17,790	19,498	9,972	4,897	5,075	19,567	9,472	10,095	7,749	3,421	4,328
1 month or less	2,467	1,278	1,189	847	412	435	1,102	584	518	518	282	236
2 to 3 months	8,482	4,357	4,125	2,187	1,125	1,062	4,276	2,198	2,078	2,019	1,034	985
4 to 5 months	15,031	7,106	7,925	3,930	1,937	1,993	8,031	3,853	4,178	3,070	1,316	1,754
6 months or more	11,308	5,049	6,259	3,008	1,423	1,585	6,158	2,837	3,321	2,142	789	1,353
Tennessee	63,283	30,756	32,527	15,442	7,629	7,813	33,722	16,583	17,139	14,119	6,544	7,575
1 month or less	5,278	2,766	2,512	1,482	768	714	2,465	1,304	1,161	1,331	694	637
2 to 3 months	25,392	12,871	12,521	6,144	3,053	3,091	13,061	6,709	6,352	6,187	3,109	3,078
4 to 5 months	14,770	7,162	7,608	3,702	1,788	1,914	7,946	3,866	4,080	3,122	1,454	1,668
6 months or more	17,843	8,017	9,826	4,114	2,020	2,094	10,250	4,710	5,540	3,479	1,287	2,192
Alabama	72,656	34,704	37,952	16,478	8,004	8,474	39,893	19,325	20,568	16,285	7,375	8,910
1 month or less	5,750	2,969	2,781	1,426	691	735	2,842	1,478	1,364	1,482	800	682
2 to 3 months	41,542	20,302	21,240	9,130	4,529	4,601	22,600	11,162	11,437	9,812	4,610	5,202
4 to 5 months	11,727	5,392	6,335	2,708	1,299	1,409	6,599	3,105	3,494	2,420	988	1,432
6 months or more	13,637	6,041	7,596	3,214	1,485	1,729	7,852	3,579	4,273	2,571	977	1,594
Mississippi	124,453	61,421	63,032	34,854	17,305	17,549	62,679	31,072	31,607	26,920	13,044	13,876
1 month or less	10,850	5,599	5,251	3,619	1,756	1,863	4,910	2,553	2,357	2,321	1,290	1,031
2 to 3 months	35,599	18,187	17,412	9,356	4,691	4,665	17,619	9,036	8,583	8,624	4,410	4,214
4 to 5 months	64,287	31,403	32,884	18,182	9,079	9,103	32,890	16,143	16,747	13,215	6,181	7,034
6 months or more	13,717	6,282	7,435	3,697	1,779	1,918	7,260	3,340	3,920	2,760	1,163	1,597
Louisiana	42,851	20,997	21,854	12,882	6,462	6,420	24,037	11,934	12,103	5,932	2,601	3,331
1 month or less	4,640	1,955	2,685	1,372	671	701	2,698	1,009	1,089	570	275	295
2 to 3 months	12,466	6,146	6,320	3,492	1,738	1,754	6,718	3,399	3,319	2,256	1,009	1,247
4 to 5 months	8,517	4,268	4,249	2,658	1,376	1,282	4,771	2,400	2,302	1,088	483	605
6 months or more	17,828	8,628	9,200	5,360	2,677	2,683	10,450	5,117	5,383	2,018	834	1,184
Texas	79,775	38,656	41,119	18,124	8,936	9,188	45,967	22,624	23,343	15,684	7,096	8,588
1 month or less	5,889	3,127	2,762	1,678	829	849	2,912	1,588	1,324	1,299	710	589
2 to 3 months	28,186	14,094	14,092	6,355	3,206	3,149	15,979	8,073	7,906	5,852	2,815	3,037
4 to 5 months	25,071	12,076	12,995	5,513	2,758	2,755	15,019	7,322	7,697	4,539	1,996	2,543
6 months or more	20,629	9,359	11,270	4,578	2,143	2,435	12,057	5,641	6,416	3,994	1,575	2,419
Oklahoma	262	135	127	62	36	26	142	71	71	58	28	30
1 month or less	19	15	4	7	6	1	11	8	3	1	1	....
2 to 3 months	95	53	42	22	12	10	53	29	24	20	12	8
4 to 5 months	42	17	25	7	4	3	21	9	12	14	4	10
6 months or more	106	50	56	26	14	12	57	25	32	23	11	12
Arkansas	47,439	23,964	23,475	11,714	5,775	5,939	23,715	12,041	11,674	12,010	6,148	5,862
1 month or less	4,971	2,615	2,356	1,279	630	649	2,285	1,190	1,095	1,407	795	612
2 to 3 months	28,522	14,632	13,890	6,650	3,326	3,324	14,221	7,316	6,905	7,651	3,990	3,661
4 to 5 months	6,111	3,078	3,033	1,622	786	836	3,111	1,625	1,486	1,378	667	711
6 months or more	7,835	3,639	4,196	2,163	1,033	1,130	4,098	1,910	2,188	1,574	696	878

a Includes all persons of negro descent.

SCHOOL ATTENDANCE.

169

TABLE 23.—NEGRO PERSONS (a) ATTENDING SCHOOL DURING THE CENSUS YEAR, CLASSIFIED BY SEX, AGE PERIODS, AND MONTHS OF SCHOOL ATTENDANCE, BY STATES AND TERRITORIES: 1890—Continued.

STATES, TERRITORIES, AND MONTHS OF SCHOOL ATTENDANCE.	ALL AGES.			UNDER 10 YEARS.			10 TO 14 YEARS.			15 YEARS AND OVER.		
	Total.	Males.	Females.	Total.	Males.	Females.	Total.	Males.	Females.	Total.	Males.	Females.
Western division:												
Montana	106	43	63	34	11	23	52	25	27	20	7	13
1 month or less	6	1	5	2	----	2	3	----	3	1	1	----
2 to 3 months	8	2	6	3	----	3	3	1	2	2	1	1
4 to 5 months	4	2	2	1	----	1	1	1	----	2	1	1
6 months or more	88	38	50	28	11	17	45	23	22	15	4	11
Wyoming	70	49	21	17	10	7	21	11	10	32	28	4
1 month or less	12	10	2	2	----	2	1	1	----	9	0	----
2 to 3 months	24	23	1	3	3	----	3	3	----	18	17	1
4 to 5 months	7	3	4	3	1	2	3	1	2	1	1	----
6 months or more	27	13	14	9	6	3	14	6	8	4	1	3
Colorado	680	320	351	232	108	124	341	174	167	107	47	60
1 month or less	30	9	21	17	4	13	9	4	5	4	1	3
2 to 3 months	38	18	20	23	12	11	8	4	4	7	2	5
4 to 5 months	51	22	29	26	10	16	14	8	6	11	4	7
6 months or more	561	280	281	166	82	84	310	158	152	85	40	45
New Mexico	223	98	125	99	27	72	77	51	26	47	20	27
1 month or less	10	4	6	5	1	4	2	2	----	3	1	2
2 to 3 months	68	33	35	18	7	11	28	17	11	22	9	13
4 to 5 months	35	14	21	14	1	13	13	10	3	8	3	5
6 months or more	110	47	63	62	18	44	34	22	12	14	7	7
Arizona	50	21	29	23	7	16	23	12	11	4	2	2
1 month or less	6	3	3	2	----	2	4	3	1	----	----	----
2 to 3 months	8	3	5	2	1	1	4	1	3	2	1	1
4 to 5 months	3	2	1	1	1	----	2	1	1	----	----	----
6 months or more	33	13	20	18	5	13	13	7	6	2	1	1
Utah	35	18	17	15	7	8	16	8	8	4	3	1
1 month or less	3	1	2	1	----	1	1	----	1	1	1	----
2 to 3 months	4	1	3	2	----	2	----	----	----	2	1	1
4 to 5 months	9	8	1	7	6	1	2	2	----	----	----	----
6 months or more	19	8	11	5	1	4	13	6	7	1	1	----
Nevada	15	9	6	8	3	5	2	2	----	5	4	1
1 month or less	----	----	----	----	----	----	----	----	----	----	----	----
2 to 3 months	2	2	----	----	----	----	----	----	----	2	2	----
4 to 5 months	1	1	----	----	----	----	----	----	----	1	1	----
6 months or more	12	6	6	8	3	5	2	2	----	2	1	1
Idaho	27	13	14	6	4	2	14	5	9	7	4	3
1 month or less	----	----	----	----	----	----	----	----	----	----	----	----
2 to 3 months	4	3	1	3	2	1	1	1	----	----	----	----
4 to 5 months	3	1	2	1	1	----	2	----	2	----	----	----
6 months or more	20	9	11	2	1	1	11	4	7	7	4	3
Washington	104	48	56	36	19	17	49	23	26	19	6	13
1 month or less	12	5	7	6	3	3	3	1	2	3	1	2
2 to 3 months	22	10	12	11	6	5	10	4	6	1	----	1
4 to 5 months	12	6	6	5	2	3	5	2	3	2	2	----
6 months or more	58	27	31	14	8	6	31	16	15	13	3	10
Oregon	148	97	51	57	46	11	73	40	33	18	11	7
1 month or less	12	7	5	2	2	----	10	5	5	----	----	----
2 to 3 months	26	21	5	12	11	1	12	8	4	2	2	----
4 to 5 months	20	15	5	7	7	----	10	6	4	3	2	1
6 months or more	90	54	36	36	26	10	41	21	20	13	7	6
California	1,619	867	752	532	284	248	821	427	394	266	156	110
1 month or less	111	61	50	41	14	27	39	19	20	31	28	3
2 to 3 months	73	49	24	27	20	7	32	18	14	14	11	3
4 to 5 months	118	56	62	40	21	19	55	23	32	23	12	11
6 months or more	1,317	701	616	424	229	195	695	367	328	198	105	93

a Includes all persons of negro descent.

STATISTICS OF POPULATION.

170

TABLE **24.**—TOTAL PERSONS IN THE UNITED STATES ATTENDING SCHOOL DURING THE CENSUS YEAR,

GENERAL NATIVITY, COLOR, AND MONTHS OF SCHOOL ATTENDANCE.	ALL AGES.			UNDER 5 YEARS.			5 TO 9 YEARS.		
	Total.	Males.	Females.	Total.	Males.	Females.	Total.	Males.	Females.
Aggregate	11,674,878	5,954,142	5,720,736	8,330	4,245	4,085	3,726,044	1,888,039	1,838,005
1 month or less	660,289	340,860	319,429	2,003	1,004	999	271,526	136,469	135,057
2 to 3 months	1,739,136	935,068	804,068	1,633	792	841	557,736	278,337	279,399
4 to 5 months	2,029,276	1,090,935	938,341	1,277	658	619	559,886	282,865	277,021
6 months or more	7,246,177	3,587,279	3,658,898	3,417	1,791	1,626	2,336,896	1,190,368	1,146,528
Total white	10,667,171	5,464,413	5,202,758	7,918	4,051	3,867	3,459,680	1,756,349	1,703,331
1 month or less	580,922	300,369	280,553	1,914	962	952	247,421	124,627	122,794
2 to 3 months	1,400,218	766,134	634,084	1,488	724	764	473,637	236,354	237,283
4 to 5 months	1,755,680	958,655	797,025	1,177	611	566	488,239	247,156	241,083
6 months or more	6,930,351	3,439,255	3,491,096	3,339	1,754	1,585	2,250,383	1,148,212	1,102,171
Native white	10,153,289	5,196,313	4,956,976	7,696	3,939	3,757	3,311,921	1,680,669	1,631,252
1 month or less	542,177	279,718	262,459	1,859	928	931	233,932	117,740	116,192
2 to 3 months	1,360,791	743,295	617,496	1,456	711	745	463,754	231,292	232,462
4 to 5 months	1,707,716	931,424	776,292	1,149	597	552	477,921	241,887	236,034
6 months or more	6,542,605	3,241,876	3,300,729	3,232	1,703	1,529	2,136,314	1,089,750	1,046,564
Native white—native parents	7,204,755	3,695,420	3,509,335	4,610	2,348	2,262	2,254,297	1,144,455	1,109,842
1 month or less	374,232	194,340	179,892	999	484	515	155,058	78,017	77,041
2 to 3 months	1,174,142	639,158	534,984	979	482	497	384,308	192,245	192,063
4 to 5 months	1,426,818	771,438	655,380	828	435	393	395,952	200,499	195,453
6 months or more	4,229,563	2,090,484	2,139,079	1,804	947	857	1,318,979	673,694	645,285
Native white—foreign parents	2,948,534	1,500,893	1,447,641	3,086	1,591	1,495	1,057,624	536,214	521,410
1 month or less	167,945	85,378	82,567	860	444	416	78,874	39,723	39,151
2 to 3 months	186,649	104,137	82,512	477	229	248	79,446	39,047	40,399
4 to 5 months	280,898	159,986	120,912	321	162	159	81,969	41,388	40,581
6 months or more	2,313,042	1,151,392	1,161,650	1,428	756	672	817,335	416,056	401,279
Foreign white	513,882	268,100	245,782	222	112	110	147,759	75,680	72,079
1 month or less	38,745	20,651	18,094	55	34	21	13,489	6,887	6,602
2 to 3 months	39,427	22,839	16,588	32	13	19	9,883	5,062	4,821
4 to 5 months	47,964	27,231	20,733	28	14	14	10,318	5,269	5,049
6 months or more	387,746	197,379	190,367	107	51	56	114,069	58,462	55,607
Total colored (a)	1,007,707	489,729	517,978	412	194	218	266,364	131,690	134,674
1 month or less	79,367	40,491	38,876	89	42	47	24,105	11,842	12,263
2 to 3 months	338,918	168,934	169,984	145	68	77	84,099	41,983	42,116
4 to 5 months	273,596	132,280	141,316	100	47	53	71,647	35,709	35,938
6 months or more	315,826	148,024	167,802	78	37	41	86,513	42,156	44,357
Negro (b)	999,324	484,969	514,355	409	192	217	264,545	130,721	133,824
1 month or less	79,020	40,269	38,751	88	42	46	23,995	11,788	12,207
2 to 3 months	338,093	168,458	169,635	143	66	77	83,877	41,869	42,008
4 to 5 months	272,809	131,823	140,986	100	47	53	71,480	35,618	35,862
6 months or more	309,402	144,419	164,983	78	37	41	85,193	41,446	43,747

a Persons of negro descent, Chinese, Japanese, and civilized Indians.

SCHOOL ATTENDANCE.

CLASSIFIED BY SEX, GENERAL NATIVITY, COLOR, AGE PERIODS, AND MONTHS OF SCHOOL ATTENDANCE: 1890.

GENERAL NATIVITY, COLOR, AND MONTHS OF SCHOOL ATTENDANCE.	10 TO 14 YEARS.			15 TO 19 YEARS.			20 YEARS AND OVER.		
	Total.	Males.	Females.	Total.	Males.	Females.	Total.	Males.	Females.
Aggregate	5,607,358	2,831,005	2,776,353	2,155,141	1,111,989	1,043,152	178,005	118,864	59,141
1 month or less	252,259	129,369	122,890	114,140	59,923	54,217	20,361	14,095	6,266
2 to 3 months	741,598	391,599	349,999	406,893	242,276	164,617	31,276	22,064	9,212
4 to 5 months	955,862	503,823	452,039	483,195	283,351	199,844	29,056	20,238	8,818
6 months or more	3,657,639	1,806,214	1,851,425	1,150,913	526,439	624,474	97,312	62,467	34,845
Total white	5,068,809	2,566,411	2,502,398	1,965,457	1,026,065	939,392	165,307	111,537	53,770
1 month or less	214,383	109,873	104,510	98,170	51,613	46,566	19,025	13,294	5,731
2 to 3 months	562,722	301,487	261,235	334,939	207,669	127,270	27,432	19,900	7,532
4 to 5 months	807,884	431,411	376,473	431,983	260,651	171,332	26,397	18,826	7,571
6 months or more	3,483,820	1,723,640	1,760,180	1,100,356	506,132	594,224	92,453	59,517	32,936
Native white	4,771,009	2,414,508	2,356,561	1,907,261	993,085	914,176	155,342	104,112	51,230
1 month or less	195,835	100,389	95,446	94,188	49,375	44,813	16,363	11,286	5,077
2 to 3 months	544,163	291,304	252,859	325,093	200,986	124,107	26,325	19,002	7,323
4 to 5 months	781,317	416,910	364,407	421,867	253,913	167,954	25,462	18,117	7,345
6 months or more	3,249,754	1,605,905	1,643,849	1,066,113	488,811	577,302	87,192	55,707	31,485
Native white—native parents	3,345,072	1,694,627	1,650,445	1,472,714	767,972	704,742	128,062	86,018	42,044
1 month or less	132,980	68,641	64,339	72,510	38,483	34,027	12,685	8,715	3,970
2 to 3 months	487,342	260,283	227,059	278,515	169,725	108,790	22,998	16,423	6,575
4 to 5 months	659,013	348,961	310,052	348,973	205,976	142,997	22,052	15,567	6,485
6 months or more	2,065,737	1,016,742	1,048,995	772,716	353,788	418,928	70,327	45,313	25,014
Native white—foreign parents	1,425,937	719,881	706,116	434,547	225,113	209,434	27,280	18,094	9,186
1 month or less	62,855	31,748	31,107	21,678	10,892	10,786	3,678	2,571	1,107
2 to 3 months	56,821	31,021	25,800	46,578	31,261	15,317	3,327	2,579	748
4 to 5 months	122,304	67,949	54,355	72,894	47,937	24,957	3,410	2,550	860
6 months or more	1,184,017	589,163	594,854	293,397	135,023	158,374	16,865	10,394	6,471
Foreign white	297,740	151,903	145,837	58,196	32,980	25,216	9,965	7,425	2,540
1 month or less	18,548	9,484	9,064	3,991	2,238	1,753	2,662	2,008	654
2 to 3 months	18,559	10,183	8,376	9,846	6,683	3,163	1,107	898	209
4 to 5 months	26,567	14,501	12,066	10,116	6,738	3,378	935	709	226
6 months or more	234,066	117,735	116,331	34,243	17,321	16,922	5,261	3,810	1,451
Total colored (a)	538,549	264,594	273,955	189,684	85,924	103,760	12,698	7,327	5,371
1 month or less	37,876	19,496	18,380	15,961	8,310	7,651	1,336	801	535
2 to 3 months	178,876	90,112	88,764	71,954	34,607	37,347	3,844	2,164	1,680
4 to 5 months	147,978	72,412	75,566	51,212	22,700	28,512	2,659	1,412	1,247
6 months or more	173,819	82,574	91,245	50,557	20,307	30,250	4,859	2,950	1,909
Negro (b)	534,864	262,575	272,289	187,464	84,672	102,792	12,042	6,809	5,233
1 month or less	37,755	19,419	18,336	15,890	8,261	7,629	1,292	759	533
2 to 3 months	178,525	89,912	88,613	71,748	34,482	37,266	3,800	2,129	1,671
4 to 5 months	147,600	72,213	75,387	51,016	22,571	28,445	2,613	1,374	1,239
6 months or more	170,984	81,031	89,953	48,810	19,358	29,452	4,337	2,547	1,790

b Includes all persons of negro descent.

ILLITERACY.

BY STATES AND TERRITORIES: 1890.

TABLE 31.—TOTAL ILLITERATE POPULATION 10 YEARS OF AGE AND OVER, CLASSIFIED BY GENERAL NATIVITY AND COLOR.

TABLE 32.—TOTAL ILLITERATE POPULATION 10 YEARS OF AGE AND OVER, CLASSIFIED BY SEX AND DEGREE OF ILLITERACY.

TABLE 33.—ILLITERATE WHITE POPULATION 10 YEARS OF AGE AND OVER, CLASSIFIED BY SEX AND DEGREE OF ILLITERACY.

TABLE 34.—ILLITERATE NATIVE WHITE POPULATION 10 YEARS OF AGE AND OVER, CLASSIFIED BY SEX AND DEGREE OF ILLITERACY.

TABLE 35.—ILLITERATE NATIVE WHITE POPULATION OF NATIVE PARENTAGE 10 YEARS OF AGE AND OVER, CLASSIFIED BY SEX AND DEGREE OF ILLITERACY.

TABLE 36.—ILLITERATE NATIVE WHITE POPULATION OF FOREIGN PARENTAGE 10 YEARS OF AGE AND OVER, CLASSIFIED BY SEX AND DEGREE OF ILLITERACY.

TABLE 37.—ILLITERATE FOREIGN WHITE POPULATION 10 YEARS OF AGE AND OVER, CLASSIFIED BY SEX AND DEGREE OF ILLITERACY.

TABLE 38.—ILLITERATE COLORED POPULATION 10 YEARS OF AGE AND OVER, CLASSIFIED BY SEX AND DEGREE OF ILLITERACY.

TABLE 39.—ILLITERATE NEGRO POPULATION 10 YEARS OF AGE AND OVER, CLASSIFIED BY SEX AND DEGREE OF ILLITERACY.

TABLE 40.—TOTAL ILLITERATE POPULATION 10 YEARS OF AGE AND OVER, CLASSIFIED BY SEX AND AGE PERIODS.

TABLE 41.—ILLITERATE WHITE POPULATION 10 YEARS OF AGE AND OVER, CLASSIFIED BY SEX AND AGE PERIODS.

TABLE 42.—ILLITERATE NATIVE WHITE POPULATION 10 YEARS OF AGE AND OVER, CLASSIFIED BY SEX AND AGE PERIODS.

TABLE 43.—ILLITERATE NATIVE WHITE POPULATION OF NATIVE PARENTAGE 10 YEARS OF AGE AND OVER, CLASSIFIED BY SEX AND AGE PERIODS.

TABLE 44.—ILLITERATE NATIVE WHITE POPULATION OF FOREIGN PARENTAGE 10 YEARS OF AGE AND OVER, CLASSIFIED BY SEX AND AGE PERIODS.

TABLE 45.—ILLITERATE FOREIGN WHITE POPULATION 10 YEARS OF AGE AND OVER, CLASSIFIED BY SEX AND AGE PERIODS.

TABLE 46.—ILLITERATE COLORED POPULATION 10 YEARS OF AGE AND OVER, CLASSIFIED BY SEX AND AGE PERIODS.

TABLE 47.—ILLITERATE NEGRO POPULATION 10 YEARS OF AGE AND OVER, CLASSIFIED BY SEX AND AGE PERIODS.

FOR THE UNITED STATES: 1890.

TABLE 48.—TOTAL ILLITERATE POPULATION 10 YEARS OF AGE AND OVER, CLASSIFIED BY DEGREE OF ILLITERACY, GENERAL NATIVITY, COLOR, SEX, AND AGE PERIODS.

FOR CITIES HAVING 25,000 INHABITANTS OR MORE: 1890.

TABLE 49.—TOTAL ILLITERATE POPULATION 10 YEARS OF AGE AND OVER, CLASSIFIED BY SEX AND DEGREE OF ILLITERACY.

TABLE 50.—ILLITERATE NATIVE WHITE POPULATION OF NATIVE PARENTAGE 10 YEARS OF AGE AND OVER, CLASSIFIED BY SEX AND DEGREE OF ILLITERACY.

TABLE 51.—ILLITERATE NATIVE WHITE POPULATION OF FOREIGN PARENTAGE 10 YEARS OF AGE AND OVER, CLASSIFIED BY SEX AND DEGREE OF ILLITERACY.

TABLE 52.—ILLITERATE FOREIGN WHITE POPULATION 10 YEARS OF AGE AND OVER, CLASSIFIED BY SEX AND DEGREE OF ILLITERACY.

TABLE 53.—ILLITERATE COLORED POPULATION 10 YEARS OF AGE AND OVER, CLASSIFIED BY SEX AND DEGREE OF ILLITERACY.

TABLE 54.—TOTAL ILLITERATE POPULATION 10 YEARS OF AGE AND OVER, CLASSIFIED BY SEX AND AGE PERIODS.

TABLE 55.—ILLITERATE NATIVE WHITE POPULATION OF NATIVE PARENTAGE 10 YEARS OF AGE AND OVER, CLASSIFIED BY SEX AND AGE PERIODS.

TABLE 56.—ILLITERATE NATIVE WHITE POPULATION OF FOREIGN PARENTAGE 10 YEARS OF AGE AND OVER, CLASSIFIED BY SEX AND AGE PERIODS.

TABLE 57.—ILLITERATE FOREIGN WHITE POPULATION 10 YEARS OF AGE AND OVER, CLASSIFIED BY SEX AND AGE PERIODS.

TABLE 58.—ILLITERATE COLORED POPULATION 10 YEARS OF AGE AND OVER, CLASSIFIED BY SEX AND AGE PERIODS.

ILLITERACY.

195

TABLE **31.**—TOTAL ILLITERATE POPULATION 10 YEARS OF AGE AND OVER, CLASSIFIED BY GENERAL NATIVITY AND COLOR, BY STATES AND TERRITORIES: 1890.

STATES AND TERRITORIES.	Aggregate.	Total white.	NATIVE WHITE.			Foreign white.	COLORED.		
			Total.	Native parents.	Foreign parents.		Total.	Negro. (a)	Chinese, Japanese, and civilized Indians.
The United States..........	6,324,702	3,212,574	2,065,003	1,890,723	174,280	1,147,571	3,112,128	3,042,668	69,460
North Atlantic division..............	859,980	810,091	229,897	167,686	62,211	580,194	49,898	46,756	3,142
Maine......................	29,587	29,108	11,443	7,438	4,005	17,665	479	155	324
New Hampshire	21,476	21,340	3,679	2,332	1,347	17,661	136	115	21
Vermont....................	18,154	17,986	7,211	3,395	3,816	10,775	168	149	19
Massachusetts.............	114,468	111,442	9,727	4,228	5,499	101,715	3,026	2,607	419
Rhode Island	27,525	26,355	4,087	1,646	2,441	22,268	1,170	1,106	64
Connecticut...............	32,194	30,536	4,300	2,553	1,747	26,236	1,658	1,532	126
New York	266,911	255,498	57,362	36,739	20,623	198,136	11,413	10,017	1,396
New Jersey	74,321	63,163	21,351	17,309	4,042	41,812	11,158	10,860	298
Pennsylvania..............	275,353	254,063	110,737	92,046	18,691	143,926	20,090	20,215	475
South Atlantic division..............	1,981,888	595,952	571,899	564,502	7,397	24,053	1,385,936	1,384,632	1,304
Delaware	18,878	8,186	6,068	5,839	220	2,118	10,692	10,675	17
Maryland	125,376	44,653	32,105	28,907	3,198	12,548	80,723	80,644	79
District of Columbia.......	24,884	3,495	1,803	1,596	207	1,692	21,389	21,346	43
Virginia	365,736	105,058	103,265	102,669	596	1,793	260,678	260,599	79
West Virginia	79,180	68,188	65,420	64,017	1,403	2,768	10,992	10,985	7
North Carolina.............	409,703	173,722	173,545	173,129	416	177	235,981	235,238	743
South Carolina.............	360,705	59,443	59,063	58,782	281	380	301,262	301,169	93
Georgia	518,706	114,691	113,945	113,884	561	746	404,015	403,925	90
Florida	78,720	18,516	16,685	16,179	506	1,831	60,204	60,051	153
North Central division..............	964,268	849,843	436,328	366,492	69,836	413,515	114,425	107,395	7,030
Ohio	149,843	132,244	82,673	70,796	11,877	49,571	17,599	17,496	103
Indiana	105,829	94,334	78,638	71,848	6,790	15,696	11,495	11,407	88
Illinois...................	152,634	140,219	64,380	55,930	8,450	75,839	12,415	12,111	304
Michigan	95,914	91,076	27,016	16,627	10,389	64,060	4,838	2,306	2,532
Wisconsin	84,745	82,984	15,613	5,227	10,386	67,371	1,761	379	1,382
Minnesota	58,057	56,966	7,112	2,466	4,646	49,854	1,091	386	705
Iowa......................	52,061	49,828	20,649	16,388	4,261	29,179	2,233	2,177	56
Missouri	181,368	133,806	112,938	105,477	7,461	20,868	47,562	47,333	229
North Dakota...............	7,743	7,528	929	295	634	6,599	215	83	132
South Dakota..............	9,974	9,564	1,811	934	877	7,753	410	91	319
Nebraska	24,021	21,575	7,412	5,744	1,668	14,163	2,446	1,367	1,079
Kansas	42,079	29,719	17,157	14,760	2,397	12,562	12,360	12,259	101
South Central division	2,318,871	817,031	754,935	729,468	25,467	62,096	1,501,840	1,498,584	3,256
Kentucky..................	294,381	183,851	178,159	175,308	2,851	5,692	110,530	110,507	23
Tennessee	340,140	172,169	170,318	169,089	1,229	1,851	167,971	167,881	90
Alabama...................	438,535	107,335	106,235	105,394	841	1,100	331,200	330,703	497
Mississippi	360,613	45,755	44,987	44,284	703	768	314,858	313,573	1,285
Louisiana	364,184	80,039	72,013	68,663	3,350	8,026	283,245	282,670	575
Texas.....................	308,873	132,389	89,829	74,637	15,192	42,560	176,484	175,882	602
Oklahoma..................	2,400	1,503	1,342	1,251	91	161	897	881	16
Arkansas	209,745	93,990	92,052	90,842	1,210	1,938	116,655	116,487	168
Western division	199,686	139,657	71,944	62,575	9,369	67,713	60,029	5,301	54,728
Montana...................	5,884	4,232	1,020	705	315	3,212	1,652	153	1,499
Wyoming	1,630	1,408	427	275	152	981	222	147	75
Colorado..................	17,180	15,474	9,235	8,610	625	6,239	1,706	940	766
New Mexico	50,070	43,265	40,065	38,484	1,581	3,200	6,805	722	6,083
Arizona...................	10,785	8,956	2,056	940	1,116	6,900	1,829	245	1,584
Utah......................	8,232	7,407	2,219	1,150	1,069	5,188	825	132	693
Nevada	4,897	1,356	173	121	52	1,183	3,541	86	3,455
Idaho	3,225	2,119	867	631	236	1,252	1,106	42	1,064
Washington	11,778	8,261	2,467	1,882	585	5,794	3,517	255	3,262
Oregon....................	10,103	6,946	3,302	2,824	478	3,644	3,157	171	2,986
California.................	75,902	40,233	10,113	6,953	3,160	30,120	35,669	2,408	33,261

a Includes all persons of negro descent.

STATISTICS OF POPULATION.

TABLE 32.—TOTAL ILLITERATE POPULATION 10 YEARS OF AGE AND OVER, CLASSIFIED BY SEX AND DEGREE OF ILLITERACY, BY STATES AND TERRITORIES: 1890.

STATES AND TERRITORIES.	AGGREGATE.			NUMBER WHO CAN READ BUT CAN NOT WRITE.			NUMBER WHO CAN NEITHER READ NOR WRITE.		
	Total.	Males.	Females.	Total.	Males.	Females.	Total.	Males.	Females.
The United States	6,324,702	3,008,222	3,316,480	1,167,853	502,969	664,884	5,156,849	2,505,253	2,651,596
North Atlantic division	859,989	407,186	452,803	169,384	63,889	105,495	690,605	343,297	347,308
Maine	26,367	15,002	10,055	5,955	3,498	2,697	24,533	13,504	11,028
New Hampshire	21,476	11,643	9,833	3,221	1,498	1,723	18,255	10,145	8,110
Vermont	18,154	10,230	7,924	3,087	1,574	1,513	15,067	8,656	6,411
Massachusetts	114,468	47,348	67,120	17,004	5,530	11,474	97,464	41,818	55,646
Rhode Island	27,525	12,240	15,285	6,240	2,273	3,967	21,285	9,967	11,318
Connecticut	32,194	15,233	16,961	6,124	2,488	3,636	26,070	12,745	13,325
New York	266,911	124,443	142,468	46,071	18,281	27,790	220,840	106,162	114,678
New Jersey	74,321	35,413	38,908	18,530	7,540	10,990	55,791	27,873	27,918
Pennsylvania	275,353	134,704	140,649	64,052	22,277	41,775	211,301	112,427	98,874
South Atlantic division	1,981,888	926,096	1,055,792	300,691	132,513	168,178	1,681,197	793,583	887,614
Delaware	18,878	9,274	9,604	2,409	992	1,417	16,469	8,282	8,187
Maryland	125,376	59,526	65,850	18,549	7,804	10,745	106,827	51,722	55,105
District of Columbia	24,884	9,821	15,063	3,112	1,203	1,909	21,772	8,618	13,154
Virginia	365,736	177,043	188,693	47,584	21,559	26,025	318,152	155,484	162,668
West Virginia	79,180	37,579	41,601	23,608	9,569	14,039	55,572	28,010	27,562
North Carolina	409,703	184,506	225,197	76,144	30,279	45,865	333,559	154,227	179,332
South Carolina	360,705	167,120	193,585	46,843	22,417	24,426	313,862	144,703	169,159
Georgia	518,706	244,944	273,762	70,359	32,962	37,397	448,347	211,982	236,365
Florida	78,720	36,283	42,437	12,083	5,728	6,355	66,637	30,555	36,082
North Central division	964,268	457,793	506,475	275,598	112,222	163,376	688,670	345,571	343,099
Ohio	149,843	69,924	79,919	42,876	16,553	26,323	106,967	53,371	53,596
Indiana	105,829	49,505	56,324	32,452	12,695	19,757	73,377	36,810	36,567
Illinois	152,634	70,548	82,086	38,823	15,588	23,235	113,811	54,960	58,851
Michigan	95,914	51,522	44,392	22,199	10,566	11,633	73,715	40,956	32,759
Wisconsin	84,745	39,517	45,228	23,620	9,472	14,148	61,125	30,045	31,080
Minnesota	58,057	25,993	32,064	22,070	8,076	13,994	35,987	17,917	18,070
Iowa	52,061	24,125	27,936	17,800	6,764	11,036	34,261	17,361	16,900
Missouri	181,368	86,530	94,838	50,246	21,920	28,326	131,122	64,610	66,512
North Dakota	7,743	3,650	4,093	2,980	1,151	1,829	4,763	2,499	2,264
South Dakota	9,974	4,816	5,158	3,542	1,419	2,123	6,432	3,397	3,035
Nebraska	24,021	11,753	12,268	6,470	2,855	3,615	17,551	8,898	8,653
Kansas	42,079	19,910	22,169	12,520	5,163	7,357	29,559	14,747	14,812
South Central division	2,318,871	1,098,755	1,220,116	396,738	181,297	215,441	1,922,133	917,458	1,004,675
Kentucky	294,381	141,999	152,382	64,812	28,400	36,412	229,569	113,599	115,970
Tennessee	340,140	155,869	184,271	81,288	33,578	47,710	258,852	122,291	136,561
Alabama	438,535	206,362	232,173	62,214	29,071	33,143	376,321	177,291	199,030
Mississippi	360,613	170,761	189,852	53,609	26,556	27,053	307,004	144,205	162,799
Louisiana	364,184	172,847	191,337	31,076	15,565	15,511	333,108	157,282	175,826
Texas	308,873	151,852	157,021	50,768	24,549	26,219	258,105	127,303	130,802
Oklahoma	2,400	1,286	1,114	599	313	286	1,801	973	828
Arkansas	209,745	97,779	111,966	52,372	23,265	29,107	157,373	74,514	82,859
Western division	199,686	118,392	81,294	25,442	13,048	12,394	174,244	105,344	68,900
Montana	5,884	4,330	1,554	854	552	302	5,030	3,778	1,252
Wyoming	1,630	1,070	560	366	188	178	1,264	882	382
Colorado	17,180	9,808	7,372	2,552	1,380	1,172	14,628	8,428	6,200
New Mexico	50,070	20,969	29,101	6,634	2,845	3,789	43,436	18,124	25,312
Arizona	10,785	6,027	4,758	665	303	362	10,120	5,724	4,396
Utah	8,232	3,778	4,454	2,605	997	1,608	5,627	2,781	2,846
Nevada	4,897	3,127	1,770	261	193	68	4,636	2,934	1,702
Idaho	3,225	2,336	889	645	359	286	2,580	1,977	603
Washington	11,778	7,639	4,139	2,111	1,225	886	9,667	6,414	3,253
Oregon	10,103	6,634	3,469	2,347	1,369	978	7,756	5,265	2,491
California	75,902	52,674	23,228	6,402	3,637	2,765	69,500	49,037	20,463

ILLITERACY.

TABLE 33.—ILLITERATE WHITE POPULATION 10 YEARS OF AGE AND OVER, CLASSIFIED BY SEX AND DEGREE OF ILLITERACY, BY STATES AND TERRITORIES: 1890.

STATES AND TERRITORIES.	AGGREGATE.			NUMBER WHO CAN READ BUT CAN NOT WRITE.			NUMBER WHO CAN NEITHER READ NOR WRITE.		
	Total.	Males.	Females.	Total.	Males.	Females.	Total.	Males.	Females.
The United States	8,212,574	1,517,722	1,694,852	802,481	322,717	479,764	2,410,093	1,195,005	1,215,088
North Atlantic division	810,091	382,672	427,419	159,647	59,832	99,815	650,444	322,840	327,604
Maine	29,108	15,664	13,444	5,002	2,404	2,598	24,106	13,260	10,846
New Hampshire	21,340	11,568	9,772	3,197	1,489	1,708	18,143	10,079	8,064
Vermont	17,986	10,122	7,864	3,058	1,561	1,497	14,928	8,561	6,367
Massachusetts	111,442	45,833	65,609	16,443	5,312	11,131	94,999	40,521	54,478
Rhode Island	26,355	11,748	14,607	5,930	2,168	3,762	20,425	9,580	10,845
Connecticut	30,536	14,408	16,128	5,722	2,327	3,395	24,814	12,081	12,733
New York	255,498	118,810	136,688	43,856	17,388	26,468	211,642	101,422	110,220
New Jersey	63,163	30,101	33,062	16,155	6,542	9,613	47,008	23,559	23,449
Pennsylvania	254,663	124,418	130,245	60,284	20,641	39,643	194,379	103,777	90,602
South Atlantic division	595,952	273,946	322,006	148,961	58,250	90,711	446,991	215,696	231,295
Delaware	8,186	4,027	4,159	1,190	470	720	6,996	3,557	3,439
Maryland	44,653	21,429	23,224	8,763	3,280	5,483	35,890	18,149	17,741
District of Columbia	3,495	1,237	2,258	621	204	417	2,874	1,033	1,841
Virginia	105,058	51,954	53,104	23,451	9,816	13,635	81,607	42,138	39,469
West Virginia	68,188	31,339	36,849	21,966	8,716	13,250	46,222	22,623	23,599
North Carolina	173,722	75,726	97,996	47,023	17,126	29,897	126,699	58,600	68,099
South Carolina	58,843	27,052	31,791	12,836	5,368	7,468	46,607	22,284	24,323
Georgia	114,691	51,927	62,764	29,506	11,771	17,735	85,185	40,156	45,029
Florida	18,516	8,655	9,861	3,605	1,499	2,106	14,911	7,156	7,755
North Central division	849,843	402,177	447,666	256,882	103,345	153,537	592,961	298,832	294,129
Ohio	132,244	61,131	71,113	39,413	14,982	24,431	92,831	46,149	46,682
Indiana	94,334	43,816	50,518	30,497	11,755	18,742	63,837	32,061	31,776
Illinois	140,219	64,475	75,744	36,650	14,538	22,121	103,560	49,937	53,623
Michigan	91,076	49,087	41,989	21,468	10,211	11,257	69,608	38,876	30,732
Wisconsin	82,984	38,601	44,383	23,517	9,425	14,092	59,467	29,176	30,291
Minnesota	56,966	25,469	31,497	21,977	8,029	13,948	34,989	17,440	17,549
Iowa	49,828	22,962	26,866	17,378	6,576	10,802	32,450	16,386	16,064
Missouri	133,806	63,846	69,960	42,874	18,403	24,471	90,932	45,443	45,489
North Dakota	7,528	3,529	3,999	2,968	1,145	1,823	4,560	2,384	2,176
South Dakota	9,564	4,598	4,966	3,515	1,395	2,120	6,049	3,203	2,846
Nebraska	21,575	10,549	11,026	6,211	2,716	3,495	15,364	7,833	7,531
Kansas	29,719	14,114	15,605	10,405	4,170	6,235	19,314	9,944	9,370
South Central division	817,031	386,081	430,950	214,511	90,353	124,158	602,520	295,728	306,792
Kentucky	183,851	87,358	96,493	51,057	21,818	29,239	132,794	65,540	67,254
Tennessee	172,169	76,631	95,538	54,563	20,803	33,760	117,606	55,828	61,778
Alabama	107,335	49,549	57,786	28,346	11,776	16,570	78,989	37,773	41,216
Mississippi	45,755	22,103	23,652	12,594	5,718	6,876	33,161	16,385	16,776
Louisiana	80,989	39,257	41,682	7,608	3,511	4,152	73,276	35,746	37,530
Texas	132,389	67,590	64,799	28,018	13,385	14,633	104,371	54,205	50,166
Oklahoma	1,503	824	679	503	265	238	1,000	559	441
Arkansas	93,090	42,769	50,321	31,767	13,077	18,690	61,323	29,692	31,631
Western division	139,657	72,846	66,811	22,480	10,937	11,543	117,177	61,909	55,268
Montana	4,232	2,953	1,279	794	510	284	3,438	2,443	995
Wyoming	1,408	899	509	338	172	166	1,070	727	343
Colorado	15,474	8,588	6,886	2,333	1,257	1,076	13,141	7,331	5,810
New Mexico	43,265	17,406	25,859	5,829	2,427	3,402	37,436	14,979	22,457
Arizona	8,956	4,715	4,241	615	267	348	8,341	4,448	3,893
Utah	7,407	3,195	4,212	2,563	966	1,597	4,844	2,229	2,615
Nevada	1,356	965	391	210	149	61	1,146	816	330
Idaho	2,119	1,332	787	605	330	275	1,514	1,002	512
Washington	8,261	5,286	2,975	1,962	1,109	853	6,299	4,177	2,122
Oregon	6,946	4,031	2,915	2,064	1,122	942	4,882	2,909	1,973
California	40,233	23,476	16,757	5,167	2,628	2,539	35,066	20,848	14,218

STATISTICS OF POPULATION.

198

TABLE 34.—ILLITERATE NATIVE WHITE POPULATION 10 YEARS OF AGE AND OVER, CLASSIFIED BY SEX AND DEGREE OF ILLITERACY, BY STATES AND TERRITORIES: 1890.

STATES AND TERRITORIES.	AGGREGATE.			NUMBER WHO CAN READ BUT CAN NOT WRITE.			NUMBER WHO CAN NEITHER READ NOR WRITE.		
	Total.	Males.	Females.	Total.	Males.	Females.	Total.	Males.	Females.
The United States...........	2,065,003	978,408	1,086,595	579,827	238,356	341,471	1,485,176	740,052	745,124
North Atlantic division...............	229,897	112,168	117,729	68,508	26,364	42,144	161,389	85,804	75,585
Maine........................	11,443	6,836	4,607	2,358	1,237	1,141	9,045	5,579	3,466
New Hampshire..............	3,679	2,163	1,516	789	434	355	2,890	1,729	1,161
Vermont....................	7,211	4,364	2,847	1,540	874	666	5,671	3,490	2,181
Massachusetts..............	9,727	4,696	5,031	2,011	846	1,165	7,716	3,850	3,866
Rhode Island	4,087	1,992	2,095	1,325	584	741	2,762	1,408	1,354
Connecticut	4,300	2,334	1,966	1,244	639	605	3,056	1,695	1,361
New York	57,362	31,556	25,806	14,757	7,173	7,584	42,605	24,383	18,222
New Jersey.................	21,351	11,222	10,129	6,537	2,001	3,036	14,814	8,321	6,493
Pennsylvania...............	110,737	47,005	63,732	37,907	11,656	26,251	72,830	35,349	37,481
South Atlantic division...............	571,899	263,024	308,875	144,904	56,725	88,179	426,995	206,299	220,696
Delaware	6,068	3,049	3,019	883	358	525	5,185	2,691	2,494
Maryland...................	32,105	16,053	16,052	6,747	2,618	4,129	25,358	13,435	11,923
District of Columbia	1,803	895	908	334	134	200	1,469	761	708
Virginia....................	103,265	50,772	52,493	23,180	9,645	13,535	80,085	41,127	38,958
West Virginia..............	65,420	29,907	35,513	21,389	8,474	12,915	44,031	21,433	22,598
North Carolina	173,545	75,611	97,934	46,981	17,105	29,876	126,564	58,506	63,058
South Carolina	59,063	27,467	31,596	12,779	5,340	7,439	46,284	22,127	24,157
Georgia.....................	113,945	51,555	62,390	29,379	11,721	17,658	84,566	39,834	44,732
Florida	16,685	7,715	8,970	3,232	1,330	1,902	13,453	6,385	7,068
North Central division...............	436,328	215,277	221,051	145,568	61,480	84,088	290,760	153,797	136,963
Ohio........................	82,673	39,188	43,485	28,511	10,893	17,618	54,162	28,295	25,867
Indiana.....................	78,638	37,105	41,533	26,402	10,293	16,109	52,236	26,812	25,424
Illinois.....................	64,380	31,388	32,992	20,818	8,627	12,191	43,562	22,761	20,801
Michigan...................	27,016	15,566	11,450	7,811	4,217	3,594	19,205	11,349	7,856
Wisconsin..................	15,613	8,315	7,298	4,080	2,047	2,033	11,533	6,268	5,265
Minnesota..................	7,112	3,915	3,197	1,965	990	975	5,147	2,925	2,222
Iowa.......................	20,649	10,528	10,121	7,601	3,153	4,448	13,048	7,375	5,673
Missouri...................	112,938	55,027	57,911	38,420	16,718	21,702	74,518	38,309	36,209
North Dakota..............	929	482	447	263	128	135	666	354	312
South Dakota..............	1,811	1,007	804	568	282	286	1,243	725	518
Nebraska...................	7,412	4,066	3,346	2,633	1,327	1,306	4,779	2,739	2,040
Kansas	17,157	8,690	8,467	6,496	2,805	3,691	10,661	5,885	4,776
South Central division................	754,935	355,044	399,891	208,832	88,044	120,788	546,103	267,000	279,103
Kentucky	178,159	84,956	93,203	49,919	21,407	28,512	128,240	63,549	64,691
Tennessee	170,318	75,749	94,569	54,232	20,659	33,573	116,086	55,090	60,996
Alabama....................	106,235	48,918	57,317	28,150	11,678	16,472	78,085	37,240	40,845
Mississippi.................	44,987	21,660	23,327	12,456	5,647	6,809	32,531	16,013	16,518
Louisiana..................	72,013	34,743	37,270	6,959	3,287	3,672	65,054	31,456	33,598
Texas......................	89,829	46,073	43,756	25,112	12,160	12,952	64,717	33,913	30,804
Oklahoma..................	1,342	745	597	465	248	217	877	497	380
Arkansas..................	92,052	42,200	49,852	31,539	12,958	18,581	60,513	29,242	31,271
Western division................	71,944	32,895	39,049	12,015	5,743	6,272	59,929	27,152	32,777
Montana....................	1,020	686	334	245	149	96	775	537	238
Wyoming	427	265	162	112	66	46	315	199	116
Colorado...................	9,235	4,584	4,651	1,287	697	590	7,948	3,887	4,061
New Mexico................	40,065	15,721	24,344	5,464	2,272	3,192	34,601	13,449	21,152
Arizona	2,056	1,101	955	245	117	128	1,811	984	827
Utah	2,219	1,188	1,031	780	407	373	1,439	781	658
Nevada....................	173	122	51	39	29	10	134	93	41
Idaho......................	867	525	342	338	199	139	529	326	203
Washington	2,467	1,409	1,058	842	445	397	1,625	964	661
Oregon	3,302	1,811	1,491	1,199	599	600	2,103	1,221	882
California	10,113	5,483	4,630	1,464	772	692	8,649	4,711	3,938

ILLITERACY.

TABLE 35.—ILLITERATE NATIVE WHITE POPULATION OF NATIVE PARENTAGE 10 YEARS OF AGE AND OVER, CLASSIFIED BY SEX AND DEGREE OF ILLITERACY, BY STATES AND TERRITORIES: 1890.

STATES AND TERRITORIES.	AGGREGATE.			NUMBER WHO CAN READ BUT CAN NOT WRITE.			NUMBER WHO CAN NEITHER READ NOR WRITE.		
	Total.	Males.	Females.	Total.	Males.	Females.	Total.	Males.	Females.
The United States	1,890,723	888,415	1,002,308	536,444	218,416	318,028	1,354,279	669,999	684,280
North Atlantic division	167,036	79,607	88,079	52,730	19,091	33,639	114,956	60,516	54,440
Maine	7,438	4,464	2,974	1,736	929	807	5,702	3,535	2,167
New Hampshire	2,332	1,437	895	570	318	252	1,762	1,110	643
Vermont	3,395	2,195	1,200	862	527	335	2,533	1,668	865
Massachusetts	4,228	2,273	1,955	906	428	478	3,322	1,845	1,477
Rhode Island	1,646	820	826	489	217	272	1,157	603	554
Connecticut	2,553	1,465	1,088	731	398	333	1,822	1,067	755
New York	36,739	20,652	16,087	10,157	4,984	5,173	26,582	15,668	10,914
New Jersey	17,309	9,076	8,233	5,095	2,171	2,924	12,214	6,905	5,309
Pennsylvania	92,046	37,225	54,821	32,184	9,119	23,065	59,862	28,106	31,756
South Atlantic division	564,502	259,315	305,187	142,867	55,860	87,007	421,635	203,455	218,180
Delaware	5,830	2,926	2,913	825	327	498	5,014	2,599	2,415
Maryland	28,907	14,511	14,396	5,971	2,326	3,645	22,936	12,185	10,751
District of Columbia	1,596	800	796	277	112	165	1,319	688	631
Virginia	102,660	50,429	52,240	23,025	9,573	13,452	79,644	40,856	38,788
West Virginia	64,017	29,218	34,799	20,899	8,263	12,636	43,118	20,955	22,163
North Carolina	173,129	75,402	97,727	46,842	17,041	29,801	126,287	58,361	67,926
South Carolina	58,782	27,312	31,470	12,698	5,293	7,405	46,084	22,019	24,065
Georgia	113,384	51,289	62,095	29,193	11,642	17,551	84,191	39,647	44,544
Florida	16,179	7,428	8,751	3,137	1,283	1,854	13,042	6,145	6,897
North Central division	366,492	179,435	187,057	125,587	52,425	73,162	240,905	127,010	113,895
Ohio	70,796	33,659	37,137	24,567	9,413	15,154	46,229	24,246	21,983
Indiana	71,848	33,829	38,019	24,205	9,436	14,769	47,643	24,393	23,250
Illinois	55,930	27,036	28,894	18,503	7,568	10,935	37,427	19,468	17,959
Michigan	16,627	9,497	7,130	5,195	2,746	2,449	11,432	6,751	4,681
Wisconsin	5,227	2,905	2,322	1,627	791	836	3,600	2,114	1,486
Minnesota	2,466	1,523	943	636	342	294	1,830	1,181	649
Iowa	16,388	8,313	8,075	6,242	2,571	3,671	10,146	5,742	4,404
Missouri	105,477	51,343	54,134	36,240	15,762	20,478	69,237	35,581	33,656
North Dakota	295	155	140	81	41	40	214	114	100
South Dakota	934	549	385	310	148	162	624	401	223
Nebraska	5,744	3,166	2,578	2,186	1,089	1,097	3,558	2,077	1,481
Kansas	14,760	7,460	7,300	5,795	2,518	3,277	8,965	4,942	4,023
South Central division	729,468	342,305	387,163	205,156	86,325	118,831	524,312	255,980	268,332
Kentucky	175,308	83,470	91,838	49,186	21,065	28,121	126,122	62,405	63,717
Tennessee	169,089	75,116	93,973	53,850	20,495	33,355	115,239	54,621	60,618
Alabama	105,304	48,519	56,875	27,906	11,577	16,329	77,488	36,942	40,546
Mississippi	44,284	21,297	22,987	12,271	5,552	6,719	32,013	15,745	16,268
Louisiana	68,668	33,058	35,605	6,535	3,093	3,442	62,128	29,965	32,163
Texas	74,637	38,597	36,040	23,810	11,543	12,267	50,827	27,054	23,773
Oklahoma	1,251	697	554	437	235	202	814	462	352
Arkansas	90,842	41,551	49,291	31,161	12,765	18,396	59,681	28,786	30,895
Western division	62,575	27,753	34,822	10,104	4,715	5,389	52,471	23,038	29,433
Montana	705	481	224	174	108	66	531	373	158
Wyoming	275	182	93	66	42	24	209	140	69
Colorado	8,610	4,228	4,382	1,126	600	526	7,484	3,628	3,856
New Mexico	38,484	14,945	23,539	5,126	2,150	2,976	33,358	12,795	20,563
Arizona	940	492	448	146	69	77	794	423	371
Utah	1,150	578	572	420	190	230	730	388	342
Nevada	121	87	34	23	19	4	98	68	30
Idaho	631	379	252	247	138	109	384	241	143
Washington	1,882	1,059	823	671	341	330	1,211	718	493
Oregon	2,824	1,553	1,271	1,043	509	534	1,781	1,044	737
California	6,053	2,769	3,284	1,062	549	513	5,891	3,220	2,671

200

STATISTICS OF POPULATION.

TABLE 36.—ILLITERATE NATIVE WHITE POPULATION OF FOREIGN PARENTAGE 10 YEARS OF AGE AND OVER, CLASSIFIED BY SEX AND DEGREE OF ILLITERACY, BY STATES AND TERRITORIES: 1890.

STATES AND TERRITORIES.	AGGREGATE.			NUMBER WHO CAN READ BUT CAN NOT WRITE.			NUMBER WHO CAN NEITHER READ NOR WRITE.		
	Total.	Males.	Females.	Total.	Males.	Females.	Total.	Males.	Females.
The United States	174,280	90,993	84,287	43,383	19,940	23,443	130,897	70,053	60,844
North Atlantic division	62,211	32,561	29,650	15,778	7,273	8,505	46,433	25,288	21,145
Maine	4,005	2,372	1,633	662	328	334	3,343	2,044	1,300
New Hampshire	1,347	726	621	219	116	103	1,128	610	518
Vermont	3,816	2,169	1,647	678	347	331	3,138	1,822	1,316
Massachusetts	5,499	2,423	3,076	1,105	418	687	4,394	2,005	2,389
Rhode Island	2,441	1,172	1,269	836	367	469	1,605	805	800
Connecticut	1,747	869	878	513	241	272	1,234	628	606
New York	20,623	10,904	9,719	4,600	2,189	2,411	16,023	8,715	7,308
New Jersey	4,042	2,146	1,896	1,442	730	712	2,600	1,416	1,184
Pennsylvania	18,691	9,780	8,911	5,723	2,537	3,186	12,968	7,243	5,725
South Atlantic division	7,397	3,709	3,688	2,037	865	1,172	5,360	2,844	2,516
Delaware	229	123	106	58	31	27	171	92	79
Maryland	3,198	1,542	1,656	776	292	484	2,422	1,250	1,172
District of Columbia	207	95	112	57	22	35	150	73	77
Virginia	596	343	253	155	72	83	441	271	170
West Virginia	1,403	689	714	490	211	279	913	478	435
North Carolina	416	209	207	139	64	75	277	145	132
South Carolina	281	155	126	81	47	34	200	108	93
Georgia	561	266	295	186	79	107	375	187	188
Florida	506	287	219	95	47	48	411	240	171
North Central division	69,836	35,842	33,994	19,981	9,055	10,926	49,855	26,787	23,068
Ohio	11,877	5,529	6,348	3,944	1,480	2,464	7,933	4,049	3,884
Indiana	6,790	3,276	3,514	2,197	857	1,340	4,593	2,419	2,174
Illinois	8,450	4,352	4,098	2,315	1,059	1,256	6,135	3,293	2,842
Michigan	10,380	6,069	4,329	2,616	1,471	1,145	7,773	4,598	3,175
Wisconsin	10,386	5,410	4,976	2,453	1,256	1,197	7,933	4,154	3,779
Minnesota	4,646	2,392	2,254	1,329	648	681	3,317	1,744	1,573
Iowa	4,261	2,215	2,046	1,359	582	777	2,902	1,633	1,269
Missouri	7,461	3,684	3,777	2,180	956	1,224	5,281	2,728	2,553
North Dakota	634	327	307	182	87	95	452	240	212
South Dakota	877	458	419	258	134	124	619	324	295
Nebraska	1,668	900	768	447	238	209	1,221	662	559
Kansas	2,307	1,290	1,167	701	287	414	1,696	943	753
South Central division	25,467	12,739	12,728	3,676	1,719	1,957	21,791	11,020	10,771
Kentucky	2,851	1,486	1,365	733	342	391	2,118	1,144	974
Tennessee	1,229	633	596	382	164	218	847	469	378
Alabama	841	399	442	244	101	143	507	298	290
Mississippi	703	363	340	185	95	90	518	268	250
Louisiana	3,350	1,685	1,665	424	194	230	2,926	1,491	1,435
Texas	15,102	7,476	7,715	1,302	617	685	13,800	6,859	7,031
Oklahoma	91	48	43	28	13	15	63	35	28
Arkansas	1,210	649	561	378	193	185	832	456	376
Western division	9,369	5,142	4,227	1,911	1,028	883	7,458	4,114	3,344
Montana	315	205	110	71	41	30	244	164	80
Wyoming	152	83	69	46	24	22	106	59	47
Colorado	625	356	269	161	97	64	464	259	205
New Mexico	1,581	776	805	338	122	216	1,243	654	589
Arizona	1,116	609	507	99	48	51	1,017	561	456
Utah	1,069	610	459	360	217	143	709	393	316
Nevada	52	35	17	16	10	6	36	25	11
Idaho	236	146	90	91	61	30	145	85	60
Washington	585	350	235	171	104	67	414	246	168
Oregon	478	258	220	156	81	75	322	177	145
California	3,160	1,714	1,446	402	223	179	2,758	1,491	1,267

ILLITERACY.

201

TABLE 37.—ILLITERATE FOREIGN WHITE POPULATION 10 YEARS OF AGE AND OVER, CLASSIFIED BY SEX AND DEGREE OF ILLITERACY, BY STATES AND TERRITORIES: 1890.

STATES AND TERRITORIES.	AGGREGATE.			NUMBER WHO CAN READ BUT CAN NOT WRITE.			NUMBER WHO CAN NEITHER READ NOR WRITE.		
	Total.	Males.	Females.	Total.	Males.	Females.	Total.	Males.	Females.
The United States..........	1,147,571	539,314	608,257	222,654	84,361	138,293	924,917	454,953	469,964
North Atlantic division...........	580,194	270,504	309,690	91,139	33,468	57,671	489,055	237,036	252,019
Maine	17,665	8,828	8,837	2,604	1,147	1,457	15,061	7,681	7,380
New Hampshire..................	17,601	9,405	8,256	2,408	1,055	1,353	15,253	8,350	6,903
Vermont......................	10,775	5,758	5,017	1,518	687	831	9,257	5,071	4,186
Massachusetts................	101,715	41,137	60,578	14,432	4,466	9,966	87,283	36,671	50,612
Rhode Island	22,268	9,756	12,512	4,605	1,584	3,021	17,663	8,172	9,491
Connecticut	26,236	12,074	14,162	4,478	1,688	2,790	21,758	10,386	11,372
New York	198,186	87,254	110,882	29,099	10,215	18,884	169,037	77,039	91,998
New Jersey	41,812	18,879	22,933	9,618	3,641	5,977	32,194	15,238	16,956
Pennsylvania................	143,926	77,413	66,513	22,377	8,985	13,392	121,549	68,428	53,121
South Atlantic division................	24,053	10,922	13,131	4,057	1,525	2,532	19,996	9,397	10,599
Delaware	2,118	978	1,140	307	112	195	1,811	866	945
Maryland.....................	12,548	5,376	7,172	2,016	662	1,354	10,532	4,714	5,818
District of Columbia	1,692	342	1,350	287	70	217	1,405	272	1,133
Virginia.....................	1,793	1,182	611	271	171	100	1,522	1,011	511
West Virginia................	2,768	1,432	1,336	577	242	335	2,191	1,190	1,001
North Carolina	177	115	62	42	21	21	135	94	41
South Carolina	380	185	195	57	28	29	323	157	166
Georgia......................	746	372	374	127	50	77	619	322	297
Florida	1,831	940	891	373	169	204	1,458	771	687
North Central division................	413,515	186,900	226,615	111,314	41,865	69,449	302,201	145,035	157,166
Ohio.........................	49,571	21,943	27,628	10,902	4,089	6,813	38,669	17,854	20,815
Indiana......................	15,696	6,711	8,985	4,095	1,462	2,633	11,601	5,249	6,352
Illinois	75,839	33,087	42,752	15,841	5,911	9,930	59,998	27,176	32,822
Michigan.....................	64,060	33,521	30,539	13,657	5,994	7,663	50,403	27,527	22,876
Wisconsin....................	67,371	30,286	37,085	19,437	7,378	12,059	47,934	22,908	25,026
Minnesota....................	49,854	21,554	28,300	20,012	7,039	12,973	29,842	14,515	15,327
Iowa.........................	29,179	12,434	16,745	9,777	3,423	6,354	19,402	9,011	10,391
Missouri.....................	20,868	8,819	12,049	4,454	1,685	2,769	16,414	7,134	9,280
North Dakota................	6,599	3,047	3,552	2,705	1,017	1,688	3,894	2,030	1,864
South Dakota................	7,753	3,591	4,162	2,947	1,113	1,834	4,806	2,478	2,328
Nebraska.....................	14,163	6,483	7,680	3,578	1,389	2,189	10,585	5,094	5,491
Kansas	12,562	5,424	7,138	3,909	1,365	2,544	8,653	4,059	4,594
South Central division................	62,096	31,037	31,059	5,679	2,809	3,870	56,417	28,728	27,689
Kentucky	5,692	2,402	3,290	1,138	411	727	4,554	1,991	2,563
Tennessee	1,851	882	969	331	144	187	1,520	738	782
Alabama	1,100	631	469	196	98	98	904	533	371
Mississippi	768	443	325	138	71	67	630	372	258
Louisiana....................	8,926	4,514	4,412	704	224	480	8,222	4,290	3,932
Texas........................	42,560	21,517	21,043	2,906	1,225	1,681	39,654	20,292	19,362
Oklahoma	161	79	82	38	17	21	123	62	61
Arkansas.....................	1,038	569	469	228	119	109	810	450	360
Western division................	67,713	39,951	27,762	10,465	5,194	5,271	57,248	34,757	22,491
Montana......................	3,212	2,267	945	549	361	188	2,663	1,906	757
Wyoming......................	981	634	347	226	106	120	755	528	227
Colorado.....................	6,239	4,004	2,235	1,046	560	486	5,193	3,444	1,749
New Mexico	3,200	1,685	1,515	365	155	210	2,835	1,530	1,305
Arizona......................	6,900	3,614	3,286	370	150	220	6,530	3,464	3,066
Utah.........................	5,188	2,007	3,181	1,783	559	1,224	3,405	1,448	1,957
Nevada.......................	1,183	843	340	171	120	51	1,012	723	289
Idaho........................	1,252	807	445	267	131	136	985	676	309
Washington	5,794	3,877	1,917	1,120	664	456	4,674	3,213	1,461
Oregon	3,644	2,220	1,424	865	532	333	2,779	1,688	1,091
California...................	30,120	17,993	12,127	3,703	1,856	1,847	26,417	16,137	10,280

STATISTICS OF POPULATION.

.202

TABLE 38.—ILLITERATE COLORED POPULATION (a) 10 YEARS OF AGE AND OVER, CLASSIFIED BY SEX AND DEGREE OF ILLITERACY, BY STATES AND TERRITORIES: 1890.

STATES AND TERRITORIES.	AGGREGATE.			NUMBER WHO CAN READ BUT CAN NOT WRITE.			NUMBER WHO CAN NEITHER READ NOR WRITE.		
	Total.	Males.	Females.	Total.	Males.	Females.	Total.	Males.	Females.
The United States	3,112,128	1,490,500	1,621,628	365,372	180,252	185,120	2,746,756	1,310,248	1,436,508
North Atlantic division	49,898	24,514	25,384	9,737	4,057	5,680	40,161	20,457	19,704
Maine	479	268	211	53	24	29	426	244	182
New Hampshire	136	75	61	24	9	15	112	66	46
Vermont	168	108	60	29	13	16	139	95	44
Massachusetts	3,026	1,515	1,511	561	218	343	2,465	1,297	1,168
Rhode Island	1,170	492	678	310	105	205	860	387	473
Connecticut	1,658	825	833	402	161	241	1,256	664	592
New York	11,413	5,633	5,780	2,215	893	1,322	9,198	4,740	4,458
New Jersey	11,158	5,312	5,846	2,375	998	1,377	8,783	4,314	4,469
Pennsylvania	20,690	10,286	10,404	3,768	1,636	2,132	16,922	8,650	8,272
South Atlantic division	1,385,936	652,150	733,786	151,730	74,263	77,467	1,234,206	577,887	656,319
Delaware	10,692	5,247	5,445	1,219	522	697	9,473	4,725	4,748
Maryland	80,723	38,097	42,626	9,786	4,524	5,262	70,937	33,573	37,364
District of Columbia	21,389	8,584	12,805	2,491	999	1,492	18,898	7,585	11,313
Virginia	260,678	125,089	135,589	24,133	11,743	12,390	236,545	113,346	123,199
West Virginia	10,992	6,240	4,752	1,642	853	789	9,350	5,387	3,963
North Carolina	235,981	108,780	127,201	29,121	13,153	15,968	206,860	95,627	111,233
South Carolina	301,262	139,468	161,794	34,007	17,049	16,958	267,255	122,419	144,836
Georgia	404,015	193,017	210,998	40,853	21,191	19,662	363,162	171,826	191,336
Florida	60,204	27,628	32,576	8,478	4,229	4,249	51,726	23,399	28,327
North Central division	114,425	55,616	58,809	18,716	8,877	9,839	95,709	46,739	48,970
Ohio	17,599	8,793	8,806	3,463	1,571	1,892	14,136	7,222	6,914
Indiana	11,495	5,689	5,806	1,955	940	1,015	9,540	4,749	4,791
Illinois	12,415	6,073	6,342	2,164	1,050	1,114	10,251	5,023	5,228
Michigan	4,838	2,435	2,403	731	355	376	4,107	2,080	2,027
Wisconsin	1,761	916	845	103	47	56	1,658	869	789
Minnesota	1,091	524	567	93	47	46	998	477	521
Iowa	2,233	1,163	1,070	422	188	234	1,811	975	836
Missouri	47,562	22,684	24,878	7,372	3,517	3,855	40,190	19,167	21,023
North Dakota	215	121	94	12	6	6	203	115	88
South Dakota	410	218	192	27	24	3	383	194	189
Nebraska	2,446	1,204	1,242	259	139	120	2,187	1,065	1,122
Kansas	12,360	5,796	6,564	2,115	993	1,122	10,245	4,803	5,442
South Central division	1,501,840	712,674	789,166	182,227	90,944	91,283	1,319,613	621,730	697,883
Kentucky	110,530	54,641	55,889	13,755	6,582	7,173	96,775	48,059	48,716
Tennessee	167,971	79,238	88,733	26,725	12,775	13,950	141,246	66,463	74,783
Alabama	331,200	156,813	174,387	33,868	17,295	16,573	297,332	139,518	157,814
Mississippi	314,858	148,658	166,200	41,015	20,838	20,177	273,843	127,820	146,023
Louisiana	283,245	133,590	149,655	23,413	12,054	11,359	259,832	121,536	138,296
Texas	176,484	84,262	92,222	22,750	11,164	11,586	153,734	73,098	80,636
Oklahoma	897	462	435	96	48	48	801	414	387
Arkansas	116,655	55,010	61,645	20,605	10,188	10,417	96,050	44,822	51,228
Western division	60,029	45,546	14,483	2,962	2,111	851	57,067	43,435	13,632
Montana	1,652	1,377	275	60	42	18	1,592	1,335	257
Wyoming	222	171	51	28	16	12	194	155	39
Colorado	1,706	1,220	486	219	123	96	1,487	1,097	390
New Mexico	6,805	3,563	3,242	805	418	387	6,000	3,145	2,855
Arizona	1,829	1,312	517	50	36	14	1,779	1,276	503
Utah	825	583	242	42	31	11	783	552	231
Nevada	3,541	2,162	1,379	51	44	7	3,490	2,118	1,372
Idaho	1,106	1,004	102	40	29	11	1,066	975	91
Washington	3,517	2,353	1,164	149	116	33	3,368	2,237	1,131
Oregon	3,157	2,603	554	283	247	36	2,874	2,356	518
California	35,669	29,198	6,471	1,235	1,009	226	34,434	28,189	6,245

a Persons of negro descent, Chinese, Japanese, and civilized Indians.

ILLITERACY.

203

TABLE 39.—ILLITERATE NEGRO POPULATION (a) 10 YEARS OF AGE AND OVER, CLASSIFIED BY SEX AND DEGREE OF ILLITERACY, BY STATES AND TERRITORIES: 1890.

STATES AND TERRITORIES.	AGGREGATE.			NUMBER WHO CAN READ BUT CAN NOT WRITE.			NUMBER WHO CAN NEITHER READ NOR WRITE.		
	Total.	Males.	Females.	Total.	Males.	Females.	Total.	Males.	Females.
The United States..........	3,042,668	1,438,923	1,603,745	362,654	178,208	184,446	2,680,014	1,260,715	1,419,299
North Atlantic division...............	46,756	21,679	25,077	9,560	3,916	5,644	37,196	17,763	19,433
Maine.................	155	84	71	46	21	25	109	63	46
New Hampshire	115	55	60	24	9	15	91	46	45
Vermont.................	149	92	57	28	12	16	121	80	41
Massachusetts...............	2,607	1,106	1,501	533	195	338	2,074	911	1,163
Rhode Island	1,106	446	660	303	99	204	803	347	456
Connecticut	1,532	714	818	394	157	237	1,138	557	581
New York	10,017	4,334	5,683	2,140	833	1,307	7,877	3,501	4,376
New Jersey...............	10,860	5,021	5,839	2,355	980	1,375	8,505	4,041	4,464
Pennsylvania...............	20,215	9,827	10,388	3,737	1,610	2,127	16,478	8,217	8,261
South Atlantic division	1,384,632	651,436	733,196	151,634	74,215	77,419	1,232,998	577,221	655,777
Delaware...............	10,675	5,230	5,445	1,217	520	697	9,458	4,710	4,748
Maryland...............	80,644	38,622	42,022	9,778	4,517	5,261	70,866	33,505	37,361
District of Columbia	21,346	8,545	12,801	2,490	999	1,491	18,856	7,546	11,310
Virginia...............	260,599	125,041	135,558	24,115	11,736	12,379	236,484	113,305	123,179
West Virginia...............	10,985	6,233	4,752	1,640	851	789	9,345	5,382	3,963
North Carolina...............	235,238	108,452	126,786	29,069	13,132	15,937	206,169	95,320	110,849
South Carolina...............	301,169	139,428	161,741	34,002	17,048	16,954	267,167	122,380	144,787
Georgia...............	403,925	192,952	210,973	40,846	21,184	19,662	363,079	171,768	191,311
Florida	60,051	27,533	32,518	8,477	4,228	4,249	51,574	23,305	28,269
North Central division...............	107,395	51,934	55,461	18,456	8,729	9,727	88,939	43,205	45,734
Ohio...............	17,496	8,704	8,792	3,453	1,565	1,888	14,043	7,139	6,904
Indiana...............	11,407	5,637	5,770	1,939	933	1,006	9,468	4,704	4,764
Illinois...............	12,111	5,792	6,319	2,149	1,036	1,113	9,962	4,756	5,206
Michigan...............	2,306	1,241	1,065	604	286	318	1,702	955	747
Wisconsin...............	379	205	174	83	34	49	296	171	125
Minnesota...............	386	202	184	78	40	38	308	162	146
Iowa...............	2,177	1,118	1,059	419	185	234	1,758	933	825
Missouri...............	47,333	22,471	24,862	7,366	3,512	3,854	39,967	18,959	21,008
North Dakota...............	83	49	34	12	6	6	71	43	28
South Dakota...............	91	75	16	16	16	....	75	59	16
Nebraska...............	1,367	711	656	237	131	106	1,130	580	550
Kansas...............	12,250	5,729	6,530	2,100	985	1,115	10,159	4,744	5,415
South Central division...............	1,498,584	710,783	787,801	182,111	90,883	91,228	1,316,473	619,900	696,573
Kentucky...............	110,507	54,623	55,884	13,753	6,581	7,172	96,754	48,042	48,712
Tennessee...............	167,881	79,186	88,695	26,712	12,771	13,941	141,169	66,415	74,754
Alabama...............	330,703	156,585	174,118	33,849	17,284	16,565	296,854	139,301	157,553
Mississippi...............	313,573	148,003	165,570	40,980	20,817	20,163	272,593	127,186	145,407
Louisiana...............	282,670	133,222	149,448	23,397	12,041	11,356	259,273	121,181	138,092
Texas...............	175,882	83,835	92,047	22,729	11,156	11,573	153,153	72,679	80,474
Oklahoma...............	881	447	434	95	48	47	786	399	387
Arkansas...............	116,487	54,882	61,605	20,596	10,185	10,411	95,891	44,697	51,194
Western division	5,301	3,091	2,210	893	465	428	4,408	2,626	1,782
Montana...............	153	93	60	33	17	16	120	76	44
Wyoming...............	147	103	44	23	14	9	124	89	35
Colorado...............	940	498	442	186	94	92	754	404	350
New Mexico...............	722	412	310	164	80	84	558	332	226
Arizona...............	245	192	53	37	25	12	208	167	41
Utah...............	132	86	46	16	10	6	116	76	40
Nevada...............	86	41	45	10	6	4	76	35	41
Idaho...............	42	19	23	11	4	7	31	15	16
Washington...............	255	165	90	40	26	14	215	139	76
Oregon...............	171	112	59	38	21	17	133	91	42
California...............	2,408	1,370	1,038	335	168	167	2,073	1,202	871

a Includes all persons of negro descent.

204

STATISTICS OF POPULATION.

TABLE 40.—TOTAL ILLITERATE POPULATION 10 YEARS OF AGE AND OVER,

	STATES AND TERRITORIES.	10 TO 14 YEARS.			15 TO 19 YEARS.			20 TO 24 YEARS.			25 TO 34 YEARS.		
		Total.	Males.	Females.	Total.	Males.	Females.	Total.	Males.	Females.	Total.	Males.	Females.
1	The United States...	731,688	396,489	335,109	653,554	351,336	302,218	671,667	326,303	345,364	1,172,057	556,284	615,773
2	North Atlantic division......	29,810	16,921	12,889	55,215	31,461	23,754	82,071	45,813	37,158	174,083	95,358	78,725
3	Maine................	1,517	856	661	3,340	1,941	1,399	3,567	2,039	1,528	5,476	3,114	2,362
4	New Hampshire..........	1,090	594	496	2,705	1,529	1,176	2,986	1,864	1,122	4,191	2,456	1,735
5	Vermont..............	768	453	385	1,040	600	457	1,692	1,018	675	3,104	1,871	1,233
6	Massachusetts..........	1,591	786	805	6,654	3,567	3,087	10,841	5,704	5,137	21,506	10,477	11,029
7	Rhode Island..........	1,267	700	567	2,412	1,354	1,058	2,750	1,518	1,232	4,917	2,336	2,581
8	Connecticut............	799	456	343	2,199	1,200	999	3,133	1,773	1,360	6,143	3,405	2,738
9	New York..............	7,669	4,085	3,584	16,115	8,147	7,968	25,887	12,708	13,179	55,077	29,600	26,377
10	New Jersey............	3,056	1,683	1,373	4,300	2,518	1,782	6,713	3,690	3,023	14,753	7,868	6,885
11	Pennsylvania..........	12,053	7,302	4,751	16,150	10,322	5,828	25,401	15,499	9,902	58,016	34,231	23,785
12	South Atlantic division........	300,758	162,561	138,197	241,366	128,231	113,135	218,949	100,641	118,308	350,460	150,000	200,460
13	Delaware.............	1,677	890	787	1,520	863	657	1,715	916	799	3,520	1,793	1,736
14	Maryland.............	10,981	5,944	5,037	11,057	6,127	4,930	11,002	5,572	5,430	22,018	10,185	11,833
15	District of Columbia......	1,232	716	516	1,490	753	737	1,902	768	1,134	4,046	1,417	2,629
16	Virginia..............	50,116	27,566	22,550	40,539	23,195	17,344	36,746	17,732	19,014	62,608	27,596	35,012
17	West Virginia..........	10,582	5,631	4,951	8,093	4,677	3,416	8,491	4,606	3,885	13,869	6,587	7,282
18	North Carolina...........	67,833	36,285	31,548	50,167	26,592	23,575	42,353	18,125	24,228	69,406	28,085	41,321
19	South Carolina..........	64,725	34,606	30,119	50,584	25,537	25,047	43,162	18,775	24,387	62,298	25,488	36,810
20	Georgia..............	84,731	46,058	38,673	70,246	36,927	33,319	63,612	29,434	34,178	97,040	42,216	54,833
21	Florida..............	8,881	4,865	4,016	7,670	3,560	4,110	9,966	4,713	5,253	15,646	6,633	9,013
22	North Central division........	47,883	26,299	21,584	54,943	32,296	22,647	71,969	39,804	32,165	107,466	88,235	79,231
23	Ohio.................	4,270	2,240	2,030	7,050	4,079	2,971	10,455	5,961	4,494	25,168	13,774	11,394
24	Indiana..............	4,851	2,763	2,088	5,532	3,372	2,160	6,991	4,012	2,979	16,757	8,963	7,794
25	Illinois..............	5,027	2,662	2,365	7,743	4,465	3,278	12,136	6,307	5,829	29,504	15,102	14,402
26	Michigan.............	4,030	2,296	1,734	5,803	3,545	2,258	7,842	4,779	3,063	18,560	10,841	7,719
27	Wisconsin.............	3,101	1,629	1,472	4,876	2,455	1,921	5,376	2,964	2,412	13,625	6,975	6,650
28	Minnesota.............	2,486	1,344	1,142	2,796	1,498	1,298	3,996	2,211	1,785	9,574	4,941	4,633
29	Iowa................	1,672	946	726	2,080	1,354	726	3,018	1,758	1,260	7,061	3,800	3,261
30	Missouri..............	17,414	9,625	7,789	15,128	8,978	6,150	16,195	8,602	7,593	33,274	16,624	16,650
31	North Dakota...........	779	411	368	487	256	231	646	342	304	1,430	760	670
32	South Dakota..........	857	447	410	519	284	235	748	435	313	1,717	903	814
33	Nebraska.............	1,452	813	639	1,480	805	675	2,020	1,056	964	4,401	2,361	2,040
34	Kansas...............	1,944	1,123	821	1,949	1,205	744	2,546	1,377	1,169	6,835	3,131	3,204
35	South Central division........	341,275	184,550	156,725	287,873	151,813	136,060	276,135	127,228	148,907	432,120	192,522	239,598
36	Kentucky.............	34,364	18,766	15,598	32,157	18,191	13,966	33,431	16,761	16,670	56,711	27,029	29,682
37	Tennessee............	44,386	24,214	20,172	38,713	21,215	17,498	37,505	17,531	19,974	62,391	26,934	35,457
38	Alabama.............	74,036	39,901	34,135	59,341	31,017	28,324	53,546	24,009	29,537	78,305	33,574	44,731
39	Mississippi...........	48,475	26,440	22,035	45,928	23,926	22,002	44,973	20,147	24,826	69,075	29,891	39,184
40	Louisiana............	62,282	32,512	29,770	52,312	25,687	26,625	46,779	21,162	25,617	63,814	29,014	34,800
41	Texas...............	43,293	24,037	19,256	34,226	18,678	15,548	36,344	17,221	19,123	62,060	29,052	33,008
42	Oklahoma............	565	336	229	173	119	54	124	65	59	306	142	164
43	Arkansas.............	33,874	18,344	15,530	25,023	12,980	12,043	23,433	10,332	13,101	39,458	16,886	22,572
44	Western division............	11,962	6,158	5,804	14,157	7,535	6,622	21,643	12,817	8,826	47,919	30,169	17,750
45	Montana.............	296	171	125	335	228	107	789	580	209	1,847	1,436	411
46	Wyoming.............	168	98	70	112	70	42	154	124	30	416	305	111
47	Colorado.............	916	451	465	1,116	541	575	2,036	1,149	887	4,753	2,862	1,871
48	New Mexico...........	4,333	2,012	2,321	5,024	1,886	3,138	6,364	2,451	3,913	10,778	4,037	6,741
49	Arizona..............	1,174	646	528	1,184	614	570	1,323	798	525	2,738	1,632	1,106
50	Utah................	925	504	421	549	326	223	566	341	225	1,306	680	626
51	Nevada..............	291	143	148	379	225	154	483	288	195	1,124	741	383
52	Idaho...............	315	198	117	159	109	50	223	174	49	600	446	154
53	Washington...........	650	387	263	665	427	238	1,386	981	405	3,261	2,332	929
54	Oregon..............	585	332	253	463	302	161	884	603	281	2,425	1,780	645
55	California............	2,309	1,216	1,093	4,171	2,807	1,364	7,435	5,328	2,107	18,671	13,898	4,773

ILLITERACY.

CLASSIFIED BY SEX AND AGE PERIODS, BY STATES AND TERRITORIES: 1890.

35 TO 44 YEARS.			45 TO 54 YEARS.			55 TO 64 YEARS.			65 YEARS AND OVER.			AGE UNKNOWN.			
Total.	Males.	Females.	Total.	Males.	Females.	Total.	Males.	Females.	Total.	Males.	Females.	Total.	Males.	Females.	
1,056,693	476,807	579,886	871,205	393,420	477,785	589,219	259,859	329,360	535,955	224,653	311,302	42,664	23,071	19,593	1
155,986	75,252	80,734	144,333	60,469	83,864	108,299	40,593	67,706	103,296	37,599	65,697	5,996	3,720	2,276	2
4,763	2,552	2,211	4,021	2,073	1,948	3,205	1,539	1,666	3,538	1,718	1,820	160	100	60	3
3,440	1,826	1,614	3,030	1,460	1,570	2,169	1,019	1,150	1,738	812	926	127	83	44	4
3,205	1,783	1,422	2,780	1,508	1,272	2,372	1,177	1,195	2,800	1,440	1,300	152	91	61	5
21,249	8,625	12,624	22,872	8,257	14,615	16,299	5,361	10,938	12,810	4,251	8,559	646	320	326	6
5,188	2,222	2,966	4,969	1,966	3,003	3,398	1,251	2,147	2,489	811	1,678	135	82	53	7
5,793	2,701	3,092	6,026	2,474	3,552	4,110	1,555	2,555	3,484	1,324	2,160	507	345	162	8
49,071	23,821	25,250	43,981	18,679	25,302	34,132	13,463	20,669	32,686	13,061	19,625	1,393	879	514	9
14,356	6,748	7,608	13,204	5,689	7,515	9,144	3,628	5,516	8,103	3,144	4,959	692	445	247	10
48,921	24,974	23,947	43,450	18,363	25,087	33,470	11,600	21,870	35,648	11,038	24,610	2,184	1,375	809	11
322,542	137,510	185,032	244,452	108,338	136,114	153,772	71,527	82,245	138,690	62,166	76,524	10,890	5,122	5,768	12
3,507	1,717	1,790	2,890	1,322	1,568	1,959	901	1,058	1,925	805	1,120	156	67	89	13
24,075	10,992	13,083	20,293	9,437	10,856	12,567	5,526	7,041	11,841	4,844	6,997	1,542	899	643	14
5,757	2,099	3,658	4,982	2,085	2,897	2,728	1,040	1,688	2,296	738	1,558	451	205	246	15
64,392	28,832	35,560	48,483	21,923	26,560	31,366	15,106	16,260	29,451	14,154	15,297	2,035	939	1,096	16
12,838	5,772	7,066	9,943	4,113	5,830	7,200	2,902	4,858	7,322	2,780	4,542	782	511	271	17
63,740	25,029	38,711	50,795	22,054	28,741	33,401	15,005	18,396	30,342	12,631	17,711	1,666	700	966	18
54,659	22,968	31,691	39,142	17,297	21,845	23,918	11,847	12,071	21,068	10,133	10,935	1,149	469	680	19
79,614	34,326	45,288	56,861	24,886	31,975	34,749	16,432	18,317	29,454	13,656	15,798	2,390	1,009	1,381	20
13,960	5,775	8,185	11,063	5,221	5,842	5,824	2,768	3,056	4,991	2,425	2,566	719	323	396	21
170,263	82,491	87,777	163,504	72,389	91,115	138,860	56,791	82,069	143,532	56,101	87,431	5,843	3,387	2,456	22
26,634	13,341	13,293	25,890	11,323	14,567	22,696	8,907	13,789	26,641	9,708	16,933	1,039	591	448	23
18,718	9,228	9,490	18,362	8,051	10,311	16,285	6,404	9,881	17,658	6,372	11,286	675	340	335	24
28,486	13,571	14,915	26,587	11,583	15,004	21,770	8,676	13,094	20,766	7,806	12,960	555	316	239	25
17,434	9,702	7,732	15,884	8,045	7,839	12,624	6,013	6,611	13,325	6,016	7,309	412	285	127	26
13,629	6,484	7,145	14,070	6,199	7,871	13,916	5,797	8,119	16,362	6,841	9,521	290	173	117	27
8,972	3,877	5,095	10,199	3,999	6,200	9,954	3,952	6,002	9,572	3,836	5,736	508	425	83	28
7,769	3,684	4,085	9,735	4,195	5,540	9,655	3,876	5,779	10,848	4,362	6,486	223	150	73	29
33,650	15,773	17,877	27,262	11,776	15,486	19,432	7,724	11,708	17,334	6,584	10,750	1,679	844	835	30
1,322	599	723	1,140	513	627	1,004	402	602	898	351	547	37	16	21	31
1,645	789	856	1,594	716	878	1,415	625	790	1,399	567	832	80	50	30	32
4,451	2,182	2,269	4,046	1,869	2,177	3,238	1,453	1,785	2,812	1,140	1,672	121	74	47	33
7,558	3,261	4,297	8,735	4,120	4,615	6,871	3,052	3,819	5,917	2,518	3,399	224	123	101	34
366,285	155,671	210,614	290,296	135,731	154,565	170,450	80,916	89,534	138,628	62,819	75,809	15,809	7,505	8,304	35
50,367	23,107	27,260	37,556	16,572	20,984	24,773	10,747	14,026	22,518	9,495	13,023	2,504	1,331	1,173	36
54,695	21,599	33,096	46,088	20,354	25,734	29,024	12,830	16,194	24,122	9,821	14,301	3,216	1,371	1,845	37
61,812	23,916	37,896	55,871	27,556	28,315	29,324	14,075	15,249	23,979	11,140	12,839	2,321	1,174	1,147	38
59,667	26,066	33,601	40,969	17,595	23,374	27,780	14,934	12,846	21,677	10,901	10,776	2,069	861	1,208	39
53,550	24,166	29,384	40,765	19,075	21,690	23,781	11,507	12,274	19,610	9,081	10,529	1,291	643	648	40
51,381	22,845	28,536	40,662	20,484	20,178	21,400	10,204	11,196	16,684	7,936	8,748	2,823	1,395	1,428	41
385	161	224	391	211	180	276	153	123	167	90	77	13	9	4	42
34,428	13,811	20,617	27,994	13,884	14,110	14,092	6,466	7,626	9,871	4,355	5,516	1,572	721	851	43
41,612	25,883	15,729	28,620	16,493	12,127	17,838	10,032	7,806	11,809	5,968	5,841	4,126	3,337	789	44
1,217	911	306	808	611	197	329	210	119	180	107	73	83	76	7	45
335	235	100	262	156	106	104	53	51	75	28	47	4	1	3	46
3,603	2,076	1,527	2,258	1,254	1,004	1,240	624	616	772	382	390	488	440	37	47
9,422	3,842	5,580	6,947	3,163	3,784	4,343	2,124	2,219	2,726	1,392	1,334	133	62	71	48
2,160	1,187	973	1,310	704	606	598	301	297	285	138	147	13	7	6	49
1,329	616	713	1,105	453	712	1,013	347	666	1,261	429	832	118	82	36	50
1,076	742	334	747	472	275	364	255	109	215	125	90	218	136	82	51
677	507	170	587	445	142	347	248	99	215	112	103	102	97	5	52
2,267	1,509	758	1,545	890	655	935	511	424	648	300	348	421	302	119	53
2,025	1,389	636	1,492	945	547	1,059	601	458	885	421	464	285	261	24	54
17,501	12,869	4,632	11,409	7,400	4,099	7,506	4,758	2,748	4,547	2,534	2,013	2,203	1,864	399	55

STATISTICS OF POPULATION.

TABLE **41.**—ILLITERATE WHITE POPULATION 10 YEARS OF AGE AND OVER,

	STATES AND TERRITORIES.	10 TO 14 YEARS.			15 TO 19 YEARS.			20 TO 24 YEARS.			25 TO 34 YEARS.		
		Total.	Males.	Females.	Total.	Males.	Females.	Total.	Males.	Females.	Total.	Males.	Females.
1	The United States...	316,498	174,256	142,242	277,613	155,457	122,156	303,247	157,733	145,514	602,977	306,139	296,838
2	North Atlantic division........	28,058	16,001	12,057	52,667	30,021	22,646	78,394	43,167	35,227	164,006	90,080	73,926
3	Maine....................	1,507	852	655	3,306	1,921	1,385	3,520	2,010	1,510	5,373	3,055	2,318
4	New Hampshire	1,004	600	404	2,669	1,500	1,172	2,973	1,856	1,117	4,175	2,447	1,728
5	Vermont	761	456	305	1,327	875	452	1,616	1,008	608	3,073	1,850	1,223
6	Massachusetts	1,550	766	784	6,518	3,477	3,041	10,608	5,555	5,053	20,847	10,090	10,757
7	Rhode Island.............	1,248	686	562	2,376	1,333	1,043	2,683	1,485	1,198	4,730	2,258	2,481
8	Connecticut	761	433	328	2,140	1,176	964	2,993	1,693	1,300	5,859	3,247	2,612
9	New York................	7,287	3,883	3,404	15,573	7,835	7,738	24,878	12,100	12,778	53,573	28,342	25,231
10	New Jersey	2,589	1,436	1,153	3,659	2,162	1,497	5,656	3,109	2,547	12,644	6,815	5,829
11	Pennsylvania	11,271	6,899	4,872	15,075	9,722	5,353	23,467	14,351	9,116	53,723	31,976	21,747
12	South Atlantic division........	97,857	53,900	43,957	65,905	36,583	29,322	57,934	28,230	29,704	106,701	48,702	57,999
13	Delaware.................	498	275	223	481	288	193	652	378	274	1,527	826	701
14	Maryland	3,176	1,809	1,367	3,353	1,928	1,425	3,491	1,894	1,597	7,404	3,802	3,602
15	District of Columbia......	181	119	62	160	96	64	212	101	111	401	167	234
16	Virginia.................	16,426	9,192	7,234	11,539	6,693	4,846	10,438	5,525	4,913	19,181	9,475	9,706
17	West Virginia............	9,613	5,100	4,513	6,909	3,856	3,053	6,853	3,445	3,408	11,804	5,439	6,365
18	North Carolina..........	30,018	16,232	13,786	19,461	10,491	8,970	16,582	7,525	9,057	31,313	13,431	17,882
19	South Carolina..........	13,157	7,231	5,926	8,135	4,431	3,704	6,461	3,075	3,386	10,517	4,724	5,793
20	Georgia	21,841	12,214	9,627	14,121	7,829	6,292	11,359	5,371	5,988	20,771	9,146	11,625
21	Florida	2,947	1,728	1,219	1,746	971	775	1,886	916	970	3,783	1,692	2,091
22	North Central division........	41,876	22,985	18,891	48,553	28,677	19,876	63,304	35,344	27,960	147,028	78,392	68,636
23	Ohio	3,847	2,029	1,818	6,396	3,704	2,692	9,390	5,367	4,023	22,318	12,306	10,012
24	Indiana	4,455	2,554	1,901	5,021	3,072	1,949	6,180	3,570	2,610	14,641	7,920	6,721
25	Illinois.................	4,613	2,448	2,165	7,220	4,148	3,072	11,301	5,882	5,419	27,482	14,134	13,348
26	Michigan	3,737	2,132	1,605	5,458	3,369	2,089	7,414	4,551	2,863	17,690	10,402	7,288
27	Wisconsin	2,992	1,571	1,421	4,243	2,390	1,853	5,211	2,880	2,331	13,305	6,794	6,511
28	Minnesota	2,389	1,289	1,100	2,717	1,466	1,251	3,903	2,162	1,741	9,373	4,837	4,536
29	Iowa....................	1,613	909	704	2,016	1,310	706	2,857	1,678	1,179	6,689	3,605	3,084
30	Missouri	13,770	7,603	6,170	11,651	7,014	4,637	11,972	6,454	5,518	24,100	12,325	11,775
31	North Dakota.............	753	392	361	468	245	223	616	321	295	1,387	736	651
32	South Dakota.............	829	433	396	503	275	228	707	412	295	1,627	852	775
33	Nebraska................	1,353	755	598	1,367	748	619	1,831	970	861	3,881	2,091	1,790
34	Kansas..................	1,516	870	646	1,493	936	557	1,922	1,097	825	4,535	2,390	2,145
35	South Central division........	139,441	76,632	62,809	100,253	55,169	45,084	88,217	42,737	45,480	153,322	71,587	81,735
36	Kentucky................	22,958	12,507	10,451	21,371	12,009	9,362	21,259	10,571	10,688	34,877	16,656	18,221
37	Tennessee...............	24,181	13,213	10,968	19,927	10,783	9,144	18,740	8,865	9,875	32,081	14,005	18,076
38	Alabama.................	23,203	12,774	10,429	13,816	7,535	6,281	10,719	5,005	5,714	19,397	8,668	10,729
39	Mississippi.............	8,013	4,292	3,721	5,669	3,279	2,390	4,662	2,315	2,347	8,677	4,174	4,503
40	Louisiana...............	16,859	8,847	8,012	12,093	6,249	5,844	9,491	4,589	4,952	15,150	7,467	7,683
41	Texas...................	24,748	13,891	10,857	15,563	8,821	6,742	13,823	7,055	6,768	25,662	13,015	12,647
42	Oklahoma................	500	289	211	146	103	43	91	50	41	189	100	89
43	Arkansas	18,379	10,219	8,160	11,668	6,390	5,278	9,432	4,337	5,095	17,289	7,502	9,787
44	Western division.............	9,266	4,738	4,528	10,235	5,007	5,228	15,398	8,255	7,143	31,920	17,378	14,542
45	Montana.................	250	138	112	211	138	73	610	425	185	1,351	1,009	342
46	Wyoming.................	162	95	67	108	67	41	135	109	26	340	249	91
47	Colorado................	897	438	459	1,067	504	563	1,866	1,019	847	4,278	2,538	1,740
48	New Mexico..............	3,526	1,618	1,908	4,211	1,498	2,713	5,388	1,945	3,443	9,330	3,246	6,084
49	Arizona.................	961	521	440	990	498	492	1,070	608	462	2,215	1,223	992
50	Utah....................	877	477	400	488	289	199	487	282	205	1,110	530	580
51	Nevada..................	20	11	9	64	50	14	116	88	28	325	254	71
52	Idaho	303	190	113	137	90	47	180	140	40	420	289	131
53	Washington..............	478	275	203	419	263	156	1,010	730	280	2,345	1,640	705
54	Oregon..................	490	281	209	325	205	120	588	375	213	1,407	893	514
55	California..............	1,302	694	608	2,215	1,405	810	3,948	2,534	1,414	8,799	5,507	3,292

ILLITERACY.

207

CLASSIFIED BY SEX AND AGE PERIODS, BY STATES AND TERRITORIES: 1890.

35 TO 44 YEARS.			45 TO 54 YEARS.			55 TO 64 YEARS.			65 YEARS AND OVER.			AGE UNKNOWN.			
Total.	Males.	Females.	Total.	Males.	Females.	Total.	Males.	Females.	Total.	Males.	Females.	Total.	Males.	Females.	
541,617	255,259	286,358	458,709	194,212	264,497	353,585	136,555	217,030	342,309	128,337	213,972	16,019	9,774	6,245	1
144,936	69,961	74,975	135,533	56,264	79,269	103,223	38,370	64,853	98,066	35,487	62,579	5,208	3,321	1,887	2
4,665	2,500	2,165	3,946	2,030	1,916	3,157	1,507	1,650	3,479	1,693	1,786	155	96	59	3
3,413	1,814	1,599	3,009	1,449	1,560	2,151	1,010	1,141	1,722	805	917	120	77	43	4
3,178	1,763	1,415	2,755	1,491	1,264	2,353	1,162	1,191	2,773	1,427	1,346	150	90	60	5
20,496	8,271	12,225	22,285	7,987	14,298	16,012	5,235	10,777	12,516	4,151	8,365	610	301	309	6
4,882	2,097	2,785	4,709	1,850	2,859	3,278	1,210	2,068	2,330	701	1,509	110	68	42	7
5,405	2,510	2,895	5,717	2,322	3,395	3,910	1,461	2,449	3,272	1,229	2,043	479	337	142	8
46,567	22,629	23,938	42,049	17,736	24,313	32,921	12,973	19,948	31,406	12,524	18,882	1,244	788	456	9
11,993	5,701	6,292	11,217	4,763	6,454	8,000	3,094	4,906	6,886	2,652	4,234	519	369	150	10
44,337	22,076	21,661	39,846	16,636	23,210	31,441	10,718	20,723	33,682	10,245	23,437	1,821	1,195	626	11
95,828	42,743	53,085	68,238	26,302	41,936	50,452	17,932	32,520	50,656	18,234	32,422	2,381	1,320	1,061	12
1,471	745	726	1,377	594	783	1,070	472	598	1,083	434	649	27	15	12	13
7,997	3,871	4,126	7,559	3,400	4,159	5,440	2,187	3,253	5,583	2,109	3,474	650	429	221	14
598	221	377	717	211	506	604	152	452	548	128	420	74	42	32	15
17,124	8,401	8,723	11,885	5,046	6,839	8,897	3,648	5,249	9,266	3,822	5,444	302	152	150	16
10,992	4,852	6,140	8,483	3,394	5,089	6,418	2,467	3,951	6,633	2,461	4,172	483	325	158	17
27,788	11,501	16,287	18,992	6,813	12,179	14,514	4,752	9,762	14,625	4,807	9,818	429	174	255	18
8,455	3,777	4,678	5,277	1,900	3,377	3,738	1,201	2,537	3,606	1,280	2,326	97	33	64	19
18,007	7,883	10,124	11,697	4,026	7,671	8,398	2,555	5,843	8,261	2,798	5,463	236	105	131	20
3,396	1,492	1,904	2,251	918	1,333	1,373	498	875	1,051	395	656	83	45	38	21
145,494	71,337	74,157	142,163	62,087	80,076	125,544	50,204	75,340	131,871	50,649	81,222	4,010	2,502	1,508	22
22,684	11,427	11,257	22,336	9,566	12,770	20,254	7,697	12,557	24,231	8,574	15,657	788	461	327	23
16,029	8,014	8,015	16,063	6,896	9,167	14,908	5,708	9,200	16,553	5,834	10,719	484	248	236	24
25,626	12,290	13,336	23,967	10,310	13,657	20,165	7,843	12,322	19,458	7,188	12,270	387	232	155	25
16,614	9,290	7,324	15,122	7,681	7,441	12,030	5,785	6,295	12,657	5,682	6,975	354	245	109	26
13,255	6,298	6,957	13,802	6,050	7,752	13,726	5,703	8,023	16,169	6,744	9,425	281	171	110	27
8,772	3,784	4,988	10,030	3,917	6,113	9,853	3,814	6,039	9,449	3,786	5,663	480	414	66	28
7,268	3,441	3,827	9,192	3,920	5,272	9,390	3,732	5,658	10,012	4,234	6,878	191	133	58	29
23,537	11,254	12,283	19,074	8,817	11,957	14,897	5,617	9,280	13,422	4,835	8,587	774	427	347	30
1,267	573	694	1,123	505	618	991	395	596	888	347	541	35	15	20	31
1,568	746	822	1,518	674	844	1,369	603	766	1,373	558	815	70	45	25	32
3,847	1,901	1,946	3,627	1,665	1,962	2,988	1,323	1,665	2,584	1,035	1,549	97	61	36	33
5,027	2,319	2,708	5,709	2,586	3,123	4,978	2,034	2,939	4,475	1,832	2,643	69	50	19	34
128,402	57,164	71,238	92,137	39,238	52,899	60,223	22,773	37,450	51,919	19,202	32,717	3,117	1,579	1,538	35
30,157	13,897	16,260	22,042	9,173	12,869	15,791	6,339	9,452	14,767	5,880	8,887	629	326	303	36
27,231	10,909	16,322	21,379	8,574	12,805	14,495	5,276	9,219	13,212	4,605	8,607	923	401	522	37
15,374	6,421	8,953	11,282	4,658	6,624	6,893	2,221	4,672	6,898	2,128	4,270	253	139	114	38
7,444	3,473	3,971	4,465	1,670	2,795	3,170	1,164	2,006	2,907	1,074	1,833	148	62	86	39
11,460	5,676	5,784	7,456	3,288	4,168	4,695	1,843	2,852	3,581	1,272	2,309	154	76	78	40
21,338	10,436	10,902	15,016	7,438	7,578	8,939	3,794	5,145	6,612	2,722	3,890	688	418	270	41
173	80	93	191	93	98	137	74	63	71	32	39	5	3	2	42
15,225	6,272	8,953	10,306	4,344	5,962	6,103	2,062	4,041	4,371	1,480	2,882	317	154	163	43
26,957	14,054	12,903	20,698	10,321	10,317	14,143	7,276	6,867	9,797	4,765	5,032	1,303	1,052	251	44
780	545	235	558	393	165	263	158	105	151	93	58	58	54	4	45
259	173	86	227	128	99	101	51	50	73	26	47	3	1	2	46
3,226	1,833	1,393	2,056	1,130	926	1,159	588	571	730	364	366	195	174	21	47
8,261	3,235	5,026	6,068	2,660	3,408	3,928	1,909	2,019	2,432	1,240	1,192	121	55	66	48
1,764	896	868	1,144	578	566	549	270	279	252	115	137	11	6	5	49
1,139	475	664	1,072	383	689	968	320	648	1,237	415	822	29	24	5	50
319	226	93	289	182	107	137	98	39	76	48	28	10	8	2	51
363	229	134	313	185	128	210	119	91	185	82	103	8	8	....	52
1,506	991	515	1,140	659	481	742	399	343	479	211	268	142	118	24	53
1,262	747	515	1,082	592	490	894	483	411	815	385	430	83	70	13	54
8,078	4,704	3,374	6,089	3,431	3,258	5,192	2,881	2,311	3,367	1,786	1,581	643	534	109	55

STATISTICS OF POPULATION.

208

TABLE 42.—ILLITERATE NATIVE WHITE POPULATION 10 YEARS OF AGE AND

	STATES AND TERRITORIES.	10 TO 14 YEARS.			15 TO 19 YEARS.			20 TO 24 YEARS.			25 TO 34 YEARS.		
		Total.	Males.	Females.	Total.	Males.	Females.	Total.	Males.	Females.	Total.	Males.	Females.
1	The United States...	292,963	161,728	131,235	224,927	127,471	97,456	206,402	105,046	101,356	377,509	182,091	195,418
2	North Atlantic division.......	17,133	10,076	7,057	21,020	13,217	7,803	20,833	11,985	8,848	40,088	21,066	19,022
3	Maine..........	907	539	368	1,486	929	557	1,431	891	540	2,103	1,300	803
4	New Hampshire	298	162	136	478	275	198	424	259	165	644	411	233
5	Vermont..........	561	344	217	882	593	289	887	554	833	1,549	956	593
6	Massachusetts..........	568	293	275	1,202	673	529	1,270	633	637	2,341	1,076	1,265
7	Rhode Island	403	238	165	674	388	286	551	293	258	811	351	460
8	Connecticut	300	171	129	585	336	249	541	303	238	867	466	401
9	New York	4,200	2,420	1,780	5,400	3,359	2,041	5,649	3,294	2,355	11,244	6,251	4,993
10	New Jersey	1,677	966	711	1,816	1,198	618	1,769	1,075	694	3,686	2,017	1,609
11	Pennsylvania	8,219	4,943	3,276	8,502	5,466	3,036	8,811	4,683	3,628	16,843	8,238	8,605
12	South Atlantic division.......	97,259	53,559	43,700	64,956	36,099	28,857	56,318	27,354	28,964	102,931	46,694	56,237
13	Delaware..........	474	260	214	420	255	165	487	283	204	1,119	578	541
14	Maryland	2,839	1,631	1,208	2,782	1,659	1,123	2,621	1,474	1,147	5,339	2,801	2,538
15	District of Columbia......	164	110	54	136	90	46	133	76	57	255	121	134
16	Virginia..........	16,384	9,162	7,222	11,484	6,650	4,834	10,326	5,436	4,890	18,891	9,256	9,635
17	West Virginia	9,566	5,071	4,495	6,850	3,818	3,032	6,753	3,366	3,387	11,513	5,244	6,269
18	North Carolina..........	30,013	16,229	13,784	19,458	10,488	8,970	16,573	7,518	9,055	31,292	13,418	17,874
19	South Carolina..........	13,141	7,224	5,917	8,125	4,428	3,697	6,434	3,060	3,374	10,465	4,695	5,770
20	Georgia	21,821	12,197	9,624	14,088	7,809	6,279	11,297	5,335	5,962	20,056	9,079	11,577
21	Florida..........	2,857	1,675	1,182	1,613	902	711	1,694	806	888	3,401	1,502	1,899
22	North Central division.......	34,514	19,137	15,377	35,377	21,703	13,674	38,188	22,141	16,047	79,234	43,223	36,011
23	Ohio..........	3,429	1,830	1,599	5,232	3,125	2,107	6,557	3,864	2,693	14,491	8,136	6,355
24	Indiana	4,302	2,463	1,839	4,741	2,909	1,832	5,685	3,300	2,385	13,153	7,179	5,974
25	Illinois..........	3,526	1,896	1,630	4,484	2,805	1,679	5,641	3,266	2,375	12,685	6,860	5,816
26	Michigan..........	2,382	1,400	982	2,911	1,916	995	2,696	1,699	997	4,773	2,836	1,937
27	Wisconsin..........	2,015	1,077	938	2,448	1,400	1,048	2,003	1,130	873	3,628	1,892	1,736
28	Minnesota..........	1,260	664	596	1,030	571	459	870	509	361	1,473	806	667
29	Iowa..........	1,269	739	530	1,328	906	422	1,580	995	585	3,289	1,964	1,325
30	Missouri..........	13,467	7,432	6,035	11,177	6,780	4,397	10,958	6,008	4,950	21,274	10,908	10,366
31	North Dakota..........	308	160	148	134	74	60	105	53	52	165	79	86
32	South Dakota..........	414	212	202	170	100	70	187	125	62	326	175	151
33	Nebraska..........	827	497	330	598	369	229	648	405	243	1,281	791	490
34	Kansas..........	1,315	767	548	1,124	748	376	1,258	787	471	2,696	1,588	1,108
35	South Central division........	136,233	74,964	61,269	96,411	53,322	43,089	82,051	39,337	42,714	140,450	64,846	75,604
36	Kentucky..........	22,885	12,464	10,421	21,282	11,955	9,327	21,088	10,475	10,613	34,403	16,403	18,000
37	Tennessee..........	24,133	13,189	10,944	19,874	10,754	9,120	18,646	8,815	9,831	31,831	13,872	17,959
38	Alabama..........	23,134	12,734	10,400	13,778	7,509	6,269	10,659	4,970	5,689	19,189	8,542	10,647
39	Mississippi	8,599	4,880	3,719	5,651	3,271	2,380	4,618	2,287	2,331	8,577	4,112	4,465
40	Louisiana	16,527	8,663	7,864	11,703	6,017	5,686	8,919	4,200	4,719	13,438	6,396	7,042
41	Texas..........	22,147	12,567	9,580	12,368	7,353	5,015	9,267	4,834	4,433	15,698	8,017	7,681
42	Oklahoma..........	485	283	202	139	100	39	83	46	37	162	87	75
43	Arkansas	18,323	10,184	8,139	11,616	6,363	5,253	9,371	4,310	5,061	17,152	7,417	9,735
44	Western division..........	7,824	3,992	3,832	7,163	3,130	4,033	8,412	3,629	4,783	14,806	6,262	8,544
45	Montana	189	108	81	79	53	26	87	62	25	234	170	64
46	Wyoming	125	71	54	48	28	20	39	30	9	68	51	17
47	Colorado	778	379	399	829	372	457	1,160	548	612	2,228	1,089	1,139
48	New Mexico	3,440	1,572	1,868	4,064	1,413	2,651	5,095	1,801	3,294	8,599	2,867	5,732
49	Arizona..........	498	269	229	375	204	171	275	146	129	360	203	157
50	Utah..........	672	383	289	284	183	101	223	131	92	373	206	167
51	Nevada	14	8	6	14	8	6	13	7	6	40	30	10
52	Idaho	254	162	92	75	46	29	60	49	11	122	66	56
53	Washington..........	386	230	156	167	105	62	197	131	66	482	303	179
54	Oregon	429	249	180	194	127	67	207	124	83	425	269	156
55	California	1,039	561	478	1,034	591	443	1,056	600	456	1,875	1,008	867

ILLITERACY.

209

OVER, CLASSIFIED BY SEX AND AGE PERIODS, BY STATES AND TERRITORIES: 1890.

35 TO 44 YEARS.			45 TO 54 YEARS.			55 TO 64 YEARS.			65 YEARS AND OVER.			AGE UNKNOWN.			
Total.	Males.	Females.	Total.	Males.	Females.	Total.	Males.	Females.	Total.	Males.	Females.	Total.	Males.	Females.	
333,037	154,770	178,267	245,612	103,667	141,945	184,126	69,700	114,426	191,118	68,632	122,486	9,309	5,303	4,006	1
37,459	18,683	18,776	30,214	13,420	16,794	26,316	10,269	16,047	35,271	12,556	22,715	1,563	896	667	2
1,815	1,095	720	1,206	737	469	920	522	398	1,488	767	721	87	56	31	3
581	348	233	394	234	160	323	190	133	512	268	244	30	16	14	4
1,396	773	623	827	500	327	453	269	184	595	335	260	61	40	21	5
1,633	783	850	1,011	455	556	646	336	310	983	412	571	73	35	38	6
580	263	317	367	170	197	275	134	141	406	147	259	20	8	12	7
589	301	288	482	249	233	344	199	145	532	264	268	60	45	15	8
10,045	5,548	4,407	7,173	3,827	3,346	5,746	2,981	2,765	7,555	3,667	3,888	350	209	141	9
3,619	1,902	1,717	2,998	1,466	1,532	2,535	1,160	1,375	3,098	1,337	1,761	153	101	52	10
17,201	7,670	9,531	15,756	5,782	9,974	15,074	4,478	10,596	20,102	5,359	14,743	729	386	343	11
91,826	40,887	50,939	63,603	24,421	39,182	46,455	16,440	30,015	46,706	16,052	30,114	1,785	918	867	12
1,098	575	523	950	436	514	729	343	386	782	316	466	9	3	6	13
5,820	2,888	2,932	5,177	2,445	2,732	3,512	1,505	2,007	3,691	1,407	2,284	324	243	81	14
336	168	168	300	140	160	213	87	126	201	65	136	56	38	18	15
16,863	8,223	8,640	11,563	4,861	6,702	8,565	3,451	5,114	8,910	3,598	5,312	279	135	144	16
10,595	4,660	5,935	7,916	3,139	4,777	5,871	2,240	3,631	6,011	2,171	3,840	315	168	147	17
27,766	11,488	16,278	18,966	6,794	12,172	14,467	4,724	9,743	14,582	4,779	9,803	428	173	255	18
8,388	3,742	4,646	5,205	1,867	3,338	3,670	1,172	2,498	3,538	1,240	2,292	97	33	64	19
17,913	7,831	10,082	11,554	3,967	7,587	8,249	2,502	5,747	8,143	2,730	5,404	224	96	128	20
3,047	1,312	1,735	1,933	742	1,191	1,179	416	763	908	331	577	53	29	24	21
75,111	38,870	36,241	61,361	27,855	33,506	52,035	20,360	31,675	57,855	20,312	37,543	2,653	1,676	977	22
14,215	7,478	6,737	12,319	5,388	6,931	11,234	4,276	6,958	14,655	4,777	9,878	541	314	227	23
13,892	7,104	6,788	12,624	5,534	7,090	11,282	4,253	7,029	12,558	4,157	8,401	401	206	195	24
12,105	6,243	5,862	9,696	4,428	5,268	7,951	3,012	4,939	8,044	2,707	5,337	248	162	86	25
4,245	2,549	1,696	3,374	1,845	1,529	2,891	1,494	1,397	3,583	1,715	1,868	161	112	49	26
2,136	1,150	986	1,173	603	570	893	450	443	1,210	534	676	107	79	28	27
887	445	442	516	272	244	360	173	187	393	175	218	323	300	23	28
3,218	1,807	1,411	3,061	1,493	1,568	2,906	1,160	1,746	3,912	1,405	2,507	86	59	27	29
19,954	9,688	10,266	14,535	6,283	8,252	10,964	4,097	6,867	9,965	3,483	6,482	644	348	296	30
93	44	49	57	34	23	22	13	9	32	17	15	13	8	5	31
260	154	106	144	80	64	131	71	60	139	62	77	40	28	12	32
1,212	707	505	1,023	529	494	909	405	504	878	340	538	36	23	13	33
2,894	1,501	1,393	2,839	1,366	1,473	2,492	956	1,536	2,486	940	1,546	53	37	16	34
116,238	50,931	65,307	81,085	33,670	47,415	52,686	19,264	33,422	46,529	16,816	29,713	2,652	1,294	1,358	35
29,334	13,533	15,801	20,647	8,665	11,982	14,405	5,783	8,622	13,525	5,364	8,161	590	314	276	36
26,929	10,778	16,151	20,950	8,372	12,578	14,127	5,106	9,021	12,934	4,472	8,462	894	391	503	37
15,199	6,313	8,886	11,054	4,529	6,525	6,732	2,144	4,588	6,263	2,062	4,201	227	115	112	38
7,302	3,387	3,915	4,316	1,587	2,729	3,003	1,075	1,928	2,779	1,003	1,776	142	58	84	39
9,731	4,627	5,104	5,713	2,463	3,250	3,826	1,867	1,959	2,520	943	1,577	136	67	69	40
12,559	6,048	6,511	8,207	3,781	4,426	5,058	1,780	3,278	4,179	1,499	2,680	346	194	152	41
147	68	79	152	76	76	112	57	55	57	25	32	5	3	2	42
15,037	6,177	8,860	10,046	4,197	5,849	5,923	1,952	3,971	4,272	1,448	2,824	312	152	160	43
12,403	5,399	7,004	9,349	4,301	5,048	6,634	3,367	3,267	4,607	2,206	2,401	656	519	137	44
164	99	65	108	78	30	69	44	25	47	32	15	43	40	3	45
60	41	19	53	30	23	19	9	10	13	4	9	2	1	1	46
1,742	849	893	1,188	622	566	735	387	348	460	239	221	115	99	16	47
7,521	2,870	4,651	5,464	2,325	3,139	3,578	1,710	1,868	2,230	1,123	1,107	74	40	34	48
255	131	124	148	76	72	99	52	47	46	20	26	....	....	....	49
240	124	116	183	72	111	101	41	60	126	34	92	17	14	3	50
23	17	6	25	20	5	25	21	4	14	8	6	5	3	2	51
126	75	51	89	52	37	56	36	20	80	34	46	5	5	....	52
340	197	143	318	154	164	284	141	143	214	86	128	79	62	17	53
461	250	211	500	255	245	513	269	244	540	245	295	33	23	10	54
1,471	746	725	1,273	617	656	1,155	657	498	927	471	456	283	232	51	55

STATISTICS OF POPULATION.

TABLE 43.—ILLITERATE NATIVE WHITE POPULATION OF NATIVE PARENTAGE 10 YEARS OF

	STATES AND TERRITORIES.	10 TO 14 YEARS.			15 TO 19 YEARS.			20 TO 24 YEARS.			25 TO 34 YEARS.		
		Total.	Males.	Females.	Total.	Males.	Females.	Total.	Males.	Females.	Total.	Males.	Females.
1	The United States...	267,410	147,622	119,788	198,867	112,032	86,835	184,206	92,589	91,617	337,642	161,525	176,117
2	North Atlantic division	10,373	6,017	4,356	11,450	7,191	4,259	12,377	7,160	5,217	24,652	13,186	11,466
3	Maine	481	298	183	730	467	263	812	507	305	1,229	761	468
4	New Hampshire	109	65	44	159	100	59	203	134	69	363	255	108
5	Vermont	257	171	86	340	240	100	070	070	100	691	491	200
6	Massachusetts	176	103	73	281	183	98	355	194	161	730	398	332
7	Rhode Island	84	56	28	107	63	44	106	62	44	208	109	99
8	Connecticut	117	76	41	182	114	68	208	130	78	398	235	163
9	New York	2,234	1,296	938	2,699	1,706	993	2,931	1,747	1,184	5,875	3,428	2,447
10	New Jersey	1,070	630	440	1,162	759	403	1,210	740	470	2,647	1,478	1,169
11	Pennsylvania	5,845	3,322	2,523	5,784	3,559	2,225	6,179	3,393	2,786	12,581	6,101	6,480
12	South Atlantic division	96,314	52,994	43,320	64,183	35,629	28,554	55,639	26,991	28,648	101,409	45,917	55,492
13	Delaware	457	250	207	396	239	157	461	264	197	1,061	549	512
14	Maryland	2,548	1,462	1,086	2,449	1,471	978	2,297	1,304	993	4,577	2,427	2,150
15	District of Columbia	141	94	47	119	76	43	115	69	46	203	104	99
16	Virginia	16,270	9,092	7,187	11,429	6,615	4,814	10,279	5,412	4,867	18,789	9,199	9,590
17	West Virginia	9,411	4,983	4,428	6,707	3,718	2,989	6,640	3,311	3,329	11,236	5,090	6,146
18	North Carolina	29,041	16,189	13,752	19,419	10,466	8,953	16,536	7,494	9,042	31,241	13,387	17,854
19	South Carolina	13,067	7,181	5,886	8,093	4,410	3,683	6,415	3,050	3,365	10,428	4,676	5,752
20	Georgia	21,710	12,142	9,577	14,035	7,777	6,258	11,260	5,318	5,942	20,567	9,036	11,531
21	Florida	2,751	1,601	1,150	1,536	857	679	1,636	769	867	3,307	1,449	1,858
22	North Central division	26,140	14,664	11,482	26,103	16,235	9,028	29,592	17,210	12,382	62,490	34,428	28,062
23	Ohio	2,879	1,563	1,316	4,296	2,596	1,700	5,437	3,257	2,180	11,727	6,628	5,099
24	Indiana	3,858	2,214	1,644	4,209	2,596	1,613	5,063	2,923	2,140	11,624	6,377	5,247
25	Illinois	2,819	1,514	1,305	3,541	2,187	1,354	4,528	2,630	1,898	10,321	5,655	4,666
26	Michigan	955	593	362	1,167	798	369	1,291	800	491	2,624	1,600	1,024
27	Wisconsin	360	214	146	373	245	128	396	242	154	859	504	355
28	Minnesota	198	114	84	145	101	44	192	115	77	408	265	143
29	Iowa	793	465	328	790	551	239	1,021	676	345	2,262	1,413	849
30	Missouri	12,668	7,004	5,664	10,365	6,280	4,085	10,090	5,546	4,544	19,361	9,978	9,383
31	North Dakota	57	32	25	20	8	12	37	21	16	54	27	27
32	South Dakota	133	79	54	73	50	23	75	59	16	138	78	60
33	Nebraska	448	289	159	330	224	106	466	303	163	933	592	341
34	Kansas	978	583	395	854	599	255	996	638	358	2,179	1,311	868
35	South Central division	128,926	71,150	57,776	91,493	50,747	40,746	79,513	38,323	41,190	136,199	62,796	73,403
36	Kentucky	22,583	12,289	10,294	20,938	11,727	9,211	20,779	10,283	10,496	33,675	16,032	17,643
37	Tennessee	23,945	13,084	10,861	19,730	10,665	9,065	18,529	8,744	9,785	31,634	13,773	17,861
38	Alabama	22,923	12,611	10,312	13,681	7,456	6,225	10,592	4,942	5,650	19,067	8,484	10,583
39	Mississippi	8,469	4,812	3,657	5,559	3,226	2,333	4,556	2,247	2,309	8,458	4,042	4,416
40	Louisiana	15,872	8,309	7,563	11,210	5,724	5,486	8,474	3,963	4,511	12,732	6,063	6,669
41	Texas	16,676	9,761	6,915	8,707	5,599	3,108	7,243	3,858	3,385	13,488	6,096	6,492
42	Oklahoma	456	267	189	124	90	34	77	44	33	151	81	70
43	Arkansas	18,002	10,017	7,985	11,454	6,260	5,194	9,263	4,242	5,021	16,994	7,325	9,669
44	Western division	5,651	2,797	2,854	5,578	2,230	3,348	7,085	2,905	4,180	12,892	5,198	7,694
45	Montana	101	60	41	49	28	21	62	44	18	161	120	41
46	Wyoming	58	34	24	25	15	10	27	23	4	51	42	9
47	Colorado	652	307	345	733	319	414	1,091	507	584	2,093	1,013	1,080
48	New Mexico	3,172	1,429	1,743	3,743	1,263	2,480	4,785	1,649	3,136	8,251	2,701	5,550
49	Arizona	105	58	47	111	60	51	128	74	54	204	114	90
50	Utah	250	143	107	93	52	41	84	56	28	175	88	87
51	Nevada	4	3	1	10	5	5	7	3	4	23	18	5
52	Idaho	149	97	52	53	34	19	39	37	2	87	46	41
53	Washington	265	163	102	107	71	36	139	100	39	386	203	183
54	Oregon	338	202	136	150	107	43	161	95	66	333	217	116
55	California	557	301	256	504	276	228	562	317	245	1,178	636	542

ILLITERACY.

211

AGE AND OVER, CLASSIFIED BY SEX AND AGE PERIODS, BY STATES AND TERRITORIES: 1890.

35 TO 44 YEARS.			45 TO 54 YEARS.			55 TO 64 YEARS.			65 YEARS AND OVER.			AGE UNKNOWN.			
Total.	Males.	Females.	Total.	Males.	Females.	Total.	Males.	Females.	Total.	Males.	Females.	Total.	Males.	Females.	
305,161	141,430	163,731	230,423	96,845	133,578	176,118	66,269	109,849	182,023	65,025	116,998	8,873	5,078	3,795	1
26,311	13,408	12,903	24,644	10,996	13,648	23,691	9,217	14,474	32,788	11,613	21,175	1,400	819	581	2
1,160	720	440	873	552	321	727	417	310	1,347	689	658	79	53	26	3
388	257	131	302	188	114	289	166	123	400	250	234	29	16	13	4
531	329	202	385	255	130	319	198	121	515	293	222	48	35	13	5
693	405	288	535	295	240	504	288	216	891	379	512	63	28	35	6
250	131	110	248	125	123	240	125	115	386	144	242	17	5	12	7
379	216	103	385	209	176	319	188	131	509	255	254	56	42	14	8
5,920	3,494	2,435	5,067	2,875	2,192	4,850	2,576	2,274	6,852	3,344	3,508	302	186	116	9
2,988	1,629	1,359	2,724	1,354	1,370	2,379	1,109	1,270	2,984	1,281	1,703	145	96	49	10
13,993	6,227	7,766	14,125	5,143	8,982	14,064	4,150	9,914	18,814	4,972	13,842	661	358	303	11
90,549	40,277	50,272	62,711	24,015	38,696	45,945	16,230	29,715	46,008	16,368	29,640	1,744	894	850	12
1,052	553	499	923	423	500	716	338	378	764	307	457	9	3	6	13
5,160	2,585	2,575	4,747	2,255	2,492	3,340	1,435	1,905	3,487	1,340	2,147	302	232	70	14
305	150	155	275	128	147	194	80	114	188	61	127	56	38	18	15
16,783	8,174	8,609	11,494	4,820	6,674	8,512	3,424	5,083	8,828	3,560	5,263	276	133	143	16
10,372	4,557	5,815	7,777	3,097	4,680	5,762	2,195	3,567	5,810	2,110	3,700	302	157	145	17
27,711	11,468	16,243	18,924	6,772	12,152	14,425	4,707	9,718	14,505	4,746	9,750	427	173	254	18
8,356	3,722	4,634	5,188	1,857	3,331	3,649	1,159	2,490	3,430	1,224	2,206	96	33	63	19
17,850	7,794	10,056	11,490	3,941	7,549	8,189	2,484	5,705	8,050	2,701	5,349	224	96	128	20
2,960	1,274	1,686	1,893	722	1,171	1,158	408	750	886	319	567	52	29	23	21
63,299	33,149	30,150	54,659	24,904	29,755	48,296	18,735	20,561	53,344	18,530	34,814	2,503	1,580	923	22
11,826	6,378	5,448	10,614	4,729	5,885	10,220	3,890	6,330	13,287	4,321	8,966	510	297	213	23
12,478	6,442	6,036	11,632	5,139	6,493	10,722	4,040	6,682	11,885	3,908	7,977	377	190	187	24
10,531	5,483	5,048	8,850	4,040	4,804	7,537	2,846	4,601	7,566	2,522	5,044	237	153	84	25
2,632	1,644	988	2,432	1,353	1,079	2,325	1,174	1,151	8,058	1,435	1,023	143	100	43	26
778	476	302	711	387	324	678	346	332	981	425	556	91	66	25	27
342	200	142	312	177	135	259	122	137	300	136	164	310	293	17	28
2,535	1,500	1,035	2,683	1,317	1,366	2,673	1,061	1,612	3,548	1,274	2,274	83	56	27	29
18,484	9,004	9,480	13,768	5,954	7,814	10,589	3,935	6,654	9,530	3,304	6,226	622	338	284	30
49	25	24	30	17	13	17	11	6	24	10	14	7	4	3	31
142	90	52	105	58	47	113	59	54	116	49	67	39	27	12	32
1,006	602	404	909	471	438	834	367	467	783	295	488	35	23	12	33
2,496	1,305	1,191	2,613	1,256	1,357	2,329	884	1,445	2,266	851	1,415	49	33	16	34
113,652	49,740	63,912	79,675	32,953	46,722	51,914	18,932	32,982	45,499	16,385	29,114	2,597	1,279	1,318	35
28,847	13,311	15,536	20,372	8,538	11,834	14,253	5,719	8,534	13,275	5,258	8,017	586	313	273	36
26,775	10,707	16,068	20,813	8,310	12,503	14,012	5,051	8,961	12,763	4,894	8,869	888	388	500	37
15,096	6,271	8,825	10,967	4,484	6,483	6,666	2,121	4,545	6,175	2,035	4,140	227	115	112	38
7,194	3,327	3,867	4,243	1,555	2,688	2,959	1,061	1,898	2,706	969	1,737	140	58	82	39
9,220	4,397	4,823	5,460	2,336	3,124	3,201	1,325	1,876	2,360	875	1,485	134	66	68	40
11,523	5,572	5,951	7,757	3,526	4,231	4,859	1,678	3,181	3,987	1,423	2,564	307	184	123	41
131	62	69	147	73	74	108	54	54	52	23	29	5	3	2	42
14,866	6,093	8,773	9,916	4,131	5,785	5,856	1,923	3,933	4,181	1,408	2,773	310	152	158	43
11,350	4,856	6,494	8,734	3,977	4,757	6,272	3,155	3,117	4,384	2,129	2,255	629	506	123	44
118	73	45	74	51	23	58	39	19	40	26	14	42	40	2	45
43	31	12	43	26	17	16	6	10	11	4	7	1	1	....	46
1,643	794	849	1,137	591	546	714	373	341	435	227	208	112	97	15	47
7,328	2,778	4,550	5,392	2,290	3,102	3,533	1,688	1,845	2,212	1,110	1,102	68	37	31	48
158	73	85	117	59	58	78	36	42	39	18	21	....	....	3	49
171	96	75	155	61	94	97	41	56	110	29	81	15	12	3	50
18	13	5	19	16	3	23	10	4	12	7	5	5	3	2	51
102	59	43	76	41	35	50	30	20	70	30	40	5	5	....	52
262	155	107	259	119	140	254	120	134	182	67	115	78	61	17	53
403	223	180	489	226	213	467	241	226	502	221	281	31	21	10	54
1,104	561	543	1,023	497	526	982	562	420	771	390	381	272	229	43	55

212

STATISTICS OF POPULATION.

TABLE 44.—ILLITERATE NATIVE WHITE POPULATION OF FOREIGN PARENTAGE 10 YEARS OF

	STATES AND TERRITORIES.	10 TO 14 YEARS.			15 TO 19 YEARS.			20 TO 24 YEARS.			25 TO 34 YEARS.		
		Total.	Males.	Females.	Total.	Males.	Females.	Total.	Males.	Females.	Total.	Males.	Females.
1	The United States...	25,553	14,106	11,447	26,060	15,439	10,621	22,196	12,457	9,739	39,867	20,566	19,301
2	North Atlantic division	6,760	4,059	2,701	9,570	6,026	3,544	8,456	4,825	3,631	15,436	7,880	7,556
3	Maine	426	241	185	756	462	294	619	384	235	874	539	335
4	New Hampshire	189	97	92	314	175	139	221	125	96	281	156	125
5	Vermont	304	173	131	536	353	183	514	301	213	928	535	393
6	Massachusetts	392	190	202	921	490	431	915	439	476	1,011	678	633
7	Rhode Island	319	182	137	567	325	242	445	231	214	603	242	361
8	Connecticut	183	95	88	403	222	181	333	173	160	469	231	238
9	New York	1,966	1,124	842	2,701	1,653	1,048	2,718	1,547	1,171	5,369	2,823	2,546
10	New Jersey	607	336	271	654	439	215	559	335	224	1,039	539	500
11	Pennsylvania	2,374	1,621	753	2,718	1,907	811	2,132	1,290	842	4,262	2,137	2,125
12	South Atlantic division	945	565	380	773	470	303	679	363	316	1,522	777	745
13	Delaware	17	10	7	24	16	8	26	19	7	58	29	29
14	Maryland	291	169	122	333	188	145	324	170	154	762	374	388
15	District of Columbia	23	16	7	17	14	3	18	7	11	52	17	35
16	Virginia	105	70	35	55	35	20	47	24	23	102	57	45
17	West Virginia	155	88	67	143	100	43	113	55	58	277	154	123
18	North Carolina	72	40	32	39	22	17	37	24	13	51	31	20
19	South Carolina	74	43	31	32	18	14	19	10	9	37	19	18
20	Georgia	102	55	47	53	32	21	37	17	20	89	43	46
21	Florida	106	74	32	77	45	32	58	37	21	94	53	41
22	North Central division	8,368	4,473	3,895	9,214	5,468	3,746	8,596	4,931	3,665	16,744	8,795	7,949
23	Ohio	550	267	283	936	529	407	1,120	607	513	2,764	1,508	1,256
24	Indiana	444	249	195	532	313	219	622	377	245	1,529	802	727
25	Illinois	707	382	325	943	618	325	1,113	636	477	2,364	1,214	1,150
26	Michigan	1,427	807	620	1,744	1,118	626	1,405	899	506	2,149	1,236	913
27	Wisconsin	1,655	863	792	2,075	1,155	920	1,607	888	719	2,769	1,388	1,381
28	Minnesota	1,062	550	512	885	470	415	678	394	234	1,065	541	524
29	Iowa	476	274	202	538	355	183	559	319	240	1,027	551	476
30	Missouri	799	428	371	812	500	312	868	462	406	1,913	930	983
31	North Dakota	251	128	123	114	66	48	68	32	36	111	52	59
32	South Dakota	281	133	148	97	50	47	112	66	46	188	97	91
33	Nebraska	379	208	171	268	145	123	182	102	80	348	199	149
34	Kansas	337	184	153	270	149	121	262	149	113	517	277	240
35	South Central division	7,307	3,814	3,493	4,918	2,575	2,343	3,138	1,614	1,524	4,251	2,050	2,201
36	Kentucky	302	175	127	344	228	116	309	192	117	728	371	357
37	Tennessee	188	105	83	144	89	55	117	71	46	197	99	98
38	Alabama	211	123	88	97	53	44	67	28	39	122	58	64
39	Mississippi	130	68	62	92	45	47	62	40	22	119	70	49
40	Louisiana	655	354	301	493	293	200	445	237	208	706	333	373
41	Texas	5,471	2,806	2,665	3,571	1,754	1,817	2,024	976	1,048	2,210	1,021	1,189
42	Oklahoma	29	16	13	15	10	5	6	2	4	11	6	5
43	Arkansas	321	167	154	162	103	59	108	68	40	158	92	66
44	Western division	2,173	1,195	978	1,585	900	685	1,327	724	603	1,914	1,064	850
45	Montana	88	48	40	30	25	5	25	18	7	73	50	23
46	Wyoming	67	37	30	23	13	10	12	7	5	17	9	8
47	Colorado	126	72	54	93	50	43	69	41	28	135	76	59
48	New Mexico	268	143	125	321	150	171	310	152	158	348	166	182
49	Arizona	393	211	182	264	144	120	147	72	75	156	89	67
50	Utah	422	240	182	191	131	60	139	75	64	198	118	80
51	Nevada	10	5	5	4	3	1	6	4	2	17	12	5
52	Idaho	105	65	40	22	12	10	21	12	9	35	20	15
53	Washington	121	67	54	60	34	26	58	31	27	146	100	46
54	Oregon	91	47	44	44	20	24	46	29	17	92	52	40
55	California	482	260	222	530	315	213	494	283	211	697	372	325

ILLITERACY.

AGE AND OVER, CLASSIFIED BY SEX AND AGE PERIODS, BY STATES AND TERRITORIES: 1890.

35 TO 44 YEARS.			45 TO 54 YEARS.			55 TO 64 YEARS.			65 YEARS AND OVER.			AGE UNKNOWN.			
Total.	Males.	Females.	Total.	Males.	Females.	Total.	Males.	Females.	Total.	Males.	Females.	Total.	Males.	Females.	
27,876	13,340	14,586	15,189	6,822	8,367	8,008	3,431	4,577	9,095	3,607	5,488	436	225	211	1
11,148	5,275	5,873	5,570	2,424	3,146	2,625	1,052	1,573	2,483	943	1,540	163	77	86	2
655	375	280	333	185	148	193	105	88	141	78	63	8	3	5	3
193	91	102	92	46	46	34	24	10	22	12	10	1	....	1	4
865	444	421	442	245	197	134	71	63	80	42	38	13	5	8	5
940	378	562	476	160	316	142	48	94	92	33	59	10	7	3	6
330	132	198	119	45	74	35	9	26	20	3	17	3	3	....	7
210	85	125	97	40	57	25	11	14	23	9	14	4	3	1	8
4,116	2,054	2,062	2,106	952	1,154	896	405	491	703	323	380	48	23	25	9
631	273	358	274	112	162	156	51	105	114	56	58	8	5	3	10
3,208	1,443	1,765	1,631	639	992	1,010	328	682	1,288	387	901	68	28	40	11
1,277	610	667	892	406	486	510	210	300	758	284	474	41	24	17	12
46	22	24	27	13	14	13	5	8	18	9	9	....	....	....	13
660	303	357	430	190	240	172	70	102	204	67	137	22	11	11	14
31	18	13	34	12	22	19	7	12	13	4	9	....	....	....	15
80	49	31	69	41	28	53	27	26	82	38	44	3	2	1	16
223	103	120	169	72	97	109	45	64	201	61	140	13	11	2	17
55	20	35	42	22	20	42	17	25	77	33	44	1	....	1	18
32	20	12	17	10	7	21	13	8	48	22	26	1	....	1	19
63	37	26	64	26	38	60	18	42	93	38	55	....	....	....	20
87	38	49	40	20	20	21	8	13	22	12	10	1	....	1	21
11,812	5,721	6,091	6,702	2,951	3,751	3,739	1,625	2,114	4,511	1,782	2,729	150	96	54	22
2,389	1,100	1,289	1,705	659	1,046	1,014	386	628	1,368	456	912	31	17	14	23
1,414	662	752	992	395	597	560	213	347	673	249	424	24	16	8	24
1,574	760	814	846	382	464	414	166	248	478	185	293	11	9	2	25
1,613	905	708	942	492	450	566	320	246	525	280	245	18	12	6	26
1,358	674	684	462	216	246	215	104	111	229	109	120	16	13	3	27
545	245	300	204	95	109	101	51	50	93	39	54	13	7	6	28
683	307	376	378	176	202	233	99	134	364	131	233	8	3	....	29
1,470	684	786	767	329	438	375	162	213	435	179	256	22	10	12	30
44	19	25	27	17	10	5	2	3	8	7	1	6	4	2	31
118	64	54	39	22	17	18	12	6	28	18	10	1	1	....	32
206	105	101	114	58	56	75	38	37	95	45	50	1	....	1	33
398	196	202	226	110	116	163	72	91	220	89	131	4	4	....	34
2,586	1,191	1,395	1,410	717	693	772	332	440	1,030	431	599	55	15	40	35
487	222	265	275	127	148	152	64	88	250	106	144	4	1	3	36
154	71	83	137	62	75	115	55	60	171	78	93	6	3	3	37
103	42	61	87	45	42	66	23	43	88	27	61	....	....	....	38
108	60	48	73	32	41	44	14	30	73	34	39	2	....	2	39
511	230	281	253	127	126	125	42	83	160	68	92	2	1	1	40
1,036	476	560	450	255	195	199	102	97	192	76	116	39	10	29	41
16	6	10	5	3	2	4	3	1	5	2	3	....	....	....	42
171	84	87	130	66	64	67	29	38	91	40	51	2	....	2	43
1,053	543	510	615	324	291	362	212	150	313	167	146	27	13	14	44
46	26	20	34	27	7	11	5	6	7	6	1	1	....	1	45
17	10	7	10	4	6	3	3	....	2	....	2	1	....	1	46
99	55	44	51	31	20	21	14	7	25	12	13	3	2	1	47
193	92	101	72	35	37	45	22	23	18	13	5	6	3	3	48
97	58	39	31	17	14	21	16	5	7	2	5	....	....	....	49
69	28	41	28	11	17	4	....	4	16	5	11	2	2	....	50
5	4	1	6	4	2	2	2	....	2	1	1	....	....	....	51
24	16	8	18	11	2	6	6	....	10	4	6	....	....	....	52
78	42	36	59	35	24	30	21	9	32	19	13	1	1	....	53
58	27	31	61	29	32	46	28	18	38	24	14	2	2	....	54
367	185	182	250	120	130	173	95	78	156	81	75	11	3	8	55

214

STATISTICS OF POPULATION.

TABLE 45.—ILLITERATE FOREIGN WHITE POPULATION 10 YEARS OF AGE AND OVER,

	STATES AND TERRITORIES.	10 TO 14 YEARS.			15 TO 19 YEARS.			20 TO 24 YEARS.			25 TO 34 YEARS.		
		Total.	Males.	Females.	Total.	Males.	Females.	Total.	Males.	Females.	Total.	Males.	Females.
1	The United States...	23,535	12,528	11,007	52,686	27,986	24,700	96,845	52,687	44,158	225,468	124,048	101,420
2	North Atlantic division	10,925	5,925	5,000	31,647	16,804	14,843	57,561	31,182	26,379	123,918	69,014	54,904
3	Maine	600	313	287	1,820	992	828	2,089	1,119	970	3,270	1,755	1,515
4	New Hampshire	786	428	358	2,220	1,245	975	2,549	1,597	952	3,531	2,036	1,495
5	Vermont	200	112	88	445	282	163	729	454	275	1,524	894	630
6	Massachusetts	982	473	509	5,316	2,804	2,512	9,338	4,922	4,416	18,506	9,014	9,492
7	Rhode Island	845	448	397	1,702	945	757	2,132	1,192	940	3,928	1,907	2,021
8	Connecticut	461	262	199	1,555	840	715	2,452	1,390	1,062	4,992	2,781	2,211
9	New York	3,087	1,463	1,624	10,173	4,476	5,697	19,229	8,806	10,423	42,329	22,091	20,238
10	New Jersey	912	470	442	1,843	964	879	3,887	2,034	1,853	8,958	4,798	4,160
11	Pennsylvania	3,052	1,956	1,096	6,573	4,256	2,317	15,156	9,668	5,488	36,880	23,738	13,142
12	South Atlantic division	598	341	257	949	484	465	1,616	876	740	3,770	2,008	1,762
13	Delaware	24	15	9	61	33	28	165	95	70	408	248	160
14	Maryland	337	178	159	571	269	302	870	420	450	2,065	1,001	1,064
15	District of Columbia	17	9	8	24	6	18	79	25	54	146	46	100
16	Virginia	42	30	12	55	43	12	112	89	23	290	219	71
17	West Virginia	47	29	18	59	38	21	100	79	21	291	195	96
18	North Carolina	5	3	2	3	3	......	9	7	2	21	13	8
19	South Carolina	16	7	9	10	3	7	27	15	12	52	29	23
20	Georgia	20	17	3	33	20	13	62	36	26	115	67	48
21	Florida	90	53	37	133	69	64	192	110	82	382	190	192
22	North Central division	7,362	3,848	3,514	13,176	6,974	6,202	25,116	13,203	11,913	67,794	35,169	32,625
23	Ohio	418	199	210	1,164	579	585	2,833	1,503	1,330	7,827	4,170	3,657
24	Indiana	153	91	62	280	163	117	495	270	225	1,488	741	747
25	Illinois	1,087	552	535	2,736	1,343	1,393	5,660	2,616	3,044	14,797	7,265	7,532
26	Michigan	1,355	732	623	2,547	1,453	1,094	4,718	2,852	1,866	12,017	7,566	5,351
27	Wisconsin	977	494	483	1,795	990	805	3,208	1,750	1,458	9,677	4,902	4,775
28	Minnesota	1,129	625	504	1,687	895	792	3,033	1,653	1,380	7,900	4,031	3,869
29	Iowa	344	170	174	688	404	284	1,277	633	504	3,400	1,641	1,759
30	Missouri	312	171	141	474	234	240	1,014	446	568	2,820	1,417	1,409
31	North Dakota	445	232	213	334	171	163	511	268	243	1,222	657	565
32	South Dakota	415	221	194	333	175	158	520	287	233	1,301	677	624
33	Nebraska	526	258	268	769	379	390	1,183	565	618	2,600	1,300	1,300
34	Kansas	201	103	98	369	188	181	664	310	354	1,839	802	1,037
35	South Central division	3,208	1,668	1,540	3,842	1,847	1,995	5,566	2,800	2,766	12,872	6,741	6,131
36	Kentucky	73	43	30	89	54	35	171	96	75	474	253	221
37	Tennessee	48	24	24	53	29	24	94	50	44	250	133	117
38	Alabama	69	40	29	38	26	12	60	35	25	208	126	82
39	Mississippi	14	12	2	18	8	10	44	28	16	100	62	38
40	Louisiana	332	184	148	390	232	158	572	339	233	1,712	1,071	641
41	Texas	2,601	1,324	1,277	3,195	1,468	1,727	4,556	2,221	2,335	9,964	4,998	4,966
42	Oklahoma	15	6	9	7	3	4	8	4	4	27	13	14
43	Arkansas	56	35	21	52	27	25	61	27	34	137	85	52
44	Western division	1,442	746	696	3,072	1,877	1,195	6,986	4,626	2,360	17,114	11,116	5,998
45	Montana	61	30	31	132	85	47	523	363	160	1,117	839	278
46	Wyoming	37	24	13	60	39	21	96	79	17	272	198	74
47	Colorado	119	59	60	238	132	106	706	471	235	2,050	1,449	601
48	New Mexico	86	46	40	147	85	62	293	144	149	731	379	352
49	Arizona	463	252	211	615	294	321	795	462	333	1,855	1,020	835
50	Utah	205	94	111	204	106	98	264	151	113	737	324	413
51	Nevada	6	3	3	50	42	8	103	81	22	285	224	61
52	Idaho	49	28	21	62	44	18	120	91	29	298	223	75
53	Washington	92	45	47	252	158	94	813	599	214	1,863	1,337	526
54	Oregon	61	32	29	131	78	53	381	251	130	982	624	358
55	California	263	133	130	1,181	814	367	2,892	1,934	958	6,924	4,499	2,425

ILLITERACY.

CLASSIFIED BY SEX AND AGE PERIODS, BY STATES AND TERRITORIES: 1890.

35 TO 44 YEARS.			45 TO 54 YEARS.			55 TO 64 YEARS.			65 YEARS AND OVER.			AGE UNKNOWN.			
Total.	Males.	Females.	Total.	Males.	Females.	Total.	Males.	Females.	Total.	Males.	Females.	Total.	Males.	Females.	
208,580	100,489	108,091	213,097	90,545	122,552	169,459	66,855	102,604	151,191	59,705	91,486	6,710	4,471	2,239	1
107,477	51,278	56,199	105,319	42,844	62,475	76,907	28,101	48,806	62,795	22,931	39,864	3,645	2,425	1,220	2
2,850	1,405	1,445	2,740	1,293	1,447	2,237	985	1,252	1,991	926	1,065	68	40	28	3
2,832	1,466	1,366	2,615	1,215	1,400	1,828	820	1,008	1,210	537	673	90	61	29	4
1,782	900	792	1,928	991	937	1,900	893	1,007	2,178	1,092	1,086	89	50	39	5
18,863	7,488	11,375	21,274	7,532	13,742	15,366	4,899	10,467	11,533	3,739	7,794	537	266	271	6
4,302	1,834	2,468	4,342	1,680	2,662	3,003	1,076	1,927	1,924	614	1,310	90	60	30	7
4,816	2,209	2,607	5,235	2,073	3,162	3,566	1,262	2,304	2,740	965	1,775	419	292	127	8
36,522	17,081	19,441	34,876	13,909	20,967	27,175	9,992	17,183	23,851	8,857	14,994	894	579	315	9
8,374	3,799	4,575	8,219	3,297	4,922	5,465	1,934	3,531	3,788	1,315	2,473	366	268	98	10
27,136	15,006	12,130	24,090	10,854	13,236	16,367	6,240	10,127	13,580	4,886	8,694	1,092	809	283	11
4,002	1,856	2,146	4,635	1,881	2,754	3,997	1,492	2,505	3,890	1,582	2,308	596	402	194	12
373	170	203	427	158	269	341	129	212	301	118	183	18	12	6	13
2,177	983	1,194	2,382	955	1,427	1,928	682	1,246	1,892	702	1,190	326	186	140	14
262	53	209	408	71	337	391	65	326	347	63	284	18	4	14	15
261	178	83	322	185	137	332	197	135	356	224	132	23	17	6	16
397	192	205	537	225	312	547	227	320	622	290	332	168	157	11	17
22	13	9	26	19	7	47	28	19	43	28	15	1	1	....	18
67	35	32	72	33	39	68	29	39	68	34	34	....	....	....	19
94	52	42	143	59	84	149	53	96	118	59	59	12	9	3	20
349	180	169	318	176	142	194	82	112	143	64	79	30	16	14	21
70,383	32,467	37,916	80,802	34,232	46,570	73,509	29,844	43,665	74,016	30,337	43,679	1,357	826	531	22
8,469	3,949	4,520	10,017	4,178	5,839	9,020	3,421	5,599	9,576	3,797	5,779	247	147	100	23
2,137	910	1,227	3,439	1,362	2,077	3,626	1,455	2,171	3,995	1,677	2,318	83	42	41	24
13,521	6,047	7,474	14,271	5,882	8,389	12,214	4,831	7,383	11,414	4,481	6,933	139	70	69	25
12,369	6,741	5,628	11,748	5,836	5,912	9,139	4,241	4,898	9,074	3,967	5,107	193	133	60	26
11,119	5,148	5,971	12,629	5,447	7,182	12,833	5,253	7,580	14,959	6,210	8,749	174	92	82	27
7,885	3,339	4,546	9,514	3,645	5,869	9,493	3,641	5,852	9,056	3,611	5,445	157	114	43	28
4,050	1,634	2,416	6,131	2,427	3,704	6,484	2,572	3,912	6,700	2,829	3,871	105	74	31	29
3,583	1,566	2,017	5,139	2,034	3,105	3,933	1,520	2,413	3,457	1,352	2,105	130	79	51	30
1,174	529	645	1,066	471	595	969	382	587	856	330	526	22	7	15	31
1,308	592	716	1,374	594	780	1,238	532	706	1,234	496	738	30	17	13	32
2,635	1,194	1,441	2,604	1,136	1,468	2,079	918	1,161	1,706	695	1,011	61	38	23	33
2,133	818	1,315	2,870	1,220	1,650	2,481	1,078	1,403	1,989	892	1,097	16	13	3	34
12,164	6,233	5,931	11,052	5,568	5,484	7,537	3,509	4,023	5,390	2,386	3,004	465	285	180	35
823	364	459	1,395	508	887	1,386	550	830	1,242	516	726	39	12	27	36
302	131	171	420	202	227	368	170	198	278	133	145	29	10	19	37
175	108	67	228	129	99	161	77	84	135	66	69	26	24	2	38
142	86	56	149	83	66	167	89	78	128	71	57	6	4	2	39
1,729	1,049	680	1,743	825	918	1,369	476	893	1,061	329	732	18	9	9	40
8,779	4,388	4,391	6,809	3,657	3,152	3,881	2,014	1,867	2,433	1,223	1,210	342	224	118	41
26	12	14	39	17	22	25	17	8	14	7	7	....	....	....	42
188	95	93	260	147	113	180	110	70	99	41	58	5	2	3	43
14,554	8,655	5,899	11,289	6,020	5,269	7,509	3,909	3,600	5,100	2,469	2,631	647	533	114	44
616	446	170	450	315	135	194	114	80	104	61	43	15	14	1	45
199	132	67	174	98	76	82	42	40	60	22	38	1	....	1	46
1,484	984	500	808	503	360	424	201	223	270	125	145	80	75	5	47
740	365	375	604	335	269	350	199	151	202	117	85	47	15	32	48
1,509	765	744	996	502	494	450	218	232	206	95	111	11	6	5	49
809	351	548	889	311	578	867	279	588	1,111	381	730	12	10	2	50
296	209	87	264	162	102	112	77	35	62	40	22	5	5	....	51
237	154	83	224	133	91	154	83	71	105	48	57	3	3	....	52
1,166	794	372	822	505	317	458	258	200	265	125	140	63	56	7	53
801	497	304	582	337	245	381	214	167	275	140	135	50	47	3	54
6,607	3,958	2,649	5,416	2,814	2,602	4,037	2,224	1,813	3,440	1,315	1,125	360	302	58	55

STATISTICS OF POPULATION.

216

TABLE 46.—ILLITERATE COLORED POPULATION (a) 10 YEARS OF AGE AND OVER,

	STATES AND TERRITORIES.	10 TO 14 YEARS.			15 TO 19 YEARS.			20 TO 24 YEARS.			25 TO 34 YEARS.		
		Total.	Males.	Females.	Total.	Males.	Females.	Total.	Males.	Females.	Total.	Males.	Females.
1	The United States...	415,100	222,233	192,957	375,941	195,879	180,062	368,420	168,570	199,859	569,080	250,145	318,935
2	North Atlantic division	1,752	920	832	2,548	1,440	1,108	4,577	2,646	1,931	10,077	5,278	4,799
3	Maine	10	4	6	34	20	14	47	29	18	103	59	44
4	New Hampshire	6	4	2	12	9	3	13	8	5	16	9	7
5	Vermont	7	3	4	13	8	5	17	10	7	31	21	10
6	Massachusetts	41	20	21	136	90	46	233	149	84	659	387	272
7	Rhode Island	19	14	5	36	21	15	67	33	34	178	78	100
8	Connecticut	38	23	15	59	24	35	140	80	60	284	158	126
9	New York	382	202	180	542	312	230	1,009	608	401	2,404	1,258	1,146
10	New Jersey	467	247	220	641	356	285	1,057	581	476	2,109	1,053	1,056
11	Pennsylvania	782	403	379	1,075	600	475	1,994	1,148	846	4,293	2,255	2,038
12	South Atlantic division	202,901	108,661	94,240	175,461	91,648	83,813	161,015	72,411	88,604	243,768	101,298	142,470
13	Delaware	1,179	615	564	1,039	575	464	1,063	538	525	2,002	967	1,035
14	Maryland	7,805	4,135	3,670	7,704	4,199	3,505	7,511	3,678	3,833	14,614	6,383	8,231
15	District of Columbia	1,051	597	454	1,330	657	673	1,690	667	1,023	3,615	1,250	2,395
16	Virginia	33,690	18,374	15,316	29,060	16,592	12,498	26,308	12,207	14,101	43,427	18,121	25,306
17	West Virginia	969	531	438	1,184	821	363	1,638	1,161	477	2,065	1,148	917
18	North Carolina	37,815	20,053	17,762	30,706	16,101	14,605	25,771	10,600	15,171	38,093	14,654	23,439
19	South Carolina	51,568	27,375	24,193	42,449	21,106	21,343	36,701	15,700	21,001	51,781	20,764	31,017
20	Georgia	62,890	33,844	29,046	56,125	29,098	27,027	52,253	24,063	28,190	76,278	33,070	43,208
21	Florida	5,934	3,137	2,797	5,924	2,589	3,335	8,080	3,797	4,283	11,803	4,941	6,922
22	North Central division	6,007	3,314	2,693	6,390	3,619	2,771	8,665	4,460	4,205	20,438	9,843	10,595
23	Ohio	423	211	212	654	375	279	1,065	594	471	2,850	1,468	1,382
24	Indiana	396	209	187	511	300	211	811	442	369	2,116	1,043	1,073
25	Illinois	414	214	200	523	317	206	835	425	410	2,082	1,028	1,054
26	Michigan	293	164	129	345	176	169	428	228	200	870	439	431
27	Wisconsin	109	58	51	133	65	68	165	84	81	320	181	139
28	Minnesota	97	55	42	79	32	47	93	49	44	201	104	97
29	Iowa	59	37	22	64	44	20	161	80	81	372	195	177
30	Missouri	3,635	2,022	1,613	3,477	1,964	1,513	4,223	2,148	2,075	9,174	4,299	4,875
31	North Dakota	26	19	7	19	11	8	30	21	9	43	24	19
32	South Dakota	28	14	14	16	9	7	41	23	18	90	51	39
33	Nebraska	99	58	41	113	57	56	189	86	103	520	270	250
34	Kansas	428	253	175	456	269	187	624	280	344	1,800	741	1,059
35	South Central division	201,834	107,918	93,916	187,620	96,644	90,976	187,918	84,491	103,427	278,798	120,935	157,863
36	Kentucky	11,406	6,259	5,147	10,786	6,182	4,604	12,172	6,190	5,982	21,834	10,373	11,461
37	Tennessee	20,205	11,001	9,204	18,786	10,432	8,354	18,765	8,666	10,099	30,310	12,929	17,381
38	Alabama	50,833	27,127	23,706	45,525	23,482	22,043	42,827	19,004	23,823	58,908	24,906	34,002
39	Mississippi	39,862	21,548	18,314	40,259	20,647	19,612	40,311	17,832	22,479	60,398	25,717	34,681
40	Louisiana	45,423	23,665	21,758	40,219	19,438	20,781	37,288	16,623	20,665	48,664	21,547	27,117
41	Texas	18,545	10,146	8,399	18,683	9,857	8,806	22,521	10,166	12,355	36,398	16,037	20,361
42	Oklahoma	65	47	18	27	16	11	83	15	18	117	42	75
43	Arkansas	15,495	8,125	7,370	13,355	6,590	6,765	14,001	5,995	8,006	22,169	9,384	12,785
44	Western division	2,696	1,420	1,276	3,922	2,528	1,394	6,245	4,562	1,683	15,999	12,791	3,208
45	Montana	46	33	13	124	90	34	179	155	24	496	427	69
46	Wyoming	6	3	3	4	3	1	19	15	4	76	56	20
47	Colorado	19	13	6	49	37	12	170	130	40	475	344	131
48	New Mexico	807	394	413	813	388	425	976	506	470	1,448	791	657
49	Arizona	213	125	88	194	116	78	253	190	63	523	409	114
50	Utah	48	27	21	61	37	24	79	59	20	196	150	46
51	Nevada	271	132	139	315	175	140	367	200	167	799	487	312
52	Idaho	12	8	4	22	19	3	43	34	9	180	157	23
53	Washington	172	112	60	246	164	82	376	251	125	916	692	224
54	Oregon	95	51	44	138	97	41	296	228	68	1,018	887	131
55	California	1,007	522	485	1,956	1,402	554	3,487	2,794	693	9,872	8,391	1,481

a Persons of negro descent, Chinese, Japanese, and civilized Indians.

ILLITERACY.

217

CLASSIFIED BY SEX AND AGE PERIODS, BY STATES AND TERRITORIES: 1890.

35 TO 44 YEARS.			45 TO 54 YEARS.			55 TO 64 YEARS.			65 YEARS AND OVER.			AGE UNKNOWN.			
Total.	Males.	Females.	Total.	Males.	Females.	Total.	Males.	Females.	Total.	Males.	Females.	Total.	Males.	Females.	
515,076	221,548	293,528	412,496	199,208	213,288	235,634	123,304	112,330	193,646	96,316	97,330	26,645	13,297	13,348	1
11,050	5,291	5,759	8,800	4,205	4,595	5,076	2,223	2,853	5,230	2,112	3,118	788	399	389	2
98	52	46	75	43	32	48	32	16	59	25	34	5	4	1	3
27	12	15	21	11	10	18	9	9	16	7	9	7	6	1	4
27	20	7	25	17	8	19	15	4	27	13	14	2	1	1	5
753	354	399	587	270	317	287	126	161	294	100	194	36	19	17	6
306	125	181	260	116	144	120	41	79	159	50	109	25	14	11	7
388	191	197	309	152	157	200	94	106	212	95	117	28	8	20	8
2,504	1,192	1,312	1,932	943	989	1,211	490	721	1,280	537	743	149	91	58	9
2,363	1,047	1,316	1,987	926	1,061	1,144	534	610	1,217	492	725	173	76	97	10
4,584	2,298	2,286	3,604	1,727	1,877	2,020	882	1,147	1,966	793	1,173	363	180	183	11
226,714	94,767	131,947	176,214	82,036	94,178	103,320	53,595	49,725	88,034	43,932	44,102	8,509	3,802	4,707	12
2,036	972	1,064	1,513	728	785	889	429	460	842	371	471	129	52	77	13
16,078	7,121	8,957	12,734	6,037	6,697	7,127	3,339	3,788	6,258	2,735	3,523	892	470	422	14
5,159	1,878	3,281	4,265	1,874	2,391	2,124	888	1,236	1,748	610	1,138	377	163	214	15
47,268	20,431	26,837	36,598	16,877	19,721	22,469	11,458	11,011	20,185	10,332	9,853	1,733	787	946	16
1,846	920	926	1,490	749	741	842	435	407	689	319	370	299	186	113	17
35,952	13,528	22,424	31,803	15,241	16,562	18,887	10,253	8,634	15,717	7,824	7,893	1,237	526	711	18
46,204	19,191	27,013	33,805	15,397	18,408	20,180	10,646	9,534	17,462	8,853	8,609	1,052	436	616	19
61,607	26,443	35,164	45,164	20,860	24,304	26,351	13,877	12,474	21,193	10,858	10,335	2,154	904	1,250	20
10,564	4,283	6,281	8,812	4,303	4,509	4,451	2,270	2,181	3,940	2,030	1,910	636	278	358	21
24,774	11,154	13,620	21,341	10,302	11,039	13,316	6,587	6,729	11,661	5,452	6,209	1,833	885	948	22
3,950	1,914	2,036	3,554	1,757	1,797	2,442	1,210	1,232	2,410	1,134	1,276	251	130	121	23
2,689	1,214	1,475	2,299	1,155	1,144	1,377	696	681	1,105	538	567	191	92	99	24
2,860	1,281	1,579	2,620	1,273	1,347	1,605	833	772	1,308	618	690	168	84	84	25
820	412	408	762	364	398	594	278	316	668	334	334	58	40	18	26
374	186	188	268	140	110	190	94	96	193	97	96	9	2	7	27
200	93	107	169	82	87	101	48	53	123	50	73	28	11	17	28
501	243	258	543	275	268	265	144	121	236	128	108	32	17	15	29
10,113	4,519	5,594	7,588	3,459	4,129	4,535	2,107	2,428	3,912	1,749	2,163	905	417	488	30
55	26	29	17	8	9	13	7	6	10	4	6	2	1	1	31
77	43	34	76	42	34	46	22	24	26	9	17	10	5	5	32
604	281	323	419	204	215	250	130	120	228	105	123	24	13	11	33
2,531	942	1,589	3,026	1,534	1,492	1,898	1,018	880	1,442	686	756	155	73	82	34
237,883	98,507	130,376	198,150	96,493	101,666	110,227	58,143	52,084	86,709	43,617	43,092	12,692	5,926	6,766	35
20,210	9,210	11,000	15,514	7,399	8,115	8,982	4,408	4,574	7,751	3,615	4,136	1,875	1,005	870	36
27,464	10,690	16,774	24,709	11,780	12,929	14,529	7,554	6,975	10,910	5,216	5,694	2,203	970	1,323	37
46,438	17,495	28,943	44,589	22,898	21,691	22,431	11,854	10,577	17,581	9,012	8,569	2,068	1,035	1,033	38
52,223	22,593	29,630	36,504	15,925	20,579	24,610	13,770	10,840	18,770	9,827	8,943	1,921	799	1,122	39
42,030	18,490	23,600	33,309	15,787	17,522	19,086	9,664	9,422	16,020	7,800	8,220	1,137	567	570	40
30,043	12,409	17,634	25,646	13,046	12,600	12,461	6,410	6,051	10,072	5,214	4,858	2,135	977	1,158	41
212	81	131	200	118	82	130	70	60	96	58	38	8	6	2	42
10,203	7,539	11,664	17,688	9,540	8,148	7,989	4,404	3,585	5,500	2,866	2,634	1,255	567	688	43
14,655	11,829	2,826	7,982	6,172	1,810	3,695	2,756	939	2,012	1,203	809	2,823	2,285	538	44
437	366	71	250	218	32	66	52	14	29	14	15	25	22	3	45
76	62	14	35	28	7	3	2	1	2	2	....	1	....	1	46
377	243	134	202	124	78	81	36	45	42	18	24	291	275	16	47
1,101	607	554	879	503	376	415	215	200	294	152	142	12	7	5	48
396	291	105	166	126	40	49	31	18	33	23	10	2	1	1	49
190	141	49	93	70	23	45	27	18	24	14	10	89	58	31	50
757	516	241	458	290	168	227	157	70	130	77	62	208	128	80	51
314	278	36	274	260	14	137	129	8	30	30	....	94	89	5	52
761	518	243	405	231	174	193	112	81	169	89	80	279	184	95	53
763	642	121	410	353	57	165	118	47	70	36	34	202	191	11	54
9,423	8,165	1,258	4,810	3,969	841	2,314	1,877	437	1,180	748	432	1,620	1,330	290	55

STATISTICS OF POPULATION.

TABLE 47.—ILLITERATE NEGRO POPULATION (a) 10 YEARS OF AGE AND OVER.

	STATES AND TERRITORIES.	10 TO 14 YEARS.			15 TO 19 YEARS.			20 TO 24 YEARS.			25 TO 34 YEARS.		
		Total.	Males.	Females.	Total.	Males.	Females.	Total.	Males.	Females.	Total.	Males.	Females.
1	The United States...	411,726	220,414	191,312	371,076	192,853	178,223	360,887	163,107	197,780	550,551	235,420	315,131
2	North Atlantic division.......	1,724	900	824	2,377	1,291	1,086	4,086	2,178	1,908	8,863	4,115	4,748
3	Maine.....................	4	....	4	18	11	7	11	6	5	25	12	13
4	New Hampshire	6	4	2	9	6	3	10	5	5	9	2	7
5	Vermont	6	2	4	11	6	5	17	10	7	24	14	10
6	Massachusetts	41	20	21	99	53	46	160	76	84	489	218	271
7	Rhode Island	18	13	5	31	17	14	57	25	32	160	61	99
8	Connecticut...............	37	23	14	54	19	35	118	58	60	240	114	126
9	New York	366	190	176	476	257	219	797	403	394	1,834	705	1,129
10	New Jersey	466	246	220	622	338	284	1,006	530	476	1,971	915	1,050
11	Pennsylvania	780	402	378	1,057	584	473	1,910	1,065	845	4,111	2,074	2,037
12	South Atlantic division.......	202,773	108,596	94,177	175,331	91,578	83,753	160,857	72,316	88,541	243,464	101,125	142,339
13	Delaware..................	1,179	615	564	1,039	575	464	1,060	535	525	1,990	955	1,035
14	Maryland	7,804	4,135	3,669	7,702	4,197	3,505	7,498	3,665	3,833	14,583	6,352	8,231
15	District of Columbia......	1,051	597	454	1,330	657	673	1,683	660	1,023	3,631	1,238	2,393
16	Virginia	33,688	18,373	15,315	28,995	16,499	12,496	26,299	12,198	14,101	43,416	18,113	25,303
17	West Virginia	969	531	438	1,184	821	363	1,636	1,159	477	2,061	1,144	917
18	North Carolina...........	37,736	20,014	17,722	30,617	16,056	14,561	25,684	10,563	15,121	37,932	14,599	23,333
19	South Carolina...........	51,548	27,366	24,182	42,441	21,102	21,339	36,694	15,697	20,997	51,763	20,755	31,008
20	Georgia	62,888	33,843	29,045	50,118	23,092	27,026	52,243	24,055	28,188	76,258	33,053	43,205
21	Florida...................	5,910	3,122	2,788	5,905	2,579	3,326	8,060	3,784	4,276	11,830	4,916	6,914
22	North Central division.......	5,515	3,042	2,473	5,837	3,346	2,491	7,940	4,046	3,894	18,903	8,027	9,976
23	Ohio	422	211	211	643	366	277	1,054	583	471	2,819	1,438	1,381
24	Indiana	395	209	186	505	295	210	805	438	367	2,090	1,023	1,067
25	Illinois...................	413	214	199	504	302	202	798	391	407	1,949	897	1,052
26	Michigan	86	53	33	120	77	43	133	71	61	337	180	157
27	Wisconsin	11	2	9	14	6	8	13	5	8	48	30	18
28	Minnesota	17	11	6	5	1	4	22	9	13	70	43	27
29	Iowa	55	34	21	59	41	18	154	75	79	354	180	174
30	Missouri..................	3,634	2,022	1,612	3,465	1,953	1,512	4,184	2,110	2,074	9,074	4,203	4,871
31	North Dakota.............	4	....	4	4	4	....	16	13	3	22	12	10
32	South Dakota.............	3	2	1	3	3	....	13	10	3	29	26	3
33	Nebraska.................	48	31	17	70	37	33	132	66	66	332	174	158
34	Kansas	427	253	174	445	261	184	617	275	342	1,779	721	1,058
35	South Central division........	201,451	107,713	93,738	187,284	96,483	90,801	187,525	84,275	103,250	278,074	120,506	157,568
36	Kentucky.................	11,405	6,259	5,146	10,785	6,181	4,604	12,171	6,189	5,982	21,825	10,366	11,459
37	Tennessee	20,201	10,999	9,202	18,779	10,429	8,350	18,755	8,661	10,094	30,290	12,919	17,371
38	Alabama..................	50,749	27,074	23,675	45,490	23,469	22,021	42,773	18,986	23,787	58,785	24,852	33,933
39	Mississippi	39,670	21,446	18,224	40,081	20,566	19,515	40,156	17,759	22,397	60,149	25,601	34,548
40	Louisiana	45,379	23,645	21,734	40,162	19,413	20,749	37,212	16,577	20,635	48,552	21,477	27,075
41	Texas	18,497	10,125	8,372	18,619	9,829	8,790	22,456	10,120	12,336	36,236	15,905	20,331
42	Oklahoma.................	65	47	18	27	16	11	30	12	18	111	36	75
43	Arkansas	15,485	8,118	7,367	13,341	6,580	6,761	13,972	5,971	8,001	22,126	9,350	12,776
44	Western division.............	263	163	100	247	155	92	479	292	187	1,247	747	500
45	Montana	24	21	3	3	2	1	6	3	3	38	25	13
46	Wyoming.................	5	2	3	2	1	1	18	14	4	57	39	18
47	Colorado	16	11	5	27	16	11	87	47	40	281	160	121
48	New Mexico	78	54	24	52	23	29	75	36	39	155	93	62
49	Arizona..................	2	1	1	7	5	2	50	45	5	102	85	17
50	Utah.....................	15	9	6	19	10	9	19	17	2	32	22	10
51	Nevada...................	1	1	....	7	6	1	2	....	2	11	1	10
52	Idaho....................	3	1	2	4	4	....	2	....	2	8	2	6
53	Washington	5	2	3	16	11	5	29	19	10	69	47	22
54	Oregon...................	22	14	8	7	6	1	19	10	9	15	11	4
55	California	92	47	45	103	71	32	172	101	71	479	262	217

a Includes all persons of negro descent.

ILLITERACY.

CLASSIFIED BY SEX AND AGE PERIODS, BY STATES AND TERRITORIES: 1890.

35 TO 44 YEARS.			45 TO 54 YEARS.			55 TO 64 YEARS.			65 YEARS AND OVER.			AGE UNKNOWN.			
Total.	Males.	Females.	Total.	Males.	Females.	Total.	Males.	Females.	Total.	Males.	Females.	Total.	Males.	Females.	
498,667	208,451	290,216	403,634	192,520	211,114	231,490	120,399	111,091	190,899	94,806	96,093	23,738	10,953	12,785	1
10,286	4,587	5,699	8,568	4,030	4,538	4,982	2,160	2,822	5,141	2,073	3,063	729	340	389	2
28	14	14	29	20	9	8	5	3	30	15	15	2	1	1	3
23	8	15	20	11	9	18	9	9	14	5	9	6	5	1	4
25	19	6	20	14	6	17	13	4	27	13	14	2	1	1	5
649	252	397	566	252	314	284	123	161	290	100	190	29	12	17	6
296	116	180	255	113	142	116	40	76	148	47	101	25	14	11	7
358	163	195	299	147	152	194	91	103	204	91	113	28	8	20	8
2,149	856	1,293	1,839	866	973	1,184	473	711	1,258	528	730	114	56	58	9
2,310	994	1,316	1,968	908	1,060	1,140	531	609	1,209	488	721	168	71	97	10
4,448	2,165	2,283	3,572	1,699	1,873	2,021	875	1,146	1,961	791	1,170	355	172	183	11
226,433	94,639	131,844	176,054	81,948	94,106	103,237	53,555	49,682	87,935	43,886	44,049	8,498	3,793	4,705	12
2,035	971	1,064	1,512	727	785	889	429	460	842	371	471	129	52	77	13
16,055	7,099	8,956	12,731	6,035	6,696	7,121	3,334	3,787	6,258	2,735	3,523	892	470	422	14
5,145	1,865	3,280	4,264	1,873	2,391	2,124	888	1,236	1,746	609	1,137	372	158	214	15
47,247	20,415	26,832	36,582	16,871	19,711	22,458	11,454	11,004	20,181	10,331	9,850	1,733	787	946	16
1,845	919	926	1,460	719	741	842	435	407	689	319	370	299	186	113	17
35,834	13,482	22,352	31,708	15,188	16,520	18,840	10,234	8,606	15,650	7,790	7,860	1,237	526	711	18
46,193	19,188	27,005	33,849	15,391	18,458	20,175	10,642	9,533	17,455	8,851	8,604	1,051	436	615	19
61,591	26,432	35,159	45,150	20,849	24,301	26,345	13,874	12,471	21,181	10,852	10,329	2,151	902	1,249	20
10,538	4,268	6,270	8,798	4,295	4,503	4,443	2,265	2,178	3,933	2,028	1,905	634	276	358	21
23,489	10,508	12,981	20,402	9,842	10,560	12,625	6,259	6,366	10,917	5,115	5,802	1,767	849	918	22
3,027	1,893	2,084	3,538	1,744	1,794	2,437	1,208	1,229	2,405	1,131	1,274	251	130	121	23
2,676	1,207	1,469	2,284	1,151	1,133	1,364	690	674	1,097	532	565	191	92	99	24
2,777	1,204	1,573	2,605	1,259	1,346	1,595	828	767	1,306	617	689	164	80	84	25
426	243	183	449	232	217	347	165	182	371	193	178	38	27	11	26
84	42	42	86	50	36	54	27	27	62	41	21	7	2	5	27
110	58	52	84	42	43	41	21	20	32	15	17	5	2	3	28
488	232	256	538	271	267	264	143	121	233	125	108	32	17	15	29
10,060	4,470	5,590	7,572	3,446	4,126	4,532	2,105	2,427	3,910	1,748	2,162	902	414	488	30
18	9	9	6	2	4	6	5	1	6	3	3	1	1	--------	31
25	24	1	15	0	6	1	--------	1	1	1	--------	1	--------	1	32
386	195	191	219	113	106	94	53	41	65	30	35	21	12	9	33
2,512	931	1,581	3,006	1,523	1,483	1,890	1,014	876	1,429	679	750	154	72	82	34
237,235	98,089	139,146	197,760	96,236	101,524	110,047	58,049	51,998	86,503	43,512	43,021	12,645	5,890	6,755	35
20,207	9,208	10,999	15,508	7,393	8,115	8,981	4,407	4,574	7,751	3,615	4,130	1,874	1,005	869	36
27,449	10,676	16,773	24,093	11,771	12,322	14,521	7,550	6,971	10,900	5,211	5,689	2,293	970	1,323	37
46,336	17,444	28,892	44,524	22,867	21,657	22,409	11,853	10,556	17,569	9,005	8,564	2,068	1,035	1,033	38
51,902	22,474	29,518	36,382	15,852	20,530	24,533	13,724	10,809	18,692	9,783	8,909	1,918	798	1,120	39
41,957	18,383	23,574	33,215	15,718	17,497	19,057	9,648	9,409	16,001	7,796	8,205	1,135	505	570	40
29,913	12,311	17,602	25,575	12,995	12,580	12,433	6,394	6,039	10,059	5,212	4,847	2,094	944	1,150	41
209	78	131	198	116	82	138	78	60	95	58	37	8	6	5	42
19,172	7,515	11,657	17,665	9,524	8,141	7,975	4,395	3,580	5,496	2,862	2,634	1,255	567	688	43
1,174	628	546	850	464	386	599	376	223	343	185	158	99	81	18	44
33	14	19	24	15	9	13	9	4	10	4	6	2	--------	2	45
40	30	10	21	15	6	1	--------	1	2	2	--------	1	--------	1	46
252	130	122	159	85	74	69	27	42	40	17	23	9	5	4	47
160	91	69	122	70	52	51	32	19	25	11	14	4	2	2	48
60	42	18	17	11	6	3	1	2	2	1	1	2	1	1	49
14	7	7	13	9	4	7	5	2	1	1	--------	12	6	6	50
26	15	11	18	4	14	13	12	1	8	2	6	--------	--------	--------	51
10	3	7	9	6	3	2	--------	2	3	3	--------	1	--------	1	52
51	39	12	44	24	20	29	13	16	9	7	2	3	3	--------	53
17	6	11	50	41	9	26	16	10	10	3	7	5	5	--------	54
511	251	260	373	184	189	385	261	124	233	134	99	60	59	1	55

220

STATISTICS OF POPULATION.

TABLE **48.**—TOTAL ILLITERATE POPULATION 10 YEARS OF AGE AND OVER IN THE UNITED STATES,

	DEGREE OF ILLITERACY, GENERAL NATIVITY, AND COLOR.	10 TO 14 YEARS.			15 TO 19 YEARS.			20 TO 24 YEARS.			25 TO 34 YEARS.		
		Total.	Males.	Females.	Total.	Males.	Females.	Total.	Males.	Females.	Total.	Males.	Females.
1	All illiterates..................	731,688	396,489	335,199	653,554	351,336	302,218	671,667	326,303	345,364	1,172,057	556,284	615,773
2	Total white.........................	316,498	174,256	142,242	277,613	155,457	122,156	303,247	157,733	145,514	602,977	306,139	296,838
3	Native white..................	292,963	161,728	131,235	224,927	127,471	97,456	206,402	105,046	101,356	377,509	182,091	195,418
4	Native parents............	267,410	147,622	119,788	198,867	112,032	86,835	184,206	92,589	91,617	337,642	161,525	176,117
5	Foreign parents............	25,553	14,106	11,447	26,060	15,439	10,621	22,196	12,457	9,730	39,867	20,566	19,301
6	Foreign white.................	23,535	12,528	11,007	52,686	27,986	24,700	96,845	52,687	44,158	225,468	124,048	101,420
7	Total colored (a)	415,190	222,233	192,957	375,941	195,879	180,062	368,420	168,570	199,850	569,080	250,145	318,935
8	Persons of negro descent......	411,726	220,414	191,312	371,076	192,853	178,223	360,887	163,107	197,780	550,551	235,420	315,131
9	Illiterates who can read but can not write.	104,905	56,956	47,949	127,065	67,430	59,635	119,036	53,695	65,941	219,070	94,381	124,689
10	Total white	62,881	35,062	27,819	66,938	37,668	29,270	63,923	30,207	33,716	134,628	58,380	76,248
11	Native white...................	60,052	33,555	26,497	60,859	34,579	26,280	52,732	24,815	27,917	104,244	43,841	60,403
12	Native parents............	55,528	30,956	24,572	55,382	31,175	24,207	48,138	22,218	25,920	94,304	39,275	55,029
13	Foreign parents............	4,524	2,599	1,925	5,477	3,404	2,073	4,594	2,597	1,997	9,940	4,566	5,374
14	Foreign white.................	2,829	1,507	1,322	6,079	3,089	2,990	11,191	5,392	5,799	30,384	14,539	15,845
15	Total colored (a)	42,024	21,894	20,130	60,127	29,762	30,365	55,713	23,488	32,225	84,442	36,001	48,441
16	Persons of negro descent..........	41,870	21,818	20,052	59,924	29,630	30,294	55,352	23,225	32,127	83,725	35,422	48,303
17	Illiterates who can neither read nor write.	626,783	339,533	287,250	526,489	283,906	242,583	552,631	272,608	279,423	952,987	461,903	491,084
18	Total white	253,617	139,194	114,423	210,675	117,789	92,886	239,324	127,526	111,798	468,349	247,759	220,590
19	Native white...................	232,911	128,173	104,738	164,068	92,892	71,176	153,670	80,231	73,439	273,265	138,250	135,015
20	Native parents............	211,882	116,666	95,216	143,485	80,857	62,628	136,068	70,371	65,697	243,338	122,250	121,088
21	Foreign parents............	21,029	11,507	9,522	20,583	12,035	8,548	17,602	9,860	7,742	29,927	16,000	13,927
22	Foreign white.................	20,706	11,021	9,685	46,607	24,897	21,710	85,654	47,295	38,359	195,084	109,509	85,575
23	Total colored (a)	373,166	200,339	172,827	315,814	166,117	149,697	312,707	145,082	167,625	484,638	214,144	270,494
24	Persons of negro descent..........	369,856	198,596	171,260	311,152	163,223	147,929	305,535	139,882	165,653	466,826	199,998	266,828

a Persons of negro descent, Chinese, Japanese, and civilized Indians.

527

ILLITERACY.

CLASSIFIED BY DEGREE OF ILLITERACY, GENERAL NATIVITY, COLOR, SEX, AND AGE PERIODS: 1890.

35 TO 44 YEARS.			45 TO 54 YEARS.			55 TO 64 YEARS.			65 YEARS AND OVER.			AGE UNKNOWN.			
Total.	Males.	Females.	Total.	Males.	Females.	Total.	Males.	Females.	Total.	Males.	Females.	Total.	Males.	Females.	
1,050,603	476,807	570,886	871,205	393,420	477,785	589,219	259,859	329,360	535,955	224,653	311,302	42,664	23,071	19,593	1
541,017	255,259	286,358	458,709	194,212	264,497	353,585	136,555	217,030	342,309	128,337	213,972	16,019	9,774	6,245	2
333,037	154,770	178,267	245,612	103,667	141,945	184,126	69,700	114,426	191,118	68,632	122,486	9,309	5,303	4,006	3
305,161	141,430	163,731	230,423	96,845	133,578	176,118	66,269	109,849	182,023	65,025	116,998	8,873	5,078	3,795	4
27,876	13,340	14,536	15,189	6,822	8,367	8,008	3,431	4,577	9,095	3,607	5,488	436	225	211	5
208,580	100,489	108,091	213,007	90,545	122,552	169,459	66,855	102,604	151,191	59,705	91,486	6,710	4,471	2,239	6
515,076	221,548	293,528	412,496	199,208	213,288	235,634	123,304	112,330	193,646	96,316	97,330	26,645	13,297	13,348	7
498,667	208,451	290,216	403,634	192,520	211,114	231,490	120,399	111,091	190,899	94,806	96,093	23,738	10,953	12,785	8
194,386	83,526	110,860	100,753	65,054	95,699	122,541	42,868	79,673	115,164	36,788	78,876	4,333	2,271	2,062	9
135,775	54,243	81,532	125,349	43,301	82,048	106,188	32,349	73,839	104,760	30,523	74,237	2,039	984	1,055	10
97,835	39,654	58,181	76,486	26,659	49,827	61,600	17,587	44,013	64,564	17,000	47,564	1,455	666	789	11
89,871	36,457	53,414	71,755	24,931	46,824	58,816	16,698	42,118	61,267	16,077	45,190	1,383	629	754	12
7,964	3,197	4,767	4,731	1,728	3,003	2,784	889	1,895	3,297	923	2,374	72	37	35	13
37,940	14,589	23,351	48,863	16,642	32,221	44,588	14,762	29,826	40,196	13,523	26,673	584	318	266	14
58,611	29,283	29,328	35,404	21,753	13,651	16,353	10,519	5,834	10,404	6,265	4,139	2,294	1,287	1,007	15
58,041	28,832	29,209	35,070	21,510	13,560	16,196	10,412	5,784	10,332	6,220	4,112	2,144	1,139	1,005	16
862,307	393,281	469,026	710,452	328,366	382,086	466,678	216,991	249,687	420,791	187,865	232,926	38,331	20,800	17,531	17
405,842	201,016	204,826	333,360	150,911	182,449	247,397	104,206	143,191	237,549	97,814	139,735	13,980	8,790	5,190	18
235,202	115,116	120,086	169,126	77,008	92,118	122,526	52,113	70,413	126,554	51,032	74,022	7,854	4,637	3,217	19
215,290	104,973	110,317	158,668	71,914	86,754	117,302	49,571	67,731	120,756	48,948	71,808	7,490	4,449	3,041	20
19,912	10,143	9,769	10,458	5,094	5,364	5,224	2,542	2,682	5,798	2,684	3,114	364	188	176	21
170,640	85,900	84,740	164,234	73,903	90,331	124,871	52,093	72,778	110,995	46,182	64,813	6,126	4,153	1,973	22
456,465	192,265	264,200	377,002	177,455	199,637	219,281	112,785	106,496	183,242	90,051	93,191	24,351	12,010	12,341	23
440,626	179,619	261,007	368,504	171,010	197,554	215,294	109,987	105,307	180,567	88,586	91,981	21,594	9,814	11,780	24

CAN NOT SPEAK ENGLISH.

TABLE 59.—TOTAL PERSONS 10 YEARS OF AGE AND OVER WHO CAN NOT SPEAK ENGLISH, CLASSIFIED BY GENERAL NATIVITY AND COLOR, BY STATES AND TERRITORIES: 1890.

TABLE 60.—TOTAL PERSONS 10 YEARS OF AGE AND OVER WHO CAN NOT SPEAK ENGLISH, CLASSIFIED BY SEX, GENERAL NATIVITY, AND COLOR, BY STATES AND TERRITORIES: 1890.

TABLE 61.—TOTAL PERSONS 10 YEARS OF AGE AND OVER WHO CAN NOT SPEAK ENGLISH, CLASSIFIED BY SEX AND AGE PERIODS, BY STATES AND TERRITORIES: 1890.

TABLE 62.—WHITE PERSONS 10 YEARS OF AGE AND OVER WHO CAN NOT SPEAK ENGLISH, CLASSIFIED BY SEX AND AGE PERIODS, BY STATES AND TERRITORIES: 1890.

TABLE 63.—NATIVE WHITE PERSONS 10 YEARS OF AGE AND OVER WHO CAN NOT SPEAK ENGLISH, CLASSIFIED BY SEX AND AGE PERIODS, BY STATES AND TERRITORIES: 1890.

TABLE 64.—NATIVE WHITE PERSONS OF NATIVE PARENTAGE 10 YEARS OF AGE AND OVER WHO CAN NOT SPEAK ENGLISH, CLASSIFIED BY SEX AND AGE PERIODS, BY STATES AND TERRITORIES: 1890.

TABLE 65.—NATIVE WHITE PERSONS OF FOREIGN PARENTAGE 10 YEARS OF AGE AND OVER WHO CAN NOT SPEAK ENGLISH, CLASSIFIED BY SEX AND AGE PERIODS, BY STATES AND TERRITORIES: 1890.

TABLE 66.—FOREIGN WHITE PERSONS 10 YEARS OF AGE AND OVER WHO CAN NOT SPEAK ENGLISH, CLASSIFIED BY SEX AND AGE PERIODS, BY STATES AND TERRITORIES: 1890.

TABLE 67.—COLORED PERSONS 10 YEARS OF AGE AND OVER WHO CAN NOT SPEAK ENGLISH, CLASSIFIED BY SEX AND AGE PERIODS, BY STATES AND TERRITORIES: 1890.

TABLE 68.—TOTAL PERSONS 10 YEARS OF AGE AND OVER WHO CAN NOT SPEAK ENGLISH, CLASSIFIED BY GENERAL NATIVITY AND COLOR, FOR CITIES HAVING 25,000 INHABITANTS OR MORE: 1890.

TABLE 69.—TOTAL PERSONS 10 YEARS OF AGE AND OVER WHO CAN NOT SPEAK ENGLISH, CLASSIFIED BY SEX, GENERAL NATIVITY, AND COLOR, FOR CITIES HAVING 25,000 INHABITANTS OR MORE: 1890.

TABLE 70.—TOTAL PERSONS 10 YEARS OF AGE AND OVER WHO CAN NOT SPEAK ENGLISH, CLASSIFIED BY SEX AND AGE PERIODS, FOR CITIES HAVING 25,000 INHABITANTS OR MORE: 1890.

254 STATISTICS OF POPULATION.

TABLE 59.—TOTAL PERSONS 10 YEARS OF AGE AND OVER WHO CAN NOT SPEAK ENGLISH, CLASSIFIED BY GENERAL NATIVITY AND COLOR, BY STATES AND TERRITORIES: 1890.

STATES AND TERRITORIES.	Aggregate.	Total white.	NATIVE WHITE.			Foreign white.	Total colored. (a)
			Total.	Native parents.	Foreign parents.		
The United States	1,718,406	1,609,069	238,025	168,149	69,876	1,371,044	109,427
North Atlantic division	567,106	562,868	53,198	41,699	11,499	509,670	4,238
Maine	19,329	19,291	5,371	2,466	2,905	13,920	38
New Hampshire	17,874	17,818	508	59	449	17,310	56
Vermont	4,045	4,024	223	28	195	3,801	21
Massachusetts	56,066	55,378	1,345	192	1,153	54,033	688
Rhode Island	13,175	13,117	389	16	373	12,728	58
Connecticut	18,475	18,341	442	38	404	17,899	134
New York	220,850	218,874	3,764	442	3,322	215,110	1,976
New Jersey	41,726	41,349	442	48	394	40,907	377
Pennsylvania	175,566	174,676	40,714	38,410	2,304	133,962	890
South Atlantic division	28,825	26,364	1,099	450	649	25,265	2,461
Delaware	1,085	1,070	4	1	3	1,066	15
Maryland	15,516	15,397	505	205	300	14,892	110
District of Columbia	563	522	19	10	9	503	41
Virginia	1,621	1,595	61	42	19	1,534	26
West Virginia	1,837	1,834	89	60	29	1,745	3
North Carolina	797	166	56	51	5	110	631
South Carolina	206	182	20	20	....	162	24
Georgia	393	346	39	39	....	307	47
Florida	6,807	5,252	306	22	284	4,946	1,555
North Central division	730,752	725,071	34,315	4,741	29,574	690,756	5,681
Ohio	68,264	68,175	2,683	880	1,704	65,492	89
Indiana	20,982	20,924	3,216	1,103	2,113	17,708	58
Illinois	135,916	135,460	4,136	648	3,488	131,324	456
Michigan	84,449	82,648	2,985	574	2,411	79,663	1,801
Wisconsin	143,124	142,155	10,228	454	9,774	131,927	969
Minnesota	98,910	98,517	3,398	111	3,287	95,119	393
Iowa	52,734	52,690	1,719	158	1,561	50,971	44
Missouri	30,778	30,531	2,462	544	1,918	28,069	247
North Dakota	15,239	15,086	440	47	393	14,646	153
South Dakota	20,661	20,282	1,019	23	996	19,263	379
Nebraska	37,502	36,465	1,028	74	954	35,437	1,037
Kansas	22,193	22,138	1,001	116	885	21,137	55
South Central division	170,173	152,936	60,982	48,146	21,836	82,954	17,237
Kentucky	5,565	5,539	285	99	186	5,254	26
Tennessee	1,486	1,435	244	61	183	1,191	51
Alabama	1,044	774	52	35	17	722	270
Mississippi	1,056	416	115	106	9	301	640
Louisiana	66,499	51,146	42,886	41,390	1,496	8,260	15,353
Texas	92,504	91,688	26,277	6,403	19,874	65,411	816
Oklahoma	235	225	23	11	12	202	10
Arkansas	1,784	1,713	100	41	59	1,613	71
Western division	221,640	141,830	79,431	73,113	6,318	62,399	79,810
Montana	3,937	2,271	51	21	30	2,220	1,666
Wyoming	1,667	1,293	29	22	7	1,264	374
Colorado	17,688	16,648	9,032	8,871	161	7,616	1,040
New Mexico	73,271	66,429	62,316	59,778	2,538	4,113	6,842
Arizona	13,009	11,472	2,637	999	1,638	8,835	1,537
Utah	4,476	3,498	41	27	14	3,457	978
Nevada	3,051	677	18	11	7	659	2,374
Idaho	2,185	928	5	1	4	923	1,257
Washington	9,462	5,790	90	41	49	5,700	3,672
Oregon	11,105	3,474	80	40	40	3,394	7,631
California	81,789	29,350	5,132	3,302	1,830	24,218	52,439

a Persons of negro descent, Chinese, Japanese, and civilized Indians.

CAN NOT SPEAK ENGLISH.

255

TABLE 60.—TOTAL PERSONS 10 YEARS OF AGE AND OVER WHO CAN NOT SPEAK ENGLISH, CLASSIFIED BY SEX, GENERAL NATIVITY, AND COLOR, BY STATES AND TERRITORIES: 1890.

STATES AND TERRITORIES.	AGGREGATE.		TOTAL WHITE.		TOTAL NATIVE WHITE.		NATIVE WHITE—NATIVE PARENTS.		NATIVE WHITE—FOREIGN PARENTS.		FOREIGN WHITE.		TOTAL COLORED. (a)	
	Males.	Females.	Males.	Females.	Males.	Females.	Males.	Females.	Males.	Females.	Males.	Females.	Males.	Females.
The United States....	858,889	859,607	773,029	836,040	106,533	131,492	75,874	92,275	30,659	39,217	666,496	704,548	85,860	23,567
North Atlantic division......	293,759	273,347	289,819	273,049	21,877	31,321	16,762	24,937	5,115	6,384	267,942	241,728	3,940	298
Maine	8,300	11,029	8,264	11,027	2,584	2,767	1,168	1,298	1,416	1,469	5,680	8,240	36	2
New Hampshire	7,338	10,536	7,303	10,515	228	280	30	29	198	251	7,075	10,235	35	21
Vermont	1,830	2,215	1,811	2,213	75	148	11	17	64	131	1,736	2,065	19	2
Massachusetts	25,559	30,507	24,992	30,386	522	823	81	111	441	712	24,470	29,563	567	121
Rhode Island	5,465	7,710	5,418	7,699	127	262	8	8	119	254	5,291	7,437	47	11
Connecticut	9,987	8,488	9,854	8,487	203	239	15	23	188	216	9,651	8,248	133	1
New York	108,377	112,473	106,479	112,395	1,658	2,106	174	268	1,484	1,838	104,821	110,289	1,898	78
New Jersey	23,034	18,692	22,665	18,684	197	245	28	20	169	225	22,468	18,439	369	8
Pennsylvania	103,869	71,697	103,033	71,643	16,283	24,431	15,247	23,163	1,036	1,268	86,750	47,212	836	54
South Atlantic division......	15,298	13,527	13,921	12,443	522	577	222	228	300	349	13,399	11,866	1,377	1,084
Delaware	684	401	670	400	3	2	1	....	1	2	663	393	14	1
Maryland	7,382	8,134	7,266	8,131	241	264	100	105	141	159	7,025	7,867	116	3
District of Columbia	256	307	220	302	5	14	4	6	1	8	215	288	36	5
Virginia	1,299	322	1,275	320	32	29	20	22	12	7	1,243	291	24	2
West Virginia	1,185	652	1,182	652	50	39	35	25	15	14	1,132	613	3	....
North Carolina	419	378	98	68	31	25	27	24	4	1	67	43	321	310
South Carolina	106	100	93	89	9	11	9	11	....	....	84	78	13	11
Georgia	226	167	189	157	18	21	18	21	....	....	171	136	37	10
Florida	3,741	3,066	2,928	2,324	134	172	8	14	126	158	2,794	2,152	813	742
North Central division......	321,745	403,007	318,803	400,268	13,732	20,583	1,888	2,853	11,844	17,730	305,071	385,685	2,942	2,739
Ohio	32,083	36,181	32,000	36,175	955	1,728	299	590	656	1,138	31,045	34,447	83	6
Indiana	8,773	12,209	8,718	12,206	1,276	1,940	449	654	827	1,286	7,442	10,266	55	3
Illinois	60,456	75,460	60,021	75,439	1,621	2,515	274	374	1,347	2,141	58,400	72,924	435	21
Michigan	40,753	43,696	40,050	42,598	1,257	1,728	238	336	1,019	1,392	38,793	40,870	703	1,098
Wisconsin	59,405	83,719	59,096	83,149	4,130	6,098	209	245	3,921	5,853	54,876	77,051	309	570
Minnesota	41,764	57,146	41,594	56,923	1,372	2,026	47	64	1,325	1,962	40,222	54,897	170	223
Iowa	23,023	29,711	22,984	29,706	726	993	64	94	662	899	22,258	28,713	39	5
Missouri	13,330	17,448	13,091	17,440	920	1,542	204	340	716	1,202	12,171	15,898	239	8
North Dakota	6,530	8,709	6,447	8,639	184	256	17	30	167	226	6,263	8,383	83	70
South Dakota	9,063	11,598	8,854	11,428	426	593	7	16	419	577	8,428	10,835	209	170
Nebraska	17,010	20,492	16,536	19,929	441	587	35	39	406	548	16,095	19,342	474	563
Kansas	9,555	12,638	9,502	12,636	424	577	45	71	379	506	9,078	12,059	53	2
South Central division......	82,281	87,860	74,504	78,342	31,605	38,377	21,231	26,915	10,374	11,462	42,980	39,965	7,690	9,547
Kentucky	2,604	2,961	2,585	2,954	143	142	54	45	89	97	2,442	2,812	19	7
Tennessee	780	706	740	695	126	118	31	30	95	88	614	577	40	11
Alabama	554	490	439	335	28	24	19	16	9	8	411	311	115	155
Mississippi	497	559	216	200	27	88	27	79	....	9	189	112	281	359
Louisiana	30,090	36,409	23,522	27,624	18,625	24,261	18,066	23,324	559	937	4,897	3,363	6,568	8,785
Texas	46,768	45,736	46,177	45,511	12,598	13,679	3,008	3,395	9,590	10,284	33,579	31,832	591	225
Oklahoma	107	128	97	128	13	10	9	2	4	8	84	118	10	....
Arkansas	881	900	818	895	45	55	17	24	28	31	773	840	66	5
Western division......	145,803	75,837	75,892	65,938	38,797	40,634	35,771	37,343	3,026	3,292	37,095	25,304	69,911	9,899
Montana	3,086	851	1,609	662	28	23	12	9	16	14	1,581	639	1,477	189
Wyoming	1,359	308	985	308	25	4	21	1	4	3	960	304	374	....
Colorado	10,843	6,845	9,849	6,799	4,636	4,396	4,566	4,305	70	91	5,213	2,403	994	46
New Mexico	36,509	36,762	32,880	33,549	30,538	31,778	29,228	30,550	1,310	1,228	2,342	1,771	3,629	3,213
Arizona	7,022	5,987	5,945	5,527	1,356	1,281	553	446	803	835	4,589	4,246	1,077	460
Utah	2,174	2,302	1,408	2,090	18	23	16	11	2	12	1,390	2,067	766	212
Nevada	2,347	704	531	146	10	8	5	6	5	2	521	138	1,816	558
Idaho	1,822	363	611	317	1	4	....	1	1	3	610	313	1,211	46
Washington	6,405	3,057	3,544	2,246	41	49	19	22	22	27	3,503	2,197	2,861	811
Oregon	9,087	2,018	1,835	1,639	31	49	19	21	12	28	1,804	1,590	7,252	379
California	65,149	16,640	16,695	12,655	2,113	3,019	1,332	1,970	781	1,049	14,582	9,636	48,454	3,985

a Persons of negro descent, Chinese, Japanese, and civilized Indians.

256

STATISTICS OF POPULATION.

TABLE 61.—TOTAL PERSONS 10 YEARS OF AGE AND OVER WHO CAN NOT SPEAK

	STATES AND TERRITORIES.	10 TO 14 YEARS.			15 TO 19 YEARS.			20 TO 24 YEARS.			25 TO 34 YEARS.		
		Total.	Males.	Females.	Total.	Males.	Females.	Total.	Males.	Females.	Total.	Males.	Females.
1	The United States	98,704	49,222	49,482	137,747	69,754	67,993	195,383	103,682	91,701	409,049	222,450	186,599
2	North Atlantic division	26,644	13,178	13,466	54,134	26,702	27,432	82,442	44,070	38,372	155,426	89,894	65,532
3	Maine	2,817	1,378	1,439	3,735	1,608	2,127	3,004	1,268	1,736	3,595	1,430	2,165
4	New Hampshire	1,807	798	1,009	3,631	1,413	2,218	3,360	1,463	1,897	3,389	1,371	2,018
5	Vermont	243	108	135	367	217	150	552	322	230	861	435	426
6	Massachusetts	3,528	1,596	1,932	8,692	3,938	4,754	9,730	4,760	4,970	12,890	6,430	6,460
7	Rhode Island	1,552	665	887	2,146	834	1,312	1,950	875	1,075	2,511	1,033	1,478
8	Connecticut	1,045	541	504	2,299	1,168	1,131	3,107	1,752	1,355	4,782	2,883	1,899
9	New York	6,724	3,243	3,481	17,664	8,116	9,548	31,088	14,773	16,315	63,780	34,283	29,506
10	New Jersey	1,319	674	645	3,007	1,634	1,373	5,858	3,279	2,579	12,676	7,627	5,049
11	Pennsylvania	7,609	4,175	3,434	12,593	7,774	4,819	23,793	15,578	8,215	50,933	34,402	16,531
12	South Atlantic division	1,392	756	636	2,893	1,252	1,141	3,413	1,835	1,578	6,995	4,078	2,917
13	Delaware	39	21	18	65	41	24	166	99	67	402	277	125
14	Maryland	478	249	229	1,060	520	540	1,596	740	856	3,489	1,837	1,652
15	District of Columbia	18	10	8	52	20	32	69	34	35	134	75	59
16	Virginia	52	32	20	103	80	23	197	166	31	531	458	73
17	West Virginia	50	27	23	75	48	27	182	138	44	416	289	127
18	North Carolina	110	55	55	93	58	35	89	49	40	177	82	95
19	South Carolina	16	6	10	17	9	8	20	11	9	36	19	17
20	Georgia	17	11	6	33	18	15	51	30	21	105	64	41
21	Florida	612	345	267	895	458	437	1,043	568	475	1,705	977	728
22	North Central division	28,044	13,674	14,370	39,275	20,480	18,795	63,012	31,624	31,388	154,276	70,497	83,779
23	Ohio	1,273	653	620	3,158	1,682	1,476	6,064	3,182	2,882	15,309	8,135	7,174
24	Indiana	896	441	455	1,033	524	509	1,319	655	664	3,287	1,451	1,836
25	Illinois	3,590	1,748	1,842	7,548	3,845	3,703	14,116	6,636	7,480	34,749	16,539	18,210
26	Michigan	3,765	1,825	1,940	4,854	2,536	2,318	8,776	4,928	3,848	21,519	11,131	10,388
27	Wisconsin	5,840	2,789	3,051	6,614	3,285	3,329	9,090	4,064	5,026	26,335	10,605	15,730
28	Minnesota	4,106	1,940	2,166	5,061	2,633	2,428	8,232	4,351	3,881	19,119	7,912	11,207
29	Iowa	1,508	786	722	3,058	1,853	1,205	4,207	2,272	1,935	9,034	3,971	5,063
30	Missouri	958	471	487	1,376	696	680	2,176	1,073	1,103	5,807	2,882	2,925
31	North Dakota	1,248	640	608	1,044	530	514	1,628	810	818	3,338	1,268	2,070
32	South Dakota	1,941	965	976	1,672	832	840	2,050	1,028	1,022	4,129	1,664	2,465
33	Nebraska	1,773	850	923	2,614	1,469	1,145	3,631	1,843	1,788	7,630	3,333	4,297
34	Kansas	1,146	566	580	1,243	595	648	1,723	782	941	4,020	1,606	2,414
35	South Central division	27,204	13,632	13,572	22,876	10,702	12,174	19,824	9,312	10,512	33,094	16,232	16,862
36	Kentucky	141	64	77	265	168	97	381	209	172	952	505	447
37	Tennessee	112	60	52	113	65	48	139	77	62	287	166	121
38	Alabama	84	51	33	65	33	32	104	53	51	237	123	114
39	Mississippi	137	62	75	109	41	68	95	42	53	205	91	114
40	Louisiana	13,450	6,642	6,808	10,367	4,826	5,541	7,798	3,435	4,363	11,600	5,172	6,428
41	Texas	13,173	6,695	6,478	11,836	5,510	6,326	11,139	5,415	5,724	19,398	9,974	9,424
42	Oklahoma	11	4	7	10	6	4	25	10	15	61	34	27
43	Arkansas	96	54	42	111	53	58	143	71	72	354	167	187
44	Western division	15,420	7,982	7,438	19,069	10,618	8,451	26,692	16,841	9,851	59,253	41,749	17,509
45	Montana	68	42	26	228	168	60	583	464	119	1,262	1,006	256
46	Wyoming	11	7	4	73	47	26	286	236	50	609	502	107
47	Colorado	1,222	614	608	1,471	736	735	2,584	1,600	984	5,356	3,478	1,878
48	New Mexico	10,142	5,208	4,934	9,805	4,609	5,196	9,625	4,517	5,108	14,723	6,993	7,730
49	Arizona	1,742	938	804	1,619	772	847	1,606	878	728	3,283	1,880	1,403
50	Utah	71	37	34	160	94	66	269	162	107	760	443	317
51	Nevada	117	53	64	189	130	59	271	188	83	864	696	168
52	Idaho	28	13	15	82	61	21	165	142	23	450	390	60
53	Washington	255	151	104	562	389	173	1,289	941	348	2,915	2,102	813
54	Oregon	155	77	78	358	239	119	971	753	218	3,806	3,236	570
55	California	1,609	842	767	4,522	3,373	1,149	9,043	6,960	2,083	25,230	21,023	4,207

CAN NOT SPEAK ENGLISH. 257

ENGLISH, CLASSIFIED BY SEX AND AGE PERIODS, BY STATES AND TERRITORIES: 1890.

35 TO 44 YEARS.			45 TO 54 YEARS.			55 TO 64 YEARS.			65 YEARS AND OVER.			AGE UNKNOWN.			
Total.	Males.	Females.	Total.	Males.	Females.	Total.	Males.	Females.	Total.	Males.	Females.	Total.	Males.	Females.	
805,106	156,487	148,619	230,171	106,366	123,805	167,706	71,472	96,234	162,925	70,136	92,789	11,705	9,320	2,385	1
98,113	53,170	44,943	66,242	31,382	34,860	42,246	17,296	24,950	37,960	14,895	23,065	3,899	3,172	727	2
2,526	966	1,560	1,784	772	1,012	1,121	494	627	691	340	351	56	44	12	3
2,396	923	1,473	1,801	710	1,091	952	405	547	475	209	266	63	46	17	4
609	206	403	447	157	290	358	109	249	494	173	321	24	13	11	5
8,631	3,621	5,010	6,627	2,735	3,892	3,454	1,393	2,061	2,168	818	1,350	346	268	78	6
2,092	824	1,268	1,627	661	966	814	346	468	417	174	243	66	53	13	7
3,070	1,637	1,433	2,052	1,004	1,048	1,031	446	585	747	277	470	342	279	63	8
41,128	21,563	19,565	27,330	12,816	14,514	17,211	6,963	10,248	14,645	5,625	9,020	1,271	995	276	9
7,923	4,634	3,289	5,162	2,646	2,516	3,008	1,280	1,728	2,320	869	1,451	453	391	62	10
29,648	18,706	10,942	19,412	9,881	9,531	14,207	5,800	8,437	16,003	6,410	9,593	1,278	1,083	195	11
4,966	2,802	2,164	3,751	1,911	1,840	2,623	1,112	1,511	2,600	1,036	1,564	692	516	176	12
231	147	84	95	58	37	51	23	28	32	14	18	4	4	......	13
2,599	1,342	1,257	2,244	1,014	1,230	1,701	732	1,059	1,892	735	1,157	367	213	154	14
99	48	51	74	30	44	57	19	38	59	19	40	1	1	......	15
356	299	57	187	138	49	77	46	31	84	46	38	34	34	......	16
302	193	109	213	130	83	169	62	107	210	85	125	220	213	7	17
129	62	67	83	55	28	46	22	24	66	33	33	4	3	1	18
39	21	18	36	21	15	27	12	15	15	7	8	......	......		19
56	37	19	52	27	25	34	15	19	34	14	20	11	10	1	20
1,155	653	502	767	438	329	371	181	190	208	83	125	51	38	13	21
128,877	54,023	74,854	114,592	46,213	68,379	96,509	38,695	57,814	104,318	45,308	59,010	1,849	1,231	618	22
11,972	5,799	6,173	10,259	4,445	5,814	8,889	3,868	5,521	11,102	4,654	6,448	238	165	73	23
3,028	1,193	1,835	3,295	1,211	2,084	3,298	1,261	2,037	4,752	1,992	2,760	74	45	29	24
25,540	11,393	14,147	19,632	8,093	11,539	15,021	5,706	9,315	15,386	6,243	9,143	334	253	81	25
15,833	7,419	8,414	11,014	5,207	6,617	8,540	3,537	5,003	8,975	3,873	5,102	273	207	66	26
25,187	10,029	15,158	23,106	8,669	14,437	21,616	8,529	13,087	25,091	11,293	13,798	245	142	103	27
17,491	6,438	11,053	16,469	6,377	10,092	14,339	5,869	8,470	13,866	6,117	7,749	227	127	100	28
8,052	2,979	5,073	9,187	3,538	5,649	8,127	3,322	4,805	9,437	4,212	5,225	124	90	34	29
5,212	2,330	2,882	5,336	2,160	3,176	4,648	1,650	2,998	5,118	1,965	3,153	147	103	44	30
2,729	1,020	1,709	1,966	802	1,164	1,757	770	987	1,495	672	823	34	18	16	31
3,418	1,307	2,111	2,919	1,225	1,694	2,331	1,028	1,303	2,152	988	1,164	49	26	23	32
6,594	2,679	3,915	6,342	2,605	3,737	4,735	2,229	2,506	4,097	1,958	2,139	86	44	42	33
3,821	1,437	2,384	4,167	1,791	2,376	3,208	1,426	1,782	2,847	1,341	1,506	18	11	7	34
25,841	12,608	13,233	19,214	9,460	9,754	11,925	5,552	6,373	9,249	4,103	5,146	946	683	263	35
917	460	457	939	425	514	937	352	585	1,011	406	605	22	15	7	36
268	127	141	244	131	113	164	76	88	147	72	75	12	6	6	37
220	116	104	139	72	67	92	42	50	66	28	38	37	36	1	38
178	91	87	124	70	54	90	44	46	109	50	59	9	6	3	39
9,235	4,203	5,032	6,528	2,775	3,753	3,896	1,582	2,314	3,366	1,265	2,101	259	190	69	40
14,657	7,444	7,213	10,813	5,771	5,042	6,503	3,330	3,173	4,381	2,201	2,180	604	428	176	41
38	18	20	49	19	30	23	10	13	18	6	12	......	......		42
328	149	179	378	197	181	220	116	104	151	75	76	3	2	1	43
47,309	33,884	13,425	26,372	17,400	8,972	14,403	8,817	5,586	8,798	4,794	4,004	4,319	3,718	601	44
822	669	153	463	374	89	147	100	47	72	37	35	292	226	66	45
400	353	47	188	158	30	58	41	17	42	15	27	......	......		46
3,247	2,059	1,188	1,772	1,032	740	995	571	424	620	353	267	421	400	21	47
12,202	6,114	6,088	8,351	4,374	3,977	5,131	2,829	2,302	3,154	1,794	1,360	138	71	67	48
2,443	1,343	1,100	1,422	740	682	664	345	319	219	120	99	11	6	5	49
782	435	347	655	290	365	730	280	450	933	354	579	116	79	37	50
848	705	143	444	354	90	193	144	49	108	68	40	17	9	8	51
514	445	69	458	384	74	266	220	46	135	82	53	87	85	2	52
1,859	1,265	594	1,102	697	405	550	284	266	455	211	244	475	365	110	53
3,160	2,758	402	1,526	1,278	248	586	362	224	300	152	148	243	232	11	54
21,032	17,738	3,294	9,991	7,719	2,272	5,083	3,641	1,442	2,760	1,608	1,152	2,519	2,245	274	55

POP. PT. 2 — 17

STATISTICS OF POPULATION.

TABLE 62.—WHITE PERSONS 10 YEARS OF AGE AND OVER WHO CAN NOT SPEAK

'258

	STATES AND TERRITORIES.	10 TO 14 YEARS.			15 TO 19 YEARS.			20 TO 24 YEARS.			25 TO 34 YEARS.		
		Total.	Males.	Females.	Total.	Males.	Females.	Total.	Males.	Females.	Total.	Males.	Females.
1	The United States	92,156	45,880	46,276	129,941	64,870	65,071	184,090	95,222	88,868	377,792	195,728	182,064
2	North Atlantic division	26,605	13,159	13,446	53,856	26,467	27,389	81,748	43,409	38,339	153,672	88,213	65,459
3	Maine	2,817	1,378	1,439	3,730	1,604	2,126	2,997	1,261	1,736	3,579	1,414	2,165
4	New Hampshire	1,802	796	1,006	3,620	1,406	2,214	3,353	1,459	1,894	3,879	1,863	2,016
5	Vermont	243	108	135	365	215	150	549	319	230	852	426	426
6	Massachusetts	3,514	1,590	1,924	8,610	3,874	4,736	9,612	4,655	4,957	12,624	6,199	6,425
7	Rhode Island	1,550	663	887	2,141	829	1,312	1,937	865	1,072	2,494	1,021	1,473
8	Connecticut	1,045	541	504	2,290	1,159	1,131	3,080	1,725	1,355	4,720	2,821	1,899
9	New York	6,714	3,240	3,474	17,571	8,035	9,536	30,790	14,480	16,310	62,922	33,433	29,489
10	New Jersey	1,317	672	645	2,931	1,608	1,373	5,795	3,217	2,578	12,520	7,473	5,047
11	Pennsylvania	7,603	4,171	3,432	12,548	7,737	4,811	23,635	15,428	8,207	50,582	34,063	16,519
12	South Atlantic division	1,150	632	518	2,063	1,059	1,004	3,001	1,062	1,429	6,356	3,700	2,656
13	Delaware	38	20	18	64	40	24	105	98	07	394	269	125
14	Maryland	477	249	228	1,056	516	540	1,577	721	856	3,437	1,786	1,651
15	District of Columbia	17	10	7	49	17	32	59	25	34	119	61	58
16	Virginia	51	31	20	101	78	23	193	162	31	519	448	71
17	West Virginia	50	27	23	75	48	27	182	138	44	413	286	127
18	North Carolina	24	12	12	12	8	4	19	13	6	32	18	14
19	South Carolina	14	5	9	13	7	6	18	9	9	29	18	11
20	Georgia	15	10	5	27	12	15	44	26	18	91	52	39
21	Florida	464	268	196	666	333	333	834	470	364	1,322	762	560
22	North Central division	27,563	13,421	14,142	38,832	20,264	18,568	62,424	31,284	31,140	153,034	69,737	83,297
23	Ohio	1,272	652	620	3,151	1,675	1,476	6,050	3,169	2,881	15,272	8,100	7,172
24	Indiana	895	441	454	1,031	523	508	1,310	646	664	3,258	1,422	1,836
25	Illinois	3,589	1,747	1,842	7,531	3,830	3,701	14,041	6,567	7,474	34,547	16,345	18,202
26	Michigan	3,538	1,709	1,829	4,663	2,459	2,204	8,587	4,856	3,731	21,219	11,015	10,204
27	Wisconsin	5,733	2,735	2,998	6,526	3,243	3,283	8,989	4,021	4,968	26,163	10,530	15,633
28	Minnesota	4,067	1,921	2,146	5,020	2,616	2,404	8,202	4,332	3,870	19,046	7,880	11,166
29	Iowa	1,506	784	722	3,054	1,849	1,205	4,200	2,266	1,934	9,020	3,960	5,060
30	Missouri	958	471	487	1,361	683	678	2,132	1,029	1,103	5,710	2,787	2,923
31	North Dakota	1,224	621	603	1,022	519	503	1,613	802	811	3,303	1,248	2,055
32	South Dakota	1,919	955	964	1,657	825	832	2,018	1,010	1,008	4,044	1,619	2,425
33	Nebraska	1,718	821	897	2,580	1,454	1,126	3,570	1,815	1,755	7,447	3,240	4,207
34	Kansas	1,144	564	580	1,236	588	648	1,712	771	941	4,005	1,591	2,414
35	South Central division	23,602	11,882	11,720	20,156	9,425	10,731	17,804	8,434	9,370	30,279	14,046	15,833
36	Kentucky	139	62	77	262	165	97	377	208	169	844	398	446
37	Tennessee	109	57	52	110	63	47	132	74	58	273	153	120
38	Alabama	52	31	21	54	29	25	74	43	31	164	87	77
39	Mississippi	20	12	8	15	4	11	33	17	16	80	37	43
40	Louisiana	10,068	5,000	5,068	7,839	3,637	4,202	5,986	2,669	3,317	9,256	4,207	5,049
41	Texas	13,113	6,668	6,445	11,760	5,472	6,288	11,052	5,360	5,692	19,171	9,786	9,385
42	Oklahoma	11	4	7	9	5	4	23	8	15	56	29	27
43	Arkansas	90	48	42	107	50	57	127	55	72	335	149	186
44	Western division	13,236	6,786	6,450	15,034	7,655	7,379	19,023	10,433	8,590	34,451	19,132	15,319
45	Montana	44	23	21	137	90	47	437	334	103	858	635	223
46	Wyoming	11	7	4	61	35	26	269	219	50	493	386	107
47	Colorado	1,202	595	607	1,452	718	734	2,477	1,495	982	5,061	3,194	1,867
48	New Mexico	9,266	4,746	4,520	8,915	4,190	4,725	8,623	3,985	4,638	13,307	6,202	7,095
49	Arizona	1,526	811	715	1,436	665	771	1,420	748	672	2,860	1,551	1,309
50	Utah	27	12	15	99	54	45	185	94	91	519	241	278
51	Nevada	6	5	1	56	45	11	99	79	20	231	195	36
52	Idaho	23	10	13	51	33	18	114	93	21	242	192	50
53	Washington	132	74	58	329	221	108	886	628	258	1,893	1,213	680
54	Oregon	99	47	52	192	112	80	430	269	161	1,007	550	457
55	California	900	456	444	2,306	1,492	814	4,083	2,489	1,594	7,900	4,773	3,217

CAN NOT SPEAK ENGLISH. 259

ENGLISH, CLASSIFIED BY SEX AND AGE PERIODS, BY STATES AND TERRITORIES: 1890.

35 TO 44 YEARS.			45 TO 54 YEARS.			55 TO 64 YEARS.			65 YEARS AND OVER.			AGE UNKNOWN.			
Total.	Males.	Females.	Total.	Males.	Females.	Total.	Males.	Females.	Total.	Males.	Females.	Total.	Males.	Females.	
278,109	133,386	144,723	217,219	95,996	121,223	162,265	67,594	94,671	159,777	68,503	91,274	7,720	5,850	1,870	1
97,121	52,231	44,890	65,946	31,129	34,817	42,189	17,258	24,931	37,936	14,880	23,056	3,795	3,073	722	2
2,520	961	1,559	1,784	772	1,012	1,120	493	627	691	340	351	53	41	12	3
2,383	914	1,469	1,796	709	1,087	950	404	546	473	207	266	62	45	17	4
694	292	402	446	157	289	357	108	249	491	172	291	24	13	11	5
8,500	3,512	4,988	6,574	2,699	3,875	3,443	1,388	2,055	2,165	816	1,349	336	259	77	6
2,077	809	1,268	1,625	660	965	812	345	467	416	174	242	65	52	13	7
3,042	1,609	1,433	2,047	1,000	1,047	1,030	445	585	747	277	470	340	277	63	8
40,648	21,099	19,549	27,195	12,691	14,504	17,191	6,948	10,243	14,637	5,619	9,018	1,206	934	272	9
7,837	4,551	3,286	5,132	2,617	2,515	3,005	1,277	1,728	2,318	863	1,450	444	382	62	10
29,420	18,484	10,936	19,347	9,824	9,523	14,281	5,850	8,431	15,995	6,406	9,589	1,265	1,070	195	11
4,519	2,550	1,969	3,498	1,762	1,736	2,508	1,058	1,450	2,511	999	1,512	668	499	169	12
229	145	84	94	57	37	50	23	27	32	14	18	4	4	.....	13
2,568	1,311	1,257	2,237	1,008	1,229	1,788	729	1,059	1,892	735	1,157	365	211	154	14
88	80	10	74	30	44	57	19	38	50	10	40	.....	.....		15
351	294	57	186	137	49	76	45	31	84	46	38	34	34	.....	16
302	193	109	213	130	83	169	62	107	210	85	125	220	213	7	17
23	15	8	20	12	8	15	8	7	18	9	9	3	3		18
35	18	17	33	19	14	26	11	15	14	6	8				19
46	29	17	47	23	24	33	15	18	34	14	20	9	8	1	20
877	506	371	594	346	248	294	146	148	168	71	97	33	26	7	21
127,849	53,504	74,345	113,861	45,862	67,999	95,987	38,472	57,515	103,742	45,075	58,667	1,779	1,184	595	22
11,952	5,780	6,172	10,253	4,440	5,813	8,886	3,366	5,520	11,101	4,653	6,448	238	165	73	23
3,019	1,184	1,835	3,290	1,207	2,083	3,298	1,261	2,037	4,751	1,991	2,760	72	43	29	24
25,424	11,278	14,146	19,602	8,066	11,536	15,017	5,702	9,315	15,384	6,242	9,142	325	244	81	25
15,577	7,339	8,238	11,702	5,223	6,479	8,367	3,470	4,888	8,729	3,768	4,961	266	202	64	26
24,992	9,959	15,033	22,997	8,627	14,370	21,518	8,490	13,028	24,993	11,260	13,733	244	141	103	27
17,442	6,415	11,027	16,421	6,356	10,065	14,295	5,854	8,441	13,814	6,101	7,713	210	119	91	28
8,047	2,975	5,072	9,177	3,528	5,649	8,127	3,322	4,805	9,436	4,211	5,225	123	89	34	29
5,151	2,273	2,878	5,321	2,145	3,176	4,644	1,646	2,998	5,118	1,965	3,153	136	92	44	30
2,698	1,007	1,691	1,956	796	1,160	1,750	767	983	1,486	669	817	34	18	16	31
3,359	1,273	2,086	2,837	1,168	1,669	2,286	1,005	1,281	2,130	980	1,150	32	19	13	32
6,376	2,592	3,784	6,148	2,524	3,624	4,591	2,154	2,437	3,953	1,894	2,059	82	42	40	33
3,812	1,429	2,383	4,157	1,782	2,375	3,208	1,426	1,782	2,847	1,341	1,506	17	10	7	34
23,500	11,618	11,882	17,521	8,752	8,769	10,963	5,192	5,771	8,284	3,750	4,534	827	595	232	35
914	457	457	935	422	513	937	352	585	1,009	406	603	22	15	7	36
255	116	139	236	124	112	163	76	87	145	71	74	12	6	6	37
156	83	73	113	64	49	76	41	35	48	25	23	37	36	1	38
71	44	27	67	37	30	58	31	27	68	32	36	4	2	2	39
7,260	3,446	3,814	5,016	2,185	2,831	3,017	1,259	1,758	2,486	945	1,541	218	174	44	40
14,494	7,319	7,175	10,735	5,712	5,023	6,471	3,309	3,162	4,361	2,191	2,170	531	360	171	41
36	16	20	49	19	30	23	10	13	18	6	12				42
314	137	177	370	189	181	218	114	104	149	74	75	3	2	1	43
25,120	13,483	11,637	16,393	8,491	7,902	10,618	5,614	5,004	7,304	3,799	3,505	651	499	152	44
415	297	118	228	149	79	90	51	39	58	27	31	4	3	1	45
249	202	47	124	94	30	44	27	17	42	15	27	.....	.....		46
3,037	1,860	1,177	1,698	963	735	976	554	422	613	347	266	132	123	9	47
11,095	5,535	5,560	7,509	3,891	3,618	4,730	2,624	2,106	2,861	1,640	1,221	133	67	66	48
2,133	1,119	1,014	1,284	635	649	617	315	302	187	97	90	9	4	5	49
510	204	306	545	200	345	688	253	435	908	340	568	17	10	7	50
141	108	33	66	50	16	47	30	17	27	16	11	4	3	1	51
154	102	52	147	80	67	98	56	42	96	43	53	3	2	1	52
1,099	649	450	675	376	299	385	181	204	331	148	183	60	54	6	53
653	329	324	466	238	228	359	155	204	240	112	128	28	23	5	54
5,634	3,078	2,556	3,651	1,815	1,836	2,584	1,368	1,216	1,941	1,014	927	261	210	51	55

STATISTICS OF POPULATION.

260

TABLE **63.**—NATIVE WHITE PERSONS 10 YEARS OF AGE AND OVER WHO CAN NOT SPEAK

	STATES AND TERRITORIES.	10 TO 14 YEARS.			15 TO 19 YEARS.			20 TO 24 YEARS.			25 TO 34 YEARS.		
		Total.	Males.	Females.	Total.	Males.	Females.	Total.	Males.	Females.	Total.	Males.	Females.
1	The United States.....	48,561	24,203	24,358	38,031	17,735	20,296	28,546	12,788	15,758	41,642	17,431	24,211
2	North Atlantic division.........	7,413	3,732	3,681	6,468	3,189	3,279	4,771	2,196	2,575	7,348	2,942	4,406
3	Maine....................	1,384	724	660	1,199	592	607	806	395	411	892	385	507
4	New Hampshire.............	188	89	99	138	61	77	76	27	49	46	20	20
5	Vermont	40	17	23	48	16	82	40	11	29	38	10	28
6	Massachusetts.............	314	125	189	394	158	236	224	86	138	211	78	133
7	Rhode Island	143	52	91	120	37	83	57	18	39	38	7	31
8	Connecticut..............	116	58	58	141	73	68	70	32	38	63	27	36
9	New York...............	894	442	452	764	381	383	542	245	297	793	295	498
10	New Jersey..............	113	48	65	106	56	50	69	28	41	82	39	43
11	Pennsylvania.............	4,221	2,177	2,044	3,558	1,815	1,743	2,887	1,354	1,533	5,185	2,081	3,104
12	South Atlantic division.........	248	137	111	225	111	114	137	67	70	154	63	91
13	Delaware	......	......	......	1	......	1	1	......	1	1	1	......
14	Maryland	55	36	19	93	56	37	73	34	39	89	43	46
15	District of Columbia.......	4	1	3	4	1	3	2	......	2	4	1	3
16	Virginia	14	6	8	8	4	4	9	5	4	11	6	5
17	West Virginia.............	14	9	5	7	5	2	10	6	4	16	2	14
18	North Carolina............	15	8	7	3	3	......	8	5	3	7	4	3
19	South Carolina............	4	1	3	1	1	......	4	1	3	3	......	3
20	Georgia................	4	3	1	6	3	3	2	1	1	8	4	4
21	Florida.................	138	73	65	102	38	64	28	15	13	15	2	13
22	North Central division.........	10,461	5,002	5,459	6,698	3,020	3,678	4,107	1,663	2,444	6,405	2,085	4,320
23	Ohio	262	130	132	327	166	161	276	122	154	544	203	341
24	Indiana	611	306	305	493	222	271	343	143	200	670	241	429
25	Illinois.................	923	445	478	791	364	427	576	217	359	908	308	600
26	Michigan	1,006	500	506	611	290	321	306	130	176	474	161	313
27	Wisconsin...............	3,219	1,544	1,675	2,295	1,028	1,267	1,343	545	798	2,156	645	1,511
28	Minnesota...............	1,472	675	797	781	328	453	421	152	269	446	142	304
29	Iowa...................	486	235	251	435	215	220	263	121	142	284	88	196
30	Missouri................	467	232	235	377	169	208	344	134	210	599	198	401
31	North Dakota.............	243	108	135	85	36	49	31	12	19	42	12	30
32	South Dakota.............	719	332	387	154	56	98	37	17	20	55	7	48
33	Nebraska................	491	226	265	222	95	127	100	41	59	125	48	77
34	Kansas.................	562	269	293	127	51	76	67	29	38	102	32	70
35	South Central division.........	18,810	9,420	9,390	13,751	6,347	7,404	9,103	4,027	5,076	11,684	4,938	6,746
36	Kentucky................	32	13	19	50	27	23	38	26	12	80	37	43
37	Tennessee...............	60	33	27	40	20	20	31	20	11	62	32	30
38	Alabama................	22	14	8	5	1	4	4	2	2	4	1	3
39	Mississippi..............	15	8	7	10	2	8	11	1	10	25	5	20
40	Louisiana...............	9,782	4,836	4,946	7,397	3,378	4,019	5,325	2,258	3,067	7,449	3,053	4,396
41	Texas..................	8,863	4,498	4,365	6,228	2,910	3,318	3,680	1,713	1,967	4,043	1,803	2,240
42	Oklahoma...............	5	1	4	4	3	1	5	3	2	4	4	......
43	Arkansas................	31	17	14	17	6	11	9	4	5	17	3	14
44	Western division.............	11,629	5,912	5,717	10,889	5,068	5,821	10,428	4,835	5,593	16,051	7,403	8,648
45	Montana................	11	8	3	8	3	5	7	4	3	14	8	6
46	Wyoming................	......	......	......	1	......	1	6	5	1	12	12	......
47	Colorado	1,062	514	548	1,045	474	571	1,245	636	609	2,109	1,041	1,068
48	New Mexico..............	9,123	4,672	4,451	8,681	4,060	4,621	8,225	3,779	4,446	12,311	5,638	6,673
49	Arizona.................	813	427	386	536	250	286	329	154	175	459	252	207
50	Utah...................	5	3	2	11	5	6	12	4	8	5	3	2
51	Nevada.................	2	2	......	2	......	2	2	1	1	4	2	2
52	Idaho..................	......	......	......	2	......	2	......	......	......	......	......	......
53	Washington..............	14	5	9	9	4	5	14	7	7	21	11	10
54	Oregon.................	15	7	8	9	5	4	9	3	6	16	6	10
55	California...............	584	274	310	585	267	318	579	242	337	1,100	430	670

CAN NOT SPEAK ENGLISH.

ENGLISH, CLASSIFIED BY SEX AND AGE PERIODS, BY STATES AND TERRITORIES : 1890.

35 TO 44 YEARS.			45 TO 54 YEARS.			55 TO 64 YEARS.			65 YEARS AND OVER.			AGE UNKNOWN.			
Total.	Males.	Females.	Total.	Males.	Females.	Total.	Males.	Females.	Total.	Males.	Females.	Total.	Males.	Females.	
29,766	12,743	17,023	21,000	8,774	12,226	15,148	6,491	8,657	14,526	5,827	8,699	805	541	264	1
6,200	2,296	3,904	6,331	2,210	4,121	6,277	2,221	4,056	8,156	2,943	5,213	234	148	86	2
539	234	305	302	139	163	150	64	86	97	49	48	2	2	.....	3
24	12	12	14	5	9	6	4	2	1	.....	1	15	10	5	4
28	11	17	9	1	8	11	5	6	7	3	4	2	1	1	5
104	35	69	50	00	00	28	15	13	16	3	13	4	1	3	6
21	8	13	6	3	3	1	1	.....	3	1	2				7
29	6	23	8	4	4	7	1	6	5	2	3	3	.....	3	8
403	144	259	147	51	96	77	23	54	71	19	52	73	58	15	9
36	16	20	21	8	13	5	.....	5	7	.....	7	3	2	1	10
5,016	1,830	3,186	5,772	1,976	3,796	5,994	2,110	3,884	7,949	2,866	5,083	132	74	58	11
99	37	62	68	28	40	46	16	30	76	25	51	46	38	8	12
.....	.....	.....	.....	.....	.....	.....	.....	.....	1	1	.....				13
60	17	43	36	13	23	33	12	21	47	17	30	19	13	6	14
1	1	.....	3	1	2	1	.....	1							15
9	6	3	2	1	1	2	1	1	4	1	3	2	2	.....	16
8	2	6	7	3	4	3	2	1	2	.....	2	22	21	1	17
7	3	4	5	5	.....	3	.....	3	6	1	5	2	2	.....	18
2	2	.....	3	3	.....	1	.....	1	2	1	1				19
4	4	.....	7	1	6	2	1	1	5	1	4	1	.....	1	20
8	2	6	5	1	4	1	.....	1	9	3	6				21
3,347	1,022	2,325	1,420	402	1,018	742	191	551	1,054	303	751	81	44	37	22
432	131	301	351	84	267	188	45	143	290	67	223	13	7	6	23
538	187	351	242	83	159	114	35	79	198	57	141	7	2	5	24
500	160	340	236	75	161	78	15	63	112	29	83	12	8	4	25
230	70	160	132	35	97	94	28	66	120	39	81	12	4	8	26
848	250	598	147	35	112	78	20	58	130	54	76	12	9	3	27
155	36	119	48	14	34	37	7	30	31	12	19	7	6	1	28
144	41	103	31	9	22	28	6	22	43	8	35	5	3	2	29
369	104	265	152	43	109	69	16	53	75	19	56	10	5	5	30
19	7	12	11	4	7	4	2	2	5	3	2	.....	.....	.....	31
18	2	16	15	5	10	11	6	5	8	1	7	2	.....	2	32
39	14	25	23	7	16	20	7	13	7	3	4	1	.....	1	33
55	20	35	32	8	24	21	4	17	35	11	24	.....	.....	.....	34
7,407	3,176	4,231	4,571	1,808	2,763	2,542	1,050	1,492	1,894	690	1,204	220	149	71	35
42	16	26	25	16	9	10	5	5	7	3	4	1	.....	1	36
29	13	16	13	6	7	4	.....	4	4	2	2	1	.....	1	37
4	1	3	2	.....	2	1	1	.....	2	.....	2	8	8	.....	38
14	4	10	13	2	11	11	1	10	16	4	12				39
5,523	2,330	3,193	3,669	1,387	2,282	2,076	804	1,272	1,609	553	1,056	56	26	30	40
1,781	806	975	841	393	448	433	234	199	254	126	128	154	115	39	41
3	1	2	1	.....	1	.....	.....	.....	1	1	.....				42
11	5	6	7	4	3	7	5	2	1	1	.....				43
12,713	6,212	6,501	8,610	4,326	4,284	5,541	3,013	2,528	3,346	1,866	1,480	224	162	62	44
6	3	3	3	1	2	2	1	1	.....	.....	.....				45
4	4	.....	5	3	2	1	1	.....							46
1,507	768	739	1,010	547	463	641	382	259	346	214	132	67	60	7	47
10,147	5,007	5,140	6,794	3,461	3,333	4,327	2,382	1,945	2,626	1,490	1,136	82	49	33	48
265	144	121	129	71	58	76	42	34	29	16	13	1	.....	1	49
1	1	.....	2	1	1	.....	.....	.....	4	.....	4	1	1	.....	50
.....	.....	.....	4	2	2	2	2	.....	1	.....	1	1	1	.....	51
.....	.....	.....	1	1	.....	.....	.....	.....	2	.....	2				52
14	5	9	6	3	3	3	1	2	2	.....	2	7	5	2	53
7	2	5	8	3	5	8	1	7	4	1	3	4	3	1	54
762	278	484	648	233	415	481	201	280	332	145	187	61	43	18	55

STATISTICS OF POPULATION.

TABLE 64.—NATIVE WHITE PERSONS OF NATIVE PARENTAGE 10 YEARS OF AGE AND OVER WHO CAN

	STATES AND TERRITORIES.	10 TO 14 YEARS.			15 TO 19 YEARS.			20 TO 24 YEARS.			25 TO 34 YEARS.		
		Total.	Males.	Females.	Total.	Males.	Females.	Total.	Males.	Females.	Total.	Males.	Females.
1	The United States.....	26,340	13,229	13,111	22,347	10,482	11,865	19,113	8,643	10,470	29,486	12,841	16,645
2	North Atlantic division.........	4,593	2,369	2,229	3,700	1,849	1,851	3,040	1,410	1,630	5,347	2,130	3,217
3	Maine......................	636	324	312	497	244	253	392	189	203	.428	174	254
4	New Hampshire.............	7	4	3	6	5	1	9	3	6	8	3	5
5	Vermont....................				2		2	.10	4	6	6	3	3
6	Massachusetts.............	20	10	10	37	13	24	33	16	17	36	16	20
7	Rhode Island.............	1		1	4	2	2	1	1		2		2
8	Connecticut...............				6	2	4	8	6	2	9	3	6
9	New York..................	95	36	59	53	24	29	51	19	32	108	37	71
10	New Jersey................	4	2	2	10	7	3	10	7	3	8	5	3
11	Pennsylvania.............	3,835	1,993	1,842	3,035	1,552	1,533	2,526	1,165	1,361	4,742	1,889	2,853
12	South Atlantic division.........	59	31	28	49	32	17	57	31	26	64	26	38
13	Delaware..................												
14	Maryland..................	21	11	10	23	17	6	26	14	12	22	13	9
15	District of Columbia........	2	1	1	3	1	2	1		1	1		1
16	Virginia..................	7	2	5	5	3	2	7	4	3	8	3	5
17	West Virginia.............	7	6	1	6	4	2	7	5	2	11	2	9
18	North Carolina............	14	7	7	2	2		7	4	3	7	4	3
19	South Carolina............	4	1	3	1	1		4	1	3	3		3
20	Georgia...................	4	3	1	6	3	3	2	1	1	8	4	4
21	Florida...................				3	1	2	3	2	1	4		4
22	North Central division...........	883	450	433	585	273	312	438	190	248	734	299	435
23	Ohio.....................	87	45	42	88	39	49	66	26	40	130	55	75
24	Indiana...................	255	131	124	154	69	85	102	43	59	148	56	92
25	Illinois...................	106	57	49	89	38	51	65	24	41	113	53	60
26	Michigan..................	72	45	27	47	29	18	55	22	33	110	47	69
27	Wisconsin.................	172	85	87	81	47	34	39	22	17	65	19	46
28	Minnesota.................	30	13	17	7	3	4	13	5	8	22	12	10
29	Iowa......................	20	8	12	21	13	8	15	9	6	25	9	16
30	Missouri..................	125	60	65	74	25	49	55	23	32	72	29	43
31	North Dakota..............	5	2	3	7	1	6	4	2	2	14	5	9
32	South Dakota..............	4		4				1	1		2	1	1
33	Nebraska..................	4	3	1	8	2	6	15	10	5	10	5	5
34	Kansas....................	3	1	2	9	7	2	8	3	5	17	8	9
35	South Central division.........	10,839	5,323	5,516	8,428	3,865	4,563	6,085	2,615	3,470	8,498	3,543	4,955
36	Kentucky..................	17	7	10	15	7	8	14	9	5	18	8	10
37	Tennessee.................	17	11	6	8	5	3	6	2	4	8	4	4
38	Alabama...................	10	7	3	4	1	3	3	1	2	4	1	3
39	Mississippi...............	14	8	6	10	2	8	10	1	9	23	5	18
40	Louisiana.................	9,529	4,715	4,814	7,201	3,283	3,918	5,155	2,194	2,961	7,175	2,964	4,211
41	Texas.....................	1,251	575	676	1,184	563	621	890	405	485	1,252	555	697
42	Oklahoma..................				1	1		3	2	1	.4	4	
43	Arkansas..................	1		1	5	3	2	4	1	3	14	2	12
44	Western division...............	9,961	5,056	4,905	9,585	4,463	5,122	9,493	4,397	5,096	14,843	6,843	8,000
45	Montana...................	2	2		4	1	3	2	1	1	6	5	1
46	Wyoming...................				1		1	4	4		10.	10	
47	Colorado..................	1,033	500	533	1,023	469	.554	1,228	631	597	2,070	1,024	1,046
48	New Mexico................	8,494	4,336	4,158	8,101	3,784	4,317	7,800	3,560	4,240	11,833	5,398	6,435
49	Arizona...................	141	82	59	166	90	76	123	65	58	236	137	99
50	Utah......................	2	2		6	4	2	10	4	6	4	3	1
51	Nevada....................				2		2	1		1	3	2	1
52	Idaho.....................												
53	Washington................	4	1	3	5	2	3	7	5	2	5	2	3
54	Oregon....................	5	3	2	4	3	1	6	2	4	10	5	5
55	California................	280	130	150	273	110	163	312	125	187	666	257	409

CAN NOT SPEAK ENGLISH.

263

NOT SPEAK ENGLISH, CLASSIFIED BY SEX AND AGE PERIODS, BY STATES AND TERRITORIES: 1890.

35 TO 44 YEARS.			45 TO 54 YEARS.			55 TO 64 YEARS.			65 YEARS AND OVER.			AGE UNKNOWN.			
Total.	Males.	Females.	Total.	Males.	Females.	Total.	Males.	Females.	Total.	Males.	Females.	Total.	Males.	Females.	
24,010	10,711	13,299	13,733	7,975	10,758	14,009	6,106	7,903	13,485	5,455	8,030	626	432	194	1
5,163	1,896	3,267	5,827	2,034	3,793	5,982	2,131	3,851	7,883	2,850	5,033	159	93	66	2
269	118	151	133	63	70	63	29	34	46	25	21	2	2	.....	3
7	2	5	5	2	3	4	2	2	.....	.....	.....	13	9	4	4
3	1	2	3	1	2	2	1	1	1	.....	1	1	1	.....	5
21	7	14	21	11	10	11	6	5	11	2	9	2	.....	2	6
2	2	.....	2	1	1	1	1	.....	3	1	2	.....	.....	.....	7
5	1	4	2	1	1	4	1	3	4	1	3	.....	.....	.....	8
52	18	34	29	14	15	16	7	9	15	4	11	23	15	8	9
4	2	2	7	4	3	2	.....	2	2	.....	2	1	1	.....	10
4,800	1,745	3,055	5,625	1,937	3,688	5,879	2,084	3,795	7,801	2,817	4,984	117	65	52	11
51	26	25	50	24	26	36	13	23	63	21	42	21	18	3	12
.....	.....	.....	.....	.....	.....	.....	.....	.....	1	1	.....	.....	.....	.....	13
25	8	17	21	9	12	26	10	16	36	14	23	5	4	1	14
1	1	.....	2	1	1	.....	.....	.....	.....	.....	.....	.....	.....	.....	15
7	5	2	2	1	1	1	.....	1	4	1	3	1	1	.....	16
5	2	3	7	3	4	3	2	1	2	.....	2	12	11	1	17
6	3	3	5	5	.....	3	.....	3	5	.....	5	2	2	.....	18
2	2	.....	3	3	.....	1	.....	1	2	1	1	.....	.....	.....	19
4	4	.....	7	1	6	2	1	1	5	1	4	1	.....	1	20
1	1	.....	3	1	2	.....	.....	.....	3	3	.....	.....	.....	.....	21
574	231	343	452	139	313	366	111	255	655	162	493	54	33	21	22
111	36	75	80	18	62	98	27	71	220	47	173	9	6	3	23
149	59	90	93	34	59	58	19	30	142	37	105	2	1	1	24
63	31	32	81	30	51	42	12	30	77	21	56	12	8	4	25
83	31	52	68	20	48	53	19	34	71	22	49	9	3	6	26
29	13	16	20	5	15	15	6	9	29	9	20	4	3	1	27
14	5	9	6	1	5	11	1	10	3	2	1	5	5	.....	28
19	11	8	14	5	9	16	5	11	25	2	23	3	2	1	29
71	28	43	51	18	33	41	12	29	47	9	38	8	5	3	30
8	3	5	4	1	3	2	1	1	3	2	1	.....	.....	.....	31
1	1	.....	6	2	4	3	2	1	4	.....	4	2	.....	2	32
11	6	5	9	3	6	13	5	8	4	1	3	.....	.....	.....	33
15	7	8	20	7	13	14	2	12	30	10	20	.....	.....	.....	34
6,115	2,641	3,474	4,070	1,578	2,492	2,273	928	1,345	1,653	604	1,049	185	134	51	35
13	7	6	12	11	1	5	3	2	4	2	2	1	.....	1	36
11	5	6	7	3	4	2	.....	2	1	1	.....	1	.....	1	37
3	1	2	2	.....	2	.....	.....	.....	1	.....	1	8	8	.....	38
13	4	9	12	2	10	10	1	9	14	4	10	.....	.....	.....	39
5,312	2,262	3,050	3,521	1,331	2,190	1,973	778	1,195	1,471	515	956	53	24	29	40
753	356	397	512	229	283	279	143	136	160	80	80	122	102	20	41
1	1	.....	1	.....	1	.....	.....	.....	1	1	.....	.....	.....	.....	42
9	5	4	3	2	1	4	3	1	1	1	.....	.....	.....	.....	43
12,107	5,917	6,190	8,334	4,200	4,134	5,352	2,923	2,429	3,231	1,818	1,413	207	154	53	44
4	2	2	2	.....	2	1	1	.....	.....	.....	.....	.....	.....	.....	45
4	4	.....	2	.....	2	1	1	.....	.....	.....	.....	.....	.....	.....	46
1,476	749	727	1,000	545	455	635	377	258	339	211	128	67	60	7	47
9,884	4,865	5,019	6,712	3,411	3,301	4,272	2,352	1,920	2,606	1,476	1,130	76	46	30	48
152	81	71	100	56	44	56	27	29	24	15	9	1	.....	1	49
1	1	.....	2	1	1	.....	.....	.....	1	.....	1	1	1	.....	50
.....	.....	.....	2	1	1	1	1	.....	1	.....	1	1	1	.....	51
.....	.....	.....	.....	.....	.....	.....	.....	.....	1	.....	1	.....	.....	.....	52
5	1	4	4	2	2	2	1	1	2	.....	2	7	5	2	53
2	.....	2	5	2	3	2	1	1	3	1	2	3	2	1	54
579	214	365	505	180	325	382	162	220	254	115	139	51	39	12	55

264

STATISTICS OF POPULATION.

TABLE **65.**—NATIVE WHITE PERSONS OF FOREIGN PARENTAGE 10 YEARS OF AGE AND OVER WHO CAN

	STATES AND TERRITORIES.	10 TO 14 YEARS.			15 TO 19 YEARS.			20 TO 24 YEARS.			25 TO 34 YEARS.		
		Total.	Males.	Females.	Total.	Males.	Females.	Total.	Males.	Females.	Total.	Males.	Females.
1	The United States	22,221	10,974	11,247	15,684	7,253	8,431	9,433	4,145	5,288	12,156	4,590	7,566
2	North Atlantic division	2,815	1,363	1,452	2,768	1,340	1,428	1,731	786	945	2,001	812	1,189
3	Maine	748	400	348	702	348	354	414	206	208	464	211	253
4	New Hampshire	181	85	96	132	56	76	67	24	43	38	17	21
5	Vermont	40	17	23	46	16	30	30	7	23	32	7	25
6	Massachusetts	294	115	179	357	145	212	191	70	121	175	62	113
7	Rhode Island	142	52	90	116	35	81	56	17	39	36	7	29
8	Connecticut	116	58	58	135	71	64	62	26	36	54	24	30
9	New York	799	406	393	711	357	354	491	226	265	685	258	427
10	New Jersey	109	46	63	96	49	47	59	21	38	74	34	40
11	Pennsylvania	386	184	202	473	263	210	361	189	172	443	192	251
12	South Atlantic division	189	106	83	176	79	97	80	36	44	90	37	53
13	Delaware	....	....	....	1	....	1	1	....	1	1	1	....
14	Maryland	34	25	9	70	39	31	47	20	27	67	30	37
15	District of Columbia	2	....	2	1	....	1	1	....	1	3	1	2
16	Virginia	7	4	3	3	1	2	2	1	1	3	3	....
17	West Virginia	7	3	4	1	1	....	3	1	2	5	....	5
18	North Carolina	1	1	....	1	1	....	1	1	....	....	....	....
19	South Carolina	....	....	....	....	....	....	....	....	....	....	....	....
20	Georgia	....	....	....	....	....	....	....	....	....	....	....	....
21	Florida	138	73	65	99	37	62	25	13	12	11	2	9
22	North Central division	9,578	4,552	5,026	6,113	2,747	3,366	3,669	1,473	2,196	5,671	1,786	3,885
23	Ohio	175	85	90	239	127	112	210	96	114	414	148	266
24	Indiana	356	175	181	339	153	186	241	100	141	522	185	337
25	Illinois	817	388	429	702	326	376	511	193	318	795	255	540
26	Michigan	934	455	479	564	261	303	251	108	143	358	114	244
27	Wisconsin	3,047	1,459	1,588	2,214	981	1,233	1,304	523	781	2,091	626	1,465
28	Minnesota	1,442	662	780	774	325	449	408	147	261	424	130	294
29	Iowa	466	227	239	414	202	212	248	112	136	259	79	180
30	Missouri	342	172	170	303	144	159	289	111	178	527	169	358
31	North Dakota	238	106	132	78	35	43	27	10	17	28	7	21
32	South Dakota	715	332	383	154	56	98	36	16	20	53	6	47
33	Nebraska	487	223	264	214	93	121	85	31	54	115	43	72
34	Kansas	559	268	291	118	44	74	59	26	33	85	24	61
35	South Central division	7,971	4,097	3,874	5,323	2,482	2,841	3,018	1,412	1,606	3,186	1,395	1,791
36	Kentucky	15	6	9	35	20	15	24	17	7	62	29	33
37	Tennessee	43	22	21	32	15	17	25	18	7	54	28	26
38	Alabama	12	7	5	1	....	1	1	1	....	....	....	....
39	Mississippi	1	....	1	....	....	....	1	....	1	2	....	2
40	Louisiana	253	121	132	196	95	101	170	64	106	274	89	185
41	Texas	7,612	3,923	3,689	5,044	2,347	2,697	2,790	1,308	1,482	2,791	1,248	1,543
42	Oklahoma	5	1	4	3	2	1	2	1	1	....	....	....
43	Arkansas	30	17	13	12	3	9	5	3	2	3	1	2
44	Western division	1,668	856	812	1,304	605	699	935	438	497	1,208	560	648
45	Montana	9	6	3	4	2	2	5	3	2	8	3	5
46	Wyoming	....	....	....	....	....	....	2	1	1	2	2	....
47	Colorado	29	14	15	22	5	17	17	5	12	39	17	22
48	New Mexico	629	336	293	580	276	304	425	219	206	478	240	238
49	Arizona	672	345	327	370	160	210	206	89	117	223	115	108
50	Utah	3	1	2	5	1	4	2	....	2	1	....	1
51	Nevada	2	2	....	....	....	....	1	1	....	1	....	1
52	Idaho	....	....	....	2	....	2	....	....	....	....	....	....
53	Washington	10	4	6	4	2	2	7	2	5	16	9	7
54	Oregon	10	4	6	5	2	3	3	1	2	6	1	5
55	California	304	144	160	312	157	155	267	117	150	434	173	261

CAN NOT SPEAK ENGLISH.

265

NOT SPEAK ENGLISH, CLASSIFIED BY SEX AND AGE PERIODS, BY STATES AND TERRITORIES: 1890.

35 TO 44 YEARS.			45 TO 54 YEARS.			55 TO 64 YEARS.			65 YEARS AND OVER.			AGE UNKNOWN.			
Total.	Males.	Females.	Total.	Males.	Females.	Total.	Males.	Females.	Total.	Males.	Females.	Total.	Males.	Females.	
5,756	2,032	3,724	2,267	790	1,468	1,139	385	754	1,041	372	669	179	109	70	1
1,037	400	637	504	176	328	295	90	205	273	93	180	75	55	20	2
270	116	154	169	76	93	87	35	52	51	24	27	...	...	...	3
17	10	7	9	3	6	2	2	...	1	...	1	2	1	1	4
25	10	15	6	...	6	9	4	5	6	3	3	1	...	1	5
83	28	55	31	12	19	15	7	8	5	1	4	2	1	1	6
19	6	13	4	2	2	...	...	...	...	...	...	...	...	...	7
24	5	19	6	3	3	3	...	3	1	1	...	3	...	3	8
351	126	225	118	37	81	61	16	45	56	15	41	50	43	7	9
32	14	18	14	4	10	3	...	3	5	...	5	2	1	1	10
216	85	131	147	39	108	115	26	89	148	49	99	15	9	6	11
48	11	37	18	4	14	10	3	7	13	4	9	25	20	5	12
															13
35	9	26	15	4	11	7	2	5	11	3	8	14	9	5	14
			1	...	1	1	...	1							15
2	1	1	...	...	...	1	1	...				1	1	...	16
3	...	3	...	...	...							10	10	...	17
1	...	1	...	...	...				1	1	...				18
															19
															20
7	1	6	2	...	2	1	...	1	1	...	1				21
2,773	791	1,982	968	263	705	376	80	296	399	141	258	27	11	16	22
321	95	226	271	66	205	90	18	72	70	20	50	4	1	3	23
389	128	261	149	49	100	56	16	40	56	20	36	5	1	4	24
437	129	308	155	45	110	36	3	33	35	8	27	...	...	...	25
147	39	108	64	15	49	41	9	32	49	17	32	3	1	2	26
819	237	582	127	30	97	63	14	49	101	45	56	8	6	2	27
141	31	110	42	13	29	26	6	20	28	10	18	2	1	1	28
125	30	95	17	4	13	12	1	11	18	6	12	2	1	1	29
298	76	222	101	30	71	28	4	24	28	10	18	2	...	2	30
11	4	7	7	3	4	2	1	1	2	1	1	...	...	...	31
17	1	16	9	3	6	8	4	4	4	1	3	...	...	...	32
28	8	20	14	4	10	7	2	5	3	2	1	1	...	1	33
40	13	27	12	1	11	7	2	5	5	1	4	...	...	...	34
1,292	535	757	501	230	271	269	122	147	241	86	155	35	15	20	35
29	9	20	13	5	8	5	2	3	3	1	2	...	...	...	36
18	8	10	6	3	3	2	...	2	3	1	2	...	...	...	37
1	...	1	...	...	...	1	1	...	1	...	1	...	...	...	38
1	...	1	1	...	1	1	...	1	2	...	2	...	...	...	39
211	68	143	148	56	92	103	26	77	138	38	100	3	2	1	40
1,028	450	578	329	164	165	154	91	63	94	46	48	32	13	19	41
2	...	2	...	...	...										42
2	...	2	4	2	2	3	2	1	...	...	...				43
606	295	311	276	126	150	189	99	90	115	48	67	17	8	9	44
2	1	1	1	1	...	1	...	1							45
...	...	...	3	1	2										46
31	19	12	10	2	8	6	5	1	7	3	4	...	...	...	47
263	142	121	82	50	32	55	30	25	20	14	6	6	3	3	48
113	63	50	29	15	14	20	15	5	5	1	4	...	...	...	49
									3	...	3				50
			2	1	1	1	1	...							51
			1	1	...				1	...	1				52
9	4	5	2	1	1	1	...	1							53
5	2	3	3	1	2	6	...	6	1	...	1	1	1	...	54
183	64	119	143	53	90	99	39	60	78	30	48	10	4	6	55

266

STATISTICS OF POPULATION.

TABLE 66.—FOREIGN WHITE PERSONS 10 YEARS OF AGE AND OVER WHO CAN NOT SPEAK

	STATES AND TERRITORIES.	10 TO 14 YEARS.			15 TO 19 YEARS.			20 TO 24 YEARS.			25 TO 34 YEARS.		
		Total.	Males.	Females.	Total.	Males.	Females.	Total.	Males.	Females.	Total.	Males.	Females.
1	The United States......	43,595	21,677	21,918	91,910	47,135	44,775	155,544	82,434	73,110	336,150	178,297	157,853
2	North Atlantic division.........	19,192	9,427	9,765	47,388	23,278	24,110	76,977	41,213	35,764	146,324	85,271	61,053
3	Maine....................	1,433	654	779	2,531	1,012	1,519	2,191	866	1,325	2,687	1,029	1,658
4	New Hampshire	1,614	707	907	3,482	1,345	2,137	3,277	1,432	1,845	3,333	1,343	1,990
5	Vermont	203	91	112	317	199	118	509	308	201	814	416	398
6	Massachusetts...............	3,200	1,465	1,735	8,216	3,716	4,500	9,388	4,569	4,819	12,413	6,121	6,292
7	Rhode Island...............	1,407	611	796	2,021	792	1,229	1,880	847	1,033	2,456	1,014	1,442
8	Connecticut................	929	483	446	2,149	1,086	1,063	3,010	1,693	1,317	4,657	2,794	1,863
9	New York..................	5,820	2,798	3,022	16,807	7,654	9,153	30,248	14,235	16,013	62,129	33,138	28,991
10	New Jersey	1,204	624	580	2,875	1,552	1,323	5,726	3,189	2,537	12,438	7,434	5,004
11	Pennsylvania	3,382	1,994	1,388	8,990	5,922	3,068	20,748	14,074	6,674	45,397	31,982	13,415
12	South Atlantic division.........	902	495	407	1,838	948	890	2,954	1,595	1,359	6,202	3,637	2,565
13	Delaware	38	20	18	63	40	23	164	98	66	393	268	125
14	Maryland..................	422	213	209	963	460	503	1,504	687	817	3,348	1,743	1,605
15	District of Columbia........	13	9	4	45	16	29	57	25	32	115	60	55
16	Virginia	37	25	12	93	74	19	184	157	27	508	442	66
17	West Virginia	36	18	18	68	43	25	172	132	40	397	284	113
18	North Carolina.............	9	4	5	9	5	4	11	8	3	25	14	11
19	South Carolina.............	10	4	6	12	6	6	14	8	6	26	18	8
20	Georgia	11	7	4	21	9	12	42	25	17	83	48	35
21	Florida....................	326	195	131	564	295	269	806	455	351	1,307	760	547
22	North Central division.........	17,102	8,419	8,683	32,134	17,244	14,890	58,317	29,621	28,696	146,629	67,652	78,977
23	Ohio.....................	1,010	522	488	2,824	1,509	1,315	5,774	3,047	2,727	14,728	7,897	6,831
24	Indiana...................	284	135	149	538	301	237	967	503	464	2,588	1,181	1,407
25	Illinois...................	2,666	1,302	1,364	6,740	3,466	3,274	13,465	6,350	7,115	33,639	16,037	17,602
26	Michigan..................	2,532	1,209	1,323	4,052	2,169	1,883	8,281	4,726	3,555	20,745	10,854	9,891
27	Wisconsin	2,514	1,191	1,323	4,231	2,215	2,016	7,646	3,476	4,170	24,007	9,885	14,122
28	Minnesota.................	2,595	1,246	1,349	4,239	2,288	1,951	7,781	4,180	3,601	18,600	7,738	10,862
29	Iowa.....................	1,020	549	471	2,619	1,634	985	3,937	2,145	1,792	8,736	3,872	4,864
30	Missouri..................	491	239	252	984	514	470	1,788	895	893	5,111	2,589	2,522
31	North Dakota..............	981	513	468	937	483	454	1,582	790	792	3,261	1,236	2,025
32	South Dakota..............	1,200	623	577	1,503	769	734	1,981	993	988	3,989	1,612	2,377
33	Nebraska	1,227	595	632	2,358	1,359	999	3,470	1,774	1,696	7,322	3,192	4,130
34	Kansas...................	582	295	287	1,109	537	572	1,645	742	903	3,903	1,559	2,344
35	South Central division.........	4,792	2,462	2,330	6,405	3,078	3,327	8,701	4,407	4,294	18,595	10,008	8,587
36	Kentucky..................	107	49	58	212	138	74	339	182	157	864	461	403
37	Tennessee.................	49	24	25	70	43	27	101	54	47	211	121	90
38	Alabama..................	30	17	13	49	28	21	70	41	29	160	86	74
39	Mississippi...............	5	4	1	5	2	3	22	16	6	55	32	23
40	Louisiana.................	286	164	122	442	259	183	661	411	250	1,807	1,154	653
41	Texas....................	4,250	2,170	2,080	5,532	2,562	2,970	7,372	3,647	3,725	15,128	7,983	7,145
42	Oklahoma.................	6	3	3	5	2	3	18	5	13	52	25	27
43	Arkansas	59	31	28	90	44	46	118	51	67	318	146	172
44	Western division	1,607	874	733	4,145	2,587	1,558	8,595	5,598	2,997	18,400	11,729	6,671
45	Montana..................	33	15	18	129	87	42	430	330	100	844	627	217
46	Wyoming.................	11	7	4	60	35	25	263	214	49	481	374	107
47	Colorado.................	140	81	59	407	244	163	1,232	859	373	2,952	2,153	799
48	New Mexico...............	143	74	69	234	130	104	398	206	192	986	564	422
49	Arizona..................	713	384	329	900	415	485	1,091	594	497	2,401	1,299	1,102
50	Utah.....................	22	9	13	88	49	39	173	90	83	514	238	276
51	Nevada...................	4	3	1	54	45	9	97	78	19	227	193	34
52	Idaho....................	23	10	13	49	33	16	114	93	21	242	192	50
53	Washington	118	69	49	320	217	103	872	621	251	1,872	1,202	670
54	Oregon...................	84	40	44	183	107	76	421	266	155	991	544	447
55	California.................	316	182	134	1,721	1,225	496	3,504	2,247	1,257	6,890	4,343	2,547

CAN NOT SPEAK ENGLISH.

ENGLISH, CLASSIFIED BY SEX AND AGE PERIODS, BY STATES AND TERRITORIES: 1890.

35 TO 44 YEARS.			45 TO 54 YEARS.			55 TO 64 YEARS.			65 YEARS AND OVER.			AGE UNKNOWN.			
Total.	Males.	Females.	Total.	Males.	Females.	Total.	Males.	Females.	Total.	Males.	Females.	Total.	Males.	Females.	
248,343	120,643	127,700	196,210	87,222	108,997	147,117	61,103	86,014	145,251	62,676	82,575	6,915	5,309	1,606	1
90,921	49,935	40,986	59,615	28,919	30,696	35,912	15,037	20,875	29,780	11,937	17,843	3,561	2,925	636	2
1,981	727	1,254	1,482	633	849	970	429	541	594	291	303	51	39	12	3
2,359	902	1,457	1,782	704	1,078	944	400	544	472	207	265	47	35	12	4
666	281	385	437	156	281	346	103	243	487	170	317	22	12	10	5
8,396	3,477	4,919	6,522	2,676	3,846	3,417	1,375	2,042	2,149	813	1,336	332	258	74	6
2,056	801	1,255	1,619	657	962	811	344	467	413	173	240	65	52	13	7
3,013	1,603	1,410	2,039	996	1,043	1,023	444	579	742	275	467	337	277	60	8
40,245	20,955	19,290	27,048	12,640	14,408	17,114	6,925	10,189	14,566	5,600	8,966	1,133	876	257	9
7,801	4,535	3,266	5,111	2,609	2,502	3,000	1,277	1,723	2,311	868	1,443	441	380	61	10
24,404	16,654	7,750	13,575	7,848	5,727	8,287	3,740	4,547	8,046	3,540	4,506	1,133	996	137	11
4,420	2,513	1,907	3,430	1,734	1,696	2,462	1,042	1,420	2,435	974	1,461	622	461	161	12
229	145	84	94	57	37	50	23	27	31	13	18	4	4	....	13
2,508	1,294	1,214	2,201	995	1,206	1,755	717	1,038	1,845	718	1,127	346	198	148	14
87	38	49	71	29	42	56	19	37	59	19	40	....	....	....	15
342	288	54	184	136	48	74	44	30	80	45	35	32	32	....	16
294	191	103	206	127	79	166	60	106	208	85	123	198	192	6	17
16	12	4	15	7	8	12	8	4	12	8	4	1	1	....	18
33	16	17	30	16	14	25	11	14	12	5	7	....	....	....	19
42	25	17	40	22	18	31	14	17	29	13	16	8	8	....	20
869	504	365	589	345	244	293	146	147	159	68	91	33	26	7	21
124,502	52,482	72,020	112,441	45,460	66,981	95,245	38,281	56,964	102,688	44,772	57,916	1,608	1,140	558	22
11,520	5,649	5,871	9,902	4,356	5,546	8,698	3,321	5,377	10,811	4,586	6,225	225	158	67	23
2,481	997	1,484	3,048	1,124	1,924	3,184	1,226	1,958	4,553	1,934	2,619	65	41	24	24
24,924	11,118	13,806	19,366	7,991	11,375	14,939	5,687	9,252	15,272	6,213	9,059	313	236	77	25
15,347	7,269	8,078	11,570	5,188	6,382	8,273	3,451	4,822	8,600	3,720	4,880	254	198	56	26
24,144	9,709	14,435	22,850	8,592	14,258	21,440	8,470	12,970	24,863	11,206	13,657	232	132	100	27
17,287	6,379	10,908	16,373	6,342	10,031	14,258	5,847	8,411	13,783	6,089	7,694	203	113	90	28
7,903	2,934	4,969	9,146	3,519	5,627	8,099	3,316	4,783	9,303	4,203	5,100	118	86	32	29
4,782	2,169	2,613	5,109	2,102	3,007	4,575	1,630	2,945	5,043	1,946	3,097	126	87	39	30
2,679	1,000	1,679	1,945	792	1,153	1,746	765	981	1,481	666	815	34	18	16	31
3,341	1,271	2,070	2,822	1,163	1,659	2,275	999	1,276	2,122	979	1,143	30	19	11	32
6,337	2,578	3,759	6,125	2,517	3,608	4,571	2,147	2,424	3,946	1,891	2,055	81	42	39	33
3,757	1,409	2,348	4,125	1,774	2,351	3,187	1,422	1,765	2,812	1,330	1,482	17	10	7	34
16,093	8,442	7,651	12,950	6,944	6,006	8,421	4,142	4,279	6,390	3,060	3,330	607	446	161	35
872	441	431	910	406	504	927	347	580	1,002	403	599	21	15	6	36
226	103	123	223	118	105	159	76	83	141	69	72	11	6	5	37
152	82	70	111	64	47	75	40	35	46	25	21	29	28	1	38
57	40	17	54	35	19	47	30	17	52	28	24	4	2	2	39
1,737	1,116	621	1,347	798	549	941	455	486	877	392	485	162	148	14	40
12,713	6,513	6,200	9,894	5,319	4,575	6,038	3,075	2,963	4,107	2,065	2,042	377	245	132	41
33	15	18	48	19	29	23	10	13	17	5	12	....	....	....	42
303	132	171	363	185	178	211	109	102	148	73	75	3	2	1	43
12,407	7,271	5,136	7,783	4,165	3,618	5,077	2,601	2,476	3,958	1,933	2,025	427	337	90	44
409	294	115	225	148	77	88	50	38	58	27	31	4	3	1	45
245	198	47	119	91	28	43	26	17	42	15	27	....	....	....	46
1,530	1,092	438	688	416	272	335	172	163	267	133	134	65	63	2	47
948	528	420	715	430	285	403	242	161	235	150	85	51	18	33	48
1,868	975	893	1,155	564	591	541	273	268	158	81	77	8	4	4	49
509	203	306	543	199	344	688	253	435	904	340	564	16	9	7	50
141	108	33	62	48	14	45	28	17	26	16	10	3	2	1	51
154	102	52	146	79	67	98	56	42	94	43	51	3	2	1	52
1,085	644	441	669	373	296	382	180	202	329	148	181	53	49	4	53
646	327	319	458	235	223	351	154	197	236	111	125	24	20	4	54
4,872	2,800	2,072	3,003	1,582	1,421	2,103	1,167	936	1,609	869	740	200	167	33	55

STATISTICS OF POPULATION.

TABLE 67.—COLORED PERSONS (a) 10 YEARS OF AGE AND OVER WHO CAN NOT SPEAK

	STATES AND TERRITORIES.	10 TO 14 YEARS.			15 TO 19 YEARS.			20 TO 24 YEARS.			25 TO 34 YEARS.		
		Total.	Males.	Females.	Total.	Males.	Females.	Total.	Males.	Females.	Total.	Males.	Females.
1	The United States.....	6,548	3,342	3,206	7,806	4,884	2,922	11,293	8,460	2,833	31,257	26,722	4,535
2	North Atlantic division.........	39	19	20	278	235	43	604	661	33	1,754	1,681	73
3	Maine............	...	...	...	5	4	1	7	7	...	16	16	...
4	New Hampshire............	5	2	3	11	7	4	7	4	3	10	8	2
5	Vermont............	...	...	...	2	2	...	3	3	...	9	9	...
6	Massachusetts............	14	6	8	82	64	18	118	105	13	266	231	35
7	Rhode Island............	2	2	...	5	5	...	13	10	3	17	12	5
8	Connecticut............	...	...	...	9	9	...	27	27	...	62	62	...
9	New York............	10	3	7	93	81	12	298	293	5	867	850	17
10	New Jersey............	2	2	...	26	26	...	63	62	1	156	154	2
11	Pennsylvania............	6	4	2	45	37	8	158	150	8	351	339	12
12	South Atlantic division.........	242	124	118	330	193	137	322	173	149	639	378	261
13	Delaware............	1	1	...	1	1	...	1	1	...	8	8	...
14	Maryland............	1	...	1	4	4	...	19	19	...	52	51	1
15	District of Columbia.........	1	...	1	3	3	...	10	9	1	15	14	1
16	Virginia.........	1	1	...	2	2	...	4	4	...	12	10	2
17	West Virginia.........	...	...	...	...	...	...	...	...	...	3	3	...
18	North Carolina............	86	43	43	81	50	31	70	36	34	145	64	81
19	South Carolina............	2	1	1	4	2	2	2	2	...	7	1	6
20	Georgia.........	2	1	1	6	6	...	7	4	3	14	12	2
21	Florida............	148	77	71	229	125	104	209	98	111	383	215	168
22	North Central division.........	481	253	228	443	216	227	588	340	248	1,242	760	482
23	Ohio............	1	1	...	7	7	...	14	13	1	37	35	2
24	Indiana.........	1	...	1	2	1	1	9	9	...	29	29	...
25	Illinois.........	1	1	...	17	15	2	75	69	6	202	194	8
26	Michigan.........	227	116	111	191	77	114	189	72	117	300	116	184
27	Wisconsin.........	107	54	53	88	42	46	101	43	58	172	75	97
28	Minnesota.........	39	19	20	41	17	24	30	19	11	73	32	41
29	Iowa.........	2	2	...	4	4	...	7	6	1	14	11	3
30	Missouri.........	...	...	...	15	13	2	44	44	...	97	95	2
31	North Dakota.........	24	19	5	22	11	11	15	8	7	35	20	15
32	South Dakota.........	22	10	12	15	7	8	32	18	14	85	45	40
33	Nebraska.........	55	29	26	34	15	19	61	28	33	183	93	90
34	Kansas.........	2	2	...	7	7	...	11	11	...	15	15	...
35	South Central division.........	3,602	1,750	1,852	2,720	1,277	1,443	2,020	878	1,142	2,815	1,286	1,529
36	Kentucky.........	2	2	...	3	3	...	4	1	3	8	7	1
37	Tennessee.........	3	3	...	3	2	1	7	3	4	14	13	1
38	Alabama.........	32	20	12	11	4	7	30	10	20	73	36	37
39	Mississippi.........	117	50	67	94	37	57	62	25	37	125	54	71
40	Louisiana.........	3,382	1,642	1,740	2,528	1,189	1,339	1,812	766	1,046	2,344	965	1,379
41	Texas.........	60	27	33	76	38	38	87	55	32	227	188	39
42	Oklahoma.........	...	...	...	1	1	...	2	2	...	5	5	...
43	Arkansas.........	6	6	...	4	3	1	16	16	...	19	18	1
44	Western division.........	2,184	1,196	988	4,035	2,963	1,072	7,669	6,408	1,261	24,807	22,617	2,190
45	Montana.........	24	19	5	91	78	13	146	130	16	404	371	33
46	Wyoming.........	...	...	...	12	12	...	17	17	...	116	116	...
47	Colorado.........	20	19	1	19	18	1	107	105	2	295	284	11
48	New Mexico.........	876	462	414	890	419	471	1,003	532	470	1,426	791	635
49	Arizona.........	216	127	89	183	107	76	186	130	56	423	329	94
50	Utah.........	44	25	19	61	40	21	84	68	16	241	202	39
51	Nevada.........	111	48	63	133	85	48	172	109	63	633	501	132
52	Idaho.........	5	3	2	31	28	3	51	49	2	208	198	10
53	Washington.........	123	77	46	233	168	65	403	313	90	1,022	889	133
54	Oregon.........	56	30	26	166	127	39	541	484	57	2,799	2,686	113
55	California.........	709	386	323	2,216	1,881	335	4,960	4,471	489	17,240	16,250	990

a Persons of negro descent, Chinese, Japanese, and civilized Indians.

CAN NOT SPEAK ENGLISH.   269

ENGLISH, CLASSIFIED BY SEX AND AGE PERIODS, BY STATES AND TERRITORIES: 1890.

35 TO 44 YEARS.			45 TO 54 YEARS.			55 TO 64 YEARS.			65 YEARS AND OVER.			AGE UNKNOWN.			
Total.	Males.	Females.	Total.	Males.	Females.	Total.	Males.	Females.	Total.	Males.	Females.	Total.	Males.	Females.	
26,997	23,101	3,896	12,952	10,370	2,582	5,441	3,878	1,503	3,148	1,633	1,515	3,985	3,470	515	1
992	939	53	296	253	43	57	38	19	24	15	9	104	99	5	2
6	5	1	....	....		1	1					3	3	....	3
13	9	4	5	1	4	2	1	1	2	2	....	1	1	....	4
5	4	1	1	....	1	1	1	....							5
131	109	22	53	36	17	11	5	6	3	2	1	10	9	1	6
15	15	....	2	1	1	2	1	1	1	....	1	1	1	....	7
28	28	....	5	4	1	1	1					2	2		8
480	464	16	135	125	10	20	15	5	8	6	2	65	61	4	9
86	83	3	30	29	1	3	3	....	2	1	1	9	9	....	10
228	222	6	65	57	8	16	10	6	8	4	4	13	13	....	11
447	252	195	253	149	104	115	54	61	89	37	52	24	17	7	12
2	2	....	1	1	....	1		1							13
31	31	....	7	6	1	3	3					2	2		14
11	9	2	....	....	....							1	1		15
5	5	....	1	1	....	1	1								16
....															17
106	47	59	63	43	20	31	14	17	48	24	24	1	....	1	18
4	3	1	3	2	1	1	1		1	1	....				19
10	8	2	5	4	1	1		1				2	2		20
278	147	131	173	92	81	77	35	42	40	12	28	18	12	6	21
1,028	519	509	731	351	380	522	223	299	576	233	343	70	47	23	22
20	19	1	6	5	1	3	2	1	1	1	....				23
9	9	....	5	4	1	....			1	1		2	2		24
116	115	1	30	27	3	4	4	....	2	1	1	9	9	....	25
256	80	176	212	74	138	173	58	115	246	105	141	7	5	2	26
195	70	125	109	42	67	98	39	59	98	33	65	1	1	....	27
49	23	26	48	21	27	44	15	29	52	16	36	17	8	9	28
5	4	1	10	10	....				1	1		1	1		29
61	57	4	15	15	....	4	4		....	....		11	11		30
31	13	18	10	6	4	7	3	4	9	3	6	....			31
59	34	25	82	57	25	45	23	22	22	8	14	17	7	10	32
218	87	131	194	81	113	144	75	69	144	64	80	4	2	2	33
9	8	1	10	9	1							1	1		34
2,341	990	1,351	1,693	708	985	962	360	602	965	353	612	119	88	31	35
3	3	....	4	3	1				2	....	2				36
13	11	2	8	7	1	1	....	1	2	1	1	....			37
64	33	31	26	8	18	16	1	15	18	3	15	....			38
107	47	60	57	33	24	32	13	19	41	18	23	5	4	1	39
1,975	757	1,218	1,512	590	922	879	323	556	880	320	560	41	16	25	40
163	125	38	78	59	19	32	21	11	20	10	10	73	68	5	41
2	2	....	....												42
14	12	2	8	8	....	2	2	....	2	1	1	....			43
22,189	20,401	1,788	9,979	8,909	1,070	3,785	3,203	582	1,494	995	499	3,668	3,219	449	44
407	372	35	235	225	10	57	49	8	14	10	4	288	223	65	45
151	151	....	64	64	....	14	14								46
210	199	11	74	69	5	19	17	2	7	6	1	289	277	12	47
1,107	579	528	842	483	359	401	205	196	293	154	139	5	4	1	48
310	224	86	138	105	33	47	30	17	32	23	9	2	2	....	49
272	231	41	110	90	20	42	27	15	25	14	11	99	69	30	50
707	597	110	378	304	74	146	114	32	81	52	29	13	6	7	51
360	343	17	311	304	7	168	164	4	39	39	....	84	83	1	52
760	616	144	427	321	106	165	103	62	124	63	61	415	311	104	53
2,507	2,429	78	1,060	1,040	20	227	207	20	60	40	20	215	209	6	54
15,398	14,660	738	6,340	5,904	436	2,499	2,273	226	819	594	225	2,258	2,035	223	55

CITIZENSHIP OF FOREIGN BORN MALES 21 YEARS OF AGE AND OVER.

CITIZENSHIP OF FOREIGN BORN MALES.   281

TABLE 71.—FOREIGN BORN MALES 21 YEARS OF AGE AND OVER, CLASSIFIED ACCORDING TO CITIZENSHIP, BY STATES AND TERRITORIES: 1890.

STATES AND TERRITORIES.	Foreign born males 21 years of age and over.	ALIENS.			Naturalized.	First naturalization papers filed.	Unknown.
		Total.	Can speak English.	Can not speak English.			
The United States	4,348,459	1,189,452	801,260	388,192	2,545,753	236,061	377,193
North Atlantic division	1,679,850	578,523	410,626	167,897	912,575	54,752	134,000
Maine	30,470	15,670	12,959	2,711	11,128	558	3,114
New Hampshire	26,047	13,037	9,431	3,606	10,131	688	2,191
Vermont	10,686	8,120	7,103	1,017	9,243	496	1,827
Massachusetts	257,604	118,508	102,650	15,858	112,504	6,541	19,541
Rhode Island	40,185	20,004	16,966	3,038	15,605	1,554	3,022
Connecticut	78,419	28,639	22,408	6,231	38,730	2,098	8,952
New York	685,462	193,046	129,734	63,312	416,372	22,737	53,307
New Jersey	145,047	41,877	27,561	14,316	87,466	4,993	10,711
Pennsylvania	397,440	139,622	81,814	57,808	211,396	15,087	31,335
South Atlantic division	102,178	26,607	18,809	7,798	61,325	3,040	11,206
Delaware	6,152	2,094	1,579	515	3,494	115	449
Maryland	42,589	11,083	7,341	3,742	26,322	1,394	3,790
District of Columbia	9,242	1,833	1,688	145	5,617	163	1,629
Virginia	11,313	3,056	2,177	879	6,730	175	1,343
West Virginia	9,780	1,822	1,186	636	6,320	204	1,437
North Carolina	2,081	419	384	35	1,338	48	276
South Carolina	3,406	736	688	48	2,261	59	350
Georgia	6,954	1,716	1,578	138	4,129	171	938
Florida	10,652	3,848	2,188	1,660	5,099	711	994
North Central division	1,921,101	360,732	246,205	114,527	1,243,914	139,413	177,042
Ohio	218,841	38,672	24,971	13,701	153,789	5,495	20,883
Indiana	73,358	5,187	3,833	1,354	55,670	3,467	9,028
Illinois	399,317	95,729	66,779	28,950	242,487	16,947	35,154
Michigan	248,317	58,895	42,412	16,483	145,901	22,134	21,357
Wisconsin	244,384	37,844	21,864	15,980	158,149	23,368	20,023
Minnesota	221,300	37,297	24,519	12,778	140,902	25,720	17,380
Iowa	155,670	26,283	17,699	8,584	107,236	6,929	15,222
Missouri	120,737	22,151	16,963	5,188	80,886	4,153	13,547
North Dakota	36,314	9,633	7,603	2,030	17,747	7,376	1,538
South Dakota	42,014	5,573	3,722	1,851	28,644	5,073	3,024
Nebraska	95,875	15,328	10,070	5,258	61,815	8,334	10,398
Kansas	73,065	8,140	5,770	2,370	50,682	4,817	9,426
South Central division	164,537	40,284	22,337	17,947	96,777	6,728	20,748
Kentucky	29,816	4,601	3,595	1,006	20,933	541	3,736
Tennessee	11,047	2,240	1,960	280	6,500	347	1,951
Alabama	8,125	1,772	1,548	224	4,865	338	1,150
Mississippi	5,031	1,104	958	146	3,079	97	751
Louisiana	25,351	7,597	4,644	2,953	13,975	991	2,788
Texas	75,248	21,638	8,538	13,100	40,956	4,036	8,618
Oklahoma	1,659	123	111	12	1,217	70	249
Arkansas	8,260	1,209	974	226	5,247	308	1,505
Western division	480,793	183,306	103,283	80,023	231,162	32,128	34,197
Montana	29,073	8,360	6,332	2,028	14,950	4,787	1,876
Wyoming	9,192	2,802	1,770	1,032	4,378	1,076	936
Colorado	50,340	12,446	8,569	3,877	29,449	3,662	4,783
New Mexico	6,757	2,393	1,103	1,290	3,574	307	483
Arizona	10,031	5,179	1,882	3,297	3,893	222	737
Utah	24,525	6,437	5,075	1,362	14,021	1,509	1,898
Nevada	10,770	4,277	2,678	1,599	5,824	264	405
Idaho	11,705	3,641	2,144	1,497	6,465	845	754
Washington	57,950	16,677	12,766	3,911	29,649	6,862	4,762
Oregon	37,415	13,422	5,870	7,552	17,795	2,677	3,521
California	232,135	107,672	55,094	52,578	100,564	9,857	14,042

OCCUPATIONS.

(For designations of Tables, see the two following pages.)

302

STATISTICS OF POPULATION.

TABLE 77.—TOTAL PERSONS 10 YEARS OF AGE AND OVER ENGAGED IN GAINFUL OCCUPATIONS

	STATES AND TERRITORIES.	POPULATION 10 YEARS OF AGE AND OVER.			PERSONS ENGAGED IN GAINFUL OCCUPATIONS.			PERSONS ENGAGED IN AGRICULTURE, FISHERIES, AND MINING.		
		Total.	Males.	Females.	Total.	Males.	Females.	Total.	Males.	Females.
1	The United States	47,413,559	24,352,659	23,060,900	22,735,661	18,821,090	3,914,571	9,013,336	8,333,813	679,523
2	North Atlantic division	13,888,377	6,904,566	6,983,811	6,971,460	5,543,041	1,428,419	1,265,950	1,245,102	20,848
3	Maine	541,662	271,787	269,875	257,096	212,033	45,063	86,296	84,831	1,465
4	New Hampshire	315,497	155,928	159,569	164,703	127,845	36,858	42,982	42,360	622
5	Vermont	271,173	137,899	133,274	129,771	108,904	10,007	50,100	55,504	010
6	Massachusetts	1,839,607	887,063	952,544	982,444	719,166	263,278	81,100	80,163	937
7	Rhode Island	281,959	135,955	146,004	155,878	113,164	42,714	12,606	12,422	184
8	Connecticut	609,830	300,675	309,155	317,014	245,634	71,380	48,676	47,909	767
9	New York	4,822,392	2,385,622	2,436,770	2,435,725	1,921,785	513,940	410,132	401,529	8,603
10	New Jersey	1,143,123	568,585	574,538	570,738	459,467	111,271	74,889	73,477	1,412
11	Pennsylvania	4,063,134	2,061,052	2,002,082	1,959,001	1,635,143	323,948	453,086	446,877	6,209
12	South Atlantic division	6,415,921	3,178,769	3,237,152	3,118,056	2,431,787	686,269	1,714,318	1,466,832	247,486
13	Delaware	131,967	67,309	64,658	64,286	53,938	10,348	18,702	18,395	307
14	Maryland	798,605	392,485	406,120	393,267	308,515	84,752	105,396	102,669	2,727
15	District of Columbia	188,567	88,703	99,864	101,119	68,992	32,127	1,886	1,829	57
16	Virginia	1,211,934	598,677	613,257	551,839	445,473	106,366	271,745	255,009	16,736
17	West Virginia	549,538	281,576	267,962	223,788	202,081	21,707	129,887	126,631	3,256
18	North Carolina	1,147,446	559,764	587,682	537,363	422,171	115,192	374,359	318,711	55,648
19	South Carolina	802,406	395,466	406,940	440,854	311,423	129,431	328,017	239,567	88,450
20	Georgia	1,302,208	647,922	654,286	668,713	508,790	159,923	418,128	347,601	70,527
21	Florida	283,250	146,867	136,383	136,827	110,404	26,423	66,198	56,420	9,778
22	North Central division	16,909,613	8,828,083	8,081,530	7,673,838	6,661,149	1,012,689	3,239,103	3,158,833	80,270
23	Ohio	2,858,659	1,442,430	1,416,229	1,272,786	1,088,609	184,177	429,019	418,806	10,213
24	Indiana	1,674,028	855,368	818,660	724,058	639,156	84,902	330,569	322,221	8,348
25	Illinois	2,907,671	1,507,159	1,400,512	1,353,559	1,153,249	200,310	456,488	443,559	12,929
26	Michigan	1,619,035	851,163	767,872	759,575	663,627	95,948	308,501	302,398	6,103
27	Wisconsin	1,258,390	657,968	600,422	576,290	495,229	81,061	242,099	236,168	5,931
28	Minnesota	962,350	523,342	439,008	469,086	403,461	65,625	195,422	191,596	3,826
29	Iowa	1,441,308	755,134	686,174	631,835	551,418	80,417	330,390	322,296	8,094
30	Missouri	1,995,638	1,037,994	957,644	884,379	771,554	112,825	404,665	392,245	12,420
31	North Dakota	129,452	74,442	55,010	67,771	59,956	7,815	43,055	43,131	824
32	South Dakota	236,208	133,252	102,956	114,093	102,635	11,458	70,839	69,429	1,410
33	Nebraska	771,659	426,815	344,844	368,060	325,416	42,644	170,574	167,117	8,457
34	Kansas	1,035,215	563,016	492,199	452,346	406,839	45,507	256,582	249,867	6,715
35	South Central division	7,799,487	3,977,614	3,821,873	3,635,814	2,973,045	662,769	2,347,204	2,023,282	323,922
36	Kentucky	1,360,031	689,572	670,459	590,324	506,946	83,378	326,085	314,212	11,873
37	Tennessee	1,276,031	640,077	635,954	553,753	473,171	80,582	336,886	313,076	23,810
38	Alabama	1,069,545	531,941	537,604	541,602	411,627	129,975	380,852	299,861	80,991
39	Mississippi	902,028	451,788	450,240	462,739	337,931	124,808	360,049	270,684	89,365
40	Louisiana	794,683	394,815	399,868	423,074	314,293	108,781	240,780	185,266	55,464
41	Texas	1,564,755	830,783	733,972	696,208	610,193	86,015	432,318	398,140	34,178
42	Oklahoma	44,701	25,811	18,890	20,906	19,849	1,057	13,928	13,617	311
43	Arkansas	787,113	412,227	374,886	347,208	299,035	48,173	256,356	228,432	27,924
44	Western division	2,400,161	1,463,627	936,534	1,336,493	1,212,068	124,425	446,761	439,764	6,997
45	Montana	107,811	75,596	32,215	72,223	67,587	4,636	25,780	25,584	196
46	Wyoming	47,755	32,675	15,080	30,630	28,736	1,894	11,201	11,128	73
47	Colorado	327,896	202,719	125,177	191,943	172,796	19,147	59,243	58,548	635
48	New Mexico	112,541	61,885	50,656	54,151	50,217	3,934	26,611	26,190	421
49	Arizona	46,076	29,736	16,340	26,416	24,847	1,569	10,528	10,427	101
50	Utah	147,227	79,747	67,480	66,901	59,825	7,076	24,083	23,510	573
51	Nevada	38,225	25,370	12,855	23,415	21,501	1,824	10,536	10,404	132
52	Idaho	62,721	40,276	22,445	35,172	33,278	1,894	18,814	18,612	202
53	Washington	275,639	170,965	95,074	164,696	153,581	11,115	47,943	47,291	652
54	Oregon	244,374	146,406	97,968	126,781	115,988	10,793	50,980	50,080	900
55	California	989,896	589,252	400,644	544,165	483,622	60,543	161,042	157,990	3,052

OCCUPATIONS.

303

AND IN EACH CLASS OF OCCUPATIONS, CLASSIFIED BY SEX, BY STATES AND TERRITORIES: 1890.

PERSONS ENGAGED IN PROFESSIONAL SERVICE.			PERSONS ENGAGED IN DOMESTIC AND PERSONAL SERVICE.			PERSONS ENGAGED IN TRADE AND TRANSPORTATION.			PERSONS ENGAGED IN MANUFACTURING AND MECHANICAL INDUSTRIES.			
Total.	Males.	Females.	Total.	Males.	Females.	Total.	Males.	Females.	Total.	Males.	Females.	
944,333	632,646	311,687	4,360,577	2,692,879	1,667,698	3,326,122	3,097,701	228,421	5,091,293	4,064,051	1,027,242	1
299,468	192,797	106,671	1,523,513	946,721	576,792	1,316,779	1,201,302	115,477	2,565,750	1,957,119	608,631	2
12,364	6,007	6,357	41,091	26,908	14,183	37,291	34,850	2,441	80,054	59,437	20,617	3
6,831	3,529	3,302	23,711	14,428	9,283	19,771	18,339	1,432	71,408	49,189	22,219	4
6,276	3,029	3,247	22,059	11,805	10,254	14,551	13,834	717	29,702	24,602	5,100	5
43,247	26,248	16,999	185,938	99,755	86,183	196,513	174,239	22,274	475,646	338,761	136,885	6
5,446	3,447	1,999	28,906	17,747	11,159	27,372	24,709	2,663	81,548	54,839	26,709	7
12,485	7,509	4,976	60,073	35,166	24,907	49,383	44,457	4,926	146,397	110,593	35,804	8
115,376	76,484	38,892	554,437	327,552	226,885	527,564	481,790	45,774	828,216	634,430	193,786	9
22,363	15,000	6,763	129,522	81,334	48,188	120,072	111,385	8,687	223,892	177,671	46,221	10
75,080	50,944	24,136	477,776	332,026	145,750	324,262	297,699	26,563	628,887	507,597	121,290	11
92,361	66,791	25,570	591,812	282,173	309,639	308,751	291,228	17,523	410,814	324,763	86,051	12
2,213	1,505	708	16,222	10,313	5,909	9,045	8,331	714	18,104	15,394	2,710	13
14,576	10,144	4,432	102,301	54,455	47,846	68,979	63,233	5,746	102,015	78,014	24,001	14
7,308	5,689	1,619	39,723	19,143	20,580	28,891	23,900	4,991	23,311	18,431	4,880	15
17,695	11,965	5,730	126,259	58,545	67,714	58,526	56,649	1,877	77,614	63,305	14,309	16
8,602	6,397	2,265	31,424	19,427	11,997	22,973	22,239	734	30,842	27,387	3,455	17
12,296	8,971	3,325	71,264	29,087	42,177	28,799	28,171	628	50,645	37,231	13,414	18
8,193	5,970	2,223	51,772	22,335	29,437	21,735	21,024	711	31,137	22,527	8,610	19
15,969	11,907	4,062	120,852	49,395	71,457	54,770	53,054	1,716	58,994	46,833	12,161	20
5,449	4,243	1,206	31,995	19,473	12,522	15,033	14,627	406	18,152	15,641	2,511	21
371,847	236,730	134,617	1,379,151	905,238	473,913	1,151,139	1,076,163	74,976	1,533,098	1,284,185	248,913	22
61,913	41,783	20,130	255,289	173,384	81,905	195,578	180,978	14,600	330,987	273,658	57,329	23
34,519	24,104	10,415	127,118	88,076	39,042	92,344	87,059	5,285	139,508	117,696	21,812	24
63,122	41,176	21,946	268,105	175,161	92,944	246,704	227,246	19,458	319,140	266,107	53,033	25
33,490	20,445	13,045	152,210	106,915	45,295	103,276	95,991	7,285	162,098	137,878	24,220	26
24,278	13,545	10,733	111,998	73,196	38,802	68,620	63,830	4,790	129,295	108,490	20,805	27
22,707	14,000	8,707	94,693	57,976	36,717	72,456	68,185	4,271	83,748	71,644	12,104	28
37,762	18,962	18,800	85,932	52,916	33,016	88,097	83,666	4,431	89,654	73,578	16,076	29
39,465	27,963	11,502	147,296	91,005	56,291	140,046	132,083	7,963	152,907	128,258	24,649	30
3,058	1,945	1,113	9,282	4,407	4,875	6,679	6,505	174	4,797	3,968	829	31
5,995	3,613	2,382	13,911	8,232	5,679	12,850	12,461	389	10,498	8,900	1,598	32
19,539	12,294	7,245	59,272	38,745	20,527	62,883	59,355	3,528	55,792	47,905	7,887	33
25,439	16,840	8,599	54,045	35,225	18,820	61,606	58,804	2,802	54,674	46,103	8,571	34
114,263	86,914	27,349	535,709	288,575	247,134	315,818	304,860	10,958	323,320	269,914	58,406	35
22,150	16,135	6,015	98,269	51,964	46,305	61,145	57,940	3,205	82,075	66,695	15,380	36
19,450	14,988	4,467	85,339	43,480	41,859	53,906	52,126	1,780	58,172	49,512	8,660	37
11,952	9,180	2,772	73,480	34,840	38,640	36,299	35,388	911	39,019	32,358	6,661	38
10,862	7,587	3,275	49,774	21,507	28,267	22,417	21,817	600	19,637	16,336	3,301	39
10,026	7,196	2,830	90,068	51,217	38,851	40,586	38,483	2,103	41,664	32,131	9,533	40
28,123	22,226	5,897	100,669	63,459	37,210	77,033	75,209	1,824	58,065	51,159	6,906	41
1,017	843	174	1,718	1,344	374	2,075	2,025	50	2,168	2,020	148	42
10,683	8,764	1,919	36,392	20,764	15,628	21,857	21,372	485	21,920	19,703	2,217	43
66,894	49,414	17,480	330,392	270,172	60,220	234,135	224,648	9,487	258,311	228,070	30,241	44
2,900	2,294	606	20,336	17,653	2,683	11,443	11,219	224	11,764	10,837	927	45
1,203	953	250	8,334	7,169	1,165	5,258	5,172	86	4,634	4,314	320	46
9,830	7,458	2,372	42,952	32,656	10,296	40,538	38,779	1,759	39,380	35,355	4,025	47
1,712	1,386	326	16,852	14,331	2,521	4,979	4,903	76	3,997	3,407	590	48
1,095	928	167	8,322	7,371	951	3,738	3,705	33	2,733	2,416	317	49
2,843	2,135	708	15,535	12,037	3,498	11,088	10,548	540	13,352	11,595	1,757	50
1,060	730	330	5,450	4,526	924	3,308	3,251	57	3,061	2,680	381	51
1,295	1,004	291	6,718	5,788	930	4,358	4,273	85	3,087	2,701	386	52
8,214	6,598	1,616	42,291	36,692	5,599	29,266	28,421	845	36,982	34,579	2,403	53
6,926	5,007	1,919	26,542	21,847	4,695	19,373	18,534	839	22,960	20,520	2,440	54
29,816	20,921	8,895	137,060	110,102	26,958	100,786	95,843	4,943	115,461	98,766	16,695	55

304

STATISTICS OF POPULATION.

TABLE 78.—TOTAL PERSONS 10 YEARS OF AGE AND OVER IN THE UNITED STATES ENGAGED IN EACH SPECIFIED OCCUPATION, CLASSIFIED BY SEX: 1890.

OCCUPATIONS.	Total.	Males.	Females.	OCCUPATIONS.	Total.	Males.	Females.
All occupations	22,735,661	18,821,090	3,914,571	**Trade and transportation—Continued.**			
				Brokers (commercial)	5,960	5,950	10
Agriculture, fisheries, and mining	9,013,336	8,333,813	679,523	Clerks and copyists (i)	557,358	493,139	64,219
				Commercial travelers	58,691	58,080	611
Agricultural laborers (a)	3,004,061	2,556,957	447,104	Draymen, hackmen, teamsters, etc	368,499	368,265	234
Apiarists	1,773	1,728	45	Foremen and overseers	36,084	35,109	975
Dairymen and dairywomen	17,895	16,161	1,734				
Farmers, planters, and overseers (b)	5,281,557	5,055,130	226,427	Hostlers	54,036	54,014	22
Fishermen and oystermen (c)	60,162	59,899	263	Hucksters and peddlers	59,083	56,824	2,259
				Livery stable keepers	26,757	26,710	47
Gardeners, florists, nurserymen, and vine growers.	72,601	70,186	2,415	Locomotive engineers and firemen (j)	79,463	79,459	4
Lumbermen and raftsmen	60,856	60,838	18	Merchants and dealers in drugs and chemicals (retail).	46,375	45,641	734
Miners (coal)	208,545	208,330	215				
Miners (not otherwise specified)	141,047	140,914	133	Merchants and dealers in dry goods (retail).	42,527	40,349	2,178
Quarrymen	87,656	87,628	28	Merchants and dealers in groceries (retail).	114,997	108,638	6,359
Stock raisers, herders, and drovers	70,729	70,047	682	Merchants and dealers in wines and liquors (retail).	10,078	9,942	136
Wood choppers	33,697	33,665	32	Merchants and dealers in wines and liquors (wholesale).	3,643	3,605	38
Other agricultural pursuits (d)	17,747	17,330	417	Merchants and dealers, not specified (retail).	446,262	430,314	15,948
Professional service	944,333	632,646	311,687	Merchants and dealers (wholesale), importers, and shipping merchants.	27,443	27,285	158
				Messengers and errand and office boys	51,355	48,446	2,909
Actors	9,728	5,779	3,949	Newspaper carriers and newsboys	5,288	5,216	72
Architects	8,070	8,048	22	Officials of banks and of insurance, trade, transportation, trust, and other companies. (k)	39,900	39,683	217
Artists and teachers of art	22,496	11,681	10,815	Packers and shippers	24,946	18,426	6,520
Authors and literary and scientific persons.	6,714	3,989	2,725				
Chemists, assayers, and metallurgists	4,503	4,464	39	Pilots	4,259	4,258	1
				Porters and helpers (in stores and warehouses).	24,356	24,002	354
Clergymen	88,203	87,060	1,143	Sailors (g)	55,899	55,882	17
Dentists	17,498	17,161	337	Salesmen and saleswomen	264,394	205,943	58,451
Designers, draftsmen, and inventors	9,391	9,086	305				
Engineers (civil, mechanical, electrical, and mining) and surveyors.	43,239	43,115	124	Steam railroad employés (not otherwise specified). (l)	382,750	381,312	1,438
Journalists	21,849	20,961	888	Stenographers and typewriters	33,418	12,148	21,270
				Street railway employés	37,434	37,423	11
Lawyers	89,630	89,422	208	Telegraph and telephone operators	52,214	43,740	8,474
Musicians and teachers of music	62,155	27,636	34,519				
Officers of United States army and navy	2,926	2,926		Telegraph and telephone linemen and electric light and power company employés.	11,134	10,465	669
Officials (government) (e)	79,664	74,789	4,875	Undertakers	9,891	9,808	83
Physicians and surgeons	104,805	100,248	4,557	Weighers, gaugers, and measurers	3,860	3,842	18
				Other persons in trade and transportation.	3,883	3,080	803
Professors in colleges and universities	5,392	4,697	695				
Teachers	341,952	96,581	245,371	**Manufacturing and mechanical industries**	5,091,293	4,064,051	1,027,242
Theatrical managers, showmen, etc.	18,055	17,421	634				
Veterinary surgeons	6,494	6,492	2	Agricultural implement makers (not otherwise classified). (m)	3,755	3,731	24
Other professional service	1,569	1,090	479	Apprentices (blacksmiths)	4,244	4,242	2
				Apprentices (boot and shoe makers)	1,031	1,004	27
Domestic and personal service	4,360,577	2,692,879	1,667,698	Apprentices (carpenters and joiners)	6,760	6,751	9
				Apprentices (carriage and wagon makers).	852	851	1
Barbers and hairdressers	84,982	82,157	2,825				
Bartenders	55,806	55,660	146	Apprentices (dressmakers)	4,340		4,340
Boarding and lodging house keepers	44,349	11,756	32,593	Apprentices (leather curriers, etc.)	421	421	
Engineers and firemen (not locomotive)	139,765	139,718	47	Apprentices (machinists)	9,738	9,726	12
Hotel keepers	44,076	38,800	5,276	Apprentices (masons)	1,027	1,026	1
				Apprentices (milliners)	1,204		1,204
Housekeepers and stewards (f)	92,036	5,947	86,089				
Hunters, trappers, guides, and scouts	2,534	2,515	19	Apprentices (painters)	2,321	2,314	7
Janitors	21,556	18,776	2,780	Apprentices (plumbers)	4,624	4,622	2
Laborers (not specified) (a)	1,913,373	1,858,558	54,815	Apprentices (printers)	4,635	4,483	152
Launderers and laundresses	248,462	31,831	216,631	Apprentices (tailors)	2,625	1,925	700
				Apprentices (tinsmiths)	2,037	2,034	3
Nurses and midwives	47,586	6,190	41,396				
Restaurant keepers	19,283	16,867	2,416	Apprentices (not otherwise specified)	35,698	34,156	1,542
Saloon keepers	71,385	69,110	2,275	Artificial flower makers	3,046	503	2,543
Servants	1,454,791	238,152	1,216,639	Bakers	60,197	57,910	2,287
				Basket makers	5,225	4,514	711
Sextons	4,982	4,954	28	Blacksmiths	205,337	205,279	58
Soldiers, sailors, and marines (United States). (g)	27,919	27,919					
Watchmen, policemen, and detectives	74,629	74,350	279	Bleachers, dyers, and scourers	14,210	12,503	1,707
Other domestic and personal service	13,063	9,619	3,444	Bone and ivory workers	1,691	1,469	222
				Bookbinders	23,858	12,298	11,560
Trade and transportation	3,326,122	3,097,701	228,421	Boot and shoe makers and repairers	218,544	179,867	38,677
				Bottlers and mineral and soda water makers.	7,230	6,681	549
Agents (claim, commission, real estate, insurance, etc.) and collectors.	174,582	169,707	4,875				
Auctioneers	3,205	3,203	2				
Bankers and brokers (money and stocks)	30,008	29,508	500				
Boatmen and canalmen	16,716	16,683	33				
Bookkeepers and accountants (h)	159,374	131,602	27,772				

a In agricultural districts "agricultural laborers" are often reported simply as "laborers".

b Farmers' wives, sons, and daughters, working in common and without stated remuneration, especially in the southern states, are often reported as "farmers", and so tabulated.

c Frequently returned as "sailors". In many cases where the avocation is followed for only a portion of the year they are reported under some other branch of industry.

d Includes "turpentine farmers and laborers", principally found in a few of the southern states.

e Includes national, state, county, city, and town governments.

f Includes paid housekeepers in private families, hotels, etc., matrons in public and private institutions, and stewards and stewardesses.

g "Sailors" at sea are liable to be omitted unless they are actual members of families which are enumerated.

h Includes bookkeepers and accountants of all kinds, irrespective of where they may happen to be employed.

i Includes clerks and copyists of all kinds, irrespective of where they may happen to be employed. See "Stenographers and typewriters".

j See "Steam railroad employés (not otherwise specified)".

k Includes officials of mining and quarrying companies, classified in 1880 with officials of manufacturing companies.

l See "Locomotive engineers and firemen".

m Generally reported as blacksmiths, carpenters, iron and steel workers, machinists, painters, wood workers, etc.

OCCUPATIONS.

305

TABLE 78.—TOTAL PERSONS 10 YEARS OF AGE AND OVER IN THE UNITED STATES ENGAGED IN EACH SPECIFIED OCCUPATION, CLASSIFIED BY SEX: 1890—Continued.

OCCUPATIONS.	Total.	Males.	Females.	OCCUPATIONS.	Total.	Males.	Females.
Manufacturing and mechanical industries—Continued.				**Manufacturing and mechanical industries—Continued.**			
Box makers (paper)	17,757	4,714	13,043	Mill and factory operatives (not specified). (k)	93,596	51,603	41,993
Box makers (wood)	10,883	9,572	1,311	Millers (flour and grist)	52,841	52,747	94
Brass workers (not otherwise specified). (a)	17,265	16,352	913	Milliners	60,482	395	60,087
Brewers and maltsters (b)	20,362	20,294	68	Model and pattern makers	10,300	10,159	141
Brick and tile makers and terra cotta workers. (b)	60,214	60,070	144	Molders	66,289	66,243	46
Britannia workers	904	787	117	Musical instrument makers (not otherwise specified). (l)	652	629	23
Broom and brush makers	10,115	8,940	1,160	Nail and tack makers (m)	4,583	4,106	477
Builders and contractors	45,988	45,978	10	Oil well employés	9,147	9,137	10
Butchers	105,456	105,339	117	Oil works employés	5,624	5,527	37
Butter and cheese makers	11,211	10,808	403	Painters, glaziers, and varnishers	219,912	218,646	1,266
Button makers	2,601	1,011	1,590	Paper hangers	12,369	12,315	54
Cabinet makers	85,915	85,891	24	Paper mill operatives	27,817	18,856	8,961
Candle, soap, and tallow makers	3,450	3,051	399	Photographers	20,040	17,839	2,201
Carpenters and joiners	611,482	611,293	189	Piano and organ makers and tuners (n)	14,683	14,367	316
Carpet makers (c)	22,302	11,546	10,756	Plasterers	39,002	38,987	15
Carriage and wagon makers (not otherwise classified). (d)	34,538	34,308	230	Plumbers and gas and steam fitters	56,607	56,563	44
Charcoal, coke, and lime burners	8,704	8,689	15	Potters	14,928	12,939	1,989
Chemical works employés (b)	3,628	2,613	1,015	Powder and cartridge makers	1,385	963	422
Clock and watch makers and repairers	25,252	20,556	4,696	Printers, lithographers, and pressmen. (o)	86,893	81,154	5,739
Compositors (e)	30,060	23,745	6,315	Print works operatives (p)	6,701	5,162	1,539
Confectioners	23,251	17,577	5,674	Publishers of books, maps, and newspapers.	6,284	6,210	74
Coopers	47,486	47,438	48	Roofers and slaters	7,043	7,040	3
Copper workers	3,384	3,377	7	Rope and cordage makers	8,001	4,896	3,105
Corset makers	6,533	733	5,800	Rubber factory operatives	16,162	9,706	6,456
Cotton mill operatives (f)	173,142	80,177	92,965	Sail, awning, and tent makers	3,257	3,006	251
Distillers and rectifiers (b)	3,314	3,305	9	Salt works employés	1,765	1,662	103
Door, sash, and blind makers (g)	5,041	5,031	10	Saw and planing mill employés (g)	133,637	133,355	282
Dressmakers	289,164	836	288,328	Seamstresses (r)	150,044	4,001	146,043
Electroplaters	2,756	2,644	112	Sewing machine makers (not otherwise classified). (s)	880	850	30
Electrotypers and stereotypers (e)	1,471	1,466	5	Sewing machine operators (t)	7,126	1,104	6,022
Engravers	8,320	8,017	303	Ship and boat builders	22,951	22,948	3
Fertilizer makers (b)	732	726	6	Shirt, collar, and cuff makers (u)	21,107	5,132	15,975
Fish curers and packers (h)	1,279	1,084	195	Silk mill operatives (v)	34,855	14,192	20,663
Gas works employés (b)	5,224	5,219	5	Starch makers	746	566	180
Glass workers	34,282	32,572	1,710	Steam boiler makers	21,339	21,333	6
Glove makers	6,416	2,741	3,675	Stove, furnace, and grate makers (m)	8,932	8,912	20
Gold and silver workers	20,263	16,914	3,349	Straw workers	3,666	1,243	2,423
Gunsmiths, locksmiths, and bell hangers	9,158	9,069	89	Sugar makers and refiners	2,616	2,612	4
Hair workers	1,254	684	570	Tailors and tailoresses (u)	185,400	121,591	63,809
Harness and saddle makers and repairers	43,480	42,647	833	Tinners and tinware makers	55,488	54,589	899
Hat and cap makers	24,013	17,319	6,694	Tobacco and cigar factory operatives	111,625	83,634	27,991
Hosiery and knitting mill operatives (c)	29,555	8,745	20,810	Tool and cutlery makers (not otherwise classified). (d)	17,985	17,449	536
Iron and steel workers (i)	144,921	142,585	2,336	Trunk, valise, leather-case, and pocket-book makers	6,279	5,458	821
Lace and embroidery makers	5,256	821	4,435	Umbrella and parasol makers	3,403	1,465	1,938
Lead and zinc workers	4,616	4,413	203	Upholsterers	25,666	23,918	1,748
Leather curriers, dressers, finishers, and tanners	39,332	39,040	292	Well borers	4,854	4,853	1
Machinists	177,090	176,951	139	Wheelwrights	12,856	12,855	1
Manufacturers and officials of manufacturing companies.	101,610	101,280	330	Whitewashers	3,996	3,987	9
Marble and stone cutters	61,070	61,012	58	Wire workers	12,319	11,238	1,081
Masons (brick and stone)	158,918	158,878	40	Wood workers (not otherwise specified)	67,360	63,600	3,760
Meat and fruit packers, canners, and preservers. (j)	5,830	4,419	1,411	Woolen mill operatives (w)	84,109	47,638	36,471
Mechanics (not otherwise specified)	15,485	15,472	13	Other persons in manufacturing and mechanical industries.	76,714	60,806	15,908
Metal workers (not otherwise specified)	16,694	15,837	857				

a See "Molders" and "Metal workers (not otherwise specified)".
b The unskilled workmen are often reported as common laborers.
c See "Woolen mill operatives" and "Mill and factory operatives (not specified)".
d Generally reported as blacksmiths, carpenters, iron and steel workers, machinists, painters, wood workers, etc.
e See "Printers, lithographers, and pressmen".
f See "Print works operatives" and "Mill and factory operatives (not specified)".
g See "Saw and planing mill employés".
h See "Meat and fruit packers, canners, and preservers".
i Includes employés of foundries, furnaces, and rolling mills. See "Metal workers (not otherwise specified)", "Molders", "Nail and tack makers", and "Stove, furnace, and grate makers".
j See "Fish curers and packers".
k Includes textile mill operatives (not otherwise specified), and also mill and factory hands for whom the specific branch of industry was not reported.
l See "Piano and organ makers and tuners".
m See "Iron and steel workers" and "Metal workers (not otherwise specified)".
n See "Musical instrument makers (not otherwise specified)".
o See "Compositors" and "Electrotypers and stereotypers".
p See "Cotton mill operatives" and "Mill and factory operatives (not specified)".
q See "Door, sash, and blind makers".
r See "Sewing machine operators", "Shirt, collar, and cuff makers", and "Tailors and tailoresses".
s Generally reported as cabinet makers, iron and steel workers, machinists, wood workers, etc.
t See "Seamstresses", "Shirt, collar, and cuff makers", and "Tailors and tailoresses".
u See "Seamstresses" and "Sewing machine operators".
v See "Mill and factory operatives (not specified)".
w See "Carpet makers", "Hosiery and knitting mill operatives", and "Mill and factory operatives (not specified)".

POP—PT 2——20

306

STATISTICS OF POPULATION.

TABLE 79.—TOTAL PERSONS 10 YEARS OF AGE AND OVER ENGAGED IN EACH SPECIFIED

	OCCUPATIONS.	THE UNITED STATES.			ALABAMA.			ARIZONA.		
		Total.	Males.	Fe-males.	Total.	Males.	Fe-males.	Total.	Males.	Fe-males.
1	All occupations	22,735,661	18,821,090	3,914,571	541,602	411,627	129,975	26,416	24,847	1,569
2	Agriculture, fisheries, and mining	9,013,336	8,333,813	679,523	380,852	299,861	80,991	10,528	10,427	101
3	Agricultural laborers (a)	3,004,061	2,556,957	447,104	186,607	118,798	67,809	1,516	1,502	14
4	Apiarists	1,773	1,728	45	3	3		12	12	
5	Dairymen and dairywomen	17,895	16,161	1,734	192	164	28	26	25	1
6	Farmers, planters, and overseers (a)	5,281,557	5,055,130	226,427	181,865	168,791	13,074	2,172	2,121	51
7	Fishermen and oystermen (a)	60,162	59,899	263	397	391	6	1	1	
8	Gardeners, florists, nurserymen, and vine growers	72,601	70,186	2,415	751	705	46	105	104	1
9	Lumbermen and raftsmen	65,866	65,838	28	1,035	1,032	3	67	67	
10	Miners (coal)	208,545	208,330	215	5,094	5,085	9			
11	Miners (not otherwise specified)	141,047	140,914	133	2,881	2,881		3,561	3,560	1
12	Quarrymen	37,656	37,628	28	434	434		24	24	
13	Stock raisers, herders, and drovers	70,729	70,047	682	151	149	2	2,712	2,679	33
14	Wood choppers	33,697	33,665	32	1,225	1,224	1	298	298	
15	Other agricultural pursuits (a)	17,747	17,330	417	217	204	13	4	4	
16	Professional service	944,333	632,646	311,687	11,952	9,180	2,772	1,095	928	167
17	Actors	9,728	5,779	3,949	28	20	8	4	4	
18	Architects	8,070	8,048	22	78	78		7	7	
19	Artists and teachers of art	22,496	11,681	10,815	131	59	72	8	3	5
20	Authors and literary and scientific persons	6,714	3,989	2,725	38	28	10	9	7	2
21	Chemists, assayers, and metallurgists	4,503	4,464	39	30	30		48	48	
22	Clergymen	88,203	87,060	1,143	1,856	1,846	10	49	49	
23	Dentists	17,498	17,161	337	212	212		22	22	
24	Designers, draftsmen, and inventors	9,391	9,086	305	21	21		2	2	
25	Engineers (civil, mechanical, electrical, and mining) and surveyors	43,239	43,115	124	465	465		100	100	
26	Journalists	21,849	20,961	888	194	186	8	36	36	
27	Lawyers	89,630	89,422	208	1,313	1,311	2	159	158	1
28	Musicians and teachers of music	62,155	27,636	34,519	435	151	284	76	57	19
29	Officers of United States army and navy	2,926	2,926		11	11		82	82	
30	Officials (government) (a)	79,664	74,789	4,875	1,072	993	79	157	151	6
31	Physicians and surgeons	104,805	100,248	4,557	1,846	1,826	20	93	89	4
32	Professors in colleges and universities	5,392	4,697	695	89	76	13	3	3	
33	Teachers	341,952	96,581	245,371	4,045	1,789	2,256	215	86	129
34	Theatrical managers, showmen, etc	18,055	17,421	634	72	62	10	21	20	1
35	Veterinary surgeons	6,494	6,492	2	15	15		4	4	
36	Other professional service	1,569	1,090	479	1	1				
37	Domestic and personal service	4,360,577	2,692,879	1,667,698	73,480	34,840	38,640	8,322	7,371	951
38	Barbers and hairdressers	84,982	82,157	2,825	646	642	4	110	109	1
39	Bartenders	55,806	55,660	146	503	502	1	112	112	
40	Boarding and lodging house keepers	44,349	11,756	32,593	624	138	486	74	25	49
41	Engineers and firemen (not locomotive)	139,765	139,718	47	1,442	1,442		230	230	
42	Hotel keepers	44,076	38,800	5,276	322	238	84	82	69	13
43	Housekeepers and stewards (a)	92,036	5,947	86,089	1,392	54	1,338	133	7	126
44	Hunters, trappers, guides, and scouts	2,534	2,515	19	19	19		20	20	
45	Janitors	21,556	18,776	2,780	78	72	6	11	10	1
46	Laborers (not specified) (a)	1,913,373	1,858,558	54,815	30,256	25,218	5,038	3,720	3,694	26
47	Launderers and laundresses	248,462	31,831	216,631	10,787	220	10,567	528	269	259
48	Nurses and midwives	47,586	6,190	41,396	511	55	456	15	5	10
49	Restaurant keepers	19,283	16,867	2,416	154	113	41	55	48	7
50	Saloon keepers	71,385	69,110	2,275	279	275	4	164	163	1
51	Servants	1,454,791	238,152	1,216,639	25,463	4,865	20,598	1,165	709	456
52	Sextons	4,982	4,954	28	59	58	1	2	2	
53	Soldiers, sailors, and marines (United States) (a)	27,919	27,919		118	118		1,860	1,860	
54	Watchmen, policemen, and detectives	74,629	74,350	279	731	730	1	28	28	
55	Other domestic and personal service	13,063	9,619	3,444	96	81	15	13	11	2
56	Trade and transportation	3,326,122	3,097,701	228,421	36,299	35,388	911	3,738	3,705	33
57	Agents (claim, commission, real estate, insurance, etc.) and collectors	174,582	169,707	4,875	1,537	1,506	31	111	111	
58	Auctioneers	3,205	3,203	2	32	32		1	1	
59	Bankers and brokers (money and stocks)	30,008	29,508	500	252	248	4	46	45	1
60	Boatmen and canalmen	16,716	16,683	33	223	222	1	1	1	
61	Bookkeepers and accountants (a)	159,374	131,602	27,772	1,294	1,248	46	155	151	4
62	Brokers (commercial)	5,960	5,950	10	127	127		7	7	
63	Clerks and copyists (a)	557,358	493,139	64,219	5,306	5,052	254	354	349	5
64	Commercial travelers	58,691	58,080	611	325	322	3	16	16	
65	Draymen, hackmen, teamsters, etc	368,499	368,265	234	3,917	3,908	9	676	676	
66	Foremen and overseers	36,084	35,109	975	484	482	2	75	75	
67	Hostlers	54,036	54,014	22	437	437		53	53	
68	Hucksters and peddlers	59,083	56,824	2,259	440	402	38	28	28	
69	Livery stable keepers	26,757	26,710	47	201	201		44	44	
70	Locomotive engineers and firemen (a)	79,463	79,459	4	1,127	1,127		188	188	
71	Merchants and dealers in drugs and chemicals (retail)	46,375	45,641	734	400	400		33	33	
72	Merchants and dealers in dry goods (retail)	42,527	40,349	2,178	785	768	17	39	37	2
73	Merchants and dealers in groceries (retail)	114,997	108,638	6,359	1,210	1,128	82	86	84	2
74	Merchants and dealers in wines and liquors (retail)	10,078	9,942	136	56	56		7	7	
75	Merchants and dealers in wines and liquors (wholesale)	3,643	3,605	38	23	23		6	6	

a See explanatory notes in Table 78.

OCCUPATIONS.

OCCUPATION, CLASSIFIED BY SEX, BY STATES AND TERRITORIES: 1890.

ARKANSAS Total	Males	Females	CALIFORNIA Total	Males	Females	COLORADO Total	Males	Females	CONNECTICUT Total	Males	Females	DELAWARE Total	Males	Females	DIST. OF COLUMBIA Total	Males	Females	#
347,208	299,035	48,173	544,165	483,622	60,543	191,943	172,796	19,147	317,014	245,634	71,380	64,286	53,938	10,348	101,119	68,992	32,127	1
256,356	228,432	27,924	161,042	157,990	3,052	59,243	58,548	695	48,676	47,909	767	18,702	18,395	307	1,886	1,829	57	2
87,678	69,803	17,875	51,799	51,532	267	9,981	9,926	55	15,193	15,131	62	8,004	7,951	53	582	567	15	3
15	15	....	249	247	2	22	18	4	7	7	....	2	2	....	....	....	....	4
113	96	17	4,314	4,253	61	401	382	19	76	64	12	27	12	15	194	177	17	5
165,463	155,472	9,991	61,808	59,356	2,452	20,234	19,697	537	28,347	27,664	683	9,861	9,628	233	275	270	5	6
184	182	2	1,946	1,921	25	13	13	....	1,817	1,817	....	409	408	1	98	98	....	7
423	397	26	5,404	5,298	106	876	854	22	1,449	1,441	8	203	199	4	647	627	20	8
1,039	1,039	....	3,972	3,972	....	391	391	....	128	128	....	17	17	....	20	20	....	9
500	500	....	674	674	....	3,591	3,589	2	70	70	....	28	28	....	....	....	....	10
274	274	....	21,310	21,291	19	16,476	16,471	5	163	163	....	14	14	....	10	10	....	11
52	52	....	596	596	....	894	893	1	1,530	1,529	1	64	64	....	26	26	....	12
166	156	10	5,978	5,868	110	5,297	5,247	50	39	39	....	8	8	....	26	26	....	13
438	438	....	2,829	2,825	4	1,057	1,057	....	353	353	....	63	63	....	7	7	....	14
11	8	3	163	157	6	10	10	....	4	3	1	2	1	1	1	1	....	15
10,083	8,764	1,919	29,816	20,921	8,895	9,830	7,458	2,372	12,485	7,509	4,976	2,213	1,505	708	7,308	5,689	1,619	16
15	11	4	666	443	223	283	154	129	88	58	30	6	4	2	72	51	21	17
30	30	....	425	424	1	164	164	....	115	114	1	10	10	....	145	145	....	18
106	51	55	1,025	471	554	308	139	169	372	185	187	52	10	42	258	115	143	19
17	13	4	350	241	109	75	51	24	171	100	71	13	9	4	186	157	29	20
8	8	....	272	270	2	223	222	1	61	61	....	7	7	....	46	46	....	21
1,807	1,804	3	1,931	1,896	35	596	581	15	1,192	1,166	26	268	264	4	390	384	6	22
133	133	....	716	700	16	158	151	7	332	330	2	56	47	9	153	152	1	23
9	8	1	276	275	1	64	64	....	291	280	11	63	62	1	229	227	2	24
225	225	....	1,964	1,953	11	1,085	1,085	....	698	698	....	146	146	....	444	443	1	25
171	169	2	947	896	51	818	804	14	298	289	9	49	48	1	272	249	23	26
1,082	1,082	....	3,228	3,217	11	1,266	1,260	6	833	832	1	176	176	....	1,408	1,401	7	27
417	160	257	2,710	1,284	1,426	799	486	313	970	428	542	153	56	97	407	266	231	28
8	8	....	106	106	....	28	28	....	30	30	....	2	2	....	260	260	....	29
876	826	50	2,792	2,654	138	1,034	988	46	900	821	79	199	191	8	767	714	53	30
2,289	2,264	25	3,119	2,844	275	966	907	59	1,178	1,089	89	245	233	12	729	689	40	31
18	16	2	119	100	19	43	40	3	119	105	14	9	8	1	42	40	2	32
3,386	1,872	1,514	7,954	1,964	5,990	2,129	555	1,574	4,558	667	3,891	710	184	526	1,315	259	1,056	33
67	66	1	890	884	6	221	216	5	190	182	8	33	33	....	69	66	3	34
15	15	....	175	175	....	56	56	....	60	60	....	14	14	....	23	23	....	35
4	3	1	61	34	27	14	7	7	29	14	15	2	1	1	3	2	1	36
36,302	20,764	15,628	137,060	110,102	26,958	42,952	32,656	10,296	60,073	35,166	24,907	16,222	10,313	5,909	39,723	19,143	20,580	37
531	524	7	3,248	3,083	165	1,017	974	43	1,180	1,138	42	268	261	7	622	586	36	38
339	339	....	2,600	2,596	4	775	775	....	836	836	....	99	99	....	330	329	1	39
499	169	330	1,939	672	1,267	1,229	339	890	674	159	515	114	13	101	329	42	287	40
1,084	1,084	....	4,114	4,112	2	1,785	1,783	2	1,960	1,959	1	465	463	2	599	599	....	41
494	364	130	2,334	2,015	319	673	556	117	483	433	50	90	88	2	112	98	14	42
748	19	729	2,518	418	2,100	705	67	638	2,399	135	2,264	515	22	493	532	62	470	43
40	40	....	305	299	6	41	41	....	4	4	....	6	6	....	....	....	....	44
61	58	3	637	567	70	238	227	11	401	382	19	49	39	10	251	231	20	45
15,903	14,534	1,369	58,421	58,022	399	20,751	20,662	89	24,358	23,793	565	8,222	8,148	74	10,550	10,193	357	46
3,351	144	3,207	9,302	7,795	1,507	1,798	1,069	729	1,785	410	1,375	397	52	345	5,846	214	5,632	47
218	15	203	1,860	279	1,581	439	56	383	1,243	133	1,110	164	8	156	816	156	660	48
127	108	19	1,043	919	124	306	237	69	199	173	26	44	38	6	407	339	68	49
289	281	8	4,924	4,799	125	1,265	1,250	15	1,155	1,127	28	118	109	9	259	237	22	50
12,040	2,435	9,605	39,066	19,880	19,186	10,669	3,381	7,288	21,705	2,872	18,833	5,355	658	4,697	17,291	4,294	12,997	51
31	31	....	121	121	....	27	27	....	127	127	....	24	24	....	67	67	....	52
91	91	....	1,939	1,939	....	612	612	....	101	101	....	5	5	....	605	605	....	53
432	431	1	2,012	2,011	1	518	517	1	1,270	1,269	1	260	260	....	1,020	1,020	....	54
114	106	8	677	575	102	104	83	21	193	115	78	24	15	9	87	71	16	55
21,857	21,372	485	100,786	95,843	4,943	40,538	38,779	1,759	49,383	44,457	4,926	9,045	8,331	714	28,891	23,900	4,991	56
1,071	1,047	24	6,228	6,075	153	2,889	2,824	65	2,133	2,060	73	357	347	10	1,095	1,060	35	57
15	15	....	121	121	....	39	39	....	31	31	....	16	16	....	20	20	....	58
139	137	2	2,559	2,433	126	620	603	17	285	285	....	27	27	....	145	144	1	59
56	56	....	193	193	....	14	14	....	122	122	....	49	49	....	72	71	1	60
889	836	53	6,077	5,468	609	1,847	1,667	180	3,384	2,679	705	291	213	78	688	522	166	61
23	23	....	136	134	2	62	62	....	63	63	....	9	9	....	71	71	....	62
2,842	2,709	133	16,927	15,815	1,112	5,551	5,003	548	8,741	7,494	1,247	1,394	1,227	167	12,496	8,988	3,508	63
347	345	2	1,184	1,166	18	416	401	15	792	784	8	50	50	....	119	115	4	64
2,417	2,416	1	11,582	11,571	11	5,806	5,803	3	5,633	5,632	1	667	667	....	3,331	3,330	1	65
297	297	....	797	791	6	740	738	2	433	416	17	77	77	....	75	74	1	66
277	277	....	1,990	1,990	....	542	542	....	1,141	1,141	....	207	207	....	461	458	3	67
150	143	7	1,782	1,741	41	279	273	6	1,278	1,268	10	133	130	3	410	397	13	68
228	228	....	1,124	1,120	4	455	455	....	480	478	2	71	71	....	98	93	5	69
605	605	....	1,511	1,511	....	1,592	1,591	1	712	712	....	245	245	....	185	185	....	70
530	528	2	1,489	1,484	5	592	586	6	557	543	14	143	140	3	290	285	5	71
706	702	4	778	730	48	308	298	10	390	381	9	117	92	25	116	98	18	72
863	848	15	3,136	3,009	127	923	887	36	1,908	1,843	65	393	355	38	1,066	916	150	73
46	46	....	495	491	4	112	111	1	150	146	4	30	29	1	46	44	2	74
17	17	....	249	247	2	39	38	1	60	60	....	4	4	....	21	20	1	75

STATISTICS OF POPULATION.

TABLE 79.—TOTAL PERSONS 10 YEARS OF AGE AND OVER ENGAGED IN EACH SPECIFIED

	OCCUPATIONS.	THE UNITED STATES.			ALABAMA.			ARIZONA.		
		Total.	Males.	Females.	Total.	Males.	Females.	Total.	Males.	Females.
	Trade and transportation—Continued.									
76	Merchants and dealers, not specified (retail)	446,262	430,314	15,948	5,432	5,265	167	508	500	8
77	Merchants and dealers (wholesale), importers, and shipping merchants.	27,443	27,285	158	232	229	3	7	7	......
78	Messengers and errand and office boys	51,355	48,446	2,909	394	387	7	8	8	......
79	Newspaper carriers and newsboys	5,288	5,216	72	35	35	......	3	3	......
80	Officials of banks and of insurance, trade, transportation, trust, and other companies. (a)	39,900	39,683	217	542	541	1	84	84	......
81	Packers and shippers	24,946	18,426	6,520	50	46	4	119	119	......
82	Pilots	4,259	4,258	1	60	60	......	1	1	......
83	Porters and helpers (in stores and warehouses)	24,356	24,002	354	687	655	2	7	7	......
84	Sailors (a)	55,899	55,882	17	283	282	1	12	12	......
85	Salesmen and saleswomen	264,394	205,943	58,451	2,176	2,040	136	177	174	3
86	Steam railroad employés (not otherwise specified). (a)	382,750	381,312	1,438	7,274	7,250	24	783	780	3
87	Stenographers and typewriters	33,418	12,148	21,270	124	78	46	13	12	1
88	Street railway employés	37,434	37,423	11	140	140	......	......	......	......
89	Telegraph and telephone operators	52,214	43,740	8,474	467	436	31	80	76	4
90	Telegraph and telephone linemen and electric light and power company employés.	11,134	10,465	669	115	115	......	4	4	......
91	Undertakers	9,891	9,808	83	47	47	......	5	5	......
92	Weighers, gaugers, and measurers	3,860	3,842	18	52	52	......	1	1	......
93	Other persons in trade and transportation	3,883	3,080	803	13	11	2	......	......	......
94	**Manufacturing and mechanical industries**	5,091,293	4,064,051	1,027,242	39,019	32,358	6,661	2,733	2,416	317
95	Agricultural implement makers (not otherwise classified). (a)	3,755	3,731	24	18	18	......	......	......	......
96	Apprentices (blacksmiths)	4,244	4,242	2	36	36	......	3	3	......
97	Apprentices (boot and shoe makers)	1,031	1,004	27	2	2	......	......	......	......
98	Apprentices (carpenters and joiners)	6,760	6,751	9	40	40	......	3	3	......
99	Apprentices (carriage and wagon makers)	852	851	1	1	1	......	......	......	......
100	Apprentices (dressmakers)	4,340	......	4,340	3	......	3	......	......	......
101	Apprentices (leather curriers, etc.)	421	421	......	2	2	......	1	1	......
102	Apprentices (machinists)	9,738	9,726	12	54	54	......	4	4	......
103	Apprentices (masons)	1,927	1,926	1	8	8	......	......	......	......
104	Apprentices (milliners)	1,204	......	1,204	17	......	17	......	......	......
105	Apprentices (painters)	2,321	2,314	7	14	14	......	2	2	......
106	Apprentices (plumbers)	4,624	4,622	2	14	14	......	......	......	......
107	Apprentices (printers)	4,635	4,483	152	23	23	......	2	2	......
108	Apprentices (tailors)	2,625	1,925	700	3	1	2	......	......	......
109	Apprentices (tinsmiths)	2,037	2,034	3	7	7	......	2	2	......
110	Apprentices (not otherwise specified)	35,698	34,156	1,542	133	129	4	7	7	......
111	Artificial flower makers	3,046	503	2,543	......	......	......	......	......	......
112	Bakers	60,197	57,910	2,287	234	225	9	87	84	3
113	Basket makers	5,225	4,514	711	28	27	1	......	......	......
114	Blacksmiths	205,337	205,279	58	2,254	2,253	1	294	294	......
115	Bleachers, dyers, and scourers	14,210	12,503	1,707	59	53	6	8	8	......
116	Bone and ivory workers	1,691	1,469	222	......	......	......	......	......	......
117	Bookbinders	23,858	12,298	11,560	30	22	8	2	2	......
118	Boot and shoe makers and repairers	213,544	179,867	33,677	683	672	11	77	77	......
119	Bottlers and mineral and soda water makers	7,230	6,681	549	20	19	1	0	0	......
120	Box makers (paper)	17,757	4,714	13,043	4	......	4	......	......	......
121	Box makers (wood)	10,883	9,572	1,311	64	63	1	......	......	......
122	Brass workers (not otherwise specified) (a)	17,265	16,352	913	13	13	......	1	1	......
123	Brewers and maltsters (a)	20,362	20,294	68	43	43	......	20	20	......
124	Brick and tile makers and terra cotta workers (a)	60,214	60,070	144	672	671	1	43	43	......
125	Britannia workers	904	787	117	......	......	......	......	......	......
126	Broom and brush makers	10,115	8,949	1,166	22	22	......	......	......	......
127	Builders and contractors	45,988	45,978	10	703	703	......	36	36	......
128	Butchers	105,456	105,339	117	512	512	......	160	159	1
129	Butter and cheese makers	11,211	10,808	403	9	9	......	......	......	......
130	Button makers	2,601	1,011	1,590	......	......	......	......	......	......
131	Cabinet makers	35,915	35,891	24	106	106	......	6	6	......
132	Candle, soap, and tallow makers	3,450	3,051	399	4	4	......	......	......	......
133	Carpenters and joiners	611,482	611,293	189	6,835	6,833	2	530	530	......
134	Carpet makers (a)	22,302	11,546	10,756	5	......	5	......	......	......
135	Carriage and wagon makers (not otherwise classified). (a)	34,538	34,308	230	166	166	......	12	12	......
136	Charcoal, coke, and lime burners	8,704	8,689	15	794	791	3	3	3	......
137	Chemical works employés (a)	3,628	2,613	1,015	......	......	......	......	......	......
138	Clock and watch makers and repairers	25,252	20,556	4,696	106	106	......	11	11	......
139	Compositors (a)	30,060	23,745	6,315	98	84	14	39	32	7
140	Confectioners	23,251	17,577	5,674	86	81	5	12	12	......
141	Coopers	47,486	47,438	48	148	147	1	4	4	......
142	Copper workers	3,384	3,377	7	24	24	......	3	3	......
143	Corset makers	6,533	733	5,800	1	......	1	......	......	......
144	Cotton mill operatives (a)	173,142	80,177	92,965	1,948	960	988	......	......	......
145	Distillers and rectifiers (a)	3,314	3,305	9	55	55	......	......	......	......
146	Door, sash, and blind makers (a)	5,041	5,031	10	18	18	......	......	......	......
147	Dressmakers	289,164	836	288,328	1,314	......	1,314	103	......	103
148	Electroplaters	2,756	2,644	112	2	2	......	......	......	......
149	Electrotypers and stereotypers (a)	1,471	1,466	5	2	2	......	......	......	......
150	Engravers	8,320	8,017	303	13	13	......	1	1	......
151	Fertilizer makers (a)	732	726	6	2	2	......	......	......	......
152	Fish curers and packers (a)	1,279	1,084	195	......	......	......	......	......	......

a See explanatory notes in Table 78.

OCCUPATIONS.

309

OCCUPATION, CLASSIFIED BY SEX, BY STATES AND TERRITORIES: 1890—Continued.

ARKANSAS			CALIFORNIA			COLORADO			CONNECTICUT			DELAWARE			DISTRICT OF COLUMBIA			
Total	Males	Females	Total	Males	Females	Total	Males	Females	Total	Males	Females	Total	Males	Females	Total	Males	Females	
4,116	4,051	65	15,639	15,123	516	8,917	8,829	88	5,949	5,766	183	1,388	1,297	91	2,289	2,101	188	76
89	89		891	887	4	272	270	2	294	293	1	60	59	1	109	109		77
105	103	2	961	943	18	242	224	18	580	559	21	215	212	3	1,106	1,034	22	78
22	22		185	184	1	47	47		85	82	3	9	9		93	93		79
174	173	1	1,439	1,427	12	984	980	4	819	815	4	119	119		157	156	1	80
23	23		588	512	76	117	114	3	1,091	468	623	48	32	16	17	10	7	81
25	25		82	82		4	4		73	73		55	55		24	24		82
282	282		716	709	7	124	124		178	168	10	24	24		470	465	5	83
95	95		3,956	3,954	2	44	44		979	979		510	510		171	171		84
1,767	1,667	100	5,897	4,961	936	2,060	1,751	309	5,105	3,772	1,333	619	398	221	1,777	1,216	561	85
3,038	3,034	4	7,568	7,556	12	7,921	7,904	17	3,875	3,851	24	1,308	1,299	9	382	367	15	86
77	36	41	1,152	359	793	538	206	332	471	161	310	66	33	33	448	215	233	87
88	88		1,628	1,627	1	408	408		417	415	2	51	50	1	639	639		88
335	308	27	1,136	847	289	697	603	94	540	359	181	190	177	13	248	203	45	89
32	32		143	142	1	215	215		362	306	56	32	32		48	48		90
45	45		245	243	2	59	59		191	188	3	62	62		77	77		91
14	14		90	87	3	31	31		16	10		6	6		3	3		92
12	10	2	112	110	2	32	31	1	65	48	17	3	2	1	33	28	5	93
21,920	19,703	2,217	115,461	98,766	16,695	39,380	35,355	4,025	146,397	110,593	35,804	18,104	15,394	2,710	23,311	18,431	4,880	94
			14	14					146	146		1	1					95
12	12		173	173		31	31		76	76		28	28		60	60		96
			32	29	3	2	2		14	14		4	4		7	7		97
17	17		166	166		22	22		145	145		48	48		77	77		98
1	1		11	11		2	2		26	26		15	15		4	4		99
4		4	110		110	14		14	72		72	11		11	72		72	100
2	2		13	13					4	4		6	6					101
4	4		195	195		51	51		899	839		83	83		47	47		102
2	2		25	25		14	14		46	46		5	5		32	32		103
1		1	23		23	7		7	18		18	4		4	13		13	104
2	2		62	62		15	15		28	28		21	21		31	31		105
10	10		108	108		40	40		83	83		21	21		86	86		106
17	16	1	111	110	1	38	34	4	79	76	3	41	41		69	63	6	107
1	1		49	35	14	4	4		12	11	1	8	4	4	16	14	2	108
3	3		43	43		5	5		27	27		12	12		31	31		109
49	48	1	958	887	71	182	168	14	595	571	24	265	256	9	342	330	12	110
			18	6	12				3		3	1		1	3		3	111
121	118	3	2,161	2,005	156	629	591	38	1,073	1,028	45	182	180	2	522	510	12	112
12	12		86	48	38	2	1	1	62	58	4	50	50		20	20		113
2,037	2,037		6,641	6,638	3	2,137	2,137		3,490	3,487	3	814	814		731	730	1	114
15	12	3	156	135	21	26	22	4	516	451	65	91	91		61	50	11	115
			8	8					392	340	52							116
22	15	7	526	296	230	130	89	41	258	161	97	19	9	10	539	338	201	117
380	378	2	4,611	4,270	341	711	706	5	2,641	2,357	284	365	349	16	566	562	4	118
5	5		211	210	1	80	76	4	149	147	2	13	13		60	57	3	119
1		1	101	10	91	13	5	8	1,413	349	1,064				6		6	120
24	24		876	863	13	28	27	1	262	172	90	5	5		13	13		121
5	5		214	214		28	28		4,485	3,953	532	16	16		41	41		122
4	4		877	873	4	254	254		169	169		37	37		72	72		123
358	358		1,216	1,216		1,724	1,724		810	809	1	226	226		532	532		124
			1	1					440	394	46							125
28	28		115	110	5	51	51		95	79	16	10	10		15	15		126
285	285		1,699	1,698	1	1,008	1,008		771	771		291	291		436	436		127
463	463		4,230	4,229	1	1,126	1,126		1,589	1,588	1	375	375		581	577	4	128
3	3		165	164	1	24	24		162	159	3	15	15		19	19		129
			2	2					403	116	287							130
94	94		840	840		198	198		519	519		109	109		198	198		131
			106	101	5	21	21		110	94	16	2	2		8	8		132
4,375	4,372	3	17,115	17,105	10	8,106	8,100	6	9,530	9,528	2	1,950	1,950		2,079	2,079		133
7		7	52	38	14	30	17	13	237	144	93	24	19	5	4		4	134
188	188		726	726		225	225		889	885	4	164	164		74	74		135
3	3		161	161		135	135		77	77		27	27		19	19		136
			11	10	1	1		1	64	60	4	9	9		6	6		137
62	62		484	476	8	137	137		2,556	1,998	558	42	42		69	69		138
93	85	8	1,194	881	313	247	212	35	426	328	98	49	37	12	616	592	24	139
89	82	7	651	549	102	268	197	71	279	230	49	71	61	10	220	170	50	140
133	133		929	928	1	73	73		200	200		60	60		60	60		141
6	6		81	81		16	16		212	212		12	11	1	16	16		142
			16	4	12	5		5	2,921	351	2,570							143
84	58	26	136	67	69				11,012	5,797	5,215	593	254	339				144
31	31		80	80					32	32		2	2		3	3		145
3	3		143	142	1	6	6		108	108		75	75		3	3		146
679		679	8,884	28	8,856	2,310	6	2,304	5,620	4	5,616	1,118		1,118	2,542		2,542	147
			23	23		11	11		347	309	38	2	2		8	8		148
									30	30					40	40		149
1	1		183	181	2	36	35	1	305	292	13	6	6		95	94	1	150
7	7		81	81					14	14		6	6		3	3		151
									10	10		1	1		2	2		152

STATISTICS OF POPULATION.

310

TABLE 79.—TOTAL PERSONS 10 YEARS OF AGE AND OVER ENGAGED IN EACH SPECIFIED

	OCCUPATIONS.	THE UNITED STATES.			ALABAMA.			ARIZONA.		
		Total.	Males.	Females.	Total.	Males.	Females.	Total.	Males.	Females.
	Manufacturing and mechanical industries—Cont'd.									
153	Gas works employés (a)	5,224	5,219	5	41	41	....	....	....	....
154	Glass workers	34,282	32,572	1,710	8	8	....	2	2	....
155	Glove makers	6,416	2,741	3,675	....	....	....	....	....	....
156	Gold and silver workers	20,263	16,914	3,349	51	51	....	10	10	....
157	Gunsmiths, locksmiths, and bell hangers	9,158	9,069	89	70	70	....	14	14	....
158	Hair workers	1,254	684	570	8	....	8	58	58	....
159	Harness and saddle makers and repairers	43,480	42,647	833	145	144	1	1	1	....
160	Hat and cap makers	24,013	17,319	6,694	....	....	....	....	....	....
161	Hosiery and knitting mill operatives (a)	29,555	8,745	20,810	247	90	157	15	15	....
162	Iron and steel workers (a)	144,921	142,585	2,336	2,792	2,782	10	....	....	....
163	Lace and embroidery makers	5,256	821	4,435	7	....	7	1	....	1
164	Lead and zinc workers	4,616	4,413	203	3	3	....	....	....	....
165	Leather curriers, dressers, finishers, and tanners	39,332	39,040	292	51	51	....	5	5	....
166	Machinists	177,090	176,951	139	1,342	1,341	1	126	126	....
167	Manufacturers and officials of manufacturing companies	101,610	101,280	330	764	761	3	32	32	....
168	Marble and stone cutters	61,070	61,012	58	233	233	....	15	15	....
169	Masons (brick and stone)	158,918	158,878	40	1,871	1,870	1	213	213	....
170	Meat and fruit packers, canners, and preservers (a)	5,830	4,419	1,411	11	9	2	....	....	....
171	Mechanics (not otherwise specified)	15,485	15,472	13	689	689	....	4	4	....
172	Metal workers (not otherwise specified)	16,694	15,837	857	78	78	....	44	44	....
173	Mill and factory operatives (not specified)(a)	93,596	51,603	41,993	1,384	730	654	12	12	....
174	Millers (flour and grist)	52,841	52,747	94	1,021	1,019	2	29	29	....
175	Milliners	60,482	395	60,087	804	3	801	21	....	21
176	Model and pattern makers	10,300	10,159	141	70	70	....	....	....	....
177	Molders	66,289	66,243	46	377	377	....	13	13	....
178	Musical instrument makers (not otherwise specified). (a)	652	629	23	....	....	....	....	....	....
179	Nail and tack makers (a)	4,583	4,106	477	2	2	....	....	....	....
180	Oil well employés	9,147	9,137	10	....	....	....	....	....	....
181	Oil works employés	5,624	5,587	37	83	83	....	....	....	....
182	Painters, glaziers, and varnishers	219,912	218,646	1,266	1,219	1,214	5	89	89	....
183	Paper hangers	12,369	12,315	54	40	40	....	3	3	....
184	Paper mill operatives	27,817	18,856	8,961	....	....	....	....	....	....
185	Photographers	20,040	17,839	2,201	127	118	9	21	21	....
186	Piano and organ makers and tuners (a)	14,683	14,367	316	20	20	....	4	4	....
187	Plasterers	39,002	38,987	15	306	305	1	27	27	....
188	Plumbers and gas and steam fitters	56,607	56,563	44	207	207	....	11	11	....
189	Potters	14,928	12,939	1,989	69	69	....	....	....	....
190	Powder and cartridge makers	1,385	963	422	....	....	....	....	....	....
191	Printers, lithographers, and pressmen (a)	86,893	81,154	5,739	493	482	16	82	74	8
192	Print works operatives (a)	6,701	5,162	1,539	....	....	....	....	....	....
193	Publishers of books, maps, and newspapers	6,284	6,210	74	30	30	....	8	8	....
194	Roofers and slaters	7,043	7,040	3	20	20	....	....	....	....
195	Rope and cordage makers	8,001	4,896	3,105	13	13	....	....	....	....
196	Rubber factory operatives	16,162	9,706	6,456	....	....	....	2	2	....
197	Sail, awning, and tent makers	3,257	3,006	251	8	8	....	....	....	....
198	Salt works employés	1,765	1,662	103	....	....	....	....	....	....
199	Saw and planing mill employés (a)	133,637	133,355	282	2,850	2,829	21	82	82	....
200	Seamstresses (a)	150,044	4,001	146,043	2,404	6	2,398	167	....	167
201	Sewing machine makers (not otherwise classified). (a)	880	850	30	1	1	....	....	....	....
202	Sewing machine operators (a)	7,126	1,104	6,022	3	....	3	....	....	....
203	Ship and boat builders	22,951	22,948	3	112	112	....	5	5	....
204	Shirt, collar, and cuff makers (a)	21,107	5,132	15,975	7	2	5	....	....	....
205	Silk mill operatives (a)	34,855	14,192	20,663	....	....	....	....	....	....
206	Starch makers	746	566	180	....	....	....	....	....	....
207	Steam boiler makers	21,339	21,333	6	191	191	....	21	21	....
208	Stove, furnace, and grate makers (a)	8,932	8,912	20	25	25	....	....	....	....
209	Straw workers	3,666	1,243	2,423	....	....	....	....	....	....
210	Sugar makers and refiners	2,616	2,612	4	....	....	....	....	....	....
211	Tailors and tailoresses (a)	185,400	121,591	63,809	307	230	77	46	40	6
212	Tinners and tinware makers	55,488	54,589	899	240	240	....	46	46	....
213	Tobacco and cigar factory operatives	111,625	83,634	27,991	139	134	5	5	5	....
214	Tool and cutlery makers (not otherwise classified). (a)	17,985	17,449	536	20	20	....	1	1	....
215	Trunk, valise, leather-case, and pocket-book makers	6,279	5,458	821	18	18	....	....	....	....
216	Umbrella and parasol makers	3,403	1,465	1,938	....	....	....	....	....	....
217	Upholsterers	25,666	23,918	1,748	73	72	1	11	11	....
218	Well borers	4,854	4,853	1	17	17	....	4	4	....
219	Wheelwrights	12,856	12,855	1	111	111	....	21	21	....
220	Whitewashers	3,996	3,987	9	47	47	....	....	....	....
221	Wire workers	12,319	11,238	1,081	7	5	2	....	....	....
222	Wood workers (not otherwise specified)	67,360	63,600	3,760	246	245	1	2	2	....
223	Woolen mill operatives (a)	84,109	47,638	36,471	52	26	26	....	....	....
224	Other persons in manufacturing and mechanical industries	76,714	60,806	15,908	493	446	47	32	32	....

a See explanatory notes in Table 78.

OCCUPATIONS.

311

OCCUPATION, CLASSIFIED BY SEX, BY STATES AND TERRITORIES: 1890—Continued.

ARKANSAS.			CALIFORNIA.			COLORADO.			CONNECTICUT.			DELAWARE.			DISTRICT OF COLUMBIA.			
Total.	Males.	Fe-males.	Total.	Males.	Fe-males.	Total.	Males.	Fe-males.	Total.	Males.	Fe-males.	Total.	Males.	Fe-males.	Total.	Males.	Fe-males.	
6	6		156	156		19	19		85	85	16	15	15		71	71		153
4	4		186	186		100	100		140	124	16	45	45		11	11		154
			291	124	167	6	6		13	6	7	2		2				155
29	29		256	251	5	82	82		1,474	1,298	176	25	24	1	42	41	1	156
63	63		268	268		51	51		1,553	1,486	67	18	18		51	51		157
			19	12	7	2		2	27	5	22				3	2	1	158
100	100		1,532	1,513	19	410	410		680	657	23	80	80		113	113		159
2	2		122	95	27	9	8	1	5,150	3,798	1,352	7	5	2	11	10	1	160
17		17	28	8	20				1,212	400	812	5	2	3	5	2	3	161
97	97		1,090	1,084	6	1,042	1,042		5,728	5,304	424	1,282	1,281	1	150	150		162
7		7	77	5	72	17		17	88	26	62	8		8	15		15	163
1	1		57	55	2	2	2		45	34	11							164
122	122		1,040	1,039	1	32	32		337	337		1,028	1,008	20	22	22		165
767	766	1	3,957	3,953	4	1,383	1,383		7,737	7,728	9	973	973		701	700	1	166
432	431	1	2,087	2,033	4	494	494		2,644	2,642	2	374	374		182	178	4	167
191	191		1,194	1,192	2	1,093	1,092	1	1,579	1,577	2	137	137		323	323		168
696	696		1,915	1,914	1	2,726	2,725	1	3,107	3,107		385	385		1,125	1,125		169
5	4	1	389	291	98	26	23	3	68	62	6	44	34	10	1		1	170
415	415		234	234		109	109		939	938	1	39	39		27	27		171
5	5		143	141	2	612	609	3	3,612	3,333	279	33	32	1	36	35	1	172
197	174	23	655	578	77	144	121	23	2,763	1,498	1,265	366	185	181	30	30	6	173
650	649	1	888	882	6	288	288		360	360		249	249		63	63		174
387		387	1,531	11	1,520	418		418	1,104	6	1,098	181		181	185		185	175
16	10		252	251	1	83	83		454	452	2	60	60		57	55	2	176
77	77		1,213	1,211	2	356	356		3,780	3,778	2	244	244		109	109		177
			4	4					1	1					5	5		178
8	8		114	114		12	12		90	58	38	5	5		1	1		179
			33	33		3	3											180
76	76		63	63		49	49		28	28		3	3					181
802	802		6,230	6,206	24	1,946	1,942	4	5,064	4,990	74	953	892	61	1,270	1,270		182
27	27		277	277		102	102		94	93	1	59	59		193	193		183
			190	177	13	14	14		1,642	996	646	158	107	51				184
167	158	9	750	671	79	261	242	19	338	284	54	30	28	2	129	117	12	185
16	16		201	201		32	32		887	845	42	8	8		38	38		186
197	197		973	971	2	907	907		121	121		99	99		533	533		187
117	117		2,309	2,306	3	781	780	1	1,269	1,269		195	195		711	710	1	188
74	74		132	132		15	15		117	106	11	8	8		29	29		189
			80	78	2				537	245	292	28	28		1	1		190
406	391	15	2,710	2,532	178	1,178	1,123	55	1,346	1,156	190	177	161	16	1,648	1,336	312	191
			2	2					136	98	38	4	4					192
85	85		211	209	2	81	79	2	75	75		11	11		32	32		193
7	7		130	130		48	48		112	112		28	28		32	32		194
			200	198	2				172	93	79	8	6	2				195
			22	22					2,762	1,533	1,229	2	2					196
4	4		172	165	7	18	12	6	48	43	5	9	9		27	23	4	197
			22	22														198
3,663	3,662	1	3,315	3,313	2	534	534		353	353		182	182		81	81		199
999	29	970	2,212	94	2,118	718	8	710	1,301	296	1,005	225	3	222	1,072		1,072	200
			6	6		1	1		66	66								201
			160	94	66	1		1	318	30	288	3		3				202
20	20		1,166	1,166		14	14		553	553		482	482		65	65		203
			729	543	186	12	5	7	454	70	384	3		3	7		7	204
			98	36	62				4,066	1,425	2,641	26	7	19	1	1		205
									12	10	2	13	13					206
64	64		713	710	3	228	228		222	222		154	154		31	31		207
32	32		64	64		30	30		74	74		7	7		6	6		208
			26	9	17				130	73	57	1	1					209
			177	177					1	1								210
210	190	20	5,619	4,609	1,010	813	681	132	1,947	1,507	440	293	143	150	554	410	144	211
181	181		1,281	1,263	18	441	441		881	850	31	279	275	4	379	378	1	212
59	54	5	3,869	3,281	88	356	337	19	967	893	74	81	66	15	173	173		213
87	87		130	130		20	20		2,770	2,671	99	28	28		24	24		214
20	20		123	114	9	23	23		115	81	34	4	4		12	12		215
			8	8					105	102	3	1	1		6	6		216
25	25		874	857	17	180	178	2	520	499	21	209	187	22	182	181	1	217
39	39		224	224		45	45		6	6		2	2					218
49	49		296	296		87	87		250	250		163	163		71	71		219
24	24		44	44		13	13		24	24		7	7		133	133		220
4	4		170	170		7	7		772	671	101	12	12		7	7		221
246	246		964	949	15	215	215		1,419	1,332	87	254	202	52	120	114	6	222
16	12	4	425	368	57	2		2	8,050	5,019	3,031	213	130	83				223
212	210	2	1,494	1,362	132	516	497	19	5,046	2,926	2,120	572	514	58	633	505	128	224

312

STATISTICS OF POPULATION.

TABLE 79.—TOTAL PERSONS 10 YEARS OF AGE AND OVER ENGAGED IN EACH SPECIFIED

	OCCUPATIONS.	FLORIDA.			GEORGIA.			IDAHO.		
		Total.	Males.	Fe-males.	Total.	Males.	Fe-males.	Total.	Males.	Fe-males.
1	All occupations..............	136,827	110,404	26,423	668,713	508,790	159,923	35,172	33,278	1,894
2	Agriculture, fisheries, and mining..........	66,108	56,420	9,778	418,128	347,601	70,527	18,814	18,612	202
3	Agricultural laborers (a)............	23,562	16,783	6,770	214,030	154,541	59,489	2,862	2,847	15
4	Apiarists.....................	18	17	1	5	5	....			
5	Dairymen and dairywomen.........	51	47	4	216	137	79	49	42	7
6	Farmers, planters, and overseers (a)...	38,196	35,241	2,955	189,933	179,123	10,810	8,634	8,467	167
7	Fishermen and oystermen (a)......	991	983	8	394	379	15	13	13	
8	Gardeners, florists, nurserymen, and vinegrowers.	641	625	16	800	766	64	101	100	4
9	Lumbermen and raftsmen..........	821	819	2	745	744	1	205	205	
10	Miners (coal)...................	....	....		130	130	....			
11	Miners (not otherwise specified)....	837	837	....	981	979	2	5,201	5,200	1
12	Quarrymen....................	4	4	....	855	855	....	4	4	
13	Stock raisers, herders, and drovers.	333	330	3	116	109	7	1,553	1,545	8
14	Wood choppers.................	719	719	....	1,675	1,670	5	168	168	
15	Other agricultural pursuits (a).....	525	515	10	8,748	8,663	85	1	1	
16	Professional service............	5,449	4,243	1,206	15,969	11,907	4,062	1,295	1,004	291
17	Actors......................	4	2	2	29	24	5	7	2	5
18	Architects...................	31	31	....	86	85	1	2	2	
19	Artists and teachers of art.......	67	33	34	178	99	79	14	7	7
20	Authors and literary and scientific persons......	20	13	7	67	41	26	3	2	1
21	Chemists, assayers, and metallurgists.	18	18	....	21	21	....	22	22	
22	Clergymen....................	927	919	8	2,525	2,517	8	80	79	1
23	Dentists.....................	134	134	....	282	280	2	20	20	
24	Designers, draftsmen, and inventors.	11	11	....	20	20	....	1	1	
25	Engineers (civil, mechanical, electrical, and mining) and surveyors.	258	257	1	428	428	....	109	109	
26	Journalists..................	115	108	7	314	309	5	34	33	1
27	Lawyers.....................	574	574	....	1,731	1,730	1	176	176	
28	Musicians and teachers of music....	194	56	138	634	190	444	58	22	36
29	Officers of United States army and navy.	34	34	....	21	21	....	64	64	
30	Officials (government) (a).........	743	689	54	1,561	1,478	83	170	161	9
31	Physicians and surgeons..........	649	632	17	2,425	2,383	42	117	112	5
32	Professors in colleges and universities.	20	18	2	93	83	10	1	1	
33	Teachers....................	1,601	667	934	5,441	2,087	3,354	341	121	220
34	Theatrical managers, showmen, etc..	31	30	1	64	62	2	60	60	0
35	Veterinary surgeons............	15	15	....	34	34	....	1	1	
36	Other professional service........	3	2	1	6	6	....			
37	Domestic and personal service..........	31,995	19,473	12,522	120,852	49,395	71,457	6,718	5,788	930
38	Barbers and hairdressers........	354	347	7	1,005	985	20	108	106	2
39	Bartenders...................	188	188	....	605	605	....	134	134	
40	Boarding and lodging house keepers.	382	87	295	907	179	728	84	34	50
41	Engineers and firemen (not locomotive).	592	592	....	1,744	1,741	3	208	208	
42	Hotel keepers.................	208	149	59	386	275	111	130	118	18
43	Housekeepers and stewards (a)....	331	33	298	1,398	81	1,317	73	7	66
44	Hunters, trappers, guides, and scouts.	112	111	1	9	9	....	30	30	
45	Janitors.....................	32	29	3	162	153	9	9	9	
46	Laborers (not specified) (a).......	16,183	14,874	1,309	42,348	35,238	7,110	3,716	3,695	21
47	Launderers and laundresses......	4,730	160	4,570	30,237	280	29,957	234	176	58
48	Nurses and midwives...........	213	26	187	795	90	705	38	2	36
49	Restaurant keepers............	147	113	34	287	176	111	40	33	7
50	Saloon keepers...............	144	137	7	317	298	19	279	274	5
51	Servants....................	7,470	1,736	5,734	38,655	7,335	31,320	1,360	693	667
52	Sextons.....................	20	20	....	87	86	1	1	1	
53	Soldiers, sailors, and marines (United States) (a)..	451	451	....	211	211	....	236	236	
54	Watchmen, policemen, and detectives.	376	376	....	1,524	1,520	4	30	30	
55	Other domestic and personal service.	62	44	18	175	133	42	2	2	....
56	Trade and transportation.............	15,033	14,627	406	54,770	53,054	1,716	4,358	4,273	85
57	Agents (claim, commission, real estate, insurance, etc.) and collectors.	692	683	9	2,319	2,275	44	142	137	5
58	Auctioneers..................	14	14	....	24	24	....	1	1	
59	Bankers and brokers (money and stocks).........	92	92	....	325	321	4	31	29	2
60	Boatmen and canalmen..........	366	366	....	118	118	....	17	17	
61	Bookkeepers and accountants (a)..	520	493	27	2,135	2,017	118	134	127	7
62	Brokers (commercial)...........	9	9	....	157	157	....			
63	Clerks and copyists (a).........	2,146	2,028	118	7,659	7,249	410	489	464	25
64	Commercial travelers..........	115	115	....	1,100	1,097	3	36	35	1
65	Draymen, hackmen, teamsters, etc.	1,500	1,500	....	5,697	5,688	9	570	570	
66	Foremen and overseers.........	202	202	....	531	529	2	123	123	
67	Hostlers....................	150	150	....	720	720	....	37	37	
68	Hucksters and peddlers.........	150	145	5	689	528	161	19	19	
69	Livery stable keepers..........	99	99	....	317	317	....	66	66	
70	Locomotive engineers and firemen (a).	423	423	....	1,977	1,977	....	282	282	
71	Merchants and dealers in drugs and chemicals (retail).	248	243	5	517	513	4	66	64	2
72	Merchants and dealers in dry goods (retail)	178	171	7	904	883	21	42	37	5
73	Merchants and dealers in groceries (retail)........	543	522	21	1,894	1,807	87	57	56	1
74	Merchants and dealers in wines and liquors (retail).	26	26	....	74	73	1	19	19	
75	Merchants and dealers in wines and liquors (wholesale).	5	5	....	48	48	....	6	6	

a See explanatory notes in Table 78.

OCCUPATIONS.

OCCUPATION, CLASSIFIED BY SEX, BY STATES AND TERRITORIES: 1890—Continued.

ILLINOIS Total	ILLINOIS Males	ILLINOIS Females	INDIANA Total	INDIANA Males	INDIANA Females	IOWA Total	IOWA Males	IOWA Females	KANSAS Total	KANSAS Males	KANSAS Females	KENTUCKY Total	KENTUCKY Males	KENTUCKY Females	
1,353,559	1,153,249	200,310	724,058	639,156	84,902	631,835	551,418	80,417	452,346	406,839	45,507	590,324	506,940	83,378	1
456,488	443,559	12,929	330,569	322,221	8,348	330,390	322,296	8,094	256,582	249,867	6,715	326,085	314,212	11,873	2
125,964	125,137	827	84,638	84,074	564	74,156	73,753	403	48,199	47,965	234	105,007	103,136	1,871	3
164	159	5	61	61	....	162	155	7	23	23	....	15	15	....	4
589	554	35	530	490	40	490	412	78	360	339	21	407	372	35	5
297,529	285,644	11,885	232,838	225,194	7,644	243,853	236,338	7,515	198,839	192,452	6,387	211,782	201,902	9,880	6
759	757	2	314	314	....	217	216	1	119	119	....	253	252	1	7
4,604	4,460	144	1,999	1,904	95	1,900	1,828	72	1,465	1,416	49	1,264	1,183	81	8
521	521	....	904	904	....	215	214	1	148	148	....	950	948	2	9
21,389	21,370	19	6,279	6,278	1	6,755	6,748	7	4,445	4,438	7	4,128	4,128	....	10
825	825	....	199	199	....	993	990	3	1,019	1,019	....	963	963	....	11
1,983	1,981	2	1,548	1,548	....	368	368	....	340	340	....	550	549	1	12
1,448	1,445	3	432	431	1	948	941	7	1,565	1,551	14	240	240	....	13
626	626	....	722	722	....	270	270	....	37	37	....	504	504	....	14
87	80	7	105	102	3	57	57	....	23	20	3	22	20	2	15
63,122	41,176	21,946	34,519	24,104	10,415	37,762	18,962	18,800	25,439	16,840	8,599	22,150	16,135	6,015	16
778	446	332	150	89	61	96	62	34	58	39	19	44	25	19	17
743	741	2	107	107	....	110	110	....	98	98	....	95	95	....	18
1,850	1,031	819	557	260	297	539	195	344	346	142	204	328	187	141	19
466	277	189	148	76	72	146	80	66	101	65	36	72	48	24	20
250	249	1	57	57	....	15	15	....	24	24	....	41	40	1	21
5,207	5,066	141	3,160	3,122	38	3,253	3,219	34	2,665	2,634	31	2,559	2,548	11	22
1,142	1,108	34	594	575	19	553	540	13	361	349	12	804	804	....	23
749	735	14	172	169	3	59	58	1	52	52	....	68	68	....	24
2,271	2,252	19	752	751	1	653	648	5	404	404	....	709	707	2	25
1,549	1,473	76	679	651	28	735	709	26	619	587	32	342	332	10	26
5,789	5,769	20	3,208	3,199	9	2,800	2,779	21	2,964	2,944	20	2,356	2,353	3	27
4,693	2,022	2,671	1,981	660	1,321	1,839	490	1,349	1,268	371	897	972	364	608	28
42	42	....	16	16	....	7	7	....	152	152	....	19	19	....	29
5,007	4,685	322	2,778	2,597	181	2,418	2,175	243	2,145	1,962	183	2,104	1,978	126	30
6,594	6,207	387	4,714	4,571	143	3,051	2,923	128	2,773	2,673	100	3,323	3,256	67	31
290	262	28	254	216	38	186	165	21	179	161	18	125	114	11	32
23,322	6,536	16,786	18,971	5,818	13,153	20,112	3,610	16,502	10,484	3,455	7,029	7,876	2,892	4,984	33
1,585	1,516	69	893	853	40	672	663	9	410	399	11	732	729	3	34
681	680	1	305	305	....	482	482	....	229	229	....	73	73	....	35
114	79	35	23	12	11	86	82	4	47	40	7	8	3	5	36
268,105	175,161	92,944	127,118	88,076	39,042	85,932	52,916	33,016	54,045	35,225	18,820	98,269	51,964	46,305	37
6,539	6,293	246	8,370	8,288	82	2,436	2,387	49	1,753	1,729	24	1,395	1,362	33	38
4,104	4,087	17	1,758	1,752	6	412	411	1	48	48	....	950	947	3	39
3,063	654	2,409	987	280	707	774	277	497	614	231	383	847	232	615	40
10,284	10,278	6	4,977	4,974	3	2,133	2,132	1	1,767	1,767	....	2,530	2,530	....	41
2,038	1,760	278	1,033	931	102	1,575	1,454	121	1,243	1,115	128	612	508	104	42
4,144	272	3,872	2,528	80	2,448	1,875	62	1,813	1,257	46	1,211	1,904	92	1,812	43
71	71	....	23	23	....	35	35	....	18	18	....	11	11	....	44
1,836	1,732	104	482	433	49	453	437	16	338	332	6	308	275	33	45
120,129	119,051	1,078	67,683	67,182	501	39,784	39,486	298	24,197	24,049	148	37,422	36,763	659	46
7,788	1,582	6,206	3,545	367	3,178	1,848	278	1,570	2,206	317	1,889	9,177	222	8,895	47
2,853	407	2,446	694	99	595	714	116	598	444	101	343	646	93	553	48
1,557	1,379	178	424	397	27	1,065	987	78	720	642	78	167	145	22	49
7,627	7,488	139	3,043	2,992	51	1,108	1,093	15	262	261	1	1,120	1,082	38	50
88,396	12,683	75,713	34,489	3,331	31,158	30,517	2,600	27,917	16,948	2,372	14,576	39,405	6,009	33,396	51
279	270	....	125	125	....	100	100	....	51	50	1	95	94	1	52
201	201	....	54	54	....	10	10	....	1,291	1,291	....	87	87	....	53
6,261	6,258	3	1,615	1,585	30	883	882	1	731	730	1	1,462	1,360	102	54
935	686	249	228	183	45	210	169	41	157	126	31	191	152	39	55
246,704	227,246	19,458	92,344	87,059	5,285	88,097	83,666	4,431	61,606	58,804	2,802	61,145	57,940	3,205	56
14,874	14,424	450	5,229	5,016	213	5,727	5,599	128	4,471	4,363	108	3,028	2,911	117	57
218	218	....	109	109	....	120	120	....	75	75	....	59	59	....	58
2,120	2,080	40	467	463	4	1,161	1,138	23	1,187	1,169	18	326	318	8	59
307	304	3	164	164	....	83	83	....	19	19	....	212	212	....	60
13,314	10,470	2,844	3,483	2,764	719	3,143	2,476	667	1,867	1,532	335	2,500	2,239	261	61
295	295	....	72	72	....	49	49	....	41	41	....	113	113	....	62
44,793	37,998	6,795	12,953	11,014	1,939	11,895	10,304	1,591	7,689	6,726	963	9,294	8,368	926	63
5,295	5,220	75	2,420	2,394	26	2,758	2,729	29	1,137	1,131	6	1,072	1,067	5	64
25,663	25,644	19	10,282	10,282	....	7,914	7,909	5	4,418	4,415	3	6,762	6,761	1	65
8,274	8,174	100	1,070	1,060	10	1,639	1,630	9	1,368	1,363	5	563	560	....	66
3,224	3,224	....	1,660	1,660	....	1,184	1,184	....	822	822	....	1,395	1,391	4	67
4,394	4,259	135	1,490	1,469	21	866	845	21	383	377	6	835	796	39	68
1,797	1,794	3	1,073	1,073	....	1,377	1,375	2	1,295	1,292	3	505	505	....	69
5,234	5,234	....	3,237	3,237	....	3,374	3,373	1	2,379	2,370	....	1,382	1,382	....	70
3,278	3,221	57	2,144	2,116	28	1,805	1,778	27	1,563	1,545	18	1,131	1,110	21	71
2,946	2,837	109	1,793	1,753	40	1,740	1,707	33	1,283	1,264	19	1,534	1,462	72	72
7,623	7,385	238	4,412	4,264	148	2,987	2,945	42	2,303	2,270	33	2,988	2,822	166	73
372	371	1	79	79	....	47	46	1	17	17	....	126	125	1	74
277	276	1	57	55	2	33	33	....	6	6	....	92	91	1	75

314　　　　　　　　　　STATISTICS OF POPULATION.

TABLE **79.**—TOTAL PERSONS 10 YEARS OF AGE AND OVER ENGAGED IN EACH SPECIFIED

	OCCUPATIONS.	FLORIDA.			GEORGIA.			IDAHO.		
		Total.	Males.	Females.	Total.	Males.	Females.	Total.	Males.	Females.
	Trade and transportation—Continued.									
76	Merchants and dealers, not specified (retail)	2,404	2,828	76	7,198	6,972	226	569	562	7
77	Merchants and dealers (wholesale), importers, and shipping merchants.	81	81		308	307	1	8	8	
78	Messengers and errand and office boys	125	124	1	794	776	18	8	8	
79	Newspaper carriers and newsboys	12	11	1	76	75	1	2	2	
80	Officials of banks and of insurance, trade, transportation, trust, and other companies. (a)	155	154	1	575	575		129	129	
81	Packers and shippers	40	37	3	147	102	45	61	60	1
82	Pilots	123	123		72	72		1	1	
83	Porters and helpers (in stores and warehouses)	216	211	5	1,517	1,510	7	3	3	
84	Sailors (a)	948	948		273	273		10	10	
85	Salesmen and saleswomen	775	705	70	3,507	3,225	282	112	98	14
86	Steam railroad employés (not otherwise specified). (a)	2,247	2,236	11	11,307	11,251	56	1,209	1,209	
87	Stenographers and typewriters	60	36	24	336	243	93	13	5	8
88	Street railway employés	73	72	1	368	368				
89	Telegraph and telephone operators	232	211	21	758	654	104	73	66	7
90	Telegraph and telephone linemen and electric light and power company employés.	25	25		182	182		10	10	
91	Undertakers	23	23		68	67	1	2	2	
92	Weighers, gaugers, and measurers	3	3		47	47		2	2	
93	Other persons in trade and transportation	13	13		32	23	9	2	2	
94	**Manufacturing and mechanical industries**	18,152	15,641	2,511	58,994	46,833	12,161	3,987	3,601	386
95	Agricultural implement makers (not otherwise classified). (a)	3	3		31	31				
96	Apprentices (blacksmiths)	7	7		63	63		6	6	
97	Apprentices (boot and shoe makers)	1	1		10	10				
98	Apprentices (carpenters and joiners)	24	24		109	109		2	2	
99	Apprentices (carriage and wagon makers)	1	1		5	5				
100	Apprentices (dressmakers)				25		25	2		2
101	Apprentices (leather curriers, etc.)				3	3		1	1	
102	Apprentices (machinists)	20	20		99	99		7	7	
103	Apprentices (masons)	6	6		38	38				
104	Apprentices (milliners)				5		5			
105	Apprentices (painters)	3	3		29	29				
106	Apprentices (plumbers)	5	5		26	26				
107	Apprentices (printers)	14	13	1	29	27	2	3	2	1
108	Apprentices (tailors)	2	2		18	17	1			
109	Apprentices (tinsmiths)	1	1		69	69				
110	Apprentices (not otherwise specified)	161	154	7	288	284	4	10	9	1
111	Artificial flower makers				1		1	1		1
112	Bakers	191	178	13	318	305	13	41	41	
113	Basket makers	3	3		51	49	2	4	4	
114	Blacksmiths	470	470		2,883	2,882	1	424	424	
115	Bleachers, dyers, and scourers	17	15	2	99	84	15	2	2	
116	Bone and ivory workers	1		1						
117	Bookbinders	19	15	4	122	59	63			
118	Boot and shoe makers and repairers	228	225	3	1,188	1,174	14	110	110	
119	Bottlers and mineral and soda water makers	9	9		42	40	2	6	6	
120	Box makers (paper)	1		1	69	7	62			
121	Box makers (wood)	18	12	6	48	46	2	1	1	
122	Brass workers (not otherwise specified) (a)	2	2		19	19		4	4	
123	Brewers and maltsters (a)	1	1		100	100		54	54	
124	Brick and tile makers and terra cotta workers (a)	118	118		1,123	1,119	4	48	48	
125	Britannia workers									
126	Broom and brush makers	4	4		32	32				
127	Builders and contractors	246	246		645	645		87	87	
128	Butchers	290	290		784	782	2	200	200	
129	Butter and cheese makers	1	1		25	22	3	7	7	
130	Button makers									
131	Cabinet makers	62	62		291	291		11	11	
132	Candle, soap, and tallow makers				8	6	2			
133	Carpenters and joiners	3,488	3,488		10,107	10,105	2	999	999	
134	Carpet makers (a)							2		2
135	Carriage and wagon makers (not otherwise classified). (a)	59	59		222	222		15	15	
136	Charcoal, coke, and lime burners	118	117	1	69	69		53	53	
137	Chemical works employés (a)				27	25	2			
138	Clock and watch makers and repairers	48	47	1	136	133	3	15	15	
139	Compositors (a)	76	66	10	280	254	26	22	20	2
140	Confectioners	51	48	3	190	172	18	13	13	
141	Coopers	64	64		600	600		10	10	
142	Copper workers	4	4		33	33		4	4	
143	Corset makers (a)				1		1			
144	Cotton mill operatives (a)	19	19		7,246	3,364	3,882			
145	Distillers and rectifiers (a)	18	18		233	233		1	1	
146	Door, sash, and blind makers (a)	1	1		28	28				
147	Dressmakers	564		564	2,358	2	2,356	150		150
148	Electroplaters	1	1		3	3				
149	Electrotypers and stereotypers (a)				15	15				
150	Engravers	1	1		24	24				
151	Fertilizer makers (a)	4	4		20	20				
152	Fish curers and packers (a)									

a See explanatory notes in Table 78.

OCCUPATIONS.

OCCUPATION, CLASSIFIED BY SEX, BY STATES AND TERRITORIES: 1890—Continued.

	ILLINOIS.			INDIANA.			IOWA.			KANSAS.			KENTUCKY.			
	Total.	Males.	Females.	Total.	Males.	Females.	Total.	Males.	Females.	Total.	Males.	Females.	Total.	Males.	Females.	
	30,436	29,569	867	12,678	12,460	218	14,892	14,692	200	10,569	10,425	144	8,712	8,476	236	76
	2,918	2,902	16	542	540	2	513	511	2	304	301	3	341	340	1	77
	4,481	4,070	411	551	529	22	333	325	8	230	218	12	712	691	21	78
	545	529	16	128	127	1	48	47	1	40	40		162	159	3	79
	2,745	2,727	18	863	860	3	1,290	1,265	25	1,103	1,083	20	658	656	2	80
	1,930	1,597	333	473	414	59	599	531	68	264	249	15	316	274	42	81
	131	131		110	110		89	89		9	9		145	145		82
	960	948	12	307	297	10	90	90		111	110	1	835	830	5	83
	3,486	3,483		400	399	1	148	148		25	25		299	239		84
	19,125	15,771	3,354	7,330	6,246	1,084	5,559	4,814	745	4,216	3,636	580	4,310	3,470	840	85
	26,976	26,858	118	12,418	12,379	39	13,601	13,576	25	9,705	9,684	21	8,267	8,236	31	86
	3,778	1,044	2,734	804	268	536	898	305	593	658	274	384	507	185	322	87
	3,444	3,442	2	542	542		337	337		302	302		664	663	1	88
	4,333	3,785	548	2,217	2,077	140	1,819	1,607	182	1,350	1,248	102	757	685	72	89
	751	667	84	272	262	10	176	176		124	123	1	162	162		90
	578	577	1	408	405	3	159	158	1	128	128		249	248	1	91
	460	458	2	68	68		81	81		58	58		90	90		92
	329	257	72	39	33	6	33	31	2	27	25	2	42	39	3	93
	319,140	266,107	53,033	139,508	117,696	21,812	89,654	73,578	16,076	54,674	46,103	8,571	82,675	66,695	15,980	94
	1,047	1,026	21	273	273		82	82		18	18		83	83		95
	257	257		117	117		116	116		76	76		74	74		96
	69	66	3	8	8		8	8		3	3		30	29	1	97
	516	514	2	114	114		117	117		30	30		106	106		98
	74	74		23	23		18	18		10	10		7	7		99
	333		333	43		43	74		74	34		34	75		75	100
	24	24		8	8		9	9		8	8		20	20		101
	694	693	1	229	229		101	101		78	78		123	123		102
	127	127		23	23		19	19		16	16		12	12		103
	118		118	20		20	39		39	24		24	13		13	104
	235	235		54	54		33	33		16	16		24	24		105
	322	322		55	55		24	24		13	13		36	36		106
	362	344	18	86	84	2	109	107	2	50	45	5	43	42	1	107
	337	192	145	49	45	4	28	25	3	7	7		51	35	16	108
	149	149		41	41		32	32		16	16		38	38		109
	2,748	2,594	154	842	811	31	491	469	22	253	233	20	630	605	25	110
	55	32	23	10		10	1		1	2		2	1		1	111
	4,163	3,982	181	1,452	1,416	36	882	838	44	702	686	16	778	742	36	112
	200	190	10	174	142	32	36	29	7	14	12	2	97	91	6	113
	13,460	13,454	6	8,142	8,142		5,647	5,645	2	3,864	3,863	1	5,146	5,143	3	114
	281	257	24	104	101	3	79	71	8	48	40	8	77	69	8	115
	19	19		7	7		8	8								116
	2,200	963	1,237	308	178	130	293	188	105	162	107	55	293	153	140	117
	7,684	6,990	694	3,182	3,114	68	2,127	2,055	72	1,255	1,250	5	2,278	2,046	227	118
	301	274	27	116	107	9	88	86	2	38	38		43	39	4	119
	669	86	583	79	20	59	59		59	11		11	66	7	59	120
	1,022	935	87	140	120	20	84	68	16	41	41		213	203	10	121
	1,040	1,019	21	78	77	1	66	66		20	20		246	246		122
	1,714	1,714		444	441	3	214	213	1	26	26		335	335		123
	4,371	4,333	38	1,804	1,804		1,218	1,218		476	476		899	896	3	124
																125
	849	785	64	867	838	29	261	254	7	186	186		113	113		126
	3,164	3,163	1	1,234	1,234		1,017	1,017		741	741		718	718		127
	8,934	8,929	5	3,447	3,441	6	2,915	2,915		2,163	2,162	1	1,416	1,415	1	128
	853	843	10	138	134	4	1,485	1,475	10	200	197	3	41	41		129
	39	26	13										1	1		130
	3,943	3,942	1	1,875	1,874	1	546	545	1	339	339		616	615	1	131
	331	303	28	29	29		34	34		21	20	1	36	29	7	132
	43,600	43,583	17	22,719	22,716	3	16,201	16,199	2	10,990	10,985	5	11,795	11,794	1	133
	604	308	296	451	111	340	376	140	236	173	49	124	86	45	41	134
	2,876	2,858	18	2,043	2,025	18	1,268	1,257	11	616	616		773	772	1	135
	135	135		154	154		68	68		18	18		40	40		136
	131	69	62	23	15	8	4	4		5	3	2	18	12	6	137
	4,440	3,001	1,439	294	293	1	242	240	2	175	175		289	276	13	138
	2,346	1,890	456	743	597	146	880	607	273	708	533	175	414	385	29	139
	1,683	1,157	526	423	374	49	334	275	59	301	281	20	390	309	81	140
	3,923	3,915	8	2,806	2,803	3	1,024	1,024		423	422	1	1,753	1,753		141
	167	167		54	54		28	28		13	13		53	53		142
	530	54	476	8		8	1		1	1		1	2		2	143
	263	121	142	903	295	608	40	25	15	1	1		595	239	356	144
	211	211		41	41		9	9		3	3		712	709	3	145
	221	221		38	38		150	146	4	10	10		5	5		146
	19,617	45	19,572	8,126	9	8,117	8,140	5	8,135	4,388	5	4,383	4,228	10	4,218	147
	265	250	15	27	25	2	7	7		2	2		21	21		148
	191	189	2	9	9		14	14		16	16		16	16		149
	649	631	18	60	56	4	81	80	1	21	20	1	112	111	1	150
	25	25		3	3		6	6					7	7		151
	23	23		37	37		2	2								152

316   STATISTICS OF POPULATION.

TABLE **79.**—TOTAL PERSONS 10 YEARS OF AGE AND OVER ENGAGED IN EACH SPECIFIED

	OCCUPATIONS.	FLORIDA.			GEORGIA.			IDAHO.		
		Total.	Males.	Females.	Total.	Males.	Females.	Total.	Males.	Females.
	Manufacturing and mechanical industries—Cont'd.									
153	Gas works employés (a)	7	7		58	58				
154	Glass workers	8	8		105	105		2	2	
155	Glove makers				1		1	1		1
156	Gold and silver workers	21	21		69	69		2	2	
157	Gunsmiths, locksmiths, and bell hangers	17	17		71	71		9	9	
158	Hair workers	8		8	1		1			
159	Harness and saddle makers and repairers	41	41		825	825		61	61	
160	Hat and cap makers	7	8	4	6	4	2	1	1	
161	Hosiery and knitting mill operatives (a)	6	1	5	991	97	104			
162	Iron and steel workers (a)	44	44		537	537		38	38	
163	Lace and embroidery makers	3		8	14		14			
164	Lead and zinc workers	1	1		4	4				
165	Leather curriers, dressers, finishers, and tanners	3	3		182	181	1	7	7	
166	Machinists	456	456		1,706	1,706		244	244	
167	Manufacturers and officials of manufacturing companies.	333	333		1,353	1,350	3	39	39	
168	Marble and stone cutters	22	22		799	797	2	44	44	
169	Masons (brick and stone)	381	379	2	1,912	1,912		112	112	
170	Meat and fruit packers, canners, and preservers (a)				8	8		1	1	
171	Mechanics (not otherwise specified)	150	150		771	771		9	9	
172	Metal workers (not otherwise specified)	7	7		22	20	2	1	1	
173	Mill and factory operatives (not specified) (a)	226	217	9	1,303	901	402	19	19	
174	Millers (flour and grist)	199	196	3	1,205	1,197	8	85	85	
175	Milliners	169		169	763	3	760	79		79
176	Model and pattern makers	10	10		46	46		2	2	
177	Molders	34	34		375	375		13	13	
178	Musical instrument makers (not otherwise specified). (a)	2	2							
179	Nail and tack makers (a)	2	2							
180	Oil well employés				1	1				
181	Oil works employés	1	1		98	98				
182	Painters, glaziers, and varnishers	648	648		2,004	2,003	1	152	152	
183	Paper hangers	11	11		57	57		8	8	
184	Paper mill operatives				96	66	30			
185	Photographers	103	99	4	183	172	11	24	24	
186	Piano and organ makers and tuners (a)	11	11		52	52				
187	Plasterers	121	121		526	526		27	27	
188	Plumbers and gas and steam fitters	59	59		389	389		21	21	
189	Potters	8	8		94	94				
190	Powder and cartridge makers									
191	Printers, lithographers, and pressmen (a)	290	275	15	875	842	33	75	72	3
192	Print works operatives (a)	2	2		11	11				
193	Publishers of books, maps, and newspapers	13	13		50	50		9	9	
194	Roofers and slaters	1	1		22	22		2	2	
195	Rope and cordage makers				15	13	2			
196	Rubber factory operatives	1	1		5	5				
197	Sail, awning, and tent makers	26	26		5	5				
198	Salt works employés									
199	Saw and planing mill employés (a)	1,744	1,696	48	4,510	4,502	8	237	237	
200	Seamstresses (a)	924		924	3,675	6	3,669	135		135
201	Sewing machine makers (not otherwise classified). (a)				4	4				
202	Sewing machine operators (a)				1		1			
203	Ship and boat builders	124	124		53	53		5	5	
204	Shirt, collar, and cuff makers (a)				23	11	12			
205	Silk mill operatives (a)	1		1						
206	Starch makers	31	9	22						
207	Steam boiler makers	30	30		128	128		34	34	
208	Stove, furnace, and grate makers (a)	1	1		35	35		1	1	
209	Straw workers	1	1							
210	Sugar makers and refiners	38	38							
211	Tailors and tailoresses (a)	163	133	30	647	437	210	51	48	3
212	Tinners and tinware makers	150	150		394	394		47	47	
213	Tobacco and cigar factory operatives	4,756	4,125	631	107	94	13	10	10	
214	Tool and cutlery makers (not otherwise classified). (a)	19	19		39	39		2	2	
215	Trunk, valise, leather-case, and pocket-book makers.	5	5		74	74		2	2	
216	Umbrella and parasol makers				3	3				
217	Upholsterers	33	33		198	170	19	6	6	
218	Well borers	23	23		23	23		2	2	
219	Wheelwrights	69	69		289	289		12	12	
220	Whitewashers	11	11		162	162				
221	Wire workers	2	2		36	34	2			
222	Wood workers (not otherwise specified)	54	51	3	603	541	68	8	8	
223	Woolen mill operatives (a)	6	6		191	100	91			
224	Other persons in manufacturing and mechanical industries.	105	87	18	1,166	1,068	98	27	27	

a See explanatory notes in Table 73.

OCCUPATIONS.

317

OCCUPATION, CLASSIFIED BY SEX, BY STATES AND TERRITORIES: 1890—Continued.

	ILLINOIS.			INDIANA.			IOWA.			KANSAS.			KENTUCKY.		
Total.	Males.	Females.	Total.	Males.	Females.	Total.	Males.	Females.	Total.	Males.	Females.	Total.	Males.	Females.	
337	336	1	135	135	....	36	36	....	27	27	....	50	50	....	153
2,073	2,019	54	2,002	1,925	77	13	13	....	12	12	....	163	162	1	154
250	102	148	8	8	....	37	16	21	3	2	1	....	....	....	155
560	499	61	172	171	1	67	66	1	35	35	....	149	147	2	156
685	685	....	205	205	....	127	127	....	101	101	....	158	158	....	157
74	28	46	17	13	4	4	2	2	2	....	2	2	....	2	158
8,260	8,241	19	1,772	1,756	16	2,134	2,129	5	1,246	1,246	....	1,158	1,144	14	159
263	195	68	43	29	14	30	17	13	18	14	4	47	35	12	160
942	195	747	852	44	808	26	5	21	14	8	6	17	3	14	161
9,064	8,928	136	3,209	3,174	35	375	368	7	321	321	....	2,083	2,066	17	162
264	52	212	36	....	36	24	....	24	21	....	21	21	....	21	163
1,036	956	80	11	11	....	8	8	....	858	858	....	15	13	2	164
1,621	1,618	3	848	848	....	64	64	....	33	33	....	519	519	....	165
12,798	12,784	14	4,862	4,861	1	2,296	2,294	2	1,553	1,552	1	2,307	2,301	6	166
6,655	6,626	29	3,485	3,472	13	1,331	1,326	5	675	671	4	1,340	1,336	4	167
3,044	3,042	2	1,565	1,565	....	695	695	....	735	735	....	944	943	1	168
10,102	10,095	7	4,252	4,251	1	4,104	4,103	1	3,299	3,290	....	2,686	2,682	4	169
1,009	846	163	155	113	42	194	174	20	97	83	14	37	26	11	170
559	559	....	506	505	1	268	268	....	117	117	....	447	447	....	171
971	923	48	150	140	10	40	38	2	153	153	....	71	71	....	172
1,449	848	601	1,407	718	689	473	233	230	232	93	139	993	553	440	173
2,503	2,488	15	2,372	2,368	4	1,398	1,393	5	1,306	1,305	1	1,638	1,635	3	174
4,364	16	4,348	2,578	7	2,571	2,309	3	2,306	1,390	....	1,390	1,272	24	1,248	175
813	809	4	258	257	1	69	69	....	64	64	....	126	126	....	176
5,972	5,964	8	2,168	2,168	....	591	590	1	455	454	1	1,061	1,059	2	177
82	82	....	25	25	....	2	2	....	....	....	....	1	1	....	178
322	247	75	201	198	3	1	1	....	1	1	....	74	73	1	179
1	1	....	41	41	....	....	....	....	....	....	....	5	5	....	180
90	88	2	37	37	....	36	36	....	12	12	....	19	19	....	181
18,454	18,365	89	7,895	7,867	28	4,882	4,863	19	2,931	2,918	13	3,451	3,443	8	182
943	941	2	557	555	2	176	174	2	119	119	....	352	350	2	183
694	560	134	433	357	76	95	79	16	13	13	....	100	66	34	184
1,431	1,235	196	782	700	82	801	684	117	510	442	68	350	328	22	185
980	964	16	246	245	1	84	84	....	42	42	....	77	77	....	186
3,426	3,425	1	2,370	2,370	....	1,319	1,318	1	1,256	1,256	....	861	861	....	187
4,427	4,425	2	1,099	1,098	1	569	569	....	371	371	....	507	507	....	188
1,001	963	38	671	629	42	287	286	1	50	50	....	136	119	17	189
27	18	9	....	....	....	....	....	....	12	12	....	....	....	....	190
7,039	6,674	365	2,020	1,861	168	1,964	1,857	107	1,430	1,320	110	1,269	1,211	58	191
52	51	1	28	28	....	6	6	....	....	....	....	....	....	....	192
815	806	9	135	134	1	211	207	4	196	195	1	51	51	....	193
469	469	....	111	111	....	96	96	....	23	23	....	55	55	....	194
278	170	108	28	27	1	20	16	4	4	4	....	234	194	40	195
131	128	3	5	5	....	3	3	....	....	....	....	....	....	....	196
160	121	39	18	17	1	10	10	....	3	2	1	14	11	3	197
39	39	....	....	....	....	1	1	....	158	146	12	....	....	....	198
4,833	4,830	3	4,083	4,081	2	3,179	3,162	17	177	177	....	2,591	2,589	2	199
9,338	206	9,132	5,097	9	5,088	2,777	2	2,775	1,497	2	1,495	5,765	15	5,750	200
96	95	1	84	84	....	13	5	8	2	2	....	6	6	....	201
241	41	200	56	22	34	63	8	55	5	....	5	30	1	29	202
514	514	....	288	288	....	91	91	....	17	17	....	176	176	....	203
594	205	389	232	49	183	63	48	15	73	34	39	145	102	43	204
146	54	92				4	1	3	4	1	3	11	6	5	205
29	25	4	105	149	16	119	82	37	....	....	....	....	....	....	206
1,551	1,551	....	896	896	....	478	478	....	359	359	....	185	185	....	207
653	650	3	337	337	....	66	66	....	68	68	....	309	308	1	208
29	17	12	32	27	5	4	....	4	13	13	....	1	....	1	209
328	327	1	1	1	....	1	1	....	....	....	....	....	....	....	210
17,281	11,325	5,956	3,361	2,212	1,149	2,231	1,778	453	1,088	817	271	3,304	1,925	1,379	211
4,189	4,084	105	1,543	1,532	11	1,250	1,241	9	897	894	3	1,037	1,030	7	212
5,241	4,575	666	1,740	1,524	216	1,308	1,117	191	493	469	24	3,557	3,041	516	213
458	445	13	320	315	5	171	159	12	13	13	....	216	214	2	214
277	263	14	49	49	....	28	28	....	8	8	....	201	184	17	215
27	22	5	7	7	....	1	1	....	....	....	....	3	1	2	216
2,601	2,502	99	729	689	40	393	372	21	156	152	4	344	335	9	217
264	264	....	237	237	....	515	515	....	159	159	....	33	33	....	218
283	283	....	350	350	....	137	137	....	70	70	....	166	166	....	219
368	368	....	132	132	....	39	39	....	17	17	....	179	179	....	220
972	908	64	178	178	....	85	83	2	27	27	....	136	133	3	221
6,393	6,207	186	3,790	3,624	166	693	671	22	191	191	....	1,066	1,051	15	222
822	514	308	1,347	610	737	279	186	93	13	12	1	1,158	452	706	223
5,470	4,548	922	1,598	1,486	112	1,275	1,073	202	595	558	37	1,174	1,059	115	224

STATISTICS OF POPULATION.

318

TABLE 79.—TOTAL PERSONS 10 YEARS OF AGE AND OVER ENGAGED IN EACH SPECIFIED

	OCCUPATIONS.	LOUISIANA.			MAINE.			MARYLAND.		
		Total.	Males.	Fe-males.	Total.	Males.	Fe-males.	Total.	Males.	Fe-males.
1	All occupations..............	423,074	314,293	108,781	257,096	212,033	45,063	393,267	308,515	84,752
2	Agriculture, fisheries, and mining............	240,730	185,266	55,464	86,290	84,831	1,405	105,396	102,669	2,727
3	Agricultural laborers (a)............	146,096	97,041	49,055	17,058	16,965	93	45,611	44,570	1,041
4	Apiarists................	14	14	....	7	7	....	9	9	....
5	Dairymen and dairywomen........	496	419	77	52	45	7	492	410	82
6	Farmers, planters, and overseers (a)......	88,098	81,930	6,168	60,887	59,535	1,352	42,584	41,076	1,508
7	Fishermen and oystermen (a)........	1,564	1,557	7	3,666	3,664	2	9,196	9,179	17
8	Gardeners, florists, nurserymen, and vine growers	1,414	1,315	99	448	439	9	1,801	1,733	68
9	Lumbermen and raftsmen............	1,401	1,399	2	2,314	2,313	1	941	941	....
10	Miners (coal)....................	....	....	....	28	28	....	3,323	3,323	....
11	Miners (not otherwise specified)......	70	70	....	28	28	....	772	770	2
12	Quarrymen..............	5	5	....	1,318	1,318	....	804	804	....
13	Stock raisers, herders, and drovers......	213	199	14	40	40	....	153	153	....
14	Wood choppers.............	1,139	1,134	5	463	463	....	332	331	1
15	Other agricultural pursuits (a)......	220	183	37	15	14	1	78	70	8
16	Professional service..........	10,026	7,196	2,830	12,364	6,007	6,357	14,576	10,144	4,432
17	Actors..................	93	42	51	53	33	20	135	89	46
18	Architects................	66	66	....	27	27	....	76	76	....
19	Artists and teachers of art........	114	69	45	249	72	177	292	142	150
20	Authors and literary and scientific persons......	28	19	9	99	34	65	114	77	37
21	Chemists, assayers, and metallurgists......	38	37	1	16	16	....	81	81	....
22	Clergymen............	1,170	1,163	7	968	956	12	1,489	1,475	14
23	Dentists..............	183	182	1	278	275	3	295	292	3
24	Designers, draftsmen, and inventors......	29	29	....	56	56	....	130	127	3
25	Engineers (civil, mechanical, electrical, and mining) and surveyors.	512	512	....	356	356	....	721	718	3
26	Journalists............	200	196	4	187	172	15	269	262	7
27	Lawyers............	1,071	1,070	1	751	750	1	1,484	1,484	....
28	Musicians and teachers of music......	615	350	265	676	202	474	1,114	616	498
29	Officers of United States army and navy......	28	28	....	24	24	....	48	48	....
30	Officials (government) (a)......	1,010	942	68	1,022	926	96	1,248	1,184	64
31	Physicians and surgeons........	1,275	1,250	25	1,121	1,046	75	1,762	1,700	62
32	Professors in colleges and universities......	114	92	22	63	53	10	145	136	9
33	Teachers............	3,332	1,018	2,314	6,254	848	5,406	4,832	1,305	3,527
34	Theatrical managers, showmen, etc........	112	99	13	124	123	1	239	238	1
35	Veterinary surgeons..........	26	26	....	28	28	....	84	84	....
36	Other professional service........	10	6	4	12	10	2	18	10	8
37	Domestic and personal service..........	90,068	51,217	38,851	41,091	26,908	14,183	102,301	54,455	47,846
38	Barbers and hairdressers............	1,048	992	56	871	859	12	1,613	1,547	66
39	Bartenders..............	960	957	3	72	72	....	809	798	11
40	Boarding and lodging house keepers......	601	91	510	519	205	314	800	119	690
41	Engineers and firemen (not locomotive)......	1,603	1,602	1	1,382	1,382	....	2,236	2,234	2
42	Hotel keepers............	216	142	74	539	484	55	426	385	41
43	Housekeepers and stewards (a)......	1,466	135	1,331	2,099	103	1,996	2,307	299	2,008
44	Hunters, trappers, guides, and scouts......	132	132	....	82	82	....	24	24	....
45	Janitors..............	97	74	23	139	137	2	379	284	95
46	Laborers (not specified) (a)......	46,235	40,397	5,838	20,821	20,693	128	38,028	36,740	1,288
47	Launderers and laundresses......	9,929	248	9,681	787	216	571	9,538	349	9,189
48	Nurses and midwives............	551	41	510	691	89	602	1,169	88	1,081
49	Restaurant keepers............	188	149	39	131	114	17	453	400	53
50	Saloon keepers............	729	694	35	232	223	9	1,622	1,504	118
51	Servants..............	24,905	4,175	20,730	11,755	1,303	10,452	40,134	7,117	33,017
52	Sextons..............	56	53	3	42	42	....	180	178	2
53	Soldiers, sailors, and marines (United States) (a).	100	100	....	189	189	....	491	491	....
54	Watchmen, policemen, and detectives......	1,149	1,147	2	642	642	....	1,783	1,779	4
55	Other domestic and personal service......	103	88	15	98	73	25	300	209	91
56	Trade and transportation..........	40,586	38,483	2,103	37,291	34,850	2,441	68,979	63,233	5,746
57	Agents (claim, commission, real estate, insurance, etc.) and collectors.	1,694	1,656	38	1,245	1,196	49	2,675	2,627	48
58	Auctioneers..............	38	38	....	8	8	....	64	64	....
59	Bankers and brokers (money and stocks)........	223	213	10	141	141	....	269	263	6
60	Boatmen and canalmen............	260	208	1	175	174	1	397	397	....
61	Bookkeepers and accountants (a)......	1,609	1,543	66	1,501	1,034	467	2,424	2,203	221
62	Brokers (commercial)............	219	219	....	39	39	....	140	140	....
63	Clerks and copyists (a)......	10,260	9,884	376	5,319	4,365	954	13,205	12,194	1,011
64	Commercial travelers............	460	457	3	643	633	10	946	938	8
65	Draymen, hackmen, teamsters, etc......	3,746	3,737	9	4,332	4,330	2	7,306	7,299	7
66	Foremen and overseers............	246	241	5	240	232	8	416	394	22
67	Hostlers..............	1,052	1,051	1	836	836	....	1,341	1,339	2
68	Hucksters and peddlers............	911	783	128	639	631	8	1,869	1,750	119
69	Livery stable keepers............	119	118	1	394	394	....	278	276	2
70	Locomotive engineers and firemen (a)......	441	441	....	538	538	....	1,184	1,184	....
71	Merchants and dealers in drugs and chemicals (retail).	524	514	10	439	430	9	786	767	19
72	Merchants and dealers in dry goods (retail)......	448	395	53	488	452	36	671	586	85
73	Merchants and dealers in groceries (retail)........	1,846	1,550	296	1,810	1,778	32	2,445	1,890	555
74	Merchants and dealers in wines and liquors (retail)......	59	58	1	26	26	....	179	173	6
75	Merchants and dealers in wines and liquors (wholesale).	18	18	....	12	12	....	93	91	2

a See explanatory notes in Table 78.

OCCUPATIONS.

OCCUPATION, CLASSIFIED BY SEX, BY STATES AND TERRITORIES: 1890—Continued.

	MASSACHUSETTS.			MICHIGAN.			MINNESOTA.			MISSISSIPPI.			MISSOURI.		
	Total.	Males.	Females.	Total.	Males.	Females.	Total.	Males.	Females.	Total.	Males.	Females.	Total.	Males.	Females.	
	982,444	719,166	263,278	759,575	663,627	95,948	469,086	403,461	65,625	462,739	337,931	124,808	884,379	771,554	112,825	1
	81,100	80,163	937	308,501	302,398	6,103	195,422	191,596	3,826	360,049	270,684	89,365	404,665	392,245	12,420	2
	27,488	27,359	129	72,369	71,818	551	52,158	51,701	457	180,520	107,368	73,152	92,441	91,666	775	3
	13	13	......	104	102	2	43	43	......	4	4	......	94	89	5	4
	171	147	24	307	289	18	517	463	54	112	78	34	1,043	976	67	5
	37,139	36,421	718	198,258	192,803	5,455	133,868	130,607	3,261	176,885	160,811	16,074	290,616	279,199	11,417	6
	9,254	9,247	7	1,021	1,619	2	874	873	1	384	384	......	348	348	......	7
	4,080	4,024	56	2,589	2,525	64	1,075	1,033	42	560	519	41	2,706	2,575	131	8
	204	204	......	11,467	11,465	2	3,677	3,673	4	642	642	......	1,190	1,189	1	9
	42	42	......	788	788	......							5,602	5,591	11	10
	282	282	......	18,167	18,165	2	1,859	1,858	1	7	7	......	7,367	7,357	10	11
	1,802	1,802	......	300	300	......	898	898	......	93	87	6	1,147	1,146	1	12
	136	136	......	299	294	5	549	543	6				788	788	......	13
	408	408	......	2,118	2,118	......	377	377	......	444	443	1	1,284	1,283	1	14
	81	78	3	114	112	2	27	27	......	398	341	57	30	38	1	15
	43,247	26,248	16,999	33,490	20,445	13,045	22,767	14,060	8,707	10,862	7,587	3,275	39,465	27,963	11,502	16
	509	312	197	271	185	86	192	111	81	10	8	2	341	207	134	17
	620	617	3	179	179	......	242	241	1	17	17	......	434	433	1	18
	1,667	803	864	676	308	368	500	261	239	84	39	45	749	402	347	19
	891	352	539	211	113	98	133	83	50	27	11	16	204	139	65	20
	296	289	7	119	117	2	37	37	......	11	11	......	127	127	......	21
	2,883	2,798	85	3,025	2,981	44	1,935	1,905	30	1,810	1,803	7	3,874	3,841	33	22
	983	972	11	563	547	16	357	342	15	189	189	......	602	586	16	23
	1,040	1,000	40	227	224	3	173	170	3	7	7	......	256	253	3	24
	3,028	3,012	16	1,481	1,477	4	1,242	1,241	1	161	161	......	1,475	1,472	3	25
	1,299	1,201	98	636	605	31	566	550	16	142	135	7	893	867	26	26
	2,589	2,587	2	2,648	2,638	10	2,142	2,135	7	898	898	......	3,954	3,951	3	27
	4,387	1,986	2,401	2,123	779	1,344	1,267	603	664	309	78	231	2,389	1,019	1,370	28
	92	92	......	41	41	......	44	44	......	8	8	......	27	27	......	29
	4,122	3,859	263	2,966	2,795	171	2,130	2,048	82	823	739	84	3,526	3,376	150	30
	3,848	3,378	470	3,529	3,335	194	1,513	1,401	112	1,671	1,658	13	5,373	5,253	120	31
	340	244	96	203	188	15	152	132	20	67	63	4	233	213	20	32
	13,566	1,770	11,787	13,418	2,786	10,632	9,456	2,085	7,371	4,636	1,772	2,864	14,002	4,821	9,181	33
	749	715	34	742	724	18	375	370	5	32	31	1	769	754	15	34
	202	202	......	899	899	......	225	225	......	12	12	......	195	195	......	35
	136	50	86	33	24	9	86	76	10	3	2	1	42	27	15	36
	185,938	99,755	86,183	152,210	106,915	45,295	94,693	57,976	36,717	49,774	21,507	28,267	147,296	91,005	56,291	37
	4,531	4,366	165	2,910	2,797	113	1,576	1,544	32	447	442	5	3,775	3,644	131	38
	1,979	1,979	......	1,887	1,887	......	1,387	1,387	......	268	267	1	2,358	2,356	2	39
	3,499	683	2,816	1,411	476	935	1,006	367	639	472	110	362	2,095	605	1,490	40
	6,934	6,933	1	7,007	7,097	......	3,235	3,235	......	641	641	......	5,407	5,407	......	41
	1,221	1,055	166	1,938	1,775	163	1,293	1,191	102	304	194	110	1,097	783	314	42
	7,081	434	6,647	2,489	137	2,352	1,525	77	1,448	861	34	827	2,646	177	2,469	43
	16	16	......	126	126	......	96	96	......	20	20	......	67	67	......	44
	2,007	1,883	124	618	577	41	629	606	23	41	36	5	820	755	65	45
	63,845	63,062	783	81,445	80,727	718	40,736	40,548	188	19,099	15,561	3,538	60,594	59,872	722	46
	7,175	1,640	5,535	2,530	465	2,065	2,185	341	1,844	6,907	125	6,782	9,352	719	8,633	47
	4,200	455	3,745	1,378	269	1,109	1,112	103	1,009	282	29	253	1,303	187	1,116	48
	1,029	876	153	384	338	46	350	305	45	87	63	24	755	673	82	49
	800	760	40	2,980	2,930	50	1,840	1,827	13	281	277	4	2,687	2,650	37	50
	74,997	9,367	65,630	41,097	4,305	37,632	35,790	4,476	31,314	19,539	3,214	16,325	50,548	9,416	41,132	51
	246	245	1	161	161	......	73	73	......	42	41	1	124	123	1	52
	398	398	......	394	394	......	333	333	......	17	17	......	452	452	......	53
	5,048	5,040	8	2,144	2,142	2	1,338	1,338	......	344	343	1	2,735	2,731	4	54
	932	563	369	321	252	69	189	129	60	93	122	29	481	388	93	55
	196,513	174,239	22,274	103,276	95,991	7,285	72,456	68,185	4,271	22,417	21,817	600	140,046	132,083	7,963	56
	8,359	8,037	322	5,804	5,575	229	6,250	6,144	106	920	903	17	7,942	7,746	196	57
	187	187	......	78	78	......	72	72	......	5	5	......	139	139	......	58
	1,106	1,104	2	780	752	28	797	785	12	96	94	2	1,284	1,250	34	59
	190	190	......	234	234	......	124	124	......	75	75	......	283	283	......	60
	14,703	9,177	5,526	5,402	4,272	1,130	4,072	3,421	651	902	873	29	5,831	5,134	697	61
	444	444	......	53	53	......	85	85	......	30	30	......	182	181	1	62
	32,617	27,417	5,200	15,815	13,020	2,795	12,023	10,431	1,592	3,159	3,001	158	23,154	21,180	1,974	63
	3,697	3,658	39	2,951	2,921	30	1,779	1,764	15	351	346	5	3,521	3,497	24	64
	25,706	25,693	13	11,861	11,857	4	7,985	7,980	5	1,828	1,828	......	16,624	16,616	8	65
	1,317	1,236	81	1,272	1,256	16	1,158	1,147	11	248	248	......	1,384	1,370	14	66
	4,740	4,740	......	1,385	1,385	......	976	976	......	875	874	1	2,174	2,174	......	67
	4,249	4,157	92	1,838	1,804	34	768	748	20	207	186	21	1,763	1,685	78	68
	1,213	1,211	2	1,007	1,005	2	609	607	2	184	184	......	1,361	1,361	......	69
	2,170	2,170	......	2,743	2,743	......	2,244	2,244	......	565	565	......	3,238	3,238	......	70
	1,992	1,957	35	1,893	1,861	32	1,059	1,044	15	383	378	5	2,588	2,561	27	71
	1,442	1,241	201	1,366	1,307	59	684	670	14	621	607	14	2,208	2,123	85	72
	6,439	6,144	295	3,909	3,786	123	1,708	1,678	30	628	570	58	4,713	4,560	153	73
	575	571	4	90	90	......	70	70	......	28	28	......	161	160	1	74
	156	153	3	74	74	......	60	60	......	6	6	......	130	129	1	75

820

STATISTICS OF POPULATION.

TABLE 79.—TOTAL PERSONS 10 YEARS OF AGE AND OVER ENGAGED IN EACH SPECIFIED

	OCCUPATIONS.	LOUISIANA.			MAINE.			MARYLAND.		
		Total.	Males.	Females.	Total.	Males.	Females.	Total.	Males.	Females.
	Trade and transportation—Continued.									
76	Merchants and dealers, not specified (retail)......	5,851	5,354	497	4,994	4,893	101	9,293	8,457	836
77	Merchants and dealers (wholesale), importers, and shipping merchants.	872	868	4	373	370	8	905	900	5
78	Messengers and errand and office boys..........	494	490	4	182	180	2	1,684	1,652	32
79	Newspaper carriers and newsboys	87	86	1	19	19		172	170	2
80	Officials of banks and of insurance, trade, transportation, trust, and other companies. (a)	321	319	2	352	349	3	686	686	
81	Packers and shippers	198	170	28	244	165	79	1,169	638	531
82	Pilots	218	218		61	61		110	110	
83	Porters and helpers (in stores and warehouses)...	478	473	5	29	27	2	1,245	1,225	20
84	Sailors (a)	1,458	1,457	1	6,466	6,466		3,481	3,481	
85	Salesmen and saleswomen	2,406	1,998	408	2,262	1,812	450	5,409	3,482	1,927
86	Steam railroad employés (not otherwise specified). (a)	3,110	3,094	16	2,568	2,559	9	5,405	5,364	41
87	Stenographers and typewriters	199	103	96	172	51	121	348	202	146
88	Street railway employés	366	366		144	144		923	923	
89	Telegraph and telephone operators	335	309	26	348	257	91	809	739	70
90	Telegraph and telephone linemen and electric light and power company employés	79	79		104	104		186	186	
91	Undertakers	65	60	5	110	109	1	265	263	2
92	Weighers, gaugers, and measurers	145	141	4	30	30		123	123	
93	Other persons in trade and transportation	222	214	8	8	5	3	78	57	21
94	**Manufacturing and mechanical industries**	41,664	32,131	9,533	80,054	59,437	20,617	102,015	78,014	24,001
95	Agricultural implement makers (not otherwise classified). (a)	5	5		72	72		16	16	
96	Apprentices (blacksmiths)	95	95		56	56		150	150	
97	Apprentices (boot and shoe makers)	23	23		4	3	1	30	30	
98	Apprentices (carpenters and joiners)	110	110		60	60		151	151	
99	Apprentices (carriage and wagon makers)	5	5		10	10		24	24	
100	Apprentices (dressmakers)	28		28	25		25	157		157
101	Apprentices (leather curriers, etc.)	3	3					17	17	
102	Apprentices (machinists)	51	51		46	46		226	226	
103	Apprentices (masons)	27	27		19	19		35	35	
104	Apprentices (milliners)	11		11	14		14	35		35
105	Apprentices (painters)	16	16		19	19		61	61	
106	Apprentices (plumbers)	12	12		14	14		78	78	
107	Apprentices (printers)	27	27		46	42	4	166	162	4
108	Apprentices (tailors)	9	7	2	9	7	2	261	232	29
109	Apprentices (tinsmiths)	16	16		16	16		108	108	
110	Apprentices (not otherwise specified)	540	521	19	177	173	4	1,495	1,437	58
111	Artificial flower makers	11	1	10				9	3	6
112	Bakers	1,150	1,082	68	317	302	15	1,792	1,724	68
113	Basket makers	41	31	10	121	63	58	228	206	22
114	Blacksmiths	2,019	2,017	2	2,656	2,656		3,987	3,986	1
115	Bleachers, dyers, and scourers	35	27	8	638	602	36	162	143	19
116	Bone and ivory workers				1	1		6	6	
117	Bookbinders	103	94	9	107	63	44	265	170	95
118	Boot and shoe makers and repairers	1,747	1,720	27	7,541	5,417	2,124	4,255	3,944	311
119	Bottlers and mineral and soda water makers	45	45		31	30	1	173	165	8
120	Box makers (paper)	26		26	349	105	244	343	41	302
121	Box makers (wood)	97	97		214	198	16	509	478	31
122	Brass workers (not otherwise specified) (a)	18	18		42	42		444	432	12
123	Brewers and maltsters (a)	103	102	1	9	9		443	441	2
124	Brick and tile makers and terra cotta workers (a)	337	329	8	633	632	1	1,899	1,894	5
125	Britannia workers				1	1				
126	Broom and brush makers	114	110	4	74	65	9	369	355	14
127	Builders and contractors	316	316		206	206		621	621	
128	Butchers	1,343	1,334	9	632	632		2,528	2,519	9
129	Butter and cheese makers	11	11		50	48	2	76	75	1
130	Button makers				4	4		18	10	8
131	Cabinet makers	313	313		240	240		903	901	2
132	Candle, soap, and tallow makers	40	39	1	26	26		40	40	
133	Carpenters and joiners	5,965	5,961	4	8,263	8,263		9,620	9,619	1
134	Carpet makers (a)				50	31	19	154	127	27
135	Carriage and wagon makers (not otherwise classified). (a)	89	89		403	403		409	409	
136	Charcoal, coke, and lime burners	56	54	2	206	206		193	190	3
137	Chemical works employés	11	10	1	13	12	1	70	51	19
138	Clock and watch makers and repairers	115	114	1	161	126	35	285	266	19
139	Compositors (a)	162	151	11	384	126	258	294	279	15
140	Confectioners	186	155	31	226	207	19	771	562	209
141	Coopers	1,762	1,761	1	811	811		1,034	1,034	
142	Copper workers	73	73		6	6		129	129	
143	Corset makers	7	1	6	9		9	16		16
144	Cotton mill operatives (a)	684	377	307	12,030	5,317	6,713	3,466	1,320	2,146
145	Distillers and rectifiers (a)	17	17					78	77	1
146	Door, sash, and blind makers (a)	28	28		111	111		53	53	
147	Dressmakers	1,582	5	1,577	3,819		3,819	6,120	10	6,110
148	Electroplaters				5	5		42	42	
149	Electrotypers and stereotypers (a)	2	2		2	2		22	22	
150	Engravers	85	85		13	13		98	97	1
151	Fertilizer makers (a)	1		1	2	2		98	97	1
152	Fish curers and packers (a)				494	327	167	60	60	

a See explanatory notes in Table 78.

OCCUPATIONS.

OCCUPATION, CLASSIFIED BY SEX, BY STATES AND TERRITORIES: 1890—Continued.

MASSACHUSETTS			MICHIGAN			MINNESOTA			MISSISSIPPI			MISSOURI			
Total.	Males.	Females.	Total.	Males.	Females.	Total.	Males.	Females.	Total.	Males.	Females.	Total.	Males.	Females.	
23,787	22,877	910	13,122	12,774	348	9,172	9,031	141	4,231	4,108	123	17,284	16,908	376	76
2,369	2,355	14	628	626	2	721	718	3	82	78	4	1,461	1,457	4	77
4,178	3,786	392	773	722	51	521	508	13	181	177	4	1,887	1,776	111	78
257	253	4	104	101	3	105	104	1	8	8	......	455	453	2	79
2,093	2,076	17	1,159	1,154	5	944	941	3	144	144	......	1,675	1,664	11	80
2,722	1,973	749	805	692	113	550	498	52	17	16	1	978	792	186	81
146	146	......	36	36	......	56	56	......	54	54	......	155	155	......	82
957	917	40	254	239	15	200	199	1	407	407	......	1,824	1,811	13	83
4,059	4,057	2	3,729	3,726	3	483	483	......	520	520	......	575	575	......	84
23,183	17,285	5,898	7,154	5,870	1,284	4,781	4,124	657	1,784	1,695	89	12,205	9,981	2,224	85
11,832	11,740	92	12,571	12,545	26	8,632	8,612	20	3,912	3,893	19	15,340	15,289	51	86
1,919	439	1,480	934	336	598	1,185	440	745	44	18	26	1,895	608	1,287	87
3,587	3,587	......	881	881	......	809	809	......	13	13	......	2,403	2,403	......	88
1,503	960	543	1,762	1,427	335	1,307	1,147	160	326	309	17	2,276	1,893	383	89
1,564	1,352	212	858	856	2	266	266	......	25	25	......	427	422	5	90
579	571	8	312	310	2	90	90	......	27	27	......	213	212	1	91
165	165	......	36	36	......	51	51	......	28	28	......	179	179	......	92
311	213	98	103	87	16	60	58	2	3	1	2	134	118	16	93
475,646	338,761	136,885	162,098	137,878	24,220	83,748	71,644	12,104	19,637	16,336	3,301	152,907	128,258	24,049	94
146	146	......	115	115	......	42	42	......	18	18	......	76	76	......	95
137	137	......	92	92	......	69	69	......	11	11	......	169	169	......	96
85	81	4	15	15	......	20	19	1	1	1	......	52	50	2	97
385	385	......	139	139	......	48	48	......	14	14	......	241	240	1	98
109	108	1	20	20	......	5	5	......	1	1	......	40	40	......	99
267	......	267	125	......	125	48	......	48				201	......	201	100
58	58	......	33	33	......	8	8	......				20	20	......	101
934	934	......	153	153	......	80	80	......	15	15	......	254	254	......	102
158	158	......	31	31	......	18	18	......	3	3	......	67	67	......	103
76	......	76	45	......	45	12	......	12				65	......	65	104
119	119	......	48	47	1	25	25	......	5	5	......	120	120	......	105
478	478	......	72	72	......	97	97	......	1	1	......	167	167	......	106
351	343	8	142	138	4	68	60	8	4	4	......	222	217	5	107
126	104	22	62	46	16	16	15	1	2	2	......	93	66	27	108
81	81	......	41	41	......	34	33	1	4	4	......	101	101	......	109
1,781	1,713	68	852	823	29	461	445	16	48	43	......	1,544	1,441	103	110
13	1	12	7	6	1	2	2	......				16	1	15	111
3,685	3,467	218	1,457	1,400	57	681	646	35	138	134	4	2,081	2,017	64	112
277	249	28	309	240	69	29	29	......	53	27	26	171	148	23	113
8,328	8,327	1	7,816	7,816	......	4,855	4,855	......	1,412	1,412	......	8,747	8,742	5	114
2,407	2,194	213	88	80	8	71	53	18	21	19	2	118	108	10	115
631	556	75	7	7	......	1	1	......				21	21	......	116
2,345	1,104	1,241	514	286	228	335	208	127	7	5	2	887	460	427	117
68,873	52,307	16,566	3,532	3,301	231	2,412	2,195	217	332	329	3	4,676	3,999	677	118
581	542	39	173	154	19	97	96	1	4	4	......	247	235	12	119
3,264	972	2,292	214	26	188	64	5	59				233	36	197	120
1,080	1,004	76	556	505	51	101	88	13	3	3	......	477	466	11	121
1,523	1,481	42	395	383	12	30	30	......	3	3	......	230	230	......	122
467	467	......	572	572	......	508	508	......				1,340	1,340	......	123
2,155	2,152	3	1,328	1,323	5	777	777	......	376	376	......	1,721	1,720	1	124
324	262	62													125
719	464	255	427	333	94	98	98	......	10	10	......	451	444	7	126
1,961	1,961	......	1,345	1,345	......	1,679	1,678	1	191	191	......	2,065	2,064	1	127
2,434	2,434	......	3,648	3,645	3	2,249	2,249	......	875	874	1	4,142	4,138	4	128
191	183	8	272	265	7	349	341	8	5	5	......	143	139	4	129
669	203	466	1	......	1	554	554	......	45	45	......	1,408	1,408	......	130
2,396	2,393	3	1,770	1,767	3	81	69	12				166	131	35	131
873	820	53	49	44	5										132
32,783	32,731	2	23,699	23,693	6	15,187	15,185	2	3,938	3,934	4	22,046	22,041	5	133
2,811	1,195	1,616	386	163	223	136	66	70				217	122	95	134
1,007	972	35	1,734	1,700	34	686	686	......	105	105	......	1,805	1,804	1	135
89	89	......	243	243	......	51	51	......	299	299	......	195	194	1	136
443	377	66	420	114	306	17	14	3				128	101	27	137
3,510	2,186	1,324	403	360	43	261	261	......	61	61	......	521	518	3	138
2,811	1,588	1,223	804	585	219	727	558	169	93	79	14	1,385	1,116	269	139
1,638	1,103	535	550	414	136	561	425	136	86	76	10	1,180	877	303	140
1,517	1,516	1	2,811	2,808	3	1,431	1,428	3	71	71	......	2,122	2,122	......	141
458	457	1	817	817	......	35	35	......	6	6	......	73	73	......	142
828	119	709	401	23	378	12	......	12				70	1	69	143
61,550	28,775	32,775	65	54	11	87	80	7	463	233	230	170	97	73	144
61	61	......	10	10	......	25	25	......	26	26	......	87	85	2	145
325	325	......	193	193	......	214	214	......	8	8	......	33	33	......	146
20,111	24	20,087	11,017	6	11,011	6,460	6	6,454	513	......	513	8,065	11	8,054	147
264	259	5	58	56	2	16	16	......				56	55	1	148
165	165	......	36	36	......	31	31	......				55	55	......	149
788	760	28	102	100	2	77	77	......				259	257	2	150
113	112	1	2	2	......	1	1	......				2	2	......	151
303	275	28	9	9	......	6	6	......				1	1	......	152

POP—PT 2——21

322 STATISTICS OF POPULATION.

TABLE 79.—TOTAL PERSONS 10 YEARS OF AGE AND OVER ENGAGED IN EACH SPECIFIED

	OCCUPATIONS.	LOUISIANA.			MAINE.			MARYLAND.		
		Total.	Males.	Females.	Total.	Males.	Females.	Total.	Males.	Females.
	Manufacturing and mechanical industries—Cont'd.									
153	Gas works employés (a)	39	39		29	29		88	88	
154	Glass workers	1	1		9	9		924	872	52
155	Glove makers				4	3	1	50	11	39
156	Gold and silver workers	41	41		45	44	1	235	207	28
157	Gunsmiths, locksmiths, and bell hangers	106	106		21	21		191	191	
158	Hair workers	6	1	5	6	1	5	249	190	59
159	Harness and saddle makers and repairers	289	287	2	535	525	10	782	763	19
160	Hat and cap makers	10	9	1	109	72	37	396	210	186
161	Hosiery and knitting mill operatives (a)	17	4	13	56	7	69	957	41	916
162	Iron and steel workers (a)	243	232	11	437	437		1,299	1,285	14
163	Lace and embroidery makers	11		11	6		6	65	10	55
164	Lead and zinc workers	2	2		1	1		71	68	3
165	Leather curriers, dressers, finishers, and tanners	54	54		687	686	1	522	506	16
166	Machinists	766	766		1,815	1,814	1	2,591	2,590	1
167	Manufacturers and officials of manufacturing companies	484	468	16	1,585	1,583	2	1,862	1,856	6
168	Marble and stone cutters	130	130		2,773	2,773		1,183	1,183	
169	Masons (brick and stone)	1,157	1,157		1,757	1,757		2,340	2,340	
170	Meat and fruit packers, canners, and preservers (a)	16	16		49	32	17	697	301	396
171	Mechanics (not otherwise specified)	300	300		119	119		100	100	
172	Metal workers (not otherwise specified)	22	21	1	32	31	1	177	168	9
173	Mill and factory operatives (not specified) (a)	545	422	123	1,918	1,282	636	638	336	302
174	Millers (flour and grist)	180	180		657	657		1,285	1,285	
175	Milliners	458		458	974	2	972	1,102	2	1,100
176	Model and pattern makers	39	39		85	85		193	188	5
177	Molders	184	184		426	426		1,177	1,176	1
178	Musical instrument makers (not otherwise specified) (a)				2	2		14	13	1
179	Nail and tack makers (a)	2	2					16	15	1
180	Oil well employés									
181	Oil works employés	261	255	6	2	2		22	22	
182	Painters, glaziers, and varnishers	1,539	1,535	4	2,646	2,632	14	3,963	3,915	48
183	Paper hangers	56	56		65	64	1	520	519	1
184	Paper mill operatives	7	4	3	1,308	1,109	199	407	305	102
185	Photographers	154	145	9	207	188	19	199	183	16
186	Piano and organ makers and tuners (a)	48	48		101	100	1	386	381	5
187	Plasterers	414	413	1	87	87		707	707	
188	Plumbers and gas and steam fitters	189	188	1	330	330		1,016	1,014	2
189	Potters	23	23		44	44		398	379	19
190	Powder and cartridge makers	1	1		10	10				
191	Printers, lithographers, and pressmen (a)	716	695	21	643	538	105	1,497	1,433	64
192	Print works operatives (a)				24	19	5	51	51	
193	Publishers of books, maps, and newspapers	26	26		50	49	1	67	67	
194	Roofers and slaters	198	197	1	45	45		82	82	
195	Rope and cordage makers	20	15	5	67	44	23	84	42	42
196	Rubber factory operatives				10	3	7	2		2
197	Sail, awning, and tent makers	50	50		225	221	4	189	184	5
198	Salt works employés				6	6		6	6	
199	Saw and planing mill employés (a)	2,106	2,104	2	4,106	4,104	2	872	870	2
200	Seamstresses (a)	5,780	21	5,759	1,482	8	1,474	5,918	75	5,843
201	Sewing machine makers (not otherwise classified) (a)	3	3		3	3		2	2	
202	Sewing machine operators (a)	4		4	68	19	49	116	2	114
203	Ship and boat builders	403	403		2,582	2,581	1	1,020	1,020	
204	Shirt, collar, and cuff makers (a)	46	27	19	90	34	56	1,179	188	991
205	Silk mill operatives (a)				79	34	45	32	13	19
206	Starch makers									
207	Steam boiler makers	240	240		151	151		544	544	
208	Stove, furnace, and grate makers (a)	25	25		33	33		184	184	
209	Straw workers				103	4	99	125	34	91
210	Sugar makers and refiners	242	242		2	2		21	21	
211	Tailors and tailoresses (a)	1,079	697	382	2,285	717	1,568	7,778	4,784	2,994
212	Tinners and tinware makers	483	481	2	978	974	4	3,012	2,877	135
213	Tobacco and cigar factory operatives	1,377	990	387	146	131	15	3,005	2,335	670
214	Tool and cutlery makers (not otherwise classified) (a)	48	48		174	174		77	77	
215	Trunk, valise, leather-case, and pocket-book makers	20	20		42	41	1	89	88	1
216	Umbrella and parasol makers	5	4	1				64	29	35
217	Upholsterers	230	219	11	176	168	8	681	626	55
218	Well borers	13	13		10	10		23	23	
219	Wheelwrights	200	200		173	173		688	688	
220	Whitewashers	60	60		6	6		461	458	3
221	Wire workers	14	14		42	42		63	63	
222	Wood workers (not otherwise specified)	168	165	3	896	800	96	926	886	40
223	Woolen mill operatives (a)	71	40	31	3,822	2,519	1,303	459	273	186
224	Other persons in manufacturing and mechanical industries	621	566	55	1,071	973	98	1,370	1,130	240

a See explanatory notes in Table 78.

OCCUPATIONS.

OCCUPATION, CLASSIFIED BY SEX, BY STATES AND TERRITORIES: 1890—Continued.

MASSACHUSETTS			MICHIGAN			MINNESOTA			MISSISSIPPI			MISSOURI			
Total.	Males.	Fe-males.	Total.	Males.	Fe-males.	Total.	Males.	Fe-males.	Total.	Males.	Fe-males.	Total.	Males.	Fe-males.	
482	482	....	101	101	....	54	54	....	15	15	....	181	181	....	153
886	810	70	132	131	1	89	89	....	....	....	....	652	648	4	154
91	39	52	21	8	13	27	15	12	....	....	....	24	15	9	155
4,483	3,547	936	135	129	6	75	75	....	35	35	....	267	258	9	156
336	331	5	181	181	....	77	77	....	38	38	....	346	344	2	157
149	68	81	14	4	10	13	3	10	....	....	....	18	4	14	158
2,248	2,010	238	1,682	1,629	53	1,126	1,116	10	92	92	....	2,285	2,282	3	159
1,704	1,081	623	86	46	40	34	20	14	....	....	....	131	102	29	160
2,826	774	2,052	401	76	325	105	9	96	5	....	5	57	10	47	161
5,911	5,725	186	2,495	2,480	15	625	625	....	66	66	....	2,094	2,025	69	162
236	37	199	54	....	54	23	....	23	8	....	8	51	2	49	163
214	180	34	26	25	1	17	16	1	....	....	....	578	562	16	164
8,976	8,923	53	622	618	4	212	212	....	18	18	....	601	600	1	165
18,904	18,896	8	5,169	5,159	10	2,376	2,374	2	563	562	1	4,716	4,706	10	166
9,581	9,555	26	4,020	4,004	16	1,450	1,450	....	317	316	1	3,394	3,375	19	167
5,530	5,525	5	860	859	1	1,269	1,268	1	28	28	....	2,220	2,215	5	168
9,361	9,360	1	5,619	5,619	....	4,218	4,218	....	577	577	....	5,985	5,984	1	169
349	264	85	114	78	36	41	39	2	3	3	....	223	170	53	170
457	457	....	265	265	....	228	228	....	429	429	....	469	468	1	171
1,400	1,340	60	312	305	7	86	86	....	2	2	....	360	355	5	173
18,163	8,891	9,272	2,441	2,052	389	468	362	106	990	497	493	977	467	510	173
536	536	....	2,132	2,129	3	2,212	2,209	3	517	515	2	3,190	3,188	2	174
3,355	17	3,338	2,353	3	2,350	1,290	....	1,290	426	....	426	2,493	17	2,476	175
823	816	7	410	410	....	96	96	....	5	5	....	276	274	2	176
4,446	4,446	....	2,461	2,460	1	553	553	....	40	49	....	1,914	1,913	1	177
119	112	7	3	3	....	8	8	....	....	....	....	5	5	....	178
969	725	244	13	12	1	19	19	....	....	....	....	40	40	....	179
															180
149	140	9	18	18	....	88	88	....	154	152	2	53	53	....	181
16,003	15,904	99	7,933	7,896	37	4,150	4,141	9	603	602	1	8,094	8,069	25	182
926	923	3	207	206	1	245	244	1	9	9	....	700	699	1	183
8,398	4,487	3,911	751	545	206	85	63	22	....	....	....	159	98	61	184
1,139	916	223	880	768	112	634	565	69	94	84	10	835	742	93	185
3,230	3,107	123	378	378	....	96	95	1	9	9	....	168	166	2	186
946	946	....	817	817	....	955	954	1	135	135	....	2,312	2,311	1	187
4,884	4,882	2	1,141	1,141	....	1,310	1,310	....	39	39	....	1,764	1,764	....	188
269	230	39	111	104	7	170	168	2	59	59	....	279	278	1	189
154	79	75	46	46	....										190
5,487	4,956	531	2,306	2,175	131	1,827	1,741	86	268	241	27	3,593	3,354	239	191
2,254	1,605	649	19	19	....	10	10	....				28	28	....	192
423	418	5	196	194	2	163	162	1	16	15	1	273	268	5	193
763	763	....	162	162	....	46	46	....	1	1	....	261	261	....	194
2,344	1,338	1,006	23	21	2	3	3	....				96	74	22	195
6,772	3,778	2,994	6	....	6	7	7	....				1	....	1	196
430	305	25	51	48	3	16	16	....	3	3	....	76	52	24	197
19	14	5	470	460	10	1	1	....				3	3	....	198
1,555	1,553	2	18,289	18,277	12	5,209	5,204	5	2,818	2,817	1	3,338	3,333	5	199
6,461	167	6,294	2,975	18	2,957	2,302	75	2,227	1,457	4	1,453	6,769	25	6,744	200
89	89	....	8	8	....				2	2	....	5	3	2	201
931	125	806	76	13	63	41	1	40	1	....	1	84	....	84	202
1,739	1,730	....	1,305	1,305	....	397	397	....	98	98	....	203	203	....	203
1,374	184	1,190	130	46	84	114	49	65	1	....	1	352	194	158	204
2,752	845	1,907	225	34	191	1	....	1				14	11	3	205
40	40	....													206
791	791	....	892	892	....	438	438	....	54	54	....	622	622	....	207
492	490	2	776	767	9	40	46	....				580	580	....	208
2,337	752	1,585	61	24	37							2	1	1	209
233	233	....	3	2	1							7	7	....	210
10,003	5,312	4,691	4,266	2,617	1,649	2,315	2,072	243	114	104	10	4,776	3,341	1,435	211
2,342	2,274	68	1,556	1,553	3	1,074	1,066	8	165	165	....	2,256	2,240	16	212
2,586	1,915	671	3,143	2,161	982	964	843	121	9	9	....	3,551	2,549	1,002	213
2,372	2,237	135	624	622	2	128	128	....	13	13	....	210	209	1	214
483	320	163	143	135	8	44	44	....	5	5	....	150	156	3	215
91	34	57	26	12	14	8	8	....				17	15	2	216
2,347	2,129	218	654	625	29	311	298	13	37	36	1	883	864	19	217
26	26	....	202	202	....	264	264	....	35	35	....	100	100	....	218
853	853	....	858	858	....	108	108	....	57	57	....	143	143	....	219
132	132	....	44	44	....	37	37	....	34	34	....	282	281	1	220
2,777	2,494	283	342	327	15	36	36	....	2	2	....	349	346	3	221
7,403	6,874	529	5,831	5,571	260	863	850	13	174	170	4	2,013	1,837	176	222
22,261	12,980	9,281	467	247	220	228	130	98	70	34	36	273	188	85	223
4,549	3,368	1,181	2,340	2,085	255	824	750	74	157	144	13	2,428	2,131	297	224

STATISTICS OF POPULATION.

324

TABLE **79.**—TOTAL PERSONS 10 YEARS OF AGE AND OVER ENGAGED IN EACH SPECIFIED

	OCCUPATIONS.	MONTANA.			NEBRASKA.			NEVADA.		
		Total.	Males.	Fe-males.	Total.	Males.	Fe-males.	Total.	Males.	Fe-males.
1	All occupations	72,223	67,587	4,636	368,060	325,416	42,644	23,415	21,591	1,824
2	Agriculture, fisheries, and mining	25,780	25,584	196	170,574	167,117	3,457	10,536	10,404	132
3	Agricultural laborers (a)	3,217	3,210	7	34,771	34,596	175	2,242	2,229	13
4	Apiarists	1	1		24	23	1	1	1	
5	Dairymen and dairywomen	64	59	5	325	275	50	43	39	4
6	Farmers, planters, and overseers (a)	5,775	5,629	146	132,292	129,106	3,186	1,643	1,588	55
7	Fishermen and oystermen (a)	11	11		81	81		26	26	
8	Gardeners, florists, nurserymen, and vino growers	149	146	3	944	917	27	164	152	12
9	Lumbermen and raftsmen	809	809		129	129		80	80	
10	Miners (coal)	711	711		39	39				
11	Miners (not otherwise specified)	9,795	9,791	4	49	48	1	4,844	4,802	42
12	Quarrymen	156	156		235	235		3	3	
13	Stock raisers, herders, and drovers	4,458	4,427	31	1,619	1,603	16	1,049	1,043	6
14	Wood choppers	909	909		54	54		431	431	
15	Other agricultural pursuits (a)	34	34		12	11	1	4	4	
16	Professional service	2,900	2,294	606	19,539	12,294	7,245	1,060	730	330
17	Actors	111	58	53	90	61	29	3	3	
18	Architects	46	46		165	165		2	2	
19	Artists and teachers of art	58	30	28	313	120	193	13	3	10
20	Authors and literary and scientific persons	25	22	3	67	34	33	3	3	
21	Chemists, assayers, and metallurgists	90	90		43	43		50	50	
22	Clergymen	144	144		1,774	1,750	24	34	34	
23	Dentists	68	65	3	322	321	1	20	20	
24	Designers, draftsmen, and inventors	19	19		93	88	5	3	3	
25	Engineers (civil, mechanical, electrical, and mining) and surveyors	294	294		597	597		103	103	
26	Journalists	105	103	2	574	564	10	22	22	
27	Lawyers	343	342	1	2,453	2,434	19	100	100	
28	Musicians and teachers of music	222	163	59	1,070	428	642	56	21	35
29	Officers of United States army and navy	60	60		69	69				
30	Officials (government) (a)	319	292	27	1,432	1,333	99	182	165	17
31	Physicians and surgeons	232	227	5	1,721	1,636	85	81	78	3
32	Professors in colleges and universities	11	10	1	75	67	8	5	4	1
33	Teachers	579	160	419	7,906	1,830	6,076	323	65	263
34	Theatrical managers, showmen, etc	152	150	2	519	503	16	49	43	1
35	Veterinary surgeons	17	17		236	236		2	2	
36	Other professional service	5	2	3	20	15	5	1	1	
37	Domestic and personal service	20,330	17,653	2,683	59,272	38,745	20,527	5,450	4,526	924
38	Barbers and hairdressers	343	334	9	1,729	1,683	46	120	119	1
39	Bartenders	496	496		961	961		144	144	
40	Boarding and lodging house keepers	295	116	179	807	316	491	130	53	77
41	Engineers and firemen (not locomotive)	938	938		1,384	1,384		220	220	
42	Hotel keepers	311	260	51	999	908	91	140	121	19
43	Housekeepers and stewards (a)	172	26	146	853	36	817	56	4	52
44	Hunters, trappers, guides, and scouts	53	53		19	19		71	68	3
45	Janitors	47	44	3	367	356	11	10	10	
46	Laborers (not specified) (a)	9,909	9,888	21	25,324	25,190	134	2,117	2,077	40
47	Launderers and laundresses	830	677	153	1,549	440	1,109	494	340	154
48	Nurses and midwives	99	10	89	500	40	460	40	7	33
49	Restaurant keepers	93	85	8	390	354	36	29	22	7
50	Saloon keepers	818	835	13	1,177	1,171	6	236	225	11
51	Servants	3,826	1,818	2,008	20,731	3,439	17,292	1,513	990	523
52	Sextons	10	10		24	24		2	2	
53	Soldiers, sailors, and marines (United States) (a)	1,885	1,885		1,596	1,596		1	1	
54	Watchmen, policemen, and detectives	151	151		663	662	1	111	111	
55	Other domestic and personal service	30	27	3	199	166	33	16	12	4
56	Trade and transportation	11,443	11,219	224	62,883	59,355	3,528	3,308	3,251	57
57	Agents (claim, commission, real estate, insurance, etc.) and collectors	558	544	14	4,732	4,658	74	78	74	4
58	Auctioneers	15	15		70	70				
59	Bankers and brokers (money and stocks)	232	231	1	1,357	1,342	15	48	48	
60	Boatmen and canalmen	27	27		54	54				
61	Bookkeepers and accountants (a)	550	535	15	3,075	2,642	433	173	164	9
62	Brokers (commercial)	7	7		83	83		1	1	
63	Clerks and copyists (a)	1,484	1,414	70	11,294	10,022	1,272	381	370	11
64	Commercial travelers	96	96		1,608	1,594	14	13	13	
65	Draymen, hackmen, teamsters, etc	2,088	2,088		5,292	5,289	3	704	704	
66	Foremen and overseers	241	240	1	921	916	5	78	78	
67	Hostlers	146	146		1,173	1,173		53	53	
68	Hucksters and peddlers	80	79	1	558	544	14	26	25	1
69	Livery stable keepers	135	135		1,068	1,068		43	43	
70	Locomotive engineers and firemen (a)	454	454		1,718	1,718		182	182	
71	Merchants and dealers in drugs and chemicals (retail)	121	120	1	1,334	1,298	36	24	24	
72	Merchants and dealers in dry goods (retail)	44	40	4	795	782	13	52	52	
73	Merchants and dealers in groceries (retail)	193	191	2	1,361	1,340	21	100	99	1
74	Merchants and dealers in wines and liquors (retail)	50	50		73	73		5	5	
75	Merchants and dealers in wines and liquors (wholesale)	21	21		39	39		5	4	1

a See explanatory notes in Table 78.

OCCUPATIONS.

OCCUPATION, CLASSIFIED BY SEX, BY STATES AND TERRITORIES: 1890—Continued.

NEW HAMPSHIRE.			NEW JERSEY.			NEW MEXICO.			NEW YORK.			NORTH CAROLINA.			
Total.	Males.	Females.	Total.	Males.	Females.	Total.	Males.	Females.	Total.	Males.	Females.	Total.	Males.	Females.	
164,703	127,845	36,858	570,738	459,467	111,271	54,151	50,217	3,934	2,435,725	1,921,785	513,940	537,363	422,171	115,192	1
42,982	42,360	622	74,889	73,477	1,412	26,611	26,190	421	410,132	401,529	8,603	374,359	318,711	55,648	2
11,578	11,527	51	28,686	28,528	158	5,991	5,946	45	132,596	131,967	629	171,796	129,448	42,348	3
6	6		6	4	2	3	3		271	268	3	6	5	1	4
51	41	10	352	293	59	29	28	1	1,152	902	250	105	67	38	5
29,286	28,731	555	35,146	34,041	1,105	10,256	9,943	313	249,010	241,648	7,862	192,551	179,476	13,075	6
173	172		3,595	3,594	1	11	11		4,674	4,669	5	2,586	2,542	44	7
276	272	4	3,668	3,606	62	124	120	4	10,884	10,567	317	515	449	66	8
382	382		107	107		156	156		2,004	2,004		1,725	1,723	2	9
						804	804		148	147	1	97	97		10
46	46		1,825	1,824	1	2,168	2,167	1	2,911	2,909	2	717	715	2	11
485	484	1	866	866		24	24		4,858	4,853	5	148	148		12
52	52		149	148	1	6,832	6,775	57	558	558		88	84	4	13
587	586	1	332	332		212	212		833	833		1,087	1,037		14
61	61		157	134	23	1	1		233	204	29	2,938	2,870	68	15
6,831	3,529	3,302	22,363	15,600	6,763	1,712	1,386	326	115,376	76,484	38,892	12,296	8,971	3,325	16
22	10	12	190	131	59	15	7	8	3,269	1,867	1,402	8	3	5	17
24	24		897	897		10	10		1,597	1,593	4	35	35		18
157	56	101	819	530	289	14	6	8	4,891	2,976	1,915	98	51	47	19
67	28	39	239	134	105	16	15	1	1,235	786	449	56	40	16	20
15	15		309	308	1	24	24		835	821	14	28	28		21
674	657	17	2,018	2,000	18	161	159	2	7,532	7,322	210	2,252	2,240	12	22
162	161	1	443	435	8	23	23		2,269	2,234	35	105	105		23
55	54	1	487	475	12	1	1		1,934	1,801	133	8	8		24
238	237	1	1,812	1,803	9	112	112		6,546	6,518	28	304	304		25
127	126	1	699	678	21	48	47	1	3,360	3,209	151	184	179	5	26
417	416	1	2,159	2,157	2	239	239		11,194	11,177	17	992	992		27
405	155	250	1,818	897	921	216	174	42	10,557	5,844	4,713	204	96	108	28
14	14		29	29		51	51		539	539		20	20		29
470	422	48	1,740	1,672	68	202	189	13	8,688	8,356	332	1,436	1,321	115	30
673	639	84	2,044	1,929	115	154	150	4	11,139	10,446	693	1,560	1,534	26	31
44	34	10	120	112	8	3	3		538	462	76	63	50	13	32
3,102	335	2,767	6,336	1,235	5,101	398	152	246	84,711	6,269	28,442	4,701	1,817	2,884	33
100	100		472	463	9	18	17	1	3,283	3,096	187	47	44	3	34
35	35		186	186		6	6		887	887		11	11		35
30	11	19	46	29	17	1	1		372	281	91	4	3	1	36
23,711	14,428	9,283	129,522	81,334	48,188	16,852	14,331	2,521	554,437	327,552	226,885	71,264	29,087	42,177	37
506	498	8	2,085	2,025	60	93	93		13,153	12,473	680	545	532	13	38
103	102	1	1,040	1,029	11	129	129		13,364	13,327	37	318	318		39
472	179	293	1,395	220	1,175	103	33	70	5,425	1,234	4,191	352	94	258	40
766	766		5,543	5,541	2	162	162		18,787	18,780	7	1,138	1,138		41
422	396	26	1,573	1,431	142	108	91	17	7,544	7,068	476	309	235	74	42
1,850	51	1,799	2,742	192	2,550	164	11	153	12,466	1,211	11,255	1,606	65	1,541	43
18	18		12	12		12	12		384	384		44	44		44
84	80	4	557	477	80	13	9	4	5,258	3,912	1,346	73	71	2	45
10,595	10,539	56	54,825	54,424	401	11,642	11,363	279	196,109	194,493	1,616	25,610	21,126	4,484	46
448	147	301	4,377	853	3,524	868	171	697	22,097	4,294	17,803	8,247	118	8,129	47
410	33	377	1,741	160	1,581	39	7	32	9,619	1,444	8,175	594	41	553	48
75	64	11	492	446	46	57	50	7	2,943	2,681	262	167	119	48	49
309	292	17	3,070	2,845	225	253	249	4	11,842	11,278	564	180	105	75	50
7,010	637	6,373	44,499	6,278	38,221	2,033	777	1,256	213,748	34,309	179,439	31,354	4,299	27,055	51
81	81		236	236		1	1		770	766	4	62	62		52
12	12		57	57		1,089	1,089		3,929	3,926		26	26		53
492	492		3,120	3,113	7	75	75		13,560	13,527	33	581	579	2	54
48	31	17	658	495	163	6	4	2	3,402	2,445	957	69	55	14	55
19,771	18,339	1,432	120,072	111,385	8,687	4,970	4,903	76	527,564	481,790	45,774	28,799	28,171	628	56
774	735	39	5,815	5,668	147	163	159	4	25,189	24,418	771	1,081	1,048	33	57
36	36		90	90		8	8		476	474	2	44	44		58
98	97	1	1,025	1,023	2	53	53		5,866	5,831	35	109	109		59
21	21		1,918	1,916	2	9	9		6,212	6,190	22	204	204		60
901	516	385	6,674	5,911	763	188	177	11	28,611	23,993	4,618	812	762	50	61
16	16		391	391		2	2		1,681	1,676	5	55	55		62
3,072	2,592	480	22,713	20,643	2,070	692	673	19	103,752	94,220	9,532	3,696	3,532	164	63
306	301	5	1,196	1,189	7	13	12	1	7,981	7,903	78	399	395	4	64
2,943	2,942	1	12,206	12,200	6	534	534		55,849	55,808	41	3,226	3,225	1	65
220	217	3	1,245	1,171	74	80	80		4,079	3,738	341	375	374	1	66
611	611		1,696	1,696		48	48		8,042	8,039	3	443	443		67
336	330	6	2,150	2,105	45	58	57	1	13,648	13,179	469	287	244	43	68
233	233		590	588	2	55	55		2,700	2,689	11	183	183		69
589	589		2,097	2,097		235	235		7,723	7,723		540	540		70
287	280	7	1,140	1,124	16	64	63	1	4,961	4,861	100	348	347	1	71
261	245	16	1,142	1,004	138	61	61		4,766	4,384	382	707	698	9	72
828	817	11	4,527	4,100	427	135	134	1	17,249	16,094	1,155	1,166	1,141	25	73
9	9		495	481	14	13	13		4,614	4,548	66	62	61	1	74
8	7	1	157	157		8	8		819	809	10	18	17	1	75

326

STATISTICS OF POPULATION.

TABLE **79.**—TOTAL PERSONS 10 YEARS OF AGE AND OVER ENGAGED IN EACH SPECIFIED

	OCCUPATIONS.	MONTANA.			NEBRASKA.			NEVADA.		
		Total.	Males.	Females.	Total.	Males.	Females.	Total.	Males.	Females.
	Trade and transportation—Continued.									
76	Merchants and dealers, not specified (retail)......	1,298	1,280	18	8,981	8,905	76	341	330	11
77	Merchants and dealers (wholesale), importers, and shipping merchants.	27	27		563	561	2	7	7	
78	Messengers and errand and office boys	69	69		513	502	11	22	22	
79	Newspaper carriers and newsboys	8	8		146	143	3	2	2	
80	Officials of banks and of insurance, trade, transportation, trust, and other companies. (a)	291	288	3	989	978	11	100	100	
81	Packers and shippers	63	63		280	232	48	26	26	
82	Pilots	5	5		8	8				
83	Porters and helpers (in stores and warehouses)	25	25		135	133	2	13	13	
84	Sailors (a)	63	63		99	93		10	10	
85	Salesmen and saleswomen	354	340	14	3,980	3,381	599	71	67	4
86	Steam railroad employés (not otherwise specified). (a)	2,299	2,295	4	7,416	7,394	22	640	640	
87	Stenographers and typewriters	94	42	52	1,089	372	717	7	3	4
88	Street railway employés	48	48		605	604	1			
89	Telegraph and telephone operators	262	238	24	1,168	1,036	132	64	53	11
90	Telegraph and telephone linemen and electric light and power company employés.	23	23		205	205		10	10	
91	Undertakers	15	15		73	73		5	5	
92	Weighers, gaugers, and measurers	3	3		53	53		1	1	
93	Other persons in trade and transportation	5	5		48	44	4			
94	**Manufacturing and mechanical industries**	11,764	10,837	927	55,792	47,905	7,887	3,001	2,680	381
95	Agricultural implement makers (not otherwise classified). (a)	1	1		9	9				
96	Apprentices (blacksmiths)	8	8		47	47		4	4	
97	Apprentices (boot and shoe makers)				4	4				
98	Apprentices (carpenters and joiners)	4	4		57	55	2	1	1	
99	Apprentices (carriage and wagon makers)				3	3				
100	Apprentices (dressmakers)	1		1	27		27	3		3
101	Apprentices (leather curriers, etc.)				3	3				
102	Apprentices (machinists)	10	10		74	74		2	2	
103	Apprentices (masons)	2	2		15	15				
104	Apprentices (milliners)	1		1	18		18	1		1
105	Apprentices (painters)	2	2		21	21		4	4	
106	Apprentices (plumbers)	8	8		53	53				
107	Apprentices (printers)	7	7		64	62	2	4	4	
108	Apprentices (tailors)				11	10	1			
109	Apprentices (tinsmiths)	2	2		14	14				
110	Apprentices (not otherwise specified)	30	27	3	271	263	8	8	8	
111	Artificial flower makers				1		1			
112	Bakers	158	153	5	698	667	31	38	35	3
113	Basket makers	1	1		18	17	1	3	3	
114	Blacksmiths	915	915		3,194	3,191	3	364	364	
115	Bleachers, dyers, and scourers	7	6	1	35	35		2	2	
116	Bone and ivory workers				1	1				
117	Bookbinders	16	10	6	203	146	57	2	1	1
118	Boot and shoe makers and repairers	180	179	1	1,068	1,037	16	93	93	
119	Bottlers and mineral and soda water makers	18	17	1	55	54	1	4	4	
120	Box makers (paper)				31		31			
121	Box makers (wood)	1	1		20	20				
122	Brass workers (not otherwise specified) (a)	2	2		22	22		3	3	
123	Brewers and maltsters (a)	98	97	1	196	196		2	2	
124	Brick and tile makers and terra cotta workers (a)	185	185		1,195	1,192	3	43	43	
125	Britannia workers							12	12	
126	Broom and brush makers	1	1		127	127				
127	Builders and contractors	301	301		1,110	1,109	1	25	25	
128	Butchers	464	464		2,113	2,111		105	105	
129	Butter and cheese makers	7	7		203	200	8	7	7	
130	Button makers									
131	Cabinet makers	26	26		268	268				
132	Candle, soap, and tallow makers				19	17	2	9	9	
133	Carpenters and joiners	2,690	2,689	1	11,214	11,205	9	474	473	1
134	Carpet makers (a)				118	49	69	1	1	
135	Carriage and wagon makers (not otherwise classified). (a)	46	46		458	458		23	23	
136	Charcoal, coke, and lime burners	70	70		6	6		18	18	
137	Chemical works employés (a)				1		1			
138	Clock and watch makers and repairers	35	34	1	227	227		22	22	
139	Compositors (a)	60	55	5	712	593	119	45	42	3
140	Confectioners	39	34	5	291	254	37	6	6	
141	Coopers	23	23		308	308		8	8	
142	Copper workers	6	6		20	20		3	3	
143	Corset makers									
144	Cotton mill operatives (a)				8	7	1			
145	Distillers and rectifiers (a)	2	2		45	45				
146	Door, sash, and blind makers (a)	4	4		7	7				
147	Dressmakers	564		564	4,003		3,990	105		105
148	Electroplaters				10	10				
149	Electrotypers and stereotypers (a)									
150	Engravers				12	12				
151	Fertilizer makers (a)	1	1		50	50				
152	Fish curers and packers (a)				1	1		1	1	

a See explanatory notes in Table 78.

OCCUPATIONS.

OCCUPATION, CLASSIFIED BY SEX, BY STATES AND TERRITORIES: 1890—Continued.

NEW HAMPSHIRE			NEW JERSEY			NEW MEXICO			NEW YORK			NORTH CAROLINA			
Total.	Males.	Females.	Total.	Males.	Females.	Total.	Males.	Females.	Total.	Males.	Females.	Total.	Males.	Females.	
2,023	2,564	59	16,433	15,492	941	824	813	11	67,671	64,389	3,282	5,284	5,209	75	76
98	98		1,470	1,465	5	23	23		5,293	5,260	33	134	133	1	77
92	92		1,995	1,939	56	23	23		13,737	12,582	1,155	331	325	6	78
13	13		163	161	2	1	1		697	680	17	10	10		79
192	189	3	1,491	1,485	6	76	76		5,400	5,381	19	274	273	1	80
104	83	21	917	697	220	201	201		4,431	3,119	1,312	78	45	33	81
11	11		359	358	1	2	2		960	960		97	97		82
26	23	3	422	411	11	23	23		5,677	5,574	103	242	241	1	83
112	112		2,774	2,773	1	6	6		8,424	8,421	3	697	697		84
1,551	1,274	277	9,007	6,732	2,275	149	143	6	48,598	33,144	15,454	2,187	2,071	116	85
2,849	2,840	9	12,018	11,953	65	1,107	1,104	3	34,974	34,814	160	5,041	5,019	22	86
81	28	53	1,170	371	799	14	11	3	6,449	2,331	4,118	48	31	17	87
95	95		1,212	1,212					8,044	8,044		72	72		88
212	162	50	1,811	1,425	386	93	78	15	7,080	4,987	2,093	380	362	18	89
67	67		712	555	157	7	7		1,872	1,787	85	55	55		90
80	78	2	525	521	4	11	11		2,097	2,075	22	57	56	1	91
4	4		125	125		3	3		751	754		45	45		92
12	12		201	156	45	2	2		1,188	911	277	7	3	4	93
71,408	49,189	22,210	223,892	177,671	46,221	3,997	3,407	590	828,216	634,430	193,786	50,645	37,231	13,414	94
31	31		13	13					660	658	2	3	3		95
20	20		158	158		6	6		514	513	1	37	37		96
2	2		59	57	2				257	251	6	3	3		97
16	16		580	577	3	2	2		1,094	1,094		52	52		98
9	9		21	21					103	103		6	6		99
5		5	186		186	1		1	1,220		1,220	2		2	100
4	4		19	19					24	24		2		2	101
64	64		547	544	3	16	16		1,434	1,430	4	41	41		102
8	8		217	216	1				390	390		14	14		103
2		2	25		25				255		255	2		2	104
8	8		136	136		1	1		401	399	2	9	9		105
14	14		370	370		1	1		1,341	1,340	1	3	3		106
30	28	2	216	213	3	9	7	2	800	774	26	20	20		107
7	6	1	99	57	42	1	1		677	455	222	1	1		108
9	9		72	71	1	1	1		327	327		5	5		109
137	131	6	2,051	1,989	62	26	25	1	6,159	5,853	306	148	145	3	110
			129	31	98				2,374	377	1,997				111
309	303	6	3,092	3,016	76	73	69	4	13,466	13,070	396	114	106	8	112
54	48	6	223	210	12				1,327	1,139	188	92	77	15	113
1,725	1,725		5,649	5,648	1	413	413		22,327	22,319	8	2,102	2,100	2	114
325	316	9	1,001	913	88	1	1		2,050	1,425	625	60	56	4	115
			78	63	15				285	234	51				116
56	38	18	895	592	303				7,795	3,765	4,030	44	27	17	117
10,582	8,161	2,421	8,089	6,764	1,325	181	181		27,928	24,133	3,795	1,068	1,058	10	118
60	54	6	483	450	33	5	5		2,042	1,856	186	16	16		119
321	147	174	1,366	504	862				5,316	1,601	3,715	32	25	7	120
231	215	16	357	325	32				2,222	1,825	397	52	51	1	121
104	104		1,115	1,052	63	1	1		3,844	3,718	126				122
151	151		780	774	6	27	27		4,576	4,572	4	18	18		123
1,488	1,487	1	5,234	5,231	3	26	26		8,633	8,610	23	552	549	3	124
			11	11					78	72	6	16	16		125
46	40	6	356	285	71				2,403	2,006	397	16	16		126
134	134		1,601	1,601		62	62		6,999	6,997	2	234	234		127
450	450		4,793	4,791	2	139	139		10,379	10,355	24	420	420		128
61	56	5	170	162	8	1		1	3,100	2,876	224	12	9	3	129
			618	274	344				558	191	367				130
326	326		954	954		6	6		6,666	6,661	5	257	257		131
26	26		222	199	23				674	606	68				132
5,182	5,182		21,101	21,181	10	811	811		73,022	72,987	35	7,113	7,110	3	133
114	43	71	658	478	180	1		1	6,936	3,147	3,789				134
238	238		544	544		15	15		4,847	4,820	27	380	380		135
11	11		153	153		13	13		355	355		9	9		136
18	13	5	268	231	37				976	753	223	18	18		137
100	94	6	999	879	120	23	23		3,441	3,130	311	89	89		138
225	102	123	990	837	153	57	49	8	5,551	4,659	892	175	166	9	139
123	92	31	989	733	256	9	7	2	4,983	3,465	1,518	88	86	2	140
414	414		1,481	1,480	1	1	1		7,472	7,458	14	775	775		141
11	11		199	199		2	2		532	579	8	19	19		142
14	8	6	997	60	937				521	78	443				143
15,772	6,649	9,123	3,463	1,288	2,175				5,523	2,357	3,166	7,792	3,473	4,319	144
1	1		67	65	2				269	269		302	302		145
209	209		389	389					1,680	1,678	2	29	29		146
2,414		2,414	10,303	35	10,268	205		205	59,550	518	59,032	1,052		1,052	147
5	5		258	250	8				768	673	35				148
									461	460	1				149
1	1		60	60		1		1	2,465	2,402	63	3	3		150
25	23	2	897	814	23				57	57		47	47		151
2	2		43	42	1				41	41		8	8		152

828

STATISTICS OF POPULATION.

TABLE 79.—TOTAL PERSONS 10 YEARS OF AGE AND OVER ENGAGED IN EACH SPECIFIED

	OCCUPATIONS.	MONTANA.			NEBRASKA.			NEVADA.		
		Total.	Males.	Females.	Total.	Males.	Females.	Total.	Males.	Females.
	Manufacturing and mechanical industries—Cont'd.									
153	Gas works employés (a)	3	3		39	39		1	1	
154	Glass workers	9	9		35	33	2	1	1	
155	Glove makers	3	3		6		6	2	1	1
156	Gold and silver workers	11	11		36	36		116	116	
157	Gunsmiths, locksmiths, and bell hangers	8	8		117	117		12	12	
158	Hair workers				3		3			
159	Harness and saddle makers and repairers	101	101		1,231	1,231		41	41	
160	Hat and cap makers	1		1	40	30	10	2	2	
161	Hosiery and knitting mill operatives (a)				13	10	3			
162	Iron and steel workers (a)	488	488		438	436	2	15	15	
163	Lace and embroidery makers	1		1	13		13			
164	Lead and zinc workers	18	18		14	14				
165	Leather curriers, dressers, finishers, and tanners	13	13		49	49		3	3	
166	Machinists	433	433		1,659	1,658	1	119	119	
167	Manufacturers and officials of manufacturing companies	113	113		612	612		21	21	
168	Marble and stone cutters	143	143		587	587		12	12	
169	Masons (brick and stone)	625	624	1	3,115	3,114	1	82	82	
170	Meat and fruit packers, canners, and preservers (a)				130	128	2	9	9	
171	Mechanics (not otherwise specified)	17	17		139	139		5	5	
172	Metal workers (not otherwise specified)	870	869	1	106	106		48	46	2
173	Mill and factory operatives (not specified) (a)	91	86	5	158	71	87	128	128	
174	Millers (flour and grist)	55	55		918	918		26	26	
175	Milliners	123		123	1,351	8	1,343	60		60
176	Model and pattern makers	7	7		62	61	1	2	2	
177	Molders	98	98		530	527	3	33	33	
178	Musical instrument makers (not otherwise specified). (a)				2	2				
179	Nail and tack makers (a)				5	5				
180	Oil well employés	1	1							
181	Oil works employés				20	20				
182	Painters, glaziers, and varnishers	411	410	1	3,514	3,493	21	106	105	1
183	Paper hangers	18	18		184	183	1	3	3	
184	Paper mill operatives				31	20	11			
185	Photographers	89	81	8	431	392	39	17	17	
186	Piano and organ makers and tuners (a)	6	6		46	46		3	3	
187	Plasterers	137	137		1,334	1,334		19	19	
188	Plumbers and gas and steam fitters	165	165		885	883	2	27	27	
189	Potters	1	1		106	105	1			
190	Powder and cartridge makers									
191	Printers, lithographers, and pressmen (a)	269	266	3	1,860	1,790	70	46	43	3
192	Print works operatives (a)									
193	Publishers of books, maps, and newspapers	23	23		165	162	3	2	2	
194	Roofers and slaters	5	5		52	52				
195	Rope and cordage makers	9	9		10	10				
196	Rubber factory operatives				1	1				
197	Sail, awning, and tent makers	3	3		16	16		1	1	
198	Salt works employés							2	2	
199	Saw and planing mill employés (a)	508	508		409	409		133	133	
200	Seamstresses (a)	161		161	1,527	8	1,519	92		92
201	Sewing machine makers (not otherwise classified). (a)				1	1				
202	Sewing machine operators (a)	1		1	3		3			
203	Ship and boat builders	7	7		18	18		4	4	
204	Shirt, collar, and cuff makers (a)	4	3	1	22	13	9			
205	Silk mill operatives (a)									
206	Starch makers				14	10	4			
207	Steam boiler makers	58	58		240	240		18	18	
208	Stove, furnace, and grate makers (a)				29	29				
209	Straw workers				1		1			
210	Sugar makers and refiners				4	4				
211	Tailors and tailoresses (a)	214	195	19	1,361	1,209	152	60	58	2
212	Tinners and tinware makers	123	123		936	934	2	41	41	
213	Tobacco and cigar factory operatives	60	57	3	653	606	47	3	3	
214	Tool and cutlery makers (not otherwise classified). (a)	11	11		15	15		1	1	
215	Trunk, valise, leather-case, and pocket-book makers				22	22		1	1	
216	Umbrella and parasol makers							1		1
217	Upholsterers	28	28		186	184	2	55	55	
218	Well borers	4	4		178	178		6	6	
219	Wheelwrights	26	26		71	70	1	8	8	
220	Whitewashers	3	3		15	15		1	1	
221	Wire workers				20	20		2	2	
222	Wood workers (not otherwise specified)	38	37	1	211	206	5	12	12	
223	Woolen mill operatives (a)				20	17	3			
224	Other persons in manufacturing and mechanical industries.	156	155	1	1,011	933	78	52	52	

a See explanatory notes in Table 78.

OCCUPATIONS.

329

OCCUPATION, CLASSIFIED BY SEX, BY STATES AND TERRITORIES: 1890—Continued.

	NEW HAMPSHIRE.			NEW JERSEY.			NEW MEXICO.			NEW YORK.			NORTH CAROLINA.			
	Total.	Males.	Females.	Total.	Males.	Females.	Total.	Males.	Females.	Total.	Males.	Females.	Total.	Males.	Females.	
	49	49	—	220	219	1	5	5	—	1,078	1,076	2	20	20	—	153
	13	11	2	4,298	4,221	77				4,516	4,241	275	2	2	—	154
	183	120	63	164	47	117				4,999	2,111	2,848	1	—	1	155
	95	91	4	1,498	1,117	379	48	48	—	3,839	3,234	605	41	41	—	156
	39	37	2	398	395	3	5	5	—	1,678	1,678	—	42	42	—	157
	5	3	2	23	10	13				268	121	147				158
	403	385	18	1,678	1,543	136	37	37	—	4,511	4,406	105	250	250	—	159
	14	11	3	6,137	4,745	1,392	1	1	—	6,472	4,503	1,990	8	8	—	160
	2,271	813	1,458	1,019	361	658				9,547	3,506	6,041	191	29	162	161
	754	652	102	5,974	5,859	115	54	54	—	14,240	14,007	239	148	146	2	162
	10	—	10	469	108	361	2	—	2	2,713	477	2,236	10	—	10	163
	1	1	—	212	210	2				506	477	29				164
	505	503	2	2,647	2,588	59	4	4	—	6,460	6,403	57	107	107	—	165
	1,800	1,799	1	9,034	9,030	4	160	160	—	25,565	25,543	22	955	954	1	166
	1,226	1,225	1	4,728	4,720	8	50	49	1	18,054	17,974	80	1,035	1,035	—	167
	1,328	1,328	—	1,602	1,598	4	88	88	—	11,257	11,236	21	234	234	—	168
	1,268	1,268	—	6,767	6,766	1	215	215	—	24,867	24,856	11	1,341	1,341	—	169
	1	1	—	162	140	22				784	544	240	12	8	4	170
	107	107	—	208	208	—	14	14	—	2,087	2,081	6	770	770	—	171
	53	50	3	582	526	56	86	86	—	2,526	2,391	135	84	81	3	172
	3,887	1,543	2,344	5,419	2,745	2,674	5	5	—	8,558	3,051	4,607	1,627	1,037	590	173
	237	237	—	974	972	2	78	78	—	4,264	4,258	6	1,747	1,734	13	174
	562	—	562	1,441	6	1,435	92	—	92	8,732	213	8,519	603	—	603	175
	75	75	—	452	449	3	3	3	—	1,809	1,725	84	14	13	1	176
	575	575	—	2,803	2,801	2	16	16	—	11,185	11,174	11	188	188	—	177
				87	85	2				227	218	9				178
	8	8	—	239	238	1				249	201	48				179
	9	9	—	9	9	—				574	573	1				180
	1	1	—	384	380	4				1,041	1,037	4	32	32	—	181
	2,133	2,122	11	9,439	9,375	64	122	121	1	40,533	40,260	273	1,029	1,026	3	182
	50	48	2	506	504	2	3	3	—	1,812	1,800	12	13	13	—	183
	681	544	137	817	721	96				5,166	3,912	1,254	41	30	11	184
	191	147	44	464	435	29	26	24	2	2,632	2,375	257	96	92	4	185
	78	78	—	600	590	10	1	1	—	4,930	4,867	63	19	19	—	186
	40	40	—	526	525	1	47	47	—	3,876	3,875	1	198	198	—	187
	201	201	—	3,085	3,083	2	26	25	1	15,000	14,980	20	82	82	—	188
	19	19	—	3,801	2,978	823	13	6	7	879	747	132	67	58	9	189
				61	57	4				121	104	17	1	1	—	190
	380	344	36	3,375	3,261	114	79	79	—	18,162	17,055	1,107	461	451	10	191
	455	374	81	843	714	129				1,142	863	279				192
	45	43	2	285	284	1	6	6	—	1,128	1,118	10	15	15	—	193
	39	39	—	432	432	—				1,706	1,704	2	7	7	—	194
	9	2	7	162	131	31				1,700	1,048	652	2	2	—	195
	8	6	2	2,178	1,595	583				1,528	1,023	595	13	13	—	196
	14	14	—	147	137	10				880	818	62				197
				22	22	—				786	710	76				198
	1,639	1,639	—	974	974	—	113	113	—	7,402	7,397	5	3,410	3,407	3	199
	611	—	611	2,927	86	2,841	235	2	233	22,004	2,466	19,533	4,231	4	4,227	200
				335	323	12				78	76	2	3	3	—	201
	113	8	105	593	60	533				3,327	604	2,723	6	3	3	202
	74	74	—	1,406	1,406	—	1	1	—	4,733	4,731	2	99	99	—	203
	19	6	13	1,952	524	1,428				10,783	2,156	8,627				204
	3	3	—	15,149	7,561	7,588	15	—	15	5,922	2,417	3,505	42	20	22	205
	1	1	—	2	2	—				134	89	45				206
	89	89	—	992	992	—	29	29	—	3,183	3,181	2	29	29	—	207
	15	15	—	125	125	—				1,622	1,619	3	4	4	—	208
	4	—	4	105	34	71				431	131	300				209
				276	276	—				642	640	2				210
	982	360	622	5,718	3,602	2,116	77	71	6	61,291	41,908	19,383	375	231	144	211
	315	315	—	2,092	2,056	36	44	44	—	9,916	9,703	213	253	248	5	212
	145	139	6	3,111	2,242	869	4	4	—	25,652	18,526	7,126	5,719	3,754	1,965	213
	292	283	9	1,315	1,294	21				2,665	2,572	93	22	22	—	214
	30	29	1	1,128	999	129	3	3	—	1,308	1,079	229				215
	1	1	—	271	176	95				1,218	484	734	2	2	—	216
	125	122	3	964	908	56	5	5	—	5,411	4,913	498	90	86	4	217
				58	58	—	4	4	—	205	205	—	5	5	—	218
	188	188	—	969	969	—	13	13	—	1,681	1,681	—	265	265	—	219
	9	9	—	87	87	—	2	1	1	383	380	3	33	33	—	220
	31	31	—	1,285	1,138	147	2	2	—	1,811	1,615	196	2	2	—	221
	1,045	929	116	1,696	1,604	92	5	5	—	10,541	10,065	476	442	431	11	222
	3,541	2,195	1,346	2,946	1,661	1,285	31	29	2	8,018	4,040	3,978	200	131	69	223
	509	460	49	5,201	3,683	1,518	41	19	2	14,219	9,463	4,756	631	559	72	224

330-

STATISTICS OF POPULATION.

TABLE 79.—TOTAL PERSONS 10 YEARS OF AGE AND OVER ENGAGED IN EACH SPECIFIED

	OCCUPATIONS.	NORTH DAKOTA.			OHIO.			OKLAHOMA.		
		Total.	Males.	Females.	Total.	Males.	Females.	Total.	Males.	Females.
1	All occupations	67,771	59,956	7,815	1,272,786	1,088,609	184,177	20,906	19,849	1,057
2	Agriculture, fisheries, and mining	43,955	43,131	824	429,019	418,806	10,213	13,928	13,617	311
3	Agricultural laborers (a)	12,273	12,157	116	107,691	106,932	759	1,067	1,057	10
4	Apiarists				95	92	3	2	2	
5	Dairymen and dairywomen	24	19	5	1,424	1,309	115	14	13	1
6	Farmers, planters, and overseers (a)	30,890	30,109	691	284,342	275,221	9,121	12,411	12,117	294
7	Fishermen and oystermen (a)	19	19		944	944		1	1	
8	Gardeners, florists, nurserymen, and vine growers	94	91	2	4,551	4,375	170	26	24	2
9	Lumbermen and raftsmen	33	33		800	800		12	11	
10	Miners (coal)	36	36		22,037	22,012	25	4	4	
11	Miners (not otherwise specified)	8	8		2,429	2,423	6	10	10	
12	Quarrymen	6	6		3,380	3,377	3	2	2	
13	Stock raisers, herders, and drovers	693	684	9	573	573		378	374	4
14	Wood choppers	8	8		612	610	2	1	1	
15	Other agricultural pursuits (a)	1	1		141	138	3			
16	Professional service	3,058	1,945	1,113	61,913	41,783	20,130	1,017	843	174
17	Actors	2	1	1	368	221	147	2	1	1
18	Architects	6	6		350	347	3	7	7	
19	Artists and teachers of art	12	2	10	1,474	688	786	9	1	8
20	Authors and literary and scientific persons	6	4	2	326	189	137	2	2	
21	Chemists, assayers, and metallurgists	1	1		204	202	2			
22	Clergymen	342	340	2	5,075	4,988	87	83	82	1
23	Dentists	29	29		1,113	1,095	18	21	20	1
24	Designers, draftsmen, and inventors	3	3		617	604	13	1	1	
25	Engineers (civil, mechanical, electrical, and mining) and surveyors	45	45		2,399	2,395	4	40	40	
26	Journalists	81	81		1,264	1,207	57	30	30	
27	Lawyers	337	337		5,336	5,324	12	264	264	
28	Musicians and teachers of music	94	46	48	4,074	1,668	2,406	39	13	26
29	Officers of United States army and navy	43	43		29	29		8	8	
30	Officials (government) (a)	357	337	20	4,636	4,283	353	74	68	6
31	Physicians and surgeons	190	184	6	7,034	6,747	287	217	211	6
32	Professors in colleges and universities	7	7		368	314	54	4	2	2
33	Teachers	1,395	380	1,015	25,544	9,841	15,703	197	75	122
34	Theatrical managers, showmen, etc.	67	60	7	1,165	1,124	41	13	12	1
35	Veterinary surgeons	36	36		477	477		6	6	
36	Other professional service	2	1	1	60	40	20			
37	Domestic and personal service	9,282	4,407	4,875	255,289	173,384	81,905	1,718	1,344	374
38	Barbers and hairdressers	152	151	1	5,943	5,775	168	92	90	2
39	Bartenders	105	105		2,991	2,984	7	24	23	1
40	Boarding and lodging house keepers	75	27	48	2,198	547	1,651	32	19	13
41	Engineers and firemen (not locomotive)	245	245		9,897	9,894	3	29	29	
42	Hotel keepers	263	243	20	1,879	1,658	221	61	49	12
43	Housekeepers and stewards (a)	354	9	345	5,835	232	5,603	21	1	20
44	Hunters, trappers, guides, and scouts	36	36		30	30		2	2	
45	Janitors	44	43	1	1,362	1,187	175	4	4	
46	Laborers (not specified) (a)	2,021	2,011	10	129,792	128,610	1,182	705	692	13
47	Launderers and laundresses	206	48	158	7,069	818	6,251	97	42	55
48	Nurses and midwives	69	13	56	1,882	272	1,610	2		2
49	Restaurant keepers	44	41	3	954	862	92	37	33	4
50	Saloon keepers	151	148	3	6,844	6,555	289	72	72	
51	Servants	4,562	338	4,224	73,009	8,501	64,508	396	144	252
52	Sextons	1	1		287	287		2	2	
53	Soldiers, sailors, and marines (United States) (a)	874	874		671	671		130	130	
54	Watchmen, policemen, and detectives	65	65		4,042	4,030	12	10	10	
55	Other domestic and personal service	15	9	6	604	471	133	2	2	
56	Trade and transportation	6,679	6,505	174	195,578	180,978	14,600	2,075	2,025	50
57	Agents (claim, commission, real estate, insurance, etc.) and collectors	641	636	5	10,638	10,254	384	332	329	3
58	Auctioneers	6	6		245	245		8	8	
59	Bankers and brokers (money and stocks)	113	113		960	947	13	41	41	
60	Boatmen and canalmen	10	10		606	605	1	1	1	
61	Bookkeepers and accountants (a)	259	244	15	9,650	7,928	1,722	36	29	7
62	Brokers (commercial)	7	7		198	197	1			
63	Clerks and copyists (a)	697	650	47	30,334	25,697	4,637	202	188	14
64	Commercial travelers	98	98		5,153	5,101	52	12	12	
65	Draymen, hackmen, teamsters, etc.	304	304		22,123	22,112	11	144	144	
66	Foremen and overseers	207	207		1,952	1,917	35	17	17	
67	Hostlers	155	155		3,027	3,025	2	24	24	
68	Hucksters and peddlers	32	31	1	4,664	4,497	167	8	6	2
69	Livery stable keepers	119	119		1,678	1,676	2	61	61	
70	Locomotive engineers and firemen (a)	332	332		5,700	5,700		8	8	
71	Merchants and dealers in drugs and chemicals (retail)	143	143		2,894	2,849	45	112	112	
72	Merchants and dealers in dry goods (retail)	122	119	3	2,785	2,678	107	46	46	
73	Merchants and dealers in groceries (retail)	97	97		8,754	8,235	339	164	160	4
74	Merchants and dealers in wines and liquors (retail)	5	5		345	341	4	10	10	
75	Merchants and dealers in wines and liquors (wholesale)	1	1		253	252	1	1	1	

a See explanatory notes in Table 78.

OCCUPATIONS.

OCCUPATION, CLASSIFIED BY SEX, BY STATES AND TERRITORIES: 1890—Continued.

OREGON.			PENNSYLVANIA.			RHODE ISLAND.			SOUTH CAROLINA.			SOUTH DAKOTA.			
Total.	Males.	Fe-males.	Total.	Males.	Fe-males.	Total.	Males.	Fe-males.	Total.	Males.	Fe-males.	Total.	Males.	Fe-males.	
126,781	115,988	10,793	1,959,091	1,635,143	323,948	155,878	113,164	42,714	440,854	311,423	129,431	114,093	102,635	11,458	1
50,980	50,080	900	453,086	446,877	6,209	12,606	12,422	184	328,017	239,567	88,450	70,839	69,429	1,410	2
10,605	10,521	84	100,326	99,290	1,036	4,842	4,801	41	195,267	116,952	78,315	12,373	12,256	117	3
11	11	....	69	68	1	....	....	....	3	3	....	5	5	....	4
184	171	13	996	875	121	7	6	1	61	46	15	40	38	2	5
30,057	29,313	744	208,044	203,281	4,763	5,930	5,798	132	127,225	117,156	10,069	54,686	53,409	1,277	6
1,478	1,473	5	827	825	2	782	782	....	507	501	6	28	28	....	7
609	592	17	5,807	5,680	127	756	749	7	284	261	23	137	130	7	8
1,818	1,818	....	9,016	9,011	5	18	18	....	269	269	....	77	77	....	9
146	146	....	103,280	103,161	119	51	51	....	....	....	....	42	42	....	10
2,165	2,162	3	13,611	13,595	16	15	15	....	782	782	....	1,947	1,947	....	11
62	62	....	6,495	6,484	11	128	128	....	200	200	....	317	317	....	12
3,105	3,071	34	740	740	....	16	16	....	84	82	2	886	879	7	13
737	737	....	3,671	3,670	1	53	53	....	779	776	3	289	289	....	14
3	3	....	204	197	7	8	5	3	2,556	2,539	17	12	12	....	15
6,926	5,907	1,010	75,080	50,944	24,136	5,446	3,447	1,999	8,103	5,970	2,223	5,935	3,613	2,382	16
221	148	73	541	345	196	52	33	10	4	3	1	21	10	11	17
68	68	....	532	528	4	87	87	....	20	20	....	19	19	....	18
191	85	106	1,899	1,016	883	213	108	105	62	30	32	44	18	26	19
36	26	10	487	318	169	78	44	34	21	12	9	19	13	6	20
19	19	....	653	646	7	36	36	....	22	22	....	17	17	....	21
553	545	8	6,580	6,512	68	424	419	5	1,028	1,023	5	630	621	9	22
129	129	....	1,828	1,779	49	116	109	7	138	138	....	60	59	1	23
48	48	....	1,364	1,322	42	212	205	7	5	5	....	8	8	....	24
474	474	....	4,614	4,607	7	375	373	2	236	236	....	197	197	....	25
188	182	6	1,701	1,640	61	129	125	4	102	100	2	199	196	3	26
662	661	1	6,735	6,728	7	283	283	....	772	771	1	740	737	3	27
450	232	218	5,522	2,385	3,137	492	229	263	246	82	164	214	65	149	28
5	5	....	120	120	....	85	85	....	10	10	....	19	19	....	29
607	569	38	5,553	5,146	407	514	484	30	732	685	47	510	476	34	30
736	696	40	8,356	7,978	378	526	469	57	1,140	1,129	11	409	395	14	31
59	52	7	458	387	71	28	24	4	66	61	5	34	29	5	32
2,212	838	1,404	26,223	7,645	18,578	1,712	265	1,447	2,953	1,008	1,945	2,739	618	2,121	33
186	183	3	1,133	1,088	45	83	82	1	25	24	1	54	54	....	34
44	44	....	596	596	....	26	26	....	7	7	....	62	62	....	35
8	3	5	185	158	27	25	11	14	4	4	....	....	....	....	36
26,542	21,847	4,695	477,770	332,026	145,750	28,906	17,747	11,159	51,772	22,335	29,437	13,911	8,232	5,679	37
526	497	29	8,499	8,239	260	705	683	22	421	414	7	305	300	5	38
507	506	1	4,394	4,381	13	441	436	5	231	231	....	73	73	....	39
351	108	243	3,281	830	2,451	382	93	289	277	46	231	160	87	73	40
1,167	1,167	....	18,706	18,697	9	1,245	1,235	....	679	679	....	357	357	....	41
497	401	96	4,741	4,370	371	219	193	26	161	111	50	406	372	34	42
440	61	379	9,506	576	8,930	933	61	872	1,001	64	937	332	18	314	43
77	68	9	32	32	....	4	4	....	3	3	....	13	13	....	44
80	73	7	1,836	1,527	309	241	235	6	70	64	6	50	46	4	45
14,435	14,365	70	262,224	260,095	2,129	11,231	11,088	143	20,798	16,003	4,795	5,197	5,171	26	46
1,239	1,075	164	8,422	1,814	6,608	1,154	151	1,003	7,797	128	7,669	379	146	233	47
210	29	181	4,497	575	3,922	522	70	452	548	46	503	128	20	108	48
117	102	15	1,752	1,584	168	150	145	5	122	67	55	108	90	18	49
749	740	9	2,722	2,584	138	419	415	4	123	114	9	156	154	2	50
5,711	2,235	3,476	135,815	15,720	120,095	9,816	1,539	8,277	18,810	3,653	15,157	5,416	558	4,858	51
28	28	....	772	766	6	46	46	....	56	56	....	9	9	....	52
18	18	....	526	526	....	330	330	....	11	11	....	742	742	....	53
297	297	....	9,135	9,116	19	944	944	....	613	613	....	66	66	....	54
84	68	16	916	594	322	134	79	55	51	32	19	14	10	4	55
19,373	18,534	839	324,262	297,699	26,563	27,372	24,709	2,663	21,735	21,024	711	12,850	12,461	389	56
1,493	1,443	50	13,804	13,379	425	1,067	1,032	35	823	815	8	1,144	1,133	11	57
15	15	....	357	357	....	35	35	....	21	21	....	5	5	....	58
530	510	20	1,386	1,381	5	139	136	3	99	97	2	316	311	5	59
98	98	....	2,051	2,051	....	61	61	....	163	163	....	20	20	....	60
1,026	923	103	12,722	10,594	2,128	2,001	1,394	607	682	656	26	406	362	44	61
14	14	....	567	567	....	57	57	....	63	63	....	10	10	....	62
2,849	2,593	256	53,636	47,141	6,495	4,408	3,806	602	3,147	2,997	150	1,391	1,260	131	63
478	476	2	2,930	2,876	54	411	404	7	238	238	....	162	158	4	64
2,205	2,203	2	39,673	39,647	26	3,852	3,850	2	2,007	2,006	1	1,119	1,118	1	65
210	208	2	3,203	3,030	173	183	178	5	266	265	1	288	283	....	66
341	341	....	4,808	4,808	....	769	769	....	357	357	....	190	180	1	67
104	99	5	6,418	6,200	218	779	765	14	318	217	101	59	55	1	68
240	240	....	1,822	1,818	4	185	185	....	117	117	....	280	280	....	69
423	423	....	9,861	9,861	....	207	207	....	484	484	....	320	320	....	70
419	414	5	4,099	3,996	103	329	324	5	237	232	5	264	260	4	71
209	204	5	3,130	2,793	337	195	168	27	333	321	12	149	145	4	72
375	363	12	10,974	9,996	978	1,175	1,147	28	803	767	36	304	303	1	73
35	35	....	532	515	17	252	250	2	37	37	....	17	17	....	74
29	29	....	451	442	9	65	65	....	13	13	....	5	5	....	75

332

STATISTICS OF POPULATION.

TABLE **79.**—TOTAL PERSONS 10 YEARS OF AGE AND OVER ENGAGED IN EACH SPECIFIED

	OCCUPATIONS.	NORTH DAKOTA.			OHIO.			OKLAHOMA.		
		Total.	Males.	Females.	Total.	Males.	Females.	Total.	Males.	Females.
	Trade and transportation—Continued.									
76	Merchants and dealers, not specified (retail)	1,158	1,150	8	23,653	23,024	629	475	468	7
77	Merchants and dealers (wholesale), importers, and shipping merchants	18	18	...	1,469	1,466	3	14	14	...
78	Messengers and errand and office boys	26	26	...	2,501	2,390	111	6	6	...
79	Newspaper carriers and newsboys	8	8	...	398	396	2	1	1	...
80	Officials of banks and of insurance, trade, transportation, trust, and other companies. (a)	108	106	2	2,216	2,207	9	27	27	...
81	Packers and shippers	8	8	...	1,518	1,070	448			
82	Pilots	6	6	...	161	161	...	2	2	...
83	Porters and helpers (in stores and warehouses)	4	4	...	1,088	1,069	19	1	1	...
84	Sailors (a)	12	12	...	1,745	1,744	1	0	2	...
85	Salesmen and saleswomen	533	484	49	16,157	12,507	3,650	163	158	5
86	Steam railroad employés (not otherwise specified). (a)	1,210	1,208	2	21,918	21,838	80	102	101	1
87	Stenographers and typewriters	56	26	30	2,482	928	1,554	19	12	7
88	Street railway employés				2,304	2,303	1			
89	Telegraph and telephone operators	173	161	12	4,182	3,703	479	29	29	...
90	Telegraph and telephone linemen and electric light and power company employés	5	5	...	660	651	9	3	3	...
91	Undertakers	8	8	...	882	878	4	3	3	...
92	Weighers, gaugers, and measurers	1	1	...	223	223	...			
93	Other persons in trade and transportation	2	2	...	242	164	78			
94	**Manufacturing and mechanical industries**	4,797	3,968	829	330,987	273,658	57,329	2,168	2,020	148
95	Agricultural implement makers (not otherwise classified). (a)				283	282	1	2	2	...
96	Apprentices (blacksmiths)	13	13	...	804	804	...			
97	Apprentices (boot and shoe makers)				118	116	2			
98	Apprentices (carpenters and joiners)	1	1	...	864	864	...			
99	Apprentices (carriage and wagon makers)	1	1	...	101	101	...			
100	Apprentices (dressmakers)	8	...	8	277	...	277	2	...	2
101	Apprentices (leather curriers, etc.)				29	29	...			
102	Apprentices (machinists)	1	1	...	879	878	1			
103	Apprentices (masons)				76	76	...			
104	Apprentices (milliners)	1	...	1	79	...	70			
105	Apprentices (painters)				144	142	2			
106	Apprentices (plumbers)	3	3	...	170	170	...			
107	Apprentices (printers)	1	1	...	312	298	14			
108	Apprentices (tailors)	2	2	...	195	165	30			
109	Apprentices (tinsmiths)	1	1	...	145	145	...			
110	Apprentices (not otherwise specified)	17	15	2	2,461	2,363	98			
111	Artificial flower makers				8	...	8			
112	Bakers	53	48	5	3,894	3,763	131	58	53	...
113	Basket makers				434	390	44			
114	Blacksmiths	591	591	...	16,059	16,056	3	185	185	...
115	Bleachers, dyers, and scourers	1	1	...	290	252	38	3	3	...
116	Bone and ivory workers				19	19	...			
117	Bookbinders	20	16	4	1,274	665	609	1	...	1
118	Boot and shoe makers and repairers	124	124	...	10,446	9,013	1,433	55	55	...
119	Bottlers and mineral and soda water makers	9	9	...	271	261	10	2	2	...
120	Box makers (paper)				536	55	481			
121	Box makers (wood)				609	514	95	1	1	...
122	Brass workers (not otherwise specified) (a)	2	2	...	1,662	1,630	32			
123	Brewers and maltsters (a)	25	25	...	1,971	1,970	1			
124	Brick and tile makers and terra cotta workers (a)	44	44	...	3,020	3,013	7	43	43	...
125	Britannia workers				1	1	...			
126	Broom and brush makers	3	3	...	988	925	63			
127	Builders and contractors	52	52	...	2,970	2,969	1	38	38	...
128	Butchers	226	226	...	7,268	7,265	3	84	84	...
129	Butter and cheese makers	10	10	...	597	587	10			
130	Button makers				2	2	...			
131	Cabinet makers	14	14	...	3,119	3,115	4	15	15	...
132	Candle, soap, and tallow makers				460	375	85	1	1	...
133	Carpenters and joiners	1,052	1,052	...	39,415	39,404	11	753	753	...
134	Carpet makers (a)	11	...	11	922	419	503			
135	Carriage and wagon makers (not otherwise classified). (a)	40	40	...	4,036	3,992	44	24	24	...
136	Charcoal, coke, and lime burners				338	338	...			
137	Chemical works employés (a)				138	113	25			
138	Clock and watch makers and repairers	20	20	...	2,339	1,807	532	6	6	...
139	Compositors (a)	88	71	17	1,783	1,428	355	21	19	2
140	Confectioners	21	20	1	1,196	912	281	29	28	1
141	Coopers	11	11	...	4,472	4,470	2	4	4	...
142	Copper workers	3	3	...	139	139	...			
143	Corset makers				47	10	37			
144	Cotton mill operatives (a)				504	202	302			
145	Distillers and rectifiers (a)				225	224	1			
146	Door, sash, and blind makers (a)				126	126	...			
147	Dressmakers	475	...	475	20,615	21	20,594	90	...	90
148	Electroplaters				186	183	3			
149	Electrotypers and stereotypers (a)				78	78	...			
150	Engravers				443	434	9			
151	Fertilizer makers (a)				19	19	...			
152	Fish curers and packers (a)				34	34	...			

a See explanatory notes in Table 78.

OCCUPATIONS.

OCCUPATION, CLASSIFIED BY SEX, BY STATES AND TERRITORIES: 1890—Continued.

	OREGON.			PENNSYLVANIA.			RHODE ISLAND.			SOUTH CAROLINA.			SOUTH DAKOTA.		
	Total.	Males.	Females.	Total.	Males.	Females.	Total.	Males.	Females.	Total.	Males.	Females.	Total.	Males.	Females.
76	2,797	2,745	52	42,923	40,285	2,638	4,097	3,847	250	3,422	3,288	134	2,470	2,444	26
77	75	75		1,951	1,924	27	211	210	1	129	128	1	85	85	
78	153	150	3	7,636	7,345	291	579	566	13	187	186	1	26	26	
79	16	16		684	679	5	21	21		32	32		2	2	
80	328	326	2	4,513	4,501	12	300	299	1	225	225		234	231	3
81	102	102		2,943	1,987	956	338	133	205	34	30	4	22	22	
82	25	25		268	268		83	83		63	63		3	3	
83	59	59		953	927	26	107	105	2	533	530	3	9	8	1
84	792	792		1,770	1,770		389	389		400	409		29	29	
85	1,038	920	118	30,167	21,205	8,962	2,692	2,073	619	1,927	1,756	171	672	609	63
86	2,015	2,014	1	42,704	42,525	179	1,213	1,203	10	4,040	4,017	23	2,433	2,430	3
87	227	72	155	2,571	1,144	1,427	128	31	97	62	49	13	126	61	65
88	105	105		3,037	3,036	1	478	478		94	94		18	18	
89	369	323	46	6,079	5,115	964	227	125	102	289	270	19	238	220	18
90	43	43		935	912	23	159	137	22	24	24		22	22	
91	33	33		1,252	1,233	19	104	104		41	41		12	12	
92	3	3		578	570	8	12	12		11	11		1	1	
93	10	10		224	171	53	24	20	4	5	5		4	4	
94	22,960	20,520	2,440	628,887	507,597	121,290	81,548	54,839	26,709	31,137	22,527	8,610	10,498	8,900	1,598
95	2	2		251	251		27	27		8	8		4	4	
96	20	20		681	681		38	38		51	50	1	10	10	
97	2	2		94	92	2	6	6		2	2				
98	16	16		1,123	1,122	1	74	74		90	90		6	6	
99	2	2		119	119		5	5		4	4				
100	6		6	569		569	42		42	47		47	12		12
101	2	2		62	62		3	3					4	4	
102	13	13		1,855	1,852	3	227	227		32	32		3	3	
103	8	8		293	293		24	24		21	21		4	4	
104	5		5	141		141	12		12	8		8	2		2
105	4	4		408	408		27	26	1	10	10		4	4	
106	23	23		519	518	1	51	51		2	2				
107	4	4		647	634	13	34	34		25	24	1	20	20	
108	2	1	1	312	232	80	23	13	10	29	27	2			
109	5	5		329	329		19	19		8	8				
110	78	73	5	6,386	6,129	257	879	854	25	153	149	4	43	42	1
111				857	43	814	1		1						
112	251	248	3	8,676	8,393	283	481	449	32	272	249	23	90	90	0
113	4	4		446	434	12	17	15	2	27	24	3			
114	1,362	1,362		23,326	23,321	5	1,366	1,366		1,380	1,379	1	1,001	1,001	
115	19	17	2	2,842	2,743	99	1,953	1,663	290	24	21	3	5	5	
116				182	154	28	24	24							
117	72	37	35	2,869	1,423	1,446	104	61	43	41	26	15	24	14	10
118	378	276	2	18,656	16,720	1,936	612	583	29	575	568	7	230	229	1
119	21	20	1	1,063	1,030	33	70	68	2	7	7		9	9	
120	7		7	2,202	583	1,619	426	69	357	2		2	1	1	
121	54	53	1	962	724	238	128	115	13	2	2		1	1	
122	11	11		1,047	1,006	41	81	81							
123	130	130		1,984	1,978	6	56	56		18	18		26	26	
124	367	367		6,807	6,784	23	157	157		333	333		123	123	
125				40	37	3	8	8							
126	20	20		1,196	1,113	83	65	36	29	2	2		18	18	
127	415	415		4,715	4,715		276	276		214	214		164	164	
128	641	640	1	12,541	12,510	31	513	513		432	431	1	411	411	
129	24	23	1	605	581	24	34	34		9	9		50	48	2
130				221	149	72	62	31	31						
131	196	196		3,756	3,756		206	206		93	93		31	31	
132	13	13		317	285	32	82	79	3	3	3				
133	5,287	5,285	2	60,739	60,728	11	4,825	4,823	2	4,708	4,705	3	2,457	2,457	
134	17	9	8	7,142	4,540	2,602	100	78	22	4		4	7		7
135	152	152		3,383	3,361	22	102	102		111	111		111	111	
136	16	16		3,342	3,338	4	5	5		13	13		1	1	
137	1		1	549	407	142	101	70	31	13	13				
138	87	85	2	1,988	1,734	254	159	144	15	82	82		31	31	
139	170	110	60	2,423	2,222	201	175	128	47	143	128	15	201	150	51
140	129	102	27	3,166	2,342	824	146	125	21	47	38	9	44	39	5
141	129	129		3,405	3,399	6	94	93	1	467	467		35	35	
142	3	3		306	304	2	36	36		17	17				
143	1		1	98	15	83	21	9	12						
144				8,736	4,057	4,679	18,360	8,790	9,570	6,800	3,580	3,220			
145	6	6		317	317					83	83				
146	28	28		200	200		38	38		39	39				
147	1,301	2	1,299	34,166	40	34,126	3,080	5	3,075	1,791		1,791	924		924
148	6	6		268	265	3	80	80		3	3				
149				158	156	2	14	14							
150	22	21	1	1,033	910	123	295	290	5	5	5				
151				28	28		11	11		162	160	2			
152	134	134		17	17		6	6							

334

STATISTICS OF POPULATION.

(TABLE **79.**—TOTAL PERSONS 10 YEARS OF AGE AND OVER ENGAGED IN EACH SPECIFIED

	OCCUPATIONS.	NORTH DAKOTA.			OHIO.			OKLAHOMA.		
		Total.	Males.	Females.	Total.	Males.	Females.	Total.	Males.	Females.
	Manufacturing and mechanical industries—Cont'd.									
153	Gas works employés (a)	1	1		377	377				
154	Glass workers				4,318	3,998	320			
155	Glove makers				19	10	9			
156	Gold and silver workers	7	7		741	690	51	4	4	
157	Gunsmiths, locksmiths, and bell hangers	6	6		580	579	1	5	5	
158	Hair workers				86	53	33			
159	Harness and saddle makers and repairers	146	146		3,360	3,295	65	35	35	
160	Hat and cap makers				276	154	122	1	1	
161	Hosiery and knitting mill operatives (a)	1		1	871	172	699			
162	Iron and steel workers (a)	4	4		18,973	18,731	242	4	4	
163	Lace and embroidery makers	2		2	170	2	168			
164	Lead and zinc workers				168	160	8			
165	Leather curriers, dressers, finishers, and tanners	4	4		1,379	1,372	7			
166	Machinists	145	145		14,389	14,365	24	16	16	
167	Manufacturers and officials of manufacturing companies	56	56		8,318	8,290	28	37	36	1
168	Marble and stone cutters	14	14		3,283	3,279	4	32	32	
169	Masons (brick and stone)	159	159		10,517	10,517		145	145	
170	Meat and fruit packers, canners, and preservers(a)	2	2		248	201	47			
171	Mechanics (not otherwise specified)	13	13		717	717		4	4	
172	Metal workers (not otherwise specified)	1	1		949	872	77			
173	Mill and factory operatives (not specified) (a)	12	5	7	1,913	1,186	727	1	1	
174	Millers (flour and grist)	129	129		3,329	3,327	2	19	19	
175	Milliners	118		118	4,384	27	4,357	31		31
176	Model and pattern makers	1	1		1,012	1,005	7	1	1	
177	Molders	7	7		7,507	7,502	5	3	3	
178	Musical instrument makers (not otherwise specified). (a)				14	14				
179	Nail and tack makers (a)				824	790	34			
180	Oil well employés				1,159	1,157	2			
181	Oil works employés				603	599	4			
182	Painters, glaziers, and varnishers	200	199	1	16,673	16,561	114	121	121	
183	Paper hangers	7	7		981	968	13	1	1	
184	Paper mill operatives				1,904	1,275	629			
185	Photographers	62	57	5	1,382	1,228	154	16	15	1
186	Piano and organ makers and tuners (a)	3	3		431	431				
187	Plasterers	29	29		3,471	3,470	1	44	44	
188	Plumbers and gas and steam fitters	17	17		2,856	2,854	2	7	7	
189	Potters				3,967	3,375	592			
190	Powder and cartridge makers				112	102	10			
191	Printers, lithographers, and pressmen (a)	129	125	4	5,243	4,804	439	59	57	2
192	Print works operatives (a)				34	34				
193	Publishers of books, maps, and newspapers	23	23		295	290	5	6	6	
194	Roofers and slaters				467	467				
195	Rope and cordage makers				816	513	303			
196	Rubber factory operatives				545	373	172			
197	Sail, awning, and tent makers	2	2		104	93	11			
198	Salt works employés				53	53				
199	Saw and planing mill employés (a)	50	50		4,231	4,231		31	31	
200	Seamstresses (a)	150		150	11,451	40	11,411	12		12
201	Sewing machine makers (not otherwise classified). (a)				52	52				
202	Sewing machine operators (a)				103	27	76			
203	Ship and boat builders	2	2		963	963		1	1	
204	Shirt, collar, and cuff makers (a)				214	92	122			
205	Silk mill operatives (a)				40	24	16			
206	Starch makers				176	126	50			
207	Steam boiler makers	35	35		1,972	1,972				
208	Stove, furnace, and grate makers (a)				1,169	1,168	1			
209	Straw workers				45	37	8			
210	Sugar makers and refiners				23	23				
211	Tailors and tailoresses (a)	119	106	13	13,441	7,666	5,775	25	22	3
212	Tinners and tinware makers	84	84		3,971	3,923	48	32	32	
213	Tobacco and cigar factory operatives	52	51	1	6,983	4,825	2,158	14	13	1
214	Tool and cutlery makers (not otherwise classified). (a)	1	1		1,123	1,103	20			
215	Trunk, valise, leather-case, and pocket-book makers				329	326	3	5	5	
216	Umbrella and parasol makers				67	49	18			
217	Upholsterers	2	2		2,158	2,049	109	5	5	
218	Well borers	19	19		673	672	1	24	24	
219	Wheelwrights	7	7		637	637		2	2	
220	Whitewashers	1	1		523	523				
221	Wire workers	1	1		1,263	1,242	21	1	1	
222	Wood workers (not otherwise specified)	6	6		5,967	5,624	343			
223	Woolen mill operatives (a)				1,096	570	526			
224	Other persons in manufacturing and mechanical industries.	18	15	3	4,204	3,333	871	7	6	1

a See explanatory notes in Table 78.

OCCUPATIONS.

OCCUPATION, CLASSIFIED BY SEX, BY STATES AND TERRITORIES: 1890—Continued.

	OREGON.			PENNSYLVANIA.			RHODE ISLAND.			SOUTH CAROLINA.			SOUTH DAKOTA.			
	Total.	Males.	Females.	Total.	Males.	Females.	Total.	Males.	Females.	Total.	Males.	Females.	Total.	Males.	Females.	
	6	6	....	982	981	1	90	90	....	27	27	....	....	....	....	153
	7	7	....	12,428	11,760	659	26	26	....	....	....	....	8	8	....	154
	1	....	1	60	38	22	4	1	3	....	....	....	....	....	....	155
	21	21	....	1,770	1,383	387	3,155	2,460	695	26	26	....	37	37	....	156
	47	47	....	802	797	5	31	30	1	27	27	....	13	13	....	157
	....	....	....	119	76	43	108	82	26	....	....	....	....	....	....	158
	317	317	....	3,610	3,568	42	256	232	24	111	111	....	276	276	....	159
	8	7	1	2,545	1,900	645	85	63	22	5	5	....	....	....	....	160
	3	1	2	6,548	1,546	5,002	693	230	463	11	....	11	....	....	....	161
	116	116	....	52,497	52,122	375	2,006	1,727	279	85	85	....	20	20	....	162
	8	....	8	694	102	592	16	....	16	12	....	12	....	....	....	163
	....	....	....	506	500	6	7	7	....	4	4	....	....	....	....	164
	53	53	....	7,221	7,169	52	169	169	....	25	25	....	16	16	....	165
	684	684	....	24,013	24,003	10	4,399	4,398	1	572	572	....	132	132	....	166
	464	464	....	12,269	12,240	29	1,264	1,264	....	363	361	2	158	158	....	167
	163	163	....	7,052	7,048	4	798	798	....	238	238	....	258	258	....	168
	563	563	....	19,170	19,167	3	1,560	1,559	1	1,061	1,061	....	649	649	....	169
	443	433	10	254	160	94	44	42	2	3	3	....	....	....	....	170
	120	120	....	595	592	3	75	75	....	321	321	....	23	23	....	171
	17	17	....	2,349	2,248	101	184	148	36	10	9	1	1	1	....	172
	103	82	21	20,616	11,284	9,332	6,375	3,179	3,196	1,401	901	500	42	22	20	173
	416	416	....	5,680	5,679	1	72	72	....	579	579	....	245	245	....	174
	346	2	344	5,773	15	5,758	456	....	456	377	....	377	277	....	277	175
	48	48	....	1,716	1,699	17	200	198	2	19	19	....	1	1	....	176
	186	186	....	9,724	9,718	6	897	897	....	67	67	....	20	20	....	177
	....	....	....	90	86	4	....	....	....	....	....	....	....	....	....	178
	....	....	....	864	838	26	22	22	....	....	....	....	....	....	....	179
	....	....	....	7,055	7,048	7	....	....	....	....	....	....	....	....	....	180
	2	2	....	1,835	1,831	4	32	31	1	43	43	....	....	....	....	181
	1,165	1,158	7	20,165	20,036	129	2,297	2,293	4	783	783	....	459	459	....	182
	32	32	....	2,258	2,253	5	99	99	....	4	4	....	15	15	....	183
	16	14	2	2,642	1,825	817	111	89	22	20	14	6	....	....	....	184
	175	148	27	1,870	1,676	194	129	111	18	75	71	4	107	95	12	185
	26	26	....	718	693	25	85	84	1	15	15	....	13	13	....	186
	236	236	....	5,171	5,169	2	179	179	....	135	135	....	122	122	....	187
	300	299	1	6,177	6,175	2	653	653	....	78	77	1	55	55	....	188
	45	45	....	1,071	963	108	34	33	1	20	20	....	1	1	....	189
	....	....	....	168	158	10	1	....	1	....	....	....	....	....	....	190
	580	533	47	8,710	8,049	661	510	478	32	314	299	15	326	312	14	191
	....	....	....	724	563	161	816	629	187	....	....	....	....	....	....	192
	29	29	....	586	569	17	22	22	....	9	9	....	45	45	....	193
	3	3	....	1,354	1,354	....	46	46	....	11	11	....	1	1	....	194
	27	26	1	1,433	842	591	44	25	19	....	....	....	....	....	....	195
	3	3	....	423	264	159	1,650	920	730	....	....	....	....	....	....	196
	14	14	....	278	260	18	42	37	5	14	14	....	1	1	....	197
	1	1	....	78	78	....	....	....	....	....	....	....	....	....	....	198
	1,941	1,934	7	7,957	7,955	2	118	118	....	826	824	2	194	194	....	199
	347	9	338	14,776	262	14,514	574	3	571	2,317	....	2,317	217	....	217	200
	1	1	....	44	40	4	14	13	1	....	....	....	....	....	....	201
	1	....	1	618	36	582	46	6	40	4	....	4	....	....	....	202
	190	190	....	2,159	2,150	....	118	118	....	109	109	....	5	5	....	203
	7	7	....	1,817	326	1,491	70	11	59	7	....	7	1	....	1	204
	....	....	....	5,882	1,570	4,312	166	65	101	1	1	....	....	....	....	205
	....	....	....	9	9	....	....	....	....	....	....	....	....	....	....	206
	95	95	....	3,582	3,581	1	196	106	....	49	49	....	16	16	....	207
	7	7	....	1,651	1,650	1	69	69	....	5	5	....	....	....	....	208
	3	2	1	113	55	58	10	6	4	3	3	....	....	....	....	209
	....	....	....	590	590	....	6	6	....	1	1	....	....	....	....	210
	605	535	70	20,491	12,089	8,402	1,038	635	403	326	269	57	200	175	25	211
	819	819	....	6,294	6,194	100	354	354	....	207	203	4	179	179	....	212
	118	100	18	18,161	12,882	5,279	239	124	115	36	35	1	88	85	3	213
	23	23	....	3,201	3,128	73	660	619	41	....	....	....	1	1	....	214
	11	11	....	709	521	188	9	9	....	....	....	....	1	1	....	215
	3	3	....	1,452	483	969	9	8	1	2	2	....	....	....	....	216
	121	112	9	2,981	2,611	370	216	203	13	70	65	5	12	12	....	217
	13	13	....	688	688	....	3	3	....	9	9	....	55	55	....	218
	43	43	....	1,906	1,906	....	137	137	....	169	169	....	18	18	....	219
	2	2	....	224	224	....	44	44	....	33	33	....	1	1	....	220
	....	....	....	....	....	....	....	....	....	....	....	....	....	....	....	221
	10	8	2	1,422	1,331	91	205	69	136	4	4	....	13	13	....	222
	171	170	1	6,381	5,752	629	440	411	29	158	152	6	9	6	3	223
	155	114	41	13,432	7,135	6,297	11,143	6,088	5,055	36	24	12	42	40	2	224
	275	266	9	9,012	7,693	1,319	651	478	173	1,485	1,376	109	....	....	....	

336   STATISTICS OF POPULATION.

TABLE 79.—TOTAL PERSONS 10 YEARS OF AGE AND OVER ENGAGED IN EACH SPECIFIED

	OCCUPATIONS.	TENNESSEE.			TEXAS.			UTAH.		
		Total.	Males.	Females.	Total.	Males.	Females.	Total.	Males.	Females.
1	All occupations	553,753	473,171	80,582	696,203	610,193	86,015	66,901	59,825	7,076
2	Agriculture, fisheries, and mining	336,886	313,070	23,816	432,318	398,140	34,178	24,083	23,510	573
3	Agricultural laborers (a)	120,009	107,388	12,621	129,553	111,469	18,084	4,462	4,430	32
4	Apiarists	14	14		44	40	4	12	12	
5	Dairymen and dairywomen	375	323	52	530	506	24	54	37	17
6	Farmers, planters, and overseers (a)	207,279	196,230	11,049	279,351	263,548	15,803	12,340	11,854	486
7	Fishermen and oystermen (a)	835	835		431	429	2	23	23	
8	Gardeners, florists, nurserymen, and vine growers	982	897	85	1,105	1,050	55	528	505	23
9	Lumbermen and raftsmen	1,066	1,066		1,050	1,050		140	140	
10	Miners (coal)	3,436	3,434	2	653	653		521	521	
11	Miners (not otherwise specified)	1,455	1,455		245	242	3	3,120	3,117	3
12	Quarrymen	825	825		373	373		121	121	
13	Stock raisers, herders, and drovers	221	217	4	17,819	17,626	193	2,418	2,409	9
14	Wood choppers	863	862	1	1,038	1,038		151	151	
15	Other agricultural pursuits (a)	26	24	2	126	116	10	193	190	3
16	Professional service	19,450	14,983	4,467	28,123	22,226	5,897	2,843	2,135	708
17	Actors	28	19	9	269	136	133	57	20	37
18	Architects	99	99		155	155		70	69	1
19	Artists and teachers of art	310	168	142	310	148	162	87	69	23
20	Authors and literary and scientific persons	56	30	26	89	65	24	22	15	7
21	Chemists, assayers, and metallurgists	20	20		59	59		49	49	
22	Clergymen	2,684	2,674	10	3,363	3,354	9	123	119	4
23	Dentists	353	352	1	405	398	7	93	89	4
24	Designers, draftsmen, and inventors	45	45		58	57	1	26	26	
25	Engineers (civil, mechanical, electrical, and mining) and surveyors	637	634	3	887	886	1	280	280	
26	Journalists	314	304	10	538	520	18	86	84	2
27	Lawyers	2,064	2,064		3,555	3,552	3	315	315	
28	Musicians and teachers of music	832	228	604	1,558	667	891	186	104	82
29	Officers of United States army and navy	6	6		228	228		19	19	
30	Officials (government) (a)	1,712	1,638	74	2,953	2,808	145	297	261	36
31	Physicians and surgeons	3,436	3,385	51	4,381	4,340	41	242	226	16
32	Professors in colleges and universities	100	85	15	113	107	6	10	9	1
33	Teachers	6,478	2,970	3,508	8,848	4,415	4,433	794	309	485
34	Theatrical managers, showmen, etc	214	204	10	205	275	20	71	66	5
35	Veterinary surgeons	46	45	1	46	46		13	13	
36	Other professional service	16	13	3	13	10	3	3	3	
37	Domestic and personal service	85,339	43,480	41,859	100,669	63,459	37,210	15,535	12,037	3,498
38	Barbers and hairdressers	1,178	1,158	20	1,913	1,891	22	227	216	11
39	Bartenders	722	721	1	1,578	1,575	3	236	236	
40	Boarding and lodging house keepers	871	190	681	1,547	376	1,171	149	44	105
41	Engineers and firemen (not locomotive)	2,253	2,252	1	1,962	1,962		413	413	
42	Hotel keepers	490	395	95	1,258	928	330	153	114	39
43	Housekeepers and stewards (a)	1,644	81	1,563	1,535	70	1,465	196	15	181
44	Hunters, trappers, guides, and scouts	13	13		51	51		33	33	
45	Janitors	213	202	11	211	202	9	39	33	6
46	Laborers (not specified) (a)	31,177	29,799	1,378	43,326	41,448	1,878	8,529	8,465	64
47	Launderers and laundresses	11,773	287	11,486	11,536	812	10,724	450	233	217
48	Nurses and midwives	626	65	561	570	79	491	195	8	187
49	Restaurant keepers	172	138	34	474	405	69	60	48	12
50	Saloon keepers	681	673	8	1,879	1,842	37	264	263	1
51	Servants	31,994	6,033	25,961	29,313	8,329	20,984	3,634	967	2,667
52	Sextons	78	77	1	81	81		15	15	
53	Soldiers, sailors, and marines (United States) (a)	14	14		1,796	1,796		766	766	
54	Watchmen, policemen, and detectives	1,198	1,171	27	1,405	1,405		149	149	
55	Other domestic and personal service	242	211	31	234	207	27	27	19	8
56	Trade and transportation	53,906	52,126	1,780	77,033	75,209	1,824	11,088	10,548	540
57	Agents (claim, commission, real estate, insurance, etc.) and collectors	2,776	2,706	70	4,679	4,578	101	1,080	1,055	25
58	Auctioneers	31	31		39	39		8	8	
59	Bankers and brokers (money and stocks)	359	354	5	832	807	25	205	201	4
60	Boatmen and canalmen	228	228		138	138		1	1	
61	Bookkeepers and accountants (a)	2,134	2,008	126	3,000	2,868	132	562	531	31
62	Brokers (commercial)	88	88		78	78		10	10	
63	Clerks and copyists (a)	7,164	6,667	497	10,242	9,804	448	1,757	1,546	211
64	Commercial travelers	1,116	1,100	7	1,456	1,442	14	157	151	6
65	Draymen, hackmen, teamsters, etc	6,793	6,783	10	7,020	7,009	11	1,568	1,565	3
66	Foremen and overseers	526	523	3	1,073	1,072	1	160	159	1
67	Hostlers	856	854	2	1,024	1,023	1	94	94	
68	Hucksters and peddlers	773	752	21	946	913	33	119	114	5
69	Livery stable keepers	384	384		769	768	1	69	68	1
70	Locomotive engineers and firemen (a)	1,340	1,340		2,777	2,775	2	416	416	
71	Merchants and dealers in drugs and chemicals (retail)	787	777	10	1,560	1,555	5	123	122	1
72	Merchants and dealers in dry goods (retail)	1,619	1,588	31	1,735	1,702	33	83	77	6
73	Merchants and dealers in groceries (retail)	2,208	2,054	154	3,061	2,970	91	164	154	10
74	Merchants and dealers in wines and liquors (retail)	50	50		100	100		34	34	
75	Merchants and dealers in wines and liquors (wholesale)	39	39		57	57		8	8	

a See explanatory notes in Table 78.

OCCUPATIONS.

OCCUPATION, CLASSIFIED BY SEX, BY STATES AND TERRITORIES: 1890—Continued.

VERMONT.			VIRGINIA.			WASHINGTON.			WEST VIRGINIA.			WISCONSIN.			WYOMING.			
Total.	Males.	Females.	Total.	Males.	Females.	Total.	Males.	Females.	Total.	Males.	Females.	Total.	Males.	Females.	Total.	Males.	Females.	
128,771	108,804	19,967	551,880	445,473	106,866	164,696	153,581	11,115	223,788	202,081	21,707	576,290	495,229	81,061	30,630	28,736	1,894	1
56,183	55,534	649	271,745	255,009	16,736	47,943	47,291	652	129,887	126,631	3,256	242,099	236,108	5,931	11,201	11,128	73	2
18,090	18,012	78	117,692	108,008	9,684	8,224	8,173	51	35,066	34,587	479	60,983	60,400	583	1,142	1,139	3	3
23	23	......	12	12	......	4	4	......	7	6	1	107	104	3	1	1	......	4
27	25	2	218	176	42	151	148	3	104	71	33	323	286	37	17	15	2	5
34,873	34,310	563	138,298	131,430	6,868	27,571	27,032	539	83,152	80,434	2,718	166,704	161,460	5,244	2,571	2,524	47	6
43	43	......	7,699	7,640	59	1,202	1,162	40	51	51	......	794	792	2	10	10	......	7
284	279	5	1,037	971	66	550	542	8	268	253	15	1,598	1,449	59	33	29	4	8
401	401	......	655	655	......	4,826	4,826	......	1,050	1,050	......	7,211	7,209	2	21	21	......	9
......	......	......	605	605	......	2,181	2,179	2	8,979	8,972	7	......	......	......	1,877	1,874	3	10
133	133	......	3,261	3,259	2	926	926	......	633	633	......	3,042	3,042	......	1,151	1,150	1	11
2,068	2,068	......	793	792	1	140	140	......	250	249	1	604	604	......	71	71	......	12
46	46	......	199	196	3	1,044	1,036	8	69	68	1	203	202	1	4,147	4,134	13	13
192	191	1	1,176	1,171	5	1,121	1,121	......	243	243	......	509	599	......	157	157	......	14
3	3	......	40	34	6	3	2	1	15	14	1	21	21	......	3	3	......	15
6,276	3,629	3,247	17,695	11,965	5,730	8,214	6,598	1,616	8,662	6,397	2,265	24,278	13,545	10,733	1,203	953	250	16
5	4	1	63	28	35	276	137	130	13	11	2	151	93	58	15	8	7	17
14	14	......	48	48	......	225	225	......	23	23	......	156	156	......	5	5	......	18
99	39	60	149	80	69	221	119	102	119	55	64	441	201	240	23	9	14	19
40	19	21	68	51	17	34	23	11	15	12	3	106	58	48	12	10	2	20
7	7	......	28	28	......	45	45	......	23	23	......	44	44	......	14	14	......	21
620	614	6	2,180	2,164	16	525	518	7	988	987	1	2,134	2,116	18	63	62	1	22
131	130	1	284	284	......	149	140	......	119	118	1	431	412	19	10	10	......	23
25	25	......	79	79	......	81	81	......	24	23	1	179	175	4	2	2	......	24
107	106	1	792	791	1	1,109	1,100	......	360	360	......	808	808	......	125	125	......	25
82	76	6	196	192	4	326	320	6	118	117	1	487	469	18	25	23	2	26
457	457	......	1,650	1,649	1	1,204	1,195	9	937	937	......	1,691	1,686	5	131	131	......	27
332	99	233	547	261	286	527	307	220	277	90	187	1,464	621	843	87	65	22	28
7	7	......	137	137	......	65	65	......	7	7	......	10	10	......	117	117	......	29
412	355	57	1,847	1,754	93	698	671	27	564	522	42	2,031	1,929	102	128	121	7	30
640	614	26	1,978	1,931	47	777	739	38	1,046	1,026	20	1,800	1,733	67	90	87	3	31
37	31	6	120	120	......	24	20	4	36	30	6	155	149	6	1	......	1	32
3,130	306	2,824	7,350	2,210	5,140	1,612	567	1,045	3,921	1,986	1,935	11,552	2,260	9,292	236	49	187	33
92	92	......	111	107	4	259	258	1	48	47	1	337	329	8	104	100	4	34
20	20	......	40	40	......	20	20	......	17	17	......	281	281	......	6	6	......	35
10	5	5	13	11	2	28	21	7	7	6	1	22	17	5	3	3	......	36
22,050	11,805	10,254	126,259	58,545	67,714	42,291	36,692	5,599	31,424	19,427	11,997	111,998	73,196	38,802	8,334	7,169	1,165	37
347	342	5	1,001	983	18	784	768	16	439	436	3	1,810	1,740	70	108	107	1	38
23	23	......	729	720	9	966	965	1	161	161	......	1,458	1,453	5	139	138	1	39
186	58	128	631	146	485	520	247	273	221	59	162	892	438	454	45	18	27	40
572	572	......	2,069	2,069	......	1,888	1,888	......	1,160	1,160	......	3,515	3,512	3	228	228	......	41
306	286	20	461	383	78	698	622	76	344	282	62	1,734	1,628	100	84	75	9	42
1,380	41	1,339	2,643	136	2,507	551	128	423	883	25	858	1,861	54	1,807	86	16	70	43
16	16	......	40	40	......	78	78	......	11	11	......	134	134	......	41	41	......	44
55	53	2	240	225	15	106	102	4	74	60	14	412	389	23	34	34	......	45
9,331	9,244	87	45,172	42,070	3,102	24,100	24,041	59	15,091	14,971	120	54,873	54,398	475	4,794	4,785	9	46
362	79	283	13,153	237	12,916	1,194	820	374	922	57	865	1,729	309	1,420	108	77	31	47
366	48	318	1,165	95	1,070	233	29	204	185	31	154	958	151	807	30	6	24	48
58	51	7	203	147	56	296	259	37	64	50	14	280	233	47	27	26	1	49
46	46	......	280	266	14	1,092	1,084	8	276	267	9	4,004	3,940	64	159	156	3	50
8,733	677	8,056	55,777	8,390	47,387	8,154	4,048	4,106	11,040	1,339	9,701	36,609	3,206	33,403	1,569	642	927	51
29	29	......	145	140	5	25	25	......	29	29	......	95	95	......	8	8	......	52
......	......	......	1,323	1,323	......	1,097	1,097	......	2	2	......	27	27	......	754	754	......	53
232	232	......	1,008	1,002	6	432	432	......	461	458	3	1,371	1,369	2	52	52	......	54
17	8	9	159	113	46	77	59	18	61	29	32	176	120	56	8	6	2	55
14,551	13,834	717	58,526	56,649	1,877	29,260	28,421	845	22,973	22,239	734	68,620	63,830	4,790	5,258	5,172	86	56
521	505	16	2,260	2,245	24	3,091	3,057	34	671	658	13	4,205	4,098	107	166	158	8	57
14	14	......	95	95	......	41	41	......	26	26	......	38	38	......	1	1	......	58
129	128	1	211	210	1	798	785	13	60	60	......	504	499	5	60	60	......	59
34	34	......	565	565	......	100	100	......	227	227	......	196	195	1	3	3	......	60
577	442	135	1,490	1,427	63	1,554	1,451	103	507	469	38	3,454	2,862	592	165	155	10	61
12	12	......	102	102	......	29	28	1	15	15	......	47	47	......	1	1	......	62
2,072	1,818	254	9,105	8,597	508	3,251	3,006	245	2,815	2,538	277	10,817	8,825	1,992	706	679	27	63
288	286	2	654	648	6	208	206	2	329	327	2	1,729	1,714	15	85	85	......	64
2,403	2,403	......	5,085	5,084	1	3,779	3,778	1	2,409	2,408	1	8,218	8,217	1	782	782	......	65
223	221	2	641	639	2	885	885	......	332	332	......	1,018	1,007	11	137	137	......	66
341	341	......	871	870	1	299	298	1	246	246	......	1,101	1,101	......	83	82	......	67
287	280	7	609	549	60	109	104	5	246	243	3	890	863	27	9	9	......	68
194	194	......	261	260	1	306	305	1	97	97	......	739	739	......	34	34	......	69
584	584	......	1,375	1,375	......	670	670	......	1,225	1,225	......	2,050	2,050	......	487	487	......	70
187	183	4	586	582	4	467	465	2	248	244	4	1,137	1,111	26	54	54	......	71
226	224	2	825	800	25	267	264	3	479	470	9	885	860	25	24	23	1	72
467	459	8	1,829	1,710	119	715	707	8	644	605	39	1,944	1,850	94	50	48	2	73
2	2	......	102	102	......	115	115	......	22	21	1	154	151	3	15	15	......	74
1	1	......	27	27	......	50	49	1	7	7	......	65	65	......	4	4	......	75

338

STATISTICS OF POPULATION.

TABLE **79.**—TOTAL PERSONS 10 YEARS OF AGE AND OVER ENGAGED IN EACH SPECIFIED

	OCCUPATIONS.	TENNESSEE.			TEXAS.			UTAH.		
		Total.	Males.	Females.	Total.	Males.	Females.	Total.	Males.	Females.
	Trade and transportation—Continued.									
76	Merchants and dealers, not specified (retail)......	7,169	7,061	108	11,224	10,982	242	1,372	1,328	44
77	Merchants and dealers (wholesale), importers, and shipping merchants.	340	338	2	340	338	2	54	54	
78	Messengers and errand and office boys............	456	441	15	483	472	11	116	114	2
79	Newspaper carriers and newsboys..............	91	90	1	94	94	....	6	6	
80	Officials of banks and of insurance, trade, transportation, trust, and other companies. (a)	660	656	4	687	686	1	184	184	
81	Packers and shippers......................	125	110	15	214	211	3	77	77	
82	Pilots.........................	82	82	....	36	36	....			
83	Porters and helpers (in stores and warehouses)....	1,289	1,283	6	679	676	3	20	19	1
84	Sailors (a).........................	304	304	....	895	895	....	21	21	....
85	Salesmen and saleswomen............	3,874	3,479	395	5,645	5,304	341	636	544	92
86	Steam railroad employés (not otherwise specified). (a)	8,457	8,425	32	13,490	13,443	47	1,568	1,564	4
87	Stenographers and typewriters............	321	138	183	385	243	142	72	33	39
88	Street railway employés...............	420	420	....	570	570	....	104	104	....
89	Telegraph and telephone operators...........	710	632	78	1,243	1,111	132	188	134	54
90	Telegraph and telephone linemen and electric light and power company employés.	94	93	1	115	115		28	28	
91	Undertakers..................	160	160	....	83	83	....	19	19	....
92	Weighers, gaugers, and measurers...........	34	34	....	86	86	....	4	4	....
93	Other persons in trade and transportation.....	49	45	4	18	16	2	1	1	....
94	Manufacturing and mechanical industries...........	58,172	49,512	8,660	58,065	51,159	6,906	13,352	11,595	1,757
95	Agricultural implement makers (not otherwise classified). (a)	36	36	....	29	29	....	2	2	....
96	Apprentices (blacksmiths)...........	38	38	....	57	57	....	12	12	....
97	Apprentices (boot and shoe makers)........	2	2	....	4	4	....			
98	Apprentices (carpenters and joiners).......	66	66	....	95	95	....	29	29	....
99	Apprentices (carriage and wagon makers)......	9	9	....	3	3	....	1	1	....
100	Apprentices (dressmakers)............	5	....	5	4	....	4	17	....	17
101	Apprentices (leather curriers, etc.).......	1	1	....	5	5	....	1	1	....
102	Apprentices (machinists)............	51	51	....	74	74	....	3	3	....
103	Apprentices (masons)............	14	14	....	7	7	....	16	16	....
104	Apprentices (milliners)............	3	....	3	6	....	6	2	....	2
105	Apprentices (painters)............	5	5	....	25	25	....	10	9	1
106	Apprentices (plumbers)............	28	28	....	10	10	....	20	20	....
107	Apprentices (printers)............	28	27	1	30	30	....	20	18	2
108	Apprentices (tailors)............	5	5	....	10	10	....	1	1	....
109	Apprentices (tinsmiths)............	31	31	....	20	20	....	1	1	....
110	Apprentices (not otherwise specified)........	225	223	2	229	225	4	60	58	2
111	Artificial flower makers............	1	....	1	2	....	2	1	....	1
112	Bakers............	333	323	10	735	716	10	136	131	5
113	Basket makers............	90	75	15	17	17	....	12	10	2
114	Blacksmiths............	4,126	4,125	1	4,147	4,146	1	800	800	....
115	Bleachers, dyers, and scourers........	51	44	7	51	46	5	14	13	1
116	Bone and ivory workers............							1	1	....
117	Bookbinders............	161	85	76	120	91	38	45	27	18
118	Boot and shoe makers and repairers........	1,231	1,211	10	1,225	1,215	10	519	482	37
119	Bottlers and mineral and soda water makers.......	29	29	....	44	44	....	14	14	....
120	Box makers (paper)............	26	2	24	4	....	4	4	1	3
121	Box makers (wood)............	128	128	....	9	9	....			
122	Brass workers (not otherwise specified) (a).....	25	25	....	13	13	....	9	9	....
123	Brewers and maltsters (a)............	79	79	....	110	110	....	70	70	....
124	Brick and tile makers and terra cotta workers (a).	1,120	1,116	4	932	930	2	433	432	1
125	Britannia workers............									
126	Broom and brush makers............	84	84	....	73	70	3	18	18	....
127	Builders and contractors............	759	759	....	1,046	1,046	....	395	395	....
128	Butchers............	804	804	....	2,091	2,090	1	344	344	....
129	Butter and cheese makers............	25	25	....	15	15	....	8	7	1
130	Button makers............							2	1	1
131	Cabinet makers............	450	450	....	264	264	....	62	62	....
132	Candle, soap, and tallow makers............	33	29	4	18	18	....	3	2	1
133	Carpenters and joiners............	10,694	10,693	1	13,259	13,252	7	2,996	2,992	4
134	Carpet makers (a)............	52	11	41	14	....	14	53	23	30
135	Carriage and wagon makers (not otherwise classified). (a)	507	507	....	238	238	....	54	54	....
136	Charcoal, coke, and lime burners........	234	234	....	80	80	....	33	33	....
137	Chemical works employés (a)............	30	20	10	13	11	2			
138	Clock and watch makers and repairers........	135	135	....	225	225	....	62	62	....
139	Compositors (a)............	296	285	11	487	430	57	90	61	29
140	Confectioners............	232	209	23	396	366	30	51	43	8
141	Coopers............	640	639	1	154	154	....	29	29	....
142	Copper workers............	35	35	....	38	38	....	10	10	....
143	Corset makers............									
144	Cotton mill operatives (a)............	1,774	751	1,023	459	350	109			
145	Distillers and rectifiers (a)............	109	109	....	14	14	....			
146	Door, sash, and blind makers (a)............	35	35	....	6	6	....			
147	Dressmakers............	1,993	4	1,989	2,115	....	2,115	975	2	973
148	Electroplaters............	3	3	....	2	2	....	1	1	....
149	Electrotypers and stereotypers (a)............	11	11	....	9	9	....			
150	Engravers............	32	32	....	22	22	....	10	10	....
151	Fertilizer makers (a)............									
152	Fish curers and packers (a)............				6	6	....			

a See explanatory notes in Table 78.

OCCUPATIONS.

OCCUPATION, CLASSIFIED BY SEX, BY STATES AND TERRITORIES: 1890—Continued.

VERMONT.			VIRGINIA.			WASHINGTON.			WEST VIRGINIA.			WISCONSIN.			WYOMING.			
Total.	Males.	Females.	Total.	Males.	Females.	Total.	Males.	Females.	Total.	Males.	Females.	Total.	Males.	Females.	Total.	Males.	Females.	
1,974	1,943	31	8,666	8,363	303	3,440	3,390	50	3,316	3,245	71	9,839	9,581	258	382	375	7	76
65	65	......	459	457	2	201	200	1	87	86	1	441	439	2	9	9	......	77
77	77	......	669	656	13	178	175	3	136	131	5	576	556	20	23	23	......	78
11	11	......	59	58	1	20	20	......	29	20	......	79	78	1	3	3	......	79
315	313	2	575	575	......	431	429	2	260	259	1	717	715	2	88	88	......	80
58	55	3	134	108	26	56	51	5	137	95	42	505	360	145	9	9	......	81
7	7	......	101	101	......	33	33	......	102	102	......	55	55	......	......	......	......	82
12	12	......	784	778	6	52	52	......	72	72	......	201	195	6	9	8	1	83
41	41	......	1,789	1,789	......	1,012	1,011	1	120	120	......	1,454	1,453	1	14	14	......	84
937	801	136	3,385	2,884	501	1,707	1,551	156	1,170	1,019	151	3,986	3,205	781	112	101	11	85
2,015	2,010	5	13,488	13,436	52	4,161	4,157	4	6,016	6,003	13	8,701	8,688	13	1,617	1,616	1	86
98	31	67	210	110	100	300	153	147	72	42	30	677	218	459	21	11	10	87
69	69	......	303	303	......	144	144	......	295	205	......	364	364	......	26	26	......	88
223	183	40	892	836	56	423	367	56	428	396	32	1,360	1,196	164	163	155	8	89
31	31	......	97	97	......	114	114	......	32	32	......	151	150	1	8	8	......	90
46	46	......	150	150	......	38	38	......	50	50	......	135	135	......	5	5	......	91
2	2	......	45	45	......	3	3	......	39	38	1	50	50	......	3	3	......	92
8	6	2	18	16	2	23	23	......	7	7	......	78	40	38	1	1	......	93
29,702	24,602	5,100	77,614	63,305	14,309	36,982	34,579	2,403	30,842	27,387	3,455	129,295	108,490	20,805	4,634	4,314	320	94
15	15	......	20	20	......				2	2	......	151	151	......				95
35	35	......	87	87	......	11	11	......	32	32	......	133	133	......	1	1	......	96
2	2	......	7	7	......	4	4	......	5	5	......	40	40	......				97
27	27	......	164	164	......	13	13	......	50	50	......	140	140	......	3	3	......	98
2	2	......	7	7	......	1	1	......	3	3	......	30	30	......	1	1	......	99
13	......	13	4	......	4	7	......	7	6	......	6	140	......	146	1	......	1	100
			2	2	......				3	3	......	17	17	......				101
41	41	......	108	108	......	24	24	......	111	111	......	231	231	......	10	10	......	102
15	15	......	32	32	......	5	5	......	6	6	......	20	20	......				103
7	......	7	2	......	2	5	......	5	4	......	4	68	......	68				104
9	9	......	36	36	......	8	8	......	9	9	......	58	58	......	2	2	......	105
15	15	......	30	30	......	29	29	......	11	11	......	93	93	......	2	2	......	106
28	26	2	69	68	1	23	23	......	25	25	......	110	108	2	7	6	1	107
3	1	2	15	14	1	4	3	1	5	5	......	57	41	16	3	3	......	108
11	11	......	20	20	......	2	2	......	13	13	......	112	111	1	4	4	......	109
181	177	4	380	380	......	80	85	4	182	170	3	1,141	1,104	37	8	8	......	110
1	......	1	2	......	2							15	15	......				111
133	128	5	480	466	14	420	412	8	194	189	5	1,144	1,075	69	53	52	1	112
33	33	......	145	86	59	6	5	1	25	23	2	175	168	7				113
1,577	1,577	......	4,514	4,514	......	1,622	1,622	......	2,311	2,311	......	6,099	6,097	2	428	427	1	114
56	40	16	74	60	14	23	21	2	29	27	2	111	102	9	9	9	......	115
												4	4	......				116
46	21	25	134	75	59	78	58	20	24	12	12	329	206	123	10	7	3	117
614	550	64	2,378	2,322	56	479	477	2	867	862	5	4,418	3,804	614	94	93	1	118
10	9	1	38	37	1	51	50	1	19	19	......	350	212	138	2	2	......	119
50	28	22	303	21	282				21	......	21	125	9	116				120
120	112	8	200	181	19	8	8	......	18	18	......	372	325	47				121
31	31	......	10	10	......	12	12	......	4	4	......	301	270	31	3	3	......	122
5	5	......	38	38	......	169	168	1	68	68	......	1,887	1,849	38	22	22	......	123
175	175	......	1,467	1,464	3	1,175	1,175	......	503	503	......	1,254	1,253	1	67	67	......	124
																		125
23	22	1	51	50	1	20	20	......	31	27	4	161	160	4				126
113	113	......	587	586	1	1,077	1,077	......	324	323	1	881	881	......	91	91	......	127
339	339	......	827	826	1	899	897	2	478	478	......	2,955	2,955	......	144	143	1	128
198	192	6	54	49	5	20	20	......	14	14	......	1,736	1,690	46	1	1	......	129
																		130
1	1	......																131
126	126	......	867	867	......	253	252	1	195	195	......	765	763	2	19	19	......	132
9	9	......	12	12	......	12	11	1	5	5	......	95	80	15	2	2	......	133
3,912	3,912	......	13,131	13,126	5	10,783	10,770	4	5,073	5,072	1	17,164	17,163	1	1,061	1,060	1	134
31	10	21	18	8	10	5	......	5	29	11	18	264	144	120				134
120	120	......	501	500	1	160	160	......	258	258	......	1,618	1,604	14	18	18	......	135
58	58	......	93	93	......	62	62	......	464	463	1	121	121	......	3	3	......	136
13	8	5	20	19	1				5	5	......	63	40	23				137
62	61	1	151	151	......	129	128	1	53	53	......	339	336	3	16	16	......	138
165	78	87	222	217	5	344	300	44	94	72	22	628	437	191	24	21	3	139
32	26	6	243	223	20	147	130	17	77	74	3	494	379	115	14	14	......	140
254	254	......	935	935	......	165	165	......	513	513	......	1,914	1,913	1	5	5	......	141
7	7	......	35	35	......	9	9	......	12	12	......	52	52	......	8	8	......	142
												5	......	5				143
609	305	304	1,605	778	827	1	1	......				431	186	245				144
									25	25	......	32	32	......				145
1	1	......	80	80	......	4	4	......				293	290	3				146
50	50	......	38	38	......	78	78	......										147
1,735	......	1,735	2,274	......	2,274	1,473	11	1,462	1,114	......	1,114	8,727	9	8,718	196	......	196	147
22	22	......	3	3	......	7	7	......	2	2	......	31	31	......	1	1	......	148
												13	13	......				149
6	5	1	23	23	......	14	14	......	16	16	......	94	93	1	6	6	......	150
1	1	......	20	20	......				1	1	......	1	1	......				151
			12	12	......	61	61	......				4	4	......				152

340

STATISTICS OF POPULATION.

TABLE 79.—TOTAL PERSONS 10 YEARS OF AGE AND OVER ENGAGED IN EACH SPECIFIED

	OCCUPATIONS.	TENNESSEE.			TEXAS.			UTAH.		
		Total.	Males.	Females.	Total.	Males.	Females.	Total.	Males.	Females.
	Manufacturing and mechanical industries—Cont'd.									
153	Gas works employés (a)	70	70	....	24	24	....	3	3	....
154	Glass workers	13	13	....	6	6	....	10	10	....
155	Glove makers	....	....	....	....	....	....	4	1	3
156	Gold and silver workers	72	72	....	88	88	....	12	12	....
157	Gunsmiths, locksmiths, and bell hangers	81	81	....	147	147	....	28	28	....
158	Hair workers	2	....	2	2	....	2	....	....	....
159	Harness and saddle makers and repairers	672	670	2	1,166	1,162	4	204	204	....
160	Hat and cap makers	9	7	2	10	10	....	7	6	1
161	Hosiery and knitting mill operatives (a)	30	1	29	19	2	17	23	2	21
162	Iron and steel workers (a)	1,339	1,335	4	253	249	4	64	64	....
163	Lace and embroidery makers	7	....	7	18	....	18	6	....	6
164	Lead and zinc workers	7	7	....	....	....	....			
165	Leather curriers, dressers, finishers, and tanners.	438	438	....	81	81	....	31	31	....
166	Machinists	1,495	1,495	....	1,891	1,891	....	393	392	1
167	Manufacturers and officials of manufacturing companies.	1,131	1,128	3	879	874	5	169	169	....
168	Marble and stone cutters	896	895	1	588	588	....	238	238	....
169	Masons (brick and stone)	2,594	2,594	....	2,386	2,385	1	972	972	....
170	Meat and fruit packers, canners, and preservers. (a)	22	16	6	20	16	4			
171	Mechanics (not otherwise specified)	735	734	1	668	668	....	36	36	....
172	Metal workers (not otherwise specified)	35	35	....	89	89	....	90	89	1
173	Mill and factory operatives (not specified) (a)	716	468	248	808	830	68	208	152	56
174	Millers (flour and grist)	1,933	1,929	4	1,026	1,023	3	233	232	1
175	Milliners	764	....	764	1,101	....	1,101	212	....	212
176	Model and pattern makers	60	60	....	44	44	....	10	10	....
177	Molders	713	713	....	237	237	....	89	89	....
178	Musical instrument makers (not otherwise specified). (a)	....	....	....	2	2	....	1	1	....
179	Nail and tack makers (a)	26	26	....	2	2	....			
180	Oil well employés	....	....	....	....	....	....	2	2	....
181	Oil works employés	83	82	1	124	124	....	2	2	....
182	Painters, glaziers, and varnishers	2,262	2,257	5	2,906	2,898	8	625	625	....
183	Paper hangers	119	118	1	77	77	....	35	35	....
184	Paper mill operatives	21	13	8	....	....	....			
185	Photographers	243	233	10	454	431	23	81	77	4
186	Piano and organ makers and tuners (a)	41	41	....	57	57	....	3	3	....
187	Plasterers	678	678	....	336	336	....	222	222	....
188	Plumbers and gas and steam fitters	415	415	....	347	347	....	168	168	....
189	Potters	87	87	....	60	60	....	8	8	....
190	Powder and cartridge makers	5	5	....	....	....	....			
191	Printers, lithographers, and pressmen (a)	1,016	975	41	1,505	1,445	60	262	251	11
192	Print works operatives (a)	....	....	....	....	....	....	2	2	....
193	Publishers of books, maps, and newspapers	52	52	....	97	97	....	14	14	....
194	Roofers and slaters	35	35	....	30	30	....	10	10	....
195	Rope and cordage makers	3	1	2	12	12	....	3	3	....
196	Rubber factory operatives	....	....	....	....	....	....			
197	Sail, awning, and tent makers	1	1	....	17	17	....	15	14	1
198	Salt works employés	....	....	....	3	3	....	6	6	....
199	Saw and planing mill employés (a)	3,443	3,439	4	4,257	4,256	1	151	151	....
200	Seamstresses (a)	3,485	6	3,479	2,975	....	2,975	202	3	199
201	Sewing machine makers (not otherwise classified). (a)	2	2	....	3	3	....			
202	Sewing machine operators (a)	6	1	5	4	....	4	4	....	4
203	Ship and boat builders	36	36	....	87	87	....	8	8	....
204	Shirt, collar, and cuff makers (a)	79	52	27	31	19	12	4	3	1
205	Silk mill operatives (a)	....	....	....	....	....	....	16	10	6
206	Starch makers	....	....	....	....	....	....			
207	Steam boiler makers	172	172	....	245	245	....	57	57	....
208	Stove, furnace, and grate makers (a)	153	153	....	3	3	....	1	1	....
209	Straw workers	....	....	....	1	1	....	7	....	7
210	Sugar makers and refiners	....	....	....	3	3	....			
211	Tailors and tailoresses (a)	739	550	189	881	812	69	348	308	40
212	Tinners and tinware makers	802	796	6	825	821	4	145	145	....
213	Tobacco and cigar factory operatives	694	539	155	184	180	4	63	60	3
214	Tool and cutlery makers (not otherwise classified). (a)	52	52	....	90	90	....	4	3	1
215	Trunk, valise, leather-case, and pocket-book makers.	82	82	....	24	24	....	8	8	....
216	Umbrella and parasol makers	....	....	....	....	....	....	1	1	....
217	Upholsterers	162	151	11	171	166	5	34	33	1
218	Well borers	68	68	....	210	210	....	24	24	....
219	Wheelwrights	111	111	....	294	294	....	37	37	....
220	Whitewashers	106	106	....	21	21	....	13	13	....
221	Wire workers	28	28	....	16	16	....	2	2	....
222	Wood workers (not otherwise specified)	840	824	16	275	270	5	65	63	2
223	Woolen mill operatives (a)	567	289	278	105	71	34	101	69	32
224	Other persons in manufacturing and mechanical industries.	690	603	87	670	628	42	107	103	4

a See explanatory notes in Table 78.

OCCUPATIONS.

OCCUPATION, CLASSIFIED BY SEX, BY STATES AND TERRITORIES: 1890—Continued.

| Vermont | | | Virginia | | | Washington | | | West Virginia | | | Wisconsin | | | Wyoming | | | |
Total	Males	Females	Total	Males	Females	Total	Males	Females	Total	Males	Females	Total	Males	Females	Total	Males	Females	
9	9		52	52		23	23		28	28		85	85					153
10	10		7	7		7	7		865	776	89	151	146	5	2	2		154
2		2	47	12	35	3	2	1	9	5	4	85	40	45				155
22	22		80	80		36	36		58	58		82	82		4	4		156
14	14		65	65		55	55		40	40		152	149	3	9	9		157
8		8	4	1	3							19	5	14				158
286	286		495	495		302	302		318	318		1,888	1,383	5	72	72		159
8	6	2	36	21	15	9	8	1	11	11		140	62	78	1	1		160
454	178	276	148	62	86	1		1	13	3	10	843	113	730				161
416	410	6	1,848	1,833	15	195	195		1,861	1,853	8	1,955	1,943	12	181	181		162
4		4	13		13	8		8				35		35	3		3	163
3	3		124	123	1							96	89	7				164
107	107		560	559	1	39	39		355	355		1,954	1,940	14	6	6		165
1,076	1,076		1,973	1,973		975	974	1	866	866		3,794	3,794		534	534		166
974	973	1	1,230	1,225	5	612	612		479	470		2,473	2,466	7	82	81	1	167
2,979	2,977	2	789	789		854	854		497	497		1,052	1,052		32	32		168
809	809		2,709	2,708	1	1,697	1,697		1,212	1,212		4,742	4,742		312	312		169
1	1		18	10	8	82	81	1	8	8		50	39	11				170
135	135		472	472		99	99		87	87		209	209		29	29		171
43	43		89	87	2	26	26		115	111	4	71	67	4	1	1		172
506	384	122	1,010	615	395	187	182	5	163	109	54	1,764	1,410	354	7	5	2	173
346	346		2,295	2,293	2	349	348	1	960	960		1,938	1,937	1	24	24		174
437		437	580		580	342	5	337	406		406	1,881	5	1,876	48		48	175
24	24		94	92	2	54	54		31	31		253	253		1	1		176
809	809		686	686		292	292		186	186		1,870	1,870		11	11		177
1	1								1	1		4	4					178
29	28	1	71	71					329	328	1	22	19	3				179
			1	1					292	292								180
2	2		14	14					174	174		15	15		5	5		181
1,836	1,831	5	2,239	2,235	4	1,899	1,897	2	945	936	9	5,421	5,381	40	203	203		182
20	20		116	116		94	94		21	20	1	146	146		9	9		183
427	353	74	68	48	20	64	63	1	83	70	13	1,175	819	356				184
131	123	8	152	152		232	211	21	122	118	4	692	595	97	22	21	1	185
339	311	28	39	39		24	24		9	9		81	81		4	4		186
12	12		1,008	1,007	1	742	742		800	800		531	530	1	71	71		187
129	129		414	414		676	676		141	141		875	875		43	43		188
19	19		47	45	2	28	28		525	390	135	90	88	2	1	1		189
			5	3	2							15	15					190
228	205	23	882	842	40	807	775	32	338	325	13	1,736	1,631	105	263	259	4	191
19	10	0							11	11		19	19					192
16	16		36	36		60	60		16	16		125	123	2	12	12		193
75	75		28	28		12	12		17	17		59	59					194
1	1		1		1	4	4		1		1	156	57	99				195
												96	33	63				196
8	8		57	55	2	29	28	1				47	33	14				197
			43	43					46	40	2							198
2,270	2,270		3,996	3,987	9	3,660	3,656	4	1,892	1,890	2	13,325	13,217	108	50	50		199
542		542	5,010	7	5,003	814		814	1,058		1,058	8,268	36	8,232	48		48	200
8	3											3	3					201
28	1	27	6		6	6		6	1		1	54	2	52				202
19	19		547	547		430	430		75	75		427	427		1	1		203
270	20	250	55	18	37	5	4	1	8	6	2	72	31	41				204
4	3	1	158	51	107				1		1	1	1					205
												1		1				206
23	22		356	356		106	106		210	210		497	497		74	74		207
6	6		79	79		11	11		52	52		85	85		2	2		208
7		7										84	31	53				209
8	8											1	1		1	1		210
401	197	204	848	578	270	579	510	69	521	332	189	4,101	2,980	1,181	68	64	4	211
320	319	1	810	807	3	402	402		329	327	2	1,552	1,502	50	42	42		212
84	74	10	9,361	5,882	3,479	219	213	6	630	473	157	2,180	1,906	274	30	30		213
68	68		32	32		60	60		73	72	1	360	352	8	2	2		214
2	2		165	164	1	9	9		8	8		481	461	20				215
			3	3					2	1	1	3	3					216
65	59	6	215	211	4	99	99		36	34	2	589	549	40	13	13		217
			16	16		22	22		51	51		236	236		17	17		218
289	289		773	773		50	50		60	60		188	188		11	11		219
7	6	1	158	158		4	4		10	10		61	61					220
8	8		7	7		8	8		3	3		148	135	13				221
669	639	30	480	462	18	241	240	1	193	193		2,907	2,670	237	20	20		222
1,409	770	639	261	176	85				104	70	34	709	331	378	6	6		223
279	246	33	1,547	1,173	374	353	348	5	277	248	29	1,483	1,335	148	20	20		224

342   STATISTICS OF POPULATION.

TABLE 80.—TOTAL PERSONS 10 YEARS OF AGE AND OVER ENGAGED IN GAINFUL OCCUPATIONS AND IN EACH CLASS OF OCCUPATIONS, CLASSIFIED BY GENERAL NATIVITY AND COLOR, BY STATES AND TERRITORIES: 1890.

ALL OCCUPATIONS.

STATES AND TERRITORIES.	Total white.	NATIVE WHITE.			Foreign white.	Total colored. (a)	Persons of negro descent.
		Total.	Native parents.	Foreign parents.			
The United States	19,542,188	14,437,431	10,895,023	3,542,408	5,104,757	3,193,473	3,073,164
North Atlantic division	6,827,709	4,628,589	3,110,562	1,518,027	2,199,120	143,751	136,143
Maine	256,192	213,295	189,847	23,448	42,897	904	551
New Hampshire	164,288	120,701	105,118	15,583	43,587	415	349
Vermont	128,289	104,899	83,537	21,362	23,390	482	401
Massachusetts	970,255	589,195	378,888	210,307	381,060	12,189	11,028
Rhode Island	152,017	89,036	53,672	35,964	62,981	3,861	3,699
Connecticut	310,614	204,996	135,715	69,281	105,618	6,400	6,028
New York	2,395,422	1,517,056	869,252	647,804	878,366	40,303	36,936
New Jersey	546,156	362,665	239,488	123,177	183,491	24,582	23,831
Pennsylvania	1,904,476	1,426,146	1,055,045	371,101	478,330	54,615	53,239
South Atlantic division	1,772,368	1,658,553	1,540,464	118,089	113,815	1,345,688	1,344,140
Delaware	51,897	44,475	37,758	6,717	7,422	12,389	12,350
Maryland	297,227	245,793	186,102	59,691	51,434	96,040	95,811
District of Columbia	61,015	50,771	39,754	11,017	10,244	40,104	40,007
Virginia	310,487	300,296	291,718	8,578	10,191	241,352	241,095
West Virginia	209,669	199,171	184,616	14,555	10,498	14,110	14,101
North Carolina	320,277	318,045	315,578	2,467	2,232	217,080	216,590
South Carolina	151,197	147,418	143,510	3,908	3,779	289,657	289,550
Georgia	299,330	291,835	284,989	6,846	7,495	369,383	369,265
Florida	71,269	60,749	56,439	4,310	10,520	65,558	65,371
North Central division	7,491,829	5,317,726	3,782,479	1,535,247	2,173,603	182,509	175,757
Ohio	1,236,659	996,674	720,477	276,197	239,985	36,127	35,876
Indiana	705,004	626,635	522,581	104,054	78,369	19,054	18,858
Illinois	1,328,813	871,551	580,415	291,136	457,262	24,746	23,983
Michigan	751,199	465,885	311,118	154,767	285,314	8,376	6,394
Wisconsin	574,104	308,012	121,754	186,258	266,092	2,186	1,060
Minnesota	466,553	209,434	102,606	106,828	257,119	2,533	2,102
Iowa	627,407	454,489	325,347	129,142	172,918	4,428	4,345
Missouri	823,285	688,245	544,274	143,971	135,040	61,094	60,655
North Dakota	67,512	24,494	13,728	10,766	43,018	259	169
South Dakota	113,432	64,919	42,326	22,593	48,513	661	327
Nebraska	362,511	251,544	197,154	54,390	110,967	5,549	4,699
Kansas	434,850	355,844	300,699	55,145	79,006	17,496	17,289
South Central division	2,231,058	2,048,201	1,888,355	159,846	182,857	1,404,756	1,401,944
Kentucky	482,602	449,877	401,853	48,024	32,725	107,722	107,666
Tennessee	387,896	375,822	364,604	11,218	12,074	165,857	165,734
Alabama	247,993	239,126	231,710	7,416	8,867	203,609	203,406
Mississippi	157,955	152,747	146,993	5,754	5,208	304,784	303,637
Louisiana	179,324	150,832	114,917	35,915	28,492	243,750	243,157
Texas	525,393	440,460	397,738	42,722	84,933	170,815	170,085
Oklahoma	19,793	18,100	16,597	1,503	1,693	1,113	1,083
Arkansas	230,102	221,237	213,943	7,294	8,805	117,106	116,976
Western division	1,219,724	784,362	573,163	211,199	435,362	116,769	15,175
Montana	68,528	38,580	27,078	11,502	29,948	3,095	1,111
Wyoming	29,527	19,733	14,373	5,360	9,794	1,103	638
Colorado	186,937	131,450	104,748	26,702	55,487	5,006	3,583
New Mexico	49,744	42,691	38,724	3,967	7,053	4,407	1,044
Arizona	23,634	13,536	10,051	3,485	10,098	2,782	1,102
Utah	65,650	38,045	20,041	18,004	27,005	1,251	349
Nevada	19,217	10,579	6,889	3,690	8,638	4,198	152
Idaho	33,206	22,076	16,060	6,016	10,530	1,966	104
Washington	159,297	99,281	77,260	22,021	60,016	5,399	1,055
Oregon	116,850	85,593	71,710	13,883	31,257	9,931	635
California	467,134	281,598	185,629	95,969	185,536	77,631	5,342

a Persons of negro descent, Chinese, Japanese, and civilized Indians.

OCCUPATIONS.

343

TABLE 80.—TOTAL PERSONS 10 YEARS OF AGE AND OVER ENGAGED IN GAINFUL OCCUPATIONS AND IN EACH CLASS OF OCCUPATIONS, CLASSIFIED BY GENERAL NATIVITY AND COLOR, BY STATES AND TERRITORIES: 1890—Cont'd.

AGRICULTURE, FISHERIES, AND MINING.

STATES AND TERRITORIES.	Total white.	NATIVE WHITE.			Foreign white.	Total colored. (a)	Persons of negro descent.
		Total.	Native parents.	Foreign parents.			
The United States	7,222,925	5,917,024	5,122,613	794,411	1,305,901	1,790,411	1,757,403
North Atlantic division	1,251,574	1,004,699	850,362	154,337	246,875	14,376	13,916
Maine	86,104	78,891	72,937	5,954	7,213	193	106
New Hampshire	42,920	38,721	37,054	1,667	4,199	62	60
Vermont	56,061	48,120	41,087	7,033	7,941	122	113
Massachusetts	80,440	55,605	48,448	7,157	24,835	660	635
Rhode Island	12,317	9,362	8,651	731	2,935	289	272
Connecticut	47,759	36,673	32,688	3,985	11,086	917	833
New York	406,988	330,080	265,518	64,562	76,908	3,144	3,055
New Jersey	70,673	56,923	50,179	6,744	13,750	4,216	4,195
Pennsylvania	448,312	350,304	293,800	56,504	98,008	4,774	4,629
South Atlantic division	948,270	930,435	913,153	17,302	17,824	766,039	765,441
Delaware	14,510	13,826	13,298	528	684	4,192	4,192
Maryland	75,137	68,466	61,919	6,547	6,671	30,259	30,257
District of Columbia	1,317	983	808	175	334	569	563
Virginia	167,751	165,433	163,850	1,583	2,318	103,994	103,913
West Virginia	125,047	121,541	117,231	4,310	3,506	4,840	4,840
North Carolina	233,648	233,008	231,955	1,053	640	140,711	140,287
South Carolina	104,489	103,866	102,963	903	617	223,534	223,496
Georgia	191,525	190,725	189,542	1,183	800	226,603	226,570
Florida	34,861	82,607	31,587	1,020	2,254	31,337	31,318
North Central division	3,199,057	2,361,700	1,836,660	525,040	837,357	40,046	27,480
Ohio	422,683	371,406	306,862	64,544	51,277	6,336	6,307
Indiana	327,208	299,972	263,594	36,378	27,236	3,361	3,310
Illinois	452,017	348,312	266,610	81,702	103,705	4,471	4,457
Michigan	306,130	198,472	143,195	55,277	107,658	2,371	1,592
Wisconsin	241,263	122,180	50,377	71,899	119,077	836	172
Minnesota	195,189	75,040	32,604	42,362	120,143	233	74
Iowa	329,398	229,576	166,586	62,990	99,822	992	934
Missouri	388,572	353,767	316,778	36,980	34,805	16,003	16,079
North Dakota	43,911	13,448	7,409	6,039	30,463	44	35
South Dakota	70,677	36,267	23,359	12,908	34,410	162	34
Nebraska	169,759	110,713	86,349	24,364	59,046	815	245
Kansas	252,260	202,535	172,877	29,658	49,715	4,822	4,281
South Central division	1,407,291	1,346,285	1,305,415	40,870	61,006	939,013	938,407
Kentucky	286,610	280,401	272,747	7,654	6,209	39,475	39,464
Tennessee	252,023	249,511	246,948	2,563	2,512	84,863	84,824
Alabama	168,258	165,580	163,746	1,834	2,678	212,594	212,485
Mississippi	113,358	112,017	110,248	1,769	1,341	246,691	245,021
Louisiana	79,192	73,793	70,335	3,458	5,399	161,538	161,244
Texas	325,563	287,234	267,767	19,467	38,329	106,755	106,587
Oklahoma	13,274	12,308	11,447	861	966	654	652
Arkansas	169,013	165,441	162,177	3,264	3,572	87,343	87,290
Western division	410,724	273,885	217,023	56,862	142,839	30,937	2,099
Montana	25,229	14,102	10,417	3,685	11,127	551	41
Wyoming	10,758	6,924	5,321	1,603	3,834	443	141
Colorado	58,951	40,327	33,210	7,117	18,624	292	184
New Mexico	23,707	20,902	19,529	1,373	2,805	2,904	166
Arizona	10,002	6,203	4,835	1,368	3,799	526	29
Utah	23,922	13,799	6,682	7,117	10,123	161	21
Nevada	9,180	4,594	3,126	1,468	4,586	1,356	42
Idaho	17,822	12,506	9,475	3,031	5,316	992	17
Washington	46,676	30,044	24,556	5,488	16,632	1,267	252
Oregon	49,503	38,055	33,265	4,790	11,448	1,477	103
California	140,974	86,429	66,607	19,822	54,545	20,063	1,093

a Persons of negro descent, Chinese, Japanese, and civilized Indians.

344   STATISTICS OF POPULATION.

TABLE 80.—TOTAL PERSONS 10 YEARS OF AGE AND OVER ENGAGED IN GAINFUL OCCUPATIONS AND IN EACH CLASS
OF OCCUPATIONS, CLASSIFIED BY GENERAL NATIVITY AND COLOR, BY STATES AND TERRITORIES: 1890—Cont'd.

PROFESSIONAL SERVICE.

| STATES AND TERRITORIES. | Total white. | NATIVE WHITE. | | | Foreign white. | Total colored. (a) | Persons of negro descent. |
		Total.	Native parents.	Foreign parents.			
The United States	909,186	795,073	640,785	154,288	114,113	35,147	33,994
North Atlantic division	297,157	254,425	197,107	57,318	42,732	2,311	2,219
Maine	12,349	11,707	10,901	806	642	15	10
New Hampshire	6,826	6,399	5,954	405	427	5	5
Vermont	6,271	5,831	5,147	684	440	5	3
Massachusetts	43,017	37,476	30,608	6,868	5,541	230	219
Rhode Island	5,389	4,691	3,875	816	698	57	56
Connecticut	12,409	11,182	9,241	1,941	1,227	76	71
New York	114,624	92,318	64,141	28,177	22,306	752	706
New Jersey	21,992	18,332	14,068	4,264	3,660	371	369
Pennsylvania	74,280	66,489	53,132	13,357	7,791	800	780
South Atlantic division	79,464	74,985	69,193	5,792	4,470	12,897	12,872
Delaware	2,081	1,970	1,708	262	111	132	129
Maryland	13,660	12,211	9,976	2,235	1,449	910	914
District of Columbia	6,581	5,759	4,873	886	822	727	725
Virginia	15,123	14,540	14,050	490	583	2,572	2,566
West Virginia	8,432	8,185	7,569	616	247	230	229
North Carolina	10,106	9,925	9,726	199	181	2,190	2,181
South Carolina	6,143	5,961	5,656	305	182	2,050	2,048
Georgia	12,888	12,495	12,014	481	393	3,081	3,078
Florida	4,450	3,939	3,621	318	511	999	999
North Central division	367,199	318,845	246,625	72,220	48,354	4,148	4,012
Ohio	61,038	55,506	44,766	10,740	5,532	875	863
Indiana	34,045	31,983	27,847	4,136	2,062	474	456
Illinois	62,512	52,418	39,308	13,110	10,094	610	602
Michigan	33,291	26,681	19,402	7,279	6,610	199	151
Wisconsin	24,227	19,408	10,422	8,986	4,810	51	38
Minnesota	22,692	17,488	11,297	6,191	5,204	75	70
Iowa	37,670	34,171	25,757	8,414	3,499	92	80
Missouri	38,225	34,014	28,559	5,455	4,211	1,240	1,234
North Dakota	3,049	2,043	1,383	660	1,006	9	7
South Dakota	5,982	5,049	3,760	1,289	933	13	8
Nebraska	19,459	17,072	14,128	2,944	2,387	80	70
Kansas	25,009	23,012	19,996	3,016	1,997	430	426
South Central division	99,687	93,555	86,652	6,903	6,182	14,576	14,549
Kentucky	20,319	19,231	17,579	1,652	1,088	1,831	1,826
Tennessee	17,119	16,565	15,880	685	554	2,331	2,328
Alabama	9,990	9,601	9,180	421	880	1,962	1,961
Mississippi	8,113	7,902	7,561	341	211	2,749	2,745
Louisiana	8,417	7,217	5,561	1,656	1,200	1,699	1,696
Texas	25,523	23,233	21,557	1,676	2,290	2,600	2,595
Oklahoma	991	937	859	78	54	26	25
Arkansas	9,215	8,869	8,475	394	346	1,468	1,463
Western division	65,679	53,263	41,208	12,055	12,416	1,215	342
Montana	2,863	2,284	1,800	484	579	37	29
Wyoming	1,141	960	740	211	181	62	59
Colorado	9,731	8,282	6,904	1,378	1,449	99	88
New Mexico	1,692	1,392	1,208	184	300	20	10
Arizona	1,088	856	695	161	232	7	3
Utah	2,836	2,106	1,381	725	730	7	1
Nevada	1,020	846	577	269	174	40	....
Idaho	1,291	1,095	855	240	196	4	....
Washington	8,189	6,670	5,479	1,191	1,519	25	17
Oregon	6,776	5,823	4,978	845	953	150	28
California	29,052	22,949	16,582	6,367	6,103	764	107

a Persons of negro descent, Chinese, Japanese, and civilized Indians.

OCCUPATIONS. 345

TABLE 80.—TOTAL PERSONS 10 YEARS OF AGE AND OVER ENGAGED IN GAINFUL OCCUPATIONS AND IN EACH CLASS OF OCCUPATIONS, CLASSIFIED BY GENERAL NATIVITY AND COLOR, BY STATES AND TERRITORIES: 1890—Cont'd.

DOMESTIC AND PERSONAL SERVICE.

STATES AND TERRITORIES.	Total white.	NATIVE WHITE.			Foreign white.	Total colored. (a)	Persons of negro descent.
		Total.	Native parents.	Foreign parents.			
The United States	3,334,184	1,959,117	1,342,028	617,089	1,375,067	1,026,393	963,080
North Atlantic division	1,425,735	733,382	473,655	259,727	692,353	97,778	91,420
Maine	40,649	29,193	24,639	4,554	11,456	442	302
New Hampshire	23,485	14,507	12,187	2,320	8,978	220	105
Vermont	21,776	16,203	11,353	4,850	5,573	283	245
Massachusetts	177,720	66,760	39,946	26,814	110,960	8,218	7,210
Rhode Island	26,463	10,183	6,064	4,119	16,280	2,443	2,330
Connecticut	56,070	24,677	14,612	10,065	31,393	4,003	3,700
New York	525,938	237,697	124,065	113,632	288,241	28,499	25,596
New Jersey	113,831	53,785	33,999	19,786	60,046	15,691	15,057
Pennsylvania	439,803	280,377	206,790	73,587	159,426	37,973	36,809
South Atlantic division	177,583	149,611	131,904	17,707	27,972	414,229	413,467
Delaware	9,677	6,881	5,626	1,255	2,796	6,545	6,509
Maryland	50,654	36,075	26,283	9,792	14,579	51,647	51,431
District of Columbia	10,213	6,841	5,219	1,622	3,372	29,510	29,421
Virginia	30,767	28,973	27,819	1,154	1,794	95,492	95,383
West Virginia	25,431	23,461	21,226	2,235	1,970	5,993	5,977
North Carolina	19,225	18,998	18,828	170	227	52,039	51,986
South Carolina	6,956	6,356	6,046	310	600	44,816	44,775
Georgia	16,455	15,205	14,624	581	1,250	104,307	104,330
Florida	8,205	6,821	6,233	588	1,384	23,790	23,655
North Central division	1,270,239	774,767	504,991	269,776	495,472	108,912	105,356
Ohio	233,319	165,100	113,824	51,276	68,219	21,970	21,774
Indiana	115,206	98,278	80,358	17,920	16,928	11,912	11,709
Illinois	252,480	129,596	79,483	50,113	122,893	15,016	14,927
Michigan	147,756	78,179	47,597	30,582	69,577	4,454	3,507
Wisconsin	110,978	53,289	17,481	35,808	57,689	1,020	642
Minnesota	92,851	33,583	13,310	20,273	59,208	1,842	1,601
Iowa	83,223	55,850	36,902	18,948	27,373	2,700	2,638
Missouri	112,390	80,965	55,835	25,130	31,425	34,900	34,517
North Dakota	9,092	3,233	1,408	1,825	5,859	190	112
South Dakota	13,590	7,591	4,299	3,292	5,999	321	150
Nebraska	55,409	34,053	25,562	8,491	21,356	3,863	3,621
Kansas	43,936	35,050	28,932	6,118	8,886	10,109	9,975
South Central division	192,117	153,621	127,432	26,189	38,496	343,592	342,474
Kentucky	46,656	39,736	32,401	7,335	6,920	51,613	51,577
Tennessee	29,321	27,209	25,071	1,232	2,118	56,018	55,963
Alabama	14,582	13,477	12,663	814	1,105	58,898	58,819
Mississippi	6,745	6,065	5,508	557	680	43,029	42,939
Louisiana	26,912	19,774	11,259	8,515	7,138	63,156	62,911
Texas	51,953	32,927	26,192	6,735	19,026	48,716	48,202
Oklahoma	1,360	1,164	1,015	149	196	358	333
Arkansas	14,588	13,275	12,423	852	1,313	21,804	21,733
Western division	268,510	147,736	104,046	43,690	120,774	61,882	10,363
Montana	17,688	8,655	5,585	3,070	9,033	2,648	937
Wyoming	7,816	5,001	3,408	1,593	2,815	518	384
Colorado	39,244	24,700	19,142	5,558	14,544	3,708	2,444
New Mexico	15,493	13,483	12,327	1,156	2,010	1,359	801
Arizona	6,298	2,625	1,705	920	3,673	2,024	1,101
Utah	14,667	8,335	4,066	4,269	6,332	868	296
Nevada	3,207	1,540	922	618	1,667	2,243	85
Idaho	5,973	3,730	2,525	1,205	2,243	745	78
Washington	30,006	20,187	14,935	5,252	18,819	3,285	615
Oregon	20,438	13,011	10,516	2,495	7,427	6,104	409
California	98,680	46,469	28,915	17,554	52,211	38,380	3,213

a Persons of negro descent, Chinese, Japanese, and civilized Indians.

346

STATISTICS OF POPULATION.

TABLE 80.—TOTAL PERSONS 10 YEARS OF AGE AND OVER ENGAGED IN GAINFUL OCCUPATIONS AND IN EACH CLASS OF OCCUPATIONS, CLASSIFIED BY GENERAL NATIVITY AND COLOR, BY STATES AND TERRITORIES: 1890—Cont'd.

TRADE AND TRANSPORTATION.

STATES AND TERRITORIES.	Total white.	NATIVE WHITE.			Foreign white.	Total colored. (a)	Persons of negro descent.
		Total.	Native parents.	Foreign parents.			
The United States	3,169,624	2,457,066	1,722,462	734,604	712,558	156,498	145,717
North Atlantic division	1,301,982	984,768	642,233	342,535	317,214	14,797	14,488
Maine	37,219	32,935	29,393	3,542	4,284	72	70
New Hampshire	19,747	16,175	14,253	1,922	3,572	24	24
Vermont	14,518	12,323	9,844	2,479	2,195	83	82
Massachusetts	195,013	148,626	105,204	43,422	46,387	1,500	1,436
Rhode Island	26,811	20,405	14,247	6,158	6,406	561	549
Connecticut	48,728	38,517	27,431	11,086	10,211	655	641
New York	523,108	365,116	194,735	170,381	157,992	4,456	4,284
New Jersey	117,915	90,513	61,576	28,937	27,402	2,157	2,136
Pennsylvania	318,923	260,158	185,550	74,608	58,765	5,339	5,315
South Atlantic division	241,780	218,340	187,945	30,395	23,440	66,971	66,931
Delaware	8,393	7,514	6,466	1,048	879	652	652
Maryland	61,291	52,518	37,767	14,751	8,773	7,688	7,682
District of Columbia	23,921	21,285	17,351	3,934	2,636	4,970	4,969
Virginia	42,610	39,926	37,472	2,454	2,684	15,916	15,907
West Virginia	20,884	18,979	16,327	2,652	1,905	2,089	2,088
North Carolina	21,130	20,507	19,994	513	623	7,669	7,668
South Carolina	14,684	13,262	11,884	1,378	1,422	7,051	7,043
Georgia	37,997	35,299	32,653	2,646	2,698	16,773	16,764
Florida	10,870	9,050	8,031	1,019	1,820	4,163	4,158
North Central division	1,136,828	869,239	591,405	277,834	267,589	14,311	14,122
Ohio	192,510	159,342	106,677	52,665	33,168	3,063	3,006
Indiana	90,892	80,576	64,089	16,487	10,316	1,452	1,448
Illinois	244,634	170,910	104,907	66,003	73,724	2,070	2,035
Michigan	102,767	69,717	44,738	24,979	33,050	509	454
Wisconsin	68,512	45,524	20,310	25,214	22,988	108	75
Minnesota	72,225	45,569	26,789	18,780	26,656	231	221
Iowa	87,806	70,403	52,050	18,353	17,403	291	290
Missouri	135,119	111,435	78,669	32,766	23,684	4,927	4,905
North Dakota	6,668	3,767	2,374	1,393	2,901	11	10
South Dakota	12,712	9,258	6,325	2,933	3,454	138	122
Nebraska	62,548	50,318	40,592	9,726	12,230	385	337
Kansas	60,435	52,420	43,885	8,535	8,015	1,171	1,109
South Central division	266,188	229,719	191,009	38,710	36,469	49,180	49,019
Kentucky	53,696	47,055	37,487	10,168	6,641	7,449	7,448
Tennessee	42,828	39,530	36,227	3,303	3,298	11,078	11,076
Alabama	27,011	24,809	22,509	2,300	2,202	9,288	9,285
Mississippi	16,629	14,913	13,143	1,770	1,716	5,783	5,745
Louisiana	34,385	26,674	15,450	11,224	7,711	6,201	6,173
Texas	70,548	57,059	48,774	8,285	13,489	6,485	6,452
Oklahoma	2,046	1,851	1,643	208	195	29	29
Arkansas	19,045	17,228	15,776	1,452	1,817	2,812	2,811
Western division	222,846	155,000	109,870	45,130	67,846	11,289	1,157
Montana	11,090	7,271	5,183	2,088	3,819	853	46
Wyoming	5,199	3,637	2,608	1,029	1,562	59	34
Colorado	40,092	31,088	24,838	6,250	9,004	446	411
New Mexico	4,909	3,898	3,202	696	1,011	70	40
Arizona	3,556	2,339	1,759	580	1,217	182	13
Utah	10,899	7,496	4,287	3,209	3,403	189	15
Nevada	2,935	1,912	1,224	688	1,023	373	13
Idaho	4,147	2,809	2,020	789	1,338	211	8
Washington	23,855	19,967	15,427	4,540	8,888	411	69
Oregon	18,262	13,861	11,137	2,724	4,401	1,111	43
California	92,902	60,722	38,185	22,537	32,180	7,884	460

a Persons of negro descent, Chinese, Japanese, and civilized Indians.

OCCUPATIONS. 347

TABLE 80.—TOTAL PERSONS 10 YEARS OF AGE AND OVER ENGAGED IN GAINFUL OCCUPATIONS AND IN EACH CLASS OF OCCUPATIONS, CLASSIFIED BY GENERAL NATIVITY AND COLOR, BY STATES AND TERRITORIES: 1890—Cont'd.

MANUFACTURING AND MECHANICAL INDUSTRIES.

STATES AND TERRITORIES.	Total white.	NATIVE WHITE.			Foreign white.	Total colored. (a)	Persons of negro descent.
		Total.	Native parents.	Foreign parents.			
The United States	4,906,269	3,309,151	2,067,135	1,242,016	1,597,118	185,024	172,970
North Atlantic division	2,551,261	1,651,315	947,205	704,110	899,946	14,489	14,105
Maine	79,871	60,569	51,977	8,592	19,302	183	66
New Hampshire	71,310	44,899	35,630	9,269	26,411	98	95
Vermont	29,663	22,422	16,106	6,316	7,241	39	37
Massachusetts	474,065	280,728	154,682	126,046	193,337	1,581	1,558
Rhode Island	81,037	44,975	20,835	24,140	36,062	511	492
Connecticut	145,648	93,947	51,743	42,204	51,701	749	730
New York	824,764	491,845	220,793	271,052	332,919	3,452	3,204
New Jersey	221,745	143,112	79,666	63,446	78,633	2,147	2,127
Pennsylvania	623,158	468,818	315,773	153,045	154,340	5,729	5,706
South Atlantic division	325,262	285,162	238,269	46,893	40,100	85,552	85,429
Delaware	17,236	14,284	10,660	3,624	2,952	868	868
Maryland	96,485	76,523	50,157	26,366	19,962	5,530	5,527
District of Columbia	18,983	15,903	11,503	4,400	3,080	4,328	4,324
Virginia	54,236	51,424	48,527	2,897	2,812	23,378	23,326
West Virginia	29,875	27,005	22,263	4,742	2,870	967	967
North Carolina	36,168	35,607	35,075	532	561	14,477	14,465
South Carolina	18,931	17,973	16,961	1,012	958	12,200	12,188
Georgia	40,465	38,111	36,156	1,955	2,354	18,529	18,523
Florida	12,883	8,332	6,967	1,365	4,551	5,269	5,241
North Central division	1,518,006	993,175	602,798	390,377	524,831	15,092	14,787
Ohio	327,109	245,320	148,348	96,972	81,789	3,878	3,866
Indiana	137,653	115,826	86,693	29,133	21,827	1,855	1,845
Illinois	317,161	170,315	90,107	80,208	146,846	1,979	1,962
Michigan	161,255	92,836	56,186	36,650	68,419	843	637
Wisconsin	129,124	67,605	23,164	44,441	61,519	171	133
Minnesota	83,596	37,748	18,546	19,202	45,848	152	136
Iowa	89,310	64,489	44,052	20,437	24,821	344	344
Missouri	148,979	108,064	64,433	43,631	40,915	3,928	3,920
North Dakota	4,792	2,003	1,154	849	2,789	5	5
South Dakota	10,471	6,754	4,583	2,171	3,717	27	18
Nebraska	55,336	39,388	30,523	8,865	15,948	456	433
Kansas	53,220	42,827	35,009	7,818	10,393	1,454	1,438
South Central division	265,775	225,021	177,847	47,174	40,754	57,545	57,435
Kentucky	75,321	62,854	41,639	21,215	12,467	7,354	7,351
Tennessee	46,605	43,013	39,578	3,435	3,592	11,567	11,546
Alabama	28,152	25,659	23,612	2,047	2,493	10,867	10,856
Mississippi	13,110	11,850	10,533	1,317	1,260	6,527	6,487
Louisiana	30,418	23,374	12,312	11,062	7,044	11,246	11,223
Texas	51,806	40,007	33,448	6,559	11,799	6,259	6,249
Oklahoma	2,122	1,840	1,633	207	282	46	44
Arkansas	18,241	16,424	15,092	1,332	1,817	3,679	3,679
Western division	245,965	154,478	101,016	53,462	91,487	12,346	1,214
Montana	11,658	6,268	4,093	2,175	5,390	106	58
Wyoming	4,613	3,211	2,287	924	1,402	21	20
Colorado	38,919	27,053	20,654	6,399	11,866	461	456
New Mexico	3,943	3,016	2,458	558	927	54	27
Arizona	2,690	1,513	1,057	456	1,177	43	16
Utah	13,326	6,909	3,625	3,284	6,417	26	16
Nevada	2,875	1,687	1,040	647	1,188	186	7
Idaho	3,973	2,536	1,785	751	1,437	14	1
Washington	36,571	22,413	16,863	5,550	14,158	411	102
Oregon	21,871	14,843	11,814	3,029	7,028	1,089	47
California	105,526	65,029	35,340	29,689	40,497	9,935	464

a Persons of negro descent, Chinese, Japanese, and civilized Indians.

		Same House			No		Yes	–	–	–		1	40	–	Foreman
		Same House			No		No	No	No	No	H				
		Same House			No		No	No	No	No	S				
		Same House			No		Yes	–	–	–		1	–	–	Laborer

General

Bender, Thomas. *Toward an Urban Vision: Ideas and Institutions in Nineteenth Century America.* Baltimore: Johns Hopkins University Press, 1982.

Berthoff, Rowland. *An Unsettled People: Social Order and Disorder in American History.* New York: Harper & Row, 1971.

Boyer, Paul. *Urban Masses and Moral Order in America: 1820-1920.* Cambridge, MA: Harvard University Press, 1978.

Brands, H. W. *The Reckless Decade: America in the 1890s.* New York: St. Martin's, 1995.

Calhoun, Charles W., ed. *The Gilded Age: Essays on the Origins of Modern America.* Wilmington, DE: Scholarly Resources, 1996.

Cashman, Sean D. *America and the Gilded Age: From the Death of Lincoln to the Rise of Theodore Roosevelt,* 3d ed. New York: New York University Press, 1993.

Hamilton, Richard F. *America's New Empire: The 1890s and Beyond.* New Brunswick, NJ: Transaction, 2010.

Harris, Neil, ed. *The Land of Contrasts: 1880-1901.* New York: G. Braziller, 1970.

Jones, Howard Mumford. *The Age of Energy: Varieties of American Experience, 1865-1915.* New York: Viking, 1971.

Keller, Morton. *Affairs of State: Public Life in Late Nineteenth-Century America.* Cambridge, MA: Belknap Press of Harvard University Press, 1977.

LaFeber, Walter. *The New Empire: An Interpretation of American Expansion, 1860-1898.* 1963; reprint, Ithaca, NY: Cornell University Press, 1998.

Morgan, H. Wayne, ed. *The Gilded Age,* 2d ed. Syracuse, NY: Syracuse University Press, 1963.

Painter, Nell Irwin. *Standing at Armageddon: The United States, 1877-1919.* New York: Norton, 1987.

Paterson, Thomas, and Stephen G. Rabe, eds. *Imperial Surge: The United States Abroad, the 1890s-Early 1900s.* Lexington, MA: D.C. Heath, 1992.

Schlup, Leonard, and Stephen H. Paschen, eds. *The 1890s in America: Documenting the Maturation of a Nation.* Lewiston, NY: E. Mellen, 2006.

Smith, Susan Harris, and Melanie Dawson, eds. *The American 1890s: A Cultural Reader.* Durham, NC: Duke University Press, 2000.

Trachtenberg, Alan. *The Incorporation of America: Culture and Society in the Gilded Age.* New York: Hill and Wang, 1982.

Wiebe, Robert. *The Search for Order, 1877-1920.* 1967; reprint, Westport, CT: Greenwood, 1980.

African Americans

Curtis, Edward E., IV, and Danielle Brune Sigler, eds. *The New Black Gods: Arthur Huff Fauset and the Study of African American Religions.* Bloomington: Indiana University Press, 2009.

Dickerson, Dennis C. *African Methodism and Its Wesleyan Heritage: Reflections on AME Church History.* Nashville, TN: AMEC Sunday School Union, 2009.

Gatewood, Willard B., Jr. *Black Americans and the White Man's Burden, 1898-1903.* Urbana: University of Illinois Press, 1975.

Gatewood, Willard R. *Aristocrats of Color: The Black Elite, 1880-1920.* 1990; reprint, Fayetteville: University of Arkansas Press, 2000.

Gilmore, Glenda Elizabeth. *Gender and Jim Crow: Women and the Politics of White Supremacy in North Carolina, 1896-1920.* Chapel Hill: University of North Carolina Press, 1996.

Harlan, Louis R. *Booker T. Washington: The Making of a Black Leader, 1856-1901,* vol. 1 of *Booker T. Washington,* 2 vols. New York: Oxford University Press, 1972, 1983.

Hochman, Barbara. *Uncle Tom's Cabin and the Reading Revolution: Race, Literacy, Childhood, and Fiction, 1851-1911.* Amherst: University of Massachusetts Press, 2011.

Jeffrey, Julie Roy. *Abolitionists Remember: Antislavery Autobiographies and the Unfinished Work of Emancipation.* Chapel Hill: University of North Carolina Press, 2008.

Johnson, Berman E. *The Dream Deferred: A Survey of Black America, 1840-1896,* 2d ed. Dubuque, Iowa : Kendall/Hunt, 1996.

Kennedy-Nolle, Sharon. *Writing Reconstruction: Race, Gender, and Citizenship in the Postwar South.* Chapel Hill: University of North Carolina Press, 2015.

Leonard, Elizabeth. *Men of Color to Arms! Black Soldiers, Indian Wars, and the Quest for Equality.* New York: Norton, 2010.

Lewis, David Levering. *W. E. B. Du Bois, 1868-1919: The Biography of a Race,* vol. 1 of *W. E. B. Du Bois,* 2 vols. New York: H. Holt, 1993, 2000.

McCaskill, Barbara, and Caroline Gebhard, eds. *Post-Bellum, Pre-Harlem: African American Literature and Culture, 1877-1919.* New York : New York University Press, 2006.

Meltzer, Milton, ed. *In Their Own Words: A History of the American Negro, 1865-1916,* vol. 3 of *In Their Own Words: A History of the American Negro,* 3 vols. New York: Crowell, 1964-1967.

National Association for the Advancement of Colored People (NAACP). *Thirty Years of Lynching in the United States, 1889-1918.* 1919; reprint, Clark, NJ: Lawbook Exchange, 2012.

Nieman, Donald G., ed. *From Slavery to Sharecropping: White Land and Black Labor in the Rural South, 1865-1900.* New York: Garland, 1994.

Willis, Deborah. *Posing Beauty: African American Images, from the 1890s to the Present.* New York: Norton, 2009.

Zamir, Shamoon. *Dark Voices: W.E.B DuBois and American Thought, 1888-1903.* Chicago: University of Chicago Press, 1995.

Arts

American Art Posters of the 1890s in the Metropolitan Museum of Art, including the Leonard A. Lauder Collection. Catalogue by David W. Kiehl; essays by Phillip Dennis Cate, Nancy Finlay, and David W. Kiehl. New York: Metropolitan Museum of Art, 1987.

Argyle, Ray. *Scott Joplin and the Age of Ragtime.* Jefferson, NC: McFarland, 2009.

Chang, Gordon H., Mark Dean Johnson, et al., eds. *Asian American Art, 1850-1970.* Stanford, CA: Stanford University Press, 2008.

Crawford, Richard. *America's Musical Life: A History.* 2001; reprint, New York: Norton, 2005.

DesRochers, Rick. *The New Humor in the Progressive Era: Americanization and the Vaudeville Comedian.* New York: Palgrave Macmillan, 2014.

Faucett, Bill F. *George Whitefield Chadwick: The Life and Music of the Pride of New England.* Boston: Northeastern University Press, 2012.

Gale, Robert L. *The Gay Nineties in America: A Cultural Dictionary of the 1890s.* Westport, CT: Greenwood, 1992.

Goddu, Joseph. *American Art Posters of the 1890s: November 25, 1989 to January 6, 1990.* New York: Hirschl & Adler Galleries, 1990.

Hills, Patricia. *The Painters' America: Rural and Urban Life, 1810-1910.* New York: Praeger, 1974.

Hohman, Valleri J. *Russian Culture and Theatrical Performance in America, 1891-1933.* New York: Palgrave Macmillan, 2011.

Kimbrough, Sara Dodge. *Drawn from Life: The Story of Four American Artists Whose Friendship and Work Began in Paris during the 1880s.* Jackson: University Press of Mississippi, 1976.

Lasser, Michael. *America's Songs II: Songs from the 1890s to the Post-War Years.* New York: Routledge, 2014.

Miller, Worth Robert. *Populist Cartoons: An Illustrated History of the Third-Party Movement in the 1890s.* Kirksville, MA: Truman State University Press, 2011.

Moon, Krystyn R. *Yellowface: Creating the Chinese in American Popular Music and Performance, 1850s-1920s.* New Brunswick, NJ: Rutgers University Press, 2005.

Mumford, Lewis. *The Brown Decades: A Study of the Arts of America 1865-1895,* 2d rev. ed. New York: Dover, 1955.

Rainey, Sue. *Creating a World on Paper: Harry Fenn's Career in Art.* Amherst: University of Massachusetts Press, 2013.

Scherer, Barrymore Laurence. *A History of American Classical Music.* Naperville, IL: Sourcebooks, 2007.

Slout, William L., ed. *Life upon the Wicked Stage: A Visit to the American Theatre of the 1860s, 1870s, and 1880s, as Seen in the Pages of the New York Clipper.* San Bernardino, CA: Borgo, 1996.

Trachtenberg, Alan. *Brooklyn Bridge: Fact and Symbol,* 2d ed. Chicago: University of Chicago Press, 1979.

Tucker, Amy. *The Illustration of the Master: Henry James and the Magazine Revolution.* Stanford, CA: Stanford University Press, 2010.

Willis, Deborah. *Posing Beauty: African American Images, from the 1890s to the Present.* New York: Norton, 2009.

Economics and Business

Alexander, Benjamin F. *Coxey's Army: Popular Protest in the Gilded Age.* Baltimore: Johns Hopkins University Press, 2015.

Atherton, Lewis. *The Cattle Kings.* 1961; reprint, Greenwood, 1984.

Barber, William J., ed. *The Development of the National Economy: The United States from the Civil War through the 1890s.* London: Pickering & Chatto, 2004.

Bentley, Amy. *Inventing Baby Food: Taste, Health, and the Industrialization of the American Diet.* Oakland: University of California Press, 2014.

Card, David, and Craig Olson. "Bargaining Power, Strike Durations, and Wage Outcomes: An Analysis of Strikes in the 1880s." *Journal of Labor Economics* 13, no. 1 (January 1995): 32-61.

Clanton, Gene. *Congressional Populism and the Crisis of the 1890s.* Lawrence: University Press of Kansas, 1998.

Cochran, Thomas C., and William Miller. *The Age of Enterprise,* rev. ed. New York: Harper, 1961.

Degler, Carl. *The Age of Economic Revolution, 1876-1900,* 2d ed. Glenview, IL: Scott, Foresman, 1977.

Ettinger, Roseann. *Men's Clothing and Fabrics in the 1890s: Price Guide.* Atglen, PA: Schiffer, 1998.

Galambos, Louis. *The Creative Society-and the Price Americans Paid for It.* New York: Cambridge University Press, 2012.

Grant, H. Roger. *Self-Help in the 1890s Depression.* Ames: Iowa State University Press, 1983.

Gressley, Eugene. *Bankers and Cattlemen.* New York: Knopf, 1966.

Greever, William S. *The Bonanza West: The Story of the Western Mining Rushes 1848-1900.* 1963; reprint, Moscow, ID: University of Idaho Press, 1990.

Higgs, Robert. *The Transformation of the American Economy, 1865-1914: An Essay in Interpretation.* New York: Wiley, 1971.

Kirk, Neville. *Comrades and Cousins: Globalization, Workers and Labour Movements in Britain, the USA and Australia from the 1880 to 1914.* London: Merlin, 2003.

Lamoreaux, Naomi R., and Kenneth L. Sokoloff, eds. *Financing Innovation in the United States, 1870 to the Present.* Cambridge, MA: MIT Press, 2007.

Letwin, William. *Law and Economic Policy in America: The Evolution of the Sherman Antitrust Act.* New York: Random House, 1965.

Pletcher, David M. *The Diplomacy of Trade and Investment: American Economic Expansion in the Hemisphere, 1865-1900.* Columbia: University of Missouri Press, 1998.

Prechel, Harland. *Big Business and the State: Historical Transitions and Corporate Transformation, 1880s-1890s.* Albany: State University of New York Press, 2000.

Reitano, Joanne. *The Tariff Question in the Gilded Age.* University Park: Pennsylvania University Press, 1994.

Rosenbloom, Joshua L. "Strikebreaking and the Labor Market in the United States, 1881-1894." *Journal of Economic History* 58, no. 1 (March 1998): 183-205.

Schmidt, James D. *Industrial Violence and the Legal Origins of Child Labor.* New York: Cambridge University Press, 2010.

Schneirov, Richard. *Labor and Urban Politics: Class Struggle and the Origins of Modern Liberalism in Chicago, 1864-1897.* Urbana: University of Illinois Press, 1998.

Schröter, Harm G. *Americanization of the European Economy: A Compact Survey of American Economic Influence in Europe since the 1880s.* Norwell, MA: Springer, 2005.

Shannon, Fred A. *The Centennial Years, a Political and Economic History of America from the Late 1870s to the Early 1890s,* ed. by Robert Huhn Jones. Garden City, NY: Doubleday, 1967.

Sklar, Martin J. *The Corporate Reconstruction of American Capitalism, 1890-1916: The Market, the Law, and Politics*. New York: Cambridge University Press, 1988.

Skrabec, Quentin R., Jr. *The Carnegie Boys: The Lieutenants of Andrew Carnegie That Changed America*. Jefferson, NC: McFarland, 2012.

Taillon, Paul Michel. *Good, Reliable, White Men: Railroad Brotherhoods, 1877-1917*. Urbana: University of Illinois Press, 2009.

Trachtenberg, Alan. *The Incorporation of America: Culture and Society in the Gilded Age*. New York: Hill and Wang, 1982.

Woloch, Nancy. *Politics and Society in Twentieth-Century America: Protective Laws for Women Workers, 1890s-1990s*. Princeton, NJ: Princeton University Press, 2015.

Zeff, Stephen A., ed. *The U.S. Accounting Profession in the 1890s and Early 1900s*. New York: Garland, 1988.

Government, Politics, and the Presidency

Ayers, Edward L. *The Promise of the New South: Life after Reconstruction*. New York: oxford University Press, 1992.

Blomberg, Thomas G., and Karol Lucken, *American Penology: A History of Control*, 2d ed. New Brunswick, NJ: Aldine Transaction, 2010.

Brands, H. W. *Bound to Empire: The United States and the Philippines*. New York: Oxford University Press, 1992.

Burnham, John C. *Health Care in America: A History*. Baltimore: Johns Hopkins University Press, 2015.

Calhoun, Charles W. *Conceiving a New Republic: The Republican Party and the Southern Question, 1869-1900*. Lawrence: University Press of Kansas, 2006.

Clanton, Gene. *Congressional Populism and the Crisis of the 1890s*. Lawrence: University Press of Kansas, 1998.

Dobson, John M. *Politics in the Gilded Age: A New Perspective on Reform*. New York: Praeger, 1972.

Durden, Robert F. *The Climax of Populism: The Election of 1896*. Lexington: University of Kentucky Press, 1965.

Gerlach, Murney. *British Liberalism and the United States: Political and Social Thought in the Late Victorian Age*. New York: Palgrave, 2001.

Glad, Paul W. *McKinley, Bryan, and the People*. Philadelphia: Lippincott, 1964.

Goodwyn, Lawrence. *Democratic Promise: The Populist Moment in America*. New York: Oxford University Press, 1976. [Abridged ed.: *The Populist Moment: A Short History of the Agrarian Revolt in America*. New York: Oxford University Press, 1978.]

Gould, Lewis L. *The Presidency of William McKinley*. Lawrence: Regents' Press of Kansas, 1980.

Healy, David. *US Expansionism: The Imperialist Urge in the 1890s*. Madison: University of Wisconsin Press, 1970.

Hicks, John D. *The Populist Revolt: A History of the Farmers' Alliance and the People's Party*. 1931; reprint, Westport, CT: Greenwood, 1981.

Holmes, William, ed. *American Populism*. New York: Hill and Wang, 1994.

Hunt, Michael H. *The Making of a Special Relationship: The United States and China to 1914*. New York: Columbia University Press, 1983.

Janney, Caroline E. *Remembering the Civil War: Reunion and the Limits of Reconciliation*. Chapel Hill: University of North Carolina Press, 2013.

Jones, Stanley L. *The Presidential Election of 1896*. Madison: University of Wisconsin Press, 1964.

Kahn, Ronald, and Ken I. Kersch, eds. *The Supreme Court and American Political Development*. Lawrence: University Press of Kansas, 2006.

Karnow, Stanley. *In Our Image: America's Empire in the Philippines*. New York: Random House, 1989.

Kleppner, Paul. "Voters and Parties in the Western States, 1876-1900." *Western Historical Quarterly* 14 (January 1983): 49-68.

Koenig, Louis W. *Bryan: A Political Biography of William Jennings Bryan*. New York: Putnam, 1971.

Marcus, Robert D. *Grand Old Party: Political Structure in the Gilded Age, 1880-1896*. New York: Oxford University Press, 1971.

Mattox, Henry E. *The Twilight of Amateur Diplomacy: The American Foreign Service and Its Senior Officers in the 1890s*. Kent, OH: Kent State University Press, 1989.

McGerr, Michael E. *The Decline of Popular Politics: The American North, 1865-1928*. New York: Oxford University Press, 1986.

McMath, Robert C. *American Populism: A Social History, 1877-1898*. New York: Hill and Wang, 1993.

McSeveney, Samuel T. *The Politics of Depression: Political Behavior in the Northeast, 1893-1896*. New York: Oxford University Press, 1972.

Mitrani, Sam. *The Rise of the Chicago Police Department: Class and Conflict, 1850-1894*. Urbana: University of Illinois Press, 2013.

Morgan, H. Wayne. *William McKinley and His America*, rev. ed. Kent, OH: Kent State University Press, 2003.

Ninkovich, Frank. *The United States and Imperialism*. Malden, MA: Blackwell, 2001.

Orr, Brooke Speer. *The "People's Joan of Arc": Mary Elizabeth Lease, Gendered Politics and Populist Party Politics in Gilded-Age America*. New York: P. Lang, 2014.

Osborne, Thomas J. *"Empire Can Wait": American Opposition to Hawaiian Annexation, 1893-1898*. Kent, OH: Kent State University Press, 1981.

Ostler, Jeffrey. *Prairie Populism: The Fate of Agrarian Radicalism in Kansas, Nebraska, and Iowa, 1880-1892*. Lawrence: University Press of Kansas, 1993.

Paterson, Thomas G., and Stephen G. Rabe, eds. *Imperial Surge: The United States Abroad, the 1890s-Early 1900s*. Lexington, MA: D.C. Heath, 1992.

Phillips, Michael. *The Lochner Court, Myth and Reality: Substantive Due Process from the 1890s to the 1930s*. Westport, CT: Praeger, 2001.

Pletcher, David M. *The Awkward Years: American Foreign Relations under Garfield and Arthur*. Columbia, MO: University of Missouri Press, 1998.

Pletcher, David M. *The Diplomacy of Trade and Investment: American Economic Expansion in the Hemisphere, 1865-1900*. Columbia, MO: University of Missouri Press, 1998.

Postel, Charles. *The Populist Vision*. New York: Oxford University Press, 2007.

Salvatore, Nick. *Eugene Debs, Citizen and Socialist*. Urbana: University of Illinois Press, 1982.

Schoonover, Thomas. *Uncle Sam's War of 1898 and the Origins of Globalization*. Lexington: University Press of

Skocpol, Theda. *Protecting Soldiers and Mothers: The Political Origins of Social Policy in the United States*. Cambridge, MA: Belknap Press of Harvard University Press, 1992.

Shannon, Fred A. *The Centennial Years, a Political and Economic History of American from the Late 1870s to the Early 1890s*, ed. by Robert Huhn Jones. Garden City, NY: Doubleday, 1967.

Spillane, Joseph F., and David B. Wolcott. *A History of Modern American Criminal Justice*. Thousand Oaks, CA: SAGE, 2013.

Welch, Richard E., Jr., *The Presidencies of Grover Cleveland*. Lawrence: University Press of Kansas, 1988.

White, Richard. *"It's Your Misfortune and None of My Own:: A New History of the American West*. Norman: University of Oklahoma Press, 1991.

Williams, R. Hal. *The Years of Decision: American Politics in the 1890s*. New York: Wiley, 1978.

Woodward, C. Vann. *Origins of the New South, 1877-1913*, with a critical essay on recent works by Charles B. Dew. Baton Rouge: Louisiana State University Press, 1971.

Woodward, C. Vann. *Tom Watson, Agrarian Rebel*. 1938; reprint, New York: Oxford University Press, 1963.

Wyatt-Brown, Bertram. *The Shaping Southern Culture: Honor, Grace, and War, 1760s-1890s*. Chapel Hill: University of North Carolina Press, 2001.

Immigration

Alexander, June Granatir. *Daily Life in Immigrant America, 1870-1920: How the Second Great Wave of Immigrants Made Their Way in America*, rev. ed. Chicago: I. Dee, c2009.

Bergland, Betty A., and Lori Ann Lahlum, eds. *Norwegian American Women: Migration, Communities, and Identities*. St. Paul: Minnesota Historical Society Press, 2011.

Bergquist, James M. *Daily Life in Immigrant America, 1820-1870: How the First Great Wave of Immigrants Made Their Way in America*, rev. ed. Chicago: I. Dee, 2009.

Blake, Angela M. *How New York Became American, 1890-1924*. Baltimore: Johns Hopkins University Press, 2006.

Bodnar, John. *The Transplanted: A History of Immigrants in Urban America*. Bloomington: Indiana University Press, 1985.

Daniels, Roger. *Coming to America: A History of Immigration and Ethnicity in American Life*. New York: HarperCollins, 1990.

Davis, Graham, ed. *In Search of a Better Life: British and Irish Migration*. Stroud, Gloucestershire, UK: The History Press, 2011.

Dinnerstein, Leonard, Roger L. Nichols, and David M. Reimers. *Natives and Strangers: A History of Ethnic Americans*, 6th ed. New York: Oxford University Press, 2014.

Dublin, Thomas, ed. *Immigrant Voices: New Lives in America, 1773-2000*, 2d ed. Urbana: University of Illinois Press, 2014.

Ettinger, Patrick. *Imaginary Lines: Border Enforcement and the Origins of Undocumented Immigration, 1882-1930*. Austin: University of Texas Press, 2009.

Frost, Helen. *German Immigrants, 1820-1920*. Mankato, MN: Capstone, 2002,

Green, Nancy L., and François Weil, eds. *Citizenship and Those Who Leave: The Politics of Emigration and Expatriation*. Urbana: University of Illinois Press, 2007.

Gyory, Andrew. *Closing the Gate: Race, Politics, and the Chinese Exclusion Act*. Chapel Hill: University of North Carolina Press, 1998.

Hoerder, Dirk, ed. *American Labor and Immigration History, 1877-1920s: Recent European Research*. Urbana: University of Illinois Press, 1983.

Irving, Katrina. *Immigrant Mothers: Narratives of Race and Maternity, 1890-1925*. Urbana: University of Illinois Press, 2000.

Klapper, Melissa R. *Small Strangers: The Experiences of Immigrant Children in America, 1880-1925*. Chicago: I. Dee, 2007.

Soennichsen, John. *The Chinese Exclusion Act of 1882*. Santa Barbara, CA: Greenwood, 2011.

Literature

Berthoff, Warner. *The Ferment of Realism: American Literature, 1884-1919*. 1965; reprint, New York: Cambridge University Press, 1981.

Bierce, Ambrose. *Skepticism and Dissent: Selected Journalism from 1898-1901*, ed. by Lawrence I. Berkove. Ann Arbor, MI: Delmas, 1980.

Doyle, James. *The Fin de Siècle Spirit: Walter Blackburn Harte and the American-Canadian Literary Milieu of the 1890s*. Toronto: ECW, 1995.

Frederick, Peter J. *Knight of the Golden Rule: The Intellectual as Christian Social Reformer in the 1890s*. Lexington: University Press of Kentucky, 1976.

Hochman, Barbara. *Uncle Tom's Cabin and the Reading Revolution: Race, Literacy, Childhood, and Fiction, 1851-1911*. Amherst: University of Massachusetts Press, 2011.

Jeffrey, Julie Roy. *Abolitionists Remember: Anitslavery Autobiographies and the Unfinished Work of Emancipation*. Chapel Hill: University of North Carolina Press, 2008.

Kennedy-Nolle, Sharon. *Writing Reconstruction: Race, Gender, and Citizenship in the Postwar South*. Chapel Hill: University of North Carolina Press, 2015.

Kieniewicz, Teresa. *Men, Wmen, and the Novelist: Face and Fiction in the American Novel of the 1870s and 1880s*. Washington, DC: University Press of America, 1982.

Lears, T. J. Jackson. *No Place of Grace: Antimodernism and the Transformation of American Culture, 1880-1920*. 1981; reprint, Chicago: University of Chicago Press, 1994.

Mariani, Giorgio. *Spectacular Narratives: Representations of Class and War in Stephen Crane and the American 1890s*. New York: P. Lang, 1992.

Martin, Jay. *Harvests of Change: American Literature, 1865-1914*. Englewood Cliffs, NJ: Prentice-Hall, 1974.

McCaskill, Barbara, and Caroline Gebhard, eds. *Post-Bellum, Pre-Harlem: African American Literature and Culture, 1877-1919*. New York : New York University Press, 2006.

Mielke, Robert. *The Riddle of the Painful Earth: Suffering and Society in W. D. Howells' Major Writings of the Early 1890s*. Kirksville, MO: Thomas Jefferson Press, Northeast Missouri State University, 1994.

Mindich, David T. Z. *Just the Facts: How "Objectivity" Came to Define American Journalism*. New York: New York University Press, 1998.

Schlereth, Wendy Clauson. The Chap-book: *A Journal of American Intellectual Life in the 1890s*. Ann Arbor: UMI Research Press, 1982.

Spencer, David R. *The Yellow Journalism: The Press and America's Emergence as a World Power*. Evanston, IL: Northwestern University Press, 2007.

Tucker, Amy. *The Illustration of the Master: Henry James and the Magazine Revolution*. Stanford, CA: Stanford University Press, 2010.

Popular Culture

Alexander, Benjamin F. *Coxey's Army: Popular Protest in the Gilded Age*. Baltimore: Johns Hopkins University Press, 2015.

Algeo, Matthew. *Pedestrianism: When Watching People Walk Was America's Favorite Spectator Sport*. Chicago: Chicago Review Press, 2014.

American Art Posters of the 1890s in the Metropolitan Museum of Art, including the Leonard A. Lauder Collection. Catalogue by David W. Kiehl; essays by Phillip Dennis Cate, Nancy Finlay, and David W. Kiehl. New York: Metropolitan Museum of Art, 1987.

Bentley, Amy. *Inventing Baby Food: Taste, Health, and the Industrialization of the American Diet*. Oakland: University of California Press, 2014.

Blake, Angela M. *How New York Became American, 1890-1924*. Baltimore: Johns Hopkins University Press 2006.

Brands, H. W. *The Reckless Decade: America in the 1890s*. New York: St. Martin's, 1995.

Butterick Publishing Company. *Metropolitan Fashions of the 1880s: From the 1885 Butterick Catalog*. Mineola, NY: Dover, 1997.

Crawford, Richard. *America's Musical Life: A History*. 2001; reprint, New York: Norton, 2005.

Cremin, Lawrence. The Transformation of the School: Progressivism in American Education, 1870-1957. 1961; reprint, New York: Vintage, 1994.

Danna, Sammy R. *Lydia Pinkham: The Face That Launched a Thousand Ads*. Lanham, MD: Scarecrow, 2014.

DesRochers, Rick. *The New Humor in the Progressive Era: Americanization and the Vaudeville Comedian*. New York: Palgrave Macmillan, 2014.

Ettinger, Roseann. *Men's Clothing and Fabrics in the 1890s: Price Guide*. Atglen, PA: Schiffer, 1998.

Fahs, Alice, and Joan Waugh, eds. *The Memory of the Civil War in American Culture*. Chapel Hill: University of North Carolina Press, 2004.

Finnegan, Margaret Mary. *Selling Suffrage: Consumer Culture and Votes for Women*. New York: Columbia University Press, 1999.

Fischer, Roger A. *Them Damned Pictures: Explorations in American Political Cartoon Art*. North Haven, CT: Shoe String/Archon, 1996.

Foy, Jessica H., and Thomas J. Schlereth, eds. *American Home Life, 1880-1930: A Social History of Spaces and Services*. Knoxville: University of Tennessee Press, 1992.

Gale, Robert L. *The Gay Nineties in America: A Cultural Dictionary of the 1890s*. Westport, CT: Greenwood, 1992.

Garvey, Ellen Gruber. *The Adman in the Parlor: Magazines and the Gendering of Consumer Culture, 1880s to 1910s*. New York: Oxford University Press, 1996.

Gidlow, Liette. *The Big Vote: Gender, Consumer Culture, and the Politics of Exclusion, 1890s-1920s*. Baltimore: Johns Hopkins University Press, 2004.

Goddu, Joseph. *American Art Posters of the 1890s: November 25, 1989 to January 6, 1990*. New York: Hirschl & Adler Galleries, 1990.

Grant, H. Roger. *Self-Help in the 1890s Depression*. Ames: Iowa State University Press, 1983.

Harris, Kristina, ed. *Authentic Victorian Fashion Patterns: A Complete Lady's Wardrobe*. Mineola, NY: Dover, 1999.

Harzig, Christiane, and Dirk Hoerder, eds. *The Press of Labor Migrants in Europe and North America 1880s to 1930s*. Bremen: Universität Bremen, 1985.

Hoerder, Dirk, gen. ed. *Essays on the Scandanavian-North American Radical Press, 1880s-1930s*. Bremen: Labor Newspaper Preservation Project, Universität Bremen, 1984.

Jasper, Joanne. *Turn of the Century American Dinnerware, 1880s to 1920s*. Paducah, KY: Collector Books, 1996.

Keith, Jeanette. *Fever Season: The Story of a Terrifying Epidemic and the People Who Saved a City*. New York: Bloomsbury, 2012.

Lasser, Michael. *America's Songs II: Songs from the 1890s to the Post-War Years*. New York: Routledge, 2014.

Miller, Worth Robert. *Populist Cartoons: An Illustrated History of the Third-Party Movement in the 1890s*. Kirksville, MO: Truman State University Press, 2011.

Mindich, David T. Z. *Just the Facts: How "Objectivity" Came to Define American Journalism*. New York: New York University Press, 1998.

Moon, Krystyn R. *Yellowface: Creating the Chinese in American Popular Music and Performance, 1850s-1920s*. New Brunswick, NJ: Rutgers University Press, 2005.

Nevins, Allan, and Frank Weitenkampf. *A Century of Political Cartoons: Caricature in the United States from 1800 to 1900*. 1944; reprint, New York: Octagon, 1975.

Schlereth, Wendy Clauson. The Chap-book: *A Journal of American Intellectual Life in the 1890s*. Ann Arbor, MI: UMI Research, 1982.

Schoonover, David E., ed. *The Ladies' Etiquette Hand-Book: The Importance of Being Refined in the 1880s*. Iowa City: University of Iowa press, 2001.

Smith, Susan Harris, and Melanie Dawson, eds. *The American 1890s: A Cultural Reader*. Durham, NC: Duke University Press, 2000.

Smith, Timothy B. *The Golden Age of Battlefield Preservation: The Decade of the 1890s and the Establishment of America's First Five Military Parks*. Knoxville: University of Tennessee press, 2008.

Spencer, David R. *The Yellow Journalism: The Press and America's Emergence as a World Power*. Evanston, IL: Northwestern University Press, 2007.

Trachtenberg, Alan. *Brooklyn Bridge: Fact and Symbol*, 2d ed. Chicago: University of Chicago Press, 1979.

Warner, Patricia. *When the Girls Came Out to Play: The Birth of American Sportswear*. Amherst: University of Massachusetts Press, 2006.

Willis, Deborah. *Posing Beauty: African American Images, from the 1890s to the Present*. New York: Norton, 2009.

Wyatt-Brown, Bertram. *The Shaping of Southern Culture: Honor, Grace, and War, 1760s-1890s*. Chapel Hill: University of North Carolina Press, 2001.

Progressivism

Ashby, LeRoy. *Saving the Waifs: Reformers and Dependent Children, 1890-1917*. Philadelphia: Temple University Press, 1984.

Brown, Victoria Bissell. *The Education of Jane Addams: Politics and Culture in Modern America*. Philadelphia: University of Pennsylvania Press, 2004.

Cremin, Lawrence. *The Transformation of the School: Progressivism in American Education, 1870-1957*. 1961; reprint, New York: Vintage, 1994.

Crunden, Robert M. *Ministers of Reform: The Progressives' Achievement in American Civilization, 1889-1920*. New York: Basic Books, 1982.

Danbom, David. *"The World of Hope": Progressives and the Search for an Ethical Public Life*. Philadelphia: Temple University Press, 1987.

Diliberto, Gioia. *A Useful Woman: The Early Life of Jane Addams*. New York: Scribners, 1999.

Filler, Louis. *Appointment at Armageddon: Muckraking and Progressivism in the American Tradition*. Westport, CT: Greenwood, 1976.

Flanagan, Maureen A. *America Reformed: Progressives and Progressivisms, 1890s-1920s*. New York: Oxford University Press, 2007.

Gilmore, Glenda Elizabeth, comp. *Who Were the Progressives? Readings*. Boston: Bedford/St Martin's, 2002.

Grantham, Dewey W. *Southern Progressivism: The Reconciliation of Progress and Tradition*. Knoxville: University of Tennessee Press, 1983.

Jensen, Richard. *The Winning of the Midwest: Social and Political Conflict, 1888-1896*. Chicago: University of Chicago Press, 1971.

Link, William A. *The Paradox of Southern Progressivism, 1880-1930*. Chapel Hill: University of North Carolina Press, 1992.

Knight, Louise W. (2005). *Citizen: Jane Addams and the Struggle for Democracy*. Chicago, IL: University of Chicago Press,

Sklar, Kathryn Kish. *Florence Kelley and the Nation's Work*. New Haven: Yale University Press, 1995.

Wiebe, Robert H. *Businessmen and Reform: A Study of the Progressive Movement.* 1962; reprint, Chicago: I. Dee, 1988.

Religion

Blum, Edward J. *Reforging the White Republic: Race, Religion, and American Nationalism, 1865-1898.* Baton Rouge: Louisiana State University Press, 2005.

Creech, Joe. *Righteous Indignation: Religion and the Populist Revolution.* Urbana: University of Illinois Press, 2006.

Curtis, Edward E., IV, and Danielle Brune Sigler, eds. *The New Black Gods: Arthur Huff Fauset and the Study of African American Religions.* Bloomington: Indiana University press, 2009.

Curtis, Susan. *A Consuming Faith: The Social Gospel and Modern American Culture.* Columbia, MO: University of Missouri Press, 2001.

Dickerson, Dennis C. *African Methodism and Its Wesleyan Heritage: Reflections on AME Church History.* Nashville, TN: AMEC Sunday School Union, 2009.

Frederick, Peter J. *Knights of the Golden Rule: The Intellectual as Christian Social Reformer in the 1890s.* Lexington: University Press of Kentucky, 1976.

Green, Steven K. *The Second Disestablishment: Church and State in Nineteenth-Century America.* New York: Oxford University Press, 2010.

Hill, Patricia R. *The World Their Household: The American Woman's Foreign Mission Movement and Cultural Transformation, 1870-1920.* Ann Arbor: University of Michigan Press, 1985.

Hopkins, Charles Howard. *The Rise of the Social Gospel in American Protestantism, 1865-1915.* 1940; reprint, New York: AMS Press, 1982.

Jonas, Thomas J. *The Divided Mind: American Catholic Evangelists in the 1890s.* New York: Garland, 1988.

Tyrell, Ian. *Reforming the World: The Creation of America's Moral Empire.* Princeton, NJ: Princeton University Press, 2010.

Weston, William J. *Presbyterian Pluralism: Competition in a Protestant House.* Knoxville: University of Tennessee Press, 1997.

Spanish-American War

Blow, Michael. *A Ship to Remember: The Maine and the Spanish-American War.* New York: Morrow, 1992.

Bradford, James C., ed. *Crucible of Empire: The Spanish-American War and Its Aftermath.* Annapolis: Naval Institute Press, 1993.

Challener, Richard D. *Admirals, Generals, and American Foreign Policy, 1889-1914.* Princdton, NJ: Princeton University Press, 1973.

Cosmas, Graham A. *An Army for Empire: The United States Army in the Spanish-American War.* 1971; reprint, Shippensburg, PA: White Mane, 1994.

Damiani, Brian P. *Advocates of Empire: William McKinley, the Senate, and American Expansion, 1898-1899.* New York : Garland Pub., 1987.

Foner, Philip S. *The Spanish-Cuban-American War and the Birth of American Imperialism, 1895-1902,* 2 vols. New York: Monthly Review, 1972.

Freidel, Frank. *The Splendid Little War.* Boston: Little, Brown, 1958.

Gatewood, Willard B., Jr. *Black Americans and the White Man's Burden, 1898-1903.* Urbana: University of Illinois Press, 1975.

Healy, David. *US Expansionism: The Imperialist Urge in the 1890s.* Madison: University of Wisconsin Press, 1970.

Jeffers, H. Paul. *Colonel Roosevelt: Theodore Roosevelt Goes to War, 1897-1898.* New York: Wiley, 1996.

Linderman, Gerald F. *The Mirror of War: American Society and the Spanish-American War.* Ann Arbor: University of Michigan Press, 1974.

Morris, Edmund. *The Rise of Theodore Roosevelt.* 1979; reprint, New York: Modern Library, 2001.

Musicant, Ivan. *Empire by Default: The Spanish-American War and the Dawn of the American Century.* 1998; reprint, H. Holt, 2008.

Offner, John L. *An Unwanted War: The Diplomacy of the United Sates and Spain over Cuba, 1895-1898.* Chapel Hill: University of North Carolina Press, 1992.

Ninkovich, Frank. *The United States and Imperialism.* Malden, MA: Blackwell, 2001.

Paterson, Thomas G., and Stephen G. Rabe, eds. *Imperial Surge: The United States Abroad, The 1890s-Early 1900s.* Lexington, MA: D.C. Heath, 1992.

Pérez, Louis A., Jr. *The War of 1898: The United States and Cuba in History and Historiography.* Chapel Hill: University of North Carolina Press, 1998.

Schoonover, Thomas. *Uncle Sam's War of 1898 and the Origins of Globalization.* Lexington: University Press of Kentucky, 2003.

Spencer, David R. *The Yellow Journalism: The Press and America's Emergence as a World Power.* Evanston, IL: Northwestern University Press, 2007.

Trask, David F. *The War with Spain in 1898.* 1981; reprint, Lincoln: University of Nebraska Press, 1996.

Sports

Alexander, George E. *Lawn Tennis: Its Founders and Its Early Days.* Lynn, MA: H. O. Zimman, 1974.

Algeo, Matthew. *Pedestrianism: When Watching People Walk Was America's Favorite Spectator Sport.* Chicago: Chicago Review Press, 2014.

Baltzell, E. Digby. *Sporting Gentlemen: Men's Tennis from the Age of Honor to the Cult of the Superstar.* 1995; reprint, New Brunswick, NJ: Transaction, 2013.

Finison, Lorenz J. *Boston's Cycling Craze, 1880-1900: A Story of Race, Sport, and Society.* Amherst: University of Massachusetts Press, 2014.

Fleitz, David L. *The Irish in Baseball: An Early History.* Jefferson, NC: McFarland, 2009.

Holm, Ed, ed. *Yachting's Golden Age: 1880-1905.* New York: Knopf, 1999.

Klein, Christopher. *Strong Boy: The Life and Times of John L. Sullivan, America's First Sports Hero.* Guilford, CT: Lyons, 2013.

Laing, Jeffrey Michael. *Bud Fowler: Baseball's First Black Professional.* Jefferson, NC: McFarland, 2013.

Pollack, Adam J. *John L. Sullivan: The Career of the First Gloved Heavyweight Champion.* Jefferson, NC: McFarland, 2006.

Putney, Clifford. *Muscular Christianity: Manhood and Sports in Protestant America, 1880-1920.* Cambridge, MA: Harvard University Press, 2003.

Schwartz, Gary H. *The Art of Tennis, 1874-1940: Timeless, Enchanting Illustrations and Narrative of Tennis' Formative Years.* Tiburon, CA: Wood River, 1990.

Thorn, John. *Baseball in the Garden of Eden.* New York: Simon & Schuster, 2011.

Warner, Patricia. *When the Girls Came Out to Play: The Birth of American Sportswear.* Amherst: University of Massachusetts Press, 2006.

Webb, Bernice Larson. *The Basketball Man, James Naismith.* Lawrence: University Press of Kansas, 1973.

Women's History

Baker, Paula. "The Domestication of Politics: Women and American Political Society, 1780-1920." *American Historical Review* 89 (1984): 620-647.

Beeton, Beverly. *Women Vote in the West: The Woman Suffrage Movement, 1869-1896.* New York: Garland, 1986.

Bentley, Amy. *Inventing Baby Food: Taste, Health, and the Industrialization of the American Diet.* Oakland: University of California Press, 2014.

Blair, Karen J. *The Clubwoman as Feminist: True Womanhood Defined, 1868-1914.* New York: Holmes & Meier, 1980.

Bolt, Christine. *Sisterhood Questioned? Race, Class, and Internationism in the American and British Women's Movements, c. 1880s-1970s.* New York: Routledge, 2004.

Bordin, Ruth. *Woman and Temperance: The Quest for Power and Liberty, 1873-1900.* Philadelphia: Temple University Press, 1981.

Buhle, Mari Jo. *Women and Socialism, 1870-1920.* Urbana: University of Illinois Press, 1981.

Clemens, Elisabeth S. "Securing Political Returns to Social Capital: Women's Associations in the United States, 1880s-1920s." *Journal of Interdisciplinary History* 29 (1999): 613-638.

Cunningham, Patricia A. *Reforming Women's Fashion, 1850-1920.* Kent, OH: Kent State University Press, 2003.

Edwards, Rebecca. *Angels in the Machinery: Gender and American Party Politics from the Civil War to the Progressive Era.* New Nork: Oxford University Press, 1997.

Finnegan, Margaret Mary. *Selling Suffrage: Consumer Culture and Votes for Women.* New York: Columbia University Press, 1999.

Gidlow, Lietta. *The Big Vote: Gender, Consumer Culture, and the Politics of Exclusion, 1890s-1920s.* Baltimore: Johns Hopkins University Press, 2004.

Gilmore, Glenda Elizabeth. *Gender and Jim Crow: Women and the Politics of White Supremacy in North Carolina, 1896-1920.* Chapel Hill: University of North Carolina Press, 1996.

Hill, Patricia R. *The World Their Household: The American Woman's Foreign Mission Movement and Cultural Transformation, 1870-1920.* Ann Arbor: University of Michigan Press, 1985.

Hunter, Jane. *The Gospel of Gentility: American Women Missionaries in Turn-of-the-Century China.* New Haven: Yale University Press, 1985.

Kraditor, Aileen. *The Ideas of the Woman Suffrage Movement, 1890-1920.* New York: Columbia University Press, 1965.

Orr, Brooke Speer. *The "People's Joan of Arc": Mary Elizabeth Lease, Gendered Politics and Populist Party Politics in Gilded-Age America.* New York: P. Lang, 2014.

Scott, Anne Firor. *Natural Allies: Women's Associations in American History.* Champaign: University of Illinois Press, 1992.

Tilly, Louise A., and P. Gurin, eds. *Women, Politics, and Change.* New York: Russell Sage Foundation, 1990.

Woloch, Nancy. *Politics and Society in Twentieth-Century America: Protective Laws for Women Workers, 1890s-1900s.* Princeton, NJ: Princeton University Press, 2015.

RESIDENCE, APRIL 1, 1935 — **PERSONS 14 YEARS OLD AND O[VER]**

17	18	19	20	D	21	22	23	24	25	E	26	27	28
Same House			No		Yes	–	–	–	–		40	–	Foreman
Same House			No		No	No	No	No	H		–	–	
Same House			No		No	No	No	No	S		–	–	
Same House			No		Yes	–	–	–	–			–	Labor[er]